Environmental Economics
and Policy

Environmental Economics and Policy

Tom Tietenberg
Colby College

HarperCollins*College*Publishers

Acquisitions Editor: Bruce Kaplan
Project Editor: David Nickol
Design Supervisor: Mary McDonnell
Cover Design: Kay Petronio
Production Manager: Mike Kemper
Printer and Binder: R. R. Donnelley & Sons Company
Cover Printer: The Lehigh Press,Inc.

Environmental Economics and Policy

Library of Congress Cataloging-in-Publication Data

Tietenberg, Thomas H.
    Environmental economics and policy / Tom Tietenberg.
        p.   cm.
    Includes index.
    ISBN 0-673-46974-3
    1. Environmental economics.   I. Title.
HD75.6.T54   1994
333.7--dc20   93-42324
                                                                              CIP

95 96 97 9 8 7 6 5 4 3

Contents

Preface

About two decades ago, while on a plane heading for a conference, I struck up a conversation with the passenger next to me. During the course of that conversation he asked me what I did for a living. After mulling my response that I was an environmental economist, he asked, "Isn't that a contradiction in terms?"

He had a point. The economy has been a major source of environmental degradation. Developers pave over wetlands. Timber companies denude the forests. Fishermen deplete the oceans. Industries pollute the waters. And on and on.

Recently, however, those same powerful forces that have historically been associated with environmental degradation have been enlisted in the struggle to protect the environment. Buying and selling quotas have helped restore New Zealand fisheries. Pharmaceutical companies are investing in biodiversity preservation. Peak-load and congestion pricing have encouraged the better use of existing power plants and roads rather than the building of new ones. By-the-bag charging for solid waste has stimulated recycling and reduced the volume of waste. Green fees are raising revenue for environmental improvement while discouraging environmentally destructive behavior. The list goes on

The success of these approaches in providing a politically feasible and effective means of changing environmentally destructive behavior has attracted much wider interest in the field of environmental economics. Environmental groups, states, local governments, national governments, and even international organizations are beginning to enlist the principles and techniques of environmental economics in their effort to preserve and protect the environment.

But environmental economics is not a naturally hospitable field. Most of the economic principles that underlie these approaches flow from some intimidating mathematical models, making them inaccessible to all but those who were willing to invest the time and effort to learn the underlying mathematics. This lack of accessible textbooks has created a void. This book is designed specifically to fill that void. It was written to communicate the powerful insights of the field to those taking courses designed for nonmajors or, more generally, to an audience with little or no training in economics.

With its strong emphasis on public policy this book shows how economics can be used both to understand the behavioral sources of environmental problems and to provide the foundation for innovative solutions. Chapters 1–4 of the book describe the basic economic approach to the environment, laying out the underlying values as well as the procedures used to translate those values into policy-relevant principles. Chapters 5–18 deal with natural resource economics (analyzing the flow of materials and energy from the environment into the economy) and environmental economics (analyzing the flow of waste products into the environment. Chapters 19–21 focus on sustainable development, reflecting the demonstrated, current global interest in finding new environmentally compatible means of lifting the world's poor out of poverty. Throughout, how the principles can be applied is illustrated by a host of specific international examples. Considerable attention has been paid to environmental problems and policies in Eastern and Western Europe, Japan, and the developing nations as well as the United States.

Topics covered in this book include the following: the economics of recycling; the causes, consequences, and potential solutions for global deforestation; economic incentive policies, including the actual experience with their use in France, Sweden, the Netherlands, and Japan; new applications in the United States (acid rain and ozone depletion), and potential applications to global warming and declining biodiversity; oil spills and ocean dumping; the economics of limited liability for oil spills; the Gaia hypothesis; informal arrangements for restricting access to common property resources; nuclear power around the world; new approaches by electric utilities to internalize environmental costs; the economics of renewable energy sources; the magnitude of subsidies for irrigation water; emerging water markets in the United States; sustainable agriculture in the United States and Europe; economics of populations in Zimbabwe; indoor air pollution; results from the National Acid Rain Precipitation Assessment Program; the London agreement on ozone depletion; citizen suits and the private enforcement of environmental laws; cost/benefit analysis of global warming; the cost effectiveness of alternative automobile fuels; joint and several liability doctrine for hazardous wastes; deficiencies of national income accounting from the point of view of sustainable development; examples of industrial waste reduction; and strategies for preserving biodiversity.

This is an economics book but it goes beyond economics. Insights from the natural and physical sciences, literature and political science, as well as other disciplines are scattered liberally through the text. In some cases these references raise unresolved issues that economic analysis can help resolve, while in others they affect the structure of the economic analysis or provide a contrasting point of view.

Tom Tietenberg

Environmental Economics
and Policy

CHAPTER 1

Visions of the Future

From the arch of the bridge to which his guide has carried him, Dante now sees the Diviners . . . coming slowly along the bottom of the fourth Chasm. By help of their incantations and evil agents, they had endeavored to pry into the future which belongs to the almighty alone, and now their faces are painfully twisted the contrary way; and being unable to look before them, they are forced to walk backwards.

DANTE ALIGHIERI, *DIVINE COMEDY: THE INFERNO,* TRANSLATED BY CARLYLE
(1867)

INTRODUCTION

The Self-Extinction Premise

About the time the American colonies became independent, Edward Gibbon completed his monumental work, *The History of the Decline and Fall of the Roman Empire.* In a particularly poignant passage that opens the last chapter of his opus, he re-creates a scene in which the learned Poggius, a friend, and two servants ascend the Capitoline Hill after the fall of Rome. They are awed by the contrast between what Rome once was and what Rome had become:

> In the time of the poet it was crowned with the golden roofs of a temple; the temple is overthrown, the gold has been pillaged, the wheel of fortune has accomplished her revolution, and the sacred ground is again disfigured with thorns and brambles. . . . The forum of the Roman people, where they assembled to enact their laws and elect their magistrates is now enclosed for the cultivation of potherbs, or thrown open for the reception of swine and buffaloes. The public and private edifices, that were founded for eternity lie prostrate, naked, and broken, like the limbs of a mighty giant; and the ruin is the more visible, from the stupendous relics that have survived the injuries of time and fortune. [Vol. 6, pp. 650–51]

What could cause the demise of such a grand and powerful society? Gibbon weaves a complex thesis to answer this question, suggesting ultimately that the seeds for Rome's destruction were sown by the Empire itself.[1] Though Rome finally succumbed to such external forces as fires and invasions, its vulnerability was based upon internal weakness.

The premise that societies germinate the seeds of their own destruction has long fascinated scholars. In one historically significant study in the early nineteenth century, Thomas Malthus foresaw a time when the urge to reproduce would create a situation in which population growth would outstrip the growth of food supply, resulting in starvation and death.

The 1970s and 1980s have ushered in a revival of interest in Malthus's premise, mainly because of the growing number of writers who believe that modern society has embarked on a path that leads to self-destruction. Modern ecologists, for example, have suggested that the environment possesses a unique "carrying capacity" to support humans; once that capacity is exceeded, widespread ecological disruption occurs with disastrous consequences for humanity. The focus is no longer on individual societies, but rather on the survival of the planet.

Sources of concern are not difficult to find. Since mid-century the world has lost nearly one fifth of the topsoil from its cropland, a fifth of its tropical rain forests, and tens of thousands of plant and animal species. Human activity has increased carbon dioxide levels to the point where the global climate is being affected. The protective ozone shield is being depleted. Dead forests and lakes are common in parts of Europe.[2]

Writers have begun to suggest that we have reached a turning point. Bill McKibben put it this way:

> We can no longer imagine that we are part of something larger than ourselves. . . . now we make the world, affect every operation. . . . This is, I suppose, the victory we have been pointing to at least since the eviction from Eden—the domination some have always dreamed of. But it is the story of King Midas writ large—the power looks nothing like we thought it would. It is a brutish, cloddish power, not a creative one.[3]

Humans have negotiated the transition from "adapting to" nature to "managing" nature.[4] The scale of activity has become so large that we affect the life processes of the planet. Where will it all lead?

---

[1]Rome does not provide the only historical example of a powerful society that followed a path to self-extinction. It has been suggested, for example, that the classic Maya civilization succumbed when its concentrated population proved too large to be supported by the soils around it. See Jeremy A. Sabloff, "The Collapse of Classic Maya Civilization," in *Patient Earth,* John Harte and Robert H. Socolow, eds. (New York: Holt, Rinehart and Winston, 1971): 16–27; Lester R. Brown, "World Population Growth, Soil Erosion, and Food Security," *Science* 214 (November 27, 1981): 995–1002.

[2]For an up-to-date examination of the earth's vital signs see the first chapter of the current edition of *State of the World* (New York: W. W. Norton), an annual published by the staff of the Worldwatch Institute in Washington, DC.

[3]Bill McKibben, *The End of Nature* (New York: Random House, 1989): 83–84.

[4]Symptomatic of this transition was the title of the September 1989 issue of *Scientific American.* This special issue on the environment was titled "Managing Planet Earth."

Environmental and Natural Resource Economics

For several decades economists have been concerned with topics such as exhaustible resources and pollution, but during the last two decades, the frequency of related books and articles has accelerated rapidly.[5] Consequently, we've come to better understand the relationship between humanity and the environment and how that relationship affects, and is affected by, economic and political institutions.

This knowledge has allowed political leaders to forge new solutions to old problems. Economic principles underlie fundamentally new approaches to pollution control policy, making better use of scarce water supplies, stemming deforestation, and limiting climate change—to name but a few of the areas that have been transformed. In this book you will be introduced to these economic principles and the entire spectrum of economic approaches to producing better environmental outcomes derived from them.

Thinking About the Future

The two visions presented in this chapter (the basic pessimist model and the basic optimist model) demonstrate areas of concern that will be given closer scrutiny later in this text. They also highlight the key relationships that motivate the conclusions drawn by authors of those visions so that we can assess the adequacy of these relationships as guides to reality.

As Example 1.1 points out, speculating about the future is a risky business. The pessimist and optimist visions we examine were chosen from the literally hundreds that exist because they define, in some sense, the end points of a spectrum. We shall, of course, want to explore not only these end points, but the vast intervening territory as we proceed through the book.

THE BASIC PESSIMIST MODEL

One end of the spectrum is defined by an ambitious study published in 1972 under the title *The Limits to Growth* and subsequently updated and revised in 1992 under the title *Beyond the Limits*. Based on a technique known as *systems dynamics,* developed by Professor Jay Forrester at MIT, a large-scale computer model was constructed to simulate likely future outcomes of the world economy. The most prominent feature of systems dynamics is the use of feedback loops to explain behavior. The *feedback loop* is a closed path that connects an action to its effect on the surrounding conditions, which in turn can influence further action. As the examples presented subsequently in this chapter demonstrate, depending on how the relationships are described, a wide variety of complex behavior can be described by this technique.

---

[5]One article that is generally credited with sparking a renewed interest in natural resource problems is John Krutilla, "Conservation Reconsidered," *The American Economic Review* 57 (September 1968): 777–786.

EXAMPLE 1.1

The Dangers of Prognostication

Our view of the future can be limited by our understanding of the past and present, as well as of the technological possibilities that lie around the corner. Often that understanding is not what it should be, and the forecasts based on it can seem rather absurd in retrospect.

In 1486, for example, a committee headed by Fray Hernando de Talavera was established by King Ferdinand and Queen Isabella to advise them on the merits of funding Christopher Columbus's plan to sail to the West Indies. Following four years of work, the committee reported its conclusion that a voyage of the type contemplated was impossible because (1) the Western Ocean was infinite and probably not navigable; (2) even if the Antipodes (the expected landfall) were reached, the return journey would be impossible; and (3) there probably were no Antipodes to be reached because most of the world was presumably covered by water; St. Augustine said so.

In 1835 Thomas Tredgold, a British railroad designer, declared, "Any general system of conveying passengers—at a velocity exceeding 10 miles an hour, or thereabouts—is extremely improbable."

The chief geologist of the U.S. Geological Survey reported in 1920 that only seven billion barrels of petroleum remained to be recovered with existing techniques. He predicted that, at the contemporary annual rate of consumption of a half billion barrels, American oil resources would be exhausted in fourteen years—by 1934. However, when that fateful year arrived, twelve, not seven, billion barrels had been produced and there was an additional twelve billion barrels of proved reserves.

Economists are certainly not immune from the dangers of prognostication. In *The Coal Question: An Inquiry Concerning the Progress of the Nation and the Probable Exhaustion of our Coal Mines,* published in 1865, Stanley Jevons concluded that the rapid increase in coal consumption coupled with the finite nature of the supply of coal would cause progress to stop in the near future. In his discussion of Jevons's work, John Maynard Keynes notes in passing that Jevons had a similar fear of an increasing scarcity of paper. Jevons apparently acted on those fears for, some fifty years after his death, his children had not used up the stock of paper he had accumulated.

Sources: Glenn Hueckel, "A Historical Approach to Future Economic Growth," *Science* 191 (March 14, 1975): 925–31; Harry U. Spiegel, ed., *The Development of Economic Thought* (New York: Wiley, 1952): 490–525; Edward Cornish et al., *The Study of the Future* (Washington, DC: World Future Society, 1977): 106–08.

Conclusions of the Pessimist Model

Three main conclusions were reached by this study. The first suggests that within a time span of less than a hundred years with no major change in the physical, economic, or social relationships that have traditionally governed world development, society will run out of the nonrenewable resources on which the industrial base depends. When the resources have been depleted, a precipitous collapse of the economic system will result, manifested in massive

FIGURE 1.1 The Limits-to-Growth Standard Run

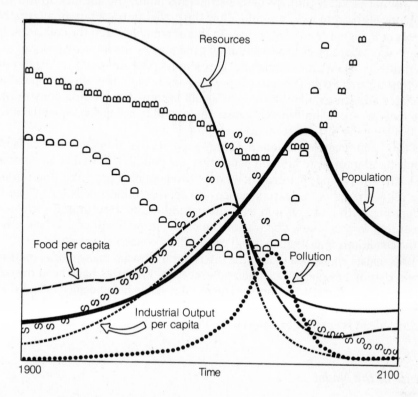

Key: Births = B, Deaths = D, and Services = S.

The "standard" world model run assumes no major change in the physical, economic, or social relationships that have governed the development of the world system. All variables plotted here follow historical values from 1900 to 1970. Food, industrial output, and population grow exponentially until the rapidly diminishing resource base forces a slowdown in industrial growth. Because of natural delays in the system, both population and pollution continue to increase for some time after the peak of industrialization. Population growth is finally halted by a rise in the death rate due to decreased food and medical services.

Source: Donella Meadows et al. *The Limits to Growth* (New York: Universe Books, 1972), p. 129.

unemployment, decreased food production, and a decline in population as the death rate soars. There is no smooth transition, no gradual slowing down of activity; rather, the economic system consumes successively larger amounts of the depletable resources until suddenly they are gone. The characteristic behavior of the system is overshoot and collapse (see Figure 1.1).

The second conclusion of the study is that piecemeal approaches to solving the individual problems will not be successful. To demonstrate this point, the authors arbitrarily double their estimates of the resource base and allow the model to trace out an alternative vision based on this new, higher level of resources. In this alternative vision the collapse still occurs, but this time it is caused by excessive pollution generated by the increased pace of industrialization permitted by the greater availability of resources. The authors then suggest that if the depletable resource and pollution problems were somehow jointly solved, population would grow unabated and the availability of food would become the binding constraint. In this model the removal of one limit merely causes the system to bump subsequently into another one, usually with more dire consequences.

As its third and final conclusion, the study suggests that overshoot and collapse can be avoided only by an immediate limit on population and pollution as well as a cessation of economic growth. The portrait painted shows only two possible outcomes: the termination of growth by self-restraint and conscious policy—an approach that avoids the collapse—or the termination of growth by a collision with the natural limits, resulting in societal collapse. Thus, according to this study, one way or the other, growth will cease. The only issue is whether the conditions under which it will cease will be congenial or hostile.

The 1992 update concluded that in the intervening 20 years many of the limits identified in the earlier study have been reached and exceeded. Fisheries have been overexploited; forests are being cut down at an unprecedented rate; soil is being depleted, and the air over some cities cannot be breathed without causing damage to the respiratory system. Still, the authors conclude, it is possible to avoid the collapse if we make the right choices now.

The Nature of the Model

Why were these conclusions reached? Clearly they depend on the structure of the model. By identifying the characteristics that yield these conclusions, we can then, in subsequent chapters of this book, examine the realism of those characteristics. The dominant characteristic of the model is exponential growth coupled with fixed limits. Exponential growth in any variable (for example, 3 percent per year) implies that the absolute increases in that variable will be greater and greater each year.[6] Furthermore, the higher the rate of growth in resource consumption, the faster a fixed stock of it will be exhausted. Suppose, for example, current reserves of a resource are 100 times current use and the supply of reserves cannot be expanded. If consumption were not growing, this stock would last 100 years. However, if consumption were to grow at 2 percent per year, the reserves would be exhausted in 55 years, and if growth increased to 10 percent per year, exhaustion would occur after only 24 years.

Several resources are held in fixed supply by the model. These include the amount of available land and the stock of depletable resources. In addition, the supply of food is fixed relative to the supply of land. The combination of exponential growth in demand and fixed sources of supply necessarily implies that, at some point, resource supplies must be ex-

---

[6]Suppose, for example, that in some initial year there are 100 units of a specific variable. If that variable is growing at 10 percent per year then it will grow by 10 units during the first year and 11 units the second year.

hausted. The extent to which those resources are essential thus creates the conditions for collapse.

This basic structure of the model is in some ways reinforced and in some ways tempered by the presence of a large number of positive and negative feedback loops. *Positive feedback loops* are those in which secondary effects tend to reinforce the basic trend. An example of a positive feedback loop is the process of capital accumulation. New investment generates greater output, which, when sold, generates profits. These profits, in turn, can be used to fund additional new investments. This example suggests a manner in which the growth process is self-reinforcing.

Positive feedback loops may also be involved in global warming. Scientists believe that the relationship between emissions of methane and global warming, for example, may be described as a positive feedback loop. Because methane is a greenhouse gas, increases in methane emissions contribute to global warming. As the planetary temperature rises, however, it could release extremely large quantities of methane currently trapped in the permafrost; the larger quantities of methane would trigger further temperature increases, which could release more methane, and so on.

Human responses can intensify environmental problems. When shortages of a commodity are imminent, consumers typically begin to hoard the commodity. Hoarding intensifies the shortage. Similarly, people faced with shortages of food commonly eat the seed that is the key to more plentiful food in the future. Situations giving rise to this kind of downward spiral are particularly troublesome.

A *negative feedback loop* is self-limiting rather than self-reinforcing, as illustrated by the role of death rates in limiting population growth in the model. As growth occurs, it causes larger increases in industrial output, which in turn cause more pollution. The increase in pollution triggers a rise in death rates, retarding population growth. From this example it can be seen that negative feedback loops can provide a tempering influence on the growth process, though not necessarily a desirable one.

Perhaps the best-known example of negative feedback on a planetary scale is provided in a theory advanced by James Lovelock, an English scientist. Called the *Gaia hypothesis* after the Greek concept for Mother Earth, this view of the world suggests that the earth is a living organism with a complex feedback system that seeks an optimal physical and chemical environment. Deviations from this optimal environment trigger natural, nonhuman response mechanisms that restore the balance. According to the Gaia hypothesis, the planetary environment is (at least in part) a self-regulating process.

The model of the world envisioned by the Gaia hypothesis is incompatible with that envisioned by the *Limits to Growth* team. Because of the dominance of positive feedback loops, coupled with fixed limits on essential resources, the structure of the *Limits to Growth* model preordains its conclusion that human activity is on a collision course with nature. Although the values assumed for various parameters (the size of the stock of depletable resources, for example) affect the timing of the various effects, they do not substantially affect the nature of the outcome.

The dynamics implied by the notion of a feedback loop is helpful in a more general sense than the specific relationships embodied in this model. As we proceed with our investigation, the degree to which our economic and political institutions serve to intensify or to limit emerging environmental problems will be a key concern.

THE BASIC OPTIMIST MODEL

Is the portrait of the fate of the world economy painted by the *Limits to Growth* model an accurate one? Because Herman Kahn and his associates did not think so, they presented an alternative vision in a book titled *The Next 200 Years: A Scenario for America and the World.*[7] This vision is an optimistic one based in large part on the continuing evolution of a form of technological progress that serves to push back the natural limits until they are no longer limiting.

Conclusions of the Optimist Model

The basic conclusion reached by this study is stated in the opening pages of the book:

> 200 years ago almost everywhere human beings were comparatively few, poor and at the mercy of the forces of nature, and 200 years from now, we expect, almost everywhere they will be numerous, rich and in control of the forces of nature. [p. 1]

The future path of population growth is expected by Kahn and his associates to approximate an S-shaped logistic curve. This image suggests that in 1976, an omniscient observer looking backward through time and then forward into the future would see rather different things. The retrospective glance would reveal a period of exponential population growth, whereas the glance into the future would reveal continued growth, but with steadily declining growth rates, until, at the end of the next 200-year period, growth would automatically come to a halt. By that time, however, the population would have increased to four times its current level and the average person in the world economy would be earning $20,000 a year (in constant dollars)—a far cry from the 1976 average of $1300 (see Figure 1.2).

To Kahn and his associates, interference with this natural evolution of society would not only be unwarranted, it would be unethical. As they see it, tampering with the growth process would consign the residents of the poorest developing countries—and indeed, the poorest residents of the developed countries—to a life of poverty, a life without hope. In contrast, they see continued growth as providing continued betterment for both groups (although, due to an expected decline in the gap between the rich nations and the poor, those in the poorest nations would benefit most from continued growth).

The Nature of the Model

The Kahn model is more qualitative than the *Limits to Growth* model, so its structure is less specific. It is not a computer program that simulates the future. Rather, Kahn and his associates devised scenarios they believed to be plausible and then verified that the various components of these scenarios were consistent with each other. The book is filled with reasons why the chosen scenario is reasonable. These lists of reasons frequently include new technologies

---

[7]Herman Kahn, William Brown, and Leon Martel, *The Next 200 Years: A Scenario for America and the World* (New York: William Morrow, 1976).

FIGURE 1.2   The Kahn Perspective on Prospects of Humanity (in fixed 1975 dollars)

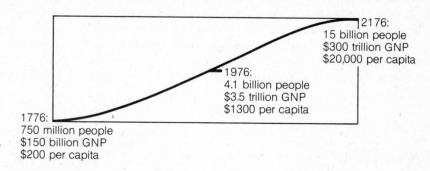

2176:
15 billion people
$300 trillion GNP
$20,000 per capita

1976:
4.1 billion people
$3.5 trillion GNP
$1300 per capita

1776:
750 million people
$150 billion GNP
$200 per capita

Source: Kahn et al. *The Next 200 Years: A Scenario for American and the World* (New York: William Morrow, 1976). p. 6.

that will be introduced when certain limits are reached. These technologies effectively either remove the limit or buy time until a subsequent technology can remove it.

The principles underlying Kahn's work can best be illustrated through the use of two examples: food and energy. One of the sources of collapse in the *Limits of Growth* model was the inability of food supply to keep up with consumption. Kahn, by contrast, sees food production rising so rapidly as to create an eventual abundance of food. This vision, in turn, depends on some specific sources of optimism: (1) Physical resources will not effectively limit production during the next 200 years, and (2) substantial increases can be expected in conventional foods produced by conventional means, conventional foods produced by unconventional means, and unconventional foods produced by unconventional means.

All of these sources of optimism are related to technological progress. The availability of physical resources can be expanded through the use of better (solar-powered, for example) irrigation systems. Conventional food production can be increased by the spread of better farming techniques and by the development of new hybrid seeds. If soils become depleted or scarce, then food can be raised with *hydroponics,* a process using no soil.[8] Finally, Kahn points to the development of a single-cell protein as a viable means of converting municipal waste into a food supplement.

A similar approach is taken when describing the world energy future. The authors of *The Next 200 Years* construct a list of technologies that can provide the transition to solar energy, making the case that solar energy can ultimately sustain a high level of economic activity. The list includes technologies that use coal, either directly or indirectly (such as gas produced from coal); those that exploit the vast world reserves of shale oil; nuclear power (fission, in the

[8]This technique grows plants in recirculating water, complemented by nutrient film. In the advanced versions of this technique, no soil at all is required even for stability. As an interesting aside, the technology was apparently sufficiently advanced in 1981 that it was being used to grow marijuana illegally. See "Pot Growers Turn over New Leaf, Try State-of-the-Art Hydroponics," *The Wall Street Journal* (15 January 1981): 25.

near term, replaced subsequently by fusion); and new solar technologies including windmills, photovoltaics, and ocean thermal power, to mention only a few.

When all of these lists are combined, the prevailing message is that currently recognized technologies can overcome the limitations envisioned by the *Limits to Growth* view. *The Next 200 Years* staff, then, believes that the creators of *Limits to Growth* erred in being myopic; they were too tied to conventional technologies. When the need arises, argue Kahn and his associates, these new technologies will be developed. The cliché, "Necessity is the mother of invention," captures the flavor of their belief that these technologies will be developed as they are needed.

THE ROAD AHEAD

The two models used in this chapter were developed by people trained primarily in the natural sciences rather than the social sciences. This natural-science orientation gives the models a flavor that contrasts rather markedly with the economic models presented in the rest of the book. The most striking difference is the central role that human behavior plays in the social-science models, whereas it is relegated to a rather trivial role in natural-science models.

Perhaps this distinction can best be illustrated through an analogy: When a pipe carrying water springs a leak, we plug the hole. The solution is simple, direct, and usually sufficient. However, in an economic system the most direct approach may not only be ineffective, it may be counterproductive.

Consider, for example, the manner in which the government chose to guarantee "just and reasonable" prices for natural gas, an especially important fuel. Congress imposed ceilings on the prices that pipeline companies, and ultimately producers, could charge. The evidence is now clear that this direct approach created shortages. The price ceiling lowered the quantity of natural gas available by reducing the incentives for suppliers to find new sources.[9] The failure to anticipate the effect of this policy on supplier behavior led to a situation in which the very people the law tried to protect were instead victimized by it. In order to gain a more complete understanding of what challenges to expect of the future, as well as possible solutions, we must consider the role of human behavior.

The Issues

Obviously these visions of the future present us with rather different conceptions of what the future holds, as well as different views of what policy choices should be made. They also suggest that to act as if one vision is correct, when it is not, could prove to be a costly error. Thus, it is important to determine if one of these two views or, alternatively, some third view, is correct.

In order to assess any model or view, it is necessary to address the basic issues:

---

[9]Other problems were caused by the act, as well. See Chapter 7 for a detailed examination of natural gas allocation.

1. Is the problem correctly conceptualized as exponential growth with fixed, immutable resource limits? Does the earth have a finite carrying capacity?

2. If these limits do exist, have they been measured correctly, or, as Kahn argues, has the *Limits to Growth* team been rather myopic in the way they treat resources? How can the carrying-capacity concept be operationalized? Do current levels of economic activity exceed the earth's carrying capacity?

3. How does the economic system respond to scarcities? Does the process involve mainly positive feedback loops? Would it intensify or ameliorate any initial scarcities? Is the overshoot-and-collapse syndrome an accurate portrayal of the future?

4. What is the role of the political system in controlling these problems? In what circumstances is government intervention necessary? Is this intervention uniformly benign, or can it make the situation worse? What roles are appropriate for the executive, legislative, and judicial branches?

5. Many environmental problems involve a considerable degree of uncertainty about the severity of the problem and the effectiveness of possible solutions. Can our economic and political institutions respond to this uncertainty in reasonable ways?

6. Can the economic and political systems work together to eradicate poverty while respecting our obligations to future generations? Or does our obligation to future generations inevitably conflict with the desire to raise the living standards of those currently in absolute poverty? Can short-term and long-term goals be harmonized? Is sustainable development feasible? How could it be achieved? What does it imply about the future of economic activity in the industrialized nations? in the less-industrialized nations?

The rest of the book uses economic analysis to suggest answers to these questions.

An Overview of the Book

In the following chapters you will study the rich and rewarding field of environmental and natural resource economics. The menu of topics is broad and varied. Economics provides a powerful analytical framework for examining the relationships between the environment on the one hand and the economic and political systems on the other. The study of economics can assist in identifying circumstances that give rise to environmental problems, in discovering causes of these problems, and in searching for solutions. Each chapter is an introduction to a unique topic in environmental and natural resource economics, and our overarching focus on growth in a finite environment weaves these topics together into a single theme.

We begin by comparing perspectives being brought to bear on these problems by economists and noneconomists. The manner in which scholars in various disciplines view problems and potential solutions depends on how they organize the available facts, how they interpret those facts, and what kinds of values they apply in translating these interpretations into policy. Before going into a detailed look at environmental problems, we shall compare the ideology of conventional economics to other prevailing ideologies in both the natural and social sciences. This comparison both explains why reasonable people may, upon examining the same set of facts, reach different conclusions and conveys some sense of the strengths and weaknesses of economic analysis as it is applied to environmental problems. Specific evaluation criteria are defined and examples are developed to show how economic criteria can be applied to specific environmental problems.

After examining the major perspectives shaping environmental policy, we shall then turn to the physical limits identified by *Limits to Growth,* the manner in which the economic and political institutions have dealt with the resulting problems, and the potential for improvement in the future. We begin our examination with an inquiry into the nature, causes, and consequences of population growth, a major factor in determining how rapidly the limits could be reached.

The next section of the book deals with several topics traditionally falling within natural resources economics. Energy is discussed as an example of a depletable, nonrecyclable resource. Minerals illustrate how depletable, recyclable resources are allocated over time, including the appropriate role for recycling. The degree to which the current situation approximates this ideal is assessed, with particular attention paid to aspects such as tax policy, disposal costs, and product durability.

The chapters on renewable or replenishable resources (water, food, forestry, fisheries) show that the effectiveness with which current institutions manage renewable resources depends on whether the resources are living or inanimate and whether they are treated as private or common property.

We then move on to an area of public policy—pollution control—that is coming to rely much more heavily on the use of economic incentives to produce the desired response. The overview chapter emphasizes not only the nature of the problems but also differences among policy approaches taken to resolve them. The unique aspects of local air pollution, regional and global air pollution, automobile air pollution, water pollution, and the control of toxic substances are dealt with in five subsequent individual chapters.

Following this examination of the individual environmental and natural resource problems and the policies that can be, and have been, used to ameliorate these problems, the book turns to the growth process itself. Certain questions must be asked: What are the causes and consequences of economic growth? What role do natural resources and environmental control play in the growth process? What is the likely future for economic growth? Is an immediate transition to a zero-economic-growth path (as suggested by *Limits to Growth*) necessary? Or, if unnecessary, is it desirable?

The book closes by assembling the bits and pieces of evidence accumulated in each of the preceding chapters and fusing them into an overall response to the questions posed in this chapter. That chapter also suggests some of the major unresolved issues in environmental policy that are likely to be among those commanding center stage over the next several years or decades.

SUMMARY

Is our society so myopic that it has chosen a path that can only lead to the destruction of society as we now know it? We have examined briefly two studies that provide two different answers to that question. *The Limits to Growth* responds in the affirmative, whereas Kahn and his associates respond negatively. The pessimistic view is based upon the inevitability of exceeding the carrying capacity of the planet as the population and the level of economic activity grow. The optimistic view sees initial scarcity triggering sufficiently powerful reductions in population growth and increases in technological progress that the future brings abundance, not deepening scarcity.

Our examination of these rather different visions has revealed a number of questions that must be answered if we are to assess what the future holds. Seeking answers to these questions requires that we accumulate a much better understanding about how choices are made in economic and political systems and how those choices affect, and are affected by, the natural environment. We shall begin that process in Chapter 2, where the economic approach is developed in broad terms and is contrasted with other conventional approaches.

FURTHER READING

Beckerman, Wilfred. *Two Cheers for the Affluent Society: A Spirited Defense of Economic Growth* (New York: St. Martin's Press, 1974). As the title suggests, an always spirited, frequently irreverent defense of continued economic growth.

Leontief, Wassily. *The Future of the World Economy* (New York: Oxford University Press, 1977). A major empirical study led by a Nobel Laureate in economics commissioned by the United Nations to examine the feasibility of closing the per-capita-income gap between the rich nations and the poor.

Pearce, David, Anil Markandya, and Edward B. Barbier. *Blueprint for a Green Economy* (London: Earthscan Publications, 1989). Originally written as a report for the British government, this document charts a course for the achievement of a more environmentally benign future for economic activity.

Simon, Julian L. *The Ultimate Resource* (Princeton, NJ: Princeton University Press, 1981). The tone of this optimistic study is conveyed by the title of his third chapter, "Can the Supply of Natural Resources Really Be Infinite? Yes!" Simon concludes that the ultimate resource is human imagination, a resource that knows no limit.

World Commission on Environment and Development. *Our Common Future* (Oxford: Oxford University Press, 1987). An enormously influential book that has set the tone for much current environmental activity by the United Nations, it sees third-world poverty as one fundamental cause of environmental problems and a concerted effort to reduce that poverty as a necessary component of any solution.

ADDITIONAL REFERENCES

Cole, H. S. D., ed. *Models of Doom: A Critique of the Limits to Growth* (New York: Universe Books, 1973).

Council on Environmental Quality and Department of State. *The Global 2000 Report to the President of the U.S.: Entering the 21st Century,* Vols. I–III (New York: Pergamon Press, 1980).

Hughes, Barry. *World Futures: A Critical Analysis of Alternatives* (Baltimore, MD: Johns Hopkins University Press, 1985).

Kahn, Herman, William Brown, and Leon Martel. *The Next 200 Years: A Scenario for America and the World* (New York: William Morrow, 1976).

Meadows, Donella H., et al. *Beyond the Limits: Confronting the Global Collapse Envisioning A Sustainable Future* (Post Hills, VT: Chelsea Green Publishing Company, 1992).

Meadows, Donella H., et al. *The Limits to Growth* (New York: Universe Books, 1972).

Mesarovic, Michaklo, and Edward Pestel. *Mankind at the Turning Point: The Second Report to the Club of Rome* (New York: The New American Library, 1974).

Simon, Julian L., and Herman Kahn. *The Resourceful Earth: A Response to Global 2000* (New York: Basil Blackwell, 1984).

DISCUSSION QUESTIONS

1. A central concept in *The Limits to Growth* view of the future is the finiteness of resources. In *The Ultimate Resource*, Julian Simon makes the point that calling the resource base "finite" is misleading. To illustrate this point he uses a yardstick, with its one-inch markings, as an analogy. The distance between two markings is finite—one inch—but an infinite number of points is contained within that finite space. Therefore, in one sense what lies between the markings is finite, but in another, equally meaningful sense, it is infinite. Is the concept of a finite resource base useful or not? Why or why not?

2. This chapter contains two rather different views of the future. Because the validity of these views cannot completely be tested until the time period covered by the forecast has passed (so that predictions can be matched against actual events), how can we ever hope to establish whether one is a better view than the other? What criteria might be proposed for evaluating predictions?

3. Positive and negative feedback loops lie at the core of systematic thinking about the future. As you examine the key forces shaping the future, what examples of positive and negative feedback loops can you uncover?

CHAPTER 2

The Economics Perspective

When you have eliminated the impossible, whatever remains, however improbable, must be the truth.

Sherlock Holmes, from Sir Arthur Conan Doyle's *The Sign of Four*
(1890)

INTRODUCTION

Before we examine specific environmental problems and the policy responses to them, we need to develop and clarify the economics approach so that we will have some sense of the forest before examining each of the trees. Having a feel for the underlying economic principles makes it easier to deal with individual cases and, perhaps more important, to see how they fit together into a comprehensive approach.

In this chapter we examine in some detail the relationship between human actions, as manifested through the economic system, and the environmental consequences of those actions. Based upon this relationship, criteria can then be established for judging the desirability of the outcomes of this relationship. These criteria not only provide a basis for identifying the nature and severity of environmental problems, they also provide a foundation for designing effective policies to deal with the problems identified.

Throughout this chapter the economic point of view will be contrasted with alternative points of view. These contrasts bring the economic approach into sharper focus and stimulate deeper and more critical thinking about all possible approaches.

THE HUMAN ENVIRONMENT RELATIONSHIP

The Environment as an Asset

In economics the environment is viewed as a composite asset that provides a variety of services. It is a very special asset, to be sure, because it provides the life-support systems that sustain our very existence, but it is an asset nonetheless. As with other assets, we wish to prevent

FIGURE 2.1   The Economic System and the Environment

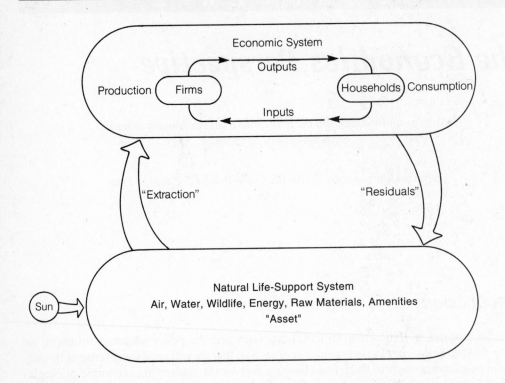

undue depreciation of the value of this asset so that it may continue to provide aesthetic and life-sustaining services.

The environment provides the economy with both raw materials, which are transformed into consumer products by the production process, and energy, which fuels this transformation. Ultimately these raw materials and energy return to the environment as waste products (see Figure 2.1).

The environment also provides services directly to consumers. The air we breathe, the nourishment we receive from food and drink, and the protection we derive from shelter and clothing are all benefits we receive either directly or indirectly from the environment. In addition, anyone who has experienced the exhilaration of white-water canoeing, the total serenity of a wilderness trek, or the breathtaking beauty of a sunset will readily recognize that the environment provides us with a variety of amenities for which no substitute exists.

If the environment is defined broadly enough, the relationship between the environment and the economic system can be considered a *closed system*. For our purposes, a closed system is one in which no inputs (energy, matter, and so on) are received from outside the system and no outputs are transferred outside the system. An *open system*, by contrast, is one in which the system imports or exports matter or energy.

If we restrict our conception of the relationship in Figure 2.1 to our planet and the atmosphere around it, then clearly we do not have a closed system. We derive most of our energy from the sun, either directly or indirectly. We have also sent spaceships well beyond the boundaries of our atmosphere. Nonetheless, for *material* inputs and outputs (not including energy), this system can be treated as a closed system because the amount of exports (such as abandoned space vehicles) and imports (moon rocks, for example) are negligible. Whether the system remains closed depends on the degree to which space exploration opens up the rest of our solar system as a source of raw materials.

The treatment of our planet and its immediate environs as a closed system has an important implication, which is summed up in the *first law of thermodynamics*—a law stating that neither energy nor matter can be created or destroyed.[1] The law implies that the mass of materials flowing into the economic system from the environment has to either accumulate in the economic system or return to the environment as waste. When accumulation stops, the mass of materials flowing into the economic system is equal in magnitude to the mass of waste flowing into the environment.

Excessive wastes can, of course, depreciate the asset; when they exceed the absorptive capacity of nature, wastes reduce the services that the asset provides.[2] Examples are easy to find: Air pollution can cause respiratory problems; polluted drinking water can cause cancer; smog obliterates scenic vistas.

The relationship of people to the environment is also conditioned by another physical law, the *second law of thermodynamics*. Known popularly as the *entropy law*, this law states that entropy increases. *Entropy* is the amount of energy not available for work.[3] Applied to energy processes, this law implies that no conversion from one form of energy to another is completely efficient and that the consumption of energy is an irreversible process. Some energy is always lost during conversion, and the rest, once used, is no longer available for further work. The second law also implies that in the absence of new energy inputs, any closed system must eventually use up its energy. Because energy is necessary for life, when energy ceases, life ceases.

We should remember that our planet is not even approximately a closed system with respect to energy; we gain energy from the sun. The entropy law does suggest, however, that this flow of solar energy establishes an upper limit on the flow of energy that can be sustained. Once the stocks of stored energy (such as fossil fuels and nuclear energy) are gone, the amount of energy available for useful work will be determined solely by this flow and by the amount that can be stored (dams, trees, and so on). Thus, over the very long run, the growth process will be limited by the availability of solar energy and our ability to put it to work.

Two different types of economic analysis can be applied to increase our understanding of the relationship between the economic system and the environment: *Positive* economics attempts to describe *what is, what was,* or *what will be. Normative* economics, by contrast,

---

[1]We know, however, from Einstein's famous equation ($E = mc^2$) that matter can be transformed into energy. This transformation is the source of energy in nuclear power.

[2]A detailed economic model, known as the materials balance model, has been constructed to integrate physical mass flows and the economic system. Description of this model is beyond the scope of this chapter, but can be found in Allen V. Kneese, Robert U. Ayers, and Ralph G. d'Arge, *Economics and the Environment: A Materials Balance Approach* (Washington, DC: Resources for the Future, 1970).

[3]For a technical description of entropy and its relationship to economics see Stuart Burness et al., "Thermodynamic and Economic Concepts as Related to Resource-Use Policies," *Land Economics* 56 (February 1980): 1–9.

deals with *what ought to be*. Disagreements within positive economics can usually be resolved by an appeal to the facts. Normative disagreements, however, involve value judgments.

Both branches are useful. Suppose, for example, we want to be precise about how the economic system treats the environmental asset. Positive economics would be used to describe the service flows and to show how those service flows would be affected by a change in the system (such as the discovery of a new production process). However, positive analysis could not be used to provide any guidance on the question of whether these service flows were optimal. That judgment would have to come from normative economics.

The essence of the normative approach in economics is to maximize the value of the asset. As long as humans exist, they cannot avoid affecting the environment. The issue, therefore, cannot be *whether* humans should have any impact on the environment; rather, the issue is to define the optimal level of impact.

Valuing the Asset

The normative approach attempts to maximize the value of the environmental asset by creating a balance between the preservation and use of that asset. To define this balance, some sort of value must be placed on the various service flows received, including the negative effects of using the environment as a receptacle for waste. In the economic point of view, this valuation is decidedly *anthropocentric,* or human-centered. Effects on the ecosphere are valued in terms of their ultimate effects on humanity. As Example 2.1 indicates, this approach is not universally accepted.

DISTINGUISHING GOOD OUTCOMES FROM BAD

Because choices concerning the treatment of the environmental asset are inevitable, a criterion for judging the desirability of various options is essential. We shall initially consider the criterion typically used to judge resource allocations at a point in time, a useful criterion when choices in various time periods are independent. We shall then expand our horizons and consider criteria for making choices that have effects not only on our generation, but on subsequent generations as well.

Static Efficiency

The chief normative economic criterion for choosing among various allocations occurring at the same point in time is called *static efficiency,* or merely *efficiency.* An allocation of resources is said to satisfy the static-efficiency criterion if the net benefit from the use of those resources is maximized by that allocation. The *net benefit* is simply the excess of benefits over costs resulting from that allocation. But how do we measure benefits and costs?

Benefits can be derived from the demand curve for the resource in question. Demand curves measure the amount of a particular good people would be willing to purchase at various prices. In a typical situation, a person will purchase less of a commodity (or environmental service) the higher its cost. In Figure 2.2, when the price is p_0, q_0 will be purchased, but if the price rises to p_1, purchases will fall to q_1.

EXAMPLE 2.1

Nature Knows Best

The view that the environment should be managed by humans is rather controversial, particularly among ecologists. In *The Closing Circle,* Barry Commoner poses what he calls the third law of ecology: Nature knows best. Commoner elaborates on this view:

> . . . living things accumulate a complex organization of compatible parts; those possible arrangements that are not compatible with the whole are screened out over the long course of evolution. Thus, the structure of a present living thing or the organization of a current natural ecosystem is likely to be "best" in the sense that it has been so heavily screened for disadvantageous components that any new one is very likely to be worse than the present one. [p.43]

"Don't interfere with the ecosystem," is the underlying message.

The conflict between the economic approach and that proposed by Commoner is perhaps best illustrated by the controversy over the Tellico Dam and the snail darter. The Tellico Dam was an ambitious water project on the Little Tennessee River authorized by Congress in 1967. During the summer of 1973, a Tennessee ichthyologist, Dr. David A. Etnier, Jr., discovered a previously unknown species of perch called the snail darter. During 1975, with the dam 75 percent complete, the Secretary of the Interior declared the snail darter an endangered species, which, under the Endangered Species Act of 1973, was sufficient to stop construction of the dam. The Supreme Court in 1978 upheld the act. The final turn of events in this twisted saga came in 1979 when Congress passed, as a rider on an energy and water appropriations bill, an exemption from the Endangered Species Act for the snail darter.

The economic approach stacks up the worth of the project against the worth of the snail darter, both as a species and as a member of the larger ecological system. The principle of minimum interference suggests that regardless of the importance of the snail darter and regardless of the cost, it should be preserved. The extinction of a species is never justified regardless of the circumstances.

Ironically, this clash of principles need not have taken place. An economic analysis showed that the dam was a poor investment, and the snail darter was subsequently successfully transplanted to the nearby Hiwasee River. Nonetheless, this issue serves to illustrate that the seemingly abstract conflict between alternative sets of values can have very practical implications.

Sources: "Endangered Species Curbs," *Congressional Quarterly Almanac* 34 (1978): 707; "Public Works Energy Development Funds," *Congressional Quarterly Almanac* 35 (1979): 223; "Endangered Species Act," *Congressional Quarterly Almanac* 35 (1979): 661; Barry Commoner, *The Closing Circle* (New York: Alfred A. Knopf, 1972).

The meaning of these demand curves can be illustrated with this hypothetical experiment: Suppose you were asked, "At a price of X dollars, how much commodity Y would you buy?" Your answer could be recorded as a point on a diagram such as Figure 2.2. By repeating the question many times for different prices, we could trace out a locus of points. Connecting

FIGURE 2.2   The Individual Demand Curve

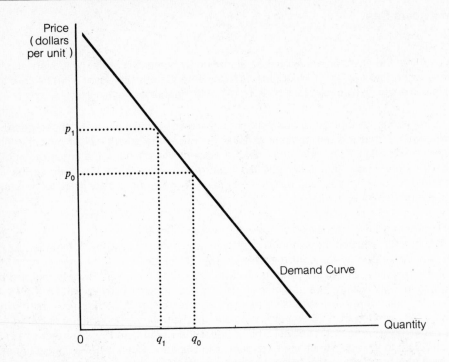

these points would yield an individual *demand curve.* Adding up all of the individual amounts demanded by all individuals at some stipulated price yields one point on the market demand curve. Connecting the points for various prices reveals the whole market demand curve.

For each quantity purchased, the corresponding point on the market demand curve represents the amount of money some person is willing to pay for the last unit of the good. The *total willingness to pay* for some quantity of this good—say, 3 units—is the sum of the willingness to pay for each of the three units. Thus the total willingness to pay for 3 units would be measured by the sum of the willingness to pay for the first, second, and third units respectively. It is now a simple extension to determine that the total willingness to pay is the area under the continuous market demand curve to the left of the allocation in question. For example, in Figure 2.3 the total willingness to pay for 5 units of the commodity is the shaded area.[4] Total willingness to pay is the concept we shall use to define total benefits. Thus *total benefits* are equal to the area under the market demand curve from the origin to the allocation of interest.

---

[4]From simple geometry it can be noticed that for linear demand curves this area is the sum of the areas of the triangle on top plus the rectangle on the bottom. The area of a right triangle is $1/2 \times$ base $\times$ height. Therefore, in our example this area is $1/2(\$5)(5)+(\$5)(5) = \$37.50$.

FIGURE 2.3   The Relationship of Demand to Willingness to Pay

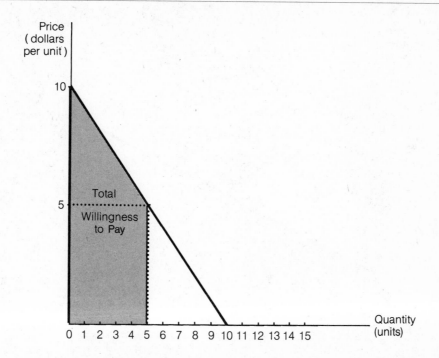

Measuring total costs on the same set of axes involves logic similar to measuring total benefits. It is important to stress that environmental services have costs even though they are produced without any human input. All costs should be measured as opportunity costs.

The opportunity cost for environmental services is the net benefit forgone because the resources providing the service can no longer be used in the next most beneficial way. Resources are not free if they can be put to alternative uses. For example, suppose a particular stretch of river can be used either for white-water canoeing or to generate electric power. Because the dam that generates the power would flood the rapids, the two uses are incompatible. The opportunity cost of saving the river for white-water canoeing is the net benefit forgone (after accounting for the cost of generation and distribution) for electricity. In graphing costs we shall use the marginal opportunity cost curve to correspond to the marginal willingness-to-pay function used earlier to graph benefits. You may remember from your introductory economics course that the *marginal opportunity cost* curve defines the additional cost of producing the last unit. In purely competitive markets, the marginal opportunity cost curve is identical to the supply curve.

Total cost is simply the sum of the marginal costs.[5] The total cost of producing 3 units is equal to the cost of producing the first unit plus the cost of producing the second unit plus the cost of producing the third unit. As with total willingness to pay, the geometric represen-

---

[5]Strictly speaking, the sum of the marginal costs is equal to total variable cost. In the short run this is smaller than total cost by the amount of the fixed cost. For our purposes this distinction is not important.

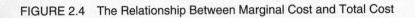

FIGURE 2.4   The Relationship Between Marginal Cost and Total Cost

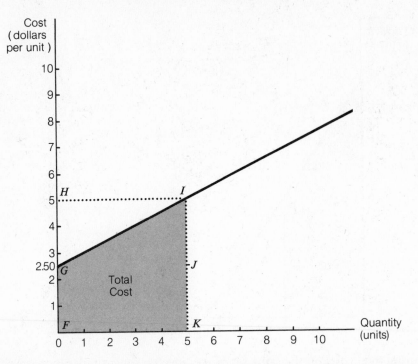

tation of the sum of the individual elements of a continuous marginal cost curve is the area under the marginal cost curve—illustrated in Figure 2.4 by the shaded area *FGIJK*.[6]

Because net benefit is defined as the excess of benefits over costs, it follows that net benefit is equal to that portion of the area under the demand curve which lies above the supply curve. Consider Figure 2.5, which combines the information in Figure 2.3 with that in Figure 2.4.

Our search for the efficient allocation begins by establishing the net benefit for an arbitrary production level—say, 4 units. At 4 units the total benefit is equal to *OLMNS* and the total cost is equal to *OKNS*. *Net benefit is therefore depicted by area KLMN.* Is 4 units an efficient allocation? It is if it maximizes the net benefit. Does 4 units maximize the net benefit?

We can answer that question by establishing whether it is possible to increase the net benefit by producing more or less of the resource. If the net benefit can be increased, clearly the original allocation could not have maximized the net benefit and therefore could not have been efficient. Consider what would happen if society were to choose 5 units instead of 4. What happens to the net benefit? It *increases* by area *MNR*. Because we can find another allocation with greater net benefit, producing 4 units is not efficient. Is producing 5 units efficient? The answer is yes. Let's see why.

---

[6]Notice again that this area is the sum of a right triangle and a rectangle. In Figure 2.4 the total variable cost of producing five units is $18.75. Can you see why?

FIGURE 2.5　The Derivation of Net Benefits

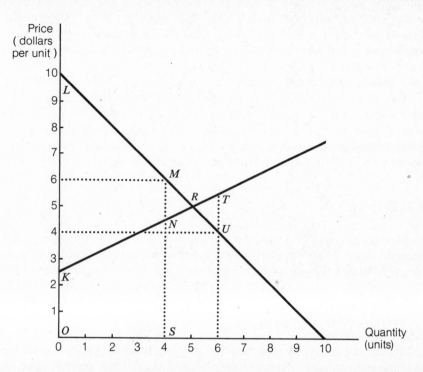

We know that 5 units convey more net benefit than 4. If this allocation is efficient, it must also be true that the net benefit is smaller for levels of production higher than 5. Notice that the additional cost of producing the sixth unit (the area under the marginal cost curve) is *larger* than the additional benefit received from producing it (the corresponding area under the demand curve). Therefore, the triangle *RTU* represents the *reduction* in net benefit that occurs if 6 units are produced rather than 5.

Because the net benefit is reduced both by producing fewer than 5 units and by producing more than 5, we conclude that 5 units is the production level that maximizes net benefit. Therefore, from our definition, a level of 5 units constitutes an efficient allocation.[7] One implication of this example, which will be very useful in succeeding chapters, is that *net benefits are maximized when the marginal benefit is equal to the marginal cost.*

The ethical basis for this criterion is derived from a concept called *Pareto optimality*, named after the Italian-born, Swiss economist Vilfredo Pareto, who first proposed it around the turn of the twentieth century. An allocation is said to be *Pareto optimal* if no rearrangement of that allocation could benefit some people without any deleterious effects on at least one other person. (A rearrangement of a resource allocation could involve changing the level produced or changing the shares received by each of the ultimate users of the resource.)

---

[7]Can you calculate the monetary worth of the net benefit? It is the sum of two right triangles and it equals $1/2(\$5)(5)$ + $1/2(\$2.50)(5)$ *or* $18.75. Can you see why?

Allocations that do *not* satisfy this definition are suboptimal. It is always possible to re-arrange suboptimal allocations so that some people are better off and no one is hurt by the re-arrangement. In any rearrangement from a suboptimal allocation to an optimal one, the gain-ers would gain more than the losers lose. Therefore, the gainers could use a portion of their gains to compensate the losers sufficiently to ensure they were at least as well off as they were prior to the reallocation.

Efficient allocations are Pareto optimal. Because net benefits are maximized by an effi-cient allocation, it is not possible to increase the net benefit by rearranging the allocation. Without an increase in the net benefit, the gainers could not sufficiently compensate the losers; the gains to the gainers would necessarily be smaller than the losses to the losers.

Inefficient allocations are inferior because they do not maximize the net benefit. Failing to maximize net benefit misses an opportunity to eliminate waste.

Dynamic Efficiency

The static-efficiency criterion is very useful for comparing resource allocations when time is not an important factor. However, many of the decisions made now affect the value of the as-set for future generations. Time *is* a factor. Exhaustible energy resources, once used, are gone. Renewable biological resources (such as fisheries or forests) can be overharvested, leaving smaller and possibly weaker populations for future generations. Persistent pollutants can ac-cumulate over time. How can we evaluate different choices when the benefits and costs may occur at different points in time?

The traditional criterion used to address this problem is called *dynamic efficiency,* a gen-eralization of the static-efficiency concept already developed. In this generalization, the crite-rion provides a way for thinking not only about the magnitude of benefits and costs, but also about timing. In order to incorporate timing, the criterion must provide a way to compare the net benefit received in one period with the net benefit received in another. The concept that allows this comparison is called present value. Therefore, before defining dynamic efficiency, we must define present value.

Present value explicitly incorporates the time value of money. A dollar today invested at 10 percent interest yields $1.10 a year from now (the return of the $1 principal plus $0.10 in-terest). The present value of $1.10 received one year from now is therefore $1 because, given $1 now, you can turn it into $1.10 a year from now by investing it at 10 percent interest. We can find the present value of any amount of money (X) received one year from now by com-puting $X/(1 + r)$, where r is the appropriate interest rate (10 percent in this example).

What could your dollar earn in two years at r percent interest? Because of compound in-terest, the amount would be $\$1(1 + r)(1 + r) = \$1.00(1 + r)^2$. It follows then that the present value of X received two years from now is $X/(1 + r)^2$.

By now the pattern should be clear. The *present value* of a *one-time* net benefit received n years from now is

$$PV[B_n] = \frac{B_n}{(1 + r)^n}$$

The present value of a *stream* of net benefits $B_0, \ldots, B_n$ received over a period of n years is computed as

$$PV[B_0, \ldots, B_n] = \sum_{i=0}^{n} \frac{B_i}{(1 + r)^i}$$

where r is the appropriate interest rate and B_0 is the amount of net benefits received immediately. The process of calculating the present value is called *discounting,* and the rate r is referred to as the *discount rate.*[8]

The number that results from a present-value calculation has a straightforward interpretation. Suppose you were investigating an allocation that would yield the following pattern of net benefits on the last day of each of the next five years: $3,000, $5,000, $6,000, $10,000, $12,000. If you use an interest rate of 6 percent ($r = 0.06$) and the formula just given, you will discover that this stream has a present value of $29,210.

What does that number mean? If you put $29,210 in a savings account earning 6 percent interest and wrote yourself checks respectively for $3,000, $5,000, $6,000, $10,000, and $12,000 on the last day of each of the next five years, your last check would just restore the account to a zero balance. Thus, you should be indifferent to receiving $29,210 now or receiving the specific five-year stream of benefits totaling $36,000; given one you can get the other. The method is called present value because it translates everything back to its current worth.

It is now possible to define dynamic efficiency. An allocation of resources across n time periods is dynamically efficient if it maximizes the present value of net benefits that could be received from all the possible ways of allocating those resources over the n periods.

To illustrate, we can use the dynamic-efficiency criterion to define an efficient allocation of a depletable, nonrecyclable resource. Dynamic efficiency assumes that society's objective is to balance the current and subsequent uses of the resources by maximizing the present value of the net benefit derived from the use of the resource.

Consider a case in which a fixed supply of a resource is to be allocated over time. Suppose further that the marginal cost of extracting this resource is constant, and that the demand curve is stable over time.

What would the efficient allocation of this resource be? The dynamically efficient allocation of this resource has to satisfy the condition that the present value of the marginal net benefit from the last unit in each period should equal the present value of the marginal net benefit in any other period. Otherwise we could increase the present value of net benefits by removing some of the resource from a period with the low marginal present value of net benefits and moving it to the period with high marginal present value of net benefits. The only time this rearrangement cannot increase the present value of net benefits is when the present values of the marginal net benefits in each period are equal.

---

[8]The discount rate should equal the social opportunity cost of capital. See Raymond Mikesell, *The Rate of Discount for Evaluating Public Projects* (Washington, DC: American Enterprise Institute for Public Policy Research, 1977) for detailed examination of the reasons for this choice and its implications. We shall examine the question of whether private firms can be expected to use the socially correct discount rate in Chapter 3 and the question of how the discount rate is chosen by the government in Chapter 4.

This immediately has an implication known as the *r-percent rule*. When the demand curve is stable over time and the marginal cost of extraction is constant, the rate of increase in the current value of the marginal net benefit is equal to r, the discount rate. Thus, in a succeeding time period, the marginal net benefit would be $1 + r$ times as large as it was in the preceding period.[9] Marginal net benefits rise at rate r in an efficient allocation in order to preserve the balance between present and future production.

Scarcity imposes an opportunity cost, which we call the *marginal user cost*. When resources are scarce, greater current use diminishes future opportunities. The marginal user cost is the present value of these forgone opportunities at the margin. Uses of those resources that would have been appropriate in the absence of scarcity may no longer be appropriate once scarcity is present. Using large quantities of water to keep lawns lush and green may be wholly appropriate for an area with sufficiently large replenishable water supplies, but quite inappropriate when it denies drinking water to future generations. Failure to take the higher scarcity value of water into account in the present will lead to an inefficiency or an extra cost to society due to the extra scarcity imposed on the future. This additional marginal value that scarcity creates is the marginal user cost.

The allocation of the resource over time is affected by the discount rate. The larger the discount rate is, the greater is the amount of the resource allocated to the earlier periods. The general conclusion is that higher discount rates tend to skew resource extraction toward the present because they give the future less weight in balancing the relative value of present and future resource use.

Sustainability

Although no generally accepted standards of fairness or justice exist, some have more prominent support than others. One such standard concerns the treatment of future generations.

What legacy should earlier generations leave to later ones? This is a particularly difficult issue because, in contrast to other groups for which we may want to insure fair treatment, future generations cannot articulate their wishes, much less negotiate with current generations. ("We'll take your radioactive wastes, if you leave us plentiful supplies of titanium.")

One starting point for intergenerational equity is provided by philosopher John Rawls in his monumental work, *A Theory of Justice*. Rawls suggests that one way to derive general principles of justice is to place, hypothetically, every person in an original position behind a "veil of ignorance." This veil of ignorance would prevent people from knowing their eventual position in society. Once behind this veil, they would decide on rules to govern the society that they would, after the decision, be forced to live in.

In our context this approach would suggest a hypothetical meeting of all members of present and future generations to decide on rules for allocating resources among generations. Because these members are prevented by the veil of ignorance from knowing the generation

---

[9]The condition that marginal user cost rises at rate r is true only when the marginal cost of extraction is constant. For a treatment of the more complicated case when marginal cost of extraction rises with the cumulative amount extracted, see T. H. Tietenberg, *Environmental and Natural Resource Economics* (New York: HarperCollins, 1992).

to which they will belong, they will not be excessively conservationist (lest they turn out to be a member of an earlier generation) or excessively exploitative (lest they become a member of a later generation).

What kind of rule would emerge from such a meeting? Perhaps the most common answer is known as the sustainability criterion. The *sustainability criterion* suggests that, at a minimum, the average individual in future generations should be left no worse off than the average individual in current generations. Allocations that impoverish future generations in order to enrich current generations are, according to this criterion, patently unfair.

One weakness of this criterion is that it does not bring sufficient clarity to the issue of population growth. Meeting the needs of future generations is obviously much harder if the population is large. What level of population is implied in the sustainability definition? That remains an open question.

In essence the sustainability criterion suggests that earlier generations are at liberty to use resources that would thereby be denied to future generations as long as the well-being of future generations remains just as high as that of all previous generations. On the other hand, diverting resources from future use would violate the sustainability criterion if it reduced the well-being of future generations below the level enjoyed by preceding generations.

One of the implications of this definition of sustainability is that it is possible to use resources (even if that denies their use to future generations) as long as the interests of future generations are protected. How could those interests be adequately protected?

One possibility involves sharing the gains from the use of the resources with future generations by investing them in capital. For example, an exhaustible oil deposit could be exploited as long as a sufficient portion of the proceeds were invested in capital (hospitals, roads, schools?), which could be used to increase the welfare of future generations.[10]

But this strategy may not go far enough. The assumption that physical capital can substitute for environmental resources is untenable for certain categories of environmental resources. Though we can contemplate the replacement of naturally breathable air with universal air conditioning in domed cities, both the expense and the artificiality of this approach make it an absurd compensation device. Clearly the issue of compensation must be approached carefully.

One distinction that has become important in thinking about compensation is the distinction between two types of capital—physical capital and natural capital. *Physical capital* incorporates the human-made stock of equipment, buildings, and so on, whereas *natural capital* refers to the stock of environmental and natural resources. These two types of capital have limited substitution possibilities. Indeed, much of the ecological economics community sees them as complements, not substitutes.[11]

To recognize the limited substitution possibilities between physical and natural capital and to provide a more operational sustainability criterion than nondeclining welfare, the defi-

---

[10]The derivation of this principle (known as the Hartwick rule) can be found in J. M. Hartwick, "Intergenerational Equity and the Investing of Rents from Exhaustible Resources," *American Economic Review* 67 (1977): 972–74.

[11]See, for example, F. Berkes and C. Folke, "A Systems Perspective on the Interrelations Between Natural, Human-Made, and Cultural Capital" *Ecological Economics* 5, No. 1 (March 1992): 1.

nition of sustainability can be further refined. To distinguish this definition from the former one, we will call this *modified sustainability*. According to the modified sustainability criterion, the value of the stock of natural capital should not decline over time. According to this modified definition, one form of natural capital could be decreased only when another form of natural capital was increased as compensation.[12]

Because of the pitfalls of treating all natural capital as homogeneous, even this definition is not above reproach. Some resources, such as air and water, are essential for sustaining life (both human and nonhuman) whereas others (such as specific minerals) are less so. This has given rise to differentiating "critical" natural capital from "other" natural capital.[13] Critical natural resources would be preserved intact. Other forms of natural capital remain open to the possibility of substitution. Although the boundary between critical and other natural capital remains subjective and therefore not completely satisfactory, most people seem to believe that the distinction has some merit.[14]

In order to be useful guides, our sustainability and efficiency criteria must be neither incompatible nor synonymous. Do these criteria meet that test?

They do. Not all sustainable allocations are sustainable and not all sustainable allocations are efficient, yet some efficient allocations satisfy the sustainability criterion and some sustainable allocations are efficient.

The juxtaposition of these criteria suggests a specific strategy for policy. Among the possible uses of resources that fulfill the sustainability criterion, choose the one that maximizes either dynamic or static efficiency as appropriate.[15] In this formulation the sustainability criterion acts as an overriding constraint on social decisions. Although this rules out nonsustainable allocations, it fails to specify which allocation among the infinite number of sustainable allocations is to be chosen. That is where the efficiency criterion comes in. It provides a means of choosing among the sustainable allocations so as to minimize waste.

This turns out to be a very helpful set of criteria in terms of policy. Many unsustainable allocations are the result of inefficient behavior. Correcting the inefficiency can either restore sustainability or move the economy a long way in that direction. Furthermore, and this is important, correcting inefficiencies can frequently produce win-win situations. Win-win situations are created when the various parties affected by the change are better off after the change than before. Win-win situations are possible because removing an inefficiency in-

---

[12]Deep ecologists believe that both the level of the current stock of environmental resources and the composition of that stock should be preserved or enhanced.

[13]See, for example, the use of this distinction to create a policy to protect wetlands in Kerry Turner and Tom Jones, eds., *Wetlands: Market and Intervention Failures* (London: Earthscan Publications, 1991).

[14]In principle this distinction could be made by economic analysis. Resources that have higher values in preservation than in use could be preserved. In practice this is difficult because many of the services provided by critical resources are very difficult to value. Although new valuation techniques have arisen to meet this need, most economists would agree that they are not yet sufficiently developed and reliable to be used for this purpose. See the discussion of this point in Chapter 4.

[15]Appropriateness in this case is determined by whether time is a crucial element in the analysis. If it is, use dynamic efficiency. If not, static efficiency will suffice.

creases the net benefits. These increased net benefits can be used to compensate those who might otherwise lose from the change. Compensating losers reduces the opposition to change, thereby making change more likely.

Do our economic and political institutions normally produce outcomes consistent with this strategy? In future chapters we provide explicit answers to this question.

SUMMARY

The relationship between humanity and the environment requires many choices. Some basis for making rational choices is absolutely necessary. If they are not made by design, decisions will be made by default.

The economics approach views the environment as a composite asset, supplying a variety of services to humanity. The intensity and composition of those services depends on the actions of humans as constrained by physical laws, such as the first and second laws of thermodynamics.

Economics has two rather different means of enhancing understanding of environmental and natural resource economics. Positive economics is useful in describing the actions of people and the impact of those actions on the environmental asset. Normative economics can provide guidance on how optimal service flows can be defined and achieved.

Normative economics suggests two precise criteria for judging the optimal level and composition of services: efficiency and sustainability. The former suggests maximizing the present value of net benefits to society. When the use of a natural resource by one generation introduces scarcity or increases the degree of scarcity of that resource in subsequent periods, the efficient allocation must take the marginal user cost into account. Failing to do this would cause a smaller than efficient amount of the resource to be conserved. The sustainability criterion allows us to judge the fairness rather than the efficiency of these intertemporal allocations. Used together these criteria provide a powerful framework for evaluating the success or failure of our social institutions in providing an appropriate balance between the desire to provide enhanced opportunities for the poor and the desire to preserve the environment. Future chapters will determine the degree to which our social institutions yield allocations that conform to these criteria.

FURTHER READING

Arrow, Kenneth J. *The Limits of Organization* (New York: W. W. Norton, 1974). In this short but pithy book, Nobel Laureate Kenneth Arrow analyzes why—and how—human beings organize their common lives to overcome the basic economic problem of allocating scarce resources. Alternative models of achieving efficient allocations are explored, including markets and governments.

Daly, Herman E., and John B. Cobb, Jr. *For the Common Good: Redirecting the Economy Toward Community, the Environment and a Sustainable Future* (Boston: Beacon Press, 1989). Written by an economist and a theologian, this powerfully argued book suggests that the world view that undergirds modern economics has some fatal flaws and suggests some redirections in this world view.

Schelling, Thomas C. *Micromotives and Macrobehavior* (New York: W. W. Norton, 1978). Through familiar and readily grasped examples, Professor Schelling demonstrates how members of a society tend to be blind to the collective consequences of their separate decisions.

ADDITIONAL REFERENCES

Butlin, J. A., ed. *The Economics of Environmental and Natural Resource Policy* (Boulder, CO: Westview Press, 1981).

Dorfman, Robert, and Nancy S. Dorfman, eds. *Economics of the Environment: Selected Readings,* 2nd ed. (New York: W. W. Norton, 1977).

Fisher, Anthony C., *Resource and Environmental Economics* (Cambridge, UK: Cambridge University Press, 1981).

Kneese, Allen V., Robert U. Ayers, and Ralph C. d'Arge. *Economics and the Environment: A Materials Balance Approach* (Washington, DC: Resources for the Future, 1970).

Kneese, Allen V. *Economics and the Environment* (New York: Penguin Books, 1977).

Krutilla, John. "Conservation Reconsidered," *The American Economic Review* 57 (September 1968): 777–86.

Rawls, John. *A Theory of Justice* (Cambridge, MA: The Belknap Press of Harvard University Press, 1971).

Siebert, Horst. *Economics of the Environment* (Lexington, MA: Lexington Books, 1981).

DISCUSSION QUESTIONS

1. It has been suggested that we should use the "net energy" criterion to make choices among various types of energy. Net energy is defined as the total energy content in the energy source minus the energy required to extract, process, and deliver energy to consumers. According to this criterion, we should use those sources with the highest net energy content first.

   Would the dynamic efficiency criterion and the net energy criterion be expected to yield the same choice? Why or why not?

2. The notion of sustainability is not the same in the natural sciences as in economics. In the natural sciences, sustainability frequently means maintaining a constant *physical* flow of each and every resource (e.g., fish or wood from the forest), whereas in economics it means maintaining the *value* of those service flows. When might the two criteria lead to different choices? Why?

CHAPTER 3

Rights, Rents, and Remedies

The charming landscape which I saw this morning, is indubitably made up of some twenty or thirty farms. Miller owns this field, Locke that, and Manning the woodland beyond. But none of them owns the landscape. There is a property in the horizon which no man has but he whose eye can integrate all the parts, that is, the poet. This is the best part of these men's farms, yet to this their land deeds give them no title.

RALPH WALDO EMERSON, NATURE (1836)

INTRODUCTION

In the last chapter we discussed specific criteria for making rational choices about the relationship between the economic system and the environment. According to those criteria, an environmental problem exists when resource allocations are either inefficient or expected to leave future generations worse off than we are.

Under what conditions would breaches of efficiency or sustainability occur? Why would individual or group interests diverge from those of society at large? What circumstances give rise to this division of interests, and what can be done about it? One useful way to examine this question is based on the concept known as a *property right*. In this chapter we will explore this concept and how it can be used to understand why the environmental asset can be undervalued by both the market and governmental policy. We shall also discuss how the government and the market can, on occasion, use knowledge of property rights and their effects on incentives to orchestrate a coordinated approach to resolving these difficulties.

PROPERTY RIGHTS

Property Rights and the Environment

The manner in which producers and consumers use environmental resources depends on the property rights governing those resources. In economics, *property rights* refers to a bundle of entitlements, privileges, and limitations defining the owner's rights to use a resource.

By examining such entitlements and how they affect human behavior, we will better understand how environmental problems arise from government and market allocations.

These property rights can be vested either with individuals, as in a capitalist economy, or with the state, as in a centrally planned socialist economy. It is not uncommon to hear that the source of environmental problems in a capitalist economy is the market system itself, or more specifically, the pursuit of profits. You may have heard this point of view expressed as, "Corporations are more interested in profits than in the needs of people." Those who espouse this view look longingly at centrally planned economies as a means of avoiding environmental excess.

Simple answers rarely suffice for complex problems; environmental and natural resource problems are not an exception. Centrally planned economies, such as the former Soviet Union, have not avoided pollution excesses (Example 3.1). On the other hand, the pursuit of profits is not inevitably inconsistent with fulfilling the needs of the people. In fact, this pursuit is often the essential ingredient in meeting people's needs. How can we tell when the pursuit of profits is consistent with societal objectives, such as efficiency and sustainability, and when it is not?

Efficient Property-Right Structures

Let's begin by describing the structure of property rights that could produce efficient allocations in a well-functioning market economy. An efficient structure has four main characteristics:

1. *Universality*. All resources are privately owned and all entitlements completely specified.
2. *Exclusivity*. All benefits and costs accrued as a result of owning and using the resources should accrue to the owner, and only to the owner, either directly or indirectly by sale to others.
3. *Transferability*. All property rights should be transferable from one owner to another in a voluntary exchange.
4. *Enforceability*. Property rights should be secure from involuntary seizure or encroachment by others.

An owner of a resource with a well-defined property right (one exhibiting these four characteristics) has a powerful incentive to use that resource efficiently because a decline in the value of that resource represents a personal loss. A farmer who owns the land has an incentive to fertilize and irrigate it because the resulting increased production raises his income level. Similarly, he has an incentive to rotate crops when that raises the productivity of his land.

When well-defined property rights are exchanged, as in a market economy, efficiency is facilitated. We can illustrate this point by examining the incentives consumers and producers face when a well-defined system of property rights is in place. Because the seller has the right to prevent the consumer from consuming the product in the absence of payment, the consumer must pay to receive the product. Given a market price, the consumer decides how

E X A M P L E   3 . 1

Pollution in Centrally Planned Economies

Because environmental problems are thought to be caused by a divergence between individual incentives and collective incentives, it is not uncommon to hear that centrally planned economies avoid environmental problems. Centralizing power in the state, as occurs in a centrally planned economy, is believed to allow collective decisions to be made at the outset.

Studies of air and water pollution in the Soviet Union and other Eastern European countries suggest that the problems found in market economies occur with equal intensity in the Eastern block. Copsa Mica, Romania, for example, is called Europe's most polluted urban area. Weakened by acid rain, monuments in Krakow, Poland, are crumbling. Women with newborn babies in some parts of Eastern Europe have priority access to bottled water because tap water is considered injurious to infant health. Some 2.3 million people in Russia still live within the area contaminated by radioactivity from the meltdown of the Chernobyl nuclear reactor in 1986.

How can this be? Goldman suggests that the centralized planning system created different, but no less potent, divergences between individual and collective incentives. For example, as of 1970, 65 percent of all factories in the largest Soviet republic, the Russian Soviet Federated Socialist Republic, discharged their waste into the water without any attempt to clean it up. They did this because the managers were being judged solely in terms of output, not in terms of the harm they caused to the environment. The central plans that set the priorities to be followed by the managers simply emphasized economic growth over the environment.

In his summary Goldman states:

Not private enterprise but industrialization is the primary cause of environmental disruption. This suggests that state ownership of all the productive resources is no cure-all.

Sources: Marshall I. Goldman, "The Convergence of Environmental Disruption," in *Ecology and Economics: Controlling Pollution in the 70's,* Marshall I. Goldman, ed. (Englewood Cliffs, NJ: Prentice-Hall, 1972): 211–24; D. Powell, "The Social Costs of Modernization: Ecological Problems in the USSR," *World Politics* 22 (1971): 327–34; Marshall I. Goldman, "Economics of Environmental and Renewable Resources in Socialist Systems," in *Handbook of Natural Resource and Energy Economics: Vol. II,* Allen V. Kneese and James L. Sweeney, eds. (Amsterdam: North-Holland, 1985): 725–45; Louis Berney, "Black Town of Transylvania Is Called Europe's Most Polluted" *The Boston Globe* (28 March 1990): 2; Hilary F. French, "Industrial Wasteland" *Worldwatch* (November/December 1988): 21–30.

much to purchase by choosing that amount which maximizes his or her individual net benefit (Figure 3.1).

The consumer's net benefit is the area under the demand curve minus the area representing cost. The cost to the consumer is the area under the price line because that area represents the expenditure on the commodity. Obviously, for a given price P^*, consumer net benefit is maximized by choosing to purchase Q_d units. Area A is then the geometric representation of the net benefit received, known as *consumer surplus,* bounded on the left by the vertical axis and on the right by the quantity of the good being considered.

FIGURE 3.1   The Consumer's Choice

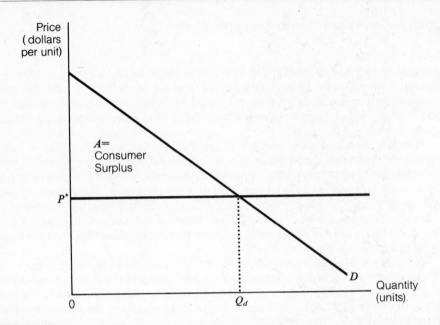

Meanwhile, sellers face a similar choice (Figure 3.2). Given price P^*, an individual seller maximizes his or her own net benefits by choosing to sell Q_s units. The net benefit received (Area B) by the seller is called *producer surplus*. It is the area under the price line that lies over the marginal cost curve, bounded on the left by the vertical axis and on the right by the quantity of the good being considered.

The price level that producers and consumers face will adjust until supply equals demand, as depicted in Figure 3.3. Given that price, consumers maximize their surplus, producers maximize their surplus, and the market clears.

Is this allocation efficient? Using our definition of static efficiency from the previous chapter, it is clear the answer is yes. The net benefit is maximized by the market allocation, and, as seen in Figure 3.3, it is equal to the sum of consumer and producer surplus. Thus we have not only established a procedure for measuring net benefits, we have also established a means of describing how the net benefits are distributed between consumers and producers.

This distribution is crucially significant. Efficiency is *not* achieved because consumers and producers are seeking efficiency. They aren't! In a system with well-defined property rights and competitive markets in which to sell those rights, producers try to maximize their surplus and consumers try to maximize their surplus. The price system, then, induces those self-interested parties to make choices that are efficient from the point of view of society as a whole. It channels the energy motivated by self-interest into socially productive paths.

Though familiarity may have dulled our appreciation, it is noteworthy that a system designed to produce a harmonious and congenial outcome could function effectively while allowing consumers and producers so much individual freedom in making choices. This is truly a remarkable accomplishment.

FIGURE 3.2   The Producer's Choice

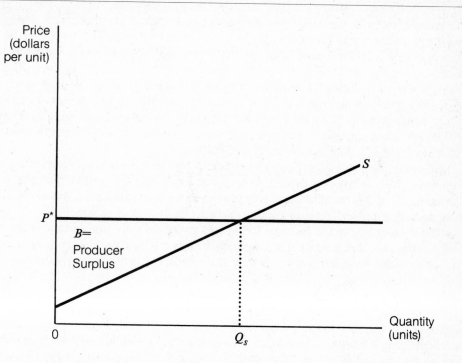

FIGURE 3.3   Market Equilibrium

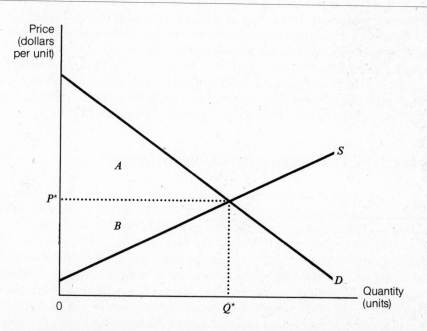

Scarcity Rent

Most natural resource industries give rise to a form of rent called *scarcity rent*. David Ricardo was the first economist to recognize the existence of scarcity rent. Ricardo suggested that the price of land was determined by the least-fertile marginal unit of land. Because the price had to be sufficiently high to allow the poorer land to be brought into production, other, more-fertile land could be farmed at an economic profit. Competition could not erode that profit because the amount of land was limited and lower prices would serve only to reduce the supply of land below demand. The only way to expand production would be to bring additional, less-fertile land (more costly to farm) into production; consequently, additional production does not lower price, as it does in a constant-cost industry.

Other circumstances also give rise to scarcity rent for natural resources. We have already shown how the allocation of depletable resources gives rise to a positive marginal user cost. The existence of this marginal user cost implies that the efficient price will exceed the marginal cost of extraction, creating a scarcity rent for those resources as well.

The scarcity rent would be equal to the area under the price line and above the marginal cost of extraction. This scarcity rent is appropriated by the owner of the resource and becomes part of his or her producer surplus as long as property rights are correctly defined. A similar scarcity rent would exist for scarce renewable resources.

It is important to clear up one possible source of confusion. Why is user cost included as part of producer surplus when other costs, such as extraction costs, are not? The distinction between these costs lies in whether or not they are actually paid. The marginal extraction cost is actually paid; it consumes resources. The marginal user cost, in contrast, is an opportunity cost, a cost that would be paid in the form of reduced profits or a reduced net benefit only if the owner of the resource should choose not to extract the last unit. When the profit-maximizing allocation is chosen, this cost is not actually borne, so the owner of the resource appropriates it as scarcity rent. This source of producer surplus is not eliminated by competition. Even when time is an important consideration in the presence of well-defined property rights, market allocations and efficient allocations coincide.

Although it can be and frequently is efficient, the economic system is not always efficient. Environmental problems represent one important class of circumstances in which it is not. If cases of inefficient depreciation of the environment are to be rectified, we must understand the circumstances that lead to inefficiency and what can be done about them.

EXTERNALITIES AS A SOURCE OF MARKET FAILURE

Exclusivity is one of the chief characteristics of an efficient property-rights structure. This characteristic is frequently violated in practice. One broad class of violations occurs when an agent making a decision does not bear all of the consequences of his or her action.

Suppose two firms are located by a river. The first produces steel; the second, somewhat downstream, operates a resort hotel. Both use the river, though in different ways. The steel firm uses it as a receptacle for waste; the resort uses it to attract customers seeking water recreation—swimming, sailing, and water skiing. If these two facilities are owned by different owners, an efficient use of the water is not likely to result. Because the steel plant does not bear the cost of reduced business at the resort that results from waste being dumped into the

FIGURE 3.4   Market Allocation With Pollution

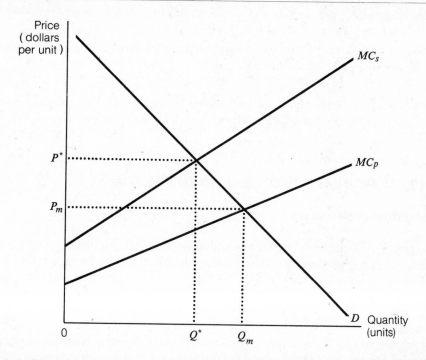

river, it is not likely to be very sensitive to that cost in its decision making. As a result, it could be expected to dump too much waste into the river and an efficient allocation of the river would not be attained.

This situation is referred to as an externality. An *externality* exists whenever the welfare of some agent, either a firm or household, directly depends not only on his or her activities, but also on activities under the control of some other agent. In the example, the increased waste in the river imposed an external cost on the resort, a cost the steel firm could not be counted upon to consider appropriately in deciding the amount of waste to dump.

The effects of this external cost on the steel industry can be seen in Figure 3.4, which depicts the market for steel. Steel production inevitably involves producing pollution as well as steel. The demand for steel is shown by the demand curve D, and the private marginal cost of producing the steel (exclusive of pollution control and damage) is depicted as MC_p. Because society considers both the cost of pollution and the cost of producing the steel, the social marginal cost function (MC_s) includes both of these costs.

If the steel industry faced no outside control on its emission levels, it would seek to produce Q_m. That choice, in a competitive setting, would maximize their private producer surplus. But that is clearly not efficient because the net benefit is maximized at Q^*, not Q_m.

With the assistance of Figure 3.4, we can draw a number of conclusions about market allocations of commodities causing pollution externalities:

1.   The output of the commodity is too large.
2.   Too much pollution is produced.

3. The prices of products responsible for pollution are too low.

4. As long as the costs are external, no incentives to search for ways to yield less pollution per unit of output are introduced by the market.

5. Recycling and reuse of the polluting substances are discouraged because release into the environment is so inefficiently cheap.

The effects of a market imperfection for one commodity end up affecting the demands for raw materials, labor, and so on. The ultimate effects are felt through the entire economy.

IMPROPERLY DESIGNED PROPERTY-RIGHTS SYSTEMS

Common-Property Resources

The first class of problems with market allocations occurs when the property rights to the resource lack one or more of the four characteristics described earlier. Perhaps the largest category of resources for which this is true is what are called common-property resources. *Common-property resources* are those that are not exclusively controlled by a single agent or source. If access to these resources is not restricted, they can be exploited on a first-come, first-served basis.

It is not difficult to derive a host of examples. Two of our important life-sustaining resources, air and water, are treated by our legal system as common-property resources. Other examples include migratory wild birds, fish, and animal populations. Even oil can, under certain circumstances, become a common-property resource. If a large subsurface "pool" of oil underlies property rights defined in terms of a surface area that is small in comparison to the geographic coverage of the pool, several different companies could end up tapping the same source of oil. Because none of these would have exclusive control over extraction from this field, the oil in this field would become a common-property resource.

Animal populations, such as the American bison, have also been treated as common property. In the early history of the United States bison were plentiful; that they were common property was not a problem. Frontier people who needed hides or meat could easily get whatever they needed; the aggressiveness of any one hunter did not affect the time and effort expended by other hunters. In the absence of scarcity, efficiency was not threatened by treating the herd as a common-property resource.

As the years slipped by, however, the demand for bison increased and scarcity became a factor. As the number of hunters increased, the time came when every additional unit of hunting activity increased the amount of time and effort required to produce a given yield of bison.

With several hunters sharing nonexclusive property rights to the bison, the resulting allocation would not be efficient. No individual hunter would have an incentive to protect that scarcity rent by restricting the hunting effort. Without exclusive rights, individual hunters would exploit the resource until profits (and net benefits) were zero. This inefficient allocation results because individual hunters cannot appropriate the scarcity rent; therefore, they ignore it. One of the losses from further exploitation that would be incorporated by exclusive owners—the opportunity cost of overexploitation—is not part of their decision-making process as long as access is not restricted.

Two characteristics of this formulation of the common-property allocation are worth noting: (1) In the presence of sufficient demand, unrestricted access will cause common-property resources to be overexploited, and (2) the scarcity rent is dissipated—no one appropriates the rent, so it is lost.

Why does this happen? Unlimited access destroys the incentive to conserve. An individual hunter who can preclude others from hunting this stock has an incentive to keep the herd at an efficient level. This restraint results in lower costs in the form of less time and effort expended to produce a given yield of bison. On the other hand, an individual hunter exploiting a common-property resource would not have any incentive to conserve because the benefits derived from restraint would, at least to some extent, be captured by other hunters. Thus unrestricted access to common-property resources promotes an inefficient allocation.

Public Goods

Resources known as *public goods* present a particularly complex category of environmental problems. Public goods are defined as those that exhibit consumption indivisibilities and, additionally, are fully accessible to all.

Consumption is said to be *indivisible* when one person's consumption of a good does not diminish the amount available for others. Several common environmental resources are public goods, including not only the "charming landscape" referred to in the chapter-opening quote by Emerson, but also clean air, clean water, and biological diversity.[1]

Biological diversity includes two related concepts: the amount of genetic variability among individuals within a single species, and the number of species within a community of organisms.

Genetic diversity, critical to species survival in the natural world, has also proved to be important in the development of new crops and livestock.[2] It enhances the opportunities for crossbreeding and thus the development of superior strains. For example, the availability of different strains was the key in developing a new disease-resistant barley.

Because of the interdependence of species within ecological communities, any particular species may have a value to the community far beyond its intrinsic value. Certain species contribute balance and stability to their ecological communities by providing food sources or holding the population of the species in check.

The richness of diversity within and among species has provided new sources of food, energy, industrial chemicals, raw materials, and medicines. Yet there is considerable evidence that biological diversity is decreasing. According to the World Resources Institute, of the 5 to 10 million species currently in existence worldwide, at least 12 percent of the bird and 15 percent of the plant species will be gone by 2000.

---

[1]Notice that public "bads" such as dirty air and dirty water are also possible.

[2]For an example of the argument that genetic diversity is important see Norman Myers, *The Sinking Ark* (New York: Pergamon Press, 1979).

FIGURE 3.5   Public Goods and Inefficiency

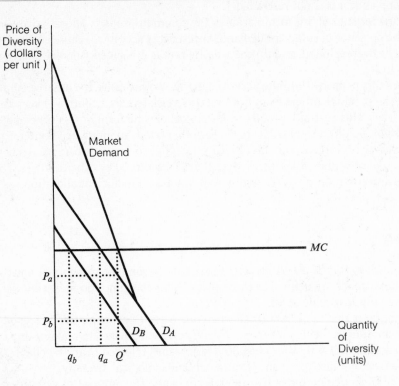

Can we rely on the private sector to produce the efficient amount of public goods such as biological diversity? Unfortunately, the answer is no! Suppose that in response to diminishing ecological diversity we decide to take up a collection to provide some means of preserving endangered species. Would the collection yield sufficient revenue to pay for an efficient level of ecological diversity? The general answer is no. Let's see why.

In Figure 3.5 we represent the demand curves for ecological diversity as determined by the preferences of two consumers, A and B. Person A values diversity more, in that her demand curve is represented by the *vertical* summation of the individual demand curve.[3] This is in contrast to a market demand curve for a divisible good, which is constructed by a *horizontal* summation of the individual demand curves. The (constant) marginal cost of providing cleanup services is represented by the MC curve.

What is the efficient level of diversity? It can be determined by a direct application of our definition of efficiency. The efficient allocation maximizes net benefits. Net benefits, in turn, are represented geometrically by the portion of the area under the market demand curve that lies above the marginal cost curve. The allocation that maximizes net benefits is Q^*, the allocation where the demand curve crosses the marginal cost curve.

---

[3]A vertical summation is necessary because everyone can simultaneously consume the same amount of ecological diversity, so we can add the amounts of money they would be willing to pay for that level of diversity.

EXAMPLE 3.2

Public Goods Privately Provided: The Nature Conservancy

Can a demand for a public good such as biological diversity be observed in practice? Would the market respond to that demand? Apparently so according to the existence of an organization called The Nature Conservancy.

The Nature Conservancy was born of an older organization called the Ecologist Union on 11 September 1950, for the purpose of establishing natural area reserves to preserve or aid in the preservation of areas, objects, and fauna and flora that have scientific, educational, or aesthetic significance. This organization purchases, or accepts as donations, land that has some unique ecological or aesthetic significance to keep it from being used for other purposes. In so doing it preserves many species by preserving the habitat.

From humble beginnings, The Nature Conservancy has, as of 1988, been responsible for the preservation of 3,643,352 acres of forests, marshes, prairies, mounds, and islands. These areas serve as home to rare and endangered species of wildlife and plants. The Conservancy owns and manages some 1,000 preserves—the largest privately owned nature preserve system in the world.

This approach has considerable merit. A private organization can move more rapidly than the public sector. Because it has a limited budget, the Nature Conservancy sets priorities and concentrates on acquiring the most ecologically unique areas. However, the theory of public goods reminds us that if this were to be the sole approach to the preservation of biological diversity, it would preserve a smaller than efficient amount.

Source: *The Nature Conservancy Magazine* 39, No. 2 (1989).

Would our collection box yield enough revenues to supply this level of diversity? The answer is no. Consider the following sequences of events: Person B comes to the collection box first and notices nothing is in it. Therefore, he chooses to contribute. How much? He contributes until his net benefits are maximized, at q_b. Not long after, person A comes along. She notices that person B has already purchased q_b. How much more will she purchase? The answer is $q_a - q_b$, because this maximizes her net benefits, given that q_b had already been purchased. The total collection, therefore, is sufficient to defray the cost of q_a units of diversity. Notice that the outcome is not efficient.

Why does this happen? Inefficiency results because each person is able to become a free rider on the other's contribution. A *free rider* is someone who derives the benefits from a commodity without contributing to its supply. Because of the consumption indivisibility and nonexcludability properties of the public good, consumers receive the benefits of any diversity purchased by other people. When this happens it tends to diminish incentives to contribute, and the contributions are not sufficiently large to finance the efficient amount of the public good; it would be undersupplied.

Notice, however, that the privately supplied amount is not zero. Some diversity would be privately supplied. Indeed, as suggested by Example 3.2, the privately supplied amount may be considerable.

FIGURE 3.6   Monopoly and Inefficiency

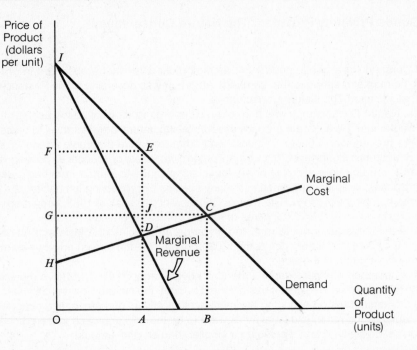

One further insight can be gained from Figure 3.5, and it is this insight that led to characterizing public-good problems as "complex" in the opening sentence of this section. The efficient market equilibrium for a public good would require different prices for each consumer. In Figure 3.5 if consumer A is charged P_a and consumer B is charged P_b, then both consumers would be satisfied with the efficient allocation (the efficient allocation would have maximized their net benefits given the prices).

Furthermore, the revenue collected would be sufficient to finance the supply of the public good (because $P_b \times Q^* + P_a \times Q^* = MC \times Q^*$). Thus, although an efficient pricing system exists, it is very difficult to implement. The efficient pricing system requires charging a different price to each consumer; in the absence of excludability, consumers may not choose to reveal the strength of their preference for this commodity. Therefore, the producer could not possibly know what prices to charge.

IMPERFECT MARKET STRUCTURES

Environmental problems also occur when one of the participants in an exchange of property rights is able to exercise an inordinate amount of power over the outcome. This can occur, for example, when a product is sold by a single seller, or *monopoly*.

It is easy to show that monopolies violate our definition of efficiency (Figure 3.6). According to our definition of static efficiency (Chapter 2), the efficient allocation would result when OB is supplied. This would yield net benefits of HIC. The monopoly, however, would produce and sell OA, where marginal revenue equals marginal cost, and would charge price

OF. At this point, producer's surplus is maximized, yet it is clearly inefficient because this choice causes society to lose net benefits equal to *EDC*.[4]

Imperfect markets clearly play some role in environmental problems. For example, the major oil-exporting countries have formed a cartel, resulting in higher than normal prices and lower than normal production. A *cartel* is a collusive agreement among producers to restrict production and raise prices. This collusive agreement allows the group to act like a monopolist.

DIVERGENCE OF SOCIAL AND PRIVATE DISCOUNT RATES

We concluded earlier that producers, in their attempt to maximize producer surplus, also maximize the present value of net benefits under the "right" conditions, such as the absence of externalities, the presence of properly defined property rights, and the presence of competitive markets within which the property rights can be exchanged.

Now let's consider one more condition. If resources are to be allocated efficiently, firms must use the same rate to discount future net benefits as is appropriate for society at large. If firms were to use a higher rate, they would extract and sell resources faster than would be efficient. Conversely, if firms were to use a lower-than-appropriate discount rate, they would be excessively conservative.

Why might private and social rates differ? As stated in the previous chapter, the social discount rate is equal to the social opportunity cost of capital. This cost of capital can be separated into two components: risk-free cost of capital and the risk premium.[5] The *risk-free cost of capital* is the rate of return earned when there is absolutely no risk of earning more or less than the expected return. The *risk premium* is an additional cost of capital required to compensate the owners of this capital when the expected and actual returns may differ. Therefore, because of the risk premium, the cost of capital is higher in risky industries.

One difference between private and social discount rates may stem from a difference between social and private risk premiums. If the risk of certain private decisions differs from the risks faced by society as a whole, then the social and private risk premiums may differ. One obvious example is the risk *caused* by the government. If the firm is afraid its assets will be taken over by the government, it may choose a higher discount rate to make its profits before nationalization occurs.[6]

From the point of view of society—as represented by government—this is not a risk, so a lower discount rate is appropriate. When private rates exceed social rates, current production is higher than is desirable to maximize the net benefits to society. Energy production and forestry have both been subject to this source of inefficiency.

Though private and social discount rates do not always diverge, they may. When those circumstances arise, market decisions are not efficient.

---

[4]Producers would lose *JDC* compared to the efficient allocation, but they would gain area *FEJG*, which is much larger. Meanwhile, consumers would be worse off because they lose the area *FECJG*. Of these, *FEJG* is merely a transfer to the monopoly whereas *EJC* is a pure loss to society. The total pure loss (*EDC*) is called a deadweight loss.

[5]This point is discussed in more detail in most principles of economics texts.

[6]This case is described in James M. Griffin and Henry B. Steele, *Energy Economics and Policy* (New York: Academic Press, 1980), 85–86.

GOVERNMENT FAILURE

Market processes are not the only sources of inefficiency. Political processes are fully as culpable. As will become clear in the chapters that follow, some environmental problems have arisen from a failure of political rather than economic institutions. To complete our study of the ability of institutions to allocate environmental resources, we must understand this source of inefficiency as well.

Government failure shares with market failure the characteristic that improper incentives are the root of the problem. Special-interest groups use the political process to engage in what has become known as rent-seeking. *Rent-seeking* is the use of resources in lobbying and other activities directed at securing protective legislation. Successful rent-seeking activity will increase the net benefits going to the special-interest group, but it will also frequently lower net benefits to society as a whole. In these instances it is a classic case of the aggressive pursuit of a larger slice of the pie leading to a smaller pie.

Why don't the losers rise up to protect their interests? One main reason is voter ignorance. Because of the high cost of keeping informed and the low probability that any single vote will be decisive, it is economically rational for voters to remain ignorant on many issues. In addition, it is difficult for diffuse groups of individuals, each of whom is affected only to a small degree, to organize a coherent, unified opposition. In a sense, successful opposition is a public good, with its attendant tendency for free-riding on the opposition of others. Opposition to special interests would normally be underfunded.

Rent-seeking can take many forms. Producers can seek protection from competitive pressures brought by imports or can seek price floors to hold prices above their efficient levels. Consumer groups can seek price ceilings or special subsidies to transfer part of their costs to the general body of taxpayers. Whatever form it takes, the existence of rent-seeking provides a direct challenge to the presumption that more direct intervention by the government automatically leads to greater efficiency.

These cases illustrate the general economic premise that environmental problems arise because of a divergence between individual and collective objectives. This is a powerful explanatory device because it not only suggests why these problems arise, it also suggests how they might be resolved—by realigning individual incentives to make them compatible with collective objectives.

Self-evident as this approach may be, it is controversial (see Example 3.3). The controversy involves whether the problem is our improper values or the improper translation of our quite proper values into action.

Economists have always been reluctant to argue that values of consumers are warped because that would necessitate dictating the "correct" set of values. Both capitalism and democracy are based on the presumption that the majority knows what it is doing, whether it is casting ballots for representatives or dollar votes for goods and services. That presumption may be wrong, but history suggests it probably isn't too far off the mark.

The Pursuit of Efficiency

We have seen that environmental problems arise when property rights are ill-defined, when these rights are exchanged under something other than competitive conditions, and when social and private discount rates diverge. We can now use our definition of efficiency to explore

EXAMPLE 3.3

Religion as the Source of Environmental Problems

One of the many alternative explanations of the source of environmental problems has been advanced by historian Lynn White, Jr. His thesis, simply put, is that the environmental crisis is due to the teachings of Judaism and Christianity, which in Western culture have created a warped view of the proper relationship between humans and their environment.

The basis for this thesis is to be found in the first book of the Old Testament:

Then God said, "Let us make man in our image, after our likeness; and let them have dominion over the fish of the sea, and over the birds of the air, and over the cattle, and over all the earth, and over every creeping thing that creeps upon the earth." [Gen. 1:26]

Two aspects of this passage are crucial to his argument: (1) God created man in His own image, and (2) man was given dominion over the other forms of life. Both of these aspects make man the dominant force on earth and, according to White, suggest that "it is God's will that man exploit nature for his proper ends." White also makes the point that, among the world's religions, this is a rather unique view of the human/environment relationship. His policy solution follows directly:

More science and more technology are not going to get us out of the present ecological crisis until we find a new religion, or rethink our old one. [p. 1205]

White believes that we must adopt new values that reject the primacy of humans and elevate the stature of nature.

This view provides a stark contrast to the economics approach, which suggests that the problem is neither the primacy of humans nor warped values but rather an imperfect translation of those values into practice.

Sources: Lynn White, Jr., "The Historical Roots of Ecologic Crisis," *Science* 155 (10 March 1967): 1203–1207; E. F. Schumacher, "Buddhist Economics," in *Small Is Beautiful* (New York: Harper Colphon Books, 1973): 50–58; Keith Thomas, *Man and the Natural World* (New York: Alfred A. Knopf, 1983): 17–25.

possible remedies, such as private negotiation, judicial remedies, and regulation by the legislative and executive branches of government.

Private Resolution Through Negotiation

The simplest means to restore efficiency occurs when the number of affected parties is small, making negotiation feasible. Suppose, for example, the noise of a stereo system shatters the tranquility of an evening. This situation is an environmental problem because the stereo owner does not exclusively bear all the costs of his or her actions. Because of the externality, an inefficiency occurs (Figure 3.7). Without considering the neighbor's welfare, the stereo owner chooses q_m decibels, a choice dictated solely by the owner's enjoyment of loud music.

FIGURE 3.7   Noise Pollution: An Example of External Cost

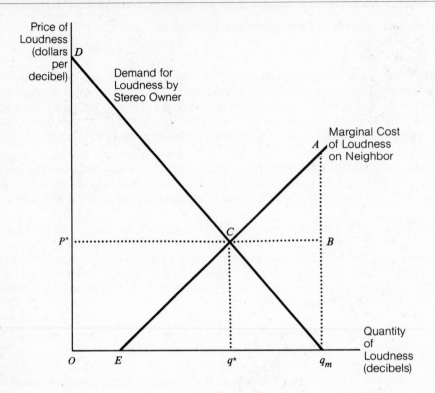

Meanwhile, the efficient level q^* is the level that maximizes the net benefit. How can efficiency be restored in this nonmarket relationship? The first possibility is individual negotiation. The neighbor could bribe the stereo owner. Suppose, for example, the neighbor offered to pay P^* for each decibel reduced. The owner should, in that case, be willing to reduce the level to q^* decibels because of the advantages. The owner loses benefits Cq_mq^* but gains revenue equal to the rectangle CBq_mq^*, which is larger.

Meanwhile, the neighbor is also better off than before. Though he or she had to pay the bribe (CBq_mq^*), the neighbor no longer bears the cost of the loud noise (ACq^*q_m), which is greater. Notice that in equilibrium it does not pay the neighbor to offer a per unit bribe either greater than P^* or less than P^*, because those bribes would, respectively, yield too much or too little reduction in noise level.

Our discussion of individual negotiations raises two particular questions: (1) Should the property right always belong to the person who gained or seized it first? (2) How can accidents be handled where prior negotiation is clearly impractical? These questions are routinely answered by the court system.

The Courts: Property Rules and Liability Rules

The court system can respond to environmental conflicts by imposing either property rules or liability rules. *Property rules* specify the initial allocation of the entitlement. The entitlements at conflict in our example are, on the one hand, the right to play a stereo loudly and, on the other, the right to peace and quiet. In applying property rules, the court merely decides which right is preeminent and places an injunction against violating that right. The injunction is removed only upon obtaining the consent of the party whose right was violated. Consent is usually obtained in return for an out-of-court monetary settlement.

Notice that in the absence of a court decision the entitlement is naturally allocated to the party who can most easily seize it. In our example the natural allocation would give the entitlement to the party who likes loud music. The courts must decide whether to overturn this natural allocation.

How would they decide? Would the court decision be efficient? In a classic article published in 1960, economist Ronald Coase held that as long as negotiation costs are negligible and affected consumers can negotiate freely with each other (when the number of affected parties is small), the court could allocate the entitlement to *either* party and an efficient allocation would result. The only effect of the court's decision is to change the distribution of costs and benefits among the affected parties. This remarkable conclusion has come to be known as the *Coase Theorem*.

We have already shown (in Figure 3.7) that if the stereo owner has the property right, it is in the neighbor's interest to offer a bribe of P^* per decibel of noise reduction, resulting in the desired level of q^*. Now suppose the neighbor had the property right instead. To play the stereo loudly, the owner must bribe the neighbor. It would be advantageous to offer the neighbor P^* per decibel allowed, and upon receiving this offer, the neighbor would maximize personal net benefit by accepting q^* decibels.

The difference between these two allocations lies in how the cost of obtaining the efficient decibel level is shared between the parties. When the property right is assigned to the owner of the stereo, the cost is borne by the neighbor. When the property right is assigned to the neighbor, the cost is borne by the owner. In either case the efficient decibel level results. The Coase Theorem shows that the very existence of an inefficiency triggers pressures for improvements. Furthermore, the existence of this pressure does not depend on the assignment of property rights.

This is an important point. As we shall see in succeeding chapters, private efforts triggered by inefficiency can frequently prevent the worst excesses of environmental degradation.[7]

The importance of this theorem should not be overstated, however. Both theoretical and practical objections can be raised. The chief theoretical qualification concerns the implicit assumption of zero wealth effects. The decision to confer the property right on a particular party results in a transfer of wealth to that party. This transfer might shift the demand curve out, as long as the income elasticity of demand is not zero. Thus, giving the property right to the stereo owner in Figure 3.7 would shift the demand curve to the right, whereas giving it to the neighbor would shift the cost curve to the left. Whenever wealth effects are significant, the type of property rule affects the outcome.

Wealth effects normally are small, so the zero wealth effect assumption is probably not a fatal flaw. However, some serious practical flaws do mar the usefulness of the Coase Theorem.

---

[7]See, for example, how lobster harvesters have evolved elaborate rules to prevent this common-property resource from being fished to extinction in J. M. Acheson, *The Lobster Gangs of Maine* (University Press of New England, 1988).

The first involves the incentives for noisemaking that result when the property right is assigned to the stereo owner. Because noise production would become a profitable activity with this assignment, other neighbors might be encouraged to turn their stereos up in order to earn the bribes. That certainly would not be efficient.

Negotiation is also difficult to apply when the number of people affected by the noise is large. You may have already noticed that in the presence of several affected parties, noise reduction is a public good.[8] The free-rider problem would make it difficult for the group to offer an efficient bribe.

When individual negotiation is not practical for one reason or another, the courts can turn to *liability rules.* These are rules that award monetary damages, after the fact, to the injured party. The amount of the award is designed to correspond to the amount of damage inflicted. Thus, to return to Figure 3.7, an efficient liability rule would impose damages equal to the area under *ECA* from *E* to the chosen decibel level. Suppose, for example, the stereo owner persisted in transmitting q_m decibels. If the court decided that damages were appropriate, it would award an amount equal to EAq_m.

The owner might initially be tempted now to play the music softer than *OE,* but, upon reflection, he would certainly resist that temptation. The owner would derive additional benefits beyond *OE* that would be greater than the costs of the damages. Knowing the damages to be paid (equal to the area formed under the line *ECA* from *E* to the chosen decibel level), the owner would choose q^*. More benefits would be lost for further reductions than would be gained in reduced damages paid. (Why doesn't he decide to increase the decibel level beyond q^*?) Thus, appropriately designed liability rules can also correct inefficiencies by forcing those who cause damage to bear the cost of that damage.

Liability rules are interesting from an economics point of view because early decisions create precedents for later ones. Imagine, for example, how the incentives to prevent oil spills facing an oil company are transformed once it has had to clean up after an oil spill and to compensate fishermen for reduced catches. It quickly becomes evident that accident prevention is cheaper than retrospectively dealing with the damage once it has occurred.

This approach also has its limitations, however. It relies on a case-by-case determination based on the unique circumstances for each case. Administratively, such a determination is very expensive. Expenses, such as court time, lawyers' fees, and so on, fall into a category called *transaction costs* by economists. In the present context, these are the administrative costs incurred in attempting to correct the inefficiency.

Legislative and Executive Regulation

When the number of parties involved in a dispute is large and the circumstances are common, we are tempted to correct the inefficiency by statutes or regulations rather than court decisions. These remedies can take several forms. The legislature could dictate that no one should play his or her stereo louder than q^*. This dictum might then be backed up with sufficiently

---

[8] In this case our graph would reflect the situation by vertically summing the individual marginal cost curves to obtain a curve reflecting the total damage to all parties.

large jail sentences or fines to deter potential violators. Alternatively, the legislature could impose a tax on decibels. A decibel tax of P^* per unit, for example, would induce the stereo owner to reduce the noise to q^* (Figure 3.7).

Legislatures could also establish rules to permit greater flexibility and yet reduce damage. For example, some apartment buildings for young singles might allow louder stereos whereas others, catering to older folks or couples with young children needing large amounts of sleep, could enforce stricter silence standards. With this approach, those who like loud music could pick the former building, those who do not, the latter.

AN EFFICIENT ROLE FOR GOVERNMENT

Although the economic approach suggests that government action could well be used to restore efficiency, it also suggests that inefficiency is not a sufficient condition to justify government intervention. Any corrective mechanism involves transaction costs. If these transaction costs are high enough, and the benefit to be derived from correcting the inefficiency small enough, then it is best simply to live with the inefficiency.

Consider, for example, the pollution problem. Woodstoves, which were widely used for cooking and heat in the late 1800s in the United States, were sources of pollution, but because of the enormous capacity of the air to absorb the emissions, no regulation resulted. Today, however, the resurgence of demand for woodstoves, precipitated in part by high oil prices, has resulted in strict regulations for woodstove emissions.

As society has evolved, the scale of economic activity (and emissions) has expanded. Cities are experiencing severe problems with many air and water pollutants because of the clustering of activities. Both the expansion and the clustering have increased the amount of emissions per unit volume of air or water. As a result, pollutant concentrations have caused perceptible problems with human health, vegetation growth, and aesthetics.

Historically, as incomes have risen, the demand for leisure activities has also risen. Many of these leisure activities, such as canoeing and backpacking, take place in unique, pristine environmental areas. With the number of these areas declining as a result of conversion to other uses, the value of remaining areas has increased. Thus, the benefits from protecting some areas from pollution and/or development have risen over time until they have exceeded the transaction costs.

By increasing pollution problems and driving up the demand for clean air and pristine areas, the level and concentration of economic activity have created the preconditions for government action. Can government respond, or will rent-seeking prevent efficient political solutions? We shall devote a good deal of the rest of this book to a search for the answer to that question.

SUMMARY

How producers and consumers use the resources making up the environmental asset depends on the nature of the property rights governing resource use. When property-right systems are universal, exclusive, transferable, and enforceable, the owner of a resource has a powerful incentive to use that resource efficiently because failing to do so results in a personal loss.

For scarce natural resources, the owners derive a scarcity rent. In properly specified property-right systems, this rent is not dissipated by competition. It serves the social purpose of allowing owners to efficiently balance their extraction and conservation decisions.

The economic system will not always sustain efficient allocations, however. Specific circumstances that could lead to inefficient allocations include externalities; improperly defined property-right systems (such as common-property resources and public goods); imperfect markets for trading the property rights to the resources (monopoly); and the divergence of social and private discount rates (under the threat of nationalization). When these circumstances arise, market allocations do not maximize the present value of the net benefit.

Due to rent-seeking behavior by special-interest groups or the less-than-perfect implementation of efficient plans, the political system can produce inefficiencies as well. Voter ignorance on many issues, coupled with the public-good nature of any results of political activity, tend to create an environment in which private, but not social, net benefits are maximized.

The efficiency criterion can be used to assist in identifying circumstances in which our political and economic institutions lead us astray. It can also assist in the search for remedies by facilitating the design of regulatory, judicial, or legislative solutions.

FURTHER READINGS

Anderson, Terry L., and P. J. Hill. "The Evolution of Property Rights: A Study of the American West," *The Journal of Law and Economics* XVIII (April 1975): 163–79. An interesting test of the proposition that as the efficiency losses from common-property resources in the West rose, individuals increased the amount of time and resources devoted to definition and enforcement of rights to land, water, and livestock.

Bromley, Daniel W. "Property Rules, Liability Rules and Environmental Economics," *Journal of Economic Issues* XII (March 1978): 43–60. An elaboration of the role of property rules and liability rules in solving environmental problems.

"Coase Theorem Symposium: Part I," *Natural Resources Journal* XIII (October 1973): 557–716; "Coase Theorem Symposium: Part II," *Natural Resources Journal* XIV (January 1974): 1–54. A wide-ranging, penetrating series of essays on the limits and implications of the Coase Theorem.

Cropper, Maureen L., and Wallace E. Oates. "Environmental Economics: A Survey," *Journal of Economic Literature* 30 (1992): 675-740. A review of the environmental economics field by two prominent practitioners.

Goldfarb, Theodore D., ed. *Taking Sides: Clashing Views on Environmental Issues,* 3rd ed. (Guilford, CT: Dushkin Publishing Group, 1989). A provocative collection of pairs of opposing views on 19 aspects of environmental policy.

Stavins, Robert N. "Harnessing Market Forces to Protect the Environment" *Environment* 31 (1989): 4–7, 28–35. An excellent, nontechnical review of the many ways in which the creative use of economic policies can produce superior environmental outcomes.

ADDITIONAL REFERENCES

Bolotin, Frederic N. *International Public Policy Sourcebook, Vol. 2: Education and Environment* (Boulder, CO: Greenwood Press, 1989).

Bromley, Daniel W. *Economic Interests and Institutions: The Conceptual Foundations of Public Policy* (Oxford: Basil Blackwell, 1989).

Coase, Ronald. "The Problem of Social Cost," *The Journal of Law and Economics* 3 (October 1960): 1–44.

Johnson, Stanley P. *The Environmental Policy of the European Communities* (London: Graham & Trotman, 1989).

OECD. *Environment and Economics* (Paris: Organization for Economic Co-operation and Development, 1985).

Mercuro, Nicholas, and Warren J. Samuels. "The Role and Resolution of the Compensation Principle in Society, I," *Research in Law and Economics* 1 (Greenwich, CT: JAI Press, 1979): 157–94; and "The Role and Resolution of the Compensation Principle in Society, II," *Research in Law and Economics* 2 (Greenwich, CT: JAI Press, 1980): 103–28.

Ross, Lester. *Environmental Policy in China* (Bloomington, IN: Indiana University Press, 1988).

Pryde, Philip R. "The 'Decade of the Environment' in the U.S.S.R.," *Science* 220 (15 April 1983): 274–79.

DISCUSSION QUESTIONS

1. In a well-known legal case, *Miller v Schoene* (287 U.S. 272), a classic conflict of property rights was featured. Red cedar trees, used only for ornamental purposes, carried a disease that could destroy apple orchards within a radius of two miles. There was no known way of curing the disease except by destroying the cedar trees or by ensuring that apple orchards were at least two miles away from the cedar trees. Apply the Coase Theorem to this situation. Does it make any difference to the outcome whether the cedar tree owners are entitled to retain their trees or the apple growers are entitled to be free of them? Why or why not?

2. In primitive societies the entitlements to use land were frequently possessory rights rather than ownership rights. Those on the land could use it as they wished but could not transfer it to anyone else. One could acquire a new plot by simply occupying and using it, leaving the old plot available for someone else. Would this type of entitlement system cause more or less incentive to conserve the land than an ownership entitlement? Why? Would a possessory entitlement system be more efficient in a modern society or a primitive society? Why?

CHAPTER 4

Valuing the Environment

Cost-benefit analysis is valuable in regulatory decision making, but unless we recognize its shortcomings we are likely to force a superficial quantification of issues that cannot wholly be grasped by the reassuringly precise embrace of numbers. [If this technique is used inappropriately] we shall be guided by a bright light in the wrong place, and the result will be not only bad cost-benefit analysis, but bad decisions.

DOUGLAS M. COSTLE (1981), EPA ADMINISTRATOR DURING
CARTER ADMINISTRATION

INTRODUCTION

Soon after the *Exxon Valdez* oil tanker ran aground on the Bligh Reef in Prince William Sound off the coast of Alaska on 24 March 1989, the Exxon corporation accepted liability for the damage caused by the leaking oil. This liability consisted of two parts: (1) the cost of clearing up the spilled oil and restoring the site in so far as possible, and (2) compensation for the damage caused to the local ecology. From an economic point of view, imposing this liability makes sense, for it internalizes a cost that would otherwise be externalized. Internalizing the cost, in turn, provides incentives to exercise greater care in the future.

However, implementing this principle was a far from trivial exercise. How much damage was caused? How much compensation was appropriate? Although the costs of cleaning up were fairly transparent (specific bills for labor, materials, and equipment appeared at Exxon corporate headquarters with great regularity), estimating the damage was more complex. To arrive at a reasonable answer, the courts turned to economists.

A series of special techniques have been developed to value the benefits from environmental improvement or, conversely, to value the damage done by environmental degradation. Special techniques were necessary because most of the normal valuation techniques that have been used over the years cannot be applied to environmental resources. Demand curves for normal commodities such as bread or automobiles can be estimated from readily available market data, but no such data exist for environmental resources which do not pass through markets. It is not possible to check your local grocery store for the current price of clean air.

The special valuation techniques are now used in two related yet different contexts. On the one hand, they are used in *ex post* settings such as the oil spill just described. In this case the damage has already happened, and the purpose of the valuation exercise is to establish the appropriate level of compensation. On the other hand, these techniques are also used in *ex ante* settings, where the purpose of valuation is facilitate the process of deciding what good policy actions might be. Valuation has been used, for example, to assess the desirability of specific government investments in environmental improvement and to assess the desirability of new regulations to protect certain aspects of the environment from further degradation. It has also been used to rank the seriousness of environmental problems to provide guidance to environmental agencies as they decide how to focus their efforts.

In this chapter we shall examine these valuation methods. We begin with an examination of benefit/cost analysis, the primary *ex ante* technique that uses environmental valuation. In this section we identify and discuss the various valuation techniques that are used to value environmental resources in both *ex ante* and *ex post* settings. This is followed by a discussion of the strategies that exist for using economics to protect the environment when valuation information cannot reliably be obtained. One of these strategies, cost-effectiveness analysis, has become extremely important in guiding pollution control policy. It is popular not only for the very practical consideration that it can be a valuable component of the policy process even when reliable valuation estimates cannot be obtained, but also because it responds to the concerns of those who reject the anthropomorphic basis for economic valuation. It has become the technique of choice for those who recognize the importance of economics for protecting the environment but are skeptical of any efforts to monetize the value of environmental resources.

BENEFIT/COST ANALYSIS

The most ambitious of the techniques is benefit/cost analysis. Though it makes the most precise statements about which policy choices are efficient, it also imposes the largest requirement for information in order to provide those statements. It is fairly easy for most people to accept the general premise that the benefits and costs of actions should be weighed before deciding on a particular policy choice. The technique becomes more controversial, however, when specific numbers are attached to the anticipated benefits, and costs and specific decision rules for translating these numbers into a decision are followed.

The Decision Rules

We start our investigation by discussing how the benefit and cost information is used once it is available. Three main decision rules are commonly used, and they are *not* equivalent.

The *maximum net-present-value criterion* is the empirical counterpart to the present value of net benefits criterion used to define dynamic efficiency. This criterion suggests that resources should be committed to those uses maximizing the present value of net benefits received. If accomplished properly, this analysis will correctly identify an efficient allocation.

In practice, however, two other frequently used criteria do not guarantee that the efficient allocation will be identified. These are the *benefit/cost ratio criterion* and the *positive net-present-value criterion*. The decision rule for the former criterion implies that an activity should be undertaken if the ratio of the present value of benefits to the present value of costs exceeds 1.0. The decision rule for the second criterion implies that an activity should be undertaken whenever the present value of net benefits is greater than zero. Although both of these techniques guarantee that no activity that confers more costs on society than benefits will be undertaken, they do not guarantee efficiency. The point can be illustrated most easily using our definition of static efficiency.

Recall from Chapter 2 that efficiency is attained when the *marginal* benefit equals the *marginal* cost. Neither a benefit/cost ratio greater than 1.0 nor a positive net benefit insures that these marginal conditions will hold. In fact, when the benefit/cost ratio is equal to 1.0 (or, equivalently, the net benefit is equal to 0.0), this ensures that total benefit equals total cost (Figure 4.1).

The net benefit is maximized when Q_1 is supplied. At this point the marginal benefit is equal to the marginal cost, so total benefits exceed total costs by the largest possible amount. In fact, the net benefit is equal to E, which is considerably greater than zero.[1]

At what allocation would net benefit equal zero? In Figure 4.1 the answer is Q_2. The figure is drawn such that area A equals area B. Because area B represents net cost (or, equivalently, negative net benefit) and area A represents positive net benefit, the net benefit from allocation Q_2 is zero. This implies that *average* benefits equal *average* costs, *total* benefits equal *total* costs, and the benefit/cost ratio equals 1.0.[2]

This result suggests that whenever the benefit/cost ratio or positive net-present-value criteria are used, the government may choose inefficient activities. Only the maximum net-present-value approach is completely compatible with efficiency.

Measuring Benefits

For many resource problems, measurement of benefits is relatively uncomplicated because the resource in question is a marketed commodity and information on prices and quantities consumed can be used to derive the demand curve. Once the demand curve is defined, it can be used to quantify the willingness to pay, the concept used to measure benefits.

Greater difficulties are encountered when the resource in question is not handled through normal markets. One classic example arises when we compare the value of preserving an environmental resource, such as a unique canyon, with that of developing the resource, such as hydroelectric power. We must compare the benefits without development to the power benefits with development.

Economists recognize two broad classes of value conferred by environmental resources: use value and nonuse value. Use value is created by the current use of resources either directly

---

[1]Total benefits are $A + C$; total costs are equal to C.

[2]Average benefits are equal to $(A + C + D) \div Q$, and average costs are equal to $(B + C + D) \div Q$. Therefore, as long as $A = B$, average benefits equal average costs.

FIGURE 4.1   Benefit/Cost Analysis and Efficiency

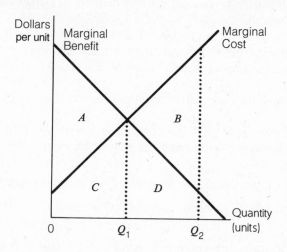

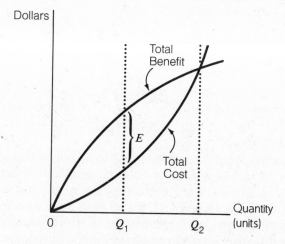

or indirectly. The direct-use value of a stream, for example, would be created by the recreational opportunities it affords, its use for irrigating agriculture, and its use as a source of drinking water, to name but a few value-creating activities. Indirect benefits might include its role in supporting ecological functions, such as providing a habitat for fish or other wildlife. Nonuse values are created by the desire to assure continued provision of this resource for others in the future.

Use Values

Recreation Benefits. One common direct-use value is created by the recreational opportunities afforded by environmental resources. Recreation benefits could be estimated from the recreational demand curve for that resource, if it were known. However, because visitors normally are not charged anything but nominal fees for using publicly owned recreation areas, it is difficult to know what the true demand is. Market prices do not prevail, and demands are not revealed.

To get around this problem, a technique called the *Clawson-Knetsch method* was developed for estimating the recreational demand for a particular site when market prices are not available.[3] This technique uses travel costs to measure how much people would be willing to pay to come to the area.

The simplest version of the procedure is as follows:[4]

1. For a given recreation site, the surrounding area is divided into concentric circular zones for the purpose of measuring the travel cost from each zone to the site and return.

2. Visitors at the site are sampled to determine their zones of origin.

3. Visitation rates, defined as visitor days per capita, are calculated for each zone of origin.

4. A travel-cost measure is constructed to indicate the cost of travel from the origin zone to the recreation site and back.

5. Using a statistical technique known as regression analysis, visitation rates are then related to travel costs and socioeconomic variables such as average income, median educational attainment, and the like.

6. The observed total visitation for the site from all travel-cost zones represents one point on the demand curve for that site; that is, the intersection of the present horizontal price line (either at a zero price or the typical nominal fee) with the true economic demand curve.

7. Other points on the demand curve are found by assuming that visitors will respond to a $1 increase in admission price in the same way that they would respond to a $1 increase in computed travel cost. To find the point on the demand curve for the site where the admission price rises by $1, the estimated visitation-rate equation is used to compute visitation rates and total visits for all travel-cost zones with the existing travel cost plus $1. Visits are summed across travel-cost zones to determine the predicted total visitation at the higher price. These calculations are repeated for higher and higher hypothetical admission prices until the full demand curve is traced out.

The next difficulty in comparing preservation and development involves forecasting how the benefits from these alternative uses will change over time. The demand for recreational

---

[3]This is described in detail in Marion Clawson and Jack Knetsch, *Economics of Outdoor Recreation* (Baltimore, MD: Johns Hopkins University Press, for Resources for the Future, 1966); Jack L. Knetsch, "Economics of Including Recreation as a Purpose of Eastern Water Projects," *Journal of Farm Economics* 46 (December 1964): 1148–57.

[4]This description is taken from A. Myrick Freeman, III, *The Benefits of Environmental Improvement: Theory and Practice* (Baltimore, MD: The Johns Hopkins Press, for Resources for the Future, 1979): 201–209. Some newer approaches are discussed in R. Mendelsohn and G. M. Brown, Jr., "Revealed Preference Approaches to Valuing Outdoor Recreation," *Natural Resources Journal* 23, No. 3 (July 1983): 607–18.

activity has a positive income elasticity, which implies that the demand curve will shift out over time as income increases. The benefits of the preservation alternative will necessarily increase over time as well. If benefits of preservation increase faster than costs, then the net benefits of preservation increase over time. Preservation may be the preferred alternative, even if the benefits from preservation in the current year are lower than the benefits from development, as long as benefits are growing faster than costs. Furthermore, as is clear from Example 4.1, the dominance of the preservation alternative may turn out to be relatively insensitive to the specific estimate of recreational benefits, a comforting finding in light of the difficulty of obtaining precise estimates.

Pollution Damages and Pollution Control Benefits.   Some of the most difficult problems of benefit estimation are raised by the search for an efficient level of pollution control. The benefits derived from pollution control are the damages prevented. The benefit derived from more control over pollution is the difference between the level of damage when emissions are controlled at one level and the lower level of damage that would result from greater control. Our measurement of benefits, then, depends upon our ability to estimate the damage that results from various levels of pollution.

In the United States, damage estimates have also become important in the courts. Under the Comprehensive Environmental Response, Compensation, and Liability Act, local, state, or federal governments can seek monetary compensation from responsible parties for natural resources that are injured or destroyed by spills and releases of hazardous wastes. Some basis for deciding the magnitude of the award is necessary.[5]

The damage caused by pollution can take many different forms. The first, and probably most obvious, is the effect on the health of humans. Polluted air and water can cause disease when ingested. Other forms of damage include loss of enjoyment from outdoor activities and damage to vegetation, animals, and materials.

Assessing the magnitude of this damage requires (1) identifying the affected categories, (2) estimating the physical relationship between the pollutant emissions (including natural sources) and the damage caused to the affected categories, (3) estimating the responses by the affected parties toward averting or mitigating some portion of the damage, and (4) placing a monetary value on the physical damages. Each of these steps is typically difficult to accomplish.

Because the experiments used to track down causal relationships are uncontrolled, identifying the affected categories is a complicated matter. Obviously we cannot run large numbers of people through controlled experiments. If people were subjected to different levels of some pollutant, such as carbon monoxide, so that we could study the short-term and long-term effects, some might become ill and even die. Ethical concern precludes human experimentation of this type.

This leaves us essentially two choices: We can try to infer the impact on humans from controlled laboratory experiments on animals,[6] or we can do an after-the-fact statistical analy-

---

[5]The rules for determining these damages are defined in Department of Interior regulations. See 40 Code of Federal Regulations 300.72–74.

[6]Extrapolation from animal studies is used mainly in determining the toxicity of chemicals and has not been used to any appreciable degree in determining the effects of "conventional" pollutants.

EXAMPLE 4.1

Preservation versus Development: The Hell's Canyon Case

Hell's Canyon, on the Snake River separating Oregon from Idaho, is the deepest canyon on the North American continent. It affords a visitor some of the most spectacular vistas in the country and provides a natural habitat for a variety of wildlife. It also offers one of the best remaining sites for the development of hydroelectric power.

During the 1970s a major controversy developed concerning whether a portion of this canyon should be dedicated to the production of hydroelectric power through the construction of the High Mountain Sheep Dam or preserved in its natural state. If the dam were developed, a large lake would be formed behind it, changing the character of the canyon.

During this controversy several economists from an organization called Resources for the Future, Inc., a respected Washington think tank, performed a benefit/cost analysis on the choice. The issues were relatively clear. As an environmental resource supporting recreational activities, this canyon was unique in the area. The demand for those activities was increasing at a very rapid rate, but the construction of the dam would diminish the value of the site for those purposes. On the other hand, the electricity produced by the dam would also be valuable.

In contrast to the use of the resource as a natural area, which, due to its uniqueness, has very few substitutes, electricity could be produced by other methods. Unfortunately, these other methods would be more expensive. The benefit of the dam, then, would be the costs saved by generating electricity in this manner rather than by the next cheapest source (nuclear), and the cost would include the opportunity cost of the recreational activities forgone.

What did the analysis suggest? The authors concluded that the net benefits from preservation were rising rapidly over time, so even though current benefits from preservation were less than the current benefits from producing electricity, in present-value terms the preservation option yielded higher net benefits. The analysis indicated that if the current annual value of recreational activities exceeded $80,000, then the efficient decision would be to preserve the site. Their estimate of the current annual value of recreational activities at that site was approximately $900,000. Even though the data on which this latter estimate was based were not very solid, $900,000 is more than ten times higher than needed to justify preservation. The likelihood that the "true" estimate, if it were known, would be less than $80,000 is very low. Therefore they recommended preservation. On the basis of this recommendation and other considerations, Congress voted to prohibit further development of this section of the river.

Source: Anthony C. Fisher, John V. Krutilla, and Charles J. Chicchetti, "Alternative Uses of Natural Environments: The Economics of Environmental Modification," in *Natural Environments: Studies in Theoretical and Applied Analysis*, John V. Krutilla, ed. (Washington, DC: Johns Hopkins University Press, for Resources for the Future, 1972): 18–53.

sis of differences in mortality or disease rates for various human populations living in polluted environments to see the extent to which they are correlated with pollution concentrations. Neither approach is completely acceptable.

Animal experiments are expensive, and the extrapolation from effects on animals to effects on humans is tenuous at best. Many of the significant effects do not appear for a long time. To determine these effects in a reasonable period of time, test animals must be subjected to large doses for a relatively short period of time. The researcher then extrapolates from the results of these high-dosage, short-duration experiments to estimate the effects of lower doses over a longer period of time on a human population. Because these extrapolations move well beyond the range of experimental experience, many scientists disagree on how they should be accomplished.

Statistical studies, on the other hand, deal with human populations subjected to low doses for long periods but, unfortunately, have another set of problems—correlation does not imply causation. To illustrate, the fact that death rates are higher in cities with higher pollution levels does not prove that the higher pollution *caused* the higher death rates. Perhaps those same cities had older populations, which would tend to lead to higher death rates. Or perhaps they had more smokers. The existing studies have been sophisticated enough to account for many of these other possible influences, but, due to the relative paucity of data, they have not been able to cover them all.

The problems discussed so far arise when identifying *whether* or not a particular effect results from pollution. The next step is to estimate *how strong* the relationship is between the effect and the pollution concentrations. In other words, it is necessary not only to discover whether pollution causes an increased incidence of respiratory disease but also to estimate how much reduction in respiratory illness could be expected from a given reduction in pollution.

The nonexperimental nature of the data makes this a difficult task. It is not uncommon for researchers analyzing the same data to come to remarkably different conclusions.[7] Diagnostic problems are compounded when the effects are *synergistic,* that is, when the effect depends in a nonadditive way on what other elements are in the surrounding air or water at the time of the analysis.

Once physical damages have been identified, the next step is to place a monetary value on them. It is not difficult to see how complex an undertaking this is. Consider, for example, the difficulties in assigning a value to extending a human life by several years or to the pain, suffering, and grief borne by a cancer victim and his or her family.

Economists have used several different approaches to place a monetary value on reductions in physical damages. The first method, the *contingent valuation* approach, relies on surveys to ascertain how much respondents would be willing to pay to preserve the environment, to reduce the amount of man-made injury to it, or to lower the various types of environmental risk posed by modern industrial society. To name but a few of the large numbers of existing

---

[7]For example, in their often-cited study based on a large volume of data, *Air Pollution and Human Health* (Baltimore, MD: Johns Hopkins University Press, 1977), economists Lester B. Lave and Eugene P. Seskin concluded that a 50 percent reduction in air pollution nationally would lead to a 4.7 percent reduction in mortality. Working with the same data, a pair of mathematicians with General Motors Research Corporation came to the conclusion that a 50 percent reduction in air pollution would drop mortality by only 0.43 percent. This controversy is described in "New Perspective on Air Pollution," *Science News* CXIX: 152.

studies, this approach has been used to value visibility,[8] the recreational use of two rivers in Maine,[9] reductions in nuclear plant injuries,[10] and migratory waterfowl in the Pacific flyway.[11]

The major concern with the use of the contingent valuation method has been the potential for survey respondents to give biased answers. Four types of potential bias have been the focus of a large amount of research: (1) *strategic bias,* (2) *information bias,* (3) *starting point bias,* and (4) *hypothetical bias.*

Strategic bias arises when the respondent provides a biased answer in order to influence a particular outcome. If a decision to preserve a stretch of river for fishing, for example, depends on whether or not the survey produces a sufficiently large value for fishing, the respondents who enjoy fishing may be tempted to provide an answer that assures a high value, rather than a lower value that reflects their true valuation.

Information bias may arise whenever respondents are forced to value attributes with which they have little or no experience. For example, the valuation by a recreationist of a loss in water quality in one body of water may be based on the ease of substituting recreation on another body of water. If the respondent has no experience using the second body of water, the valuation will be based on an entirely false perception.

Starting-point bias may arise in those survey instruments in which a respondent is asked to check off his or her answers from a predefined range of possibilities. How that range is defined by the designer of the survey may affect the resulting answers. A range of $0 to $100 may produce a different valuation by respondents, for example, than a range of $10 to $100, even if no bids are in the $0 to $10 range.

The final source of bias, hypothetical bias, can enter the picture because the respondent is being confronted by a contrived, rather than an actual, set of choices. Because he or she will not have to actually pay the estimated value, the respondent may treat the survey casually, providing ill-considered answers.

A large amount of experimental work has now been done on contingent valuation to determine how serious a problem these biases may present.[12] In general the results seem to suggest that although these biases certainly exist, they can be kept acceptably small with suitably designed survey instruments.

---

[8]Robert D. Rowe and Lauraine G. Chestnut, *The Value of Visibility: Economic Theory and Applications for Air Pollution Control* (Cambridge, MA: Abt Books, 1982).

[9]William O'Neil and Kristin Hallberg, *Estimating the Value of River-Related Recreational Activities: A Comparison of Two Approaches Based on Case Studies of the West Branch of the Penobscot River and the Saco River* (Orono, ME: Maine Land and Water Resources Center, 1985).

[10]Patricia J. Mulligan, "Willingness-to-Pay for Decreased Risks of Nuclear Accidents," Working Paper Number 3, Energy Extension Programs, Pennsylvania State University, 1977.

[11]Gardener Mallard Brown, Jr. and Judd Hammock, "A Preliminary Investigation of the Economics of Migratory Waterfowl," in *Natural Environments: Studies in Theoretical and Applied Analysis,* John V. Krutilla, ed. (Baltimore, MD: Johns Hopkins University Press, for Resources for the Future, Inc., 1972).

[12]For a comprehensive survey of the state of the art see Ronald G. Cummings et al. (1986),*Valuing Environmental Good: An Assessment of the Contingent Valuation Method* (Totowa, NJ: Rowman and Littlefield, 1986).

A quite different approach involves inferring the valuation of an environmental attribute that is not directly observable from related markets where values are directly observable. Common examples include the housing and labor markets.

Housing market studies, also called property-value studies, start from the presumption that the purchaser's willingness to pay for property takes the quality of the local environment into account. All other things being equal, for example, one would expect houses in neighborhoods with clean air to command higher prices than houses in neighborhoods with polluted air. By statistically comparing the market values of similar houses in neighborhoods with different levels of air quality, these studies attempt to decompose the value of housing into its component parts. Because one of those component parts is a premium paid for clean air, this premium can serve as a measure of the value of clean air.

For labor markets the presumption is that workers facing higher levels of environmental risk (such as an exposure to a potentially hazardous substance) have to be compensated in order to accept that risk. Wages can be decomposed into their component parts and the environmental risk premium isolated. This premium can then be used to value the benefits that would be conferred by a reduction in this risk.

In general the statistical studies support the basic common premise behind these two approaches—property values and wages do indeed reflect the existence of pollution as well as other forms of environmental risk—but they have also indicated that we still have a lot to learn about risk valuation. In particular, it now seems clear that environmental risk valuations are sensitive to the context in which they arise; valuations derived in one context (such as the risk of contracting lung cancer from smoking) cannot automatically be transferred to another context (such as the risk of contracting lung cancer through exposure to a radioactive substance). Furthermore, the type of risk, such as whether the exposure is voluntary or involuntary, seems to make quite a difference in the value placed on reducing that risk.[13]

It may be surprising, but these rather different approaches yield quite similar valuations, as can be illustrated by an explicit comparison of the property-value and contingent-valuation methods for providing a measure of the benefits derived from reducing pollution in the Los Angeles area.[14] Based on the statistical analysis, the property-value approach found that the average household would be willing to pay $42 to achieve a 30-percent improvement in its air quality. According to the mean bid in the contingent-valuation survey, the average household should be willing to pay $29 for that improvement. Considering the very different bases for deriving these numbers, they are rather close.

Valuing Human Life.   One fascinating public policy area where these various approaches have been applied is in the valuation of human life. Many government programs, from those controlling hazardous pollutants in the workplace or drinking water to those improving nuclear power plant safety, are designed to save human life as well as to reduce illness. How

[13]See the discussion of context in environmental risk valuation in V. Kerry Smith, "The Valuation of Environmental Risks Using Hedonic Wage Models" in *Horizontal Equity, Uncertainty, and Economic Well-Being,* Martin David and Timothy Smeeding, eds. (Chicago: University of Chicago Press, 1985).

[14]Brookshire et al., "Valuing Public Goods: A Comparison of Survey and Hedonic Approaches," *The American Economic Review* 72 (March 1982): 165-77.

resources should be allocated among these programs depends crucially on the value of human life. How is life to be valued?

The simple answer, of course, is that life is priceless, but that turns out to be not very helpful. Because the resources used to prevent loss of life are scarce, choices must be made. The economic approach to valuing life-saving reductions in environmental risk is to calculate the change in the probability of death resulting from the reduction in environmental risk and to place a value on the change. Thus it is not life itself that is being valued but rather a reduction in the probability that some segment of the population could be expected to die earlier than otherwise.

It is possible to translate the value derived from this procedure in an "implied value of human life." This is accomplished by dividing the amount each individual is willing to pay for a specific reduction in the probability of death by the probability reduction. Suppose, for example, that a particular environmental policy could be expected to reduce the average concentration of a toxic substance to which one million people are exposed. Suppose further that this reduction in exposure could be expected to reduce the risk of death from 1 out of 100,000 to 1 out of 150,000. This implies that the number of expected deaths would fall from 10 to 6.67 in the exposed population as a result of this policy. If each of the one million persons exposed is willing to pay $5 for this risk reduction (for a total of $5 million), then the implied value of a life is approximately $1.5 million ($5 million divided by 3.33).

What actual values have been derived from these methods? A recent survey of a large number of studies examining reductions in a number of life-threatening risks found that most implied values for human life (in 1986 dollars) were between $1.6 million and $8.5 million.[15] This same survey went on to suggest that the most appropriate estimates were probably closer to the $1.6 million estimate. In other words, all government programs resulting in risk reductions costing less than $1.6 million would be justified in benefit/cost terms. Those costing more might or might not be justified, depending on the appropriate value of a life saved in the particular risk context being examined.

Nonuse Values

Nonuse values, those that derive from motivations other than personal use, are obviously less tangible than use values. It is therefore not surprising that they are more controversial. Indeed, when the Department of Interior drew up its regulations on the appropriate procedures for performing natural resource damage assessment, it prohibited the inclusion of nonuse values unless use values for the incident under consideration were zero.[16]

However, the evidence that existence values exist seems quite persuasive. Certain behavioral actions of people reveal strong support for environmental resources even when those re-

---

[15]Ann Fisher et al., "The Value of Reducing Risks of Death: A Note on New Evidence," *Journal of Policy Analysis and Management* 8, No. 1 (1989): 96.

[16]A subsequent court decision reversed this initial ruling. For a fuller treatment of this process see R. Dunford, "Natural Resource Damages from Oil Spills," in *Innovation in Environmental Policy*, T. H. Tietenberg, ed. (Cheltenham, UK: Edward Elgar, 1992): 165–93.

E X A M P L E   4 . 2

Valuing the Northern Spotted Owl

The northern spotted owl lives in an area of the Pacific Northwest where its habitat is threatened by logging. Its significance derives both from its designation under the Endangered Species Act as a threatened species and from its role as an indicator of the overall health of the Pacific Northwest's old-growth forest.

In 1990 an interagency scientific committee presented a plan to withdraw certain forested areas from harvesting and preserve them as "habitat conservation areas." Would preserving these areas represent an efficient choice?

To answer this question, a national contingent-valuation survey was conducted to estimate the (nonuse) value of preservation in this case. Conducted by mail, the survey went to 1,000 households.

The results suggested that the benefits of preservation outweighed the costs by at least 3 to 1, regardless of the assumptions made to resolve such issues as how to treat the nonresponding households. (One calculation, for example, included them all as a zero nonuse value.) Under the assumptions most favorable to preservation, the ratio of benefits to costs was 43 to 1. In this case the nonuse values were large enough to indicate that preservation was the efficient choice.

The authors also point out, however, that the distributional implications of this choice should not be ignored. Although the benefits of preservation are distributed widely throughout the entire population, the costs are concentrated on a relatively small group of people in one geographic region. Perhaps the public should be willing to share some of the preservation benefits by allocating tax dollars to this area to facilitate the transition and to reduce the hardship.

Source: Daniel A. Hagen, James W. Vincent, and Patrick G. Welle, "Benefits of Preserving Old-Growth Forests and the Spotted Owl," *Contemporary Policy Issues* 10 (April 1992): 13–26.

sources provide no direct or even indirect benefit. One example is provided by the millions of dollars contributed each year by large numbers of people to environmental organizations.

The fact that these values exist does not mean that they are easy to monetize. Contingent valuation is the main technique used to get at nonuse values. People are simply asked questions in structured surveys that induce them to reveal nonuse values. As Example 4.2 indicates, these values can be quite large.

Approaches to Cost Estimation

Estimating costs is generally easier than estimating benefits, but it is not easy. One major problem for both derives from the fact that benefit/cost analysis is forward-looking and thus requires an estimate of what a particular strategy *will* cost, which is much more difficult than tracking down what an existing strategy *does* cost.

Another frequent problem is posed by collecting cost information when availability of that information is controlled by a firm having an interest in the outcome. Pollution control is an obvious example. Two rather different approaches have been used to deal with this problem.

The Survey Approach. One way to discover the costs associated with a policy is to ask those who bear the costs, and presumably know the most about them, to reveal the magnitude of the costs to policymakers. Polluters, for example, could be asked to provide control-cost estimates to regulatory bodies.

The problem with this approach is the strong incentive not to be truthful. An overestimate of the costs can trigger less-stringent regulation; therefore, it is financially advantageous to provide overinflated estimates.

The Engineering Approach. The engineering approach bypasses the source being regulated by using general engineering information to catalogue the possible technologies that could be used to meet the objective and to estimate the costs of purchasing and using those technologies. The final step in the engineering approach is to assume that the sources would use technologies that minimize cost. This produces a cost estimate for a "typical," well-informed firm.

This approach has its own problems. The expertise needed to develop these estimates is limited. Furthermore, these estimates may not approximate the actual cost of any particular firm. Unique circumstances may cause the costs of that firm to be higher, or lower, than estimated; the firm, in short, may not be typical.

The Combined Approach. To circumvent these problems, analysts frequently use a combination of survey and engineering approaches. The survey approach collects information on possible technologies as well as special circumstances facing the firm. Engineering approaches are used to derive the actual costs of those technologies, given the special circumstances. This combined approach attempts to balance information best supplied by the source with that best derived independently.

In the cases described so far, the costs are relatively easy to quantify and the problem is simply finding a way to acquire the best information. This is not always the case, however. Some costs are not easy to quantify, though economists have developed some ingenious ways to secure monetary estimates even for those costs.

Take, for example, a policy designed to conserve energy by forcing more people to carpool. If the effect of this is simply to increase the average time of travel, how is this cost to be measured?

For some time, transportation analysts have recognized that people do value their time, and quite a literature has now grown up to provide estimates of this valuation. The basis for this valuation is opportunity cost—how the time might be used if it weren't being consumed in travel. Although the results of these studies depend on the amount of time involved, individuals seem to value their time at a rate not more than half their wage rates.[17]

---

[17]See M. E. Beesley, *Urban Transport: Studies in Economic Policy* (London: Butterworth, 1973): 160, 179.

The Treatment of Risk

For many environmental problems, it is not possible to state with certainty what consequences a particular policy will have, because scientific estimates are often imprecise. Determining the efficient exposure to potentially toxic substances requires obtaining results at high doses and extrapolating to low doses, as well as extrapolating from animal studies to humans. It also requires relying upon epidemiological studies, which infer a pollution-induced adverse human-health impact from correlations between indicators of health in human populations and recorded pollution levels.

Another illustration of the significance of scientific uncertainty is afforded by the global warming problem. Certain gases, when emitted into the atmosphere, are suspected of causing the planetary temperature to rise. If this suspicion is correct, it could have very serious implications. Among other things, it could trigger a rise in the sea level and could result in the deaths of large numbers of plants no longer suited for the temperatures to which they would be subjected. The conjecture that increased emissions of carbon dioxide and other greenhouse gases are causing a rise in temperature is based upon a computer model that has only partially been validated. This is a prototypical example of a problem that is poorly understood but, if the conjectures are true, could pose a significant risk.

The treatment of risk in the policy process involves two major dimensions: (1) identifying and quantifying the risks, and (2) deciding how much risk is acceptable. The former is primarily scientific and descriptive, the latter more evaluative or normative.

Benefit/cost analysis grapples with the evaluation of risk in several ways. Suppose, for example, that we have a range of policy options *A, B, C, D* and a range of possible outcomes *E, F, G* for each of these policies, depending on how the economy evolves over the future. For example, these outcomes might depend on whether the demand growth for the resource is low, medium, or high. Thus, if we choose policy *A,* we might end up with outcomes *AE, AF,* or *AG.* Each of the other policies has three possible outcomes as well, yielding a total of twelve possible outcomes.

We could conduct a separate benefit/cost analysis for each of the twelve possible outcomes. Unfortunately, the policy that maximizes net benefits for *E* may differ from the policy that maximizes net benefits for *F* or *G.* If we only knew which outcome would prevail, we could select the policy that maximized net benefits; the problem is that we don't. Furthermore, choosing the policy that is best if outcome *E* prevails may be disastrous if *G* results instead.

When a dominant policy emerges, this problem is avoided. A *dominant policy* is one that confers higher net benefits for every outcome. In this case, the existence of risk concerning the future is not relevant for the policy choice. Though this fortuitous circumstance is exceptional rather than common, it can occur.[18]

Other options exist even when dominant solutions do not emerge. Suppose, for example, that we were able to assess the likelihood that each of the three possible outcomes would occur. We might expect outcome *E* to occur with probability 0.5, *F* with probability 0.3, and *G*

---

[18]For one example see Dennis Epple and Lester Lave, "Helium: Investments in the Future," *The Bell Journal of Economics* 11 (Autumn 1980): 617–30.

with probability 0.2. Armed with this information, we can estimate the expected present value of net benefits. The *expected present value of net benefits* for a particular policy is defined as the sum of the outcomes of the present value of net benefits for that policy, where each outcome is weighted by its probability of occurrence. Symbolically this is expressed as

$$EPVNB_j = \sum_{i=1}^{I} P_i PVNB_{ij} \quad j = 1, \ldots, J$$

where $EPVNB_j$ = the expected value of net benefits for policy j

P_i = the probability of the ith outcome occurring

$PVNB_{ij}$ = is the present value of net benefits for policy j, if outcome i prevails

J = the number of policies being considered

I = the number of outcomes being considered

Once this calculation has been made, the final step is to select the policy with the highest expected present value of net benefits.

This approach has the substantial virtue that it weighs higher probability outcomes more heavily. However, it also makes a specific assumption about society's preference for risk. This approach is appropriate if society is risk neutral. *Risk neutrality* can be defined most easily by the use of an example. Suppose you were allowed to choose between being given a definite $50 or entering a lottery in which you had a 50 percent chance of winning $100 and a 50 percent chance of winning nothing. (Notice that the expected value of this lottery is $50 = 0.5($100) + 0.5($0).) You would be said to be risk neutral if you would be indifferent between these two choices. If you view the lottery as more attractive, you would be exhibiting *risk-loving* behavior, and a preference for the definite $50 would suggest *risk-averse* behavior. Using the expected present value of net benefits approach implies that society is risk-neutral.

Is this a valid assumption? The evidence is mixed. The existence of gambling suggests that at least some members of society are risk lovers; the existence of insurance suggests that, at least for some risks, others are risk-averse. Because the same people may gamble and own insurance policies, it's likely that the type of risk may be important.

Even if individuals were demonstrably risk-averse, this would not be a sufficient condition for the government to forsake risk neutrality in evaluating public investments. One famous article argues that risk neutrality is appropriate because "when the risks of a public investment are publicly borne, the total cost of risk-bearing is insignificant and, therefore, the government should ignore uncertainty in evaluating public investments."[19] The logic behind this result suggests that as the number of risk bearers (and the degree of diversification of risks) increases, the amount of risk borne by any individual diminishes to zero.

When the decision is irreversible, considerably more caution is appropriate.[20] Irreversible decisions may subsequently be regretted, but the option to change courses will be lost forever.

---

[19]Kenneth J. Arrow and Robert C. Lind, "Uncertainty and the Evaluation of Public Investment Decisions," *American Economic Review* 60, No. 3 (June, 1970): 366.

[20]K. J. Arrow and A. C. Fisher, "Preservation, Uncertainty, and Irreversibility," *Quarterly Journal of Economics* 87 (1974): 312–19.

Extra caution also affords an opportunity to learn more about alternatives to a decision and its consequences before acting. Isn't it comforting to know that procrastination can occasionally be optimal?

There is a movement in national policy in both the courts and the legislature to search for imaginative ways to define acceptable risk.[21] In general, the policy approaches reflect a case-by-case approach. As we shall see in subsequent chapters, current policy reflects a high degree of risk aversion regarding a number of environmental problems.

Choosing the Discount Rate

In the previous chapter we discussed how the discount rate could be defined conceptually as the social opportunity cost of capital. This cost of capital can be divided further into two components: (1) the riskless cost of capital, and (2) the risk premium.

As Example 4.3 indicates, this has been (and continues to be) an important issue. When the public sector uses a discount rate lower than that in the private sector, the public sector will find more projects with longer payoff periods worthy of authorization. And as we have already seen, the discount rate is a major determinant of the allocation of resources among generations as well.

Traditionally, economists have used long-term interest rates on government bonds as one measure of the cost of capital, adjusted by a risk premium that would depend on the riskiness of the project considered. Unfortunately, the choice of how large an adjustment to make has been left to the discretion of the analysts. This ability to affect the desirability of a particular project or policy by the choice of discount rate led to a situation in which government agencies were using a variety of discount rates to justify programs or projects they supported. One set of hearings conducted by Congress during the 1960s discovered that, at that time, agencies were using discount rates ranging from zero percent to 20 percent.[22]

During the early 1970s the Office of Management and Budget came out with a circular that required all government agencies, with some exceptions,[23] to use a discount rate of 10 percent in their benefit/cost analysis.[24] This standardization reduces biases by eliminating the agency's ability to choose a discount rate that justifies a predetermined conclusion. It also allows a project to be considered without regard to fluctuations in the true social cost of capital

---

[21]An excellent collection of essays on this subject is contained in Theodore S. Glickman and Michael Gough, eds., *Readings in Risk* (Washington, DC: Resources for the Future, 1990).

[22]Senator William Proxmire, "PPB, The Agencies and the Congress," in *The Analysis and Evaluation of Public Expenditures: The PPB System,* U.S. Congress, Joint Economic Committee, Subcommittee on Economy in Government (Washington, DC: Government Printing Office, 1969): xiii.

[23]The main exception involves water resources projects. The discount rates used for these projects are computed once each year by the U.S. Treasury Department and transmitted to the Water Resources Council, an independent, executive coordinating agency. See Charles W. Howe, *Natural Resources Economics: Issues, Analysis, and Policy* (New York: John Wiley & Sons, 1979), 158.

[24]Circular No. A-94, as revised 27 March 1972.

EXAMPLE 4.3

The Importance of the Discount Rate

For years the United States and Canada had been discussing the possibility of constructing a tidal-power project in the Passamaquoddy Bay between Maine and New Brunswick. This project would have heavy initial capital costs but low operating costs, which presumably would hold for a long time into the future. As part of their analysis of the situation, a complete inventory of costs and benefits was completed in 1959.

Using the same benefit and cost figures, Canada concluded that the project should not be built, the United States that it should. Because these conclusions were based on the same benefit/cost data, the differences can be attributed solely to the use of different discount rates. The United States used 2.5 percent; their Canadian counterparts used 4.125 percent. The higher discount rate makes the initial cost weigh much more heavily in the calculation, leading to the Canadian conclusion that the project yields a negative net benefit. Because the lower discount rate weights the lower future operating costs relatively more heavily, the Americans saw the net benefit as positive.

There are a number of other examples, as well. During 1962, Congress authorized a number of water projects that had been justified by benefit/cost analysis using a discount rate of 2.63 percent. Upon examining these projects, economists Fox and Herfindahl found that, at an 8 percent rate of discount, only 20 percent of the projects would have had favorable benefit/cost ratios.

The choice of the discount rate even played a major role during a highly publicized dispute between President Jimmy Carter and Congress. President Carter wanted to rescind authorization from many previously approved water projects that he viewed as wasteful. The President based his conclusions on a discount rate of 6.38 percent, whereas Congress was using a lower one.

Far from being an esoteric subject, the choice of the discount rate is fundamentally important in defining the role of the public sector, the types of projects undertaken, and the allocation of resources across generations.

Sources: Edith Stokey and Richard Zeckhauser, *A Primer for Policy Analysis* (New York: W. W. Norton, 1978): 164–65; Raymond Mikesell, *The Rate of Discount for Evaluating Public Projects* (Washington, DC: The American Enterprise Institute for Public Policy Research, 1977): 3–5; Irving K. Fox and Orris C. Herfindahl, "Attainment of Efficiency in Satisfying Demands for Water Resources," *American Economic Review* 54 (May 1964): 202.

---

due to cycles in the behavior of the economy. On the other hand, when the social opportunity cost of capital differs from this administratively determined level, the benefit/cost analysis generally will not define the efficient allocation.[25]

---

[25]For a detailed treatment of current discounting practices in the U.S. government, see the special issue of the *Journal of Environmental Economics and Management* 18, No. 2, Part 2 (March 1990), which is devoted to this subject.

A Critical Appraisal

The approaches to benefit estimation are sophisticated, but most observers feel that the resulting estimates are not yet sufficiently reliable that they could be used to fine-tune policy. One well-known survey of the field, commissioned by the Council on Environmental Quality, a government body, concluded:

> This report makes two points quite clear. First, in spite of recent advances, the estimation of certain kinds of environmental benefits is still in need of much additional refinement. . . . Second, where state-of-the art analyses of environmental benefits have been undertaken—as exemplified by the studies in this report—they strongly suggest that environmental protection is good economics.[26]

Although the estimates are certainly good enough to tell us that the benefits from environmental control are large and worth pursuing, they are not reliable enough to use in picking a single pollution level as the efficient one.

Similar concerns can be raised about costs. The Environmental Protection Agency (EPA) commissioned a study to examine just how accurate cost forecasts were. The study compared actual capital outlays by firms responding to the pollution-control laws to the forecasts of those same costs made earlier by both the EPA and by affected industries. When issued in June 1980, the report found that "both EPA and industry forecasts tend to overestimate compliance costs more often than they underestimate these costs."[27] Further, the report found that some of these overestimates were substantial. For the oil-refining industry, for example, both EPA and the industry projected capital costs of $1.4 billion. The actual costs were around $590 million, less than half of the projected total.

We have seen that it is sometimes, though not always, difficult to estimate benefits and costs. When this estimation is difficult or unreliable, it limits the value of a benefit/cost analysis. This problem would be particularly disturbing if biases tended to systematically increase or decrease net benefits. Do such biases exist?

In the early 1970s, economist Robert Haveman did a major study that sheds some light on this question. Focusing on Army Corps of Engineers water projects, such as flood control, navigation, and hydroelectric power generation, Haveman compared the *ex ante* (before the fact) estimates of benefits and costs with their *ex post* (after the fact) counterparts. Thus he was able to address the issues of accuracy and bias. His conclusions were:

> In the empirical case studies presented, *ex post* estimates of benefits often showed little relationship to their *ex ante* counterparts. On the basis of the few cases and the *a priori* analysis presented here, one could conclude that there is a serious bias incorporated into agency *ex ante* evaluation procedures, resulting in persistent overstatement of expected benefits. Similarly in the analysis of project construction costs, enormous variance was found among projects in the relationship between estimated and realized costs. Although no persistent bias in estimation was apparent, nearly

[26]A. Myrick Freeman, III, *The Benefits of Air and Water Pollution Control: A Review and Synthesis of Recent Estimates,* a report prepared for the Council on Environmental Quality (December 1979): xi–xii.

[27]Cited in "Antipollution Costs Were Overestimated by Government and Industry, Study Says," *The Wall Street Journal,* 19 June 1980, p. 7.

50 percent of the projects displayed realized costs that deviated by more than plus or minus 20 percent from *ex ante* projected costs.[28]

In the cases examined by Haveman, at least, the notion that benefit/cost analysis is purely a scientific exercise was clearly not consistent with the evidence; the biases of the analysts were merely translated into numbers.

Another shortcoming of benefit/cost analysis is that it does not really address the question of who reaps the benefits and who pays the cost. It is quite possible for a particular course of action to yield high net benefits, but to have the benefits borne by one group of society and the costs borne by another.(Remember Example 4.2?) This admittedly extreme case does serve to illustrate a basic principle—insuring that a particular policy is efficient provides an important, but not always the sole, basis for public policy. Other aspects, such as who reaps the benefit or bears the burden, are also important.

In summary, on the positive side, benefit/cost analysis is frequently a very useful part of the policy process. Even when the underlying data are not strictly reliable, the outcomes may not be sensitive to that unreliability. In other circumstances, the data may be reliable enough to give indications of the consequences of broad policy directions, even when they are not reliable enough to "fine-tune" those policies. When done correctly, benefit/cost analysis can provide a useful complement to the other influences on the political process by clarifying what choices yield the highest net benefits to society.

On the negative side, benefit/cost analysis has been attacked as seeming to promise more than it can actually deliver, particularly in the absence of solid benefit information. There have been two responses to this kind of concern. First, regulatory processes have been developed that can be implemented with very little information and yet have desirable economic properties. The recent reforms in air-pollution control, which we shall cover in Chapter 13, provide a powerful example.

The second approach involves techniques that supply useful information to the policy process without relying on controversial techniques to monetize environmental services, which are difficult to value. The rest of this chapter deals with the two most prominent of these—cost-effectiveness analysis and impact analysis.

Even when benefits are difficult or impossible to quantify, economic analysis has much to offer. Policymakers should know, for example, how much various policy actions will cost and what their impacts on society will be, even if the efficient policy choice cannot be identified with any certainty. Cost-effectiveness analysis and impact analysis both respond to this need, albeit in different ways.

COST-EFFECTIVENESS ANALYSIS

What can be done to guide policy when the requisite valuation for benefit/cost analysis is either unavailable or not sufficiently reliable? Without a good measure of benefits, making an efficient choice is no longer possible.

---

[28]Robert H. Haveman, *The Economic Performance of Public Investments: An* Ex Post *Evaluation of Water Resources Investments* (Baltimore, MD: Johns Hopkins University Press, for Resources for the Future, 1972).

In such cases it frequently is possible, however, to set a policy target on some other basis. One example is pollution control. What level of pollution should be established as the maximum acceptable level? In many countries that level has been determined by studies on human health. Studies of the effects of a particular pollutant on human health are assembled. Researchers attempt to find a threshold level below which no damage seems to occur. That threshold is then further lowered to provide a margin of safety, and the new threshold becomes the pollution target.

Other approaches could be used to decide on very different kinds of policy targets. Ecologists could help to define the critical numbers of certain species or the specific critical wetlands resources that should be preserved.

Once that objective is specified, however, economic analysis can have a great deal to say about the cost consequences of choosing a means of achieving that objective. The cost consequences are important in order to assure that wasteful expenditures do not trigger a political backlash.

Typically, several means of achieving the specified objective are available; some will be relatively cheap, but others turn out to be very expensive. The problems are frequently complicated enough that identifying the cheapest manner of achieving an objective cannot be accomplished without analyzing the situation.

Cost-effectiveness analysis frequently involves an optimization procedure. An *optimization procedure,* in this context, is merely a systematic method for finding the least expensive way to accomplish the objective. This procedure does not generally produce an efficient allocation because the predetermined objective may not be efficient. All efficient policies are cost effective, but not all cost-effective policies are efficient.[29]

In our pollution control example, cost-effectiveness can be used to find the least-cost means of meeting a particular standard and its associated cost. Using this cost as a benchmark case, we can estimate how much costs could be expected to increase from this minimum level if policies that are not cost effective are implemented. Cost-effectiveness analysis can also be used to determine how much compliance costs can be expected to change if the EPA chooses a more-stringent or less-stringent standard. The case study presented in Example 4.4 not only illustrates the use of cost-effectiveness analysis, it also shows that costs can be very sensitive to the regulatory approach chosen by the EPA.

IMPACT ANALYSIS

What can be done when the information needed to perform a benefit/cost analysis or a cost-effectiveness analysis is not available? The analytical technique designed to deal with this problem is called impact analysis. An *impact analysis,* whether it focuses on economic impact or environmental impact or both, attempts to quantify the consequences of various actions.

---

[29]You may recognize an analogy from your introductory economics course. A firm that uses the cheapest possible method for producing a given output will not be maximizing profits unless the chosen output level is the one that maximizes profits. Thus, profit maximization implies cost minimization, but the converse is not necessarily true.

EXAMPLE 4.4

NO$_2$ Control in Chicago: An Example of Cost-Effectiveness Analysis

As part of its mandate to implement and enforce the Clean Air Act, the Environmental Protection Agency, a part of the executive branch of the federal government, commissioned a study to examine, among other things, the cost consequences of implementing two different air quality standards by a variety of regulatory approaches. The final report, issued on 17 September 1979, shows just how sensitive costs in this area are to the regulatory approach.

The authors of the report used information on the cost of control for each of 797 stationary sources of nitrogen oxide emissions in the city of Chicago for various degrees of control. A total of 100 receptors measured the air quality at 100 different locations within the city. The relationship between ambient air quality at those receptors and emissions from the 797 sources was then modeled using mathematical equations. Once these equations were estimated, the model was calibrated to ensure that it was capable of re-creating the actual situation in Chicago. Following successful calibration, this model was used to simulate what would happen if EPA were to take various regulatory actions.

The first issue addressed was, "How much would costs increase, in the least cost solution, if the ambient air quality standard were changed from 500 micrograms to 250 micrograms per cubic meter?" Note that the latter implies much cleaner air than the former. The analysis indicated that the least-cost means of meeting the more stringent standard would cost about $24 million a year, whereas the cost of meeting the 500 microgram per cubic meter standard would be only $1 million. In other words, the stricter standard implies an annual cost some 24 times as high. Note that this analysis does not give any hint as to whether the additional expenditure is efficient. One would need the benefit estimates to decide that.

The second issue addressed was the sensitivity of control costs for meeting the more stringent 250 microgram per cubic meter standard to the regulatory approach chosen by EPA. The study considered several possibilities, two of which were (1) equal percentage reductions in all sources and (2) the least-cost solution. The results were striking. In order to ensure that the standard was met by all receptors under the equal-percentage reduction approach, all sources were required to cut back their emissions by 90 percent at an annual cost of $254 million. The least-cost solution, which targets the greatest reductions at those firms capable of achieving them most cheaply, was estimated to cost only $24 million per year.

Conclusions such as these have triggered a series of major reforms in air-pollution control that are designed to reduce costs without sacrificing air quality. These reforms have reduced some of the conflict between environmentalists and industrialists. We shall cover these in some detail in Chapter 13.

Source: Robert J. Anderson, Jr., Robert O. Reid, and Eugene P. Seskin, *An Analysis of Alternative Policies for Attaining and Maintaining a Short-Term NO$_2$ Standard* (Princeton, NJ: MATHTECH, Inc., 1979).

In contrast to benefit/cost analysis, a pure impact analysis makes no attempt to convert all these consequences into a one-dimensional measure, such as dollars, to ensure comparability. In contrast to both benefit/cost analysis and cost-effectiveness analysis, impact analysis does not necessarily attempt to optimize. Impact analysis places a large amount of relatively undigested information at the disposal of the policymaker. It is up to the policymaker to assess the importance of the various consequences and act accordingly.

On January 1, 1970, President Nixon signed the National Environmental Policy Act of 1969. This act, among other things, directed all agencies of the Federal Government to

> include in every recommendation or report on proposals for legislation and other major Federal actions significantly affecting the quality of the human environment, a detailed statement by the responsible official on—
>
> (i) the environmental impact of the proposed action,
>
> (ii) any adverse environmental effects which cannot be avoided should the proposal be implemented,
>
> (iii) alternatives to the proposed action,
>
> (iv) the relationship between local short-term uses of man's environment and the maintenance and enhancement of long-term productivity, and
>
> (v) any irreversible and irretrievable commitments of resources which would be involved in the proposed action should it be implemented.[30]

This was the beginning of the environmental impact statement, which is now a familiar, if controversial, part of environmental policy making.

Current environmental impact statements are more sophisticated than their early predecessors and may contain a benefit/cost analysis or a cost-effectiveness analysis in addition to other more traditional impact measurements. In the past, however, the tendency has been to issue huge environmental impact statements that are virtually impossible to comprehend in their entirety.

In response, the Council on Environmental Quality, which, by law, administers the environmental impact statement process, has set content standards that are now resulting in shorter, more concise statements. To the extent that they merely quantify consequences, statements can avoid the problem of "hidden value judgments" that sometimes plague benefit/cost analysis, but they do so only by bombarding the policymakers with masses of noncomparable information. All three of the techniques discussed in this chapter are useful, but none of them can stake a claim as being universally the "best" approach. The nature of the information that is available and its reliability make a difference.

SUMMARY

In this chapter, we have examined the most prominent, but certainly not the only, economic techniques available to supply policymakers with the information needed to implement environmental policy. We have seen that benefit/cost analysis offers the most concrete guidance.

---

[30] 83 STAT 853.

For some functions, such as choosing the efficient level of pollution control, it is difficult to implement. Even so, the exercise of identifying the costs and benefits, as well as assessing their importance, can be an extremely valuable part of the policy process.

Even when benefits are difficult to calculate, economic analysis in the form of cost-effectiveness can be valuable. This technique can establish the least expensive ways to accomplish predetermined policy goals and to assess the extra costs involved when policies other than the least-cost policy are chosen. What it cannot do is answer the question of whether those predetermined policy goals are efficient.

At the end of the spectrum is impact analysis, which merely identifies and quantifies the impacts of particular policies without any pretense of optimality or even comparability of the information generated. Impact analysis does not guarantee an efficient outcome.

This chapter has examined a major issue that will recur throughout the book—the role of information in structuring an appropriate relationship between humankind and the environment. We have seen information problems at many levels—the absence of knowledge about the consequences of various courses of action; inability to compare different types of information in an uncontroversial way, even when we can identify impacts; and possible biases in the structuring of information, as well as in the process of transmitting it to policymakers. We must remain cognizant of these issues as we examine specific environmental problems. We begin that investigation in the next chapter with population growth, which is a major influence on both the timing and the intensity of many other environmental problems.

FURTHER READING

Barde, Jean-Philippe, and David W. Pearce. *Valuing the Environment: Six Case Studies* (London: Earthscan Publications, 1991). A series of essays describing the use of economic valuation of environmental resources to inform public policy. Includes case studies from Germany, Italy, the Netherlands, Norway, the United Kingdom, and the United States.

Cummings, Ronald G., David S. Brookshire, and William D. Schulze. *Valuing Environmental Goods: An Assessment of the Contingent Valuation Method* (Totowa, NJ: Rowman and Littlefield, 1986). A critical evaluation of the contingent valuation method by both practitioners and impartial reviewers.

Dixon, John A., and Maynard M. Hufschmidt. *Economic Valuation Techniques for the Environment* (Baltimore, MD: Johns Hopkins University Press, 1986). Several case studies on the application of valuation techniques to environmental problems in less developed countries.

Kelman, Steven. "Cost-Benefit Analysis—An Ethical Critique," *Regulation* (January/February 1981), 33–40. Kelman suggests that attempts to expand the use of benefit/cost analysis in the areas of environmental, health, and safety regulation raise troubling ethical questions.

Kneese, Allen V. *Measuring the Benefits of Clean Air and Water* (Washington, DC: Resources for the Future, 1984). An accessible introduction to a large number of studies that attempt to quantify the benefits of cleaner air and water.

Lave, Lester B., ed. *Quantitative Risk Assessment in Regulation* (Washington, DC: The Brookings Institution, 1982). This book examines the requirements for quantitative risk assessment and the role it has played in the recent decisions of several regulatory agencies. The authors of the essays see a much larger possible role for quantitative risk assessment.

Mitchell, Robert Cameron, and Richard T. Carson. *Using Surveys to Value Public Goods: The Contingent Valuation Method* (Washington, DC: Resources for the Future, 1989). A comprehensive examination of contingent valuation research with brief summaries of representative studies.

Smith, V. Kerry, ed. *Environmental Policy under Reagan's Executive Order: The Role of Benefit-Cost Analysis* (Chapel Hill: University of North Carolina Press, 1984). Written by leading practitioners, this collection of essays takes stock of how President Reagan's Executive Order requiring benefit/cost analysis of proposed regulations has affected the making of policy.

ADDITIONAL REFERENCES

Boyle, Kevin J., and Richard C. Bishop. "Valuing Wildlife in Benefit-Cost Analysis: A Case Study Involving Endangered Species," *Water Resources Research* 23, No. 5 (May 1987): 943–50.

Brookshire, D. S., M. A. Thayer, W. D. Schulze, and R. C. d'Arge. "Valuing Public Goods: A Comparison of Survey and Hedonic Approaches," *The American Economic Review* 72 (March 1982): 165–77.

Clawson, Marion, and Jack Knetsch. *Economics of Outdoor Recreation* (Baltimore: Johns Hopkins University Press, for Resources for the Future, 1966).

Fisher, Ann. "The Value of Reducing Risks of Death: A Note on New Evidence" *Journal of Policy Analysis and Management* 8, No. 1 (1989): 88–100.

Fisher, Anthony C., John V. Krutilla, and Charles J. Chicchetti. "Alternative Uses of Natural Environments: The Economics of Environmental Modification," in John V. Krutilla, ed., *Natural Environments: Studies in Theoretical and Applied Analysis* (Washington, DC: Johns Hopkins University Press, for Resources for the Future, 1972): 18–53.

Freeman, A. Myrick, III. *The Benefits of Environmental Improvement: Theory and Practice* (Baltimore, MD: Johns Hopkins University Press, for Resources for the Future, 1979).

Freeman, A. Myrick, III. *Air and Water Pollution Control: A Benefit-Cost Assessment* (New York: John Wiley & Sons, 1982).

Freeman, A. Myrick, III. *The Benefits of Air and Water Pollution Control: A Review and Synthesis of Recent Estimates,* a report prepared for the Council on Environmental Quality (December 1979).

Haveman, Robert H. *The Economic Performance of Public Investments: An* Ex Post *Evaluation of Water Resource Investments* (Baltimore, MD: Johns Hopkins University Press, for Resources for the Future, 1972).

Hufschmidt, Maynard, David E. James, Anton D. Meister, Blair T. Bower, and John A. Dixon. *Environment, Natural Systems, and Development: An Economic Valuation Guide* (Baltimore, MD: Johns Hopkins University Press, 1983).

Lave, Lester B., and Eugene P. Seskin. *Air Pollution and Human Health* (Baltimore, MD: Johns Hopkins University Press, 1977).

Lave, Lester B., ed. *Quantitative Risk Assessment in Regulation* (Washington, DC: The Brookings Institution, 1982).

Mikesell, Raymond. *The Rate of Discount for Evaluating Public Projects* (Washington, DC: The American Enterprise Institute for Public Policy Research, 1977).

Rowe, R. D., R. d'Arge, and D. S. Brookshire. "An Experiment on the Economic Value of Visibility," *Journal of Environmental Economics and Management* 7 (March 1980): 1–19.

Smith, V. Kerry, ed. *Environmental Resources and Applied Welfare Economics: Essays in Honor of John V. Krutilla* (Washington, DC: Resources for the Future, 1988).

DISCUSSION QUESTIONS

1. Is risk neutrality an appropriate assumption for cost/benefit analysis? Why or why not? Does it seem more appropriate for some environmental problems than others? If so, which ones? If you were evaluating the desirability of locating a hazardous waste incinerator in a particular town, would the Arrow-Lind rationale for risk neutrality be appropriate? Why or why not?

2. Was the executive order issued by President Reagan mandating a heavier use of cost/benefit analysis in regulatory rulemaking a step toward establishing a more rational regulatory structure, or was it a subversion of the environmental policy process? Why?

3. Certain environmental laws prohibit the EPA from considering the costs of meeting various standards when the levels of the standards are set. Is this a good example of "putting first things first" or simply an unjustifiable waste of resources? Why?

CHAPTER 5

The Population Problem

The 1990s will be a crucial decade. The choices of the next ten years will decide the speed of population growth for much of the next century;. . . they will decide whether the pace of damage to the environment speeds up or slows down;. . . they may decide the future of the earth as habitation for humans.

DR. NAFIS SADIK, EXECUTIVE DIRECTOR OF THE UN POPULATION FUND
THE STATE OF THE WORLD POPULATION 1990

INTRODUCTION

In the first chapter of this book we examined two strikingly different views of what the future holds for the world economic system. At the heart of those views lie rather divergent views of the world population problem. Meadows and her team see population growth as continuing relentlessly, putting enormous pressure on food and environmental resources. Kahn, on the other hand, sees the world as being in a period of transition from high rates of natural increase to strikingly lower ones, culminating eventually in zero population growth. Because of abundant technological possibilities for satisfying the temporarily increasing, but eventually stable, population, Kahn maintains an optimistic outlook.

These views are symptomatic of a debate that has deep historical roots. Thomas Malthus, a turn-of-the-century classical economist, concluded that population growth posed a trap for nations seeking to develop. Temporary increases in income were seen as triggering increases in population until the land could no longer supply adequate food. Paul Ehrlich has brought this Malthusian argument into the twentieth century by arguing that the very existence of all forms of life on the planet is jeopardized by population growth. In his provocatively titled book, *The Population Bomb,* he argues that population is not merely *an* important problem, it is *the* problem in ensuring long-term survival of the species.

Contrasting views are held by representatives of third-world countries and some prominent population economists—such as Julian Simon. Simon maintains that Ehrlich has not only overstated the seriousness of the problem, he also fails to recognize that population growth in many of the developing countries is desirable. It should be clear from this brief review that no consensus exists either on the seriousness of the problem or, indeed, whether the problem exists at all.

TABLE 5.1   Annual Average Rate of World Population Growth 1965–70, 1975–80, 1985–90 (percent)

	1965–70	*1975–80*	*1985–90*
World	2.04	1.75	1.63
Africa	2.62	2.97	3.02
Asia	2.43	1.86	1.63
Europe	0.64	0.42	0.27
South America	2.45	2.27	2.08
United States	1.08	1.06	0.86

Source: From *World Resources 1988–89.* Copyright © 1988 by World Resources and the International Institute for Environment and Development. Reprinted by permission of Basic Books, a division of HarperCollins Publishers, Inc.

In this chapter we shall examine the macroeconomic issues relating to population and economic growth, as well as the microeconomic issues dealing with economic determinants of fertility. We shall briefly examine the effects that population growth and economic growth each have on the other and shall follow this by a consideration of the economic approach to population growth and that approach can be used to facilitate population control.

HISTORICAL PERSPECTIVE

World Population Growth

It has been estimated that at the beginning of the Christian era, A.D. 1, world population stood at about 250 million people and was growing at 0.04 percent per year (not 4 percent!). Not long ago, the world's population passed 4 billion and was growing at an annual rate around 2.0 percent per year. If that 2.0 percent growth rate were to continue unabated, the world's population would double in only 35 years. Since the beginning of time, the population has grown to over 5 billion people; at a 2.0 percent growth rate, the next 5 billion could take only 35 years.

In recent years, with the notable exception of Africa, the average rate of population growth has declined(Table 5.1). This slowdown has been experienced in both developed and less-developed countries, although rates remain higher in the less-developed countries.

The World Fertility Survey, a multinational survey of some 400,000 women in 61 countries, revealed a significant downward trend in fertility rates and birthrates over the last decade. This tendency appears in both developing and developed nations, with only African nations bucking the trend.[1] The survey found several apparent causes, including increased use of contraception, a growing preference for fewer children, and couples marrying later.

Although the trend toward falling birthrates is pervasive, the fact remains that most developing countries still have, and can be expected to have in the future, substantial increases

---

[1]For an analysis of the factors underlying the tendency of African nations to be experiencing increases in fertility rates, see John C. Caldwell, "Fertility in Africa," in *Fertility Decline in the Less Developed Countries,* Nick Eberstadt, ed. (New York: Praeger, 1981): 97–118.

in their populations. Some 90 percent of the population growth between 1980 and 2000 is expected to occur in the poorer countries.

For example, in 1985–1990, Honduras, Kenya, Liberia, Zimbabwe, and Nicaragua all had annual average growth rates in excess of 3.0 percent. During the same period, East Germany, Italy, and Belgium all experienced annual average growth rates of less than one tenth of one percent. Austria, Denmark, Sweden, and West Germany all currently have declining populations.[2]

Population Growth in the United States

As seen in Table 5.1, population growth in the United States has followed the general declining pattern of most of the developed world, although in most periods American growth rates have exceeded the average for Europe by a substantial margin. These large reductions in American population growth rates have primarily been due to declines in the birthrate, which fell from a high of 55.2 live births per thousand population in 1820 to only 14.6 live births per thousand in 1975, the lowest recorded birthrate in the period covered by the data. By 1987 the birthrate had climbed back to 15.7 (Figure 5.1).

Birthrates provide a rather crude measure of the underlying population trends, however, primarily because they do not account for age structure. To understand the effect of age structure, let's separate the birthrate experience into two components: (1) the number of persons in the childbearing years, and (2) the number of children those persons are bearing.

To quantify the second of these components, the Census Bureau uses a concept known as the *total fertility rate,* which is the number of live births an average woman has in her lifetime if, at each year of age, she experiences the average birthrates occurring in the general population of similarly aged women. This concept can be used to determine what level of fertility would, if continued, lead to a stationary population. A *stationary population* is one in which age- and sex-specific fertility rates yield a birthrate that is constant and equal to the death rate, so the growth rate is zero. The level of the total fertility rate that is compatible with a stationary population is called the *replacement rate.* Rates higher than the replacement rate would lead to population growth; rates lower would lead to population declines. Once the replacement fertility rate is reached, the World Bank estimates that it takes approximately 25 years for the population to stabilize, due to the large numbers of families in the childbearing years. As the age structure reaches its older equilibrium, the growth rate declines until a stationary population is attained.

In the United States, the replacement rate is 2.11. The two children replace the mother and her mate, and the extra 0.11 is to compensate for those women who do not survive the childbearing years and for the fact that slightly more than 50 percent of births are males. The United States total fertility rate dropped below the replacement rate in 1972 and has remained below it ever since (Figure 5.2). In 1986 (the latest year for which data were available) the rate stood at 1.84. If it were to remain at this level for 25 years, the U.S. population could be expected to decline at a rate of 5.2 percent per year.

This introduction to the population situation serves to raise two questions: (1) What is the relationship between population growth and economic growth? and (2) How can the rate

---

[2]The comparative population-growth-rate figures can be found in World Resources Institute, *World Resources: 1990–91* (New York: Oxford University Press, 1990): 254–55.

FIGURE 5.1   U.S. Birthrates from 1880–1987

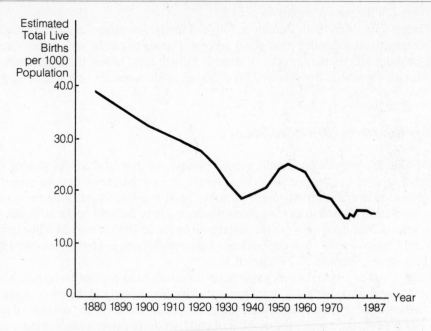

Sources: U.S. Bureau of the Census, *Historical Statistics of the United States, Colonial Times to 1970,* Part 1, Series B5–B10, p. 49; *Statistical Abstract of the United States, 1989,* p. 61; U.S. National Center for Health Statistics, *Vital Statistics of the United States,* annual; unpublished data.

of population growth be altered when alteration is appropriate? The first question lays the groundwork for considering the effect of population growth on quality of life, including the effects of a stationary population. The second allows us to consider public policies geared toward manipulating the rate of population growth when desirable.

EFFECTS OF POPULATION GROWTH ON ECONOMIC GROWTH

A number of questions guide our inquiry. Does population growth enhance or inhibit the opportunities of a country's citizens? Does the answer depend on the stage of development? Given that several countries are now entering a period of declining population growth, what are the possible effects of this decline on economic growth?

Population growth affects economic growth, and, as long as each person contributes something, those effects generally are positively correlated. As long as their marginal product is positive, additional people mean additional output. This is not a very restrictive condition, so it should usually hold true.

However, the existence of a positive marginal product is not a very appropriate test of the desirability of population growth! Perhaps a better one is to ask whether population growth positively affects the average citizen. Whenever the marginal product of an additional person

FIGURE 5.2   Total U.S. Fertility Rate, 1940–1986

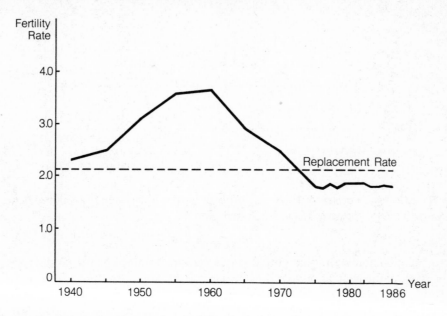

Sources: U.S. Bureau of the Census, *Historical Statistics of the United States, Colonial Times to 1970,* Part 1, B11, p. 50; *Statistical Abstract of the United States, 1989,* p. 64; U.S. National Center for Health Statistics, *Vital Statistics of the United States,* annual; and unpublished data.

is lower than the average product, adding more people simply reduces the welfare of the average citizen. Can you see why?

For a range of marginal productivities, between zero and the average product, economic growth measured in aggregate terms would increase, but measured in per capita terms would decrease. Similarly, for another range of marginal productivities—those greater than the average product—where economic growth increases regardless of whether it is measured in aggregate or per capita terms. Whether or not the material status of the average citizen is improved by population growth becomes a question of whether the marginal product of additional people is higher or lower than the average product.

To facilitate our examination of the population-related determinants of economic growth, let's examine a rather simple definition of output:

$$O = LX$$

where O is the output level, X is the output per worker, and L is the number of workers. This equation can be expressed in per capita terms by dividing both sides by population, denoted as P:

$$\frac{O}{P} = \frac{L}{P} X$$

FIGURE 5.3   Age Structure of Two Populations

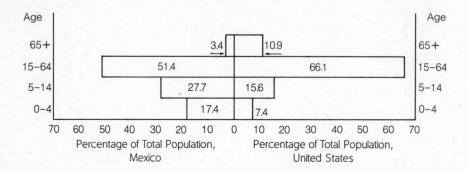

Source: Nancy Birdsall, "Population Growth and Poverty in the Developing World," *Population Bulletin* 35, No. 5 (Washington, DC: Population Reference Bureau, 1980).

This equation now states that output per capita is determined by the product of two factors: the share of the population that is in the labor force, and the output per worker. Each of these two factors provides a channel through which population growth affects economic growth.

The most direct effect of population growth on the percentage of the population employed, the *age structure effect,* results from induced changes in the age distribution. Suppose we were to compare two populations—one rapidly growing and one slowly growing. The one with the rapid growth would contain a much larger percentage of younger persons (Figure 5.3).

Due to its slow growth, the U.S. population is in general older. Whereas approximately 45 percent of Mexico's population is 14 years of age or younger, the comparable figure for the United States is 23 percent. This is reinforced at the other end of the age structure, where some 10.9 percent of the U.S. population is 65 or older as compared to only 3.4 percent in Mexico.

These differences in the age structure have mixed effects on the percentage of the labor force available to be employed. The abundance of youth in a rapidly growing population creates a large supply of people too young to work, a situation referred to as the *youth effect.* On the other hand, a country characterized by slow population growth has a rather larger percentage of persons who have reached, or are past, the traditional retirement age of 65, a situation referred to as the *retirement effect.* Some developing countries are experiencing both effects simultaneously as better public-health policies reduce death rates while birthrates remain high. How do the youth and retirement effects interact to determine the percentage of the population in the labor force? Does the youth effect dominate the retirement effect?

Examine the percentage of population in the prime working ages, 15–64. As Figure 5.3 shows, this percentage is much higher for the United States. A larger percentage of the population is in the working force in the United States than in Mexico. For Mexico the youth effect dominates.

This dominance of the youth effect generalizes to other countries. For example, in 1990 the African countries had an average of 51.7 percent of the population in the prime working age whereas European countries averaged 66.9 percent.[3] High population growth retards per capita economic growth by decreasing the percentage of the population in the labor force.

How about possible relationships between population growth and the second factor, the amount of output produced by the average worker? The most common way to enhance productivity is through the accumulation of capital. As the capital stock is augmented (for example, through the introduction of assembly lines or production machinery), workers become more productive. Can a connection between population growth and capital accumulation be established?[4]

The main connection examined by researchers has been between savings and capital accumulation. The availability of savings determines the level of additions to the capital stock. Availability of savings, in turn, is affected in part by the age structure of the population. Older populations are presumed to save more because less is spent directly on the care and nurturing of children. Therefore, all other things being equal, societies with rapidly growing populations could be expected to save proportionately less. This lowered availability of savings would lead to lower amounts of capital stock augmentation and lower productivity per worker.

A final model suggesting a negative effect of population growth on economic growth involves the presence of some fixed essential factor for which limited substitution possibilities exist (land or raw materials, for example). In this case, the *law of diminishing marginal productivity* applies. This law states that in the presence of a fixed factor (land), successively larger additions of a variable factor (labor) will eventually lead to a decline in the marginal productivity of the variable factor. It suggests that in the presence of fixed factors, successive increases in labor will drive the marginal product down. When it falls below the average product, per capita income will decline with further increases in the population.

Not all arguments suggest that growth in output per capita will be restrained by population growth. Perhaps the most compelling arguments for the view that population growth enhances per capita growth are those involving technological progress and *economies of scale* (Figure 5.4).

The vertical axis shows marginal productivity measured in units of output. The horizontal axis describes various levels of labor employed on a fixed amount of land. Population growth implies an increase in the labor force, which is recorded on the graph as a movement to the right on the horizontal axis.

The curve labeled $P(t_1)$ shows the functional relationship between the marginal product of labor and the amount of labor employed on a fixed plot of land at a particular point in time (t_1). Different curves represent different points in time because in each period of time there exists a unique state of the art in the knowledge of how to use the labor most effectively. Thus, as time passes, technological progress occurs, advancing the state of the art and shifting the productivity curves outward, as demonstrated by $P(t_2)$ *and* $P(t_3)$.

Three particular situations are demonstrated by Figure 5.4. At time t_1, an application of $L(t_1)$ yields a marginal product of $M(t_1)$. At times t_2 and t_3, the application of $L(t_2)$ and $L(t_3)$ units of labor respectively yield $M(t_2)$ *and* $M(t_3)$ marginal units of output. Marginal products have increased as larger amounts of labor were added.

---

[3]World Resources Institute, *World Resources: 1990–91* (New York: Oxford University Press, 1990): 256–57.

[4]This connection is clearly articulated in Ansley J. Coale and Edgar M. Hoover, *Population Growth and Economic Development in Low Income Countries* (Princeton, NJ: Princeton University Press, 1958).

FIGURE 5.4 Technological Progress and the Law of Diminishing Returns

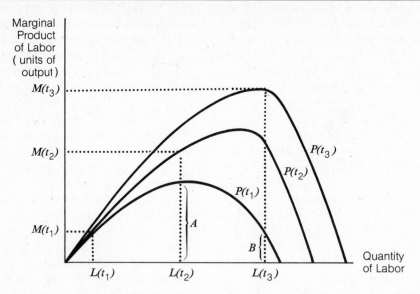

Consider what would have happened, however, if the state of technical knowledge had not increased. The increase in labor from $L(t_2)$ to $L(t_3)$ would have been governed by the $P(t_1)$ curve, and the marginal product would have declined from A to B. This is precisely the result anticipated by the law of diminishing marginal productivity. Technological progress provides one means of escaping the law of diminishing marginal productivity.

The second source of increase in output per worker is economies of scale. Economies of scale occur when increases in inputs lead to a more than proportionate increase in output. By increasing demand for output, population growth allows these economies of scale to be exploited. In the United States, at least, this has been a potent source of growth. Edward Dennison, in a major study of U.S. economic growth, concluded that economies of scale accounted for slightly over 10 percent of the growth in total potential national income per unit input in the 1929–1969 period.[5] Although it seems clear that the population level in the United States is already sufficient to exploit economies of scale, the same is not necessarily true for all developing countries.

In the absence of trade restrictions, however, the relevant market now is the global market, not the domestic market. The level of domestic population has little to do with the ability to exploit economies of scale in the modern global economy unless tariffs, quotas, or other trade barriers prevent the exploitation of foreign markets. If trade restrictions are a significant barrier, the appropriate remedy would be reducing trade restrictions, not boosting the local population.

Because these *a priori* arguments suggest that population growth could either enhance or retard economic growth, it is necessary to rely on empirical studies to sort out the relative importance of these effects. Several researchers have attempted to validate the premise that population growth inhibits per capita economic growth. Their attempts were based on the no-

---

[5]Edward Dennison, *Accounting for United States Economic Growth, 1929–1969* (Washington, DC: The Brookings Institution, 1974): 128–30.

tion that if the premise were true, one should be able to observe lower growth in per capita income in countries with higher population growth rates, all other things being equal.

A study for the National Research Council conducted an intensive review of the evidence.[6] Does the evidence support the expectations? Their major conclusions were:

1. Little evidence exists to support the expectation that the average savings rate depends on growth rates or the age structure of the population.

2. Slower population growth would raise the amount of capital per worker and, hence, the productivity per worker.

3. Slower population growth is unlikely to result in a net reduction in agricultural productivity and might well raise it.

4. There is no significant relation between national population density and economies of scale.

5. Rapid population growth puts more pressure on both depletable and renewable resources.

Rapid population growth may also increase the inequality of income. Perhaps the clearest statement of this argument comes from Peter Lindert.[7] He believes that high population growth increases the degree of inequality for a variety of reasons, but the most important involve a depressing effect on the earning capacity of children and on wages.

The ability to provide for the education and training of children, given fixed budgets of time and money, is a function of the number of children in the family—the fewer the children, the higher the proportion of income (and wealth, such as land) available to develop each child's earning capacity. Because low-income families tend to have larger families than high-income families do, the offspring from low-income families are usually more disadvantaged. The result is a growing gap between the rich and the poor.

Thomas Espenshade has provided some revealing estimates of parental expenditures on childrearing in the United States that tend to confirm certain key aspects of this argument.[8] The average expenditure to raise a child to age 18 depends crucially on income level and the size of the family, ranging from an expenditure of $135,700 (in constant 1981 dollars) for high-income families including two wage earners and only one child to $58,300 spent on the average child by a lower-income family including a single wage earner and three children. Adding in college expenditures where appropriate would boost these figures considerably.

Espenshade also examines the proportion of the typical family's income spent on childrearing as well as the sensitivity of this proportion to the number of children in the family. According to his analysis, families with only one child commit about 30 percent of total family expenditures to their child. This percentage rises to between 40 and 45 percent for two-

[6]Working Group on Population Growth and Economic Development, National Research Council, *Population Growth and Economic Development: Policy Questions* (Washington, DC: National Academy Press, 1986).

[7]Peter Lindert. *Fertility and Scarcity in America* (Princeton, NJ: Princeton University Press, 1978).

[8]Thomas J. Espenshade, *Investing in Children: New Estimates of Parental Expenditures* (Washington, DC: The Urban Institute Press, 1984).

child families and nearly 50 percent in three-child families. The detailed data in this study make clear that average expenditures per child consistently decline as the number of children in a family increases.

Another link between population growth and income inequality results from the effect of population growth on the labor supply. High population growth could increase the supply of labor faster than otherwise, depressing wage rates vis-à-vis profit rates. Because low-income groups have a higher relative reliance on wages for their income than do the rich, this effect would also increase the degree of inequality.

After an extensive review of the historical record for the United States, Lindert concludes:

> There seems to be good reason for believing that extra fertility affects the size and "quality" of the labor force in ways that raise income inequalities. Fertility, like immigration, tends to reduce the average "quality" of the labor force, by reducing the amounts of family and public school resources devoted to each child. The retardation in the historic improvement in labor force quality has in turn held back the rise in the incomes of the unskilled relative to those enjoyed by skilled labor and wealth-holders. [p. 258]

Lindert's interpretation of the American historical record does seem to be valid for developing countries. The National Research Council study found that slower population growth would decrease income inequality and raise the education and health levels of the children. This link between rapid population growth and income inequality provides an additional powerful motivation for controlling population. Slower population growth reduces income inequality.

At the level of individual countries, some powerful evidence is beginning to emerge on the negative environmental effects of population density when coupled with poverty. In Africa forestlands are declining as trees are cut down to provide fuel for cooking for an expanding population. Due to a shortage of land, peasants in Bangladesh settle on islands formed from the silt deposited by soil erosion. Several thousand were drowned when a cyclone hit the area in 1985. In Brazil and Southeast Asia, peasants are forced to farm marginal lands, which rapidly erode and lose their nutrients. Forced to sacrifice long-term objectives merely to survive, the poor are becoming both a major source of environmental problems and the major victims of them. Population growth bears some responsibility for both the degree of poverty and the intensity of the problems it triggers.

EFFECTS OF ECONOMIC GROWTH ON POPULATION GROWTH

Up to this point, we have considered the effect of population growth on economic growth. We have now to examine the converse relationship. Does economic growth affect population growth? Table 5.1 suggests that it may, because the higher-income countries are characterized by lower population growth rates.

This suspicion is reinforced by some further evidence. Most of the industrialized countries have passed through three stages of population growth. The conceptual framework that organizes this evidence is called the *theory of demographic transition*. This theory suggests that as nations develop they eventually reach a point where birthrates fall (Figure 5.5).

During Stage 1, the period immediately prior to industrialization, birthrates are stable and slightly higher than death rates, ensuring population growth. During Stage 2, the period

FIGURE 5.5   The Demographic Transition

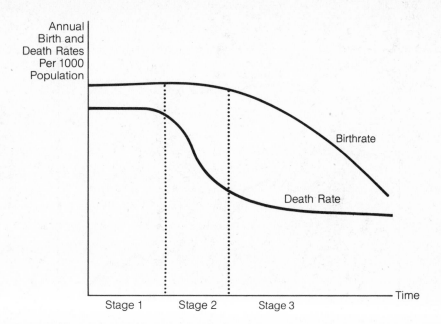

immediately following the initiation of industrialization, death rates fall dramatically with no accompanying change in birthrates. This decline in mortality results in a marked increase in life expectancy and a rise in the population-growth rate. In Western Europe, Stage 2 is estimated to have lasted somewhere around fifty years.

Stage 3, the period of demographic transition, involves large declines in the birthrate that exceed the continued declines in the death rate. Thus, the period of demographic transition involves further increases in life expectancy, but rather smaller population growth rates than characterized the second stage. The Chilean experience with the demographic transition is illustrated in Figure 5.6. Can you identify the stages?

The theory of demographic transition is useful because it suggests that reductions in population growth might accompany rising standards of living, at least in the long run. However, it also leaves many questions unanswered. Why does the fall in birthrates occur? Can the process be speeded up? Will lower-income countries automatically experience demographic transition as living standards improve? Are industrialization or better designed agricultural production systems possible solutions to "the population problem"?

To answer these questions it is necessary to begin to look more deeply into the sources of change behind the demographic transition. Once these sources are identified and understood, they can be manipulated in such a way as to produce the maximum social benefit.

THE ECONOMIC APPROACH TO POPULATION CONTROL

Is the current rate of population growth efficient? Is it sustainable? The issue of sustainability is most easily dealt with in specific natural resource settings (such as the ability to produce

FIGURE 5.6   Annual Birthrates, Death Rates, and Rates of Natural Population Increase in
Chile, 1929–1970

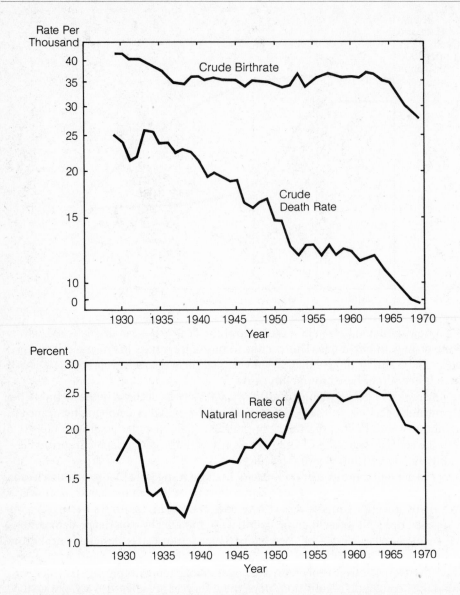

Sources: Michael C. Keeley, ed., *Population, Public Policy, and Economic Development,* p. 52 (New York: Praeger, 1976) an imprint of Greenwood Publishing Group, Inc., Westport CT.

sufficient food), so intensive consideration of that question will be deferred until succeeding chapters.

The efficiency question can be attacked in two ways. The first is to conduct a benefit/cost analysis of population control to see whether some government control would maximize effi-

EXAMPLE 5.1

The Value of an Averted Birth

If population growth tends to reduce average income, then the nation experiencing this population growth would have an incentive to spend money on population control. Determining how much money should be spent depends upon a comparison of the costs of the population control program with the value of an averted birth.

Enke and Zind developed a simulation model to assess the value of an averted birth. The model allowed for substitution among capital and labor, the restraining effect of the dependency ratio, and the effect of an age structure and income on saving. To obtain the value of averted births, they compared a scenario with no birth control to one in which a reduction in fertility over a 30-year period was compatible with 50 percent of all women in each age group practicing contraception. The implied terminal fertility rate was approximately 23 per 1,000.

On the basis of this simulation they concluded:

A modest birth control programme, costing perhaps 30 cents a year per head of national population, can raise average income over only 15 years by almost twice the percentage that it would rise without birth control. . . . The value of permanently preventing the birth of a marginal infant is about twice an LDC's annual income per head. [p. 41]

This is a controversial finding because there is not uniform agreement that the simulated mechanisms approximate those that would actually prevail in developing countries, particularly if the population growth is moderate rather than rapid. Nonetheless, it does suggest that for those countries that are experiencing very rapid population growth, the potential payoff to instituting means of controlling that population growth could be substantial.

Sources: S. Enke and R. Zind, "Effect of Fewer Births on Average Income," *Journal of Biosocial Science* 1 (1969): 41–55; Julian L. Simon, *The Economics of Population Growth* (Princeton, NJ: Princeton University Press, 1977).

---

ciency. Such a study was conducted by Enke and Zind (Example 5.1). Focused purely on the effects of additional population on output per capita, the study found that intensified population control measures would increase net benefits.

The demonstration that population growth reduces per capita income, however, is not sufficient to prove that an inefficiency exists. If the reduced output is borne entirely by the families of the children, this reduction may represent a conscious choice by parents to sacrifice production in order to have more children. The net benefit gained from having more children (not measured by Enke and Zind) would exceed the net benefit lost as output per person declined.

To establish whether or not population control is efficient, we must discover whether or not there are potential behavioral biases toward overpopulation. Will parents always make efficient childbearing decisions?

A negative response seems appropriate for several reasons. The first is derived from the previously discussed evidence that high population growth may exacerbate income inequality.

Income equality is a public good. The population as a whole cannot be excluded from the degree of income equality which exists. Furthermore, it is an indivisible good because, in a given society, the prevailing income distribution is the same for all the citizens of that society.

Why should individuals care about inequality *per se* as opposed to simply caring about their own income? Aside from a pure humane concern for others, particularly the poor, people care about inequality because it can create social tensions. When these social tensions exist, society is a less-pleasant place to live.[9]

The demand to reduce income inequality clearly exists in modern society, as evidenced by the large number of private charitable organizations created to fulfill this demand. Because the reduction of income inequality is a public good, we also know that these organizations cannot be relied upon to reduce inequality as much as would be socially justified. Similarly, for the same reason we know that parents will not take it sufficiently into account when they make their childbearing decisions. They will have too many children and will exacerbate income inequality in the process.

Two other externalities are apparent as well: (1) the cost of food and (2) the cost of education. It is common for developing countries to subsidize food by holding prices below market levels. Lower-than-normal food prices artificially lower the cost of children as long as the quantities of food available are maintained by government subsidy.[10]

The second area in which the costs of children are not fully borne by the parents is education. Primary education is usually financed by the state with the funds collected by taxes. The point is *not* that parents do not pay these costs; in part they do. The point is rather that their level of contribution is not usually sensitive to the number of children they have. The school taxes paid are generally the same whether parents have two children, ten children, or even no children. Thus the marginal educational expenditure for a parent—the additional cost of education due to the birth of a child—is certainly lower than the true social cost of educating that child.

Unfortunately, very little has been accomplished on assessing the empirical significance of these externalities. Despite this lack of evidence, the interest in controlling population is clear. The task is a difficult one. The right to bear children is considered in many countries, if not most, as an inalienable right, immune to influences outside the family. Indira Gandhi, the Prime Minister of India, lost an election in the late 1970s due principally to her aggressive and direct approach to population control. Though she subsequently regained her position, political figures in other democratic countries are not likely to miss the message. Dictating that no family can have more than two children is not politically palatable at this time. Such a dictum is seen as an unethical infringement on the rights of those who are mentally, physically, and monetarily equipped to care for larger families. Yet population control measures can provide a higher quality of life for the smaller number of individuals born while reducing the human impact on the planet. What, then, is a democratic country to do? How can it gain control over

---

[9] See Linda Feldman, "Study Correlates Population Rise, Political Instability," *The Christian Science Monitor* (26 June 1989): 8.

[10] Notice, however, that if the food is domestically produced and the effect of price controls is to lower the prices farmers receive for their crops, the consequence is to lower the demand for children in the agricultural sector. Can you see why?

FIGURE 5.7   The Demand for Children

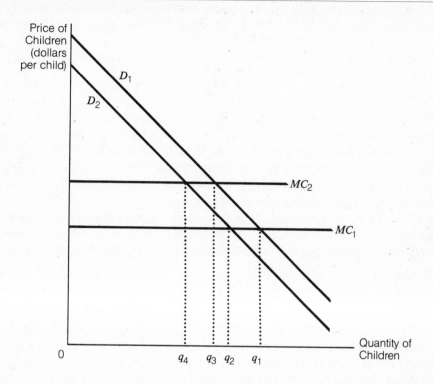

population growth while allowing individual families considerable flexibility in choosing their family size?

Successful population control involves two components: (1) lowering the desired family size, and (2) providing sufficient access to contraceptive methods and family planning information to allow that size family to be realized.

The economic approach to population control *indirectly* controls population by lowering the desired family size. This is accomplished by identifying those factors that affect desired family size and changing them. In order to use the economic approach, we need to know how fertility decision making is affected by the economic environment experienced by the family.

The major model attempting to assess the determinants of childbirth decision making from an economic viewpoint is called the *microeconomic theory of fertility*. The point of departure for this theory is viewing children as consumer durables. The key insight is that the demand for children will, as with more conventional commodities, be downward sloping. All other things being equal, the more expensive children become, the fewer will be demanded.

With this point of departure, childbearing decisions can be modeled within a traditional demand-and-supply framework (Figure 5.7). We shall designate the initial situation, prior to the imposition of any controls as the point where demand, designated by D_1, and marginal cost, designated by MC_1, are equal. The desired number of children at this point is given as q_1. Notice that, according to the analysis, the desired number of children can be reduced by an inward shift of the demand curve to D_2, or an upward shift in the marginal cost of children to MC_2, or both. What would cause these to shift?

Let's consider the demand curve. Why might it have shifted inward during the demographic transition? Several sources of this change have emerged:

1. The shift from an agricultural to an industrial economy reduces the productivity of children. In an agricultural economy, extra hands are useful, but in an industrial economy, child labor laws result in children contributing substantially less to the family. Therefore, the investment demand for children is reduced.

2. In countries with primitive savings systems, one of the very few ways a person can provide for old-age security is to have plenty of children to provide for him or her in the twilight years. One would not, at first glance, think of children as social security systems, but in many societies they are precisely that. When alternative means of providing for old-age security are developed, the demand for children decreases.

3. In some countries a woman's status is almost exclusively defined in terms of the number of children she bears. If personal status is positively correlated with desired family size, this will increase the demand for children.

4. A decrease in infant mortality can also cause the demand curve to shift inward. When infant mortality is high, it takes a large number of births to produce the desired number of children at the ages when they are needed. Support for this argument was obtained during an attempt to reduce infant mortality in one of the southern states of India. Apparently, this program did have the side effect of reducing the birthrate.[11]

5. Some evidence also suggests that the amount the demand curve shifts inward as a result of economic growth depends on the manner in which the increased employment associated with development is shared among the members of society. Those countries that have typically entered into a phase of sustained fertility decline in spite of low levels of average per capita income levels are usually characterized by a relatively equal distribution of income and a relatively widespread participation in the benefits of growth. (See Example 5.2.)

Desired family size is also affected by changes in the cost of children. The costs of raising children can be changed as a means of controlling population.

1. One of the main components of the cost of children is the opportunity cost of the mother's time. By increasing the educational and labor-market opportunities for women, the opportunity cost of raising children is increased. This can affect the observed fertility rate both by deferring the time of marriage and by causing a reduction in the number of children desired.

---

[11]A detailed exploration of the relationship between fertility and urbanization can be found in David Goldberg, "Residential Location and Fertility," in *Population and Development: The Search for Selective Intervention,* Ronald Ridker, ed. (Baltimore, MD: Johns Hopkins University Press, 1976): 387–428. Urban fertility rates generally are lower.

EXAMPLE 5.2

Fertility Decline in Korea: A Case Study

The dramatic fertility decline in the Republic of Korea that occurred during the period from 1960 to 1974 has been one of the fastest ever recorded. Therefore, it provides a unique opportunity to study the forces that led to this decline and the extent to which they might be applicable to other countries.

The period prior to the dramatic decline contained a series of shattering events, including the Korean War. Culturally homogeneous to start with, Korea emerged from this period as a relatively egalitarian society. During the fertility decline, Korea experienced very rapid economic growth, stimulated to a large extent by imported capital and technology. Because the development approach focused on labor-intensive technologies, the fruits of this development were spread rather uniformly throughout the economy. Rising real wages and an expanded demand for labor served to preserve the relatively equal income distribution that had been inherited from the 1950s.

This combination of rapid economic growth and widespread participation in that growth among various sectors of the economy produced a dramatic fertility decline in almost all groups of society. Birthrates started to decline simultaneously in all regions, classes, and categories of households.

The changes in economic institutions that accompanied economic growth reinforced the tendency toward declining fertility rates. This period saw the rise, for example, of savings institutions, the widespread ownership of property (which permitted the accumulation of some wealth), and social insurance. These tended to provide alternative mechanisms for assuring old-age security.

A substantial increase also occurred in the percentage of females in the labor force, resulting in an increase in the age of marriage and a reduction in the fertility rate of married women. At the same time, education levels of women rose, which also contributed to the decline.

Though the degree of income and cultural equality in Korea was unusual, many of the other factors contributing to fertility decline, such as pursuing a development plan that reduced income inequality as the nation grew, providing alternative social security systems, and assuring expanding labor-market opportunities for women, are available to other nations.

Source: Robert Repetto, *Economic Equality and Fertility in Developing Countries* (Baltimore, MD: Johns Hopkins University Press, 1979): 69–120.

---

2. As societies urbanize and industrialize, housing space becomes more expensive due to the concentrated demands in specific locations.[12] Thus although the cost of extra space for children may be low in rural settings, it is much higher in urban settings.

3. The cost of children to parents may also be affected to a large extent by the cost of education. As nations struggle to improve their literacy rates by universal compulsory

---

[12]Michael T. Kaufman, "South India Success Story: Small Families the Norm," *The New York Times* (6 March 1980): 2:3.

education, they may simultaneously raise the cost of children. These costs rise not only because of direct additional parental expenditures on education but also because of the earnings that are forgone when the children are in school rather than working.

4. As development occurs, parents generally demand more and higher-quality education for their children. Depending on the system for financing education, providing this higher-quality education may raise the cost of every child even if the cost of a given quality of education is not rising.

All of this provides a menu of opportunities for population control. The reasons listed here represent potent forces for change, yet these methods should be used with care. Inducing a family to have fewer children without assisting the family in satisfying the basic needs the children were fulfilling (such as old-age security) would be inequitable.

Policies in China illustrate just how far economic incentives can be carried.[13] In announced regulations, one-child parents received subsidized health expenditures; priority in education, health care and housing; and additional subsidized food. Meanwhile, parents who have more than two children received a reduction of 5 percent in their total income for the third child, 6 percent for the fourth, and so on. Also, families were denied access to further subsidized grain beyond that which they would already receive for their two previous children.

Initially these policies did bring about a rather dramatic fall in the birthrate in China, but recently the birthrate has taken an upturn. Although China's fertility rate had dipped as low as 2.1, by 1986 it had risen to 2.4. The policies are so draconian as to precipitate a degree of resistance sufficient to undermine the effort.

Countries seeking to reduce fertility do not have to resort to extreme measures. Policies such as enhancing the status of women, providing alternative sources of old-age security, and supplying employment opportunities that equalize income distribution are both humane and effective.

Vernon Ruttan has summarized some of the studies that have evaluated the effects of this type of approach: (a) Greater family wealth sustains higher education levels and better health; (b) a rise in the value of the mother's time has a positive effect of the demand for contraceptive services and a negative effect on fertility; (c) a rise in the value of the father's earnings has a positive effect on completed family size, child health, and child education; and (d) increases in mother's schooling has a negative effect on fertility and infant mortality and a positive effect on nutrition and children's schooling.[14]

In terms of population growth, child nutrition, and health these studies indicate a large payoff to making women fuller partners in the quest for improved living standards in the Third World. In the words of Dr. Nafis Sadik, Executive Director of the United Nations Population Fund:

---

[13]For a detailed investigation of China's policies see Karen Hardee-Cleaveland and Judith Banister, "Fertility Policy and Implementation in China, 1986–88" *Population and Development Review* 14, No. 2 (June 1988): 245–86.

[14]Vernon W. Ruttan, "Perspectives on Population and Development," *Indian Journal of Agricultural Economics* 39, No. 4 (October/December 1984): 636. Ruttan in turn credits Robert E. Evenson, "Notes on the New Home Economics," in *Home Economics and Agriculture in Third World Countries,* Miriam Seltzer, ed. (St. Paul, MN: University of Minnesota College of Home Economics Center for Youth Development and Research, 1980).

The extent to which women are free to make decisions affecting their lives may be the key to the future, not only of the poor countries, but the rich ones too. As mothers; producers or suppliers of food, fuel and water; traders and manufacturers; political and community leaders, women are at the centre of the process of change.[15]

The desire to reduce family size, however, is not sufficient if access to birth control information and contraceptives is inadequate. One study found that the adequacy of family planning programs varied markedly among the countries within a continent.[16] Where access was very good, fertility was declining, particularly when access was coupled with better education and opportunities for women.

SUMMARY

World population growth has slowed considerably in recent years, with only African nations resisting the trend. Population declines are already occurring in East Germany and are expected in the near future in a number of Northern European countries. The United States' total fertility rate is now below the replacement level. If maintained for a number of years, this fertility behavior would usher in an era of zero or negative population growth for the United States as well.

Those countries experiencing declines in their population growth will also experience a rise in the average age of their population. This transition to an older population should boost the growth of per capita income by increasing the share of the population in the labor force and by allowing more family wealth to be concentrated on the nutrition, health, and education of the children.

Slower population growth should also help to reduce income inequality. Because they typically have larger families, on average this effect will be felt most strongly in lower-income families. This tendency for incomes of lower-income families to increase faster than those of higher-income families should be reinforced by the effects on labor supply. By preventing an excess supply of labor, which holds wages down, slower population growth benefits wage earners. Wages are a particularly important source of income for lower-income families.

Although it is certainly premature to proclaim, as some have, an end to the population explosion,[17] it is similarly premature to label population growth as an insoluble problem. The evidence of the last few years suggests that steps to defuse *the population bomb* have been undertaken and are meeting with success.

---

[15]Nafis Sadik, *The State of World Population 1989* (New York: United Nations Population fund, 1989): 3.

[16]Robert J. Lapham and W. Parker Mauldin, "Contraceptive Prevalence: The Influence of Organized Family Planning Programs" *Studies in Family Planning* 16, No. 3 (1985): 123–24.

[17]For an articulation of this position, see Donald J. Bogue, "The End of the Population Explosion," *Public Interest* (Spring 1967): 11–20. For a critical appraisal, see Paul Demeny, "On the End of the Population Explosion," *Population and Development Review* 5 (March 1979): 141–62.

FURTHER READING

Commission on Population Growth and the American Future. *Research Reports,* Elliot R. Morss and Richie H. Reed, eds. (Washington, DC: Government Printing Office, 1972).

Vol. I	Demographic and Social Aspects of Population Growth
Vol. II	Economic Aspects of Population Change
Vol. III	Population Resources and the Environment
Vol. IV	Governance and Population: The Governmental Implications of Populatio Change
Vol. V	Population Distribution
Vol. VI	Aspects of Population Growth Policy
Vol. VII	Statements at Public Hearings

An excellent survey of population issues as they relate to the American future. Volumes II and III are particularly relevant to the theme of this book.

Easterlin, Richard A. "The Economics and Sociology of Fertility: A Synthesis," in Charles Tilly, ed., *Historical Studies of Changing Fertility* (Princeton, NJ: Princeton University Press, 1978): 57–133. One of the very few comprehensive surveys of the literature accessible to readers who are not mathematically adept.

Easterlin, Richard A., ed. *Population and Economic Change in Developing Countries* (Chicago: The University of Chicago Press, 1980). An excellent collection of essays on subjects ranging from child costs and economic development to an examination of the population explosion in preindustrial England.

Kelly, Allen C. "Economic Consequences of Population Change in the Third World," *Journal of Economic Literature* 26 (December 1988): 1685–1728. Excellent review of a complex literature with a detailed bibliography.

"New Economic Approaches to Fertility," a special supplement of the *Journal of Political Economy* 81, No. 2 (March/April 1973). A highly technical collection of essays that refine and test the economic theory of fertility. An excellent bibliography is included.

Schultz, T. Paul. *Economics of Population* (Reading, MA: Addison-Wesley, 1981). A useful intensive introduction to the field that is intended for undergraduates. Gives a sense of the controversies existing in the field.

Simon, Julian L. *The Economics of Population Growth* (Princeton, NJ: Princeton University Press, 1977). A comprehensive survey of the literature plus original work; proposes the idea that moderate population growth (as opposed to zero or high) may be helpful to developing countries.

ADDITIONAL REFERENCES

Becker, Gary. "An Economic Analysis of Fertility," in *Demographic and Economic Changes in Developed Countries,* National Bureau of Economic Research (Princeton, NJ: Princeton University Press, 1960): 209–31.

Davis, Kingsley, et al. *Below Replacement Fertility in Industrial Societies: Causes, Consequences, Policies* (New York: Cambridge University Press, 1987).

Easterlin, Richard A. *Population, Labor Force and Long Swings in Economic Growth* (New York: Columbia University Press, 1968).

Eberstadt, Nick. *Fertility Decline in the Less Developed Countries* (New York: Praeger Publishers, 1981).

Johnson, D. Gale, and Ronald D. Lee. *Population Growth and Economic Development: Issues and Evidence* (Madison, WI: University of Wisconsin Press, 1987).

Kuznets, Simon. *Population, Capital, and Growth: Selected Essays* (New York: W. W. Norton, 1973).

Lee, Ronald D., et al. eds. *Population, Food, and Rural Development* (New York: Oxford University Press, 1988).

Mahadevan, K. *Fertility Policies of Asian Countries* (Newbury Park, CA: SAGE Publications, 1988).

Repetto, Robert. "The Effects of Income Distribution on Fertility in Developing Countries" in Nick Eberstadt, ed., *Fertility Decline in the Less Developed Countries* (New York: Praeger Publishers, 1981): 254–73.

Ridker, Ronald, ed. *Population and Development: The Search for Selective Interventions* (Baltimore, MD: The Johns Hopkins University Press, 1976).

Simmons, Ozzie C. *Perspectives on Development and Population* (New York: Plenum, 1988).

DISCUSSION QUESTIONS

1. Fertility rates vary widely among various ethnic groups in the United States. Black and Spanish-speaking Americans have above-average rates, for example, whereas Jews have below-average fertility rates. This may be due to different ethnic beliefs, but it may also be due to economic factors. How could you use economics to explain these fertility rate differences? What tests could you devise to see whether this explanation has validity?

2. The microeconomic theory of fertility provides an opportunity to determine how public policies that were designed for quite different purposes could affect fertility rates. Identify some public policies (e.g., subsidies to people who own their own home, or subsidized day care) that could have an effect on fertility rates, and describe the relationship.

CHAPTER 6

Natural Resource Economics: An Overview

*The whole machinery of our intelligence, our general ideas and laws,
fixed and external objects, principles, persons, and gods, are so many
symbolic, algebraic expressions. They stand for experience; experience
which we are incapable of retaining and surveying in its multitudi-
nous immediacy. We should flounder hopelessly, like the animals, did
we not keep ourselves afloat and direct our course by these intellectual devices. Theory helps us to bear our ignorance of fact.*

SANTAYANA, *THE SENSE OF BEAUTY* (1896)

INTRODUCTION

In the *Limits to Growth* vision of the future, society's demand for resources suddenly exceeds
their availability. Rather than anticipating a smooth transition to a steady state, this vision estimates that the system will overshoot the resource base, precipitating a collapse. Is this realistic? Is profit maximization inconsistent with smooth adjustments to increasing scarcity?

We begin with the simple but useful *resource taxonomy* (classification system), used to
distinguish various measures of resource availability. Confusing these categories and thereby
using published information incorrectly can cause, and has caused, considerable mischief.

We then turn to the question of how markets allocate these resources over time. Whether
or not the market is capable of yielding a dynamically efficient allocation in the presence or
absence of a renewable substitute provides a focal point for the analysis. Succeeding chapters
will use these principles both to examine the allocation of energy, food, and water resources
and as a basis for developing more elaborate models of renewable biological populations such
as fisheries and forests.

A RESOURCE TAXONOMY

Three separate concepts are used to classify the stock of depletable resources: (1) *current reserves*, (2) *potential reserves*, and (3) *resource endowment*. In the United States the
Geological Survey (USGS) has the official responsibility for keeping records of the U.S. resource base, and they have developed the classification system described in Figure 6.1.

FIGURE 6.1   A Categorization of Resources

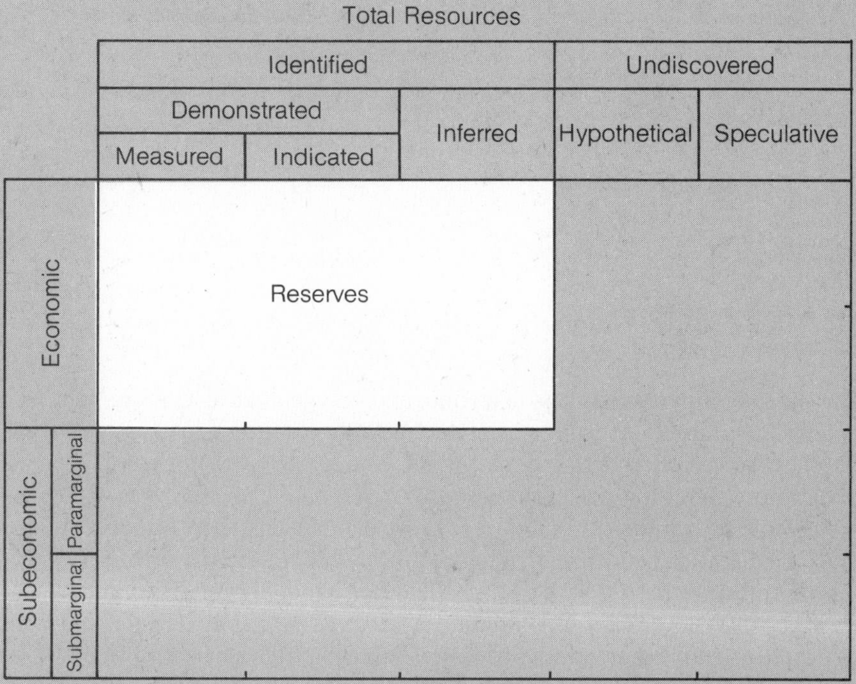

Terms

Identified resources: specific bodies of mineral-bearing material whose location, quality, and quantity are known from geological evidence, supported by engineering measurements.

Measured resources: material for which quantity and quality estimates are within a margin of error of less than 20 percent, from geologically well-known sample sites.

Indicated resources: material which quantity and quality have been estimated partly from sample analyses and partly from reasonable geological projections.

Inferred resources: material in unexplored extensions of demonstrated resources based on geological projections.

Undiscovered resources: unspecified bodies of mineral-bearing material surmised to exist on the basis of broad geological knowledge and theory.

Hypothetical resources: undiscovered materials reasonably expected to exist in a known mining district under known geological conditions.

Speculative resources: undiscovered materials that may occur either in known types of deposits in favorable geological settings where no discoveries have been made, or in yet unknown types of deposits that remain to be recognized.

SOURCE: U.S. Bureau of Mines and the U.S. Geological Survey. "Principle of the Mineral Resource Classification System of the U.S. Bureau of Mines and the U.S. Geological Survey," *Geological Survey Bulletin* 1450-A, 1976.

TABLE 6.1   Estimates of Ultimately Recoverable Oil from Enhanced Oil Recovery with 10 Percent Minimum Rate of Return (price in constant 1976 dollars)

Price per Barrel	Ultimate Recovery (10^9 barrels)
$11.62	21.2
$13.75	29.4
$22.00	41.6
$30.00	49.2
More than $30.00	51.1

Source: U.S. Congress, Office of Technology Assessment, *Enhanced Oil Recovery Potential in the United States* (Washington, DC: OTA, 1978): 7.

Notice the two dimensions—one economic and one geological. A movement from top to bottom represents movement from cheaply extractable resources to those extracted at substantially higher prices. By contrast, a movement from left to right represents increasing geological uncertainty about the size of the resource base.

Current reserves (white area in Figure 6.1) are defined as known resources that can profitably be extracted at current prices. The magnitude of these current reserves can be expressed as a number. *Potential reserves,* on the other hand, are most accurately defined as a function rather than a number. The amount of reserves potentially available depends upon the price people are willing to pay for those resources—the higher the price, the larger the potential reserves. For example, Congress conducted a study on the amount of additional oil that could be recovered from existing oil fields using enhanced recovery techniques such as injecting solvents or steam into the well to lower the density of the oil. These techniques, more expensive than conventional ones, allow greater amounts of oil to be recovered. As price is increased, the amount of oil that can be economically recovered also increases (Table 6.1).

The *resource endowment* represents the natural occurrence of resources in the earth's crust. Because prices have nothing to do with the size of the resource endowment, it is a geological rather than an economic concept. This concept is important because it represents an upper limit on the availability of terrestrial resources.

The distinctions among these three concepts are significant. One common mistake in failing to respect these distinctions is using data on current reserves as if it represented the maximum potential reserves. As Example 6.1 indicates, this fundamental error can lead to conclusions wide of the mark.

A second common mistake is to assume that the entire resource endowment can be made available as potential reserves at some price people would be willing to pay. Clearly, if an infinite price were possible, then the entire resource endowment could be exploited. However, an infinite price is not likely.

Certain mineral sources are so costly to extract that it is inconceivable any current or future society would be willing to pay the price necessary to extract them. Thus, it seems likely that the maximum feasible size of the potential reserves is smaller than the resource endowment. Exactly how much smaller cannot yet be determined with any degree of certainty.

Other distinctions among resource categories are also useful. The first category includes all depletable, recyclable resources, such as copper. A *depletable resource* is one for which the natural-replenishment feedback loop can safely be ignored. The rate of replenishment for these resources is so low that it does not offer a potential for augmenting the stock in any reasonable time frame.

EXAMPLE 6.1

The Pitfalls in Misusing Reserve Data

The number of years a given resource will last is commonly estimated by computing what is known as the *static reserve index,* the ratio of current reserves to current consumption. The result of the calculation is supposed to be interpreted as the number of years remaining until the resource is exhausted. This is a correct calculation of the time to exhaustion *if and only if* (1) the consumption of the resource remains at current levels until the time of exhaustion (it can neither increase nor decrease) and (2) no additions to the reserves occur in the intervening period (current reserves and potential reserves are assumed equal for the prices that can be expected to prevail).

These assumptions generally are not even approximately accurate. For example, in 1934 the static index for copper was 40, indicating that the reserves would be exhausted in 40 years. In 1974, 40 years later, the index stood at 57. A similar calculation for crude oil, iron oil, and lead would reveal the same pattern: The static index tends to underestimate the time until exhaustion.

The *Limits to Growth* study used an index called the *exponential reserve index,* which tends to underestimate the time to exhaustion by an even greater amount than the static index. This index assumes that consumption will grow over time at a constant rate of growth. No correction is made for additions to reserves or for the effects of higher prices on demand. It is therefore neither very surprising, nor very interesting, that their time of exhaustion estimates are so proximate.

Sources: Paul R. Ehrlich and Anne H. Ehrlich, *Population Resources Environment,* 2nd ed. (San Francisco: W. H. Freeman, 1972): 70–72; Earl Cook, "Limits to Exploitation of Nonrenewable Resources," *Science* 191 (20 February 1976): 667–82.

A recyclable *resource* is one that, although currently being used for some particular purpose, exists in a form allowing its mass to be recovered once that purpose is no longer necessary or desirable. For example, copper wiring from an automobile can be recovered after the car has been shipped to the junk yard. The degree to which a resource is recycled is determined by economic conditions, a subject covered in subsequent chapters.

The current reserves of a depletable, recyclable resource can be augmented by economic replenishment as well as by recycling. Economic replenishment takes many forms, all sharing the characteristic that they turn previously unrecoverable resources into recoverable ones. One obvious stimulant for this replenishment is price. As price rises, producers find it profitable to explore more widely, dig more deeply, use lower-concentration ores, and so on.

Higher prices also stimulate technological progress. Technological progress simply means an advancement in the state of knowledge that allows us to do things we were not able to do before. One profound, if controversial, example can be found in the successful harnessing of nuclear power.

The other side of the coin for depletable, recyclable resources is that their potential reserves can be exhausted. The depletion rate is affected by the demand for and durability of the products built with the resource and by the ability to reuse the products. Except where demand is totally price inelastic (that is, insensitive to price), higher prices tend to reduce the quantity demanded. Durable products last longer, reducing the need for newer ones. Reusable products provide a substitute for new products. In the commercial sector, reusable soft-drink bottles provide one example; flea markets (where secondhand items are sold) provide an example for the household sector.

For some resources, the size of the potential reserves depends explicitly on our ability to store the resource. For example, helium generally is found commingled with natural gas in common fields. Unless the helium is simultaneously captured and stored as the natural gas is extracted and stored, it diffuses into the atmosphere. This results in such low concentrations that extraction of helium from the air is not economical at current or even likely future prices. Thus, the useful stock of helium depends crucially on how much we decide to store.

Not all depletable resources permit recycling or reuse. Depletable energy resources such as coal, oil, and gas are consumed as they are used. Once they are combusted and turned into heat energy, the heat dissipates into the atmosphere and becomes nonrecoverable.

The endowment of depletable resources is of finite size. Current use of depletable, nonrecyclable resources precludes future use; hence, the issue of how they should be shared among generations is raised in the starkest, least forgiving, form.

Depletable, recyclable resources raise this same issue, though somewhat less starkly. Recycling and reuse make the useful stock last longer, all other things being equal. It is tempting to suggest that depletable recyclable resources could last forever with 100 percent recycling, but unfortunately the physical theoretical upper limit on recycling is less than 100 percent—an implication of a version of the entropy law defined in Chapter 2. Some of the mass is always lost during recycling.

For example, copper pennies can be melted down to recover the copper, but the amount rubbed off during circulation would never be recovered. As long as less than 100 percent of the mass is recycled, the useful stock must eventually decline to zero. Even for recyclable depletable resources, the cumulative useful stock is finite, and current consumption patterns still have an effect on future generations.

Renewable resources are differentiated from depletable resources primarily by the fact that natural replenishment augments the flow of renewable resources at a nonnegligible rate. Solar energy, water, cereal grains, fish, forests, and animals are all examples of renewable resources. Thus it is possible, though not inexorable, that a flow of these resources could be maintained perpetually.[1]

For some renewable resources, the continuation and volume of their flow depend crucially on humans. Soil erosion and nutrient depletion reduce the flow of food. Excessive fishing reduces the stock of fish, which in turn reduces the rate of natural increase of the fish population. Newsprint can be recycled. Other examples abound. For other renewable resources, such as solar energy, the flow is independent of humans. The amount consumed by one generation does not reduce the amount that can be consumed by subsequent generations.

Some renewable resources can be stored; others cannot. For those that can, storage provides a valuable way to manage the allocation of the resource over time. We are not left simply at the mercy of natural ebbs and flows of the source. Without proper care, food perishes rapidly, but with storage, it can be used to feed the hungry in times of famine. Unstored solar energy radiates off the earth's surface and dissipates into the atmosphere. Although solar en-

[1]Even renewable resources are ultimately finite, because their renewability is dependent on energy from the sun and the sun is expected to serve as an energy source for only the next five or six billion years. That fact does not eliminate the need to manage resources effectively until that time. Furthermore, the finiteness of renewable resources is sufficiently far into the future to make the distinction useful.

ergy can be stored in many forms, the most common natural form of storage occurs when it is converted to biomass by photosynthesis.

Storage of renewable resources usually performs a different service than storage of depletable resources. Storing depletable resources extends their economic life; storing renewable resources, on the other hand, can serve as a means of smoothing out the cyclical imbalances of supply and demand. Surpluses are stored for later time periods when deficits may occur. Food stockpiles and the use of dams to store hydropower are two familiar examples.

Managing renewable resources presents a different challenge than managing depletable resources, though an equally significant one. The challenge for depletable resources involves allocating dwindling stocks among generations while meeting the ultimate transition to renewable resources. In contrast, the challenge for managing renewable resources involves the maintenance of an efficient sustainable flow. The next six chapters deal with how the economic and political sectors have responded to these challenges for particularly significant types of resources.

EFFICIENT INTERTEMPORAL ALLOCATIONS

If we are to judge the adequacy of market allocations, we must define what is meant by efficiency in relation to the management of depletable- and renewable-resource allocations. Because allocation over time is the crucial issue, dynamic efficiency becomes the core concept.

The dynamic-efficiency criterion assumes that society's objective is to maximize the present value of net benefits coming from the resource. With fixed and finite supplies of depletable resources, production of a unit today precludes production of that unit tomorrow. Therefore, production decisions today must take forgone future net benefits into account. Marginal user cost is the opportunity cost measure that allows balancing to take place.

The Allocation Over N Periods

When the demand curve is stable over time and the marginal cost of extraction is constant, the rate of increase in the current value of the marginal user cost is equal to r, the discount rate. Thus, in any future period in which the resource is being extracted, the marginal user cost would be $1 + r$ times as large as it was in the previous period.[2] Marginal user cost rises at rate r in an efficient allocation in order to preserve the balance between present and future production.

Figure 6.2(a) demonstrates how the efficient quantity extracted varies over time, and Figure 6.2(b) shows the behavior of the marginal user cost and the marginal cost of extraction. Total marginal cost refers to the sum of the two. The marginal cost of extraction is represented by the lower line, and the marginal user cost is depicted as the vertical distance between the marginal cost of extraction and the total marginal cost. To avoid confusion, you

---

[2]The condition that marginal user cost rise at rate r is true only when the marginal cost of extraction is constant. For the more complicated case see T. H. Tietenberg, *Environmental and Natural Resource Economics* (New York: HarperCollins, 1992): Chapter 6.

FIGURE 6.2(a)   Constant Marginal Extraction Cost with No Substitute Resource:
Quantity Profile

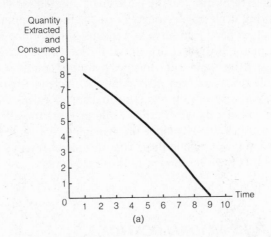

FIGURE 6.2(b)   Constant Marginal Extraction Cost with No Substitute Resource:
Marginal-Cost Profile

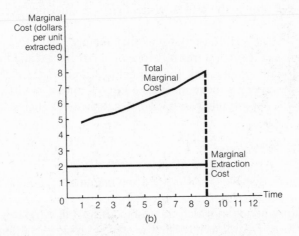

should note that the horizontal axis is defined in terms of time, not quantity (the more conventional designation).

Several trends are worth noting. First, the efficient marginal user cost rises steadily (at rate r) in spite of the fact that the marginal cost of extraction remains constant. This rise in the efficient marginal user cost reflects increasing scarcity and the accompanying rise in the opportunity cost of current consumption.

In response to these rising costs over time, the quantity extracted falls over time until it finally goes to zero, which occurs precisely at the moment when the total marginal cost equals the maximum price consumers are willing to pay. An efficient allocation envisions a smooth transition to the exhaustion of a resource. The resource does not "suddenly" run out, although in this case it does run out.

Transition to a Renewable Substitute

So far we have discussed the allocation of a depletable resource when no substitute is available to take its place. However, suppose we consider the nature of an efficient allocation when a substitute renewable resource is available at constant marginal cost. This could describe the efficient allocation of oil or natural gas with a solar substitute, for example, or the efficient allocation of exhaustible groundwater with a surface-water substitute. How could we define an efficient allocation in this circumstance?

Because this problem is very similar to the one already discussed, we can use what we have already learned as a foundation for mastering this new situation. The depletable resource would be exhausted in this case, just as it was in the previous case, but that will be less of a problem because we will merely switch to the renewable one at the appropriate time.

The total marginal cost for the depletable resource would never exceed the marginal cost of the substitute because society could always use the renewable resource instead, whenever it was cheaper. Thus, although the maximum willingness to pay (the *choke price*) sets the upper limit on total marginal cost when no substitute is available, the marginal cost of extraction of the substitute sets the upper limit when one is available at a marginal cost lower than the choke price.

In this efficient allocation, the transition is once again smooth. Quantity extracted is gradually reduced as the marginal use cost rises until the switch is made to the substitute. No abrupt change is evident in either marginal cost or quantity profiles.

Because the renewable resource is available, more of the depletable resource would be extracted in the earlier periods than would be without a renewable resource (as was the case in our previous numerical example). As a result, the depletable resource would be exhausted sooner than it would have been without the renewable-resource substitute.

At the transition point, called the *switch point,* consumption of the renewable resource begins. Prior to the switch point, only the depletable resource is consumed, whereas after the switch point only the renewable resource is consumed. This sequencing of consumption patterns results from the cost patterns. Prior to the switch point, the depletable resource is cheaper. At the switch point, the marginal cost of the depletable resource (including the marginal user cost) rises to meet the marginal cost of the substitute and the transition occurs.

Exploration and Technological Progress

The search for new resources is expensive. As easily discovered resources are exhausted, we must search in less-rewarding environments, such as the bottom of the ocean or locations deep within the earth. This suggests that the *marginal cost of exploration,* which is the marginal cost of finding additional units of the resource, should be expected to rise over time, just as the marginal cost of extraction does.

As the total marginal cost for a resource rises over time, society should actively explore possible new sources of that resource. The higher the marginal cost of extraction for known sources is expected to rise, the larger is the potential increase in net benefits from exploration.

Some of this exploration would be successful: New sources of the resource would be discovered. If the marginal extraction cost of the newly discovered resources is low enough, these discoveries could lower, or at least retard, the increase in the total marginal cost of production. As a result, the new finds would tend to encourage more consumption. Successful exploration would cause a smaller and slower decline in consumption while dampening the rise in total marginal cost.

It is also not difficult to expand our concept of efficient resource allocations to include technological progress, the general term economists give to advances in the state of knowledge. In the present context, technological progress would be manifested as reductions in the cost of extraction. For a resource that can be extracted at constant marginal cost, a one-time breakthrough lowering the marginal cost of extraction would move the time of transition further into the future. Furthermore, for an increasing-cost resource, more of the total available resource would be recovered in the presence of technological progress than would be recovered without it. (Can you see why?)

The most pervasive effects of technological progress involve continuous downward shifts in the cost of extraction over some time period. The total marginal cost of the resource could actually fall over time if the cost-reducing nature of technological progress became so potent that, in spite of increasing reliance on inferior ore, the marginal cost of extraction decreased (Example 6.2). With a finite amount of this resource, the fall in total marginal cost would be transitory, because ultimately it would have to rise. This period of transition can last quite a long time, however.

MARKET ALLOCATIONS

In the preceding sections we have examined in detail how the efficient allocation of substitutable depletable and renewable resources over time would be defined in a variety of circumstances. We must now address the question of whether actual markets can be expected to produce an efficient allocation. Can the private market involving millions of consumers and producers each reacting to his or her own unique preferences *ever* result in a dynamically efficient allocation? Is profit maximization compatible with dynamic efficiency?

Appropriate Property-Right Structures

The most common misconception of those who believe that even a perfect market could never achieve an efficient allocation is a belief that producers want to extract and sell the resources as fast as possible because that is how they derive the value from the resource. This misconception makes people see markets as myopic and unconcerned about the future.

As long as the property rights governing natural resources have the characteristics of exclusivity, universality, transferability, and enforceability (Chapter 3), the markets in which those resources are bought and sold will not necessarily lead to myopic choices. When bearing the marginal user cost, the producer acts in an efficient manner. A resource in the ground has two potential sources of value to its owner: (1) a use value when it is sold (the only source considered by those diagnosing inevitable myopia), and (2) an asset value when it remains in the ground. As long as the price of a resource continues to rise, the resource in the ground is becoming more valuable. However, the owner of this resource accrues this capital gain only if the resource is conserved. A producer who sells all resources in the earlier periods loses the chance to take advantage of higher prices in the future.

EXAMPLE 6.2

Technological Progress in the Iron Ore Industry

The term "technological progress" plays an important role in the economic analysis of mineral resources. Yet, at times, it can appear abstract, even mystical. It shouldn't! Far from being a blind faith detached from reality, technological progress refers to a host of ingenious ways in which people have reacted to impending shortages with sufficient imagination that the available supply of resources has been greatly expanded at reasonable cost. To illustrate how concrete a notion technological progress is, let's discuss one example of how it has worked in the past.

In 1947 the president of Republic Steel, C. M. White, calculated the expected life of the Mesabi range of northern Minnesota (the source of some 60 percent of iron ore consumed during World War II) as being in the range from five to seven years. By 1955, only eight years later, *U.S. News and World Report* was able to conclude that worry over the scarcity of iron ore could be forgotten. The source of this remarkable transformation of a problem of scarcity into one of abundance was the discovery of a new technique, called *pelletization*, of preparing iron ore.

Prior to pelletization, the standard ores from which iron was derived contained from 50 to more than 65 percent iron in crude form. There was a significant percentage of taconite ore available containing less than 30 percent iron in crude form, but no one knew how to produce it at reasonable cost. Pelletization is a process by which these ores are processed and concentrated at the mine site prior to shipment to the blast furnaces. The advent of pelletization allowed the profitable use of the taconite ores.

While expanding the supply of iron ore, pelletization reduced its cost in spite of the inferior grade being used. There were several sources of the cost reduction. First, substantially *less* energy was used: The shift in ore technology toward pelletization produced net energy savings of 17 percent in spite of the fact that the pelletization process itself required more energy. The reduction came from the discovery that the blast furnaces could be operated much more efficiently using pelletization inputs. The process also reduced labor requirements per ton by some 8.2 percent while increasing the output of the blast furnaces. A blast furnace owned by Armco Steel in Middletown, Ohio, which had a rated capacity of approximately 1500 tons of molten iron per day, was able by 1960 to achieve production levels of 2700 and 2800 tons per day when fired with 90 percent pellets. Pellets nearly doubled the blast furnace productivity!

Sources: Peter J. Kakela, "Iron Ore: Energy Labor and Capital Changes with Technology," *Science* 202 (15 December 1978): 1151–57; "Iron Ore: From Depletion to Abundance," *Science* 212 (10 April 1981): 132–36.

A prescient, profit-maximizing producer attempts to balance present and future production in order to maximize the value of the resource. Because higher prices in the future provide an incentive to conserve, a producer who ignores this incentive would not be maximizing the value of the resource. We would expect the resource to then be bought by someone willing to conserve and prepared to maximize its value. As long as social and private discount rates coincide, property-right structures are well-defined, and reliable information about future prices is available, a producer who selfishly pursues maximum profits simultaneously provides the maximum present value of net benefits for society.

The implication of this analysis is that, in prescient competitive resource markets, the price of the resource equals the total marginal cost of extracting and using the resource.

Environmental Costs

One of the most important situations in which property-right structures may not be well defined is that in which the extraction of a natural resource imposes an environmental cost on society not internalized by the producers. The aesthetic costs of strip mining, the health risks associated with uranium tailings, and the acids leached into streams from mine operations are all examples of associated environmental costs. Not only is the presence of environmental costs empirically important, it is also conceptually important because it forms one of the bridges between the traditionally separate fields of environmental economics and natural resource economics.

Suppose, for example, that the extraction of the depletable resource caused some damage to the environment not adequately reflected in the costs faced by the extracting firms. This would be an external cost. The cost of getting the resource out of the ground, as well as processing and shipping it, is borne by the resource owner and considered in the calculation of how much of the resource to extract. The environmental damage, however, is not borne by the owner and, in the absence of any outside attempt to internalize that cost, will not be part of the extraction decision. How would the market allocation, based on only the former cost, differ from the efficient allocation, which is based on both?

The inclusion of environmental costs results in higher prices, which tend to dampen demand. This lowers the rate of consumption of the resource, which, all other things being equal, would make it last longer.

What can we learn about the allocation of depletable resources over time when environmental side effects are not borne by the agent determining the extraction rate? The price of the depletable resource would be too low and the resource would be extracted too rapidly. This once again shows the interdependencies among the various decisions we have to make about the future. Environmental and natural resource decisions are intimately and inextricably linked.

SUMMARY

The efficient allocation of substitutable depletable and renewable resources depends on the circumstances. When the resource can be extracted at a constant marginal cost, the efficient quantity of the depletable resource extracted declines over time. If no substitute is available, the quantity declines smoothly to zero. If a renewable constant-cost substitute is available, the quantity of the depletable resource extracted will decline smoothly to the quantity available from the renewable resource. In both cases, all of the available depletable resource would be eventually used up and marginal user cost would rise over time, reaching a maximum when the last unit of depletable resource was extracted.

Introducing technological progress and exploration activity tends to delay the transition to renewable resources. Exploration expands the size of current reserves; technological progress keeps marginal extraction cost from rising as much as it otherwise would. If these effects are sufficiently potent, marginal cost could actually decline for some period of time, causing the quantity extracted to rise.

When property-right structures are properly defined, market allocations of depletable resources can be efficient. Self-interest and efficiency are not necessarily incompatible.

When the extraction of resources imposes an external environmental cost, however, market allocations will not generally be efficient. The market price of the depletable resource would be too low, and too much of the resource would be extracted too rapidly.

In an efficient market allocation, the transition from depletable to renewable resources is smooth and exhibits none of the overshoot and collapse characteristics of the *Limits to Growth* view of the world. Whether the actual market allocations of these various types of resources are efficient remains to be seen. To the extent they are, a laissez-faire policy would represent an appropriate response by the government. On the other hand, if the market is not capable of yielding an efficient allocation, then some form of government intervention may be necessary. In the next few chapters we shall examine these questions for a number of different types of depletable and renewable resources.

FURTHER READING

Bohi, Douglas R., and Michael A. Toman. *Analyzing Nonrenewable Resource Supply* (Washington, DC: Resources for the Future, 1984). A reinterpretation and evaluation of existing research that attempts to weave together theoretical, empirical, and practical insights concerning the management of depletable resources.

Chapman, Duane. "Computation Techniques for Intertemporal Allocation of Natural Resources," *American Journal of Agricultural Economics* 69, No. 1 (February 1987): 134–42. Shows how to find numerical solutions for the types of depletable resource problems considered in this chapter.

Conrad, Jon M., and Colin W. Clark. *Natural Resource Economics: Notes and Problems* (Cambridge, UK: Cambridge University Press, 1987). This book reviews techniques of dynamic optimization and shows how they can be applied to the management of various resource systems.

Fisher, Anthony C. *Resource and Environmental Economics* (Cambridge, UK: Cambridge University Press, 1981). This volume presents a careful heuristic development of the major mathematical results in optimal resource use for depletable and renewable resources. It also has chapters on preserving natural environments and on pollution. This text is written for graduate students or upper-level undergraduates.

Toman, Michael A. "'Depletion Effects' and Nonrenewable Resource Supply," *Land Economics* 62 (November 1986): 341–53. An excellent, nontechnical discussion of the increasing cost case with and without exploration and additions to reserves.

Williams, Stephen F. "Running Out: The Problem of Exhaustible Resources," *The Journal of Legal Studies* VII (January 1978): 165–99. An excellent, nontechnical introduction to the basic ideas contained in this chapter by a natural resource lawyer.

ADDITIONAL REFERENCES

Anders, Gerhard, W. Philip Gramm, S. Charles Maurice, and Charles W. Smithson. *The Economics of Mineral Extraction* (New York: Praeger Publishers, 1980).

Dasgupta, P. S., and G. M. Heal. *Economic Theory and Exhaustible Resources* (Cambridge, UK: Cambridge University Press, 1979).

Dasgupta, Partha. *The Control of Resources* (Cambridge, MA: Harvard University Press, 1982).

Kneese, Allen V., and James L. Sweeney, eds. *Handbook of Natural Resource and Energy Economics: Vol. III* (Amsterdam: North-Holland, 1986).

Peterson, Frederick M. and Anthony C. Fisher. "The Exploitation of Extractive Resources: A Survey," *Economic Journal* LXXXVIII (December 1977): 681–721.

Scott, Anthony, ed. *Progress in Natural Resource Economics* (Oxford: Clarendon Press, 1985).

DISCUSSION QUESTIONS

1. Identify any external costs that might be associated with the following activities: (1) extracting timber from public lands, (2) extracting timber from one's own land, (3) harvesting fish from the ocean, and (4) taking water from a shared groundwater source. How would these external costs affect the extraction of these resources over time?
2. What causes technical progresss? Can the rate of technical progress be influenced by the government? Why or why not?

CHAPTER 7

Energy

If it ain't broke, don't fix it!

OLD MAINE PROVERB

INTRODUCTION

Energy is one of our most critical resources; without it, life would cease. We derive energy from the food we eat. Through photosynthesis, the plant life we consume—both directly and indirectly when we eat meat—depends on energy from the sun. The materials we use to build our houses and produce the goods we consume are extracted from the earth's crust, then transformed into finished products with expenditures of energy.

Currently, most industrialized countries depend on oil and natural gas for most of their energy needs. In the United States, for example, these two resources together supply 67 percent of all energy consumed. Both are depletable, nonrecyclable sources of energy. Crude oil proven reserves peaked during the 1970s, natural gas peaked in the 1980s in the United States and Europe, and since that time, the amount extracted has exceeded additions to reserves[1] (see Figures 7.1 and 7.2).

Because they are depletable resources, oil and natural gas would be transition fuels in an efficient allocation. They would be used until the marginal cost of further use exceeded the marginal cost of substitute resources—either more abundant depletable resources, such as coal, or renewable sources, such as solar energy.[2] In an efficient market path, the transition to these alternative sources would be smooth and harmonious. Have the allocations of the last several decades been efficient or not?

In a 1977 speech to the nation, U.S. President Jimmy Carter suggested that the resolve needed to solve our energy problems was "the moral equivalent of war." The existence of a crisis atmosphere suggests that the allocations have not been efficient. Why not? Is the market mechanism flawed in its allocation of depletable recyclable resources? If so, is the flaw fatal? If not, what caused the inefficient allocations? Is the problem correctable?

---

[1]In contrast, world reserves of oil and gas have continued to increase during the 1980s. See U.S. Energy Information Administration, *International Energy Annual* (Washington, DC: U.S. Government Printing Office): various issues.

[2]When used for other purposes, oil can be recycled. Waste lubricating oil is now routinely recycled.

FIGURE 7.1   United States and Western Europe Estimated Crude Oil Reserves Over Time

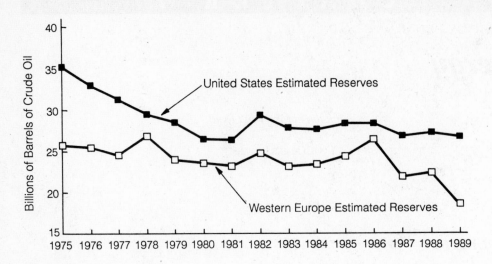

FIGURE 7.2   United States and Western Europe Estimated Natural Gas Reserves Over Time

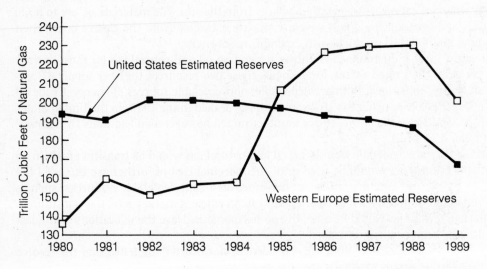

Source: U.S. Energy Information Administration, *International Energy Annual* (Washington, DC: Government Printing Office): annual.

In this chapter we shall examine some of the major issues associated with the allocation of energy resources over time and see how economic analysis can clarify our understanding of both the sources of the problems and their solution. Because energy is too complex a subject to treat comprehensively in one chapter, however, additional references are provided.

NATURAL GAS: PRICE CONTROLS

In the United States during the winter of late 1974 and early 1975, serious shortages of natural gas developed. Customers who had contracted and were willing to pay for natural gas were unable to get as much as they wanted. The shortage (or curtailments as the Federal Energy Regulatory Commission calls them) amounted to 2.0 trillion cubic feet of natural gas in 1974–1975, which represented roughly 10 percent of the marketed production in 1975.[3] In an efficient allocation, shortages of that magnitude would never have happened. Why did they?

The source of the problem can be traced directly to government controls over natural-gas prices. This story begins, oddly enough, with the rise of the automobile, which traditionally has not used natural gas as a fuel. The increasing importance of the automobile for transportation created a rising demand for gasoline, which in turn stimulated a search for new sources of crude oil. This exploration activity uncovered large quantities of natural gas (known as associated gas), in addition to large quantities of crude oil, which was the object of the search.

As natural gas was discovered, it replaced manufactured gas—and some coal—in the geographic areas where it was found. Then, as a geographically dispersed demand developed for this increasingly available gas, a long-distance system of gas pipelines was designed and constructed. In the period following World War II, natural gas became an important source of energy for the United States.

The regulation of natural gas began in 1938 with the passage of the Natural Gas Act. This act transformed the Federal Power Commission (FPC) into a federal regulatory agency charged with maintaining "just" prices. In 1954, a Supreme Court decision in *Phillips Petroleum Co.* v *Wisconsin* forced the FPC to extend their price control regulations to the producer. Prior to that time, they had merely limited their regulation to pipeline companies.

Because the process of setting price ceilings proved cumbersome, the hastily conceived initial "interim" ceilings remained in effect for almost a decade before the Commission was able to impose more carefully considered ceilings.[4] What was the effect of this regulation?

The ceilings prevented prices from reaching their normal levels. Because price increases are the source of the incentive to conserve, the lower prices caused more of the resource to be used in earlier years. Consumption levels in those years was higher under price controls than without them. Attracted by artificially low prices, consumers would invest in equipment to use natural gas, only to discover—after the transition—that natural gas was no longer available.

Price controls may cause other problems as well. Up to this point, we have discussed permanent controls. Not all price controls are permanent; they can change at the whim of the political process in unpredictable ways. The fact that prices could suddenly rise when the ceil-

---

[3]The curtailment figure comes from Federal Energy Administration, *National Energy Outlook* (Washington, DC: 1976): 121; the marketed figure is from U.S. Department of Energy, *Monthly Energy Review: April 1978* (Washington, DC: U.S. Government Printing Office, 1978): 24.

[4]For an excellent discussion of this period, see Stephen G. Breyer and Paul W. MacAvoy, *Energy Regulation by the Federal Power Commission* (Washington, DC: The Brookings Institution, 1974).

ing is lifted also creates unfortunate incentives. If producers expect a large price increase in the near future, they have an incentive to stop production and wait for the higher prices. Needless to say, this circumstance could cause severe problems for consumers.

For legal reasons the price controls on natural gas were placed solely on gas shipped across state lines. Gas consumed within the states where it was produced could be priced at what the market would bear. As a result, gas produced and sold within the state received a higher price than that sold in other states. Consequently, the share of gas in the interstate market fell over time as producers found it more profitable to commit reserve additions to the *intrastate,* rather than the *interstate,* market. In the 1964–1969 period, about 33 percent of the average annual reserve additions were committed to the interstate market. By 1970–1974, this commitment had fallen to a little less than 5 percent.

The practical effect of charging less for gas destined for the interstate market was to cause the shortages to be concentrated in states served by pipeline and dependent on the interstate shipment of gas. As a result, the damage caused was greater than it would have been if all consuming areas had shared somewhat more equitably in the shortfall. The price-control system not only caused the damage, it intensified it!

Natural-gas allocations not only hastened the time of transition to a substitute resource, it also caused a transition to an inefficient substitute. The reason for this substitution bias and its implications are explored in Example 7.1.

It seems fair to conclude that, by sapping the economic system of its ability to respond to changing conditions, price controls on natural gas created a significant amount of turmoil. If this kind of political control is likely to recur with some regularity, perhaps some of the *Limits to Growth* concerns may be valid, though for different reasons. The overshoot and collapse syndrome in this case would be caused by government interference rather than any pure market behavior. If so, the proverb that opens this chapter becomes particularly relevant!

Why did Congress embark on such a counterproductive policy? The answer is found in rent-seeking behavior that can be explained through the use of our consumer- and producer-surplus model. Let's examine the political incentives in a simple model.

Consider Figure 7.3. An efficient market allocation would result in Q^* supplied at price P^*. The net benefits received by the country would be represented by the total geometric area encompassed by the areas denoted as A and B. Of these net benefits, area A would be received by consumers as consumer surplus and B would be received by producers as a producer surplus.

Now suppose that a price ceiling were established. From the preceding discussion we know that this ceiling would reduce the marginal user cost because higher future prices would no longer be possible. In Figure 7.3, this has the effect for current producers of lowering the perceived supply curve, due to the lower marginal user cost. As a result of this shift in the perceived supply curve, current production would expand to Q_c and price would fall to P_c. Current consumers would unambiguously be better off because consumer surplus would be area $A + B + C$ instead of area A. They would have gained a net benefit equal to $B + C$.

It may appear that producers could also gain if $D > B$, but that is not correct. Because producers would be overproducing, they would be giving up the scarcity rent they could have gotten without price controls. Area D measures only current profits without considering scarcity rent. When the loss in scarcity rent is considered, producers unambiguously lose net benefits.

Meanwhile, some future consumers are also worse off. Because the supplies are used more rapidly, the point when the price to future consumers is higher than it would be otherwise will eventually be reached. The higher price implies lower consumer surplus.

EXAMPLE 7.1

Price Controls and Substitution Bias

Faced with shortages, pipeline companies looked for alternative sources of supply. Two that they discovered were liquid natural gas (LNG), shipped from abroad in pressurized ships, and synthetic natural gas (SNG), manufactured from various petroleum products. These sources were both very expensive.

Pipeline companies induced consumers to use these substitutes by using average cost pricing. The artificially cheap natural gas was blended with the synthetic gas and sold at the average cost of the two depending on the proportions. Thus, if they used 90 percent natural gas at $1 per unit and 10 percent other sources at $5 per unit, the cost of the combined gas was $1.40 per unit (0.90 × $1 + 0.10 × $5). Thus, instead of paying the high marginal cost of the substitute for additional units consumed, as efficiency would dictate, consumers paid the much lower average cost. The pricing system sent them the wrong signal.

This system of pricing created a bias toward substitutes that could be blended with natural gas and away from substitutes that could not. In this case the bias was particularly unfortunate; not only did it create additional demand for imported energy sources (LNG) at a time when the official policy was to discourage such imports, it also encouraged lower levels of thermodynamic efficiency in the use of our diminishing oil resources. The conversion to gas caused some of the potential energy to be lost. Substitutes rendered noneconomic in certain parts of the country by this pricing system included heat pumps and residential solar space heating.

Because this system of average cost pricing encouraged pipeline companies to accept high-cost sources of imported or synthetic gas that could be commingled with the artificially cheap natural gas during the 1970s, the price rise was especially rapid and sharp when natural gas prices began to be decontrolled in the early 1980s. The large base of artificially low-cost natural gas no longer provided a cushion to counterbalance the very high cost of the new sources. Average residential prices for natural gas rose from $2.98 per thousand cubic feet in 1979 to $6.06 in 1983. Since that time prices have stabilized, with the 1989 price being $5.63; the excess demand in the natural gas market had been eliminated by higher prices.

Sources: Thomas H. Tietenberg, "Substitution Bias in a Depletable Resource Model with Administered Prices," in *Erschöpfbare Ressourcen* (Berlin: Duncker and Humlot, 1980): 522–29; Energy Information Administration, *Monthly Energy Review* (January 1989): 105.

Congress may view scarcity rent as a possible source of revenue to transfer from producers to consumers. As we have seen, however, scarcity rent is an opportunity cost that serves a distinct purpose—the protection of future consumers. When government attempts to reduce this scarcity rent through price controls, the result is an overallocation to current consumers and an underallocation to future consumers. Thus, what appears to be a transfer from producers to consumers is, in large part, also a transfer from future consumers to present consumers. Because current consumers mean current votes and future consumers may not know whom to blame by the time shortages appear, price controls are politically attractive. Unfortunately, they are also inefficient: The losses to future consumers and producers are greater than the gains to current consumers. Because they distort the allocation toward the

FIGURE 7.3   The Effect of Price Controls

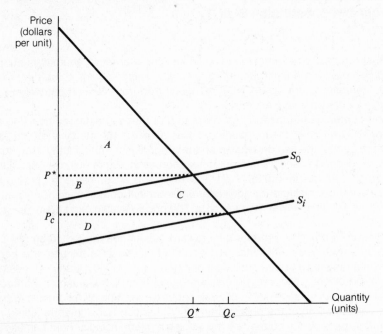

present, controls are also unfair. Thus, markets in the presence of price controls are indeed myopic, but the problem lies with the controls, not the market.

Over the long run, price controls end up harming consumers rather than helping them. Scarcity rent plays an important role in the allocation process, and attempts to eliminate it can create more problems than are solved. After long debating the price-control issue, Congress passed the Natural Gas Policy Act on 9 November 1978. This act initiated the eventual phased decontrol of natural-gas prices. Included among its other provisions was a movement away from the average-cost pricing of substitute gas for industrial customers and the imposition of price controls for the first time on intrastate gas, until such time as all prices are decontrolled. On 27 July 1989 President George Bush signed a bill removing in stages all remaining controls on natural gas. By January 1993, no sources of natural gas were subject to price controls.

OIL: THE CARTEL PROBLEM

Inasmuch as we have considered similar effects on natural gas, we shall merely note that price controls have been responsible for much mischief in the oil market as well.[5] A second source of misallocation in the oil market, however, deserves further consideration. Most of the world's oil is produced by a cartel called the Organization of Petroleum Exporting Countries (OPEC). The members of this organization collude to exercise power over oil production and prices. Seller power over resources due to a lack of effective competition leads to an inefficient

---

[5]The price controls on oil were similar to, but not the same as, price controls on natural gas. For a discussion on the effects on those controls, see Kenneth J. Arrow and Joseph P. Kalt, *Petroleum Price Regulation: Should We Decontrol?* (Washington, DC: American Enterprise Institute, 1979).

allocation. Sellers with market power can restrict supply and thus force prices higher than otherwise.

A monopolist can extract more scarcity rent from a depletable resource base than competitive suppliers can, simply by restricting supply. The monopolistic transition results in slower production and higher prices. The monopolistic transition to a substitute therefore occurs later than a competitive transition. It also reduces the net benefit society receives from these resources.

The cartelization of the oil suppliers has been very effective. Why? Were the conditions that made it profitable unique to oil, or could oil cartelization be the harbinger of a wave of natural resource cartels? To answer these questions, we must isolate the factors that make cartelization possible. Though many factors are involved, four stand out: (1) the price elasticity of demand for OPEC oil in both the long run and the short run, (2) the income elasticity of demand for oil, (3) the supply responsiveness of the oil producers who are not OPEC members, and (4) the compatibility of interests among members of OPEC.

Price Elasticity of Demand

The elasticity of demand is an important ingredient because it determines how responsive demand is to price. When demand elasticities are less than 1.0, price increases lead to increased revenue. Exactly how much revenue would increase when prices increase depends on the price elasticity of demand. In general, the lower the price elasticity of demand the larger the gains to be derived from forming a cartel.

The price elasticity of demand for oil depends on the opportunities for conservation as well as on the availability of substitutes. As storm windows cut heat losses, the same temperature can be maintained with less heating oil. Smaller automobiles reduce the amount of gasoline needed to travel a given distance. The larger the set of these opportunities and the smaller the cash outlays required to exploit them, the more price elastic the demand. This suggests that the price elasticity of demand in the long run (when sufficient time has passed to allow adjustments) will be greater, perhaps significantly, than in the short run.

The availability of substitutes is important because it limits the degree to which prices can be raised by a producer cartel. Abundant quantities of substitutes available at prices not far above competitive oil prices can set an upper limit on the cartel price. Unless OPEC controls those sources as well—and it doesn't—any attempts to raise prices above those limits would cause the consuming nations to simply switch to these alternative sources; OPEC would have priced itself out of the market.

Alternative sources clearly exist, although they are expensive and the time of transition is long. One extensive survey of world energy resources, for example, concluded that about as much petroleum could be extracted from unconventional sources—such as deep offshore wells, wells in the polar seas, heavy oils, enhanced recovery techniques, oil shales, tar sands, and synthetic oils—as is currently available from conventional petroleum reserves. It further concludes, however, that those sources wouldn't make much of a dent in the oil market until the end of the twentieth century and then only at very high cost. This report conjectured that the high cost of these sources would confine their use to transportation and chemicals.[6]

---

[6]World Energy Conference, *World Energy Resources: 1985–2020* (New York: IPC Science and Technology Press, 1978): 2–3.

EXAMPLE 7.2

Are Soft Energy Paths Doomed?

In 1976 a young physicist named Amory Lovins published an article in *Foreign Affairs* that built an immediate following for him and his ideas. His thesis, boldly stated, was that we could follow two paths to our energy future. One, dubbed by Lovins as the "hard path," consisted of an increasing reliance on large-scale, centralized technologies, whereas the second, the "soft path," relied more on smaller, decentralized technologies. The former is epitomized by nuclear-power plants, whereas solar home heating, windmills, and small dams provide examples of the latter. Furthermore, Lovins argued, these paths are mutually exclusive and the existing system is biased toward the former. If valid, this argument would cast a dark shadow over any expectation that the transition to the soft path would be efficient and smooth.

Lovins suggests that the current system of relying upon centralized power has allowed the buildup of vested interests having a stake in maintaining the status quo. One way this dominance could be perpetuated is for the utilities to refuse to purchase excess power from the soft-path producers. With no market or distribution system, producers would have less incentive to produce power by these means.

Whatever validity that argument may have had at the time it was made, it seems to have been weakened by congressional action. In 1978 Congress passed the Public Utility Regulatory Policies Act to encourage the production of electricity from renewable resources and from cogeneration systems. *Cogeneration* is the combined production of electricity and useful thermal energy. Among other provisions, this act (1) requires utilities to purchase excess power at a price equal to what it would have cost the utilities to generate the power themselves, (2) requires utilities to provide backup power to those producers at average cost (usually lower than the price utilities pay the producers for excess power), and (3) stipulates that the qualifying small-production units cannot be owned by utilities. Though this is a controversial piece of legislation, undoubtedly it has spurred the development of small, renewable, energy sources for producing electricity.

Source: Amory B. Lovins, "Energy Strategy: The Road Not Taken?" *Foreign Affairs* LV (October 1976): 65–98. The importance of this act to potential investors in renewable resources is described in Colin Norman, "Renewable Power Sparks Financial Interest," *Science* CCXII (26 June 1981): 1479–81.

Although coal is clearly a substitute for some uses and is available in large supplies, as we shall see in the next section, coal use triggers a number of environmental problems.

Clearly, the ultimate substitute is solar energy, and it is the cost of solar energy that will set the long-run upper limit on the ability of OPEC to raise its prices. Because in many parts of the United States solar energy for space and hot-water heating is currently cost competitive, that limit is probably not substantially higher than recent OPEC prices. Although it will take a significant amount of time for these new technologies to get all the bugs worked out and begin to penetrate the market on a massive scale, the transition seems to be proceeding smoothly. As Example 7.2 indicates, this transition has extended to electricity production as well, which some observers felt would resist that change.

Income Elasticity of Demand

The income elasticity of oil demand is important because it indicates how sensitive oil demand is to growth in the world economy. At constant prices, as income grows, oil demand should grow. This continual increase in demand fortifies the ability of OPEC to raise its prices. High income elasticities of demand support the cartelization of oil. All other things being equal, the higher the income elasticity of demand, the higher the price would have to rise to bring demand to zero (in the absence of substitutes) or the more rapidly it would rise to the level of the substitute resource when one is available.

The income elasticity of demand is also important because it registers how sensitive demand is to the business cycle. The higher the income elasticity of demand, the more sensitive demand is. This is a major source of the weakening of the cartel that occurred during 1983. A recession caused a large reduction in the demand for oil, putting new pressure on the cartel to absorb these demand reductions.

Non-OPEC Suppliers

Another key factor in the ability of producer nations to exercise power over a natural resource market is their ability to prevent new suppliers, not part of the cartel, from entering the market and undercutting the price. OPEC currently produces about two thirds of the world's oil. If the remaining producers were able, in the face of higher prices, to expand their supply dramatically, they would increase the amount of oil supplied and cause the prices to fall, decreasing OPEC's market share. If this response were large enough, the allocation of oil would approach the competitive allocation.

Currently only Mexico appears to have large enough reserves to make an individual difference in the world oil market, but because both the size of its reserves and its production profile are uncertain, it is difficult to assess Mexico's ultimate impact on the future world market.

This does not mean that non-OPEC members collectively do not have an impact on price. They do. The cartel must take the nonmembers into account when setting prices. The impact of this competitive fringe on OPEC behavior was dramatically illustrated by events in the 1985–1986 period. In 1979, OPEC accounted for approximately 50 percent of world oil production, but in 1986 this had fallen to approximately 30 percent. Total world oil production during this period was down over 10 percent for all producers, so the pressures on the cartel mounted and prices ultimately fell. The average cost of crude oil imports in the United States fell from $36.52 per barrel in 1981 to $25.94 in January 1986. OPEC simply was not able to hold the line on prices because the necessary reductions in production were too large for the individual cartel members to sustain.

Compatibility of Member Interests

The final factor we shall consider in determining the potential for cartelization of natural resource markets is the internal cohesion of the cartel. When there is only one seller, the objective of that seller can be pursued without worrying about alienating others who could undermine the profitability of the enterprise. In a cartel composed of many sellers, that freedom is

TABLE 7.1   The World's Largest Oil Reserves as of January 1, 1989

Country	Reserves (in billions of barrels)
Saudi Arabia	255.0
Iraq	100.0
United Arab Emirates	98.1
Kuwait	94.5
Iran	92.9
USSR	58.5
Venezuela	58.1
Mexico	54.1
United States	26.8
China	23.6

Source: *Oil and Gas Journal,* 26 Dec 1988, pp. 48–49, as cited in United States Energy Information Administration, *International Energy Annual 1988* (Washington, DC: U.S. Government Printing Office).

no longer as wide-ranging. The incentives of each member and the incentives of the group as a whole may diverge.

Cartel members have a strong incentive to cheat. A cheater, if undetected by the other members, could surreptitiously lower its price and steal part of the market away from the others. Formally, the price elasticity of demand facing an individual member is substantially higher than that for the group as a whole because some of the increase in individual sales at a lower price represents sales reductions for other members. With a higher price elasticity, lower prices maximize profits. Thus, successful cartelization presupposes a means for detecting cheating and enforcing the collusive agreement.[7]

In addition to cheating, however, there is another threat to the stability of cartels—the degree to which members fail to agree on pricing and output decisions. Oil provides an excellent example of how these dissensions can arise. Since the 1974 rise of OPEC as a world power, Saudi Arabia has exercised a moderating influence on the pricing decisions of OPEC. Why?

One highly significant reason is the size of Saudi Arabia's oil reserves (see Table 7.1). Saudi Arabia holds approximately 33 percent of the OPEC proved reserves; its reserves are larger than those of any other member. Because of this, Saudi Arabia has an incentive to preserve the value of those resources. It is worried about setting prices so high as to undercut the future demand for its oil. As was stated earlier, the demand for oil in the long run is more price elastic than in the short run. Meanwhile, the countries with smaller reserves know that in the long run their reserves will be gone and are more concerned about the near future. Because alternative sources of supply are not much of a threat in the near future due to long development times, other countries want to extract as much rent as possible now.

---

[7]During February, 1985, OPEC hired a large Dutch accounting firm to help it detect cheating among its members. See "Dutch Accountants Take on a Formidable Task: Ferreting Out 'Cheaters' in the Ranks of OPEC," *The Wall Street Journal* (26 February 1985): 39.

The size of Saudi Arabia's production also gives it the potential to make its influence felt. Its capacity to produce is so large that it can unilaterally affect world prices. In January 1981, for example, it was producing approximately 10.3 million barrels of crude oil a day—representing about 41 percent of all OPEC production.

Cartelization is not an easy path to pursue for producers, but when possible, it can be very profitable. When the resource is a strategic and pervasive raw material, cartelization can be very costly for consuming nations.

Strategic-material cartelization also confers on the members political, as well as economic, power. Economic power can become political power when the revenue is used to purchase weapons or the capacity to produce weapons. The producer nations can also use an embargo of the material as a lever to cajole reluctant adversaries into foreign policy concessions.

TRANSITION FUELS: ENVIRONMENTAL PROBLEMS

Currently the industrialized world depends on oil and gas for most of our energy. In the distant future we shall make a transition to renewable sources of energy. How about the intermediate time period?

Though some observers believe the transition to renewable sources will proceed so rapidly that no transition fuels will be necessary, most believe that transition fuels will probably play a significant role. Though other contenders, such as natural gas from deep wells, are clearly present, the fuels receiving the most attention as transition fuels are coal and uranium.

Domestic coal is abundantly available. Coal resources are approximately 22 times as large as oil and gas resources combined on a heat-equivalent basis. Neither availability nor dependency on foreign countries is an issue with coal.

Resource availability is a problem with uranium as long as we depend on conventional reactors. However, if the United States moves to the new generation of breeder reactors, which can use a wider range of fuels, availability will cease to be an important issue. On a heat-equivalent basis, domestic uranium resources are 4.2 times as great as domestic oil and gas resources if they are used in conventional reactors. With breeder reactors, the United States uranium base is 252 times the size of its oil and gas base.

The main issue defining the role for these two fuels involves their environmental impact. Coal's main drawback is its contribution to air pollution. Its high sulfur content makes it a potentially large source of sulfur dioxide emissions, one of the chief culprits in the acid-rain problem. It is also a major source of particulate emissions and carbon dioxide, one of the greenhouse gases implicated in global warming. Because a detailed analysis of these environmental problems follows in subsequent chapters, we shall not consider them any further here except to note that if those who burn coal fail to consider these environmental costs, the market will foster an excessive reliance on coal.

The other main transition fuel, uranium, used in nuclear electrical generation stations, has its own limitations, principally safety. Two sources of concern stand out: (1) nuclear accidents, and (2) the storage of radioactive waste. Is the market likely to make the correct decisions on these questions? In both cases the answer is no, given the current decision-making environment. Let's consider these issues one by one.

The production of electricity by nuclear reactors requires radioactive elements. If these elements escape into the atmosphere and come in contact with humans in sufficient concentrations, they produce birth defects, cancer, and death. Some radioactive elements may also escape during the normal operation of a plant, but the greatest risk of nuclear power is still the threat of nuclear accidents.

Nuclear accidents may inject large doses of radioactivity into the environment. The most dangerous of these possibilities is the core meltdown. Unlike other types of electrical generation, nuclear processes continue to generate heat even after the reactor is turned off. This means that the nuclear fuel must be continuously cooled or the heat levels will escalate beyond the design capacity of the reactor shield. If, in this case, the reactor vessel should fracture, clouds of radioactive gases and particulates would be released into the atmosphere.

For some time conventional wisdom had held that nuclear accidents involving a core meltdown were a remote possibility. On 25 April 1986, however, a serious core meltdown occurred at the Chernobyl nuclear plant in the Soviet Union. Though safety standards are generally conceded to be much higher in the Western industrialized world than in the Soviet Union, this incident has added yet another burden for an already troubled industry to bear.

Nuclear power has been beset by economic as well as political forces. New nuclear power plant construction has become much more expensive, in part due to the increasing regulatory requirements designed to provide a safer system. Its economic advantage over coal has dissipated, and the demand for new nuclear plants has been eliminated. In the United States, for example, in 1973, 219 nuclear power plants were either planned or in operation. By the end of 1986 that number had fallen to 130, the difference being explained by cancellations. No new applications for nuclear plants are pending.

Not all nations are making the same choice with respect to the nuclear option. Sweden not only has pledged not to build any new nuclear plants, but also plans to shut down those currently in operation early in the twenty-first century. In France and Japan, however, standardized plant design and regulatory stability have resulted in electricity generating costs for nuclear power which are lower than for coal. Both countries are expanding the role of nuclear power.[8]

An additional concern relates to storing nuclear wastes. The waste-storage issue relates to both ends of the nuclear-fuel cycle—the disposal of uranium tailings from the mining process and spent fuel from the reactors, though the latter receives most of the publicity. Uranium tailings contain several elements, the most prominent being thorium-230, which decays with a half-life of 78,000 years to a radioactive, chemically inert gas, radon-222. Once formed, this gas has a very short half-life (38 days).

The spent fuel from nuclear reactors contains a variety of radioactive elements with quite different half-lives. In the first few centuries, the dominant contributors to radioactivity are fission products, principally strontium-90 and cesium-137. After approximately 1,000 years, most of these elements will have decayed, leaving the transuranic elements having substantially longer half-lives. These remaining elements would remain a risk for up to 240,000 years. Thus, decisions made today affect not only the level of risk borne by the current generation—

---

[8]For a survey of the global situation for nuclear power see Christopher Flavin, *Nuclear Power: The Market Test* (Washington, DC: Worldwatch Institute Paper #57, 1983).

in the form of nuclear accidents—but also that borne by a host of succeeding generations (due to the longevity of radioactive risk from the disposal of spent fuel).

Can we expect the market to make the correct choice with respect to nuclear power? Because this seems to be a clear case of externalities, we might expect the answer for the problem of nuclear accidents to be no. Third parties, those living near the reactor, would receive the brunt of the damage from a nuclear accident. Would the utility have an incentive to choose the efficient level of precaution?

If the utility had to compensate fully for all the damages caused, then the answer would be yes. In the United States full compensation is not paid by the individual utilities for two reasons: (1) the role of the government in sharing the risk, and (2) the role of insurance.

When the government first allowed private industry to use atomic power to generate electricity, there were no takers. No utility could afford the damages if an accident occurred. No insurance company would underwrite the risk. Then in 1957, with the passage of the Price-Anderson Act, the government underwrote the liability. That act provided for a liability ceiling of $560 million (once that amount had been paid out, no more claims would be honored), of which the government would bear $500 million. The industry would pick up the remaining $60 million. The Act was originally designed to expire in ten years, at which time the industry would assume full responsibility for the liability.

The Act didn't expire, though over time a steady diminution of the government's share of the liability has occurred. Currently the liability ceiling still exists, albeit at a higher level; the amount of private insurance has increased; and a system has been set up to assess all utilities by retrospective premium in the event an accident occurs.

The effect of the Price-Anderson Act is to reduce the expected cost of nuclear power to the utility choosing to use it. Both the liability ceiling and the portion of the liability borne by government reduce the potential compensation the utility would have to pay. As the industry assumes an increasing portion of the liability burden, the risk sharing embodied in the retrospective premium system (the means by which it assumes that burden) breaks the link between precautionary behavior by the individual utility and the compensation it might have to pay. Under this system, increased safety by the utility does not reduce its premiums.

The individual utilities pay into a fund that compensates victims. The important point is that the actual cost of an accident to the utility is not sensitive to the level of precautions it takes. The cost to all utilities, whether they have accidents or not, is the premium paid both before and after any accident. These premiums do not reflect the amount of precautionary measures taken by an individual plant; therefore, individual utilities have little incentive to provide an efficient amount of safety.[9]

In recognition of the utilities' lower-than-efficient concern for safety, the federal government has established the Nuclear Regulatory Commission to oversee the safety of nuclear reactors, among its other responsibilities. In the aftermath of the nuclear accident at Three Mile Island on 28 March 1979, a Presidential Commission was established to provide an independent evaluation of this system of safety regulation. Their final report,[10] issued on 30

---

[9]For further discussion of this point see Jeffrey A. Dubin and Geoffry S. Rothwell, "Subsidy to Nuclear Power Through Price-Anderson Liability Limit," *Contemporary Policy Issues* (July 1990).

[10]The President's Commission on the Accident at Three Mile Island, *The Need for Change: The Legacy of TMI* (New York: Pergamon Press, 1979).

October 1979, was highly critical of the existing system and made a series of recommendations to improve it. Though the problem of nuclear accidents is manageable in principle, it may or may not be manageable in practice.

Both the operating safety and the nuclear-waste storage issue can be viewed as a problem of determining appropriate compensation. Those who gain from nuclear power should be forced to compensate those who lose. If they can't, in the absence of externalities, the net benefits from adopting nuclear power are not positive. If nuclear power is efficient, by definition the gains to the gainers will exceed the losses to the losers. Nonetheless, it is important that this compensation actually be paid because without compensation, the losers can block the efficient allocation.

A compensation approach is already being taken in those countries still expanding the role of nuclear power. The French government, for example, has announced a policy of reducing electricity rates by roughly 15 percent for those living near nuclear stations. And in Japan during 1980, the Tohoku Electric Power Company paid the equivalent of $4.3 million to residents of Ojika, in northern Japan, to get them to withdraw their opposition to a nuclear power plant being built there.

This approach could also help resolve the current political controversy over the location of nuclear-waste disposal sites. Most plans currently focus on burying the waste in some geologically stable formation. Current and future generations of people living near the chosen sight would have a tendency to oppose nuclear power because the costs to them appear to outweigh the benefits. To others, however, who may enjoy nuclear-produced electricity and may live far from the sites, the benefits might exceed the costs. This rationale prompted a number of states to pass laws permitting nuclear power but prohibiting the permanent storage of waste in their state.

Under a compensation scheme, those consuming nuclear power should be taxed to compensate those who live in the areas of the disposal site. If the compensation is adequate to induce them to accept the site, then nuclear power is a viable option and the costs of disposal are ultimately borne by the consumers. Some towns, such as Naturita, Colorado, are actively seeking to become disposal sites. If taxes to obtain a sufficient number of disposal sites are so high that nuclear energy becomes noncompetitive, then nuclear energy is not an efficient source.

Are future generations adequately represented in this transaction? The quick answer is no, but that answer is not correct. Those living around the sites will experience declines in the market value of land reflecting the increased risk of living or working there. The payment system is designed to compensate those who experience the reduction, the current generation. Future generations, should they decide to live near a disposal site, would be compensated by lower land values. If the land values were not cheap enough to compensate them, they would not have to live there. As long as full information on the risks posed is available, those who do bear the cost of locating near the sites do so only if they are willing to accept the risk in return for lower land values.[11]

---

[11]For further discussion of possible compensation schemes see Robert Cameron Mitchell and Richard T. Carson, "Property Rights, Protest, and the Siting of Hazardous Waste Facilities," and Howard Kunreuther and Paul R. Kleindorfer, "A Sealed-Bid Auction Mechanism for Siting Noxious Facilities," *American Economic Review* 76, No. 2 (May 1986): 285–90, 295–99.

CONSERVATION AND LOAD MANAGEMENT

As the previous discussion indicated, environmental problems associated with the transition fuels present particular difficulties for generating electrical power. Although alternative fuels and solar power will eventually play an increasing role, most experts seem to feel that they will penetrate the market slowly as they become more familiar and accessible. How then is the transition to these long-term solutions to be managed by the electrical utilities sector in light of the problems associated with the transition fuels?

For a number of utilities, conservation has assumed an increasing role. To a major extent, conservation has already been stimulated by market forces. High oil and natural gas prices, coupled with the rapidly increasing cost of both nuclear and coal-fired generating stations, have reduced electrical demand significantly. Yet many Public Utilities Commissions, the state bodies charged with regulating the production, transmission, and sale of electricity, are coming to the conclusion that more conservation is needed.

Perhaps the most significant role for conservation is its ability to defer capacity expansion. Each new electrical generating plant tends to cost more than the last, and frequently the cost increase is substantial. When the new plants come on line, rate increases to finance the new plant are necessary. By reducing the demand for electricity, conservation delays the date when the new capacity is needed to satisfy the higher demand. Delays in the need to construct new plants translate into delays in rate increases as well.

The dominant electricity pricing system is ill-designed to stimulate the efficient amount of conservation. Average-cost pricing is common. This pricing system implies that the new higher-cost sources are averaged in with the lower-cost sources, yielding a rate that is substantially lower than the true marginal cost of the power being generated. Thus the consumer considering investing in conservation would save less money by conserving with average-cost pricing than would be the case if the energy saved were priced at its true marginal cost. Less than an efficient amount of conservation would be the expected outcome.

Utilities are reacting to this situation in a number of ways. One is to consider investing in conservation, rather than in new plants, when conservation is the cheaper alternative. The thrust of these programs can be illustrated by referring to a few of the programs instituted by the Pacific Gas and Electric Company (PG&E), a leader in the field, which has established a system of rebates for residential customers to install conservation measures in their homes, has provided free home weatherization to qualified low-income homeowners, has offered owners of multifamily residential buildings incentives for installing solar water-heating systems, and has provided subsidized energy audits to inform customers about money-saving conservation opportunities. Similar incentives have been provided to the commercial, agricultural, and industrial sectors. Though the costs of these investments must also be recovered from customers, PG&E reports that the savings have been dramatic and customer satisfaction has been high. Less power consumed means available energy supplies last longer.

The total amount of electrical energy demanded in a given year is not the only concern utilities have. They are also concerned with how that energy demand is spread out over the year. The capacity of the system must be high enough to satisfy the demand during the periods when the energy demand is highest (called peak periods). During other periods, much of the capacity remains underutilized.

Demand during the peak period imposes two rather special costs on utilities. First, the peaking units, those generating facilities fired up only during the peak periods, produce electricity at a much higher marginal cost than do base-load plants, those fired up virtually all the time. Peaking units are typically cheaper to build than base-load plants, but they have higher operating costs. Second, it is the growth in peak demand that frequently triggers the need for capacity expansion. Slowing down the growth in peak demand may delay the need for new expensive capacity expansion so that a higher proportion of the power needs can be met by the most efficient generating plants.

Utilities are also responding to this problem by adopting load-management techniques to produce a more balanced use of this capacity over the year. One economic load-management technique is called *peak-load pricing.* Peak-load pricing attempts to impose the full (higher) marginal cost of supplying peak power on those consuming peak power by charging higher prices during the peak period.

Although many utilities have now begun to use simple versions of this approach, some are experimenting with very innovative ways of implementing rather refined versions of this system. One innovative system, for example, transmits electricity prices every five minutes over regular power lines. In a customer's household the lines attached to one or more appliances can be controlled by switches that turn the power off any time the prevailing price exceeds a limit established by the customer. Other less-sophisticated pricing systems simply inform consumers in advance what prices will prevail in predetermined peak periods.

A study by economists at the Rand Corporation in California indicates that even the rudimentary versions of peak-load pricing work.[12] Based on the actual experience with time-of-day rates by more than 6,000 commercial and industrial customers, they found that business customers saved themselves and utilities on average $1,000 per year for an added metering cost of only $50. Working with an additional sample of over 3,000, the authors found that residential customers also saved by shifting some of their demand to less expensive periods. The greatest shifts were registered by the largest residential customers and those with several electric appliances.

It is interesting that this study found the gains from peak-load pricing in the United States to be somewhat lower than those reported for European customers, who have been exposed to peak-load pricing for a longer period of time. Attributing the large European response in part to the longer time Europeans have had to adapt to this system, the authors speculate that the longer-term response by U.S. customers could turn out to be quite a bit greater than already recorded.

A third innovation in the utility sector involves procedures for internalizing the environmental costs. Those who have typically been assigned the responsibility for regulating utility prices have focused almost exclusively on holding prices down by choosing the cheapest sources of power. Unfortunately, only generating and distribution costs were considered; the damage caused by emissions was ignored. The resulting choices turned out not to be the cheapest when all costs were considered.

To rectify this imbalance in the procedures for choosing generating sources, some states have begun explicitly incorporating environmental costs in their decision-making process. New York State, for example, adds 1.4 cents/kwh to the estimated cost of electricity produced

---

[12]Jan Paul Acton, et al., "Time-of-Day Electricity Rates for the United States," Report #R-3086-HF (Santa Monica, CA: Rand Corporation, 1983); Rolla Edward Park and Jan Paul Acton, *Response to Time-of-Day Electricity Rates by Large Business Customers: Initial Analysis of Data from Ten U.S. Utilities* (Santa Monica, CA: Rand Corporation Report No. R-3080-HF/MD/RC, 1983).

from fossil fuel sources to account for the various negative environmental effects. By creating a more level playing field for competing sources, this technique has increased the competitiveness of renewable power sources such as hydro, solar, and wind.

THE LONG RUN

Ultimately our energy needs will have to be fulfilled from renewable energy sources, either because the depletable energy sources have been exhausted or, as is more likely, because the environmental costs of using the depletable sources have become so high that renewable sources were cheaper.

Depending on how the scientific uncertainty is resolved, the most compelling case for the transition may well be made by the mounting evidence that the global climate is being jeopardized by current and prospective energy consumption patterns. If the Third World were to follow the energy-intensive, fossil-fuel based, path to development pioneered by the industrialized nations, the amount of carbon dioxide emissions injected into the air would be unprecedented. Currently, one half of all developing nations rely on imported oil for more than 75 percent of their commercial energy needs.[13] A transition away from fossil fuels to other energy forms in both the industrialized and third-world nations would be an important ingredient in any strategy to reduce carbon dioxide emissions. Can our institutions manage that transition in a timely and effective manner?

Renewable energy comes in many different forms. Hydro power can be derived from flowing water; biomass can be burned; solar energy can be used to produce heat used to drive steam turbines or converted directly into electricity by means of photovoltaics; wind energy can drive turbines; hydrogen extracted from the air by solar energy could fuel cars or furnaces; and geothermal energy can be captured from the bowels of the earth and put to useful work.

The extent to which these sources will penetrate the market will depend upon their relative cost and consumer acceptance. Relative cost will no doubt change over time as research uncovers better ways to harness the power of renewable sources. Perhaps the best example of how research can lower costs is provided by the experience with photovoltaics.

Photovoltaics involve the direct conversion of solar energy to electricity (as opposed to indirect conversions such as when steam energy is used to drive a turbine). Anticipating a huge potential market, private industry has been very interested in photovoltaics and has poured a lot of research dollars into improving its commercial viability. The research has paid off. In 1976, the average market price for a photovoltaic module was $44 per peak watt installed and 0.5 megawatts were sold. Only a decade later, costs were down eightfold (in constant 1986 dollars) to $5.25 and shipments had climbed to 24.7 megawatts.[14] Rural electrification projects using photovoltaics are slowly spreading into the Third World.

---

[13]U.S. Agency for International Development, *Decentralized Hydropower in AID's Development Assistance Program* (Washington, DC: AID, 1986).

[14]Cited in Cynthia Pollock Shea, "Shifting to Renewable Energy," *State of the World: 1988* (New York: W. W. Norton, 1988): 74.

Somewhat lower down the scale in terms of commercial viability is using hydrogen as a fuel. If an electric current (produced by photovoltaics, for example) is conducted through a reservoir of water, the liquid splits into its constituent elements—hydrogen and oxygen. When burned with oxygen, hydrogen creates a single by-product—drinkable water.

Hydrogen has many potential uses including serving as a fuel for automobiles. Prototype cars that use this fuel have already been built. Although the costs of supplying and using this fuel have declined in response to recent research, the declines are not yet sufficiently large to make it a competitor in the near future.

Consumer acceptance is an important ingredient in the transition to any alternative source of energy. New systems are usually less reliable and more expensive than old systems. Once they become heavily used, their reliability normally increases and cost declines; experience is a good teacher. Because the early consumers, the pioneers, experience both lower reliability and higher costs, procrastination can be an optimal individual strategy. If every consumer procrastinates about switching, however, the industry will not be able to operate at a sufficient scale and will not be able to gain enough experience to produce the reliability and lower cost that will assure a large, stable market. How can this initial consumer reluctance be overcome?

One strategy, the one used in the United States, involves using tax dollars to subsidize purchases by the pioneers. Once the market is sufficiently large that it can begin to take advantage of economies of scale and can eliminate the initial sources of unreliability, the subsidies can be eliminated. The available empirical evidence suggests that the tax-credit approach has significantly increased the degree of market penetration of solar equipment in the United States.[15]

The penetration would have been even greater if the cartel had been able to sustain the very high oil prices which were in effect at the beginning of the 1980s. As oil prices fell in real terms, both residential and commercial enthusiasm for making the transition to solar energy was undermined. Because saving money is a primary motivation for making the switch and low oil prices translate into relatively low or even negative savings, uncertainty associated with the path of future oil and natural-gas prices could continue to be a barrier to the transition.

SUMMARY

We have seen that the relationship between government and the market is not always a harmonious and efficient one. In the past, price controls have tended to reduce energy conservation, to discourage exploration and supply, to cause biases in the substitution among fuel types, and to penalize future consumers. This important area makes a clear case for less, not more, regulation.

---

[15]Catherine A. Durham, Bonnie G. Colby, and Molly Longstreth, "The Impact of State Tax Credits and Energy Prices on Adoption of Solar Energy Systems," *Land Economics* 64 (November 1988): 347–55; Gene R. Fry, "The Economics of Home Solar Water Heating and the Role of Solar Tax Credits," *Land Economics* 62 (May 1986): 134–44.

This is not universally true, however. Other dimensions of the energy problem suggest the need for some government role. The government should ensure that the costs of energy fully reflect the potentially large environmental costs and that fluctuating resource prices do not undermine the transition to appropriate renewable energy resources that make sense in the long run. Government should also oversee nuclear reactor safety and should ensure that communities forced to accept nuclear-waste disposal sites are fully compensated. Given the environmental difficulties with both of the traditional transition fuels (coal and uranium), conservation and load-management techniques are now playing and will continue to play a larger role in the electric utilities sector. Two economic measures that have been instrumental in ushering in this greater role are subsidizing conservation where it is cheaper for the utility than capacity expansion and peak-load pricing. The potential for an efficient allocation of energy resources by the economic and political institutions clearly exists, even if it has not always occurred in the past.

FURTHER READING

Griffin, James M., and Henry B. Steele. *Energy Economics and Policy,* 2nd ed. (New York: Academic Press, 1986). A very readable textbook on energy economics aimed at undergraduates with one course in the principles of economics. Covers OPEC, environmental issues, national security, conservation, price controls, and market structure regulations, as well as energy research and development.

Landsberg, Hans H., ed. *Energy: The Next Twenty Years* (Cambridge, MA: Ballinger, 1979). A comprehensive report combining the effort of 19 experts across the country funded by the Ford Foundation. Contains nine recommendations including decontrol of oil and natural-gas prices, development of an effective oil stockpile program, improving the acceptability of coal, vigorous pursuit of conservation, and removal of impediments to the use of solar power.

Schurr, Sam H., et al. *Energy in America's Future: The Choice Before Us* (Baltimore, MD: Johns Hopkins University Press, for Resources for the Future, 1979). A monumental, twenty-chapter book attempting to synthesize what is known and not known about energy demand, supply, health, safety, and environmental issues and the process of making energy choices. Concludes that "it will be possible to fulfill the expansionist requirement that enough energy will be available to support economic growth while meeting the conservationist demand that energy use be lessened substantially from what previously was thought to be the necessary minimum."

Shea, Cynthia Pollock. "Shifting to Renewable Energy," in Lester R. Brown et al., eds., *State of the World: 1988* (New York: W. W. Norton, 1988): 62–82. A wealth of information on how the transition to renewable resources is shaping up around the world.

Stobaugh, Robert, and Daniel Yergin, eds. *Energy Future: Report of the Energy Project at the Harvard Business School* (New York: Random House, 1979). A nontechnical, almost chatty collection of essays concerning the near-term energy choices for America written by persons associated with the Harvard Business School as students or faculty. Concludes the only viable program that would politically reduce dependence on foreign oil is for the government to give financial incentives to encourage conservation and the use of solar energy.

Walton, A. L., and E. H. Warren, Jr. *The Solar Alternative: An Economic Perspective* (Englewood Cliffs, NJ: Prentice-Hall, 1982). A short, uncomplicated introduction to the economics of solar energy including chapters on market distortions and the equity issues associated with a transition to solar power.

Webb, Michael G., and Martin J. Ricketts. *The Economics of Energy* (New York: John Wiley & Sons, 1980). Written by two British economists and aimed at undergraduates who have had intermediate microeconomic theory, this textbook is particularly rich in examples drawn from the British experience.

ADDITIONAL REFERENCES

Adelman, M. A. *The World Petroleum Market* (Baltimore, MD: Johns Hopkins University Press, for Resources for the Future, 1972).

Arrow, Kenneth J., and Joseph P. Kalt. *Petroleum Price Regulation: Should We Decontrol?* (Washington, DC: American Enterprise Institute, 1979).

Bhatia, Ramesh, and Armand Pereira. *Socioeconomic Aspects of Renewable Energy Technologies* (New York: Praeger Publishers, 1988).

Bohi, Douglas R., and Milton Russell. *Limiting Oil Imports: An Economic History and Analysis* (Baltimore, MD: Johns Hopkins University Press, for Resources for the Future, 1978).

Cropper, M. L. "Pollution Aspects of Nuclear Energy Use," *Journal of Environmental Economics and Management* 7 (December 1980): 334–52.

Griffin, James M. "OPEC Behavior: A Test of Alternative Hypotheses," *The American Economic Review* 75, No. 5 (December 1985): 954–63.

Hall, Darwin C., ed. "Social and Private Costs of Alternative Energy Technologies," a special issue of *Contemporary Policy Issues* (July 1990).

Lerner, A. P. "OPEC—A Plan—If You Can't Beat Them, Join Them," *Atlantic Economic Journal* 8 (September 1980): 1–3.

Toman, Michael, and Molly K. Macauley. "Risk Aversion and the Insurance Value of Strategic Oil Stockpiling," *Resources and Energy* 8 (1986): 151–65.

Lind, Robert C., et al. *Discounting for Time and Risk in Energy Policy* (Washington, DC: Resources for the Future, 1982).

West, Ronal E., and Frank Kreith. *Economic Analysis of Solar Thermal Energy Systems* (Cambridge, MA: MIT Press, 1988)

DISCUSSION QUESTIONS

1. Should benefit/cost analysis play the dominant role in deciding the proportion of American electrical energy to be supplied by nuclear power? Why or why not?

2. One economist (Lerner [1980]) proposed that the United States impose a tariff on oil imports equal to 100 percent of the import price. This tariff is designed to reduce dependence on foreign sources as well as to discourage OPEC from raising prices (because, due to the tariff, the delivered price would rise twice as much as the OPEC increase, causing a large subsequent reduction in consumption). Should this proposal become public policy? Why or why not?

CHAPTER 8

Water

You'll never miss the water
Till your well runs dry.

WILLIAM CHRISTOPHER HANDY, "JOE TURNER'S BLUES" (1915)

INTRODUCTION

To the red country and part of the gray country of Oklahoma, the last rains came gently, and they did not cut the scarred earth. . . . The sun flared down on the growing corn day after day until a line of brown spread along the edge of each green bayonet. The clouds appeared and went away, and in awhile they did not try anymore.

With these words John Steinbeck sets the scene for his powerful novel *The Grapes of Wrath*. Drought and poor soil conservation practices combined to destroy the agricultural institutions that had provided nourishment and livelihood to Oklahoma residents since settlement in that area had begun. In desperation, those who had worked that land were forced to abandon not only their possessions, but their past. Moving to California to seek employment, they were uprooted only to be caught up in a web of exploitation and hopelessness.

Based on an actual situation, the novel demonstrates how the social fabric can tear when subject to tremendous stress, such as an inadequate availability of water, and how painful those tears can be. Clearly problems such as these should be anticipated and prevented as much as possible.

Water is one of the essential elements of life. We humans depend not only on an intake of water to replace the continual loss of body fluids but also on food sources that themselves need water to survive. This resource deserves special attention.

In this chapter we shall examine how our economic and political institutions have allocated this important resource in the past and how they might improve on its allocation in the future. We initiate our inquiry by examining the likelihood and severity of water scarcity. Turning to the management of our water resources, we will define the efficient allocation of ground and surface water over time and compare these allocations to current practice, particularly in the United States. Finally, we will examine the menu of opportunities for meaningful institutional reform.

FIGURE 8.1 The Hydrologic Cycle

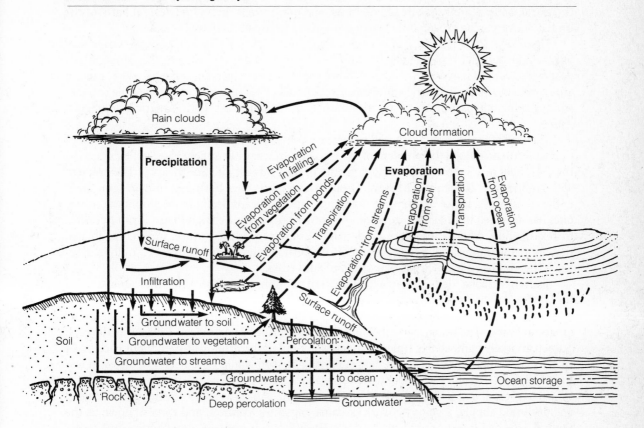

THE POTENTIAL FOR WATER SCARCITY

The earth's renewable supply of water is governed by the hydrologic cycle, a system of continuous water circulation (Figure 8.1). Enormous quantities of water are cycled each year through this system, though only a fraction of circulated water is available each year for human use.

Available supplies are derived from two rather different sources—surface water and groundwater. As the name implies, *surface water* consists of the fresh water in rivers, lakes, and reservoirs that collects and flows on the earth's surface. By contrast, groundwater collects in porous layers of underground rock known as aquifers. Though some groundwater is renewed by percolation of rain or melted snow, most was accumulated over geologic time and, because of its location, cannot be recharged once it is depleted. Of the 16,000 trillion gallons of groundwater estimated to be available for extraction in the United States, only about 400 trillion gallons are available on a renewable basis. The rest is a finite, depletable resource.

If we were simply to add up the available supply of fresh water (total runoff) on a global scale and compare it with the demand for it, we would discover that the supply is currently about 10 times demand. Though comforting, that statistic is also misleading because it masks the impact of growing demand and the rather severe excess-demand situations that already exist in certain parts of the world. Taken together, these insights suggest that in many parts of the world water scarcity is already upon us, and other areas, including several parts of the United States, can be expected to experience water scarcity in the next few decades.

The Global 2000 Report estimates that by the year 2000, worldwide available water supplies will be only 3.5 times demand because of population growth.[1] Due to the temporal and geographic variation in both water availability and population growth, some parts of the world are expected to be particularly vulnerable. Areas noted as being especially susceptible to water shortages include part of Africa, North America, the Middle East, Latin America, and South Asia.

The United States is not expected to escape water scarcity problems. The Water Resources Council estimates that "the problem of inadequate surface water supply is or will be severe by the year 2000 in 17 subregions located mainly in the Midwest and Southwest."[2] The problem with groundwater is even more severe. Groundwater levels have been declining in some areas of the country as a result of intensive pumping, and significant depletion of groundwater supplies has occurred in three major regions—southern Arizona, the High Plains (from Nebraska to Texas), and California. Kenneth Frederick of Resources for the Future, Inc., has estimated that annual withdrawals exceed recharge in Western aquifers by more than 22 million acrefeet.[3] The number is even larger in particularly dry years.

Tucson, Arizona, demonstrates how western communities cope. Until the completion of the Central Arizona Project, which diverts water from the Colorado River, Tucson, which averages about 11 inches of rain a year, was the largest city in the United States to rely entirely on groundwater. The water levels in some wells in Tucson have dropped 100 feet in 10 years. Tucson annually pumped five times as much water out of the ground as nature put back in. At *current* consumption rates the aquifers supplying Tucson would have been exhausted in less than 100 years. Despite the rate at which its water supplies were being depleted, Tucson continued to grow at a rapid rate. To head off this looming gap between increasing water demand and declining supply, a giant network of dams, pipelines, tunnels, and canals known as the Central Arizona Project was constructed to transfer water from the Colorado River to Tucson. Water diversion has been a common, but increasingly unavailable, policy response.

Though the discussion thus far has focused on the quantity of water, that is not the only problem. Quality is also a problem. Much of the available water is polluted with chemicals, radioactive materials, salt, or bacteria. Though we shall reserve for subsequent chapters a detailed look at the water pollution problem, it is important to keep in mind that water scarcity has an important qualitative dimension that further limits the supply of potable water.

This brief survey of the evidence suggests that in certain parts of the world groundwater supplies are being depleted to the potential detriment of future users. Supplies, which for all practical purposes will never be replenished, are being "mined" to satisfy current needs. Once used, they are gone. Is this allocation efficient, or are there demonstrable sources of ineffi-

---

[1]Gerald O. Barney, *The Global 2000 Report to the President of the U.S.: Entering the 21st Century: Volume 1, The Summary Report* (New York: Pergamon Press, 1980): 155.

[2]U.S. Water Resources Council, *The Nation's Water Resources, 1975–2000,* Volume 1 (Washington, DC: Government Printing Office, 1978): 56.

[3]Kenneth D. Frederick, "Water Supplies," in Paul Portney, ed., *Current Issues in Natural Resources Policy* (Washington, DC: Resources for the Future, 1982): 227.

ciency? Answering this question requires us to be quite clear about what is meant by an efficient allocation of surface and groundwater.

THE EFFICIENT ALLOCATION OF SCARCE WATER

What efficiency means for the allocation of water depends crucially on whether surface water or groundwater is being tapped. In the absence of storage, the problem with surface water is to allocate a renewable supply among competing users. Intergenerational effects are less important, as future supplies depend on natural phenomena (such as precipitation) rather than on current withdrawal practices. For groundwater, on the other hand, withdrawing water now does affect the resources available to future generations. In this case, the allocation over time is a crucial aspect of the analysis. Because it represents a somewhat simpler analytical case, we shall start by considering the efficient allocation of surface water.

Surface Water

An efficient allocation of surface water (1) must strike a balance among a host of competing users and (2) must supply an acceptable means of handling the year-to-year variability in surface water flow. The former issue is acute because so many different potential users have legitimate competing claims: Some (such as municipal drinking water suppliers or farmers) withdraw the water for consumption; others (such as swimmers or boaters) use but do not consume the water. The latter challenge arises because surface water supplies are not constant from year to year or month to month. Because precipitation, runoff, and evaporation all change from year to year, less water will be available to be allocated in some years than in others. Not only must a system for allocating the average amount of water be in place, above-average and below-average flows must also be anticipated and allocated.

With respect to the first problem, the dictates of efficiency are quite clear—the water should be allocated so that the marginal net benefit is equalized for all uses. (Remember that the marginal net benefit is the vertical distance between the demand curve for water and the marginal cost of extracting and distributing that water for the last unit of water consumed.) To demonstrate why efficiency requires marginal net benefits, consider a situation in which the marginal net benefits are *not* equal. We shall show that in this situation it is always possible to find some reallocation of the water that increases net benefits. Because net benefits could be increased by this reallocation, the initial allocation could not have maximized net benefits. Inasmuch as an efficient allocation maximizes net benefits, the allocation through which net benefits are not equalized could not have been efficient.

If marginal net benefits have not been equalized, it is always possible to increase net benefits by transferring water from those uses with low net marginal benefits to those with higher net marginal benefits. By transferring the water to the users who value the marginal water more, the net benefits of the water use are increased; those losing water are giving up less than those receiving the additional water are gaining. When the marginal net benefits are equalized, no such transfer is possible without lowering net benefits.

Marginal scarcity rent would be zero if water were not scarce. All users would get all they want. Their marginal net benefits would still be equal, but in this case they would be zero.

Groundwater

When withdrawals exceed recharge from a particular aquifer, the resource will be mined over time until supplies are exhausted or until the marginal cost of pumping additional water becomes prohibitive. The marginal extraction cost (the cost of pumping the last unit to the surface) would rise over time as the water table fell. Pumping would stop either (1) when the water table ran dry or (2) when the marginal cost of pumping was either greater than the marginal benefit of the water or greater than the marginal cost of acquiring water from some other source.

Abundant surface water in proximity to the location of the groundwater could serve as a substitute for groundwater, effectively setting an upper bound on the marginal cost of extraction. The user would not pay more to extract a unit of groundwater than it would cost to acquire surface water. Unfortunately in many parts of the country where groundwater overdrafts are particularly severe, the competition for surface water is already keen; a cheap source of surface water doesn't exist.

In efficient groundwater markets, the water price would rise over time. The rise would continue until the point of exhaustion, the point at which the marginal pumping cost becomes prohibitive or when the marginal cost of pumping becomes equal to the next-least-expensive source of water. At that point the marginal pumping cost and the price would be equal.

THE CURRENT ALLOCATION SYSTEM

Riparian and Prior Appropriation Doctrines

Within the United States the means of allocating water differ from one geographic area to the next, particularly with respect to the legal doctrines that govern conflicts. In this section we shall focus on the allocation systems that prevail in the arid Southwest, which must cope with the most potentially serious and imminent scarcity of water.

In the earliest days of settlement in the American Southwest and West, the government had a minimal presence. Residents were pretty much on their own in creating a sense of order. Property rights played a very important role in reducing conflicts in this potentially volatile situation.

As water was always a significant factor in the development of an area, the first settlements were usually oriented near bodies of water. The property rights that evolved, called *riparian rights,* allocated the right to use the water to the owner of the land adjacent to the water. This was a practical solution because by virtue of their location, these owners had easy access to the water. Furthermore, there were enough sites with access to water that virtually all who sought water could be accommodated.

With population growth and the consequent rise in the demand for land, this allocation system became less appropriate. As demand increased, the amount of land adjacent to water became scarce, forcing some spillover onto land which was not adjacent to water. The owners of this land began to seek means of acquiring water to make their land more productive.

About this time, with the discovery of gold in California, mining became an important source of employment. With the advent of mining came a need to divert water away from streams to other sites. Unfortunately, riparian property rights made no provision for water to be diverted to other locations. The rights to the water were tied to the land and could not be separately transferred.

This situation created a demand for a change in the property-right structure from riparian rights to one which was more congenial to the need for transferability. The waste resulting from the lack of transferability became so great that it outweighed any transition costs of changing the system of property rights. The evolution that took place in the mining camps became the forerunner of what has become known as the *prior appropriation* doctrine.

The miners established the custom that the first person to arrive had the superior claim on the water.[4] In practice, this severed the relationship that had existed under the riparian doctrine between the rights to land and the rights to water. As this new doctrine became adopted in legislation, court rulings, and seven state constitutions, widespread diversion of water based on prior appropriation became possible. Stimulated by the profits that could be made in shifting water to more valuable uses, private companies were formed to construct irrigation systems, and to transport water from surplus to deficit areas. Agriculture flourished.

Although prior to 1860 the role of the government was rather minimal, after 1860 that began to change—slowly at first, but picking up momentum as the twentieth century began. The earliest incursions involved establishing the principle that the ownership of water properly belonged to the state. Claimants were accorded on the right to use, known as a *usufruct right,* rather than an ownership right. The establishment of this principle of public ownership was followed in short order by establishing state control over the rates charged by the private irrigation companies, imposing restrictions on the ability to transfer water out of the district, and creating a centralized bureaucracy to administer the process.

This was only the beginning. The demand for land in the arid West and Southwest was still growing, creating a complementary demand for water to make the desert bloom. The tremendous profits to be made from large-scale water diversion created the political climate necessary for the federal government to get involved.

The federal role in water resources originated in the early 1800s, largely out of concern for the nation's regional development and economic growth. Toward these ends, the federal government built a network of inland waterways to provide transportation. Since 1902, the federal government has built almost 700 dams to provide water and power to help settle the West.

To promote growth and regional development, the federal government has paid an average of 70 percent of the combined construction and operating costs of such projects, leaving states localities, and private users to carry the remaining 30 percent. Such subsidies have even been extended to cover some of the costs of providing marketable water services. For example, the federal government pays 81 percent of the cost of supplying irrigation water and 64 percent of municipal water costs.[5]

---

[4]For a detailed treatment of this evolution, see Charles W. McCurdy, "Stephen J. Field and Public Land Law Development in California, 1850–1866: A Case Study of Judicial Resource Allocation in Nineteenth Century America," *Law and Society* (Winter 1976): 235–66.

[5]Kenneth Rubin, *Efficient Investments in Water Resources: Issues and Options* (Washington, DC: Congressional Budget Office, 1983): xii.

This, in a nutshell, is the current situation for water. Both the state and federal governments play a large role. Though the prior appropriation doctrine stands as the foundation of this allocation system, it is heavily circumscribed by government regulations and direct government appropriation of a substantial amount of water.

Sources of Inefficiency

The current system is not efficient. The prime source of inefficiency involves restrictions that have been placed on water transfers, preventing their gravitation to the highest-valued use. Other sources, such as charging inefficiently low prices, must bear some of the responsibility.

Restrictions on Transfers.   To achieve an efficient allocation of water, the marginal net benefits have to be equalized across all uses of the water. With a well-structured system of water property rights, this equalization could be a direct result of the transferability of the rights. Users receiving low marginal net benefits from their current allocation would trade their rights to those who would receive higher net benefits. Both parties would be better off. The payment received by the seller would exceed the net benefits forgone, and the payment made by the buyer would be less than the value of the water acquired.

Unfortunately, the existing mixed system of prior appropriation rights coupled with quite restrictive regulations has diminished the degree of transferability that can take place. Diminished transferability in turn reduces the market pressures toward equalization of the marginal net benefits. By itself this indictment is not sufficient to demonstrate that the existing system is inefficient. If it could be shown that this regulatory system was able to substitute some bureaucratic process for finding and maintaining this equalization, efficiency would still be possible. Unfortunately, that has not been the case, as can be seen by examining in more detail the specific nature of these restrictions. The allocation is inefficient.

One of the earliest restrictions required that users put their water to "beneficial use" or lose their rights to it. It is not difficult to see what this "use it or lose it" principle does to the incentive to conserve. Particularly careful users who, at their own expense, find ways to use less water would find their allocations reduced accordingly. The regulations strongly discourage conservation.

A second restriction, known as "preferential use," attempts to establish bureaucratically a value hierarchy of uses. With this doctrine, the government attempts to establish allocation priorities across categories of water. Within categories (irrigation for agriculture, for example) the priority is determined by prior appropriation ("first in time—first in right"), but among categories the preferential use doctrine governs.

The preferential use doctrine supports three rather different kinds of inefficiencies. First it substitutes a bureaucratically determined set of priorities for market priorities, resulting in a lower likelihood that marginal net benefits would be equalized. Second, it reduces the incentive to make investments that complement water use in lower-preference categories for the simple reason that their water could be withdrawn as the needs in higher level categories grow. Finally, it allocates the risk of shortfalls in an inefficient way

Although the first two inefficiencies are rather self-evident, the third merits further explanation. Because water supplies fluctuate over time, unusual scarcities can occur in any particular year. With a well-specified system of property rights, damage caused by this risk would be minimized by allowing those most damaged by a shortfall to purchase a larger share of the diminished amount of water available during a drought from those less hurt by the increased shortfall.

Diminishing, and in some cases eliminating, the ability to transfer rights from so-called "high preferential use" categories to "lower preferential use" categories during times of acute need, makes the damage caused by shortfalls higher than necessary. In essence, the preferential use doctrine fails to adequately consider the marginal damage caused by temporary shortfalls, something a well-structured system of property rights would do automatically.

Inhibiting transfers has very practical implications. Due to low energy costs and the federal subsidies, agricultural irrigation has become the dominant use of water in the West. Currently about 5 of every 6 gallons withdrawn and 9 out of every 10 gallons consumed go for the irrigation of nearly 50 million acres in 17 western states,[6] yet the marginal net benefits from agricultural uses are lower, sometimes substantially lower, than the marginal net benefits of water use by municipalities and industry.[7] A transfer of water from irrigated agriculture to these other uses would raise net benefits, but regulatory restrictions inhibit these transfers.[8]

Federal Reclamation Projects.   By providing subsidies to approved projects, federal reclamation projects have diverted water to these projects even when the net benefits were negative. Why was this done? What motivated the construction of inefficient projects?

Some work by Professor Chuck Howe of the University of Colorado provides a possible explanation.[9] He examined the benefits and costs of constructing the Big Thompson project in northeastern Colorado. With this project the water is pumped to an elevation that allows it to flow through a tunnel to the eastern side of the mountains. On that side, electric power is produced at several points. At lower elevations, the water is channeled into natural streams and feeder canals for distribution.

Howe calculated that the **national** net benefits for this project, which includes all benefits and costs, were either –$341.4 million or –$237.0 million, depending on the number of years included in the calculations. The project cost substantially more to construct than it returned in benefits. However, **regional** net benefits for the geographic region served by the facility were strongly positive ($766.9 million or $1,187 million respectively). This facility was an extraordinary boon for the local area because a very large proportion of the total cost had been passed on to national taxpayers despite the fact that the benefits were local. The local political pressure was able to secure project approval despite its inherent inefficiency.

---

[6]Kenneth D. Frederick and Allen V. Kneese, "Competition for Water" in Ernest A. Engelbert with Ann Foley Scheuring, eds., *Water Scarcity* (Berkeley: University of California Press, 1984): 82.

[7]See the estimates in Diana C. Gibbons, *The Economic Value of Water* (Washington, DC: Resources for the Future, 1986).

[8]Although regulatory restrictions inhibit these transfers, they do not completely eliminate them. Several transfers from agricultural uses to municipalities have successfully overcome the regulatory hurdles. See Bonnie C. Saliba, " Do Water Markets 'Work'? Market Transfers and Trade-offs in the Southwestern States," *Water Resources Research* 23, No. 7 (July 1987): 1117.

[9]Charles W. Howe, "Project Benefits and Costs from National and Regional Viewpoints: Methodological Issues and Case Study of the Colorado–Big Thompson Project" *Natural Resources Journal* 26 (Winter 1986).

Although the very existence of these facilities is a source of inefficiency, yet another is the manner in which the water is priced. The subsidies have been substantial. Ken Frederick has reported on some work done by the Natural Resources Defense Council to calculate the subsidies to irrigated agriculture in the Westlands Water District (one of the world's richest agricultural areas), located on the west side of California's San Joaquin Valley.[10] In recent years the Westlands Water District has paid about $10 to $12 per acre-foot, less than 10% of the unsubsidized cost of delivering water to the district. (An acre-foot is the amount of water it would take to flood an acre of level land to a depth of one foot.) The resulting subsidy was estimated to be $217 per irrigated acre or $500,000 per year for the average size farm.

Water Pricing. Restrictions on transfer are not the only source of inefficiency in the current allocation system. The prices charged by water distribution utilities do not promote efficiency of use.

Both the level of prices and the rate structure are at fault. In general, the price level is too low and the rate structure does not adequately reflect the costs of providing service to different types of customers.

In part, perhaps because water is considered an essential commodity, the prices charged by public water companies are too low. For surface water the rates are too low for two rather distinct reasons: (1) historic average costs are used to determine rates, and (2) marginal scarcity rent is rarely included.

Efficient pricing requires the use of marginal cost, not average cost. To adequately balance conservation with use, the customer should be paying the marginal cost of supplying the last unit of water, yet these regulated utilities typically are allowed to charge prices just high enough to cover the costs of running the operation (as is revealed by figures from the recent past). Because average costs are not lower than marginal costs and historic costs are lower than current or prospective costs, prices are understated.

The second source of the problem is the failure of regulators overseeing the operations of water distribution companies to allow a marginal user cost to be incorporated in the calculation of the appropriate price, a problem that is even more severe when groundwater is involved. One study by Martin and others found that due to a failure to include a user cost, rates in Tucson, Arizona, were about 58 percent too low despite some recent increases.[11]

Average cost pricing and ignoring the marginal user cost means an excessive demand for water. Simple actions, such as fixing leaky faucets, are easy to overlook when water is excessively cheap. Yet in a city such as New York leaky faucets can account for a significant amount of wasted water.

Current pricing policies also fail to provide the proper signals to migrants. New residents moving into the area are not forced to bear the full cost of their move. As a result, arid locations appear more attractive than they should. One automatic dampening mechanism that

---

[10]The estimates are in Kenneth Frederick, "Water Resource Management and the Environment: The Role of Economic Incentives" in OECD, *Renewable Natural Resources: Economic Incentives for Improved Management* (Paris: Organization for Economic Co-operation and Development, 1989): 33. The original NRDC report was Phillip E. LaVeen and Laura B. King, *Turning Off the Tap off Federal Water Subsidies: Volume 1, The Central Valley Project* (San Francisco: Natural Resources Defense Council, 1985).

[11]William E. Martin, Helen M. Ingram, Nancy K. Laney, and Adrian H. Griffin, *Saving Water in a Desert City* (Washington, DC: Resources for the Future, 1984).

the market provides to prevent excessive population growth in areas of water scarcity is thwarted.

Common Property Problems.   The allocation of groundwater must confront one additional problem. When many users tap the same aquifer, that aquifer becomes a common-property resource. Tapping a common-property resource will tend to deplete it too rapidly; users lose the incentive to conserve. The marginal scarcity rent will be ignored.

The incentive to conserve a groundwater resource in an efficient market is created by the desire to prevent pumping costs from rising too rapidly and the desire to capitalize on the higher prices that could reasonably be expected in the future. With common-property resources, neither of these desires translates into conservation for the simple reason that water conserved by one party may simply be used by someone else because the conserver has no exclusive right to the water that is saved. Water saved by one party to take advantage of higher prices can easily be pumped out by another user before the higher prices ever materialize.

For common-property resources, pumping costs would rise too rapidly, initial prices would be too low, and too much water would be consumed by the earliest users. The burden of this waste would not be shared uniformly. Because the typical aquifer is bowl-shaped, users on the periphery of the aquifer would be particularly hard hit. When the water level declines, the edges go dry first, whereas the center can continue to supply water for substantially longer periods. Future users would also be hard hit relative to current users.

POTENTIAL REMEDIES

Economic analysis points the way to a number of possible means of remedying the current water situation in the Southwestern United States. These reforms would promote efficiency of water use while affording more protection to the interests of future generations of water users.

The first reform would reduce the number of restrictions on water transfers. The "use it or lose it" component of the beneficial use doctrine can promote the extravagant use of water and discourage conservation. Typically, water saved by conservation is forfeited.[12] Allowing users to capture the value of water saved by permitting them to sell it would stimulate water conservation and allow the water to flow to higher-valued uses (see Example 8.1).

One serious problem with the current water use doctrine in the Western and Southwestern United States is that it fails to provide adequate protection for the instream uses of water, such as habitat for wildlife or for fishing and boating. As the competition for water increases, the pressure to allocate larger amounts of the stream for consumptive uses increases as well. Eventually the water level becomes too low to support aquatic life and recreation activities.

Though they do exist (see Example 8.2), water rights for instream flow maintenance are few in number relative to rights for consumptive purposes. Those few instream rights that do exist typically have a low priority relative to the more senior consumptive rights. As a practical matter this means that in periods of low water flow, the instream rights lose out and the

---

[12]In *Salt River User's Association* v *Kavocovich* [411 P.2d 201 (1966)], the Arizona Court of Appeals ruled that irrigators who lined their ditches could not apply "saved" water to adjacent land.

████████████████ E X A M P L E   8 . 1 ████████████████

Using Economic Principles to Conserve Water in California

In 1977 when California governor Jerry Brown negotiated a deal to settle one of the state's perennial water fights by building a new water diversion project, environmental groups were opposed. The opposition was expected. What was not expected was the form it took. Rather than simply block every imaginable aspect of the plan, the Environmental Defense Fund (EDF) set out to show project supporters how the water needs could be better supplied by ways that put no additional pressure on the environment.

According to this strategy, if the owners of the agricultural lands to the west of the water district seeking the water could be convinced to reduce their water use by adopting new, water-saving irrigation techniques, the conserved water could be transferred to the district in lieu of the project. But the growers had no incentive to conserve because conserving the water required the installation of costly new equipment and as soon as the water was saved it would be forfeited under the "use it, or lose it" regulations. What could be done?

On 17 January 1989, largely through the efforts of EDF, an historic agreement was negotiated between the growers association, a major user of irrigation water, and the Metropolitan Water District (MWD) of California, a public agency that supplies water to the Los Angeles area. Under that agreement the MWD will bear the capital and operating costs, as well as the indirect costs (such as reduced hydro power), of a huge program to reduce seepage losses as the water is transported to the growers and to install new water-conserving irrigation techniques in the fields. In return they will get all of the conserved water. Everyone gains. The district gets the water it needs at a reasonable price; the growers retain virtually the same amount of irrigation benefits without being forced to bear large additional expenditures.

Because the existing regulatory system created a very large inefficiency, moving to a more efficient allocation of water necessarily increased the net benefits. By using those additional net benefits in creative ways, it was possible to eliminate a serious environmental threat.

Source: Robert E. Taylor, *Ahead of the Curve: Shaping New Solutions to Environmental Problems* (New York: Environmental Defense Fund, 1990).

water is withdrawn for consumptive uses. As long as the definition of "beneficial use" requires diversion, as it does in many states, water left for fish habitat or recreation is undervalued.

This undervaluation of instream uses is not inevitable, however, as some enterprising fishermen have discovered.[13] In the Yellowstone River Valley in Montana, several spring creeks are wholly contained within the boundaries of property owned by a single landowner. Because these creeks are not subject to the same legal restrictions as waterways crossing property

---

[13]These examples were drawn from Terry L. Anderson, *Water Crisis: Ending the Policy Drought* (Washington, DC: Cato Institute, 1983): 81–85.

EXAMPLE 8.2

Protecting Instream Uses Through Acquiring Water Rights

Attempts by environmental groups to protect instream water uses must confront two problems. First, any acquired rights are usually public goods, implying that others can free-ride on their provision without contributing to the cause. Consequently the demand for instream rights will be inefficiently low. This is not a sufficient remedy. Second, once the rights have been acquired, their use to protect instream flows may not be considered "beneficial use" (and therefore could be confiscated and granted to others for consumptive use) or may be so junior to other rights as to be completely ineffective in times of low flow, the times when they would most be needed.

Some movement toward protecting instream rights is occurring, however. In 1979, in what was then a precedent-setting action, The Nature Conservancy, an environmental, public-interest organization, applied to Arizona's Department of Water Resources for an permit for "instream flow" at the Ramsey Canyon Preserve, asking essentially for both the right to use a certain amount of water and the right to simply leave it in the stream. When the permit was approved in 1983, this was the first legal recognition in Arizona of the right to appropriate water for wildlife and recreational uses without diverting water from a streambed. As of mid-1987, over twenty-five minimum instream flow permit applications were pending and an Instream Task Force had been appointed to assist the Arizona authority in formulating new criteria and procedures for granting permits.

What worked at Ramsey Canyon was simple and straightforward, but it is not an adequate protection device in many places. Under the prior appropriation doctrine, any rights that predate the 1983-granted instream flow right would have entitled the holder to priority for the water.

Another approach has been followed in Colorado. Several years ago, a subsidiary of the Chevron corporation gave the Nature Conservancy a gift entitling it to 300 cubic feet/second flow rate of water in the Black Canyon of Colorado's Gunnison River. Because Colorado law stipulates that instream flow rights can be held only by the state, the Conservancy was faced with the "use it, or lose it" rule under the prior appropriation doctrine. Taking the only step available, the Conservancy negotiated a transfer of the instream flow rights to the state.

Sources: Ken Wiley, "Untying the Western Water Knot," *The Nature Conservancy* 40, No. 2 (March/April 1990): 5–13; Bonnie Colby Saliba and David B. Bush, *Water Markets in Theory and Practice: Market Transfers and Public Policy* (Boulder, CO: Westview Press, 1987): 74–77.

---

boundaries, landowners can sell the daily fishing rights. The revenues from these sales provide owners with an incentive to develop spawning beds, protect the fish habitat, and in general, make the fishing experience as desirable as possible. By limiting the number of fishermen, the owners prevent overexploitation of the resource.

In England and Scotland, markets are relied upon to protect instream uses more than they are in the United States. Private angling associations have been formed to purchase fishing rights from landowners. Once these rights have been acquired, the associations charge for

FIGURE 8.2   Increasing Block Rate Structure

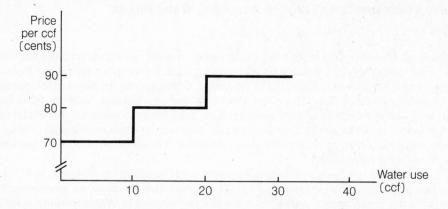

fishing, using some of the revenues to preserve and to improve the fish habitat. Because fishing rights in England sell for as much as $220,000, the holders of these rights have a substantial incentive to protect their investments. One of the forms this protection takes is illustrated by the Anglers Cooperative Association, which has taken on the responsibility of monitoring the streams for pollution and alerting the authorities to any potential problems.

Another set of changes that would enhance efficiency involves reforming the water pricing policies followed by public water distribution utilities. The traditional practice of recovering only the costs of distributing water and treating the water itself as a free good should be abandoned in favor of a marginal cost pricing system that includes a scarcity value for water in the price. Because scarce water is not in any meaningful sense a free good, the user cost of that water must be imposed on current users. Only in this way will the property incentive for conservation be created and the interests of future generations of water users be preserved.

Including this user cost in water prices is rather more difficult than it may first appear. Water utilities are typically regulated because they have a monopoly in the local area. One typical requirement for the rate structure of a regulated monopoly is that it earn only a "fair" rate of return. Excess profits are not permitted. Charging a uniform price for water to all users that includes a user cost would generate profits for the seller. (Remember the discussion of scarcity rent in Chapter 3?) The scarcity rent accruing to the seller as a result of incorporating the user cost would represent revenue in excess of operating and capital costs.

One way that water utilities are attempting to respect the rate of return requirement while promoting water conservation is through the use of an increasing block rate. Under this system the price per unit of water consumed rises as the amount consumed rises (Figure 8.2).

In this example, the first 10 ccf of water cost $.70 per ccF.[14] The next 10 ccf cost $.80 per ccf, and the third cost $.90 per ccf. A customer using 26 ccf would pay a bill for the month of $20.40 (10 × $.70 + 10 × $.80 + 6 × $.90).

This type of structure encourages conservation by ensuring that the marginal cost of consuming additional water is high. At the margin, where the consumer decides how much extra water to use, quite a bit of money can be saved by being frugal with water use. However, it also holds revenue down by charging a lower price for the first units consumed. This has the added

---

[14]A ccf is one hundred cubic feet. One hundred cubic feet corresponds to 748 gallons.

TABLE 8.1   Water Rate Structures Used by U.S. Public and Private Utilities (1982)

	Number of Utilities					
	Small (500–1000)		Medium (25,000–50,000)		Large (500,000–1,000,000)	
Rate Structure	*Public*	*Private*	*Public*	*Private*	*Public*	*Private*
Flat Fee[a]	13	26	4	0	5	0
Flat Rate[b]	6	0	15	0	15	0
Flat Fee plus Flat Rate	29	26	28	15	10	0
Declining Block[c]	38	22	40	64	35	43
Increasing Block[d]	4	2	4	3	0	14
Other	8	20	8	18	35	43

[a]Flat fee paid monthly or annually, not based on water use
[b]Constant flat rate per unit of water use
[c]Charge per unit of water declines with increasing water use
[d]Charge per unit of water increases with increasing water use

Source: Congressional Budget Office from Environmental Protection Agency, Office of Drinking Water, *Survey of Operating and Financial Characteristics of Community Water Systems* (prepared by Temple, Barker, and Sloan, Inc., October 1982) as cited in Congressional Budget Office, *Financing Municipal Water Supply Systems* (May 1987). pp. 6, 7

virtue that those who need some water, but cannot afford the marginal price paid by more extravagant users, can have access to water without placing their budget in as much jeopardy as would be the case with a uniform price.

How many U.S. utilities are using increasing block pricing? As Table 8.1 indicates, not many. Some evidence from Europe suggests that increasing block pricing is not common there either.[15]

A surprisingly large number of U.S. utilities are using a flat fee, which from a scarcity point of view is the worst possible form of pricing. With a flat fee the marginal cost of additional water consumption is zero. *Zero!* Water use by individual customers is not even metered.

Although more complicated versions of a flat fee system are certainly possible, they do not solve the incentive to conserve problem. At least until the late 1970s, Denver, Colorado used eight different factors (including number of rooms, number of persons, number of bathrooms, etc.) to calculate the monthly bill. Despite the complexity of this billing system, because the amount of the bill was unrelated to actual volume used (water use was not metered), the marginal cost of additional water consumed was still zero.

Declining block pricing, another inefficient pricing system, is much more prevalent than increasing block pricing. By charging customers a higher marginal cost for low levels of water consumption and a lower marginal cost for higher levels, regulators are placing an undue financial burden on low-income people who consume little water and confronting high-income people with a marginal cost that is too low to provide adequate incentives to conserve.

---

[15]Paul Harrington, *Pricing of Water Services* (Paris: Organization for Economic Co-operation and Development, 1987):40.

Other aspects of the rate structure are important as well. Efficiency dictates that prices equal the marginal cost of provision (including marginal user cost when appropriate). Several practical corollaries follow from this theorem. First, prices during peak demand periods should exceed prices during off-peak periods. It is peak use that strains the capacity of the system and therefore triggers the needs for expansion. Therefore, peak users should pay the extra costs associated with system expansion by being charged higher rates. Few current water pricing systems satisfy this condition in practice.

When it costs a water utility more to serve one class of customers than another, each class of customers should bear the costs associated with its service. Typically this implies, for example, that those farther away from the source or at higher elevations (requiring more pumping) should pay higher rates. In practice utility water rates make fewer distinctions among customer classes than would be efficient. As a result, higher-cost water users are in effect subsidized; they receive too little incentive to conserve and too little incentive to locate in parts of the city that can be served at lower cost.

A somewhat more subtle, but no less important violation of this rule occurs in rapidly expanding areas where population growth necessitates system expansion. Suppose, for example, that due to rapid population growth, a particular city has to build a rather large water project to import water from another area. Efficiency dictates that these new users should pay higher rates to cover the additional costs of expanding the system; because the expansion would not be needed in the absence of population growth, existing residents should not have to foot the bill.

The efficiency condition is typically violated in practice in two different ways. First, the federal or state governments can usually be counted on to pick up a portion of the tab, so state or federal taxpayers end up paying for some costs that should be borne by new residents. Second, local areas often attempt to mitigate the adverse effects on growth that this system would trigger by prorating the expansion costs over all residents—existing and new. In essence, all customers pay an average cost rather than the marginal cost of supplying their water.[16]

These principles suggest a much more complicated rate structure for water than merely charging everyone the same price. As Example 8.3 demonstrates, the political consequences of introducing these changes may be rather drastic.

SUMMARY

Though on a global scale the supply of available water exceeds demand, at particular times and in particular locations water scarcity is already a serious problem. In a number of locations, the current use of water exceeds replenishable supplies, implying that aquifers are being irreversibly drained.

Efficiency dictates that replenishable water be allocated so as to equalize the marginal net benefits of water use even when supplies are higher or lower than normal. The efficient allocation of groundwater requires that the user cost of that depletable resource be considered.

---

[16]Notice the parallel between this water price problem and the synfuels price problem discussed in Example 7.1.

EXAMPLE 8.3

Politics and the Pricing of Scarce Water

Just as economics can make specific recommendations about the level and structure of water prices, politics can provide insights on the implementation of those recommendations. The implementation process is not always smooth or predictable, as the people of Tucson, Arizona, found out.

In 1976, the city of Tucson faced what it perceived as a water crisis. The development of its service capacity had not kept pace with rapid population growth, and artificially low prices reduced the incentive to conserve. The groundwater supplies on which the city depended were being depleted.

Assisted by a newly-elected city council, the utility instituted a new rate structure involving higher water prices overall and more attention to the cost of service in determining the rate structure. An unexpectedly dry year (creating an abnormally high demand), coupled with a newly implemented increasing block rate structure, conspired to ensure that water bills increased tremendously soon after the change. The resulting anger of the residents spawned a recall campaign in which the councillors responsible for the rate increase were retired from office.

Are major changes in prices politically infeasible? The authors of the Tucson study believe not, though they do believe that feasible increases also have to be implemented with greater care. In particular, they believe that local politicians must be willing to take risks, that local residents must be convinced that a real problem exists, and the burden of the increases must be distributed so no one group is asked to bear too large a share.

Source: William E. Martin, Helen M. Ingram, Nancy K. Laney, and Adrian H. Griffin, *Saving Water in a Desert City* (Washington, DC: Resources for the Future, 1984).

When marginal cost pricing (including marginal user cost) is used, water consumption patterns strike an efficient balance between present and future uses. Typically, the marginal pumping cost would rise over time until it exceeds the marginal benefit received from that water or the reservoir runs dry.

In earlier times in the United States, markets played the major role in allocating water, but in more recent times, governments have begun to play a much larger role in allocating this crucial resource.

Several sources of inefficiency are evident in the current system of water allocation in the southwestern United States. Transfers of water among various users are restricted so that the water remains in low-valued uses while high-valued uses are denied. Instream uses of water are actively discouraged in many western states. Prices charged for water by public suppliers typically do not cover costs, and the rate structures are not designed to promote efficient use of the resource. For groundwater, user cost is rarely included, and for all sources of water, the rate structure does not usually reflect the costs of services. These deficiencies combine to produce a situation in which we are not getting the most out of the water we are using and we are not conserving sufficient amounts for the future.

Reforms are possible. Allowing conservers to capture the value of water saved by selling it would stimulate conservation. Creating separate fishing rights that can be sold or allowing environmental groups to acquire and retain instream water rights would provide some incentive to protect streams as fish habitats. More utilities could adopt increasing block pricing as a means of forcing users to realize and to consider all of the costs of supplying the water. To the extent that more fundamental change is politically possible, a set of transferable water deeds can be instituted to provide for more efficiency in the consumptive uses of groundwater.

Water scarcity is not merely a problem to be faced at some distant time in the future. In many parts of the world it is already a serious problem, and unless preventive measures are taken, it will get worse. The problem is not insoluble, though to date the steps necessary to solve it have not yet been taken.

FURTHER READING

Anderson, Terry L. *Water Crisis: Ending the Policy Drought* (Washington, DC: The Cato Institute, 1983). A provocative survey of the political economy of water, concluding that we have to rely more on the market to solve the crisis.

Anderson, Terry L., ed. *Water Rights: Scarce Resource Allocation, Bureaucracy, and The Environment* (Cambridge, MA: Ballinger, 1983). Nine essays examining the causes, consequences, and possible solutions to water scarcity in the southwestern United States from a property-rights point of view.

Gibbons, Diana. *The Economic Value of Water* (Washington, DC: Resources for the Future, 1986). A detailed survey and synthesis of existing studies on the economic value of water in various uses.

Herrington, Paul. *Pricing of Water Services* (Organization for Economic Co-operation and Development, 1987). An excellent survey of the water pricing practices in the OECD countries.

Martin, William E., Helen M. Ingram, Nancy K. Laney, and Adrian H. Griffin. *Saving Water in a Desert City* (Washington, DC: Resources for the Future, 1984). A detailed look at the political and economic ramifications of an attempt by Tucson, Arizona, to improve the pricing of its diminishing supply of water.

Saliba, Bonnie Colby and David B. Bush. *Water Markets in Theory and Practice: Market Transfers and Public Policy* (Boulder, CO: Westview Press, 1987): 74–77. A highly recommended, accessible study of the way western water markets work in practice in United States.

U.S. Water Resources Council. *The Nation's Water Resources 1975–2000* (Washington, DC: U.S. Government Printing Office, 1978). A multivolume series examining on a location-by-location basis the present and future supply of and demand for water.

ADDITIONAL REFERENCES

Custodio, E., and A. Gurgui, eds. *Groundwater Economics: Selected Papers from a United Nations Symposium held in Barcelona, Spain* (New York: Elsevier, 1989).

Frederick, K. D. "Water Supplies," in Paul R. Portney, ed., *Current Issues in Natural Resource Policy* (Washington, DC: Resources for the Future, 1982): 216–52.

Frederick, K. D. *Scarce Water and Institutional Change* (Washington, DC: Resources for the Future, 1986).

Livingston, Marie L., and Thomas A. Miller. "The Impact of Instream Water Rights on Choice Domains," *Land Economics* 62, No. 3 (August 1986): 269–77.

OECD. *Renewable Natural Resources: Economic Incentives for Improved Management* (Paris: Organization for Economic Co-operation and Development, 1987).

Postel, Sandra. "Saving Water for Agriculture," in Lester Brown et al., eds., *State of the World: 1990* (New York: W. W. Norton, 1990)

Smith, Vernon L. "Water Deeds: A Proposed Solution to the Water Valuation Problem," *Arizona Review* 26 (January 1977): 7–10.

Sheridan, David (for the Council on Environmental Quality). *Desertification of the United States* (Washington, DC: U.S. Government Printing Office, 1981).

Torell, L. Allen, James D. Libbin, and Michael D. Miller. "The Market Value of Water in the Ogallala Aquifer," *Land Economics* 66, No. 2 (May 1990): 163–75.

Wahl, Richard W. *Markets for Federal Water: Subsidies, Property Rights, and the Bureau of Reclamation* (Washington, DC: Resources for the Future, 1989)

DISCUSSION QUESTIONS

1. Who stands to gain and who to lose compared to the current system if the Smith system of water deeds were to be instituted? Politically, where might the support for or opposition to such a proposal come from?

2. What pricing system identified in Table.8.1 best describes the pricing system used to price the water you use at your college or university? Does this pricing system effect your behavior about water use (length of showers, etc.)? How? could you recommend a better pricing system in this circumstance? What would it be?

3. What system is used in your home town to price the publicly supplied water? Why was that pricing system chosen?

4. Suppose you come from a part of the world that is blessed with abundant water. Demand never comes close to the available amount. Should you be careful about the amount you use or should you simply use whatever you want whenever you want it? Why?

CHAPTER 9

Agriculture

The Commission's assessment of the future prospects for overcoming world hunger has led to one conclusion . . . the outcome of the war on hunger, by the year 2000 and beyond, will not be determined by forces beyond human control, but, rather, by decision and actions well within the capability of nations working individually and together.

PRESIDENTIAL COMMISSION ON WORLD HUNGER, *OVERCOMING WORLD HUNGER: THE CHALLENGE AHEAD* (1980)

INTRODUCTION

In Chapter 1, food was a point of contention between Kahn and the *Limits to Growth* team. The *Limits to Growth* team foresaw the demand for food (driven by population growth) outstripping the supply (primarily due to a decline in the availability of arable land), suggesting a resulting famine as one source of societal collapse. Kahn, on the other hand, foresaw population growth as diminishing, and a tremendous expansion in food supplies forthcoming from the applications of new technologies. Which vision seems more accurate?

Chronic malnourishment already exists on a large scale. The International Fund for Agricultural Development has reported that:[1]

- About 340 million people worldwide are currently chronically ill from malnutrition.
- Over 500 million do not get enough calories to do a full day's labor.
- At a time when enough grain is being produced to provide everyone in the world with twice the daily minimum caloric requirements, global hunger is at an all-time high.

Though some may quarrel with the specific numbers, recognition that a substantial proportion of the world's population is currently malnourished seems universal.

Why has this situation arisen? Cereal grain, the world's chief supply of food, is a renewable private-property resource that, managed effectively, could be sustained as long as we re-

---

[1]International Fund for Agricultural Development, *The State of Rural World Poverty* (New York: New York University Press, 1992).

ceive energy from the sun. Are current agricultural practices sustainable? Are they efficient? Because land is typically not a common-property resource, farmers have an incentive to invest in irrigation and other means of increasing yield because they can appropriate the additional revenues generated. On the surface, a flaw in the market process is not apparent. We must dig deeper to uncover the sources of the problem.

In this chapter we shall explore the validity of three common hypotheses used to explain widespread malnourishment: (1) a persistent global scarcity of food, (2) a maldistribution of that food both among nations and within nations, and (3) temporary shortages caused by weather or other natural causes. These hypotheses are not mutually exclusive: They could all be valid sources of a portion of the problem. As we shall see later in the chapter, it is important to distinguish among these sources and assess their relative importance because each implies a different policy approach.

GLOBAL SCARCITY

A number of commentators see the problem as an absolute global scarcity—a case of too many people chasing too little food.[2] Garrett Hardin, a human ecologist, has suggested the situation is so desperate that our conventional ethics, which involve sharing the available resources, are not only insufficient, they are counterproductive. He argues that we must replace these dated notions of sharing wealth with more-stern "lifeboat ethics."[3]

The allegory he invokes involves a lifeboat adrift in the sea that can safely hold 50 or, at most, 60 persons. Hundreds of other persons are swimming about, clamoring to get into the lifeboat, their only chance for survival. Hardin suggests that if passengers in the boat were to follow conventional ethics and allow swimmers into the boat, it would eventually sink, taking everyone to the bottom of the sea. In contrast, he argues, lifeboat ethics would suggest a better resolution of the dilemma; the 50 or 60 should row away, leaving the others to certain death, but saving those fortunate enough to gain entry to the lifeboat. The implication is that food sharing is counterproductive. It encourages more population growth and ultimately would cause inevitable and even more serious shortages in the future.

The existence of a global scarcity of food is the premise that underlies this view; when famine is inevitable, sharing is counterproductive. In the absence of global scarcity (the lifeboat has a large enough capacity for all), a worldwide famine can be avoided by a sharing of resources. How accurate is the premise of global scarcity?

Examining Global Scarcity

Most authorities seem to agree that an adequate amount of food is currently being produced. Studies made by the Food and Agricultural Organization of the United Nations, which report that the available supplies of food are more than adequate to supply the nutritional needs of all the world, are typical.

---

[2]See, for example, Lester R. Brown, *In the Human Interest* (New York: W. W. Norton, 1974); and William Paddock and Paul Paddock, *Famine—1975!* (Boston, MA: Little, Brown, 1967).

[3]Garrett Hardin, "Living on a Lifeboat," *Bioscience* XXIV (October 1974): 561–68.

FIGURE 9.1   The Market for Food

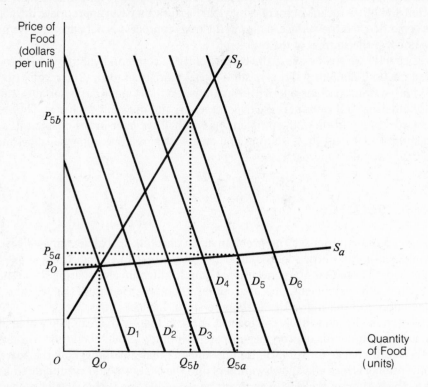

Because this evidence is limited to a single point in time, however, it provides no sense of whether scarcity is decreasing or increasing. If we are to identify and evaluate trends, we must develop more precise, measurable notions of how the market allocates food.

As a renewable resource, cereal grains could be produced indefinitely, if managed correctly. However, two facets of the world hunger problem have to be taken into account. First, although population growth has slowed down, it has not stopped. Therefore, it is reasonable to expect the rising demand for food to continue. Second, the primary input for growing food is land, and land is ultimately fixed in supply. Thus, our analysis must explain how a market reacts in the presence of rising demand for a renewable resource that is produced using a fixed factor of production!

A substantial and dominant proportion of the Western world's arable land is privately owned. Access to this land is restricted: The owners have the right to exclude others and can reap what they sow. The typical owner of farmland has sufficient control over the resource to prevent undue depreciation, but not enough control over the market as a whole to raise the specter of monopoly profits.

What kind of outcome could we expect from this market in the face of rising demand and a fixed supply of land? What do we mean by scarcity and how could we perceive its existence? The answer depends crucially on the nature of the supply curve (Figure 9.1).

Suppose the market is initially in equilibrium with quantity Q_O supplied at price P_O. Let the passage of time be recorded as shifts outward in the demand curve.

Consider what would happen in the fifth time period. If the supply curve were S_a, the quantity would rise to Q_{5a}. However, if the supply curve were Sb, the quantity supplied would only rise to Q_{5b}, but price would rise P_{5b}.

This analysis sheds light on what is meant by scarcity in the world food market. It does not mean a shortage. Even under the relatively adverse supply circumstances pictured by the supply curve S_b, the amount of food supplied would equal the amount demanded. As prices rose, potential demand would be choked off and additional supplies would be called forth.

Some critics argue that the demand for food is not price sensitive. Because food is a necessary commodity for survival, they say, its demand is inflexible and doesn't respond to prices. Although it is a necessary commodity, not all food fits that category. We don't have to gaze very long at an average vending machine in a developed country to conclude that some food is far from a necessity.

Examples of food purchases being price responsive abound. One occurred during the 1960s, when the price of meat skyrocketed for what turned out to be a relatively short period. It wasn't long before hamburger substitute, made entirely out of soybean meal, appeared in supermarkets. The result was a striking reduction in meat consumption. This is a particularly important example because the raising of livestock for meat in Western countries consumes an enormous amount of grain. This evidence suggests that the balance between the direct consumption of cereal grains and the indirect consumption through meat is affected by prices.

But enough about the demand side; what do we know of the supply side? What factors would determine whether S_a or S_b is a more adequate representation of the past and the future?

Although rising prices certainly stimulate a supply response, the question is, How much? As the demand for food rises, the supply can be increased either by expanding the amount of land under cultivation, by increasing the yields on the land already under cultivation, or by some combination of the two. Historically, both sources have been important.

Typically, the most fertile land is cultivated first. That land is then farmed more and more intensively until it is cheaper, at the margin, to bring additional, less-fertile land into production. Because it is less fertile, the additional land is brought into production only if prices rise high enough to make farming it profitable. Thus, the supply curve for arable land (and hence for food, as long as land remains an important factor of production) can be expected to slope upward.

Two forms of global scarcity can materialize. In the most serious case, per capita food production can decline. In terms of Figure 9.1, this could occur if the slope of the supply curve was sufficiently steep that production could not keep pace with increases in demand brought about by population growth. Declining per capita food consumption could provide some support for lifeboat ethics.

Even in the absence of declining per capita consumption, however, the global scarcity hypothesis can exist. If the supply curve is sufficiently steeply sloped that food prices increase more rapidly than other prices in general, the relative price of food can rise over time. Per capita welfare would decline, even if consumption was rising. This form of scarcity is related more to the cost of food than the availability of food: As supplies of food increase, the cost of food rises relative to the cost of other goods.

The evidence for per capita production is clear (Figure 9.2). Food production has increased faster than population in both the developed and developing countries since 1970,

FIGURE 9.2   Index of Per Capita Food Production for the World and Developing Countries (1974–1988)

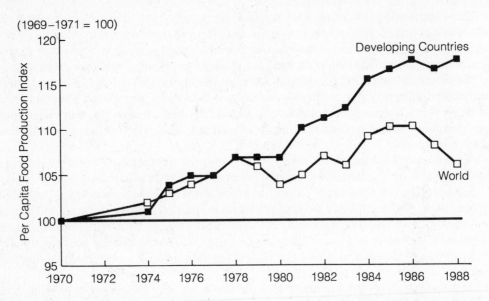

Source: FAO, The State of Food and Agriculture, 1979, 1981, 1985, and 1989: (Rome, United Nations).

though the most recent experience has not been as favorable. Per capita production has increased, although the increase has been small.

Have relative agricultural prices risen? Harold Barnett, a noted resource economist, published the results of a preliminary study on trends in resource prices, including agricultural prices.[4] Specifically, he examined the ratio of an index of agricultural prices to the general wholesale price index for a variety of countries over two different time periods (1950–1962 and 1961–1972). A total of 53 cases were examined. He discovered that for 23 of those cases agriculture prices rose at a statistically significant higher rate than wholesale prices in general. Using only the later time period (involving 31 countries), he found that some 15 countries experienced rises in agricultural prices that significantly exceed rises in wholesale prices.

According to this evidence, the supply curve for agricultural products is more steeply sloped than the supply curve for products in general in about half the countries. In those countries, at least, some global scarcity is apparent. Because not all market prices are efficient, as we shall see later in this chapter, we must not place too much faith in these numbers. Even so, the evidence suggests that agricultural supplies have increased faster than population but at an increasingly relative cost.

---

[4]Harold J. Barnett, "Scarcity and Growth Revisited," in *Scarcity and Growth Reconsidered,* V. Kerry Smith, ed. (Baltimore, MD: Johns Hopkins University Press, for Resources for the Future, 1979): 163–217.

Outlook for the Future

What factors will influence the future relative costs of food? A continuation of past trends would suggest an increasing role for the developing nations as they expand production to meet their increasing shares of population while the nations of the north continue their exports. The ability of developing nations to expand their role is considered in the next section as a part of the food-distribution problem. In this section, therefore, we shall deal with forces affecting productivity in the industrialized nations of the north to ascertain the sustainability of historic trends.

Rather dramatic historic increases in crop productivity were stimulated by improvement in machinery; increasing utilization of commercial fertilizers, pesticides, and herbicides; developments in plant and animal breeding; expanding use of irrigation water; and adjustments in location of crop production. In the United States their combined effect doubled average yield per acre from 1910 to 1977.[5] Will history repeat itself?

Technological Progress.   Technological progress provides the main source of support for optimism about continued productivity increases. Three techniques appear particularly promising: (1) recombinant DNA, which permits recombining genes from one species with those of another; (2) tissue culture, which allows whole plants to be grown from single cells; and (3) cell fusion, which involves uniting the cells of species that would not normally mate to create new types of plants different from "parent" cells. One knowledgeable reviewer in the field suggested several applications for these generic engineering techniques, including:

1. Making food crops more resistant to diseases and insect pests.
2. Creating hardy new crop plants capable of surviving in marginal soils.
3. Giving staple food crops such as corn, wheat, and rice the ability to make their own nitrogen-rich fertilizers by using solar energy to make ammonia from nitrogen in the air.
4. Increasing crop yields by improving the way plants use the sun's energy during photosynthesis.[6]

The World Bank has estimated that these techniques could increase yields at least 30 percent beyond those achieved with the best previously available seeds.[7]

The outlook is not uniformly bright, however. Four concerns have arisen regarding the ability of the industrial nations to achieve further productivity gains: the declining share of

---

[5]Melvin L. Cotner, Nelson L. Bills, and Robert F. Boxley, "An Economic Perspective of Land Use," in *Economics, Ethics, Ecology: Roots of Productive Conservation,* Water E. Jeske, ed. (Ankeny, IA: Soil Conservation Society of America, 1981): 31.

[6]Robert Cooke, "Engineering a New Agriculture," *Technology Review* 85 (May/June 1982): 24–25.

[7]The World Bank, *World Development Report, 1982* (Washington, DC: International Bank for Reconstruction and Development, 1982).

land allocated to agricultural use, the rising cost of energy, the rising environmental cost of traditional forms of agriculture, and the role of price distortions in agricultural policy.[8] A close examination of these concerns reveals that current agricultural practices in the industrial nations may be neither efficient nor sustainable and a transition to efficient sustainable agriculture could involve lower productivity levels.

Allocation of Agricultural Land.   During 1920 in the United States, 958 million acres were used for farming. By 1974 the comparable figure was 465 million acres.[9] Some 50 percent of the agricultural land in 1920 had been converted to nonagricultural purposes by 1974. A simple extrapolation of this trend would certainly raise questions about our ability to increase productivity at historical rates. Is a simple extrapolation reasonable? What determines the allocation of land between agricultural and nonagricultural uses?

Agricultural land will be converted to nonagricultural land when its profitability in nonagricultural uses is higher. If we are to explain the historical experience, we must be able to explain why the relative value of land in agriculture has declined.

Two factors stand out. First, an increasing urbanization and industrialization of society rapidly raised the value of nonagricultural land. Second, rising productivity of the remaining land allowed the smaller amount of land to produce a lot more food. Less land was needed in agriculture to meet the demand for food.

It seems unlikely that simple extrapolation of the decline in agricultural land of the magnitude since 1920 would be accurate. Since the middle of the 1970s, the urbanization process has diminished to the point that many urban areas are experiencing declining population. This shift is not entirely explained by suburbia spilling beyond the boundaries of what was formerly considered urban. For the first time in our history, a significant amount of population has moved from urban to rural areas.

Furthermore, as increases in food demand are accompanied by increased prices of food, the value of agricultural land should increase. Higher food prices would tend to slow conversion and possibly even reverse the trend. To make this impact even greater, several states have now allowed agricultural land either to escape the property tax (until it is sold for some nonagricultural purpose) or to pay lower rates. Confirming evidence for this generally optimistic assessment can be found in the fact that most of the conversion to nonagricultural uses actually occurred prior to World War II.[10]

Energy Costs.   Agricultural production in the industrial nations is very energy intensive. Some major portion of the productivity gains resulted from energy using mechanization and

---

[8]See, for example, Lester R. Brown, "World Population Growth, Soil Erosion, and Food Security," *Science* 214 (27 November 1981): 995–1002.

[9]See Melvin L. Cotner, Nelson L. Bills, and Robert F. Boxley, "An Economic Perspective of Land Use," in *Economics, Ethics, Ecology: Roots of Productive Conservation,* Walter E. Jeske, ed. (Ankeny, IA: Soil Conservation Society of America, 1981): 31.

[10]The decline in crop land since 1949 has involved only 13 of more than 400 million acres converted since 1920. For more details on this, see Melvin L. Cotner, Nelson L. Bills, and Robert F. Boxley, "An Economic Perspective of Land Use," in *Economics, Ethics, Ecology: Roots of Productive Conservation,* Walter E. Jeske, ed. (Ankeny, IA: Soil Conservation Society of America, 1981): 31–36.

the increased use of pesticides and fertilizers, which are derived from petroleum feedstocks and natural gas. The costs of petroleum and natural gas have risen substantially and probably can be expected to continue to rise in real terms over the long run as the available supplies of fossil fuels are exhausted or global warming concerns diminish their use. To the extent that energy-intensive producers cannot develop cheaper substitutes, the supply curve must shift to the left to reflect the increasing costs of doing business.

One economist investigating this question notes that energy and capital are complements in agriculture.[11] Due to this complementary relationship, energy price increases could be expected to trigger some reduction in capital as well as some reduction in energy on the typical energy-intensive farm, reducing the yield per acre. Furthermore, because d'Arge found that farm wage rates have risen less rapidly than either energy costs or the costs of borrowing (as reflected by interest rates), he expects a readjustment of American agriculture in the future as labor is substituted for capital. A shift toward smaller, family-operated units would trigger a consequent reduction in the agricultural productivity growth rate.

Environmental Costs.   At least some of the past productivity gains have come by depreciating the asset. Soil erosion provides a case in point. Some soil erosion is natural, of course, and within certain tolerance limits does not harm productivity. The concern arises because some farm practices partially responsible for increasing productivity (continuous cropping rather than rotation with pasture or other soil-retaining crops) have tended to exacerbate soil erosion. The fears are further intensified by the belief that these losses are irreversible within one generation.

If increased soil erosion is taking place, why would a property owner allow this depletion? In the past, soil conservation simply did not pay. The techniques to avoid it were expensive, and the ready availability of cheap fertilizer to replace lost nutrients meant that the cost of soil depletion was low. Further, the damage caused to rivers and streams by this eroding soil was not borne by the farmers, who could best control it.

The barriers that prevented erosion from being checked are now disappearing. As the level of topsoil reaches lower tolerance limits, the fertility of the land is affected. Rising cost is making fertilizers a less desirable substitute for soil erosion, and public policy has begun to subsidize soil erosion techniques. In 1985, the U.S. Congress authorized the Conservation Reserve Program, which was designed to reduce soil erosion and stimulate tree planting. As of 1990 farmers had enrolled about 34 million acres of land in this program, and it has become one of the largest federally sponsored tree planting programs ever. It is expected to reduce soil erosion by hundreds of millions of tons per year, to decrease sediment in reservoirs and streams, to increase the protection of recreational resources, and to preserve the long-term productivity of the land.[12] In the near future we may see more soil conservation techniques practiced because they are becoming profitable.

Some past agricultural practices have caused environmental damage, and continuing these would cause rising environmental costs. In recent years the frequency and quantity of

---

[11]Ralph C. d'Arge, "The Energy Squeeze and Agricultural Growth," in *Economics, Ethics, Ecology: The Roots of Productive Conservation,* Walter E. Jeske, ed. (Ankeny, IA: Soil Conservation Society of America, 1981): 99–105.

[12]U.S. General Accounting Office, *1990 Farm Bill: Opportunities for Change* (Washington, DC: U.S. Government Printing Office, 1990): 23.

agricultural chemicals has increased dramatically.[13] Over the past 25 years, for example, nitrogenous fertilizer use increased by 150 percent in the Netherlands, by 225 percent in Denmark, and by 300 percent in the United States. Serious drinking water problems have emerged. In 1979 some 179 German water authorities were supplying drinking water with nitrate concentrations exceeding the standards. Four years later the number of communities violating the standards had increased four times to 807. Some of the nutrients from fertilizers leak into lakes and stimulate the excessive growth of algae. Aside from the aesthetic cost to a body of water choked with plant life, this nutrient excess can deprive other aquatic life forms of the oxygen they need to survive.

Pesticide use has also increased. Since 1975, for example, the quantity of pesticides used in Germany has increased by 30 percent and in Denmark by 69 percent. A great deal of pest control in the past has relied upon pesticides. Many of these persist in the environment, and there is an increasing recognition that some toxicity extends to species other than the target population. The herbicides and pesticides can contaminate water supplies, rendering them unfit for drinking and for supporting normal populations of fish.

Throughout all OECD countries, "sustainable agriculture" is being increasingly associated with the reduced use of pesticides and mineral fertilizers, and policies have been established to facilitate the transition. Denmark and Sweden are pursuing ambitious agricultural chemical reduction targets. In Austria, Finland, the Netherlands, and Sweden a variety of input taxes and input levies have recently been reduced. The charges provide an incentive to use fewer agricultural chemicals while the revenue is used to ease the transition by funding research on alternative approaches and the dissemination of information. Many OECD countries expect little effect on crop yields, though production levels are lower.[14]

Irrigation, a traditional source of productivity growth, is running into limits as well, particularly in the western United States. Some traditionally important underground sources used to supply water are not being replenished at a rate sufficient to offset the withdrawals. Encouraged by enormous subsidies that transfer the cost to the taxpayers, these water supplies are being exhausted. Those that remain are subject to rising levels of salt. Irrigation of soils with naturally occurring salts causes a concentration of the salts near the surface. This salty soil is less productive and, in extreme cases, kills the crops.

One sign that a transition is underway is the rise of organic farming. Although at present only 1 percent of U.S. produce is organically grown, experts in the field predict as much as 10 percent will be by the end of the century. The transition would not be immediate or easy. It takes from one to five years to convert from conventional agriculture to organic farming. Studies comparing organic farms with comparable conventional farms have found that the organic farms had lower yields, but they also had lower costs with the result that income was about the same as that for comparable conventional agriculture farms.[15]

---

[13]The data in this section are from M. D. Young, *Agriculture and the Environment: OECD Policy Experiences and American Opportunities* (Washington, DC: United States Environmental Protection Agency, 1990).

[14]Organization for Economic Co-operation and Development, *Agriculture and Environment: Opportunities for Integration* (Paris: OECD, 1988). See the most recent evidence on the retarding effects on food production in the industrialized countries in Lester R. Brown et al., *Vital Signs: 1992* (New York: W. W. Norton, 1992): 24, 40.

[15]Pierre Crosson and Janet Ekey, "Alternative Agriculture: a Review and Assessment of the Literature," Discussion Paper ENR88-01 (Washington, DC: Resources for the Future, 1988); and Patrick Madden, "Can Sustainable Agriculture Be Profitable?" *Environment* 29, No. 4 (May 1987): 19–34.

A recent source of encouragement for organic farms has been the demonstrated willingness of consumers to pay a premium for organically grown fruits and vegetables. Because it would be relatively easy for producers to claim their produce was organically grown, even if it was not, organic growers need a reliable certification process to assure the consumers that they are indeed getting what they pay for. In some areas growers associations handle the testing and labeling, but in others it is handled by new organizations that have sprung up specifically to provide this service.[16] In California, where labeling of organic produce has become routine, retail sales of organics grew from $1 million in 1979 to $50 million in 1987.

The Role of Agricultural Policies

Past gains in agricultural productivity have come at a large environmental cost. Why? Part of the answer, of course, can be found in an examination of the externalities associated with agriculture. Many of the costs of farming are borne not by the farmers, but by others subjected to contaminated groundwater and polluted streams. But that is not the whole story. Government policies must bear some of the responsibility as well.

Government policies have completely subverted the normal functioning of the price system. Three types of agricultural policies are involved: (1) subsidies for specific farming inputs such as equipment, fertilizers, or pesticides; (2) guaranteed prices for outputs; and (3) trade barriers to protect against competition from imports.

Subsidies have helped to create a dependence on purchased inputs. One study examined whether the size of the farm subsidy (as measured by its proportion to total income) across countries was correlated with fertilizer use in those countries.[17] It was. Countries with the largest subsidies used considerably more fertilizer than those with little or no subsidies. The subsidies made it possible to use inefficient and unsustainable levels of fertilizer.

Guaranteed prices have the effect of increasing the profitability of agriculture, making it possible to convert inappropriate land to agricultural purposes. New Zealand provides an interesting example. Frustrated with the high levels of subsidies that were being poured into the agricultural sector, the government in New Zealand eliminated most agricultural subsidies over a three-year period. Not only did fertilizer use fall 55 percent, but it turned out that the resulting shakeout in the agricultural sector resulted in a much higher proportion of smaller farms, which have a less adverse impact on the environment. The subsidies had propped up the larger farms.[18]

Other countries have not been eager to follow New Zealand's lead. The subsidies have become an important component of farm income, making them difficult to eliminate. Agricultural subsidies in the United States and the European Economic Community are responsible for about one third and one half of all farm income, respectively. In Japan farmers

---

[16]The first such organization, NutriClean, uses a complex evaluation procedure to establish whether the produce meets their "no detected residue" standard. If so, the produce is allowed to display the NutriClean label. The farmer pays for the service with a fee depending on the sales volume.

[17]Richard Blackhurst and Kym Anderson, "The Greening of World Trade as cited in 'Agriculture Survey'," *The Economist* (12 December 1992): 17.

[18]"Agriculture Survey," *The Economist* (12 December 1992): 15.

earn twice as much income from subsidies as from the practice of agriculture. In Switzerland the comparable figure is four times agricultural income.

Recently, however, governments have begun to encourage sustainable agriculture, not only by discouraging the harmful side effects of traditional agriculture, but by learning more about sustainable practices and disseminating the information derived from this research. In the United States, for example, the Food, Agriculture, Conservation, and Trade Act of 1990 expanded a program of research on sustainable agriculture first established under the Food Security Act of 1985. Reportedly about $265.1 million was being spent annually on sustainable agriculture research during the early 1990s.[19]

A Summing Up

Agricultural productivity in the industrialized countries can be expected to rise in the future, but at lower rates. Part of the large historic increases in agricultural productivity were based upon unsustainable, inefficient, and environmentally destructive agricultural practices, which were supported and encouraged by agricultural subsidies. In the future we can expect that as farmers become less insulated from the energy and environmental costs as subsidies are removed, some of the expected gains from technological progress will be offset.

In addition to changes in the productivity of agriculture in the future, we can also expect changes in agricultural practices. A transition to alternative agriculture appears to be underway. What would be the effects of this transition if it were to penetrate deeply into traditional agriculture? According to a national study based upon a large model of U.S. agriculture, widespread adoption of organic farming methods in the United States would increase national net farm income, but would also increase consumer food costs and decrease agricultural export levels.[20]

DISTRIBUTION OF FOOD RESOURCES

Imperfections in food distribution, particularly those associated with inadequate purchasing power, provide a second source of the malnourishment problem. According to this point of view the basic problem is poverty. We would expect, therefore, that the poorest segments of society would be the most malnourished and the poorest countries would contain the largest number of malnourished people.

If accurate, this representation suggests a very different policy orientation than that suggested by global scarcity. If the problem is maldistribution rather than shortage, this issue is how to get the food to the poorest people. The alleviation of poverty, increasing the ability to pay for food, is a strategy that could alleviate the problem. If the problem were a lack of food, this strategy would be totally ineffectual.

---

[19]United States General Accounting Office, *Sustainable Agriculture: Program Management, Accomplishments, and Opportunities,* Report # GAO/RCED-92-233 (September 1992). This report also noted that despite the fact that the responsibilities for implementing this program were fragmented, it had in fact been quite successful in promoting sustainable agriculture.

[20]Kent D. Olson, James Langley, and Earl O. Heady, "Widespread Adoption of Organic Farming Practices: Estimated Impacts on U.S. Agriculture," *Journal of Soil and Water Conservation* 37, No. 1 (January/February, 1982).

TABLE 9.1   Daily Per Capita Calorie Supply as Percent of Requirements

	1969–71	1974–76	1978–80	1977	1978	1979	1980
Developing market economies	95.5	95.5	99.2	96.3	99.2	99.8	98.6
Africa	93.5	93.1	93.7	94.3	93.9	93.3	94.0
Far East	92.8	90.8	95.7	91.1	96.0	96.9	94.1
Latin America	105.8	106.7	108.9	107.5	108.4	108.7	109.4
Near East	97.2	106.2	111.0	108.5	109.7	111.3	112.1
Other developing market economies	100.0	101.5	105.7	102.8	105.7	106.3	105.3
Asian centrally planned economies	90.7	97.7	104.3	99.1	101.3	105.0	106.6
Total developing countries	93.9	96.3	100.9	97.2	99.9	101.5	101.2
Least developed countries	88.3	84.1	84.1	82.9	84.3	83.1	85.0
Total developed countries	128.4	130.8	133.1	131.2	132.2	133.7	133.4
World	104.8	106.5	109.8	107.0	109.1	110.4	110.0

Source: Food and Agricultural Organization, *The State of Food and Agriculture: 1982* (Rome: United Nations, 1983), Table1.1, p. 5.

Defining the Problem

There is considerable and persuasive evidence that the problem is a distribution one (Table 9.1). The information in this table is constructed by the Food and Agriculture Organization (FAO) in several steps. First, they calculated a minimum number of calories that will allow normal activity and good health in adults and will permit children to reach normal body weight and intelligence in the absence of disease. Though these vary by country, they are generally in the neighborhood of 2,400 kilocalories per day.

In the second step, the FAO calculated the number of kilocalories the average citizen of that country receives from food intake. The final step involves calculating the ratio of actual intake to minimum desired intake and multiplying that ratio by 100. The results are portrayed in Table 9.1. An index equal to 100 means that the caloric intake is just sufficient for the average citizen to avoid nutritional deficiency. A number lower than 100 means the average citizen of the country is subject to nutritional deficiencies.

Though the data are far from perfect,[21] a number of interesting conclusions can be drawn. Looking at the bottom line first, we find that the average member of the world population has a sufficient caloric intake. This reinforces our conclusion that the problem is not one of global scarcity. It is also clear, however, that the food is not uniformly distributed among the world's peoples. During 1979, for example, the diet of the average citizen in developing countries was barely adequate. The average diet in Africa was nutritionally deficient in every year covered by

---

[21]Dealing only with calories, these data ignore other kinds of nutritional deficiencies, such as insufficient vitamin or protein intake. Concentrating solely on the average ignores the nutritional problems of the very poorest citizens. Considerable hunger can exist in a country where the average citizen is well fed.

the table. For the least developed countries, the average diet contained fewer calories than the nutritional deficiency threshold. Meanwhile, nutritional levels in developed countries on average were well in excess of the minimum.

Equally interesting, however, is the trend. Clear progress is being made in the developing countries as a whole. The change from the 1966–1968 period to the 1975–1977 period is strikingly positive. These very positive results, however, are tempered considerably by the results for the least developed nations. For those countries, the average diet was woefully inadequate at the beginning of the period, and the situation has deteriorated during the intervening ten years.

Those countries that seem the most resistant to improvement in their nutritional situation seem to share two characteristics: (1) high population growth, and (2) low per capita income. Of the 46 countries included in the FAO most seriously affected group, all but four have population growth rates in excess of 2.0 percent,[22] and all but four of them had GNP per capita ratios of less than $500 per year. These figures compare with an average population growth rate of 0.7 percent and an average GNP per capita of $8,070 in the industrialized countries.[23]

As we stated in the chapter on population growth, these characteristics may well be related. High poverty levels are generally conducive to high population growth, and high population growth rates may increase the degree of income inequality. Thus, extreme poverty may perpetuate itself. Inasmuch as we have examined population-control strategies in Chapter 5, we shall now focus on strategies to increase the amount of food available to the poorest people. What can be done?

Domestic Production in LDCs

The first issue to be addressed concerns the relative merits of increasing domestic production in the less-developed countries as opposed to importing more from abroad. There are several reasons for believing that many developing countries can profitably increase the percentage of their consumption domestically produced. One of the most important is that food imports use up precious foreign exchange.

Most developing countries cannot pay for imports with their own currencies. They must pay in an internationally accepted currency, such as the American dollar, earned through the sale of exports. As more foreign exchange is used for agricultural imports, less is available for imports such as capital goods, which could raise the productivity (and hence incomes) of local workers.

The lack of foreign exchange has been exacerbated by the rapid rise in oil prices. Many developing nations must spend large portions of export earnings merely to import energy. In 1986 the average low-income country spent 17 percent of its export earnings on energy, up from 7 percent in 1965. For some countries the situation is even more dismal. Ethiopia, for

---

[22]Food and Agriculture Organization, *The State of Food and Agriculture: 1979* (Rome: Food and Agriculture Organization of the United Nations, 1980): 1–5.

[23]The World Bank, *World Development Report, 1980* (Washington, DC: International Bank for Reconstruction and Development, 1980): 110–111, 142.

TABLE 9.2 A Hypothetical Example of the Law of Comparative Advantage

	Hours to Produce One Unit of Textiles	*Hours to Produce One Unit of Wheat*
Less-Developed Country	1	3
Developed Country	1	1

example, spent 36 percent of its export earnings for energy imports.[24] That leaves little for capital goods or agricultural imports.

Although this pressure on foreign exchange suggests a need for greater reliance on domestic agricultural production, it would be incorrect to carry that argument to its logical extreme by suggesting that all nations should become self-sufficient in food. The reason why self-sufficiency is not always efficient is suggested by *the law of comparative advantage.*

Nations are better off specializing in those products for which they have a comparative advantage. If its comparative advantage is not in food but in textiles, for example, the country would be better off by producing and exporting textiles, using the earnings to purchase food (Table 9.2). The opportunity costs of producing textiles and wheat (measured in hours of labor per unit output) are given for a hypothetical less-developed country (LDC) and a developed country (DC).

Suppose we are considering an eight-hour day in each country. If the average worker in each country were to spend four hours of each day on each activity, then eight units of textile (four by the LDC and four by the DC) and five and one-third units of wheat (one and one-third by the LDC and four by the DC) would be produced by the two countries each day. (Be sure you can see how these numbers can be derived from the table.)

Suppose, however, that the LDC in this case were to specialize in textiles (by allocating all eight hours to textile production) while the DC specialized in wheat. It is easy to verify that the total world production would now be eight units of textiles and eight units of wheat. *When countries specialize in those products in which they have a comparative advantage, total production can increase!*

Why did this happen in our example? It happened because the opportunity cost of making textiles in the LDC (in terms of foregone wheat) was lower than in the DC, whereas the opportunity cost of growing wheat in the DC (in terms of foregone textile production) was lower than that in the LDC. By freeing labor in the DC from making textiles, the LDC would be able to reap some of the benefits of the increased wheat production.

Although this example is hypothetical, the principle it conveys is real. Total self-sufficiency in food for all nations is not an appropriate goal. Those nations with a comparative advantage in agriculture due to climate, soil type, available land, and so on, such as the United States, should be net exporters, whereas those nations, such as Japan, with comparative advantage in other commodities should remain net food importers. This balance should not be allowed to get out of line, however, by creating an excessive reliance on either domestic production or imports.

Have the low-income countries as a group been reducing the share of their food consumption that comes from imports? Historically the answer was no. The World Bank (1980)

---

[24]Ibid. p. 240.

computed an index of food production per capita by country. The index was constructed in such a manner that it took on the value 100 for a domestic production per capita level equal to that achieved by the country on average during the 1969–1971 period. Therefore, values of less than 100 indicated a fall in food production per capita. The average value for low-income countries for the 1976–1978 period was 97, whereas it was 108 for industrialized market economies. Since 1979 the low-income countries have apparently barely kept pace with population growth.[25] The obvious implication was that low-income countries as a group are having trouble even keeping up with population growth, much less making headway in reducing imports.

The Undervaluation Bias

Why has food production in the developing countries barely kept pace with population growth for so many years? Agriculture in the low-income countries has been undervalued, implying that the rate of return on investment in agriculture is well below what it would be if agricultural output were allowed to receive its full social value. As a result, investments in agriculture were lower than they would otherwise have been and productivity has suffered.

Before investigating the sources and consequences of this problem, let's discuss one enduring myth that tends to distort thinking on the subject of agricultural incentives. According to the myth, peasant farmers do not respond to prices for cash crops because they are too ignorant, and they do not respond to prices for subsistence crops because they consume them rather than sell them. Therefore, the myth concludes, supply in peasant economies is not price elastic. Population included increases in demand would cause higher prices but not increased supplies. As one of many studies, Example 9.1 indicates this argument has one fatal flaw. It is not true!

Governments have used many mechanisms having the undesirable side effect of undervaluing agriculture and destroying incentives in the process. Two stand out—marketing boards and export taxes.

National marketing boards have been established in many developing countries to stabilize agricultural prices and hold food prices down to protect the poor from malnutrition. Typically, a marketing board sells food at subsidized prices. As the subsidy grows, the board looks around for ways to reduce the amount of subsidy.

Two strategies regularly employed by marketing boards are the wholesale importation of artificially cheap food from the United States (available under the food aid program originally designed to get rid of wheat surpluses) and holding down prices paid to domestic farmers. Both, of course, have the long-term effect of disrupting local production. The perniciousness of this process is shown in Example 9.2.

The effects of holding prices down can be illustrated by what happened to farmers in Mali in 1979–1980. Although it cost Malian farmers 83 francs per kilo to produce their irrigated rice, the government paid them only 60 francs per kilo. During that period most Malian rice

---

[25]Ibid. p. 234.

EXAMPLE 9.1

The Price Responsiveness of Supply: Thailand

The market response to an increasing demand for food resulting from population growth is rising prices. This increase in prices is then presumed to call forth further increases in supply. The more price responsive is the supply, the smaller the price increases needed to satisfy a given level of demand, so the question of agricultural production responsiveness to prices is of major importance.

There is considerable debate about whether we should expect farmers to respond to prices. Those who believe that prices are important see farmers as rational, calculating individuals seizing the opportunities presented to them in the form of higher prices. The other camp generally believes that small farmers are ignorant and so set in their ways as to be oblivious to what happens in the markets for their products.

Jere Behrman, an economist on the faculty of the University of Pennsylvania, has investigated this question. He published a major empirical study assessing the price responsiveness of four major annual crop supplies in Thailand over the period 1937–1963. Three (cassava, corn, and *kenaf*) were cash crops; the fourth (rice) was a subsistence crop where only the surplus was marketed.

Using sophisticated econometric models, he found a substantial amount of price responsiveness in the supply of all four commodities. He found the substantial price responses found for kenaf are particularly noteworthy because this crop had been adopted by near-subsistence farmers who previously were, at most, marginal participants in the national market. Behrman also discovered that Thai farmers were risk-averse; production could be increased by lowering the risk even if the expected price remained the same. In Thailand, at least, policies allowing prices to rise and reducing the risk have had a substantial impact. We should not sell small-scale peasant farmers short!

*Kenaf is a fiber used to manufacture gunny sacks and, to a lesser extent, rope and paper.

Source: Jere Behrman, *Supply Response in Underdeveloped Agriculture* (Amsterdam: Holland Publishing, 1968).

---

was smuggled across the border to Senegal, Niger, and Upper Volta, where it received market prices. A World Bank study during the period found that farmers in 13 surveyed countries received less than half of the value of their crops.[26]

Many developing countries depend on export taxes, levied on all goods shipped abroad, as a principal source of revenue. Some of these taxes fall on cash-crop food exports (bananas, coca beans, coffee, and so on). The impact of export taxes is to raise the cost to foreign purchasers, reducing the amount of demand. A reduction in demand generally means lower

---

[26]This information came from a study by agricultural economist Carl Eicher reported in Janet Raloff, "Africa's Famine: The Human Dimension, *Science News* 127 (11 May 1985): 300.

EXAMPLE 9.2

Perverse Government Intervention: The Case of Colombia

The failure of the market to increase productivity in the agricultural sector or to reduce the incidence of poverty sometimes has been due to government policies. The experience in Colombia is relatively typical.

Marketing of wheat in Colombia is controlled by the huge Colombia Institute for Agricultural Marketing, operated by the government. In 1951–1954, wheat production averaged 140,000 metric tons a year. By 1971, this production level had fallen to 49,000 tons. During this same period, consumption of wheat in Colombia rose from 179,000 tons to 434,000 tons. The difference, of course, had to be made up by imports.

Why did this happen? There seemed to be two reasons, both of which had the effect of lowering the real price of wheat received by the Colombian farmer—who, as expected, reacted by cutting production. The first reason was a massive inflow of surplus grain from the United States, which was subsidized by the United States government as part of our food aid program. This artificially cheap wheat simply stole much of the market normally supplied by domestic producers.

The second cause was a decision by the marketing institute to hold wheat prices constant in the 1968–1971 period in spite of an annual inflation rate approaching 10 percent. The intended purpose, of course, was to hold prices down for consumers, which it temporarily did. The unintended side effect was to discourage domestic production and to increase the losses of the marketing institute, which had to pay the difference between what the imported wheat cost and the lower price offered to consumers.

Is there a moral to the story? Possibly. The supply side has to be kept continually in mind as governments attempt to raise the nutrition levels of their citizens.

Sources: Reed Hertford, "Government Price Policies for Wheat, Rice and Tractors in Colombia," in *Distortions of Agricultural Incentives,*" Theodore W. Schultz, ed. (Bloomington: Indiana University Press, 1978): 121–39; World Bank, *World Development Report, 1980* (Washington DC: International Bank for Reconstruction and Development, 1980): 87.

---

prices and lower incomes for the farmers. Thus, this strategy also impairs food production incentives.

Government policies in the Third World affect not only the level of agricultural production, they affect the techniques employed as well. A 1987 study by the World Bank reported that in nine developing countries pesticide subsidies ranged from 15 to 90 percent of full retail cost, with a median of 44 percent.[27] Agricultural mechanization is another target for subsidies. As a result of this distortion of prices, farmers have been encouraged to rely heavily on

---

[27]Development Committee, *Environment, Growth and Development* (Washington, DC: World Bank, 1987): 20.

pesticides and to embrace mechanization where possible, strategies which make little sense in the long run.

Having become dependent on the subsidies, it becomes difficult for these farmers to make the transition to sustainable agricultural practices.

Feeding the Poor

The undervaluation bias was caused by a misguided attempt to use price controls as the way to provide the poor with access to an adequate diet. It backfired because the price controls served to reduce the availability of food. Is there a way to reduce the nutritional gap among the poor while maintaining adequate supplies of food?

Some countries (such as Sri Lanka, Colombia, and the United States) are using food stamp programs to subsidize food purchases by the poor. In Colombia this is being accomplished by issuing food coupons to low-income women and children who are particularly vulnerable to nutritional deficiency. The coupons can be used by recipients to purchase a number of high-nutrition, low-cost foods. About 200,000 households were reached in 1980. By boosting the purchasing power of those with the greatest need, these programs provide access to food while protecting the incentives of farmers. Those countries lowering food prices to everyone need substantially higher payments by the government to finance the programs. When governments look around for ways to finance these subsidies, they are tempted to try to reduce the subsidy by paying below-market prices to farmers or relying more heavily on artificially low-cost imported food aid. In the long run, either of these strategies can be self-defeating.

Targeting the assistance to those who need it is one strategy that works. Another approach to feeding the poor is an attempt to ensure that the income distribution effects of agricultural policies benefit the poor. One great hope associated with the "green revolution" was that new varieties of seeds produced by scientific research would expand the supply of food, holding down prices and making a better diet accessible to the poor while providing expanding employment opportunities for the poor to supply more grain. How did it work out?

The green revolution started with maize hybrids adapted in the 1950s from the United States and Rhodesia and later spread across large parts of Central America and East Africa. Since the mid-1960s, short-stalk, fertilizer-responsive varieties of rice have spread throughout East Asia and of wheat have spread through Mexico and the Indian and Pakistan Punjabs.

In many areas with access to these hybrids, productivity has doubled or tripled over a thirty-year period. Short-duration varieties have allowed many farmers to harvest two crops a year where only one was formerly possible. The transformation was unprecedented.

The effects were impressive.[28] In most areas with access to these modern varieties, small farmers adopted them no less widely, intensively, or productively than others. Labor use per acre was increased, with a consequent increase in the wage bill received by the poor. Poor people's consumption and nutrition were better with the new varieties than without them.

---

[28]For the evidence see Michael Lipton and Richard Longhurst, *New Seeds and Poor People* (Baltimore, MD: Johns Hopkins University Press, 1989)

E X A M P L E   9 . 3

The Distribution Dilemma: India's Green Revolution

India illustrates the trade-off between efficiency and equity sometimes faced by developing countries. India achieved substantial increases in its production of wheat (and subsequently of rice) through the introduction of new hybrid seed. Distributed through a limited budget, the new seed could either be given to small farmers in the poorer regions or to the richer Punjab area, where the preconditions for rapid-yield expansion were present. India chose the latter strategy.

Several barriers existed to substantially increased yields among the poorer farmers. The smaller farmers did not have the savings or the access to capital markets to put in the complementary inputs (principally irrigation) required to gain the maximum productivity increase from the new seed. In addition, their land holdings were not typically large enough to utilize the optimum scale of the complementary inputs.

Two main developments resulted. Food products increased substantially, but the gains were captured by larger farms. Francine Frankel estimates that the majority of Indian farmers experienced a relative decline in their economic position (small rice farmers received 75 to 80 percent of the gains received by the larger farmers), and some smaller percentage of them actually experienced an absolute decline. For this latter category, the effect of the green revolution was to make them worse off, not better off.

Source: Francine Frankel, *India's Green Revolution: Economic Gains and Political Costs* (Princeton, NJ: Princeton University Press, 1971).

However, the adoption of these varieties has had a darker side as well. Reliance on a few species of hybrid cereal grains increases the risk from diseases and pests. Every Wall Street portfolio manager knows that risk can be lowered by holding a diverse collection of stocks. The security offered by diversity of agricultural species has diminished as larger and larger areas are planted in these new varieties. In other areas, those without access to the new varieties have probably lost out as large quantities of new grain enter the market, eliminating by competition some of the more traditional sources. Small farmers were not always the beneficiaries of these new agricultural hybrids (see Example 9.3).

We are now in a position to define the role for aid from the developed nations. Temporary food aid is helpful when traditional sources are completely inadequate (natural disasters) or when the food aid does not interfere with the earnings of domestic producers. In the long run, developed nations could provide both appropriate technologies (such as solar-powered irrigation systems) and the financial capital to get farmer-owned local cooperatives off the ground. These cooperatives would then provide some of the advantages of scale (such as risk sharing and distribution) while maintaining the existing structure of small-scale farms. Coupled with effective population-control efforts and a balanced development program designed to raise the general standard of living, this approach could provide a solution to the distributional portion of the world food problem.

Industrialized nations could also open their markets to agricultural products from the developing countries by eliminating subsidies and by removing trade barriers. These acts would level the agricultural playing field, would remove some of the undervaluation bias that is due to external factors, and would provide a source of income to some of the poorest farmers in developing countries.

FEAST AND FAMINE CYCLES

The remaining dimension of the world food problem concerns the year-to-year fluctuations in food availability caused by vagaries of weather and planting decisions. Even if the average level of food availability were appropriate, the fact that the average consists of a sequence of overproduction and underproduction years means that society as a whole can benefit from smoothing out the fluctuations.

The point is vividly depicted by an analogy. If a person were standing in two buckets of water—the first containing boiling hot water, the second, ice-cold water—his misery would not be assuaged in the least by a friend telling him that on average the temperature was perfect. The average does not tell the whole story.

The fluctuations of supplies for food seem to be rather large, and the swings in prices even larger. Why? One characteristic of the farming sector suggests that farmers' production decisions may actually make the fluctuations worse or at least prolong them. This tendency is explored via the *cobweb model.*

Suppose, due to a weather-induced shortage, the price rises. For the next growing season, farmers have to plant well in advance of harvest time. Their decisions about how much to plant will depend on the price they expect to receive. Let us suppose they use this year's price as their guess of what next year's price will be.

They will plan to supply a larger amount. Because the market cannot absorb that much of the commodity, the price falls. If farmers use this new lower price to plan the following year's crop, they will produce less. This will cause the price to rise again, and so on.

The fluctuations that occur normally produce a damped oscillation. In the absence of further supply shocks, the amplitude of price and quantity fluctuations decreases over time until the equilibrium price and quantity are obtained.[29]

The demand for food tends to be price inelastic, particularly in developing countries. This has some important implications. The more price inelastic the demand curve, the higher the price has to go in order to bring the demand into line with supply when a weather-induced shortage occurs. One conclusion is immediately obvious—the more inelastic the demand curve, the more likely farmers as a group are to gain from the shortfall. As long as the demand curve is price inelastic in the relevant range (a condition commonly satisfied in the short run by food products), farmers as a group will be better off by supply shortfalls.[30]

---

[29]Theoretically, undamped oscillations, which increase in amplitude over time are possible under certain conditions, but this pattern does not seem to characterize existing food markets.

[30]This is not necessarily true for every farmer, of course. If the supply reduction is concentrated on a few, they will unambiguously be worse off whereas the remaining farmers will be better off. The point is that the revenue gains received by the latter group will exceed the losses suffered by the former group.

On the consumer side of this issue, a quite different picture emerges. Consumers are unambiguously hurt by shortfalls and helped by situations with excess supply. The more price inelastic the demand curve, the greater is the loss in consumer surplus from shortfalls and the greater is the gain in consumer surplus from excess supply.

This creates some interesting (and from the policy point of view, difficult) incentives. Producers as a group do not have any particular interest in protecting against supply shortfalls, but they have a substantial interest in protecting against excess supply. Consumers, on the other hand, have no quarrel with excess supply but want to guard against supply shortfalls.

Although society as a whole would gain from the stabilization of prices and quantities, the different segments of society have rather different views of how that stabilization should come about. Farmers will be delighted with price stabilization as long as the average price is high; consumers will be delighted if the average price is kept low.

The main means of attempting to stabilize prices and quantities is by creating stockpiles. These can be drawn down during periods of scarcity and built up during periods of excess supply. Currently, two different types of food stockpiles exist. The first is a special internationally held emergency stockpile that would be used to alleviate the hunger caused by natural disasters (such as drought). Established in 1975 by the Seventh Special Session of the United Nations General Assembly, with an annual target of 500,000 tons, the World Emergency Stockpile has the potential to greatly reduce suffering without having any noticeable disruptive effect on the world grain market (involving some 70 million tons traded). Unfortunately, its full potential has not yet been reached. Contributions in 1979, for example, totaled 314,000 tons, considerably short of the annual target. The bulk of accumulated reserves was distributed to needy nations in that same year, leaving little in reserve.

The second kind of stockpile represents the stocks held individually by the various countries. It was hoped that these stockpiles would be internationally coordinated. Despite intensive negotiations, by 1979 the mechanism for coordinating these stocks had not yet been agreed upon, much less implemented. However, the level of the stocks was adequate. The FAO Secretariat estimates the minimum safe level of world carryover stocks for cereals to be between 17 and 18 percent of world consumption. After a rather precipitous decline in 1973, by 1977 the stocks had been rebuilt to the minimum safe levels. Almost two thirds of the stockpile is controlled by the exporting countries.

The process has started to increase food security on a worldwide basis but has not yet reached the point of solving the problem. Significant difficult political decisions on stockpile management, such as timing purchases and sales, have yet to be agreed upon. Until that time, because the interests of producers and consumer nations are no different, it is unlikely that any uncoordinated system will be fully effective.

SUMMARY

The world hunger problem is upon us and it is real. Serious malnutrition is currently being experienced in many parts of the world. The root of the chronic problem is poverty—an inability to afford the rising costs of food, though solving the problem will become more difficult as past unsustainable agricultural practices are eliminated and food prices rise. The harm caused by poverty and rising food prices is intensified by fluctuations in the availability of food.

These problems are not insoluble. The FAO has concluded that developing countries *could* increase their food production by around 4 percent per year through the 1990s, well in excess of population growth. They conclude, however, that this will occur only if the developed nations share technology and provide the developing countries access to their markets and if the developing countries show a willingness to adopt pricing policies that do not restrict output. This can be accomplished without jeopardizing the poor by using direct food-purchase subsidies (such as a food-stamp program) rather than price controls.

Because a major part of the world hunger problem is poverty, it is not enough to simply produce more food. The ability of the poor to afford food has also to be improved. Reducing poverty can be accomplished by bolstering nonfarm employment opportunities as well as by enhancing the returns of smaller-scale farmers. Small-scale farming can compete effectively, given access to credit markets and new improved technologies.

Food stockpiles—the key element in a program to provide food security—exist but are not yet fully effective. The emergency stockpile has not achieved its designed capacity and the system of national stockpiles is large but not effectively managed. The light is at the end of the tunnel and the train is moving, but the journey is distressingly slow.

FURTHER READING

Crosson, Pierre R., and Sterling Brubaker. *Resource and Environmental Effects of U.S. Agriculture* (Baltimore, MD: Johns Hopkins University Press, for Resources for the Future, 1982). This book identifies the environmental costs associated with future increases in production and suggests measures to deal with them.

Meier, Gerald M. *Leading Issues in Economic Development,* 3rd ed. (New York: Oxford University Press, 1976). A highly regarded extensive collection of integrated short articles on various aspects of the development process. Contains an excellent section on agricultural development with an extensive bibliography.

Presidential Commission on World Hunger. *Overcoming World Hunger: The Challenge Ahead* (Washington, DC: U.S. Government Printing Office, 1980).

Streeten, Paul. *What Price Food? Agricultural Policies in Developing Countries* (New York: St. Martin's Press, 1987). An excellent study of agricultural policies in developing countries.

ADDITIONAL REFERENCES

Alexandros, Nikos, ed. *World Agriculture: Towards 2000* (New York: New York University Press, 1988).

Browder, John O., ed. *Fragile Lands of Latin America: Strategies for Sustainable Development* (Boulder, CO: Westview Press, 1988).

Cobia, David. *Cooperatives in Agriculture* (Englewood Cliffs, NJ: Prentice-Hall, 1988).

Collins, Robert A., and J. C. Headley. "Optimal Investment to Reduce the Decay of an Income Stream: The Case of Soil Conservation," *Journal of Environmental Economics and Management* 10 (March 1983): 60–71.

Crosson, Pierre R. *The Cropland Crisis: Myth or Reality?* (Washington, DC: Resources for the Future, 1982).

Crosson, Pierre R. *Productivity Effects of Cropland Erosion in the United States* (Washington, DC: Resources for the Future, 1983).

Hall, Darwin C., et al. "Organic Food and Sustainable Agriculture," *Contemporary Policy Issues* VII, No. 4 (October 1989): 47–72.

Regev, Uri, Haim Shalit, and A. P. Gutteirrez. "On the Optimal Allocation of Pesticides with Increasing Resistance: The Case of Alfalfa Weevil," *Journal of Environmental Economics and Management* 10 (March 1983): 86–100.

DISCUSSION QUESTIONS

1. "By applying modern technology to agriculture, the United States has become the most productive food-producing nation in the world. The secret to solving the world food problem lies in transferring this technology to developing countries." Discuss.
2. Under Public Law 480, the United States sells surplus grains to developing countries, which pay in local currencies. Because the United States rarely spends all of these currencies, much of this grain transfer is *de facto* an outright gift. Is this an equitable and efficient way for the U.S. to dispose of surplus grain? Why or why not?

CHAPTER 10

Forests

There is nothing more difficult to carry out, nor more doubtful of success, nor more dangerous to handle, than to initiate a new order of things. For the reformer has enemies in all who profit by the old order, and only lukewarm defenders in all those who would profit from the new order. The lukewarmness arises partly from fear of their adversaries who have law in their favor; and partly from the incredulity of mankind, who do not truly believe in anything new until they have had actual experience of it.

MACHIAVELLI, *THE PRINCE* (1513)

INTRODUCTION

Forests provide a variety of products and services. The raw materials for housing and many products made out of wood are extracted from the forest. In many parts of the world wood is an important fuel. Paper products are derived from wood fiber. Trees cleanse the air by absorbing carbon dioxide and adding oxygen. Forests provide shelter and sanctuary for wildlife, and they play an important role in the ecology of watersheds that supply much of our drinking water.

Although the contributions that trees make to our everyday life are easy to overlook, even the most rudimentary calculations indicate their significance. Slightly less than one third of the land in the United States is covered by forests, the largest category of land use with the exception of pasture and grazing land. For Maine, an example of a heavily forested state, 95 percent of the land area is covered by forest. In 1980 the comparable figure for the world was 31.3 percent.[1]

Managing these forests is no easy task. In contrast to cereal grains, which are planted and harvested on an annual cycle, forests mature very slowly. The manager must decide not only how to maximize yields on a given amount of land but also when to harvest and replant. A delicate balance must be established among the various possible uses of forests. Because harvesting the resource diminishes other values (such as protecting the aesthetic value of forested

---

[1] OECD, *OECD Environmental Data: Compendium 1985* (Paris: Organization for European Co-operation and Development, 1985): 103.

vistas), establishing the proper balance requires some means of comparing the values of potentially conflicting uses. The efficiency criterion is one obvious method.

A glance at some of the vital signs of the forest resource does not inspire confidence that it is being managed either efficiently or sustainably. Deforestation is currently proceeding at an unprecedented rate. In 1990 the World Resources Institute reported that 40 to 50 million acres of tropical forests, an area about the size of the state of Washington, are being destroyed each year as trees are cut for timber and to clear land for agriculture and development.[2] This estimate, which was based upon remote sensing data from satellites, was 50 percent higher than the previous global estimate prepared by the United Nations Food and Agricultural Organization in 1980.

Deforestation is a serious problem because it has intensified global warming, has decreased biodiversity, has caused agricultural productivity to decline, has increased soil erosion and desertification, and has precipitated the decline of traditional cultures of people indigenous to the forests. Instead of being used on a sustainable basis to provide for the needs of subsequent generations as well as current generations, the forests are being "cashed in." According to a 1989 study for the International Tropical Timber Organization, a 69-member trade group based in Yokohama, Japan, less than 0.1 percent of tropical logging was done sustainably.[3] Current forestry practices seem to violate both the sustainability and efficiency criteria. Why is this occurring and what can be done about it?

In the remainder of this chapter we shall explore how economics can be combined with forest ecology to assist in efficiently managing this important resource. We begin by characterizing what is meant by an efficient allocation of the forest resource when the value of the harvested timber is the only concern. Starting simply, we first model the efficient decision to cut a single stand or cluster of trees with a common age by superimposing economic considerations on a biological model of tree growth. This model is then expanded to demonstrate how the multiple values of the forest resource should influence the harvesting decision. Turning to matters of institutional adequacy, we shall then examine the inefficiencies that have resulted or can be expected to result from both public and private management decisions and strategies for restoring efficiency.

DEFINING EFFICIENT MANAGEMENT

Special Attributes of the Forest

Although forests share many characteristics with other living resources, they also have some unique aspects. Trees provide a saleable commodity when they are harvested, but left standing they are a capital asset, providing for increased growth the following year and a stream of

---

[2]World Resources Institute and International Institute for Environment and Development, *World Resources: 1990–91* (New York: Basic Books, 1990).

[3]In this context sustainability refers to harvesting no more than would be replaced by growth; sustainable harvest would preserve the interests of future generations by assuring that the volume of remaining timber was not declining over time. This is a somewhat stronger sustainability criterion than introduced in Chapter 2, which only requires that future generations be as well off. It would conceivably be possible to make future generations better off even if the volume of wood were declining over time by providing a compensating amount of some commodity or service they value even more.

environmental services such as watershed protection and wildlife habitat. Each year, the forest manager must decide whether to harvest a particular stand of trees or to wait. In contrast to many other living resources, however, the time period between initial investment (planting) and recovery of that investment (harvesting) is especially long. Intervals of 25 years or more are common in forestry, but not in many other industries. Finally, most of the environmental services provided by the forest are externalities, which plays havoc with incentives, reducing the ability of institutions to manage forestlands efficiently and sustainably.

The Biological Dimension

Tree growth is measured on a volume basis, typically by cubic feet on a particular site. This measurement is taken of the trunks, exclusive of bark and limbs, between the stump and a 4-inch top. For larger trees, the stump is 24 inches from the ground. Only standing trees are measured; those toppled by wind or age are not included. In this sense the volume is measured in net rather than gross terms.

Based on this measurement of volume, the data reveal that tree stands go through distinct growth phases. Initially, when the trees are very young, growth is rather slow in volume terms, though the tree may experience a considerable increase in height. A period of sustained, rapid growth follows, with volume increasing considerably. Finally, slower growth sets in as the stand fully matures, until growth stops or even reverses.

The actual growth of a stand of trees depends on many factors, including the weather, the fertility of the soil, susceptibility to insects or disease, the type of tree, the amount of care devoted to the trees, and vulnerability to forest fire or air pollution. Thus, there is a tremendous amount of variability of tree growth from stand to stand. Some of these growth-enhancing or growth-retarding factors are under the influence of foresters; others are not.

Abstracting from these differences, it is possible to develop a hypothetical but realistic biological model of the growth of a stand of trees. In this case our model (Figure 10.1) is based on the growth of a stand of Douglas fir trees in the Pacific Northwest.[4]

Notice that the figure is consistent with the growth phases mentioned earlier. Following an early period of limited growth, the stand experiences rapid growth in the middle ages with growth ceasing after 135 years.

When should this stand be harvested? Foresters have come up with a calculation called the *mean annual increment* (MAI), which provides the basis for a biological approach to answering this question. Developing this concept provides a useful contrast to the economic approach, which is presented in subsequent sections.

The MAI is calculated by dividing the cumulative volume of the stand at the end of each decade by the cumulative number of years the stand has been growing up to that decade. For growth patterns like the ones represented by Figure 10.1, the MAI rises during the early ages and then falls during the later ages (Table 10.1).

According to the biological decision rule, the forest should be harvested at the age when the MAI is maximized. According to our Douglas fir example, this occurs when the stand is

---

[4]The numerical model in the text is based loosely on the data presented in Marion Clawson, "Decision Making in Timber Production, Harvest, and Marketing," Research Paper R-4 (Washington DC: Resources for the Future, 1977), Table 1, p. 13. The mathematical function relating volume to age of the stand in Figure 10.1 is a third-degree polynomial of the form $v = a + bt + ct^2 + dt^3$, where v = volume in cubic feet, t = the age of the stand in years, and a, b, c, and d are parameters that take on the values 0, 40, 3.1, and –0.016, respectively.

FIGURE 10.1   Model of Tree Growth in a Stand of Douglas Fir

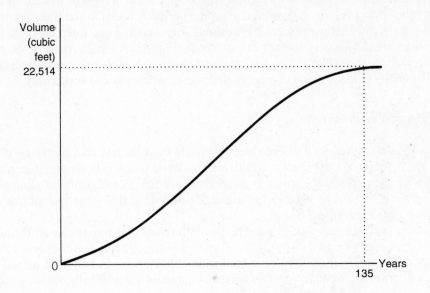

100 years old. Column 4 in Table 10.1 helps us to understand what is special about this age. Annual incremental growth rises until the trees are about 70 years old, declining thereafter. The MAI rises for the first 100 years because the annual incremental growth is above the MAI during that period; it falls in the following years because the annual incremental growth is below the MAI.

The Economics of Forest Harvesting

To an economist, this biological criterion seems rather arbitrary; it fails to consider any of the factors (such as the value of the timber, the time value of money, or costs associated with planting and harvesting) that would play a central role in an efficient harvesting decision. However, it is possible to use the basic biological model of growth portrayed in Figure 10.1 as the basis for an economic model of the harvesting decision.

From the definition of efficiency, the optimal time to harvest this stand would be that time which maximizes the present value of the net benefits from the wood. The size of the net benefits from the wood depends on whether the land will be perpetually committed to forestry or left to natural processes after harvest. For our first model, we will assume that the stand will be harvested once and the land will be left as is following the harvest. This model will serve to illustrate how the economic principles of forestry can be applied to the simplest case while it provides the background necessary to move to more complicated and more realistic examples.

Two costs are presumed to be important in this decision: planting costs and harvesting costs. Apart from their magnitudes, these costs differ in one significant characteristic—the

TABLE 10.1   The Biological Harvesting Decision: Douglas Fir

Age (Years) (1)	Volume[a] (Cubic Feet) (2)	MAI[b] (Cubic Feet) (3)	Annual Incremental Growth[c] (Cubic Feet) (4)
10	694	6.9	6.9
20	1,912	95.6	121.8
30	3,558	118.6	164.6
40	5,536	138.4	198.8
50	7,750	155.0	221.4
60	10,104	168.0	235.4
70	12,502	178.6	239.8
80	14,848	185.6	234.6
90	17,046	189.4	219.8
100	19,000	190.0	195.4
110	20,614	187.4	161.4
120	21,792	181.6	117.8
130	22,438	172.6	64.6
135	22,514	166.8	11.6

[a]Calculated from the formula used to produce Figure 10.1. See footnote 3.

[b]Column 2 divided by Column 1.

[c]Change over intervening period in Column 1 divided by change in number of years in Column 1.

time at which they are borne. Planting costs are borne immediately, whereas harvesting costs are borne at the time of harvest. In a present-value calculation, harvesting costs are discounted (as is the value of the wood) because they are paid (received) in the future, whereas planting costs are not discounted because they are paid immediately. For the sake of our example, assume that planting this stand costs $1,000 and harvesting costs $0.30 per cubic foot of wood harvested.

With these additions to the model, it is now possible to calculate the present value of net benefits that would be derived from harvesting this stand at various ages (Table 10.2). The net benefits are calculated by subtracting the present value of costs from the value of the timber at that age. Two different discount rates are used to illustrate the influence of discounting on the harvesting decision. The undiscounted calculations ($r = 0.0$) simply indicate the actual values that would prevail at each age; the positive discount rate takes the time value of money into account.

An interesting conclusion can be gleaned from Table 10.2. Discounting shortens the time until the stand is harvested. Whereas the maximum undiscounted net benefits occur at 135 years, when a discount rate of only 0.02 is used, the maximum occurs at 68 years, roughly half the time of the undiscounted case. Higher discount rates would yield even shorter harvesting times.

TABLE 10.2   Economic Harvesting Decision: Douglas Fir

Age (Years)	Volume (Cu. Ft.)	Undiscounted (r = 0.0)			Discounted (r = 0.02)		
		Value of Timber ($)	Cost ($)	Net Benefits ($)	Value of Timber ($)	Cost ($)	Net Benefits ($)
10	694	694	1,208	−514	567	1,171	−604
20	1,912	1,912	1,574	338	1,288	1,386	−98
30	3,558	3,558	2,067	1,491	1,964	1,589	375
40	5,536	5,536	2,661	2,875	2,507	1,752	755
50	7,750	7,750	3,325	4,425	2,879	1,864	1,015
60	10,104	10,104	4,031	6,073	3,080	1,924	1,156
68	12,023	12,023	4,607	7,416	3,128	1,938	1,190
70	12,502	12,502	4,751	7,751	3,126	1,938	1,118
80	14,848	14,848	5,454	9,394	3,046	1,914	1,132
90	17,046	17,046	6,114	10,932	2,868	1,860	1,008
100	19,000	19,000	6,700	12,300	2,623	1,787	836
110	20,614	20,614	7,184	13,430	2,334	1,700	634
120	21,792	21,792	7,538	14,254	2,024	1,607	417
130	22,438	22,438	7,731	14,707	1,710	1,513	197
135	22,514	22,514	7,754	14,760	1,449	1,466	−17

Notes:
Volume of Timber from Table 10.1.
Value of Timber $= \text{Price} \times \text{Volume}/(1 + r)^t$
Cost $= \$1,000 + \$0.30 \times \text{Volume}/(1 + r)^t$
Net Benefits $=$ Value of Timber $-$ Cost

Higher discount rates imply shorter harvesting periods because they are less tolerant of the slow timber growth that occurs as the stand reaches maturity. The use of a positive discount rate implies a direct comparison between the increase in the value of the timber that occurs prior to harvesting and the increase in value that would occur if the forest were harvested and the money from the sale invested at rate r. In the undiscounted case, the opportunity cost of capital is zero, so it pays to leave the money invested in trees as long as some growth is occurring. As long as r is positive, however, the trees will be harvested as soon as the growth rate is low enough that more will be earned from financial investments.

Sustainable Forestry

Is economic efficiency compatible with sustainable forestry? The answer depends on what is meant by sustainable forestry. If the possibility of compensation is entertained along with the "nondeclining welfare among generations" definition, then efficiency is fully compatible with sustainability as long as the economic gains from harvest are invested and shared with future generations. In this case even when efficiency resulted in some deforestation, future generations would not suffer.

Suppose, however, that we consider sustainable forestry to be realized only when the forests are sufficiently protected that harvests can be realized perpetually. Under this definition sustainable forestry would occur as long as harvests were limited to the growth of the forest, leaving the volume of wood unaffected over some specified time scale.

Efficiency is not necessarily compatible with this definition of sustainable forestry. Maximizing the present value involves an implicit comparison between the increase in value from delaying harvest (largely due to the growth in volume) and the increase in value from harvesting the timber and investing the earnings (largely a function of r, the interest rate earned on invested savings). With slow-growing species the growth rate in volume is small; maximizing the present value may well involve harvest volumes higher than the net growth of the forest.

The search for sustainable forestry practices that are also economically sustainable has led to the development of rapidly growing tree species and plantation forestry. Rapidly growing species raise the attractiveness of replanting because the invested funds are tied up for a shorter period of time. These species are raised in plantations, where they can be harvested and replanted at a low cost. Forest plantations have been established for such varied purposes as supplying fuelwood in developing countries to supplying pulp for paper mills in both the industrialized and developing countries.

Plantation forestry is controversial. Not only do plantation forests typically involve a single species of tree, which provides poor wildlife habitat, they also require large inputs of fertilizer and pesticides.

In some parts of the world the natural resilience of the forest ecosystem is sufficiently high that sustainability is ultimately achieved despite decades of unsustainable levels of harvest. In the United States, for example, sometime during the 1940s the net growth of the nation's timberlands exceeded timber removals. The four surveys conducted since that time confirm that net growth has exceeded harvests in spite of a rather large and growing demand for timber. The total volume of forest in the United States has been growing since at least World War II; the harvests during that period have been sustainable in terms of forest volume, although the harvests of specific species in specific locations may not have been.[5]

SOURCES OF INEFFICIENCY

The rather harmonious view of an efficiently harvested forest contrasts sharply with the reality of rapid deforestation. Why are forests being harvested so rapidly, in apparent violation of both efficiency and sustainability criteria?

Global Inefficiencies

The first source of deforestation involves external costs that transcend national borders. Because the costs transcend national borders, it is unrealistic to expect national policy to solve the problem. Some international action would normally be necessary.

---

[5]Roger Sedjo, "The Nation's Forest Resources," Discussion Paper ENR90-07 (Washington, DC: Resources for the Future, 1990): 72.

Biodiversity.   Due to species extinction, the diversity of the forms of life that inhabit the planet is diminishing at an unprecedented rate. This extinction of species is an irreversible process. Deforestation, particularly the destruction of the tropical rain forests, is a major source of species extinction because it destroys the most biologically active habitats. In particular Amazonia has been characterized by Norman Myers as the "single richest region of the tropical biome."[6] The quantity of bird, fish, plant, and insect life that is unique to that region is unmatched anywhere else on the planet.

One of the tragic ironies of the situation is that these extinctions are occurring at precisely the moment in history when we would be most able to take advantage of the gene pool this biodiversity represents. Modern techniques now make it possible to transplant desirable genes from one species into another, creating species with new characteristics such as enhanced disease or pest resistance. But the gene pool must be diverse to serve as a source of donor genes. Tropical forests have already contributed genetic material to increase disease resistance of cash crops such as coffee and cocoa, and they have been the source of some entirely new foods. Approximately one quarter of all prescription drugs have been derived from substances found in tropical plants. Future discoveries, however, are threatened by deforestation's deleterious effect on habitat.

Global Warming.   Deforestation also contributes to global warming. Because trees absorb carbon dioxide, a major greenhouse gas, deforestation eliminates a potentially significant means of ameliorating the rise in carbon dioxide emissions. Furthermore burning trees, an activity commonly associated with agricultural land clearing, adds carbon dioxide to the air, by liberating the carbon sequestered within the trees. Why is deforestation occurring so rapidly when the benefits conferred by a standing forest are so significant by virtually anyone's reckoning? The concept of externalities provides the key to resolving this paradox. Both the global warming and biodiversity benefits are largely external to the nation containing the forest, whereas the costs of preventing deforestation are largely internal. The loss of biodiversity precipitated by deforestation is perhaps most deeply felt by the industrialized world, not the countries that control the forests. Currently, the technologies to exploit the gene pool this diversity represents are in widest use in the industrialized countries. Similarly, most of the damage from global warming would be felt outside the borders of the country being deforested, yet stopping deforestation means giving up the jobs and income derived from harvesting the wood or harvesting the land made available by clearing the forests. It is therefore not surprising that the most vociferous opposition to the loss of biodiversity is mounted in the industrialized nations, not the tropical forest nations. Global externalities provide not only a clear rationale for market failure, but also a clear reason why the governments involved cannot be expected to solve the problem by themselves.

Poverty and Debt

Poverty and debt are also major sources of pressure on the forests. Peasants see unclaimed forest land as an opportunity to own land. Nations confronted with masses of peasants see unowned or publicly owned forests as a politically more viable source of land for the landless than taking it forcibly from the rich. Without land, larger numbers of peasants descend upon

---

[6]Norman Myers, *The Primary Source: Tropical Forests and Our Future* (New York: W. W. Norton, 1984): 50.

the urban areas in search of jobs than can be accommodated by urban labor markets. Politically explosive tensions, created and nourished by the resulting atmosphere of frustration and hopelessness, force governments to open up forested lands to the peasants, or at least to look the other way as peasants stake their claim.

In eastern and southern Africa, positive feedback loops have created a downward cycle in which poverty and deforestation reinforce each other. Most natural forests have long since been cut down for timber, fuelwood, and cleared land for agricultural purposes. As forests disappear, the rural poor divert more time toward locating fuelwood. When fuelwood is no longer available, animal waste is burned, thereby eliminating it as a source of fertilizer to nourish depleted soils. Fewer trees hasten soil erosion. Depleted soils lead to diminished nutrition, as does an inability to find or afford fuelwood or animal waste for cooking and for boiling unclean water. Lower nutrition saps energy, increases susceptibility to disease, and reduces productivity. Survival strategies may necessarily sacrifice long-term goals simply to ward off starvation or death; the forests are typically an early casualty.

Poverty at the national level takes the form of staggering levels of debt to service in comparison to the capacity to generate foreign exchange earnings. In periods of high real interest rates, servicing these debts commands most if not all foreign exchange earnings. Using these foreign exchange earnings to service the debt eliminates the possibility of using them to finance imports for sustainable activities to alleviate poverty.

The large debts owed by many developing countries also encourage these countries to overexploit their resource endowments to raise the necessary foreign exchange. Timber exports represent a case in point. As Gus Speth, the president of the World Resources Institute points out, "By an accident of history and geography, half of the Third World external debt and over two-thirds of global deforestation occur in the same fourteen developing countries."

Perverse Incentives

Profit maximization does not produce efficient outcomes when the pattern of incentives facing decision-makers is perverse. Forestry provides an unfortunately large number of situations where perverse incentives have produced very inefficient and unsustainable outcomes.

Privately owned forests are a significant force all over the world, but in some countries, such as the United States, they are the dominant force. In the United States some 72 percent of forested land is privately owned, and some 15 percent of forested land is owned by the forest industry, while the remaining privately owned 57 percent is held by farmers or other landowners. These latter parcels tend to be small in size.

Bearing external costs is another problem faced by private managers. Private forest decisions are plagued by externally generated costs of various types. Yields are adversely affected by externally imposed costs, such as air pollution (Example 10.1). When heavy investments in forested lands can be wiped out by factors totally out of the control of the owners, the incentive to invest is undermined.

Providing a sustainable flow of timber is not the sole purpose of the forest, however. When the act of harvesting timber imposes costs on other valued aspects of the forest (such as watershed maintenance, prevention of soil erosion, protection of biodiversity, etc.), these may not (and normally will not) be adequately considered in the decision.

The value of the standing forest as wildlife habitat or as a key element in the local ecosystem is one external cost that can lead to an inefficient harvesting decision. The controversy that erupted in the Pacific Northwest of the United States between environmentalists and log-

E X A M P L E   1 0 . 1

Externalities in Forest Management: *Waldsterben*

When the first signs of forest death began to show up in the forests of West Germany, it was widely assumed that it was the spreading of a white fir decline that had been periodically decimating fir forests in Central Europe for the past 250 years. By the late 1970s, however, when Norway spruce began dying as well, it became apparent to scientists that they were being faced with an unprecedented situation of mass devastation, a situation known in German as *Waldsterben*.

It is spreading rapidly. In 1982, the government of the Federal Republic of Germany estimated that about 8 percent of its forests were damaged. By 1985, a repeat survey discovered that some 52 percent of the stands were affected. Among white firs more than 60 years old, some 95 percent exhibit visible symptoms of decline. The damage is particularly acute in the Black and Bavarian Forests. In 1985, the Union of German Forest Owners estimated the annual costs of *Waldsterben* at some $1 billion a year if present trends continue as expected.

Based on the perplexing array of symptoms, as well as the rapidity with which it is moving through forests, scientists now believe that multiple causes are involved. Early speculation that it was acid rain now seems too simple to explain the magnitude of the destruction. Most current scientific hypotheses about the causes involve the interactions of several pollutants, including nitrogen and sulfur compounds, ozone, aluminum, and a variety of organic chemicals such as ethylene or aniline.

Waldsterben is a good example of the policymaker's dilemma. The destruction is widespread and increasing rapidly, but considerable scientific uncertainty exists about the specific causes. Although the costs of inaction are apparently very high, with so many suspects to choose from, it is hard to formulate an effective control strategy. Meanwhile foresters helplessly watch as their resource bases dwindle due to factors entirely beyond their control.

Source: Don Hinrichsen, "Waldsterben: Forest Death Syndrome," *The Amicus Journal* (Spring 1986): 23—27.

gers can in part be explained by the different values these two groups put on habitat destruction. This region contains a number of old-growth Douglas firs, which can reach a height of thirty stories. These two-hundred-year-old trees would be very valuable sources of timber, but they are also important components of the local ecosystem. (Among other ecosystem contributions, these trees provide a home for the endangered northern spotted owl.)

Perverse incentives can be created by governments as well. The rapid rate of deforestation in Brazil is in no small part due to perverse incentives created by the Brazilian government.[7]

The Brazilian government has reduced taxes on income derived from agriculture by as much as 90 percent. This tax discrimination overvalues agriculture and makes it profitable to cut down forests and convert the land to agriculture even when, in the absence of discrimina-

---

[7]For further details on the Brazilian situation see Hans P. Binswanger, "Brazilian Policies that Encourage Deforestation in the Amazon," Working Paper No. 16 (Washington, DC: The World Bank, 1989); and Dennis J. Mahar, *Government Policies and Deforestation on Brazil's Amazon Region* (Washington, DC: The World Bank, 1989).

tory tax relief, agriculture in these regions would not be profitable. In addition, land taxes discriminate against forests. A farm containing forests is taxed at a higher rate than one containing only pastures or cropland.[8] This system of taxation encourages higher than efficient rates of conversion of land from forests to pasture or cropland and subsidizes an activity that, in the absence of tax discrimination, would not normally be economically viable. In essence, Brazilian taxpayers are subsidizing deforestation.

The system of property rights over land also is at fault. How do individuals establish a solid claim to unclaimed land in Brazil? Acquiring land by squatting has been formally recognized since 1850. A squatter acquires a usufruct right (the right to continue using the land) by living on a plot of unclaimed public land and using it "effectively" for at least a year and a day. If these two conditions are met for five years, the squatter acquires ownership of the land, including the right to transfer it to others. A claimant gets title for an amount of land up to three times the amount cleared of forest; the more deforestation the squatter engages in, the larger the amount of land he acquires! In effect deforestation is a necessary step for landless peasants to acquire land.

In the Far East and the United States, perverse incentives take another form. Logging is the major source of deforestation in both regions. Why don't loggers act efficiently? The sources of inefficiency can be found in the concession agreements, which define the terms under which public forests can be harvested.

To loggers, existing forests have a substantial advantage over new forests: They can be harvested immediately. This advantage is reflected in the economic rent (called stumpage value in the industry) associated with a standing forest. In principle governments have a variety of policy instruments at their disposal to extract this rent from the concessionaires, but they have typically given out the concessions to harvest this timber without capturing anywhere near all of the rent.[9] The result is that the cost of harvesting is artificially reduced and loggers can afford to harvest much more forestland than would be efficient. The failure of government to capture this rent also means that the wealth tied up in these forests has typically gone to a few, now wealthy, individuals and corporations rather than to the government to be used for the alleviation of poverty or other worthy social objectives.

Because forest concessions are typically for limited terms, the concession holders have little incentive to replant, to exercise care in their logging procedures, or even to conserve younger trees until they reach the efficient harvest age. The future value of the forest will not be theirs to capture. The resulting logging practices destroy a multiple of the number of trees represented by the high-value species due to the destruction of surrounding species by the construction of access roads, the felling and dragging of the trees, and the elimination of the

---

[8]Much of this land is apparently used to raise beef for export to the United States for use in fast-food hamburgers. For more on the hamburger connection, see J. O. Browder, "The Social Costs of Rain Forest Destruction: A Critique and Analysis of the Hamburger Debate," *InterCiencia* 13, No. 2 (1988): 115–20; and C. Uhl, "Our Steak in the Jungle," *Bioscience* 35 (1986): 642.

[9]One way for the government to capture this rent would be to put timber concessions up for bid. Bidders would have an incentive to pay up to the stumpage value for these concessions. The more competitive the bidding was, the higher the likelihood that the government would capture all of the rent. In practice, many of the concessions have been given to those with influence in the government at far below market rates. See Jeffrey R. Vincent, "Rent Capture and the Feasibility of Tropical Forest Management," *Land Economics* 66, No. 2 (May 1990): 212–23.

protective canopy. Although sustainable forestry would be possible for many of these nations, concession agreements such as these make it unlikely.[10]

The list of losers from inefficient forestry practices frequently includes indigenous peoples who have lived in and derived their livelihood from these forests for a very long time. As the loggers and squatters push deeper and deeper into forests, the indigenous people, who lack the power to stem the tide, are forced to relocate farther and farther away from their traditional lands.

IMPLEMENTING EFFICIENT MANAGEMENT

Does ownership of forest by the government provide an answer? With the large amount of resources at its disposal, plus the ability to acquire land through eminent domain proceedings, the government can achieve the efficient scale rather easily. Furthermore, because it is not obligated to maximize profits, it can more easily take external effects on wildlife or recreation into account. Unfortunately, if the U.S. experience is typical, the potential to solve these problems by public ownership is more illusory than real.

Public ownership of lands in the United States started even before the fledgling nation had a constitution. The first public land, much of it forestland, was accepted as a donation by the Confederation of Congress on 29 October 1782. Though these lands were owned by the government, they were not managed by the government until more than a century later. The forest was treated as common property.

By the second half of the nineteenth century, a number of voices began to decry the apparent wanton destruction of the forests and to call for more enlightened use of the resource. The first piece of legislation designed to respond to this outcry was the Forest Reserve Act of 1891, which authorized the first permanent system of forest reserves. No provision for private harvesting of trees on the forest reserves was included. It was not until 1897, with the passage of a general administration bill, that Congress provided the funds and a process to manage this system. This act authorized private harvesting on forest reserves under other restrictive conditions.

The management for these reserves was transferred in 1905 to the U.S. Department of Agriculture's Forest Service. The Weeks Act, passed in 1911, enabled the Forest Service to acquire new forestland, which ultimately became a major part of the national forests in the eastern part of the United States.

The ambitious chief of the USDA Forest Service at that time, Gifford Pinchot, was to have an enormous influence over Forest Service management for several decades. Unlike other contemporaries such as John Muir, who wanted to withdraw these lands from use, Pinchot vigorously pursued a philosophy that they should be used. Focusing first on timber produc-

---

[10]Currently foresters believe that the sustainable yield for closed tropical rainforests is zero, because they have not yet learned how to regenerate the species in a harvested area. Destroying the thick canopy, thereby allowing the light to penetrate, so changes the growing conditions and the nutrient levels of the soil that even replanting is unlikely to regenerate the types of trees included in the harvest.

TABLE 10.3   Major U.S. Forest Legislation

Date and Citation	Popular Name	Major Provisions
March 3, 1891 26 Stat. 1095	Forest Reserve Act of 1891	Authorized first system of national permanent forest reserves.
June 12, 1960 74 Stat. 215	Multiple Use–Sustained Yield Act	Provided legislative mandate for multiple use of forestlands. No guidance on policy issues or management strategies.
Sept. 3, 1964 78 Stat. 890	The Wilderness Act of 1964	Designated initial areas to be included as wilderness areas and set stringent rules governing use.
Aug. 17, 1974 88 Stat. 476	Forest and Rangeland Renewable Resources Planning Act	A planning act, requiring an assessment of all renewable resources every ten years and a program for the national forests every five years.

tion, his goal was the promotion of a sustainable level of harvest from the national forests. Concern over wildlife and recreation would come much later.

The desire to maintain a sustained level of harvest gave rise to the acceptance of a number of operational procedures by the Forest Service that were explicitly biologically based. Chief among these were the maximum average annual increment described earlier and the requirement to keep the allowable cut on the national forests steady through time to reduce the potential instability that would be faced by private forest owners if the market were flooded with timber from the public lands.

Although the Forest Service had to some extent followed a multiple-use philosophy since its inception, in the period following World War II public interest in nontimber uses grew sufficiently that the rather *ad hoc* methods of the Forest Service for achieving a balance were no longer deemed sufficient. During the 1960s and 1970s, a significant amount of new legislation was passed (Table 10.3).

The Multiple Use–Sustained Yield Act mandated a multiple-use philosophy without giving a lot of guidance on how to implement that philosophy. In part, this act had been sought by the Forest Service to protect its multiple-use philosophy from attack by those seeking congressional or judicial support for single interests. However, subsequent legislation would force the Forest Service to be much more systematic in how it sought to define and implement a multiple-use philosophy.

The Wilderness Act set aside specific forest areas to be preserved in their pristine state. No roads were permitted, and timber harvests were prohibited in wilderness areas. Although initially limited to designating specific areas that had by tradition not been harvested, the act has in fact been the basis of a significant amount of judicial and agency interpretation, with the ultimate effect that it has ushered in much more wilderness land than was envisioned by those discussing it in Congress at the time the bill was passed.

Though the management of public forests in the United States has been evolving since 1782, it has not yet reached the point where it yields efficient outcomes. Harvests from the public forests are subsidized by taxpayers.[11] The benefits of the forests to wildlife and recreation are inadequately protected.[12] Too many political pressures influence the process. Other policy approaches offer the prospect of a more rapid transition to efficiency.

One such approach involves restoring efficient incentives. Concessionaires should pay the full cost for their rights to harvest publicly controlled lands, including compensating for damage to the forests surrounding the trees of interest. The magnitude of land transferred to squatters should not be a multiple of the amount of cleared forest. The rights of indigenous peoples should be respected.

Most of these changes could be implemented by individual nations to protect their own forests, and to do so would be in their interests. By definition, inefficient practices cost more than the benefits received. The move to a more efficient set of policies would necessarily generate more net benefits, which could be shared in ways that build political support for the change. But what about the global inefficiencies? How can those be resolved?

Several economic strategies exist. They share the characteristic that they all involve compensating the nations conferring external benefits so as to encourage conservation actions consistent with global efficiency.

Debt–Nature Swaps.   One strategy involves reducing the pressure on the forests caused by the international debt owed by many developing countries. Private banks hold most of the debt, and they are not typically motivated by a desire to protect biodiversity. Nonetheless, it is possible to find some common ground for negotiating strategies to reduce the debt. Banks realize that complete repayment of the loans is probably not possible. Rather than completely write off the loans, an action that not only causes harm to the income statement but also creates adverse incentives for repayment of future loans, they are willing to consider alternative strategies.

One of the more innovative policies that explores common ground in international arrangements has become known as the debt–nature swap. It is innovative in two senses: (1) the uniqueness of the policy instrument, and (2) the direct involvement of nongovernmental organizations in implementing the policy. A debt–nature swap involves the purchase (at a discounted value in the secondary debt market) of a developing country debt, usually by a nongovernmental environmental organization (NGO). The new holder of the debt, the NGO, offers to cancel the debt in return for an environmentally related action on the part of the debtor nation. In July 1987, for example, an American environmental organization purchased $650,000 worth of Bolivia's foreign debt from a private bank at a discounted price of $100,000.

---

[11]A review of several studies estimating the size of these subsidies can be found in Robert Repetto, *The Forest for the Trees? Government Policies and the Misuse of Forest Resources* (Washington, DC: World Resources Institute, 1988): 90–98.

[12]The below-cost sale of timber to harvesters is usually justified by the Forest Service in terms of the associated public benefits of harvesting (enhanced recreation opportunities and wildlife protection). This argument is difficult to accept because, as Robert Repetto puts it in *The Forest for the Trees? Government Policies and the Misuse of Forest Resources*, " The supposed beneficiaries, including both environmental groups and fish and wildlife agencies in affected states, loudly oppose and are suing the Forest Service to stop it from providing the benefits they are allegedly receiving." (Washington, DC: World Resources Institute, 1988): 97.

It then swapped the face value of the debt with the government of Bolivia in return for an agreement to put together a public–private partnership. This partnership would develop a program that combines ecosystem conservation and regional development planning in 3.7 million acres of designated tropical forestland. The agreement also includes a $250,000 fund in local currency for establishing and administering a system for protecting the forest reserve.

Other arrangements involving different governments and different environmental organizations have since followed this lead. The main advantage of these arrangements to the debtor nation is that a significant foreign exchange obligation can be paid off with domestic currency. Debt–nature swaps offer a realistic possibility to turn what has been a major force for unsustainable economic activity (the debt crisis) into a force for resource conservation.

Extractive Reserves.   One strategy designed to protect the indigenous people of the forest as well as to prevent deforestation involves the establishment of extractive reserves. These areas would be reserved for the indigenous people to engage in their traditional hunting and gathering activities.

Extractive reserves have already been established in the Acre region of Brazil. Acre's main activity comes from the thousands of men who tap the rubber trees scattered throughout the forest, a practice dating back 100 years. Because of the activities of Chico Mendes, a leader of the tappers who was subsequently assassinated, the Brazilian government established four extractive reserves in June 1988 to protect the rubber tappers from encroaching development.

Establishing Conservation Easements.   A common global fund could be established to receive and dispense revenue raised in the industrialized nations for the purpose of protecting biodiversity. Controlled by representatives of these signatory nations, this fund could conceivably dispense monies for acquiring conservation easements for ecologically valuable sites. Conservation easements restrict the activities that can be permitted on the land. In the context of a tropical forest, a conservation easement would allow traditional uses of the forest by indigenous people, but clear-cutting would be prohibited. The easement could be granted in perpetuity or for a very long time.

One specific proposal on how this might be accomplished has been put forward by Katzman and Cale.[13] Five characteristics undergird their proposal:

1.   Tropical nations would establish a legal distinction between conservation easements and other claims of ownership to forests to assure enforceability of the easement.

2.   Industrialized nations would prioritize and evaluate habitats globally to assure that the expended funds achieved the maximum net benefits.

3.   Each tropical nation would establish an offering price for conservation easements on various habitats; in essence they would compete for the limited funds.

4.   Industrialized nations would agree to a budget for the acquisition of easements and for enforcement, and to a means for financing that budget.

---

[13]Martin T. Katzman and William G. Cale, Jr., "Tropical Forest Preservation Using Economic Incentives," *Bioscience* 40, No. 11 (December 1990): 827–32.

EXAMPLE 10.2

Success Stories in Conserving Tropical Forests

It is easy to lose sight of the positive steps that are being taken while concentrating on the problem of tropical deforestation, but some successes are apparent as well. These include

- UNESCO's Man and Biosphere Program, which protects 244 Biosphere Reserves in 65 countries, 59 of them in 29 tropical countries
- Brazil's protected area system, which includes more than 12 million hectares of parks, biological reserves, forest reserves, hunting parks, game farms, and private reserves
- More than 500 conservation areas in Indonesia
- Peru's system of more than 20 parks and other protected areas adding up to more than 4.3 million hectares, with four of the largest conservation areas in tropical forests
- Private reserve systems modeled after those in the developed countries (see Example 3.2) that are now beginning in several developing countries such as Venezuela, Indonesia, and Costa Rica

Source: Laural Tangley, "Saving Tropical Forests," *Bioscience* 36, No. 1 (January 1986): 4–8.

5. A foundation would be established in each tropical nation to administer the financial transfer and to oversee the administration of the easement. (Unlike extractive reserves, where the easement is implicitly held by the tropical state, the conservation easement is granted to a foundation.)

One interesting precedent that shares some, but not all, of the elements of proposal is the World Heritage Convention. This convention established a World Heritage Fund, which is used to protect environments of "outstanding universal value." Each signatory is required to contribute at least 1 percent of its contribution to the regular budget of UNESCO to the fund every two years. In practice this means that the fund is financed almost entirely by the industrial nations, but smaller nations can tap its resources. Some 57 natural sites are currently within this system, 25 of them in the tropics.

Some 90 nations have signed this agreement, suggesting that the fund arrangements have successfully exploited some common interests. Because subscribing to the agreement apparently confers benefits on the signatories, it is essentially self-enforcing. Other groups are pursuing similar objectives (see Example 10.2).

Debt-nature swaps, extractive reserves, and conservation easements all involve a recognition of the fact that resolving the global externalities component of deforestation requires a rather different approach than does resolving the other aspects of the deforestation problem. In general this approach involves financial transfers from the industrialized nations to the tropical nations, transfers that are constructed so as to incorporate global interests into decisions about the future of tropical forests.

SUMMARY

Tree stands typically go through three distinct growth phases—slow growth in volume in the early stage, followed by rapid growth in the middle years and slower growth as the stand reaches full maturity. The owner who harvests the timber receives the income from its sale, but the owner who delays harvest will receive additional growth. The amount of growth depends on the part of the growth cycle the stand is in.

From an economic point of view, the efficient time to harvest a stand of timber is when the net benefits are maximized. The net benefits are maximized when the marginal gain from delaying the harvest one more year is equal to the marginal cost of the delay. For longer-than-efficient delays, the additional costs outweigh the increased benefits, whereas for earlier-than-efficient harvests, more benefits (in terms of the increased value of the timber) are given up than costs are saved. Typically the efficient age at harvest is 25 years or older.

The efficient harvest age depends on the circumstances the owner faces. In general, the larger the discount rate the earlier the harvest. If standing timber provides amenity services (such as for recreation or wildlife management) in proportion to the volume of the standing timber, the efficient rotation will be longer than it would be in the absence of any amenity services.

Profit maximization can be compatible with both efficient and sustainable forest management under the right circumstances, but this is not always so. In particular, profit-maximizing private owners have an incentive to adopt the efficient rotation when amenity services are small and to undertake investments that increase the yield of the forest. Efficient behavior is consistent with sustainability of a particular forest when the growth rate of the forest is larger than the discount rate.

In reality, not all private firms will follow efficient forest management practices because externalities may create inefficient incentives. When amenity values are large and not captured by the forest owner, the private rotation period may fail to consider these values, leading to an inefficiently short rotation period.

Inefficient deforestation has been encouraged by a failure to incorporate global benefits from standing forests; by concession agreements that provide incentives to harvest too much, too soon, and fail to provide adequate incentives to protect the interests of future generations; by land property-right systems that make the amount of land acquired by squatters a multiple of cleared forestland; and by tax systems that discriminate against standing forests.

Substantial strides toward restoring efficiency as well as sustainability can be achieved simply by recognizing and correcting the perverse incentives. Some corrective actions can be and should be taken by the tropical forest nations themselves as they are in their own interests. But these domestic actions will not, by themselves, provide adequate protection for the global interests in the tropical forests. Three schemes designed to internalize some of these benefits—debt–nature swaps, extractive reserves, and conservation easements—have already begun to be implemented.

FURTHER READING

Bowes, Michael D., and John V. Krutilla. "Multiple Use Management of Public Forestlands," in Allen V. Kneese and James L. Sweeney, eds., *Handbook of Natural Resource and Energy Economics* (Amsterdam: North-Holland 1985). Excellent analytical treatment of the multiple-use strategy as it applies to U.S. forest policy. Somewhat mathematical.

Clawson, Marion. *The Federal Lands Revisited* (Washington, DC: Resources for the Future, 1983). A comprehensive overview of current policy issues related to federally owned lands in the United States, including but not limited to national forests.

Clawson, Marion. "Private Forests," in Paul R. Portney, ed., *Current Issues in Natural Resource Policy* (Washington, DC: Resources for the Future, 1982): 283–92. A short summary of the problems of and the prospects for U.S. private forests.

Deacon, R. T. "The Simple Analytics of Forest Economics," in R. T. Deacon and M. B. Johnson, eds., *Forestlands: Public and Private* (San Francisco: Pacific Institute for Public Policy Research, 1985). An especially accessible treatment of forestry economics.

Gregory, G. Robinson. *Resource Economics for Foresters* (Somerset, NJ: John Wiley & Sons, 1987). Undergraduate text in forest economics that could be used to go beyond the material in this chapter.

Irland, Lloyd C. *Wilderness Economics and Policy* (Lexington, MA: Lexington Books, 1979). An overview of wilderness policy in the United States and how economic analysis can contribute to a clearer understanding of the issues.

Price, Colin. *The Theory and Application of Forest Economics* (Oxford: Basil Blackwell, 1989). A text aimed at "students of forestry and of natural resource management at both undergraduate and graduate levels."

Repetto, Robert. *The Forest for the Trees? Government Policies and the Misuse of Forest Resources* (Washington, DC: World Resources Institute, 1988). A highly recommended study of forestry practices in several different countries.

ADDITIONAL REFERENCES

Berck, P. "Optimal Management of Renewable Resources with Growing Demand and Stock Externalities," *Journal of Environmental Economics and Management* 8 (1981): 105–117.

Clawson, Marion. *America's Land and Its Uses* (Washington, DC: Resources for the Future, 1972).

Clawson, Marion. "Decision-Making in Timber Production, Harvest, and Marketing," Research Paper R-4 (Washington, DC: Resources for the Future, 1977).

Clawson, Marion., *Forests for Whom and for What?* (Washington, DC: Resources for the Future, 1975).

Hartman, R. "The Harvesting Decision When a Standing Forest Has Value," *Economic Inquiry* 14 (1976): 52–58.

Hyde, William F. *Timber Supply, Land Allocation, and Economic Efficiency* (Washington, DC: Resources for the Future, 1980).

Johansson, Per-Olov. *Economics of Forestry and Natural Resources* (New York: Basil Blackwell, 1985).

Merrifield, David E., and Richard W. Hayes. "The Adjustment of Product and Factor Markets: An Application to the Pacific Northwest Forest Products Industry," *American Journal of Agricultural Economics* 66, No. 1 (February 1984): 79–87.

Repetto, R. and M. Gillis, eds. *Public Policy and the Misuse of Forest Resources* (Cambridge, UK: Cambridge University Press, 1988).

Samuelson, Paul A. "Economics of Forestry in an Evolving Society," *Economic Inquiry* 14 (1976): 466–92.

DISCUSSION QUESTIONS

1. Should the U.S. national forests become "privatized" (sold to private owners)? Why or why not?
2. In his book *The Federal Lands Revisited*, Marion Clawson proposed what he called the "pullback concept":

> Under the pullback concept any person or group could apply, under applicable law, for a tract of federal land, for any use they chose; but any other person or group would have a limited time between the filing of the initial application and granting other lease or the making of the sale in which to "pull back" a part of the area applied for. . . . The user of the pullback provision would become the applicant for the area pulled back, required to meet the same terms applicable to the original application, . . . but the use could be what the applicant chose, not necessarily the use proposed by the original applicant. [p. 216].

Evaluate the "pullback concept" as a means for conservationists to prevent some mineral extraction or timber harvesting on federal lands.

CHAPTER 11

Wildlife

In an overpopulated (or overexploited) world, a system of the commons leads to ruin. . . . Even if an individual fully perceives the ultimate consequences of his actions he is most unlikely to act in any other way, for he cannot count on the restraint his conscience might dictate being matched by a similar restraint on the part of all others.

GARRETT HARDIN, *CARRYING CAPACITY AS AN ETHICAL CONCEPT* (1967)

INTRODUCTION

Humans share the planet with many other living species. How those biological resources are treated depends on whether they are commercially valuable and the incentives of those who are best positioned to protect those species.

One major threat to wildlife is the destruction of its habitat. It follows that one important means of protecting wildlife is to protect the habitat in which it lives. We have seen in previous chapters how agricultural subsidies can cause excessive conversion of productive habitat to agriculture and how perverse incentives cause the destruction of forested ecosystems. Changing these perverse incentives can serve as a means of protecting wildlife habitat.

Protecting habitat is not enough, however, when the species becomes commercially valuable. Commercially valuable species are like a double-edged sword. On the one hand, the value of the species to humans provides a reason for human concern about its future. On the other hand, commercially exploited biological resources can also be depleted if not managed effectively. If, through human activities, the population is drawn down beyond a critical threshold, even commercially valuable species can become extinct.

Extinction, though important, is not the only critical renewable-resource-management issue. If it were, public policy could concentrate on avoiding extinction and not concern itself with any other outcome. Biological populations belong to a class of renewable resources we will call *interactive resources,* wherein the size of the resource stock (population) is determined jointly by biological considerations and by actions taken by society. The size of the population, in turn, determines the availability of resources for the future. Thus, humanity's actions determine the flow of these resources over time. Because this flow is not purely a natural phenomenon, a second crucial dimension is the optimum rate of use across time and across generations. What is the efficient rate of use of interactive renewable resources? In the absence of outside influences, can the market be relied upon to achieve and sustain this rate?

FIGURE 11.1 The Relationship Between the Fish Stock and Growth

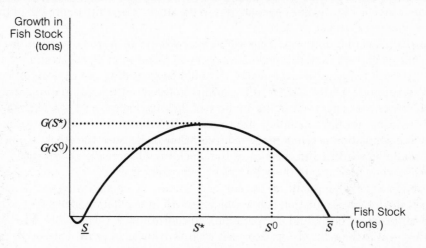

Using the fishery as a case study, we begin by defining what is meant by the efficient level of harvest from a fishery; we can then examine how well our economic and political institutions meet the efficiency test. We then consider how economic incentive systems can be used to assure sustainable harvests. Finally, we examine how another type of commercial opportunity, that associated with ecotourism, can be used for protection of certain specific types of wildlife.

EFFICIENT HARVESTS

The Biological Dimension

Like many other studies, our characterization of the fishery rests on a biological model originally proposed by Schaefer.[1] The Schaefer model posits a particular average relationship between the growth of the fish population and the size of the fish population. This is an average relationship in the sense that it abstracts from such influences as water temperature and the age structure of the population. The model therefore does not attempt to characterize the fishery on a day-to-day basis, but rather in terms of some long-term average in which these various random influences tend to counterbalance each other (Figure 11.1).

The size of the population is represented on the horizontal axis and the growth of the population on the vertical axis. The graph suggests that there is a range of population sizes ($\underline{S}$ to S^*) where population growth increases as the population increases and a range (S^* to $\overline{S}$) where initial increases in population lead to eventual declines in growth.

We can shed further light on this relationship by examining more closely the two points ($\underline{S}$ and $\overline{S}$) where the function intersects the horizontal axis and therefore growth in the stock

---

[1]M. D. Schaefer, "Some Considerations of Population Dynamics and Economics in Relation to the Management of Marine Fisheries," *Journal of the Fisheries Research Board of Canada* XIV (1957): 669–81.

is zero. $\bar{S}$ is known as the *natural equilibrium* because it is the population size that would persist in the absence of outside influences. Reductions in the stock due to mortality or out-migration would be exactly offset by increases in the stock due to births, growth of the fish in the remaining stock, and in-migration.

This natural equilibrium would persist because it is stable. A *stable equilibrium* is one in which movements away from this population level set forces in motion to restore it. If, for example, the stock temporarily exceeded $\bar{S}$, it would be exceeding the capacity of its habitat (called the carrying capacity). As a result, mortality rates or out-migration would increase until the stock was once again within the confines of the carrying capacity of its habitat at $\bar{S}$.

This tendency for the population size to return to $\bar{S}$ works in the other direction as well. Suppose the population is temporarily reduced below $\bar{S}$. Because the stock is now smaller, growth would be positive and the size of the stock would increase. Over time, the fishery would move along the curve to the right until $\bar{S}$ is reached again.

What about the other points on the curve? $\underline{S}$, known as the *minimum viable population*, represents the level of population below which growth in population is negative (deaths and out-migration exceed births and in-migration). In contrast to $\bar{S}$, this equilibrium is unstable. Population sizes to the right of $\underline{S}$ lead to positive growth and a movement along the curve to $\bar{S}$ and away from $\underline{S}$. When the population moves to the left of S, the population declines until it eventually becomes extinct. In this region no forces act to return the population to a viable level.

A catch level is said to represent a *sustainable yield* whenever it equals the growth rate of the population because it can be maintained forever. As long as the population size remains constant, the growth rate (and hence, the catch) will remain constant as well.

S^* is what is known in biology as the *maximum sustainable yield* population, defined as that population size which yields the maximum growth; hence, the maximum sustainable yield is equal to this maximum growth, and it represents the largest catch that can be perpetually sustained. If the catch is equal to the growth, the sustainable yield for any population size (between $\underline{S}$ and $\bar{S}$ can be determined by drawing a vertical line from the stock size of interest on the horizontal axis to the point where it intersects the function and then drawing a horizontal line over to the vertical axis. The sustainable yield is the growth in the biomass defined by the intersection of this line with the vertical axis. Thus, in terms of Figure 11.1, $G(S^0)$ is the sustainable yield for population size S^0. Because the catch is equal to the growth, population size (and next year's growth) remains the same.

It should now be clear why $G(S^*)$ is the maximum sustainable yield. Larger catches would be possible in the short run, but these could not be sustained; they would lead to reduced population sizes and eventually, if the population were drawn down to a level smaller than S, to the extinction of the species.

Static-Efficient Sustained Yield

Is the maximum sustainable yield synonymous with efficiency? The answer is no. Efficiency, it may be remembered, is associated with maximizing the net benefit from the use of the resource. If we are to define the efficient allocation, we must include the costs of harvesting as well as the benefits.

FIGURE 11.2 The Efficient Sustainable Yield for a Fishery

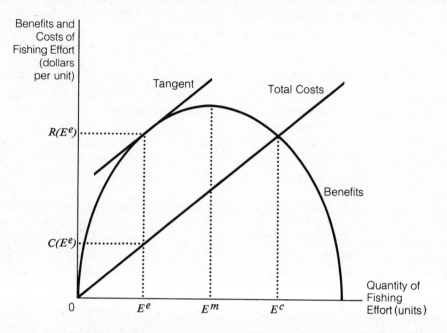

Let's begin by defining the efficient sustainable yield without worrying about discounting. The static-efficient sustainable yield is that catch level which, if maintained perpetually, would produce the largest annual net benefit. We shall refer to this as the *static-efficient* sustainable yield to distinguish it from the *dynamic-efficient* sustainable yield, which incorporates discounting. The initial use of this static concept enables us to fix the necessary relationships firmly in mind before dealing with the more difficult role discounting plays. Subsequently, we shall raise the question of whether or not efficiency always results in a sustainable yield as opposed to a catch that changes over time.

We shall condition our analysis on three assumptions that simplify the analysis without sacrificing too much realism: (1) The price of fish is constant and does not depend on the amount sold; (2) the marginal cost of a unit of fishing effort is constant; and (3) the amount of fish caught per unit of effort expended is proportional to the size of fish population (the smaller the population, the fewer fish caught per unit of effort).

In any sustainable yield, catches, population, effort levels, and net benefits remain constant over time. The static-efficient sustainable yield allocation maximizes the constant net benefit.

In Figure 11.2, the benefits (revenues) and costs are portrayed as a function of fishing effort and can be measured in vessel years, hours of fishing, or some other convenient metric. The shape of the revenue function is dictated by the shape of the function in Figure 11.1 because the price of fish is assumed constant. To avoid confusion, notice that increasing fishing effort in Figure 11.1 would result in smaller population sizes and would be recorded as a movement from right to left. Because the variable on the horizontal axis in Figure 11.2 is effort, not population, an increase in fishing effort is recorded as a movement from left to right.

As sustained levels of effort are increased, eventually a point is reached (E^m) where further effort reduces the sustainable catch and revenue for all years. That point, of course, corresponds to the maximum sustainable yield in Figure 11.2, which involves identical population and growth levels. Every effort level portrayed in Figure 11.2 corresponds to a population level in Figure 11.1.

The net benefit is presented in the diagram as the difference (vertical distance) between benefits (prices times the quantity caught) and costs (the constant marginal cost of effort times the units of effort expended). The efficient level of effort is E^e, that point in Figure 11.2 where the vertical distance between benefits and costs is maximized.

E^e is the efficient level of effort because it is where marginal benefit (which graphically is the slope of the total-benefit curve) is equal to marginal cost (the *constant* slope of the total cost curve). Levels of effort higher than E^e are inefficient because the additional cost associated with them exceeds the value of the fish obtained. Can you see why lower levels of effort are inefficient?

Now we are armed with sufficient information to determine whether or not the maximum sustainable yield is efficient. The answer is clearly no. The maximum sustainable yield is efficient only if the marginal cost of additional effort is zero. Can you see why? (Hint: What is the marginal benefit at the maximum sustainable yield?) Because this is not the case, the efficient level of effort is *less* than that necessary to harvest the maximum sustainable yield. Thus, the static efficient level of effort leads to a *larger* fish population than does the maximum sustainable yield level of effort.

To fix these concepts firmly in mind, consider what would happen to the static efficient sustainable yield if a technological change were to occur (e.g., sonar detection), lowering the marginal cost of fishing. The lower marginal cost would result in a rotation of the total cost curve to the right. With this new cost structure, the old level of effort is no longer efficient. The marginal cost of fishing (slope of the total-cost curve) is now lower than the marginal benefit (slope of the total-benefit curve). Because the marginal cost is constant, the equality of marginal cost and marginal benefit can only result from a decline in marginal benefits. This implies an increase in effort. The new static-efficient sustainable yield equilibrium implies more effort, a lower population level, a larger catch, and a higher net benefit for the fishery.

APPROPRIABILITY AND MARKET SOLUTIONS

We have now defined an efficient allocation of the fishery. The next step is to characterize the normal market allocation and to contrast these two allocations. Where they differ we can entertain the possibility of various public-policy corrective means.

Let's first consider the allocation resulting from a fishery managed by a competitive sole owner. A sole owner would have a well-defined property right to the fish.

A sole owner would want to maximize his or her profits. Ignoring discounting for the moment, the owner can increase profits by increasing fishing effort until marginal revenue equals marginal cost. Clearly this is effort level E^e, the static-efficient sustainable yield. This will yield positive profits equal to the difference between $R(E^e)$ and $C(E^e)$.

In ocean fisheries, however, sole owners are not normal. Ocean fisheries are typically common-property resources—no one exercises complete control over them. Because the property rights to the fishery are not conveyed to any single owner, no single fisherman can keep others from exploiting the fishery. Sometimes common-property resources can coexist in the same market as private-property fisheries (Example 11.1).

What problems arise when access to the fishery is completely unrestricted? Free-access resources create two kinds of externalities: a contemporaneous externality and an intergenerational externality. The contemporaneous externality, which is borne by the current generation, involves the overcommitment of resources to fishing—too many boats, too many fishermen, too much effort. As a result, current fishermen earn a substantially lower rate of return on their efforts. The intergenerational externality, borne by future generations, occurs because overfishing reduces the stock, which in turn lowers future profits from fishing.[2]

Once too many fishermen have unlimited access to the same common-property fishery, the property rights to the fish are no longer efficiently defined. At the efficient level, each boat would receive a profit equal to its share of the scarcity rent. However, this rent serves as a stimulus for new fishermen to enter, drawing up costs and eliminating the rent. Open access results in overexploitation.

The sole owner chooses not to expend more effort than E^e because to do so would reduce the profits of the fishery, resulting in a personal loss. When access to the fishery is unrestricted, a decision to expend effort beyond E^e reduces profits to the fishery as a whole but not to that individual fisherman. Most of the decline in profits falls on the other fishermen.

In a free-access resource, the individual fisherman has an incentive to expend further effort until profits are zero. In Figure 11.2 that point is at effort level E^c, where net benefits are zero. It is now easy to see the contemporaneous externality—too much effort is being expended to catch too few fish, and the cost is substantially higher than it would be in an efficient allocation. If this point seems abstract, it shouldn't. Many fisheries are currently plagued by precisely these kinds of problems.

In a productive fishery in the Bering Sea and Aleutian Islands, for example, one study found significant overcapitalization.[3] Although the efficient number of motherships (used to take on and process the catch at sea so that the catch boats do not have to return to port as often) was estimated to be 9, the current level was 140. As a result, a significant amount of net benefits ($124 million a year) were lost. Had the fishery been harvested more slowly, the same catch could have been achieved with fewer boats used closer to their capacity.

An intergenerational externality occurs because the size of the population is reduced, causing future profits to be lower than would otherwise be the case. As the existing population is overexploited, the free-access catch initially would be higher, but as growth rates are affected, the steady-state profit level, once attained, would be lower.

When the resource owner has exclusive property rights, the use value of the resource is balanced against the asset value. When access to the resource is unrestricted, exclusivity is lost. As a result, it is rational for the individual fisherman to ignore the asset value, because he

---

[2]This will result in fewer fish for future generations as well as smaller profits if the resulting effort level exceeds that associated with the maximum sustainable yield. If the common-property effort level is lower than the maximum-sustainable-yield effort level (when extraction costs are very high), then reductions in stock would increase the growth in the stock, thus supplying more fish (albeit lower net benefits) to future generations.

[3]Daniel D. Huppert, "Managing Alaska's Groundfish Fisheries: History and Prospects," Working Paper (University of Washington Institute for Marine Resources, 1990).

E X A M P L E   1 1 . 1

Property Rights and Fisheries: Oysters

The oyster industry provides a unique opportunity to study the effect of property-right structures on incentives because it contains both private-property and common-property oyster beds. In some cases these private-property and common-property beds compete with each other in the same market. This allows us to compare the price and quantity behavior of markets supplied by fishermen operating under both property-right systems to markets that depend solely on one or the other.

What would we expect to find?

1. Common-property resources should be harvested earlier in the season because there is less incentive to conserve common-property resources.

2. Common-property fishermen should earn lower average incomes because the economic rent is dissipated.

3. The markets served purely by private-property fisheries should have higher prices because private-property fishermen can respond to market conditions whereas common-property fishermen are driven to catch and sell as many fish as early as possible.

What was revealed by examining data from Maryland, Virginia, Louisiana, and Mississippi?

1. From 1945 to 1970 the ratio of the harvest in the earlier part of the harvesting season to the later part was 1.35 for the common-property resource state (Maryland) and 1.01 for the contiguous private-property state (Virginia).

2. The average annual incomes over the period 1950–1969 of fishermen in Virginia was $2,453, whereas that for Maryland was $1,606. Another comparison revealed that fishermen in the private-property state of Louisiana earned $3,207, whereas their counterparts in the contiguous common-property state of Mississippi earned $870.

3. Over the period 1966–1969, the mean price per pound of oysters in markets served purely by private oyster beds was $.94, whereas the mean price per pound for oysters from the common-property resource averaged only $.73 per pound. In addition, in a comparison of contiguous private- and common-property states, the private-property states all experienced higher prices.

Though these results do not come from carefully controlled experiments and therefore cannot be regarded as definitive, they are completely compatible with our understanding of the way in which property-right structures influence decisions.

Source: Richard J. Agnello and Lawrence P. Donnelly, "Prices and Property Rights in the Fisheries," *Southern Economic Journal* XL (October 1979): 253–62.

can never appropriate it, and simply maximize the use value. In the process, all the scarcity rent is dissipated. The allocation that results from allowing unrestricted access to the fishery

EXAMPLE 11.2

Harbor Gangs of Maine

Because free access to common-property resources reduces net benefits so drastically, this loss encourages those harvesting the resource to restrict access if possible. The Maine lobster fishery is one setting where informal arrangements have served to limit access.

Key among these arrangements is a system of territories that establishes boundaries between fishing areas. Particularly near the offshore islands, these territories tend to be exclusively harvested by close-knit, disciplined gangs. These gangs restrict access to their territory by various covert means such as cutting the lines to lobster traps owned by new entrants, rendering them unretrievable. The income and catch levels achieved by the members of these gangs exceed those for comparable gangs lobstering less-exclusive territories.

Although it would be a mistake to assume that all common-property resources are characterized by unlimited access, it would also be a mistake to assume that these informal arrangements automatically provide sufficient social means for producing efficient harvests, thereby eliminating any need for public policy. The Maine lobster stock is also protected by regulations limiting the size of lobsters that can be taken and prohibiting the harvest of bearing females. Because estimates suggest that over 95 percent of legally harvestable lobsters are in fact harvested, these regulations apparently afford significant protection to the stock. The main role for the informal arrangements has been to prevent the overcapitalization problem. When fewer fishermen harvest the available yield, income levels for those fishermen are higher.

Source: James M. Acheson, *The Lobster Gangs of Maine* (Hanover, NH: University Press of New England, 1988).

---

is identical to that resulting from a dynamic-efficient sustainable yield when an infinite discount rate is used.

Free-access resources do not automatically lead to a stock lower than that maximizing the sustained yield. We can draw a cost function with a slope sufficiently steep that it intersects the benefit curve at a point to the left of E^m. Nonetheless, it is not unusual for mature free-access common-property fisheries to be exploited well beyond the point of maximum sustainable yield.

Are free-access resources and common-property resources synonymous concepts? They are not. On the one hand, governments can restrict entry, a topic we shall address in the next section. On the other hand, informal arrangements among those harvesting the common-property resource can also serve to limit access[4] (see Example 11.2).

Common-property resources generally violate both the efficiency and sustainability criteria. If these criteria are to be fulfilled, some restructuring of the decision-making environment is necessary. How that could be done is the subject of the next section.

---

[4]For other examples of these arrangements, see F. Berkes, D. Feeny, B. J. McCay, and J. M. Acheson, "The Benefits of the Commons," *Nature* 340, No. 6229 (July 1989): 91–93.

PUBLIC POLICY TOWARD FISHERIES

What can be done? A variety of public-policy responses are possible. Perhaps it is appropriate to start with allowing the market to work.

Aquaculture

Having demonstrated that inefficient management of the fishery results from treating it as common, rather than private, property, we have one obvious solution—allowing some fisheries to be privately, rather than commonly, held. This approach can work when the fish are not very mobile (such as lobsters), when they can be confined by artificial barriers, or when they instinctively return to their place of birth to spawn.

The advantages of such a move go well beyond the ability to preclude overfishing. The owner is encouraged to invest in the resource and undertake measures that will increase the productivity (yield) of the fishery.[5] This movement toward controlled raising and harvesting of fish is called *aquaculture,* and there are some noteworthy examples of success.[6] Probably the highest yields ever attained through aquaculture resulted from using rafts to raise mussels. Some 300,000 kg/hectare of mussels, for example, have been raised in this manner in the Galician bays of Spain.[7] This productivity level approximates those achieved in poultry farming, widely regarded as one of the most successful attempts to increase the productivity of farm-produced animal protein.

In the United States aquaculture has been thwarted by treating bodies of water as common property. This need not be the case, of course. In Example 11.1 we saw that some oysters are raised in the United States in common-property beds and others are raised in private beds. As fish in the common-property resource become more scarce, triggering price increases, aquaculture probably would become more profitable and prevalent.

In some ways Japan, as a densely populated country depending heavily on fish for protein, has reached the point where merely harvesting what the sea offers is no longer sufficient to satisfy the market at low cost. Consequently, Japan has become a leader in aquaculture, undertaking some of the most advanced aquaculture ventures in the world. The government there has been supportive, mainly by creating private-property rights for waters formerly held commonly. The prefecture governments (comparable to states in the United States) initiate the process by designating the areas to be used for aquaculture. The local fishermen's cooperative associations then partition these areas and allocate the subareas to individual fishermen for exclusive use. This exclusive control allows the owner to invest in the resource and to manage it effectively and efficiently.

Another market approach to aquaculture involves fish ranching rather than fish farming.[8] Whereas fish farming involves cultivating fish over their lifetime in a controlled environment, fish ranching involves holding them in captivity only for the first few years of their lives.

---

[5]For example, adding certain nutrients to the water or controlling the temperature can markedly increase the yields of some species.

[6]The examples of aquaculture in this chapter are drawn from John E. Bardach, John H. Ryther, and William O. McClarney, *Aquaculture: The Farming and Husbandry of Freshwater and Marine Organisms* (New York: Wiley Interscience, 1972).

[7]A hectare is a measure of surface area equal to 10,000 square meters or 2.471 acres.

[8]See L. Stokes, "The Economics of Salmon Ranching," *Land Economics* 58, No. 4 (November 1982): 464–77.

Fish ranching relies on the strong homing instincts in certain fish such as Pacific salmon or ocean trout to permit their ultimate capture. The young salmon or ocean trout are hatched and confined in a convenient catch area for approximately two years. When released they migrate to the ocean. Upon reaching maturity, they return by instinct to the place of their births where they are harvested. Brown estimates that 193,000 metric tons of salmon were harvested by the United States, the Soviet Union, and Japan in 1984.[9]

Aquaculture is certainly not the answer for all fish. Although it works well for shellfish, catfish, salmon, and some other species, some fish, such as tuna, will probably never be harvested domestically at a profit. Nonetheless, it is comforting to note that aquaculture can provide a safety valve in some regions and for some fish.[10]

Raising the Real Cost of Fishing

Perhaps one of the best ways to illustrate the virtues of using economic analysis to help design policies is to show the harsh effects of policy approaches that ignore it. Because the earliest approaches to fishery management had a single-minded focus on attaining the maximum sustainable yield with little or no thought given to maximizing the net benefit, they provide a useful contrast.

Perhaps the best concrete example is the set of policies originally designed to deal with overexploitation of the Pacific salmon fishery in the United States.[11] The Pacific salmon is particularly vulnerable to overexploitation, and even extinction, because of its migration patterns. Pacific salmon are spawned in the gravel beds of rivers. As juvenile fish they migrate to the ocean, only to return as adults to spawn in the rivers of their birth. After spawning, they die. When the adults swim upstream with an instinctual need to return to their native streams, they can easily be captured by traps, nets, or other catching devices.

Recognizing the urgency of the problem, the government took action. To reduce the catch, it raised the cost of fishing. Initially this was accomplished by preventing the use of any barricades on the rivers and by prohibiting the use of traps (the most efficient catching devices) in the most productive areas. These measures proved insufficient because mobile techniques (trolling, nets, and so on) proved quite capable, by themselves, of overexploiting the resource. Officials then began to close designated fishing areas and suspend fishing in other areas for certain periods of time. In Figure 11.3 these measures would be reflected as a rotation of the cost curve to the left until it intersected the benefits curve at a level of effort equal to E^e. The aggregate of all these regulations had the desired effect of curtailing the yield of salmon.

Were these policies efficient? They were not and would not have been even had they resulted in the efficient catch! This statement may seem inconsistent, but it is not. Efficiency

---

[9]Brown, Lester R., "Maintaining World Fisheries," in *State of the World: 1985,* Lester Brown et al. (New York: W. W. Norton, 1985): 90.

[10]In another example, Frederick Bell shows that the social welfare losses from the overexploitation of common-property wild crawfish were reduced by an estimated $1,068,933 in 1978 by the existence of private-property crawfish farms. Without them social welfare losses would have been 4.16 times greater. See Frederick W. Bell, "Mitigating the Tragedy of the Commons," *Southern Economic Journal* 52, No. 3 (January 1986): 653–64.

[11]An excellent, detailed analysis of these policies can be found in J. A. Crutchfield and G. Pontecovo, *The Pacific Salmon Fisheries: A Study of Irrational Conservation* (Baltimore, MD: Johns Hopkins University Press for Resources for the Future, 1969).

FIGURE 11.3 The Effect of Regulation

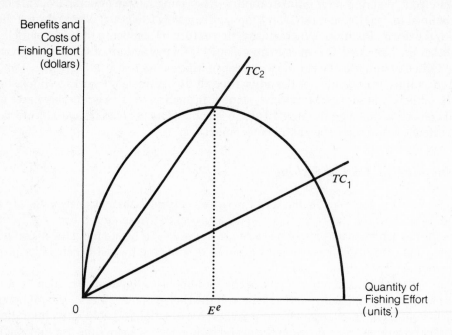

implies both that the catch must be at the efficient level and that it must also be extracted at the lowest possible cost. This latter condition was violated by these policies (see Figure 11.3).

In Figure 11.3 are reflected the total cost in an efficient allocation (TC_1) and the total cost after these policies were imposed (TC_2). The net benefit received from an efficient policy is shown graphically as the vertical distance between total cost and total benefit. After the policy, however, the net benefit was reduced to zero; the net benefit (represented by vertical distance) was lost to society. Why?

The net benefit was wasted due to the use of excessively expensive means to catch the desired yield of fish. Traps would reduce the cost of catching the desired number of fish, but traps were prohibited, so larger expenditures on capital and labor were required to catch the same number of fish. This additional capital and labor represents one source of the waste.

The limitations on fishing times and fishing areas had a similar effect on cost. Rather than being allowed to fish those areas and times where capital and labor would be most productively applied (while insuring that the target yields were not exceeded), fishermen were forced to use less productive areas and times. The additional time, energy, and equipment were also wasted resources.

Regulation imposed other costs as well. It was soon discovered that although the preceding regulations were adequate to protect the depletion of the fish population, they had no effect on the incentive for individual fishermen to increase their share of the take. Even though the profits would be small because of high costs, new technological change would allow adopters to increase their share of the market and put others out of business. To protect themselves, the fishermen were successful in introducing bans on new technology. These restrictions took various forms, but two seem particularly noteworthy. The first was the banning of the use of thin-stranded, monofilament net. The course-stranded net it would have replaced was visible to the salmon in the daytime and therefore could be avoided by them. As a result, it was useful only at night. By contrast, the thinner monofilament nets could be successfully used during the daylight hours as well. The monofilament nets were banned in both Canada and the United States soon after they appeared.

The most flagrantly inefficient regulation was one in Alaska that barred gill-netters in Bristol Bay from using engines to propel their boats. This regulation lasted until the 1950s and heightened the public's awareness of the anachronistic nature of this regulatory approach. The world's most technologically advanced nation was reaping its harvest from the Bering Sea in sailboats while the rest of the world—particularly Japan and the Soviet Union—was modernizing its fishing fleets at a torrid pace!

Time-restriction regulations had a similar effect. Limiting fishing time provides an incentive to use that time as intensively as possible. Huge boats facilitate large harvests within the period and therefore are attractive, but they are very inefficient: The same harvest could have been achieved with fewer, smaller boats used to their optimum capacity.

Guided by a narrow focus on the maximum sustainable yield that ignored costs, these policies led to a substantial loss in the net benefit received from the fishery. Costs are an important dimension of the problem: When they are ignored, the incomes of fishermen suffer. When incomes suffer, further conservation measures become more difficult to implement and incentives to violate the regulations are intensified.

Taxes

Is it possible to provide incentives for cost reduction while assuring that the yield is reduced to the efficient level? Can a more efficient policy be devised? Economists who have studied the question believe that more efficient policies are possible.

Consider a tax on effort. In Figure 11.3 taxes on effort would also be represented as a rotation of the TC line, and the after-tax cost to the fishermen would be adequately represented by line TC_2. Because the after-tax curve coincides with TC_2, the cost curve for all those inefficient regulations, doesn't this imply that the tax system is just as inefficient? No! The key to understanding the difference is the distinction between *transfer costs* and *real-resource costs.*

Under a regulation system of the type described earlier in this chapter, all of the costs included in TC_2 are real-resource costs, which involve utilization of resources. Transfer costs, by contrast, involve transfers of resources (from one part of society to another) rather than their use. Transfer costs apply to that part of society bearing them but are exactly offset by the gain received by the recipients. Resources are not used up; they are merely transferred. Thus, the calculation of the size of the net benefit should subtract real-resource costs, but not transfer costs, from benefits. For society as a whole, transfer costs are retained as part of the net benefit.

In Figure 11.3 the net benefit under a tax system is identical to that under an efficient allocation. The net benefit represents a transfer cost to the fisherman that is exactly offset by the revenues, received by the tax collector. This discussion should not obscure the fact that, as far as the individual fisherman is concerned, these are very real costs. Rent normally received by a sole owner is now received by the government. Because the tax revenues involved can be substantial (Example 11.3), fishermen wishing to have the fishery efficiently managed may object to this particular way of doing it. They would prefer a policy that restricts catches while allowing them to keep the rents. Is that possible?

Efficient versus Market Exploitation of Lobsters

Two economists, Henderson and Tugwell [1979], set out to quantify the degree of overexploitation characterizing two particular Maritime Canadian common-property lobster fishing ports: Port Maitland and Miminegash. They estimated the relationship between effort and sustainable catch for each of the two fishing grounds and also the costs of various levels of fishing effort. Using these functions, they derived both the optimal and free-market solutions, which could then be compared to each other and to the maximum sustainable yield. These calculations could also be used to derive the tax required to force the market solution to converge to the efficient solution.

	Port Maitland			Miminegash		
		Actual			Actual	
	Optimal Solution	Free Entry	Average 1959–63	Optimal Solution	Free Entry	Average 1959–63
Lobster stock (1000 lb.)	3,050	2,490	2,467	2,450	1,125	1,273
Lobster catch (1000 lb.)	745	1,330	1,183	801	936	1,094
Effort (100 traps)	112	454	—	122	365	—
Ratio: catch/stock	0.25	0.53	0.48	0.33	0.83	0.86
Optimal tax/1000 lb. catch	270	NA	NA	255	NA	NA
Annual resource savings: value of trap savings less value of reduced catch	$202,173	NA	NA	$180,470	NA	NA

	Port Maitland	Miminegash
Maximum sustainable yield stock	1,766	1,629
Lobster price/1000 lb	$485	$370
Opportunity cost/100 traps	$1,421	$950

Several features are noteworthy in these tables. The "free-entry" or market solutions for catch are remarkably close to the actual averages in spite of the uncertainty of estimating the underlying equations. The "free entry" catch levels are substantially greater than the optimal levels due to an inefficiently high level of effort (traps). The last entries in the first table indicate that the welfare losses (compared to the optimum level) run about $202,000 in Port Maitland and $180,000 in Miminegash *each year.* For Port Maitland this represents a loss of some 62 percent of the net benefits obtainable under an efficient program!

The first table also presents the optimum tax level that would cause the free access and optimum to converge. For Port Maitland this amounts to $270 per thousand pounds of lobster, approximately 56 percent of the current price ($485). If this tax were levied, some fishermen would exit and the catch would rise, but the remaining fishermen would not have received higher profits. The increased net benefits would be appropriated by the government. It is not difficult to understand why fishermen do not generally support tax policies, even though these policies could prevent overexploitation.

Source: J. V. Henderson and M. Tugwell, "Exploitation of the Lobster Fishery: Some Empirical Results," *Journal of Environmental Economics and Management* VI (December 1979): 287–96.

Individual Transferable Quotas

One policy making it possible is a properly designed quota on the number of fish that can be taken from the fishery. The "properly designed" caveat is important because there are many different types of quota schemes and not all are of equal merit. An efficient quota system has several identifiable characteristics:

1. The quotas entitle the holder to catch a specified weight of a specified type of fish.
2. The total amount of fish authorized by the quotas held by all fishermen should be equal to the efficient catch for the fishery.
3. The quotas should be freely transferable among fishermen.

Each of these three characteristics plays an important role in obtaining an efficient allocation. Suppose, for example, the quota were defined in terms of the right to own and use a fishing boat rather than in terms of catch—not an uncommon type of quota. Such a quota is not efficient, because under this type of quota an inefficient incentive still remains for each boat owner to build larger boats, to place extra equipment on them, and to spend more time fishing. These actions would expand the capacity of each boat and cause the actual catch to exceed the target (efficient) catch. In a nutshell, the boat quota limits the number of boats fishing but does not limit the amount of fish caught by each boat. If we are to reach and sustain an efficient allocation, it is the catch which must ultimately be limited.

Although the purpose of the second condition is obvious, the role of transferability deserves more consideration. With transferability, the entitlement to fish flows naturally to those gaining the most benefit from it because their costs are lower. Because it is valuable, the transferable quota commands a positive price. Those who have quotas but also have high costs find they make more money selling the quotas than using them. Meanwhile, those who have lower costs find they can purchase more quotas and still make money.

Transferable quotas also encourage technological progress. Adopters of new cost-reducing technologies can make more money on their existing quotas and make it profitable to purchase new quotas from others who have not adopted the technology.

Therefore, in marked contrast to the earlier regulatory methods used to raise costs, both the tax system and the transferable quota system encourage low extraction rates.

How about the distribution of the rent? In a quota system the distribution of the rent depends crucially on how the quotas are initially allocated. There are many possibilities with different outcomes. The first possibility is for the government to auction these quotas off. But the government would then appropriate all the rent and the outcome would be very similar to the outcome of the tax system. If the fishermen do not like the tax system, they would not like the auction system either.

In an alternative approach, the government could give the quotas to the fishermen, say in proportion to their historical catch. The fishermen could then trade among themselves until a market equilibrium is reached. All the rent would be retained only by the *current* generation of fishermen. Fishermen who might want to enter the market would have to purchase the quotas from existing fishermen. Competition among the potential purchasers would drive up the price of the transferable quotas until it reflected the market value of future rents, appropriately discounted.[12]

Thus this type of quota system allows the rent to remain with the fishermen, but only the current generation of fishermen. Future generations see little difference between this quota system and a tax system; in either case, they have to pay to enter the industry, whether it be through the tax system or by purchasing the quotas.

In 1983 a limited individual transferable quota system was established in New Zealand to protect its deepwater trawl fishery.[13] Because this fishery was newly developed, allocating the quotas proved relatively easy. The total allowable catches for the seven basic species were divided into individual transferable quotas and were allocated to existing firms on the basis of investment in harvesting equipment, investment in onshore production equipment, and recent onshore production. The rights to harvest were denominated in terms of a specific amount of fish but were only granted for a ten-year period.

At the same time the deep-sea fishery policy was being considered, the inshore fishery began to fall on hard times. Too many participants were chasing too many fish. Some particularly desirable fish species were being seriously overfished. Although the need to reduce the amount of pressure being put on the population was rather obvious, how to accomplish that reduction was not at all obvious. It was relatively easy to prevent new fishermen from entering the fisheries, but it was harder to figure out how to reduce the pressure from those who had been fishing in the area for years or even decades. Because fishing is characterized by economies of scale, simply reducing everyone's catch proportionately wouldn't make much sense. That would simply place higher costs on everyone and waste a great deal of fishing capacity as all boats sat around idle for a significant proportion of time. A better solution would clearly be to have fewer boats harvesting the stock. That way, each boat could be used closer to its full capacity without depleting the population. Which fisherman should be asked to give up their livelihood and leave the industry?

The economic incentive approach addressed this problem by imposing an annual fee on fishermen for their catch quotas. The revenues derived from this fee were used to buy out fishermen who were willing to forgo any future fishing for the species in jeopardy. Essentially, each fisherman stated the lowest price that he or she would accept for leaving the industry; the regulators selected those who could be induced to leave at the lowest price, paid the stipulated amount from the tax revenues, and retired their licenses to fish for this species. It wasn't long before a sufficient number of licenses had been retired and the population was protected. Because the program was voluntary, those who left the industry only did so when they felt they had been adequately compensated. Meanwhile, those who paid the fee realized that this small investment would benefit them greatly in the future as the population recovered. A dif-

---

[12]This occurs because the maximum bid any potential entrant would make is the value to be derived from owning that permit. This value is equal to the present value of future rents (the difference between price and marginal cost for each unit of fish sold). Competition will force the purchaser to bid near that maximum value, lest he or she lose the quota.

[13]Lee G. Anderson, "Property Rights in Fisheries: Lessons from the New Zealand Experience," Working Paper No. 89-22 (Bozeman, MT: Political Economy Research Center, 1989).

ficult and potentially dangerous pressure on a valuable natural resource had been avoided by the creative use of an approach that changed the economic incentives.[14]

The 200-Mile Limit

The final policy dimension concerns the international aspects of the fishery problem. Obviously the various policy approaches to effective management of fisheries requires some governing body to have jurisdiction over a fishery so that it can enforce its regulations.

This is not currently the case for many of the ocean fisheries. Much of the open water of the oceans is a common-property resource to governments as well as to individual fishermen. Therefore, no single body can exercise control over it. As long as that continues to be the case, the corrective action will be difficult to implement. In recognition of this fact there is an evolving law of the sea defined by international treaties. One of the concrete results of this law has been some limited restrictions on whaling. Whether or not this process ultimately yields a consistent and comprehensive system of management remains to be seen.

Countries bordering the sea have declared that their ownership rights extend some 200 miles out to sea. Within these areas, the countries have exclusive jurisdiction and can proceed to implement effective management policies. These declarations have been upheld and are now firmly entrenched in international law. Thus, very rich fisheries in coastal waters can be protected while those in the open waters await the outcome of an international negotiations process.

EXTENSIONS TO OTHER SPECIES

Space does not permit a detailed treatment of other biological populations, but it is important to demonstrate that at least some of the principles derived from a close examination of both fisheries management and forest management are transferable to other species. In particular, rearranging economic incentives can be a key to restoring efficient, sustainable management.

A rather different use of economic incentives is at work in Africa protecting the elephant herds in Zimbabwe.[15] African elephants have long been treated as common property. As might be expected, elephant populations are being threatened, but different African countries are having rather different experiences.

The elephant populations of Zimbabwe, Botswana, Namibia, and South Africa are increasing, whereas those in Kenya are decreasing. These Southern African countries all support conservation through utilization, allowing safari hunting and tourism on private, state, and communal lands, but limiting access. Hunting rights are severely limited and are granted to

---

[14]This concept is spreading to other fisheries. In the United States, for example, the Mid-Atlantic Fishery Management Council has applied it to the Atlantic surf clam and ocean quahog fishery. See Amendment #8, Fishery Management Plan for the Atlantic Surf Clam and Ocean Quahog Fishery (Dover, DE: Mid-Atlantic Fishery Management Council, 1989).

[15]Randy T. Simmons and Urs P. Keuter, "Herd Mentality: Banning Ivory Sales is No Way to Save the Elephant," *Policy Review* 50 (Fall 1989): 46–49.

local communities of indigenous peoples. Because many safaris hunt with cameras, tourism can be an additional source of income without killing elephants. When animals (such as rogue elephants) are eliminated by National Parks personnel, the ivory and hides of these animals belong to the members of the local communities.

Tourism and the sale of both hunting rights and elephant products provide a significant source of income to local communities. Two dozen peasant villages in Zimbabwe earned $5 million from safari owners in 1990 by selling elephant hunting rights on their communal lands. Giving local communities a large stake in herd preservation also facilitates strict enforcement of poaching laws. Poachers are shot on sight.

Kenya, a country with large declines in its elephant population, has no such system. Whereas in Zimbabwe villagers have a very large stake in protecting the source of this income, the elephant herd, Kenyans have little stake in their protection. The potential revenue that could be used to institutionalize a protection system is enormous. Economists have estimated that some $25 million per year would be available in Kenya from tourists seeking to view and photograph elephants.[16]

One approach to the protection of biological species is to rearrange the economic incentives so that local groups have an economic interest in their preservation. Unlimited access to common-property resources undermines those incentives.

SUMMARY

Unrestricted access to commercially valuable species will generally result in overexploitation. In the case of fisheries characterized by particularly low extraction costs (the Pacific-salmon fishery), extinction is a definite possibility in the absence of outside control. Where extraction costs are higher, extinction is unlikely even with unrestricted access.

Both the private and public sectors have moved to ameliorate the problems associated with past mismanagement of wildlife populations. The reassertion of private-property rights in Japan and other countries has stimulated the development of aquaculture. Governments in Canada and the United States have moved to limit overexploitation of the Pacific salmon. International agreements have been reached to place limits on whaling. It is doubtful that these programs fully satisfy the efficiency criterion, although it does seem clear that sustainable catches will result.

An increasing reliance on individual transferable quotas, as evidenced in both New Zealand and the United States, offers the chance to preserve stocks without jeopardizing the incomes of those men and women currently harvesting fish from the sea. Approaches to the preservation of elephants that give local communities a stake in herd preservation similarly recognize the necessity of building political coalitions to support conservation. Creative strategies for sharing the gains from moving to an efficient level of use could prove to be a significant weapon in the arsenal of techniques designed to protect biological resources from overexploitation.

---

[16]Gardner Brown Jr. and Wes Henry, "The Economic Value of Elephants," Working Paper No. 89-12 (London Environmental Economics Centre, 1989).

It would be folly to ignore barriers to further action, such as the reluctance of individual fishermen to submit to many forms of regulation, the lack of a firm policy governing open ocean waters, and the difficulties of enforcing various approaches. Whether these barriers will fall before the pressing need for effective management remains to be seen.

FURTHER READING

Anderson, Lee G. *The Economics of Fisheries Management* (Baltimore, MD: Johns Hopkins University Press, 1977). A highly recommended text for those wishing to go into the material in this chapter in greater depth.

Bell, Frederick W. *Food From the Sea: The Economics and Politics of Ocean Fisheries* (Boulder, CO: Westview Press, 1978). A comprehensive and comprehensible treatment of the actual and potential management of fisheries by an academic economist who was previously chief of economic research for the National Marine Fisheries Service, U.S. Department of Commerce. Full examples of actual regulation.

Clark, Colin. *Mathematical Bioeconomics: The Optimal Management of Renewable Resources* (New York: Wiley Interscience, 1976). Accessible only to those with strong undergraduate backgrounds in math, this is an excellent introduction to the use of mathematics to formulate optimal management policies. Focused almost entirely on fisheries.

ADDITIONAL REFERENCES

Campbell, H. F., and R. K. Lindner. "The Production of Fishing Effort and the Economic Performance of License Limitation Programs," *Land Economics* 66, No. 1 (February 1990): 56–66.

Clark, C. W. "Profit Maximization and the Extinction of Animal Species," *Journal of Political Economy* 81 (August 1973): 950–60.

Crutchfield, J. A., and G. Pontecovo. *The Pacific Salmon Fisheries: A Study of Irrational Conservation* (Baltimore, MD: Johns Hopkins University Press, for Resources for the Future, 1969).

Dupont, Diane P. "Rent Dissipation in Restricted Access Fisheries," *Journal of Environmental Economics and Management* 19, No. 1 (July 1990): 26–44.

Gallastegui, Carmen. "An Economic Analysis of Sardine Fishing in the Gulf of Valencia (Spain)," *Journal of Environmental Economics and Management* 10 (June 1983): 138–50.

Henderson, J. V., and M. Tugwell. "Exploitation of the Lobster Fishery: Some Empirical Results," *Journal of Environmental Economics and Management* VI (December 1979): 287–96.

Munro, G. R. "Fisheries, Extended Jurisdiction, and the Economics of Common Property Resources," *Canadian Journal of Economics* 15 (August 1982): 405–25.

Stokes, R. L. "The Economics of Salmon Ranching," *Land Economics* 58 (November 1982): 464–77.

Swanson, Timothy M. "International Regulation of the Ivory Trade," Working Paper No. 89-04 (London Environmental Economics Centre, 1989).

DISCUSSION QUESTIONS

1. Is the establishment of the 200-mile limit a sufficient form of government intervention to ensure that the tragedy of the commons does not occur for fisheries within the 200-mile limit? Why or why not?
2. With discounting it is possible for the efficient fish population to fall below the level required to produce the maximum sustained yield. Does this violate the sustainability criterion? Why or why not?

CHAPTER 12

Environmental Economics: An Overview

Democracy is not a matter of sentiment, but of foresight. Any system that doesn't take the long run into account will burn itself out in the short run.

CHARLES YOST, *THE AGE OF TRIUMPH AND FRUSTRATION*

INTRODUCTION

In the last few chapters we have dealt extensively with achieving a balanced set of mass and energy flows; it now remains to discuss how a balance can be achieved in the reverse flow of waste products back to the environment. Because the waste flows are inexorably intertwined with the flow of mass and energy into the economy, establishing a balance for waste flows will have feedback effects on the input flows as well.

Two questions must be addressed: (1) What is the appropriate level of waste flow? (2) How should the responsibility for achieving this flow level be allocated among the various sources of the pollutant when reductions are needed?

In this chapter we shall lay the foundation for understanding the policy approach to controlling pollution. We define efficient and cost-effective levels of control for a variety of pollutant types, compare these control levels with those achieved by market forces, and demonstrate how these insights can be used to design desirable policy responses. This overview is then followed by a series of chapters that show how these principles have been applied to the design of pollution-control policies in various countries around the world.

A POLLUTANT TAXONOMY

The amount of waste products emitted determines the load upon the environment. The damage done by this load depends on the capacity of the environment to assimilate the waste products (Figure 12.1). We shall refer to this ability of the environment to absorb pollutants

FIGURE 12.1 The Relationship Between Emissions and Pollution Damage

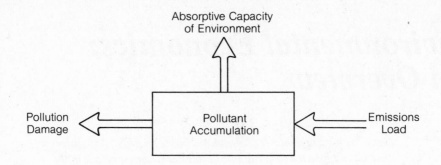

as its *absorptive capacity*. If the emissions load exceeds the absorptive capacity, then the pollutant accumulates in the environment.

Pollutants for which the environment has little or no absorptive capacity are called *stock pollutants*. Stock pollutants accumulate over time as emissions enter the environment. Examples of stock pollutants include nonbiodegradable bottles tossed by the roadside; heavy metals, such as lead, which accumulate in the soils near the emission source; and persistent synthetic chemicals such as dioxin and PCBs (polychlorinated biphenyls).

Pollutants for which the environment has some absorptive capacity are called *fund pollutants*. As long as the emission rate does not exceed the absorptive capacity of the environment, these pollutants do not accumulate. Examples of fund pollutants are easy to find. Many organic pollutants injected into an oxygen-rich stream will be transformed by the resident bacteria into less-harmful inorganic matter. Carbon dioxide is absorbed by plant life and the oceans.

The point is *not* that the mass is destroyed: The law of conservation of mass suggests this cannot be the case. Rather, when fund pollutants are injected into the air or water, they may be transformed into substances that are not considered harmful to people or to the ecological system, or they may be so diluted or dispersed that the resulting concentrations are not harmful.

Pollutants can also be classified by their zone of influence, defined both horizontally and vertically. The horizontal dimension deals with the domain over which damage from an emitted pollutant is experienced. The damage caused by *local* pollutants is experienced near the source of emission, whereas the damage from *regional* pollutants is experienced at greater distances from the source of emission. The local and regional categories are not mutually exclusive; it is possible for a pollutant to be both. Sulfur oxides and nitrogen oxides, for example, are both local and regional pollutants.

The vertical zone of influence describes whether the damage is caused mainly by ground-level concentrations of an air pollutant or by concentrations in the upper atmosphere. When the damage caused by a pollutant is determined mainly by concentrations of the pollutant near the earth's surface, it is called a *surface pollutant*. When the damage is related more to the pollutant's concentration in the upper atmosphere, the substance is called a *global pollutant*.

Water pollutants are obviously surface pollutants, but air pollutants can be surface pollutants, global pollutants, or both. One common global pollutant, carbon dioxide injected into the atmosphere as a product of fossil-fuel combustion, has been implicated in rising world temperatures via the "greenhouse effect." In addition, chlorofluorocarbon emissions are currently suspected of playing a role in the destruction of the ozone that protects the earth's surface from harmful solar radiation. As we shall see, the appropriate policy responses for global and surface pollutants are quite different.

This taxonomy will prove useful in designing policy responses to these various types of pollution problems. Each type of pollutant requires a unique policy response. The failure to recognize these distinctions leads to counterproductive policy.

DEFINING THE EFFICIENT ALLOCATION OF POLLUTION

Pollutants are the residuals of production and consumption. These residuals must eventually be returned to the environment in one form or another. Because their presence in the environment may depreciate the service flows received, an efficient allocation of resources must take this cost into account. What is meant by the efficient allocation of pollution depends on the nature of the pollutant.

Fund Pollutants

To the extent that the emission of fund pollutants exceeds the assimilative capacity of the environment, they accumulate. When the emission rate is low enough, however, the discharges can be assimilated by the environment, with the result that the link between present emissions and future damage may be broken.

When this happens, current emissions cause current damage and future emissions cause future damage, but the level of future damage is independent of current emissions. This independence of allocations among time periods allows us to explore the efficient allocation of fund pollutants using the concept of static, rather than dynamic, efficiency. Because the static concept is simpler, this affords us the opportunity to incorporate more dimensions of the problem without unnecessarily complicating the analysis.

The normal starting point for the analysis would be to maximize the net benefit from the waste flows. However, pollution is more easily understood if we deal with an equivalent formulation involving the minimization of two rather different types of costs: damage costs and control or avoidance costs.

In order to examine the efficient allocation graphically, we need to know something about how control costs vary with the degree of control and how the damages vary with the amount of pollution emitted. Though our knowledge in these areas is far from complete, economists generally agree on the shapes of these relationships.

Generally, the marginal damage caused by a unit of pollution increases with the amount emitted. When small amounts of the pollutant are emitted, the marginal damage is quite small. However, when large amounts are emitted, the marginal unit can cause significantly more damage. It is not hard to understand why. Small amounts of pollution are easily diluted

FIGURE 12.2 The Efficient Allocation of a Fund Pollutant

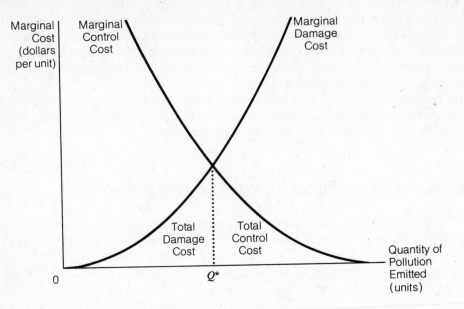

in the environment, and the body can tolerate small quantities of substances. However, as the amount in the atmosphere increases, dilution is less effective and the body is less tolerant.

Marginal control costs commonly increase with the amount controlled. For example, suppose a source of pollution tries to cut down on its particulate emissions by purchasing an electrostatic precipitator that captures 80 percent of the particulates as they flow past in the stack. If the source wants further control, it can purchase another precipitator and place it in the stack above the first one. This second precipitator captures 80 percent of the remaining 20 percent or 16 percent of the uncontrolled emissions. Thus, the first precipitator would achieve an 80 percent reduction from uncontrolled emissions, whereas the second precipitator, which costs the same as the first, would achieve only a further 16 percent reduction. Obviously, each unit of emission reduction costs more for the second precipitator than for the first.

In Figure 12.2 we use these two pieces of information on the shapes of the relevant curves to derive the efficient allocation. A movement from right to left refers to greater control and less pollution emitted. The efficient allocation is represented by Q^*, the point at which the damage caused by the marginal unit of pollution is exactly equal to the marginal cost of avoiding it.[1]

Greater degrees of control (points to the left of Q^*) are inefficient because the further increase in avoidance costs would exceed the reduction in damages. Hence, total costs would rise. Similarly, levels of control lower than Q^* would result in a lower cost of control, but the increase in damage costs would be even larger, yielding an increase in total cost. Either in-

---

[1]At this point we can see why this formulation is equivalent to the net-benefit formulation. Since the benefit is damage reduction, another way of stating this proposition is to state that marginal benefit must equal marginal cost. That is, of course, the familiar proposition derived by maximizing net benefits.

creasing or decreasing the amount controlled causes an increase in total costs. Hence Q^* must be efficient.

The diagram suggests that, under the conditions presented, the optimal level of pollution is not zero. If you find this disturbing, remember that we confront this principle every day. Take the damage caused by automobile accidents, for example. Obviously, a considerable amount of damage is caused by automobile accidents. Yet we do not reduce that damage to zero because the cost of doing so would be too high.

The point is *not* that we do not know how to stop automobile accidents. All we would have to do is eliminate automobiles! Rather, the point is because we value the benefits of automobiles, we take steps to reduce accidents (using speed limits) only to the extent that the costs of accident reduction are commensurate with the damage reduction achieved; the efficient level of automobile accidents is not zero.

The second point to be made is that in some circumstances the optimal level of pollution *may* be zero or close to it. This situation occurs when the damage caused by even the first unit of pollution is so severe that it is higher than the marginal cost of controlling the last unit of pollution. This would be reflected in Figure 12.2 as a leftward shift of the damage cost curve of sufficient magnitude that its intersection with the vertical axis would lie above the point where the marginal cost curve intersects the vertical axis. This circumstance seems to characterize the treatment of highly dangerous radioactive pollutants such as plutonium.

Insights besides the one that a zero level of pollution is not normally efficient are easily derived from our characterization of the efficient allocation. For example, it should be clear from Figure 12.2 that the optimal level of pollution generally is not the same for all parts of the country. Areas that have higher population levels or are particularly sensitive to pollution should have lower levels, whereas areas that have lower population levels or are less sensitive should have more.

Examples of ecological sensitivity are not hard to find. For instance, some natural settings are less sensitive to acid rain than others because the local geological strata neutralize moderate amounts of the acid. Thus, the marginal damage caused by a unit of acid rain is lower in those fortunate regions than in others less tolerant. It can also be argued that pollutants affecting visibility are more damaging in national parks and other areas where visibility is an important part of the aesthetic experience than in other, more industrial, areas.

MARKET ALLOCATION OF POLLUTION

Because air and water are treated in our legal system as common-property resources, it should surprise no one at this point in the book that the market misallocates them. Our general conclusion that common-property resources are overexploited certainly applies here. Air and water resources have been overexploited as waste repositories. However, this conclusion only scratches the surface; much more can be learned about market allocations of pollution.

When firms create products, rarely does the process of converting raw material into outputs use 100 percent of the mass. Some of the mass, called a *residual,* is left over. If the residual is valuable, it is simply reused. However, if it is not valuable, the firm has an incentive to deal with it in the cheapest manner possible.

The typical firm has several alternatives. It can control the amount of the residual by using inputs more completely so that less is left over. It can also produce less output, so that smaller amounts of the residual are generated. Recycling the residual is sometimes a viable option, as is removing the most damaging components of the waste stream and disposing of the rest.

Because damage costs are externalities but control costs are not, what is cheapest for the firm is not always cheapest for society as a whole. When pollutants are injected into water courses or the atmosphere, they cause damages to those firms and consumers downstream or downwind of the source. These costs are *not* borne by the emitting source and therefore not considered by it, although they certainly are borne by society at large.[2] As with other services that are systematically undervalued, the disposal of wastes into the air or water becomes inefficiently attractive. As we saw in Chapter 3, inefficient pollution-control choices lead to further inefficiencies in product and input markets.

In the case of stock pollutants, the problem is particularly severe. Uncontrolled markets would lead to an excessive production of X, too few resources committed to pollution control, and an inefficiently large amount of the stock pollutant in the environment. Thus, the burden on future generations caused by the presence of this pollutant would be inefficiently large.

There are important differences between this case and the previously discussed inefficiencies associated with the extraction or production of minerals, energy, and food. For private-property resources, the market forces provide automatic signals of impending scarcity. These forces may be understated, but they operate in the correct direction. Even when some resources are treated as common property (fisheries), the possibility for a private-property alternative (fish farming) is enhanced. As we saw with Example 11.1, when private-property and common-property resources sell in the same market, the private-property owner tends to ameliorate the excesses of those who exploit common properties. Efficient firms are rewarded with higher profits.

No comparable automatic amelioration mechanism is evident with pollution.[3] Because this cost is borne partially by consumers, rather than producers, it does not find its way into product prices. Firms that attempt to control their pollution unilaterally are placed at a competitive disadvantage; due to the added expense, their costs of production are higher than those of their less conscientious competitors. Not only does the unimpeded market fail to generate the efficient level of pollution control, it penalizes those firms that might attempt to control an efficient amount. Hence the case for some sort of government intervention is particularly strong for pollution control.

EFFICIENT POLICY RESPONSES

Our use of the efficiency criterion has helped in demonstrating why markets fail to produce an efficient level of pollution control and in tracing out the effects of this less-than-optimal degree of control on the markets for related commodities. It can also be used to define efficient policy responses.

Efficiency is achieved when the marginal cost of control is equal to the marginal damage caused by the pollution for each emitter. One way to achieve this equilibrium would be to im-

---

[2]Actually the source certainly considers some of the costs if only to avoid adverse public relations. The point, however, is that this consideration is likely to be incomplete; the source is unlikely to internalize all of the damag

[3]Affected parties do have an incentive to negotiate among themselves, a topic covered in Chapter 3. As pointed out in that chapter, however, that approach only works well in cases where the number of affected parties is small.

pose a legal limit on the amount of pollution allowed by each emitter. If the limit were chosen precisely at the level of pollution where marginal control cost equals marginal damage (Q^* in Figure 12.2) efficiency would have been achieved.

An alternative approach would be to internalize the marginal damage caused by each unit of emissions by means of a tax or charge on each unit of emissions. This per unit charge could either increase with the level of pollution (following the marginal damage curve for each succeeding unit of emission) or be constant, as long as the rate is equal to the marginal social damage at the point where the marginal social damage and marginal control costs cross (see Figure 12.2). Because the emitter is paying the marginal social damage when confronted by these fees, pollution costs would be internalized. The efficient choice would also be the cost-minimizing choice for the emitter.[4]

However, although the efficient levels of these policy instruments can be easily defined in principle, they are very difficult to implement in practice. To implement either of these policy instruments, it is necessary to know the level of pollution at which the two marginal cost curves cross for every emitter. That is a tall order, one that imposes an unrealistically high information burden on control authorities. Control authorities typically have very poor information on control costs and little reliable information on marginal damage functions.

How can environmental authorities allocate pollution-control responsibility in a reasonable manner when the information burdens are apparently so unrealistically large? One approach, the approach now chosen by a number of countries including the United States, is to select specific legal levels of pollution based upon some other criterion such as providing adequate margins of safety for human or ecological health. Once these thresholds have been established by whatever means, half of the problem has been resolved. The other half deals with deciding how to allocate the responsibility for meeting predetermined pollution levels among the large numbers of emitters.

This is precisely where the cost-effectiveness criterion comes in. Once the objective is stated in terms of meeting the predetermined pollution level at minimum cost, it is possible to derive the conditions that any cost-effective allocation of the responsibility must satisfy. These conditions can then be used as a basis for choosing among various kinds of policy instruments that impose more reasonable information burdens on control authorities.

COST-EFFECTIVE POLICIES FOR EMISSION REDUCTION

Defining a Cost-Effective Allocation

Suppose that the regulatory authorities are interested in controlling the total weight of emissions in a manner that minimizes the cost of control. What can we say about the cost-effective allocation of control responsibility for reducing emissions by a predetermined amount?

Consider a simple example. Assume two emission sources are currently emitting a total of 30 units of emissions. Assume further that the control authority determines that the environment can assimilate 15 units, making a reduction of 15 units necessary. How should this 15-unit reduction be allocated between the two sources in order to minimize the total cost of the reduction?

---

[4]Another policy choice is to remove the people from the polluted area. The government has used this strategy for heavily contaminated toxic waste sites such as Times Beach, Missouri, and Love Canal, New York.

FIGURE 12.3 A Cost-Effective Reduction in Emissions

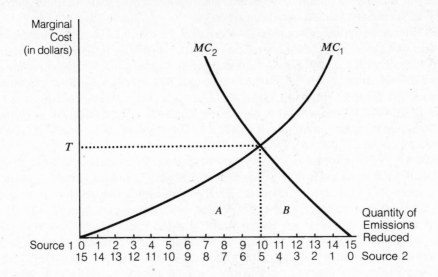

With the aid of Figure 12.3 we can demonstrate the answer. Figure 12.3 is drawn by mea-suring the marginal cost of control for the first source from the left-hand axis (MC_1) and the marginal cost of control for the second source from the right-hand axis (MC_2). Notice that a total of 15 units of reduction is achieved for every point on this graph; each point represents some different combination of reduction by the two sources. Drawn in this manner, the dia-gram represents all possible allocations of the 15-unit reduction between the two sources. The left-hand axis, for example, represents an allocation of the entire reduction to the second source; the right-hand axis represents a situation in which the first source bears the entire re-sponsibility. All points in between represent different degrees of shared responsibility. What allocation minimizes the cost of control?

In the cost-effective allocation, the first source cleans up 10 units; the second source cleans up 5 units. The total variable cost of control of this particular assignment of the re-sponsibility for the reduction is represented by area A plus area B. Area A is the cost of control for the first source, area B the cost of control for the second. Any other allocation would result in a higher total control cost (convince yourself that this is true).

Figure 12.3 also demonstrates one of the most important propositions in the economics of pollution control. *The cost of achieving a given reduction in emissions will be minimized if and only if the marginal costs of control are equalized for all emitters.*[5] This is demonstrated by the fact that the marginal cost curves cross at the cost-effective allocation.

---

[5]This statement is true when marginal cost increases with the amount of emissions reduced (Figure 12.3). Suppose that for some pollutants the marginal cost were to decrease with the amount of emissions reduced. What would be the cost-effective allocation in that admittedly unusual situation?

Cost-Effective Pollution-Control Policies

This proposition can be used as a basis for choosing among the various policy instruments that the control authority might use to achieve this allocation. Sources have a large menu of options for controlling the amount of pollution they inject into the environment. The cheapest method of control will differ widely, not only among industries, but also among plants in the same industry. Selecting the cheapest method requires detailed information on the possible control techniques and their associated costs.

Plant managers are generally able to acquire this information for their plants when it is in their interest to do so. However, the government authorities responsible for meeting pollution targets are not likely to have this information. Because the degree to which these plants would be regulated depends on cost information, it is unrealistic to expect the plant managers to transfer unbiased information to the government. Plant managers have a strong incentive to overstate control costs in hopes of reducing their ultimate burden.

This situation poses a difficult dilemma for control authorities. The cost of incorrectly assigning the control responsibility among various polluters is likely to be large, yet the control authorities do not have the information at their disposal to make a correct allocation. Those who have the information—the plant managers—are not inclined to share it. Can the cost-effective allocation be found? The answer depends on the particular approach taken by the control authority.

Emission Standards

We start our investigation of this question by supposing that the control authority pursues a traditional legal approach by imposing a separate emission standard on each source. In the economics literature this approach is referred to as the "command-and-control" approach. An *emission standard* is a legal limit on the amount of the pollutant an individual source is allowed to emit. In our example it is clear that the two standards should add up to the allowable 15 units, but it is not clear how, in the absence of information on control costs, these 15 units are to be allocated between the two sources. The easiest method of resolving this dilemma— and the one chosen in the earliest days of pollution control—would be to allocate each source an equal reduction. As is clear from Figure 12.3, this strategy would not be cost effective. Although the first source would have lower costs, this cost reduction would be substantially smaller than the increase faced by the second source; compared to a cost-effective allocation, total costs would increase if both sources were forced to clean up the same amount.

When emission standards are used, there is no reason to believe that the authority will assign the responsibility for emission reduction in a cost-minimizing way. This is probably not surprising. Who would have believed otherwise?

Nonetheless, some policy instruments do allow the authority to allocate the emission reduction in a cost-effective manner even when it has no information on the magnitude of control costs. These policy approaches rely on economic incentives to produce the desired outcome. The two most common approaches are known as emission charges and transferable emission permits.

FIGURE 12.4 Cost-Minimizing Control of Pollution with an Emission Charge

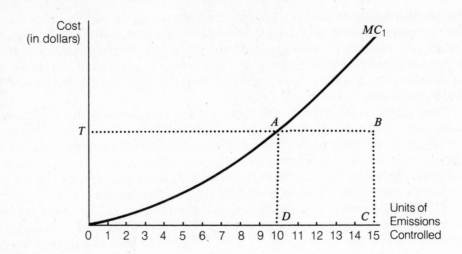

Emission Charges

An *emission charge* is a fee, collected by the government, levied on each unit of pollutant emitted into the air or water. The total payment any source would make to the government could be found by multiplying the fee times the amount of pollution emitted. Emission charges reduce pollution because pollution costs the firm money. To save money, the source seeks ways to reduce its pollution.

How much pollution control would the firm choose to purchase? A profit-maximizing firm would control, rather than emit, pollution whenever it proved cheaper to do so. We can illustrate the firm's decision with Figure 12.4. The level of uncontrolled emission is 15 units, and the emission charge is T. Thus, if the firm were to decide against controlling any emissions, it would have to pay T times 15, represented by area $OTBC$.

Is this the best the firm can do? Obviously not, because it can control some pollution at a lower cost than paying the emission charge. It would pay the firm to reduce emissions until the marginal cost of reduction is equal to the emission charge. The firm would minimize its cost by choosing to clean up 10 units of pollution and emitting 5 units. At this allocation the firm would pay control costs equal to area OAD and total emission charge payments equal to area $ABCD$, for a total cost of $OABC$. This is clearly less than $OTBC$, the amount the firm would pay if it chose not to clean up any pollution.

Let's carry this one step further. Suppose that we levied the same emission charge on both sources discussed in Figure 12.3. Each source would then control its emissions until its marginal control cost equaled the emission charge. (Faced with an emission charge T, the second source would clean up 5 units.) Because they both are facing the same emission charge, they will *independently* choose levels of control consistent with equal marginal control costs. This is precisely the condition that yields a cost-minimizing allocation.

This is a rather remarkable finding. We have shown that as long as the control authority imposes the same emission charge on all sources, the resulting reduction allocation *automatically* minimizes the costs of control. This is true in spite of the fact that the control authority may not have any knowledge of control costs.

FIGURE 12.5 Cost Savings from Technological Change: Charges vs. Standards

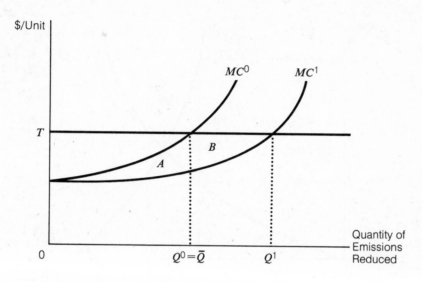

However, we have not yet dealt with the issue of how the appropriate level of the emission charge is determined. Each level of a charge will result in *some* level of emission reduction. Furthermore, the responsibility for meeting that reduction will be allocated in a manner that minimizes control costs. How high should the charge be set to ensure that the resulting emission reduction is the *desired* level of emission reduction?

Without knowing the cost of control, the control authority cannot establish the correct tax rate on the first try. It is possible, however, to develop an iterative, trial-and-error process to find the appropriate charge rate. This process is initiated by choosing an arbitrary charge rate and observing the amount of reduction that occurs when that charge is imposed. If the observed reduction is larger than desired, the charge should be lowered; if the reduction is smaller, the charge should be raised. The new reduction that results from the adjusted charge can then be observed and compared with the desired reduction. Further adjustments in the charge can be made as needed. This process can be repeated until the actual and desired reductions are equal. At that point, the correct emission charge would have been found.

The charge system not only causes sources to choose a cost-effective allocation on the control responsibility, it also stimulates the development of newer, cheaper means of controlling emissions as well as promoting technological progress. This is illustrated in Figure 12.5.

The reason for this is rather straightforward. Control authorities base the emission standards on specific technologies. As new technologies are discovered by the control authority, the standards are tightened. These more strict standards force firms to bear higher costs. Therefore, with emissions standards, firms have an incentive to hide technological changes from the control authority.

With an emissions charge system the firm saves money by adopting cheaper new technologies. As long as the firm can reduce its pollution at a marginal cost lower than T, it pays to adopt the new technology. In Figure 12.5 the firm saves A and B by adopting the new technology and voluntarily reduces its emissions from Q^0 to Q^1.

FIGURE 12.6   Cost Effectiveness and the Emission Permit System

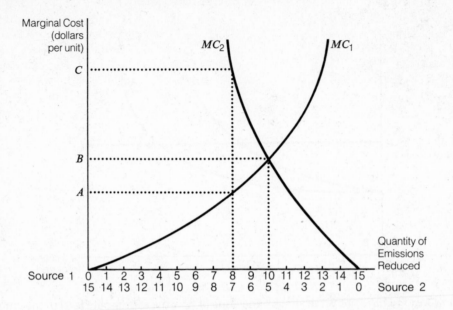

With an emissions charge, the minimum cost allocation of meeting a predetermined emission reduction can be found by a control authority even when it has no information on control costs. An emission charge also stimulates technological advances in emission reduction. Unfortunately, the process for finding the appropriate rate would take some experimenting. During the trial-and-error period of finding the appropriate rate, sources would be faced with a volatile emission charge. Changing emission charges would make planning for the future difficult. Investments that would make sense under a high emission charge might not make sense when it falls. From either a policymaker's or business manager's perspective, this process leaves much to be desired.

Transferable Emission Permits

Is it possible for the control authority to find the cost-minimizing allocation without going through a trial-and-error process? It is possible if a *transferable emission permit system* is used to control pollution. Under this system, all sources are required to have permits to emit. Each permit specifies exactly how much the firm is allowed to emit. The permits are freely transferable. The control authority issues exactly the number of permits needed to produce the desired emission level. Any emissions by a source in excess of those allowed by its permit would cause the source to face severe monetary sanctions.

Why this system automatically leads to a cost-effective allocation can be seen in Figure 12.6, which treats the same set of circumstances as in Figure 12.3. Suppose that somehow the first source found itself with 7 permits. Because it has 15 units of uncontrolled emissions, this would mean it must control 8 units. Similarly, suppose that the second source has the remaining 8 permits, meaning that it would have to clean up 7 units. Notice that both firms have an incentive to trade. The marginal cost of control for the second source (C) is substantially higher than that for the first (A). The second source could lower its cost if it could buy a permit from the first source at a price lower than C. Meanwhile, the first source would be better off if it could sell a permit for a price higher than A. Because C is greater than A, grounds for trade certainly exist.

A transfer of permits would take place until the first source had only 5 permits left (and is controlling 10 units), while the second source had 10 permits (and was controlling 5 units). At this point, the permit price would equal B, because that is the marginal value of that permit to both sources, and neither source would have any incentive to trade further. The permit market would be in equilibrium.

Notice that the market equilibrium for an emission-permit system is the cost-effective allocation! Simply by issuing the appropriate number of permits (15) and letting the market do the rest, the control authority can achieve a cost-effective allocation without having even the slightest knowledge about control costs. This system allows the government to meet its policy objective while allowing greater flexibility in how that objective is met.

The incentives created by this system ensure that sources use this flexibility to achieve the objective at the lowest possible cost. As we shall see in the next two chapters, this remarkable property has been responsible for the prominence of this type of approach in current attempts to reform the regulatory process.

OTHER POLICY DIMENSIONS

Two main pollution-control policy instruments rely on economic incentives—charges and transferable permits. Both of these allow the control authority to distribute the responsibility for control in a cost-effective manner. The major difference between them we have discussed so far is that the appropriate charge can be determined only by an iterative trial-and-error process over time, whereas the permit price can be determined immediately by the market. Can other differences be identified?

One major additional difference concerns the manner in which these two systems react to changes in external circumstances in the absence of further decisions by the control authority. This is an important consideration because bureaucratic procedures are notoriously sluggish and changes in policies are usually rendered rather slowly.[6] We shall consider three such circumstances— growth in the number of sources, inflation, and technological progress.

If the number of sources were to increase in a permit market, the demand for permits would shift to the right. Given a fixed supply of permits, the price would rise, as would the control costs, but the amount of emissions or pollution concentrations (in the case of the ambient permit system) would remain the same. If charges were being used, in the absence of additional action by the control authority the charge level would remain the same. This implies that the existing sources would control only what they would control in the absence of growth. Therefore, the arrival of new sources would cause a deterioration of air or water quality in the region. The costs of abatement would rise, because the costs of control paid by the new sources must be considered, but by a lesser amount than in a permit market because of

---

[6]This is probably particularly true when the modification involves a change in the rate at which firms are charged for their emissions.

the lower amount of pollution being controlled. If the choice is between a fixed fee and a fixed number of permits in a growing economy, the dominance of the permit system over the fixed fee system increases over time.[7]

With a permit system, inflation in the cost of control would automatically result in higher permit prices, but with a charge system it would result in lower control. Essentially the real charge (the nominal charge adjusted for inflation) declines with inflation if the nominal charge remains the same.

However, we should not conclude that, over time, charges always result in less control than permits. Suppose, for example, that technological progress in designing pollution-control equipment were to cause the marginal cost of abatement to fall. In a permit system this would result in lower prices and lower abatement costs but the same aggregate degree of control. With a charge system, the amount controlled would actually increase and would therefore result in more control than a permit system that, prior to the fall in costs, controlled the same amount.

If the control authority were to adjust the charge in each of these cases appropriately, the outcome would be identical to that achieved by a permit market. The permit market reacts automatically to these changes in circumstances, whereas the charge system requires a conscious administrative act to achieve the same result.

The second major difference between permits and charges involves the cost of being wrong. Suppose that we have very imprecise information on damages caused and avoidance costs incurred by various levels of pollution, yet we have to choose either a charge level or a permit level and live with it. What can be said about the relative merits of permits versus charges in the face of this uncertainty?

The answer depends upon the circumstances.[8] Permits offer a great deal of certainty about the quantity of emissions; charges confer more certainty about the marginal cost of control. Therefore, permits are the only system that allows an ambient standard or an aggregate emission standard to be met with certainty. In other cases, however, when the objective is to minimize total costs (the sum of damage cost and control costs), permits would be preferred when the costs of being wrong are more sensitive to changes in the quantity of emission than to changes in the marginal cost of control. Charges would be preferred when control costs were more important. When would that be the case?

When the marginal damage curve is steeply sloped and the marginal cost curve is rather flat, certainty about emissions is more important than certainty about control costs. Smaller deviations of actual emissions from expected emissions can cause a rather large deviation in damage costs, whereas control costs would be relatively insensitive to the degree of control. Permits would prevent large fluctuations in these damage costs and would therefore yield a lower cost of being wrong than charges.

Now suppose that the marginal control cost curve was steeply sloped, but the marginal damage curve was flat. Small changes in the degree of control would have a large effect on

[7]See Richard V. Butler and Michael D. Maher, "The Control of Externalities in a Growing Economy," *Economic Inquiry* 20, No. 1 (January 1982): 155–63.

[8]A more formal and mathematical treatment of this issue can be found in M. Weitzman, "Prices vs. Quantities," *Review of Economic Studies* XLI (1974): 447–91. A specific application to pollution control is presented in Z. Adar and J. M. Griffin, "Uncertainty and Choice in Pollution Control Instruments," *Journal of Environmental Economics and Management* III (1976): 178–88.

E X A M P L E   1 2 . 1

Energy-Demand Uncertainty and the Cost of Being Wrong: Permits vs. Charges

The Four Corners area (where Utah, Arizona, New Mexico, and Colorado intersect) poses a classic confrontation between energy development and preserving the environment. Though sparsely populated, it is near several unique parks and wilderness areas and serves as the base for several large electrical generating stations, which provide power to a large number of southwestern and western states.

One of the uncertainties affecting the air quality of the region is the amount that electricity demand will grow over the next several years. The higher the growth in demand, the more uncontrolled emissions. The higher the level of uncontrolled emissions, the more control that has to be placed on each source in order to preserve air quality. If, in incorrect anticipation of too high growth, the regulators impose too stringent a degree of control, then control costs will be excessively high. If controls are established at too low a level, damage costs would be too high. There are costs associated with each type of mistake.

In a doctoral dissertation submitted at Stanford, Charles Kolstad [1982] used this setting to investigate whether regulators would be better off using a permit system or an emission charge system to protect air quality in the face of this uncertainty. Capturing the control-cost and damage functions in a computer simulation model, he calculated the cost of being wrong if regulators chose permits or if they chose charges. His findings were completely in accord with our analysis:

For constant or declining marginal damage, emissions [charges] yield total costs (including damage) 5–10% lower than for [permits]. However, for even slightly upward sloping marginal damage, [permits] yield roughly 20% lower costs than emissions [charges].[p. 206]

Because the increasing-marginal-cost case is probably the most likely for sulfur oxide emissions, the use of permits in the Four Corners would seem preferable.

Source: Charles Kolstad, *"Economic and Regulatory Efficiency,"* Report #LA-9458-T(Thesis) (Los Alamos, NM: Los Alamos National Laboratory, 1982).

abatement costs but would not affect damages very much. In this case it makes sense to rely on charges to give more precise control over control costs, accepting the less-dire consequences from possible fluctuations in damage costs.

These cases suggest that a preference either for permits or for charges in the face of uncertainty is not universal, it depends on the circumstances. Theory is not strong enough to dictate a choice. Empirical studies are necessary to establish a preference for particular situations. Example 12.1 discusses one such empirical study.

SUMMARY

In this chapter we developed the conceptual framework needed to evaluate current approaches to pollution-control policy. The efficient amount of a fund pollutant was defined as the amount that minimizes the sum of damage and control costs. Using this definition we were able to derive two propositions of interest: (1) The efficient level of pollution would vary from region to region, and (2) the efficient level of pollution would not generally be zero, though in some particular circumstances it might.

Because pollution is a classic externality, markets will generally produce more than the efficient amount of both fund pollutants and stock pollutants. For both pollutants, this will imply higher-than-efficient damages and lower-than-efficient control costs. For stock pollutants, an excessive amount of pollution would build up in the environment, imposing a detrimental externality on future generations as well as on current generations.

The market would not provide any automatic ameliorating response to the accumulation of pollution as it would in the case of natural-resource scarcity. Firms unilaterally attempting to control their pollution are placed at a competitive disadvantage. Hence the case for some sort of government intervention is particularly strong for pollution control.

Although policy instruments could in principle be defined to achieve an efficient level of pollution for every emitter, in practice it is very difficult because the amount of information required by the control authorities is unrealistically high.

Cost-effectiveness analysis provides a way out of this dilemma. When the objective is defined in terms of reducing emissions by a predetermined amount, uniform emission charges or an emission-permit system could be used to attain the cost-effective allocation even when the control authority has no information whatsoever on either control costs or damage costs. Uniform emission standards would not, except by coincidence, be cost effective. In addition, either permits or charges would stimulate more technological progress in pollution control than would emission standards.

The permit approach and the charge approach respond differently to growth in the number of sources, to inflation, to technological change, and to uncertainty. As we shall see in the next few chapters, some countries (primarily in Europe) have chosen to rely on emission charges whereas others (primarily the United States) have chosen to rely on permits. We can now use this framework to evaluate the rather different policy approaches that have been taken toward the major sources of pollution.

FURTHER READING

Baumol, W. J., and W. E. Oates. *The Theory of Environmental Policy* (Englewood Cliffs, NJ: Prentice-Hall, 1975). A classic on the economic analysis of externalities. Accessible only to those with a thorough familiarity with multivariable calculus.

Hahn, Robert W. "Economic Prescriptions for Environmental Problems: How the Patient Followed the Doctor's Orders," *Journal of Economic Perspectives* 3, No. 2 (Spring 1989): 95–114. Chronicles the experience with both marketable permits and emission charges in the United States and Europe.

Organization for Economic Co-operation and Development. *Pollution Charges in Practice* (Paris: OECD, 1980). A comprehensive survey of the application of pollution charges for air and water pollution control primarily, but not exclusively, in Western Europe.

Organization for Economic Co-operation and Development. *Economic Instruments for Environmental Protection* (Paris: OECD, 1989). A survey of how economic incentive approaches to pollution control have been used in the industrialized nations that belong to the OECD.

Portney, Paul, ed. *Public Policies for Environmental Protection* (Washington, DC: Resources for the Future, 1990). A collection of essays reviewing problems of environmental regulation from the perspective of the late 1980s.

Tietenberg, T. H. *Emissions Trading: An Exercise in Reforming Pollution Policy* (Washington, DC: Resources for the Future, 1985). An examination of the use of marketable permits to control pollution in principle and in practice.

ADDITIONAL REFERENCES

Anderson, Frederick R., et al. *Environmental Improvement Through Economic Incentives* (Baltimore, MD: Johns Hopkins University Press, for Resources for the Future, 1977).

Barnett, Andy H., and Bruce Yandle, Jr. "Allocating Environmental Resources," *Public Finance* 28 (1973): 11–19.

Collinge, R. A., and W. E. Oates. "Efficiency in Pollution Control in the Short and Long Runs: A System of Rental Emission Permits," *Canadian Journal of Economics* 15 (May 1982): 347–54.

Dales, J. H. *Pollution, Property and Prices* (Toronto, Canada: Toronto University Press, 1968).

Hahn, Robert W. and Robert G. Noll. "Designing a Market for Tradable Emissions Permits," in Wesley A. Magat, ed., *Reform of Environmental Regulation* (Cambridge, MA: Ballinger, 1982).

Kneese, Allen V., and Charles L. Schultz. *Pollution, Prices, and Public Policy* (Washington, DC: The Brookings Institution, 1975).

Lyon, R. M. "Auctions and Alternative Procedures for Allocating Pollution Rights," *Land Economics* 58 (February 1982): 16–32.

Milliman, Scott R., and Raymond Prince. "Firm Incentives to Promote Technological Change in Pollution Control," *Journal of Environmental Economics and Management* 17, No. 3, (November 1989): 247–65.

Montgomery, David W. "Markets in Licenses and Efficient Pollution Control Programs," *Journal of Economic Theory* 5 (December 1982): 395–418.

Orr, Lloyd. "Incentive for Innovation as the Basis for Effluent Charge Strategy," *The American Economic Review* 66 (May 1976): 441–47.

Plourde, C. G. "A Model of Waste Accumulation and Disposal," *Canadian Journal of Economics* V (February 1982): 119–25.

Stavins, Robert N. "Harnessing Market Forces to Protect the Environment," *Environment* 31, No. 1 (January/February 1989): 4–7, 28–35.

Weitzman, M. "Prices vs. Quantities," *Review of Economic Studies* XLI (1974): 447–91.

DISCUSSION QUESTIONS

1. In his book *(What Price Incentives?)* Steven Kelman suggests that from an ethical point of view, the use of economic incentives (such as emission charges or emission permits) in environmental policy is undesirable. He argues that transforming our mental image of the environment from a sanctified preserve to a marketable commodity has detrimental effects not only on our use of the environment but also on our attitude toward it. His point is that applying economic incentives to environmental policy weakens and cheapens our traditional values with regard to the environment.

   a. Consider the effects of economic-incentive systems on prices paid by the poor, on employment, and on the speed of compliance with pollution-control laws—as well as the Kelman arguments. Are economic-incentive systems more or less ethically justifiable than the traditional regulatory approach?

   b. Kelman seems to feel that because emission permits automatically prevent environmental degradation, they are more ethically desirable than emission charges. Do you agree? Why or why not?

CHAPTER 13

Stationary-Source Local Air Pollution

When choosing between two evils, I always like to try the one I've never tried before.

MAE WEST, ACTRESS

INTRODUCTION

Attaining and maintaining clean air is an exceedingly difficult policy task. In the United States, for example, an estimated 27,000 major stationary sources of air pollution, as well as hundreds of thousands of more minor sources, are subject to control. Many distinct production processes emit many different types of pollutants. The resulting damages range from minimal effects on plants and vegetation to the possible modification of the earth's climate.

The policy response to this problem has been continually evolving. The U.S. experience is not atypical. Congress enacted the first legislation to grapple with these problems in 1955. Called the Air Pollution Control Act of 1955, that law mainly subsidized research into air-pollution problems. The following fourteen years ushered in a period of vigorous legislative activity.

However, the amount of legislation is a misleading indicator of what was actually accomplished. It was not until 1967 that the federal government began to play much of a role other than subsidizing research, and even the 1967 law was mainly an attempt to cajole the states into action. The common thread woven by the statutes during this period was a reliance on cooperation from the states.

By 1970 the national government had discovered that this reliance was misplaced: State cooperation was not forthcoming. Fearing that the imposition of strict controls on industrial sources would place them at a competitive disadvantage in their quest for increases in employment and taxable industrial property, states were unwilling to take the lead in air-pollution control policy.

In this atmosphere of frustration, the Clean Air Act Amendments of 1970 were passed. They set a bold new direction, which has been retained and refined by subsequent acts. By virtue of that act, the federal government assumed a much larger and much more vigorous direct role. The U.S. Environmental Protection Agency (EPA) was created to implement and oversee this massive attempt to control the injection of substances into our air. Individually tailored strategies were created to deal with mobile and stationary sources. These strategies depend in part on whether the type of pollutant being controlled is a "conventional" pollutant or a "hazardous" pollutant.

CONVENTIONAL POLLUTANTS

Conventional pollutants are relatively common substances, found in almost all parts of the country, and are presumed to be dangerous only in high concentrations. In the United States these pollutants are called *criteria pollutants* because the Act requires EPA to produce "criteria documents" to be used in setting acceptable standards for these pollutants. These documents summarize and evaluate all of the existing research on the various health and environmental effects associated with these pollutants. The central focus of air-pollution control during the 1970s was on criteria pollutants.

The Command-and-Control Policy Framework

In the preceding chapter, several possible approaches to controlling pollution were described and analyzed in theoretical terms. The historical approach to air-pollution control has been based primarily on emission standards. It has been a traditional command-and-control (CAC) approach. In this section we shall outline the specific nature of this approach, analyze it from an efficiency and cost-effectiveness perspective, and how a series of recent reforms based on economic incentives has worked to rectify some of these deficiencies.

For each of the conventional pollutants, the typical first step is to establish ambient air-quality standards. These standards set legal ceilings on the allowable concentration of the pollutant in the outdoor air averaged over a specified time period. Many pollutants have the standard defined in terms on a long-term average (defined normally as an annual average) and a short-term average (such as a three-hour average). These short-term averages can usually be exceeded no more than once a year. These standards have to be met everywhere, though as a practical matter they are monitored at a large number of specific locations. As Example 4.3 pointed out, control costs can be quite sensitive to the level of these short-term averages.

In the United States two ambient standards are defined.[1] The *primary standard* is designed to protect human health. This is the first standard to be determined, and it has the earliest deadlines for compliance. All pollutants have a primary standard. The *secondary standard* is designed to protect other aspects of human welfare from those pollutants having separate effects. Currently only sulfur oxides and particulates have separate secondary stan-

---

[1]We shall discuss the U.S. approach in some detail to show how abstract command-and-control concepts can be translated into specific policy. Many industrialized countries have rather similar policies. For more detail on the environmental policies of some European countries and Japan, see Frederic N. Bolotin, ed., *International Public Policy Sourcebook: Volume 2, Education and Environment* (New York: Greenwood Press, 1989). The Japanese approach, which is rather different, will be treated in more detail subsequently in this chapter.

TABLE 13.1 National Primary and Secondary Ambient Air Quality Standards

Pollutant	Primary Standard[a]	Secondary Standard[a]
Sulfur Oxides	a. 80 µg/m3 (0.03 ppm) annual arithmetic mean b. 365 µg/m3 (0.14 ppm) maximum 24-hour concentration not to be exceeded more than once a year	1300 µg/m3 (0.5 ppm) 3-hour concentration not to be exceeded more than once a year.
Particulate Matter[b]	a. 50 µg/m^3 annual arithmetic mean b. 150 µg/m^3 maximum 24-hour concentration not to be exceeded more than once per year	Same as primary standard
Carbon Monoxide	a. 10 mg/m^3 (9 ppm) maximum 8-hour concentration not to be exceeded more than once per year b. 40 mg/m^3 (35 ppm) maximum 1-hour concentration not to be exceeded more than once per year	No secondary standard
Ozone	235 µg/m^3 (0.12 ppm) maximum average hourly concentration not to be exceeded more than once per year	Same as primary standard
Nitrogen Dioxide	100 µg/m^3 (0.05 ppm) annual arithmetic mean	Same as primary standard
Lead	1.5 µg/m^3 arithmetic mean averaged over a calendar quarter	Same as primary standard

[a] Guide to measurements: µg/m^3 is micrograms per cubic meter; mg/m^3 is milligrams per cubic meter; and ppm is parts per million.

[b] TSP was the indicator pollutant for the original particulate matter standards. This standard was replaced with a new standard in 1987. The new standard tracks particles less than 10 µ in diameter as the new indicator pollutant.

Source: *Code of Federal Regulations,* Volume 40, Parts 50.4, 50.6, 50.8, 50.9, 50.11, and 50.12 (1989).

dards. Protection is afforded by the secondary standard for aesthetics (particularly visibility), physical objects (houses, monuments, and so on), and vegetation. When a separate secondary standard exists, both it and the primary standard must be met. The existing primary and secondary standards are given in Table 13.1.

The ambient standards are required by statute to be determined without any consideration given to the costs of meeting them. They are supposed to be set at a level sufficient to protect even the most sensitive members of the population.

Although the EPA is responsible for defining the ambient standards, the primary responsibility for ensuring that the ambient air-quality standards are met falls on the state control agencies. They exercise this responsibility by developing and executing an acceptable state implementation plan (SIP), which must be approved by the EPA. This plan divides the state up into separate air-quality control regions. There are special procedures for handling regions that cross state borders, such as Metropolitan New York.

The SIP spells out for each control region the procedures and timetables for meeting local ambient standards and for abatement of the effects of locally emitted pollutants on other states. The degree of control required depends on the severity of the pollution problem in each of the control regions.

By 1975 it had become apparent that, despite some major gains in air quality, many areas had not met and would not meet the ambient standards by the statutory deadlines. Therefore, in the 1977 Amendments to the Clean Air Act, Congress extended the deadline for attainment of all primary (health-related) ambient standards to 1982, with further extensions to 1987 possible for ozone and carbon monoxide. The amendments also required the EPA to designate all areas not meeting the original deadlines as *nonattainment regions*.

The areas receiving this designation were subjected to particularly stringent controls. After the 1977 Amendments were passed, all portions of state implementation plans applying to nonattainment regions had to be revised by the state control authorities to ensure compliance with the new deadlines. To prod the states into action, Congress gave the EPA the power to halt the construction of major new or modified pollution sources and to deny federal sewage and transportation grants for any state not submitting a plan showing precisely how and when attainment would be reached.

State implementation plans in nonattainment regions must include a permit program for newly constructed large sources or large sources that have undergone some major modification. Permits cannot be granted to these sources unless the state can demonstrate that emissions resulting from commencing or expanding operations would not jeopardize the region's progress toward attainment. The state can satisfy this requirement by controlling existing sources to a sufficiently high degree that progress can be demonstrated even with the new sources in operation.

A second condition for the permit to be issued stipulates that all major new or modified sources in nonattainment areas must also control their own emissions to the *lowest achievable emission rate* (LAER). The LAER is defined as the lowest emission rate included in any state implementation plan *whether or not any source is currently achieving that rate*. This part of the law was designed to ensure that only the most stringent controls would be used by any source locating in a nonattainment area. It is controversial because it implies that new sources could be forced to use technologies that have never been commercially tested.

Regions with air quality at least as high as the standards by the original deadline were subject to another set of controls known collectively as the PSD policy. This policy derives its name from its objective, namely the *prevention of significant deterioration* of the air in cleaner regions. The origin of this policy is found in the preamble to the 1970 Clean Air Act, which stated as an objective: "to protect and enhance the quality of the nation's air."

In 1972 the EPA was successfully sued by the Sierra Club for promulgating regulations that did not ensure that this objective would be met. The system of ambient standards prevented the deterioration of the air *beyond* the standard, but air significantly cleaner than the standard would normally have deteriorated until it reached the standard. Following the court's decision, the EPA adopted a PSD program in 1974, and the 1977 Amendment to the Clean Air Act continued a modified version of that program.

The PSD regulations specify the maximum allowable increases or increments in pollution concentration beyond some baseline. To allow some variability in the size of these increments, Congress specified that PSD regions be subdivided into three types of areas, with each type allowed a different increment. Class I areas include national parks and wilderness areas. The increments for these regions are the smallest. Practically any degradation in these areas is considered significant and is disallowed.

All other areas were initially designated as Class II regions, where a modest increment is allowed. States may redesignate any Class II region as a Class I region (thus allowing less future deterioration) or as a Class III region (allowing more). Class III regions are allowed the largest increment. In no case, however, can pollutant concentrations in any PSD region rise above the governing ambient standard.

New sources seeking to locate in PSD regions must secure permits. As a condition of securing their permits, these sources must install the *best available control technology* (BACT). The specific technologies that satisfy their requirement are determined by states on a case-by-case basis. Each new permitted source consumes a portion of the allowable increment. Once the increment has been completely consumed, no further deterioration of the air is allowed in that area, even if the air is cleaner than required by the prevailing ambient standard. Thus, where the PSD increments are binding, for all practical purposes they define a tertiary standard varying in magnitude from region to region.

In addition to defining the ambient standards and requiring states to define BACT and LAER emission standards, the EPA itself has established national uniform emission standards for new sources of criteria pollutants or major modifications of existing sources.

The progress in defining those standards has been very slow. The standards governing new and modified sources of criteria pollutants are called the *New Source Performance Standards* (NSPS), and they were designed only to serve as a floor for BACT and LAER determinations by the states. Congress wanted to ensure that all sources would have to meet a minimum standard regardless of where it was located. This was seen as a way to prevent states from caving in as industry tried to play one state off against another in its attempt to seek the lowest possible emission standards. Neither LAER nor BACT can be lower than the new-source performance standards.

Simply stating the regulations is not enough. They must be enforced with appropriate sanctions whenever noncompliance occurs. Prior to the 1977 amendments, noncompliance was a significant problem, with delays of up to six years being common. Because of this situation, in 1977 Congress established the *noncompliance penalty* as a means of reducing the profitability in delaying compliance.

Without sanctions, the source benefits from delaying compliance. The equipment purchases necessary to ensure compliance are expensive and add nothing to profits. In addition, court action is slow and sometimes sympathetic toward business. The noncompliance penalty is designed to harmonize these private incentives with the social objectives pursued by the Act.

Patterned after a system first used in Connecticut, the magnitude of the noncompliance penalty is determined by the economic value of delay to the source. Any economic gains received by the source as a result of noncompliance are included in the penalty and are transferred to the EPA; they no longer accrue to the source. The initial indications are that the existence of this penalty has cut delays by 30 to 40 percent.[2]

The final characteristic of the Clean Air Act that we shall discuss is that it rules out tailoring the degree of control to the prevailing meteorological conditions. All strategies must achieve better air quality through emission reductions stringent enough to ensure compliance in quite adverse conditions.

---

[2]See Sue Anne Batey Blackman and William J. Baumol, "Modified Fiscal Incentives in Environmental Policy," *Land Economics* 56 (November 1980): 419.

The Efficiency of the Command-and-Control Approach

Efficiency presumes that the ambient standards are set at efficient levels. To ascertain whether or not the current standards are efficient, it is necessary to inquire into five aspects of the standard-setting process: (1) the threshold concept on which the standards are based, (2) the level of the standard, (3) the choice of uniform standards over standards more tailored to the regions involved, (4) the timing of emission flows, and (5) the failure to incorporate the degree of human exposure in the standard-setting process.

The Threshold Concept.   Some basis is needed for setting the ambient standard. Because the Clean Air Act prohibits the balancing of costs and benefits, some alternative criterion must be used. For the primary (health-related) standard, this criterion is known as the *health threshold*. The standard is to be defined with a margin of safety sufficiently high that no adverse health effects would be suffered by any member of the population as long as the air quality was at least as good as the standards. This approach presumes the existence of a threshold such that concentrations above that level produce adverse health effects, but concentrations below it produce none.

If the threshold concept were valid, the marginal damage function would be zero until the threshold was reached and would be positive at higher concentrations. The belief that the actual damage function has this shape is not consistent with the evidence, because we are now learning that adverse health effects can occur at pollution levels lower than the ambient standards.[3] The standard that produces no adverse health effects among the general population (which, of course, includes especially susceptible groups) is probably zero or close to it. It is certainly lower than the established ambient standards. What the standards purport to accomplish and what they actually accomplish are rather different.

The Level of the Ambient Standard.   The absence of a defensible threshold complicates the analysis. Some other basis must be used for determining the level at which the standard should be established. Efficiency would dictate setting the standard in order to maximize the net benefit, which includes a consideration of costs as well as benefits.

The current policy explicitly excludes costs from consideration in setting the ambient standards. Costs are allowed to enter the process only when the policy instruments used to meet ambient standards are being defined. It is difficult to imagine that the process of setting the ambient standard would yield an efficient outcome when it is prohibited from considering one of the key elements of that outcome!

Unfortunately, for reasons which were discussed in some detail in Chapter 4, our current benefit measurements are not sufficiently reliable to permit the identification of the efficient level with any confidence. Freeman, for example, in his extensive 1982 survey of the evidence concludes that the benefits (in 1978 dollars) derived from controlling stationary sources lie somewhere in the interval from $4.8 billion to $49.4 billion per year with a most likely point

---

[3]See, for example, Lester B. Lave and Eugene P. Seskin, *Air Pollution and Human Health* (Baltimore, MD: Johns Hopkins University Press, 1977), which discovered a positive association between pollution and mortality even in those cities meeting the primary standards.

estimate of $21.4 billion per year.[4] This can be compared to a cost of stationary-source control of around $9.0 billion per year. These figures suggest that a high degree of confidence can be attached to the belief that government intervention is justified, but they provide no evidence whatsoever on whether current policy is efficient. A similar fate met a recent attempt to use benefit/cost analysis to ascertain the efficiency of the particulate standard (Example 13.1).

Uniformity.   The same primary and secondary standards apply to all parts of the country. No account is taken of the number of people exposed, the sensitivity of the local ecology, or the costs of compliance in various areas. All of these would have some effect on the efficient standard, and efficiency would therefore dictate different standards for different regions. In general, the evidence suggests that the inefficiencies associated with uniformity are greatest in rural areas, but we shall leave a full description and interpretation of that evidence for later in the book.

The PSD program does introduce some variability by establishing more stringent standards for regions with the cleanest air. If national parks and other Class I areas are especially sensitive to pollution, that portion of the program could represent a move toward efficiency. Because states have some flexibility in choosing which portions of their area would be designated as Class II and Class III regions, it is conceivable, but by no means obvious, that they would make efficient choices.

Furthermore, it remains true that no area is allowed to experience air-quality levels worse than the primary and secondary standards for any longer than necessary to reach those standards.

Timing of Emission Flows.   Because concentrations are important for criteria pollutants, the timing of emissions is an important policy concern. Emissions clustered in time are as troublesome as emissions clustered in space. How do we handle those relatively rare but devastating occasions when thermal inversions prevent the normal dispersion and dilution of the pollutants? From an economic efficiency point of view, the most obvious approach is to tailor the degree of control to the circumstances. Stringent control would be exercised when meteorological conditions were relatively stagnant; less control would be applied under normal circumstances. The strong stand against intermittent controls in the Clean Air Act, however, rules this out.

It turns out that a reliance on a constant degree of control, rather than allowing intermittent controls, raises compliance costs substantially, particularly when the required degree of control is high. In perhaps the earliest empirical study soundly based on economic theory, Teller examined the costs of controlling sulfur dioxide in Nashville, Tennessee, through fuel substitution.[5] He specifically examined two strategies: constant abatement, which requires the same degree of control over time, and forecasted abatement, which allows the degree of control to be tailored to forecasted weather conditions.

---

[4]A. Myrick Freeman III, *Air and Water Pollution Control: A Benefit-Cost Assessment* (New York: John Wiley & Sons, 1982).

[5]Azriel Teller, "Air Pollution Abatement: Economic Rationality and Reality," in *America's Changing Environment*, Roger Revelle and Hans H. Landsberg, eds. (Boston, MA: Beacon Press, 1970).

EXAMPLE 13.1

Net Benefit Analysis of the Particulate Ambient Standard

Although the EPA is precluded from considering benefit/cost analysis in setting ambient standards, it is not precluded from having the studies done. One such study was done as part of the process of considering whether to change the stringency or the form of the particulate ambient standard.

The purpose of the study was to aggregate on a national basis estimates of various forms of damage that would be done by particulate emissions (including health effects, soiling and materials damage, and visibility effects) under various regulatory regimes. The aggregation brought together a number of different studies, each relying on different data and different valuation techniques. These aggregate benefit estimates were then combined with cost information to produce net benefit information for each of the considered options.

Aggregating these rather different studies posed some problems. First, they were not all of equal quality. Some had gone through extensive peer review; others had not. Second, it was not clear whether estimates from the various studies could legitimately be added together without double-accounting some of the benefits. For example, the property and wage studies may indirectly be valuing the health effects that are more directly valued by epidemiological studies.

To grapple with these problems, Mathtech, Inc., the contractor on the study, did the net benefit analysis on a variety of regulatory options separately for each of six aggregation procedures. Unfortunately, they discovered that the ranking of standards in terms of economic efficiency was very sensitive to the different benefit estimation procedures employed. For the most restrictive accounting of benefits, all changes would lead to lower net benefits than merely continuing the current policy. For less restrictive benefit aggregation procedures, net benefits were highest for much more stringent standards.

The study also compared the net benefits from some of the more restrictive ambient standards depending upon whether the implementation deadline was 7 years or 9 years. For this aspect the results were conclusive—the 9-year implementation period produced higher net benefits.

Two insights on the use of benefit/cost analysis can be carried away from this specific example. First, the application of benefit/cost techniques to discover the efficient set of ambient standards is subject to a large number of uncertainties; the notion that analysts can derive a single, generally agreed-upon net benefit calculation for a specific regulatory option is naive. Second, despite these uncertainties, a great deal can be learned from the analysis even if it does not produce a single definitive answer. In this specific case, not only was the evidence on the implementation deadline unambiguous, but the analysis found that some regulatory options were dominated by others; armed with this evidence serious consideration can be focused on the undominated options.

Source: Mathtech, Inc., "Benefit and Net Benefit Analysis of Alternative National Ambient Air Quality Standards for Particulate Matter," Volume I of a report prepared for the Benefits Analysis Program of the U.S. Environmental Protection Agency (March 1983).

Both strategies achieve compliance with the ambient standards, but forecasted control requires less total emission reduction. His results indicate that constant abatement would be five times more expensive than forecasted abatement.

Concentration Versus Exposure. Present ambient standards are defined in terms of pollutant concentrations in the outdoor air, yet health effects are more closely related to human exposure to pollutants. (Exposure is determined both by the concentrations of air pollutants in each of the places in which people spend time and by the amount of time spent in each place.) Because only about 10 percent of the population's person-hours are spent outdoors, indoor air becomes very important in designing strategies to improve the health risk of pollutants.[6] Recent studies have suggested that exposure to pollutants is several times higher indoors than it is outdoors.[7] To date, despite its apparent importance, very little attention has been focused on controlling indoor air pollution.[8]

Cost Effectiveness of the Command-and-Control Approach

Though the ambient standards are not efficient, determining the magnitude of the inefficiency is plagued by uncertainties. It is not possible to state definitively just how inefficient they are.

Cost effectiveness is based on somewhat more solid evidence. Though it does not allow us to shed any light on whether a particular ambient standard is efficient or not, cost-effectiveness studies do allow us to see whether the command-and-control policy described earlier has resulted in the ambient standards being met in the least costly manner possible.

As we have seen, the CAC strategy will normally not be cost effective, but general principles are not enough to establish the degree to which this strategy diverges from the least-cost ideal. If the divergence is small, the proponents of reform would not likely be able to overcome the inertia of the status quo. If the divergence is large, the case for reform is stronger.

The cost effectiveness of the CAC approach depends on local circumstances such as prevailing meteorology, the locational configuration of sources, stack heights, and how costs vary with the amount controlled. Several simulation models capable of dealing with these complexities have now been constructed for a number of different pollutants in a variety of airsheds (Table 13.2).

For a number of reasons the estimated costs cannot be directly compared across studies, so it is appropriate to develop a means of comparing them that minimizes the comparability problems. One such technique, the one we have chosen, involves calculating the ratio of the CAC allocation costs to the lowest cost of meeting the same objective for each study. A ratio equal to 1.0 implies that the CAC allocation is cost effective. By subtracting 1.0 from the ratio in the table, it is possible to interpret the remainder as the percentage increase in cost from the least-cost ideal due to relying on the CAC system.

Of the nine reported comparisons, eight find that the CAC policy costs at least 78 percent more than the least-cost allocation. If we omit the Hahn and Noll [1982] study (for reasons discussed in the next two paragraphs), the study involving the *smallest* cost savings (sulfur dioxide control in the Lower Delaware Valley) finds that the CAC allocation results in abatement costs that are 78 percent higher than necessary to meet the standards. In the Chicago

---

[6]This estimate is for the United States.

[7]Kirk R. Smith, "Air Pollution: Assessing Total Exposure in the United States," *Environment* 30, No. 8 (October 1988): 10–15; 33–38.

[8]The one major policy response to indoor air pollution has been the large number of states which have passed legislation requiring "smoke free" areas in public places to protect nonsmokers.

TABLE 13.2 Empirical Studies of Air-Pollution Control

Study and Year	Pollutants Covered	Geographic Area	CAC benchmark	Assumed pollutant type	Ratio of CAC cost to least cost
Atkinson and Lewis (1974)	Particulates	St. Louis Metropolitan Area	SIP regulations	Nonuniformly mixed	6.00
Roach et al. (1981)	Sulfur dioxide	Four Corners in Utah, Colorado, Arizona and New MeFxico	SIP regulations	Nonuniformly mixed	4.25
Hahn and Noll (1982)	Sulfates	Los Angeles standards	California emission	Nonuniformly mixed	1.07
Krupnick (1983)	Nitrogen dioxide	Baltimore regulations	Proposed RACT	Nonuniformly mixed	5.96
Seskin, Anderson and Reid (1983)	Nitrogen dioxide	Chicago	Proposed RACT regulations	Nonuniformly mixed	14.40
McGartland (1984)	Particulates	Baltimore	SIP regulations	Nonuniformly mixed	4.18
Spofford (1984)	Sulfur dioxide	Lower Delaware Valley	Uniform percentage reduction	Nonuniformly mixed	1.78
	Particulates	Lower Delaware Valley	Uniform percentage reduction	Nonuniformly mixed	22.00
Maloney and Yandle (1984)	Hydrocarbons	All domestic Du Pont plants	Uniform percentage reduction	Uniformly mixed	4.15

Definitions: CAC = Command and control, the traditional regulatory approach
 SIP = State implementation plan
 RACT = Reasonably available control technologies, a set of standards imposed on existing sources in nonattainment areas.

study, the CAC costs are estimated to be 14 times as expensive as necessary, and in the Lower Delaware Valley they are estimated to be 22 times more expensive than necessary.

The Hahn and Noll finding that the CAC strategy was close to being cost effective was somewhat unique in a couple of respects. Because we can learn something from this study about the conditions under which CAC policies may not be far off the mark, it is worth subjecting it to close scrutiny.

The city studied by Hahn and Noll, Los Angeles, has a large sulfate problem, necessitating a very high degree of control. In effect, virtually every source is forced to control as much as is economically feasible. All policies must ultimately arrive at this allocation.[9]

Does the degree of cost excess associated with the CAC approach depend on the stringency of the ambient standard being met? The evidence seems to suggest that it does depend on the stringency, but in rather well-defined ways. Atkinson and Lewis [1974] find, for example, that within a middle range of possible ambient standards, the divergence between the CAC allocation and the least-cost allocation becomes larger as the ambient standard target becomes harder to meet. However, two authors concentrating on the most stringent range of control (as opposed to the middle ranges of control examined by Atkinson and Lewis) have found that the relative divergence between the CAC and least-cost allocations declines as the ambient standard becomes tougher to meet. Spofford finds this to be the case for both particulates and sulfur oxides; Maloney and Yandle find it to be true for hydrocarbon control.[10] Apparently the CAC air-pollution policy approximates the least-cost allocation only at sufficiently high degrees of control that any control flexibility is effectively eliminated.

Air Quality

Despite the deficiencies of this approach, it has produced better air quality in the United States. A 1990 U.S. EPA Report reveals that since 1979 particulate emissions are down 22 percent, sulfur dioxide emissions by 17 percent, carbon dioxide emissions by 25 percent, nitrogen dioxide emissions by 8 percent, volatile organic compounds (precursors for ozone formation) by 17 percent, and lead by 93 percent.[11]

How typical has the U.S. experience been? Is pollution declining on a worldwide basis? The Global Environmental Monitoring System, operating under the auspices of the World Health Organization and the United Nations Environment Program, monitors air quality

---

[9]Hahn and Noll also suggest that the California Air Resources Board has specifically used its multimillion-dollar budget in part to promulgate cost-effective emission standards. Therefore, this board may be atypically cost effective in its approach to a CAC strategy due to both the amount of resources at its disposal and its inclination to use them to pursue cost-effective allocations of control responsibility.

[10]See W. O. Spofford, Jr., "Efficiency Properties of Alternative Source Control Policies for Meeting Ambient Air Quality Standards: An Empirical Application to the Lower Delaware Valley," Discussion Paper D-118 (Washington, DC: Resources for the Future, 1984); and M. T. Maloney and B. Yandle, "Estimation of the Cost of Air Pollution Control Regulation," *Journal of Environmental Economics and Management* 11, (1984): 244–63.

[11]Office of Air Quality Planning and Standards, *National Air Quality and Emission Trends: 1988* (Raleigh, NC: U.S. Environmental Protection Agency, 1990).

around the globe. Scrutiny of its reports reveals that the U.S. experience is rather typical for the industrialized nations, which have generally reduced pollution (both in terms of emissions and ambient outdoor air quality).[12] Some of the reductions achieved in countries such as Japan and Norway have been spectacular. However, the air quality in most developing nations has steadily deteriorated, and the number of people exposed to unhealthy levels of pollution in those countries is frequently very high.[13] Because these countries typically are struggling merely to provide adequate employment and income to their citizens, they cannot afford to waste large sums of money on inefficient environmental policies, especially if the inefficiencies tend to subsidize the rich at the expense of the poor. Some cost-effective but fair means of improving air quality must be found.

INNOVATIVE APPROACHES

Fortunately, some innovative approaches are available. Because various versions of these approaches have now been implemented around the world, we can learn from the experience gained from their implementation.

The Emissions Trading Program

Stripped to its essentials, the command-and-control approach toward stationary sources involves the specification of emission standards (legal ceilings) on all major emission sources. These standards are imposed on a large number of specific emission points such as stacks, vents, or storage tanks.

The emissions trading program adopted in the United States attempts to inject more flexibility into the manner in which the clean air objectives are met. Sources are encouraged to change the mix of control technologies envisioned in the standards as long as air quality is improved or at least not adversely affected by the change. The program is implemented by means of four separate policies, linked by a common element known as the emission reduction credit. The emission reduction credit is the currency used in trading among emission points, whereas the offset, bubble, emissions banking, and netting policies govern how the currency can be spent.[14]

The Emission Reduction Credit.   Should any source decide to control any emission point to a higher degree than necessary to fulfill its legal obligations, it can apply to the control authority for certification of the excess control as an emission reduction credit. Certified credits can be banked or used in the bubble, offset, or netting programs. To receive certification, the emission reduction must be (1) surplus, (2) enforceable, (3) permanent, and (4) quantifiable.

---

[12]United Nations Environment Program and the World Health Organization, "Monitoring the Global Environment: An Assessment of Urban Air Quality," *Environment* 31, No. 8 (October 1989): 6–13, 26–37.

[13]For sulfur oxides, for example, the GEMS study estimates that only 30 to 35 percent of the world's population lives in areas where air is at least as clean as recommended by the World Health Organization guidelines.

[14]As described in the next chapter, these policies have recently been adopted for controlling acid rain and ozone-depleting chemicals as well.

The Offset Policy.   The offset policy was established to resolve a conflict between economic growth and progress toward meeting the ambient standards in nonattainment areas. The dilemma posed by this conflict involved how new or expanded sources could be accommodated while meeting the statutory requirement that the ambient standards be met as expeditiously as possible. Because these sources would add emission to the region, some means of offsetting them had to be found.

The offset policy allows qualified new or expanding sources to commence operations in a nonattainment area provided they acquire sufficient emission reduction credits from existing sources. Typically, they must acquire credits for 20 percent more reductions in emissions than would be added when the new facility commences operations. By buying the credits, new sources, in effect, finance emission controls undertaken by existing sources, thereby serving as a vehicle for improved air quality. Because regional emissions would be lower after the source began operations (counting the acquired emission reduction credits) than before, economic growth became the means for achieving better air quality rather than the source of further deterioration.

Major new or modified sources are qualified to participate in this program only if they control their own emissions to the degree required by the LAER standard and all existing major sources owned or operated by the applicant in the same state as the proposed source are in compliance with their legal control responsibilities.

The Bubble Policy.   The bubble policy allows existing sources to use emission reduction credits to satisfy their SIP control responsibilities. For example, existing sources in nonattainment areas can meet their assigned RACT standards either by adopting the control technology used to define the standard or by adopting some technology that emits the pollutant at a somewhat higher rate, making up the difference with acquired emission reduction credits. The sum of emission reduction credits plus actual reductions must equal the assigned reduction.

This policy derives its unusual name from its treatment of multiple emission points as if they were contained within an imaginary bubble, regulating only the amount leaving the bubble. These bubbles can be extended to include not only emission points within the same plant, but emission points in plants owned by other firms as well (Example 13.2).

Netting.   Netting allows sources undergoing modification or expansion to escape the burden of new-source review requirements so long as any net increase (counting the emission reduction credits) in plantwide emissions is insignificant. Traditionally, the test of whether a source was subject to the new-source review process or not was applied by calculating the expected increases in emission occurring after modernization or expansion. When these increases passed predetermined thresholds, the source was subject to review. Netting allows emission reduction credits earned elsewhere in the plant to offset the increases expected from the expanded, more modernized portion in order to determine whether the threshold had been exceeded. By "netting out" of review, the facility may be exempted from the need to acquire preconstruction permits as well as from meeting the associated requirements, such as modeling or monitoring the impact of the new source on air quality, installing BACT or LAER control technology, or meeting the offset requirement; it may also avoid any applicable bans on new construction. Those facilities satisfying the significant increase threshold must still meet emission limits established by the NSPS. Emission reduction credits cannot be used to avoid this national standard.

EXAMPLE 13.2

The Bubble and Offset Policies in Action

At the end of 1981, EPA had been approached by about 93 different bubble trades, and the number was growing daily. A number of these presented the prospect of saving the purchaser substantial sums of money:

1. The Narraganset Electric Company has two generating stations in Providence, Rhode Island. Under the bubble policy they were allowed to use high-sulfur oil (2.2 percent sulfur) at one plant when the second plant was burning natural gas or was not operating, instead of being required to burn 1 percent sulfur oil at both plants. This action resulted in a savings of $3 million annually, reduced the use of imported oil by 600,000 barrels per year, and reduced sulfur emissions by 30 percent.

2. The Du Pont Corporation was allowed to control five major sources of volatile organic compounds to more than 97 percent efficiency in exchange for relaxed controls on more than 200 difficult-to-control sources of fugitive emissions. The expected savings include $12 million in capital costs plus several million dollars in recurring operating costs.

3. Manufacturers of cans were allowed to comply with existing regulations for each individual can-coating line by averaging emissions of volatile organic compounds on a daily basis so long as the source did not exceed the total allowable plantwide emission per day. This is expected to save the industry $107 million in capital expenditures, $28 million per year in operating costs, and 4 trillion BTUs of natural gas per year, chiefly because expensive add-on pollution-control equipment, which would have been energy-consuming, is no longer necessary.

The exact number of offset transactions that have occurred is not known with any certainty. Some examples serve to illustrate the flexibility this system provides:

1. A cement company in Texas entered into an agreement with another local company providing for that company to install dust collectors. The cement company paid for the equipment, and the other company agreed to accept the maintenance costs, which were negligible.

2. The emissions from a 90-megawatt refuse-burning power plant to be operated by the city of Columbus, Ohio, were offset at the city's expense by installing pollution controls at two privately owned asphalt plants and by increasing the height of a smokestack at a third company.

3. A company wanting to build an oil terminal to handle 40,000 barrels a day in Contra Costa County, California, was granted a permit when it acquired, for $250,000, an offset created when a local chemical company shut down.

4. In the mid-1970s the state of Pennsylvania created an offset by altering its road-paving practices—which served to reduce hydrocarbon emissions—and used this offset to successfully induce the Volkswagen Corporation to locate its first American production facility in a depressed region in that state.

Source: These examples were taken from the National Commission of Air Quality, *To Breathe Clean Air* (Washington, DC: U.S. Government Printing Office, 1981): 136–37; and Richard A. Liroff, *Air Pollution Offsets: Trading, Selling and Banking* (Washington, DC: The Conservation Foundation, 1980): 13.

Banking.   The banking component of the emission trading program establishes procedures that allow firms to store emission reduction credits for subsequent use in the bubble, offset, or netting programs. States are authorized to design their own banking programs as long as the rules specify the ownership rights over the banked credits, the sources eligible to bank emission reduction credits, and the conditions governing the certification, holding, and use of these credits.

Smog Trading.   Because the federal statutes are permissive, states are given considerable latitude in tailoring new trading programs to their needs. Faced with one of the worst air-quality problems in the country, the Los Angeles area in California has exploited this opportunity to create a system of "smog trading" credits. Involving nitrogen oxides and sulfur oxides, this program attempts to bring under strict control the main precursors of smog. Because the costs of these controls are expected to be very high, allowing intersource trading provides a means of reducing compliance costs[15] and, it is hoped, of increasing the willingness to comply with the new regulations.

The Effectiveness of Emissions Trading

Although comprehensive data on the effects of the program do not exist because substantial proportions of it are administered by local areas and no one collects information in a systematic way, some of the major aspects of experience are clear.[16]

The program has unquestionably and substantially reduced the cost of complying with the requirements of the Clean Air Act. Most estimates place the accumulated capital savings for all components of the program at over $10 billion. This does not include the recurring savings in operating cost. On the other hand, the program has not produced the magnitude of cost savings that was anticipated by most proponents at its inception.

The level of compliance with the basic provisions of the Clean Air Act has increased. The emissions trading program expanded the possible means for compliance and sources have responded.

Somewhere between 7,000 and 12,000 trading transactions have been consummated. Each of these transactions was voluntary and for the participants represented an improvement over the traditional regulatory approach. Several of these transactions involved the introduction of innovative control technologies.

The vast majority of emissions trading transactions have involved large pollution sources trading emissions reduction credits either created by excess control of uniformly mixed pollutants (those for which the location of emission is not an important policy concern) or involv-

---

[15]Initial estimates suggested that $434 million of the expected 1994 compliance costs of $660 million could be saved by introducing trading. See "Marketable Permits Program" (Los Angeles: South Coast Air Quality Management District, 1991): Ex-3.

[16]See the evaluations of this program in D. J. Dudek and J. Palmisano, "Emissions Trading: Why Is This Thoroughbred Hobbled?" *Columbia Journal of Environmental Law*, Vol. 13, No. 2 (1988): 217-56; R. W. Hahn, "Economic Prescriptions for Environmental Problems: How the Patient Followed the Doctor's Orders," *The Journal of Economics Perspectives*, Vol. 3, No. 2 (Spring, 1989): 95-114; R. W. Hahn, and G. L. Hester, "Where Did All the Markets Go? An Analysis of EPA's Emission Trading Program," *Yale Journal of Regulation*, Vol. 6, No.1 (Winter, 1989): 109-153; and T. H. Tietenberg, "Economic Instruments for Environmental Regulation" *Oxford Review of Economic Policy* Vol. 6, No. 1 (Spring, 1990): 17-33.

ing facilities in close proximity to one another. Emissions trading seems to work especially well for uniformly mixed pollutants. No diffusion modeling is necessary to establish effects on ambient concentrations, and regulators do not have to worry about trades creating "hot spots" or localized areas of high pollution concentration. Trades can be on a 1:1 basis.

Emissions trading integrates particularly smoothly into any policy structure that is based either directly (through emission standards) or indirectly (through mandated technology or input limitations) on regulating emissions. In this case, emission limitations embedded in the operating licenses can serve as the trading benchmark.

Because emissions trading allows the issue of who will pay for the control to be separated from who will install the control, it introduces an additional degree of flexibility. This flexibility is particularly important in nonattainment areas because marginal control costs are so high. Sources that would not normally be controlled because they could not afford to implement the controls without going out of business can be controlled with emissions trading. The revenue derived from the sale of emission reduction credits can be used to finance the controls, effectively preventing bankruptcy.

Because it is quantity based, emissions trading also offers a unique possibility for leasing. Leasing is particularly valuable when the temporal pattern of emissions varies across sources. This appears to be the general case with utilities. In addition, when a firm plans to shut down one plant in the near future and to build a new one, leasing credits is a vastly superior alternative to temporarily installing equipment in the old plant that would be useless when the plant was retired. The useful life of this temporary control equipment would be wastefully short.

We have also learned that ERC transactions have higher transaction costs than we previously understood. Regulators must validate every trade. When nonuniformly mixed pollutants are involved, the transaction costs associated with estimating the air-quality effects are particularly high. Delegating responsibility for trade approval to lower levels of government may in principle speed up the approval process, but unless the bureaucrats in the lower level of government support the program, the gain may be negligible.

Emissions trading places more importance on the operating permits and emissions inventories than other approaches. To the extent that these are deficient, the potential for trades that protect air quality may be lost. Firms that have actual levels of emissions substantially below allowable emissions find themselves with a trading opportunity which, if exploited, could degrade air quality. The trading benchmark has to be defined carefully.

One question that always arises about emissions trading is the degree to which market power could undermine its desirable properties. Hahn has examined the case where permits are allocated to emitters without charge (as is done in the Emissions Trading Program) rather than allocating them by an auction.[17] His most important finding was that this initial allocation could have an effect on both the final (post-trade) allocation of permits and the permit price in the presence of market power. This finding is in direct contrast to what would happen in competitive markets (as described in Chapter 13), where both the final price and the ultimate allocation of permits would be independent of the initial allocation.

It is not hard to obtain an intuitive understanding of why the initial allocation might have an effect on the potential for price-setting behavior. Whenever a single price-setting source receives an initial allocation that is either higher than or lower than its cost-effective alloca-

[17]Robert W. Hahn, "Market Power and Transferable Property Rights," *Quarterly Journal of Economics* 99, No. 4 (November 1984): 753–65.

tion, an incentive for trading would be created. When a price-setting source receives in an initial allocation fewer permits than its cost-effective allocation, it would exercise power on the buyer's side of the market. If it received more, it would exercise power on the seller's side of the market. The farther the initial allocation diverges from the cost-effective allocation, the greater the potential for the price-setter to exercise power over the market.

Is the potential for price manipulation a serious potential flaw in permit markets? Existing simulation studies suggest that it is not. Hahn found in simulating the sulfate market in Los Angeles that the total cost function was rather flat with respect to the initial allocation unless the price-setting firm received enough permits that it was able to become virtually a monopoly seller.

In another set of published data from the Du Pont Corporation involving some 52 plants and 548 sources of hydrocarbons, Maloney and Yandle investigated the effects of cartelization of plants on the permit market.[18] Assuming that all sources receive a proportional initial distribution of the permits based on their uncontrolled emissions, they calculate the effects on control costs if plants collude. Their analysis allows collusion to take place separately among buyers and sellers and allows the number of colluding plants to vary from 10 to 90 percent of the total number of plants buying or selling.

In general, these data support the notion that high degrees of cartelization are necessary before control costs are affected to any appreciable degree and that even high degrees of cartelization do not significantly erode the large savings to be achieved from permit markets. At the 90 percent credit monopoly (achieved when the cartel controls 90 percent of all credits sold), for example, yielding a 41 percent increase in control costs, Maloney and Yandle point out that the cost savings from this severe market power situation, compared with command-and-control regulation, is still 66 (instead of 76) percent. The presence of market power does not seem to diminish the potential for cost savings very much. Even with market power, transferable permit systems seem to result in lower control costs than the command-and-control allocation.

In summary, the current regulatory reforms embodying transferable permits represent a large, but incomplete, step toward cost effectiveness.

Emission Charges

Air-pollution emission charges have been implemented by France and Japan. The French air-pollution charge was designed to encourage the early adoption of pollution control equipment, with the revenues returned to those paying the charge as a subsidy for installing the equipment. In Japan the emission charge is designed to raise revenue to compensate victims of air pollution.

The French charge system has been in effect since 1985. Originally designed to operate until 1990, it was renewed in that year. The charge is levied on all industrial firms having a power generating capacity of 50,000 watts or more, or industrial firms discharging over 2,500 tons of sulfur or nitrogen oxides per year. Only about 400 plants are affected. The charge is levied on the amount of actual sulfur oxides emitted. Some 90 percent of the charge revenue

[18]Michael T. Maloney and Bruce Yandle, "Estimation of the Cost of Air Pollution Control Regulation," *Journal of Environmental Economics and Management* 11, No. 3 (September 1984): 244–63.

is recovered by charge payers as a subsidy for pollution-control equipment; the remaining 10 percent is used for new technological developments.

Although data are limited, a few highlights seem clear. The charge level is too low to have any incentive impact. Total revenues are estimated to be about one tenth of the revenue that would result from a charge sufficient to bring French industries in line with the air-pollution control directives of the European Community.[19]

Economists typically envision two types of effluent or emissions charges. The first, an efficiency charge, is designed to produce an efficient outcome by forcing the polluter to compensate completely for all damage caused. The second, a cost-effective charge, is designed to achieve a predefined ambient standard at the lowest possible control cost. In practice the French approach fits neither of these designs.

In Japan the charge takes on a rather different function. As a result of four important legal cases where Japanese industries were forced to compensate victims for pollution damages caused, in 1973 Japan passed the Law for the Compensation of Pollution-Related Health Injury. According to this law, upon certification by a council of medical, legal, and other experts, victims of designated diseases are eligible for medical expenses, lost earnings, and other expenses; they are not eligible for other losses such as pain and suffering. Two classes of diseases are funded: specific diseases, where the specific source is relatively clear, and nonspecific respiratory diseases, where all polluters are presumed to have some responsibility.

This program is funded by an emissions charge on sulfur dioxides and from an automobile weight tax. The level of the tax is determined by the revenue needs of the compensation fund.

In contrast to emissions trading, where ERC prices respond automatically to changing market conditions, emission charges have to be determined by an administrative process. When the function of the charge is to raise revenue for a particular purpose, charge rates will be determined by the costs of achieving that purpose; when the costs of achieving the purpose rise, the level of the charge must rise to secure the additional revenue.[20]

Sometimes that process produces an unintended dynamic. In Japan, for example, the charge is calculated on the basis of the amount of compensation paid to victims of air pollution in the previous year. Although the amount of compensation has been increasing, the amount of emissions (the base to which the charge is applied) has been decreasing. As a result, unexpectedly high charge rates are necessary to raise sufficient revenue for the compensation system.

Hazardous Pollutants

Hazardous pollutants are those that pose a localized risk of severe harm to human health. They are distinguished from criteria pollutants both by the degree of harm they pose to those exposed and by the fact that emission usually occurs only at a few key locations. In recognition of these unique characteristics, the Clean Air Act sets up a special process for dealing with hazardous pollutants.

---

[19]J. B. Opschoor and Hans B. Vos, *Economic Instruments For Environmental Protection* (Paris: Organization for Economic Co-operation and Development, 1989): 34–35.

[20]Although it is theoretically possible (depending on the elasticity of demand for pollution abatement) for a rise in the tax to produce less revenue, this has typically not been the case.

The first step in the control process involves identifying those substances that are designated as hazardous and therefore must receive this special treatment. The Act requires the Administrator of EPA to make and periodically update a list of hazardous pollutants. It allows a great deal of discretion in the choice of criteria to be used in distinguishing between hazardous and criteria pollutants and in the length of time necessary to decide whether a particular substance should be listed.

Once a substance is listed, EPA must move with great speed (180 days) either to regulate emissions of the substance or to remove it from the list after finding that the evidence failed to support the tentative hazardous-substance designation. The decision to regulate a substance imposes on EPA a requirement to establish a national emission standard or workplace standard for each regulated substance. These standards must be designed to protect human health with an adequate margin of safety.

The somewhat ambiguous language in this section of the Act has led to a great deal of controversy as well as litigation concerning the meaning of this mandate. It is generally conceded that there is no safe threshold level for airborne carcinogens. Therefore, environmentalists maintain that protecting the public with an adequate margin of safety requires eliminating all exposure to listed substances. Completely eliminating emissions would, at a minimum, be very expensive and in some cases may not be possible without shutting down the operation.

The EPA has reacted to this dilemma in two ways: (1) It has moved slowly in listing pollutants, and (2) it has chosen to balance costs and risks in deciding whether to list a substance or not. By 1989, the EPA had listed only eight pollutants: asbestos (1971), beryllium (1971), mercury (1971), vinyl chloride (1975), benzene (1977), radionuclides (1979), inorganic arsenic (1980), and radon-222 (1985).

In addition to moving very slowly in listing pollutants, the agency began to incorporate risk assessment and benefit/cost analysis into their decisions. The first step in this process is to decide whether the risk posed by the substance is "significant." Substances that are not found to be posing significant risks are not listed. The second step, taken only for listed pollutants, involves identifying the level of control that will be required. This entails comparing the costs of various control possibilities with the damages to health prevented by adopting the controls.

Based on the work of Haigh, Harrison, and Nichols, it is possible to see how this kind of economic analysis can be applied to regulating hazardous pollution.[21] In their study, the authors applied benefit/cost analysis to three hazardous pollutants: benzene, coke oven emissions, and acrylonitrile. Benzene is a major industrial chemical, ranking among the top 15 in terms of production volume. Coke, produced by distilling coal in ovens, is essential to the production of steel. Acrylonitrile is an important industrial chemical used in the manufacture of a wide range of consumer products, including rugs, clothing, plastic pipe, and automobile hoses.

The analysis involved several steps. The amount and location of emission had to be identified for each substance. The number of people exposed to this risk and the amount of health risk they would experience had to be calculated. Finally, a dollar value had to be put on this

[21]John A. Haigh, David Harrison, Jr., and Albert L. Nichols, "Benefits Assessment and Environmental Regulation: Case Studies of Hazardous Air Pollutants," Discussion Paper E-83-07 (Cambridge, MA: John F. Kennedy School of Government Energy and Environment Policy Center, 1983).

TABLE 13.3   Net Benefits ($Million/Year) of Alternative Strategies for a Value of Life Saved of $1 Million

Regulatory Strategy	Maleic Anhydrite	Coke Oven Emissions	Acrylonitrile
Best Available Technology	−2.2	−8.7	−28.8
Relaxed Uniform	−1.1	−3.2	−8.0
Differential	−0.6	−2.3	−4.9

Source: From "Benefits Assessment and Environmental Regulation: Case Studies of Hazardous Air Pollutants" by John A. Haigh, David Harrison, Jr., and Albert L. Nichols. John F. Kennedy School of Government Energy and Environment Policy Center Discussion Paper E-83-07 (August 1983). Reprinted by permission.

risk so that it could be directly compared with the control costs. All of these steps had to be repeated for each considered regulatory option.

Three regulatory strategies were considered for each pollutant. The first strategy was a rather stringent set of uniformly applied emission standards designed to require the use of the "best available technology." (For benzene, the controls were applied to maleic anhydride plants, the largest source of emissions.) The second considered strategy involved a somewhat more relaxed version of the first strategy. Although the standards were still applied uniformly in this second case, the level of required control was lower. The final strategy involved differential controls based on exposure. The notion of uniform controls was dropped in this case in favor of placing heavier controls on those sources posing the greatest health risk.

The authors present their results in two main forms. The first calculates the value of human life that would be needed to justify a particular regulatory option. This form of presentation allows the reader to decide whether the regulatory option is a good idea or not by supplying his or her own sense of what the value of human life should be. The second uses a $1 million value of human life and calculates the net benefits of each option based on that assumption.

Using the $1 million figure for a human life, the results (Table 13.3) indicate that for all three pollutants the standard best available technology (BAT) strategy would yield negative net benefits. The combination of uniform standards with a very stringent level of control produces a situation where the costs exceed the benefits. A relaxed uniform standard reduces, but does not eliminate, the negative net benefits. Although lowering the uniform degree of control represents an improvement in the sense that costs are more commensurate with benefits, it still fails to target the reductions in the areas where they result in the most reduction in risk.

By configuring the controls so as to target the costs on those emitters posing the greatest risk to human health (the differential strategy), a dramatic improvement in net benefits is achieved for all three pollutants. However, for only one, coke oven emissions, are the net benefits positive. For the rest, even the differential strategy falls short of being justified by the benefits.

The significance of these data lies less in what they tell us about the correct regulatory option to choose for these specific pollutants than in the clues they provide concerning directions for policy to move in achieving greater efficiency in regulating hazardous pollutants in general. First, tailoring the strategy to the specific circumstances can produce significant re-

EXAMPLE 13.3

Efficient Regulation of Hazardous Pollutants: The Benzene Case

Regulatory approaches tend to emphasize uniform standards. As was clear from the discussion in the text, this can cause a particularly large deviation from efficiency when hazardous pollutants are involved, because both the control costs and damages are so localized.

Eight maleic anhydride plants in the United States emit more than half of the benzene from chemical manufacturing. From Table 13.3 we know that BAT uniform standards yield negative net benefits. Is there a more efficient approach?

The damage caused by these emissions (primarily an increase in the risk of leukemia) is a function both of the concentration level and the exposed population. The highest economic marginal damage estimate found by a government agency was $1 for each person exposed continuously to a concentration of one part per billion (ppb) of benzene for one year. This corresponds to a risk of 3.4 ppb for one year and a value of $360,000 placed on each life lost.

The efficient solution would be to impose an emission charge of $1 per ppb person-year exposed because this is the (high) estimate of marginal damage. Firms would respond by choosing that level of control where their marginal cost was equal to $1 per ppb person-year exposed. Because this would guarantee the equivalence of marginal cost and marginal benefit, efficiency would be achieved.

The costs of the uniform standard were not justified by the benefits. The major problem with the proposed standard was that it did not take into account either the rather large differences among the plants in control costs and number of people exposed. Some plants in isolated areas exposed very few people, whereas others in more densely populated areas clearly put more people at risk. The $1 uniform *exposure* charge solves both of these problems simultaneously. A uniform *emission* charge would take into account the differences in costs, but not the differences in exposure. Uniform emission standards take neither costs nor exposure into account and, therefore, are doubly cursed.

Source: This example is based on Albert L. Nichols, "The Importance of Exposure in Evaluating and Designing Environmental Regulations: A Case Study," *The American Economic Review* 72 (May 1982): 214–19.

ductions in cost while achieving the same risk, or it can achieve much larger risk reductions for the same cost. Uniformity, in short, imposes a large cost penalty. Second, the policies being pursued in regulating hazardous pollutants imply values for human life that differ by a factor of more than 100. This finding implies that by allocating more resources to the control of those substances which can be justified with even a lower value of life and less to those which can be justified only with a high value for life, more lives could be saved with the same expenditure of money.

How can these lessons be translated into policy? One answer is to consider the adoption of a charge levied not on emission, but rather on exposure (Example 13.3).By forcing those emitters exposing large numbers of people to a health risk to exert greater cleanup efforts than those emitters exposing fewer people to the same health risk, more lives can be saved with the same expenditure of resources. In this context, uniform exposure charges have much to recommend them.

Emissions Fees

Recognizing that the bulk of enforcement activity falls on the states and wanting to provide increased funds for that endeavor without increasing the federal budget deficit, the U.S. Congress incorporated a system of fees on polluters in Title V of the Clean Air Act.[22] Just as economists would recommend, these fees are levied annually on emissions on a per unit basis; higher emission levels trigger higher payments. Some states are planning to further differentiate the fees based on the toxicity of the substances being emitted.[23] All polluters holding permits must pay the fees to the state enforcement agencies, and the revenues must be sufficient to cover the costs of administering the program. States are free to set their own fee schedule, although the act creates a presumptive minimum annual fee of $25/ton, adjusted each year by changes in the consumer price index. In essence, this program was designed to make polluters bear the financial responsibility for the monitoring and enforcement system made necessary by their pollution. Though this fee system falls short of being fully efficient (because it is based on revenue needs, not damages), it is certainly a step in the right direction.

SUMMARY

Although air quality has improved in the industrial nations, it has deteriorated in the developing nations. Because the historical approach to air-pollution control has been a traditional command- and-control approach, it has been neither efficient nor cost effective.

The command-and-control policy has not been efficient in part because it has been based on a legal fiction, a threshold below which no health damages are inflicted on any member of the population. In fact, damages occur at levels lower than the ambient standards to especially sensitive members of the population, such as those with respiratory problems. This attempt to formulate standards without reference to control costs has been thwarted by the absence of a scientifically defensible health-based threshold. In addition, the policy fails to adequately consider the timing of emission flows. By failing to target the greatest amount of control on those periods when the greatest damage is inflicted, the current policy encourages too little control in high-damage periods and excessive control during low-damage periods. Current policy has also failed to pay sufficient attention to indoor air pollution, which may well pose larger health risks than outdoor pollution. Unfortunately, because the existing benefit estimates have large confidence intervals, the size of the inefficiency associated with these aspects of the policy has not been measured with any precision.

---

[22]Section 502(b)(3).

[23]Differentiating by toxicity is a feature of the Maine Department of Environmental Protection's proposed regulation, for example.

The policy is not cost-effective either. The allocation of responsibility among emitters for reducing pollution has resulted in control costs that are typically several times higher than necessary to achieve the air-quality objective. This has been shown to be true for a variety of pollutants in a variety of geographic settings.

Recently, the EPA has initiated the Emissions Trading Program, based on economic incentives that is designed to provide more flexibility in meeting the air-quality goals while reducing the cost and the conflict between economic growth and the preservation of air quality. These reforms, known as the bubble, offset, netting, and emissions banking programs, also promise to stimulate more rapid development of new control technologies than was possible under the traditional system.

France and Japan have both introduced emission charges as part of their approach to pollution control, but neither application fits the textbook model very well. In France the charge level is too low to have the appropriate incentive effects. In Japan the charge is designed mainly to raise revenue for compensating victims of respiratory damage caused by pollution. Only sulfur oxides are taxed.

The program to control hazardous pollutants is inefficient both in the speed with which the process is operating and in the quality of the decisions being rendered. Faced with unrealistically short deadlines for publishing standards once a hazardous substance is listed, the EPA has reacted by taking an excessively cautious approach to listing hazardous substances. Past decisions have resulted in the application of stringent standards that are uniformly applied to emitters. The evidence suggests that strategies tailored more closely to the risk posed (with emissions posing the greatest risk being reduced more) produce substantially lower risks for the same expenditure as uniformly applied standards. One reform proposal based on this analysis would impose an exposure (as opposed to an emissions) charge on emitters that would take into account not only the concentration of the emission (and the resulting health risk to each exposed person), but also the number of people exposed.

FURTHER READING

Freeman, A. Myrick, III. *Air and Water Pollution Control: A Benefit-Cost Assessment* (New York: John Wiley & Sons, 1982). A detailed survey and critical evaluation of the literature on benefit/cost analysis as it applies to air and water pollution control. Contains chapters on defining and measuring benefits associated with health of humans, vegetation, and aesthetics as well as on water recreation. Calculates a range of estimates as well as the "most likely" point estimate.

Joeres, Erhard F., and Martin H. David, eds. *Buying a Better Environment: Cost Effective Regulation through Permit Trading* (Madison, WI: The University of Wisconsin Press, 1983). An excellent collection of essays on aspects of permit trading including permit design, distributional matters, and dealing with uncertainty.

Nichols, Albert L. *Targeting Economic Incentives for Environmental Protection* (Cambridge, MA: MIT Press, 1984). An excellent review of the use of economic incentives to control pollution with a detailed treatment of the use of exposure charges to control airborne carcinogens.

Tietenberg, T. H. "Economic Instruments for Environmental Regulation," *Oxford Review of Economic Policy* 6, No. 1 (Spring 1990): 17–33. A detailed examination of the lessons to be learned from existing applications of the economic incentives approach to pollution control.

ADDITIONAL REFERENCES

Anderson, Robert J., Jr., et al. "An Analysis of Alternative Policies for Attaining and Maintaining a Short-Term NO_2 Standard," a report prepared by Mathtech, Inc., for the Council on Environmental Quality (17 September 1979).

Atkinson, Scott E., and Donald H. Lewis. "A Cost-Effective Analysis of Alternative Air Quality Control Strategies," *Journal of Environmental Economics and Management* I (November 1974): 237–50.

Blackman, Sue Anne Batey, and William J. Baumol. "Modified Fiscal Incentives in Environmental Policy," *Land Economics* 56 (November 1980): 417–31.

Hahn, Robert W., and Roger G. Noll. "Designing a Market for Tradeable Emissions Permits," in Wesley A. Magat, ed., *Reform of Environmental Regulation* (Cambridge, MA: Ballinger, 1982).

Krupnick, Alan J. "Costs of Alternative Policies for the Control of NO_2 in the Baltimore Region," Unpublished Working Paper (Resources for the Future, 1983).

Marcus, Alfred A. "Japan," in Frederic N. Bolotin, ed., *International Public Policy Sourcebook: Volume 2, Education and Environment* (New York: Greenwood Press, 1989): 275–91.

McGartland, Albert M. "Marketable Permit Systems for Air Pollution Control: An Empirical Study," Ph.D. dissertation (College Park: University of Maryland, 1984).

Oates, Wallace E., Paul R. Portney, and Albert M. McGartland. "The *Net* Benefits of Incentive-Based Regulation: A Case Study of Environmental Standard-Setting," *The American Economic Review* 79, No. 5 (December 1989): 1233–42.

Pezzey, John. "The Symmetry Between Controlling Pollution by Price and Controlling It by Quantity," *Canadian Journal of Economics* 25, No. 4 (November 1992): 983–91.

Portney, Paul R. "Air Pollution Policy" in Paul R. Portney, ed., *Public Policies for Environmental Protection* (Washington, DC: Resources for the Future, 1990): 27–96.

Roach, Fred Charles Kolstad, Allen V. Kneese, Richard Tobin, and Michael Williams. "Alternative Air Quality Policy Options in the Four Corners Region," *Southwest Review* 1, No. 2 (Summer 1981): 29–58.

Roumasset, James A., and Kirk R. Smith. "Exposure Trading: An Approach to More Efficient Air Pollution Control," *Journal of Environmental Economics and Management* 18, No. 3 (May 1990): 276–91.

Seskin, Eugene P., Robert J. Anderson, and Robert O. Reid. "An Empirical Analysis of Economic Strategies for Controlling Air Pollution," *Journal of Environmental Economics and Management*, 10, No. 2 (June 1983): 112–24.

Spofford, Walter O., Jr. "Efficiency Properties of Alternative Source Control Policies for Meeting Ambient Air Quality Standards: An Empirical Application to the Lower Delaware Valley," Unpublished Discussion Paper D-1189 (Resources for the Future, 1984).

Schelling, Thomas C., ed. *Incentives for Environmental Protection* (Cambridge, MA: MIT Press, 1983).

DISCUSSION QUESTIONS

1. As shown in Example 13.3, the efficient regulation of hazardous pollutants should take exposure into account—the more persons exposed to a given pollutant concentration, the larger is the damage caused by it and therefore the smaller is the efficient concentration level, all other things being equal. An alternative point of view would simply insure that concentrations would be held below a uniform threshold regardless of the number of people exposed. From this point of view, the public policy goal is to expose any and all people to the same concentration level—exposure is not used to establish different concentrations for different settings. What are the advantages and disadvantages of each approach? Which do you think represents the best approach? Why?

2. European countries have relied to a much greater extent on emission charges than has the United States, which seems to be moving toward a greater reliance on transferable emission permits. From an efficiency point of view, should the United States follow Europe's lead and shift the emphasis toward emission charges? Why or why not?

CHAPTER 14

Acid Rain and Atmospheric Modification

Everything should be made as simple as possible, but not simpler.

ALBERT EINSTEIN

INTRODUCTION

As the zone of influence of pollutants extends beyond local boundaries, the political difficulties of implementing comprehensive, cost-effective control measures are compounded. Pollutants crossing boundaries impose external costs; neither emitters nor the nations within which they emit have the proper incentives for controlling them.

Compounding the problem of improper incentives is the scientific uncertainty that limits our understanding of most of these problems. Our knowledge about various relationships that form the basis for our understanding of the magnitude of the problems and the effectiveness of various strategies to control them is far from complete. Unfortunately, the problems are so important and the potential consequences of inaction so drastic that procrastination is not usually an optimal strategy. To avoid having to act in the future under emergency conditions when the remaining choices are few in number, strategies that have desirable properties must be formulated now on the basis of the available information, as limited as it may be. Options must be preserved.

The costs of inaction are not limited to the damages caused. International cooperation among such traditional allies as the United States, Mexico, and Canada and the countries of Europe has been undermined by disputes over the proper control of acid rain.

In this chapter we shall survey the scientific evidence on the severity of global and regional pollution and the potential effectiveness of policy strategies designed to alleviate these problems. We shall also consider difficulties confronted by the government in implementing solutions and the role of economic analysis in understanding how to circumvent these difficulties.

REGIONAL POLLUTANTS

The primary difference between regional pollutants and local pollutants is the distance they are transported in the air. Although the damage caused by local pollutants occurs in the vicinity of emission, for regional pollutants the damage can occur at significant distances from the emission point.

The same substances can be both local pollutants and regional pollutants. Sulfur oxides, nitrogen oxides, and ozone, for example, have already been discussed as local pollutants, but they are regional pollutants as well. For example, sulfur emissions, the focal point for most acid-rain legislation, have been known to travel some 200 to 600 miles from the point of emission before returning to the earth. As the substances are being transported by the winds, they undergo a complex series of chemical reactions. Under the right conditions, both sulfur and nitrogen oxides are transformed into sulfuric and nitric acids. Nitrogen oxides and hydrocarbons can combine in the presence of sunlight to produce ozone.

Acid Rain

Acid rain, the popular term for atmospheric deposition of acidic substances, is actually a misnomer. Acidic substances are not only deposited by rain and other forms of moist air, they are also deposited as dry particles. In some parts of the world, such as the southwestern United States, dry deposition is a more important source of acidity than wet deposition.

Precipitation is normally mildly acidic, with a global background pH of 5.0 (pH is the common measurement for acidity; the lower the number, the more acidic the substance, with 7.0 being the border between acidity and alkalinity). Industrialized areas commonly receive precipitation well in excess of the global background. Rainfall in eastern North America, for example, has a typical pH of 4.4. Wheeling, West Virginia, once experienced a rainstorm with a pH of 1.5. The fact that battery acid has a pH of 1.0 may help put this event into perspective.

Though natural sources of acid deposition do exist, the evidence is quite clear that anthropogenic (human-made) sources have dominated deposition in recent years. An analysis of ice cores from Greenland, for example, covering the period from 1869 to 1984, indicates that anthropogenic sulfate has dominated sulfur deposition since the early twentieth century, and anthropogenic nitrate has dominated nitrogen deposition since about 1960.[1]

In 1980 the U.S. Congress funded a ten-year study (called the National Acid Rain Precipitation Assessment Program) to determine the causes and effects of acid rain and to make recommendations concerning its control. When completed, the report concluded that damage from current and historic levels of acid rain ranged from negligible (on crops) to modest (on aquatic life in some lakes and streams). Specific findings included the following:[2]

---

[1]P.A. Mayewski, et al., "A Detailed (1869–1984) Record of Sulfate and Nitrate Concentration from South Greenland," cited in World Resources Institute and International Institute for Environment and Development, *World Resources: 1986* (New York: Basic Books, 1986): 169.

[2]A concise summary of the findings can be found in National Acid Precipitation Assessment Program, *1989 Annual Report to the President and Congress* (Washington, DC: National Acid Precipitation Assessment Program, 1990).

EXAMPLE 14.1

Adirondack Acidification

About 180 lakes in the Adirondack Mountains of New York State, mostly at higher altitudes, which had supported natural or stocked brook trout populations in the 1930s, no longer supported these populations by the 1970s. In some cases entire communities of six or more fish species had disappeared.

The location of these lakes, some distance east of any local emission sources, makes it quite clear that most of the acid deposition is coming from outside of the region. These lakes have relatively little capacity to neutralize deposited acid because they are in areas with little or no limestone or other forms of basic rock that might serve to buffer the acid.

This is a prime recreational area, particularly for fishing. Most of the sites are within the boundary of the six million acre Adirondack Park, the last substantially undeveloped area of its size in the northeastern United States. Its remoteness, mountainous terrain, and multitude of lakes provide an accessible outdoor recreation experience for the 55 million people who live within a day's traveling distance.

Acidification has substantially reduced the recreational value of the area. Using a version of the travel cost method discussed in Chapter 4, Mullen and Menz conclude that the annual losses to New York resident anglers is in the neighborhood of at least $1 million in 1976 dollars.

One possibility for restoring these lakes would be to add lime (calcium carbonate) to buffer the effects of the acid. Would liming be efficient? In their investigation Menz and Driscoll have found that a 5-year lake neutralization program would cost in the neighborhood of $2 to $4 million. Given the $1 million estimate of *annual* losses to recreational fishing, some neutralization would apparently be efficient. The exact number of lakes to be limed would have to be determined by comparing the marginal cost of liming each lake with the marginal gain to recreation that would result. The authors are quick to point out that although liming may be used to restore damaged lakes, it is not a substitute for controlling emissions.

Sources: Government Accounting Office, *An Analysis of Issues Concerning "Acid Rain,"* Report No. GAO/RCED-85-13, 11 December 1984, p. 13; John K. Mullen and Frederic C. Menz, "The Effect of Acidification Damages on the Economic Value of the Adirondack Fishery to New York Anglers," *American Journal of Agricultural Economics* 67, No. 1 (February 1985): 112–19; Frederic C. Menz and Charles T. Driscoll, "An Estimate of the Costs of Liming to Neutralize Acidic Adirondack Surface Waters," *Water Resources Research* 19, No. 5 (October 1983): 1139–49.

1. Most species of sport fish can tolerate pH levels above 5.5, but relatively few species can sustain populations in water with a pH below 5.0. Some 9 percent of the lakes in the target population have a pH $\leq$ 5.0.

2. The regions of the United States estimated to have the highest percentage of acidified lakes are the Adirondacks in New York (Example 14.1), with 14 percent of 1,290 lakes acidified, and Florida, with 23 percent of 2,098 lakes acidified.

3. In many national parks in the East, fine sulfate particles, formed by chemical reactions of the sulfuric acid produced from emissions of SO_2, are responsible for a 50 to 60 percent degradation in visibility beyond that caused by natural influences.

4. No significant effect on crop growth was detected even at acidity levels ten times the acidity now observed in the eastern United States.

5. Acidic deposition and ozone appear to intensify the effects of natural stresses upon red spruce at eastern mountain-top locations. The cumulative effects of acidic deposition may alter the chemistry of some sensitive forest soils in the lower Midwest and the Southeast in the next 50 to 100 years, but the effect this will have on growth is unknown. The majority of American forests appear healthy.

6. Acidic deposition can increase the rate of deterioration of some construction and culturally important materials such as galvanized steel, bronze, carbonate stone, and carbonate-based paints.

These findings were significantly less dire than expected and provide a rather sharp contrast with findings of higher levels of damage in Europe. Studies have documented that Sweden has some 4,000 highly acidified lakes; in southern Norway, lakes with a total surface area of 13,000 square kilometers support no fish at all; similar reports have been received from Germany, Scotland, and Canada.[3] Furthermore, as made clear by Example 11.1, acid deposition is one of the pollution sources implicated in the massive forest death taking place in Europe.

In many countries with a federal form of government, such as the United States, the policy focus in the past has been on treating all pollutants as if they were local pollutants, overlooking the adverse regional consequences in the process. By giving local jurisdictions a large amount of responsibility for achieving the desired air quality and by measuring progress at local monitors, the stage was set for making regional pollution worse rather than better.

In the early days of pollution control, local areas adopted the motto "dilution is the solution." As implemented, this approach suggested that the way to control local pollutants was to emit from tall stacks. By the time the pollutants hit the ground, the concentrations would be diluted, making it easier to meet the ambient standards at nearby monitors.

This approach had several consequences. First, it lowered the amount of emission reduction necessary to achieve ambient standards; with tall stacks, any given amount of emission would produce lower nearby ground-level concentrations than an equivalent level of emission from a shorter-stack source. Second, the ambient standards could be met at a lower cost. Using Cleveland as a case study, Atkinson has shown that control costs would be approximately 30 percent lower but emissions would be two and one half times higher if a local, rather than a regional, strategy were followed in a marketable permit system.[4] In essence, lo-

[3]See the review in World Resources Institute and International Institute for Environment and Development, *World Resources: 1986* (New York: Basic Books, 1986): 169–70.

[4]Scott E. Atkinson, "Marketable Pollution Permits and Acid Rain Externalities," *Canadian Journal of Economics* 16, No. 4 (November 1983): 704–22.

cal areas would be able to lower their own cost by exporting emissions to other areas. By focusing its attention on local pollution, the Clean Air Act actually made the regional pollution problem worse.

By the end of the 1980s, it had become painfully clear in the United States that the Clean Air Act was ill-suited to solve regional pollution problems. Revamping the legislation to do a better job of dealing with regional pollutants, such as acid rain, became a high priority.

Politically, that was a tall order. By virtue of the fact that these pollutants are transported long distances, the set of geographic areas receiving the damage is typically not the same as the set of geographic areas responsible for most of the emission causing the damage. In many cases the recipients and the emitters are even in different countries! In this political milieu, it should not be surprising that those bearing damages should call for a large, rapid reduction in emissions, whereas those responsible for bearing the costs of that cleanup should want to proceed more slowly and with greater caution.

Economic analysis was helpful in finding a feasible path through this political thicket. In particular, a Congressional Budget Office (CBO) study helped to set the parameters of the debate by quantifying the consequences of various courses of action.[5] To analyze the economic and political consequences of various strategies designed to achieve reductions of SO_2 emissions from utilities anywhere from 8 to 12 million tons below the emission levels from those plants in 1980, the CBO used a computer-based simulation model that relates utility emissions, utility costs, and coal-market supply and demand levels to the strategies under consideration. The model, called the National Coal Model, is maintained by the Department of Energy.

The results of this modeling exercise will be presented in two segments. In the first segment we shall examine the basic available strategies, including both a traditional command-and-control strategy that simply allocates reductions on the basis of a specific formula and an emissions-charge strategy. This analysis will serve to show how sensitive costs are to various levels of emission reduction and to highlight some of the political consequences of implementing these strategies. The second segment of analysis then considers various strategies designed to mitigate the adverse political effects of the basic strategies as a means of ascertaining what is gained and lost by adopting these compromises.

In the proposed command-and-control strategies, the emission reductions were to be allocated to states on the basis of what is known as the "excess emissions" formula. For each plant, this formula subtracts from actual emissions the amount the plant would have been allowed to emit if it were forced to meet the 1979 NSPS sulfur standard for utilities. (Because that is a new source standard, plants built before that date are not automatically required to meet it.) The amount left, the excess emissions, are then summed over all the excess emission plants within each state and, finally, across states to get a national total. Each state would then be required to meet the same share of the stipulated reduction (8, 10, or 12 million tons) that it has of the total excess emissions.

[5]Congress of the United States, Congressional Budget Office, *Curbing Acid Rain: Cost, Budget, and Coal-Market Effects* (Washington, DC: U.S. Government Printing Office, 1986).

TABLE 14.1   Costs Associated with Basic Strategies to Reduce Sulfur Emissions

Strategy	Total Program Cost[a] (Billions of $)	Annual Cost to Utilities[b] (Billions of $)	Cost Effectiveness[c] ($ per ton)
8-Million-Ton Rollback	$20.4	$1.9	$270
10-Million-Ton Rollback	$34.5	$3.2	$360
12-Million-Ton Rollback	$93.6	$8.8	$779
Emissions Charge	$37.5	$7.7	$327

[a]The present value (in 1985 dollars) of additional discounted utility costs incurred (over a current policy benchmark) from 1986 to 2015, using a real discount rate of 0.03. Any emissions charges paid are not included.
[b]The additional cost to utilities of this strategy over the current policy benchmark in 1995 expressed in 1985 dollars. This value includes any emissions charges paid.
[c]The discounted program cost divided by the annual discounted SO_2 reduction measured over the 1986–2015 period.

Source: Congress of the United States, Congressional Budget Office, *Curbing Acid Rain: Cost, Budget, and Coal-Market Effects* (Washington, DC: U.S. Government Printing Office, 1986): xx, xxii, 23, and 80.

In the emissions-charge proposal each utility would be faced with a $600 per ton charge for all uncontrolled SO_2 emissions. The model assumes that utilities would minimize costs by cleaning up their emissions until the marginal cost of further cleanup is equal to $600 per ton. This results in a degree of emission reduction that is roughly comparable to the 10-million-ton command-and-control reduction.

The first implication of the analysis is that the marginal cost of additional control would rise rapidly, particularly after 10 million tons have been reduced (Table 14.1). The cost of reducing a ton of SO_2 would rise from $270 for an 8-million-ton reduction to $360 for a 10-million-ton reduction, and it would rise to a rather dramatic $779 per ton for a 12-million-ton reduction. Costs would rise much more steeply as the amount of required reduction was increased because switching to low-sulfur coal—a relatively low-cost strategy—would be insufficient, by itself, to achieve the larger reductions. At stricter standards, reliance on the more expensive scrubbers would become necessary. (Scrubbers involve a chemical process to extract or "scrub" sulfur gases before they escape into the atmosphere.)

The second insight, one that should be no surprise to readers of this book, is that the emissions charge would be more cost effective than the comparable command-and-control strategy. Whereas the command-and-control strategy could secure a 10-million-ton reduction at about $360 a ton, the emissions charge could do it for $327 a ton. The superiority of the emissions charge is due to the fact that it results in equalized marginal costs, a required condition for cost-effectiveness.[6]

It may seem a bit of a paradox that program costs are not minimized by an emissions charge because it is the most cost-effective strategy. The resolution of this paradox lies in the timing of the emission reductions achieved by an emissions-charge strategy. Because the au-

---

[6]Why, the alert reader might ask, isn't location of the emissions taken into account? Because the objective was stated as securing a reduction in emissions, not achieving an ambient standard, the cost-effective allocation is achieved when marginal control costs are equalized.

thors of this study chose in their analysis to impose the charge earlier than the command-and-control regulations, the utilities secure the reductions earlier with an emissions charge than with the command-and-control approach. Earlier reductions can only be achieved with earlier financial outlays, which, because all costs are discounted, cause higher program costs for the emissions charge. Unlike the program cost calculation, which gives no credit for early emission reduction, the construction of the particular cost-effectiveness measure chosen by the CBO takes the timing of the emissions reduction into account.

Though the emission-charge approach may be the most cost-effective policy, it is not the most popular, particularly in states with a lot of excess emissions. With an emissions-charge approach, utilities not only have to pay the higher equipment and operating costs associated with the reductions, they also have to pay a charge on all uncontrolled emissions. As Table 14.1 indicates, the additional financial burden associated with controlling acid rain by means of an emissions charge would be significant. Instead of paying the $3.2 billion for reducing 10 million tons under a command-and-control approach, utilities would be saddled with a $7.7 billion financial burden with an emissions charge. The savings from lower equipment and operating costs achieved because the emissions-charge approach is more cost-effective would be more than outweighed by the additional expense of paying the emissions charges. What is least-cost to society is not, in this case, least-cost for the utilities.

The cost of utilities could be reduced, while retaining the cost-effectiveness properties of the straight emissions charge, by instituting a sulfur-reduction emissions permit system. In such a system the excess emissions formula would be used to allocate the initial control responsibility. Utilities would then be able to create emissions-reduction credits for exceeding their assigned control; other utilities could purchase these emissions-reduction credits to help meet their own assigned control responsibilities. Compared to an emissions-charge approach, this would cut the cost to utilities almost in half by eliminating the charge on uncontrolled emissions. Another study, examining the cost savings that could be achieved within a single state (Illinois), concluded that the cost of control would be approximately one third lower if an emissions-trading approach were instituted.[7]

A version of the emissions-trading concept is an integral part of the revisions to the Clean Air Act signed in 1990. This approach would complement, not replace, the traditional approach, which was geared to the attainment of local ambient air-quality standards. As was the case with past acid rain proposals considered by Congress, under this innovative approach more-stringent emissions controls would be placed on older plants emitting precursors of acid rain as the first step.

All affected utilities would be given a limited number of sulfur dioxide allowances for each calendar year.[8] An allowance would be a federal authorization to emit a ton of SO_2 in a specific calendar year (or in a subsequent year if it was banked for later use). Only the number of tons authorized by the allowances could be legally emitted. The number of allowances would be limited, to assure that a ten-million-ton reduction from 1980 levels was achieved. Any sources of emissions contributing to acid rain with "excess" reductions (i.e., those over and above the

---

[7]Stephen L. Feldman and Robert K. Raufer, *Emissions Trading and Acid Rain: Implementing a Market Approach to Pollution Control* (Totowa, NJ: Rowman & Littlefield, 1987).

[8]The plan also envisions reducing NOx emissions by 2.5 million tons per year. To keep the exposition from getting excessively complicated, only the sulfur dioxide program is discussed here.

reductions required by law to satisfy the allowances granted) could trade their excess allowances to other utilities. These traded allowances could then be used by the purchaser to legitimize an equivalent increase in its emissions.

How tradeable emission allowances facilitate achieving the environmental goal at a lower cost is not difficult to understand. Achieving reductions of the magnitude envisioned by Congress would require some, but not all, utilities to adopt scrubbers. To force all older utilities to adopt scrubbers would be very expensive and unnecessary to achieve the desired reduction target. Yet it is politically and legally difficult under the traditional system to isolate only a few utilities to bear this additional burden for the greater good.

Emissions-allowance trading would solve this problem by allowing some utilities to voluntarily accept greater control and by providing the proper incentive to assure that some do. The emissions standards would be stringent enough that some utilities would have to choose scrubbers or some other form of overcontrol. Although all utilities would face similar, if not identical, allowable emissions standards, some utilities, presumably those for whom adopting scrubbers was the cheapest alternative, would voluntarily choose to install scrubbers. This action would automatically result in their exceeding their legal emissions-control requirements.

By purchasing sufficient allowances to satisfy their own emissions standards when combined with any other additional control, the purchasing firms would eliminate the need to install scrubbers. The process would result in sufficient, but not excessive, control and would provide a market means of selecting those utilities that would install scrubbers. It would also provide a means of sharing the costs of installing scrubbers among all utilities. Those purchasing the emissions allowances would in effect be subsidizing a portion of the selling firm's installation of the pollution-control device. Rather than isolating a few utilities to bear a disproportionate share of the control burden or requiring all utilities to bear the excessive burden of overcontrol in a misguided pursuit of fairness, emissions-allowance trading promotes voluntary cost-sharing. Fairness and efficiency can be compatible goals with the right choice of policy instruments.

It is not difficult to imagine a similar kind of scheme operating on a regional basis to control acid rain in Europe.[9] Many of the Western European nations are at the point where further control of their own emissions is very expensive. A disproportionate share of the remaining emissions affecting Western European nations are coming from Eastern European nations. However, because most of the Eastern European nations have troubled economies that can ill afford the shock of major new expenditures, they are not likely to undertake major pollution-control reductions on their own in the near future.

One solution to this problem is to seek agreement that all nations would implement some minimum level of control for all sources within their borders, allowing the Western industrialized nations to buy reductions above and beyond this minimum control level from the Eastern European nations.[10] In most Western countries, purchasing additional pollution control from Eastern Europe would represent the cheapest means of reducing acid rain, much

---

[9]This type of market has been simulated in Karl-Goran Mäler, "International Environmental Problems," *Oxford Review of Economic Policy* 6, No. 1 (Spring 1990): 80–108. The benefits from cost-effective burden sharing across borders are apparently quite large.

[10]Sweden has already negotiated an agreement of this type with Poland.

TABLE 14.2   Worldwide Cumulative Release of Two Chlorofluorocarbons, Selected Years (thousands of tons)

Year	CFC-11	CFC-12
1940	0.3	7.3
1950	14.8	148.9
1960	254.4	706.3
1970	1470.2	2961.1
1980	4375.2	6685.1
1983	5176.6	7966.0
1987	6483.2	10,087.6

Sources: Organization for European Co-operation and Development, *OECD Environmental Data* (Paris: OECD, 1985, 1989): pp. 41, 43.

cheaper than controlling their own emissions to an even higher level. The Eastern European nations would then use the revenue from the sale of emissions allowances to finance the installation of control equipment. In many cases this equipment would probably be produced and sold by the Western nations, an additional inducement to participate in cost-sharing.

GLOBAL POLLUTANTS

Ozone Depletion

In the troposphere, the portion of the atmosphere closest to the earth, ozone (O_3) is a pollutant, and its presence has been linked to agricultural damage as well as to some adverse effects on human health. More will be said about this form of tropospheric pollution in the next chapter.

However, in the stratosphere, the portion of the atmosphere lying just above the troposphere, the rather small amounts of ozone present have a crucial positive role to play in determining the quality of life on the planet. In particular, by absorbing the ultraviolet wavelengths, stratospheric ozone shields people, plants, and animals from harmful radiation, and by absorbing infrared radiation, it is a factor in determining the earth's climate.

Chlorofluorocarbons (CFCs) have been implicated in depleting this stratospheric ozone shield as a result of a complicated series of chemical reactions. These highly stable chemical compounds are used as aerosol propellants and in cushioning foams, packaging and insulating foams, industrial cleaning of metals and electronics components, food freezing, medical instrument sterilization, refrigeration for homes and food stores, and air conditioning of automobiles and commercial buildings.

The major known effect of the increased ultraviolet radiation resulting from ozone depletion is an increase in nonmelanoma skin cancer. Other potential effects, such as an increase in the more serious melanoma form of skin cancer, suppression of human immunological systems, damage to plants, eye cancer in cattle, and an acceleration of degradation in certain polymer materials, are suspected but are not as well established.

TABLE 14.3 Comparisons of Alternative Policies Having Similar Cumulative
Emissions Reductions

Policy Design	Emissions Reduction (millions of permit pounds)			Total Compliance Costs (millions of 1976 dollars)		
	1980	*1990*	*Cumulative 1980–90*	*1980*	*1990*	*Cumulative 1980–90*[a]
Mandatory controls	54.4	102.5	812.3	20.9	37.0	185.3
Permit System[b]	36.6	119.4	806.1	5.2	35.0	94.7

[a]Present value of annual compliance costs, discounted at 11 percent.
[b]Based on permit price rising from $0.25 in 1980 to $0.71 in 1990.

Source: A. R. Palmer, W. E. Mooz, T. H. Quinn, and K. A. Wolf, "Economic Implications of Regulating Chlorofluoro-carbon Emissions from Nonaerosol Applications," Report No. R-2524-EPA, prepared for the U.S. Environmental Protection Agency by the Rand Corporation (June 1980): p. 225, Table 4.7.

On 30 June 1978, the U.S. Environmental Protection Agency promulgated a regulation banning the manufacture, processing, and distribution of any "fully halogenated chlorofluo-roalkane" for those aerosol propellant uses that are subject to the Toxic Substances Control Act (which is almost all aerosol uses).[11] This ban reduced the U.S. share from about one half to about one third of worldwide production. Nonetheless worldwide release of the two principal chlorofluorocarbons—CFC-11 and CFC-12—continued to grow (see Table 14.2).

Because further progress on this issue was going to require instituting new controls on nonaerosol uses, a group of economists from the Rand Corporation was commissioned by the USEPA to model the regulatory options.[12] The resulting study collected detailed information on the costs of controlling nonaerosol applications of these gases in the United States and constructed a 10-year simulation model to capture the effects of various regulatory ap-proaches. Because chlorofluorocarbons accumulate in the atmosphere (they are expected to remain in the atmosphere for approximately a century), the desired reductions were defined in cumulative terms over the 10-year period.

In the study a system of emissions standards for producers or users of these gases that would force them to adopt specific technologies was compared to a marketable permit system. In the simulation model, both approaches were constrained to yield roughly the same cumu-lative level of emissions reduction.

The magnitude of the superiority of the permit system in this case can be seen in Table 14.3. It could produce approximately the same amount of reduction as the mandatory con-trols at about one half the cost.

The Rand study also looked at the issue of transfer costs (the payments made to the gov-ernment by the emitters for each unit of uncontrolled emissions). If the permits were auc-tioned off, firms would not only be faced with the cost of purchasing the control equipment or changing the production process, they would have to pay for the permits as well. Thus, de-pending on the relative magnitude of the cost savings from inducing cost-effective behavior

[11]This regulation can be found in 45 *Federal Register* 43721.

[12]A. R. Palmer, W. E. Mooz, T. H. Quinn, and K. A. Wolf, "Economic Implications of Regulating Chlorofluorocarbon Emissions from Nonaerosol Applications," Report No. R-2524-EPA, prepared for the U.S. Environmental Protection Agency by the Rand Corporation (June 1980).

and the additional cost imposed by the need to buy the permits, firms may or may not be better off under this type of economic incentive system than they would be under mandatory controls. This could only be determined by discovering the magnitude of the transfer costs.

The Rand study is quite clear that for this particular problem transfer costs are huge. On average, payments for permits would be some 15 times as large as the expenditures incurred in controlling emissions. Furthermore, they would be rather unequally distributed among the various industries responsible for reducing CFC emissions.

One of the aspects of this figure that is particularly noteworthy is the "other" category. This category contains some product areas (rigid insulating foams, liquid fast freezing, and sterilants) where the authors found that no control methods would be introduced, even when marketable permits are used. For these product areas, the *only* expense is the cost of the permits, and it represents a huge outlay. The manufacturers of these product lines could be expected to be unusually vociferous in the support for a policy of no action or, if action is inevitable, of traditional regulation—an approach that in all likelihood would place no controls on them at all—or a grandfathered permits system where they were given the permits free of charge.

Responding to the ozone depletion threat, 24 nations signed the Montreal Protocol during September 1988. According to this agreement, signatory nations were to restrict their production and consumption of the chief responsible gases to 50 percent of 1986 levels by 30 June 1998. Soon after the Protocol was signed, new evidence suggested that it had not gone far enough; the damage was apparently increasing more rapidly than had been thought. In response, some 59 nations signed a new ozone agreement at a conference in London in July 1990. This agreement called for the complete phaseout of halons and CFCs by the end of the twentieth century. Moreover, two other destructive chemicals (carbon tetrachloride and methyl chloroform) were added to the protocol and are scheduled to be eliminated by 2000 and 2005, respectively.

An important component of this new agreement was the establishment of a special $240 million fund over the next three years to help poorer countries switch away from ozone-depleting chemicals to more expensive but less harmful substitutes.[13] This was an important breakthrough because without this assistance, the use of ozone-depleting chemicals was expected to rise dramatically in the developing countries.[14] In China, for example, by 1980 only one out of ten households owned a refrigerator. (Refrigerators use ozone-depleting chemicals both as a coolant and as a blowing agent in the insulating foam that makes up the walls.) The government plans for every kitchen in China to be equipped with a refrigerator by 2000.

The U.S. has chosen to use a tradeable permit system to implement its responsibilities under the protocols. On 12 August 1988, the U.S. Environmental Protection Agency issued regulations implementing a tradeable permit system to achieve the targeted reductions.[15] According to these regulations, all major U.S. producers and consumers of the controlled sub-

---

[13]A panel of experts from U.S. EPA has concluded that substitutes do exist, but they would cost between $1.25 and $4.00 a pound compared to 60 to 70 cents for the traditional chemicals. *Science News* 131 (6 June 1987): 360.

[14]Daniel F. Kohler, John Haaga, and Frank Camm, "Projections of Consumption of Products Using Chlorofluorocarbons in Developing Countries," Rand Corporation Report N-2458-EPA (January 1987).

[15]53 *Federal Register* 30598 (12 August 1988). The final rules governing transfer of import and production allowances are in 54 *Federal Register* 6376 (9 February 1989).

stances were allocated baseline production or consumption allowances using 1986 levels as the basis for the proration. Each producer and consumer is allowed 100 percent of this baseline allowance initially, with smaller allowances being granted after predefined deadlines. These allowances are transferable within producer and consumer categories, and production allowances can be transferred across international borders to producers in other signatory nations provided that the transaction is approved by EPA and results in the appropriate adjustments in the buyer or seller production allowances in their respective countries. Production allowances can be augmented by demonstrating the safe destruction of an equivalent amount of controlled substances by approved means, but so far no means have been approved.

Though transfers of the production allowances are allowed, even across international borders, they are constrained rather severely. The regulations allow any producer to increase his production allowance by any means (including transfer of a portion of another producer's allowance) by a maximum of 10 percent of his apportionment before 1998 and 15 percent of his apportionment after that date.

Because the demand for these allowances is quite inelastic, supply restrictions increase revenue. By allocating allowances to the seven major domestic producers of CFCs and halons, EPA was concerned that its regulation would result in sizable windfall profits (estimated to be in the billions of dollars) for those producers. EPA handled this problem by imposing a tax to soak up the rents created by the regulation-induced scarcity. The Revenue Reconciliation Act of 1989 includes an excise tax imposed on all ozone-depleting chemicals sold or used by manufacturers, producers, or importers of these chemicals. The tax is imposed at the time the importer sells or uses the affected chemicals. It is computed by multiplying the chemical's weight by the base tax rate and the chemical's ozone-depletion factor. In addition to soaking up some of the regulation-induced scarcity rent, this tax provides incentives to switch to less harmful (and therefore untaxed) substances).

Global Warming

One class of global pollutants, greenhouse gases, absorb the long-wavelength (infrared) radiation from the earth's surface and atmosphere, trapping heat that would otherwise radiate out into space. The mix and distribution of these gases within the atmosphere is in no small part responsible for both the hospitable climate on the earth and the rather inhospitable climate on other planets. Changing the mix of these gases can modify the climate.

Though carbon dioxide is the most abundant and the most studied of these greenhouse gases, many others have similar thermal radiation properties. These include the chlorofluorocarbons, nitrous oxide, methane, and tropospheric ozone. New evidence suggests that these gases may in the future be even more important in modifying climate than the more abundant CO_2.[16]

The current concern over the effect of this class of pollutants on climate arises because emissions of these gases are increasing over time, changing their mix in the atmosphere. Evidence is mounting that by burning fossil fuels, leveling tropical forests, and injecting more

---

[16]See the description of this evidence in Michael Shepard, "The Greenhouse Effect: Earth's Climate in Transition," *EPRI Journal* 11, No. 4 (June 1986): 4–15.

of the other greenhouse gases into the atmosphere, humans are creating a thermal blanket capable of trapping enough heat to raise the temperature of the earth's surface. One National Research Council report anticipates a doubling of atmospheric CO_2 during the third quarter of the next century.[17] It further suggests that this doubling of CO_2 concentrations could result in a surface air warming of between 1.5° C and 4.5° C. A 1.5° C increase in the temperature within a century would produce the warmest climate in 6,000 years.

The report goes on to suggest the likely consequences of this trend. For the United States as a whole, the effect on agriculture is expected to be small, as positive and negative effects largely cancel each other out. For arid parts of the country, which depend on irrigation from scarce water supplies, the picture is more grim. Rising temperatures are expected to reduce the quantity and quality of available water in arid regions.

Global warming is also expected to trigger a rise in sea level. If global warming in the 3° C to 4° C range were to take place over the next hundred years, the authors conclude that a global sea-level rise of about 70 centimeters would be likely. This compares with a rise of only 15 centimeters over the last century. Much larger increases (on the order of 15 to 20 feet) could be expected if the warming caused the West Antarctic ice sheet to disintegrate, an improbable event.

The effects of climate change are expected to fall unequally on the world's people. Regions with a characteristically cold climate, such as large portions of the Soviet Union, may actually benefit from this warming trend, whereas others that are naturally somewhat arid may see marginal agricultural land become unproductive desert, triggering a diminished capacity to raise food. These differences could prove quite divisive in the search for solutions.

Global warming poses a particularly difficult challenge for our economic and political institutions. The stratosphere is a public good. Its scarcity is not reflected in rising prices; it is not automatically rationed only to the highest valued uses. The damage caused by greenhouse pollutants is an externality in both space and time. Emitters impose costs not only on residents of other countries, but on subsequent generations as well. Free-rider problems can be expected to undermine unilateral national attempts to respond. Market allocations can certainly be expected to violate the efficiency criterion and may well violate the sustainability criterion as well (see Example 14.2).

What can be done? Four strategies have been considered: (1) climatic engineering, (2) adaptation, (3) mitigation, and (4) prevention. Climate engineering envisions taking actions such as shooting particulate matter into the atmosphere to provide compensating cooling. Adaptation refers to strategies that would allow us to function effectively in warmer temperatures. Mitigation would attempt to moderate the temperature rise by strategies designed to increase the planetary capacity to absorb greenhouse gases. Prevention refers to strategies to reduce emissions of greenhouse gases. Because only the last two of these have received serious attention in public policy arenas, we shall focus on them.

The most significant prevention strategy deals with our use of fossil fuel energy. Combustion of fossil fuel energy results in the creation of carbon dioxide. Carbon dioxide

---

[17]National Research Council, *Changing Climate: Report of the Carbon Dioxide Assessment Committee* (Washington, DC: National Academy Press, 1983): p. 2.

E X A M P L E   1 4 . 2

Ethics, Risk Aversion, and the Greenhouse Effect

Can benefit/cost analysis be trusted to reach an optimal decision about strategies to control the greenhouse effect? Two sources of concern are paramount: (1) the long time period before the damage would be felt, and (2) the uncertainty about the ultimate size of the damage.

At current interest rates, a complete loss of the expected world GNP 100 years from now would have a present value of about $1 million. This is trivial in comparison to the present value of potential costs of controlling the greenhouse effect because they would be spent in the near future. Due to discounting, events that happen so far in the future have little weight in decisions where costs are borne in the present. Although maximizing the present value of net benefits guarantees that the pie to be shared among generations is as large as possible, it does not automatically guarantee that the slices of pie are actually shared equitably among generations. The logical conclusion of this form of argument is that, from an ethical point of view, future generations may be inadequately protected by benefit/cost analysis.

A second concern deals with risk aversion. As pointed out in Chapter 4, conventional benefit/cost analysis assumes risk neutrality. Is risk neutrality a credible assumption in the face of a potential catastrophe? Common sense suggests that most people react to uncertainty by acting in a cautious, risk-averse manner. Should our governments act any differently?

Concluding that conventional benefit/cost analysis is ethically flawed when applied to the greenhouse problem, d'Arge, Schultze, and Brookshire have proposed a modest alternative. In particular, they proposed to establish whether the current generation would be willing to pay some amount of money to avoid climate modification. Relying on three samples of college students as a pilot study, they did find a willingness to spend current income to avoid an environmental catastrophe, even if it would occur in all likelihood after the respondent's death. Though these samples can hardly be called representative of the population at large, the amounts per person were sufficiently large that they would justify a much larger commitment of current resources to control the problem than would be justified by a conventional benefit/cost analysis.

Sources: Ralph C. d'Arge, William D. Schultze, and David S. Brookshire, "Benefit-Cost Valuation of Long Term Effects: The Case of CO_2," a paper prepared for the Workshop on the Methodology for Economic Impact Analysis, April 24-25, 1980, Fort Lauderdale, FL; Ralph C. d'Arge, William D. Schultze, and David S. Brookshire, "Carbon Dioxide and Intergenerational Choice," *The American Economic Review* 72, No. 2 (May 1982): 251–56.

emissions can be reduced either by using less energy or by using alternative energy sources (such as wind, photovoltaics, or hydro) that produce no carbon dioxide. Because any serious reduction in carbon dioxide emissions would involve rather dramatic changes in our energy consumption patterns and a high economic cost, how vigorously this strategy is to be followed is a controversial public policy issue.[18]

Because trees absorb carbon dioxide, reforestation is a commonly mentioned mitigation strategy. If the rate of deforestation were decreased and the rate of reforestation increased, greater amounts of carbon dioxide could be absorbed.

What policy approaches are available to deal efficiently with the global warming problem? Although global warming and ozone depletion impose an environmental cost, currently that cost is not being borne, or even recognized, by those who ultimately control the magnitude of the problem. Furthermore, those choosing unilaterally to reduce their emissions expose themselves to the higher costs associated with prevention strategies.

A "carbon tax," which is currently being widely discussed in Europe and the United States, could be one component of this package.[19] Because carbon dioxide is only one of the greenhouse gases, however, taxes would necessarily be imposed on other gases as well. The appropriate level of this tax for each gas would depend upon its per unit contribution to the global warming problem; gases posing a larger per unit risk would bear higher tax rates.

Taxes on fossil fuels are not a radical concept.[20] Gasoline taxes have routinely been levied for years. Though gasoline taxes are imposed on an input to combustion rather than an emissions rate, the administrative ease with which they can be implemented and the close relationship between the composition of the fuel and the composition of the emissions makes it a popular candidate for use as one component in a package of corrective measures to reduce global warming.

Because gasoline taxes have already been implemented by nations for their own purposes, examining the degree to which these taxes deviate from the full-cost principle provides some indication of the complexity of the international negotiations to reform gasoline taxes so they would conform to the principle. To the extent that the current system of taxes approximates the ideal, conditions would appear favorable to negotiating a transition. In fact, the gasoline taxes now in use around are not efficient.

Efficient carbon taxes would reflect the damage caused by emissions, thereby fostering a reduction in emissions. In contrast, current gasoline tax rates are commonly determined by the revenue needed to build more roads; added roadway capacity ultimately translates into more emissions, not fewer. Because they are driven by the need to finance capacity expansion rather than to account for the environmental effects of combustion, gasoline taxes are currently not efficient.

Although applying the full-cost principle for global warming also requires that the tax rates be uniformly applied, that condition is a far cry from actual experience. According to the U.S. General Accounting Office, the total U.S. tax rate on gasoline was around $0.36 per gallon as of April 1991. This compares with comparable tax rates of $1.64 per gallon in Germany,

---

[18]According to research by William Nordhaus, a 10 to 20 percent reduction in carbon dioxide emissions could be achieved at a relatively low cost, but the marginal costs of larger reductions rise very rapidly. See "Greenhouse Economics: Count Before You Leap," *The Economist* (7 July 1990): 20–24.

[19]As of 1989 two countries had already unilaterally levied carbon taxes. The Netherlands carbon tax is about $2.15 per ton of carbon whereas Finland's is about $5.00 per ton of carbon.

[20]T. Sterner et al., "Tax Policy, Carbon Emissions and the Global Environment," *Journal of Transport Economics and Policy* 26, No. 2 (1992): 109–19.

$1.91 in Britain, $2.33 in France, and $3.26 in Italy.[21] When the tax rates differ by a factor of five or more, the allocation of control responsibility for reducing gasoline-related emissions does not fulfill the uniformity requirement.

The transition to a more sustainable economic system in atmospheric terms will depend upon the development of new technologies and upon much greater levels of energy efficiency than are currently being achieved. Those transitions will not occur unless the prevailing economic incentives support and encourage them. Once the greenhouse gas and ozone-depletion taxes were in effect, the incentives would be changed: Greater energy efficiency and the development of new technologies would become top-priority objectives.

Because environmental taxes would generate revenue, a common global fund could be established to receive and dispense that revenue. Controlled by representatives of the signatory nations, this fund could conceivably dispense funds for projects as diverse as reforestation or the promotion of solar-powered projects to provide income and subsistence to poor areas of the world. A fund financed by environmental taxes would help to reduce the twin causes of environmental problems: distorted market signals and poverty.[22]

One interesting precedent for this approach is the World Heritage Convention, which established a World Heritage Fund. This fund is used to protect environments of "outstanding universal value." Each signatory is required to contribute at least one percent of its contribution to the regular budget of UNESCO to the fund every two years. In practice this means that the fund is financed almost entirely by the industrial nations, but smaller nations can tap its resources. Some 90 nations have signed this agreement, suggesting that the fund arrangements have successfully exploited some common interests. Because subscribing to the agreement apparently confers benefits on the signatories, it is essentially self-enforcing.

Determining the appropriate rate for any per unit environmental tax would not be a trivial matter. Although to apply the full-cost principle correctly the rate should be equal to the marginal social damage caused by a unit of emission, current valuation techniques would not identify that level with any reasonable degree of confidence. The high degree of scientific uncertainty associated with the magnitude of the global warming threat makes precise valuation impossible. But that may not be a fatal flaw because zero, the current rate, is not correct either. Even establishing a low tax rate would be a step in the right direction; as more information is gained the rate could be adjusted.

Making explicit environmental costs that have been hidden is only one side of the coin; the other is eliminating inappropriate subsidies. Subsidies that are incompatible with the full-cost principles should be eliminated. Implicit subsidies should be targeted as well as explicit ones. For example, electricity prices should not simply be determined by historic average cost,

---

[21]United States General Accounting Office, *Energy Policy: Options to Reduce Environmental and Other Costs of Gasoline Consumption* (September 1992): 22.

[22]By substituting environmental taxes for more traditional taxes, it would also be possible to eliminate the inefficiencies associated with the traditional taxes. Some estimates suggest that using carbon taxes to replace more distortion-producing revenue sources could reduce the cost of controlling greenhouse gases substantially. See William D. Nordhaus, "A Dynamic Integrated Climate-Economy (DICE) Model of Economic Growth and Climate Change," a paper presented at the American Economics Association Meeting, Anaheim, CA, January 1993.

they should reflect the scarcity of the resource and the environmental costs imposed by generation.

Emissions trading offers an alternative approach for controlling global warming. The process would be initiated by setting transferable allowances on the amounts each nation could emit on an annual basis. Nations achieving reductions of greenhouse gases greater than required by the agreement could sell excess allowances to other nations. By purchasing these allowances, the acquiring nation could increase its emissions of greenhouse gases by an equivalent amount. The total emissions limit negotiated by the agreement would be binding: No trade leading to a net increase in aggregate emissions above this limit would be approved.

As long as the sum of emissions was equal to the total permitted annual emissions, cost effectiveness could be achieved regardless of how these emissions allowances were initially allocated across countries. An international market in emissions allowances would facilitate their movement from those countries with the capacity to create them most cheaply to those countries faced by very high costs of additional control. The capacity to achieve cost effectiveness, no matter how the initial emissions allowances are allocated, is a significant attribute of an emissions-trading approach that can be exploited for developing a market approach to cost-sharing. The potential savings from introducing trading could be large.[23]

With emissions trading as the strategy of choice, those forging new international agreements have a very large latitude in attempting to establish emissions limitations that are fair and politically feasible without jeopardizing cost effectiveness. It would be quite possible, for example, to allocate emissions allowances to nations on the basis of their population in some past year, say 1986, rather than on current energy use. This particular choice, of course, would lead to many more allowances being granted to populous third-world countries and many fewer allowances being granted to the Western industrialized world. A middle ground might reserve a significant growth increment (50 percent of their current use, for example) for the developing countries, reducing the share going to the industrialized countries sufficiently to produce the desired target. Because of the very different current emissions levels, a 50 percent growth increment for developing countries would necessitate a much smaller than 50 percent compensating reduction in the developed countries. As the Western nations acquired by purchase the necessary production allowances at market prices from those nations selling them, significant financial transfers would take place. The size of these transfers would be dictated by market forces, not by negotiation.

A precondition for the successful operation of this market is the assurance to all participants that the production allowances or emissions reduction credits are permanent, surplus, quantifiable, and enforceable.[24] This assurance can only be given if some trusted international agency is given the power to certify these transfers on a case-by-case basis. Although the potential trading partners would establish the price of the transfer between themselves, no transfer could take place until the international agency was satisfied that the offsetting reductions satisfied the four criteria.

---

[23]For one calculation see Alan S. Manne and Richard G. Richels, *Buying Greenhouse Insurance: The Economic Costs of CO_2 Emission Limits* (Cambridge, MA: MIT Press, 1992): 89–99.

[24]Some details of how such a market could be implemented can be found in Tom Tietenberg, "Implementation Issues: A General Survey," in United Nations Conference on Trade and Development, *Combatting Global Warming: Study on a Global System of Tradeable Carbon Emission Entitlements* (New York: United Nations, 1992): 127–49. A skeptical view can be found in D. G. Victor, "Limits of Market-Based Strategies for Slowing Global Warming: The Case of Tradeable Permits," *Policy Sciences* 24, No. 2 (May 1991): 199–222.

The first step in attempting to chart a course for the public sector is to discover just how serious the problem is and to ascertain the costs of being wrong, either by acting too hastily or by procrastinating. Due to the rampant uncertainties in virtually every logical link in the chain from human activities to subsequent consequences, no one at this juncture can state unequivocally how serious the damage will be. We can, however, begin to elaborate the range of possibilities and see how sensitive the outcomes are to choices before us.

The risks of being wrong are clearly asymmetric. If we control more than necessary, current generations bear a larger than necessary cost. On the other hand, if the problem turns out to be as serious as the worst predictions indicate, catastrophic and largely irreversible damage to the planet would be inflicted on future generations. How can governments respond reasonably to this uncertainty? One familiar way is by acquiring some insurance against the potential harm. In this context, acquiring insurance would take the form of undertaking prevention and mitigation strategies as a hedge against the consequences of global warming.

How much insurance should be purchased? One very interesting and provocative study was accomplished by William D. Nordhaus.[25] Based on a benefit/cost analysis of global warming, Nordhaus attempted to derive a reasonable level of carbon tax to deal with global warming. His estimates suggest that a tax of approximately $5 per ton of carbon (with equivalent taxes on other greenhouse gases) would be the most reasonable. A tax of this level would result in reductions of greenhouse gases of some 13 percent and net benefits of about $12 billion per year.

These results are controversial because many believe that benefit/cost analysis has limited applicability to global warming.[26] Because the present value component of benefit/cost analysis emphasizes short-term over long-term consequences, the application of benefit/cost analysis will weigh the current costs of controlling emissions more heavily than the distant future damages caused by global warming. Though this approach is not inherently biased against future generations, their interests will only be adequately protected if they would be willing to accept monetary compensation for a modified climate and if current generations were willing to set aside sufficient proceeds to provide this compensation. Because it is not obvious that either condition would be satisfied, the long lead times associated with this particular problem place the interests of future generations in maintaining a stable climate in jeopardy.

SUMMARY

Regional pollutants differ from local pollutants chiefly in the distance they are transported in the air. Whereas local pollutants damage the environment near the emissions site, regional pollutants can cause damage far from the site of emission. Some substances, such as sulfur oxides, nitrogen oxides, and ozone, are both local and regional pollutants.

---

[25]William D. Nordhaus, "A Perspective on Costs and Benefits," *EPA Journal* 16, No. 2 (March/April 1990): 44–45; "The Economics of the Greenhouse Effect," paper presented at MIT Workshop on Energy and Environmental Modeling and Policy Analysis (July 1989); "Economic Policy in the Face of Global Warming," photocopy, 9 March 1990. The case for a much stronger policy response based upon lower discount rates and a longer planning horizon is made in William R. Cline, *The Economics of Global Warming* (Washington, DC: Institute for International Economics, 1992).

[26]See, for example, the discussion of this controversy in Nathan J. Rosenberg and Pierre R. Crosson, "RFF Workshop on Greenhouse Warming," *Resources* (Fall 1988): 16.

As the zone of influence of pollutants extends beyond local boundaries, the political difficulties of implementing comprehensive, cost-effective control measures increase. Pollutants crossing political boundaries impose external costs; neither emitters nor the nations within which they emit have the proper incentives to institute efficient control measures.

Acid rain is a case in point. Sulfate and nitrate deposition has caused problems both between regions within countries and between countries. In the United States, the Clean Air Act has had a distinctly local focus. To control local pollution problems, state governments required the installation of tall stacks to dilute the pollution before it hit ground level. In the process a high proportion of the emissions were exported to other areas, reaching the ground hundreds of miles from the point of injection. A focus on local control made the regional problem worse.

Finding solutions to the acid rain problem has been very difficult because those bearing the costs of further control are usually not those who will benefit from the control. Economic analysis of the policy options indicates that the cost of reducing emissions rises dramatically as the amount of reduction is increased from 10 million tons to 12 million tons. The cost effectiveness of emissions trading was recognized by the inclusion of a sulfur allowance trading program in the Clean Air Act Amendments of 1990.

Chlorofluorocarbons, the first of the discussed global pollutants, are a problem because they have been implicated in the destruction of the stratospheric ozone shield that protects the earth's surface from harmful ultraviolet radiation. Studies of nonaerosol uses of CFCs indicate that a marketable permit system could achieve the emissions target at about half the cost of regulatory standards. However, these studies also indicate that forcing emitters to buy permits in an auction market would impose large additional financial burden on the emitters. (The payments for permits would be 15 times as large as the payments for controlling the pollution.) In part to avoid this financial burden, most of the U.S. trading programs have adopted a grandfathered allowance system, although the sulfur allowance program does have an auction market for a small proportion of the allowances.[27]

With regard to global warming, the emitters are separated in time from the consequence of their emissions. A doubling of carbon dioxide emissions is expected to occur well into the next century when virtually all of the current decision-makers will have passed away. The current generation bears the cost of control whereas future generations would reap the benefits. Furthermore, international agreements are made more difficult by the fact that some countries may be benefited, not harmed, by global warming, diminishing even further their incentive to control.

Economic analysis of this problem suggests that it makes sense to take some action to reduce emissions of greenhouse gases to provide insurance against the adverse, irreversible consequences if the damage tends to be higher than anticipated. Although the analysis suggests that drastic action is not called for yet, the next few years should be used fruitfully to assure that energy subsidies are removed, full costs are paid, and more knowledge about the problem is gained. The transition could be facilitated by either a system of taxes on greenhouse gases or a system of transferable emissions allowances for greenhouse gases. Some international cost-sharing is likely to be a necessary ingredient in a successful attack on the

---

[27]In September 1992 the Chicago Board of Trade was selected to run this auction market. See Jeffrey Taylor and Rose Gutfield, "CBOT Selected to Run Auction for Polluters," *The Wall Street Journal* (24 September 1992): C1, C16.

problem. During the next few decades, options must not only be preserved, they must be enhanced.

Responding in a timely and effective fashion to global and regional pollution problems will not be easy. Our political institutions are not configured in such a way to make decision making on a global scale easy. International organizations exist at the pleasure of the nations they serve. Only time will tell if the mechanism of international agreements will prove equal to the task.

ADDITIONAL REFERENCES

Adams, Donald D., and Walter P. Page. *Acid Deposition: Environmental, Economic, and Policy Issues* (New York: Plenum Publishing, 1985).

Bailey, Martin J. "Risks, Costs, and Benefits of Fluorocarbon Regulations," *The American Economic Review* 72, No. 2 (May 1982): 247–50.

Brown, Peter G. "Policy Analysis, Welfare Economics, and the Greenhouse Effect," *Journal of Policy Analysis and Management* 7 (Spring 1988):471–75.

Croker, Thomas D., ed. *Economic Perspectives on Acid Deposition Control* (Boston, MA: Butterworth Publishers, 1984).

Cumberland, John H. *Economics of Managing Chlorofluorocarbons: Stratospheric Ozone and Climate Issues* (Baltimore, MD: Johns Hopkins University Press, 1982).

Feldman, Stephen L. and Robert K. Raufer. *Emissions Trading and Acid Rain Implementing a Market Approach to Pollution Control* (Totowa, NJ: Rowman & Littlefield, 1987).

Lave, Lester B. "The Greenhouse Effect: What Government Actions Are Needed?" *Journal of Policy Analysis and Management* 7 (Spring 1988):460–70.

Meyer, Richard and Bruce Yandle. "The Political Economy of Acid Rain," *Cato Journal* 7, No. 2 (Fall 1987): 527–45.

Nordhaus, William D. "How Fast Should We Graze the Global Commons?" *The American Economic Review* 72, No. 2 (May 1982): 242–46.

Nordhaus, William D. and Gary W. Yohe. "Future Paths of Energy and Carbon Dioxide Emissions," *Changing Climate: Report of the Carbon Dioxide Assessment Committee, National Research Council* (Washington, DC: National Academy Press, 1983): 87–153.

Rosenberg, Norman J., William E. Easterling III, Pierre R. Crosson, and Joel Darmstadter, eds. *Greenhouse Warming: Abatement and Adaptation* (Washington, DC: Resources for the Future, 1989).

Streets, David G. and Thomas D. Veselka. "Economic Incentives for the Reduction of Sulfur Dioxide Emissions," *Energy Systems and Policy* 11, No. 1 (1987): 39–59.

Tietenberg, T. H. "Acid Rain Reduction Credits," *Challenge* 32, No. 2 (March/April 1989):25–29.

CHAPTER 15

Transportation

There are two things you shouldn't watch being made, sausage and law.

ANONYMOUS

INTRODUCTION

Though they emit many of the same pollutants as stationary sources, mobile sources require a different policy approach. These differences arise from the mobility of the source, the number of vehicles involved, and the role of the automobile in the American life-style.

Mobility has two major impacts on policy. On the one hand, pollution is partly caused by the temporary location of the source—a case of being in the wrong place at the wrong time. This occurs, for example, during rush hour in metropolitan areas. Because the cars have to be where the people are, relocating them—as might be done with electric power plants—is not a viable strategy. On the other hand, it is more difficult to tailor vehicle emission rates to local pollution patterns because any particular vehicle may end up in many different urban and rural areas during the course of its useful life.

Mobile sources are also more numerous than stationary sources. Although there are approximately 27,000 major stationary sources, well over 100 million vehicles travel on American roadways. Enforcement is obviously more difficult the larger the number of sources being controlled.

Whereas stationary sources generally are large and run by professional managers, automobiles are small and run by amateurs. Their small size makes it more difficult to control emissions without affecting performance, and amateur ownership makes it more likely that emission control will deteriorate over time due to a lack of dependable maintenance and care.

These complications might lead us to conclude that perhaps we should ignore mobile sources and concentrate our control efforts solely on stationary sources. Unfortunately, that is not possible. Though each individual vehicle represents a minuscule part of the problem, mobile sources collectively represent a significant proportion of three criteria pollutants—ozone, carbon monoxide, and nitrogen dioxide. (Hydrocarbons and nitrogen dioxide are precursors of ozone.)

For two of these—ozone and nitrogen dioxide—the process of reaching attainment has been particularly slow. With the increased use of diesel engines, mobile sources are becoming responsible for a rising proportion of particulate emissions, and vehicles which burn leaded gasoline were until recently a major source of airborne lead.

Because it is necessary to control mobile sources, what policy options exist? What points of control are possible, and what are the advantages and disadvantages of each? In exercising control over these sources, the government must first specify the agent charged with the responsibility for the reduction. The obvious candidates are the manufacturer and the owner-driver. The balancing of this responsibility should depend on a comparative analysis of costs and benefits, with particular reference to such factors as (1) the number of agents to be regulated, (2) the rate of deterioration while in use, (3) the life expectancy of automobiles, and (4) the availability, effectiveness, and cost of programs to reduce emissions at the point of production and at the point of use.

Although automobiles are numerous and ubiquitous, they are manufactured by a small number of firms. Because it is easier and less expensive to administer a system that controls relatively few sources, regulation at the point of production has considerable appeal.

Some problems are associated with limiting controls solely to the point of production, however. If the factory-controlled emission rate deteriorates during normal usage, control at the point of production may buy only temporary emission reduction. Though the deterioration of emission control can be combatted with warranty and recall provisions, the costs of these supporting programs have to be balanced against the costs of local control.

Because automobiles are durable, *new* vehicles make up only a relatively small percentage of the total fleet of vehicles. Therefore, control at the point of production, which affects only new equipment, takes longer to produce a given reduction in aggregate emissions because newer, controlled cars replace old vehicles very slowly. Thus, control at the point of production would produce emission reductions more slowly than a program securing emission reductions from used as well as new vehicles.

Some possible means of reducing mobile-source pollution cannot be accomplished by regulating emissions at the point of production because they involve choices made by the owner-driver. The point of production strategy is oriented toward reducing the amount of emissions *per mile driven* in a particular type of car, but only the owner can decide what kind of car to drive, as well as when and where to drive it.

These are not trivial concerns. Diesel automobiles, buses, trucks, and motorcycles emit rather different amounts of pollutants than do gasoline-powered automobiles. By changing the mix of vehicles on the road, the amount and type of emissions can be affected even if passenger miles are not changed.

Where and when the car is driven is also important. Because clustered emissions cause higher concentration levels than dispersed emissions, driving in urban areas causes more environmental damage than driving in rural areas. Local control strategies could internalize these location costs, whereas a uniform national strategy focusing solely on the point of production could not.

Timing of emissions is particularly important because conventional commuting patterns lead to a clustering of emissions during the morning and evening rush hours. Indeed, plots of pollutant concentrations in urban areas during an average day typically produce a graph with two peaks corresponding to the two rush hours.[1] Because high concentrations are more dangerous than low ones, some spreading over the 24-hour period could also prove beneficial.

---

[1]The exception is ozone formed by a chemical reaction involving hydrocarbons and nitrogen oxides in the presence of sunlight. For the evening rush-hour emissions, too few hours of sunlight remain for the chemical reactions to be completed, so graphs of daily ozone concentrations frequently exhibit a single peak.

POLICY TOWARD MOBILE SOURCES

Legislative History

Concern about mobile-source pollution originated in Southern California in the early 1950s following a path-breaking study by Dr. A. J. Haagen-Smit of the California Institute of Technology. The study by Dr. Haagen-Smit identified motor-vehicle emissions as a key culprit in forming the photochemical smog for which Southern California was becoming infamous.

During the early 1960s, while Congress held hearings, required reports, and appointed committees, California passed legislation requiring that exhaust-control devices be installed on all new cars sold in California one year after the state had certified that at least two acceptable devices were available at reasonable cost. By 1964 the state had certified four devices, and exhaust-control devices became mandatory for the 1966 model year.

The Clean Air Act Amendments of 1965 set national standards for hydrocarbon and carbon monoxide emissions from automobiles to take effect during 1968. It is interesting to note that the impetus for this act came not only from the scientific data on the effects of automobile pollution, but also from the automobile industry itself. The industry saw uniform federal standards as a way to avoid a situation in which every state passed its own unique set of emission standards, something the auto industry wanted to avoid. This pressure was successful in that the law prohibits all states except California from setting their own standards.

By 1970 there was general dissatisfaction with the slow progress being made on air-pollution control in general and automobile pollution in particular. In a "get tough" mood as it developed the Clean Air Act amendments of 1970, Congress required new emissions standards that would reduce emissions by 90 percent below their uncontrolled levels. This reduction was to have been achieved by 1975 for hydrocarbon and carbon monoxide emissions and by 1976 for nitrogen dioxide. It was generally agreed at the time the Act was passed that the technology to meet the standards did not exist. By passing this tough law, Congress hoped to force the development of an appropriate technology.

It did not work out that way. The following years ushered in a series of deadline extensions. In 1972 the automobile manufacturers requested a one-year delay in the implementation of the standards. The administrator of the EPA denied the request and was taken to court. At the conclusion of the litigation in April 1973, the administrator granted a one-year delay in the 1975 deadline for the hydrocarbon and carbon monoxide standards. Subsequently, in July 1973, a one-year delay was granted for nitrogen oxides as well.[2]

About this time two additional factors intervened. First, the OPEC embargo occurred, resulting in substantially higher crude oil prices. Second, Congress became aware of the trade-off between emissions control and fuel efficiency that characterized control devices at that time. In June 1974, an additional one-year delay in the enforcement of all emissions standards was granted by Congress as part of an energy bill, the Energy Supply and Coordination Act.

Meanwhile, manufacturers had begun installing catalytic converters in cars sold in California, to meet that state's stricter standards. The administrator of the EPA, acting on pre-

---

[2]The only legal basis for granting an extension was technological infeasibility. Only shortly before the extension was granted, the Japanese Honda CVCC engine was certified as meeting the original standards. It is interesting to speculate on what the outcome would have been if the company meeting the standards had been American rather than Japanese.

liminary research, feared that widespread introduction of catalytic converters would increase sulfur oxide emissions. As a result, he granted a further one-year delay for the attainment of the hydrocarbon and carbon monoxide emission standards. Though the EPA subsequently concluded that the sulfur oxide problem from catalytic converters was not serious, by the time that conclusion was reached, the standards had been delayed three times and the original 1975–1976 standards were scheduled for 1978. Even that schedule was not adhered to. In the Clean Air Act Amendments of 1977, Congress granted further extensions of two years while tightening the standards.

Structure of the Federal Approach

The current U.S. approach to mobile-source air pollution has served as a model for mobile-source control in many other countries (particularly in Europe). We shall therefore examine this approach in some detail.

The U.S. approach represents a blend of controlling emissions at the point of manufacture with controlling emissions from vehicles in use. New-car emission standards are administered through a certification program and an associated enforcement program.

Certification Program. The certification program tests prototypes of car models for conformity to federal standards. During the test, a prototype vehicle from each engine family is driven 50,000 miles on a test track or a dynamometer, following a mandated strict pattern of fast and slow driving, idling, and hot-and-cold starts. The manufacturers run the tests and record emission levels at 5,000-mile intervals. If the vehicle satisfies the standards over the entire 50,000 miles, it passes the deterioration portion of the certification test.

The second step in the certification process is to apply less demanding (and less expensive) tests to three additional prototypes in the same engine family. Emission readings are taken at the 0 and 4,000-mile points and then, using the deterioration rate established in the first portion of the test, are projected to the 50,000-mile point. If those projected emission levels meet the standards, then that engine family is given a certificate of conformity. Only engine families with a certificate of conformity may be sold.

Associated Enforcement Programs. The certification program is complemented by an associated enforcement program, which contains assembly-line testing, as well as recall and antitampering procedures and warranty provisions. To ensure that the prototype vehicles are representative, the EPA tests a statistically representative sample of assembly-line vehicles. If these tests reveal that more than 40 percent of the cars do not conform with federal standards, the certificate may be suspended or revoked.

The EPA has also been given the power to require manufacturers to recall and remedy manufacturing defects that cause emissions to exceed federal standards. If the EPA uncovers a defect, it usually requests the manufacturer to recall vehicles for corrective action. If the manufacturer refuses, the EPA can order a recall.

The Clean Air Act also requires two separate types of warranty provisions. These warranty provisions are designed to ensure that a manufacturer will have an incentive to produce a vehicle that, properly maintained, will meet emission standards over its useful life. The first of these provisions requires the vehicle to be free of defects that could cause it to fail to meet the standards. Under this provision, any defects discovered by consumers would be fixed at the manufacturer's expense.

The second warranty provision requires the manufacturer to bring any car that fails an inspection and maintenance test (described below) during its first 24 months or 24,000 miles (whichever occurs first) into conformance with the standards. After the 24 months or 24,000 miles, the warranty is limited solely to the replacement of devices specifically designed for emission control, such as catalytic converters. This further protection lasts sixty months.

The earliest control devices used to control pollution had two characteristics that rendered them susceptible to tampering: They adversely affected vehicle performance, and they were relatively easy to circumvent. As a result, the Clean Air Act Amendments of 1970 prohibited anyone from tampering with an emission-control system prior to the sale of an automobile, but, curiously, prohibited only dealers and manufacturers from tampering after the sale. The 1977 amendments extended the coverage of the postsale tampering prohibition to motor-vehicle repair facilities and fleet operators.

Lead.   Section 211 of the Clean Air Act provides the EPA with the authority to regulate lead and any other fuel additives used in gasoline. Under this provision, gasoline suppliers are required to make unleaded gasoline available. By ensuring the availability of unleaded gasoline, this regulation sought to reduce the amount of airborne lead and to protect the effectiveness of the catalytic converter, which is poisoned by lead.[3] Penalties are assessed on distributors (but not individual owners) for supplying catalyst-equipped vehicles with leaded gasoline.

On 7 March 1985, the EPA issued regulations imposing strict new standards on the allowable lead content in refined gasoline. These regulations required further reductions from the then existing 1.10 grams per leaded gallon (gplg) to 0.50 gplg in July 1985 and to 0.10 gplg in January 1986.[4] These actions followed a highly publicized series of medical research findings on the rather severe health and developmental consequences, particularly to small children, of even rather low levels of atmospheric lead. By 1988 unleaded gasoline accounted for 82 percent of the gasoline sales in the United States.

Local Responsibilities.   The Clean Air Act Amendments of 1977 recognized the existence of nonattainment areas. Special requirements were placed on control authorities to bring nonattainment areas into attainment. Because many of the nonattainment areas received that designation for pollutants generated by mobile sources, local authorities in those areas were required to take further actions to reduce emissions from mobile sources.

Measures that local authorities are authorized to use include requiring new cars registered in that area to satisfy the more stringent California standard (with EPA approval) and the development of comprehensive transportation plans. These plans could include measures such as on-street parking controls, road charges, and measures to reduce the number of vehicle-miles traveled.

---

[3]Three tankfuls of leaded gasoline used in a car equipped with a catalytic converter will produce a 50 percent reduction in the effectiveness of the catalytic converter.

[4]These can be found in 40 CFR 80 (1990).

In nonattainment regions that could not meet the primary standard for photochemical oxidants, carbon monoxide, or both by 31 December 1982, control authorities could delay attainments until 31 December 1987, provided they agreed to a number of additional restrictions. For the purposes of this chapter, the most important of these is the requirement that each region gaining this extension must establish a vehicle inspection and maintenance (I&M) program for emissions.

The objective of the I&M program is to identify vehicles that are violating the standards and bring them into compliance, to deter tampering, and to encourage regular routine maintenance. Because the federal test procedure used in the certification process is much too expensive to use on a large number of vehicles, shorter, less expensive tests were developed specially for the I&M programs. Because of the expense and questionable effectiveness of these programs, they are one of the most controversial components of the policy package used to control mobile-source emissions.

Alternative Fuels.   Recently the attention of policymakers has turned toward alternative fuels. In the United States, for example, under the Energy Tax Act of 1978, the federal government provided an exemption of 4 cents per gallon from the federal gasoline tax for fuels containing 10 percent or more of alcohol. Additionally, Congress passed the Alternative Motor Fuels Act of 1988 to encourage the use of methanol, ethanol, and compressed natural gas. Among its other provisions this act requires the use of alternative fuels by the maximum practical number of light-duty vehicles.

The states have also begun to take action. California, for example, has mandated the introduction of "zero emissions" vehicles (electric was what they had in mind) and vehicles that run on methanol into the fleet.

The attractiveness of alternative fuels is their ability to reduce emissions without dramatically affecting life-style. One study estimated that the widespread introduction of methane-fueled vehicles would be likely to reduce reactive hydrocarbon emissions by some 30 percent. If the vehicles were designed to burn 85 percent methanol, this same study estimated that emissions could be lowered by 50 percent.[5]

European Approaches

By the late 1980s, emission standards patterned after the 1983 American standards were introduced for all new cars in Austria, Sweden, Switzerland, Norway, and Finland. West Germany, Denmark, and the Netherlands have introduced tax incentives and lower registration fees for cleaner cars.

On 1 October 1989, the European Community's 12 member nations imposed U.S.-style emission standards on all new cars, starting with cars equipped with engines over 2 liters. Similar emission controls are scheduled to be extended to all engine sizes by 1993. The Soviet Union has, in principle, agreed to follow the example of Western Europe in introducing more

---

[5]Margaret A. Walls and Alan J. Krupnick, "Cost-effectiveness of Methanol Vehicles," *Resources,* No. 100 (Summer 1990). These numbers are controversial. The American Petroleum Institute estimates that reduction would be in the neighborhood of only 24 percent.

stringent emission controls. Because unleaded gasoline is not widely available in the Soviet Union, rapid change to catalytic converters is not expected.

The Netherlands, Norway, and Sweden are using differential tax rates to encourage consumers to purchase (and manufacturers to produce) low-emitting cars before regulations take effect requiring all cars to be low-emitting.[6] Tax differentiation confers a tax advantage (and, hence, an after-tax price advantage) on cleaner cars. The amount of the tax usually depends on (1) the emission characteristics of the car (heavier taxies being levied on heavily polluting cars), (2) the size of the car (in Germany heavier cars qualify for larger tax advantages to offset the relatively high control requirements placed upon them), and (3) the year of purchase (the tax differential is declining because all cars will eventually have to meet the standards). It apparently works. In Sweden, 87 percent of the new cars sold qualified for the tax advantage, and in Germany the comparable percentage was over 90 percent.

AN ECONOMIC AND POLITICAL ASSESSMENT

Perhaps the most glaring deficiency in the 1970 amendments occurred when an infeasible compliance schedule for meeting the ambient standards was established for mobile-source pollutants. The chief instruments to be used by local areas in meeting these standards were the new-car emission standards. Because these applied only to new cars, and because new cars make up such a small proportion of the total fleet, significant emission reductions were not experienced until well after the deadline for meeting the ambient standards. This created a very difficult situation for local areas because they were forced to meet the ambient standards prior to the time that the emission standards (the chief sources of reduction) would have much of an impact.

All they could do was to develop local strategies to make up the difference. Recognizing the difficulties the states faced, the EPA granted an extension of the deadline for submitting the transportation plans that would spell out the manner in which the standards would be reached. This extension was challenged in court by the Natural Resource Defense Council,[7] who successfully argued that the EPA did not have the authority to grant the extension. Faced with the court's decision, the EPA was forced to reject the implementation plans submitted by most states as inadequate because those plans could not ensure attainment by the deadlines. Because the law clearly states that the EPA must substitute its own plan for an inadequate plan, the EPA found itself thrust into the unfamiliar and unpleasant role of defining transportation-control plans for states with rejected SIPs.

Two main problems with this development surfaced: The EPA was not administratively equipped either in terms of staff or resources to design and implement these plans, and, because of the severity of the mismatch between deadline and implementation, the EPA could have done very little, even if the staff and resources had been available.

---

[6]For the details on these approaches see J. B. Opschoor and Hans B. Vos, *Economic Instruments for Environmental Protection* (Paris: OECD, 1989): 69–71.

[7]475 F. 2d 968 (1973).

The EPA made a valiant but futile attempt to meet its statutory responsibilities. It concluded that the best way to resolve its dilemma was to work backward from the needs to the transportation plans and, once the plans were defined, to require states to implement and enforce them. To ensure state cooperation, they set up a system of civil penalties to be applied against states that failed to cooperate.

The resulting plans were virtually unenforceable because they were so severe. For example, in order to meet the ambient standard in Los Angeles by the deadline, the plan designed by the EPA called for an 82 percent reduction in gasoline consumption in the Los Angeles basin. The reduction was to be achieved through gasoline rationing during the six months of the year when the smog problem is most severe. In publishing the plan, EPA Administrator William Ruckelshaus acknowledged that it was infeasible and would effectively destroy the economy of the state if implemented, but argued that he had no other choice under the law.

The states raised a number of legal challenges to this approach, which were never really resolved in the courts by the time Congress revised the act in 1977. The Clean Air Act Amendments of 1977 remedied the situation by extending the deadlines.

The lesson from this episode seems to be that tougher laws do not necessarily result in more rapid compliance. Because the statutory requirement could not be met, virtually nothing was accomplished as the various parties attempted to fashion a resolution through the courts.

TECHNOLOGY FORCING AND SANCTIONS

This lesson was underscored by the EPA's experience in gaining compliance with the national emission standards by the automobile manufacturers. The industry was able to obtain a number of delays in meeting those standards. The law was so tough that it was difficult to enforce within the time schedule envisioned by Congress.

This problem was intensified by the sanctions established by the act to ensure compliance. They were so brutal that the EFA was unwilling to use them; they did not represent a credible threat. For example, when an engine family failed the certification test, the law is quite specific in stating that vehicle classes not certified as conforming with the standards cannot be sold! Given the importance of the automobile industry in the American economy, this sanction was not likely to be applied. As a result there were considerable pressures on the EPA to avoid the sanctions by defining more easily satisfied procedures for certification and by setting sufficiently flexible deadlines that no manufacturer would fail to meet them.

Differentiated Regulation

In controlling the emissions of both mobile and stationary sources, the brunt of the reduction effort is borne by new sources. This raises the cost of new sources and, from the purchaser's point of view, increases the attractiveness of used cars relative to new ones. The benefit from increased control is a public good and therefore cannot to be appropriated exclusively by the new-car purchasers. One result of a strategy focusing on new sources would be to depress the demand for new cars while enhancing that for used cars.

Apparently this is precisely what happened in the United States.[8] In response to the higher cost of new cars, people held on to old automobiles longer. This has produced several unfortunate side effects. Because new cars are substantially cleaner than older cars, emission reductions have been delayed. In effect, this shift in fleet composition is equivalent to a set-back of three to four years in the timetable for reducing emissions.[9] Also, because older cars get worse gas mileage, gasoline consumption is higher than it would otherwise be. The focus on new sources is to some extent inevitable; the lesson to be drawn is that by ignoring these behavioral responses to differentiated regulation, the policymaker is likely to expect results sooner than are likely to occur.

Uniformity of Control

With the exception of the California standards, which are more stringent, the Clean Air Act requires the same emission standards on all cars. Example 15.1 shows how these standards were established. The calculations were designed to assure that required levels of control would be sufficient to meet the ambient standards in Los Angeles or in high-altitude cities such as Denver.[10] As a result, many of the costs borne by people in other parts of the country—particularly rural areas—do not yield much in the way of benefits.

This sounds like an inefficient policy because the severity of control is not tailored to the geographic need, and, indeed, most of the studies which have been accomplished indicate that this is so. One such study was accomplished by the U.S. Ad Hoc Committee on the Cumulative Regulatory Effects on the Cost of Automobile Transportation (known popularly as the RECAT report). The committee estimated annual benefits from the original 1975–1976 standards to be in the interval $3.5 to $9.1 billion, and the costs were estimated as $10.1 billion per year. A later report published by the National Academy of Sciences and the National Academy of Engineering estimated the discounted present value of benefits and costs over the period 1975–2101. They estimated the costs at $126 billion and the benefits at $137 billion. Thus, the first study found negative net benefits, whereas the second found positive but small net benefits.

Positive net benefits, of course, are not synonymous with efficiency, although negative net benefits do imply inefficiency. One study by researchers at the General Motors Research Laboratories attempted to use benefit/cost analysis to find the efficient levels of control. Their analysis suggested the following:

One clear conclusion that emerges from the foregoing is that optimal levels, from an economic standpoint, are well below the statutory values of the amended Clean Air Act: 0.94, 0.97, 0.98 for

---

[8]See Howard K. Gruenspecht, "Differentiated Regulation: The Case of Auto Emission Standards," *The American Economic Review* 72 (May 1982): 328–31.

[9]Robert W. Crandall, Howard K. Gruenspecht, Theodore E. Keeler, and Lester B. Lave, *Regulating the Automobile* (Washington, DC: The Brookings Institution, 1986): 96.

[10]Considerable evidence now suggests that in-use emission rates are substantially higher in high altitudes. See National Commission for Air Quality, *To Breathe Clean Air* (Washington, DC: U.S. Government Printing Office, 1981): 203–206.

E X A M P L E   1 5 . 1

Setting the National Automobile Emission Standards

A set of national emission standards provide the backbone of the 1970 Clean Air Act Amendments. It is natural to imagine that these standards were set after a careful weighing of the benefits and costs of various levels, but the manner in which they were established was quite different. The analysis used to justify the standards could have been accomplished on the back of an envelope.

The basic approach was developed by D. S. Barth. His calculations relied on a rollback model that simply assumes that a linear relationship exists between emission reductions and reductions in pollutant concentrations. To initiate the analysis, he needed to pick a year in which the standards would be met—1990 was chosen. He then needed to calculate how much emissions would grow in the absence of controls and in the presence of more cars, more miles traveled, and so on. He assumed emissions would grow 2.18 times between 1967 and 1990. Finally, he needed to choose an actual air-quality level in 1967. For that, he chose the highest ambient pollution-concentration reading during the year in any city. These pieces of information he then combined in a formula:

$$DER = \left[1.00 - \frac{(2.18 \times 1967\ Max) - DL}{(2.18 \times 1967\ Max) - BL} \right] \times 1967\ Rate$$

where DER is the desired emissions rate (in grams per mile), 1967 Max is the maximum ambient concentration, DL is the desired ambient concentration, BL is the background concentration level, and 1967 rate is the actual emission rate (in grams per mile) that prevailed in 1967.

Source: This example was based on D. S. Barth, "Federal Motor Vehicle Emission Goals for CO, HC and NO$_2$. Based on Desired Air Quality Levels," *Air Pollution 1970, Part 5,* U.S. Senate Committee on Public Works (Washington, DC, 1970); Eugene P. Seskin, "Automobile Air Pollution Policy," in *Current Issues in U.S. Environmental Policy,* Paul R. Portney, ed. (Baltimore, MD: Johns Hopkins University Press, 1978): 68–104.

NO$_2$, CO and HC, respectively. The highest level that emerges would put NO$_2$, CO and HC at 0.73, 0.31 and 0.82 of the 1960 values, respectively. . . . These optimal levels are relatively insensitive to the social discount rate and gasoline costs. . . . The calculated values of net benefits are dependent on the nonmarket benefits of reduced pollution levels, but the control levels are relatively insensitive.[11]

The conclusion that the costs of control exceed the benefits for automobile pollution control seems to be generally shared.[12] Large uncertainties in the benefit estimations, a theme we have explored in several previous chapters, and the failure of any of these studies to consider

---

[11]Richard C. Schwing et al. "Benefit/Cost Analysis of Automotive Emission Reductions," *Journal of Environmental Economics and Manag8ement* 7 (1980): 57–58.

[12]See the discussion in Robert W. Crandall, Howard K. Gruenspecht, Theodore E. Keeler, and Lester B. Lave, *Regulating the Automobile* (Washington, DC: The Brookings Institution, 1986): 109–116.

the role of auto emissions of carbon in global warming force us to take these results with a grain of salt. It is nonetheless interesting that because the current policy forces manufacturers to operate on a very steep portion of the marginal control cost function, benefit uncertainty does not seem to affect the conclusion that the current standards are inefficiently strict.

The Deterioration of New-Car Emission Rates

As part of its investigation of the Clean Air Act, the National Commission on Air Quality investigated the emissions of vehicles in use and compared these emission levels to the standards. Their estimates were a blend of actual measured emissions for model years already in the fleet plus forecasts for future model years based on a knowledge of the technologies to be used. The results are presented in Table 15.1. Particularly for hydrocarbons and carbon monoxide, the deterioration of emission rates in use seems pronounced.

The Commission also investigated the factors contributing to poor in-use emissions performance. It found that the principal reason for the poor performance was improper maintenance. Carburetor and ignition-timing misadjustment were key factors. Component failure and tampering were also found to affect emission levels, though to a lesser degree.

Inspection and Maintenance Programs.   The policy response to emission rate deterioration was to require I&M programs in nonattainment regions seeking extensions to the deadlines for reaching the ambient standards. There are reasons for concerns, however, as to whether this is a cost-effective response.

The first concern arises out of the change taking place in emission-control equipment. The new devices are becoming much more sophisticated. Although they will be more difficult to tamper with than earlier devices, their malfunctions will not be detected as easily by the tests used during the inspection.[13] In addition, the costs of repair may turn out to be quite high. No longer will the turn of a carburetor screw do the trick!

A second concern arises over the timing of the program. All nonattainment regions were required to put these programs in place when seeking an extension of the deadline in meeting their ambient standards, *whether the program is necessary in meeting the standards or not*. Washington, DC, for example, is a city that did not comply with the 1982 deadline but was expected to meet the 1987 deadline, whether an inspection and maintenance program was in place or not.[14] For this area and others like it, the I&M program represents an additional but unnecessary expense.

An additional concern over this program questions whether this form of reduction is the cheapest way to reach the ambient standard. Apparently the cost per ton from I&M programs turns out to be two to three times higher than that for securing an equivalent reduction from

---

[13]Reitze, for example, points out that Ford relied on a fully electronic three-way catalyst system. The short emission tests used by most inspection and maintenance systems did not detect many of the major problems with this system. In Arnold W. Reitze, Jr., "Controlling Automotive Air Pollution Through Inspection and Maintenance Programs," *The George Washington Law Review* 47 (May 1979): 726.

[14]See Arnold W. Reitze, Jr., "Controlling Automotive Air Pollution Through Inspection and Maintenance Programs," *The George Washington Law Review* 47 (May 1979): 730–31.

Table 15.1 Average Lifetime (100,000 miles) Emissions of Gasoline Automobiles

Pollutant	Year Model	Standard (g/ml)	Average Emissions (g/ml)	Ratio of Emissions to Standard
Hydrocarbons	Pre-1968	None		
	1975–76	1.5	2.41	1.6
	1977–78	1.5	2.55	1.7
	1979	1.5	1.83	1.2
	1980	0.41	0.94	2.3
	1981	0.41	0.87	2.1
	1982	0.41	0.82	2.0
	1983	0.41	0.76	2.1
	1984+	0.41	0.79	1.9
Carbon Monoxide	Pre-1968	None		
	1975–76	15.0	29.8	2.0
	1977–78	15.0	32.9	2.2
	1979	15.0	22.6	1.5
	1980	7.0	16.9	2.4
	1981	3.4	16.9	5.0
	1982	3.4	14.7	4.3
	1983	3.4	11.7	3.4
	1984+	3.4	12.4	3.6
Nitrogen Oxides	Pre-1968	None		
	1975–76	3.1	2.55	0.8
	1977–79	2.0	2.10	1.1
	1980	2.0	2.10	1.0
	1981	1.0	1.34	1.3
	1982+	1.0	1.44	1.4

Source: National Commission on Air Quality, *To Breathe Clean Air* (Washington, DC: U.S. Government Printing Office, 1981), p. 199, Table 22.

stationary sources.[15] I&M programs do have merit because they reduce other pollutants, but the current system provides little flexibility in how the program's objectives are met.

---

[15]Ibid,. p. 735.

Do vehicle inspection programs yield positive net benefits? The evidence is mixed. A comparison of the EPA studies on the costs of the program ($645/ton) with other EPA studies of the benefits for automotive pollutants ($260 to $721/ton) reveals that for some geographic areas, but not all, the programs are justified. A recent study of the Maryland inspection program, however, suggests that the EPA cost estimates may be understated by a large amount because they do not include the costs of driver time and mileage to complete the inspection and comply with the findings. Including these costs yields a benefit/cost ratio in the neighborhood of 0.125 for Maryland.[16]

It is easy to see why I&M programs are controversial. Requiring all nonattainment areas requesting an extension in the deadline to implement those standards is costly overkill. In areas such as Washington, DC, the programs are simply not needed for attainment, and the associated costs are unnecessary. In other areas the desired reductions could well be obtained more cheaply from stationary sources.

One strategy for making inspections and maintenance programs more cost effective is to target the maintenance at those cars where the emissions reduction payoff is the highest. According to studies of on-road vehicles, fewer than 10% of the cars on the road produce half of the CO exhaust fumes. Identifying and fixing those high-polluting vehicles turns out to be remarkably cost effective. One study estimates the cost at about $100/ton of reduced CO,[17] which compares very favorably to alternative sources of vehicle reduction.

Other Local Strategies.   Another possible way to counter the effects of deterioration rates of new-car emissions involves the implementation of local transportation controls, such as stimulating mass-transit usage. This approach allows the highly polluted areas to tailor the degree of control to their needs. The question of interest is whether or not these strategies are cost effective.

To examine this question and others, the National Science Foundation funded a multidisciplinary, multiuniversity study to examine the emissions payoffs and costs of implementing various local strategies. The analysis was based on a computer model that was designed to simulate the transportation system of Boston, Massachusetts, and how that system would respond to various policies available to local authorities.

The model was based on a large amount of data on the origins and destinations of trips in the Boston area. It contained equations that simulated the choice of mode (such as bus or auto) as a function of such factors as travel time, cost, and so on. Once the travel patterns were simulated, the model projected the effects of these travel patterns on aggregate emissions and finally on the concentrations of pollutants expected in each of 123 different receptor locations in the city. With this model it was possible to keep track of both the size of the emission reductions and where pollutant concentrations were reduced. This latter piece of information is important because some parts of the city are more heavily polluted than others, and reductions in those areas would make a particularly valuable contribution to meeting the ambient air-quality standards.

---

[16]Virginia D. McConnell, "Costs and Benefits of Vehicle Inspections: a Case Study of the Maryland Region," *Journal of Environmental Management* 30 (1990): 1–15.

[17]James E. Peterson and Donald H. Stedman, "Find and Fix the Polluters," *Chemtech* (January 1992): 42–53.

TABLE 15.2 Automobile Pollution Simulation

Statistic	Benchmark	Fare Reduction	Transit Extension	1980 Emission Standard
Annual vehicle miles traveled	19,818,000	19,510,000	19,799,000	19,818,000
Percentage of trips originating on transit	10.37	10.78	11.92	10.37
Average length of auto trip (mi)	9.91	9.80	10.06	9.91
Aggregate auto emissions (g/s)				
CO	19,609	19,343	19,497	4,022
HC	2,755	2,716	2,744	485
NO_2	934	919	933	401
Annual passenger miles traveled on transit by auto users who switch to transit during trip	410,400	494,300	451,500	410,400
Annual dollar resource cost (thousands)	0	$11,517	$95,083	$120,000

Source: Frank P. Grad et al., *The Automobile and the Regulation of Its Impact on the Environment* (Norman, OK: University of Oklahoma Press, 1975), Tables 5-4, 5-5, and 5-11.

As is generally true with simulation models of this sort, an enormous amount of information was generated. A small portion of this output is presented in Table 15.2 . The benchmark column represents the transportation and air-quality situation in the Boston Air-Quality Control Region in 1970. For all other simulations the population, income, and automobile fleet are assumed to be the same as for the benchmark case.

The fare reduction column portrays the effect of a 10 percent reduction in mass-transit fare, and the transit extension column gives the effect of a vigorous program of extending subway lines further into the suburbs. The 1980 emission-standard column reflects the effect of having the degree of emission control on automobiles that should have been achieved by 1980.

The fare reduction clearly dominates the system extension on grounds of cost effectiveness because it costs less and reduces pollution more, though neither strategy makes much of a difference. It is impossible to compare the other strategies, however, because the 1980 emission standards are both much more expensive and much more effective (in terms of reducing pollutants).

Most of the purely local strategies considered in this study are expensive and do not have a profound impact on air quality. Therefore, heavy reliance on traditional local strategies like those covered in this study as a substitute for control over new-car emission rates would seem misguided. Yet appropriately designed, more innovative local strategies can effectively complement new-car strategies, particularly as a means to achieve the additional control needed in those areas where the new-car standards are not sufficient to meet the ambient standards.

Demand Side Management

Perhaps the main problem with the current approach is that it focuses on cleaner vehicles, not total emissions. Total emissions can be calculated as the product of two variables: grams per mile and miles. Federal policy has focused on the former with almost no attention to the latter. As a result, miles driven have increased tremendously with the advent of new drivers, more vehicles per household, and more miles driven by each vehicle. The increase in miles driven has offset to a considerable extent the air-quality gains achieved from producing cleaner vehicles. When the resulting emission reductions are insufficient to achieve the ambient standards, controlling the number of miles driven must become a policy target as well.

Several Far Eastern cities have undertaken some innovative approaches to demand-side management. Perhaps the most innovative can be found in Singapore and Hong Kong, where the price system is used to reduce congestion and the pollution that results from that congestion (see Example 15.2).

Other, less innovative, but nonetheless interesting approaches are proliferating. Bangkok, for example, bars vehicles transporting goods from parts of the metropolitan area during various peak hours, leaving the roads to buses, cars, and motorized tricycles. In the United States reserved express bus lanes are common. (Reserved lanes for express buses lower the relative travel time for bus commuters, thereby providing an incentive for passengers to switch from cars to buses.)

Lead Banking

In the month prior to the issuance of the new, more-stringent regulations on lead in gasoline, the EPA announced the results of a benefit/cost analysis of their expected impact. The analysis concluded that the 0.10 gplg standard would result in $49 million in benefits (from reduced adverse health effects) at an estimated cost to the refining industry of $3.5 billion.

A main concern of the EPA in issuing these regulations was the rigidity of the intermediate deadlines used to implement the phasedown. Although some refineries could meet them with ease, others could do so only at a significant increase in cost. Recognizing that meeting the environmental goal did not require every refiner to meet every deadline (as long as the excess lead introduced by those complying late was offset by compensating reductions by others), the EPA initiated the lead banking program to provide additional flexibility in meeting the regulations.

Although not formally part of the emissions trading program discussed in the previous chapter, the lead banking program does have some design similarities to it. Under this program, refiners reducing lead more than required by the applicable standard in each quarter of the year can bank the credits for use or sale in some subsequent quarter. Banked credits are transferable among refiners.

EXAMPLE 15.2

Innovative Mobile Pollution Control Strategies: Singapore and Hong Kong

Mobile-source pollution is a function of the level of traffic congestion: The greater the congestion, the greater the resulting pollutant concentrations. Reducing the level of congestion is one strategy local areas can implement to reduce peak-hour concentration levels.

Singapore has successfully reduced congestion by forcing drivers to recognize the scarcity value of congested roadways. Since 1975 cars entering the city center during the morning rush hour with fewer than four people aboard have had to display a sticker. As of 1990 the sticker cost approximately $2.60 per day. Sanctions are imposed on cars found in the designated area without a sticker.

Initially the scheme reduced the number of cars entering the restricted area by three quarters. Though that magnitude of reduction has not been maintained, city streets remain relatively uncongested and pollution concentrations have been reduced.

To make further progress on reducing pollutant concentrations, Singapore felt that it must not only limit vehicular access to certain areas during rush hours, but it must begin to reduce the total number of private vehicles in operation. In 1990 it adopted a system whereby motorists have to bid for the right to own new cars, with the licenses going to the highest bidders. Only 22,000 new vehicles—about 4.3 percent of the existing car population—will be allowed on the roads in the first year of operation.

Hong Kong recently experimented with another, more precise way of charging road users for the external costs associated with road congestion. Cars were fitted with electronic number plates that identified them to various computers strategically located around the city. Based upon these computer readings, drivers were billed depending upon the intensity, location, and time of road use. Although the pilot scheme worked well, local politics prevented it from becoming permanent policy. Apparently newly elected district councils were not satisfied with the disposition of the revenue.

Source: "Traffic Jams: The City, The Commuter and The Car," *The Economist* (18 February 1989): 19–22; "Driving in Singapore," *The Wall Street Journal* (27 February 1990): A22.

The lead banking program eased the transition to the more- stringent regulatory regime.[18] Refiners had an incentive to respond quickly because lead reductions undertaken prior to the deadlines become valuable under this new program. The availability of these credits made it possible for other refiners to comply with the deadlines even in the face of equipment failures or acts of God rather than fight the deadlines in court. Designed only as a means of facilitating the transition to the point when all refiners were in compliance with the lower standards, the lead rights program ended, as scheduled, on 31 December 1987.

---

[18]For some of the details of the program as well as a description of some of the implementation difficulties, see Robert W. Hahn and Gordon L. Hester, "Marketable Permits: Lessons for Theory and Practice," *Ecology Law Quarterly* 16, No. 2 (1989): 380–91.

Alternative Fuels

Although alternative fuels have incorporated another policy option into the control picture, how effective a strategy it would be is not clear. One study examined the cost effectiveness of methanol vehicles by projecting both costs and emissions reductions for the years 2000 and 2010 and calculating a cost per ton reduced.[19]

According to these calculations, flexible-fuel vehicles would be less cost effective than vehicles dedicated to burn either 85 percent methanol or 100 percent methanol. The cost per ton for flexible-fuel vehicles would be in the neighborhood of $66,000 per ton whereas for the vehicle burning 85 percent methanol it would be $31,000 a ton.[20]

These numbers are very high, almost five times as high as alternative means of reducing hydrocarbon emissions. In 1989 the South Coast Air Quality Management District identified 120 options for reducing volatile hydrocarbons. The average cost effectiveness of the 68 measures proposed was $12,250 per ton. While early estimates such as these should not determine the outcome of the search for alternatives, they certainly do suggest that caution in proceeding too rapidly down this path would be appropriate.[21]

Air Quality

Have these policies improved air quality? In this section we shall examine the data on three pollutants for which mobile sources are very important—ozone, carbon monoxide, and lead.[22]

Ozone. Ozone continues to be the most pervasive ambient air pollution problem in the United States, with 101 areas failing to meet the ozone ambient standard for 1986–1988. Some progress was made, however. Over the 1979–1988 period, the exceedances decreased by some 10 percent. Emissions of volatile organic compounds, the precursors for ozone formation, were also down 17 percent during this period. Comparable data for other countries were not available.

Carbon Monoxide. In the United States carbon dioxide emissions declined by 25 percent over the 1979–1988 period despite a 33 percent increase in vehicle miles traveled. The

---

[19]Margaret A. Walls and Alan J. Krupnick, "Cost-effectiveness of Methanol Vehicles," *Resources,* No. 100 (Summer, 1990).

[20]Vehicles burning 100 percent fuel are estimated to produce reductions at $51,000 per ton.

[21]Mandating fuel choices is less cost effective than using economic incentives. For a specific comparison of the two approaches see Robert A. Collinge and Anne Stevens, "Targeting Methanol or Other Alternative Fuels: How Intrusive Should Policy Be?" *Contemporary Policy Issues* 8 (January 1990):54–61.

[22]In this section the data for the United States are from Office of Air Quality, *National Air Quality and Emissions Trends Report: 1988* (Washington, DC: U.S. Environmental Protection Agency, 1990) and the international data are from United Nations Environmental Program and the World Health Organization, "Monitoring the Global Environment: An Assessment of Urban Air Quality," *Environment* 31, No. 8 (October 1989): 6–13, and 26–37.

emission reductions produced a 28 percent decrease in the number of sites experiencing violations of the ambient standards and an 88 percent decrease in the number of exceedances.

Although some Western European countries have experienced stabilized emissions or a gradual decline, others show increased emissions. In the United Kingdom emissions rose by 7 percent between 1973 and 1984. In both the Netherlands and West Germany, emissions declined by 32 percent and 37 percent, respectively.

Data from Poland and Hungary suggest that CO emissions are also rising in some Eastern European countries. Experts also expect to find increasing emissions in industrializing Asian and South American countries, but current data are insufficient to confirm that conjecture.

Lead.   Declines in emissions of lead in the United States have been dramatic. From 1979 to 1988 emissions of lead dropped 93 percent and ambient concentrations dropped 89 percent.

Although relatively few countries report lead emissions, the data indicate that lead in gasoline is generally being decreased in European and Asian countries. It is generally not being decreased in Africa, or in South or Central America.[23]

POSSIBLE REFORMS

We have seen that the current approach has some salient weaknesses. Reliance on controlling emissions at the point of production has produced major improvements in cars leaving the assembly line, but emission rates deteriorate with use. The use of uniform standards has resulted in more control than necessary in rural areas and perhaps less than necessary in our most heavily polluted areas.

Manufacturers have been able to delay implementation deadlines because the sanctions for noncompliance are so severe that the EPA is reluctant to deny a certificate of conformity. Automobile users have little incentive to drive or maintain their cars in a manner that minimizes emissions. Is there a way that automobile emissions policy could be reformed to make headway on these important deficiencies?

Emission Charges

A most interesting and quite detailed proposal has been suggested by Mills and White.[24] In their proposal, emission standards are replaced by emission charges designed to provide the appropriate incentives for both manufacturers and drivers.

The chief elements of the proposal include:

1. A uniform charge levied on all new cars and paid at the time the cars are sold to dealers. The size of the charge would depend on the amounts of the three major pollu-

---

[23]Gasoline in Mexico City had the highest lead content of all sites in the global monitoring network, and volunteers from that city had the highest levels of lead in their blood.

[24]Edwin S. Mills and Lawrence J. White, "Government Policies Toward Automobile Emissions Control," in *Approaches to Control Air Pollution,* Ann F. Friedlaender, ed. (Cambridge, MA: MIT Press, 1978): 348–402.

tants emitted by the engine class during the regular EPA test. The lower the emissions are, the smaller the tax to be paid.

2. Particularly polluted areas would be permitted to augment this basic charge with another charge to reflect the greater need for clean cars in those areas. This would induce consumers in those areas to choose cleaner cars in order to avoid paying the higher fees assessed on dirty ones. Drivers in rural areas, meanwhile, would face lower emission charges in general (because no supplemental fee would be imposed), so they would not have to buy the cars with significant control overkill as they do under current policy.

3. Manufacturers would no longer be issued a certificate of conformity. All cars could be sold. Dirtier cars would pay higher emission fees. This would eliminate the current problem with sanctions that are so severe that they do not represent a credible threat, but it would provide a clear incentive for manufacturers to reduce emissions in order to hold their costs (including the charge) down.

4. An additional emission charge would be paid by drivers at their annual inspection. This fee would take into account grams per mile (as determined by the inspection) and miles driven since the last inspection. Thus a driver could reduce this fee by maintaining the car to emit less, using retrofit devices, if available, and by driving fewer miles. The incentives to keep a car clean would persist over the lifetime of the automobile, and the current incentive to hold older, dirtier cars longer would no longer persist.

In previous chapters we demonstrated that properly designed emission charges would allocate the control responsibility in a cost-minimizing way. The Mills and White proposal would appear to offer the opportunity to use this theorem as the basis for a reform of the current approach to air pollution by mobile sources.

Retirement Strategies

A final reform possibility involves strategies to accelerate the retirement of older, high-polluting vehicles. This could be accomplished either by raising the cost of holding on to older vehicles (as with higher registration fees for vehicles that pollute more) or by providing a bounty of some sort to those retiring heavily polluting vehicles early. Though probably more bureaucratically cumbersome, the subsidy approach would respond to the large number of poor households who own these older vehicles and who could ill afford to pay higher registration fees.

This approach would tend to counteract the tendency for vehicles to be used longer as a result of the new-source focus of current automotive regulations. By eliminating these heavily polluting vehicles from the fleet earlier than would otherwise be the case, greater emission reductions could be achieved at an earlier date. This approach could be applied selectively in those local areas for which it could make a significant difference.

SUMMARY

The current policy toward motor vehicle emissions blends point-of-production control with point-of-use control, but the existing blend seems quite removed from what efficiency or cost effectiveness would dictate. The history of legislation in this area has been a turbulent one, moving from a low federal profile—concerned mainly with studying the problem and assisting states—to a high federal profile involving a preemptive responsibility for emission controls.

In a period of frustration, Congress wrote such a tough law that little was accomplished during the early years. The ambient standards could not be met by the deadlines. The sanctions used for noncompliance were so severe that the EPA was reluctant to use them. Because they were not a credible threat, the sanctions did little to alter behavior.

The focus on new-source controls has caused the problem of people using older, more heavily polluting cars, delaying significant improvements in air quality. In addition, the technologies chosen by the manufacturers to meet their statutory responsibilities have failed to prevent a deterioration in operating-vehicle emission rates.

The U.S. national emission standards, which represent the core of the current approach, seem inefficient for two rather different reasons: (1) According to benefit/cost calculations they are too stringent, and (2) with the exception of California, they are uniform. These two inefficiencies are somewhat related. The controls are too stringent primarily because they require cars not contributing to nonattainment to bear the same cost of controls as those that do contribute. The current high standards cause these costs to be large. Thus, if uniform standards are to be retained, they probably should be lower.

Uniform emission standards, however, cannot be fully cost effective, whatever their level. Cost effectiveness requires higher control costs in areas having real difficulty in meeting the ambient standards than in the rest of the country. Uniform emission standards are powerless to make this crucial distinction.

Likewise, local approaches relying on inspection or maintenance are not generally cost effective. Some areas are currently required to establish these programs whether they facilitate attainment or not. Other areas could find stationary-source control cheaper, but these areas, under current rules, are not allowed to substitute one for the other. One possibility for improving the program is to identify the most heavily polluting vehicles and concentrate the maintenance requirements on them.

Despite the policy imperfections, mobile-source pollutant concentrations and emissions, with the exception of ozone, have generally improved in the industrialized nations. The picture is more bleak in developing nations, where control levels are low and increases in vehicle ownership are rapid.

For many nonattainment areas, current policy has clearly not been enough to guarantee that the ambient standards are met. In part the emissions standards themselves are at fault. Defined in terms of emissions per mile, they are powerless to prevent increases in emissions due to growth in the number of vehicles on the road and/or growth in the number of miles driven. As the population expands, carrying with it an expansion in the number of vehicles on the road, air quality necessarily deteriorates even if every car has met the standards. As suburban communities expand farther and farther from the urban center, the average number of miles driven per driver increases. Each mile driven contributes more emissions.

Appropriate regulation of emissions from mobile sources requires a great deal more than controlling emissions at the factory. Vehicle purchases, driving behavior, fuel choice, and even residential and employment locations must eventually be affected by the need to reduce mobile-source emissions. The low cost of auto travel has led to a very dispersed pattern of development. Because dispersed patterns of development make mass transit a less viable alternative, a downward spiral of population dispersal and the decline of mass transit occurs. In the long run, part of the strategy for meeting ambient standards will necessarily involve changing land use patterns to create the kind of high-density travel corridors that are compatible with effective mass transit use. That, of course will only evolve over a long period of time, but ensuring that the true social costs of transportation are borne by those making residential location and transportation decisions will start the process moving in the right direction. Affecting the choices facing automobile owners can only happen if the economic incentives associated with those choices are structured correctly.

Innovative policies aimed specifically at restructuring these incentives may fill the bill. A manufacturer's incentive to provide new types of vehicles would be greatly affected by the anticipated size of the market and the speed with which the new vehicles would penetrate that market. In the absence of some kind of economic incentive, consumers will typically wait as long as possible to adopt new technologies because of cost fears about reliability. Differential taxation, such as that used in Europe, can be used to speed up the rate of adoption.

Local approaches, such as those being implemented in Singapore, represent another point of departure. Using the price system to ration access to the central city forces drivers to internalize some of the costs of congestion, enhancing the attractiveness of public transit alternatives in the process.

In the case of mobile sources, however, the best strategy appears to be based on a carefully designed emission charge. If implemented, this approach would appear to be more cost effective and more flexible than the current approach while eliminating many of its deficiencies.

FURTHER READING

Crandall, Robert W., Howard K. Gruenspecht, Theodore E. Keeler, and Lester B. Lave. *Regulating the Automobile* (Washington, DC: The Brookings Institution, 1986). An examination of the effectiveness and efficiency of the federal regulation of automobile safety, emissions, and fuel economy in the United States.

Dewees, Donald N. *Economics and Public Policy: The Auto Pollution Case* (Cambridge, MA: MIT Press, 1974). An interesting, if somewhat dated, use of economic analysis to analyze automobile air pollution. Filled with technical detail about many of the issues covered in this chapter.

Grad, Frank P. et, al. *The Automobile and the Regulation of Its Impact on the Environment* (Norman, OK: The University of Oklahoma Press, 1975). A comprehensive multidisciplinary, multiuniversity study of automobile pollution financed by the National Science Foundation. Includes analyses by economists, engineers, and lawyers.

Mills, Edwin S., and Lawrence J. White. "Government Policies Toward Automobile Emissions Control," in Ann F. Friedlaender, ed., *Approaches to Control Air Pollution,* (Cambridge, MA: MIT Press, 1978): 348–402. A detailed, highly readable article describing the emission charge reform in detail.

ADDITIONAL REFERENCES

Gruenspecht, Howard K. "Differentiated Regulation: The Case of Auto Emission Standards," *The American Economic Review* 72 (May 1982): 328–31.

Jacoby, Henry D., et al. *Clearing the Air: Federal Policy on Automotive Emission Control* (Cambridge, MA: Ballinger Press, 1978).

Mackenzie, James J., and Michael P. Walsh. *Driving Forces: Motor Vehicle Trends and their Implications for Global Warming, Energy Strategies and Transportation Planning* (Washington, DC: World Resources Institute, 1990).

National Commission on Air Quality. *To Breathe Clean Air* (Washington, DC: U.S. Government Printing Office, 1981).

Reitze, Arnold W., Jr. "Controlling Automotive Air Pollution Through Inspection and Maintenance Programs," *The George Washington Law Review* 47 (May 1979): 735.

Seskin, Eugene P. "Automobile Air Pollution Policy," in Paul R. Portney, ed., *Current Issues in U.S. Environmental Policy* (Baltimore, MD: Johns Hopkins University Press, 1978): 68–104.

White, Lawrence J. "American Automotive Emissions Control Policy: A Review of the Reviews," *Journal of Environmental Economics and Management* 2 (1974): 231–46.

White, Lawrence J. "U.S. Automotive Emissions Controls: How Well Are They Working?" *The American Economic Review* 72 (May 1982): 332–35.

DISCUSSION QUESTIONS

1. When a threshold concentration is used as the basis for pollution control as it is for air pollution, one possibility for meeting the threshold at minimum cost is to spread the emissions out over time. One way to accomplish this is to establish a peak-hour pricing system in which emissions during peak periods are charged more. Singapore does this by forbidding from the city during rush hour all private vehicle traffic that does not conspicuously display a permit. The permits can be purchased by anyone, but they are very expensive.
   a. Would this represent a movement toward efficiency? Why or why not?
   b. What effects should this policy have on mass transit usage, gasoline sales, downtown shopping, and travel patterns?
2. The Mills and White [1978] emission charge discussed earlier in this chapter would, if implemented, represent quite a dramatic departure from existing policy. Discuss the desirability of implementing such a policy. What are the advantages and disadvantages of changing from the current approach to the Mills and White scheme?

CHAPTER 16

Water Pollution

It was the best of times, it was the worst of times, it was the age of wisdom, it was the age of foolishness, it was the epoch of belief, it was the epoch of incredulity. . . .

CHARLES DICKENS, *A TALE OF TWO CITIES* (1859)

INTRODUCTION

Although various types of pollution share common attributes, important differences are apparent as well. These differences form the basis for the elements of policy unique to each pollutant. We have seen, for example, that although the types of pollutants emitted by mobile and stationary sources are often identical, the policy approaches differ considerably.

Water pollution control has its own unique characteristics as well. Two stand out as having particular relevance for policy:

1. Recreation benefits are much more important for water pollution control than for air pollution control.[1]
2. Large economies of scale in treating sewage and other wastes create the possibility for large, centralized treatment plants as one control strategy, whereas for air pollution, on-site control is the standard approach.

These characteristics create a need for yet another policy approach. In this chapter we shall explore the problems and prospects for controlling this unique and important form of pollution.

---

[1]See Daniel Feenberg and Edwin S. Mills, *Measuring the Benefits of Water Pollution Abatement* (New York: Academic Press, 1980): 164.

NATURE OF WATER POLLUTION PROBLEMS

Types of Waste-Receiving Water

Two primary types of water are susceptible to contamination. The first, *surface water,* consists of the rivers, lakes, and oceans covering most of the earth's surface. In the past, policymakers have focused almost exclusively on preventing and cleaning up lake and river water pollution. Only recently has ocean pollution received the attention it deserves.

Groundwater, once considered a pristine resource, has been shown to be subject to considerable contamination from toxic chemicals. *Groundwater* is subsurface water that occurs beneath a water table in soils or rocks, or in geological formations that are fully saturated.

Groundwater is a vast natural resource. It has been estimated that the volume of groundwater is approximately fifty times the annual flow of surface water.[2] Though groundwater currently supplies only 25 percent of the fresh water used for all purposes in the United States, its use is increasing more rapidly than the use of surface water.

Groundwater is used primarily for irrigation and as a source of drinking water. Approximately 50 percent of the population relies on groundwater as the primary source of water for drinking. The proportion is even higher for rural areas.

Surface water also serves as a significant source of drinking water, but it has many other uses as well. Recreational benefits such as swimming, fishing, and boating are important determinants of surface-water policy in areas where the water is not used for drinking.

Sources of Contamination

Contamination of groundwater occurs when polluting substances leach into a water-saturated region. Many potential contaminants are removed by filtration and adsorption as the water moves slowly through the layers of rock and soil. Toxic organic chemicals are one major example of a pollutant that may not be filtered out during migration. Once these substances enter groundwater, very little, if any, further cleansing takes place. Moreover, because the rate of replenishment for many groundwater sources is small relative to the stock, very little mixing and dilution of the contaminants occur (see Example 16.1).

Although some contamination has been accidental, the product of unintended and unexpected waste migration to water supplies, a portion of the contamination was deliberate. Watercourses were simply a convenient place to dump municipal or private sewage and industrial wastes. Along the shoreline of many lakes or rivers, pipes dumping human or industrial wastes directly into the water were a common occurrence before laws limiting this activity were enacted and enforced.

For lake and river pollution policy purposes it is useful to distinguish between two sources of contamination—point and nonpoint sources—even though the distinction is not

---

[2]Council on Environmental Quality, *Environmental Quality—1980* (Washington, DC: U.S. Government Printing Office, 1980): 83.

E X A M P L E   1 6 . 1

Incidents of Groundwater Pollution

Traditional federal policies have paid little attention to groundwater, partly because of the high cost of testing and monitoring. Recent data, however, have shown that groundwater in many locations is contaminated by toxic chemicals. This may be posing unacceptable health risks for the public, because groundwater is widely used for drinking water. Many of the chemicals now being discovered in drinking water are either known or suspected carcinogens or mutagens.

Recently discovered incidents of groundwater contamination by toxic organic substances include the following:

1.   In 1979 a Massachusetts Legislative Commission on Water Supply found that at least one third of the 351 communities in the commonwealth were affected by chemical contamination of drinking water, and wells were restricted or closed in 22 towns.

2.   All wells in Groveland and Rowley were closed because of trichloroethylene (TCE) contamination, a known carcinogen in animals.

3.   In North Reading, TCE concentrations exceed 90 ppb in two wells supplying 30 percent of the town's water. The state maximum acceptable contamination level is 10 ppb.

4.   In January 1980, California public health officials closed 37 public wells that supplied water to 400,000 people in the San Gabriel Valley because of TCE contamination.

5.   A New York Public Interest Research Group documented that all three major aquifers under Long Island were seriously contaminated with effluent from industrial wastes, municipal treatment plants, and runoff from highways. They also found evidence of mutagenic substances in twelve groundwater sites.

Source: Council on Environmental Quality, *Environmental Quality—1980* (Washington, DC: U.S. Government Printing Office, 1980): 81–83.

always crystal clear. *Point sources* generally discharge into surface waters at a specific location through a pipe, outfall, or ditch, whereas *nonpoint sources* usually affect the water in a more indirect and diffuse way. From the policy point of view, nonpoint sources are more difficult to control and have received little legislative attention. As a result of the gains made in controlling point sources, nonpoint sources now compose over half of the waste load borne by the nation's waters.

Rivers and Lakes.   The most important nonpoint sources of pollution for rivers and lakes are agricultural activity, urban storm-water runoff, silviculture, and individual disposal systems. Contamination from agriculture includes eroded topsoil, pesticides, and fertilizer. Urban storm-water runoff contains a number of pollutants, including, typically, high quantities of lead. Forestry, if not carefully done, can contribute to soil erosion and, by removing shade cover, could have a large impact on the temperature of normally shaded streams.

Malfunctioning septic systems, more prevalent in rural areas, are estimated to be a major source of pollution for some 43 percent of the nation's river basins.

The contamination of groundwater supplies usually results from the migration of harmful substances from sites where high concentrations of chemicals can be found. These include industrial waste storage sites, landfills, and farms. Industrial wastes have been identified by the EPA as the most important source of groundwater contamination.[3]

The primary point sources are industries and municipalities. As of 1980, the EPA had identified some 59,907 point sources. Of these, 15,395 were municipal dischargers (mostly sewage treatment plants), and industrial sources made up most of the rest. Of the 7,350 "major" dischargers, responsible for well over half of all discharges, municipalities and industries were about equally represented.

Ocean Pollution.   The two primary sources of ocean pollution discussed in this chapter are oil spills and ocean dumping. Because a great deal of oil is transported over the oceans and is produced from platforms exploiting fields under the ocean, oil spills have become a more common occurrence (see Table 16.1). Various unwanted by-products of modern life have also been dumped in ocean waters based upon the mistaken belief that the vastness of the oceans allowed them to absorb large quantities of waste without suffering noticeable damage. Dumped materials have included sewage and sewage sludge, unwanted chemicals, trace metals, and even radioactive materials.

Types of Pollutants

For our purposes the large number of water pollutants can be usefully classified by means of the taxonomy we developed earlier.

Fund Pollutants.   Fund pollutants are those for which the environment has some assimilative capacity. If the absorptive capacity is high enough relative to the rate of injection, they may not accumulate at all. One type of fund water pollutant is called *degradable* because it degrades, or breaks into its component parts, within the water. Degradable wastes are normally organic residuals that are attacked and broken down by bacteria in the stream.

The process by which organic wastes are broken down into component parts consumes oxygen. The amount of oxygen consumed depends upon the magnitude of the waste load. All of the higher life forms in watercourses are *aerobic;* they require oxygen for survival. As a stream's oxygen levels fall, fish mortality increases, with the less-tolerant fish becoming the first to succumb. The oxygen level can become low enough that even the aerobic bacteria die. When this happens, the stream becomes *anaerobic* and the ecology changes drastically. This is an extremely unpleasant circumstance because the stream takes on a dark hue and the stream water stinks!

To control these waste loads, two different types of monitoring are needed: (1) monitoring the ambient conditions in the watercourse, and (2) monitoring the magnitude of emissions. The measure commonly used to keep track of ambient conditions for these conventional fund pollutants is *dissolved oxygen* (DO). The amount of dissolved oxygen in a body of water is a function of ambient conditions, such as temperature, stream flow, and the waste

---

[3]Ibid., pp. 116–120.

TABLE 16.1 Notable Oil Spills

Source and Location	Date	Tons Spilled
Ixtoc I oil well, Southern Gulf of Mexico	3 June 1979	600,000
Nowruz oil field, Persian Gulf	February 1983	600,000 (est.)
Atlantic Express and *Aegean Captain*, off Trinidad & Tobago	19 July 1979	300,000
Castillo de Beliver, off Cape Town, South Africa	6 August 1983	250,000
Amoco Cadiz, near Portsall, France	16 March 1978	223,000
Torrey Canyon, off Land's FEnd, England	18 March 1967	119,000
Sea Star, Gulf of Oman	19 December 1972	115,000
Urquiola, La Coruna, Spain	12 May 1976	100,000
Hawaiian Patriot, northern Pacific	25 February 1977[cm	99,000
Othello, Tralhavet Bay, Sweden	20 March 1970	60,000–1000,000
World Glory, off South Africa	13 June 1968	46,000
Burmah Agate, Galveston Bay, Texas	1 November 1979	36,400
Exxon Valdez, Prince William Sound, Alaska	24 March 1989	34,300

Source: Mark S. Hoffman, *The World Almanac and Book of Facts, 1990* (New York: Pharos Books, 1990).

load.[4] The measure of the oxygen demand placed on a stream by any particular volume of effluent is called the *biochemical oxygen demand* (BOD).

Using modeling techniques, emissions (measured as BOD) at a certain point can be translated into DO measures at various receptor locations along a stream. This step is necessary in order to implement an ambient permit system or an ambient emission charge.

If we were to develop a profile of dissolved oxygen readings in a stream where organic effluent is being injected, that profile would typically exhibit one or more minimum points called oxygen sags. These *oxygen sags* represent locations along the stream where the dissolved oxygen content is lower than at other points. An ambient permit or ambient charge system would be designed to reach a desired DO level at those sag points, whereas an emission permit or emission charge system would simply try to hit a particular BOD reduction target. The former would take the location of the emitter into account; the latter would not. Later in this chapter we will examine studies which model these systems on particular watercourses.

[4]The danger of anaerobic conditions is highest in the late summer and early fall, when temperatures are high and the stream is low.

A second type of fund pollutant, thermal pollution, is caused by the injection of heat into a watercourse. Typically, *thermal pollution* is caused when an industrial plant or electric utility uses surface water as a coolant, returning the heated water to the watercourse. This heat is dissipated in the receiving waters by evaporation. By raising the temperature of the water near the outfall, thermal pollution lowers the dissolved oxygen content and can result in dramatic ecological changes in that area.

Yet another example is provided by a class of pollutants, such as nitrogen and phosphorus, that are plant nutrients. These pollutants stimulate the growth of aquatic plant life, such as algae and water weeds. In excess these plants can produce odor, taste, and aesthetic problems. A lake with an excessive supply of nutrients is called *eutrophic.*

The various types of fund pollutants could be ordered on a spectrum. On one end of the spectrum would be pollutants for which the environment has a very large absorptive capacity, on the other end pollutants for which the absorptive capacity is virtually nil. The limiting case, with no absorptive capacity, are stock pollutants.

Near the end of that spectrum is a class of inorganic synthetic chemicals called persistent pollutants. These substances are called *persistent* because their complex molecular structures are not effectively broken down in the stream. Some degradation takes place, but so slowly that these pollutants can travel long distances in water in a virtually unchanged form.

These persistent pollutants accumulate, not only in the watercourses, but in the food chain as well. The concentration levels in the tissues of living organisms rise with the order of the species. Concentrations in lower life forms such as plankton may be relatively small, but, because small fish eat a lot of plankton and do not excrete the chemical, the concentrations in small fish would be higher. The magnification continues as large fish consume small fish; concentration levels in the larger fish would be even higher.

Because they accumulate in the food chain, persistent pollutants present an interesting monitoring challenge. The traditional approach would involve measurements of pollutant concentration in the water, but that is not the only variable of interest. The damage is related not only to its concentration in the water, but its concentration in the food chain as well. Although monitoring the environmental effects of these pollutants may be more compelling than monitoring other pollutants, it is also more difficult. Because effective monitoring is a prerequisite for successful policy, this suggests one major continuing role for the EPA.

A final type of fund pollutant, infectious organisms such as bacteria and viruses, is carried into surface and groundwater by domestic and animal wastes and by wastes from such industries as tanning and meat packing. These live organisms may thrive and multiply in water, or their population may decline over time, depending upon how hospitable or hostile the watercourse is for continued growth.

Accumulating Pollutants.   The most troublesome cases result when pollutants accumulate in the environment. No natural process removes or transforms stock pollutants; the watercourse cannot cleanse itself of them.

Inorganic chemicals and minerals comprise the main examples of stock pollutants. Perhaps the most notorious members of this group are the heavy metals, such as lead, cadmium, and mercury. Extreme examples of poisoning by these metals have occurred in Japan. One ocean dumping case was responsible for *Minamata Disease,* named for the location where it occurred. Some 52 people died and 150 other suffered serious brain and nerve damage. Scientists puzzled for years over the source of the ailments until they were traced to an organic form of mercury that had accumulated in the tissues of fish eaten three times a day by local residents.

In another case in Japan, known as the *Itai Itai* (literally, "ouch-ouch") *Disease,* scientists traced the source of a previously undiagnosed, extremely painful bone disease to the ingestion of cadmium. Nearby mines were the source of the cadmium, which apparently was ingested by eating contaminated rice and soybeans.

As is typical with persistent pollutants, some of the stock pollutants are difficult to monitor. Those accumulated in the food chains give rise to the same problem as is presented by persistent pollutants. Ambient sampling must be supplemented by sampling tissues from members of the food chain. To further complicate matters, the heavy metals may sink rapidly to the bottom, remaining in the sediment. Although they could be detected in sediment samples, merely drawing samples from the water itself would allow these pollutants to escape detection.

WATER POLLUTION CONTROL POLICY

U.S. policy for water pollution control considerably antedates federal air pollution control. We might suppose that the policy for water pollution control is superior because authorities had more time to profit from early mistakes. Unfortunately, that is not the case.

Early Legislation

The first federal legislation dealing with discharge into the nation's waterways occurred when Congress passed the 1899 Refuse Act. Designed primarily to protect navigation, this act focused on preventing any discharge that would interfere with using rivers as transport links. All discharges into a river were prohibited unless approved by a permit from the Chief of the U.S. Engineers. Most permits were issued to contractors dredging the rivers, and they dealt mainly with the disposal of the removed material. This act was virtually unenforced for other pollutants until 1970, when this permit program was rediscovered and used briefly (with little success) as the basis for federal enforcement actions.

The Water Pollution Control Act of 1948 represented the first attempt by the federal government to exercise some direct influence over what previously had been a state and local function. A hesitant move, because it reaffirmed that the primary responsibility for water pollution control rested with the states, it did initiate the authority of the federal government to conduct investigations, research, and surveys.

The first hints of the current approach are found in the amendments to the Water Pollution Control Act, which were passed in 1956. Two provisions of this act were especially important: (1) federal financial support for the construction of waste treatment plants and (2) direct federal regulation of waste discharges via a mechanism known as the *enforcement conference.*

The first of these provisions envisioned a control strategy based on subsidizing the construction of a particular control activity—waste treatment plants. Municipalities could receive federal grants to cover up to 55 percent of the construction of municipal sewage treatment plants. This approach not only lowered the cost to the local government of constructing these facilities, it also lowered the cost to users. Because the federal government contribution was a grant, rather than a loan, the fees charged users did not reflect the federally subsidized construction portion of the cost. The user fees were set at a lower rate that was only high enough to cover the unsubsidized portion of construction cost, as well as the operating and maintenance costs.

The 1956 Amendments envisioned a relatively narrow federal role in the regulation of discharges. Initially, only polluters contributing to interstate pollution were included, but subsequent laws have broadened the coverage. By 1961 discharges into all navigable water were covered.

The mechanism created by the Amendments of 1956 to enforce the regulation of discharges was the enforcement conference. Under this approach the designated federal control authority could call for a conference to deal with any interstate water pollution problem or could be requested to do so by the governor of an affected state. Because this authority was discretionary and not mandatory and the control authority had very few means of enforcing any decisions reached, the conferences did not achieve the intended results.

The Water Quality Act of 1965 attempted to improve the process by establishing ambient water quality standards for interstate watercourses and by requiring states to file implementation plans. This sounds like the approach currently being used in air pollution control, but there are important differences. The plans forthcoming from states in response to the 1965 act were vague and did not attempt to link specific effluent standards on discharges to the ambient standards. They generally took the easy way out and called for secondary treatment, which removes 80–90 percent of BOD and 85 percent of suspended solids. The fact that these standards bore no particular relationship to ambient quality made them difficult to enforce in the courts, since the legal authority for them was based on this relationship.

Subsequent Legislation

Point Sources. As discussed in the preceding chapters, an air of frustration regarding pollution control pervaded Washington in the 1970s. As with air pollution legislation, this frustration led to the enactment of a very tough water control law. The tone of the act is established immediately in the preamble, which calls for the achievement of two goals: (1) "that the discharge of pollutants into the navigable waters be eliminated by 1985"; and (2) "that wherever attainable, an interim goal of water quality which provides for the protection and propagation of fish, shellfish, and wildlife and provides for recreation in and on the water be achieved by June 1, 1983." The stringency of these goals represented a major departure from past policy.

This act also introduced new procedures for implementing the law. Permits were required of all dischargers (replacing the 1899 Refuse Act, which, because of its navigation focus, was difficult to enforce). The permits would be granted only when the dischargers met certain technology-based effluent standards. The ambient standards were completely bypassed, as these effluent standards were uniformly imposed and so could not depend upon local water conditions.[5]

According to the 1972 Amendments, the effluent standards were to be implemented in two stages. By 1977 industrial dischargers, as a condition of their permit, were required to meet effluent limitations based on the "best practicable control technology currently available" (BPT). In setting these national standards, the EPA was required to consider the total costs of these technologies and their relation to the benefits received, but not to consider the conditions of the individual source or the particular waters into which it was discharged. In addition, all publicly owned treatment plants were to have achieved secondary treatment by

---

[5]Actually the ambient standards were not completely bypassed. If the uniform controls were not sufficient to meet the desired standard, the effluent limitation would have to be tightened accordingly.

1977. By 1983 industrial discharges were required to meet effluent limitations based on the presumably more stringent "best available technology economically achievable" (BAT) and publicly owned treatment plants were required to meet effluent limitations that depended upon the "best practicable waste treatment technology."

The program of subsidizing municipal water treatment plants, begun in 1956, was continued in a slightly modified form by the 1972 Act. Whereas the 1965 Act allowed the federal government to subsidize up to 55 percent of the cost of construction of waste treatment plants, the 1972 Act raised the ceiling to 75 percent. The 1972 Act also increased the funds available for this program. In 1981 the federal share was reduced to 55 percent.

The 1977 Amendments continued this regulatory approach, but with some major modifications. This legislation drew a more careful distinction between the conventional and toxic pollutants, with more-stringent requirements placed on the latter, and it extended virtually all of the deadlines in the 1972 Act.

For conventional pollutants a new treatment standard was created to replace the BAT standards. The effluent limitations for these pollutants were to be based on the "best conventional technology," and the deadline for these standards was set at 1 July 1984. In setting these standards, the EPA was required to consider whether the costs of adding the pollution-control equipment were reasonable when compared with the improvement in water quality. For unconventional pollutants and toxics (any pollutant not specifically included on the list of conventional pollutants), the BAT requirement was retained but the deadline was shifted to 1984.

Other deadlines were also extended. The date for municipalities to meet the secondary treatment deadline moved from 1977 to 1983. Industrial compliance with the BPT standards was delayed until 1983 or whenever the contemplated system had the potential for application throughout the industry.

The final modification made by the 1977 Amendments involved the introduction of pretreatment standards for waste being sent to a publicly owned treatment system. These standards were designed to prevent the discharges that could inhibit the treatment process and to prevent the introduction of toxic pollutants that would not be removed by the waste treatment facility. Existing facilities were required to meet the standards three years after the date they were published, and facilities constructed later would be required to meet the pretreatment regulations upon commencement of operations.

Nonpoint Sources. In contrast to the control of point sources, the EPA was given no specific authority to regulate nonpoint sources. This type of pollution was seen by Congress as a state responsibility.

Section 208 of the Act authorized federal grants for state-initiated planning that would provide implementable plans for area-wide waste treatment management. Section 208 further specified that this area-wide plan must identify significant nonpoint sources of pollution, as well as procedures and methods for controlling them. The reauthorization of the Clean Water Act, passed over President Reagan's veto during February 1987, authorized an additional $400 million for a new program to help states control runoff, but it still left the chief responsibility for controlling nonpoint sources to the states.

The main federal role for controlling nonpoint sources has been the Conservation Reserve Program. Designed to remove some 40 to 45 million acres of highly erodible land from cultivation, this act provides subsidies to farmers for planting grass or trees. The Department of Agriculture expects that this act will result in a nationwide reduction of total erosion by 8.6 percent and a reduction in nitrogen, phosphorus, and total suspended solid loadings by between 7.8 and 9.6 percent.[6]

The Safe Drinking Water Act

The 1972 policy focused on achieving water quality sufficiently high for fishing and swimming. Because that quality is not high enough for drinking water, the Safe Drinking Water Act of 1974 issued more stringent standards for community water systems. The primary drinking water regulations set maximum allowable concentration levels for bacteria, turbidity (muddiness), and chemical/radiological contaminants. National secondary drinking water regulations were also established to protect "public welfare" from odor and aesthetic problems that might cause a substantial number of people to stop using the affected water system. The secondary standards are advisory for the states; they cannot be enforced by the EPA.

The 1986 Amendments required the EPA to issue primary standards within three years for 83 contaminants and by 1991 for at least 25 more, to set standards based on the "best available technology," and to monitor public water systems for both regulated and unregulated chemical contaminants.[7] Approximately 60,000 public water systems are subject to these regulations. Civil and criminal penalties for any violations of the standards were also increased by the amendments.

Ocean Pollution

Oil Spills. The Clean Water Act prohibits discharges of "harmful quantities" of oil into navigable waters. Because the EPA regulations define "harmful" to include all discharges that "violate applicable water quality standards or cause a film or sheen upon the surface of the water," virtually all discharges are prohibited.

Industry responsibilities include complying with Coast Guard regulations (which deal with contingency planning in case of a spill and various accident avoidance requirements)[8] and assuming the financial liability for any accident. If a spill does occur, it must be immediately reported to the Coast Guard or the EPA. Failure to report a spill can result in a fine of up to $10,000, imprisonment for not more than one year, or both.

In addition to giving notice, the discharger must either contain the spill or pay the cost of cleanup by a responsible government agency. The discharger's liability for the government's actual removal cost is limited to $50 million unless willful negligence or willful misconduct

---

[6]Marc O. Ribaudo, "Water Quality Benefits from the Conservation Reserve Program," Agricultural Economic Report No. 606 (Washington, DC: U.S. Department of Agriculture, 1989).

[7]The regulations and maximum contaminant levels can be found in 40 CFR 141.

[8]Most of the Coast Guard regulations are authorized by the Port and Safety Tanker Act of 1978 and two international conventions on oil spills to which the United States is a party.

can be proved. Successful proof of willful negligence or willful misconduct eliminates the liability limit. In addition to cleanup costs, removal costs also include compensation for damages to the natural resources. (Natural resource damages are defined as "any costs or expenses incurred by the federal government or any state government in the restoration or replacement of natural resources damaged or destroyed as a result of a discharge of oil.")

Ocean Dumping. Except for oil spills, which are covered by the Clean Water Act, discharges to the ocean are covered by the Marine Protection Research and Sanctuaries Act of 1972. This act governs all discharges of wastes to ocean waters within U.S. territorial limits and discharges of wastes in ocean waters by U.S. vessels or persons no matter where the dumping occurs. With only a few exceptions, no ocean dumping of industrial wastes or sewer sludge is now permitted.[9] Radiological, chemical, and biological warfare agents and high-level radioactive wastes are specifically prohibited by the statute. Under the amended statute, the only ocean dumping activities permitted are the disposal of dredged soil. This dumping is subject to specific regulations and is approved on a case-by-case basis.

Citizen Suits

The degree to which environmental quality is improved by public policy depends not only on the types of policies, but also on how well those policies are enforced. Policies that seem to offer promise may prove unsuitable if enforcement is difficult or lax.

The enforcement of the environmental statutes has long been the responsibility of state and federal environmental agencies. Enforcement at the state and federal level occurs through administrative proceedings or through civil and criminal judicial action. Because limited staff and resources do not enable these government agencies to fully enforce all of the environmental statutes, these methods alone do not provide the necessary level of enforcement.

During the early 1970s, a pervasive recognition that the government had neither the time nor resources to provide sufficient enforcement led Congress to create a private alternative—citizen suits. Though citizen suits are now authorized by a number of different environmental statutes, the program has been particularly successful in enforcing the Clean Water Act.

Empowered as private attorney generals, citizens are authorized to exercise oversight over government actions and to initiate civil proceedings against any private or public polluter violating the terms of its effluent standard. Environmental groups such as the Natural Resources Defense Council and the Sierra Club have become active participants in the process. Citizens may sue for an injunction (a court order requiring the illegal discharge to cease), but in addition are also given the power to "apply any appropriate civil penalties."[10] The amount of penalty can vary between $10,000 and $25,000 per day, per violation.

---

[9]Sewer sludge from New York City and its environs was the major exception, but the statute established a 1991 deadline for stopping this dumping.

[10]Clean Water Act, Section 505, 33 U.S.C. 1365.

EFFICIENCY AND COST EFFECTIVENESS

Ambient Standards and the Zero Discharge Goal

The 1956 Amendments defined ambient standards as a means of quantifying the objectives being sought. A system of ambient standards allows the control authority to tailor the quality of a particular body of water to its use. Water used for drinking would be subject to the highest standards, swimming the next highest, and so on. Once the ambient standards are defined, the control responsibility could be allocated among sources. Greater efforts to control pollution would be expended where the gap between desired and actual water quality was the largest.

Unfortunately, the early experience with ambient standards for water was not reassuring. Rather than strengthening the legal basis for the effluent standards while retaining their connection to the ambient standards, Congress chose to downgrade the importance of ambient standards by specifying a zero discharge goal. Additionally, the effluent standards were given their own legal status apart from any connection with ambient standards. The wrong inference was drawn from the early lack of legislative success. In his own inimitable style, Mark Twain put the essential point rather well:

> We should be careful to get out of an experience only the wisdom that is in it—and stop there; lest we be like the cat that sits down on a hot stove lid. She will never sit down on a hot stove lid again—and that is well; but also she will never sit down on a cold one anymore.[11]

The most fundamental problem with the current approach is that it rests on the faulty assumption that the tougher the law, the more that is accomplished. The zero discharge goal provides one example of a case in which passing a tough standard, in the hopes of actually achieving a weaker one, can backfire. Kneese and Schultze point out that in the late 1960s the French experimented with a law that required zero discharge and imposed severe penalties for violations.[12] The result was that the law was never enforced because it was universally viewed as unreasonable. Less control was accomplished under this law than would have been accomplished with a less-stringent law that could have been enforced.

Is the United States case comparable? It appears to be. In 1972 the EPA published an estimate of the costs of meeting a zero discharge goal, assuming that it is feasible. They concluded that over the decade from 1971 to 1981, removing 85 to 90 percent of the pollutants from all industrial and municipal effluents would cost $62 billion. Removing all of the pollutants would cost $317 billion, more than five times as much, and this figure probably understates the true cost.[13]

---

[11]Mark Twain, *Pudd'nhead Wilson* (New York: Harper Bros.,1897), p.125.

[12]Allen V. Kneese, and Charles L. Schultze, *Pollution, Prices, and Public Policy* (Washington, DC: The Brookings Institution, 1975).

[13]Ibid., p. 78.

Is this cost justified? Probably not for *all* pollutants, though for some it may be. Unfortunately, the zero discharge goal makes no distinction among pollutant types. For some fund pollutants it seems extreme. Perhaps the legislators realized this because when the legislation was drafted, no specific timetables or procedures were established to ensure that the zero discharge goal would be met by 1985 or, for that matter, anytime.

National Effluent Standards

The first prong in the two-pronged Congressional attack on water pollution was the national effluent standards (the other being subsidies for the construction of publicly owned waste treatment facilities). Deciding on the appropriate levels for these standards for each of the estimated 60,000 sources is not a trivial task. It is not surprising that difficulties arose.

Enforcement Problems.   Soon after passage of the 1972 Amendments, the EPA geared up to assume its awesome responsibility. Relying on a battery of consultants, it began to study the technologies of pollution control available to each industry in order to establish reasonable effluent limits. In establishing the guidelines, the EPA is required to take into account "the age of the equipment and facilities involved, the process employed, the engineering aspects of the application of various types of control techniques, process changes, nonwater quality environmental impact (including energy requirements) and such factors as the Administrator deems appropriate."

It is not clear whether this provision means that individual standards should be specified for each source, or general standards for broad categories of sources. Cost effectiveness would require the former, but in a system relying on effluent standards (but not one relying on emission charges or permits), the transaction costs associated with that approach would be prohibitively high and the delay unacceptably long. Therefore, the EPA chose the only feasible interpretation available and established general standards for broad categories of sources. Although the standards could differ among categories, they were uniformly applied to the large number of sources within each category.

The EPA inevitably fell behind the Congressional deadlines. In fact, not one effluent standard was published within the year deadline. As the standards were published, they were immediately challenged in the courts. By 1977 some 250 cases challenging the published standards were already pending.[14] Some of the challenges were successful, requiring the EPA to revise the standards. All of this took time.

By 1977 the EPA was having so much trouble defining the BPT standards that the deadlines for the BAT standards were completely unreasonable. Furthermore, for conventional pollutants, not only the deadlines but the standards themselves were irrational. Many bodies of water would have met the ambient standards without the BAT standard, whereas for others the effluent standards were not sufficient, particularly in areas with large nonpoint pollution problems. In addition, in some cases the technologies required by BPT would not be compatible (or even necessary) once the BAT standards were in effect. The situation was in a shambles.

---

[14]A. Myrick Freeman III, "Air and Water Pollution Policy," in *Current Issues in U.S. Environmental Policy*, Paul R. Portney, ed. (Baltimore, MD: Johns Hopkins University Press, for Resources for the Future, 1978): 46.

The 1977 Amendments changed both the timing of the BAT standards (delaying the deadlines) and their focus (toward toxic pollutants and away from conventional pollutants). As a result of these amendments, the EPA was required to develop industry effluent standards based on the BAT guidelines for control of 65 classes of toxic priority pollutants. In a 1979 survey the EPA discovered that all primary industries regularly discharge one or more of these toxic pollutants. As of 1980 the EPA had proposed BAT effluent limitations for control of toxic priority pollutants for nine primary industries.

The 1977 Amendments certainly improved the situation. Because toxics represent a more serious problem, it makes sense to set stricter standards for those pollutants. Extension of the deadlines was absolutely necessary; there was no alternative. However, these amendments have not resulted in a cost-effectiveness strategy. In particular, they tend to retard technological progress and to assign the responsibility for control in an unnecessarily expensive manner.

Allocating Control Responsibility.   Because the effluent standards established by the EPA are based upon specific technologies, these technologies are known to the industries. Therefore, in spite of the fact that the industry can choose any technology that keeps emissions under the limitation stated in the standard, in practice, industries tend to choose the specific equipment cited by the EPA when it established the standard. This, they reason, minimizes their risk. If anything goes wrong and they are hauled into court, they can simply argue they did precisely what the EPA had in mind when it set the standard.

The problem with this reaction is that it focuses too narrowly on a particular technology rather than on the real objective, emission reduction. The focus should be less on the purchase of a specific technology and more on doing what is necessary to hold emissions down, such as maintenance, process changes, and so on. In a field undergoing rapid technological change, tying all control efforts to a particular technology (which may become obsolete well before the standards are revised) is a poor strategy. Unfortunately, and to the detriment of securing clean water, technological stagnation has become a routine side effect of the current policy.

In allocating the control responsibility among various sources, the EPA was constrained by the inherent difficulty of making unique determinations for each source and by limitations in the act itself, such as the need to apply relatively uniform standards.[15] We know that uniform effluent standards are not cost effective, but it remains an open question whether or not the resulting increases in cost are sufficiently large to recommend an alternative approach, such as effluent charges or permits. The fact that the cost increases are large in the control of stationary-source air pollution does not automatically imply that they are large for water pollution control as well.

A number of empirical studies have investigated how closely the national effluent standards approximate the least-cost allocation (Table 16.2). These studies support the contention that the EPA standards are not cost effective, though the degree of cost ineffectiveness is typically smaller than that associated with the standards used to control air pollution.

---

[15]These limitations are spelled out in detail in C. James Koch and Robert A. Leone, "The Clean Water Act: Unexpected Impacts on Industry," *Harvard Environmental Law Review* 3 (1979): 96–104.

TABLE 16.2 Cost of Treatment under Alternative Programs: The Delaware Estuary

	Program	
Dissolved Oxygen Objective *(ppm)*	*Least Cost* *($ million/yr)*	*Uniform Treatment* *($ million/yr)*
2	1.6	5.0
3–4	7.0	20.0

Source: From *Economics and the Environment* by Allen V. Kneese. Copyright © 1977 Allen V. Kneese. Reproduced by permission of Penguin Books, Ltd. and the author.

Perhaps the most famous study examining the cost effectiveness of uniform standards in contrast with emission and ambient charges and permits was conducted on the Delaware Estuary.[16] This river basin, though small by the standards of the Mississippi or other major basins, drains an area serving a population in excess of six million people. It is a highly industrial, densely populated area.

In the study a simulation model was constructed to capture the effect on ambient dissolved oxygen content of a variety of pollutants discharged by a large number of polluters into the river at numerous locations. In addition, this model was capable of simulating the cost consequences of various methods used to allocate the responsibility for controlling effluent to meet dissolved oxygen standards.

The traditional approach was compared with the least-cost (LC) approach. Under the *uniform treatment* (UT) strategy, all discharges were faced with an effluent standard requiring them to remove a given percentage of their waste before discharging the remainder into the river. This method mirrors, in a crude way, the current EPA strategy. The least-cost (LC) strategy simply allocated the responsibility cost effectively.

For control of water pollution, this evidence suggests that the UT strategy does increase the cost substantially. For either dissolved oxygen objective, the costs are roughly three times higher.

Despite this evidence, the regulatory reform movement that played such an important role for air pollution control has not had anywhere near the same impact in water pollution control. Aside from the Fox River in Wisconsin (see Example 16.2), few examples exist.

The European Experience. Economic incentives have been important in water pollution control in Europe, where effluent charges play a prominent role in a number of countries.[17] These charge systems take a number of forms. One common approach is illustrated by Czechoslovakia, which uses charges to achieve predetermined ambient standards. Others, such as West Germany, use charges mainly to encourage firms to control more than their

---

[16]This study is described in some detail in Allen V. Kneese and Blair T. Bower, *Managing Water Quality: Economics, Technology, Institutions* (Baltimore, MD: Johns Hopkins University Press, 1968): Chapter 11; and Allen V. Kneese, *Economics and the Environment* (New York: Penguin Books, 1977).

[17]For a summary of this experience, see Frederick R. Anderson et al., *Environmental Improvement Through Economic Incentives* (Baltimore, MD: Johns Hopkins University Press, for Resources for the Future, 1977): 59–68; and J. B. Opschoor and Hans B. Vos, *Economic Instruments for Environmental Protection* (Paris: OECD, 1989).

EXAMPLE 16.2

Marketable Emission Permits on the Fox River

With the advent of the bubble and offset policies, marketable emission permits have become the centerpiece of the regulatory reform movement in air pollution control. Though no comparable scale of reform exists for control of water pollution, one attempt has been initiated in northern Wisconsin.

The Lower Fox River flows from Lake Winnebago to Green Bay, Wisconsin. Lining the banks of a key 22-mile segment of this river are ten pulp and paper mills and four municipalities that discharge effluent into the river. During the summer the desired dissolved oxygen targets are not reached at two critical sag points, even when the industrial polluters are in compliance with BPT standards and the municipal polluters are providing secondary treatment.

The Wisconsin Department of Natural Resources was faced with meeting the standards in the face of industrial resistance. To assist in choosing a policy strategy, they funded a simulation model of the river to compare traditional regulatory rules with a marketable permit system.

This model revealed significant differences among dischargers, a precondition if the market approach is to reach the environmental goals at a significantly lower cost. Under traditional abatement rules, marginal abatement costs differed by a factor of four. The study concluded that the control costs would be some 40 percent higher if the department were to rely on traditional abatement rules. The potential annual savings realized from a permit approach were estimated at $6.7 million.

In March 1981 the department approved regulations allowing dischargers on the Lower Fox River to transfer permits by approved contracts. By 1982 the first trade had already taken place, but that also proved to be the only trade prior to 1990. The system clearly has not lived up to expectations, an experience that probably will inhibit any expansion of the concept to other geographic areas.

Source: This example was drawn from William B. O'Neil, "Pollution Permits and Markets for Water Quality," an unpublished Ph.D. dissertation completed at the University of Wisconsin-Madison, 1980, and subsequent conversations with the author.

---

legal requirements. A third group, illustrated by Hungary and East Germany, shows how charge systems have been combined with effluent standards.

Czechoslovakia has used effluent charges to maintain water quality at predetermined levels for more than 15 years. A basic charge is placed on BOD and suspended solids and is complemented by a surcharge ranging from 10 to 100 percent, depending upon the contribution of the individual discharge to ambient pollutant concentrations. The basic rates can be adjusted to reflect the quality of the receiving water. This system is conceptually very close to the ambient emission charge system known to be cost effective.

The West German charge system was announced in 1976 and implemented in 1981. The level of charge is related to the degree of compliance with the standards. Firms failing to meet their required standards pay a charge on all actual emissions. If, according to the issued permit, federal emission standards (which are separately defined for each industrial sector) are met, the charge is lowered to 50 percent of the base rate and is applied to the level of discharge implied by the minimum standard. If the firm can prove the discharge to be lower than 75 percent of minimum standards, one half of the base rate is applied to the (lower) actual discharge level. The charge is waived for three years prior to the installation of new pollution control equipment promising further reductions of at least 20 percent. Revenues from the charges can be used by the administering authorities for covering administrative costs and for financial assistance to public and private pollution abatement activities.

The final approach, used in Hungary and East Germany, combines effluent charges with effluent standards. The charge is levied on discharges in excess of fixed effluent limits. In the Hungarian system the level of the charge is based on the condition of the receiving waters, among other factors. Initially, the Hungarian charges had little effect, but when the charge levels were raised, a flurry of waste treatment activity resulted.

Though these European approaches differ from one to another and are not all cost effective, their existence suggests that effluent charge systems are possible and practical. The German Council of Experts on Environmental Questions estimated the German effluent charge policy to be about one-third cheaper for the polluters as a group than an otherwise comparable uniform treatment policy. Furthermore it encouraged firms to go beyond the uniform standards when the cost such effort was justified.

Municipal Waste Treatment Subsidies

The second phase of the two-pronged water pollution control program involves subsidies for waste treatment plants. This program has run into problems as well, ranging from deficiencies in the allocation of the subsidies to the incentives created by the program.

The Allocation of Funds. Because the available funds were initially allocated on a first-come, first-served basis, it is not surprising that the funds were not spent in areas having the greatest impact. It was not uncommon, for example, for completed treatment plants to dump effluent that was significantly cleaner than the receiving water. Also, federal funds have traditionally been concentrated on smaller, largely suburban communities rather than the larger cities with the most serious pollution problems. [18]

The 1977 Amendments attempted to deal with this problem by requiring states to set priorities for funding treatment works while giving the EPA the right, after holding public hearings, not only to veto a state's priority list but to request a revised list. This tendency to ensure that the funds are allocated to projects having the highest priority was reinforced with the passage of the Municipal Wastewater Treatment Construction Grant Amendments of 1981. Under this act states are required to establish project priorities that will target funds to projects with the most significant water quality and public health consequences.

---

[18]An extended critical discussion of the manner in which these funds were allocated can be found in A. Myrick Freeman III and Robert H. Haveman, "Clean Rhetoric and Dirty Water," *The Public Interest* (Summer 1972).

Operation and Maintenance.   The current approach subsidizes the *construction* of treatment facilities but provides no incentive to *operate* them effectively. The existence of a municipal waste treatment plant does not by itself guarantee cleaner water. The EPA's annual inspection surveys of operating plants in 1976 and 1977 found only about half of the plants performing satisfactorily. More recent surveys have found that the general level of waste treatment performance has remained substantially unchanged from previous years.

When sewage treatment plants chronically or critically malfunction, the EPA may take a city to court to force compliance with a direct order or a fine. Because of various constitutional legal barriers, it is very difficult to force a city to pay a fine to the federal treasury. Without an effective and credible sanction, the EPA is in a difficult position when dealing with municipalities. Therefore, the end of the treatment plant malfunction problem cannot yet be pronounced with any assurance.

Capital Costs.   Due to the federal subsidies, local areas ended up paying only a fraction of the true cost of constructing these facilities. Because much of the money came from federal taxpayers, local communities had less incentive to hold construction costs down. One study estimated that substantially increasing the local share could reduce capital costs by as much as 30 percent.[19] Local areas are more careful with their own money.

Pretreatment Standards

To deal with hazardous wastes entering municipal waste treatment plants that cannot be treated or removed by those plants, the EPA has defined pretreatment standards regulating the quality of the wastewater flowing into the plants. These standards suffer the same deficiencies as other effluent standards; they are not cost effective (see Example 16.3). The control over wastewater flows into treatment plants provide one more aspect of environmental policy where economic incentive approaches offer an opportunity to achieve equivalent results at a lower cost.

Nonpoint Pollution

The current law does little to control nonpoint pollution, which in many areas is a significant part of the total problem. In some ways the government has tried to compensate for this uneven coverage by placing more intensive controls on point sources. Is this emphasis efficient?

It could conceivably be justified on two grounds. If the marginal damages caused by nonpoint sources are significantly smaller than those of point sources, then a lower level of control could well be justified. Because in many cases nonpoint source pollutants are not the same as point source pollutants, this is a logical possibility.

Or, if the costs of controlling nonpoint sources even to a small degree are very high, this could justify benign neglect as well. Are either of these conditions met in practice?

---

[19]Congressional Budget Office, *Efficient Investments in Wastewater Treatment Plants* (Washington, DC: U.S. Congress, 1985).

EXAMPLE 16.3

Cost-Effective Pretreatment Standards

The electroplating operations of the Rhode Island jewelry industry produce high concentrations of cyanide, copper, nickel, and zinc, which are routinely discharged into municipal sewer systems. Because the treatment plants are not designed to remove these hazardous substances, the EPA has defined pretreatment standards to prohibit excessive concentrations of these metals from entering the plants. These standards are financially burdensome, with some estimates suggesting that some 30 to 60 percent of the small firms could go out of business if the standards were imposed.

An economic analysis by Opaluch and Kashmanian (1985) of the alternative for meeting the EPA concentration objectives concludes that the EPA pretreatment standards achieve the objective at a cost almost 50 percent greater than the least-cost means of achieving the same concentration objectives. An emission permit system with a permit price of $40 per pound would, after trading, achieve the target at a cost of $12.5 million. Compared to the $19.3 million the EPA proposal would cost, this represents a considerable savings.

If the permits were auctioned off, the government would collect some $5.0 million from the sale. Although the financial burden of this auction system for allocating permits would be lower on the jewelry industry as a whole than complying with the EPA proposal, even considering this $5.0 million transfer, not every segment of the industry would better off with the auction. In particular, the permit fees paid by large firms would be sufficiently high that they would bear more financial burden under the auction scheme than with the EPA proposal. If the permits were grandfathered (allocated free of charge) rather than auctioned off, however, all existing firms would be better off under the permit system than under the EPA proposal.

Source: James J. Opaluch and Richard M. Kashmanian, "Assessing the Viability of Marketable Permit Systems: An Application in Hazardous Waste Management," *Land Economics* 61, No. 3 (August 1985): 263–71.

Costs.   Because research is in its infancy, cost information is scarce. Of the small amount of literature available, one study can give us a sense of the economic analysis. Palmini conducted an analysis of the potential effects of agricultural nonpoint policies on two small rural counties in Illinois.[20] The specific policies he examined were designed to control nitrogen (which can cause eutrophication), sediment (soil erosion), and pesticides. His model relates these policies to the choice of various farming practices, the effects of these choices on costs, and the financial return to farmers after covering variable costs.

His results indicated that rather dramatic reduction (74 percent) in soil erosion could be achieved at a cost of less than 1 percent of the earnings after variable costs were covered. A ban on selected pesticides was predicted to cause a switch to other less damaging pesticides, which would reduce the return to farmers by 0.7 percent.

---

[20]Dennis J. Palmini, "The Secondary Impact of Nonpoint Pollution Controls: A Linear Programming–Input/Output Analysis," *Journal of Environmental Economics and Management* 9 (September 1982): 263–278.

The major estimated economic impact came from policies designed to reduce nitrogen use. Palmini considered the effects of quantity restrictions (ceilings on amount used per acre) and the impact of taxes on nitrogen use. Quantity restrictions necessary to reduce pollution also substantially reduced revenues and projections. Because the demand for nitrogen is price inelastic, if nitrogen taxes were used, very high rates would be needed to reduce nitrogen use very much.

The extra expense of nitrogen control would represent a large financial burden on farmers, which they could only pass on in higher prices if all farmers were subjected to similar controls. This would make unilateral state control difficult because it would place the farmers in that state in jeopardy.

This study suggests that some nonpoint control can probably be reasonably undertaken because the costs seem low, yet it also suggests that the conclusion that all nonpoint sources can be cheaply controlled is not correct. As in other areas of environmental policy, the form and intensity of government intervention would have to be tailored to the specific problem.

The fact that point and nonpoint sources have received such different treatment from the EPA suggests the possibility that costs could be lowered by a more careful balancing of these control options. One study of phosphorus control in the Dillon Reservoir in Colorado by Industrial Economics, Inc., supports the validity of this suspicion.[21]

In this reservoir, four municipalities constitute the only point sources of phosphorus, whereas there are numerous uncontrolled nonpoint sources in the area. The combined phosphorus load on the reservoir from point and nonpoint sources is projected to exceed its assimilative capacity.

The traditional way to rescue the projected phosphorus load would be to impose even-more-stringent controls on the point sources. The study found, however, that by following a balanced program controlling both point and nonpoint sources, the desired phosphorus target could be achieved at a cost of approximately $1 million a year less than would be spent if only point sources were controlled more stringently. The more general point that should be carried away from this study is that as point sources are controlled to higher and higher degrees, rising marginal control costs will begin to make controlling nonpoint sources increasingly attractive.

Oil Spills

One of the chief characteristics of the current approach to oil spills is that it depends heavily on the ability of the legal system to internalize the costs of a spill through liability law. In principle the approach is straightforward. By forcing the owner of a vessel to pay for the costs of cleaning up the spill, including compensating for natural resource damages, a powerful incentive to exercise care is created. But is the outcome likely to be efficient in practice?

One problem with legal remedies is their high administrative cost. As Example 16.4 points out, assigning the appropriate penalties is no trivial matter. Even if the court were able to act expeditiously, the doctrines it imposes are not necessarily efficient because the financial

---

[21]Industrial Economics, Inc., *Case Studies on the Trading of Effluent Loads: Dillon Reservoir Final Report* (Cambridge, MA: Industrial Economics, 1984).

E X A M P L E   1 6 . 4

Anatomy of an Oil Spill Suit: The *Amoco Cadiz*

On 17 March 1978, the *Amoco Cadiz,* an oil transport ship traveling in a bad storm, lost steering control and, after unsuccessful towing attempts, drifted onto the rocks off the shore of Portsall, France, on the Brittany Coast. Ultimately the ship broke in two and discharged 220,000 tons of crude oil and 4,000 tons of bunker fuels along the coast of a resort area, two months prior to the opening of the tourist season.

Before the end of the year of the grounding, a mountain of claims had been filed involving France, a consortium of resort owners and fishermen, Amoco (the owner of the vessel), Bugsier (the owner of the tug), Shell oil (the owner of the oil being carried at the time), and Astilleros Espanoles (the Spanish company that built the *Amoco Cadiz*). After extensive and expensive preparations by all parties, the trial began in May 1982.

During March 1984 a preliminary opinion was issued finding Amoco and the shipbuilder jointly liable. The process then turned to the separate issue of the magnitude of the damages to be awarded. On 21 February 1989, a judgment of 670 million francs was levied against Amoco and Astilleros. The verdict was immediately appealed.

The trial judge, now retired from the bench, summed up the situation:

So here we are, twelve years after the accident, eleven years after the suit was filed, with the plaintiffs in possession of an enormous judgment and subject to enormous legal fees without one cent having changed hands. The case marches onward to the Court of Appeals with each principal party expected to appeal those aspects of the final judgment with which they disagree. This raises the possibility, almost unimaginable, but very real, that the whole case could have to be tried again.

Source: Frank J. McGarr, "Inadequacy of Federal Forum for Resolution of Oil Spill Damages," a talk given at a conference on oil spills at Newport, Rhode Island on 16 May 1990. Judge McGarr was the trial judge for the *Amoco Cadiz* case.

liability for cleaning up spills is limited by statute. The owner will minimize costs by choosing the level of precaution that equates the marginal cost of additional precaution with the resulting reduction in the marginal expected penalty. The marginal reduction in expected penalty is a function of two factors—the likelihood of a spill and the magnitude of the financial obligation it would trigger.

As long as the imposed penalty equalled the actual damage and the probability of having to pay the damage, once an accident occurred, was 1.0, this outcome would normally be efficient. The external costs would be internalized. The owner's private costs would be minimized by taking all possible cost-justified precaution measures to reduce both the likelihood and the seriousness of any resulting spill; taking precaution would simply be cheaper than paying for the cleanup.

Limited liability produces a different outcome, however. Lower levels of precaution imply damages that exceed the limit, but the vessel owner would not have to pay anything above the limit. (The only benefit to the vessel owner faced with limited liability of increasing precaution at lower levels of precaution is the reduction in the likelihood of a spill; in this range, increasing precaution does not reduce the magnitude of the financial payment should a spill occur.)

What is the effect of limited liability on the vessel owner's choice of precaution levels? As long as the liability limit is binding (which appears to routinely be the case with recent spills), the owner will chose too little precaution. Both the number and magnitude of resulting spills would be inefficiently large.

Citizen Suits[22]

Initiated during the 1970s, citizen suits add a private enforcement alternative to public enforcement in correcting environmental market failures. Public and private enforcement are partial substitutes. If government enforcement were complete, all polluters would be in compliance and citizen suits would have no role to play. Noncompliance is a necessary condition for a successful suit. In the early 1980s when public enforcement decreased, private enforcement—citizen suits—increased to take up the slack. Lax public enforcement appears to have played a significant role in the rise of citizen suits.

All attorneys' fees incurred by the citizen group in any successful action under the Clean Water Act must be reimbursed by the defendants. Reimbursement of attorneys' fees has affected both the level and focus of litigation activity. By lowering the costs of bringing citizen suits, attorney fee reimbursement has allowed citizen groups to participate far more often in the enforcement process than otherwise would have been possible. Because courts only reimburse for appropriate claims (noncompliance claims that are upheld by the court), citizen groups are encouraged to litigate only appropriate cases.

The existence of citizen suits should affect the decision-making process of the polluting firm. Adding citizen suits to the enforcement arena increases the expected penalty to the noncomplying firm by increasing the likelihood that the firm will face an enforcement action. This can be expected to increase the amount of precaution taken by the firm, but the unavailability of compliance data makes it impossible to confirm this expectation, though participants believe compliance has increased.

Although citizen suits probably do lead to greater compliance, greater compliance is not necessarily efficient. Complete compliance is not necessarily efficient if the defendant polluters face inefficiently harsh standards. If the standards are excessively high, citizen suits have the potential to promote inefficiency by forcing firms to meet standards where the marginal benefits are significantly lower than the marginal costs. However, if the effluent standards are either inefficiently low or efficient, the existence of citizen suits will necessarily create a more efficient outcome. In these cases, increasing compliance is perfectly compatible with efficiency.

---

[22]For more details on this approach see Wendy Naysnerski and Tom Tietenberg, "Private Enforcement," in T. H. Tietenberg ed., *Innovation in Environmental* Policy (Cheltenham, UK: Edward Elgar, 1992): 109–136.

An Overall Assessment

Though the benefit estimates from water pollution control are subject to much uncertainty, they do exist. While being careful not to place too much reliance on them, we can see what information can be gleaned from the studies in existence.

Freeman has summarized these studies, focusing on 1985 as a target year.[23] His survey of the field suggests that the 1985 benefit (in 1984 dollars) from conventional water pollution control policy could be as low as $5.7 billion or as high as $27.7 billion, with a most likely point estimate of $14.0 billion. This compares to estimated 1985 annual costs (in 1978 dollars) ranging from a low of $25 billion to a high of $30 billion. Thus, Freeman estimates that the net benefit from conventional control is probably negative.

Using cost-effective policies rather than the current approach, it would be possible to reduce costs substantially without affecting the benefits. Cost effectiveness would require developing better strategies for point source control and for achieving a better balance between point and nonpoint source control. The resulting reduction in costs probably would cause net benefits to become positive. That result would not necessarily make the policy efficient, however, because the level of control might still be too high or too low. Unfortunately, the evidence is not rich enough to prove whether or not the overall level of control maximizes the net benefit.

In addition to promoting current cost effectiveness, economic incentive approaches would stimulate and facilitate change better than a system of rigid, technology-based standards. Russell has attempted to assess the importance of the facilitating role by simulating the effects on the allocation of pollution control responsibility in response to regional economic growth, changing technology, and changing product mix.[24] Focusing on the steel, paper, and petroleum refining industries in the 11-county Delaware Estuary Region, his study estimated the change in permit use for three water pollutants (BOD, total suspended solids, and ammonia) that would have resulted if a marketable permit system were in place over the 1940–1978 period. The calculations assume that the plants existing in 1940 would have been allocated permits to legitimize their emissions at that time, that new sources would have had to purchase permits, and that plant shutdowns or contractions would free up permits for others to purchase.

This study found that for almost every decade and pollutant a substantial number of permits would have been made available by plant closings, capacity contractions, product-mix changes, and the availability of new technologies. In the absence of a marketable permit program, a control authority would not only have to keep abreast of all technological developments so that emission standards could be adjusted accordingly, but it would also have to assure an overall balance between effluent increases and decreases so as to preserve water quality. This tough assignment is handled completely by the market in a marketable permit system, thereby facilitating the evolution of the economy by responding flexibly and predictably to change.

---

[23]A. Myrick Freeman, III, "Water Pollution Policy," in *Public Policies for Environmental Protection,* Paul R. Portney, ed., (Washington, DC: Resources for the Future, 1990): 122–126.

[24]Clifford O. Russell, "Controlled Trading of Pollution Permits," *Environmental Science and Technology* 15, No. 1 (January 1981): 1–5.

Marketable permits encourage, as well as facilitate, this evolution. Because permits have value, in order to minimize costs firms must continually be looking for new opportunities to control emissions at lower cost. This search eventually results in the adoption of new technologies and in the initiation of changes in the product-mix that result in lower amounts of emissions. The pressure on sources to continually search for better ways to control pollution is a distinct advantage that economic incentive systems have over bureaucratically defined standards.

SUMMARY

Historically, policies for controlling water pollution have been concerned with conventional pollutants discharged into surface waters. More recently, concerns have shifted toward toxic pollutants, which apparently are more prevalent than previously believed, toward groundwater, which traditionally was thought to be an invulnerable pristine resource, and toward the oceans, which were mistakenly considered immune from most pollution problems because of their vast size.

Early attempts at controlling water pollution followed a path similar to that of air pollution control. Legislation prior to the 1970s had little impact on the problem. Frustration then led to the enactment of a tough federal law that was so ambitious and unrealistic that little progress resulted.

There the similarity ends. Whereas in air pollution a wave of recent reforms have improved the process by making it more cost effective, no parallel exists for control of water pollution. Current policy toward cleaning up rivers and lakes is based upon the subsidization of municipal waste treatment facilities and national effluent standards imposed on industrial sources.

The former approach has been hampered by delays, by problems in allocating funds, and by the fact that about half of the constructed plants are not performing satisfactorily. The latter approach has given rise to delays and to the need to define the standards in a series of court suits. In addition, effluent standards have assigned the control responsibility among point sources in a way that excessively raises cost. Nonpoint pollution sources have, until recently, been virtually ignored. Technological progress is inhibited rather than stimulated by the current approach. Benefit/cost analyses focusing on 1985 show the net benefit from the current approach to be negative.

This lack of progress could have been avoided. It did not result from a lack of toughness but from a reliance on direct regulation rather than on emission charges or emission permits, which are more flexible and cost effective in both the dynamic and static sense. In this respect the United States can perhaps take some lessons from the European experience.

The court system has assumed most of the responsibility for controlling oil spills. Those responsible for the spills are assessed the financial liability for cleaning the site up and compensating for any resulting damages to natural resources. Although in principle this approach can be efficient, in practice it has been hampered by liability limitations and the huge administrative burden an oil spill trial entails.

Enforcement is always a key to successful environmental and natural resource policy. One rather recent innovation in enforcement involves giving private citizen groups the power to bring noncomplying firms into court. By raising the likelihood that noncomplying firms would be brought before the court and assessed penalties for noncompliance, this new system can be expected to increase compliance.

FURTHER READING

Anderson, Frederick R., et al. *Environmental Improvement Through Economic Incentives* (Baltimore, MD: Johns Hopkins University Press, for Resources for the Future, 1977). This book sympathetically analyzes the political, legal, and technical problems that must be faced in a more widespread reliance on emission or effluent charges. An extensive survey of existing and proposed charge systems is included.

Freeman, A. Myrick, III. "Water Pollution Policy," in Paul R. Portney, ed., *Public Policies for Environmental Protection* (Washington, DC: Resources for the Future, 1990). An excellent, detailed analysis of control policy for water pollution, including the 1977 amendments.

Kneese, Allen V., and Blair T. Bower. *Managing Water Quality: Economics, Technology, Institutions* (Baltimore, MD: Johns Hopkins University Press, for Resources for the Future, 1968). Generally considered one of the classics in the field. Contains, among many others, chapters describing the Delaware Estuary Study and pollution-control policies in Europe.

Kneese, Allen V., and Charles L. Schultze. *Pollution, Prices, and Public Policy* (Washington, DC: The Brookings Institution, 1975). A highly readable analysis of water pollution (as well as air pollution) control policy by two highly respected economists. Does not include the 1977 air or water acts.

ADDITIONAL REFERENCES

Ashworth, John, Ivy Papps, and David Storey. " Assessing the Impact upon the British Chlor-alkali Industry of the EEC Directive on Discharges of Mercury Into Waterways," *Land Economics* 63 (February 1987): 72–78.

Bevis, Brian, and Ian Dobbs. "Firm Behavior Under Regulatory Control of Stochastic Environmental Wastes by Probabilistic Constraints," *Journal of Environmental Economics and Management* 14, No. 2 (June 1987): 112–127.

Brown, G., Jr., and R. Johnson. "Pollution Control by Effluent Charges: It Works in the Federal Republic of Germany, Why Not in the U S.?" *Natural Resources Journal* 24 (1984): 929–966.

Dinar, A., and D. Zimmerman, eds. *The Economics and Management of Water and Drainage in Agriculture* (Boston, MA: Kluwer Academic Publishers, 1991).

Eheart, J. Wayland, E. Downey Brill, Jr., and Randolph M. Lyon. "Transferable Discharge Permits for Control of BOD: An Overview," in Erhard F. Joeres and Martin H. David, eds., *Buying a Better Environment: Cost-Effective Regulation Through Permit Trading* (Madison, WI: University of Wisconsin Press, 1983): 163–195.

Feenberg, Daniel, and Edwin S. Mills. *Measuring the Benefits of Water Pollution Abatement* (New York: Academic Press, 1980).

Freeman, A. Myrick, III. *Air and Water Pollution Control: A Benefit–Cost Assessment* (New York: John Wiley & Sons, 1982).

Griffin, Ronald C. "Environmental Policy for Spatial and Persistent Pollutants," *Journal of Environmental Economics and Management* 14, No. 1 (March 1987): 41–53.

Harrington, W., A. Krupnick, and H. M. Peskin. "Policies of Nonpoint Source Water Pollution Control," *Journal of Soil and Water Conservation* 40 (Jan/Feb 1985): 27.

Koch, C. James, and Robert A. Leone. "The Clean Water Act: Unexpected Impacts on Industry," *Harvard Environmental Law Review* 3 (1979): 84–111.

Leone, Robert A., and John E. Jackson. "The Political Economy of Federal Regulatory Activity: The Case of Water Pollution Controls," in Gary Fromm, ed., *Studies in Public Regulation* (Cambridge, MA: MIT Press, 1981).

McConnell, Virginia D., John H. Cumberland, and Patrice L. Gordon. "Regional Marginal Costs and Cost Savings from Economies of Scale in Municipal Waste Treatment: An Application to the Chesapeake Bay," *Growth and Change* 19, No. 4 (Fall 1988): 1–13.

O'Neil, William B. "Pollution Permits and Markets for Water Quality," Ph.D. dissertation (University of Wisconsin–Madison, 1980).

Opaluch, James J., and Thomas A. Grigalunas. "Controlling Stochastic Pollution Events with Liability Rules: Some Evidence from OCS Leasing," *Rand Journal of Economics* 15 (1984), 142–151.

Peskin, Henry M., and Eugene P. Seskin. *Cost-Benefit Analysis and Water Pollution Control Policy* (Washington, DC: The Urban Institute, 1975).

Raucher, Robert L. "The Benefits and Costs of Policies Related to Groundwater Contamination," *Land Economics* 62, No. 1 (February 1986):33–45.

Ribaudo, Marc O. "Targeting the Conservation Reserve Program to Maximize Water Quality Benefits," *Land Economics* 65, No. 4 (November 1989): 320–32.

Rothfelder, M. "Reducing the Cost of Water Pollution Control under the Clean Water Act," *Natural Resources Journal* 22 (April 1982): 407–21.

Segerson, Kathleen. "Uncertainty and Incentives for Nonpoint Pollution Control," *Journal of Environmental Economics and Management* 15, No. 1 (March 1988): 87–98.

Spurlock, S. R., and I. D. Clifton. "Efficiency and Equity Aspects of Nonpoint Source Pollution Controls," *Southern Journal of Agricultural Economics* 14 (December 1982): 123–29.

Walker, D. J. "A Damage Function to Evaluate Erosion Control Economics," *American Journal of Agricultural Economics* 64 (November 1982): 690–98.

DISCUSSION QUESTIONS

1. "The only permanent solution to water pollution control will occur when *all* production by-products are routinely recycled. The zero discharge goal recognizes this reality and forces all dischargers to work steadily toward this solution. Less-stringent policies are at best temporary palliatives." Discuss.

2. "In exercising its responsibility to protect the nation's drinking water, the government needs to intervene only in the case of public water supplies. Private water suppliers will be adequately protected without any government intervention." Discuss.

CHAPTER 17

Solid Waste and Recycling

*The Nation is in the position of a man, who, bequeathed a fortune, has
gone on spending it recklessly, never taking the trouble to ask the
amount of his inheritance, or how long it is likely to last.*

NATIONAL CONSERVATION COMMISSION (1908)

INTRODUCTION

As the level of waste rises and the amount of space available to put it safely without contaminating groundwater declines, what can be done? The traditional answer involves the three R's: reduce, reuse, recycle.

How can economics help to assure that the three R's play an appropriate role in alleviating the solid waste problem? Is the waste level inefficiently high? Why? What measures can be taken to reduce the level of waste? What is an efficient amount of recycling? Will the market automatically generate this amount in the absence of government intervention? How does the efficient allocation over time differ between recyclable and nonrecyclable resources? The phrase *planned obsolescence* is sometimes used to suggest that industries have an incentive to produce products with a short life span. Does the market produce an efficient level of product durability? What impact does product durability have on the allocation of virgin and recycled materials?

We shall begin our investigation by describing how an efficient market in recyclable, depletable resources would work. We then use this as a benchmark to examine recycling in some detail. We close by relating our findings back to the central questions of growth in a finite environment.

EFFICIENT RECYCLING

Extraction and Disposal Cost

What determines the recycling rate? Historically, reliance has generally been on the natural inputs because they have been cheaper. As the natural inputs have become scarce relative to the demand for them, industry has begun to search for other sources.

E X A M P L E   1 7 . 1

Population Density and Recycling: The Japanese Experience

Because Japan has much greater population density than many of the other industrialized nations, it has been forced to come to grips with its solid waste disposal problems somewhat earlier. For the Japanese the solution of choice is recycling. In Tokyo enterprising firms have begun touring neighborhoods, collecting newspapers, magazines, and rags in exchange for new bathroom and facial tissue. People who want quick disposal of old refrigerators or TV sets need only to make a special call to the sanitation department for a special pickup. And although a few years ago no Japanese would touch used goods, the latest trend is garage sales and flea markets, which give secondhand wares new life.

About 40 percent of solid waste is recycled, including about half the paper, 55 percent of glass bottles and 66 percent of food and beverage cans.

Since the early 1970s, citizens have been forced to separate combustible from noncombustible trash. Burnable waste, which comprises some 72 percent of the total after recycling, is trucked to incinerators, which reduce its weight and volume. Every Japanese community has its own incinerator, totaling some 1899 garbage burning plants (compared with 155 large plants in the United States). Nonburnable garbage is separated, melted, and refabricated; ferrous metals are reclaimed. What's left, about 9 percent of the total initial waste, is deposited in a landfill.

Some problems still exist. Concern about the toxins within the trash that escape into the air from combustion and the water from landfills is mounting. Recycling peaked at about 50 percent and even declined somewhat during the 1980s.

Source: "Teeing Off on Japan's Garbage," *Newsweek* (27 November 1989): 70; "The Good News: Japan Gives Trash a Second Chance," *Time* (2 January 1989): 47.

At the same time, the costs of disposing of the products have risen as the world has experienced a large increase in the geographic concentration of people. The attraction of cities and the exodus from rural areas led an increasingly large number of people to live in urban or near-urban environments.

This concentration creates waste-disposal problems. When land was plentiful and the waste stream was less hazardous, the remnants could be buried in landfills. But as land has become scarce, burial has become increasingly expensive. In addition, concerns over environmental effects on water supplies and economic effects on the value of surrounding land have made buried waste less acceptable.[1]

The rising costs of virgin materials and of waste disposal have increased the attractiveness of recycling. By recovering and reintroducing materials into the system, recycling provides an alternative to virgin ores and also reduces the waste-disposal load (see Example 17.1).

---

[1] The U.S. EPA estimates that more than half of the existing landfills in the United States will reach their capacity by 1995. The New York State Legislative Commission on Solid Waste Management estimates that all landfills within its state will reach their capacity and close by 1995. Though the precision of these forecasts should be subject to the same healthy skepticism we have recommended elsewhere in this book for other forecasts, it is difficult to escape the conclusion that disposal is becoming both more expensive and more difficult.

EXAMPLE 17.2

New Markets For Trash: Tires

According to our model of the allocation of a depletable, recyclable resource over time, the demand for recycled waste products for use as raw materials in the production process should grow over time. Not only are communities willing to provide recycled waste products at a low cost merely to avoid disposal costs, but they can provide a steady supply. Is this expectation borne out by current trends?

Apparently it is. Take tires, for example. In the United States, car and truck drivers dispose of some 240 million tires per year. The current disposal cost is about 10 cents per pound when landfills will take them; many won't. Some 2 billion tires are stocked in remote locations, where they pose environmental hazards. (In October 1983 the 7-million-tire dump in Winchester, Virginia, caught fire; it finally burned itself out in June after blanketing the area in acrid smoke for the intervening eight months).

In 1981, a research chemist named Ed Stark developed a process for coating ground up tire particles with a polymer that "rejuvenated" the rubber, allowing it to bond together as effectively as uncured virgin material. The beauty of the process is that it makes no environmental compromises. Because it uses no water, it has no contaminated effluent to dispose of. The process does not involve combustion, so the air pollutants associated with combustion are not a problem either.

This process has since formed the basis for Tirecycle, a company set up in Babbitt, Minnesota to recycle all of Minnesota's old tires. Products made from this material include truck tire retreads, buckets, wastebaskets, gasoline tanks for lawn movers, truck bed lines, and gymnasium exercise mats. The process has proved so successful that plants are scheduled to be opened in Massachusetts and Michigan.

Source: David Morris and Neil Seidman, "Treating Trash as a Valuable Municipal Resource," *The Christian Science Monitor* (12 November 1987): 23; Peter Tonge, "Old Tires Bounce Back as New Rubber Products," *The Christian Science Monitor* (9 August 1988): 17; " Why Not Rubber Roadbeds?" *The Christian Science Monitor* (9 August 1988): 17.

Consumers as well as manufacturers play a role on both the demand and supply side of the market. On the demand side, consumers would find that products depending exclusively on virgin raw materials are subject to higher prices than those relying on recycled materials. Consequently, consumers would have a tendency to switch to products made with the cheaper, recycled raw materials, as long as quality is not adversely affected. This powerful incentive is called the *composition of demand effect*.

As long as consumers bear the cost of disposal, they have the additional incentive to return their used recyclable products to collection centers. By doing so they avoid disposal costs while reaping financial rewards for supplying a product someone wants.

For the cycle to be complete, the demand for the recycled products must be sufficiently high to justify making them available. As Example 17.2 makes clear, new markets may ultimately emerge, but the transition may prove somewhat turbulent. Simply returning recycled products to the collection centers accomplishes little if they are simply dumped into a nearby landfill[2] or if the supply is increased so much by mandatory recycling laws that prices for recycled materials fall through the floor.[3] The purity of the recycled products also plays a key role in explaining the strength of demand for them. One of the reasons for the high rate of aluminum recycling and much lower rate of plastics recycling is the differential difficulty of producing a high-quality product from scrap. Whereas bundles of aluminum cans have a relatively uniform quality, waste plastics tend to be highly contaminated with nonplastic substances, and the plastics manufacturing process has little tolerance for impurities. Remaining contaminants in metals can frequently be eliminated by high-temperature combustion, but plastics are destroyed by high temperatures.

For some materials having consumers do the separation and recovery is more costly, so it is more efficient for municipal agencies to accomplish recycling. One example is currently operating in Saugus, Massachusetts, a North Shore suburb of Boston, processing up to 1,500 tons of Boston refuse per day. From this waste, the facility annually recovers some 25,000 tons of ferrous metals and 40,000 tons of other materials suitable for use in construction. In addition, the plant is capable of producing two billion pounds of steam annually, which it sells to a nearby General Electric plant.

Recycling: A Closer Look

The model in the preceding section would lead us to expect that recycling would increase over time as virgin ore and disposal costs rose. This seems to be the case. Take copper, for example. During 1910, recycled copper accounted for about 18 percent of the total production of refined copper in the United States. By 1987, this percentage had risen to 41 percent.[4]

Though these percentages may seem low, in most cases recycling is not cheap. Transport and processing costs are usually significant. The sources of scrap are usually concentrated around cities, where the products are used, whereas the producing facilities are concentrated near the sources of the virgin materials. Scrap materials must first be transported to the production facility; then there are additional expenses in collecting, separating, and processing them. Even when there is acute scarcity, nowhere near 100 percent of the materials are recycled; costs don't permit it!

As recycling becomes cost competitive, rather dramatic changes occur in the manufacturing process. Not only do manufacturers rely more heavily on recycled inputs; they also begin to design their products to facilitate recycling. Facilitating recycling through product design is already important in industries where the connection between the manufacturer and

---

[2]In 1983 New York State ordered stores to charge a deposit on beverage containers. Although companies were eager to use the glass and aluminum cans that were returned, few knew what to do with the recycled plastic and most of it ended up in the landfill.

[3]This has happened in the Northeast as mandatory programs to recycle newspapers produced far more than could be absorbed by the market. Falling prices undercut the incentive to recycle.

[4]U.S. Department of the Interior, *Minerals Yearbook: 1987* (Washington, DC: U.S. Government Printing Office, 1987): 289.

EXAMPLE 17.3

Mercury Prices and Recycling

Mercury provides an interesting example of how a depletable recyclable resource can be allocated over time in a manner consistent with the principles discussed earlier in this chapter. Because the ratio of proved reserves to current consumption is quite low, scarcity should be a factor. In the early 1850s price did not rise very much as production rose. After the peak production in the 1870s, however, prices began to rise and production began to fall.

Very little mercury was recycled initially, but the importance of recycling rose with prices. Major sources of recycled mercury were industrial and control instruments, batteries, sludges, and dental amalgams. By 1987, the domestic production of mercury was 23,488 flasks, while 11,096 flasks came from recycling. With higher prices and diminishing supplies, recycling accounted for about 47 percent of the total amount produced during that year. The costs of recycling prevented a larger contribution, even in the face of scarcity.

---

disposal agent is particularly close. Aircraft manufacturers, which often are asked to scrap old aircraft, may stamp the alloy composition on parts during manufacturing to facilitate recycling.[5]

An efficient economic system will orchestrate a balance between the consumption of depletable and recycled materials, between disposing of used products and recycling, and between imports and domestic production. Example 17.3 shows how an efficient market can work. Mercury is an appropriate example because, according to the static reserve index, it is very scarce.

How close are we to efficiency? Have we achieved an efficient balance between imports and domestic production? Is the common pejorative notion that we are a "throwaway society" an accurate one? If so, is the market behaving efficiently—in the sense that the time for recycling has not yet come—or are there clearly identified sources of market failure, implying that the wrong price signals are being sent? The next few sections investigate these issues.

WASTE DISPOSAL AND POLLUTION DAMAGE

The treatment of waste by producers and consumers can lead to biases in the market balance between recycling and the use of virgin ores. Because disposal cost is a key ingredient in determining the efficient amount of recycling, the failure of an economic agent to bear the full cost of disposal implies a bias toward virgin materials and away from recycling. We begin by

---

[5]Council on Environmental Quality, *Environmental Quality—1980* (Washington, DC: U.S. Government Printing Office, 1980): 221.

considering how the method of financing the disposal of potentially recyclable waste affects the level of recycling.

Disposal Cost and Efficiency

We begin by being clear about the relationship of the marginal disposal cost to the efficient level of recycling. Suppose, for example, it costs a community $20/ton to recycle a particular waste product which can ultimately be sold to a local manufacturer for $10/ton. Can we conclude that this is an inefficient recycling venture because it is losing money?

No we can't! In addition to earning the $10/ton from selling the recycled product, the town is avoiding the cost of disposing of the product. This avoided marginal cost is appropriately considered a marginal benefit from recycling. Suppose the marginal avoided disposal cost were $20/ton. In this case, the benefits to the town from recycling would be $30/ton ($20/ton avoided cost plus $10/ton resale value) and the cost would be $20/ton; this would be an efficient recycling venture. Both marginal disposal costs and the prices of recycled materials directly affect the efficient level of recycling. [6]

The Disposal Decision

Potentially recyclable waste can be divided into two types of scrap: old scrap and new scrap. *New scrap* is composed of the residual materials generated during production. For example, as steel beams are formed, the small remnants of steel left over are new scrap. *Old scrap* is recovered from products used by consumers.

To illustrate the relative importance of new scrap and old scrap, consider the aluminum industry. In 1987, a total of 2,096,071 metric tons of aluminum were recovered from scrap of both kinds. Of this, 1,165,728 metric tons came from new scrap while the rest came from old, including the recycling of some 1,002,561 metric tons of aluminum cans.[7] About 38 percent of the aluminum used to make aluminum products in the United States is currently being derived from scrap.

Recycling new scrap is significantly less difficult than recycling old scrap. New scrap is already at the place of production, and with most processes it can simply be reentered into the input stream without transportation costs. Transport costs tend to be an important part of the cost of using old scrap.

Equally important are the incentives involved. Because new scrap never leaves the factory, it remains under the complete control of the manufacturer. Having the joint responsibility of creating a product and dealing with the scrap, the manufacturer now has an incentive

---

[6]In 1989 Seattle, Washington, found that its net recycling cost was $51.50 a ton, which was slightly higher than its avoided cost for landfill disposal, but it expected recycling to be cheaper within five years. See Jerome Richard, "Better Homes and Garbage," *The Amicus Journal* (Summer 1990): 50–51.

[7]U.S. Department of the Interior, *Minerals Yearbook: 1987* (Washington, DC: U.S. Government Printing Office, 1987): 85–91.

to design the product with the use of the scrap in mind. It would be advantageous to establish procedures guaranteeing the homogeneity of the scrap and minimizing the amount of processing necessary to recycle it. For all these reasons, it is likely that the market for new scrap will work efficiently and effectively.

Unfortunately, the same is not true for old scrap. The market works inefficiently because the product users do not bear the full marginal social costs of disposing of their product. As a result, the market is biased away from recycling old scrap and toward the use of virgin materials.

The key to understanding why these costs are not internalized lies in the incentives facing individual product users. Suppose you had some small aluminum products that were no longer useful to you. You could either recycle them, which usually means driving to a recycling center, or you could toss them into your trash. In comparing these two alternatives, notice that recycling imposes one cost on you (transport cost) whereas the second imposes another (disposal cost).

It is difficult for consumers to make this comparison accurately because of the way trash collection has traditionally been financed. Urban areas have generally financed trash collection with taxes, if publicly provided, or user fees, if privately provided. Neither of these approaches directly relates the size of an individual's payment to the amount of waste. The *marginal* cost to the homeowner of throwing out one more unit of trash is negligible, even when the cost to society is not.

This point can be reinforced by a numerical example. Suppose your city provides trash pickup for which you pay $150 a year in taxes. Your cost will be $150 regardless (within reasonable limits) of how much you throw out. In that year your additional (marginal) cost from throwing out these items is *zero*. Certainly the marginal cost to society is *not* zero, so the balance between these alternatives as seen by the individual homeowner is biased in favor of throwing things out.[8]

Littering is an extreme example of what we have been talking about. In the absence of some kind of government intervention, the cost to society of littering is the aesthetic loss plus the risk of damage to automobile tires and pedestrians caused by sharp edges of discarded cans or glass. Tossing used containers outside the car is relatively costless for the individual but costly for society.[9]

Disposal Costs and the Scrap Market

How would the market respond to a policy forcing product users to bear the true marginal disposal cost? The major effect would be on the supply of materials to be recycled. Consumers would now be able to avoid disposal costs and might even be paid for discarded products. This would cause the diversion of some materials to recycling centers where they could be reintegrated into the materials process. If this expanded supply allows dealers to take advantage of previously unexploited economies of scale, it could well result in a lower average cost of processing as well as more recycled materials.

---

[8]The problem is not that $150 is too low; indeed it may be too high! The point is that the cost of waste disposal does not increase with the amount of waste to be disposed.

[9]Using economic analysis, would you expect transients or residents to have a higher propensity to litter? Why?

The effect on the market is now clearly evident. The total consumption of recycled inputs increases because the price falls.

Public Policies

As Table 17.1 indicates, the current level of recycling in the United States is rather low, particularly when judged by the standards of Japan (refer back to Example 17.1). No doubt some of the responsibility for this lies in improper incentives created by inappropriate pricing. Can this misallocation resulting from the problem of inefficiently low disposal cost be corrected?

One approach would impose disposal charges reflecting the true social cost of disposal. The system in Highbridge, New Jersey, illustrates how such a scheme might work in practice.[10] In January 1988 the town replaced its flat $280 annual fee for garbage collection with a fee that varies with the amount of trash. Each 30-gallon bag or 30-gallon can set out at curbside each week must exhibit a town sticker. Each household is given 52 stickers for $140.[11] Additional stickers cost $1.25 apiece.[12]

What were the effects? The most obvious result was that the amount of trash went down by 25 percent. A number of residents began to compost food and yard wastes. Recycling programs in glass, newspapers, and cans have flourished. Neighborhood behavior has changed as people take their trash home with them from parties or bring an extra sticker. Because disposing of large pieces of used furniture can use up four stickers, the frequency of finding new homes for them has increased.

One preimplementation concern about the program was that it might impose a hardship on the poor residents of the area. Strategies based on higher prices always raise the specter that they will end up placing an intolerable burden on the poor.

That concern apparently was misplaced. Many of the town's 4,000 residents were elderly and living on relatively meager fixed incomes. Under the old system of financing trash collection, every household paid the same fee regardless of how much trash was produced. Because elderly households produce less trash, they were in effect subsidizing wealthier households under the old system. With the new system in place, elderly households paid only the flat fee because they didn't need extra stickers. The expense of these stickers was less than the average cost of disposal, the basis for the previous fee. Poor households were better off, not worse off, under the new pricing system.

Seattle, Washington, has a similar system, but with higher prices. As of 1989 residents there pay $13.75 for the first can of trash picked up per week and $9 for every additional can. Their experience has been similar to that in New Jersey. Trash disposal is down dramatically and recycling is up.

Another suggestion now being applied in many areas is the refundable deposit. Already widely accepted for beverage containers, such deposits could become a remedy for many other products

A refund system is designed to accomplish two purposes: (1) the initial charge reflects the cost of disposal and produces the desired composition of demand effect, and (2) the refund,

---

[10]Robert Hanley, "Pay-by-Bag Trash Disposal Really Pays, Town Learns," *The New York Times* (24 November 1988): B1, B7.

[11]In 1989 the base sticker rate went to $200 and the cost of additional individual stickers to $1.65.

[12]If you were running this program, would you allow these stickers to be freely transferable among Highbridge residents or not? Why?

TABLE 17.1 Recovery* of Municipal Solid Waste, 1960 to 1990 (in millions of tons and percent of total generation of each product)

Materials	Millions of Tons						
	1960	1965	1970	1975	1980	1985	1990
Paper and Paperboard	5.4	5.7	7.4	8.2	11.9	13.1	20.9
Glass	0.1	0.1	0.2	0.4	0.8	1.0	2.6
Metals							
Ferrous	0.1	0.1	0.1	0.2	0.4	0.4	1.9
Aluminum	Neg.	Neg.	Neg.	0.1	0.3	0.6	1.0
Other Nonferrous	Neg.	0.3	0.3	0.4	0.5	0.5	0.8
Total Metals	0.1	0.4	0.4	0.7	1.2	1.5	3.7
Plastics	Neg.	Neg.	Neg.	Neg.	Neg.	0.1	0.4
Rubber and Leather	0.3	0.3	0.3	0.2	0.1	0.2	0.2
Textiles	Neg.	Neg.	Neg.	Neg.	Neg.	Neg.	0.2
Wood	Neg.	Neg.	Neg.	Neg.	Neg.	Neg.	0.4
Other**	Neg.	0.3	0.3	0.4	0.5	0.5	0.8
Total Materials in Products	5.9	6.8	8.6	9.9	14.5	16.4	29.2
Total MSW Recovered - Weight	5.9	6.8	8.6	9.9	14.5	16.4	33.4

Materials	Percent of Generation of Each Material						
	1960	1965	1970	1975	1980	1985	1990
Paper and Paperboard	18.1%	15.0%	16.7%	19.1%	21.8%	21.3%	28.6%
Glass	1.5%	1.1%	1.6%	3.0%	5.3%	7.6%	19.9%
Metals							
Ferrous	1.0%	1.0%	0.8%	1.6%	3.4%	3.7%	15.4%
Aluminum	Neg.	Neg.	Neg.	9.1%	16.7%	26.1%	38.1%
Other Nonferrous	Neg.	60.0%	42.9%	44.4%	45.5%	50.0%	67.7%
Total Metals	1.0%	3.6%	2.8%	4.9%	8.3%	10.6%	23.0%
Plastics	Neg.	Neg.	Neg.	Neg.	Neg.	0.9%	2.2%
Rubber and Leather	15.0%	11.5%	9.4%	5.1%	2.3%	5.3%	4.4%
Textiles	Neg.	Neg.	Neg.	Neg.	Neg.	Neg.	4.3%
Wood	Neg.	Neg.	Neg.	Neg.	Neg.	Neg.	3.2%
Other	Neg.	100.0%	37.5%	23.5%	17.2%	14.7%	23.8%
Total Materials in Products	10.9%	10.1%	10.2%	11.3%	13.4%	13.8%	20.2%
Total MSW Recovered - %	6.7%	6.6%	7.1%	7.7%	9.6%	10.0%	17.1%

*Recovery of postconsumer varies for recycling and composing; does not include converting/fabrication scrap.
**Recovery of electrolytes in batteries; probably not recycled.

Details may not add to totals due to rounding.

Neg. = Negligible (less than 0.05 percent or 50,000 tons).

Source: Adapted from Franklin Associates, Ltd., *Characterization of Municipal Solid Waste in the United States, 1992 Update.* Prepared for the U.S. Environmental Protection Agency as cited in National Solid Wastes Management Association, *Recycling in the States: Update 1989* (Washington, DC).

EXAMPLE 17.4

Deposits as a Solution to Abandoned Automobiles

In many countries abandoned automobiles are the source of a significant visual externality. When the prices offered by junk dealers are low, for whatever reasons, discarded cars begin appearing in parking lots, meadows, forests, and even in lakes and rivers. Generally it is difficult to trace the ownership of these vehicles, so penalties are not the answer.

In Sweden a deposit-refund system was introduced in 1976 to remedy this problem. Swedish car owners who turn over their hulks to authorized junk dealers get a bonus of about $60 per car over and above whatever arrangements they could make with the junk dealer. Buyers of new cars pay a fee in the same amount. Because total deposits exceed total refunds, a surplus has accumulated. Part of this surplus has been used to finance local efforts to clean up wrecks that were abandoned before the program began.

The success of this program suggests that such an approach can work. It also suggests some pitfalls to be avoided. During the first year, there was a reduction in abandoned vehicles. After that initial period, however, the program seemed less effective. There were two main reasons: (1) the bonus payment was eroded by high inflation and therefore provided less incentive, and (2) the bottom dropped out of the market for scrapped automobiles, so dealers began charging customers to take their hulks, rather than paying them. In some areas, even with the bonus payment, the act of turning the car in may have cost the donor additional money.

A deposit system can work, providing it is flexible enough and the refund is high enough. This seems to be the experience of Norway which subsequently implemented a similar system with a higher deposit.

Source: Peter Bohm, *Deposit-Refund System: Theory and Application to Environmental, Conservation, and Consumer Policy* (Baltimore, MD: Johns Hopkins University Press, for Resources for the Future, 1981): 120–24; J. B. Opschoor and Hans B. Vos, *Economic Instruments for Environmental Protection* (Paris: Organization for Economic Co-operation and Development, 1989).

attainable upon turning the product in for recycling, helps conserve virgin materials. Such a system already is employed in Sweden and Norway to counter the problem of abandoned automobiles (Example 17.4).

The recycling of aluminum beverage cans has been one clear beneficiary of deposit-refund schemes.[13] Although not all states have passed bottle bills,[14] over 50 percent of aluminum beverage cans are now recycled in the United States.[15] As a result, scrap aluminum has become an increasingly significant component of total aluminum supplies.

Recycling aluminum saves about 95% of the energy that is needed to make new aluminum from ore. In 1987 alone, recycling aluminum can saved more than 10 billion kilowatt

---

[13]A very strong demand for aluminum scrap was also influential. In fact the price for aluminum scrap went so high in 1988 that pilferers were stealing highway signs and guardrails for their aluminum content.

[14]As of 1989 only ten states (California, Connecticut, Delaware, Iowa, Maine, Massachusetts, Michigan, New York, Oregon, and Vermont) had passed bottle bills.

[15]In Maine, a bottle bill state, 85% of aluminum beverage cans are recycled.

hours of electricity, enough to supply the residential electricity needs of New York City for more than six months. The magnitude of these energy savings has had a significant influence on the demand for recycled aluminum as cost-conscious producers search for new ways to reduce energy costs.

Beverage can recycling also reduces littering because an incentive is created to bring the bottle to a recycling center. In some cities scavenging and returning these bottles has provided a significant source of income to the homeless. One Canadian study found that recycling creates six times as many jobs as landfilling.

Deposit-refund systems are also being used for batteries and tires. New Hampshire and Maine place a surcharge on new car batteries. Consumers in these states receive a rebate if they trade in their used battery for a new one. Oklahoma places a $1.00 fee on each new tire sold and then returns 50 cents to certified processing facilities for each tire handled.

The tax system can also be used to promote recycling by taxing virgin materials and by subsidizing recycling activities. The European approach to waste oil recycling, reinforced by the high cost of imported crude oil, has been to require both residential and commercial users to recycle all waste oil they generate. Virgin lubricating oils are taxed, and the resulting income is used to subsidize the recycling industry. As a result, many countries collect up to 65 percent of the available waste oil.

In the United States, which does not subsidize waste oil recycling, the waste oil market has been rather less successful. Currently only about 15 percent of waste oil is recovered. The waste oil industry has been in a relative decline since World War II with the exception of the period immediately following the oil crisis during the 1970s, when oil prices rose dramatically.

As described briefly in Table 17.2, many states are now using tax policy to subsidize the acquisition of recycling equipment in both the public and private sectors. Frequently taking the form of sales tax exemptions or investment tax credits to private industries or loans or grants to local communities, these approaches are designed to get recycling programs off the ground with the expectation that they will ultimately be self-sustaining. The pioneers are being subsidized.

Examining Oregon's program can serve to illustrate how a tax approach works. From 1981 to 1987, to reduce energy consumption as well as to promote recycling, the Oregon Department of Energy granted tax credits to 163 projects. Being granted this credit allowed companies a five-year period in which to deduct from their taxes an amount equal to 35 percent of the cost of any equipment used solely for recycling. Oregon also offers a broader tax credit that covers equipment, land, and building purchases. Paper companies, the major recipients of both types of credits, have used them to produce the capacity to use recycled newsprint and cardboard in the papermaking process. As a result Oregon's newspaper recycling rate (65%) is twice the national average.[16]

Pollution Damage

One other situation influences the use of recycled and virgin ores. When environmental damage results from extracting and using virgin materials and not from the use of recycled mate-

---

[16]Cynthia Pollock Shea, "Building a Market for Recyclables," *Worldwatch* (May/June 1988): 12–18.

TABLE 17.2 State Incentives for Recycling

State	Incentive
California	Recycling equipment investment tax credit for individuals and corporations; development bonds for manufacturing products with recycled materials.
Colorado	Tax credits for investments in plastics recycling equipment.
Florida	Sales tax exemption on recycling machinery purchased after 1 July 1988.
Indiana	Property tax exemptions for buildings, equipment, and land involved in recycling operations.
Maine	Tax credit equal to 30% of cost of equipment and machinery; subsidies to municipalities for scrap metal transportation costs.
New Jersey	Fifty percent investment credit for recycling equipment and programs.
North Carolina	Industrial and corporate tax credits and exemptions for equipment and facilities.
Oregon	Individual and corporate income tax credits for equipment purchases and facilities.
Texas	Franchise tax exemption for sludge recycling corporations.
Wisconsin	Sales tax exemptions for equipment and facilities; business property tax exemptions for some equipment.

Source: National Solid Wastes Management Association, "Recycling in the States: Update 1989" (Washington, DC).

rials, the market allocation will be biased away from recycling. The damage might be experienced at the mine, such as the erosion and aesthetic costs of strip mining, or at the point of processing, where the ore is processed into a usable resource.

Suppose the mining industry were forced to bear the cost of this environmental damage. What difference would the inclusion of this cost have on the scrap market? The internalizing of this cost results in a leftward shift in the supply curve for the virgin ore (S_d). This would, in turn, cause a leftward shift in the total-supply curve. The market would be using less of the resource—due to higher price—while recycling more. Thus the correct treatment of these environmental costs would share with disposal costs a tendency to increase the role for recycling.

One study by Spofford examines the significance of this cost in the context of the paper industry, which, in spite of the fact it is based on a renewable resource, does rely on the recycling of used paper.[17] In his study (summarized in Figure 17.1), Spofford considers four costs: acquiring and processing virgin pulp, using scrap paper, treatment and disposal of resulting pollutants, and the external damage caused by untreated pollutants. Graphed as a function of the reuse ratio, the external damages and treatment costs are much higher with lower reuse ratios; the use of virgin materials generates most of these costs.

---

[17]W. O. Spofford, "Solid Residual Management: Some Economic Considerations," *Natural Resource Journal* 11 (July 1971): 561–89.

Spofford also differentiates the costs to society as a whole from the costs to the paper-making firm. These differ because society bears all the costs whereas the firm bears only the costs of acquiring and processing virgin pulp and the costs of using scrap paper. The private costs do not include either the treatment costs (in the absence of government control the firm would not choose to treat the pollutants) or the external damages. The major conclusion to be drawn is that the efficient reuse ratio (0.8) is significantly higher than what the market would automatically provide (0.55) due to the undervaluation of environmental damage by the market.

PRODUCT DURABILITY

In a memorable passage from *Death of a Salesman,* Willy Loman, the title character, laments:

> Once in my life I would like to own something outright before it's broken! I'm always in a race with the junkyard! I just finish paying for the car and it's on its last legs. The refrigerator consumes belts like a goddamn maniac. They time those things. They time them so when you've finally paid for them, they're used up.[18]

Willy is not alone in his anguish. In the early 1960s popular author Vance Packard came out with a book called *The Waste Makers* which suggested that Willy's plight was the product of a conscious marketing strategy by corporations. If products wear out faster, the argument goes, consumers have to buy them more often and sales are increased. Is this a valid argument? If it is, the drain on the resource base is artificially high and we have another reason for corrective measures.

Packard identifies three possible types of product obsolescence. *Functional obsolescence* occurs when a new product can perform the function in a superior manner to an older product. The vacuum tube became functionally obsolescent when it was replaced by the transistor. *Fashion obsolescence* occurs when consumers prefer a new product for reasons of taste. Wide ties and short skirts become obsolete when tastes shift to narrow ties and long skirts. *Durability obsolescence* occurs when the product can no longer perform its function because of wear and tear. A refrigerator becomes obsolete when it can no longer keep its inside temperature stable and cool. The economic implications of these three types of obsolescence are quite different.

Functional Obsolescence

Because functional obsolescence is not really a problem, we will spend little time on it. A vigorous amount of inventive activity is a natural and desirable consequence of a market economy. Those who find better ways of doing things can become wealthy from the sales of their

---

[18]Arthur Miller, "Death of a Salesman," Act II, in *Arthur Miller's Collected Plays* 1 (New York: The Viking Press, 1957): 174.

FIGURE 17.2

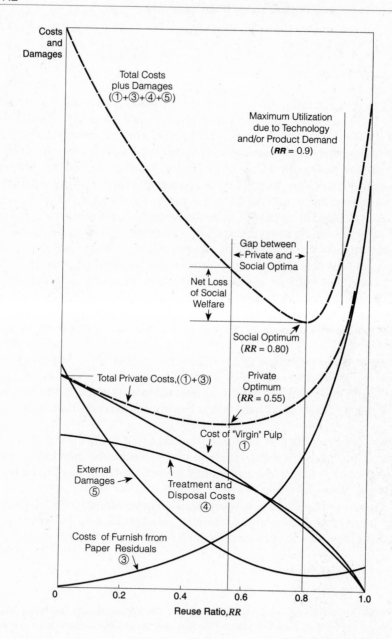

Costs and Damages

Total Costs plus Damages ((①)+(③)+(④)+(⑤))

Maximum Utilization due to Technology and/or Product Demand (**RR** = 0.9)

Gap between ←Private and → Social Optima

Net Loss of Social Welfare

Social Optimum (*RR* = 0.80)

Total Private Costs,((①)+(③))

Private Optimum (*RR* = 0.55)

Cost of "Virgin" Pulp ①

External Damages ⑤

Treatment and Disposal Costs ④

Costs of Furnish frrom Paper Residuals ③

0   0.2   0.4   0.6   0.8   1.0

Reuse Ratio, *RR*

product, whether it be a tastier way to fry chicken or a cheaper, higher-quality method of copying documents. Far from representing a problem, functional obsolescence is the natural consequence of the successful search for better products.

Fashion Obsolescence

Fashion obsolescence is trickier. On the one hand, if fashion is a valued characteristic for consumers, then it is possible to conceive fashion obsolescence as merely a special case of functional obsolescence. New fashions replace old because they are more satisfying to the consumer. In this view there is no problem with fashion obsolescence because it is merely the result of the market continually doing a superior job of satisfying consumer preference.

The opposite point of view starts from the premise that those consumer preferences being satisfied by the market are in fact *created* by the market.[19] If consumer preferences are created by producers, then it is appropriate to question whether consumers are legitimately being made better off or are merely being manipulated into believing they are better off.

The apparel industry is certainly one where fashion obsolescence plays a strong role. However, it is not clear that fashion obsolescence is as important for other products. The automobile has certainly had its share of fashion obsolescence, perhaps best epitomized by the era in the 1950s when pronounced tailfins were in vogue, yet clearly the auto industry can go only so far. It would be very difficult, for example, to explain the shift in consumer buying toward small imported automobiles in the late 1970s and early 1980s as reflecting a shift in what was fashionable.

Indeed, some observers believe that a significant portion of the malaise of the domestic auto industry in the 1980s was caused by its inability to anticipate and respond to consumer preferences. That is important because the automobile market is one in which consumer preferences were thought to be dominated by the big three American automakers.[20] Cis not the case.

Even when fashion influences consumer preferences, it is not clear that taste is dictated by the manufacturer or that it relates solely to new products. Antique furniture and antique cars are fashionable, but these fashions certainly are not created by manufacturers and do not help sell new cars or new furniture.

In looking at the totality of consumer decisions, we cannot conclude that consumer tastes are systematically manipulated by industry. Markets do exist for which a strong case can be made, but they seem to be isolated examples, rather than typical.

---

[19]For an articulation of this position, see John Kenneth Galbraith, *The Affluent Society* (New York: Houghton Mifflin, 1958). For an opposite point of view, see F. A. Hayek, "The Non Sequitur of 'Dependence Effect'," *Southern Economic Journal* 27 (April 1961): 346–52.

[20]See, for example, "How to Outmode a $4,000 Vehicle in Two Years," in Vance Packard, *The Waste Makers* (New York: David McKay, 1960).

Durability Obsolescence

We come then to the final category, the one that triggered Willy Loman's lament. For this category, we must begin to answer two questions: (1) What is an efficient level of durability, and (2) will the market supply that level?

The *efficient level of durability* is the one that maximizes the net benefit from the product. Products that last longer confer more benefits on society, but they also cost more. Therefore, it is not obvious that the most durable product is also the most efficient one. Can we trust the market to find the efficient level of durability? To examine that issue, let's look at both the demand and supply sides of the market.

On the demand side, the consumer makes his or her choices by discounting benefits and costs. The capital costs of consumer durables are borne immediately (although payments can be spread out by borrowing money), whereas the benefits (flow of services), as well as operating and maintenance costs, are accrued as a flow over time. The consumer will purchase the commodity only if the net benefit is maximized by that level of durability (the additional cost of making a more durable commodity is justified by the additional benefit received). In performing this balancing between cost and durability, will the consumer make efficient choices or, because of lack of information or some other market imperfection, will durability be undervalued or overvalued?

One way to test this is to examine a case in which the benefits and costs are relatively easy to quantify, thereby allowing a comparison of the discount rate implied by consumer purchases of durable goods with market rates. If their individual discount rates are higher than the social opportunity cost of capital (as measured by interest rates), consumers are undervaluing durability. If they use lower discount rates, they are overvaluing it.

Jerry Hausman of MIT conducted a fascinating study that relates to this issue.[21] He was able to acquire data on individual purchases of energy-using consumer durables (room air conditioners). For each of these purchases he could calculate the benefits (longer life plus energy savings resulting from higher energy efficiency) and cost (purchase price as well as expected operating and maintenance costs). From this information he could calculate the discount rates implied by the purchase made by the average consumer. High discount rates indicate a special sensitivity to the initial cost.

In his sample, the implied discount rates were higher than the market rates. Furthermore, Hausman found that discount rates were highest for the people with the lowest income, whereas they approximated the efficient rates for higher-income classes. This suggests that consumers—particularly low-income consumers— purchase less durability and less energy efficiency than are dictated by the dynamic-efficiency criterion.[22]

To be able to structure the appropriate policy response, however, the government would have to know more about the reasons for the higher implied discount rates. If the reason is in-

---

[21]Jerry Hausman, "Individual Discount Rates and the Purchase and Utilization of Energy-Using Durables," *Bell Journal of Economics* 10 (Spring 1979): 33–54.

[22]These results were subsequently corroborated by a number of other authors. For a description of these see Malcolm Gladwell, "Consumer's Choices About Money Consistently Defy Common Sense," *The Washington Post* (12 February 1990): A3.

adequate consumer information, then the appropriate policy might well be increasing the flow of reliable information through testing, labeling requirements, and so on. If it is purely that the market rate of interest is higher for low-income consumers because they have a higher probability of defaulting on loan repayments, then some means of providing easier access to capital markets might be called for. In other cases, measures such as tax subsidies or enforced standards might be appropriate.

We must also consider the supply side of the market. If they can get away with it, producers as a group have an incentive to reduce product durability below the efficient level. By doing so, they would reduce their cost per unit and they would sell many more units over time. For example a household could satisfy its demand over a ten-year period with one appliance lasting ten years, but would have to purchase two if the appliance only lasted five years. As long as the profit was higher on the sale of two, rather than one (the presumption), firms would be better off with planned obsolescence.

But the key question is whether or not they can get away with it. As long as competitive suppliers, or even potential competitive suppliers, could enter the market to supply more-durable goods, the consumer could turn to these alternative suppliers instead. In a normal market process, competition prevents individual firms from producing insufficiently durable products. Those who sell products that don't last find their markets drying up.

This market process may not work efficiently in two different cases. The first case occurs when consumers are not well informed about the differences in durability and so do not have enough information to make efficient decisions. This, remember, was one possible interpretation of the Hausman study. To the extent that they face ignorant consumers, producers would have an incentive to position themselves in the lower initial price portion of the market by lowering the durability of their products.

In recognition of the importance of this information, organizations have been set up to supply it. Consumers' Union, the publisher of *Consumer Reports,* is one such organization. It performs its own independent testing and evaluating, a service that can rectify this lack of information at reasonable cost. Its chief limitation probably relates to products undergoing rapid technological change.

For rapidly changing products, by the time the testing lab acquires the product, tests it, and reports the results, other untested but potentially superior products are already on the market. This flaw, however, is not fatal; it merely means that the rate of adoption would be rather more sluggish than would be dictated by efficiency.

The second case where a firm could profit by producing a good with an inefficiently low durability is when it does not face competition. This would require either a monopoly—which is, of course, very rare—or explicit collusion to cut corners by all the members of the industry. Because competition comes from foreign firms as well as domestic ones and from potential entrants as well as existing firms, this must be a relatively rare circumstance.

The American automobile industry provides an interesting case to examine the hypothesis that increased competition can increase durability because that industry has faced increasingly intense foreign competition. The share of the U.S. market captured by imports rose from 14.8 percent in 1976 to 29.2 percent in 1988.[23] Did this lead to increased durability?

[23]The data in this paragraph and the one that follows it came from Motor Vehicles Manufacturing Association, *Motor Vehicle Facts and Figures, 1989* (Detroit, MI: Motor Vehicles Manufacturing Association, 1989): 16, 26, 90.

According to two possible measures, it did. Durable cars should last longer and be safer. The average age of passenger cars increased from 6.2 years in 1976 to 7.6 years in 1988, and the deaths per 100 million vehicle miles traveled decreased from 3.33 in 1976 to 2.46 in 1988. Though other factors were certainly also at work, competition probably did play a major role in increasing durability.

SUMMARY

Market mechanisms automatically create pressures for recycling and reuse that are generally in the right direction, though rarely of the correct intensity. Higher disposal costs and increasing scarcity of virgin materials do create a larger demand for recycling. This is already evident for a number of products, such as those containing copper or aluminum.

However, a number of imperfections in the market suggest that the degree of recycling we are currently experiencing is less than the efficient amount. Artificially low disposal costs and tax breaks for ores combine to depress the role that old scrap can, and should, play. Severance taxes provide a limited, if poorly targeted, redress for some minerals.

One imperfection, the supposed tendency of American manufacturers to produce products less durable than efficient, seems overstated. However, the Hausman study indicates that some people purchase products less durable than efficient, implying that the market penetration of more-energy-efficient devices may be lower than efficient. This is a more limited view of product durability problems than is usually espoused by writers such as Vance Packard, but a troubling one nonetheless.

One cannot help but notice that many of these problems result from government actions. It therefore appears in this area that the appropriate role for government is selective disengagement complemented by some fine-tuning adjustments.

The most important of these fine-tuning adjustments relate to the adoption of pricing strategies for waste disposal that impose the true marginal cost on the disposers. Two elements of appropriate pricing strategies are important: (1) assuring that prices are on a per unit volume basis, and (2) incorporating the costs of environmental damage.

The commonly heard ideological prescriptions suggesting that environmental problems can be solved either by ending government interference or by increasing the amount of government control are both inaccurate. The efficient role for government in achieving a balance between the economic and environmental systems requires less control in some areas and more in others.

FURTHER READING

Bohm, Peter. *Deposit-Refund System: Theory and Application to Environmental, Conservation, and Consumer Policy* (Baltimore, MD: Johns Hopkins University Press, for Resources for the Future, 1981). A highly readable and analytically sound exploration of the experience with and potential applications for deposit-refund systems.

Curlee, T. Randall. *The Economic Feasibility of Recycling: A Case Study of Plastic Wastes* (New York: Praeger Publishers, 1986). Analyzes in nontechnical language the incentives for, and barriers to, recycling plastics.

Manthy, Robert S. *Natural Resource Commodities—A Century of Statistics* (Baltimore, MD: Johns Hopkins University Press, for Resources for the Future, 1978). A basic reference source on natural-resource prices, output, consumption, foreign trade, and employment in the United States, 1870–1973. It draws no conclusions.

Roxburgh, Nigel. *Policy Responses to Resource Depletion: The Case of Mercury* (Greenwich, CT: JAI Press, 1980). An intensive examination of the depletion experience with one particular material—mercury. Includes chapters on the resource base, extractive and scrap-metal industries, and various industries that are heavy users of mercury.

ADDITIONAL REFERENCES

Banks, Ferdinand E. *Bauxite & Aluminum: an Introduction to the Economics of Non-Fuel Minerals* (Lexington, MA: Lexington Books, 1979).

Foley, Patricia T,. and Joel P. Clark. "The Effects of State Taxation on United States Copper Supply," *Land Economics* 58 (May 1982): 153–80.

Gulley, D. A. "Severance Taxes and Market Failure," *Natural Resources Journal* 22 (July 1982): 597–617.

Harris, DeVerle P. *Mineral Resources Appraisal* (New York: Oxford University Press, 1984).

Kakela, Peter J. "Iron Ore: From Depletion to Abundance," *Science* 212 (10 April 1981): 132–36.

Lee, D. R., P. E. Graves, and R. L. Sexton. "On Mandatory Deposits, Fines, and the Control of Litter," *Natural Resources Journal* 28, No. 4 (Fall 1988): 837–47.

McClure, Charles, and Peter Mieszkowski, eds. *Fiscal Federalism and the Taxation of Natural Resources* (Lexington, MA: Lexington Books, 1983).

Mikesell, Raymond F. *Nonfuel Minerals: Foreign Dependence and National Security* (Ann Arbor, MI: University of Michigan Press, 1987).

Peck, Merton J., ed. *The World Aluminum Industry in a Changing Energy Era* (Washington, DC: Resources for the Future, 1988).

Stollery, Kenneth R. "Mineral Depletion with Cost as the Extraction Limit: A Model Applied to the Behavior of Prices in the Nickel Industry," *Journal of Environmental Economics and Management* 10 (June 1983): 151–65.

Tilton, John E, Roderick G. Eggert, and Hans H. Landsberg, eds. *World Mineral Exploration: Trends & Economic Issues* (Washington, DC: Resources for the Future, 1988).

DISCUSSION QUESTIONS

1. Glass bottles can either be recycled (crushed and remelted) or reused. The market will tend to choose the cheapest path. What factors will tend to affect the relative cost of these options? Is the market likely to make the efficient choice? Are the "bottle bills" passed by many of the states requiring deposits on bottles a move toward efficiency or not? Why?

2. Many areas have attempted to increase the amount of recycled waste lubricating oil by requiring service stations to serve as collection centers or by instituting deposit-refund systems. On what grounds, if any, is government intervention called for? In terms of the effects on the waste lubrication oil market, what differences should be noticed among those states which do nothing, those which require all service stations to serve as collection centers, and those implementing deposit-refund systems? Why?

3. What are the income distribution consequences of "fashion"? Can the need to be seen driving a new car by the rich be a boon to those with lower incomes who will ultimately purchase a better, lower-priced used car as a result?

CHAPTER 18

Toxic Substances and Hazardous Wastes

The fact that a problem will certainly take a long time to solve, and that it will demand the attention of many minds for several genera-tions, is no justification for postponing the study. Our difficulties of the moment must always be dealt with somehow, but our permanent difficulties are difficulties of every moment.

T. S. ELIOT, *CHRISTIANITY AND CULTURE* (1949)

INTRODUCTION

In one of the interesting ironies of history, the place that focused public attention in the United States on hazardous waste is called the Love Canal. *Love* is not a word any impartial observer would choose to describe the relationships among the parties to that incident.

The Love Canal typifies in many ways the dilemma posed by the creation and disposal of toxic substances. Until 1953, Hooker Electrochemical (now Hooker Chemical, a subsidiary of Occidental Petroleum Corporation) dumped waste chemicals into an old abandoned waterway known as the Love Canal, near Niagara Falls, New York.[1] At the time it seemed a reasonable solution because the chemicals were buried in what was then considered to be impermeable clay.

In 1953 Hooker deeded the Love Canal property for one dollar to the Niagara Falls Board of Education, which then built an elementary school on the site. The deed specifically excused Hooker from any damages that might be caused by the chemicals. Residential development of the area around the school soon followed.

The site became the center of controversy when, in 1978, residents complained of chemicals leaking to the surface. News reports emanating from the area included stories of spontaneous fires and vapors in basements. Medical reports suggested that the residents had experienced abnormally high rates of miscarriage, birth defects, and diseases of the liver.

Similar experiences befell Europe and Asia. In 1976 an accident at an F. Hoffman–La Roche & Co. plant in Sevesco spewed dioxin over the Italian countryside. More recently, ex-plosions in a Union Carbide plant in Bhopal, India, spread deadly gases over nearby residential

---

[1]Hooker was acquired by Occidental Petroleum in 1968.

neighborhoods with significant loss of life, and water used to quell a warehouse fire at a Sandoz warehouse near Basel, Switzerland, carried an estimated 30 tons of toxic chemicals into the Rhine River, a source of drinking water for a number of towns in the Federal Republic of Germany.

In previous chapters we touched on a few of the policy instruments used to combat toxic-substance problems. Emission standards govern the types and amounts of substances that can be injected into the air. Effluent standards regulate what can be discharged directly into water sources, and pretreatment standards control the flow of toxics into waste treatment plants. Maximum concentration levels have been established for many substances in drinking water.

This impressive array of policies is not sufficient to resolve the Love Canal problem or others having similar characteristics. When violations of the standards for drinking water are detected, for example, the water is already contaminated. Specifying maximum contaminant levels helps to identify when a problem exists, but it does nothing to prevent or contain the problem. The various standards for air and water emission that do protect against *point* sources do little to prevent contamination by *nonpoint* sources. Furthermore, most water-borne toxic pollutants are stock pollutants, not fund pollutants; they cannot be absorbed by the receiving waters. Therefore, temporally constant controls on emissions (a traditional method used for fund pollutants) is inappropriate for these toxic substances because such controls would allow a steady rise in the concentration over time. Some additional form of control is necessary to curb toxic-substance pollution.

In this chapter we shall describe and evaluate the policies that deal specifically with the creation, use, transportation, and disposal of toxic substances. Many dimensions will be considered. What are appropriate ways to dispose of hazardous materials? How can the government ensure that all waste is appropriately disposed of? How do we prevent surreptitious dumping? Who should clean up old sites? Should victims be compensated for damages caused by toxic substances under the control of someone else? If so, by whom? What are the appropriate roles for the legislature and the judiciary in creating the proper set of incentives?

NATURE OF TOXIC-SUBSTANCE POLLUTION

The main objective of the current legal system for controlling toxic substances is to protect human health, though protecting other forms of life is a secondary objective. The potential health danger depends upon the toxicity of a substance to humans and their exposure to the substance. *Toxicity* occurs when a living organism experiences detrimental effects on being exposed to a substance. In normal concentrations most chemicals are not toxic. Others, such as pesticides, are toxic by design. Yet, in excess concentrations, even a benign substance such as table salt can be toxic.

A degree of risk is involved when using any chemical substance. There are benefits as well. The task for public policy is to define an acceptable risk by balancing the costs and benefits of controlling the use of chemical substances.

Health Effects

The two main health concerns associated with toxic substances are risk of cancer and effects on reproduction.

Cancer. Since the 1900s, mortality rates have fallen for most of the major causes of death. The most conspicuous exception is cancer. Even the mortality rate for heart disease, the number one killer, has declined in recent decades. Meanwhile, the mortality rate for cancer, currently the second most common cause of death, has increased steadily through this century.

Although many suspect that this increased mortality rate for cancer may be related to increased exposure to carcinogens, proving or disproving this link is very difficult due to the latency of the disease. *Latency* refers to the state of being concealed during the period between exposure to the carcinogen and the detection of cancer. Latency periods for cancer can run from 15 to 40 years in length, but have been known to run as long as 75 years.[2]

In the United States, part of the increase in cancer has been convincingly linked to smoking, particularly among women. The proportion of women who smoke has increased, and the incidence of lung cancer has increased as well. Smoking does not account for all of the increase in cancer, however. A smaller percentage of men smoke today than in earlier decades, and modern cigarettes contain less tar. Despite this, the incidence of lung cancer among men has increased.[3]

Though it is not entirely clear what other agents may be responsible, one cause that has been suggested is the rise in the manufacture and use of synthetic chemicals since World War II.[4] A number of these chemicals have been shown in the laboratory to be carcinogenic. That does not necessarily implicate them in the rise of cancer, however, because it does not take exposure into account. The laboratory can reveal, through animal tests, the relationship between dosage and resulting effects. To track down the significance of any chemical in causing cancer in the general population would require an estimate of how large a segment of the population was exposed to various doses. Currently, our data are not extensive enough to allow these kinds of calculations to be done with any confidence.

Reproductive Effects.[5] Tracing the influence of environmental effects on human reproduction is still a new science. A growing body of scientific evidence, however, suggests that exposure to smoking, alcohol, and chemicals may contribute to infertility, may affect the viability of the fetus and the health of the infant after birth, and may cause genetic defects that can be passed on for generations.

Problems exist for both men and women. In men, exposure to toxic substances has resulted in lower sperm counts, malformed sperm, and genetic damage. In women, exposure can also result in sterility or birth defects in their children.

---

[2]Paul R. Portney, "Toxic Substance Policy and the Protection of Human Health,"in *Current Issues in U.S. Environmental Policy,* Paul R. Portney, ed. (Baltimore, MD: Johns Hopkins University Press, 1978): 100.

[3]Council on Environmental Quality, *Environmental Quality—1980* (Washington, DC: U.S. Government Printing Office, 1980): 194.

[4]Davis and Magee raise this possibility but also conclude that, because of the latency period, it is too early to tell how much, if any, of the responsibility can be assigned to the increased exposure to synthetic chemicals. See Devra Lee Davis and Brian H. Magee, "Cancer and Industrial Chemical Production," *Science* 206 (21 December 1979): 1356–58.

[5]For an excellent study of the literature, see Council on Environmental Quality, *Environmental Quality—1980* (Washington, DC; U.S. Government Printing Office, 1980): 199–205.

Policy Issues

Many aspects of the toxic substance problem make it difficult to resolve. Three important aspects are the numbers of substances involved, latency, and uncertainty.

Number of Substances.   Of the two million or so known chemical compounds, approximately 70,000 are actively used in commerce. More than 30,000 of these are in substantial use. Many exhibit little or no toxicity, and even a very toxic substance represents little risk as long as it is isolated. The trick is to identify problem substances and design appropriate policies as responses. The massive number of substances involved make that a difficult assignment. The geographic location of industrial hazardous wastes, a major component of the hazardous waste problem, is given in Table 18.1.

Latency.   The period of latency exhibited by many of these relationships compounds the problem. Two kinds of toxicity are exhibited–acute and chronic. *Acute toxicity* is present when a short-term exposure to the substance produces a detrimental effect on the exposed organisms. *Chronic toxicity* is present when the detrimental effect arises from exposure of a continued or prolonged nature.

The process of screening chemicals as potentially serious causes of chronic illness is even more complicated than that of screening for acute illness. The traditional technique for determining acute toxicity is the lethal dose determination, a relatively quick test performed on animals that calculates the dose that results in the death of 50 percent of the animal population. This test is less well suited for screening substances that exhibit chronic toxicity.

The appropriate tests for discovering chronic toxicity have typically involved subjecting animal populations to sustained low-level doses of the substance over an extended period of time. These tests are very expensive and time-consuming.[6] If all proposed chemicals were subjected to such long and detailed tests, the process itself would preclude the introduction of many new chemicals. If the EPA were to do the tests, given its limited resources, it could only test a few of the estimated 500 new chemicals introduced each year. If the industries were to do the tests, the expense could preclude the introduction of many potentially valuable new chemicals that have limited, specialized markets.

The EPA has attempted to respond by developing a series of screening tests that can be accomplished in a shorter period of time and at less expense. The chemicals identified by those screening tests as posing an unacceptable risk can be subjected to more expensive tests. As long as the short tests are sufficiently reliable for screening, the testing problem can be reduced to manageable proportions.

One particularly promising class of screening tests involves adding a chemical substance to a bacteria culture no longer capable of growth. If the substance is a mutagen, and therefore a likely carcinogen, the bacteria resume growth. Although these tests are considerably

---

[6]A two-year bioassay for carcinogenic effects of a single chemical would cost $1.25 million according to R. C. Evans, J. Bakst, and M. Dreyfus, *An Analysis of TCSA Reauthorization Proposals* (Washington, DC: EPA Office of Pesticides and Toxic Substances, 1985).

TABLE 18.1 Estimated Generation of Industrial Hazardous Waste in 1983 by State (in thousands of metric tons)

State	Quantity	Percentage of National Generation	State	Quantity	Percentage of National Generation
Alabama	6,547	2.5	Montana	662	0.2
Alaska	52	<0.1	Nebraska	739	0.3
Arizona	642	0.2	Nevada	379	0.1
Arkansas	3,729	1.4	New Hampshire	431	0.2
California	17,284	6.5	New Jersey	12,948	4.9
Colorado	1,902	0.7	New Mexico	619	0.2
Connecticut	4,328	1.6	New York	9,876	3.7
Delaware	894	0.3	North Carolina	3,954	1.5
Florida	2,981	1.1	North Dakota	269	0.1
Georgia	3,338	1.3	Ohio	19,692	7.4
Hawaii	202	0.1	Oklahoma	2,673	1.0
Idaho	1,160	0.4	Oregon	969	0.4
Illinois	14,810	5.6	Pennsylvania	18,260	6.9
Indiana	10,189	3.8	Rhode Island	1,745	0.7
Iowa	1,774	0.7	South Carolina	3,669	1.4
Kansas	2,564	1.0	South Dakota	159	0.1
Kentucky	4,647	1.7	Tennessee	12,159	4.6
Louisiana	13,801	5.2	Texas	34,866	13.1
Maine	337	0.1	Utah	1,139	0.4
Maryland	2,989	1.1	Virginia	4,038	1.5
Massachusetts	4,536	1.7	Vermont	226	0.1
Michigan	12,399	4.7	Washington	5,523	2.1
Minnesota	2,212	0.8	Wisconsin	3,297	1.2
Missouri	6,046	2.3	West Virginia	5,642	2.1
Mississippi	1,816	0.7	Wyoming	572	0.2
			Total	**265,595**	**100.0**

Projections for 1983 based on 1981 state employment shares found in Bureau of Census, U.S. Department of Commerce, *County Business Patterns 1981* (1981).

Source: Congressional Budget Office, *Hazardous Waste Management: Recent Changes and Policy Alternatives* (May 1985): 22.

cheaper to perform, the correlation between mutagens and carcinogens is not perfect. Benzene, a known carcinogen, is not a mutagen. Some carcinogens could slip through the screening process undetected.

Uncertainty.   Another dilemma inhibiting policymakers is the uncertainty surrounding the scientific evidence on which regulation is based. Effects uncovered by laboratory studies on animals are not perfectly correlated with effects on humans. Large doses administered over a three-year period may not produce the same effects as an equivalent amount spread over a twenty-year period. Some of the effects are *synergistic*—that is, their effects are compounded by other variable factors. They are either more serious or less serious in the presence of other substances or conditions than they would be in the absence of those substances or conditions.[7] Once cancer is detected, in most cases it does not bear the imprint of a particular source. Policymakers have to act in the face of limited information.

From an economic point of view, how the policy process reacts to this dilemma should depend on how well the market handles toxic substance problems. To the extent that the market generates the correct information and provides the appropriate incentives, policy may not be needed. On the other hand, when the government can best generate information or create the appropriate incentive, intervention may be called for. As the following pages demonstrate, the nature of the most appropriate policy response may depend crucially on the type of relationship existing between the polluter and the affected party or parties.

MARKET ALLOCATIONS AND TOXIC SUBSTANCES

Toxic substance contamination can arise in a variety of settings. To define the efficient policy response, we must examine what responses would be forthcoming in the normal operation of the market. Let's look at three possible relationships between the source of the contamination and the victim: employer–employee, producer–consumer, and producer–third party. The first two of these involve normal contractual relations among the parties; the latter involves non-contracting parties whose connection is defined solely by the contamination.

Occupational Hazards

Many occupations involve risk, including, for some people, exposure to toxic substances. Do employers and employees have sufficient incentives to act in concert toward achieving safety in the workplace?

The caricature of the market used by the most ardent proponents of regulation suggests not. In this view the employer's desire to maximize profits precludes spending money on

---

[7]For example, it has been shown that asbestos workers who smoke are 30 times more likely to get lung cancer than their nonsmoking fellow workers.

safety. Sick workers can simply be replaced. Therefore, the workers are powerless to do anything about it; if they complain, they are fired and replaced with others who are less vocal.

The most ardent opponents of regulation respond that this caricature omits significant market pressures and is not a particularly accurate guide. They argue that it fails to take into account employee incentives and the feedback effects of those incentives on employers.

If employees are to accept work in a potentially hazardous environment, they will do so only if appropriately compensated. Riskier occupations should call forth higher wages. The increase in wages should be sufficient to compensate the workers for the increased risk. These higher wages represent a real cost of the hazardous situation to the employer. They also produce an incentive to create a safer work environment because greater safety would result in lower wages. One cost could be balanced against the other. What was spent on safety could be recovered in lower wages.

When the marginal increased wages accurately reflect marginal damages, market equilibria are efficient. As long as this stylized view of the world is correct, the market will tailor the appropriate degree of precaution to the situation.

Proponents point out that this allocation would also allow more choices for workers than would, for example, a system requiring all workplaces to be equally safe. With varying occupational risk, those occupations with more risk (such as working with radioactive materials) would attract people who were less averse to risk. These workers would receive higher than average wages (to compensate them for the increased risk), but paying these higher wages would be cheaper to the firm (and hence, consumers) than producing a workplace safe enough for the average worker. The risk-averse workers would be free to choose less risky occupations.

Existing empirical studies make clear that wages in risky occupations do contain a risk premium. Two conclusions about these risk premiums seem clear from these studies: (1) The willingness to pay for apparently similar risk reductions varies significantly across individuals; and (2) the revealed willingness to pay for risk reduction is substantial.[8]

What is the appropriate role for the public sector in controlling contamination in the workplace? One point raised by the court system is whether or not market solutions always satisfy ethical norms. For example, if the employee is a pregnant woman and the occupational hazard involves potential damage to the fetus, does the expectant mother have the right to risk the unborn child, or is some added protection for the fetus needed? Furthermore, if the lowest-cost solution is to ban pregnant—or even fertile—women from a workplace that poses a risk to a fetus, is that an acceptable solution, or is it unfair discrimination against women? As Example 18.1 suggests, these are not idle concerns.

Ethical concerns are not the only challenges for market solutions. The ability of the worker to respond to a hazardous situation depends upon his or her knowledge of the seriousness of the danger. With toxic substances, that knowledge is likely to be incomplete. Consequently, the marginal increased wages function may be artificially rotated toward the origin: The employer would choose too little precaution. Having access to the health records of all employees, the employer may be in the best position to assess the degree of risk posed,

---

[8]See the survey of this evidence in W. Kip Viscusi, *Risk by Choice: Regulating Health and Safety in the Workplace* (Cambridge, MA: Harvard University Press, 1983): 93–113.

EXAMPLE 18.1

Susceptible Populations in the Hazardous Workplace

Some employees are especially susceptible to occupational hazards. Pregnant women and women in the childbearing years are particularly vulnerable. When an employer attempts to manage a work situation that poses a hazardous threat, either the susceptible population can be separated from the hazard or the hazard can be controlled to a sufficient level that its risk is acceptable to even the most susceptible employees.

The economic aspects of this choice are easily deduced. Removal of the susceptible population results in lower marginal risk to the workers, lower costs to the firm, and less precaution taken. But is it fair to those who are removed from their jobs?

This issue came to a head in 1978 when American Cyanamid decided to respond to an occupational risk by banning all fertile women from jobs in the section manufacturing lead chromate pigment at Willow Island, West Virginia. After reviewing the decision, the Occupational Safety and Health Administration (OSHA) cited the company under the general duty clause of the Occupational Safety and Health Act, which requires an employer to provide a workplace free of hazards, and fined it $10,000. That was not the last of it. In early 1980, the Oil, Chemical and Atomic Workers Union sued the company under the 1964 Civil Rights Act on the grounds that the company has discriminated unfairly against women.

Source: This example was taken from Council on Environmental Quality, *Environmental Quality—1980* (Washington, DC: U.S. Government Printing Office, 1980): 205.

---

but the employer also has an incentive to suppress that information. To publicize risk would mean demands for higher compensatory wages and possible lawsuits.

Information on the dangers posed by exposure to a particular toxic substance is a public good to employees; each employee has an incentive to be a *free rider* on the discoveries of others. Individual employees do not have an incentive to bear the cost of doing the necessary research to uncover the degree of risk either. Thus, it seems neither employers nor employees can be expected to produce the efficient amount of information on the magnitude of risk.[9]

As a result, the government may play a substantial role in setting the boundaries on ethical responses, in stimulating research on the nature of hazards, and in providing for the dissemination of information to affected parties. It does not necessarily follow, however, that the

---

[9]Unions would be expected to produce more efficient information flows because they represent many workers and can take advantage of economies of scale in the collection, interpretation, and dissemination of risk information. Available evidence suggests that the preponderance of wage premiums for risk have been derived from unionized workers. See W. Kip Viscusi, *Risk by Choice: Regulating Health and Safety in the Workplace* (Cambridge, MA: Harvard University Press, 1983): 55.

government should be responsible for determining the level of safety in the workplace once this information is available and the ethical boundaries are determined.

Our analysis suggesting that the market will not provide an efficient level of information on occupational risk is consistent with recent activity in state legislatures. As of 1982, New York, California, Michigan, and five other states had already enacted "Right to Know" laws, and similar measures were pending in about 20 state legislatures.[10] These laws require businesses to disclose to their employees and to the public any potential health hazards associated with toxic substances used on the job. Generally employers are required to (1) label toxic substance containers, (2) inventory all toxic substances used in the workplace, and (3) provide adequate training on the handling of these substances to all affected employees.

Product Safety

Exposure to a hazardous or potentially hazardous substance can also occur as a result of using a product, as when eating food containing chemical additives or when using pesticides. Does the market efficiently supply safe products?

One view holds that the market pressures on both parties are sufficient to yield an efficient level of safety. Safer products are generally more expensive to produce and carry a higher price tag. If consumers feel that the additional safety justifies the cost, they will purchase the safer product. Otherwise they won't. Producers supplying excessively risky products will find their market drying up because consumers will switch to competing brands that are more expensive, but safer. Similarly, producers selling excessively safe products (meaning they eliminate, at great cost, risks consumers are perfectly willing to take in return for a lower purchase price) find their markets drying up as well. Consumers will choose the cheaper, riskier product.

Economic logic suggests that the market will not (and should not) yield a uniform level of safety for all products. Different consumers will have different degrees of risk aversion. Although some consumers might purchase riskier, but cheaper, products, others might prefer safer, but more expensive, products.[11] Thus, it would be common to find products with various safety levels supplied simultaneously, reflecting and satisfying different consumer preferences for risk. Forcing all similar products to conform to a single level of risk would not be efficient. Uniform product safety is no more efficient than uniform occupational safety.

If this view of the market were completely accurate, government intervention to protect consumers would not be necessary to assure the efficient level of risk. By the force of their collective buying habits, consumers would protect themselves.

The problem with the market's ability to provide such self-regulation is the availability of information on product safety. The consumer generally acquires his or her information on a

---

[10]These laws are described in Frank Allen "Battle Building Over 'Right to Know' Laws Regarding Toxic Items Used by Workers," *The Wall Street Journal* (4 January 1983): 31. Significantly, proponents of these laws suggest that the targets are not the large chemical companies, which generally have excellent disclosure programs, but the smaller, largely nonunion plants.

[11]A classic example is provided by the manner in which Americans choose their automobiles. It is quite clear that many of the larger domestic cars are safer and more expensive than smaller, cheaper foreign cars. Some consumers are willing to pay for the safety and others are not.

product from personal experience. With toxic substances, the latency period may be so long as to preclude any effective market reaction. Even when some damage results, it is difficult for the consumer to associate it with a particular source. Although an examination of the relationships between purchasing patterns of a large number of consumers and their subsequent health might well reveal some suggestive correlations, it would be difficult for any individual consumer to deduce this correlation.

Although the government may need to assure that consumers receive adequate information on product risks, the need to dictate a prevailing level of safety is much less clear, particularly if the dictated level is uniformly applied. In situations where adequate information is available on the risks, consumers should have a substantial role in choosing the acceptable level of risk through their purchases.

Third Parties

The final case involves *third parties,* victims who have no contractual relationship to the source. When groundwater is contaminated by a neighboring waste treatment facility, by surreptitious dumping of toxic wastes, or by the improper applications of a pesticide, the victims would be third parties. In any of these situations, the affected party cannot bring any direct market pressure to bear on the source. Because these nonpoint sources are generally not controlled by the air and water regulations, the case for additional government intervention is strongest for third-party situations.

This does not necessarily imply that executive or legislative remedies are appropriate. The most appropriate response may well come from simply requiring better information on the risk or, as discussed in Chapter 3, from using the court system to impose liability.

California's Proposition 65, enacted by voter initiative on 4 November 1986, provides an example of the "better information" approach.[12] If a California business exposes anyone to a hazardous substance (other than through drinking water, which is handled separately), the business must provide a "clear and reasonable warning" unless the exposure poses "no significant risk." (Generally the courts have interpreted "no significant risk" as occurring when the business is complying with an applicable standard.) As a result, signs have begun appearing in such diverse places as bars (warning about alcohol) and gas stations (warning about fumes). Here the emphasis is on educating consumers and allowing them to make the choice about the amount of risk they will accept when no applicable standard has been developed.

Liability law provides one judicial avenue for internalizing the external costs in third-party situations. If the court finds that damage occurred, that it was caused by a toxic substance, and that a particular source was responsible for the presence of the substance, the source can be forced to compensate the victim for the damages caused. Unlike regulations that are uniformly (and hence, inefficiently) applied, a court decision can be tailored to the exact circumstances involved in the suit. Furthermore, the impact of any particular liability assignment can go well beyond the parties to that case. A decision for the plaintiff can remind other sources that they should take the efficient level of precaution now to avoid paying future damages.

---

[12]David Roe, "Barking up the Right Tree: Recent Progress in Focusing the Toxics Issue" *Columbia Journal of Environmental Law* 13, No. 2 (1988): 277–80.[13]For a

EXAMPLE 18.2

Judicial Remedies in Toxic-Substance Control: The Kepone Case

Kepone is a highly toxic substance used in the manufacture of pesticides. Kepone was produced at Hopewell, Virginia, by Life Science Products Company, a company started by former employees of Allied Chemical Corporation. The kepone produced by Life Science was sold to Allied Chemical.

Conditions at the plant and spills into the James River resulted in high contamination levels, which affected workers and people eating fish taken from the river. Allied Chemical Corporation was indicted by a grand jury on criminal charges during May 1976 and was subsequently sued by various injured parties. Eventually, it paid more than $20 million in compensation, penalties, and legal fees.

As a result of the suit, Allied and a number of other companies have begun to dramatically increase expenditures on prevention. In 1977 Allied hired Arthur D. Little, a consulting firm, to develop a broad program to anticipate and prevent further accidents. By 1981 Allied had over 400 employees concerned with environmental control.

The staff has discovered that pollution control sometimes yields unexpected benefits. In the past, Allied treated its waste, including calcium chloride, from its Baton Rouge plant and discharged it into the river. New regulations from the EPA would have raised the costs of treating the waste. Allied decided to look for a market for the calcium chloride and found one, turning a liability into an asset.

The kepone suit changed this corporation's behavior as well as the behavior of other chemical companies. They have found that anticipating can be much less costly than reacting.

Source: This example is based upon Georgette Jasen, "Like Other New-Breed Environmental Managers, Hillman of Allied Isn't Merely a Trouble Shooter," *The Wall Street Journal* (30 July 1981): 50.

In principle, liability law can force sources, including nonpoint sources, to choose efficient levels of precaution. Unlike regulation, liability law can provide compensation to the victims. How well it functions in practice remains to be seen in the rest of the chapter. Example 18.2 shows how a judicial response to one spill has transformed the way one company handles its environmental responsibilities.

CURRENT POLICY

Common Law

The common-law system is an extremely complicated approach to controlling risks. When a victim seeks recourse through the court system, a number of legal grounds can be used to pursue a claim. Not all of these may be available to every plaintiff (the person initiating the suit), because the appropriate doctrine depends partially on the legal tradition in the jurisdiction where the suit is filed. Not all jurisdictions allow a plaintiff to file on all grounds. Two of the more common legal grounds are negligence and strict liability.

Negligence.   Probably the most common legal theory used by plaintiffs to pursue claims is negligence. This body of law suggests that the defendant (the party allegedly responsible for the contamination) owes a duty to the plaintiff (the affected party) to exercise due care. If that duty has been breached, the defendant is found negligent and is forced to compensate the victim for damages caused. If the defendant is found to have exercised due care and to have performed that duty to the plaintiff, no liability is assessed. Under negligence law, the victim bears the liability unless it can be proven that the defendant was negligent.

The test conventionally applied by the courts in deciding whether or not the defendant has exercised due care, the *Learned Hand Formula,* is fundamentally an economic one. Named after the judge (*yes,* Learned Hand!) who initially formulated it, this test suggests that the defendant is guilty of negligence if the loss caused by the contamination, multiplied by the probability of contamination, exceeds the cost of preventing the contamination.[13] When correctly applied, this is simply a version of the expected-net-benefit formula developed in Chapter 4.[14] The maximization of expected net benefits is efficient as long as society is risk-neutral. Therefore, the common-law approach embodied in negligence law in principle is compatible with efficiency.

Sometimes the plaintiff can prove negligence on the part of the defendant by showing that the defendant violated a statute. In many states, any related statutory violation is taken as sufficient proof of negligence.

Strict Liability.   Strict liability can be used by plaintiffs in some states and in some circumstances. Under this doctrine the plaintiff does not have to prove negligence. As long as the activity causes damage, the defendant is declared liable even if the activity is completely legal and complies with all relevant laws.

Strict liability is usually applied in circumstances where the activity in question is inherently hazardous. Because the disposal of toxic substances is frequently considered such an activity, states are increasingly allowing toxic substance suits to be brought under this doctrine. In contrast to negligence, this strict liability transfers liability for damages to the source whether or not the source has exercised much care.

Strict liability can also be compatible with efficiency.[15] The agent dealing with toxic wastes must balance the costs of taking precautions with the likelihood of, and expected costs of, lawsuits. In cases where the precautionary expenditures are particularly high and the damages low, only limited precaution is likely to be taken. However, for truly dangerous substances it is advantageous to take extraordinary precautions and avoid large damages.

---

[13]For a detailed discussion of this formula, see Richard A. Posner, "A Theory of Negligence," *Journal of Legal Studies* 1 (1972): 29–96.

[14]For a description of necessary conditions for the formula to be applied, see J. P. Brown, "Toward an Economic Theory of Liability," *Journal of Legal Studies* 2 (June 1973): 323–39.

[15]One well-known case where strict liability will not be efficient is when the victims can influence the likelihood of contamination and the magnitude of the damage caused. With full compensation the victim's incentive to take precautions is undermined. In most toxic substance cases the role of the victim is minimal, so this potential source of inefficiency is not important.

Criminal Law

Strict liability and negligence are civil law doctrines, applied when one private party sues another. Increasingly in environmental policy, the civil law approach is being complemented by the use of criminal law in which the government serves as prosecutor, presumably acting as an agent of the people. The Kepone Case, described in Example 18.2, involved both civil and criminal law.

Criminal law affords regulators a menu of remedies that differ from those available from civil law. Financial penalties imposed under criminal law cannot be covered by insurance as civil penalties can. Jail sentences may be handed out to those found breaking the law. Corporate executives, for example, could spend up to five years in jail for particularly onerous violations of the law. Fines could also be levied against guilty parties.

Several important aspects other than remedies also differentiate the civil and criminal judicial approaches to pollution control. Criminal charges can be brought against only those charged with breaking one or more specific laws, whereas civil suits can be brought against those causing damage, whether or not a law has been violated. The burden of proof is higher in a criminal trial. To convict a person, the state must prove the defendant is guilty "beyond a reasonable doubt," whereas in civil trials, the decision is based merely upon the "preponderance of evidence." The presumption of innocence, an important part of criminal trials, has no counterpart in civil trials. Civil trials create no presumption in favor of either party.

The final major difference between civil liability law and criminal law is that *civil liability law compensates victims directly whereas criminal law does not.* Criminal law focuses on punishing the perpetrator rather than on compensating the victim.[16] Though the severity of punishment can be tailored to the amount of damage caused, the correspondence between the length of a jail sentence and the damage caused is much less indirect than forcing the defendant to pay exact monetary damages. By breaking the link between the monetary damage caused and the punishment received—the cornerstone of liability law—criminal law would be less likely than civil law to result in efficient resolutions of toxic chemical contamination problems.[17] Efficiency could result, but it would be more of a coincidence than an inherent characteristic of the process.

Statutory Law

These civil and criminal common-law remedies have been accompanied by a host of legislative remedies. The statutes have evolved over time in response to particular toxic substance problems. Each time a new problem surfaced and people were able to get legislators aroused, a new law was passed to deal with it. The result is a collage of laws on the books, each with its own unique focus. We shall cover only the main ones here.

---

[16]Criminal law remedies forcing restitution do compensate the victim, but they are the exception rather than the rule. With restitution the guilty party is forced to pay a stipulated amount of money to the victim as part of the punishment.

[17]This does not imply, however, that criminal law has no efficient role to play in enforcement. For example, falsifying official reports to the EPA is appropriately a criminal offense. Without accurate reports the entire enforcement function could be undermined. However, it would be difficult to determine the economic value of the damage caused by falsified reports, a prerequisite for assessing a financial civil penalty.

Federal Food, Drug, and Cosmetic Act.   The first concerns with toxic substances arose with *food additives* because these are ingested and potentially pose a serious and immediate threat to health. Food and drug additives are regulated under the Federal Food, Drug, and Cosmetic Act of 1938, as amended in 1958. The organization administering this act is the Food and Drug Administration (FDA).

The 1938 Act contained a general safety provision authorizing the FDA to prohibit the sale of any food that "contains any poisonous or deleterious substance which may render it injurious to health." This provision was complemented in 1958 by a provision known as the Delaney Clause after its legislative sponsor, which states that no additive should be deemed safe if it is found to induce cancer in humans or animals. Coupled with the first provision, this addition prohibits any food additive determined by the FDA to be a carcinogen in any dosage.

Manufacturers wishing to introduce new food additives or drugs must demonstrate the safety of their products through premarket testing. For cosmetics no premarket testing is required. For the FDA to take any action on cosmetics, it must bear the burden of proof to demonstrate the product is unsafe. The burden is on the manufacturer to prove the safety of food additives and drugs.

Occupational Safety and Health Act.   This 1970 act created the Occupational Safety and Health Administration (OSHA) and charged the agency with the regulatory responsibility for protecting workers from hazards in the workplace. The Act also created the National Institute for Occupational Safety and Health (NIOSH), which, among other responsibilities, must make recommendations for the OSHA regulatory standards.

In 1974, OSHA promulgated the first regulation establishing levels of pollutants that would be acceptable in the workplace atmosphere. The statute required the standards to be established at a level sufficiently stringent that no employee would suffer material impairment of health, even if that employee were exposed to the substance on a regular basis throughout his or her working life. In addition, occupational standards requiring special precautions and/or protective devices have been adopted or proposed for a number of workplace contaminants.

Carcinogens are handled more severely. Once any substance is confirmed as a carcinogen, ambient workplace standards are set, rapidly followed by the imposition of special handling requirements, protective devices, and minimum contact regulations.

The approach taken by OSHA was to specify, often in excruciating detail, acceptable contaminant levels as well as the approaches to be taken by employers to ensure the attainment of those contaminant levels.[18] In response to adverse public opinion about silly regulations, in 1978 OSHA revoked 928 previously promulgated regulations as unnecessary.

Federal Environmental Pesticide Control Act.   This 1972 act amended the Federal Insecticide, Fungicide, and Rodenticide Act. (Congress has a flair for titles!) The thrust of the legislation is to provide for the registration of all pesticides, the certification of individuals applying these pesticides, and the premarket testing of all new pesticides.

All pesticide registrations automatically expire every five years. To secure a new registration, the manufacturer must prove that the benefits derived from that pesticide will outweigh

---

[18]The humor in the situation was nicely illustrated by an ad for a political candidate opposed to OSHA. A cowboy is pictured riding off to the prairie. On the back of his horse is strapped a plastic toilet required by an OSHA regulation setting the maximum distance any employee could be from a comfort station.

its social costs. When the evidence permits, the EPA has the power to prohibit the sale of a pesticide or to restrict its use to specific applications. The EPA has used this power to dramatically decrease the use of a number of pesticides, with DDT being the earliest and most publicized example.

Certification procedures for individuals applying the pesticides represent a recognition that the danger posed depends to a large extent on how the substances are applied. With this procedure the EPA can ensure proper training for commercial applicators, and by threatening the withdrawal of certification (and the livelihood of the applicators), the EPA can influence their behavior.

Resource Conservation and Recovery Act.   To counteract the unsafe dumping of toxic wastes, Congress passed Subtitle C of the Resource Conservation and Recovery Act of 1976. This act imposes standards for handling, shipping, and disposing of toxic wastes.

The regulations implementing this act define hazardous waste and establish a cradle-to-grave management system, including standards for generators of hazardous wastes, standards for transporters, and standards and permit requirements for owners and operators of facilities that treat, store, or dispose of hazardous wastes.

The centerpiece of this rather large regulatory system is a manifest system for keeping track of the fate of the substances from their creation to their disposal. Waste generators are required to prepare a manifest for all controlled substances. If the substance is on the EPA list, it must be properly packaged and labeled, and must be delivered only to a permitted waste disposal site. Through this recording system, the EPA hopes to monitor all hazardous substances and detect any surreptitious dumping. Failure to comply with the act is punishable by civil penalties and, in certain cases, by fines and imprisonment.

In 1984 this act was amended by the Hazardous and Solid Waste Amendments of 1984. The 1984 amendments contain three major categories of changes: (1) They expanded the amount of waste covered by the regulations; (2) they limited, or in some cases, banned the use of land disposal for certain kinds of waste; and (3) they brought under regulation some activities not previously controlled, such as underground storage tanks for certain chemicals.

Toxic Substances Control Act.   This 1976 act was passed as a complement to the Resource Conservation and Recovery Act. Whereas the Resource Conservation and Recovery Act was designed to ensure safe handling and disposal of existing substances, the Toxic Substances Control Act was designed to provide a firmer basis for deciding which of the chemical substances not controlled by the existing acts should be allowed to be commercially produced.

This act requires the EPA to inventory the approximately 55,000 chemical substances in commerce, to require premanufacture notice to the EPA of all new chemical substances, and to enforce record-keeping, testing, and reporting requirements so that the EPA can assess and regulate the relative risks of chemicals. At least 90 days before manufacturing or importing a new chemical, a firm must submit test results or other information to the EPA showing that the chemical will not present "an unreasonable risk" to human health or the environment.

On the basis of the information in the premanufacture notification, the EPA may limit the manufacture, use, or disposal of the substance. The act is significant in that it represents one of the few instances where the burden of proof is on the manufacturer to prove that the product should be marketed, rather than forcing the EPA to show why it should not be marketed.

Comprehensive Environmental Response, Compensation, and Liability Act.   Known popularly as the "Superfund Act," the Comprehensive Environmental Response, Compensation, and Liability Act of 1980 created a $1.6 billion fund to be used over a five-year period to clean up existing toxic waste sites. The revenue was derived mainly from taxes on chemical industries. The Act offers compensation for the loss or destruction of natural resources controlled by the state or federal government, but it does not provide any compensation for injured individuals. A $9 billion reauthorization bill passed in 1986 significantly increased the amount of money dedicated to the cleanup of these sites.

As amended, this Act authorized federal and state government to respond quickly to incidents such as occurred in Times Beach, Missouri. Times Beach, a town of 2800 residents located about 30 miles southwest of St. Louis, had been contaminated by dioxin. Dioxin is a waste by-product created during the production of certain chemicals. One such chemical is Agent Orange, the defoliant used during the Vietnam War. The contamination occurred when a state oil hauler bought about 55 pounds of dioxin in 1971 from a now defunct manufacturer, mixed it with oil, and under contract with the local government, spread it on unpaved roads as a dust control measure. On 23 December, 1982, after soil tests revealed dangerous levels of dioxin, the Centers for Disease Control recommended total evacuation of the town.

By 22 February 1983, the federal government had authorized a transfer of some $33 million from the Superfund to cover the cost of buying out all businesses and residents and relocating them. For its part, the State of Missouri has agreed to pay ten percent of the cost—$3.3 million—into the Superfund, and fund representatives are free to attempt to recover damages from the responsible parties. By June 1983, all but 40 families had been relocated. The town is now totally vacant, an eerie reminder of the tragically high human cost that can result from the improper disposal of hazardous wastes.

The existence of the Superfund allows the governments involved to move rapidly. They are not forced to wait until the outcome of court suits against those responsible to raise the money or to face the uncertainty associated with whether the suits would ultimately be successful.

This formidable list of statutory and common-law remedies embodies a variety of approaches to the resolution of toxic substance problems. The question is whether or not these approaches are efficient or cost effective.

AN ASSESSMENT OF THE LEGAL REMEDIES

The Common Law

Judicial-Legislative Complementarity.   Common law provides a potentially useful complement to statutory law for occupational, consumer product, and third-party hazards. For all three types of toxic-substance problems, the market may create pressures preventing the flow of information about the dangers of these substances. Those employers or producers in the best position to transmit the information to parties who can best assess the risk (employees, consumers, or third parties) are not always willing to seek or relay the information. In a market where damages are not placed on the source, sources have little incentive to uncover potential problems. Uncovering health problems will only lower sales or increase wages.

Legislative remedies such as the "Right to Know" laws described earlier are not sufficient if there is too little information to be shared. Because court actions that subject sources to liability for their damages make health damage information useful to the firm, they create incentives to keep good records and to analyze the results. The failure to accurately perceive a health risk could cause an enormous financial burden on the company.[19] It is cheaper to anticipate and prevent damages before the cost becomes prohibitive.

Even premarket testing of consumer products by the government is not an adequate substitute for the judicial approach. Government has neither the staff nor the financial resources to serve as the sole source of health damage information. Some substances inevitably slip through the safety net provided by government testing. It is essential that the prime responsibility for testing fall on the producer, with the costs being passed on to the consumer as part of the price of the product. The government would then bear the responsibility for ensuring the validity of the testing process.

Judicial remedies are especially important in handling third-party contamination. Without liability, the incentive to exercise due care by the manufacturers, transporters, users, and disposers of these substances would be inefficiently low. The use of the court system to control the third-party problem was enhanced by the passage of the Resource Conservation and Recovery Act of 1976.

Because of the manifest system created by this act, good information is available to the courts on the types and quantities of substances that are sold or transported. The Act also assists in tracing responsibility so that the sources can be identified and confronted with the evidence. This record-keeping system is immensely costly, however, and may turn out, in the glare of hindsight, to be excessively ambitious. Furthermore, hazardous wastes that do not leave the facility where they were created comprise an overwhelming percentage of the total hazardous wastes, but these are not covered by the manifest system.[20] With experience, the system may evolve toward a harmonious balance between the gains from this monitoring system and the administrative burden it imposes.

Two additional features of judicial remedies make them a useful complement to legislative remedies. First, liability law usually provides the only way the victim of a toxic-substance accident can get compensated.[21] Even the "Superfund" bill does not compensate individuals for health-related damages. It only compensates for property damage.

The second attractive feature of judicial remedies is the degree to which they can be tailored to individual circumstances. We have seen in the chapters on air and water pollution the strong tendency for legislative remedies to be applied uniformly. We have also seen that uniform remedies are rarely efficient and that often the resulting loss of net benefit is substantial. When the courts impose the damage remedies correctly, an efficient allocation of precaution would automatically be tailored to the specific circumstances involved.

---

[19]During 1982, for example, the Manville Corporation faced up to $5 billion in lawsuits resulting from worker exposure to asbestos. During that same year, Monsanto was fighting a $4.7 billion class action suit for alleged prolonged worker exposure to a hazardous substance in a West Virginia plant.

[20]Roger C. Dower, "Hazardous Waste" in Public Policies for Environmental Protection, Paul R. Portney, ed. (Washington, DC: Resources for the Future, 1990): 163.

[21]Normally workers' compensation insurance provides for claims arising from proven occupational hazards. However, a study conducted by the Labor Department during 1981 found that of the two million Americans who were partially or severely disabled as a result of an occupational disease, only 5 percent received workers' compensation. Many states have disallowed claims against workers' compensation for maladies that can take 30 years to show up.

Limitations of Judicial Remedies.   The common law is far from a panacea, however. It does not cope with the largest or most complex problems, such as the emission of hazardous substances by large numbers of sources affecting large numbers of people. This was illustrated nicely in *Roger J. Diamond* v *General Motors,* a California case in which the judge ruled that the court system was not the appropriate forum to resolve the Los Angeles problem of air pollution.[22] The problem was so complex and involved so many parties that it had to be resolved by the legislature.[23] Court remedies are administratively expensive and can be used efficiently only when they are used sparingly.

The common law also currently places a large, difficult-to-meet burden of proof on the plaintiff. Generally, a plaintiff must be able to (1) identify the harmful substances, (2) demonstrate that the defendant was the source of this substance, and (3) prove that identifiable damages occurred as a result of the presence of that substance. The last two steps may be difficult to establish in practice.

Suppose for example that a well owner who discovered a harmful substance in the well simultaneously experienced a series of illnesses for which he or she had no medical history. The owner might have discovered a source emitting the same chemical nearby, but that is not enough evidence to win a lawsuit. The court would have to be convinced not only that the substance traveled from the source to the well, but also that any documented illnesses were caused by the substance and not by unrelated causes. The frequent failure to establish these links can undermine the incentive properties of common law.[24]

Japan's court system has reacted to this problem by shifting the burden of proof from the injured plaintiff to the industry. The plaintiffs in those cases have to establish the nature and cause of their diseases and the mechanism by which they were affected. To establish the link to the defendant, they are able to introduce a high statistical correlation between the defendant's activity and the incidence of the disease. Once these elements have been established, a rebuttable presumption is created that shifts the burden of proof to the defendant. The defendant is then liable unless it can be proven that its activities are not responsible for the damage.

If the American court system were to move in this direction, it would represent a radical departure from current practice.[25] The statistical approach lacks the rigor usually required by American courts because establishing a positive correlation between activity levels and the incidence of the disease does not establish causation. Other factors correlated with the activities of the defendant may be responsible.

The Japanese system does effectively raise the question of who should bear the burden of proof. If the source were to bear it, nuisance suits could arise. Nuisance suits are filed mainly

---

[22]97 Cal. Report. 639.

[23]Even when the number of sources is small, the courts can be overwhelmed if the number of plaintiffs is large. It has been estimated that asbestos suits against the Manville Corporation were being filed at the rate of 500 per month during 1982. (See "Manville May Drive Congress to Action," *Business Week* (13 September 1982, p. 35.)

[24]If it becomes too easy to prove these links, the defendant will be forced to pay liability even when the substance produced by the defendant did not cause the plaintiff's problem. In this case, efficiency would be lost because too much precaution would be taken.

[25]Some movement in this direction is now evident. A plaintiff with asbestosis, for example, may be required to prove only that the disease is more probably than not caused by any of several asbestos manufacturers. Having met this burden of proof, the plaintiff shifts the burden to the individual manufacturer to prove, it if can, that it did not cause the plaintiff's disease. See *Abel* v *Eli Lilly & Co.,* 343 N.W. 2d 164 (1984).

to harass defendants by making them spend a lot of money on defense. Such suits are without merit. As we have seen, however, if the plaintiff bears the burden of proof, the burden is particularly difficult, because the defendant generally knows so much more about the contaminating activities.

The Japanese approach gets around this problem by placing a sequential burden of proof on each party. The plaintiff is required to bear a burden sufficiently large that nuisance cases are eliminated. On the other hand, for serious cases where the plaintiff has been able to bear this initial burden of proof, the defendant (who presumably is the most knowledgeable about the subject) must then gather the information at his or her disposal.

We can quibble about whether the initial burden on the plaintiff is too low or too high under the Japanese system, but with its inherent shared responsibility, this system reduces the likelihood of nuisance suits while providing incentive for the most knowledgeable party to supply the necessary information to reach a decision.

One final concern about judicial remedies should be noted. Sometimes the source of the toxic substance problem is "judgment-proof" in the sense that it has no assets (or too few assets) to pay the damages. The marginal cost of additional damages to the source is zero, and profit-maximizing behavior leads the source to exercise too little precaution.

This problem is more serious for toxic substances than for conventional pollutants because the latency of the effects means the suits must be filed much later than other kinds of suits. By this time, the source may have gone out of business or have been transformed into a different corporate entity somewhat immune from past transgressions.

Joint and Several Liability Doctrine.   In interpreting the "Superfund" Act, the courts have allowed the government to sue "potentially responsible parties" (i.e., disposal site owners and operators, waste generators and transporters) for damages and site recovery costs under the joint and several liability doctrine.[26] Reduced to its essence, the joint and several liability doctrine makes each successfully sued defendant potentially liable for an amount up to the entire damage caused, regardless of the magnitude of its individual contribution. Because of this doctrine, the government can elect to sue only a few of the wealthiest responsible parties, thereby avoiding the higher litigation costs associated with hauling everyone into court. In one case the EPA elected to sue only 10 percent of the responsible parties, letting the others off the hook.

Successfully sued defendants retain the right of contribution, which allows parties that have made payments (either by settling out of court or in response to a court decision) to seek reimbursement from other potentially responsible parties (PRPs) that have not. This right of contribution can be exercised by those settling out of court as well as those assessed damages following a trial. Once a party signs a consent decree of either type, however, they cannot be sued for contribution by other parties.

The government enforces this act by seeking to encourage PRPs to initiate cleaning up the site on their own but is prepared to initiate the investigation and even to clean up identified hazardous waste sites on its own, if necessary, financing the effort from the several-billion-dollar Hazardous Substance Response Trust Fund created by the Act. It then seeks reimbursement from parties who are potentially responsible for the conditions at each particular

---

[26]Hooker Chemical, for example, was found liable for response costs at the Love Canal under the joint and several liability doctrine. See *United States* v *Hooker Chemical and Plastics Corporation* 18 ELR 20580.

site. The potentially responsible parties are liable for any costs of restoring the site to a safe status as well as "damages for injury to, destruction of, or loss of natural resources, including the reasonable costs of assessing such injury, destruction, or loss resulting from such a release."[27]

Any liable party who "fails without sufficient cause to properly provide removal or remedial action," may be assessed punitive damages of "three times the amount of any costs incurred by the Fund as a result of such failure to take proper action."[28]

Designed primarily as a means of raising private funds to clean up hazardous waste sites, joint and several liability has not exactly worked as smoothly as expected, even as a means of collecting revenue. Between 1986 and the end of 1988, the EPA recovered only $166 million from private parties, or roughly 7 percent of the $2.4 billion spent on Superfund cleanups during the same period.[29] Even when the suits are successful, the litigation expenses are extremely high. In one study the Rand Institute for Civil Justice in Santa Monica, California, found that nearly 90 percent of the money spent by insurers on Superfund claims went for legal and related costs rather than site cleanup.[30]

Joint and several liability has also created some perverse incentives.[31] Under the joint and several liability doctrine, the expected liability a potentially responsible party faces is very uncertain: anywhere from 0 to 100 percent of the cleanup costs regardless of the degree of precaution undertaken. Because larger firms are usually targeted by the EPA for Superfund suits, they have an incentive to take more than the efficient amount of precaution.[32] Meanwhile, smaller firms, who may expect to get off the hook because the expense of suing them exceeds the potential recovery, have little or no incentive to take appropriate precautions.

The uncertainty associated with expected damage payments has also wreaked havoc with the insurance market. Insurance companies have no idea how to set premiums, and many have left the market for environmental risks entirely. Without insurance, the probability of bankruptcy increases. Bankrupt firms contribute very little to the cleanup.

The Statutory Law

A commendable virtue of common law is that remedies can be tailored to the unique circumstances the parties find themselves in. But common law remedies are also expensive to impose, and they are ill-suited to solving widespread problems affecting large numbers of people. Thus, statutory law has a complementary role to play as well.

---

[27]42 U. S. C. §9607c.

[28]42 U. S. C. §9607c3.

[29]Roger C. Dower, "Hazardous Waste" in *Public Policies for Environmental Protection*, Paul R. Portney, ed. (Washington, DC: Resources for the Future, 1990): 185.

[30]Reported in Jonathan M. Moses, "Insurer Payouts Over Superfund Flow to Lawyers," *The Wall Street Journal* (24 April 1992):B1, B9.

[31]A formal analysis of these incentives can be found in T. H. Tietenberg, "Indivisible Toxic Torts: The Economics of Joint and Several Liability," *Land Economics* 65, No. 4 (November 1989):305–19.

[32]Cleanup and litigation costs have become so high for large companies that some of the larger chemical companies have begun voluntarily cleaning up abandoned sites. See "Environmental, Industry Groups Tackle Hazardous Waste Disposal Sites" *Chemecology* (July/August): 2.

EXAMPLE 18.3

Weighing the Risks: Saccharin

Saccharin is an artificial sweetener that has been used since the early part of the twentieth century. By the 1970s, it had become the staple of the diet food industry, particularly in soft drinks.

In the late 1960s a researcher at the University of Wisconsin reported that combinations of cholesterol and saccharin injected in the urinary bladders of mice resulted in a high incidence of bladder cancer. A special research group of the National Academy of Sciences convened to investigate the safety of saccharin and a year later declared it safe.

In January 1972, however, the FDA removed saccharin from its list of additives "generally recognized as safe." This action forced food processors to list saccharin on the ingredient label and to conform to maximum recommended dosages. Following some additional Canadian tests showing a link between bladder cancer and saccharin, in 1977 the FDA proposed a ban on the use of saccharin in all foods and beverages, citing the Delaney Clause.

Because saccharin was the only approved artificial sweetener at that time, reaction was swift and vehement. Diabetics attacked the move as denying them access to any sweetener. Groups concerned with weight gain charged that this decision increased the risk of heart attacks. In April 1977 the FDA modified its proposed ban to the extent of allowing saccharin to be labeled as an over-the-counter drug (thus escaping the Delaney Clause) and sold in tablets, powder, or liquid form. It still proposed to ban saccharin from commercially prepared foods and beverages.

Since then a number of studies have appeared, some upholding the link to cancer, others disputing it. Congress reacted by passing a series of moratoriums on the banning of saccharin, thus preventing the Delaney Clause from having its intended effect.

These actions strongly suggest that zero risk is usually not an appropriate policy goal. The objective should be to balance the risks. Provisions (such as the Delaney Clause) that prevent the balancing process are simply bad policy.

Balancing the Costs.   As currently structured, statutory law does not efficiently fulfill its potential as a complement to the common law due to the failure of current law to balance compliance costs with the damages being protected against.

The Delaney Clause, the most flagrant example, precludes any balancing of costs whatsoever in food additives. A substance that has been known to be carcinogenic in any dose cannot be used as a food additive even if the risk is counterbalanced by a considerable compensating benefit.[33] As Example 18.3 illustrates, a rule this stringent can lead to considerable political mischief as attempts are made to circumvent it.

The Delaney Clause is not the only culprit; other laws also fail to balance costs. The Resource Conservation and Recovery Act requires the standards imposed on waste generators, transporters, and disposal site operators to be high enough to protect human health and the environment. No mention is made of costs.

---

[33]It is interesting to note that a number of common foods contain natural substances that in large enough doses are carcinogenic. Radishes, for example, could probably not be licensed as a food additive because of the Delaney clause.

Even in less extreme cases, policymakers must face the question of how to balance costs. The Occupational Safety and Health Act, for example, requires standards that ensure "to the extent feasible that no employee will suffer material impairment of health or functional capacity " In changing the standard for the occupational exposure to benzene from 10 ppm to 1 ppm, the EPA had presented no data to show that even a 10 ppm standard causes leukemia. Rather, the EPA based its decision on a series of assumptions indicating that some leukemia might result from 10 ppm, so even fewer cases might result from 1 ppm.

In a case receiving a great deal of attention, the Supreme Court set aside the new benzene standard largely on the grounds that it was based on inadequate evidence.[34] In rendering their opinion the justices stated:

> "... the Secretary must make a finding that the workplaces in question are not safe. But "safe" is not the equivalent of "risk-free." A workplace can hardly be considered "unsafe" unless it threatens the workers with a significant risk of harm. [100 S. Ct. 2847]

In a concurring opinion that did not bind future decisions because it did not have sufficient support among the remaining justices, Justice Powell went even further:

> "... the statute also requires the agency to determine that the economic effects of its standard bear a reasonable relationship to the expected benefits. [100 S. Ct. 2848]

It seems clear that the notion of a risk-free environment has been repudiated by the high court, as it should have been. But what is meant by an *acceptable risk?* Efficiency clearly dictates that an acceptable risk is one that maximizes the net benefit. Thus the efficiency criterion would support Justice Powell in his approach to the benzene standard.

It is important to allay a possible source of confusion. The fact that it is difficult to set a precise standard using benefit/cost analysis because of the imprecision of the underlying data does not imply that some balancing of costs and benefits cannot, or should not, take place. It can and it should. Although benefit/cost analysis may not be sufficiently precise and reliable to suggest, for example, that a standard of 8 ppm is efficient, it usually is reliable enough to indicate clearly that 1 ppm and 15 ppm are inefficient. By failing to consider compliance cost in defining acceptable risk, statutes are probably attempting more and achieving less than we might hope for.

Degree and Form of Intervention.   The second criticism of the current statutory approach concerns both the degree of intervention and the form that intervention should take. The former issue relates to how deeply the government controls go; the latter relates to the manner in which the regulations work.

The analysis in the second section of this chapter suggested that consumer products and labor markets require less government intervention than third-party cases. The main problem in those two areas was seen as the lack of sufficient information to allow producers, consumers, employees, and employers to make informed choices. With the Delaney Clause as an obvious exception, most consumer-product-safety statutes deal mainly with research and labeling. They are broadly consistent with the results of our analysis.

---

[34]*Industrial Union Department, AFL-CIO v American Petroleum Institute, et al.,* 100 S. Ct. 2844 (1980).

This is not the case with occupational exposure, however. Government regulations have had a major and not always beneficial effect on the workplace. By covering such a large number of potential problems, OSHA has spread itself too thin and has had too little impact on problems that really count. Selective intervention, targeted at those areas where OSHA efforts could really make a difference, would get more results.

The form the OSHA regulations have taken also causes inflexibility. Not content merely to specify exposure limits, the regulations also specify the exact precautions to be taken. The contrast between this approach and the marketable permit approach in air pollution is striking.

Under the bubble policy, the EPA specifies the emission limit but allows the source great flexibility in meeting that limit. By dictating the specific activities to be engaged in or to be avoided, OSHA regulations deny this kind of flexibility. In the face of rapid technological change, inflexibility can lead to inefficiency even if the specified activities were efficient when first required. Furthermore, having so many detailed regulations makes enforcement more difficult and probably less effective.

A serious flaw in the current approach to controlling hazardous wastes is in the insufficient emphasis placed on reducing the generation and recycling of these wastes. In order to provide additional revenue to fund the cleanup, for example, the 1980 Superfund bill imposed a tax on petroleum and chemical feedstocks. Because this tax is imposed on the front end of the production process and is not calibrated by toxicity, it does not provide the appropriate incentives to switch to less-hazardous substances or to recycle the wastes.

An alternative, which is widely regarded as a superior means of raising revenue, involves the imposition of variable unit taxes (called "waste-end" taxes) on waste generated or disposed of. Waste-end taxes would not only spur industry to switch to less-toxic substances and to reduce the quantity of these substances used, it would also encourage consumers to switch away from products using large amounts of hazardous materials in the production process because higher production costs would be translated into higher product prices. As of 1985, some 20 states had already adopted some form of waste-end taxation. Unfortunately, the Superfund Amendments and Reauthorization Act of 1986 chose to replenish the Superfund with broad-based taxes rather than taxes specifically designed to reduce the generation of toxic wastes.

Scale.   The size of the hazardous waste problem dwarfs the size of the EPA staff and budget assigned to control it. The Superfund process for cleaning up existing hazardous waste sites is a good case in point. By mid-1988 the EPA had placed 1,177 sites (out of total 19,000 sites considered) on the National Priorities List for permanent cleanup. The Office of Technology Assessment (a research arm of Congress) has estimated that 10,000 sites or more will ultimately be deemed dangerous enough to be placed on the list. All agree that it is not technologically and economically feasible to permanently clean up even 2000 sites over the next few decades—even with the replenishment of the Superfund voted by the U.S. Congress in 1986.

In any case the cost is likely to be extremely high. One study has estimated that some $750 million will be needed to clean up these sites over the next thirty years.[35]

---

[35]Milton Russell, E. William Colglazier, and Mary R. English, *Hazardous Waste Remediation: The Task Ahead* (Knoxville, TN: Waste Management Research and Education Institute at the University of Tennessee, 1991): iv.

The huge scale of this undertaking has important implications for both the bureaucracy and the citizens it serves. Priorities must be established and the most serious problems attacked first. It is a fact of life that an exclusive reliance on the bureaucracy to provide complete safety is infeasible. Citizens should not abdicate their own responsibilities after being lulled into a false sense of security by the mistaken impression that the bureaucracy can and should provide adequate protection.

The scale of the problem also suggests that prevention makes excellent economic sense. Spending resources now to prevent the problem can in the long run be cheaper than attempting to clean up the mess once it has been allowed to happen.

Assurance Bonds: An Innovative Proposal

The current control system must cope with a great deal of uncertainty about magnitude of future environmental costs associated with the disposal of hazardous waste. The costs associated with collecting funds from responsible parties through litigation are very high. Many potentially responsible parties declare bankruptcy when it is time to collect cleanup costs, thereby isolating themselves from their normal responsibility.

One proposed solution would require the posting of a dated assurance bond as a necessary condition for disposing of hazardous waste.[36] The amount of the required bond would be a function of the environmental authority's estimate of the costs of environmental repair or rehabilitation if the "worst case" scenario were to come true between the posting date and the refund date. In case any site ultimately required restoration as a result of a hazardous waste leak, the funds tied up in the bond could be used to finance the work. Any unused proceeds would be redeemable at specified dates if the environmental costs turned out to be lower than predicted by the worst case.

This kind of system would create incentives for precaution; lower actual environmental costs would trigger larger refunds. Every dollar of environmental damage prevented would be a dollar earned. Assurance bonds would also make sure that the money for cleanup was readily available as soon as needed and that no lengthy and costly legal process would be necessary to secure it.

SUMMARY

The potential for contamination of the environmental asset by toxic substances is one of the most complex environmental problems. Substances that could prove toxic number in the millions. Some 55,000 of these are in active use.

---

[36]Robert Costanza and Charles Perrings, "A Flexible Assurance Bonding System for Improved Environmental Management" *Ecological Economics* 2 (1990): 57–75. A similar proposal was advanced in Clifford S. Russell, "Economic Incentives in the Management of Hazardous Waste," *Columbia Journal of Environmental Law* 13, No. 2 (1988): 257–74.

The market provides considerable pressure toward resolving toxic-substance problems as they affect employees and consumers. With reliable information at their disposal, all parties have an incentive to reduce hazards to acceptable levels. However, this pressure is absent in cases involving third parties. Here the problem frequently takes the form of an external cost imposed on innocent bystanders.

The efficient role of government can range from assuring the provision of sufficient information (so that participants in the market can make informed choices) to setting exposure limits on hazardous substances. Unfortunately, the scientific basis for decision making is weak. Only limited information on the effects of these substances is available, and the cost of acquiring complete information is prohibitive. Therefore, priorities must be established and tests developed to screen substances so that efforts can be concentrated on those that seem most dangerous.

In contrast to air and water pollution, the toxic substance problem is one in which the courts may play a particularly important role. Although screening tests will probably never be foolproof, and therefore some substances may slip through, they do provide a reasonable means for setting priorities. Liability law not only creates a market pressure for more and better information on potential damages associated with chemical substances, it also provides some incentives for manufacturers of substances, the generators of waste, the transporters of waste, and those who dispose of it to take precautions. Judicial remedies also allow the level of precaution to vary with the occupational circumstances and provide a means of compensating victims.

Judicial remedies are not sufficient, however. They are expensive and ill-suited for dealing with problems affecting large numbers of people. The burden of proof under the current American system is difficult to surmount, though in Japan some radical new approaches have been developed to deal with this problem. The joint and several liability doctrine has created some perverse incentives and has wreaked havoc on the market for environmental insurance.

Though they are clearly a positive step, the statutory responses seem to have gone too far in regulating behavior. The exposure standards in many cases seem excessively stringent, having been set without balancing the costs involved. Furthermore, OSHA and the EPA have gone well beyond the setting of exposure limits by dictating specific activities that should be engaged in or avoided. The enforcement of these standards has proved difficult and has probably spread the available resources too thin.

Reinhold Niebuhr once said, "Democracy is finding proximate solutions to insoluble problems." That seems an apt description of the institutional response to the toxic substance problem. Our political institutions have created a staggering array of legislative and judicial responses to these problems that are neither efficient nor complete. They do, however, represent a positive first step in what must be an evolutionary process.

FURTHER READING

Crandall, Robert W., and Lester B. Lave. *The Scientific Basis of Health and Safety Regulation* (Washington, DC: The Brookings Institution, 1981). For each of five health and safety regulatory actions, this book juxtaposes the views of a scientist, an economist, and a regulator on the scientific basis for the regulation and the desirability of the resulting decision. Cases considered are passive restraints in automobiles, cotton dust, saccharin, waterborne carcinogens, and sulfur dioxide.

Dower, Roger C. "Hazardous Waste" in Paul R. Portney, ed., *Public Policies for Environmental Protection* (Washington, DC: Resources for the Future, 1990): 151–94. Examines policies related to the disposal of hazardous waste.

Graham, Jon D., Laura C. Green, and Marc J. Roberts. *In Search of Safety: Chemicals and Cancer Risk* (Cambridge, MA: Harvard University Press, 1988). A detailed examination of the attempts to regulate two suspected carcinogens, benzene and formaldehyde.

Lave, Lester B. *The Strategy of Social Regulation: Decision Frameworks for Policy* (Washington, DC: The Brookings Institution, 1981). An inquiry into the ways in which the scientific foundations of regulation could be improved. Contains chapters on food additives and health, safety, and environmental regulations.

Shapiro, Michael. "Toxic Substances Policy," *Public Policies for Environmental Protection* (Washington, DC: Resources for the Future, 1990): 195–242. A comprehensive analysis of the statutes and implementation procedures used to combat environmental risks posed by toxic substances.

Viscusi, W. Kip. *Risk By Choice: Regulating Health and Safety in the Workplace* (Cambridge, MA: Harvard University Press, 1983). Examines the proper role for regulation of occupational risks in the market context where these policies must operate.

ADDITIONAL REFERENCES

Anderson, Frederick R. "Natural Resource Damages, Superfund, and the Courts," *Boston College Environmental Affairs Law Review* 16 (Spring 1989): 405–57.

Costanza, Robert and Charles Perrings. "A Flexible Assurance Bonding System for Improved Environmental Management," *Ecological Economics* 2 (1990): 57–75.

Dechert, W. Davis, and James L. Smith. "Environmental Liability and Economic Incentives for Hazardous Waste Management," *Houston Law Review* 25 (1988): 935–42.

Doniger, David D. *The Law and Policy of Toxic Substance Control: A Case Study of Vinyl Chloride* (Baltimore, MD: Johns Hopkins University Press for Resources for the Future, 1978).

Grigalunas, Thomas A., and James J. Opaluch. "Assessing Liability for Damages Under CERCLA: A New Approach for Providing Incentives for Pollution Avoidance," *Natural Resource Journal* 28 (1988): 509–33.

Johnson, Gary V., and Thomas S. Ulen. "Designing Public Policy Toward Hazardous Wastes: The Role of Administrative Regulations and Legal Liability Rules," *American Journal of Agricultural Economics,* 68 (1986): 1266–71.

Kopp, Raymond J., and V. Kerry Smith. " Benefit Estimation Goes to Court: The Case of Natural Resource Damage Assessments," *Journal of Policy Analysis and Management* 8, No. 4 (Fall 1989): 593–612.

Lave, Lester B., ed. *Quantitative Risk Assessment in Regulation* (Washington, DC: The Brookings Institution, 1982).

Mendeloff, John M. *The Dilemma of Toxic Substance Regulation* (Cambridge, MA: MIT Press, 1988).

Nichols, Albert L. "The Importance of Exposure in Evaluating and Designing Environmental Regulations: A Case Study," *The American Economic Review* 72 (May 1982): 214–19.

Russell, Clifford S. "Economic Incentives in the Management of Hazardous Waste," *Columbia Journal of Environmental Law* 13, No. 2 (1988): 257–74.

Segerson, Kathleen. "Risk and Incentives in the Financing of Hazardous Waste Cleanup,"*Journal of Environmental Economics and Management* 16, No. 1 (January 1989): 1–8.

Sullivan, Arthur M. "Liability Rules for Toxics Cleanup" *Journal of Urban Economics* 20 (1986): 191–204.

Tietenberg, T. H. " Indivisible Toxic Torts: The Economics of Joint and Several Liability," *Land Economics* 65, No. 4 (November 1989): 305–19.

DISCUSSION QUESTIONS

1. How should the courts resolve the dilemma posed in Example 18.1? Why?

2. Over the last several decades in product liability law, there has been a movement in the court system from *caveat emptor* ("buyer beware") to *caveat venditor* ("seller beware"). The liability for using and consuming risky products has been shifted from buyers to sellers. Does this shift represent a movement toward or away from an efficient allocation of risk. Why?

3. Currently it is not illegal for the industrialized countries to ship their hazardous waste to the developing countries for disposal. Should it become illegal? Why or why not?

4. How should the public sector handle a toxic gas such as radon that occurs naturally and seeps into some houses through the basement or the water supply? Is this a case of an externality or not? Does the homeowner have the appropriate incentives to take an efficient level of precaution?

CHAPTER 19

Development, Poverty, and the Environment

If there is any period one would desire to be born in, is it not the age of revolution when the old and the new stand side by side and admit of being compared? When the energies of all men are searched by fear, and by hope? When the historic glories of the old can be compensated by the rich possibilities of the new era? This time, like all times, is a very good one, if we but know what to do with it.

RALPH WALDO EMERSON, *THE AMERICAN SCHOLAR* (1873)

INTRODUCTION

In previous chapters we invested a considerable amount of time and effort in investigating individual environmental and natural resource problems and the policy responses that have been, and could have been, taken to solve them. In general, solutions are possible, and our economic and political institutions, with some exceptions, seem to be muddling through.

Our next step must be a consideration of the global economic system and the scale of the challenge it will face in the twenty-first century. Perhaps the major challenge is finding a way to deal effectively with global poverty without jeopardizing the environment or degrading the resource base passed on to future generations.

Poverty has emerged as a significant cause of environmental problems. The worst recorded air pollution is not found, as might be expected, in the highly industrialized cities of the high-income countries, but rather in the major cities of lower-income countries. Deforestation is caused in part by the migration of landless peasants into the forests, seeking a plot of land to work. Soil erosion is caused, in part, when the poor are driven to farm highly erodible land to try to survive. Dealing effectively with these environmental problems and the human suffering that lies behind them will require raising living standards.

Traditionally, this has been accomplished through economic development.[1] One model for the development of the less-industrialized countries is the path for rapid economic growth followed by the industrialized countries. How appropriate a model is this?

The two visions in Chapter 1 suggest two different answers to this question. The *Limits to Growth* view holds that exponential economic growth on a global scale will continue unabated until the physical limits are reached. At that time the global economy will overshoot its resource base and collapse. In this view economic growth is the source of the problem, not the solution. The only rational policy is to exercise direct control over the growth process itself. No other course, including the collection of individual policies discussed in the preceding chapters, would avoid the collapse.

Kahn and his associates, however, envision an automatic transition to a steady-state economy where eventually economic growth would cease, but not until all future households were significantly better off than current households. Thus, they foresee the prospect for continued development that slowly declines to zero over time. Far from being detrimental in this view, economic growth provides the vehicle for improving the welfare of future generations. As Kahn sees it, to deny that growth would consign the members of poor third-world countries to perpetual poverty. Which view of the future is correct?

Examining the appropriateness of the traditional economic growth approach to development should start by understanding that approach and its success or lack of success as a means of eliminating poverty. We will begin by defining how economic growth takes place and how the growth process is affected by increasing resource scarcity and rising environmental costs. This understanding will then be used to characterize what changes in the growth process in the industrialized nations can be expected in the future.

The relationship between growth and development in the industrialized countries is then explored. Has growth increased the well-being of the average citizen in the developed countries? Or has the evident elevated consumption of material goods made possible by economic growth merely masked large offsetting problems that would cause an appropriately measured standard of living to go down, not up?

The fate of the average citizen, of course, does not always shed light on the fate of the poor. How have the poor fared in periods of rapid economic growth? Is John Kennedy's metaphor "A rising tide lifts all ships" apt, or does a rising tide leave more people treading water?

Although the historical experience in the industrialized countries is revealing, the transferability of this experience into a third-world context is by no means obvious. To what extent can economic growth provide an answer to the crushing problems of poverty that infect the Third World? What are the barriers to achieving increased standards of living for the poor in third-world countries in a finite world?

---

[1]Herman Daly's useful distinction between growth and development is employed here. Development refers to a qualitative increase in well-being, whereas growth refers to a physical expansion in physical output of goods and services. They are related but by no means synonymous concepts. It is conceptually possible to have growth without development and development without growth, but historically the two have been inextricably entwined. See Herman E. Daly and John B. Cobb, Jr., *For the Common Good* (Boston, MA: Beacon Press, 1989).

THE GROWTH PROCESS

Nature of the Process

How does economic growth occur? It occurs in two main ways: through increases in inputs such as capital, labor, energy, and other resources, and through increases in the productivity of those resources as a result of technological progress. The former source of growth involves increasingly greater outputs, given the state of the art in production, whereas the latter source involves improvements in the state of the art.

Increases in Inputs.   The amount of growth occurring from increases in inputs is governed by two important economic concepts: economies of scale and the law of diminishing returns. The term *economies of scale* refers to the amount of increase in output obtained when all inputs are increased in the same proportion. The *law of diminishing returns* governs the relationship between inputs and output when some inputs are increased and others are held fixed.

The law of diminishing returns governs what happens when some, but not all, of the inputs are increased. Suppose, for example, that all the inputs are held fixed except for capital, which increases. As constant and successive increments of capital are added to the other fixed resources, the law of diminishing returns implies that eventually a point will be reached where each increment of input will produce smaller and smaller increments of output.

Technological Progress.   The other major source of growth, technological progress, involves the implementation of better, less wasteful ways of doing things. With technological progress, growth can occur even in the absence of increases in inputs simply because the inputs available are used more effectively. For example, with a new production technique, less energy might be wasted or fewer resources used to make a particular product.

Potential Sources of Reduced Growth

Historically, increases in factor inputs and technological progress were both important sources of growth. This does not automatically mean that they will continue to provide growth at historic levels in the future, however. A number of reasons suggest caution in extrapolating historically valid arguments into the future.

Reduced Input Flows.   Not all input flows are continuing at historic levels. Population growth has slowed considerably in most countries, which causes the growth in the labor force to slow and possibly stop. The growth fed by increasing labor is diminishing and will continue to diminish in the future.

The cost of energy and of raw materials seems to be rising, even in real terms. Producers respond to higher relative prices by cutting back on the use of these inputs, which diminishes their contribution to the growth process.

Capital formation has played a pivotal role in the past and is likely to continue doing so.[2] As workers were given more sophisticated capital equipment to work with, their productivity increased.

Capital has broken down the barriers imposed by human limitations. With the advent of bulldozers, earth moving, once limited by the strength and endurance of workers, is limited no more. The size of the market, once limited by the time and effort required to transport commodities in a horse and buggy, expanded with the advent of the railroad, the truck, and the airplane. Limits on corporate controllability imposed by the size and competence of record-keeping staffs—as they attempted to stay on top of the information and paper flows— have fallen in the face of computers providing instant access to important information compiled in the most useful format.

Although capital is a reproducible asset, some indirect limits may diminish its role in the future. These include limitations on capital's substitutability for other factors, on the productivity of future investment, and on the incentive to invest.

The ability of capital to promote historical growth rates lies in part in its ability to substitute for those factor inputs which are experiencing limits. When substitution is easy, scarcity of particular inputs should not inhibit growth, but when substitution is difficult, scarcity imposes a drag on growth.

The first substitution possibility to be considered is between capital and labor. As population growth dwindles, the growth rate in the supply of labor diminishes as well. Historically, the economic growth rate has exceeded the growth rate of labor supply, as capital was continually substituted for labor. Most studies of production have found capital and labor to be quite strong substitutes. When we think about the modern manufacturing sector, this seems quite reasonable. Therefore, dwindling population, by itself, doesn't seem a particularly large barrier.

Describing the substitution possibilities for other resources, however, becomes more complex. Studies of the capital–energy relationship over time in the United States find that capital and energy are complements, rather than substitutes.[3] Thus, capital and energy have together substituted for labor and other resources but not for each other. If one thinks of the tractor, the bulldozer, and the airplane, this seems like a natural finding.

The question of interest is whether capital and energy would remain complements in the future or whether substitution of capital for energy might be possible. This is an especially important question in light of the links between fossil fuel energy use and global warming. If the attack on global warming includes a reduction in the use of fossil fuel energy and capital is a complement with energy, global warming strategies would have the side effect of reducing the rate of capital formation.

In some energy uses substitution of capital for energy is clearly feasible because energy-saving equipment, such as computer-controlled heating and cooling, already exists. Furthermore, some capital investments will clearly hasten the transition to passive solar energy, which conserves energy by making better use of what is available.

---

[2]One of the most sophisticated studies to date on the determinants of U.S. economic growth during the period 1948–1979 finds capital formation to be the dominant force. See D. W. Jorgenson, F. M. Gollop, and B. Fraumeni, *Productivity and U.S. Economic Growth* (Cambridge, MA: Harvard University Press, 1988).

[3]Ernst R. Berndt and D. Wood, "Technology, Prices, and the Derived Demand for Energy," *Review of Economics and Statistics* 57 (August 1975): 259–68.

In other sectors such as transportation, the substitution possibilities are not quite as obvious, but that does not mean they do not exist. Bicycles are an obvious substitute for personal transportation (heavily used in many European countries, for example), as are cars powered by solar energy. To some extent communication can even substitute for transportation, as more people use home-based computer terminals and phone lines to do their jobs without leaving home. Although our historical experience would suggest limited substitution possibilities, it is not at all clear that experience is relevant for the future. Some drag on economic growth from higher energy prices appears likely.

The second possible source of growth drag relates to the future productivity of capital. As pollution concentrations rise, the amount of resources committed to combating pollution also rise. A substantial proportion of new plant and equipment expenditures is being allocated to pollution control. Unlike conventional investments, however, these investments do not cause more goods to be produced; they produce a cleaner environment. Because the value of this cleaner environment is not usually recorded in the conventional measures of economic output, conventionally measured output should rise more slowly as a larger proportion of inputs is diverted from productivity enhancement to environment enhancement.

The final source of drag concerns the incentive to invest. The amount of capital investment should depend upon the rate of return on that investment. The more profitable the investment is, the larger the amount undertaken. Yet we have already identified two related factors that reduce the rate of return on investments—the regulatory bias against new sources and the composition of investment. By focusing on new sources, the regulatory system diminishes the relative profitability of new investment while enhancing the profitability of existing capital stock. This new-source bias diminishes the incentive to invest in new capital. Meanwhile, the large proportion of new-plant and equipment expenditures going for pollution control tends to diminish the profitability of those expenditures being made, because improvements in the environment do not, in general, add to profits.

In sum, it appears that expecting increases in capital to completely compensate for reduced flows of other inputs would be risky. Some important transitions are occurring. Although they do not imply a cessation of growth catastrophically or otherwise in the near future, these transitions certainly suggest some diminution in the rate of economic growth resulting from reduced factor input flows.

Limits on Technological Progress.   Can technological progress take up the slack? If technological progress is to compensate for declining input flows, an increase in the rate of technological progress must occur. Is that likely?

Some observers are beginning to suggest that the degree to which technological progress can continue to play its historic role as a growth stimulant may be limited. Some of these limits are perceived as institutional and a matter of choice; others are perceived as natural and inexorable.

The new-source regulatory bias in pollution-control policy provides an example of an institutional limit. Because most technological progress bears fruit when it is embodied in new or modified production facilities, this new-source bias inhibits technological progress by reducing the number of these facilities.

Another institutional barrier is the decreasing commitment of resources to basic research, particularly by the public sector. Because basic research is frequently a precursor for technological progress, this trend could also diminish the rate of technological progress.

During the 1970s economic growth fell below that in earlier periods. The average rates of growth in manufacturing output were down markedly, as were growth rates in labor productivity (output divided by labor input) and technological progress. Does this dramatic decline reflect the beginning of a new era?

A number of economists have tried to isolate the sources of this decline—an assignment made difficult because so many interacting variables are involved. Nonetheless, some progress has been made and is worthy of our attention. We begin with an analysis of the effects of environmental policy on growth.

Environmental Policy

We have seen that pollution-control laws impose large compliance costs on industry. These should have some effect on inflation (by boosting output prices) and employment, as well as on growth. The question of interest is how large those impacts have been, and could be expected to be, in the future.

Generally these studies suggest that the impact of environmental policy on the rate of inflation (measured using the urban consumer price index) is very small, less than one half of a percentage point.

The effect on employment is particularly interesting because it requires balancing the losses experienced by firms that have become technologically obsolete with the gains to firms that are now producing for new markets (such as the market for pollution-control equipment). The evidence suggests that the gains to those producing the equipment more than offset the losses to those installing the equipment, resulting in more, not less, employment in the economy as a whole.

Economist Robert Haveman has surveyed the results of a range of studies conducted around the world on the effect of pollution-control expenditures on employment.[4] These studies go beyond aggregate employment effects and delve into the types of workers affected as well as into the effects of alternative ways of financing investments in pollution control. He concludes:

1. The employment demands of public sector spending for pollution control are greater than equivalent government spending for alternative purposes. About 60,000 to 70,000 jobs are created for each $1 billion of pollution-control spending. For purposes of comparison, each $1 billion of GNP generates approximately 50,000 jobs on the average.

2. Changes in the composition of employment triggered by environmental policy are likely to adversely affect low-skill, low-wage workers relative to high-skill, high-wage workers.

3. In a limited number of countries, environmental policy has been employed as a demand-inducing antirecession instrument, apparently with some success. This result is in part due to the deficit public financing of the expenditures or subsidies.

---

[4]Robert H. Haveman, "The Results and the Significance of the Employment Studies," Organization for Economic Cooperation and Development, *Employment and Environment* (Paris, France: OECD, 1978): 48–53.

4. Available evidence suggests that the adverse employment effects from plant closing attributable to environmental policy are very limited.

However, this generally positive prognosis for the impact of environmental policy on employment should not obscure the problems. Gains in employment generally benefit a different set of workers than losses do. New jobs are rarely in the same location as those lost and, as Haveman points out, rarely involve the same skill levels. Even when overall employment effects are positive, the rising costs of environmental control could cause severe localized problems.

Christiansen and Haveman have studied the effect on environmental policy on labor productivity, a major determinant of growth.[5] Their analytical approach captures, albeit crudely, the direct and indirect effects of environmental regulations. It includes whatever inhibiting effects environmental regulations may have had on capital investment and on capital–labor ratios. They conclude:

> Little evidence exists to suggest that as much as 15 percent of the slowdown can be attributed to them. A reasonable estimate would attribute, say 8 percent–12 percent of the slowdown in productivity growth to these regulations. [p. 388]

If these estimates are accurate, environmental policy cannot escape responsibility for some portion of the decline in labor productivity, but at least the degree is small.

Energy

A second possible source of growth drag is energy. Because large price increases occurred during 1973–1974, this period provides a unique opportunity to study the magnitude of the growth-inhibiting effects of energy.

What should we expect to find? Because energy and capital historically have been complements, we should find that price increases would slow down capital formation. At the same time, the fact that energy and labor are substitutes would suggest that the use of labor should be rising, which, in turn, would cause the average productivity of labor to fall.

On a general level the evidence is consistent with this set of expectations. Investment is lower, and the average productivity of labor has fallen. Work by Jorgenson and others, such as Uri and Hassanein, confirms this impression.[6]

Focusing on 1973–1976, a period characterized by rapidly increasing energy prices, Jorgenson first examined the question of whether the decline in growth was due to declines in input growth or to declines in productivity. He found that input declines were much less significant than declines in productivity. He then attempted to discover the sources of this productivity decline by looking at the specific experience of 35 different industries.

[5]Gregory B. Christiansen and Robert H. Haveman, "The Contribution of Environmental Regulations to the Slowdown in Productivity Growth," *Journal of Environmental Economics and Management* 8, No. 4 (December 1981): 381–90.

[6]Dale W. Jorgenson, "Energy Prices and Productivity Growth," *Scandinavian Journal of Economics* 83 (1981): 165–79; Noel D. Uri and Saad A. Hassanein, "Energy Prices, Labour Productivity, and Causality: An Empirical Examination," *Energy Economics* 4 (April 1982): 98–104.

Though a decline in economy-wide productivity could conceivably be caused either by a shift in resources from high-productivity industries to low-productivity industries or by a decline in productivity within each industry, Jorgenson found the latter to be far more important than the former. His analysis of the causes of these declines revealed that in 29 of the 35 sectors examined, technical change was biased toward the use of energy. This result suggests that in 1973–1976, productivity growth resulting from technical progress declined as energy prices rose.

One puzzle to be explained by those who believe energy prices have already played a significant role in productivity declines is how that could be so when the energy cost share is so small. Factors with small cost shares should in general have rather small effects on output.

One resolution to this puzzle seems consistent with the evidence.[7] Berndt and Wood suggests that in the short run the capital services provided by the capital stock are largely fixed, as are its operating characteristics. Once the capital stock is in place, the ratio of energy to capital services actually utilized is therefore fixed. Dramatic changes in energy prices therefore affect the degree to which this capital is used, with the most energy-inefficient vintages being used least. By lowering the utilization of the existing capital stock, higher energy prices reduce total factor productivity.

In this story the lower productivity does not necessarily persist. As long as new capital that uses less energy can be purchased, utilization rates rise and productivity is restored as these new machines are installed. Once the stock of capital adjusts to the new regime of higher energy prices, productivity growth rebounds.

The key to thinking about the long run is to keep straight the differences between *ex post* and *ex ante* substitution possibilities. *Ex ante* refers to the time period prior to investment, whereas *ex post* refers to the time period after the equipment is installed. Limited *ex post* substitution possibilities, which seem to have played a significant role in the slowdown of productivity growth after the major energy price increases in the 1970s and early in the 1980s, do not automatically indicate that *ex ante* substitution possibilities will be small. It is the *ex ante* substitution possibilities that will determine the future of economic growth over the long run.

Our experience with higher energy prices is quite limited. Transformations of the kind envisioned by these growth models take time to unfold. New ways of doing business are not discovered immediately, and old machines are not replaced instantaneously. Therefore, the estimates must be judged for what they are—an attempt to extract as much information as possible from a limited set of data.

OUTLOOK FOR THE NEAR FUTURE

Some of what the future portends for the United States and other developed countries is becoming clear. Because we are in a period of transition, some striking differences between our experiences in the recent past and what we will encounter in the near future are emerging.

---

[7]Ernst R. Berndt and David O. Wood, "Energy Price Shocks and Productivity Growth: A Survey," in *Energy: Markets and Regulation,* Richard L. Gordon, Henry D. Jacoby, and Martin B. Zimmerman, eds. (Cambridge, MA: MIT Press, 1987): 305–42.

Though a detailed examination would be beyond the scope of our study, we will highlight some of the emerging changes in the following discussion.

Population Impacts

The dramatic fall in fertility rates experienced by most countries of the world will have a profound impact. Inevitably, the average age of the population will rise, putting pressure on social security systems. Because the United States relies on an unfunded social security system, current payments to retirees are financed out of current payments by workers. As long as the population is growing, the ratio of workers to retirees remains high enough to provide adequate benefit levels for retirees without putting excessive strain on current workers. When population growth declines, however, as is now happening, the ratio of workers to retirees declines as well. To keep the system solvent, benefit growth has to decline and/or worker payments have to increase.

Some studies by economists and demographers suggest that labor-market implications of declining population growth will be significant.[8] One very positive effect will be a reduction in the unemployment rates of young adults. Because fewer young inexperienced workers will be entering the labor market, it will be easier to absorb those that do.

As a result of declines in population growth, the labor force will not grow as much as it has historically, creating some upward pressure on wages. These higher wages should reinforce and support the rising participation rates for women and should entice older workers to stay in the workforce longer. These enhanced job opportunities for women should keep the fertility low, reinforcing the tendency for low rates of population growth.

The work by Lindert, studied in the population chapter, suggested that periods of tight labor markets have an equalizing effect on the income distribution. If this model is accurate, and no countervailing tendencies develop, we should witness a trend toward greater income equality in the future as the rewards to labor rise relative to other factors.

The Information Economy

The importance of capital and resources in the American economy is a product of the Industrial Revolution. The Industrial Revolution ushered in an era of mass production where manufacturing replaced agriculture as the dominant source of employment and earnings. This transformation depended upon massive amounts of capital investment, and the scale of operations it brought about consumed large amounts of resources.

It now seems clear that the economy is in the midst of an equally important transformation from an industrial society to what Daniel Bell has labeled the *post industrial society.*[9] The

[8]William P. Butz et al., "Demographic Challenges in America's Future," Report No. R-2911-RC (Santa Monica, CA: The Rand Corporation, 1982); Joseph M. Anderson, "An Economic-Demographic Model of the United States Labor Market," *Research in Population Economics, Volume 4,* Julian L. Simon and Peter H. Lindert eds. (Greenwich, CT: JAI Press, 1982).

[9]Daniel Bell, *The Coming of the Post-Industrial Society: A Venture in Social Forecasting* (New York: Basic Books, 1973).

key elements of this transformation are a change from a goods-producing to a service economy, a rise in the importance of theoretical knowledge as a source of growth, and an increasing reliance on information processing.

In 1977 the Department of Commerce released a nine-volume study that tracked the progress of this transformation.[10] Until 1905 agricultural workers outnumbered industrial, service, and information workers. Porat defines an information worker as one whose income originates primarily in the manipulation of symbols or information. Industrial workers became the dominant force for the next 50 years. By 1955 information workers made up the largest category.

This transformation has profound implications for our society.[11] Computer-controlled robots will step in to fill the slots vacated by lower population growth in a direct substitution of capital for labor. Working at home will become possible for larger numbers of people as computer communication provides a substitute for transportation. Such changes will boost productivity while reducing pollution and our dependence on raw materials and energy. Intelligence will replace oil as the prime mover of the system.

This vision suggests that in the future the demand for skilled labor will rise more rapidly than the demand for unskilled labor. Education will therefore grow in importance, not only as the means of providing that skilled labor, but also as the wellspring of ideas that fuel the new growth.

THE GROWTH–DEVELOPMENT RELATIONSHIP

Has economic growth historically served as a vehicle for development? Has growth really made the average person better off? Would the lowest-income members of the United States and the world fare better with economic growth or without it?

These turn out to be difficult questions to answer in a way that satisfies everyone, but we must start somewhere. One appropriate point of departure is clarifying what we mean by growth. Some of the disenchantment with growth can be traced to how growth is measured. It is not so much that all growth is bad, but rather that increases in conventional indicators of growth are not always good. Some of the enthusiasm for zero economic growth stems from the fact that economic growth, as currently measured, can be shown to have several undesirable characteristics.

Conventional Measures

A true measure of development would increase whenever we, as a nation or as a world, were better off and decrease whenever we were worse off. Such a measure is called a *welfare measure,* and no conventional existing measure is designed to be a welfare measure.

What we currently have are *output measures,* which attempt to indicate how many goods and services have been produced, not how well off we are. Measuring output sounds fairly

---

[10]Marc Porat, *The Information Economy: Definition and Measurement* (Washington, DC: U.S. Department of Commerce, Office of Telecommunications, 1977).

[11]For a more detailed explanation, see Robert D. Hamrin, *Managing Growth in the 1980's: Toward a New Economics* (New York: Praeger, 1980).

simple, but in fact it is not. The measure of economic growth with which most are familiar is based upon the GNP, or gross national product. This number represents the sum of the outputs of goods and services in any year produced by the economy. Prices are used to weigh the importance of these goods and services in GNP. Conceptually, this is accomplished by adding up the value added by each sector of the production process until the product is sold.

Why weight by prices? Some means of comparing the value of extremely dissimilar commodities is needed. Prices provide a readily available system of weights that takes into account the value of those commodities to consumers. From early chapters we know that prices should reflect both the marginal benefit to the consumer and the marginal cost to the producer.

GNP is not a measure of welfare and was never meant to be one. One limitation of this indicator as a measure of welfare is that it includes the value of new machines that are replacing worn-out ones rather than increasing the size of the capital stock. To compensate for the fact that some investment merely replaces old machines and does not add to the size of capital stock, a new concept known as net national product (NNP) was introduced. *NNP is defined as the gross national product minus depreciation.*

NNP and GNP share the deficiency that they are both influenced by inflation. If the flow of all goods and services were to remain the same while prices doubled, both NNP and GNP would also double. Because neither welfare nor output would have increased, an accurate indicator should reflect that fact.

To resolve this problem, national income accountants present data on *constant-dollar GNP* and *constant-dollar NNP.* These numbers are derived by "cleansing" the actual GNP and NNP data to take out the effects of price rises. Conceptually, this is accomplished by defining a market basket of goods that stays the same over time. Each year this same basket is repriced. If the cost of the goods in the basket went up 10 percent, then because the quantities are held constant, we know that prices went up by 10 percent. This information is used to remove the effects of prices on the indicators; remaining increases should be due to an increased production of goods and services.

This correction does not solve all problems. For one thing, not all components of GNP contribute equally to welfare. Probably the closest component we could use in the existing system of accounts would be *consumption,* the amount of goods and services consumed by households. It leaves out government expenditures, investments, exports, and imports.

The final correction that could easily be made to the existing accounts would involve dividing real consumption by the population to get *real consumption per capita.* This correction allows us to differentiate between rises in output needed to maintain the standard of living for an increasing population and rises indicating more goods and services consumed by the average member of that population.

Real consumption per capita is about as close as we can get to a welfare-oriented output measure using readily available data, but it is a far cry from being an ideal welfare indicator.

In particular, changes in real consumption per capita fail to distinguish between economic growth resulting from a true increase in income and economic growth resulting from a depreciation in what economists have come to call "natural capital," the stock of environmentally provided assets such as the soil, the atmosphere, the forests, wildlife, and water.

The traditional definition of income was articulated by Sir John Hicks:

> The purpose of income calculations in practical affairs is to give people an indication of the amount they can consume without impoverishing themselves. Following out this idea, it would seem that

we ought to define a man's income as the maximum value which he can consume during a week, and still expect to be as well off at the end of the week as he was at the beginning.[12]

Although human-created capital (such as buildings, bridges, etc.) is treated in a manner consistent with this definition, natural capital is not. As human-created capital wears out, the accounts set aside an amount called depreciation to compensate for the decline in value as the equipment wears out. No increase in economic activity is recorded as an increase in income until depreciation has been subtracted from gross returns. That portion of the gains which merely serves to replace worn-out capital is not appropriately considered income.

No such adjustment is made for natural capital in the current national income accounting system. Depreciation of the stock of natural capital is incorrectly counted as income. Development strategies that "cash in" the endowment of natural resources are in these accounts indistinguishable from development strategies that do not depreciate the natural capital stock; the returns from both are treated as income.

Consider an analogy. Many high-quality private educational institutions in the United States have large financial endowments. In considering their budgets for the year, these institutions take the revenue from tuition and other fees and add in some proportion of the interest and capital gains earned from the endowment. Except in extraordinary circumstances, however, standard financial practice does not allow the institution to attack the principal. Drawing down the endowment and treating this increase in financial resources as income is not allowed.

However, that is precisely what the national accounts allow us to do in terms of natural resources. We can deplete our soils, cut down our forests, and douse ocean coves with oil, and the resulting economic activity is treated as income, not as a decline in the endowment of natural capital.

Because the Hicksian definition is violated for natural capital, policymakers are misled. By relying upon misleading information, policymakers are more likely to undertake unsustainable development strategies.

Adjusting the national income accounts to apply the Hicksian definition uniformly to human-made and natural capital could make quite a difference in resource-dependent countries. For example, Robert Repetto and colleagues of the World Resources Institute studied the growth rates of gross national product in Indonesia using both conventional unadjusted figures and figures adjusted to account for the depreciation of natural capital. Their study found that whereas the unadjusted gross national product increased at an average annual rate of 7.1 percent from 1971 to 1984, the adjusted estimates rose by only 4.0 percent per year.[13]

Motivated by a recognition of these serious flaws in the current system of accounts, a number of industrial countries have now proposed (or in a few cases have already set up) systems of adjusted accounts including Norway, France, Canada, Japan, the Netherlands, Germany, and the United States. Significant differences of opinion on such issues as whether the changes should be incorporated in a complementary system of accounts or in a complete revision of the standard accounts remain to be resolved.

---

[12]J. R. Hicks, *Value and Capital,* 2nd ed. (Oxford: Oxford University Press, 1947): 172.

[13]Robert Repetto, "Nature's Resources as Productive Assets," *Challenge* 32, No. 5 (September/October 1989): 16–20.

Alternative Measures

Because revised accounts are not yet available, we cannot use them to assess the relationship between growth and economic well-being. But the question won't go away, so we have to do the best we can with what information is available.

Several studies have attempted to adjust real consumption per capita figures on an *ad hoc* basis to come up with a measure that is closer to being a welfare measure. One of the first was by Nordhaus and Tobin.[14] Their first adjustment involves an attempt to account for the amount of welfare-reducing environmental damage being inflicted by pollution. Reasoning that part of the increased wages of urban workers represents compensation for having been exposed to the higher pollution concentrations, they used a portion of the income differential between urban and rural families as their measure of the monetary value of the damage caused. This estimate is then subtracted from the real consumption data.

They then adjust the data to treat consumer durables in a different way. In conventional accounts, consumer durables are incorporated by adding in their full cost at the time of purchase, in spite of the fact that services from those durable goods are received throughout its useful life. Nordhaus and Tobin subtract these durable good *purchases* and add back in an estimate of the annual *services* they provide.

The final subtraction from the conventional accounts involves excluding consumer expenditures that do not seem to raise welfare. The major expenditure they excluded was the cost of commuting to and from work. Although they are necessary expenditures, these do not themselves raise welfare.

Nordhaus and Tobin also correct for omissions that tend to bias the conventional accounts downward when interpreted in welfare terms. These include the value of leisure time and household production, neither of which is valued in conventional accounts. One benefit of growth is that productivity increases have resulted in a decline in the average workweek. This increased leisure is valued by Nordhaus and Tobin at the market wage rate that could have been earned if the time were spent working rather than in leisure activities. Household production involves the many services performed around the house. Unless there are hired servants, household production activities do not enter the conventional accounts.

The problem with the manner in which the conventional approach treats household production is nicely illustrated by an example. When a single person marries his or her housekeeper, GNP goes down, because an activity that was formerly a market activity is no longer. Yet we presume, because marriage is a voluntary arrangement, that welfare was increased. The change in the indicator sends the wrong signal. Nordhaus and Tobin correct this conventional approach by adding in an imputed value for nonmarketed household production.

Their final correction involves adding into personal consumption expenditures a value for the government services provided. Traditionally, the government sector is treated separately in the GNP and its output is valued at cost. By including this measure, Nordhaus and Tobin are correcting two problems: (1) the omission of government services from the personal consumption expenditures, and (2) valuing these services as received rather than (in the case of government durables, such as roads) at the time of purchase.

After making all these adjustments, they arrive at an indicator they call the *Measure of Economic Welfare* (MEW). The MEW per capita rose by about 42 percent between 1929 and

[14]William D. Nordhaus and James Tobin, "Is Growth Obsolete?" in *Economic Growth, Fiftieth Anniversary Colloquium, Volume 5* (New York: National Bureau of Economic Research, 1972): 4–17.

1965. This increase was only about one half of the 87.5 percent increase in real NNP per capita over the same period. According to Nordhaus and Tobin, real NNP per capita does overstate growth in economic well-being, but their estimate leaves no doubt that they believe correctly measured economic well-being has increased substantially since 1929.

Others have attempted to make different adjustments. In particular, Usher has adjusted the conventional accounts to incorporate the value of increased life expectancy and finds that this adjustment boosts the growth rate of the adjusted measure above the conventional measure.[15]

Zolotas performed a similar but somewhat more detailed set of calculations for the particular purpose of discovering whether the growth in well-being had declined over time.[16] The trends in his measure of welfare suggest that the additional increases in well-being are becoming smaller and smaller as growth continues. Similar results were subsequently obtained by Daly and Cobb.[17] They found that per capita welfare had increased 20 percent from 1951 to 1986 in the United States, but that increase was the net result of two offsetting trends. Per capita welfare had started to decline between 1970 and 1980. (Note that this is a decline in welfare, not a decline in the growth of welfare!) The estimated average annual decline during the 1970s was 0.14 percent, whereas the average annual decline during the 1980s was estimated to be 1.26 percent. If this evidence were ultimately confirmed by better designed accounts, it would show that the effects of economic growth on per capita well-being have in the past been positive but recently have turned negative. According to Daly and Cobb, further growth in the United States not only would not improve well-being, it would decrease it.

As the authors of the preceding studies would readily concede, one should be skeptical about the specific magnitude of these estimates. The procedures provide only crude approximations to those required to produce a true measure of welfare.

GROWTH AND POVERTY: THE INDUSTRIALIZED NATIONS

Conceiving of the growth–development relationship only in terms of the effects on the average citizen obscures a great deal of what may be happening in a society. Two societies may have the same per capita growth in average well-being, but if the fruits of this growth are shared uniformly in one and unequally in the second, it seems overly simplistic to argue that the increase in welfare levels would be the same in the two countries. As Example 19.1 indicates, relative income levels seem to make a difference in how well-off people feel.

Although the evidence suggests that economic growth has improved the lot of the average citizen in the developed world, it tells us nothing about how the poorest members of society fared. To determine whether the poorest citizens also benefit from growth, we must dig deeper into the nature of the growth process.

---

[15]Dan Usher, *The Measurement of Economic Growth* (New York: Columbia University Press, 1980).

[16]Xenophon Zolotas, *Economic Growth and Declining Social Welfare* (New York: New York University, 1981).

[17]Herman E. Daly and John B. Cobb, Jr., *For the Common Good* (Boston, MA: Beacon Press, 1989): 401–55.

E X A M P L E   1 9 . 1

Does Money Buy Happiness?

In a highly subjective but interesting study, economist Richard Easterlin [1973] collected data from 30 surveys conducted in 19 developed and less-developed countries that analyze the relationship between happiness and income. In every one of these surveys, the respondents were asked to rate how happy they were feeling on a scale: "very happy," "mildly happy," "mildly unhappy," and "very unhappy." Information on respondent income levels was also collected.

In analyzing these data he found:

1.   At any point in time a larger portion of high-income people are happier than low-income people—for all countries and all years.
2.   The proportion of happy and unhappy in each group remained relatively constant over time in spite of generally rising incomes. For example, in the United States, roughly the same percentage of wealthy people and poor people said they were very happy in 1940 as in 1970.

The first finding suggests that higher income is positively correlated with happiness; the second suggests that despite large increases in income, the percentage saying they were very happy did not increase. How are these apparently contradictory findings to be explained?

Easterlin explains them by suggesting that one of the components of happiness for people is their relative income. Thus, a person at the top of the heap in any particular country may be happier than he or she would be if that same income were earned in a richer country where lots of people earned that income. If this hypothesis is correct, it suggests that the average level of welfare in an economic system is an inadequate indicator of the total welfare in the society. The distribution of the fruits of economic growth makes a difference.

Source: Richard A. Easterlin, "Does Money Buy Happiness?" *The Public Interest* (Winter 1973): 3–10.

One source of information about this relationship is history. To exploit that source we shall examine the data for a period of particularly high economic growth in the United States. Did it benefit the poor or were they left behind?

The Effects on Income Inequality

Growth can help the poor, though history suggests that these beneficial effects are not inevitable. It is generally believed that income transfers are easier when the amount to be shared is growing. The donors can give up some of their gains and still be better off, whereas in a no-growth situation any sharing must come from a reduction in the real income of the donor.

On the surface many observers believe that growth has not, in fact, lived up to its billing as a means of alleviating poverty. In his survey of the situation Lee Rainwater, a Harvard sociologist, concludes

> It seems well established that income and wealth inequality have not declined significantly over the past half century, and probably have not declined at all in the past quarter century.[18]

The Effects on Poverty

The failure of economic growth to reduce economic inequality does not, as it might appear, imply that growth has not benefited the poor. In the first place, many of the published studies do not take into account the significant transfers to the poor that are rendered in kind (such as food stamps and Medicaid) rather than in cash. Therefore, published income levels may understate the positive effects on the poor. In addition, stating the problem in this relative form ignores the increases in absolute welfare that all persons, including the poor, derive.

With respect to the first point, examining the data makes it clear that transfers to the poor have been significant and have made a difference. In-kind transfer programs, such as food stamps and Medicaid, have had a significant impact on the poor. Studies such as those accomplished by Rainwater, which do not include these in-kind transfers, tend to underestimate the positive impact experienced by the poor during a growth period.

The evidence also suggests that transfers have made the difference, not growth itself. In the absence of transfers, economic growth would not have lifted many persons from below to above the poverty threshold. The linkage between growth and the poor depends more upon its effect on the willingness to transfer than on direct market effects.

By focusing on relative incomes, Rainwater was seeking to discover whether the poor are becoming better off more rapidly than the rich. His answer was no. The poor were made better off in terms of meeting basic needs, however, even if their rate of progress did not exceed that of the rich.

Although growth cannot be seen as a vehicle that inevitably creates equality of income among the rich and poor, the evidence shows that, in the United States at least, the quality of life for the poor has been improved by it. This improvement has come both from a general rising standard of living and a rise in transfers from the rich to the poor.

POVERTY IN THE LESS-INDUSTRIALIZED NATIONS

Economic growth can be a vehicle for development, and this form of development can benefit the poor as well as the rich according to the historical experience in the industrialized nations. Though the relationship between economic growth and poverty is neither inevitable nor universally effective, it does provide one possible path for dealing with poverty.

How relevant is this experience for the Third World? Can and should the traditional approach to economic growth serve as a model for those nations struggling to free themselves from the grip of poverty?

---

[18]Lee Rainwater, "Equity, Income Inequality, and the Steady State," in *The Sustainable Society,* Dennis Clark Pirages, ed. (New York: Praeger Publishers, 1977): 263.

It would be delightful to find that the poverty problem is solving itself, but that is certainly not the case. Many of the world's poor are caught in a seamless web of deteriorating conditions.[19] According to a 1988 address by World Bank President Barber Conable: "Poverty on today's scale prevents a billion people from having even minimally acceptable standards of living. . . . In sub-Sahara Africa more than 100 million people—one in four—do not get enough to eat." Agricultural productivity per capita has been declining in Africa since 1967 and in Latin America since 1981. The World Bank reports that from 1979 to 1983 life expectancy fell in nine African countries. In Zambia twice as many children died from malnutrition in 1984 as in 1980. In its 1989 annual report, the United Nations Children's Fund (UNICEF) concluded that "at least half a million young children have died in the last 12 months as a result of slowing down or the reversal of progress in the developing world."

What are the trends in incomes? Many developing countries are actually losing ground. As Inter-American Development Bank President Enrique Iglesias said in September, 1988, "The per capita income of the average Latin American is 9 percent lower today than it was in 1980. This is average. In some countries the standard of living has slipped back to where it was 20 years ago."

The picture is not totally bleak. Success against poverty is possible. Some Asian countries have done well in the 1980s, for example. Thailand has reported a 50 percent decrease in its poverty rate since 1960. The Republic of Korea, Taiwan, and Singapore have all experienced rapid industrialization and a rising standard of living.

The Appropriateness of the Traditional Model

How appropriate is the traditional economic growth model for these countries? Does it point the way out of poverty?

Scale. One of the first indicators that traditional models may be inappropriate derives from the ecological effects of the proposed global scale of economic activity necessary to eradicate poverty if the model of development followed by the industrialized nations of Asia, Europe, and Africa were adopted by the rest of the world. As Jim MacNeill, the former director of the World Commission on Environment and Development, has stated, "If current forms of development were employed, a five to ten-fold increase in economic activity would be required over the next fifty years to meet the needs and aspirations of a population twice the size of today's 5.2 billion, as well as to begin to reduce mass poverty." Whether increases of this magnitude could be accomplished while still respecting the atmospheric and ecological systems on which all economic activity ultimately depends is not at all obvious.

Increased energy consumption to support new industry would add greenhouse gases. Increased refrigeration would add more of the gases depleting the stratospheric ozone level. The industrialized nations have freely used the very large capacity of the atmosphere to absorb these gases. Little absorptive capacity is left. Most observers seem to believe that to meet the challenge we need to take an activist stance by controlling population, severely reducing emissions of these gases in the industrialized world, and discovering new forms of development that are sustainable.

---

[19]The information in this paragraph and the two that follow were obtained from Alan B. Durning, "Poverty and the Environment: Reversing the Downward Spiral," Paper No. 92 (Washington, DC: Worldwatch Institute, 1989): 15–18.

Forms of Development.   Economics can assist in the process of characterizing how the forms should differ. Appropriate development should capitalize on local strengths and stay away from weaknesses; it should be sensitive to factor prices.

Many, if not most, of the developing nations, are labor-surplus economies. It follows that their strategy for development, at least in the beginning stages, should be labor-intensive. Labor-intensive processes serve the twin purposes of capitalizing on an abundant resource and providing a source of income to large numbers of people.[20]

Although the forms of development in the industrialized nations are increasingly going to rely on a highly skilled labor force, that is inappropriate for countries where the educational systems may not currently be able to supply sufficient numbers of skilled workers to fill the need. By effectively utilizing the low-skilled workforce, developing countries can increase their incomes, decrease population growth, and ultimately create the wealth needed to support strong education system.

Development in the industrialized countries has also been very fossil-fuel dependent. Although this may be appropriate when supplies of fossil fuels are plentiful and the remaining capacity of the environment to accept the by-product gases is unlimited, it is certainly less appropriate for a future plagued by diminishing supplies and global warming.

Barriers to Development

What are the barriers to raising standards of living in the Third World? Rising populations face increasingly limited access to land, health services, education, and financial resources. Many of these problems are intensified by the current international economy. Heavy debt burdens, falling prices for their exports, and the flight of capital that could be used to create jobs and income are all significant barriers to sustainable development.

Population Growth.   Poverty begets poverty. The positive feedback loop between population growth and poverty is one powerful example. Population growth rates are typically higher, substantially higher, in low-income populations. High infant mortality causes parents to compensate with large numbers of births. Children provide one of the few available means of old age security. Knowledge about birth control techniques is sparse, and the availability of contraceptives is limited. Women frequently have low levels of education, and in some cultures large families are the only possible way for women to achieve status. Larger populations in turn tend to increase the degree of poverty by lowering wages and by spreading the resources allocated to children over a larger number.

Population growth also puts increased pressure on the natural resource base. Pushing larger numbers of people onto marginal land increases soil erosion and deforestation. Increasing population density can cause the carrying capacity of the land to be exceeded. In parts of Africa where nomadic tribes have coexisted for centuries with a fragile ecosystem, larger populations and reduced mobility have resulted in such a serious deterioration of the ecosystem that it is no longer able to satisfy basic human needs.

---

[20]Contrast this with capital-intensive processes, which use much less labor and distribute more of the returns to the owners of capital, who are typically well-off.

Land Ownership Patterns. Pressures on the land arising from population growth are exacerbated by patterns of land ownership in many of the lower-income countries. In agricultural economies access to land is a key ingredient in any attempt to eradicate poverty, but land ownership is frequently highly concentrated among a few extremely wealthy owners. Much of the undeveloped land that exists is ecologically valuable in its preserved state. Improvements in agricultural techniques can do little to raise living standards if peasants do not have access to their own land.

One common measure of the degree of inequality in land ownership is the Gini coefficient. The Gini coefficient can take on values of 0.0 (which would indicate perfect equality) to 1.0 (which would indicate perfect inequality). Perfect equality would occur if every farmer owned exactly the same amount of land. Perfect inequality would imply that all land was owned by a single farmer.

In Latin America Gini coefficients in excess of .75 are common.[21] This region has the most skewed land ownership patterns on the globe, a legacy of colonial times when colonial rulers accumulated vast amounts of land. Asian nations are somewhat better, with Gini coefficients ranging from .51 to .64, and in Africa, where collective tribal land ownership is common, the coefficients fall between .36 and .55.[22]

Trade Policies. Some of the barriers faced by third-world countries as they attempt to raise living standards have been erected by the industrialized nations. Trade policies are one example. The terms of trade for many third-world countries have deteriorated in the recent past.[23]

Some of the reasons for this deterioration are natural effects of markets rather than misguided policies. Included in this category are the import substitutions in the industrialized world (such as when optical fibers are substituted for copper in phone lines) and lower demand for third-world exports triggered by lower economic growth in the industrialized countries.

Political factors are also important. When political forces in the developed countries conspire to eliminate or substantially reduce natural markets for the developing countries, these policies not only exacerbate the poverty in the developing nations, they have a direct degrading effect on the environment.[24]

The Multi-Fiber Arrangement, originally implemented in 1974, is a case in point. Its effect has been to severely reduce developing-country exports of textiles and other products made from fibers. In developing countries, fiber products are produced by labor-intensive techniques, causing the employment impact to be high. For local sustainable agriculture the

---

[21]The land ownership data are from Alan B. Durning, "Poverty and the Environment: Reversing the Downward Spiral," Paper No. 92 (Washington, DC: Worldwatch Institute, 1989): 25.

[22]To provide one, admittedly imperfect, basis for comparison, the 1986 U.S. Gini coefficient for the distribution of income among families was .389.

[23]The terms of trade determine international purchasing power. When the terms of trade deteriorate, third-world exports purchase fewer imports. Evidence on the deteriorating terms of trade can be found in World, Bank, *World Development Report 1989* (Washington, DC: Oxford University Press, 1989): Table 14, 190–91.

[24]A study by the World Bank Staff shows that lowering tariff barriers in the European Economic Community, the United States, and Japan would permit exports from the highly indebted developing countries to increase by some $6.5 billion. World Bank, *World Debt Tables, 1988–89* (Washington, DC: World Bank, 1988): xxvii.

opportunity to provide the fiber raw materials is another source of employment. By artificially reducing the markets for these products and the fibers from which these products are manufactured, the agreement has forced some nations to substitute resource-intensive economic activities, such as timber exports, for the more environmentally congenial fiber-based manufacturing in order to earn foreign exchange.

Agricultural trade flows not only demonstrate how price distortions can be translated into unsustainable development but also show how they can exacerbate poverty. In general, price distortions and artificially supported exchange rates have resulted in a pattern of trade that involves excessive agricultural production in the developed world and too little in the developing world. Agriculture in the developed world is supported by a number of different subsidies. In the developing world, the bias operates to promote underproduction rather than overproduction. Overvalued exchange rates increase the attractiveness of importing food and decrease the attractiveness of exporting food.

By discouraging small-scale agriculture in developing countries, an activity that would provide income to a segment of the population faced with the most severe forms of poverty, biased trade flows exacerbate the poverty problem. Furthermore, because income increases targeted on this particular group typically lead to slower population growth, even some of the population pressures on the environment could ultimately be related to biases in current trade patterns.

One common stereotype of the difference between developed and less-developed countries involves their respective supplies of minerals. According to this stereotype, less-developed countries control most of the world's mineral resources, and the developed world creates the demand for them. If accurate, this view would suggest that rising mineral prices would eventually create favorable terms of trade for most developing countries.

Unfortunately, upon closer inspection this stereotype represents at best an oversimplification. Although exports of minerals have increased from less-developed to developed countries. Not all less-developed countries share these higher export levels. A few have large reserves of petroleum or nonfuel minerals, but most do not. The benefits from increasing mineral prices tend to bypass most less-developed countries.

Debt. Many third-world countries have staggering levels of debt to service. The World Bank has estimated that the total debt of all developing countries reached $1,290 billion in 1989. In 1989 poor nations sent $51.6 billion more to the industrialized nations in interest and principal repayment than they received in new capital.[25] External debt is 104.1 percent of the gross national product of the severely indebted low-income countries. These percentages reach as high as 305.1 percent for Brazil and 476.0 percent for Guyana.[26]

Unfortunately, even private capital is flowing out of the capital-poor countries, where it is desperately needed, and into the capital-rich countries. The World Bank estimates that the stock of "flight" capital held abroad by citizens of severely indebted countries equals a significant fraction of those countries' external debt.

---

[25]Even if all official development assistance and private capital flows to the developing countries were included in the total, the net outflow would still be $9.8 billion. This evidence on the debt comes from the World Bank, *World Debt Tables 1989–90 Volume 1* (Washington, DC: The World Bank, 1989): 1–9.

[26]See World Bank, *World Debt Tables 1989–90 Volume 2* (Washington, DC: The World Bank, 1989): 18, 58, 114.

In periods of high real interest rates, servicing these debts puts a significant drain on foreign exchange earnings. Using these foreign exchange earnings to service the debt eliminates the possibility of using them to finance imports for sustainable activities to alleviate poverty. One study found that in all but one of the most indebted countries, the ratio of investment to Gross Domestic Product was substantially lower in the 1982–1988 period (when the debt burden was heaviest) than in the previous six years.[27] In Argentina the ratio fell from 25 percent to 15 percent, whereas comparable figures for Venezuela indicate a fall from 33 percent to 18 percent. This fall in investment has, in turn, reduced the growth of output and exports in debtor nations and thereby further undermined their ability to repay their debts.

With the notable exception of a relatively few oil-rich nations, most developing countries import a great deal of energy. Because this demand is relatively price inelastic, their expenditures on imports have risen tremendously without similar compensating increases in receipts from the sale of exports.

The situation is reversed in many of the oil-exporting countries, which are commanding abnormally high prices for their oil. Their favorable terms of trade, however, have not always insulated them from development difficulties. Nigeria is a classic example. Buoyed by oil exports, the local wage structure and exchange rates ended up severely harming agricultural production. Resources flowed out of agricultural production and into oil production. Even the income distribution was adversely affected, becoming much more unequally distributed.[28]

The evidence suggests that although growth is no panacea for the problems of the developing world, it is probably better than no growth. However, the traditional form of growth experienced in the industrialized countries is not likely to be the most appropriate form for the less-developed countries in the future. Circumstances have changed since the industrial revolution. Furthermore, the factor endowments in third-world countries are not the same as those in the industrialized countries. Changing circumstances call for changing approaches.

SUMMARY

Historically, increases in inputs and technological progress were important sources of economic growth in the industrialized nations. In the future some factors of production, such as labor, will not increase as rapidly as they have in the past. The effect of this decline on growth depends on the interplay among the law of diminishing marginal productivity, substitution possibilities, and technological progress. The law of diminishing marginal productivity suggests slower growth rates, but technological progress and the availability of substitution possibilities counteract this drag.

Our examination of empirical evidence suggests that increased environmental control has not currently had a large impact on the economy as a whole, although certain industries have been hit quite hard. Environmental policy has triggered only a small rise in the rate of inflation and a mild reduction in growth. Environmental policy has apparently contributed more jobs than it has cost.

The situation is similar for energy. Though rather large increases in energy prices have occurred, the portion of the slowdown in economic growth during the 1970s attributed to

---

[27]"Debtors' Hangover," *The Economist* (20 May 1989): 73.

[28]Jan S. Hogendorn, *Economic Development,* 2nd ed. (New York: HarperCollins, 1992).

these increases is not large. Some diminution of growth has certainly occurred, but it seems premature to suggest that rising energy prices have already forced a transition to a period of substantially lower growth rates.

This is not to say, however, that the economy is not being transformed. It is. Two particularly important aspects of this transformation are the decline in population growth and the rise in importance of information as a driving economic force. Both aspects tend to reduce the degree to which physical limits constrain economic growth and increase the degree to which current welfare levels are sustainable.

Some crude attempts have been made to assess whether or not growth in the industrialized countries has made the citizens of those countries better off. Results of these studies suggest that because growth has ultimately generated more leisure, longer life expectancy, and more goods and services, it has been beneficial. However, more recent studies suggest that the benefits from growth have been steadily diminishing over time. One study found that further growth in the United States now lowers economic well-being of the average U.S. citizen; at this stage of affluence the negative aspects were estimated to outweigh the positive aspects.

Our examination of the evidence suggests that the notion that all of the world's people are automatically benefited by economic growth is naive. Growth has demonstrably benefited the poor in the developed countries, mainly through transfers from more well-off members of society.

The outlook for the less-industrialized nations is at best mixed. Solving many of their future environmental problems will require raising standards of living. However, following the path of development pioneered by the industrialized nations is probably not possible without triggering severe global environmental problems; the solution would become the problem. New forms of development will be necessary.

The less-industrialized countries must overcome a number of significant barriers if development is to become a reality. At the local level, rising populations face increasingly limited access to land or productive assets. At the national level, corruption and development policies discriminate against the poor. Globally their situation is worsened by rising debt burdens, falling export prices for the products they sell, and the flight of capital that could be used to create jobs and income.

How can the barriers be overcome? What new forms of development can be introduced? By what means can they be introduced? We shall deal with these questions in the next chapter.

FURTHER READING

Durning, Alan B. "Poverty and the Environment: Reversing the Downward Spiral," Paper No. 92 (Washington, DC: Worldwatch Institute, 1989). A very thorough examination of the degree of third-world poverty, the sources of that poverty, the resulting effects on the environment, and some strategies to deal with these problems.

Peskin, Henry M., Paul R. Portney, and Allen Kneese. *Environmental Regulation and the U.S. Economy* (Baltimore, MD: Johns Hopkins University Press, for Resources for the Future, 1981). Six essays on the effect of environmental regulations on the economy combined with an excellent introduction to the issues and summary of the implications of the evidence presented.

Renner, Michael. *Jobs in a Sustainable Economy* (Washington, DC: The Worldwatch Institute, 1991). Documents the point of view that "Less damaging ways of producing, consuming, and disposing of goods are fully consistent with the goal of full employment because they tend to be far more labor-intensive."

World Bank, *World Development Report: 1992* (New York: Oxford University Press, 1992). This particular edition of the well-known annual report focuses on the relationship between development in the developing countries and the environment.

ADDITIONAL REFERENCES

Dasgupta, Ajit K. *Growth, Development and Welfare: An Essay on Levels of Living* (Oxford: Basil Blackwell, 1988).

Dennison, Edward. *Accounting for United States Economic Growth, 1929–1969* (Washington, DC: The Brookings Institution, 1974).

Hirsh, Fred. *Social Limits to Growth* (Cambridge, MA: Harvard University Press, 1976).

Hueckel, Glenn. "A Historical Approach to Future Economic Growth," *Science* 191 (14 March 1975): 925–31.

Jorgenson, Dale W. "Energy and the Future U.S. Economy," *The Wharton Magazine* 3 (Summer 1979): 15–21.

Lindert, Peter. *Fertility and Scarcity in America* (Princeton, NJ: Princeton University Press, 1978).

Mesarovic, Michaklo, and Edward Pestel. *Mankind at the Turning Point: The Second Report to the Club of Rome* (New York, NY: The New American Library, 1974).

Neary, J. Peter, and Sweder Van Wijnbergen, eds. *Natural Resources and the Macroeconomy* (Cambridge, MA: MIT Press, 1986).

Perrings, Charles. *Economy and Environment: A Theoretical Essay on the Interdependence of Economic and Environmental Systems* (Cambridge, UK: Cambridge University Press, 1987).

Peskin, Henry M. "Accounting for Natural Resource Depletion and Degradation in Developing Countries," Working Paper No. 13 (Washington, DC: World Bank Environment Department, 1989).

Weintraub, Andrew, et al., eds. *The Economic Growth Controversy* (New York: International Arts and Sciences Press, 1973).

DISCUSSION QUESTIONS

1. "Economic growth has historically provided a valuable vehicle for raising the standard of living. Now that the standard of living is so high, however, further economic growth is unnecessary. When the undesirable side effects are considered, it is probably counterproductive. Economic growth is a process that has outlived its usefulness." Discuss.
2. Is affluence part of the problem or part of the solution when it comes to environmental problems? Why?

CHAPTER 20

The Quest for Sustainable Development

The challenge of finding sustainable development paths ought to provide the impetus—indeed the imperative—for a renewed search for multilateral solutions and a restructured international economic system of co-operation. These challenges cut across the divides of national sovereignty, of limited strategies for economic gain, and of separated disciplines of science.

GRO HARLEM BRUNDTLAND, FORMER PRIME MINISTER OF NORWAY, *OUR COMMON FUTURE* (1987)

INTRODUCTION

Delegations from 178 countries met in Rio de Janeiro during the first two weeks of June 1992 to begin the process of charting a sustainable development course for the future global economy. Billed by its organizers as the largest summit ever held, the United Nations Conference on Environment and Development (known popularly as the Earth Summit) sought to lay the groundwork for solving global environmental problems. The central focus for this meeting was sustainable development.

What is sustainable development? According to the Brundtland Report, which is widely credited with raising the concept to its current level of importance, "Sustainable development is development that meets the needs of the present without compromising the ability of future generations to meet their own needs."[1] However, that is far from the only possible definition.[2] A nascent concept, sustainable development is still in the process of being refined and clarified.

---

[1] The World Commission on Environment and Development, *Our Common Future* (Oxford: Oxford University Press, 1987): 43.

[2] One search for definitions produced 61, though many were very similar. See John Pezzey, "Economic Analysis of Sustainable Growth and Sustainable Development," Working Paper No. 15 (Washington, DC: World Bank Environmental Department, 1989).

FIGURE 20.1   Possible Alternative Futures

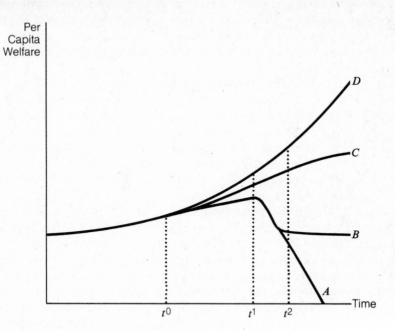

Part of the widespread appeal of the concept, according to critics, is due to its vagueness. Being all things to all people can build a large following, but it also has a rather substantial disadvantage: Close inspection may reveal the concept to be vacuous. As the emperor discovered about his new clothes, things are not always what they seem.

In this chapter we shall take a hard look at the concept of sustainable development and whether or not it is useful as a guide to the future. What are the basic principles of sustainable development? What does sustainable development imply about changes in the way our system operates? How could the transition to sustainable development be managed? Will the global economic system automatically produce sustainable development, or will policy changes be needed? What policy changes?

SUSTAINABILITY AND DEVELOPMENT

Suppose we were to map out possible future trends in the long-term welfare of the average citizen. Using a time scale measured in centuries on the horizontal axis (Figure 20.1), four basic culture trends emerge, labeled *A, B, C,* and *D,* with t_0 representing the present. *D* portrays continued exponential growth in which the future becomes a simple repetition of the past. In this scenario, not only would current welfare levels be sustainable, but growth in welfare would be sustainable. Our concern for intergenerational justice would lead us to favor current generations because they would be the poorest. Worrying about future generations would be unnecessary.

The second scenario (*C*) envisions slowly diminished growth culminating in a steady state where growth diminishes to zero. Each future generation is at least as well off as all previous generations. Current welfare levels are sustainable, though current levels of welfare growth would not be. Because the level of welfare of each generation is sustainable, artificial constraints on the process would be unnecessary. To constrain growth would injure all subsequent generations.

The third scenario (*B*) is similar in that it envisions initial growth followed by a steady state, but with an important difference—those generations between t^1 and t^2 are worse off than the generations preceding them. This is the type of scenario anticipated by Meadows and his colleagues. Neither growth nor welfare levels are sustainable at current levels, and the sustainability criterion would call for an immediate transition to sustainable welfare levels.

The final scenario (*A*) denies the existence of sustainable per capita welfare levels, suggesting that the only possible sustainable level is zero. All consumption by the current generation serves simply to hasten the end of civilization.

These scenarios suggest that three dimensions of the sustainability issue are important: (1) the existence of a positive sustainable level of welfare, (2) the magnitude of the ultimate sustainable level of welfare *vis à vis* current welfare levels, and (3) the sensitivity of the future level of welfare to actions by previous generations. The first dimension is important because if positive sustainable levels of welfare are possible, scenario *A*, which in some ways is the most philosophically difficult, is ruled out. The second is important because if the ultimately sustainable welfare level is higher than the current level, radical surgery to cut current living standards is not necessary. The final dimension raises the issue of whether the ultimate sustainable level of welfare can be increased or reduced by the actions of current generations. If so, the sustainability criterion would suggest taking these impacts into account, lest future generations be unnecessarily impoverished by involuntary wealth transfers to previous generations.

The first dimension is relatively easy to dispense with. The existence of positive sustainable welfare levels is guaranteed by the existence of renewable resources, particularly solar energy, as well as by nature's ability to assimilate a certain amount of waste.[3] Therefore we can rule out scenario *A*.

No one knows exactly what level of economic activity can ultimately be sustained, but the prediction of early societal collapse certainly seems grossly exaggerated. Because growth is slowing as a natural process, the most serious excesses of unregulated growth (such as pollution) are being mitigated, and solar energy is abundant, scenario *C* seems likely, though with current levels of information no one can completely rule out *B*.

Current generations can affect the sustainable welfare levels of future generations both positively and negatively. We could use our resources to accumulate a capital stock, providing future generations with shelter, productivity, and transportation, but our decaying inner cities illustrate that machines and buildings do not last forever. Even capital that physically stands the test of time may become economically obsolete by being ill-suited to the needs of subsequent generations.

---

[3]One study has estimated that humans are currently using approximately 19 to 25 percent of the renewable energy available from photosynthesis. On land the estimate is more like 40 percent. See Peter M. Vitousek et al., "Human Appropriation of the Products of Photosynthesis," *BioScience* 36, No. 6 (June 1986): 368–73.

Our most lasting contribution to future generations would probably come from what economists call human capital—investments in people. Though the people who receive education and training are mortal, the ideas they bring forth are not. Knowledge endures.[4]

Current actions could also reduce future welfare levels, however. Fossil fuel combustion could modify the climate to the detriment of future agriculture. By depleting the atmosphere's ozone, current chlorofluorocarbon emissions might raise the incidence of skin cancer. The storage of radioactive wastes could increase the likelihood of genetic damage in the future. The reduction of genetic diversity in the stock of plants and animals could well reduce future medical discoveries.

Suppose that high levels of sustainable welfare are feasible. Would our economic system automatically choose a growth path that produces sustainable welfare levels, or could it choose one that enriches current generations at the expense of future generations?

Market Allocations

Market imperfections—including intertemporal externalities, free-access resources, and market power—play havoc with the ability of a market to achieve sustainable outcomes. They create incentives that can interfere in important ways with the quest for sustainable development.

Allowing free access to resources promotes unsustainable allocations. Because free-access resources are overexploited by current generations, diminished stocks are left for the future. In the extreme it is even possible that the species would become extinct.

Intertemporal externalities also undermine the ability of the market to produce sustainable outcomes. Emissions of greenhouse gases impose a cost on future generations that is external to current generations. Current actions to reduce the gases will cost this generation money, but the benefits would not be felt until significantly later. Economic theory clearly forecasts that too many greenhouse gas emissions would be forthcoming for the sustainability criterion to be satisfied.

The general conclusion that market imperfections exacerbate the problem of unsustainability, however, would not be correct. For example, the existence of an oil cartel holding up prices serves to retard demand and conserve more for future generations than would otherwise be the case.

Markets can sometimes provide a safety valve to ensure sustainability when the supply of a renewable resource is threatened. Fish farming is one example where declining supplies of a renewable resource trigger the availability of an alternative renewable substitute. Even when the government intervenes detrimentally in a way that benefits current generations at the expense of future generations, as it did with natural gas, the market can limit the damage. The market for solar energy still exists as a substitute for natural gas, so the effect of government

---

[4]Although it is true that ideas can last forever, the value of those ideas may decline with time as they are supplanted by new ones. The person who conceived of horseshoes made an enormous contribution to society at the time, but the value of that insight to society has diminished along with our reliance on horses for transportation.

regulation was to make the transition significantly less smooth than it might have been, rather than preventing the transition.

The notion that left to their own devices markets would automatically provide for the future is naive, despite their apparent success in providing for generations in the past.

Efficiency and Sustainability

Suppose future governments were able to eliminate all market imperfections, restoring efficiency to the global economic system. In this idealized world, intertemporal and contemporaneous externalities would be reduced to efficient levels. Access to common resources would be restricted to efficient levels, and harvesting excess capacity would be eliminated. Competition would be restored to previously cartelized natural-resource markets. Would this package of policies be sufficient to achieve sustainability or is something more required?

One way to examine this question is to examine a number of different models that capture the essence of intertemporal resource allocation. For each model the question becomes, "Will efficient markets automatically produce sustainable development?" The conclusion to be drawn from these models is very clear: Restoring efficiency is not sufficient to produce sustainability.

Take the allocation of depletable resources over time. Imagine a simple economy where the only activity is the extraction and consumption of a single depletable resource. Even when the population is constant and the demand curves are stable, the efficient quantity profiles show declining consumption over time. In this hypothetical world, later generations would be unambiguously worse off unless current generations transferred some of the net benefits into the future. Even an efficient market allocation would not be sustainable in the absence of transfers.

The existence of an abundant renewable resource to serve as a backstop (solar energy, for example) would not solve the problem; even in this more congenial set of circumstances, the quantity profile of the depletable resource would still involve declining consumption until the backstop was reached. In the absence of compensating transfers, even efficient markets would use the depletable resources to support a higher current standard of living than could be supported indefinitely.

Dasgupta and Heal find a similar result for a slightly more realistic model.[5] They examine an economy where a single consumption good is produced by combining capital with a depletable resource. The finite supply of the depletable resource can be used to produce capital as well as be used in combination with capital to produce the consumption good. The more capital produced, the higher is the marginal product of the remaining depletable resource.

They prove that a sustainable constant consumption level exists in this model. The rising capital stock (implying a rising marginal product for the depletable resource) would compensate for the declining availability of the depletable resource. They also prove, however, that

---

[5]P. S. Dasgupta and G. M. Heal, *Economic Theory and Exhaustible Resources* (Cambridge, UK: Cambridge University Press, 1979): 299.

the use of any positive discount rate would necessarily result in declining consumption levels, a violation of the sustainability criterion. Discounting, of course, is an inherent component of dynamically efficient allocations.

In all of these models, sustainable development is possible, but it is not the choice made by efficient markets. Why not? What would it take to assure sustainable allocations? Hartwick shows that the achievement of a constant per capita consumption path (which would satisfy our definition of sustainability) results when all scarcity rent is invested in capital. None of it should be consumed by current generations.[6]

Would all scarcity rent be invested? With a positive discount rate, some of the scarcity rent is consumed by the current generation, violating the Hartwick rule. The point is profound. Restoring efficiency will typically represent a move toward sustainability, but it will not, by itself, be sufficient. Further policies must be implemented to guarantee sustainable outcomes.

How about renewable resources? At least in principle, renewable resource flows could endure forever. Are efficient market allocations of renewable resources compatible with sustainable development? John Pezzey has examined the sustainability of an allocation of a single renewable resource (such as corn) over time.[7] Sustained growth of welfare can occur in this model, but only if two conditions both hold: (1) The resource growth rate exceeds the sum of both the discount rate and the population growth, and (2) the initial food supply is sufficient for the existing population. The first condition is sometimes difficult to meet, particularly with rapid population growth and slow-growing biological resources. Sustainable development of renewable resources is very much harder in the presence of rapid population growth rates because the pressure to exceed sustainable harvest rates becomes irresistible.

Global climate change presents a rather different example where efficiency may not be sufficient for sustainability. Because the present-value component of dynamic efficiency emphasizes short- term over long-term consequences, the current costs of controlling emissions would be weighed more heavily than the distant future damages caused by global warming. Though this approach is not inherently biased against future generations, their interests would only be adequately protected if they would be willing to accept monetary compensation for a modified climate and if current generations were willing to set aside sufficient proceeds to provide this compensation. Because it is not obvious that either condition would be satisfied in practice, the long lead times associated with this particular problem place in jeopardy the interests of future generations in maintaining a stable climate.

Efficient allocations can also violate the notion of sustainability in a deeper sense. Because the definition of sustainability we have used in the immediately preceding analysis is based upon nondeclining average welfare levels, it does not require the preservation of individual resources. Harvesting fish stocks to extinction, for example, would be compatible with this definition of sustainability as long as future generations were sufficiently compensated.

However, we don't really know how much they would value the continued existence of those fish stocks. Not only is our knowledge about the ultimate ecosystem effects of the extinction of any species extremely limited, we have no idea how valuable those fish would be to

---

[6]J. M. Hartwick, "Intergenerational Equity and the Investing of Rents from Exhaustible Resources," *American Economic Review* 67 (December 1977): 972–74.

[7]John Pezzey, "Economic Analysis of Sustainable Growth and Sustainable Development," Working Paper No. 15 (Washington, DC: World Bank Environment Department, 1989): 43–46.

future generations. It is possible that they would value the continued existence of the population substantially more than we. Not only would the appropriate amount of the compensation be difficult to determine (because we don't know their preferences), but making compensation would be silly if they value the continued existence of the population more than any compensation (including accrued interest) we would be willing to pay.

One rather straightforward way to deal with this uncertainty is to include in the definition of sustainability some protection of the resources themselves. According to this logic, because it is impossible to know the value future generations place on specific renewable resources, we can only preserve their options by guaranteeing access to the resources. Efficiency would certainly not guarantee this outcome, but preserving resources would.

We must be careful to distinguish between what has been said and what has not been said. We have shown that efficient markets would not always achieve sustainable development paths. This does not mean that they would not ever or even not normally result in sustainable allocations! Indeed, the historical record reviewed in the previous chapter suggests that the incompatibility of the efficiency criterion and the sustainability criterion has been the exception, not the rule. Capital accumulation and technological progress have expanded the ways in which resources could be used and have increased subsequent welfare levels in spite of a declining resource base. Nonetheless, the two criteria are not inevitably compatible. As resource bases diminish and global externalities increase, the conflict can be expected to become more important.

A MENU OF OPPORTUNITIES

Is sustainable development just an unrealistic attempt to provide false hope in the face of a rather bleak future? Human nature being what it is, we need to have hope. When the situation is hopeless, the natural human tendency is to create scenarios that offer the illusion of hope. Is sustainable development one of those scenarios? Or can reasonable, skeptical people find grounds for believing in the existence of new forms of development that can raise living standards while respecting both the environment and the rights of future generations?

Although it is not possible in the space we have to go into detail about the various techniques that fulfill this vision, it is possible to convey a flavor[8] with the hope that this flavor will be sufficient to demonstrate that sustainable development is a pragmatic possibility, not merely an illusion.

Agriculture

Most experts believe that food supply can be expanded to meet the forecasted increases in population, but sustainable development requires this expansion to take place in a way that does not destroy the natural environment. What are the prospects?

---

[8]The material in this section comes mainly from three excellent articles: Pierre R. Crosson and Norman J. Rosenberg, "Strategies for Agriculture"; John H. Gibbons, Peter D. Blair, and Holly L. Gwin, "Strategies for Energy Use"; and Robert A. Frosch and Nicholas E. Gallopoulos, "Strategies for Manufacturing." All can be found in *Scientific American* 261, No. 3 (September 1989). Readers interested in more detail should consult those articles and the references cited at the end of each article.

Multiple cropping, which includes crop rotations, intercropping (sometimes with trees and annual crops sharing the same fields), overseeding legumes into cereals, and double cropping, is one technique that offers the potential for reduced agricultural chemicals, increased productivity, less erosion, and more effective use of water. The concept is not new. A system employed in central America since pre-Columbian times intermixes maize, beans, and squash. The maize provides a trellis for the beans; the beans enrich the soil with nitrogen; and the squash provides ground cover, reducing erosion, soil compaction, and weed growth.

Trees can be used in multiple cropping. In West Africa, leaf litter from the *Acacia alba* enriches the soil for the benefit of various grain and vegetable crops grown between them. In the American Midwest, farmers are experimenting with growing corn with other, low-growing plants. In one experiment in Nebraska, two-row corn windbreaks were spaced every 15 rows through a field of sugar beets. The wind shelter provided by the corn increased sugar production by 11 percent. The greater access to sunlight and carbon dioxide increased corn yields by 150 percent.

In Montana, tall wheatgrass, a perennial, has been used to protect winter wheat. In winter wheatgrass barriers capture snow, forming a uniform layer that insulates dormant plants from the effects of extremely low temperatures. In spring the snow melts, providing the moisture winter wheat needs for early growth. Once the winter wheat begins to grow, the wheatgrass serves as a wind barrier.

Multiple cropping can reduce the need for pesticides. In fields where crops are rotated regularly, pests (weeds, insects, and pathogens) cannot adapt themselves to a single set of environmental conditions and therefore do not increase as quickly.

Biotechnology and new irrigation techniques also offer prospects for reduced fertilizer and water use. Developing plants that "fix" nitrogen in the soil would lessen the demand for nitrogen fertilizer, and incorporating genes from pest-resistant plants into commercial crops could reduce the need for pesticides. Trickle (or drip) irrigation systems would reduce the amount of water needed by increasing the efficiency of the water used. Already widely used in Israel and part of the United States, trickle irrigation can also reduce the problems associated with salt buildup.

Energy

Prior to the 1970s, increases in the gross national product were always accompanied by proportionate increases in energy consumption. This relationship proved so stable that it was used for forecasting energy consumption. Some observers at the time took this relationship as evidence that proportionate increases in energy would be a necessary condition for growth.

Following the oil embargo and the accompanying increases in prices during the 1970s, it became clear that growth and energy consumption did not have to move in lockstep. The industrialized world's energy intensity—the amount of energy used to produce one unit of gross national product—fell by one-fifth between 1973 and 1985. In the United States, gross national product grew 40 percent while energy consumption remained constant.

Energy efficiency is the short-run key to sustainable development because it offers the opportunity to increase living standards without increasing energy consumption. Enhanced energy efficiency—which can stretch energy supplies, slow climate changes, and buy time to

TABLE 20.1 Opportunities for Greater Energy Efficiency

	Car (mi/gal)	Home (1,000J/m²)	Refrigerator (kWh/day)	Gas Furnace (million J/day)	Air Conditioner (kWh/day)
Model Average	18	190	4	210	10
New Model	27	110	3	180	7
Best Model	50	68	2	140	5
Best Prototype	77	11	1	110	3

Source: Adapted from John H. Gibbons, Peter D. Blair, and Holly L. Gwin, "Strategies for Energy Use," *Scientific American* 261, No. 3 (September 1989): 141. Copyright © 1989 by Scientific American, Inc. All rights reserved.

develop alternative energy resources—can be achieved in a variety of ways. Some of the possibilities are presented in Table 20.1.

Consider one possibility in more detail. Advanced building materials can sharply reduce loss of heat through windows, doors, and walls. In "superinsulated" homes, where normal insulation is doubled and a liner forms an airtight seal in walls, heat radiating from people, light, stoves and other appliances alone can warm the house. In comparison with the average home built in the United States, some superinsulated homes in Minnesota require 68 percent less heat; for some residences in Sweden the saving is higher. Similar savings would be possible in lighting, transportation, and manufacturing.

Waste Reduction

Sustainable development involves a more integrated approach to production than has traditionally been practiced in order to reduce raw material demands and waste discharge. In such an integrated system the consumption of energy and materials is optimized, waste generation is minimized, and the effluents of one process—whether they are spent catalysts from petroleum refining, fly and bottom ash from electric-power generators, or discarded plastic containers from consumer products—serve as raw materials for another process.

As the costs of waste disposal rise and the regulations dealing with hazardous waste disposal become more strict, examples of industries adopting this type of integrated approach become more prevalent. Meridian National, a midwestern steel-processing company, now reprocesses the sulfuric acid with which it removes scale from steel sheets and slabs, reuses the acid, and sells ferrous sulfate compounds to magnetic tape manufacturers.

At the Atlantic Richfield Company's Los Angeles refinery complex, a series of relatively low-cost changes have reduced waste volumes from about 12,000 tons a year during the early 1980s to about 3,400 tons by the end of the decade. Because disposal costs were about $300 a ton, the company saved over $2 million a year in disposal costs alone.

E X A M P L E   2 0 . 1

Sustainable Development: Three Success Stories

In Kenya, 83 percent of the urban population and 17 percent of rural households use charcoal stoves known as *jikos*. A household in Nairobi with one wage earner typically spends more than one fifth of its income on charcoal. The typical *jiko* is very energy inefficient; it represents an unnecessary drain on both income and the forests that supply the wood for charcoal.

In 1981 the government of Kenya and a local nongovernmental organization began a project disseminating a new, more energy-efficient stove. By 1985 the new stove had captured 10 percent of the market. Nationwide savings on fuel were in the neighborhood of $2 million annually.

Much of Central America is faced with declining soil fertility due to soil erosion and monocropping. Guinope, Honduras, was not an exception. Farmers were migrating out of the area, and those remaining were plagued by low incomes.

In 1981, World Neighbors, a private voluntary organization, introduced a sustainable agriculture program that relied on soil conservation practices in use elsewhere in Central America. The program included constructing drainage ditches, planting grass barriers, erecting rock walls, training farmers in fertilizing methods using chicken manure, intercropping leguminous plants, and using some chemical fertilizers. Significantly, no subsidies were involved at all. All costs were borne by the farmers.

In the first year the yields tripled and in some cases quadrupled. Nearby villages have requested training and the program is spreading rapidly.

In Brazil, some 500,000 rubber tappers (*seringueiros*) have made their living from the Amazon since the late 1800s. Recently their livelihood was threatened by the migration of large numbers of people to the forests seeking land. Encouraged by government subsidies, these migrants ultimately discovered the land to be unsuitable for agriculture once the forest canopy has been removed. One sustainable form of land use was being jeopardized by another unsustainable land use.

On 30 June 1987, the Brazilian government created an extractive reserve for the rubber tappers and in the process provided protection for the countless genetic species found in the forest. The extractive reserve allows continued extraction of rubber (as well as nuts and other renewable products) but protects the forest and its people from the ravages of deforestation.

Source: Walter V. C. Reid, "Sustainable Development: Lessons From Success," *Environment* 31, No. 4 (May 1989): 7–9, 29–35.

Markets have been found for much of Atlantic Richfield's former waste, adding further revenue. The company sells its spent alumina catalysts to Allied Chemical and its spent silica catalysts to cement makers. Alkaline carbonate sludge from a water-softening operation at the refinery goes to a sulfuric acid manufacturer a few miles away, where it neutralizes acidic wastewater.

Sustainable development frequently requires changes in how economic activities are conducted. Some of those changes are already occurring (see Example 20.1); others await additional policy changes.

MANAGING THE TRANSITION

If sustainable development is in fact possible and unfettered markets are not capable, by themselves, of managing the transition, what can be done? How can the transition to sustainable development be accomplished?

Our situation is similar to that of the thoroughly disoriented tourist, a central character in Maine folklore. Enticed by unusually brilliant fall foliage, a tourist forsook the security of the well-marked main highways for some less traveled country roads. After an hour of driving, he was no longer sure he was even headed in the right direction. Seeing a Maine native mending a fence, he pulled over to the side of the road to seek assistance. After hearing the tourist's destination, the native sadly shook his head and in his best Maine accent responded "If I was goin' they-uh, I sure wouldn't start from he-uh!"

Had we known long ago that human activities could seriously impact environmental life support systems and could deny future generations the quality of life to which our generation has become accustomed, we might have chosen a different, more sustainable, path for improving human welfare. The fact that we did not have that knowledge and therefore did not make that choice years ago means that current generations are faced with making more difficult choices with fewer options. These choices will test the creativity of our solutions and the resilience of our social institutions.

The task of managing the transition to sustainable development is made more difficult by the fact that some entrenched development paths are not only unsustainable themselves, they have so dominated sustainable strategies that switching from one to the other has become very difficult.

Southern California represents a case in point. In the Los Angeles air basin the ambient air-quality standards, designed to protect human health, are currently violated on the order of 150 out of the 365 days a year. Due to the way the city has developed, regulators in Los Angeles now face a very difficult problem. As a prime example of an automobile city, population growth in Los Angeles has spawned land-use patterns that accommodate the automobile and are, in turn, accommodated by the automobile. Responding to a massive program of highway construction and low gasoline prices, the city has become very spread out, with highly dispersed residential and employment locations. Because the efficient use of mass transit requires the existence of high-density travel corridors, an effective public transit alternative is now difficult to implement, though it could have been quite possible before the highly dispersed land use patterns became so firmly entrenched. The options left open to these regulators have steadily diminished over time. The entire fabric of life in the Los Angeles area is so interwoven with automobile access that the problem cannot be solved without envisioning fairly radical changes in lifestyle.

To meet the challenges of the next century it will be necessary to foster and support institutional change by being somewhat more creative in how we deal with environmental policy. One key to exploiting these opportunities involves harnessing the power of the marketplace and focusing that power on the reduction, or even eradication, of poverty in an environmentally sound manner.

Prospects for International Cooperation

As the scale of economic activity has proceeded steadily upward, the scope of environmental problems triggered by that activity has transcended both geographic and generational boundaries. Whereas the nation-state used to be a sufficient form of political organization for resolving environmental problems, that may no longer be the case. Whereas each generation of humans used to have the luxury of being able to satisfy its own needs without worrying about the needs of those generations to come, that is no longer the case, either. Solving problems such as poverty, global warming, ozone depletion, and the loss of biodiversity requires international cooperation. Ideally, the search for solutions would also involve intergenerational cooperation, but, of course, that is not possible. Future generations cannot speak for themselves; we must speak for them. Our policies must incorporate our obligation to future generations, however difficult or imperfect that incorporation might prove to be.

International cooperation is by no means a foregone conclusion. Global environmental problems can trigger very different effects on the countries that will sit around the negotiating table. Whereas low-lying countries could be completely submerged by the sea-level rise predicted by some global warming models or arid nations could see their marginal agricultural lands succumb to desertification, other nations may see agricultural productivity rise as warmer climates support longer growing seasons in traditionally intemperate climates.

Countries that unilaterally set out to improve the global environmental situation run the risk of making their businesses vulnerable to competition from less conscientious nations. Industrialized countries that undertake stringent environmental policies may not suffer greatly at the national level (due to offsetting employment and income increases in the industries producing pollution-control equipment), but some individual industries facing the stringent regulations will face higher costs than their competitors and can be expected to suffer accordingly. Declining market share and employment in industries confronted by especially stringent regulations are powerful political weapons that can be used to derail efforts to implement an aggressive environmental policy. The search for solutions must accommodate these concerns.

Forging new international agreements is not enough. To produce the desired effect, the agreements must be enforceable. Enforceability will be a difficult criterion to satisfy as long as the agreements infringe upon significant segments of society with legitimate claims to an alternative future. The most legitimate such claim is perhaps advanced by those currently in abject poverty.

Many individuals and institutions currently have a large stake in maintaining the status quo. Fishermen harvesting their catch from an overexploited fishery are loath to undertake any reduction in harvests, even if the reduction is necessary to conserve the stock and to return the population to a healthy level. Farmers who have come to depend on fertilizer and pesticide subsidies will be reluctant to give them up. The principle of inertia applies to politics as fully as to physical bodies: A body at rest will tend to stay at rest unless a significant outside force is introduced. Changing economic incentives can provide that force.

Opportunities for Cooperation

This list of barriers to international cooperation is certainly imposing, but the new global environmental problems also offer new opportunities for cooperation, opportunities that in some ways are unprecedented. Although the degree to which various nations are affected by these problems differ, a point made earlier, it is also true that some potential common ground exists.

One important foundation for this common ground is the inefficiency of many current economic activities. In many cases these inefficiencies are very large indeed; resources are being wasted. Whenever resources are wasted, much more environmental improvement could be obtained for current expenditures or the same improvement could be realized with a much smaller commitment of resources. By definition, moving from an inefficient policy to an efficient one creates gains to be shared. Agreements on how these gains should be shared among the cooperating parties can be used to build coalitions.

The natural reluctance of nations to impose increasingly stringent environmental policies within their borders can be diminished by assuring that the policies imposed are cost effective. We live in an age when the call for tighter environmental controls intensifies with each new discovery of yet another injury modern society is inflicting on the planet, but resistance to additional controls is growing with the recognition that the cost of compliance is also growing, as all the easy techniques become used up. Choosing cost-effective and flexible policy instruments can reduce the potential for backlash.[9]

The choice of policy instruments can also affect enforceability. In developing countries, local communities typically have the greatest accessibility to and knowledge about local biological resources. As these countries have undergone a centralization of political power, including the power to control these resources, some of the local commitment to them has been lost. Policy instruments that reestablish this commitment by offering these local communities a stake in the preservation of the resource can enhance enforceability.

With creative design of policy instruments, the incentives of local and global communities can become compatible. In some cases, being creative requires the use of conventional economic instruments in unconventional ways; in others, it requires the use of unconventional instruments in unconventional ways.

Unconventional approaches are not pipe dreams. Most of them have been successfully employed in one form or another in local communities around the globe. The experience with these instruments in their current setting provides a model for their use on an international level. How well this model fits remains an open question, but it is better to sit down for a dinner with a full menu offering some novel, but interesting, choices than one offering only a limited selection of familiar, unappetizing fare.

---

[9]One author has even suggested that nations imposing stringent environmental regulations on themselves end up gaining a competitive advantage in international markets. Using Germany and Japan to illustrate his point, Michael Porter concludes that being the first to develop new production techniques provides significant market opportunities when others subsequently adopt similar regulations and firms begin searching for the means of meeting them. See Michael E. Porter, "America's Green Strategy," *Scientific American* 264, No. 4 (April): 168.

Restructuring Incentives

How can economic incentives be used to provide the kinds of signals that will make sustainable development possible? Perhaps the best way to begin to answer this question is to recall a few examples of how this approach has worked in practice, focusing this time on how they fit into the quest for sustainable development.

Recall how the use of economic incentives was able to reduce the stress on an already overexploited New Zealand fishery. Due to their desirability and the traditional open access to the fishery, the populations of several species of fish off the coast of New Zealand were being depleted. Although the need to reduce the amount of pressure being put on the population was rather obvious, how to accomplish that reduction was not at all clear. It was relatively easy to prevent new fishermen from entering the fisheries, but it was harder to figure out how to reduce the pressure from those who had been fishing in the area for years or even decades. Because fishing is characterized by economies of scale, simply reducing everyone's catch proportionately wouldn't make much sense. That would simply place higher costs on everyone and waste a great deal of fishing capacity as all boats sat around idle for a significant proportion of time. A better solution would clearly be to have fewer boats harvesting the stock. That way each boat could be used closer to its full capacity without depleting the salmon population. Which fishermen should be asked to give up their livelihood and leave the industry?

The economic incentive approach addressed this problem by imposing transferable catch quotas on all fish harvested from the fishery. Revenues derived from the annual fee charged for renewing these quotas were used to buy out fishermen who were willing to forgo any future fishing for the relevant species. Essentially, each fisherman stated the lowest price that he or she would accept for leaving the industry; the regulators selected those who could be induced to leave at the lowest price, paid the stipulated amount from the tax revenues, and retired their catch quotas for the affected species. It wasn't long before a sufficient number of licenses had been retired and the fish population was protected. Because the program was voluntary, those who left the industry only did so when they felt they had been adequately compensated. A difficult and potentially dangerous pressure on a valuable natural resource had been avoided by the creative use of an approach that changed the economic incentives.

The fishery example shows how economic incentives can be used to reduce the conflict between economic development and the sustainable use of renewable resource. Economic incentives can also be used to make economic development the vehicle by which greater environmental protection is achieved. Recall the offset policy. Under this U.S. policy, firms already established in nonattainment areas that chose to voluntarily control their emissions more than required under the prevailing regulations had those excess emission reductions certified as "emission reduction credits." Once certified, their operating permits were tightened to assure that the reductions were permanent. These emission reduction credits could then be sold to new firms seeking to move into the nonattainment area providing that the acquiring firm bought at least 1.2 emission reduction credits for each 1.0 units of emissions added by the new plant. Air quality improved every time a new firm moved into the area. With this policy the confrontation between economic growth and environmental protection was diffused. Not only were new firms not allowed to move into polluted cities, they became one of the main vehicles for improving the quality of the air. Economic development facilitated, rather than blocked, air-quality improvement.

It now remains only to show how the entire menu of economic incentive policies can be woven together in a manner that facilitates international cooperation in the resolution of international environmental problems. Economic analysis suggests four principles that can provide the foundation for this approach.

The Full-Cost Principle.   According to full-cost principle, all users of environmental resources should pay their full cost. Those using the environment as a waste repository, for example, would be presumed responsible not only for controlling pollution to the full extent required by the law, but also for restoring environmental resources damaged beyond some *de minimus* amount and for compensating those suffering damage.

This principle is based upon the presumption that humanity has a right to a reasonably safe and healthy environment. Because this right has been held in common for the stratosphere and the international sections of the oceans, no administrative body has either the responsibility or the authority to protect that right. As a result, it has been involuntarily surrendered on a first-come, first-served basis without compensation.

Although global warming and ozone depletion impose both an international and intergenerational environmental cost, currently that cost is not being borne, or even recognized, by those who ultimately control the magnitude of the problem. Furthermore, those choosing unilaterally to reduce their emissions expose themselves to the higher costs associated with mitigating strategies. Applying the full-cost principle would send a strong signal to all users of the environment that the atmosphere is a scarce, precious resource and should be treated accordingly. Products produced by manufacturing processes that are environmentally destructive would become relatively more expensive; those produced by environmentally benign production processes would become relatively cheaper. Implementing the full-cost principle would end the implicit subsidy that all polluting activities have received since the beginning of time. When the level of economic activity was small, the corresponding subsidy was also small and therefore probably not worthy of political attention. Since the scale of economic activity has grown, however, the subsidy has become very large indeed; ignoring it leads to significant resource distortion.

What policy implications would flow from the acceptance of the full cost principle? A first implication is that emissions of harmful substances should bear an emission charge. For the global warming problem, this could take the form of a tax on all greenhouse gases emitted into the atmosphere. The "carbon tax," which is currently being widely discussed in Europe and the United States, could be one component of this package. However, because carbon dioxide is only one of the greenhouse gases, taxes would necessarily be imposed on other gases as well. The appropriate level of this tax for each gas would depend upon its per unit contribution to the global warming problem; gases posing a larger per unit risk would bear higher tax rates.

Substances contributing to ozone depletion would also be taxed according to the full-cost principle. Because the ozone depletion tax and the global warming tax would be separately assessed, substances such as CFCs that contribute to both global warming and ozone depletion would bear both taxes.

The transition to a more sustainable economic system will depend upon the development of new technologies and upon much greater levels of energy efficiency than are currently being achieved. Those transitions will not occur unless the prevailing economic incentives support and encourage them. Once the greenhouse gas and ozone depletion taxes were in effect, the incentives would be changed; greater energy efficiency and the development of new technologies would become top priority objectives.

Implications for the legal system would flow from the full-cost principle as well. For example, international laws should permit full recovery for damage caused by oil spills or other environmental incidents. Not only should the contaminated site be restored insofar as possible, but those suffering demonstrable losses should be fully compensated.

Making explicit environmental costs that have heretofore been hidden is only one side of the coin; the other is eliminating inappropriate subsidies. Subsidies that are incompatible with the full-cost principles should be eliminated. Implicit subsidies should be targeted as well as explicit ones. For example, when the pricing of environmental resources is subject to government regulation (such as water in the American Southwest), prices should not simply be determined by historic average cost, they should reflect the scarcity of the resource.

For one way to accomplish this, recall our discussion of incremental block pricing. Incremental block pricing provides a practical means of introducing the appropriate conservation incentives without jeopardizing the traditional legal constraint that water distribution utilities earn no more than a fair rate of return. With incremental block pricing, the price of additional water consumed rises with the amount consumed per unit time. Although the first units consumed per month up to some predetermined threshold would be relatively cheap, units consumed beyond the threshold would face a much higher price that truly reflects the scarcity of the resource. By assuring that the marginal units consumed were priced at full cost, adequate incentives to conserve would be introduced.

The transition to the full-cost principle could proceed gradually, beginning in certain sectors and moving to others as greater familiarity with the approach was gained. A complete, immediate transition is not an essential ingredient of a rational approach.

The Cost-Effectiveness Principle.   A policy is cost effective if it achieves the policy objective at the lowest possible cost. Cost effectiveness is an important characteristic because it can diminish political backlash by limiting wasteful expenditures.

Appropriate implementation of the full-cost principle would automatically produce cost effectiveness as a side benefit. Should acceptance of the full-cost principle falter, however, cost effectiveness could be elevated to a primary policy goal, worthy in its own right. It provides a desirable, if less than perfect, fallback position.

Political acceptance of the full-cost principle is by no means a foregone conclusion. Although taxes on greenhouse and ozone depletion gases can go a long way toward rectifying some of the current distortions in resource pricing, they will do little to reassure those whose vision of the future is defined in terms of specific limits on emissions, not correcting price distortions. It would be very difficult to establish a set of tax rates that could guarantee a specific emissions target.

If international agreements were to proceed by establishing global limits for greenhouse gases (the approach taken for ozone depleting gases), allocating the proposed reductions among the nations of the world would be one of the most difficult aspects of this alternative approach. Fairness will no doubt be one critical aspect of the negotiations, and it is likely that some form of cost-sharing will result. How are the costs to be shared?

Recall our discussion of transferable carbon emission rights. Emissions trading becomes a reasonable approach for implementing the cost-effectiveness principle while providing opportunities for cost-sharing. The process of establishing emissions trading in greenhouse gases would be initiated by setting transferable limits on the amounts each nation could emit on an annual basis. Nations achieving reductions greater than required by the agreement could receive transferable emission reduction credits that could be sold to other nations. By purchasing these credits, the acquiring nation could increase its quota by the amount covered by the emission reduction credits.

An international market in emission reduction credits would facilitate the movement of credits from those countries with the capacity to create them most cheaply to those countries faced by very high costs of additional control. The capacity to achieve cost effectiveness regardless of how the initial emission allowances are allocated is a significant attribute of an emissions trading approach that could be exploited for developing a market approach to cost-sharing. With emissions trading as the strategy of choice, those forging new international agreements would have a very large latitude in attempting to establish emission limitations that are fair and politically feasible without jeopardizing cost effectiveness. As the Western nations acquired by purchase the necessary production allowances at market prices from those nations selling them, significant financial transfers would take place. The size of these transfers would be dictated by market forces, not by negotiation.

The Property-Rights Principle.   Part of the evident loss of efficiency in modern environmental problems involves misspecified property rights, which create perverse incentives. According to the property-rights principle, local communities should have a property right over flora and fauna within their border. This property right would entitle the local community to share in any benefits created by preserving the species. Assuring that local property rights over genetic resources are defined and respected would give local communities a much larger stake in some of the global benefits to be derived from the use of those resources and would enhance the prospects for effective enforcement.

Recall our discussion of the problem of stemming the decline in the elephant population. Insofar as permitted by the migratory nature of the herd, the property-rights principle would confer the right to harvest a fixed number of elephants upon the indigenous peoples who live in the elephant's native habitat. Ownership of harvesting rights and the possibility of continued employment as long as the herd was preserved would assure an income to the local community, giving it a stake in preserving the herd. Preventing poaching would become easier because poachers would become a threat to the local community, not merely a threat to a distant national government that inspires little allegiance.

A somewhat related application of the property-rights principle could provide an additional means of resolving the diminishing supply of biologically rich tropical rain forests. One of the arguments for preserving biodiversity is that it offers a valuable gene pool for the development of future products such as medicines or food crops. Typically, however, the nations that govern the forestland containing this biologically rich gene pool have not shared in the wealth created by the products derived from it. Currently, nations cutting down their tropical forests have little incentive to protect the gene pool harbored within those forests because they are unlikely to reap any of the rewards that will ultimately result. Exploitation of the gene pool and the economic rewards that result from it typically accrue only to those nations and those companies that can afford the extensive research.

Recall our discussion of the use of royalties to provide an economic return to gene preservation. By establishing the principle that stipulated royalty payments would accrue to the nation from which the original genes were extracted, local incentives would become more compatible with global incentives.

The Sustainability Principle.   According to this principle, all resources should be used in a manner that respects the needs of future generations. Adopting the foregoing three principles would go a long way toward restoring efficiency. And restoring efficiency would set in motion the transition toward producing sustainable outcomes. As we have seen, however, restoring efficiency would not be sufficient. Other policies would be needed to satisfy the sustainability principle.

Restoring intergenerational fairness in the use of depletable resources might be an appropriate place to start. As the economic models have made clear, current incentives for sharing the wealth from the use of depletable resources are biased toward the present, even in efficient markets. Clearly this could be rectified by transferring some of the created wealth into the future, but how much?

Salah El Serafy has developed an ingenious, practical way to answer this question.[10] Calculate the present value of the net benefits received from the extraction of a depletable resource over its useful life. This becomes the wealth to be shared. Using standard annuity tables, calculate the constant annual payments that could be made from this fund forever. (In essence these payments represent the dividends and interest derived from the wealth; the principle would be left intact.) This constant annual payment is what can be consumed from the wealth created from the depletable resources. Receipts in excess of this amount (in the years the resource is being extracted and sold) must be paid into the fund. All succeeding generations receive the same annual payment; the payments continue forever.

The payments could be invested in research rather than in instruments producing a financial return. Such a strategy might envision, for example, setting aside through taxation a certain proportion of all proceeds from depletable resources for funding research on substitutes likely to be used by future generations. In the case of fossil fuels, for example, one might subsidize research into solar energy or the use of hydrogen as a fuel so that as fossil fuels are depleted, future generations would have the ability to switch to alternative sources easily without diminishing living standards in the process.

Another adjustment would confront the possibility of species extinction. Compensating future generations for extinct species (the implicit strategy in an efficient allocation) may not be adequate. Not only do we not know the appropriate level of compensation, it is possible that the preferences of future generations would be such that the value of the preserved species would exceed any possible compensation our generation would be willing to offer. Given this uncertainty about their preferences, one strategy would be to incorporate species preservation into our definition of sustainability to allow future generations to make their own valuations. With this approach, strategies that lead to species extinction would simply be infeasible, regardless of the net benefit calculations. The interests of future generations would be protected by preserving their options rather than by attempting to second-guess their preferences.

Adjusting the national income accounts would be another immediate implication of the sustainability principle. The income accounts must conform with the Hicksian definition of income. All of the costs, including the depreciation of natural capital, should be subtracted from the gross receipts in producing a national income figure. Failure to do this, as is the current practice, provides very misleading signals to the public sector. These misleading signals

---

[10]Salah El Serafy, "Absorptive Capacity, the Demand for Revenue, and the Supply of Petroleum," *The Journal of Energy and Development* 7, No. 1 (Autumn 1981): Appendix A.

provide powerful incentives for public figures to engage in economic activities that violate the sustainability principle.

Adopting the sustainability principle could also have consequences for the conduct of trade policy. Trade in commodities produced in violation of the principle could be prohibited or subject to trade sanctions.

The process to implement this change in policy is already in place. Under the General Agreement on Trade and Tariffs (GATT), current trade practices are scrutinized to ferret out those that are unfair. Dumping, defined as selling abroad at a price below the home market, is one trading practice that currently receives that scrutiny. Under U.S. antidumping statutes, when dumping is proved the U.S. Department of Commerce applies an antidumping duty as an offset and adds on a penalty. Nonsustainability could become another of the practices receiving such scrutiny without altering the current process by which the GATT agreement is enforced.

Less-targeted trade sanctions could also be used to make both signing an agreement and fulfilling its terms more attractive to reluctant signatories. The Packwood-Magnuson Amendment to the U.S. Fishery Conservation and Management Act (1976) requires the United States to retaliate whenever foreign nationals undermine the effectiveness of the International Whaling Convention. Specifically, an offending nation automatically loses half of its allocation of fish products derived from U.S. waters. Continued disregard of the convention by the foreign national leads to revocation of the right to fish in U.S. waters.

FORCED TRANSITION

Suppose that current levels of welfare were shown to be unsustainable and that an immediate transition to a new, lower standard of living were necessary to protect future generations. Suppose further that a "guided forced transition" would be less painful than a laissez-faire forced transition. How could that more abrupt transition be negotiated?

The most concrete proposals for a forced transition to the steady state come from Herman Daly, an economist with the World Bank.[11] Daly is very sympathetic with the goal of a rapid transition to sustainable development and has spent a good deal of his professional life looking into the best way to achieve that objective. We will focus on his proposals in examining how an economy might be forced to this new sustainable path more rapidly than would normally be the case.

Defining the Target

Daly begins by attempting to define the steady state, the target of his approach, and how we know when it is achieved. His definition is couched in physical, rather than value, terms. For Daly the *steady-state economy* is characterized by constant stocks of people and physical wealth maintained at some chosen, desirable level by a low rate of throughput. This through-

---

[11]Herman E. Daly, *Steady-State Economics* (San Francisco: W. H. Freeman, 1977). Expanded 2nd edition published by Island Press, 1991.

put—flows of resources and energy—provides direct consumption benefits (such as food and shelter) and investment, insofar as necessary to counteract depreciation of the capital stock.

Conceiving of the steady state in physical rather than value terms is significant because it forms an important difference between Daly and others who see the steady state as simply the absence of any development. Daly recognizes that some development would and should occur even in the steady state in spite of a constant stock of people and physical wealth. For example, as society learned more efficient ways to use energy, the value derived from the flow of energy may increase, even when the flow itself does not. Due to technological progress, the value of the services received can grow, even if the physical stocks and flows are unchanging. *The steady state and zero economic growth are not necessarily the same thing.*

Institutional Structure

Daly sees three institutional modifications as necessary for the rapid attainment of the steady state:

1. An institution for stabilizing population
2. An institution for stabilizing the stock of physical wealth and throughput
3. An institution to ensure that the stocks and flows are distributed fairly among the population

Allocation among alternative uses is handled by the market. Collective decisions are made on scale and distribution, but allocation remains with the market. Daly argues that the questions of scale, distribution, and allocation involve three separate policy goals and cannot all be served by the single instrument of prices. Market prices achieve the goal of efficient allocation; the other institutions are designed to achieve an optimal (sustainable) scale and an optimal (fair) distribution.

Population Stabilization.   According to the Daly proposals, population would be stabilized over the long run using an idea first put forth by Kenneth Boulding.[12] In this scheme each individual would be given the inalienable right to produce one (and only one!) child. Because this scheme over a generation allows each member of the current population to replace himself or herself, births would necessarily equal deaths and population stability would be achieved.

This scheme would award each person a certificate entitling the holder to have one child. Couples could pool their certificates to have two. Every time a child was born a certificate would be surrendered. Failure to produce a certificate would cause the child to be put up for adoption.

Certificates would be fully transferable. Families who placed a particularly high value on children could purchase extra certificates, whereas those who viewed parenting with something less than enthusiasm could sell certificates. As one of its virtues, this system would ensure that the overall objective of population stability would be achieved, but no family would

---

[12]Kenneth E. Boulding, *The Meaning of the Twentieth Century* (New York: Harper & Row, 1964).

be required to maintain a particular family size. Though every couple would be guaranteed the right to have two children, they could choose to have fewer or more than two.

Stock and Throughput Stabilization.   Daly suggests that *throughput* (the flow of energy and resources) should be held at some minimum level using depletion quotas for all depletable resources. These quotas would define the amount of the resource that could be extracted and used. Any extraction and use in excess of this quota would be illegal.

The size of these quotas would be determined by bureaucrats, but according to Daly, these bureaucrats would follow a specific rule. The quotas would be set at a level sufficiently stringent that the price of the resource in question would equal the price of the closest renewable substitute. When no close renewable substitute was available, the bureaucrats would be empowered to decide the most ethical level. Because the quotas would be auctioned off by the government, the government would extract all of the scarcity rent associated with the depletable resources. The quota prices would equal the scarcity rent of the covered resources.

Ensuring Distributional Fairness.   Daly also sees a need to override the normal channels for distributing income in the steady-state economy. In a growth economy, tensions between the rich and poor can be ameliorated by the opportunities for social and economic mobility that a growth economy provides. In a steady-state economy those opportunities are diminished, as the number of new jobs created is smaller.

To alleviate these tensions, Daly proposes establishing a maximum and minimum income level as well as a maximum limit on wealth. The minimum income level would be financed in part by progressive taxes with 100 percent marginal rates above the maximum income and wealth limits. Because these 100 percent tax rates would presumably yield very little revenue (the incentive to earn more having been eliminated), most of the revenue would come from the sale of depletion quotas and from lower tax rates on income levels between the minimum and maximum.

Administration

Critics point out that the Daly system would be expensive to implement. Large bureaucratic staffs would be needed to define the quotas, run the auctions, and ensure compliance. In an age where public sentiment seems to be for decreasing rather than increasing bureaucracy, this proposal would buck the trend. A universal quota system for depletable and renewable resources, in addition to being bureaucratically cumbersome, holds the potential to disrupt a smoothly operating institutional structure. Historically the only time a system such as this has been acceptable is during a war.[13]

Child certificates would also be administratively cumbersome and, in most of the industrialized world, unnecessary in light of rapidly declining fertility trends. In addition, child certificates raise moral questions. For example, this system tends to preserve the existing racial status quo. To minority groups with above-average birth rates and below-average incomes,

---

[13]In a personal communication honoring my request that he review this chapter and the one that precedes it, Herman Daly responded, "In my view the real threat to freedom and stimulus to bureaucratic control is *crisis,* and avoidance of crisis with a bit of collective action now seems a good strategy for maximizing freedom over the long run."

this looks like a policy to limit their proportion in the population. Even though that is clearly not the intended result, the suspicions raised create unnecessary tensions.

SUMMARY

Sustainable development refers to a process for providing for the needs of the present generation (particularly those in poverty) without compromising the ability of future generations to meet their own needs.

Market imperfections frequently make sustainable development less likely. Intergenerational externalities such as climate modification impose excessive costs on future generations. Free access to biological common-property resources can lead to excessive exploitation and even extinction of the species.

Even efficient markets do not necessarily produce sustainable development. Restoring efficiency is a desirable and helpful, but insufficient, means for producing sustainable welfare levels. Although in principle dynamically efficient allocations produce extraction profiles for depletable resources that are compatible with the interests of future generations, in practice this is not necessarily the case. Guaranteeing sustainability frequently requires compensation from the present to future generations, but profit-maximizing behavior produces compensation levels that are too low. Furthermore, adequate compensation levels may be difficult to define at best and it is not clear that financial payments can adequately compensate future generations for all of the options they might be asked to forgo.

New sustainable forms of development are possible, but they will not automatically be adopted. Economic incentive policies can be used to manage the transition from current practices to these new forms of development.

If it turns out that universally higher standards of living are not possible without exceeding the carrying capacity of the planet, a rapid transition to a new steady state involving levels of welfare lower than current levels would be needed. To examine how this might occur, we considered the proposals of economist Herman Daly. He sees three institutional modifications as necessary: (1) a new mechanism to control the distribution of income and wealth, (2) a system of annual quotas to govern the rate of consumption of both depletable and renewable resources, and (3) a plan to control population. The institutional modifications suggested by Daly would be implemented at a very high cost.

The search for solutions must recognize that market forces are extremely powerful. Attempts to negotiate agreements that seek to block those forces or to meet them head-on are probably doomed to failure. Nonetheless, it is possible to negotiate agreements that harness those forces and channel them in directions that enhance the possibilities of international cooperation. To take these steps will require thinking and acting in somewhat unconventional ways. Whether the world community is equal to the task remains to be seen.

FURTHER READING

Battie, Sandra S. "Sustainable Development: Challenges to the Agricultural Economics Profession," *American Journal of Agricultural Economics* 71, No. 5 (December 1989): 1083–1101. Contrasts the viewpoints of "deep ecology" sustainable development advocates with those of traditional economists and suggests some things each can learn from the other.

Costanza, Robert, et al. "The Ecological Economics of Sustainability: Making Local and Short-Term Goals Consistent with Global and Long-Term Goals," Working Paper No. 32 (Washington, DC: World Bank Environment Department, 1990). A catalogue containing abstracts of nearly 200 works in ecological economics presented at a 1990 conference on sustainability in Washington.

Pearce, David, Anil Markandya, and Edward B. Barbier. *Blueprint for a Green Economy* (London: Earthscan Publications, 1989). Seeks to answer the question, "If we accept sustainable development as a working idea, what does it mean for the way we manage a modern economy?"

Pirages, Dennis Clark, ed. *The Sustainable Society* (New York: Praeger Publishers, 1977). A multidisciplinary series of essays on the transition to a steady state.

Weiss, Edith Brown. "In Fairness to Future Generations," *Environment* 32, No. 3 (April 1990): 7–11, 30–31. A lawyer proposes a new doctrine to protect the interests of future generations and a set of principles and procedures for implementing that doctrine.

ADDITIONAL REFERENCES

Aniansson, Britt, and Uno Svedin. *Towards an Ecological Sustainable Economy* (Stockholm: Swedish Council for Planning and Coordination of Research, 1990).

Baumol, William J. "On the Possibility of Continuing Expansion of Finite Resources," *Kyklos* 39, No. 2 (1986): 167–79.

Becker, Robert A. "Intergenerational Equity: The Capital-Environment Trade-Off," *Journal of Environmental Economics and Management* 9, No. 2 (June 1982): 165–85.

Brown, Lester R., Christopher Flavin, and Sandra Postel. "Picturing a Sustainable Society," in Lester R. Brown et al., *State of the World: 1990* (New York: W. W. Norton, 1990): 173–90.

Daly, Herman E. "The Economic Growth Debate: What Some Economists Have Learned But Many Have Not," *Journal of Environmental Economics and Management* 14, No. 4 (December 1987): 323–36.

McNeeley, Jeffrey A. et al. "Strategies for Conserving Biodiversity," *Environment* 32, No. 3 (April 1990): 16–20, 36–40.

Redclift, Michael. *Sustainable Development: Exploring the Contradictions* (New York: Methuen, 1987).

Turner, R. Kery. *Sustainable Environmental Management: Principles and Practice* (Boulder, CO: Westview Press, 1988).

World Resources Institute. *Natural Endowments: Financing Resource Conservation for Development* (Washington, DC: World Resources Institute, 1989).

DISCUSSION QUESTIONS

1. Discuss the mechanism favored by Daly to control population growth. What are its advantages and disadvantages? Would it be appropriate to implement this policy now in the United States? For those who believe that it would, what are the crucial reasons? For those

who believe it is not appropriate, are there any circumstances in any countries where it might be appropriate? Why or why not?

2. "Every molecule of a nonrenewable resource used today precludes its use by future generations. Therefore, the only morally defensible policy for any generation is to use only renewable resources." Discuss.

3. "Future generations can cast neither votes in current elections nor dollars in current market decisions. Therefore, it should not come as a surprise to anyone that the interests in future generations are ignored in a market economy." Discuss.

CHAPTER 21

Visions of the Future Revisited

*Mankind was destined to live on the edge of perpetual disaster.
We are mankind because we survive. We do it in a half-assed way,
but we do it.*

PAUL ADAMSON, A FICTIONAL CHARACTER IN JAMES A. MICHENER'S *CHESAPEAKE*
(1978)

We have now come full circle. Having begun our study with two lofty visions of the future, we proceeded to dissect the details of the various components of these visions—population, the management of depletable and renewable resources, pollution, and the growth process itself. During these inquiries a number of useful insights were gained about individual environmental and natural-resource problems. Now it is time to step back and coalesce those insights into a systematic assessment of the two visions.

ADDRESSING THE ISSUES

In Chapter 1 we posed a number of questions to serve as our focus for the overarching issue of growth in a finite environment. Those questions addressed three major issues: (1) How is the problem correctly conceptualized? (2) Can our economic and political institutions respond in a timely and democratic fashion to the challenges presented? (3) Can the needs of the present generation be met without compromising the ability of future generations to meet their own need? Can short-term and long-term goals be harmonized? The next three segments of this section summarize and interpret the evidence uncovered.

Conceptualizing the Problem

At the beginning of this book we suggested that if the *Limits to Growth* team had correctly conceptualized the problem, theirs was the only conclusion that could be drawn. An exponential growth in demand coupled with a finite supply of resources implies that the resources must eventually be exhausted. If those resources are essential, society will collapse when they are exhausted.

We have seen that this is an excessively harsh characterization. The growth in the demand for resources is not insensitive to their scarcity. Though the rise in energy prices was triggered more by politics than by scarcity, it is possible to use higher energy prices as an example of how the economic system reacts.

The growth in demand following the increase in prices fell dramatically, with petroleum experiencing the largest reductions. In the United States, for example, total energy consumption in 1981 (73.8 quadrillion BTUs) was lower than it was in 1973 (74.6 quadrillion BTUs), despite increases in income and population. Petroleum consumption went from 34.8 quadrillion BTUs in 1973 to 32.0 quadrillion BTUs in 1981. Though some of this reduction was caused by sluggishness of the economy, price certainly played a major role.

Price is not the only factor that retards demand growth. Declines in population growth also play a significant role. Because the developed nations appropriate a disproportionate share of the world's resources, the dramatic decline in population growth in those countries has had a disproportionate effect on slowing the demand for resources.

Characterizing the resource base as finite—the second aspect of the model—is also excessively harsh: (1) This characterization ignores the existence of a substantial renewable resource base; (2) it focuses attention on the wrong issue; and (3) it supports ill-conceived attempts to measure the size of the resource base. We will consider each problem in turn.

In a very real sense, a significant proportion of the resource base is not finite. Plentiful supplies of renewable resources (including, significantly, energy) are available. The normal reaction to increasing scarcity of depletable resources is to switch to renewable resources. That is clearly happening. The most dramatic examples can be found in the transition to solar energy in its various forms.

Labeling the resource base as finite is also misleading because it suggests that our concern should be "running out." In fact for most resources we shall never run out. Millions of years of finite resources are left at current consumption rates. The rising cost of extracting and using those resources (including the cost to the environment), not the potential for exhausting them, is the chief threat to future standards of living. The limits on our uses of these resources are not determined by their scarcity in the crust of the earth, but rather by what we would have to sacrifice to extract and process the ores. The work by Skinner and others suggests that we may not be willing to pay the price required to extract some of the lower-grade sources of those minerals.

Ignorance of this basic point has led to a number of ill-fated attempts to measure the size of this finite resource base. The timing of the societal collapse in the *Limits to Growth* forecast was quite sensitive to the techniques used to forecast resource exhaustion. Conventional physical indicators, such as the static and the exponential reserve indices, are excessively pessimistic because they fail to take into account possibilities for expanding current reserves. Historically, no forecast based on these techniques has stood the test of time. There is no reason to expect any similar forecast to do so in the future. They are convenient because they can be readily calculated and easily interpreted, but they are also usually dead wrong.

Current reserves can be expanded in many ways. These include finding new sources of conventional materials as well as discovering new uses for unconventional materials, including what was previously considered waste. We can also stretch the useful life of these reserves by reducing the amount of materials needed to produce the products. Striking examples include the diminishing size of a typical computer system needed to process a given amount of information and the substantially diminished amount of energy needed to heat a superinsulated home.

Although our ability to assess what is happening to cost is far from perfect, two things seem clear. Historically, very little, if any, evidence supports a fear of impending scarcity of minerals. Our ability to develop lower-cost technologies for processing resources has dominated the necessity to extract lower-grade sources. As a result, in real terms, extraction costs have fallen rather than risen over time. However, the most recent evidence suggests that, for a number of minerals, a turning point has been reached in the last few years. For those resources, evidence of scarcity—in the form of rising relative prices and increased exploration activity—has appeared.

Not all errors in resource-base measurement have been committed by those having a tendency to understate the adequacy of the resource base. Errors in the other direction are committed by those who point to the abundance in the earth's crust and atmosphere of almost all substance on which we depend. Although the abundance of those substances may be supported by the evidence, the amounts we actually use will no doubt fall far short of the amounts available.

Paradoxically, some of the most obvious cases where limits are being approached, and the carrying-capacity concept has the most validity, involve renewable resources rather than depletable resources. Population growth is a key contributor to this phenomenon. Expanding populations force the cultivation of marginal lands and the deforestation of large, biologically rich tracts. The erosion of overworked soils diminishes their fertility and ultimately their productivity. Biological resources such as fisheries can be overexploited, even to the point of extinction. The problem with these resources is not their finiteness, but the way in which they have been managed.

Correct conceptualization of the resource scarcity problem suggests that both extremely pessimistic and extremely optimistic views are wrong. Impenetrable proximate physical limits on resource availability are typically not the problem; incentives and information are frequently a much more serious problem. But believing in unlimited amounts of all resources that could support continued economic growth at current rates forever is equally naive. Plenty of resources are available if we are willing to pay the price, but that price is now rising. Transitions to renewable resources, recycled resources, and less costly depletable resources have already begun.

Institutional Responses

One of the keys to understanding how society will cope with increasing resource scarcity and environmental damage lies in understanding how social institutions will react. Are market systems, with their emphasis on decentralized decision making, and democratic political systems, with their commitment to public participation and majority rule, equal to the challenge?

Our examination of the record seems to suggest that although our economic and political systems are far from infallible and some rather glaring deficiencies have become apparent, no fatal flaws have become evident.

On the positive side, markets have responded swiftly and automatically to deal with those resources experiencing higher prices. Demand has been reduced and substitution encouraged. Markets for recycling are growing, and consumer habits are changing. No one has had to oversee these responses to make sure they occur. As long as property rights are well-defined, the market system provides incentives for consumers and producers to respond to scarcity in a variety of useful ways. This characteristically rapid and smooth response illustrates none of the overshoot and collapse behavior anticipated by the *Limits to Growth* team.

Compelling as the evidence is for this point of view, it does not support the conclusion that, left to itself, the market would automatically choose a dynamically efficient or a sustainable path for the future. Market imperfections frequently make sustainable development less likely. The most serious limitations of the market become evident in how it treats common-property resources, such as the fish we eat, the air we breathe, and the water we drink. Left to its own devices, a market will overexploit common property resources, substantially lowering the net benefits received by future generations. If it is not compensated for by sufficient increases in net benefits elsewhere in the economy, such overexploitation could result in a violation of the sustainability criterion.

Even efficient markets do not necessarily produce sustainable development. Restoring efficiency is a desirable, but insufficient, means for producing sustainable welfare levels. Although in principle dynamically efficient allocations produce extraction profiles for depletable resources that are compatible with the interests of future generations, in practice this is not necessarily the case. Guaranteeing sustainability in the face of declining supplies of depletable resources requires compensation from present to future generations, but profit-maximizing behavior produces compensation levels that are too low. Furthermore, adequate compensation levels may be difficult to define at best, and it is not clear that financial payments could adequately compensate future generations for the options they might be asked to forgo.

The market has some capacity for self-correction. The decline of common-property fish catches, for example, has led to the rise of private-property fish farming. The artificial scarcity created by imperfectly defined property rights gives rise to incentives for the development of a private-property substitute.

This capacity of the market for self-healing, although comforting, is not always adequate. In some cases cheaper, more effective solutions (such as preventing the deterioration of the original natural resource base) are available. Preventive medicine is frequently superior to corrective surgery. In other cases, such as when our air is polluted, no good private substitutes are available. To provide an adequate response, it is sometimes necessary to complement market decisions with political ones.

The need for government intervention is particularly acute in controlling pollution. Uncontrolled markets not only produce too much pollution, they also tend to underprice commodities that contribute to pollution either when produced or consumed. Firms that unilaterally attempt to control their pollution run the risk of pricing themselves out of the market. Government intervention is needed to ensure that firms which neglect environmental damage in their operating decisions do not thereby gain a competitive edge.

Significant progress has been made in reducing the amount of pollution, particularly conventional air pollution. Recent regulatory innovations, such as the bubble and offset policies, represent major steps toward the development of a flexible but potential framework for controlling air pollutants. By making it less costly to achieve environmental goals, these reforms have limited the potential for a backlash against the policy. They have brought perceived costs more in line with perceived benefits. Emission charges have played a similar role for water pollution control in Europe.

It would be a great mistake, however, to assume that government intervention in resolving environmental problems has been uniformly benign. The acid rain problem was almost certainly initially made worse by a policy structure that focused on local rather than regional pollution problems. Requiring scrubbers for all new coal-fired electrical generating stations was done for purely political reasons and served to raise the cost of compliance unnecessarily.

Perhaps the most flagrant examples of counterproductive government intervention are to be found in treatment of energy and water resources. By imposing price ceilings on natural gas and oil, the government removed much of the normal resiliency of the economic system. With price controls the incentives for expanding the supply are reduced and the time profile of consumption is tilted toward the present. As was the case with natural gas, these controls can even cause biases that interfere with the transition to renewable resources. By holding water prices below the marginal cost of supply, water authorities have subsidized excess use. With price controls, resources that in a normal market would have been conserved for future generations are consumed by the current generation. When price controls are placed on normal market transactions, the overshoot syndrome anticipated by the *Limits to Growth* team can occur. The smooth transition to renewable resources that characterizes the normal market allocation is eliminated by price controls; shortages can arise.

Price controls also play a key role in the world hunger problem. By controlling the price of food, many developing countries have undervalued domestic agriculture. The long-run effect of these controls has been to increase these countries' reliance on food imports at a time when foreign exchange to pay for those imports is becoming increasingly scarce. Whereas developed countries have gone substantially down the road to price decontrol, less-developed countries have not yet been able to extricate themselves to a similar degree.

One aspect of the policy process that does not seem to have been handled well is the speed with which improvement has been sought. Public opinion polls have unambiguously shown that the general public supports environmental protection even when it raises costs and lowers employment. Policymakers have reacted to this resolve by writing very tough legislation designed to force rapid technological development.

Common sense suggests that tough legislation with early deadlines can achieve environmental goals more rapidly than weaker legislation with less tight deadlines. Common sense is frequently wrong. Writing tough legislation with early deadlines can have the opposite effect. Unreasonably tough regulations are virtually impossible to enforce. Recognizing this, polluters have repeatedly sought (and received) delays in compliance. It has frequently been better, from the polluter's point of view, to spend resources to change the regulations than to comply with them. This would not have been the case with less-stringent regulations, because the firms would have had no legally supportable grounds for delay.

In summary, the record compiled by our economic and political institutions has been mixed. It seems clear that simple prescriptions such as "leave it to the market" or "more government intervention" simply do not bear up under a close scrutiny of the record. The relationship between the economic and political sectors has to be one of selective engagement, complemented in some areas by selective disengagement. Each problem has to be treated on a case-by-case basis. As we have seen in our examination of a variety of environmental and natural resource problems, the efficiency and sustainability criteria allow such distinctions to be drawn and they provide a powerful basis for policy reform.

Sustainable Development

Historically, increases in inputs and technological progress have been important sources of economic growth in the industrialized nations. In the future some factors of production, such as labor, will not increase as rapidly as they have in the past. The effect of this decline on growth depends on the interplay among the law of diminishing marginal productivity, substitution possibilities, and technological progress. The law of diminishing marginal productivity suggests slower growth rates, whereas technological progress and the availability of substitution possibilities counteract this drag.

Our examination of empirical evidence suggests that increased environmental control has not currently had a large impact on the economy as a whole, although certain industries have been hit quite hard. Environmental policy has triggered only a small rise in the rate of inflation and a mild reduction in growth. Environmental policy has apparently contributed more jobs than it has cost. The notion that respecting the environment is incompatible with a healthy economy is demonstrably wrong.

The situation is similar for energy. Though rather large increases in energy prices have occurred, the portion of the slowdown in productivity growth during the 1970s attributed to these increases is not large. Some diminution of growth has certainly occurred, but it seems premature to suggest that rising energy prices have already forced a transition to a period of substantially lower productivity growth.

The economy is being transformed, however. It is not business as usual. Two particularly important aspects of this transformation are the decline in population growth and the rise in the importance of information as a driving economic force. Both aspects tend to reduce the degree to which physical limits constrain economic growth and increase the degree to which current welfare levels would be sustainable.

Recognizing that conventional measures of economic growth shed little light on the question, some crude attempts have been made to estimate whether or not growth in the industrialized countries has made the citizens of those countries better off. Results of these studies suggest that because growth has ultimately generated more leisure, longer life expectancy, and more goods and services, it has been beneficial. But more recent studies suggest that the benefits from growth have been steadily diminishing over time. One study found that further growth in the United States now lowers the economic well-being of the average U.S. citizen; at this stage of affluence the negative aspects were estimated to outweigh the positive aspects.

Our examination of the evidence suggests that the notion that all of the world's people are automatically benefited by economic growth is naive. Growth has demonstrably benefited the poor in the developed countries, but mainly through transfers from more well-off members of society, not exclusively from the direct effects of growth.

The future outlook for the less-industrialized nations is at best mixed. Solving many of their future environmental problems will require higher standards of living. However, following the path of development pioneered by the industrialized nations is probably not possible without triggering severe global environmental problems; the solution would become the problem. New forms of development will be necessary.

The less-industrialized countries must overcome a number of significant barriers if development is to become a reality. At the local level, rising populations face increasingly limited access to land or productive assets. At the national level, corruption and development policies discriminate against the poor. Globally their situation is worsened by rising debt burdens, falling prices for exports, and the flight of capital that could be used to create jobs and income.

New sustainable forms of development are possible and desirable, but they will not automatically be adopted in either the high-income or the low-income nations. Are cooperative solutions possible? Can any common ground be established?

The experience in the United States suggests that cooperative solutions may be possible even among traditional adversaries. Environmental regulators and lobbying groups with a special interest in environmental protection in the United States have traditionally looked upon the market system as a powerful and potentially dangerous adversary. That the market unleashed powerful forces was widely recognized and that those forces clearly acted to degrade the environment was widely lamented. Meanwhile, development proponents have traditionally seen environmental concerns as blocking projects that had the potential to raise living standards significantly. Conflict and confrontation became the *modus operandi* for dealing with this clash of objectives.

The climate for dealing effectively with both concerns has improved dramatically within the last few years. Not only have development proponents learned that in many cases short-term wealth enhancement projects that degrade the environment are ultimately counterproductive, but environmental groups have come to realize that poverty itself is a major threat to environmental protection. No longer are economic development and environmental protection seen as an "either-or" proposition. The focus has shifted toward the identification of policies or policy instruments that can promote the alleviation of poverty while protecting the environment.

In the last decade or so, the economic incentives approach to environmental and natural resource regulation has become a significant component of environmental and natural resource policy. Instead of mandating prescribed actions, such as requiring the installation of a particular piece of pollution-control equipment, this approach achieves environmental objectives by changing the economic incentives of those doing the polluting. Incentives can be changed by fees or charges, transferable permits, deposit-refund systems or even liability law. When the incentives an individual agent faces are changed, that agent can use his or her typically superior information to select the best means of meeting his or her assigned responsibility. When it is in the interest of individuals to change to new forms of development, the transformation can be amazingly rapid.

Public policy and sustainable development must proceed in a mutually supportive relationship. The government must ensure that the market is sending the right signals to all participants so that the sustainable outcome is compatible with other business objectives. Economic incentive approaches are a means of establishing that kind of compatibility. The experience with the various versions of this approach used in the United States, Europe, and Asia since the mid-1970s suggests that economic approaches in general are both feasible and effective.

How about global environmental problems? As the scale of economic activity has proceeded steadily upward, the scope of environmental problems triggered by that activity has transcended both geographic and generational boundaries. Whereas the nation-state used to be a sufficient form of political organization for resolving environmental problems, that may no longer be the case. Whereas each generation of humans used to have the luxury of being able to satisfy its own needs without worrying about the needs of those generations to come, that is no longer be the case either. Solving problems such as poverty, global warming, ozone depletion, and the loss of biodiversity requires international cooperation.

Economic incentives approaches could be helpful here as well. Emissions trading facilitates cost-sharing among participants while assuring cost-effective responses to the need for additional control. By separating the question of what control is undertaken from the question of who ultimately pays for it, the government widens the control possibilities significantly. Conferring property rights for biological populations on local communities provides an incentive for those communities to protect the populations. Strategies for reducing debt can diminish the pressure on forests and other natural resources that may be "cashed in" to pay off the debt.

The Courts are beginning to use economic incentives as well; judicial remedies for environmental problems are beginning to take their place alongside regulatory remedies. Take, for example, the problem of cleaning up already closed toxic waste sites. Current U.S. law allows the government to sue all potentially responsible parties who contributed to the contaminated site (such as waste generators or disposal site operators). These suits accomplish a double purpose: (1) They assure that the financial responsibility for contaminated sites is borne by those who directly caused the problem, and (2) they encourage those who are currently using those sites to exercise great care, lest they be forced to bear a large financial burden in the event of an incident. The traditional remedy of going to the taxpayers would have resulted in less revenue raised, fewer sites restored, and less-adequate incentives for users to exercise care.

Europe has tended to depend more on another type of economic incentive, the effluent or emission charge. This approach places a per unit fee on each unit of pollution discharged. Faced with the responsibility for paying for the damage caused by their pollution, firms recognize it as a controllable cost of doing business. This recognition triggers a search for possible ways to reduce the damage, including changing inputs, changing the production process, transforming the residuals to less harmful substances, and recycling by-products. The experience in the Netherlands, a country where the fees are higher than in most other countries, suggests that the effects can be dramatic.

Fees also raise revenue. Successful development, particularly sustainable development, requires a symbiotic partnership between the public and private sectors. To function as an equal partner the public sector must be adequately funded. If it fails to raise adequate revenue, the public sector becomes a drag on the growth process, but if it raises revenue in ways that distort incentives, that, too, can act as a drag on development. Effluent or emission charges offer the realistic opportunity to raise revenue for the public sector without producing inefficient incentives. Whereas other types of taxation discourage growth by penalizing legitimate development incentives, emission or effluent charges provide incentives for sustainable development. Some work from the United States suggests that the drag on development avoided by substituting effluent or emission charges for more traditional revenue raising devices such as capital gains, income, and sales taxes could be significant.

Incentives for forward-looking public action are as important as those for private action. The current national income accounting system provides an example of a perverse economic incentive. Though national income accounts were never intended to function as a device for measuring the welfare of a nation, in practice that is how they are used. National income per capita is a common metric for evaluating how well off a nation's people are. Yet the current construction of those accounts sends the wrong signals.

Rather than recognizing the recent *Exxon Valdez* spill for what it was, namely a decline in the value of the endowment of natural resources in the area, it is recorded as an increase in the national income. The spill boosted GNP! All the cleanup expenditures served to increase national income, but no account was taken of the consequent depreciation of the natural environment. Under the current system, the accounts make no distinction between growth that is occurring because a country is damaging its natural resource endowment, with a consequent irreversible decline in its value, and sustainable growth, where the value of the endowment remains. Only when suitable corrections are made to these accounts will governments be judged by the appropriate standards.

The power of economic incentives is certainly not inevitably channeled toward the achievement of sustainable development. They can be misapplied as well as appropriately applied. Tax subsidies to promote cattle ranching on the fragile soil in the Brazilian rain forest stimulated an unsustainable activity, which has done irreparable damage to an ecologically significant area. They must be used with care.

A Concluding Comment

Our society is currently evolving a complementary relationship among the economic system, the court system, and the legislative and executive branches of government that holds promise. We are not yet out of the woods, however. We the public must learn that part of the responsibility is ours. The government cannot solve all problems without our significant participation.

Not all behavior can be regulated. It costs too much to catch every offender. Our law enforcement system works because most people obey the law, whether anyone is watching or not. A high degree of voluntary compliance is essential if the system is to work smoothly.

The best resolution of the toxic-substance problem, for example, is undoubtedly for all makers of potentially toxic substances to be genuinely concerned about the safety of their products and to bite the bullet whenever their research raises questions. The ultimate responsibility for developing an acceptable level of risk must rest on the integrity of those who make, use, transport, and dispose of the substances. The government can assist by penalizing and controlling those few who fail to exhibit this integrity, but it can never substitute for integrity on a large scale. We cannot and should not depend purely upon altruism to solve these problems, but we should not underestimate its importance either.

The notion that we are at the end of an era may well be true, but we are also at the beginning of a new one. What the future holds is not the decline of civilization, but its transformation. As the opening quote to this chapter suggests, the road may be strewn with obstacles and our social institutions may deal with those obstacles with less grace and less finesse than we might hope for, but we are unquestionably making progress.

Index

THE THEATRE OF THE ABSURD

MARTIN ESSLIN was born in Hungary and grew up in Vienna. He majored in English and philosophy at the University of Vienna and attended the Reinhardt (Theatrical) Seminar, where he studied to be a director. Just as he was on the point of starting his theatrical career, in 1938, the Nazis moved into Vienna and he was forced to leave. He spent a year in Brussels, and then came to England, where he became a script-writer and producer for the B.B.C. He has written for the B.B.C. a large number of radio features on political, social and literary subjects and is at present head of its radio drama department. He is the author of *Brecht: The Man and His Work* (A 245).

by Martin Esslin

THE THEATRE OF THE ABSURD

ANCHOR BOOKS
Doubleday & Company, Inc., Garden City, New York

The Anchor Books edition is the first
publication of *The Theatre of the Absurd.*

Anchor Books edition: 1961

Library of Congress Catalog Card Number 61–13814
Copyright © 1961 by Martin Esslin

MME MARTIN: Quelle est la morale?
LE POMPIER: C'est à vous de la trouver.

Ionesco, *La Cantatrice Chauve*

CONTENTS

PREFACE

This is a book on a development in the contemporary theatre: the type of drama associated with the names of Samuel Beckett, Eugène Ionesco, Arthur Adamov, Jean Genet, and a number of other avant-garde writers in France, Britain, Italy, Spain, Germany, the United States, and elsewhere.

Books on theatre subjects have a tendency to be ephemeral; in most bookshops, the shelves with the autobiographies of star actors and collections of last year's hits have a tired look. I should never have written this book had I not been convinced that its subject had an importance transcending the somewhat confined world of theatre literature. For the theatre, in spite of its apparent eclipse through the rise of the mass media, remains of immense and, if anything, growing significance—precisely because of the spread of the cinema and television. These mass media are too ponderous and costly to indulge in much experiment and innovation. So, however restricted the theatre and its audience may be, it is on the living stage that the actors and playwrights of the mass media are trained and gain their experience and the material of the mass media is tested. The avant-garde of the theatre today is, more likely than not, the main influence on the mass media of tomorrow. And the mass media, in turn, shape a great deal of the thought and feeling of people throughout the Western world.

Thus the type of theatre discussed in this book is by no means of concern only to a narrow circle of intellectuals. It may provide a new language, new ideas, new approaches, and a new, vitalized philosophy to transform the modes of thought and feeling of the public at large in a not too distant future.

Moreover, an understanding of this kind of theatre, which is still misunderstood by some of the critics, should, I believe, also cast light on current tendencies of thought in other fields, or at least show how a new convention of this sort reflects the changes in science, psychology, and philosophy that have been taking place in the last half century. The theatre, an art more broadly based than poetry or abstract painting without being, like the mass media, the collective product of corporations, is the point of intersection where the deeper trends of changing thought first reach a larger public.

There has been some comment on the fact that the Theatre of the Absurd represents trends that have been apparent in the more esoteric kinds of literature since the nineteen-twenties (Joyce, Surrealism, Kafka) or in painting since the first decade of this century (Cubism, abstract painting). This is certainly true. But the theatre could not put these innovations before its wider public until these trends had had time to filter into a wider consciousness. And, as this book hopes to show, the theatre can make its own very original contribution to this new type of art.

This book is an attempt to define the convention that has come to be called the Theatre of the Absurd; to present the work of some of its major exponents and provide an analysis and elucidation of the meaning and intention of some of their most important plays; to introduce a number of lesser-known writers working in the same or similar conventions; to show that this trend, sometimes decried as a search for novelty at all cost, combines a number of very ancient and highly respectable traditional modes of literature and theatre; and, finally, to explain its significance as an expression—and one of the most representative ones—of the present situation of Western man.

It has been rightly said that what a critic wants to understand he must, at one time, have deeply loved, even if only for a fleeting moment. This book is written from the point of view of a critic who has derived some memorable experiences from watching and reading the work of the dramatists of the

Absurd; who is convinced that as a trend the Theatre of the Absurd is important, significant, and has produced some of the finest dramatic achievements of our time. On the other hand, if the concentration here on this one type of theatre gives the impression that its author is a partisan exclusively of its particular convention and cannot derive pleasure from any other type of theatre, this is due simply to his deliberate limitation to one subject for this one book. The rise of this new, original, and valuable dramatic convention certainly does not, in the opinion of this critic, wipe out all that has gone before, or invalidate the work of important dramatists, past, present, and to come, in other theatrical forms.

It is still too early to see clearly whether the Theatre of the Absurd will develop into a separate type of drama, or whether some of its formal and linguistic discoveries will eventually merge with a wider tradition, enriching the vocabulary and means of expression of the theatre at large. In either case, it deserves the most serious attention.

In writing this book I have been greatly helped by some of the authors discussed in it. The meetings I have had with these dramatists have been exhilarating experiences that, by themselves, have already richly rewarded me for writing it. I have been deeply touched by their kindness and am sincerely grateful to them, notably to Mr. Samuel Beckett; M. Arthur Adamov; M. and Mme. Eugène Ionesco; Señor Fernando Arrabal; Señor Manuel de Pedrolo; Mr. N. F. Simpson; and Mr. Harold Pinter.

I am also greatly indebted to Mr. Eric Bentley, who combines great scholarship with an inspiring enthusiasm for the theatre, and without whose encouragement and help this book might not have been written; to Dr. Herbert Blau, of the Actors' Workshop in San Francisco; Mr. Edward Goldberger; Mr. Christopher Holme; Señor F. M. Lorda; and Mr. David Tutaev for drawing my attention to writers and plays that fall within the purview of this book and for the loan of valuable books and manuscripts. My thanks are also due to Signora Connie Martellini Ricono, Mr. Charles Ricono, Miss Margery Withers, Mr. David Schendler, Mrs. Cecilia Gillie, and Mr. Robin Scott for helping me gain access to valuable

material and information, and to Miss Nancy Twist and
Messrs. Grant and Cutler for bibliographical assistance.

My wife helped me greatly by providing constructive criticism and encouragement.

MARTIN ESSLIN
London, March 1961

INTRODUCTION: THE ABSURDITY OF THE ABSURD

On November 19, 1957, a group of worried actors were preparing to face their audience. The actors were members of the company of the San Francisco Actors' Workshop. The audience consisted of fourteen hundred convicts at the San Quentin penitentiary. No live play had been performed at San Quentin since Sarah Bernhardt appeared there in 1913. Now, forty-four years later, the play that had been chosen, largely because no woman appeared in it, was Samuel Beckett's *Waiting for Godot*.

No wonder the actors and Herbert Blau, the director, were apprehensive. How were they to face one of the toughest audiences in the world with a highly obscure, intellectual play that had produced near riots among a good many highly sophisticated audiences in Western Europe? Herbert Blau decided to prepare the San Quentin audience for what was to come. He stepped onto the stage and addressed the packed, darkened North Dining Hall—a sea of flickering matches that the convicts tossed over their shoulders after lighting their cigarettes. Blau compared the play to a piece of jazz music "to which one must listen for whatever one may find in it." In the same way, he hoped, there would be some meaning, some personal significance for each member of the audience in *Waiting for Godot*.

The curtain parted. The play began. And what had bewildered the sophisticated audiences of Paris, London, and New York was immediately grasped by an audience of convicts. As the writer of "Memos of a First-Nighter" put it in the columns of the prison paper, the *San Quentin News*:

The trio of muscle-men, biceps overflowing, who parked all 642 lbs on the aisle and waited for the girls and funny stuff. When this didn't appear they audibly fumed and audibly decided to wait until the house lights dimmed before escaping. They made one error. They listened and looked two minutes too long—and stayed. Left at the end. All shook . . .¹

Or as the writer of the lead story of the same paper reported, under the headline, "San Francisco Group Leaves S.Q. Audience Waiting for Godot":

From the moment Robin Wagner's thoughtful and limbolike set was dressed with light, until the last futile and expectant handclasp was hesitantly activated between the two searching vagrants, the San Francisco company had its audience of captives in its collective hand. . . . Those that had felt a less controversial vehicle should be attempted as a first play here had their fears allayed a short five minutes after the Samuel Beckett piece began to unfold.²

A reporter from the San Francisco *Chronicle* who was present noted that the convicts did not find it difficult to understand the play. One prisoner told him, "Godot is society." Said another: "He's the outside."³ A teacher at the prison was quoted as saying, "They know what is meant by waiting . . . and they knew if Godot finally came, he would only be a disappointment."⁴ The leading article of the prison paper showed how clearly the writer had understood the meaning of the play:

It was an expression, symbolic in order to avoid all personal error, by an author who expected each member of his audience to draw his own conclusions, make his own errors. It asked nothing in point, it forced no dramatized moral on the viewer, it held out no specific hope. . . . We're still waiting for Godot, and shall continue to wait. When the scenery gets too drab and the action too slow, we'll call each other names and swear to part forever—but then, there's no place to go!⁵

It is said that Godot himself, as well as turns of phrase and characters from the play, have since become a permanent part of the private language, the institutional mythology of San Quentin.

Why did a play of the supposedly esoteric avant-garde make so immediate and so deep an impact on an audience of convicts? Because it confronted them with a situation in some ways analogous to their own? Perhaps. Or perhaps because they were unsophisticated enough to come to the theatre without any preconceived notions and ready-made expectations, so that they avoided the mistake that trapped so many established critics who condemned the play for its lack of plot, development, characterization, suspense, or plain common sense. Certainly the prisoners of San Quentin could not be suspected of the sin of intellectual snobbery, for which a sizable proportion of the audiences of *Waiting for Godot* have often been reproached; of pretending to like a play they did not even begin to understand, just to appear in the know.

The reception of *Waiting for Godot* at San Quentin, and the wide acclaim plays by Ionesco, Adamov, Pinter, and others have received, testify that these plays, which are so often superciliously dismissed as nonsense or mystification, *have* something to say and *can* be understood. Most of the incomprehension with which plays of this type are still being received by critics and theatrical reviewers, most of the bewilderment they have caused and to which they still give rise, come from the fact that they are part of a new, and still developing, stage convention that has not yet been generally understood and has hardly ever been defined. Inevitably, plays written in this new convention will, when judged by the standards and criteria of another, be regarded as impertinent and outrageous impostures. If a good play must have a cleverly constructed story, these have no story or plot to speak of; if a good play is judged by subtlety of characterization and motivation, these are often without recognizable characters and present the audience with almost mechanical puppets; if a good play has to have a fully explained theme, which is neatly exposed and finally solved, these often have neither a beginning nor an end; if a good play is to hold the mirror up to nature and portray the manners and mannerisms of the age in finely observed sketches, these seem often to be reflections of dreams and nightmares; if a good play relies on witty repartee and pointed dialogue, these often consist of incoherent babblings.

But the plays we are concerned with here pursue ends quite different from those of the conventional play and therefore use quite different methods. They can be judged only by the standards of the Theatre of the Absurd, which it is the purpose of this book to define and clarify.

It must be stressed, however, that the dramatists whose work is here presented and discussed under the generic heading of the Theatre of the Absurd do not form part of any self-proclaimed or self-conscious school or movement. On the contrary, each of the writers in question is an individual who regards himself as a lone outsider, cut off and isolated in his private world. Each has his own personal approach to both subject matter and form; his own roots, sources, and background. If they also, very clearly and in spite of themselves, have a good deal in common, it is because their work most sensitively mirrors and reflects the preoccupations and anxieties, the emotions and thinking of an important segment of their contemporaries in the Western world.

This is not to say that their works are representative of mass attitudes. It is an oversimplification to assume that any age presents a homogeneous pattern. Ours being, more than most others, an age of transition, it displays a bewilderingly stratified picture: medieval beliefs still held and overlaid by eighteenth-century rationalism and mid-nineteenth-century Marxism, rocked by sudden volcanic eruptions of prehistoric fanaticisms and primitive tribal cults. Each of these components of the cultural pattern of the age finds its characteristic artistic expression. The Theatre of the Absurd, however, can be seen as the reflection of what seems the attitude most genuinely representative of our own time's contribution.

The hallmark of this attitude is its sense that the certitudes and unshakable basic assumptions of former ages have been swept away, that they have been tested and found wanting, that they have been discredited as cheap and somewhat childish illusions. The decline of religious faith was masked until the end of the Second World War by the substitute religions of faith in progress, nationalism, and various totalitarian fallacies. All this was shattered by the war. By 1942, Albert Camus was calmly putting the question why, since life had lost all meaning, man should not seek escape in suicide. In one of the great, seminal heart-searchings of our time, *The Myth of Sisyphus*, Camus tried to diagnose the human situation in a world of shattered beliefs:

> A world that can be explained by reasoning, however faulty, is a familiar world. But in a universe that is suddenly deprived of illusions and of light, man feels a stranger. His is an irremediable exile, because he is deprived of memories of a lost homeland as much as he lacks the hope of a promised land to come. This divorce between man and his life, the actor and his setting, truly constitutes the feeling of Absurdity.[6]

"Absurd" originally means "out of harmony," in a musical context. Hence its dictionary definition: "out of harmony with reason or propriety; incongruous, unreasonable, illogical." In common usage in the English-speaking world, "absurd" may simply mean "ridiculous." But this is not the sense in which Camus uses the word, and in which it is used when we speak of the Theatre of the Absurd. In an essay on Kafka, Ionesco defined his understanding of the term as follows: "Absurd is that which is devoid of purpose. . . . Cut off from his religious, metaphysical, and transcendental roots, man is lost; all his actions become senseless, absurd, useless."[7]

This sense of metaphysical anguish at the absurdity of the human condition is, broadly speaking, the theme of the plays of Beckett, Adamov, Ionesco, Genet, and the other writers discussed in this book. But it is not merely the subject matter that defines what is here called the Theatre of the Absurd. A similar sense of the senselessness of life, of the inevitable devaluation of ideals, purity, and purpose, is also the theme of much of the work of dramatists like Giraudoux, Anouilh, Salacrou, Sartre, and Camus himself. Yet these writers differ from the dramatists of the Absurd in an important respect: They present their sense of the irrationality of the human condition in the form of highly lucid and logically constructed reasoning, while the Theatre of the Absurd strives to express its sense of the senselessness of the human condition and the

inadequacy of the rational approach by the open abandonment of rational devices and discursive thought. While Sartre
or Camus express the new content in the old convention, the
Theatre of the Absurd goes a step further in trying to achieve
a unity between its basic assumptions and the form in which
these are expressed. In some senses, the *theatre* of Sartre and
Camus is less adequate as an expression of the *philosophy* of
Sartre and Camus—in artistic, as distinct from philosophic,
terms—than the Theatre of the Absurd.

If Camus argues that in our disillusioned age the world has
ceased to make sense, he does so in the elegantly rationalistic
and discursive style of an eighteenth-century moralist, in well-
constructed and polished plays. If Sartre argues that existence
comes before essence and that human personality can be reduced to pure potentiality and the freedom to choose itself
anew at any moment, he presents his ideas in plays based on
brilliantly drawn characters who remain wholly consistent and
thus reflect the old convention that each human being has a
core of immutable, unchanging essence—in fact, an immortal
soul. And the beautiful phrasing and argumentative brilliance
of both Sartre and Camus in their relentless probing still, by
implication, proclaim a tacit conviction that logical discourse
can offer valid solutions, that the analysis of language will lead
to the uncovering of basic concepts—Platonic ideas.

This is an inner contradiction that the dramatists of the
Absurd are trying, by instinct and intuition rather than by
conscious effort, to overcome and resolve. The Theatre of the
Absurd has renounced arguing *about* the absurdity of the human condition; it merely *presents* it in being—that is, in terms
of concrete stage images of the absurdity of existence. This is
the difference between the approach of the philosopher and
that of the poet; the difference, to take an example from another sphere, between the *idea* of God in the works of Thomas
Aquinas or Spinoza and the *intuition* of God in those of St.
John of the Cross or Meister Eckhart—the difference between
theory and experience.

It is this striving for an integration between the subject matter and the form in which it is expressed that separates the
Theatre of the Absurd from the Existentialist theatre.

The Theatre of the Absurd must also be distinguished from

another important, and parallel, trend in the contemporary French theatre, which is equally preoccupied with the absurdity and uncertainty of the human condition: the "poetic avant-garde" theatre of dramatists like Michel de Ghelderode, Jacques Audiberti, Georges Neveux, and, in the younger generation, Georges Schehadé, Henri Pichette, and Jean Vauthier, to name only some of its most important exponents. This is an even more difficult dividing line to draw, for the two approaches overlap a good deal. The "poetic avant-garde" relies on fantasy and dream reality as much as the Theatre of the Absurd does; it also disregards such traditional axioms as that of the basic unity and consistency of each character or the need for a plot. Yet basically the "poetic avant-garde" represents a different mood; it is more lyrical, and far less violent and grotesque. Even more important is its different attitude toward language: the "poetic avant-garde" relies to a far greater extent on consciously "poetic" speech; it aspires to plays that are in effect poems, images composed of a rich web of verbal associations.

The Theatre of the Absurd, on the other hand, tends toward a radical devaluation of language, toward a poetry that is to emerge from the concrete and objectified images of the stage itself. The element of language still plays an important, yet subordinate, part in this conception, but what *happens* on the stage transcends, and often contradicts, the *words* spoken by the characters. In Ionesco's *The Chairs*, for example, the poetic content of a powerfully poetic play does not lie in the banal words that are uttered but in the fact that they are spoken to an ever-growing number of empty chairs.

The Theatre of the Absurd is thus part of the "anti-literary" movement of our time, which has found its expression in abstract painting, with its rejection of "literary" elements in pictures; or in the "new novel" in France, with its reliance on the description of objects and its rejection of empathy and anthropomorphism. It is no coincidence that, like all these movements and so many of the efforts to create new forms of expression in all the arts, the Theatre of the Absurd should be centered in Paris.

This does not mean that the Theatre of the Absurd is essentially French. It is broadly based on ancient strands of the

Western tradition and has its exponents in Britain, Spain, Italy, Germany, Switzerland, and the United States as well as in France. Moreover, its leading practitioners who live in Paris and write in French are not themselves Frenchmen.

As a powerhouse of the modern movement, Paris is an international rather than a merely French center: it acts as a magnet attracting artists of all nationalities who are in search of freedom to work and to live nonconformist lives unhampered by the need to look over their shoulder to see whether their neighbors are shocked. That is the secret of Paris as the capital of the world's individualists: Here, in a world of cafés and small hotels, it is possible to live easily and unmolested.

That is why a cosmopolitan of uncertain origin like Apollinaire; Spaniards like Picasso or Juan Gris; Russians like Kandinsky and Chagall; Rumanians like Tzara and Brancusi; Americans like Gertrude Stein, Hemingway, and E. E. Cummings; an Irishman like Joyce; and many others from the four corners of the world could come together in Paris and shape the modern movement in the arts and literature. The Theatre of the Absurd springs from the same tradition and is nourished from the same roots: An Irishman, Samuel Beckett; a Rumanian, Eugène Ionesco; a Russian of Armenian origin, Arthur Adamov, not only found in Paris the atmosphere that allowed them to experiment in freedom, they also found there the opportunities to get their work produced in theatres.

The standards of staging and production in the smaller theatres of Paris are often criticized as slapdash and perfunctory; that may indeed sometimes be the case; yet the fact remains that there is no other place in the world where so many first-rate men of the theatre can be found who are adventurous and intelligent enough to champion the experimental work of new playwrights and to help them acquire a mastery of stage technique—from Lugné-Poë, Copeau, and Dullin to Jean-Louis Barrault, Jean Vilar, Roger Blin, Nicolas Bataille, Jacques Mauclair, Sylvain Dhomme, Jean-Marie Serreau, and a host of others whose names are indissolubly linked with the rise of much that is best in the contemporary theatre.

Equally important, Paris also has a highly intelligent theatregoing public, which is receptive, thoughtful, and as able as it is eager to absorb new ideas. Which does not mean that the first productions of some of the more startling manifestations of the Theatre of the Absurd did not provoke hostile demonstrations or, at first, play to empty houses. What matters is that these scandals were the expression of passionate concern and interest, and that even the emptiest houses contained enthusiasts articulate enough to proclaim loudly and effectively the merits of the original experiments they had witnessed.

Yet in spite of these favorable circumstances, inherent in the fertile cultural climate of Paris, the success of the Theatre of the Absurd, achieved within a short span of time, remains one of the most astonishing aspects of this astonishing phenomenon of our age. That plays so strange and puzzling, so clearly devoid of the traditional attractions of the well-made drama, should within less than a decade have reached the stages of the world from Finland to Japan, from Norway to the Argentine, and that they should have stimulated a large body of work in a similar convention, are in themselves powerful and entirely empirical tests of the importance of the Theatre of the Absurd.

The study of this phenomenon as literature, as stage technique, and as a manifestation of the thinking of its age must proceed from the examination of the works themselves. Only then can they be seen as part of an old tradition that may at times have been submerged but one that can be traced back to antiquity, and only after the movement of today has been placed within its historical context can an attempt be made to assess its significance and to establish its importance and the part it has to play within the pattern of contemporary thought.

A public conditioned to an accepted convention tends to receive the impact of artistic experiences through a filter of critical standards, of predetermined expectations and terms of reference, which is the natural result of the schooling of its taste and faculty of perception. This framework of values, admirably efficient in itself, produces only bewildering results when it is faced with a completely new and revolutionary convention—a tug of war ensues between impressions that have undoubtedly been received and critical preconceptions that clearly exclude the possibility that any such impressions could have been felt. Hence the storms of frustration and indignation always caused by works in a new convention.

It is the purpose of this book to provide a framework of reference that will show the works of the Theatre of the Absurd within their own convention so that their relevance and force can emerge as clearly to the reader as *Waiting for Godot* did to the convicts of San Quentin.

THE THEATRE OF THE ABSURD

Chapter One

SAMUEL BECKETT: THE SEARCH FOR THE SELF

In his last will and testament, Murphy, the hero of Samuel Beckett's early novel of that name, enjoins his heirs and executors to place his ashes in a paper bag and take them to "the Abbey Theatre, Lr. Abbey Street, Dublin . . . into what the great and good Lord Chesterfield calls the necessary house, where their happiest hours have been spent, on the right as one goes down into the pit . . . and that the chain be there pulled upon them, if possible during the performance of a piece."[1] This is a symbolic act in the true irreverent spirit of the anti-theatre, but one that also reveals where the author of *Waiting for Godot* received his first impressions of the type of drama against which he reacted in his rejection of what he has called "the grotesque fallacy of realistic art—'that miserable statement of line and surface' and the penny-a-line vulgarity of a literature of notations."[2]

Samuel Beckett was born in Dublin in 1906, the son of a quantity surveyor. Like Shaw, Wilde, and Yeats, he came from the Protestant Irish middle class and was, though he later lost his faith, brought up "almost a Quaker," as he himself once put it.[3] It has been suggested that Beckett's preoccupation with the problems of being and the identity of the self might have sprung from the Anglo-Irishman's inevitable and perpetual concern with finding his own answer to the question "Who am I?" But while there may well be a grain of truth in this, it is surely far from providing a complete explanation for the deep existential anguish that is the keynote of Beckett's work and that clearly originates in levels of his personality far deeper than its social surface.

At the age of fourteen, Beckett was sent to one of the Anglo-

Irishman's traditional boarding schools, Portora Royal School at Enniskillen, County Fermanagh, founded by King James I, where Oscar Wilde had also been a pupil. It is characteristic of Beckett that he, whose writing reveals him as one of the most tormented and sensitive of human beings, and of whom it has been reported that "ever since his birth he had retained a terrible memory of his mother's womb"[4] not only became a popular and brilliant scholar but also excelled at games, batting left-handed and bowling right at cricket, and playing scrum half at Rugger.

In 1923, Beckett left Portora and entered Trinity College, Dublin, where he read French and Italian, receiving his Bachelor of Arts degree in 1927. Such was his academic distinction that he was nominated by his university as its representative in a traditional exchange of lecturers with the famous Ecole Normale Supérieure, in Paris. Accordingly, after a brief spell of teaching in Belfast, he went to Paris for a two years' stint as a *lecteur d'anglais* at the Ecole Normale in the autumn of 1928.

Thus began his lifelong association with Paris. In Paris he met James Joyce and soon became a member of his circle, contributing, at the age of twenty-three, the brilliant opening essay of that strange book entitled *Our Exagmination round his Factification for Incamination of Work in Progress,* a collection of twelve articles by twelve apostles, as a defense and exegesis of their master's as yet unnamed magnum opus. Beckett's contribution, headed "Dante . . Bruno . Vico . . Joyce," culminates in a spirited assertion of the artist's duty to express the totality and complexity of his experience regardless of the public's lazy demand for easy comprehensibility: "Here is direct expression—pages and pages of it. And if you don't understand it, Ladies and Gentlemen, it is because you are too decadent to receive it. You are not satisfied unless form is so strictly divorced from content that you can comprehend the one almost without bothering to read the other. This rapid skimming and absorption of the scant cream of sense is made possible by what I may call a continuous process of copious intellectual salivation. The form that is an arbitrary and independent phenomenon can fulfill no higher function than that of stimulus for a tertiary or quartary conditioned reflex of dribbling comprehension."[5] These are the articles of his faith that Beckett has put into practice in his own life's work as a writer, with an uncompromising consistency almost terrifying in its purity.

In a letter to Harriet Shaw Weaver dated May 28, 1929,[6] Joyce speaks of his intention of having Beckett's essay published in an Italian review. In the same letter he mentions a country picnic planned by Adrienne Monnier to celebrate the twenty-fifth anniversary of Bloomsday. This was the *Déjeuner Ulysse* held on June 27, 1929, at the Hôtel Léopold at Les Vaux-de-Cernay, near Versailles. From Richard Ellmann's biography of Joyce, we learn that Beckett was one of the guests, who included Paul Valéry, Jules Romains, Léon-Paul Fargue, Philippe Soupault, and many other distinguished names, and that on the return journey Beckett aroused the wrath of Paul Valéry and Adrienne Monnier by repeatedly prevailing upon Joyce to have the bus stopped so that they might have yet another drink at some wayside café.

During his first stay in Paris, Beckett also made his mark as a poet by winning a literary prize—ten pounds, for the best poem on the subject of time, in a competition inspired by Nancy Cunard and judged by her and Richard Aldington. Beckett's poem, provocatively entitled "Whoroscope," presents the philosopher Descartes meditating on time, hens' eggs, and evanescence. The little booklet, published in Paris by the Hours Press in an edition of a hundred signed copies at five shillings, and two hundred unsigned ones at a shilling, has become a collector's piece, with the little slip pasted on it that informs the reader of the award of the prize and that this is "Mr. Samuel Beckett's first separately published work."

For his newly found friend James Joyce, Beckett also embarked on a daring attempt at rendering the "Anna Livia Plurabelle" passage from *Work in Progress* into French. But this undertaking, in which he was assisted by Alfred Péron, had to be abandoned (and was carried to completion by Joyce, Soupault, and a number of others) in the course of 1930, when Beckett returned to Dublin to take the post of assistant to the professor of Romance languages at Trinity College.

Thus, at the age of twenty-four, Beckett seemed to be launched on a safe and brilliant academic and literary career. He obtained his Master of Arts degree. His study of Proust, commissioned by a London publisher and written while he was still in Paris, appeared in 1931. It is a penetrating interpretation of Proust's work as an exploration of time, but it also foreshadows many of Beckett's themes in the works he was still to write—the impossibility of possession in love, and the illusion of friendship: ". . . if love . . . is a function of man's sadness, friendship is a function of his cowardice; and if neither can be realised because of the impenetrability (isolation) of all that is not 'cosa mentale,' at least the failure to possess may have the nobility of that which is tragic, whereas the attempt to communicate where no communication is possible is merely a simian vulgarity, or horribly comic, like the madness that holds a conversation with the furniture."[7] For an artist therefore, "the only possible spiritual development is in the sense of depth. The artistic tendency is not expansive, but a contraction. And art is the apotheosis of solitude. There is no communication because there are no vehicles of communication."[8] Although these ideas are expositions of Proust's thought, and although today he stresses that he wrote the little book on order, not out of any deep affinity with Proust, Beckett clearly put many of his personal feelings and views into it.

To one who felt that habit and routine was the cancer of time, social intercourse a mere illusion, and the artist's life of necessity a life of solitude, the daily grind of a university lecturer's work must have appeared unbearable. After only four terms at Trinity College, he had had enough. He threw up his career and cut himself loose from all routine and social duties. Like Belacqua, the hero of his volume of short stories *More Pricks Than Kicks*, who, though indolent by nature, "enlivened the last phase of his solipsism . . . with the belief that the best thing he had to do was to move constantly from place to place,"[9] Beckett embarked on a period of *Wanderjahre*. Writing poems and stories, doing odd jobs, he moved from Dublin to London to Paris, traveled through France and Germany. It is surely no coincidence that so many of Beckett's later characters are tramps and wanderers, and that all are lonely.

More Pricks Than Kicks is set in Dublin; the next volume, a slim collection of poems, *Echo's Bones and Other Precipitates* (1935), widens its references to landmarks from Dublin

(Guiness's barges by O'Connell Bridge) to Paris (the American Bar in the Rue Mouffetard) and London (the "grand old British Museum," Ken Wood and Tower Bridge). Beckett's stay in London also left its mark on his first novel, *Murphy* (1938): the "World's End" on the fringes of Chelsea; the area around the Caledonian market and Pentonville; Gower Street.

Whenever he passed through Paris, Beckett went to see Joyce. In Richard Ellmann's words, "Beckett was addicted to silences, and so was Joyce; they engaged in conversations which consisted often in silences directed towards each other, both suffused with sadness, Beckett mostly for the world, Joyce mostly for himself. Joyce sat in his habitual posture, legs crossed, toe of the upper leg under the instep of the lower; Beckett, also tall and slender, fell into the same gesture. Joyce suddenly asked some such question as 'How could the idealist Hume write a history?' Beckett replied, 'A history of representations.' "[10] Beckett read Joyce passages from the works of Fritz Mauthner, whose *Critique of Language* was one of the first works to point to the fallibility of language as a medium for the discovery and communication of metaphysical truths. But "though he liked having Beckett with him, Joyce at the same time kept him at a distance. Once he said directly: 'I don't love anyone except my family' in a tone which suggested, 'I don't like anyone except my family either.' "[10] Once or twice Joyce, whose sight had long been failing, dictated passages from *Finnegans Wake* to Beckett. This may be the origin of the oft-repeated assertion that Beckett was at one time Joyce's private secretary. He never held such a position. If anyone ever acted as Joyce's secretary it was Paul Léon.

Richard Ellmann also tells the story of the infatuation of Joyce's unhappy daughter, Lucia, for Beckett. Beckett sometimes took Lucia, already high-strung and neurotic, to restaurants and theatres. "As her self-control began to leave her, she made less effort to conceal the passion she felt for him, and at last her feelings became so overt that Beckett told her bluntly he came to the Joyce flat primarily to see her father. He felt he had been cruel and later told Peggy Guggenheim that he was dead and had no feelings that were human; hence he had not been able to fall in love with Lucia."[11]

Peggy Guggenheim, patron of the arts and a famous collector of modern paintings, was herself, as she reports in her memoirs, "terribly in love" with Beckett a few years later. She describes him as a fascinating young man, but afflicted with an apathy that sometimes kept him in bed till midafternoon; with whom it was difficult to converse, as "he was never very animated and it took hours and lots of drink to warm him up before he finally unravelled himself."[12] Like Belacqua, who sometimes wanted "to be back in the caul on my back in the dark forever,"[13] Beckett, according to Peggy Guggenheim, "had retained a terrible memory of life in his mother's womb. He was constantly suffering from this and had awful crises, when he felt he was suffocating. He always said our life would be all right one day, but if I ever pressed him to make a decision it was fatal and he took back everything he had previously said."[12]

Murphy, published in 1938 with the help and support of Herbert Read, is to some extent concerned with an analogous situation between the hero and his girl friend Celia, who vainly tries to make him take up regular employment so they can get married, but has to see him elude her again and again.

Beckett's first play (written in French shortly after the war, but so far unpublished and unperformed), *Eleutheria*, is also concerned with a young man's efforts to cut himself loose from his family and social obligations. *Eleutheria* is in three acts; the stage is divided in the middle. On the right the hero lies in his bed, apathetic and passive. On the left his family and friends discuss his case without ever directly addressing him. Gradually, the action shifts from left to right, and eventually the hero summons up the energy to free himself from his shackles and cut himself loose from society.

Molloy and *Eleutheria* mirror Beckett's search for freedom and the right to live his own life. In fact he found himself a permanent home: in Paris. In 1937 he acquired his apartment, on the top floor of a block of flats in outer Montparnasse, which was to become his base throughout the war and postwar years.

About this time an episode occurred that might have come straight out of Beckett's own writings: he was stabbed in a Paris street by an underworld character who had accosted him for money, and had to be taken to a hospital with a perforated lung. Later, when his wound had healed, Beckett went to see his assailant in prison. He asked the apache why he had stabbed him, and received the answer, *"Je ne sais pas, Monsieur."* It might well be the voice of this man that we hear in *Waiting for Godot* and *Molloy*.

When war came, in September, 1939, Beckett was in Ireland, visiting his widowed mother. He immediately returned to Paris. He had long been a decided opponent of the National Socialist regime in Germany, appalled by its brutality and anti-Semitism. Now that war had broken out, he argued with Joyce, who regarded the war as useless and futile. Beckett firmly maintained that its objectives were indeed justified. Being a citizen of Eire, and thus a neutral, he was able to stay in Paris even after the city had been occupied by the Germans. He joined a Resistance group, and led the dangerous and precarious life of a member of the underground movement.

One day in August, 1942, he returned to his apartment and found a message informing him that some of the members of his Resistance group had been arrested. He left his home immediately and made his way into the unoccupied zone, where he found shelter and work as an agricultural laborer in a peasant's house in the Vaucluse, near Avignon. (The Vaucluse is mentioned in the French version of *Waiting for Godot*, when Vladimir argues that Estragon must know the Vaucluse country, while Estragon hotly denies ever having been anywhere except where he is at that moment, in the Merdecluse. In the English version, the Vaucluse has become "the Mâcon country," the Merdecluse the "Cackon country.")

To keep his hand in as a writer while working on the farm in the Vaucluse, Beckett began to write a novel, *Watt*. It deals with a lonely and eccentric individual who finds refuge as a servant in a house in the country ruled by a mysterious, capricious, and unapproachable master, Mr. Knott, who has some of the attributes later ascribed to the equally mysterious Mr. Godot.

After the liberation of Paris in 1945, Beckett returned there briefly before making his way to Ireland, where he volunteered for a Red Cross unit. He came back to France in the autumn of 1945 and spent some time as an interpreter and storekeeper in a field hospital at Saint-Lô. Later that winter, he finally returned to Paris, to his old apartment, which he found intact and waiting for him.

This homecoming marked the beginning of the most productive period in Beckett's life. Seized by a powerful and sustained creative impulse, he wrote in the five years that followed a succession of important works: the plays *Eleutheria, Waiting for Godot,* and *Endgame;* the novels *Molloy, Malone Dies, The Unnamable,* and the unpublished *Mercier et Camier,* as well as the short stories and fragments of prose published under the title *Nouvelles et Textes pour Rien.* All these works, some of which have become the foundation of Beckett's reputation as one of the major literary forces and influences of his time, were written in French.

This is a curious phenomenon. There have been many writers who have risen to fame with works written in a language other than their own, but usually they are compelled by circumstances to write in a foreign language: the necessities of exile; a desire to break the connection with their country of origin for political or ideological reasons; or the wish to reach a world audience, which might induce the citizen of a small language community, a Rumanian or a Dutchman, to write in French or English. But Beckett was certainly not an exile in that sense, and his mother tongue is the accepted lingua franca of the twentieth century. He chose to write his masterpieces in French because he felt that he needed the discipline that the use of an acquired language would impose upon him. As he told a student writing a thesis on his work who asked him why he used French, *"Parce qu'en français c'est plus facile d'écrire sans style."*[14] In other words, while in his own language a writer may be tempted to indulge in virtuosity of style for its own sake, the use of another language may force him to divert the ingenuity that might be expended on mere embellishments of style in his own idiom to the utmost clarity and economy of expression.

When the American director Herbert Blau suggested to Beckett that by writing in French he might be evading some part of himself, "he said yes, there were some things about himself he didn't like, that French had the right 'weakening' effect. It was a weakness he had chosen, as Melville's Bartleby 'preferred not to' live. . . ."[15] Possibly, too, Beckett wanted to avoid the tendency of English toward allusion and evocation. Yet the fact that in his own translations the English language perfectly renders his meaning and intention shows that it is not just a surface quality that he prefers in French, but the challenge and discipline it presents to his powers of expression.

Works like Beckett's, which spring from the deepest strata of the mind and probe the darkest wells of anxiety, would be destroyed by the slightest suggestion of glibness or facility; they must be the outcome of a painful struggle with the medium of their expression. As Claude Mauriac has pointed out in his essay on Beckett, anyone "who speaks is carried along by the logic of language and its articulations. Thus the writer who pits himself against the unsayable must use all his cunning so as not to say what the words make him say against his will, but to express instead what by their very nature they are designed to cover up: the uncertain, the contradictory, the unthinkable."[16] The danger of being carried along by the logic of language is clearly greater in one's mother tongue, with its unconsciously accepted meanings and associations. By writing in a foreign language, Beckett insures that his writing remains a constant struggle, a painful wrestling with the spirit of language itself. That is why he considers the radio plays and occasional pieces he has since written in English as a relaxation, a rest from this hard struggle with meaning and language. But accordingly he also attaches less importance to these works. They came too easily.

The French translation of *Murphy*, which appeared in 1947, attracted little attention, but when *Molloy* was published in 1951, it created a stir. Beckett's real triumph, however, came when *Waiting for Godot*, which had appeared in book form in 1952, was first produced on January 5, 1953, at the little Théâtre de Babylone (now defunct), on the Boulevard Raspail. Roger Blin, always at the forefront of the avant-garde in the French theatre, directed, and himself played the part of Pozzo. And against all expectations, the strange tragic farce, in which nothing happens and which had been scorned as undramatic by a number of managements, became one of the greatest successes of the postwar theatre. It ran for four hundred performances at the Théâtre de Babylone and was later transferred to another Parisian theatre. It has been translated into more than twenty languages and been performed in Sweden, Switzerland, Finland, Italy, Norway, Denmark, Holland, Spain, Belgium, Turkey, Yugoslavia, Brazil, Mexico, the Argentine, Israel, Czechoslovakia, Poland, Japan, Western Germany, Great Britain, the United States, and even in Dublin, being seen in the first five years after its original production in Paris by more than a million spectators—a truly astonishing reception for a play so enigmatic, so exasperating, so complex, and so uncompromising in its refusal to conform to any of the accepted ideas of dramatic construction.

This is not the place to trace in detail the strange stage history of *Waiting for Godot.* Suffice it to say that the play found the approval of accepted dramatists as diverse as Jean Anouilh (who described the production at the Théâtre de Babylone as equal in importance to the first performance of a Pirandello play in Paris by Pitoeff, in 1923), Thornton Wilder, Tennessee Williams, and William Saroyan (who said, "It will make it easier for me and everyone else to write freely in the theatre"); that it reached London in August, 1955, in a production that met with Beckett's disapproval but was so successful that it was transferred from the Arts Theatre Club to the West End and ran for a long time; that it reached the shores of the United States at the Miami Playhouse on January 3, 1956, where, with Bert Lahr and Tom Ewell in the parts of the tramps, it was billed as "the laugh hit of two continents" and bitterly disappointed its audience's expectations, but finally reached Broadway with Bert Lahr but without Tom Ewell, and was acclaimed by the critics.

Beckett's second play, *Endgame,* originally in two acts but later reduced to one, was to have had its world première in French under the direction of Roger Blin in Paris, but when it met with some hesitation by the management and lost its Paris venue, the Royal Court Theatre, in London, hospitably offered its stage, so that London witnessed the rare occasion of a world première in French (April 3, 1957). It later found another theatre in Paris and ran for a considerable time at the Studio des Champs Elysées. Productions in English in London (again at the Royal Court), in New York (at the Cherry Lane Theatre, off Broadway), and in San Francisco (by the Actors' Workshop) have also been notably successful.

In its original production in French, *Endgame* was coupled with the mimeplay *Act Without Words*, performed by Deryk Mendel and with music by Beckett's cousin, John Beckett. At the performance in English, *Endgame* shared the bill with the short play *Krapp's Last Tape* (October 28, 1958), which was written by Beckett in English and has since been performed in Paris, in Beckett's own translation, and in New York.

Krapp's Last Tape was directed by Donald McWhinnie, the distinguished radio producer who was instrumental in getting Beckett to write two plays especially for the B.B.C.'s Third Programme: *All That Fall* (first broadcast on January 13, 1957) and *Embers* (October 28, 1959). And so tenuous is the dividing line between Beckett's dramatic works and his later novels, which are all cast in the form of dramatic monologues, that extracts from these have also been performed on the B.B.C.'s Third Programme: *Molloy* (December 10, 1957); the fragment *From an Abandoned Work* (December 14, 1957); *Malone Dies* (June 18, 1958); and *The Unnamable* (January 19, 1959).

Samuel Beckett's rise to fame is an astonishing story of modesty and single-minded devotion to the austerest principles, rewarded by acclaim and success. Tall, slender, and youthful in his fifties, Beckett remains shy, gentle, and unassuming, completely untouched by the mannerisms of self-conscious greatness. And—what is most surprising in the author of works so filled with anguish, torment, and the deranged fantasies of human beings driven to the limits of suffering—he himself is the most balanced and serene of men. He has married, and divides his time between a small house in the country and Paris. He avoids literary coteries and is more at home among painters. He continues his exploration of the human condition, his quest for the answer to such basic questions as "Who am I?" "What does it mean when I say—I?" by writing, now more slowly and with greater difficulty than at the time of his great creative outburst. His latest novel, *Comment C'Est*, appeared in January, 1961.

When Alan Schneider, who was to direct the first American production of *Waiting for Godot*, asked Beckett who or what was meant by Godot, he received the answer, "If I knew, I would have said so in the play."[17]

This is a salutary warning to anyone who approaches Beckett's plays with the intention of discovering *the* key to their understanding, of demonstrating in exact and definite terms *what they mean*. Such an undertaking might perhaps be justified in tackling the works of an author who had started from a clear-cut philosophical or moral conception, and had then proceeded to translate it into concrete terms of plot and character. But even in such a case the chances are that the final product, if it turned out a genuine work of the creative imagination, would transcend the author's original intentions and present itself as far richer, more complex, and open to a multitude of additional interpretations. For, as Beckett himself has pointed out in his essay on Joyce's *Work in Progress*, the form, structure, and mood of an artistic statement cannot be separated from its meaning, its conceptual content; simply because the work of art as a whole *is* its meaning, *what* is said in it is indissolubly linked with the *manner* in which it is said, and cannot be said in any other way. Libraries have been filled with attempts to reduce the meaning of a play like *Hamlet* to a few short and simple lines, yet the play itself remains the clearest and most concise statement of its meaning and message, precisely because its uncertainties and irreducible ambiguities are an essential element of its total impact.

These considerations apply, in varying degrees, to all works of creative literature, but they apply with particular force to works that are essentially concerned with conveying their author's sense of mystery, bewilderment, and anxiety when confronted with the human condition, and his despair at being unable to find a meaning in existence. In *Waiting for Godot*, the feeling of uncertainty it produces, the ebb and flow of this uncertainty—from the hope of discovering the identity of Godot to its repeated disappointment—are themselves the essence of the play. Any endeavor to arrive at a clear and certain interpretation by establishing the identity of Godot through critical analysis would be as foolish as trying to discover the clear outlines hidden behind the chiaroscuro of a painting by Rembrandt by scraping away the paint.

Yet it is only natural that plays written in so unusual and baffling a convention should be felt to be in special need of an explanation that, as it were, would uncover their hidden meaning and translate it into everyday language. The source of this fallacy lies in the misconception that somehow these plays must be reducible to the conventions of the "normal" theatre, with plots that can be summarized in the form of a narrative. If only one could discover some hidden clue, it is felt, these difficult plays could be forced to yield their secret and reveal the plot of the conventional play that is hidden within them. Such attempts are doomed to failure. Beckett's plays lack plot even more completely than other works of the Theatre of the Absurd. Instead of a linear development, they present their author's intuition of the human condition by a method that is essentially polyphonic; they confront their audience with an organized structure of statements and images that interpenetrate each other and that must be apprehended in their totality, rather like the different themes in a symphony, which gain meaning by their simultaneous interaction.

But if we have to be cautious in our approach to Beckett's plays, to avoid the pitfall of trying to provide an oversimplified explanation of their meaning, this does not imply that we cannot subject them to careful scrutiny by isolating sets of images and themes and by attempting to discern their structural groundwork. The results of such an examination should make it easier to follow the author's intention and to see, if not the *answers* to his questions, at least what the *questions* are that he is asking.

Waiting for Godot does not tell a story; it explores a static situation. "Nothing happens, nobody comes, nobody goes, it's awful."[18] On a country road, by a tree, two old tramps, Vladimir and Estragon, are waiting. That is the opening situation at the beginning of Act I. At the end of Act I, they are informed that Mr. Godot, with whom they believe they have an appointment, cannot come, but that he will surely come tomorrow. Act II repeats precisely the same pattern. The same boy arrives and delivers the same message. Act I ends:

ESTRAGON: Well, shall we go?
VLADIMIR: Yes, let's go.
(*They do not move.*)

Act II ends with the same lines of dialogue, but spoken by the same characters in reversed order.

The sequence of events and the dialogue in each act are different. Each time the two tramps encounter another pair of characters, Pozzo and Lucky, master and slave, under differing circumstances; in each act Vladimir and Estragon attempt suicide and fail, for differing reasons; but these variations merely serve to emphasize the essential sameness of the situation—*plus ça change, plus c'est la même chose.*

Vladimir and Estragon—who call each other Didi and Gogo, although Vladimir is addressed by the boy messenger as Mr. Albert, and Estragon, when asked his name, replies without hesitation, Catullus—are clearly derived from the pairs of cross-talk comedians of music halls. Their dialogue has the peculiar repetitive quality of the cross-talk comedians' patter:

ESTRAGON: So long as one knows.
VLADIMIR: One can bide one's time.
ESTRAGON: One knows what to expect.
VLADIMIR: No further need to worry.[19]

And the parallel to the music hall and the circus is even explicitly stated:

VLADIMIR: Charming evening we're having.
ESTRAGON: Unforgettable.
VLADIMIR: And it's not over.
ESTRAGON: Apparently not.
VLADIMIR: It's only the beginning.
ESTRAGON: It's awful.
VLADIMIR: It's worse than being at the theatre.
ESTRAGON: The circus.
VLADIMIR: The music hall.
ESTRAGON: The circus.[20]

In accordance with the traditions of the music hall or the circus, there is an element of crudely physical humor: Estragon loses his trousers, there is a protracted gag involving three hats that are put on and off and handed on in a sequence of seemingly unending confusion, and there is an abundance of pratfalls—the writer of a penetrating thesis on Beckett, Niklaus Gessner, lists no fewer than forty-five stage directions indicating that one of the characters leaves the upright position, which symbolizes the dignity of man.[21]

As the members of a cross-talk act, Vladimir and Estragon have complementary personalities. Vladimir is the more practical of the two, and Estragon claims to have been a poet. In eating his carrot, Estragon finds that the more he eats of it the less he likes it, while Vladimir reacts the opposite way—he likes things as he gets used to them. Estragon is volatile, Vladimir persistent. Estragon dreams, Vladimir cannot stand hearing about dreams. Vladimir has stinking breath, Estragon has stinking feet. Vladimir remembers past events, Estragon tends to forget them as soon as they have happened. Estragon likes telling funny stories, Vladimir is upset by them. It is mainly Vladimir who voices the hope that Godot will come and that his coming will change their situation, while Estragon remains skeptical throughout and at times even forgets the name of Godot. It is Vladimir who conducts the conversation with the boy who is Godot's messenger and to whom the boy's messages are addressed. Estragon is the weaker of the two; he is beaten up by mysterious strangers every night. Vladimir at times acts as his protector, sings him to sleep with a lullaby, and covers him with his coat. The opposition of their temperaments is the cause of endless bickering between them and often leads to the suggestion that they should part. Yet, being complementary natures, they also are dependent on each other and have to stay together.

Pozzo and Lucky are equally complementary in their natures, but their relationship is on a more primitive level: Pozzo is the sadistic master, Lucky the submissive slave. In the first act, Pozzo is rich, powerful, and certain of himself; he represents worldly man in all his facile and shortsighted optimism and illusory feeling of power and permanence. Lucky not only carries his heavy luggage, and even the whip with which Pozzo beats him, he also dances and thinks for him, or did so in his prime. In fact, Lucky taught Pozzo all the higher values of life: "beauty, grace, truth of the first water."[22] Pozzo and

Lucky represent the relationship between body and mind, the
material and the spiritual sides of man, with the intellect subordinate to the appetites of the body. Now that Lucky's powers are failing, Pozzo complains that they cause him untold
suffering. He wants to get rid of Lucky and sell him at the
fair. But in the second act, when they appear again, they are
still tied together. Pozzo has gone blind, Lucky has become
dumb. While Pozzo drives Lucky on a journey without an apparent goal, Vladimir has prevailed upon Estragon to wait for
Godot.

A good deal of ingenuity has been expended in trying to
establish at least an etymology for Godot's name, which would
point to Beckett's conscious or subconscious intention in making him the objective of Vladimir's and Estragon's quest. It
has been suggested that Godot is a weakened form of the word
"God," a diminutive formed on the analogy of Pierre-Pierrot,
Charles-Charlot, with the added association of the Charlie
Chaplin character of the little man, who is called Charlot in
France, and whose bowler hat is worn by all four main characters in the play. It has also been noted that the title *En
Attendant Godot* seems to contain an allusion to Simone Weil's
book *Attente de Dieu,* which would furnish a further indication that Godot stands for God. Yet the name Godot may also
be an even more recondite literary allusion. As Eric Bentley
has pointed out, there is a character in a play by Balzac, a
character much talked about but never seen, and called
Godeau.[23] The play in question is Balzac's comedy *Le Fai-
seur,* better known as *Mercadet.* Mercadet is a Stock Exchange
speculator who is in the habit of attributing his financial difficulties to his former partner Godeau, who, years before, ab-
sconded with their joint capital: *"Je porte le poids du crime
de Godeau!"* On the other hand, the hope of Godeau's eventual
return and the repayment of the embezzled funds is constantly
dangled by Mercadet before the eyes of his numerous credi-
tors. *"Tout le monde a son Godeau, un faux Christophe
Colomb! Après tout Godeau . . . je crois qu'il m'a déjà rap-
porté plus d'argent qu'il ne m'en a pris!"* The plot of *Mercadet*
turns on a last, desperate speculation based on the appearance
of a spurious Godeau. But the fraud is discovered. Mercadet
seems ruined. At this moment the real Godeau is announced;

he has returned from India with a huge fortune. The play ends with Mercadet exclaiming, *"J'ai montré tant de fois Godeau que j'ai bien le droit de le voir. Allons voir Godeau!"*[24]

The parallels are too striking to make it probable that this is a mere coincidence: In Beckett's play, as in Balzac's, the arrival of Godot is the eagerly awaited event that will miraculously save the situation. And Beckett is as fond as Joyce of subtle and recondite literary allusions.

Yet whether Godot is meant to suggest the intervention of a supernatural agency, or whether he stands for a mythical human being whose arrival is expected to change the situation, or both of these possibilities combined, his exact nature is of secondary importance. The subject of the play is not Godot but waiting, the act of waiting as an essential and characteristic aspect of the human condition. Throughout our lives we always wait for something, and Godot simply represents the objective of our waiting—an event, a thing, a person, death. Moreover, it is in the act of waiting that we experience the flow of *time* in its purest, most evident form. If we are active, we tend to forget the passage of time, we *pass* the time, but if we are merely passively waiting, we are confronted with the action of time itself. As Beckett points out in his analysis of Proust, "There is no escape from the hours and the days. Neither from tomorrow nor from yesterday because yesterday has deformed us, or been deformed by us. . . . Yesterday is not a milestone that has been passed, but a daystone on the beaten track of the years, and irremediably part of us, within us, heavy and dangerous. We are not merely more weary because of yesterday, we are other, no longer what we were before the calamity of yesterday."[25] The flow of time confronts us with the basic problem of being—the problem of the nature of the self, which, being subject to constant change in time, is in constant flux and therefore ever outside our grasp. "Personality, whose permanent reality can only be apprehended as a retrospective hypothesis. The individual is the seat of a constant process of decantation, decantation from the vessel containing the fluid of future time, sluggish, pale and monochrome, to the vessel containing the fluid of past time, agitated and multicoloured by the phenomena of its hours."[26]

Being subject to this process of time flowing through us and

changing us in doing so, we are, at no single moment in our
lives, identical with ourselves. Hence "we are disappointed at
the nullity of what we are pleased to call attainment. But what
is attainment? The identification of the subject with the object
of his desire. The subject has died—and perhaps many times—
on the way."[27] If Godot is the object of Vladimir's and Estragon's desire, he seems naturally ever beyond their reach. It
is significant that the boy who acts as go-between fails to recognize the pair from day to day. The French version explicitly
states that the boy who appears in the second act is the same
boy as the one in the first act, yet the boy denies that he has
ever seen the two tramps before and insists that this is the first
time he has acted as Godot's messenger. As the boy leaves,
Vladimir tries to impress it upon him: "You're sure you saw
me, eh, you won't come and tell me tomorrow that you never
saw me before?" The boy does not reply, and we know that he
will again fail to recognize them. Can we ever be sure that
the human beings we meet are the same today as they were
yesterday? When Pozzo and Lucky first appear, neither
Vladimir nor Estragon seems to recognize them; Estragon even
takes Pozzo for Godot. But after they have gone, Vladimir
comments that they have changed since their last appearance.
Estragon insists that he didn't know them.

VLADIMIR: Yes you do know them.
ESTRAGON: No I don't know them.
VLADIMIR: We know them, I tell you. You forget everything.
(*Pause. To himself*) Unless they're not the same. . . .
ESTRAGON: Why didn't they recognize us, then?
VLADIMIR: That means nothing. I too pretended not to rec-
ognize them. And then nobody ever recognizes us.[28]

In the second act, when Pozzo and Lucky reappear, cruelly
deformed by the action of time, Vladimir and Estragon again
have their doubts whether they are the same people they met
on the previous day. Nor does Pozzo remember them:

"I don't remember having met anyone yesterday. But tomorrow I won't remember having met anyone today."[29]

Waiting is to experience the action of time, which is constant change. And yet, as nothing real ever happens, that

change is in itself an illusion. The ceaseless activity of time is self-defeating, purposeless, and therefore null and void. The more things change, the more they are the same. That is the terrible stability of the world. "The tears of the world are a constant quantity. For each one who begins to weep, somewhere else another stops."[30] One day is like another, and when we die, we might never have existed. As Pozzo exclaims in his great final outburst,

> "Have you not done tormenting me with your accursed time? . . . One day, is that not enough for you, one day like any other day he went dumb, one day I went blind, one day we'll go deaf, one day we were born, one day we'll die, the same day, the same second. . . . They give birth astride of a grave, the light gleams an instant, then it's night once more."[31]

And Vladimir, shortly afterward, agrees:

> "Astride of a grave and a difficult birth. Down in the hole, lingeringly, the gravedigger puts on the forceps."[32]

Still Vladimir and Estragon live in hope: they wait for Godot, whose coming will bring the flow of time to a stop. "Tonight perhaps we shall sleep in his place, in the warmth, dry, our bellies full, on the straw. It is worth waiting for that, is it not?"[33] This passage, omitted in the English version, clearly suggests the peace, the rest from waiting, the sense of having arrived in a haven, that Godot represents to the two tramps. They are hoping to be saved from the evanescence and instability of the illusion of time, and to find peace and permanence outside it. Then they will no longer be tramps, homeless wanderers, but will have arrived home.

Vladimir and Estragon wait for Godot although their appointment with him is by no means certain. Estragon does not remember it at all. Vladimir is not quite sure what they asked Godot to do for them. It was "nothing very definite . . . a kind of prayer . . . a vague supplication." And what had Godot promised them? "That he'd see . . . that he would think it over. . . ."[34]

When Beckett is asked about the theme of *Waiting for Godot*, he sometimes refers to a passage in the writings of St. Augustine: "There is a wonderful sentence in Augustine. I wish I could remember the Latin. It is even finer in Latin than in English. 'Do not despair: one of the thieves was saved. Do not presume: one of the thieves was damned.'" And Beckett sometimes adds, "I am interested in the shape of ideas even if I do not believe in them. . . . That sentence has a wonderful shape. It is the shape that matters."[35]

The theme of the two thieves on the cross, the theme of the uncertainty of the hope of salvation and the fortuitousness of the bestowal of grace, does indeed pervade the whole play. Vladimir states it right at the beginning: "One of the thieves was saved. . . . It's a reasonable percentage."[36] Later he enlarges on the subject: "Two thieves . . . One is supposed to have been saved and the other . . . damned. . . . And yet how is it that of the four evangelists only one speaks of a thief being saved? The four of them were there or thereabouts, and only one speaks of a thief being saved. . . . Of the other three two don't mention any thieves at all and the third says that both of them abused him."[37] There is a fifty-fifty chance, but as only one out of four witnesses reports it, the odds are considerably reduced. But, as Vladimir points out, it is a curious fact that everybody seems to believe that one witness: "It is the only version they know." Estragon, whose attitude has been one of skepticism throughout, merely comments, "People are bloody ignorant apes."[38]

It is the shape of the idea that fascinated Beckett: Out of all the malefactors, out of all the millions and millions of criminals that have been executed in the course of history, two, only two, had the chance of receiving absolution in the hour of their death in so uniquely effective a manner. One happened to make a hostile remark; he was damned. One happened to contradict that hostile remark; he was saved. How easily could the roles have been reversed. These, after all, were not well-considered judgments, but chance exclamations uttered at a moment of supreme suffering and stress. As Pozzo says about Lucky, "Remark that I might easily have been in his shoes and he in mine. If chance had not willed it otherwise. To each one his due."[39] And then our shoes might fit us one day and not the next: Estragon's boots torment him in the first act; in Act II they fit him miraculously.

Godot himself is unpredictable in bestowing kindness and

punishment. The boy who is his messenger minds the goats, and Godot treats him well. But the boy's brother, who minds the sheep, is beaten by Godot. "And why doesn't he beat you?" asks Vladimir. "I don't know, sir"—"*Je ne sais pas, Monsieur*" —the boy replies, using the words of the apache who had stabbed Beckett. The parallel to Cain and Abel is evident: There too the Lord's grace fell on one rather than on the other without any rational explanation—only that Godot beats the minder of the sheep and cherishes the minder of the goats. Here Godot also acts contrary to the Son of Man at the Last Judgment: "And he shall set the sheep on his right hand, but the goats on the left." But if Godot's kindness is bestowed fortuitously, his coming is not a source of pure joy; it can also mean damnation. When Estragon, in the second act, believes Godot to be approaching, his first thought is, "I'm accursed." And as Vladimir triumphantly exclaims, "It's Godot! At last! Let's go and meet him," Estragon runs away, shouting, "I'm in hell!"[40]

The fortuitous bestowal of grace, which passes human understanding, divides mankind into those that will be saved and those that will be damned. When, in Act II, Pozzo and Lucky return, and the two tramps try to identify them, Estragon calls out, "Abel! Abel!" Pozzo immediately responds. But when Estragon calls out, "Cain! Cain!" Pozzo responds again. "He's all mankind," concludes Estragon.[41]

There is even a suggestion that Pozzo's activity is concerned with his frantic attempt to draw that fifty-fifty chance of salvation upon himself. In the first act, Pozzo is on his way to sell Lucky "at the fair." The French version, however, specifies that it is the *"marché de Saint-Sauveur"*—the Market of the holy Saviour—to which he is taking Lucky. Is Pozzo trying to sell Lucky to redeem himself? Is he trying to divert the fifty-fifty chance of redemption from Lucky (in whose shoes he might easily have been himself) to Pozzo? He certainly complains that Lucky is causing him great pain, that he is killing him with his mere presence—perhaps because his mere presence reminds Pozzo that it might be Lucky who will be redeemed. When Lucky gives his famous demonstration of his thinking, what is the thin thread of sense that seems to underlie the opening passage of his wild, schizophrenic "word

salad?" Again it seems to be concerned with the fortuitousness
of salvation: "Given the existence . . . of a personal God . . .
outside time without extension who from the heights of divine
apathia divine athambia divine aphasia loves us dearly with
some exceptions for reasons unknown . . . and suffers . . .
with those who for reasons unknown are plunged in torment.
. . ."[42] Here again we have the personal God, with his divine
apathy, his speechlessness (aphasia), and his lack of the
capacity for terror or amazement (athambia), who loves us
dearly—with some exceptions, who will be plunged into the
torments of hell. In other words, God, who does not communicate with us, cannot feel for us, and condemns us for reasons unknown.

When Pozzo and Lucky reappear the next day, Pozzo
blind and Lucky dumb, no more is heard of the fair. Pozzo
has failed to sell Lucky; his blindness in thinking that he could
thus influence the action of grace has been made evident in
concrete physical form.

That *Waiting for Godot* is concerned with the hope of salvation through the workings of grace seems clearly established
both from Beckett's own evidence and from the text itself.
Does this, however, mean that it is a Christian, or even that
it is a religious, play? There have been a number of very ingenious interpretations in this sense. Vladimir's and Estragon's
waiting is explained as signifying their steadfast faith and hope,
while Vladimir's kindness to his friend, and the two tramps'
mutual interdependence, are seen as symbols of Christian
charity. But these religious interpretations seem to overlook a
number of essential features of the play—its constant stress on
the uncertainty of the appointment with Godot, Godot's unreliability and irrationality, and the repeated demonstration of
the futility of the hopes pinned on him. The act of waiting for
Godot is shown as essentially *absurd*. Admittedly it might be a
case of *"Credere quia absurdum est,"* yet it might even more
forcibly be taken as a demonstration of the proposition *"Absurdum est credere."*

There is one feature in the play that leads one to assume
there is a better solution to the tramps' predicament, which
they themselves both consider preferable to waiting for Godot
—that is, suicide. "We should have thought of it when the

world was young, in the nineties. . . . Hand in hand from the top of the Eiffel Tower, among the first. We were respectable in those days. Now it's too late. They wouldn't even let us up."[43] Suicide remains their favorite solution, unattainable owing to their own incompetence and their lack of the practical tools to achieve it. It is precisely their disappointment at their failure to succeed in their attempts at suicide that Vladimir and Estragon rationalize by waiting, or pretending to wait, for Godot. "I'm curious to hear what he has to offer. Then we'll take it or leave it."[44] Estragon, far less convinced of Godot's promises than Vladimir, is anxious to reassure himself that they are not tied to Godot.

> ESTRAGON: I'm asking you if we are tied.
> VLADIMIR: Tied?
> ESTRAGON: Ti-ed.
> VLADIMIR: How do you mean tied?
> ESTRAGON: Down.
> VLADIMIR: But to whom. By whom?
> ESTRAGON: To your man.
> VLADIMIR: To Godot? Tied to Godot? What an idea! No question of it. (*Pause*) For the moment.[45]

When, later, Vladimir falls into some sort of complacency about their waiting—"We have kept our appointment . . . we are not saints—but we have kept our appointment. How many people can boast as much?" Estragon immediately punctures it by retorting, "Billions." And Vladimir is quite ready to admit that they are waiting only from irrational habit. "What's certain is that the hours are long . . . and constrain us to beguile them with proceedings . . . which may at first sight seem reasonable until they become a habit. You may say it is to prevent our reason from foundering. No doubt. But has it not long been straying in the night without end of the abyssal depths?"[46]

In support of the Christian interpretation, it might be argued that Vladimir and Estragon, who are waiting for Godot, are shown as clearly superior to Pozzo and Lucky, who have no appointment, no objective, and are wholly egocentric, wholly wrapped up in their sadomasochistic relationship. Is it not their faith that puts the two tramps onto a higher plane?

It is evident that, in fact, Pozzo is naïvely overconfident and self-centered. "Do I look like a man that can be made to suffer?"[47] he boasts. Even when he gives a soulful and melancholy description of the sunset and the sudden falling of the night, we know he does not believe the night will ever fall on him—he is merely giving a performance; he is not concerned with the meaning of what he recites, but only with its effect on the audience. Hence he is taken completely unawares when night does fall on him and he goes blind. Likewise Lucky, in accepting Pozzo as his master and in teaching him his ideas, seems to have been naïvely convinced of the power of reason, beauty, and truth. Estragon and Vladimir *are* clearly superior to both Pozzo and Lucky—not because they pin their faith on Godot but because they are less naïve. They do not believe in action, wealth, or reason. They are aware that all we do in this life is as nothing when seen against the senseless action of time, which is in itself an illusion. They are aware that suicide would be the best solution. They are thus superior to Pozzo and Lucky because they are less self-centered and have fewer illusions. In fact, as a Jungian psychologist, Eva Metman, has pointed out in a remarkable study of Beckett's plays, "Godot's function seems to be to keep his dependents unconscious."[48] In this view, the hope, the habit of hoping, that Godot might come after all is the last illusion that keeps Vladimir and Estragon from facing the human condition and themselves in the harsh light of fully conscious awareness. As Dr. Metman observes, it is at the very moment, toward the end of the play, when Vladimir is about to realize he has been dreaming, and must wake up and face the world as it is, that Godot's messenger arrives, rekindles his hopes, and plunges him back into the passivity of illusion.

For a brief moment, Vladimir is aware of the full horror of the human condition: "The air is full of our cries. . . . But habit is a great deadener." He looks at Estragon, who is asleep, and reflects, "At me too someone is looking, of me too someone is saying, he is sleeping, he knows nothing, let him sleep on. . . . I can't go on!"[49] The routine of waiting for Godot stands for habit, which prevents us from reaching the painful but fruitful awareness of the full reality of being.

Again we find Beckett's own commentary on this aspect of

Waiting for Godot in his essay on Proust: "Habit is the ballast that chains the dog to his vomit. Breathing is habit. Life is habit. Or rather life is a succession of habits, since the individual is a succession of individuals. . . . Habit then is the generic term for the countless treaties concluded between the countless subjects that constitute the individual and their countless correlative objects. The periods of transition that separate consecutive adaptations . . . represent the perilous zones in the life of the individual, dangerous, precarious, painful, mysterious and fertile, when for a moment the *boredom of living* is replaced by the *suffering of being*."[50] "The suffering of being: that is the free play of every faculty. Because the pernicious devotion of habit paralyses our attention, drugs those handmaidens of perception whose coöperation is not absolutely essential."[51]

Vladimir's and Estragon's pastimes are, as they repeatedly indicate, designed to stop them from thinking. "We're in no danger of thinking any more. . . . Thinking is not the worst. . . . What is terrible is to have thought."[52]

Vladimir and Estragon talk incessantly. Why? They hint at it in what is probably the most lyrical, the most perfectly phrased passage of the play:

VLADIMIR: You are right, we're inexhaustible.
ESTRAGON: It's so we won't think.
VLADIMIR: We have that excuse.
ESTRAGON: It's so we won't hear.
VLADIMIR: We have our reasons.
ESTRAGON: All the dead voices.
VLADIMIR: They make a noise like wings.
ESTRAGON: Like leaves.
VLADIMIR: Like sand.
ESTRAGON: Like leaves.
    (Silence)
VLADIMIR: They all speak together.
ESTRAGON: Each one to itself.
    (Silence)
VLADIMIR: Rather they whisper.
ESTRAGON: They rustle.
VLADIMIR: They murmur.

ESTRAGON: They rustle.
(Silence)
VLADIMIR: What do they say?
ESTRAGON: They talk about their lives.
VLADIMIR: To have lived is not enough for them.
ESTRAGON: They have to talk about it.
VLADIMIR: To be dead is not enough for them.
ESTRAGON: It is not sufficient.
(Silence)
VLADIMIR: They make a noise like feathers.
ESTRAGON: Like leaves.
VLADIMIR: Like ashes.
ESTRAGON: Like leaves.
(Long silence)[53]

This passage, in which the cross-talk of Irish music-hall comedians is miraculously transmuted into poetry, contains the key to much of Beckett's work. Surely these rustling, murmuring voices of the past are the voices we hear in the three novels of his trilogy; they are the voices that explore the mysteries of being and the self to the limits of anguish and suffering. Vladimir and Estragon are trying to escape hearing them. The long silence that follows their evocation is broken by Vladimir, "in anguish," with the cry "Say anything at all!" after which the two relapse into their wait for Godot.

The hope of salvation may be merely an evasion of the suffering and anguish that spring from facing the reality of the human condition. There is here a truly astonishing parallel between the Existentialist philosophy of Jean-Paul Sartre and the creative intuition of Beckett, who has never consciously expressed Existentialist views. If, for Beckett as for Sartre, man has the duty of facing the human condition as a recognition that at the root of our being there is nothingness, liberty, and the need of constantly creating ourselves in a succession of choices, then Godot might well become an image of what Sartre calls "bad faith"—"The first act of bad faith consists in evading what one cannot evade, in evading what one is."[54]

While these parallels may be illuminating, we must not go too far in trying to identify Beckett's vision with any school of philosophy. It is the peculiar richness of a play like *Waiting for Godot* that it opens vistas on so many different perspectives. It is open to philosophical, religious, and psychological interpretations, yet above all it is a poem on time, evanescence, and the mysteriousness of existence, the paradox of change and stability, necessity and absurdity. It expresses what Watt felt about the household of Mr. Knott: ". . . nothing changed in Mr. Knott's establishment, because nothing remained, and nothing came or went, because all was a coming and a going."[55] In watching *Waiting for Godot*, we feel like Watt contemplating the organization of Mr. Knott's world: "But he had hardly felt the absurdity of those things, on the one hand, and the necessity of those others, on the other (for it is rare that the feeling of absurdity is not followed by the feeling of necessity), when he felt the absurdity of those things of which he had just felt the necessity (for it is rare that the feeling of necessity is not followed by the feeling of absurdity)."[56]

If *Waiting for Godot* shows its two heroes whiling away the time in a succession of desultory, and never-ending, games, Beckett's second play deals with an "endgame," the final game in the hour of death.

Waiting for Godot takes place on a terrifyingly empty open road, *Endgame* in a claustrophobic interior. *Waiting for Godot* consists of two symmetrical movements that balance each other; *Endgame* has only one act that shows the running down of a mechanism until it comes to a stop. Yet *Endgame*, like *Waiting for Godot*, groups its characters in symmetrical pairs.

In a bare room with two small windows, a blind old man, Hamm, sits in a wheelchair. Hamm is paralyzed, and can no longer stand. His servant, Clov, is unable to sit down. In two ash cans that stand by the wall are Hamm's legless parents, Nagg and Nell. The world outside is dead. Some great catastrophe, of which the four characters in the play are, or believe themselves to be, the sole survivors, has killed all living beings.

Hamm and Clov (ham actor and clown?) in some ways resemble Pozzo and Lucky. Hamm is the master, Clov the servant. Hamm is selfish, sensuous, domineering. Clov hates

Hamm and wants to leave him, but he must obey his orders. "Do this, do that, and I do it. I never refuse. Why?"[57] Will Clov have the force to leave Hamm? That is the source of the dramatic tension of the play. If he leaves, Hamm must die, as Clov is the only one left who can feed him. But Clov also must die, as there is no one else left in the world, and Hamm's store is the last remaining source of food. If Clov can muster the will power to leave, he will not only kill Hamm but commit suicide. He will thus succeed where Estragon and Vladimir have failed so often.

Hamm fancies himself as a writer—or, rather, as the spinner of a tale of which he composes a brief passage every day. It is a story about a catastrophe that caused the death of large numbers of people. On this particular day, the tale has reached an episode in which the father of a starving child asks Hamm for bread for his child. Finally the father begs Hamm to take in his child, should it still be alive when he gets back to his home. It appears that Clov might well be that very child. He was brought to Hamm when he was too small to remember. Hamm was a father to him, or, as he himself puts it, "But for me . . . no father. But for Hamm . . . no home."[58] The situation in *Endgame* is the reverse of that in Joyce's *Ulysses*, where a father finds a substitute for a lost son. Here a foster son is trying to leave his foster father.

Clov has been trying to leave Hamm ever since he was born, or as he says, "Ever since I was whelped."[59] Hamm is burdened with a great load of guilt. He might have saved large numbers of people who begged him for help. "The place was crawling with them!"[60] One of the neighbors, old Mother Pegg, who was "bonny once, like a flower of the field" and perhaps Hamm's lover, was killed through his cruelty: "When old Mother Pegg asked you for oil for her lamp and you told her to get out to hell . . . you know what she died of, Mother Pegg? Of darkness."[61] Now the supplies in Hamm's own household are running out: the sweets, the flour for the parents' pap, even Hamm's painkiller. The world is running down. "Something is taking its course."[62]

Hamm is childish; he plays with a three-legged toy dog, and he is full of self-pity. Clov serves him as his eyes. At regular intervals he is asked to survey the outside world from the two tiny windows high up in the wall. The right-hand window looks out on land, the left-hand onto the sea. But even the tides have stopped.

Hamm is untidy. Clov is a fanatic of order.

Hamm's parents, in their dustbins, are grotesquely sentimental imbeciles. They lost their legs in an accident while cycling through the Ardennes on their tandem, on the road to Sedan. They remember the day they went rowing on Lake Como—the day after they became engaged—one April afternoon (cf. the love scene in a boat on a lake in *Krapp's Last Tape*), and Nagg, in the tones of an Edwardian raconteur, retells the funny story that made his bride laugh then and that he has since repeated *ad nauseam*.

Hamm hates his parents. Nell secretly urges Clov to desert Hamm. Nagg, having been awakened to listen to Hamm's tale, scolds him: "Whom did you call when you were a tiny boy, and were frightened in the dark? Your mother? No. Me." But he immediately reveals how selfishly he ignored these calls. "We let you cry. Then we moved out of earshot, so that we might sleep in peace. . . . I hope the day will come when you'll really need to have me listen to you. . . . Yes, I hope I'll live till then, to hear you calling me like when you were a tiny little boy, and were frightened, in the dark, and I was your only hope."[63]

As the end approaches, Hamm imagines what will happen when Clov leaves him. He confirms Nagg's forecast: "There I'll be in the old shelter, alone against the silence and . . . the stillness. . . . I'll have called my father and I'll have called my . . . my son,"[64] which indicates that he does indeed regard Clov as his son.

For a last time, Clov looks out of the windows with his telescope. He sees something unusual. "A small . . . boy!" But it is not entirely clear whether he has really seen this strange sign of continuing life, "a potential procreator."[65] In some way, this is the turning point. Hamm says, "It's the end, Clov, we've come to the end. I don't need you any more."[66] Perhaps he does not believe that Clov will really be able to leave him. But Clov has finally decided that he will go: "I open the door of the cell and go. I am so bowed I only see my feet, if I open my eyes, and between my legs a little trail of black dust. I

say to myself that the earth is extinguished, though I never saw
it lit. . . . It's easy going. . . . When I fall I'll weep for happiness."[67] And as blind Hamm indulges in a last monologue
of reminiscence and self-pity, Clov appears, dressed for departure in a Panama hat, tweed coat, raincoat over his arm,
and listens to Hamm's speech, motionless. When the curtain
falls, he is still there. It remains open whether he will really
leave.

The final tableau of *Endgame* bears a curious resemblance
to the ending of a little-known but highly significant play
by the brilliant Russian dramatist and man of the theatre
Nikolai Evreinov, which appeared in an English translation as
early as 1915—*The Theatre of the Soul.*[68] This one-act play
is a monodrama that takes place *inside a human being* and
shows the constituent parts of his ego, his emotional self and
his rational self in conflict with each other. The man, Ivanov,
is sitting in a café, debating with himself whether to run away
with a night-club singer or go back to his wife. His emotional
self urges him to leave, his rational self tries to persuade him
of the advantages, moral and material, of staying with his
wife. As they come to blows, a bullet pierces the heart that
has been beating in the background. Ivanov has shot himself.
The rational and emotional selves fall down dead. A third
figure, who has been sleeping in the background, gets up. He
is dressed in traveling clothes and carries a suitcase. It is the
immortal part of Ivanov that now has to move on.

While it is unlikely that Beckett knew this old and long-
forgotten Russian play, the parallels are very striking.
Evreinov's monodrama is a purely rational construction designed to present to a cabaret audience what was then the
newest psychological trend. Beckett's play springs from genuine
depths. Yet the suggestion that *Endgame* may also be a monodrama has much to be said for it. The enclosed space with the
two tiny windows through which Clov observes the outside
world; the dustbins that hold the suppressed and despised parents, and whose lids Clov is ordered to press down when they
become obnoxious; Hamm, blind and emotional; Clov, performing the function of the senses for him—all these might
well represent different aspects of a single personality, repressed memories in the subconscious mind, the emotional and

the intellectual selves. Is Clov then the intellect, bound to serve the emotions, instincts, and appetites, and trying to free himself from such disorderly and tyrannical masters, yet doomed to die when its connection with the animal side of the personality is severed? Is the death of the outside world the gradual receding of the links to reality that takes place in the process of aging and dying? Is *Endgame* a monodrama depicting the dissolution of a personality in the hour of death?

It would be wrong to assume that these questions can be definitely answered. *Endgame* certainly was not planned as a sustained allegory of this type. But there are indications that there is an element of monodrama in the play. Hamm describes a memory that is strangely reminiscent of the situation in *Endgame:* "I once knew a madman who thought the end of the world had come. He was a painter—an engraver. . . . I used to go and see him in the asylum. I'd take him by the hand and drag him to the window. Look! There! All that rising corn! And there! Look! The sails of the herring fleet! All that loveliness! . . . He'd snatch away his hand and go back into his corner. Appalled. All he had seen was ashes. . . . He alone had been spared. Forgotten . . . It appears the case is . . . was not so . . . so unusual."[69] Hamm's own world resembles the delusions of the mad painter. Moreover, what is the significance of the picture mentioned in the stage directions? "Hanging near door, its face to wall, a picture."[70] Is that picture a memory? Is the story a lucid moment in the consciousness of that very painter whose dying hours we witness from behind the scenes of his mind?

Beckett's plays can be interpreted on many levels. *Endgame* may well be a monodrama on one level and a morality play about the death of a rich man on another. But the peculiar psychological reality of Beckett's characters has often been noticed. Pozzo and Lucky have been interpreted as body and mind; Vladimir and Estragon have been seen as so complementary that they might be the two halves of a single personality, the conscious and the subconscious mind. Each of these three pairs—Pozzo-Lucky; Vladimir-Estragon; Hamm-Clov—is linked by a relationship of mutual interdependence, wanting to leave each other, at war with each other, and yet dependent on each other. *"Nec tecum, nec sine te."* This is a frequent situation among people—married couples, for example—but it is also an image of the interrelatedness of the elements within a single personality, particularly if the personality is in conflict with itself.

In Beckett's first play, *Eleutheria*, the basic situation was, superficially, analogous to the relationship between Clov and Hamm. The young hero of that play wanted to leave his family; in the end he succeeded in getting away. In *Endgame*, however, that situation has been deepened into truly universal significance; it has been concentrated and immeasurably enriched precisely by having been freed from all elements of a naturalistic social setting and external plot. The process of contraction, which Beckett described as the essence of the artistic tendency in his essay on Proust, has here been carried out triumphantly. Instead of merely exploring a surface, a play like *Endgame* has become a shaft driven deep down into the core of being; that is why it exists on a multitude of levels, revealing new ones as it is more closely studied. What at first might have appeared as obscurity or lack of definition is later recognized as the very hallmark of the density of texture, the tremendous concentration of a work that springs from a truly creative imagination, as distinct from a merely imitative one.

The force of these considerations is brought out with particular clarity when we are confronted by an attempt to interpret a play like *Endgame* as a mere exercise in conscious or subconscious autobiography. In an extremely ingenious essay[71] Lionel Abel has worked out the thesis that in the characters of Hamm and Pozzo, Beckett may have portrayed his literary master, James Joyce, while Lucky and Clov stand for Beckett himself. *Endgame* then becomes an allegory of the relationship between the domineering, nearly blind Joyce and his adoring disciple, who felt himself crushed by his master's overpowering literary influence. Superficially the parallels are striking: Hamm is presented as being at work on an interminable story, Lucky is being made to perform a set piece of thinking, which, Mr. Abel argues, is in fact a parody of Joyce's style. Yet on closer reflection this theory surely becomes untenable; not because there may not be a certain amount of truth in it (every writer is bound to use elements of his own experience of life in his work) but because, far from illuminating the full content of a play like *Endgame*, such an interpretation reduces it to a trivial level. If *Endgame* really were nothing but a thinly disguised account of the literary, or even the human, relationship between two particular individuals, it could not possibly produce the impact it has had on audiences utterly ignorant of these particular, very private circumstances. Yet *Endgame* undoubtedly has a very deep and direct impact, which can spring only from its touching a chord in the minds of a very large number of human beings. The problems of the relationship between a literary master and his pupil would be very unlikely to elicit such a response; very few people in the audience would feel directly involved. Admittedly, a play that presented the conflict between Joyce and Beckett openly, or thinly disguised, might arouse the curiosity of audiences who are always eager for autobiographical revelations. But this is just what *Endgame* does *not* do. If it nevertheless arouses profound emotion in its audience, this can be due only to the fact that it is felt to deal with a conflict of a far more universal nature. Once that is seen, it becomes clear that while it is fascinating to argue about the aptness of such autobiographical elements, such a discussion leaves the central problem of understanding the play and exploring its many-layered meanings still to be tackled.

As a matter of fact, the parallels are by no means so close: Lucky's speech in *Waiting for Godot*, for example, is anything but a parody of Joyce's style. It is, if anything, a parody of philosophical jargon and scientific double-talk—the very opposite of what either Joyce or Beckett ever wanted to achieve in their writing. Pozzo, on the other hand, who would stand for Joyce, is utterly inartistic in his first persona, and becomes reflective in a melancholy vein only after he has gone blind. And if Pozzo is Joyce, what would be the significance of Lucky's dumbness, which comes at the same time as Pozzo's blindness? The novel that Hamm composes in *Endgame* is characterized by its attempt at scientific exactitude, and there is a clear suggestion that it is not a work of art at all, but a thinly disguised vehicle for the expression of Hamm's sense of guilt about his behavior at the time of the great mysterious calamity, when he refused to save his neighbors. Clov, on the other hand, is shown as totally uninterested in Hamm's "Work in Progress," so that Hamm has to bribe his senile father to listen to it—surely a situation as unlike that of Joyce and Beckett as can be imagined.

The experience expressed in Beckett's plays is of a far more profound and fundamental nature than mere autobiography. They reveal his experience of temporality and evanescence; his sense of the tragic difficulty of becoming aware of one's own self in the merciless process of renovation and destruction that occurs with change in time; of the difficulty of communication between human beings; of the unending quest for reality in a world in which everything is uncertain and the borderline between dream and reality is ever shifting; of the tragic nature of all love relationships and the self-deception of friendship (of which Beckett speaks in the essay on Proust), and so on. In *Endgame* we are also certainly confronted with a very powerful expression of the sense of deadness, of leaden heaviness and hopelessness, that is experienced in states of deep depression: the world outside goes dead for the victim of such states, but inside his mind there is ceaseless argument between parts of his personality that have become autonomous entities.

This is not to say that Beckett gives a clinical description of psychopathological states. His creative intuition explores the elements of experience and shows to what extent all human beings carry the seeds of such depression and disintegration within the deeper layers of their personality. If the prisoners of San Quentin responded to *Waiting for Godot*, it was because they were confronted with *their own experience* of time, waiting, hope, and despair; because they recognized the truth about *their own human relationships* in the sadomasochistic interdependence of Pozzo and Lucky and in the bickering hate-love between Vladimir and Estragon. This is also the key to the wide success of Beckett's plays: to be confronted with concrete projections of the deepest fears and anxieties, which have been only vaguely experienced at a half-conscious level, constitutes a process of catharsis and liberation analogous to the therapeutic effect in psychoanalysis of confronting the subconscious contents of the mind. This is the moment of release from deadening habit, through facing up to the suffering of the reality of being, that Vladimir almost attains in *Waiting for Godot.* This also, probably, is the release that could occur if Clov had the courage to break his bondage to Hamm and venture out into the world, which may not, after all, be so dead as it appeared from within the claustrophobic confines of Hamm's realm. This, in fact, seems to be hinted at by the strange episode of the little boy whom Clov observes in the last stages of *Endgame.* Is this boy a symbol of life outside the closed circuit of withdrawal from reality?

It is significant that in the original, French version, this episode is dealt with in greater detail than in the later, English one. Again Beckett seems to have felt that he had been too explicit. And from an artistic point of view he is surely right; in his type of theatre the half-light of suggestion is more powerful than the overtly symbolical. But the comparison between the two versions is illuminating nevertheless. In the English version, Clov, after expressing surprise at what he has discovered, merely says:

> CLOV (*dismayed*): Looks like a small boy!
>
> HAMM (*sarcastic*): A small . . . boy!
>
> CLOV: I'll go and see. (*He gets down, drops the telescope, goes towards the door, turns.*) I'll take the gaff. (*He looks for the gaff, sees it, picks it up, hastens towards the door.*)
>
> HAMM: No!
>
> (*Clov halts.*)
>
> CLOV: No? A potential procreator?
>
> HAMM: If he exists he'll die there or he'll come here. And if he doesn't . . . (*Pause.*)[72]

In the original, French version, Hamm shows far greater interest in the boy, and his attitude changes from open hostility to resignation.

> CLOV: There is someone there! Someone!
>
> HAMM: Well, go and exterminate him! (*Clov gets down from the stool.*) Somebody! (*With trembling voice*) Do your duty! (*Clov rushes to the door.*) No, don't bother. (*Clov stops.*) What distance?
>
> (*Clov climbs back on the stool, looks through the telescope.*)
>
> CLOV: Seventy . . . four meters.
>
> HAMM: Approaching? Receding?

CLOV (*continues to look*): Stationary.

HAMM: Sex?

CLOV: What does it matter? (*He opens the window, leans out. Pause. He straightens, lowers the telescope, turns to Hamm, frightened.*) Looks like a little boy.

HAMM: Occupied with?

CLOV: What?

HAMM (*violently*): What is he doing?

CLOV (*also*): I don't know what he's doing. What little boys used to do. (*He looks through the telescope. Pause. Puts it down, turns to Hamm.*) He seems to be sitting on the ground, with his back against something.

HAMM: The lifted stone. (*Pause.*) Your eyesight is getting better. (*Pause.*) No doubt he is looking at the house with the eyes of Moses dying.

CLOV: No.

HAMM: What is he looking at?

CLOV (*violently*): I don't know what he is looking at. (*He raises the telescope. Pause. Lowers the telescope, turns to Hamm.*) His navel. Or thereabouts. (*Pause.*) Why this cross-examination?

HAMM: Perhaps he is dead.[73]

After this, the French text and the English version again coincide: Clov wants to tackle the newcomer with his gaff, Hamm stops him, and, after a brief moment of doubt as to whether Clov has told him the truth, realizes that the turning point has come:

"It's the end, Clov, we've come to the end. I don't need you any more."[74]

The longer, more elaborate version of this episode clearly reveals the religious or quasi-religious symbolism of the little boy; the references to Moses and the lifted stone seem to hint that the first human being, the first sign of life discovered in the outside world since the great calamity when the earth went dead, is not, like Moses, dying within sight of the promised land, but, like Christ the moment after the resurrection, has been newly born into a new life, leaning, a babe, against the lifted stone. Moreover, like the Buddha, the little boy contemplates his navel. And his appearance convinces Hamm that the moment of parting, the final stage of the endgame, has come.

It may well be that the sighting of this little boy—undoubtedly a climactic event in the play—stands for redemption from the illusion and evanescence of time through the recognition, and acceptance, of a higher reality: the little boy contemplates his own navel; that is, he fixes his attention on the great emptiness of nirvana, nothingness, of which Democritus the Abderite has said, in one of Beckett's favorite quotations, "Nothing is more real than nothing."[75]

There is a moment of illumination, shortly before he himself dies, in which Murphy, having played a *game of chess,* experiences a strange sensation: ". . . and Murphy began to see nothing, that colorlessness which is such a rare post-natal treat, being the absence . . . not of *percipere* but of *percipi.* His other senses also found themselves at peace, an unexpected pleasure. Not the numb peace of their own suspension, but the positive peace that comes when the somethings give way, or perhaps simply add up, to the Nothing, than which in the guffaw of the Abderite naught is more real. Time did not cease, that would be asking too much, but the wheels of rounds and pauses did, as Murphy with his head among the armies [i.e., of the chessmen] continued to suck in, through all the posterns of his withered soul, the accidentless One-and-Only, conveniently called Nothing."[76]

Does Hamm, who has shut himself off from the world and killed the rest of mankind by holding on to his material possessions—Hamm, blind, sensual, egocentric—then die when Clov, the rational part of the self, perceives the true reality of the illusoriness of the material world, the redemption and resurrection, the liberation from the wheels of time that lies in union with the "accidentless One-and-Only, conveniently called Nothing"? Or is the discovery of the little boy merely a symbol of the coming of death—union with nothingness in a different, more concrete sense? Or does the reappearance of life in the outside world indicate that the period of loss of contact with the world has come to an end, that the crisis has passed and that a disintegrating personality is about to find the way back to integration, "the solemn change towards merciless

reality in Hamm and ruthless acceptance of freedom in Clov,"
as the Jungian analyst Dr. Metman puts it?[77]

There is no need to try to pursue these alternatives any
further; to decide in favor of one would only impair the
stimulating coexistence of these and other possible implications. There is, however, an illuminating commentary on
Beckett's views about the interrelation between material wants
and a feeling of restlessness and futility in the short mimeplay *Act Without Words,* which was performed with *Endgame*
during its first run. The scene is a desert onto which a man is
"flung backwards." Mysterious whistles draw his attention in
various directions. A number of more or less desirable objects,
notably a carafe of water, are dangled before him. He tries
to get the water. It hangs too high. A number of cubes, obviously designed to make it easier for him to reach the water,
descend from the flies. But however ingeniously he piles them
on top of one another, the water always slides just outside his
reach. In the end he sinks into complete immobility. The
whistle sounds—but he no longer heeds it. The water is dangled
in front of his face—but he does not move. Even the palm
tree in the shade of which he has been sitting is whisked off
into the flies. He remains immobile, looking at his hands.[78]

Here again we find man flung onto the stage of life, at first
obeying the call of a number of impulses, having his attention
drawn to the pursuit of illusory objectives by whistles from
the wings, but finding peace only when he has learned his
lesson and refuses any of the material satisfactions dangled before him. The pursuit of objectives that forever recede as they
are attained—inevitably so through the action of time, which
changes us in the process of reaching what we crave—can
find release only in the recognition of that nothingness which
is the only reality. The whistle that sounds from the wings
resembles the whistle with which Hamm summons Clov to
minister to his material needs. And the final, immobile position of the man in *Act Without Words* recalls the posture of
the little boy in the original version of *Endgame.*

The activity of Pozzo and Lucky, the driver and the driven,
always on the way from place to place; the waiting of Estragon
and Vladimir, whose attention is always focused on the promise of a coming; the defensive position of Hamm, who has

built himself a shelter from the world to hold on to his possessions, are all aspects of the same futile preoccupation with objectives and illusory goals. All movement is disorder. As Clov says, "I love order. It's my dream. A world where all would be silent and still and each thing in its last place, under the last dust."[79]

Waiting for Godot and *Endgame*, the plays Beckett wrote in French, are dramatic statements of the human situation itself. They lack both characters and plot in the conventional sense because they tackle their subject matter at a level where neither characters nor plot exist. Characters presuppose that human nature, the diversity of personality and individuality, is real and matters; plot can exist only on the assumption that events in time are significant. These are precisely the assumptions that the two plays put in question. Hamm and Clov, Pozzo and Lucky, Vladimir and Estragon, Nagg and Nell are not characters but the embodiments of basic human attitudes, rather like the personified virtues and vices in medieval mystery plays or Spanish *autos sacramentales*. And what passes in these plays are not *events* with a definite beginning and a definite end, but types of *situation* that will forever repeat themselves. That is why the pattern of Act I of *Waiting for Godot* is repeated with variations in Act II; that is why we do not see Clov actually leave Hamm at the close of *Endgame* but leave the two frozen in a position of stalemate. Both plays repeat the pattern of the old German students' song Vladimir sings at the beginning of Act II of *Waiting for Godot*, about the dog that came into a kitchen and stole some bread and was killed by the cook and buried by its fellow dogs who put a tombstone on its grave which told the story of the dog that came into the kitchen and stole some bread—and so on ad infinitum. In *Endgame* and *Waiting for Godot*, Beckett is concerned with probing down to a depth in which individuality and definite events no longer appear, and only basic patterns emerge.

In the plays he has written for the stage and for radio in English, his probing does not go quite so deep, and both individual characters and individualized plots do appear, reflecting the same patterns but reflecting them in the lives of particular human beings. *Krapp's Last Tape* deals with the flow of time and the instability of the self, *All That Fall* and *Embers* with waiting, guilt, and the futility of pinning one's hope on things or human beings.

All That Fall (the title is taken from Psalm 145: "The Lord upholdeth all that fall and raiseth up all those that be bowed down") shows an old Irishwoman, Maddy Rooney, very fat, very ill, hardly able to move, on her way to the railway station of Boghill to fetch her blind husband, Dan Rooney, who is due to arrive on the twelve-thirty train. Her progress is slow as in a nightmare. She meets a number of people with whom she wants to establish contact but fails. "I estrange them all."[80] Mrs. Rooney has lost a daughter, Minnie, more than forty years ago. When she reaches the railway station, the train is mysteriously delayed. When it arrives, it is said to have stopped for a long while on the open track. Dan and Maddy Rooney set out for home. As children jeer at them, Dan Rooney asks, "Did you ever wish to kill a child? . . . Nip some young doom in the bud?"[81] and he admits that often in winter he is tempted to attack the boy who leads him home from the station. When they are almost home, the same little boy runs after them; he is returning an object Mr. Rooney is believed to have left in his compartment on the train. It is a child's ball. The boy also knows why the train had to stop on the line: a child had fallen out of the train and been killed on the tracks. Did Dan Rooney push a child out of the train? Did his impulse to destroy young lives overcome him during the journey? And has his hatred of children something to do with Maddy's childlessness? Maddy Rooney stands for the forces of life and procreation, Dan for the death-wish that sees a young child only as a young doom that could be nipped in the bud. Does the Biblical quotation of the title support Dan Rooney's point of view? "The Lord upholdeth all that fall. . . ." Was the child who was killed and redeemed from existence saved the troubles of life and old age and thus upheld by the Lord? When the text from the psalm is mentioned as the subject of next Sunday's sermon, both Maddy and Dan Rooney break out in "wild laughter."[82] *All That Fall* touches many of the chords that are sounded in *Waiting for Godot* and *Endgame* —but in a somewhat lighter and less searching manner.

In *Krapp's Last Tape,* a one-act play that has been performed with great success on the stage in Paris, London, and New York, Beckett makes use of the tape recorder to demonstrate the elusiveness of human personality. Krapp is a very old man who throughout his adult life has annually recorded an account of the past year's impressions and events onto magnetic tape. We see him, old, decrepit, and a failure (he is a writer, but only seventeen copies of his book have been sold in the current year, "eleven at trade price to free circulating libraries beyond the seas"), listening to his own voice recorded thirty years earlier. But his voice has become the voice of a stranger to him. He even has to get a dictionary to look up one of the more elaborate words used by his former self. When the tape reaches the description of the great moment of insight that then seemed a miracle to be treasured "against the day when my work will be done," he cannot be bothered to listen to it and winds the tape on. The only description that visibly arouses his attention is one of lovemaking in a punt on a lake. Having heard his earlier self's report on his thirty-ninth year, the sixty-nine-year-old Krapp proceeds to record the current year's balance sheet. "Nothing to say, not a squeak." His only moment of happiness: "Revelled in the word spool. (*With relish*) Spoool! Happiest moment in the past half million."[83] There are memories of lovemaking with an old hag. But then Krapp returns to the old tape. Again the voice of his former self is heard describing the love scene on the lake. The old tape ends with a summing up: "Perhaps my best years are gone. When there was a chance of happiness. But I wouldn't want them back. Not with the fire in me now. No, I wouldn't want them back."[84] The curtain falls on old Krapp staring motionless before him, with the tape running on in silence.

Through the brilliant device of the autobiographical library of annual recorded statements, Beckett has found a graphic expression for the problem of the ever-changing identity of the self, which he had already described in his essay on Proust. In *Krapp's Last Tape,* the self at one moment in time is confronted with its earlier incarnation only to find it utterly strange. What, then, is the identity between Krapp now and Krapp then? In what sense are they the same? And if this is a problem with an interval of thirty years, it is surely only a difference in degree if the interval is reduced to one year, one month, one hour. Beckett at one time planned to write a long play of three Krapps: Krapp with his wife, Krapp with his wife and child, Krapp alone—further variations on the theme of the identity of the self. But he has now abandoned this project.

The radio play *Embers* resembles *Krapp's Last Tape* in that its hero is also an old man musing on the past. Against the background of the roar of the sea, Henry remembers his youth, his father who was drowned in the sea at this very spot, his father who was a sporty man and despised his son as a wash-out. It seems as if Henry wanted to establish contact with his dead father, but "he doesn't answer any more."[85] Henry's wife, Ada, although probably dead too, does respond. They remember lovemaking by the sea, their daughter's riding and music lessons, but then Ada recedes, and Henry is left alone with his thoughts, which revolve around a scene he seems to have witnessed as a child between two men at night, Bolton and Holloway, Holloway being a doctor, their family doctor, whom Bolton (Henry's father?) implored for some medical help the nature of which remains unclear. With the winter night outside and the fire dying—no more flames, only the embers glowing—Henry remains alone with his thoughts of his loneliness: "Saturday . . . nothing. Sunday . . . Sunday . . . nothing all day. . . . Nothing, all day nothing . . . Not a sound."[86]

Henry resembles the heroes of Beckett's later novels in his recall of memories in the form of "stories" and in his compulsive need to talk. As his wife, or the memory of his wife, tells him, "You should see a doctor about your talking, it's worse, what must it be like for Addie? . . . Do you know what she said to me once, when she was quite small, she said, Mummy, why does Daddy keep on talking all the time? She heard you in the lavatory, I didn't know what to answer." To which Henry replies, "I told you to tell her I was praying. Roaring prayers at God and his saints."[87]

In the two radio plays, *Embers* and *All That Fall*, this compulsion to talk that is so characteristic of all of Beckett's characters (for even the incessant writing of the crippled, legless, paralyzed heroes of his novels is a form of talk—a *monologue intérieur*) blends into a background of natural sound—the sound of the sea in *Embers*, the sounds of the road in *All That Fall*. And articulate sound, language, is somehow equated with the inarticulate sounds of nature. In a world that has lost its meaning, language also becomes a meaningless buzzing. As Molloy says at one point, ". . . the words I heard, and heard distinctly, having quite a sensitive ear, were heard a first time, then a second, and often even a third, as pure sounds, free of all meaning, and this is probably one of the reasons why conversation was unspeakably painful to me. And the words I uttered myself, and which must nearly always have gone with an effort of the intelligence, were often to me as the buzzing of an insect. And this is perhaps one of the reasons I was so untalkative, I mean this trouble I had in understanding not only what others said to me, but also what I said to them. It is true that in the end, by dint of patience, we made ourselves understood, but understood with regard to what, I ask of you, and to what purpose? And to the noises of nature too, and of the works of men, I reacted I think in my own way and without desire of enlightenment."[88]

When we hear Beckett's characters (and hence Beckett himself) using language, we often feel like Celia when she was talking to Murphy: ". . . spattered with words that went dead as soon as they sounded; each word obliterated, before it had time to make sense, by the word that came next; so that in the end she did not know what had been said. It was like difficult music heard for the first time."[89] And in fact the dialogue in Beckett's plays is often built on the principle that each line obliterates what was said in the previous line. In his thesis on Beckett, *Die Unzulänglichkeit der Sprache—The Inadequacy of Language*—Niklaus Gessner has drawn up a whole list of passages from *Waiting for Godot* in which assertions made by one of the characters are gradually qualified, weakened, and hedged in with reservations until they are completely taken back. In a meaningless universe, it is always foolhardy to make a positive statement. "Not to want to say, not to know what you want to say, not to be able to say what you think you want to say, and never to stop saying, or hardly ever, that is the thing to keep in mind, even in the heat of composition,"[90] as Molloy puts it, summing up the attitude of most of Beckett's characters.

If Beckett's plays are concerned with expressing the difficulty of finding meaning in a world subject to incessant change, his use of language probes the limitations of language both as a means of communication and as a vehicle for the expression of valid statements, an instrument of thought. When Gessner asked him about the contradiction between his writing and his obvious conviction that language could not convey meaning, Beckett replied, *"Que voulez-vous, Monsieur? C'est les mots; on n'a rien d'autre."* But in fact his use of the dramatic medium shows that he has tried to find means of expression beyond language. On the stage—witness his two mimeplays—one can dispense with words altogether, or at least one can reveal the reality behind the words, as when the actions of the characters contradict their verbal expression. "Let's go," say the two tramps at the end of each act of *Waiting for Godot*, but the stage directions inform us that "they don't move." On the stage, language can be put into a contrapuntal relationship with action, the facts behind the language can be revealed. Hence the importance of mime, knockabout comedy, and silence in Beckett's plays—Krapp's eating of bananas, the pratfalls of Vladimir and Estragon, the variety turn with Lucky's hat, Clov's immobility at the close of *Endgame*, which puts his verbally expressed desire to leave in question. Beckett's use of the stage is an attempt to reduce the gap between the limitations of language and the intuition of being, the sense of the human situation he seeks to express in spite of his strong feeling that words are inadequate to formulate it. The concreteness and three-dimensional nature of the stage can be used to add new resources to language as an instrument of thought and exploration of being.

Beckett's whole work is an endeavor to name the unnamable: "I have to speak, whatever that means. Having nothing to say, no words but the words of others, I have to speak. . . . I have the ocean to drink, so there is an ocean then."[91]

Language in Beckett's plays serves to express the breakdown, the disintegration of language. Where there is no certainty, there can be no definite meanings—and the impossibility of ever attaining certainty is one of the main themes of

Beckett's plays. Godot's promises are vague and uncertain. In *Endgame,* an unspecified something is taking its course, and when Hamm anxiously asks, "We're not beginning to . . . to . . . mean something?" Clov merely laughs. "Mean something! You and I mean something!"[92]

Niklaus Gessner has tabulated ten different modes of disintegration of language observable in *Waiting for Godot.* They range from simple misunderstandings and *double-entendres* to monologues (as signs of inability to communicate), clichés, repetitions of synonyms, inability to find the right words, and "telegraphic style" (loss of grammatical structure, communication by shouted commands) to Lucky's farrago of chaotic nonsense and the dropping of punctuation marks, such as question marks, as an indication that language has lost its function as a means for communication, that questions have turned into statements not really requiring an answer.

But more important than any merely formal signs of the disintegration of language and meaning in Beckett's plays is the nature of the dialogue itself, which again and again breaks down because no truly dialectical exchange of thought occurs in it—either through loss of meaning of single words (Godot's boy messenger, when asked if he is unhappy, replies, "I don't know, sir") or through the inability of characters to remember what has just been said (Estragon: "Either I forget immediately or I never forget").[93] In a purposeless world that has lost its ultimate objectives, dialogue, like all action, becomes a mere game to pass the time, as Hamm points out in *Endgame:* ". . . babble, babble, words, like the solitary child who turns himself into children, two, three, so as to be together and whisper together in the dark . . . moment upon moment, pattering down."[94] It is time itself that drains language of meaning. In *Krapp's Last Tape,* the well-turned idealistic professions of faith Krapp made in his best years have become empty sounds to Krapp grown old. Instead of establishing a bridge of friendliness, Mrs. Rooney's attempts to communicate with the people she meets on the road in *All That Fall* merely serve to make her more estranged from them. And in *Embers* the old man's musings are equated with the beating of the waves upon the shore.

But, if Beckett's use of language is designed to devalue lan-

guage as a vehicle of conceptual thought or as an instrument
for the communication of ready-made answers to the problems
of the human condition, his continued use of language must,
paradoxically, be regarded as an attempt to communicate on
his own part, to communicate the incommunicable. Such an
undertaking may be a paradox, but it makes sense nevertheless: it attacks the cheap and facile complacency of those who
believe that to name a problem is to solve it, that the world can
be mastered by neat classification and formulations. Such complacency is the basis of a continuous process of frustration. The
recognition of the illusoriness and absurdity of ready-made solutions and prefabricated meanings, far from ending in despair,
is the starting point of a new kind of consciousness, which
faces the mystery and terror of the human condition in the exhilaration of a new-found freedom: "For to know nothing is
nothing, not to want to know anything likewise, but to be beyond knowing anything, that is when peace enters in, to the
soul of the incurious seeker."[95]

Beckett's entire work can be seen as a search for the reality
that lies behind mere reasoning in conceptual terms. He may
have devaluated language as an instrument for the communication of ultimate truths, but he has shown himself a great
master of language as an artistic medium. *"Que voulez-vous,
Monsieur? C'est les mots; on n'a rien d'autre."* For want of
better raw material, he has molded words into a superb instrument for his purpose. In the theatre he has been able to
add a new dimension to language—the counterpoint of action,
concrete, many-faceted, not to be explained away, but making
a direct impact on an audience. In the theatre, or at least in
Beckett's theatre, it is possible to bypass the stage of conceptual thinking altogether, as an abstract painting bypasses the
stage of the recognition of natural objects. In *Waiting for
Godot* and *Endgame,* plays drained of character, plot, and
meaningful dialogue, Beckett has shown that such a seemingly
impossible tour de force can in fact be accomplished.

Chapter Two

ARTHUR ADAMOV: THE CURABLE
AND THE INCURABLE

Arthur Adamov, the author of some of the most powerful plays in the Theatre of the Absurd, now rejects all his work that might be classified under that heading. The development that led him toward this type of drama, however, and the development that led him away from it again, are of particular interest to any inquiry into its nature. Adamov, who is not only a remarkable dramatist but also a remarkable thinker, has provided us with a well-documented case history of the preoccupations and obsessions that made him write plays depicting a senseless and brutal nightmare world, the theoretical considerations that led him to formulate an aesthetic of the absurd, and, finally, the process by which he gradually returned to a theatre based on reality, the representation of social conditions, and a definite social purpose. How did it happen that a dramatist who in the late nineteen-forties so thoroughly rejected the naturalistic theatre that to use even the name of a town that could actually be found on a map would have appeared to him as "unspeakably vulgar" could by 1960 be engaged in writing a full-scale historical drama firmly situated in place and time—the Paris Commune of 1871?

Arthur Adamov, born in Kislovodsk, in the Caucasus, in 1908, the son of a wealthy oil-well proprietor of Armenian origin, left Russia at the age of four. His parents could afford to travel, and, like the children of many well-to-do Russian families, Adamov was brought up in French, a fact that explains his mastery of French literary style. The first book he ever read was Balzac's *Eugénie Grandet,* at the age of seven. The outbreak of the First World War found Adamov's family at Freudenstadt, a resort in the Black Forest. It was only through the special intervention of the King of Württemberg, who was acquainted with Adamov's father, that the family escaped internment as enemy citizens, and were given special permission to leave for Switzerland, where they settled in Geneva.

Adamov received his early education in Switzerland and later in Germany (at Mainz). In 1924, at the age of sixteen, he went to Paris and was drawn into Surrealist circles. He wrote Surrealist poetry, edited an avant-garde periodical, *Discontinuité*, became a friend of Paul Eluard, and led the life of the Parisian literary nonconformists.

Gradually he stopped writing, or at least stopped publishing what he had written. He himself later described the severe spiritual and psychological crisis that he went through in a small book that must be among the most terrifying and ruthless documents of self-revelation in the whole of world literature, *L'Aveu (The Confession)*. The earliest section of this Dostoevskian masterpiece, dated "Paris, 1938," opens with a brilliant statement of the metaphysical anguish that forms the basis of Existentialist literature and of the Theatre of the Absurd:

What is there? I know first of all that I am. But who am I? All I know of myself is that I suffer. And if I suffer it is because at the origin of myself there is mutilation, separation.

I am separated. What I am separated from—I cannot name it. But I am separated.

In a footnote Adamov adds, "Formerly it was called God. Today it no longer has any name."[1]

A deep sense of alienation, the feeling that time weighs on him "with its enormous liquid mass, with all its dark power,"[2] a deep feeling of passivity—these are some of the symptoms of his spiritual sickness.

Everything happens as though I were only one of the particular existences of some great incomprehensible and central being. . . . Sometimes this great totality of life appears to me so dramatically beautiful that it plunges me into ecstasy. But more often it seems like a monstrous beast that penetrates and surpasses me and which is everywhere, within me and outside me. . . . And terror grips and envelops me more powerfully from moment to moment. . . . My only way out is to write, to make others aware of it, so as not to have to feel all of it alone, to get rid of however small a portion of it.[3]

It is in dreams and in prayer that the writer of this haunting confession seeks escape—in dreams that are "the great silent movement of the soul through the night";[4] in prayer that is the "desperate need of man, immersed in time, to seek refuge in the only entity that could save him, the projection outward from himself of that in him which partakes of eternity."[5] Yet what is there to pray to? "The name of God should no longer come from the mouth of man. This word that has so long been degraded by usage no longer means anything. . . . To use the word God is more than sloth, it is a refusal to think, a kind of short cut, a hideous shorthand. . . ."[6] Thus the crisis of faith is also a crisis of language. "The words in our aging vocabularies are like very sick people. Some may be able to survive, others are incurable."[7]

In the next section of *L'Aveu*, dated "Paris, 1939" (it has been published in English, under the title "The Endless Humiliation")[8] Adamov gives a ruthlessly frank description of his own sickness, his desire to be humiliated by the lowest of prostitutes, his "incapacity to complete the act of carnal possession."[9] Fully aware of the nature of his neurosis—he is well versed in modern psychology and has even translated one of Jung's works into French[10]—Adamov is also aware of the *value* of neurosis, which "grants its victim a peracute lucidity, inaccessible to the so-called normal man,"[11] and which may thus give him the vision that "permits him, through the singularity of his sickness, to accede to the great general laws by which the loftiest comprehension of the world is expressed. And since the particular is always a symbolic expression of the universal, it follows that the universal is most effectively symbolized by the extreme of the particular, so that the neurosis which exaggerates a man's particularity of vision defines that much more completely his universal significance."[12]

Having given a brutally detailed description, itself a symptom of masochism by the violence of its self-humiliation, of his neurosis, with its obsessions, rites, and automatisms, Adamov returns to a diagnosis of our epoch in a section entitled "Le Temps de l'Ignominie." He defines ignominy as that which has no name, the *unnamable*, and the poet's task is not only to call each thing by its name but also to "denounce . . . the degenerated concepts, the dried-up abstractions that have usurped . . . the dead remnants of the old sacred names."[13] The degradation of language in our time becomes the expression of its deepest sickness. What has been lost is the sense of the sacred, "the unfathomable wisdom of the myths and rites of the dead old world."[14]

The disappearance of meaning in the world is clearly linked to the degradation of language, and both, in turn, to the loss of faith, the disappearance of sacred rites and sacred myths. But perhaps this degradation and despair are necessary steps toward a renewal: "Perhaps the sad and empty language that today's flabby humanity pours forth, will, in all its horror, in all its boundless absurdity, re-echo in the heart of a solitary man who is awake, and then perhaps that man, suddenly realizing that he does not understand, will begin to understand."[15] Therefore the only task left to man is to tear off all that dead skin until "he finds himself in the hour of the great nakedness."[16]

In this document of ruthless self-revelation, Adamov outlined a whole philosophy of the Theatre of the Absurd, long before he started to write his first play.

In the pages of *L'Aveu*, we can follow him through the war years—still in Paris in May and June, 1940; in Cassis in July; in Marseille by August; then, between December, 1940, and November, 1941, at the internment camp of Argelès, months passed in a stupor of dejection; back in Marseille at the end of 1941; returning to Paris in the last month of 1942. The last section of *L'Aveu* and the preface are dated 1943.

In reading this astonishing book, we are witnessing a mind laying the foundations of its salvation through self-examination and a merciless recognition of its own predicament. In his contributions to the short-lived literary review *L'Heure Nouvelle*, of which he became editor shortly after the end of the war in Europe, Adamov returned to the same themes, but already in a spirit of detachment, in the posture of a thinker called upon, at a great turning point in history, to work out a program of action for a new beginning in a new epoch.

It is a program characterized by a complete absence of illusions and easy solutions: "We are accused of pessimism, as though pessimism were but one among a number of possible attitudes, as if man were capable of choosing between two alternatives—optimism and pessimism."[17] Such a program would of necessity be destructive in its rejection of all existing dogmatisms. It insists on the artist's duty to avoid selecting just one aspect of the world—"religious, psychological, scientific, social—but to evoke behind each of these the shadow of the whole in which they must merge."[18] And again this search for wholeness, for the reality underlying the bewildering multiplicity of appearances, is seen as a search for the sacred: "the crisis of our time is essentially a religious crisis. It is a matter of life or death."[19] Yet the concept of God is dead. We are on the threshold of an era of impersonal aspects of the absolute, hence the revival of creeds like Taoism and Buddhism. This is the tragic impasse in which modern man finds himself: "From whatever point he starts, whatever path he follows, modern man comes to the same conclusion: behind its visible appearances, life hides a meaning that is eternally inaccessible to penetration by the spirit that seeks for its discovery, caught in the dilemma of being aware that it is impossible to find it, and yet also impossible to renounce the hopeless quest."[20] Adamov points out that this is not, strictly speaking, a philosophy of the absurd, because it still presupposes the conviction that the world *has* a meaning, although it is of necessity outside the reach of human consciousness. The awareness that there may be a meaning but that it will never be found is tragic. Any conviction that the world is wholly absurd would lack this tragic element.

In the social and political sphere, Adamov finds the solution in Communism. But his is a very personal form of support for the Communist cause. He finds in Communism no supernatural, sacred element. Its ideology confines itself to purely human terms, and for him it remains open to question "whether anything that confines itself to the human sphere could ever attain anything but the subhuman."[21] If this is the case, why support Communism? "If we turn to Communism nevertheless, it is merely because one day, when it will seem quite close to the realization of its highest aim—the victory over all the contradictions that impede the exchange of goods among men—it will meet, inevitably, the great 'no' of the nature of things, which it thought it could ignore in its struggle. When the material obstacles are overcome, when man will no longer be able to deceive himself as to the nature of his unhappiness, then there will arise an anxiety all the more powerful, all the more fruitful for being stripped of anything that might have hindered its realization. It goes without saying that such a purely negative hope does not seem to us to entail an adherence that, to be complete, would have to manifest itself in action."[22]

This was Adamov's position in 1946. Since then, largely as a consequence of the emergence of General de Gaulle after the events of May, 1958, he has taken a more active line in support of the extreme Left. Yet when asked in 1960 whether he had changed his attitude since 1946, Adamov confirmed that he still subscribed to what he had written fourteen years earlier.

It was toward the end of the Second World War that Adamov began to write for the theatre. He was reading Strindberg at the time, and under the influence of Strindberg's plays, notably A Dream Play, he began to discover the stuff of drama all around him, in "the most ordinary everyday happenings, particularly street scenes. What struck me above all were the lines of passers-by, their loneliness in the crowd, the terrifying diversity of their utterance, of which I would please myself by hearing only snatches that, linked with other snatches of conversation, seemed to grow into a composite entity the very fragmentariness of which became a guarantee of its symbolic truth."[23] One day he witnessed a scene that confronted him, in a sudden flash, with the dramatic reality he had wanted to express. A blind beggar passed by two pretty girls singing a refrain from some popular song: "I had closed my eyes, it was wonderful!" This gave him the idea of showing "on the stage, as crudely and as visibly as possible, the loneliness of man, the absence of communication."[24]

La Parodie, Adamov's first play, is the fruit of this idea. In a succession of rapidly sketched scenes, it shows two men infatuated with the same emptyheaded, commonplace girl, Lili. One of them, the "employee," is brisk, businesslike, and ever optimistic, while the other, "N.," is passive, helpless, and despondent. The employee, who, in a chance meeting, has gained the wholly erroneous impression that he has a date with Lili, never loses his hope and constantly turns up at imagined rendezvous. N., on the other hand, spends his time lying in the street, waiting for Lili to pass by chance. In the end the optimistic, buoyant attitude of the employee and the abject passivity of N. lead to precisely the same result—nothing. Lili cannot even tell her two rival suitors apart. The employee lands in prison, where he goes on making plans for the future and still hopes to maintain his position, although he has gone blind. N. is run over by a car and swept into the garbage by the street-cleaners. Lili is flanked by relatively successful men —a journalist with whom she seems in love and who keeps her waiting when they have a date, and the editor of his paper, who treats her as his kept mistress. The editor also takes the place, as and when the action requires it, of a number of other persons in authority—the manager of a restaurant, the director of a firm for which the employee works as a salesman, the receptionist of a hotel where he fails to get a room. While N. and the employee are seen, as it were, from their own point of view, the journalist and the editor are seen wholly from the outside, as "the other people," who, inexplicably, seem to be able to master the human situation, to whom nothing calamitous ever happens. Two identical and interchangeable couples act as a kind of chorus, the faceless crowd that surrounds us; they age as the action proceeds, but remain anonymous and interchangeable throughout.

Time is constantly evoked: the characters keep on asking each other the time without ever receiving an answer. A clock without hands is a recurring feature of the décor. The action of time is also illustrated by the gradual shrinkage of space. A dance hall shown in the beginning appears again in Scene 11 —but now the set has become much narrower.

At one point, N. is shown with a prostitute whom he begs to humiliate him. As Adamov himself has pointed out, *La Parodie* served to justify his own attitude: "Even if I am like N., I shall not be punished any more than the employee."[25]

Buoyant activity is as pointless as cringing apathy and self-humiliation.

La Parodie is an attempt to come to terms with neurosis, to make psychological states visible in concrete terms. As Adamov defines it in the introduction to the first edition, the performance of a play of this type is "the projection into the world of sensations of states of mind and images that constitute its hidden content. A stage play ought to be the point of intersection between the visible and invisible worlds, or, in other words, the display, the manifestation of the hidden, latent contents that form the shell around the seeds of drama."26

In its determined rejection of individuality in favor of schematic types—in which it resembles German Expressionist drama—*La Parodie* represents a revolt against the complexities of the psychological theatre. It is a deliberate return to primitivism. Adamov does not want to represent the world, he wants to parody it. "When I arraign the world around me, I often reproach it for being nothing more than a parody. But the sickness I admit to—is it anything more than a parody?"27 Parody is direct, harsh, and oversimplified. *La Parodie* deliberately eschews all subtleties of plot, characterization, or language. This is a theatre of gesture—N. lying in the road, the employee bustling about, the interchangeable couples going through the motions of human existence without being recognizable individuals.

Adamov felt that, having parodied the world in such simple terms, he had reached a dead end. In his next play, *L'Invasion,* he took the first steps toward portraying real characters in real human relationships. The isolated, lonely individuals of *La Parodie* are replaced by a family. It is still a family composed of lonely individuals, unable to communicate. But they are strongly linked together nevertheless—curiously enough, by a shared loyalty to a dead hero.

This hero is a dead writer, Jean, who has left an enormous mass of undeciphered papers to his friend and disciple, Pierre, the husband of the dead man's sister Agnes. The apartment where they live, together with Pierre's mother, is in a state of complete disorder, which expresses the disorder reigning in the minds of the characters. The task of deciphering Jean's literary remains is an impossible one. His writing is not only illegible but the characters themselves have faded. One can never know what he really wrote, and there is a constant danger that the literary executor will simply invent what he thinks the master ought to have written. And even if a scrap of paper, a single sentence, is finally deciphered, it still must be placed in the context of the vast mass of disordered papers.

There is another disciple of Jean's who tries to help, Tradel, but he is suspect precisely because he tends to read things into Jean's writing. The disorder within the room where the action takes place is matched by the disorder of the whole country: immigrants are streaming across the frontiers, the social structure is disintegrating. In the second act the disorder in the room, now cluttered up with furniture, has increased. Pierre finds it ever more difficult to understand the meaning of the manuscripts. A man who is looking for someone in the apartment next door enters and strikes up a conversation with Agnes. He is "the first one who comes along" with whom Agnes will run away. In the third act, this man has become a fixture in the room, and Pierre wants to retire to his own private den downstairs to work in peace. Agnes duly leaves him and goes off with the "first one who comes along." In Act IV the room has been cleaned up, the papers are neatly stacked. Order has also returned in the country. Pierre has decided to give up his work. He begins to tear up the manuscripts. Agnes appears—she wants to borrow the typewriter. Her lover is ill, she is unable to manage his business. Pierre, who has gone down to his den, is found there by Tradel; he is dead.

L'Invasion is a play about the hopeless search for meaning, the quest for a message that will make sense in a jumble of undecipherable papers; but it is concerned with order and disorder in society as well as in the family. It almost seems that Agnes stands for disorder. Has Pierre, in marrying her, not at the same time married her dead brother with his confused manuscripts? When she leaves, order returns, and disorder and business failure enter the household of the man whose mistress she has become. Yet when Pierre abandons his work on the manuscripts, he dies. He loses Agnes to the first man who comes along because he is withdrawing more and more from human contact. The disorder that Agnes brings also represents the bewildering nature of reality and of relationships with other human beings, which Pierre is unable to cope with. He withdraws from contact with others, because he finds communication more and more difficult. Language is disintegrating before his eyes: "Why does one say, 'It happens?' Who is that 'it,' what does it want from me? Why does one say 'on the ground' rather than 'at' or 'over'? I have lost too much time thinking about these things. What I want is not the meaning of words, but their volume and their moving body. I shall no longer search for anything. . . . I'll wait in silence, motionless."[28]

Pierre begs his mother, who will bring him his food in his den, never to speak to him—a sign of his complete withdrawal. It is when he abandons his attitude of withdrawal, when he decides that he wants to lead a life like everybody else, that he learns that Agnes has left him. "She left too late, or too soon. Had she had a little more patience, we could have started all over again,"[29] he says, and returns to his den —to die, just missing Agnes, who comes to ask "to borrow the typewriter," yet clearly begging to be taken back. But Pierre's mother does not, or does not want to, understand, and fails to call Pierre upstairs.

Here the tragedy turns on a misunderstanding. Had Pierre's mother not taken Agnes's demand for the typewriter literally, rather than as a symbolic request to be taken back and participate in the work of the family, Pierre might not have died rejected and unloved. Adamov has described how he thought that he had found an important new dramatic device—indirect dialogue, the characters' oblique reference to the subject under discussion, since they cannot find the courage to display their feelings openly and thereby expose themselves to tragic misunderstandings. Later he realized that he had merely reinvented a technique already used by other dramatists, notably by Chekhov.

L'Invasion is a haunting play. André Gide was deeply impressed by it; he felt that it dealt with the greatness of a dead writer and the process by which his influence and power gradually fade away—surely a curious misunderstanding on the part of the venerable old man of letters, applying the conceptions

of his own generation to the works of a new age. To a contemporary reader, the most striking feature of *L'Invasion* is
precisely the unreality of the dead hero, the fact that his much
vaunted message is essentially meaningless—absurd.

Jean Vilar, the great French director, who had produced
Adamov's adaptation of Buechner's *Danton's Death* at the
Avignon Festival of 1948, saw *L'Invasion* with the eyes of a
contemporary. He praised Adamov for renouncing "the lace
ornaments of dialogue and intrigue, for having given back to
the drama its stark purity"[30] of clear and simple stage symbols. He contrasted this stark modern theatre with that of
Claudel, "which borrows its effect from the alcohols of faith
and the grand word"[30] and, posing the alternatives Adamov
or Claudel, clearly answered—Adamov.

Gide's and Vilar's tributes to Adamov, together with comments by other distinguished literary and stage figures like
René Char, Jacques Prévert, and Roger Blin, are contained in
the slim volume in which Adamov, having failed to get them
performed on the stage, presented his first two plays to the
reading public in the spring of 1950. The response to this
publication had the desired effect; on November 14, 1950,
L'Invasion, directed by Jean Vilar, opened at the Studio des
Champs-Elysées. Three days earlier, Adamov's third play, *La
Grande et la Petite Manœuvre*, had been presented at the
Théâtre des Noctambules, directed by another of the outstanding pioneers of the French avant-garde, Jean-Marie Serreau,
and with Roger Blin in the leading part.

Adamov himself has explained the title of *La Grande et la
Petite Manœuvre* as referring to the small maneuver of the
social disorder depicted in the play, in contrast to the large
maneuver of the human condition itself, which envelops and
dwarfs the former,[31] the word "maneuver" in this context having a double military and psychological sense.

La Grande et la Petite Manœuvre combines the theme of
the parallel lives of *La Parodie* with that of the social and
political disorders in the background of *L'Invasion*. The active,
self-sacrificing struggle of a revolutionary leader is shown to
be as futile as the passivity of a tormented victim of hidden
psychological forces, who is compelled to execute the shouted
orders of invisible monitors who drive him to the gradual loss

of all his limbs. The action takes place in a country oppressed
by a brutal dictatorship. The active character, *le militant,* leads
the victorious struggle against the forces of the police state; in
the end he collapses while making a speech admitting that
the revolutionaries have been compelled to use methods of
brutal terror to gain their victory. Moreover, the *militant*
has caused the death of his own child, because the disorders
he himself had provoked made it impossible for the doctor to
reach its sickbed. Once again the activist has achieved no more
than the passive character, *le mutilé,* who, a legless, armless
cripple on a pushcart, is kicked into the road by the woman
he adores, to be crushed in the crowd.

The *mutilé,* who must obey the orders of the voices that
compel him to put his hands into the machine that will cut
them off, to walk in front of the car that will run him over, is
clearly the chief character in the play, embodying the author's
own attitude. His mutilations, like the deaths of N. and Pierre
in the earlier plays, are the direct outcome, and the expression,
of his inability to make human contact, his incapacity for love.
He himself says that if he could live with a woman and have
a child by her, the voices of his monitors would lose their
power over him;[32] the accidents in which he loses limb after
limb usually follow his repeated failures to hold the affection
of the woman he loves, Erna, who at times suggests that she
really cares for him, while at others she appears to be merely
spying on him on behalf of a secret-police agent who is her
lover.

Adamov himself has interpreted the play, which is based on
a particularly vivid and terrifying dream, as an attempt to
justify himself for his failure to take a more active part
in the political struggle of the Left. To the outside observer,
this may seem an incomplete account of the complex content
of *La Grande et la Petite Manœuvre.* The play not only argues
(as Adamov today believes, unfairly) that the efforts of the
revolutionary to eliminate political terror are vain because all
power is ultimately based on the exercise of brute force; it
also shows, very graphically, that there is an essential similarity
between the activist fighter for justice and the passive slave of
the irrational forces of his own subconscious mind. The cate-
gorical imperative that forces the *militant* to risk his life, to

leave his wife in fear and trembling and ultimately to cause the death of his sick child, is shown as springing, basically, from the same inability to love as the implacable self-destructive commands of the subconscious mind that force the *mutilé* into masochistic self-destruction. The aggressive impulses of the *militant* are merely the reverse side of the *mutilé's* aggression against himself.

The very ambivalence of possible interpretations is an indication of the power of *La Grande et la Petite Manœuvre* as a dramatic projection of an intense and tormented experience of fundamental human dilemmas. This play also shows Adamov in full command of the technical resources he needed to put his ideas into practice. The action not only moves forward in a succession of effectively contrasted scenes that follow each other with the flow of cinematic montage, it is also a perfect realization of Adamov's conception that the theatre should be able to translate ideas and psychological realities into simple and concrete images, so that "the manifestation of . . . content should literally, concretely, *corporally* coincide with that content itself."[33] This concretization of content leads to a shift of emphasis from the language of drama toward visible action. The language of the play ceases to be the main vehicle of poetry, as it is in the theatre of Claudel, with which Vilar contrasted Adamov's work. As Adamov defines this shift, "It is in this growth of gesture in its own right . . . that I see the emergence of a dimension to which language by itself would be unable to do justice, but, in turn, when language is carried along by the rhythm of bodily action that has become autonomous, the most ordinary, everyday speech will regain a power that might still be called poetry, but that I shall be content merely to call functionally effective."[34] In *La Grande et la Petite Manœuvre* the transmutation of content into visible, literal outward expression is completely realized.

The instrument he had perfected seemed available to Adamov to be used at will. Its only drawback was the narrowness of its field of application; there are relatively few basic human situations that can be expressed in such simple and general terms. Yet while his next play, *Le Sens de la Marche* (*The Direction of the March*), contains many of the elements and themes of its predecessors, Adamov again succeeded in finding a new expression for his basic preoccupation, while introducing an important new element indicating his progress in mastering his obsessions. In *Le Sens de la Marche*, the hero for the first time refuses to submit, and counterattacks. That action may not be directed against the real author of his troubles, but it is an action nevertheless. The hero, Henri, the son of a tyrannical father, goes through a number of episodes in which he confronts that father figure in a whole series of incarnations: in the commanding officer of the barracks where he goes for his military service, in the leader of a religious sect whose daughter is his fiancée for a time, in the headmaster of a school where he becomes a teacher. He submits to all these, but when he returns to his old home and finds his dead father's sinister *masseur* installed as the domestic tyrant and lover of his sister, he strangles him. As Adamov has pointed out, the idea from which he started was that "in this life of which the basic circumstances themselves are terrifying, where the same situations fatally recur, all we can do is destroy, and too late at that, what we consider, mistakenly, to be the real obstacle, but what in fact is merely the last item in a maleficent series."[35] This is a very original idea, and it is most imaginatively realized. Some of the themes of earlier plays recur, such as the revolutionaries, who are again unsuccessful; the hero's inability to love; and the sister figure.

Adamov was dissatisfied with *Le Sens de la Marche* and had put it aside for a while when another dream presented him not only with an idea for a play but with an entire, almost ready-made, play itself. And this play, *Le Professeur Taranne*, became a turning point in Adamov's development.

The professor of the title is accused of indecent exposure on a beach. He denies the allegation by indignantly pointing out that he is a distinguished scholar who has even been invited to lecture abroad, in Belgium. But the more he protests his innocence, the more deeply he becomes involved in contradictions that make his guilt more probable. A lady who comes into the police station seems to recognize him, she addresses him as Professor—but she has taken him for another professor, Menard, whom Taranne superficially resembles. The scene changes to the hotel where he is staying. Again Taranne is accused of an offense, that of having left litter in a bathing cabin at the seaside. He protests that he did not undress in a cabin at all—and thus confirms the earlier allegation. The policemen produce a notebook that has been found. Taranne eagerly recognizes it as his, but is unable to read the handwriting. What is more, the notebook consists mostly of empty pages, although Taranne insists that he had used it up entirely. A roll of paper is delivered to the professor—it is the seating plan of the dining room of an ocean liner, with his place marked at the table of honor. Jeanne, a woman relative or secretary, brings a letter that has arrived for the professor. It is from Belgium, from the rector of the University. This will confirm Taranne's claims! But in fact it is an angry refusal to invite him again. His lectures have been found to have been plagiarisms of those of the famous professor Menard. Taranne remains alone. He hangs the seating plan of the liner's dining room on a hook on the wall—it is a perfectly blank piece of paper. Slowly the professor begins to undress, performing the very act of indecent exposure of which he was accused at the beginning. Having been exposed as a fraud, he exposes himself. It is the nightmare of man trying to hold on to his identity, unable to establish conclusive proof of it.

In his dream, which the play transcribes as it was dreamed, without any attempt to "give it a general meaning, to prove anything,"[36] everything that happens to Taranne happened to Adamov himself, the only difference being that instead of shouting, "I am Professor Taranne," he exclaimed, "I am the author of *La Parodie!*"[36]

Adamov considers *Le Professeur Taranne* of particular importance in his progress as a playwright. In transcribing an actual dream he was, as it were, forced to cross a decisive threshold. For the first time in one of his plays he named an actual place, a place existing in the real world. Taranne claims that he has lectured abroad, *in Belgium,* and he receives a letter that is recognized as coming from that country by its stamp, which bears the Belgian Lion. "This looks like a trifle, but it was, nevertheless, the first time that I emerged from the no man's land of poetry and dared to call things by their name."[37]

And indeed for the tormented author of *L'Aveu,* suffering

from the sense of loneliness and separation described in that book, it is a tremendous step forward to have established a link, however tenuous, with reality, the reality of the world outside his own nightmares, even if at first it appears only in the form of the name of a real country heard within a nightmare. Of course, in *L'Aveu* itself Adamov had described real scenes from his own life. But there is a vast difference between the deliberate, humiliating *exposure* of his own suffering (reminiscent of Taranne's indecent exposure) and the ability to deal with the real world in the process of creative imaginative writing, which implies the ability to confront and master a reality outside oneself.

As Maurice Regnaut has pointed out in a penetrating essay on Adamov,[38] *Le Professeur Taranne* also marks another important stage in Adamov's development. In previous plays, to express his sense of the futility and absurdity of life, Adamov had projected the two basically contradictory attitudes that in the end amount to the same thing—namely, nothing—in pairs of characters: the employee and N., Pierre and his complacent mother, the *militant* and the *mutilé*, Henri and the revolutionaries. The dream on which *Le Professeur Taranne* is based showed him, for the first time, the way in which affirmative and self-destructive attitudes can be fused in a single character simultaneously—in the very act of asserting his worth as a citizen, his achievements as a scholar, Taranne reveals these claims to be fraudulent. And it is by no means clear whether the play is meant to show a fraud unmasked, or an innocent man confronted by a monstrous conspiracy of circumstances engineered to destroy his claims. In fact, as Adamov identifies himself with Taranne, the latter is the more tenable view; after all, in his dream Adamov cried out, "I am the author of *La Parodie*," which he undoubtedly is, and yet his claim was disproved by a succession of nightmare confrontations. Of course, if all activity is futile and absurd, then the claim to have written a play or to have lectured in Belgium is, in the final reckoning, a claim to nothing; death and oblivion will blot out all achievements. Thus, in *Le Professeur Taranne*, the hero is both an active scholar and a fraud, a respectable citizen and an exhibitionist, an optimistic hard-working paragon and a self-destructive, slothful pessimist. This opened a way for Adamov toward the creation of ambivalent, three-dimensional characters to take the place of schematic expressions of clearly defined psychological forces.

Adamov wrote *Le Professeur Taranne* in two days in 1951. It had taken him several years to complete his first two plays —a clear indication of how far he had succeeded in mastering his neurosis by harnessing it to a creative effort.

After completing *Le Sens de la Marche*, the writing of which he had interrupted to put down his nightmare of *Le Professeur Taranne*, Adamov returned to a subject that had preoccupied him before: the disorder of the times, social upheaval, and persecution. In *Tous Contre Tous*, we are again in a country that has been flooded by refugees from abroad; they are easily identifiable because they all limp. The hero, Jean Rist, loses his wife to one of the refugees and becomes a demagogue ranting against them. For a brief moment he is in power, but when the wheel of political fortune turns and the persecutors become the persecuted, he escapes arrest by assuming a limp himself and pretending to be a refugee. He lives in obscurity, upheld by the love of a refugee girl. When there is another upheaval and the refugees are again persecuted, he might perhaps escape death by declaring his true identity. But in confirming that he is the well-known hater of refugees, he would lose the love of the girl. He refuses to do so, and goes to his death.

In Jean Rist, the persecutor and the victim of persecution, Adamov has again fused two opposite tendencies in one character, not simultaneously, as in *Le Professeur Taranne*, but consecutively, in the ups and downs of the passage of time, and thus less successfully. The ending, with its self-sacrifice for the sake of love, has been criticized as a lapse into the sentimental heroics of a quite different, romantic convention of drama. This may be unjust: Jean Rist's refusal to save himself might also be interpreted as an act of resignation; of suicide in the face of an absurd, circular destiny. What the play does suffer from (in Adamov's own view) is its failure to come to grips with the reality of the problem it deals with. It is fairly obvious that this is the Jewish problem, or at least the problem of racial persecution. Yet by not situating his characters within a clearly defined social framework at one particular moment in history, at one particular point on the map, the author has deprived himself of the opportunity to do justice to the subject; he is unable to provide the background that would explain the rights and wrongs at issue: Why have the refugees taken away the jobs of the inhabitants of the country in question? Are those inhabitants justified in trying to exclude them again? Adamov himself has recognized these flaws. On the one hand, he says, he wanted to show that all sides are equally reprehensible in such a conflict, yet he acknowledges that he has made a larger number of the victims "good" characters, simply because they are made to suffer innocently. But, he adds, "I suffered from the limitation imposed on me by the vagueness of the place, the schematization of the characters, the symbolism of the situations, but I did not feel that I had the force of tackling a social conflict, and to see it as such, detached from the world of archetypes."[39]

In *Le Professeur Taranne*, he had found the courage to let in a glimpse of the real world, if only in a dream. So he decided to return to a world of dreams in two plays with very similar themes: *Comme Nous Avons Eté* (*As we were*, published in the *Nouvelle Revue Française* in March, 1953) and *Les Retrouvailles* (undated, but written circa 1952). Both plays deal with a grown man's regression to childhood, just when he is on the threshold of marriage. In *Comme Nous Avons Eté*, the character A. is having a nap in his room just before setting out to get married. Two women, mother and aunt, enter in search of a little boy who, they believe, must have wandered into the house. A. does not know them, but as the play proceeds he himself gradually turns into the little boy the two women have been looking for. In *Les Retrouvailles*, Edgar is about to leave Montpellier, where he is reading law, to return to his home near the Belgian frontier, when he encounters two ladies, one elderly, the other young, and is persuaded to stay in the house of the elderly woman while becoming engaged to the younger. He neglects his new fiancée, and she is killed in a train accident. Having finally returned home, he hears that his former fiancée, who had been waiting for him there, has also been killed in a train accident. His mother forces him into a perambulator and pushes him offstage.

These are dream plays with very obvious psychological implications; they are both attacks against the mother figure, who is trying to keep the son from establishing an adult relationship with another woman. Adamov has now completely repudiated *Comme Nous Avons Eté*, to the point of not having given it a place in the edition of his collected plays (although he allowed it to be published in an English translation in 1957.[40] *Les Retrouvailles*, technically most intriguing in the way it establishes the dream atmosphere by gradual scene changes and by the reduplication of the two pairs of mother-fiancée characters, has been published in Adamov's collected plays. But in his preface, Adamov rejects the play as a dream that he did not have but merely constructed. Yet he declares, "*Les Retrouvailles* has been most important for me; for, having finished the play, having reread it and examined it well, I understood that the time had come to put an end to the exploitation of the half-dream and the old family conflict. Or, to put it in more general terms, I think that thanks to *Les Retrouvailles* I have liquidated all that which, after having made it possible for me to write, now had become a hindrance to my writing."[41]

In other words, Adamov had reached a stage where he felt capable of writing a play that, though still an expression of his vision of the human condition, could people the stage not with mere emanations of his own psyche but with characters existing in their own right as objective human beings observed from the outside. This play is *Le Ping-Pong*, one of the masterpieces of the Theatre of the Absurd.

Le Ping-Pong presents the life story of two men—Victor, a medical student when the play starts, and Arthur, an art student. They meet at Mme. Duranty's café and play the pinball machine installed there. The machine fascinates them as a business proposition, for they observe the employee of the company coming to collect the coins that have been dropped into it; as a technical problem, for it has flaws that could surely be eliminated; and even as a challenge to their poetic instinct —the machine has a poetry of its own, flashing lights, and is in some ways a work of art. Victor and Arthur suggest an improvement in the machine. They penetrate to the headquarters of the consortium that controls it, and gradually the machine becomes the dominating influence in their lives, controlling their dreams and their emotions. If they fall in love, it is with the girl who works at the headquarters of the consortium. If they have quarrels between themselves, they are about that girl and the machine. If they fear anyone, it is the boss of the consortium. Their interest in the society around them is dictated by the relevance of political and social developments to the rise or fall of pinball machines.

And so they grow old. In the last scene we see them as two old men, playing ping-pong, a contest as childish and as futile as their lifelong preoccupation with a plaything. Victor collapses and dies. Arthur remains alone.

Le Ping-Pong, like Adamov's first play, La Parodie, is concerned with the futility of human endeavor. But while La Parodie merely asserted that whatever you do, in the end you die, Le Ping-Pong provides a powerful and closely integrated argument to back that proposition—it also shows how so much of human endeavor becomes futile, and why. It is in losing themselves to a thing, a machine that promises them power, money, influence over the woman they desire, that Victor and Arthur waste their lives in the futile pursuit of shadows. By making a machine, a means to an end, and end in itself, they pervert all those values of their lives that are genuine ends in themselves—their creative instinct, their capacity to love, their sense of being part of a community. Le Ping-Pong is a powerful image of the alienation of man through the worship of a false objective, the deification of a machine, an ambition, or an ideology.

The pinball machine in Le Ping-Pong is more than just a machine; it is the centerpiece of an organization and of a body of thought. The moment the objective—the improvement of pinball machines—becomes an ideal, it embodies itself in an organization with its own struggles for power, its own intrigues and politics, its own tactics and strategies. As such it becomes a matter of life and death for all who serve the ideal. A number of the characters in the play are destroyed in the service of the organization, or in its internal struggle for power. All this is conducted with the utmost fervor, seriousness, and intensity. And what is it all about? A childish game, a pinball machine—nothing. But are most of the objectives men devote their lives to in the real world—the world of business, politics, the arts, or scholarship—essentially different from Arthur's and Victor's dominating obsession? It is the power and beauty of *Le Ping-Pong* that it very graphically raises this very question. Adamov achieves the difficult feat of elevating the pinball machine to a convincing image of the objectives of *all* human endeavor. He does so by the poetic intensity with which he invests his characters when they talk about the most absurd aspects of that absurd apparatus with a conviction and obsessive concentration that sound utterly true.

The play contains the elements of reality and fantasy in exactly the right dosage; time and place are sufficiently real to carry conviction, yet the world in which the action takes place is hermetically sealed off from anything outside the characters' field of preoccupation. This is not because of a lack of realism on the part of the playwright; it springs directly from the obsession of the characters, which effectively confines them in so narrow a segment of the real world that we see the world through their confined field of vision.

The characters in *Le Ping-Pong* are fully realized individuals. No longer merely compelled by forces outside their control, or moving through the action like somnambulists, they have an element of freedom in determining their lives—we actually watch Arthur and Victor making the decision to devote themselves to pinball machines. And although Victor is the more practical of the two, and Arthur a poet, they are no longer merely personifications of complementary characteristics.

What is perhaps the most original feature of *Le Ping-Pong* is the way in which an inner contradiction, a dialectical relationship, is established between the action and the dialogue. This is a play that may well appear completely meaningless if it is merely read. The speeches about improvements in the construction of pinball machines may seem trivial nonsense; the meaning of the play emerges precisely at the moment when the actor delivers these nonsensical lines with a depth of conviction worthy of the loftiest flights of poetry. It is a play that has to be acted *against* the text rather than with it. This is a technique analogous to the indirect dialogue Adamov thought he had invented for *L'Invasion* and later discovered in Chekhov, but it is here raised to quite a different level. Chekhov used indirect dialogue in situations where the characters are too shy to express their real thoughts and hide their emotions behind trivial subjects. Here the characters believe in absurd propositions, with such intensity that they put forward their nonsensical ideas with the fervor of prophetic vision. In Chekhov, real feelings are suppressed behind meaningless politeness, in *Le Ping-Pong* absurd ideas are proclaimed as if they were eternal truths.

Adamov has given an interesting account of the genesis of *Le Ping-Pong.* He started with the final scene of the two old men playing ping-pong before he had even decided what the subject of the rest of the play would be. All he knew was that he wanted once more to show how, in the end, all human endeavor comes down to the same futility—senile whiling away of the remaining time before death reduces everything to final absurdity. But, Adamov says, "this peculiar method of work, paradoxically enough, saved me. Once I was sure that, as usual, I should be able to show the identity of all human destiny . . . I found myself free to make the characters act, to create situations. . . ."[42] Once he had decided to put a pinball machine into the center of the action, moreover, he was compelled to specify the time (the present) and the place (a city very much like Paris) of the action.

Nevertheless *Le Ping-Pong* belongs in the category of the Theatre of the Absurd; it shows man engaged in purposeless exertions, in a futile frenzy of activity that is bound to end in senility and death. The pinball machine has all the fascinating ambiguity of a symbol. It may stand for capitalism and big business, but it may equally well stand for any religious or political ideology that secretes its own organization and apparatus of power, that demands devotion and loyalty from its adherents.

Yet while he was working on the play, Adamov was moving away from the idea of a theatre dealing with such general human questions. He has criticized *Le Ping-Pong* on two counts—the last scene, which, having been written before the rest of the play, as it were, prejudged the issue and cramped his style; and, second, the schematic nature of the consortium, which remains, "incompletely detached from allegory. In fact, the social developments that, in the course of years, modify the internal organization of the consortium are not really indicated, so that one does not sufficiently feel the state of society on the one hand, the flow of time on the other. If I had gone so far as to tackle the 'coin-operated machine,' I had to examine the wheels of the great social machine with the same thoroughness that I examined the bumpers and flippers of the pinball machine. This is the examination I am trying to carry out in a new play, even more clearly situated in a specific time and milieu than *Le Ping-Pong*."[43] This play, which Adamov was working on at the beginning of 1955, when he wrote his introduction to the second volume of his collected plays, was *Paolo Paoli*, completed the next year and performed by Roger Planchon's brilliant young company at Lyon on May 17, 1957. It marks Adamov's abandonment of the Theatre of the Absurd and his adherence to another, equally significant movement of the modern stage—the Brechtian "epic theatre." He now regards Brecht as the greatest of contemporary playwrights and puts him next to Shakespeare, Chekhov, and Buechner among the dramatists of world literature he admires most. Having freed himself from compulsions and obsessions, he felt at liberty to follow models outside his own experience. (He had previously translated and adapted works by Buechner and Chekhov.)

Paolo Paoli is an epic drama depicting the social and political causes of the outbreak of the First World War and examining the relationship between a society based on profit and the forces of destruction to which it gives rise. The play spans the period from 1900 to 1914. Each of the twelve scenes is preceded by a survey of the social background of its period—quotations from the newspapers of the time are projected onto a screen, accompanied by current popular tunes.

The characters are most ingeniously chosen to represent a whole microcosm of the political, religious, national, and social forces involved in the origins of the First World War. Adamov's brilliance as a dramatist is shown by the astonishing ingenuity with which he has condensed all this—and extremely convincingly—into a cast of only seven characters.

Paolo Paoli is a dealer in rare butterflies; Florent Hulot-Vasseur, a collector of rare butterflies and Paolo's costumer, is an importer and manufacturer of ostrich feathers. He also becomes the lover of Paolo's German-born wife, Stella. An abbé and a captain's wife represent clericalism and chauvinist nationalism. A worker and trade unionist, Robert Marpeaux, and his young wife, Rose, complete the cast.

The role played by pinball machines in *Le Ping-Pong* is in *Paolo Paoli* taken by commodities no less absurd—butterflies and ostrich feathers. Yet these objects of trade and manufacture have far greater reality. As one of the newspaper projections before the first scene points out, ostrich feathers and products manufactured from them formed France's fourth largest export in 1900. Adamov brilliantly shows the far-reaching social and political ramifications and implications of the trade in these absurd articles: Paolo's business is founded on the fact that his father, a small Corsican civil servant, served in the public-works department on Devil's Island. This enabled the young man to organize the convicts there as part-time and ill-paid butterfly hunters. Marpeaux, the young workman who was serving a sentence for a petty theft, has escaped to the mainland and the swamps of Venezuela; he is wholly at Paolo's mercy, depending on the butterflies he catches for his livelihood. When troubles break out in China, butterfly hunting becomes more difficult there and the price of rare Chinese specimens goes up. The abbé, whose brother is a missionary in China, is able to provide Paolo with these precious goods. And so, in a few strokes, Adamov has shown the connection between the seemingly absurd object of trade and the penal system of French society, foreign politics, and the workings of the church. The same is true of Hulot-Vasseur's ostrich feathers in relation to the Boer War, and, as the plot develops, the labor and trade-union troubles of his factory and his fight against German competition are very convincingly made explicit within the narrow circle of the play.

As in *Le Ping-Pong*, the characters are obsessed with their pursuit of money and power, represented by the absurd commodities they deal in. Paolo grows rich, for a time at least, by becoming a manufacturer of knickknacks made from butterflies' wings—ashtrays, tea trays, even religious pictures, which flourish in a period of clericalism and slump when clericalism fades and German competition raises its ugly head. He loses his wife when he sets her up as a milliner, which makes her dependent for her supplies of ostrich feathers on Hulot-Vasseur, whose mistress she becomes. Stella, the German-born woman, also embodies the absurdities of European nationalism; she leaves France at the height of the anti-German feeling over Morocco, because people hate her as a German, and returns on the eve of the 1914 war, when her German neighbors persecute her as the wife of a Frenchman.

The only characters free of these obsessions are Marpeaux and his wife, Rose (though she for a time becomes Paolo's mistress). When Marpeaux returns, illegally, from Venezuela, Paolo suggests that he should spend the time till his pardon is granted by going to Morocco to hunt butterflies. (The crisis over Morocco has driven the prices up.) Of course, Morocco has become very dangerous; the French are fighting the natives. And here lies the moral of the play—the commodity that seems the object of trade is absurd, mere butterflies, but the commodity that is *really* traded is man, who has to sell his health and safety in the pursuit of butterflies. The ultimate object of trade is man, who himself becomes a commodity. (This is also the point of Adamov's very effective dramatization of Gogol's novel *Dead Souls*.) Moreover the commodities are being bought and sold in deadly earnest; trade leads to war.

Marpeaux, the victim of the social system, realizes what is at stake. After he has received his pardon (at a time when war between France and Germany seemed imminent over Morocco, and volunteers could gain amnesty), he returns to France and joins the Socialists. Working in Hulot-Vasseur's factory, he opposes the "yellow" Catholic unions managed by the abbé, and also distributes pacifist pamphlets to the soldiers in their barracks. To get rid of him, the abbé denounces him for subverting the fighting forces. As the first troops march off to war, Rose tells Paolo that Marpeaux has been arrested, and this leads to a somewhat unconvincing change of heart in Paolo, who, in the closing speech of the play, vows that henceforth he will use his money to help the hungry and needy, rather than let it circulate in the endless, iniquitous cycle of exchange, the buying and selling of useless commodities.

Paolo Paoli is a political play, brilliantly constructed and executed as drama, not very original as a political argument. (Paolo's last speech certainly makes little sense even in terms of Marxist economics: Money spent on food for the victims of Right Wing persecution is by no means effectively withdrawn from the cycle of capitalist exchange.) Nevertheless, as a tour de force the play shows Adamov as the sovereign master of his material, handling it with remarkable powers of invention, construction, and compression.

The question arises—does this piece of powerfully constructed didactic special pleading equal the haunting, dreamlike poetry of far less cleverly structured plays like *La Parodie*, *La Grande et la Petite Manœuvre* or *Le Professeur Taranne*? Is the highly explicit social framework of *Paolo Paoli*, for all the virtuosity with which it is handled, equal in depth, or even in its power to convince, to the vaguer, more general, but therefore all-embracing images of *Le Ping-Pong*?

There can be no doubt that for Adamov the development from *La Parodie* to *Paolo Paoli* represents a gradual liberation, through the artist's creative power, from the incubus of neurosis and deep personal suffering. In the whole history of literature it will be difficult to find a more triumphant example of the healing power of the creative processes of sublimation. It is fascinating to watch the gradual breaking down of the barriers that keep the writer of this series of plays from dealing with the realities of everyday life; to watch him gain the confidence that he needs to turn the nightmares that mastered him into mere material that *he* can mold and master. His early plays are, as it were, emanations of his subconscious mind, projected onto the stage as faithful transcripts of terrifying fantasies. *Paolo Paoli* is consciously planned and rationally controlled. Yet it might be argued that this gain in rationality and conscious control represents a loss of the fine frenzy, the haunting power of neurosis that gave the earlier plays their magnetic, poetical impact. What is more, by concentrating his attack on the political and social front, Adamov has narrowed his field of vision.

If in *La Grande et la Petite Manœuvre* it was the revolutionaries' futile struggle that represented the small maneuver, and the all-enveloping absurdity of the human condition dwarfing the social struggle that stood for the big maneuver, then in *Paolo Paoli* the small maneuver looms large and the large maneuver has receded into a barely perceptible background. "We all know," says the revolutionary leader in the earlier play, "that death surrounds us. But if we do not have the courage to detach ourselves from that idea, we shall retreat from the demands of the future, and all our sacrifices will have been in vain."[44] This is the argument that Paolo Paoli represents. In the earlier play, Adamov had supplied his own bitterly ironical comment on it: at the very moment when the revolutionary leader speaks these defiant words, his voice becomes lower, the pace of his delivery slows down, and he collapses.

Adamov is far too acute a thinker to be unaware of the implications of his later position. Having in his earlier phase concentrated on the absurdity of the human condition, he now maintains that "the theatre must show, simultaneously but well-differentiated, both the curable and the incurable aspect of things. The incurable aspect, we all know, is that of the inevitability of death. The curable aspect is the social one."[45]

It is precisely because it does succeed in maintaining the extremely delicate balance between the incurable and the curable aspects of the human condition that *Le Ping-Pong* must be regarded as Adamov's finest achievement to date. The pinball machine stands for all illusory objectives, material and ideological, the pursuit of which secretes ambition, self-seeking, and the urge to dominate other human beings. There is no necessity to fall victim to such illusory aims, so there *is* a social lesson in the play. And yet the absurdity of all human endeavor in the face of death is never quite forgotten, and is finally put before our eyes by a telling and compelling image. *Paolo Paoli*, on the other hand, is marred not only by the intrusion of over-simplified economic and social theories but, above all, by the introduction of a wholly positive and therefore less than human character, Marpeaux, and by the even less credible conversion of a hitherto negative character, Paolo, to provide a climax and a solution. This noble character and this noble action are clearly the consequence of the author's special pleading for the curable aspect of things, which leads to an underplaying of the incurable side of the human situation. Marpeaux's efforts, in the last resort, are as futile as those of the employee in *La Parodie*—he is arrested and the war breaks out in spite of him. Yet the author has to make this into a noble failure,

owing to the special wickedness of individual enemies, or of
social conditions, at a given period of history. And that is the
point at which the pathetic fallacy enters a politically biased
theatre. Brecht, who was well aware of this danger, avoided
similar pitfalls by foregoing all positive characters in some of
his more successful plays (*Mother Courage, Galileo*), so that
the positive message might emerge by inference rather than
by concrete demonstration—but with the result that the effect
on the audience tends to be one of a negative theatre that
concentrates on the incurable aspect of things.

In some respects, *Paolo Paoli* contains an important promise
—it shows the way in which some of the elements of the
Theatre of the Absurd can be combined with those of the
conventional well-made play to produce a very fruitful fusion
of two different traditions. In the simplicity of its construction,
the boldness of its characterization, the use of butterflies and
ostrich feathers as symbols that are at the same time perfectly
valid in the world of economic realities, *Paolo Paoli* may
contain some useful lessons for the future development of a
theatre combining elements of both the didactic epic style and
the Theatre of the Absurd.

Nor is Adamov's rejection of a nonrealistic style as complete
as it might appear. It is surely significant that in the fall of
1958, when he felt himself called upon to take an active
part in the campaign against the new Gaullist constitution,
Adamov found it easier to resort to allegorical techniques than
to make his point in the form of realistic didactic drama. Of
the three short pieces he contributed to the volume *Théâtre
de Société*, two are allegorical and only one is realistic—and an
acknowledged failure.

The most ambitious of these three sketches, *Intimité*, uses
personified collective concepts rather like those we find in medieval mystery plays—de Gaulle is caricatured as The Cause
Incarnate, the Socialists as the Cause's servile and stupid
lackey, the young blood among the Algerian *colons* as a
bullying ruffian labeled The Elite. The Cause Incarnate is
protected by a bodyguard of brutal strong-arm men; they are
called The Effects of the Cause. In the short monologue *La
Complainte du Ridicule*, the personification of ridicule laments the sad fact that it seems to have lost the power to kill

it possessed in former, happier times in France. Both these playlets, although clearly ephemeral *pièces d'occasion*, are successful as robust topical satire. The third, *Je Ne Suis Pas Français*, fails even on this level; it shows the way French parachutists in Algiers were reported to have coerced the Moslem population into demonstrating for France in May, 1958, but remains unconvincing in spite, or because, of its documentary technique. The political purpose is so obvious that the more realistically the subject is presented, the more it seems to lose the effect of reality.

Realism and fantasy are also combined in the radio play *En Fiacre* (1959), by the device of presenting a real, historically authenticated event involving characters who are demented—three old ladies who, having lost the house they lived in, spend the night in horse-drawn cabs they hire to drive around and around the streets of old-time Paris. The incident, presented as based on the casebook of a psychiatrist, and as having actually happened in February, 1902, might well have sprung from the dream world of one of Adamov's early plays. One of the three sisters is killed when she falls out of the moving cab. Has she been pushed out by the other two? And why have these three old women become homeless wanderers in the night? It appears that they learned only after their father died that the house they lived in had been the headquarters of a chain of brothels. There is also a suggestion that the dead sister, the youngest of the three, might have been in on the secret, that she might have been involved in what went on in those brothels, that she had a lover, that she was in the habit of occasionally paying the cabdrivers for those nightly journeys in currency other than mere money. But then all this may be the outcome of the fantasies of insane old women. *En Fiacre* is strictly documentary, but, in the nature of a scientific casebook, it does not seek to explain too much; it merely sets down what has been reported, leaving the motives of the action as unexplained as the solution. And while the treatment is naturalistic, the theme is madness, fantasies, dreams, irrational fears, and jealousies. The streets of Paris at night, pitiful victims of neurosis exposed to the insults of cabdrivers—this is a world not too far removed from that of *L'Aveu*.

In his latest play *Le Printemps '71* (*Spring '71*), a vast canvas of the Paris Commune in twenty-six scenes, nine interludes, and an epilogue, Adamov has finally broken through to the large-scale portrayal of historical reality. The tragic suppression of the revolutionary city government of Paris is shown in an intricate mosaic of minutely observed scenes involving dozens of characters. But even here Adamov could not do without the grotesquely allegorical element; the nine interludes, which he himself calls *guignols* (puppet shows), point the moral of the action through the grotesque cavortings of historical and allegorical personages: Bismarck, Thiers, the Commune itself, the Bank of France sitting inside her vaults, the National Assembly, a sleepy old woman knitting socks, and so on. These are the cartoons of Daumier come to life. And while the realistic action, impressive as it is, appears somewhat diffuse, these allegorical cartoon scenes are concise, witty, and make their point with astonishing force.

The two Arthur Adamovs—Adamov the dramatist of dream, neurosis, and futility, and Adamov the Brechtian epic realist —may not be so far apart as they appear. It is only too easy to understand why Adamov should repudiate his earlier plays today. They are the expression of a past he has outgrown, the fossilized remains of a former self that he is only too happy to have put behind him. Yet for that very reason he must be the last person able to pronounce a detached critical judgment on them. Kafka, whose obsessions in many ways resemble Adamov's, believed that his writings, which were the fruits of his obsessions, were not worth preserving. If he had had his way, they would have been destroyed, and the world would have lost what are undoubtedly both valuable human documents and great works of art.

Adamov today regards his plays from *La Parodie* to *Les Retrouvailles* as too schematic, crude, and lacking in a proper appreciation of the needs and prospects of remedial revolutionary action in the face of social injustice. Yet these criticisms, even if they were entirely relevant, miss the point—these plays are true and have a powerful impact because they are the genuine expressions of a soul in torment. To one who has healed himself of that torment, his past despair must inevitably appear exaggerated. It was nevertheless real when it was felt

—and it remains a very profound insight into the workings of the human mind and retains the power of all deeply felt poetic statements. It was, after all, Adamov himself, who pointed out that neurosis sharpens the perceptions and enables the sufferer to look into depths not usually open to the healthy eye. The works inspired by Adamov's neurosis may be more profound than those of an Adamov reconciled to the world, though still determined to change its institutions.

Adamov's development in many ways resembles Brecht's progress from an anarchic poet of despair to a constructive critic devoted to social progress. But Brecht never wholly succeeded in suppressing the pessimistic anarchist within himself, and it is from the tension between his two selves that his greatest poetic and dramatic power springs. Adamov, who became a dramatist much later in life than Brecht and whose despair was much deeper, more intense, and more open, may well be faced with a similar tension, a similar need to find the right balance between the curable and the incurable sides of human existence. This is a great challenge, but Adamov has shown himself capable of meeting great tasks.

Already Adamov can look back on an impressive achievement. He has shown himself a man of letters of great erudition; has translated works by Jung, Rilke, Dostoevski (*Crime and Punishment*), Strindberg (*The Father*), Gogol, Buechner, Gorki, and Chekhov; has written an excellent short monograph on Strindberg; has compiled a fascinating anthology of the Paris Commune; and is the author of one of the most brutally frank and most valuable documents of psychological autobiography. He stands in the very center of the conflicting trends and raging controversies of the contemporary avant-garde theatre, embodying as he does the two main opposing tendencies in his own person and his own *œuvre*.

Slight, dark, with piercing, probing eyes in a saturnine face, no longer a ragged figure roaming Paris in abject poverty but still preferring to live in a small Left Bank hotel and holding court in his favorite *tabac* on the Boulevard Saint-Germain, Adamov has become the main spokesman of the committed, political theatre in France. At the same time, he is regarded as one of the masters of a noncommitted, anti-political theatre of the soul. Like one of his own characters, he is the embodiment of two conflicting tendencies coexisting within the same person.

Only posterity will be able to tell which of the two was more valuable, which will have the more lasting effect.

Chapter Three

EUGÈNE IONESCO: THEATRE AND ANTI-THEATRE

The development of Arthur Adamov clearly poses the alternative between the theatre as an instrument for the expression of the individual's obsessions, nightmares, and anxiety, and the theatre as an instrument of political ideology and collective social action. Adamov has given his own emphatic answer to the question. Eugène Ionesco, who started from the same premises as Adamov and initially developed along parallel lines, has equally emphatically reached the opposite conclusions.

And Ionesco, however obscure and enigmatic he might appear in his plays, has shown that he can be highly lucid and brilliantly persuasive in expounding his ideas when he is provoked to defend himself by attacks, such as the one Kenneth Tynan, the dramatic critic of the London *Observer*, launched against him in the summer of 1958. In reviewing a revival of *The Chairs* and *The Lesson* at the Royal Court, Tynan warned his readers of the danger that Ionesco might become the messiah of the enemies of realism in the theatre. "Here at last was a self-proclaimed advocate of *anti-théâtre*: explicitly anti-realist and by implication anti-reality as well. Here was a writer ready to declare that words were meaningless and that all communication between human beings was impossible." Tynan conceded that Ionesco presented a valid personal vision, but "the peril arises when it is held up for general emulation as the gateway to the theatre of the future, that bleak new world from which the humanist heresies of faith in logic and belief in man will forever be banished." Ionesco was moving away from realism, with "characters and events [that] have traceable roots in life"—from plays such as those of Gorki,

Chekhov, Arthur Miller, Tennessee Williams, Brecht, O'Casey, Osborne, and Sartre.[1]

Tynan's attack opened one of the most interesting discussions on this subject ever conducted in public. Ionesco replied that he certainly did not see himself as a messiah, "because I do not like messiahs and I certainly do not consider the vocation of the artist or the playwright to lie in that direction. I have a distinct impression that it is Mr. Tynan who is in search of messiahs. But to deliver a message to the world, to wish to direct its course, to save it, is the business of the founders of religions, of the moralists or the politicians. . . . A playwright simply writes plays, in which he can offer only a testimony, not a didactic message. . . . Any work of art which was ideological and nothing else would be pointless . . . inferior to the doctrine it claimed to illustrate, which would already have been expressed in its proper language, that of discursive demonstration. An ideological play can be no more than the vulgarization of an ideology. . . ."[2]

Ionesco protested against the imputation that he was a deliberate anti-realist, that he maintained the impossibility of communication by language. "The very fact of writing and presenting plays is surely incompatible with such a view. I simply hold that it is difficult to make oneself understood, not absolutely impossible."[3] After a dig at Sartre (as the author of political melodramas), Osborne, Miller, Brecht, et al., as "*auteurs du boulevard*—representatives of a Left Wing conformism which is just as lamentable as the Right Wing sort," Ionesco stated his conviction that society itself formed one of the barriers between human beings, that the authentic community of man is wider than society. "No society has been able to abolish human sadness, no political system can deliver us from the pain of living, from our fear of death, our thirst for the absolute; it is the human condition that directs the social condition, not vice versa." Hence the need to break down the language of society, which "is nothing but clichés, empty formulas and slogans." That is why the ideologies with their fossilized language must be continually re-examined and "their congealed language . . . relentlessly split apart in order to find the living sap beneath."

To discover the fundamental problem common to all mankind, I must ask myself what *my* fundamental problem is, what *my* most ineradicable fear is. I am certain then to find the problems and fears of literally everyone. That is the true road into my own darkness, our darkness, which I try to bring to the light of day. . . . A work of art is the expression of an incommunicable reality that one tries to communicate—and which sometimes can be communicated. That is its paradox and its truth.[4]

Ionesco's article provoked a wide and varied response—a clear indication that both he and Tynan had touched on a vital issue. There were those who congratulated Ionesco on having written "one of the most brilliant refutations of the current theory of 'social realism,'" but added, "If only M. Ionesco were able to put some of its clarity and wisdom into his own plays, he might yet become a great playwright!" (H. F. Garten, the critic and expert on modern German drama), as well as those who agreed with Kenneth Tynan that a repudiation of politics in itself amounted to a political ideology (John Berger, the Marxist art critic). George Devine, the artistic director of the Royal Court Theatre, supported Ionesco, but insisted that Arthur Miller, John Osborne, and Brecht were by no means exclusively concerned with social purposes: "The framework of these plays is consciously social but the core of them is human," while Philip Toynbee pointed out that he considered Ionesco frivolous and thought Arthur Miller a greater dramatist anyway.

In the same issue of *The Observer*, Tynan himself took up Ionesco's challenge. His argument hinged on Ionesco's contention that artistic expression could be independent of, and in some ways superior to, ideologies and the needs of the "real world." "Art and ideology often interact on each other, but the plain fact is that both spring from a common source. Both draw on human experience to explain mankind to itself. . . . They are brothers, not child and parent." Ionesco's emphasis on introspection, the exploration of his private anxieties, Tynan argued, opened the door to subjectivism, which would make objective value judgment, and thus criticism of such plays, impossible. "Whether M. Ionesco admits it or not, every play worth serious consideration is a statement. It is a statement addressed in the first person singular to the first person plural, and the latter must retain the right to dissent. . . . If a man tells me something I believe to be an untruth, am I forbidden to do more than congratulate him on the brilliance of his lying?"[5]

The controversy raged on in the pages of the next issue of *The Observer*—with distinguished contributions from Orson Welles (mainly on the role of the critic and critical standards), Lindsay Anderson, the young dramatist Keith Johnstone, and others. Ionesco's own second riposte, however, was not published. It has since appeared in *Cahiers des Saisons*.[6] In it, Ionesco tackles the real issue behind the controversy—the problem of form and content.

"Mr. Tynan reproaches me with letting myself be seduced by the means of expressing 'objective reality' (Yet what is objective reality? That is another question) to such an extent that I forget the objective reality for the sake of the means of expression. . . . In other words, I think that I am accused of formalism." But, Ionesco maintains, the history of art, of literature, is essentially the history of modes of expression. "To approach the problem of literature through the study of its ways of expression (which is what the critic ought to do, in my opinion) amounts to approaching its basis, to fathom its essence." Thus Ionesco's own attack against fossilized forms of language, which is itself an attempt at revitalizing dead forms, appears to him to be as deeply concerned with objective reality as any social realism. "To renew the language is to renew the conception, the vision of the world. Revolution consists in bringing about a change in mental attitudes." As all really creative artistic expression is an attempt at saying new things in a new way, it cannot, by definition, merely serve for the restatement of existing ideologies. Form and structure, which must obey their own internal laws of consistency and cohesion, are as important as conceptual content. "I do not believe that there is a contradiction between creative and cognitive activity, for the structures of the mind probably reflect universal structures."

A temple or a cathedral, although not representational, reveals the fundamental laws of structure, and its value as a work of art lies in this, rather than in its utilitarian purpose. Formal experiment in art thus becomes an exploration of reality more valid and more useful (because it serves to enlarge man's understanding of the real world) than shallow works that are immediately comprehensible to the masses. Since the beginning of our century there has been a great upsurge of such creative exploration, which has transformed our understanding of the world, particularly in music and painting. "In literature, and above all in the theatre, this movement seems to have come to a stop since, perhaps, 1925. I should like to be able to hope being considered one of the modest craftsmen who have taken it up again. I have, for example, tried to exteriorize the anxiety . . . of my characters through objects; to make the stage settings speak; to translate the action into visual terms; to project visible images of fear, regret, remorse, alienation; to play with words. . . . I have thus tried to extend the language of the theatre. . . . Is this to be condemned?"

Formal experiment, Ionesco argues, is more closely concerned with reality than social realism as it was displayed at an exhibition of Soviet painting Ionesco visited. The dull representational pictures of the Soviet artists were liked by the local capitalist Philistines and, what is more, "the social-realist painters were formalists and academic precisely because they had paid insufficient attention to the formal means of expression and had thus been unable to achieve any depth." In the paintings of an artist like Masson, on the other hand, there was both truth and life:

> Because Masson, the craftsman, had left human reality alone, because he had not tried to capture it, thinking only of the act of painting, human reality and its tragic elements had revealed themselves, for that very reason, rightly, freely. Thus what Mr. Tynan calls anti-reality had become real, something incommunicable had communicated itself, and there too, behind the apparent repudiation of all human, concrete, and moral reality, its living heart had been hidden all the time, while on the other side, that of the anti-formalists, there had been only dried-up forms—empty, dead. The heart is not worn on the sleeve.[7]

The Ionesco-Tynan controversy, brilliantly conducted on

both sides, shows that Eugène Ionesco is by no means merely
the author of hilarious nonsense plays, as he is so often represented in the press, but a serious artist dedicated to the ar-
duous exploration of the realities of the human situation, fully
aware of the task that he has undertaken, and equipped with
formidable intellectual powers.

Ionesco was born in Slatina, Rumania, on November 26,
1912. His mother, whose maiden name was Thérèse Icard, was
French, and shortly after he was born, his parents went to live
in Paris. French is his first language—he had to acquire most
of his Rumanian after his return to Rumania at the age of
thirteen. His first impressions and memories are of Paris:

> When I was a child I lived near the Square de Vaugirard.
> I remember—it was so long ago!—the badly lit street on an
> autumn or winter evening. My mother held me by the hand;
> I was afraid, as children are afraid; we were out shopping
> for the evening meal. On the sidewalks sombre silhouettes in
> agitated movement, people in a hurry—phantomlike, hallu-
> cinatory shadows. When that image of that street comes to
> life again in my memory, when I think that almost all those
> people are now dead, everything seems a shadow, evanes-
> cence. I am seized by a vertigo of anxiety. . . .[8]

Evanescence, anxiety—and the theatre:

> . . . my mother could not tear me away from the Punch
> and Judy show at the Luxembourg Gardens. I stayed there,
> I could stay there, enrapt, for whole days. The spectacle
> of the Punch and Judy show held me there, as if stupefied,
> through the sight of these puppets that talked, moved,
> clubbed each other. It was the spectacle of the world itself,
> which, unusual, improbable, but truer than truth, presented
> itself to me in an infinitely simplified and caricatured form,
> as if to underline its grotesque and brutal truth. . . .[9]

After a few years at school, the local *école communale* in
Paris, the boy developed anemia and was sent to the country.
He has described how he arrived, before he had reached the
age of nine, together with his sister, who was a year younger,

at the village of La Chapelle-Anthenaise, where they were to
board with farmers.

> The falling light; my tiredness; the mysterious light of the
> countryside; the imaginary vision of the long dark corridors
> of "the castle" [which he took the steeple of the local church
> to be]; and then the thought that I was about to leave my
> mother. I could no longer resist. . . . I flung myself, crying,
> against my mother's skirts.[10]

When he revisited the village of La Chapelle-Anthenaise on
the eve of war, in 1939, Ionesco recalled fragments of memories of playing "theatre" there with other children, of his experiences in the village school and with fellow boarders at the
farm, of nightmares and strange apparitions "like figures out
of Brueghel or Bosch—large noses, distorted bodies, horrible
smiles, clubfooted. Later, back in Rumania, I was still childish
enough to have such nightmares. But now the phantoms of
my anxiety had a different appearance—they were two-dimen-
sional, sad rather than hideous, with enormous eyes. One is
led to believe that there are both Gothic and Byzantine hallucinations."[11]

He has recalled how at that time he dreamed of becoming
a saint but, reading the religious books available in the village,
he learned that it is wrong to seek after glory. So he abandoned
the idea of sainthood. Shortly afterward, he read the lives of
Turenne and Condé and decided to become a great warrior.
At the age of thirteen, back in Paris, he wrote his first play,
a patriotic drama.

The family returned to Rumania; Ionesco encountered a
rawer, more brutal world: "Shortly after my arrival in my
second homeland, I saw a man, still young, big and strong,
attack an old man with his fists and kicking him with his boots.
. . . I have no other images of the world except those of evanescence and brutality, vanity and rage, nothingness or hideous, useless hatred. Everything I have since experienced has
merely confirmed what I had seen and understood in my childhood: vain and sordid fury, cries suddenly stifled by silence,
shadows engulfed forever in the night. . . ."[12]

In Rumania, Ionesco went through school and became a
student of French at the University of Bucharest. He wrote his

first poems, elegies influenced by Maeterlinck and Francis Jammes. He also ventured into the realm of literary criticism, publishing a withering attack on three then fashionable and leading Rumanian writers—the poets Tudor Arghezi and Ion Barbu and the novelist Camil Petresco—accusing them of narrow provincialism and lack of originality. But a few days later he published a second pamphlet, praising the same authors to the skies as great and universally valid figures of Rumanian national literature. Finally he presented the two essays side by side, under the title *No!*, to prove the possibility of holding opposite views on the same subject, and the identity of contraries.

Having finished his studies, Ionesco became a teacher of French at a Bucharest *lycée*. In 1936 he married Rodica Burileano, a petite woman with an exotic cast of features not uncommon in Eastern Europe, whose Oriental beauty has given rise to the wholly unwarranted rumor that Ionesco's wife is Chinese. In 1938, Ionesco obtained a government grant to enable him to go to France to undertake research for a thesis he planned on "the themes of sin and death in French poetry since Baudelaire." He went back to France but is reputed never to have written a single line of this great work.

In the spring of 1939 he revisited La Chapelle-Anthenaise, searching for his childhood, putting down his memories in his diary. "I am writing, writing, writing. All my life I have been writing; I have never been able to do anything else.[13] . . . To whom can all this be of interest? Is my sadness, my despair communicable? It cannot have significance for anyone. No one knows me. I am nobody. If I were a writer, a public figure, it might assume some interest perhaps. And yet I am like all the others. Anyone can recognize himself in me."[14]

At the outbreak of war Ionesco was at Marseille. Later he returned to Paris, and worked in the production department of a publishing house. His daughter Marie-France was born in 1944. When the war ended, Ionesco was almost thirty-three. There was nothing to indicate that he was soon to become a famous dramatist. In fact, he disliked the theatre intensely: "I read fiction, essays, I went to the cinema with pleasure. I listened to music from time to time, I visited art galleries, but I hardly ever went to the theatre."[15]

Why did he dislike the theatre? He had loved it as a boy, but he had begun to dislike it ever since, "having acquired a critical sense, I became aware of the strings, the crude strings of the theatre." The acting of the cast embarrassed him, he felt embarrassed for the actors. "Going to the theatre to me meant going to see people, apparently serious people, making a spectacle of themselves." And yet Ionesco liked fiction, he was even convinced that the truth of fiction is superior to that of reality. Nor did he dislike acting in the cinema. But in the theatre "it was the presence on the stage of flesh-and-blood people that embarrassed me. Their material presence destroyed the fiction. I was confronted, as it were, by two planes of reality—the concrete, material, impoverished, empty, limited reality of these living, everyday human beings, moving about and talking on the stage, and the reality of the imagination, the two face to face and not coinciding, unable to be brought into relation with each other; two antagonistic worlds incapable of being unified, of merging."[16]

In spite of his dislike of the theatre, Ionesco wrote a play, almost against his will. This is how it happened: In 1948, he decided that he ought to learn English. And so he acquired an English course. Learned research, published in the august pages of the *Cahiers du Collège de Pataphysique*, has since, by close textual analysis, established that the text in question was *L'Anglais Sans Peine,* of the *Assimil* method.[17] Ionesco himself has described what happened next:

> I set to work. Conscientiously I copied whole sentences from my primer with the purpose of memorizing them. Rereading them attentively, I learned not English but some astonishing truths—that, for example, there are seven days in the week, something I already knew; that the floor is down, the ceiling up, things I already knew as well, perhaps, but that I had never seriously thought about or had forgotten, and that seemed to me, suddenly, as stupefying as they were indisputably true.[18]

As the lessons became more complex, two characters were introduced, Mr. and Mrs. Smith:

> To my astonishment, Mrs. Smith informed her husband

that they had several children, that they lived in the vicinity of London, that their name was Smith, that Mr. Smith was a clerk, that they had a servant, Mary—English, like themselves. . . . I should like to point out the irrefutable, perfectly axiomatic character of Mrs. Smith's assertions, as well as the entirely Cartesian manner of the author of my English primer; for what was truly remarkable about it was its eminently methodical procedure in its quest for truth. In the fifth lesson, the Smiths' friends the Martins arrive; the four of them begin to chat and, starting from basic axioms, they build more complex truths: "The country is quieter than the big city. . . ."[19]

Here was a comic situation, already in dialogue form: two married couples solemnly informing each other of things that must have been obvious to all of them all along. But then "a strange phenomenon took place. I don't know how—the text began imperceptibly to change before my eyes, and in spite of me. The very simple, luminously clear statements I had copied diligently into my . . . notebook, left to themselves, fermented after a while, lost their original identity, expanded and overflowed." The clichés and truisms of the conversation primer, which had once made sense although they had now become empty and fossilized, gave way to pseudo-clichés and pseudo-truisms; these disintegrated into wild caricature and parody, and in the end language itself disintegrated into disjointed fragments of words.

While writing the play (for it had become a kind of play or anti-play; that is, a parody of a play, a comedy of comedy) I felt sick, dizzy, nauseated. I had to interrupt my work from time to time and, wondering all the while what demon was prodding me on, lie down on my couch for fear of seeing my work sink into nothingness, and me with it.[20]

That is how Ionesco's first play came into being. At first he wanted to call it *L'Anglais Sans Peine*, later *L'Heure Anglaise*, but in the end it was called *La Cantatrice Chauve—The Bald Soprano*.

Ionesco read his play to a group of friends. They found it funny, although *he* believed himself to have written a very serious piece, "the tragedy of language." One of these friends, Monique Saint-Côme, who had translated novels from the Rumanian and was at that time, at the end of 1949, working with a group of avant-garde actors under the direction of Nicolas Bataille, asked Ionesco to lend her the manuscript.

Nicolas Bataille, then twenty-three years old, liked the play and wanted to meet its author. Ionesco came to see him at the little Théâtre de Poche. Nicolas Bataille has described that meeting:

> . . . tradition demands that I should tell what was the first impression I had of him. Well, to follow that usage, I shall say that he seemed to me to resemble Mr. Pickwick. I told him that we wanted to stage his play. He replied, *"Pas possible!"* He had already submitted it, without success, to, among others, Jean-Louis Barrault and . . . the Comédie Française![21]

At first the director tried to stage the play in a wildly parodistic style. But that did not work. Finally, all concerned realized that, to have its full effect, the text would have to be acted in deadly seriousness, like a play by Ibsen or Sardou. In fact, when asking Jacques Noël to design the set, Bataille did not give him the play to read. He merely told him to design the drawing room for *Hedda Gabler.* Another model the production followed was the conception of the English character conveyed by the novels of Jules Verne, whose English people have a peculiar decorum and *sang-froid*, which has been brilliantly captured by the original illustrators in the stiff, bewhiskered figures of the Editions Hetzel.

The title of the play was found during rehearsals; in the long and pointless anecdote entitled "The Headcold," which the fire chief tells, there is a reference to an *institutrice blonde*, a blonde schoolteacher. During one run-through, Henri-Jacques Huet, who played the fire chief, made a mistake and said *"cantatrice chauve"* instead. Ionesco, who was present, immediately realized that this was a far better title than *L'Heure Anglaise* or even *Big Ben Follies* (which he had considered at one time). And so the play became *The Bald Soprano.* A brief reference to the *"cantatrice chauve"* was introduced at the end of Scene 10, when the fire chief, as he is about to leave, creates general embarrassment by asking about the bald soprano, and after a painful silence receives the answer that she still wears her hair the same way.

Another important change that occurred during rehearsals concerned the end of the play. Originally Ionesco had intended that after the final quarrel between the two couples the stage should be left empty for a moment, then some extras in the audience were to start booing and protesting; this would lead to the appearance of the manager of the theatre on the stage, followed by the police. The police would "machine-gun" the audience, while the manager and the police sergeant would congratulate each other by shaking hands. But this would have necessitated a number of additional actors and thereby have increased the costs. So, as an alternative, Ionesco had planned to let the maid, at the height of the quarrel, announce, "The Author!," after which the author would appear, the actors would respectfully step aside and applaud him while the author would approach the footlights with sprightly steps, but suddenly raise his fists and shout at the audience, "You bunch of crooks! I'll get you!" But, Ionesco reports, this ending was considered "too polemical" and so eventually, as no other ending could be found, it was decided that there would be no end at all and that instead the play would start all over again from the beginning.

La Cantatrice Chauve, billed as an "anti-play," was first performed at the Théâtre des Noctambules on May 11, 1950. It was coldly received. Only Jacques Lemarchand, at that time the critic of *Combat,* and the playwright Armand Salacrou gave it favorable notices. There was little money for publicity, so the actors turned themselves into sandwich men and paraded the streets with their boards for about an hour before the performance. But the theatre remained almost empty. More than once, when there were fewer than three people in the theatre, they were given their money back and the actors went home. After about six weeks they gave up.

For Ionesco, this first encounter with the living theatre became a turning point; not only was he amazed to hear the audience laugh at what he considered a tragic spectacle of human life reduced to passionless automatism through bourgeois convention and the fossilization of language, he was also deeply moved by seeing the creatures of his imagination come to life:

> One cannot resist the desire of making appear, on a stage, characters that are at the same time real and invented. One cannot resist the need to make them speak, to make them live before our eyes. To incarnate phantasms, to give them life, is a prodigious, irreplaceable adventure, to such an extent that I myself was overcome when, during the rehearsals of my first play, I suddenly saw characters move on the stage who had come out of myself. I was frightened. By what right had I been able to do this? Was this allowed? . . . It was almost diabolical.[22]

Suddenly Ionesco realized that it was his destiny to write for the theatre. He who had been embarrassed when he saw actors trying to identify themselves with the characters they portrayed, to the point of finding such attempts indecent (as Brecht had before him), but who had been equally repelled by Brechtian acting, which "made the actor a mere pawn in a chess game" and dehumanized him, now realized what it had been that made him uneasy:

> . . . if the theatre had embarrassed me by enlarging and thereby coarsening nuances, that was merely because it had enlarged them insufficiently. What seemed too crude was not crude enough; what seemed to be not subtle enough was in fact too subtle. For if the essence of the theatre lay in the enlargement of effects, it was necessary to enlarge them even more, to underline them, to emphasize them as much as possible. To push the theatre beyond that intermediary zone that is neither theatre nor literature was to put it back into its proper framework, to its natural limits. What was needed was not to disguise the strings that moved the puppets but to make them even more visible, deliberately apparent, to go right down to the very basis of the grotesque, the realm of caricature, to transcend the pale irony of witty drawing-room comedies . . . to push everything to paroxysm, to the point where the sources of the tragic lie. To create a theatre of violence—violently comic, violently dramatic.[23]

To reach this point, Ionesco has since argued, the theatre must work with veritable shock tactics; reality itself, the consciousness of the spectator, his habitual apparatus of thought —language—must be overthrown, dislocated, turned inside out, so that he suddenly comes face to face with a new perception of reality. Thus Ionesco, the persistent critic of Brecht, is in fact postulating a far more radical, a far more fundamental alienation effect. What made him uneasy in the Brechtian style of acting was precisely that "it appeared as an unacceptable mixture of the true and the false"; that, in effect, it did not carry alienation, the abandonment of a simulation of reality, far enough.

La Cantatrice Chauve (known as *The Bald Soprano* in the United States and as *The Bald Prima Donna* in Britain) has been so widely performed and published that it is unnecessary to outline its contents in detail. Some of its features have already become proverbial: the clock that, in a spirit of contradiction, always indicates the opposite of the correct time, or the classic recognition scene between a married couple, who, after a feat of logical deduction, to their great surprise reach the conclusion that as they seem to be living in the same street, the same house, the same floor, the same room, the same bed, they must necessarily be man and wife. (This scene is said to be based on an episode when Ionesco and his wife found themselves entering the same Métro carriage by different doors and went through an elaborate pantomime of recognition.)[24]

Nor is there any doubt left of the meaning and intention of the play. Ionesco himself, who has said that he never has ideas before writing a play, but has a good many ideas about its meaning after he has completed it,[25] has explained it most convincingly. It is in fact a tragicomic picture of life in an age when "we can no longer avoid asking ourselves what we are doing here on earth and how, having no deep sense of our destiny, we can endure the crushing weight of the material world. . . . When there is no more incentive to be wicked, and everyone is good, what shall we do with our goodness, or our non-wickedness, our non-greed, our ultimate neutrality? The people in *The Bald Soprano* have no hunger, no conscious desires; they are bored stiff. They feel it vaguely, hence the final explosion—which is quite useless, as the characters and situations are both static and interchangeable, and everything ends where it started."[26]

The play is an attack against what Ionesco has called the "universal petty-bourgeoisie . . . the personification of accepted ideas and slogans, the ubiquitous conformist." What he deplores is the leveling of individuality, the acceptance of slogans by the masses, of ready-made ideas, which increasingly turn our mass societies into collections of centrally directed automata. "The Smiths, the Martins can no longer talk because they can no longer think; they can no longer think *because they can no longer be moved, can no longer feel passions.* They can no longer be; they can 'become' anybody, anything, for, having lost their identity, they assume the identity of others . . . they are interchangeable."[27]

We live in a world that has lost its metaphysical dimension, and therefore all mystery. But to restore the sense of mystery we must learn to see the most commonplace in its full horror: "To feel the absurdity of the commonplace, and of language—its falseness—is already to have gone beyond it. To go beyond it we must first of all bury ourselves in it. What is comical is the unusual in its pure state; nothing seems more surprising to me than that which is banal; the surreal is here, within grasp of our hands, in our everyday conversation."[28]

Having rediscovered his childhood passion for the theatre, Ionesco even adventured into becoming an actor. He accepted an offer from the director of *La Cantatrice Chauve*, Nicolas Bataille, and the well-known theatrical scholar and director, Akakia Viala, to play the part of Stepan Trofimovich in an adaptation of Dostoevski's *The Possessed* by Bataille and Akakia Viala. He who had always regarded the effort an actor must make as unbearable, bordering on the absurd or a kind of sainthood, now learned what it means "to take on another human being, when one finds it hard enough already to bear with oneself; to understand him with the help of the director, when one does not understand oneself."[29]

Ionesco did not like the character he had undertaken to act, "because he was another, and in allowing myself to be inhabited by him, I really had the impression of being 'pos-

sessed' or 'dispossessed,' of losing myself, of renouncing my
personality, which I don't like particularly but to which I have
at last become accustomed."[30] And yet, after many attempts
to desert, having been held back merely by the sense of his
moral obligation, suddenly the moment came when he discovered that precisely because he had lost himself in the character of Stepan Trofimovich, he was finding his own self in a
new sense. "I had learned that each of us is all the others,
that my solitude had not been real and that the actor can,
better than anyone else, understand human beings by understanding himself. In learning to act, I have also, in a certain
sense, learned to admit that the others are oneself, that you
yourself are the others, and that all lonelinesses become
identified."[31]

The run of *The Possessed* at the Théâtre des Noctambules,
which gave Ionesco these insights into the art of acting, came
to an end on February 18, 1951. Two days later, his second
play, written in June, 1950, had its first night at the tiny
Théâtre de Poche. This was *La Leçon* (*The Lesson*). As
Jacques Lemarchand has pointed out, it was a disconcerting
occasion for those who after *The Bald Soprano*—a play in
which no soprano appeared, and no bald person either—expected that in *The Lesson* there would be no question of a
lesson. To their surprise, the whole play consisted of an hour's
reproduction of a lesson, an unusual one, no doubt, but a lesson nevertheless: an aged professor giving private instruction
to an eager but obtuse girl pupil, a lesson in geography, addition, multiplication, linguistics, and other subjects—in short, as
Jacques Lemarchand put it, almost "a faithful reproduction of
a lesson given by Marshal Foch at the *école de guerre*."[32]

The Lesson, like *The Bald Soprano*, is concerned with language, and not only in the long dissertation on the neo-Spanish
language group, which includes a large number of real and
imaginary languages that are superficially all the same yet
are all distinguished by subtle differences, imperceptible to
the ear but very real nevertheless. Thus the word "*grand-mère*"
in French is pronounced "*grand-mère*" in Spanish, in Sardana-
pali, or in Rumanian as well, and yet there is a world of subtle
difference between these languages. That is, if one man says
"Grandmother" and another man says "Grandmother," they

seem to be saying the same thing, but are in fact talking about vastly different people! So, as the professor learnedly points out, if an Italian says "my country," he means Italy, but if an Oriental says "my country," he means the Orient, the same word signifying completely different things. This is a demonstration of the basic impossibility of communication—words cannot convey meanings because they leave out of account the personal associations they carry for each individual. This is one of the reasons why the professor seems unable to break through to his pupil. Their minds work along different lines and will never meet. The pupil can add but fails to grasp the possibility of subtraction, yet she can multiply astronomical figures in a flash, explaining to the baffled professor that she has merely learned all possible multiplication tables by heart. And yet, she says, she can count only to sixteen.

But there is more about language in *The Lesson* than a demonstration of the difficulties of communication. Here language is also shown as an *instrument of power*. As the play proceeds, the pupil who was eager, lively, and alert is gradually drained of her vitality, while the professor, who was timid and nervous at the beginning, gradually gains in assurance and domination. It is clear that the professor derives his progressive increase of power from his role as a giver, a very arbitrary prescriber, of meanings. Because words must have the significance *he* decides to give them, the pupil comes under his dominance, which finds its concrete, theatrical expression in her rape and murder. The maid, who in turn dominates the professor like a malignant mother figure, is immune when he attacks her with the same knife—simply because she is not one of his pupils. It is the maid who finally sums up the situation—"arithmetic leads to philology, and philology leads to crime. . . ."

The discomfiture of the pupil announces itself when she is suddenly overtaken by a violent toothache, "the final, great symptom," as the maid puts it. In some ways this toothache indicates the pupil's loss of the power to speak, her loss of the gift of language, but it also announces the victory of physical reality over that of the mind. Progressively, all the parts of her body begin to ache until, in an act of complete physical subjection, she allows the professor to plunge the knife into her, accepting the professor's final proposition—"The knife kills."

The sexual connotation of this climactic moment of the play is quite openly indicated. The pupil flops into a chair "in an immodest position . . . her legs spread wide and hanging over both sides of the chair. The professor remains standing in front of her, his back to the audience." Murderer and victim shout "Aaah!" at the same moment. In Marcel Cuvelier's production, the repeated rhythmic enunciation of the key word "couteau" by murderer and victim was equally unambiguously orgiastic.

Pierre-Aimé Touchard has argued that The Lesson expresses in caricatured form the spirit of domination always present in teacher-pupil relationships, and that the professor kills the girl because her toothache enables her to escape from having to listen to his instruction. This, according to Touchard's ingenious interpretation, is in turn a symbol for all forms of dictatorship. When dictators feel that their domination of their people is on the wane, they want to annihilate the rebellious ones, abolishing their own power in doing so.[33] This interpretation is somewhat rationalistic, although it is supported by the maid's handing the professor a swastika armband at the end of the play. The political implication of domination is certainly present in The Lesson, but it is only one, and perhaps a minor, aspect of its main proposition, which hinges on the sexual nature of all power and the relationship between language and power as the basis of all human ties. The professor dominates the pupil, but he in turn is dominated by the maid, who treats him like a fond, if disapproving, mother, spoiling her naughty child by ultimately overlooking his most flagrant pranks. The point of the play surely is that the pupils always get a toothache, and that the professor always rapes and kills them. The murder we witness is his fortieth on that single day. And the play ends with the forty-first victim arriving for her lesson.

It is all authority, therefore, which is shown up in its sexual, sadistic nature. What Ionesco is saying is that even behind so apparently harmless an exercise of authority as the teacher-pupil relationship, all the violence and domination, all the aggressiveness and possessiveness, the cruelty and lust are present that make up any manifestation of power. The technique of nonliterary theatre, which allows the author and director to treat the text of a play as expendable, enables Ionesco to bring this hidden content into the open. While the language remains on the plane of question and answer, of information asked for and imparted, the *action* can become more and more violent, sensuous, and brutal. All that remains of the elaborate body of knowledge, information (in its parodied form), and conceptual apparatus is the basic fact that the professor wants to dominate and to possess the pupil. Ionesco labeled *The Lesson* a *"drame comique."* It certainly is very funny, but it is a stark and pessimistic drama nevertheless.

Jacques, ou la Soumission (*Jack, or the Submission* in the American, *Jacques, or Obedience* in the British translation), which Ionesco completed after *The Lesson,* in the summer of 1950, has a very similar theme—the individual cowed into conformism by society and convention through the operation of the sexual instinct. Jacques at first refuses to pronounce the words that would confirm his acceptance of the standards of his family, all the members of which are called Jacques as well, thus revealing their renunciation of individuality in the same way the family of Bobby Watsons symbolized the conformity of petty-bourgeois existence in *The Bald Soprano.* Jacques resists the pressure of his family for a while; he refuses to accept the need to pronounce the fatal words and even cries out, "Oh, words, what crimes are committed in your name!" but when his sister Jacqueline points out to him that he is *"chronométrable"*—i.e. (probably), subject to the working of time, subject to the law of the clock—he collapses and finally pronounces the family creed: *"J'adore les pommes de terre au lard."* (This is translated as "I love potatoes in their jackets" in the British edition, "I adore hashed brown potatoes" in the American, but probably just means "I adore potatoes fried in bits of lard" or "potatoes with bacon," as emerges in the sequel to the play *The Future Is in Eggs,* where the bits of bacon play a part and have made the English translator, Derek Prouse, adopt the term "potatoes with bacon.")

The acceptance of the bourgeois creed by the rebellious ex-bohemian son is, according to the French tradition, the signal for settling down and marriage. Jacques is accordingly brought together with the daughter of the Robert family,

Roberte, a girl with two noses. Once more Jacques is rebellious —two noses are not enough for him; he needs three noses in his future wife, regardless of the extra expense in handkerchiefs that this implies. Although Roberte with two noses was their only daughter, the Robert family find a way out—they produce a second only daughter, Roberte II, who has three noses. But not even she at first satisfies Jacques's individualist spirit; she is not ugly enough. He cannot love her: "I have done all I could! I am what I am. . . ." And yet, when left alone with Roberte, he finally succumbs. Roberte wins him with a speech about a dream in which little guinea pigs grow out of their mother at the bottom of a bathtub; suddenly he tells her of his secret longings to be different. The conversation shifts to images of fire (rather like the maid's fiery poem in *The Bald Soprano*) and back to Roberte's description of herself in terms of humidity. Jacques cries out, "Cha-a-armant!" and this leads on to the famous passage in which the two lovers converse in a long succession of terms containing the syllable *"chat,"* with its obvious erotic implications in French —from *cha-peau* to *cha-touille* and *cha-pitre* to the point when Roberte proclaims that henceforth all concepts will be called *chat* without distinction. Jacques and Roberte embrace, the family enters and performs an obscene dance around them. Jacques and Roberte squat down on the ground, the light fades, and the stage is filled with animal noises. The stage direction insists, "All this must produce in the audience a feeling of embarrassment, awkwardness, and shame."

In fact, therefore, Jacques submits twice. He submits to the bourgeois conformism of his family, and, second and finally, to the irresistible, animal lure of the sexual impulse. And it is his second submission that is decisive. It is man's enslavement to the sexual instinct that forces him into the iron mold of bourgeois conformity.

This point is reinforced by the later play that takes up the story: *L'Avenir Est dans les Œufs, ou Il Faut de Tout pour Faire un Monde* (*The Future Is in Eggs, or It Takes All Sorts to Make a World* (written in 1951), which starts with a further orgy of *"chat"* and ends with Roberte hatching unending basketfuls of eggs destined to become the emperors, policemen, Marxists, drunkards, and so on, of the future, all to be turned into sausage meat, cannon fodder, and omelettes. "Long live production! Long live the white race!" is the despairing cry that concludes the play.

The horror of proliferation—the invasion of the stage by ever-growing masses of people or things—which appears in *The Future Is in Eggs* is one of the most characteristic images we find in Ionesco's plays. It expresses the individual's horror at being confronted with the overwhelming task of coping with the world, his solitude in the face of its monstrous size and duration. This is also the theme of *The Chairs*, written at about the same time as the second part of *Jacques* (April–June, 1951) and often considered one of Ionesco's greatest achievements.

In a circular tower on an island (very similar to that of Beckett's *Endgame*) live two old people, man and wife, aged 95 and 94 respectively; the man works as a concierge, although it seems difficult to imagine how he could do so on a lonely tower on an island. The couple is expecting the visit of a crowd of distinguished people who have been invited to listen to the message that, at the end of his life, the old man wants to pass on to posterity—the fruit of a long lifetime's experience. He himself is no orator, so he has engaged a professional orator to deliver the message. The guests arrive; they are neither heard nor seen, but the two old people are filling the stage with increasing numbers of chairs to accommodate them and pouring forth torrents of polite conversation. The crowd becomes more and more dense, the two old people have greater and greater difficulty in moving among them, finally the emperor himself arrives; the scene is set for the appearance of the orator. He comes—and is a real character. Satisfied that his message will be delivered, the old man, followed by his wife, jumps to his death into the sea. The orator faces the crowd of chairs and tries to speak, but he is deaf and dumb and can only make an inarticulate, gurgling sound. He writes something on a blackboard—it is a jumble of meaningless letters.

The power and poignancy of this situation are as great as its effectiveness as theatre. The simulation of a crowd of invisible characters is a tour de force for the actors involved, which, if it is successfully carried through, is bound to be a most impressive scenic spectacle. A play like *The Chairs* is a poetic image brought to life—complex, ambiguous, multi-dimensional. The beauty and depth of the image, as symbol and myth, transcends any search for interpretations. Of course it contains the theme of the incommunicability of a lifetime's experience; of course it dramatizes the futility and failure of human existence, made bearable only by self-delusion and the admiration of a doting, uncritical wife; of course it satirizes the emptiness of polite conversation, the mechanical exchange of platitudes that might as well be spoken into the wind. There is also a strong element of the author's own tragedy in the play—the rows of chairs resemble a theatre; the professional orator who is to deliver the message, dressed in the romantic costume of the mid-nineteenth century, is the interpretative artist who interposes his personality between that of the playwright and the audience. But the message is meaningless, the audience consists of rows of empty chairs—surely this is a powerful image of the absurdity of the artist's, the playwright's, own situation.

All these themes intertwine in *The Chairs*. But Ionesco himself has defined its basic preoccupation: "The subject of the play," he wrote to the director of the first performance, Sylvain Dhomme, "is not the message, nor the failures of life, nor the moral disaster of the two old people, but the chairs themselves; that is to say, the absence of people, the absence of the emperor, the absence of God, the absence of matter, the unreality of the world, metaphysical emptiness. The theme of the play is *nothingness* . . . the invisible elements must be more and more clearly present, more and more real (to give unreality to reality one must give reality to the unreal), until the point is reached—inadmissible, unacceptable to the reasoning mind—when the unreal elements speak and move . . . and nothingness can be heard, is made concrete. . . ."[34]

The Chairs was Ionesco's third play to reach the stage, and it did not do so without the greatest difficulties. It took Sylvain Dhomme and the two actors of the old couple, Tsilla Chelton and Paul Chevalier, three months to find the style of acting suitable for the play—a mixture of extreme naturalness of detail and the utmost unusualness of the general conception. None of the established managements in Paris wanted to risk putting on *The Chairs,* so in the end the actors themselves hired an old unused hall, the Théâtre Lancry, where they opened on April 22, 1952. Financially the venture proved a disaster. Only too often the empty chairs on the stage were matched by empty seats in the auditorium, and there were evenings when only five or six tickets were sold. Most of the critics slated the play, but, on the other hand, it did find some distinguished supporters. A defense of *The Chairs* published in the magazine *Arts* was signed by Jules Supervielle, Arthur Adamov, Samuel Beckett, Luc Estang, Clara Malraux, Raymond Queneau, and others. At the end of the last performance, the poet and playwright Audiberti was heard, in the almost empty auditorium, shouting "Bravo!" at the top of his voice.

Four years later, when Jacques Mauclair revived *The Chairs* with the same actress, Tsilla Chelton, in the part of the old woman, the climate of opinion had changed; the performance at the Studio des Champs-Elysées was a great success. The leading conservative critics, like J.-J. Gautier, of *Figaro,* still held out against Ionesco, but Jean Anouilh himself came to his defense, calling the play a masterpiece, and adding, "I believe this to be better than Strindberg, because it has its 'black' humor, à la Molière, in a manner that is at times terribly funny, because it is horrifying and laughable, poignant and always true, and because—with the exception of a bit of rather old-fashioned avant-garde at the end that I do not like— it is classical."[35]

Ionesco labeled *The Chairs* a "tragic farce," *Jacques, ou la Soumission* a "naturalistic comedy." He called his next play, *Victimes du Devoir* (*Victims of Duty*) a "pseudo-drama." This play may have been less successful than some of his earlier works, but it is certainly among his most significant statements.

Victims of Duty is a playwright's play, an argument for and against the problem drama: "All the plays that have ever been written, from Ancient Greece to the present day, have never really been anything but thrillers. Drama has always been realistic and there has always been a detective about. Every play is an investigation brought to a successful conclusion. There is a riddle and it is solved in the final scene."[36] Even the classical French tragedy, says Choubert, the hero of *Victims of Duty,* ultimately can be reduced to refined detective drama.

Choubert is a petty bourgeois spending the evening quietly with his wife, who is darning socks. His views on the theatre are immediately put to the test. A detective arrives. He is merely looking for the neighbors, but they are out. He wants to find out whether the previous tenant of Choubert's apartment spelled his name "Mallot" with a "t," or "Mallod" with a "d." The Chouberts ask the detective in; he looks such a nice young man. But before he knows where he is, Choubert is the victim of third-degree methods. He has never known Mallot, or Mallod, but he is ordered to delve into his (Choubert's) subconscious; the answer to the problem simply *must* be there. The detective is thus turned into a psychoanalyst, the identity between the detective play and the psychological drama is demonstrated.

As Choubert dives deeper and deeper into the bottomless well of his subconscious, his wife, Madeleine, changes too—into a seductress at first, then an old woman, and finally the detective's mistress. So deep down has Choubert gone that he pierces the sound and sight barriers and actually disappears from sight. When he comes to the surface again, he has become a child and Madeleine is now his mother. The detective has become his father. Again the situation changes: Choubert holds the stage, acting out the drama of his search, while Madeleine and the detective are his audience. But all he sees is a gaping hole. Attempts are made to bring him back to the surface—he has delved too deep—and is presently going up and up, higher than Mont Blanc, and in danger of becoming airborne. New characters wander in—a lady who sits silently in the corner, but to whom the others occasionally turn with a polite *"N'est-ce pas, Madame?"* and a bearded man, Nicolas d'Eu (not to be confounded with Nicolas Deux, the late Czar of Russia), who brings the conversation back to the theatre, while Choubert continues his hapless quest for Mallot.

Nicolas is for a new kind of theatre, up to date, "in harmony with the general drift of the other manifestations of the modern spirit. . . . We'll get rid of the principle of identity and unity of character. . . . As for plot and motivation, let's not mention them . . . no more drama, no more tragedy: the tragic's turning comic, the comic is tragic, and life's getting more cheerful. . . ."[37] These, of course, are the well-known points of view of Ionesco himself, only slightly parodied, and Nicolas confesses that he does not want to write—after all, "We've got Ionesco and that's enough."[38]

In the meantime, the detective is feeding Choubert enormous quantities of bread to stop the gaping hole of his memory. Nicolas d'Eu suddenly turns against the detective, who cringes in fear and pleads for his life but is pitilessly knifed by Nicolas. He dies with the cry, "Long live the white race!" Madeleine, who has been bringing cups of coffee throughout the proceedings, so that the entire stage is filled with cups, reminds them that they have not yet found Mallot. So Nicolas takes over the role of the detective and begins to feed the protesting Choubert with bread; he, like the detective, is merely doing his duty—he is a victim of duty as much as Choubert, as much as Madeleine. They are all victims of duty. What duty? In all likelihood that of finding a solution to the riddle posed at the beginning of the play. Being characters in a play, they have to find a solution at all costs; they *must* find the answer to the question whether Mallot spelled his name with a "t" or a "d." For we are here in the realm of "pseudo-drama."

Victims of Duty is one of Ionesco's favorite plays. It deals with the subject nearest to his heart, the problem of the essential tasks and limitations of the theatre. The policeman-psychoanalyst stands for the proposition that the mysteries of existence can be solved. "As for me," he says, "I remain Aristotelianly logical, true to myself, faithful to my duty, and full of respect for my bosses. . . . I don't believe in the absurd; everything hangs together, everything can be comprehended in time . . . thanks to the achievements of human thought and science."[39] But Choubert, however deeply he descends into his subconscious, can find no solution there, only a gaping hole of nothingness. Far from containing the hidden solution to the riddle of existence, the subconscious mind opens into a bottomless pit, the absolute void.

As Serge Doubrovsky has pointed out, in what is probably the most profound analysis of Ionesco's work yet made, Freudian psychoanalysis is here confronted with Sartre's Existentialist ontology and psychology. Whether intentionally or not—more probably the latter—Ionesco here illustrates Sartre's proposition that man is a "hole in Being," that he is "the being through which nothingness enters the world"[40] and that "consciousness is a being which in its being is conscious of the nothingness of its being."[41] Man *is* nothing because he has the liberty of choice and therefore is always that which he is in the process of choosing himself to be, a permanent potentiality rather than actual being. No amount of bread that the detective, and later Nicolas d'Eu, stuff into Choubert can therefore, as Doubrovsky maintains, stop the gaping hole in Choubert's consciousness or "give thought a substantial existence."[42]

But if, to quote Doubrovsky again, "consciousness is nothingness, then personality, character, disappear for good."[43] If man can choose himself anew at each instant of his life, the conception of character as the final, irreducible essence—the Platonic idea—of each individual person disappears. As Nicolas d'Eu puts it in *Victims of Duty*, "We are not ourselves. Personality doesn't exist. Within us are only forces that are either contradictory or not contradictory. . . . The characters lose their form in the formlessness of becoming. Each character is not so much himself as another." The brilliantly managed sequence of Choubert's descent into the depths and subsequent flight into the empyrean is a demonstration of this proposition. As he reaches the different levels of depth and height, Choubert turns into a bewildering variety of different, and not necessarily consistent, selves. At the same time the character of his wife also undergoes a series of changes, both in so far as *he* sees a different Madeleine at different levels of *his* self, and also as *she* becomes a different personality in responding to the changes in his character—for example, when he becomes a child, she becomes his mother, and so on.

Doubrovsky's essay is based on the assumption that Ionesco illustrates this Sartrean psychology, and parodies Freudian psychoanalysis. Yet it is possible that Ionesco might just as well be parodying both Sartre and Freud. After all, when he has killed the Freudian detective, Nicolas d'Eu, the propounder of the fluidity of character, himself resumes the search for Mallot and continues to stuff bread down Choubert's throat. In other words, the two views are interchangeable, and Choubert, the little man, suffers as much under the tyranny of the one as of the other. It is always dangerous to take Ionesco too seriously. On the other hand, much of his practice seems to follow the principles of an anti-psychological drama, renouncing ready-made solutions to the problems it purports to pose, and abandoning the sacred concept of character as the essence of personality, i.e., the view enunciated by Nicolas d'Eu. But for Ionesco, the author of *No!*, that early essay on the identity of opposites, it would not be difficult to hold a belief and to parody it at the same time.

Victims of Duty, however, is not merely a play about Ionesco's theory of the theatre (the first of a number of such essays in the tradition of Molière's *Impromptu de Versailles*). It is not merely a psychological and philosophical inquiry, or a parody of such an inquiry; it is, above all, a haunting nightmare, a deeply felt and tormented expression of its author's experience of the absurdity and cruelty of existence. Ionesco, like Kafka and Beckett, is primarily concerned with trying to communicate his own sense of being, to tell the world what it feels like, what it means for him when he says, "I am" or "I am alive." This is "the point of departure" of all his work:

> Two fundamental states of consciousness are at the root of all my plays. . . . These two basic feelings are those of evanescence on the one hand, and heaviness on the other; of emptiness and of an overabundance of presence; of the unreal transparency of the world, and of its opaqueness. . . . The sensation of evanescence results in a feeling of anguish, a sort of dizziness. But all of this can just as well become euphoric; anguish is suddenly transformed into liberty. . . . This state of consciousness is very rare, to be sure. . . . I am most often under the dominion of the opposite feeling: Lightness changes to heaviness, transparence to thickness; the world weighs heavily; the universe crushes me. A curtain, an insuperable wall, comes between me and the world, between me and myself. Matter fills everything, takes up all space, annihilates all liberty under its weight. . . . Speech crumbles . . .[44]

The proliferation of matter—chairs, eggs, furniture (in *The New Tenant*), or, in this case, Madeleine's coffee cups—is one of the manifestations of the heavy, leaden, hopeless, depressive state of consciousness. The proliferation of matter expresses "the concretization of solitude, of the victory of anti-spiritual forces."[45] And humor is the only liberation from this anguish.

Victims of Duty clearly belongs to a depressive period in Ionesco's development. The play was first performed in February, 1953, by Jacques Mauclair, the young director who later brought Ionesco his first major success with the revival of *The Chairs*. The seven short pieces which Jacques Poliéri presented in September of that year at the tiny Théâtre de la Huchette, on the other hand, were largely light, humorous, and euphoric. Only three of these (*Le Salon de l'Automobile, La Jeune Fille à Marier* and *Le Maître*) have appeared in print. The four others (*Le Connaissez-Vous, Le Rhume Onirique, La Nièce Epouse,* and *Les Grandes Chaleurs*—an adaptation from the Rumanian of Caragiale) appear to be lost, the manuscripts having gone astray.

These are slight plays, actually cabaret sketches, but nevertheless very characteristic and revealing of Ionesco's comic techniques. *Le Salon de l'Automobile*[46] is based on a confusion between motorcars and human beings. The buyer rides away in a newly acquired vehicle that is a female and that he decides to marry. The exhibition hall is filled with the farmyard noises of the exhibited vehicles. In *La Jeune Fille à Marier* the comic element is largely surprise; a lady discusses her young and innocent daughter, who has just completed her studies; an expectation of young innocence is built up. Finally the daughter appears: "She is a man, about thirty years old, robust and virile, with a bushy black mustache, wearing a gray suit."[47] The same comic principle is used again in *Le Maître*. A radio announcer and two young couples express mounting expectation to see in person a *great man* (the English translation reads, "*the leader*," but it is not quite clear whether the personality concerned might not just as well be a literary figure, more usually addressed as *Maître* in France). In tones of mounting adoration, his actions offstage are ecstatically described—he kisses babies, eats his soup, signs autographs, has his trousers ironed, and so on. When he finally appears, he is a headless body.[48]

Ionesco likes to express himself in short plays, or at least in one-act plays that can develop without interruption. He finds a division into three acts "rather artificial. The play ends, then restarts, it ends again, restarts again. . . . I don't think one should try to put too much into a play. In a three-act play there are necessarily superfluous things. The theatre needs a very simple idea: a single obsession, a simple, very clear, self-evident development."[49] His first effort to write a three-act play, *Amédée, ou Comment S'En Débarasser* (*Amédée, or How to Get Rid of It*), a comedy in three acts, may bear out his misgivings about the longer form, but it contains some of his most haunting images. The play springs from his darkest, most depressive mood, and presents what is probably his most powerful symbol of the proliferation of matter and its stifling of the spirit.

The hero of the play, Amédée Buccinioni, is, like Ionesco, a writer. He is, in fact, writing a play, a play about an old man and an old woman rather like the protagonists of *The Chairs*. But in fifteen years of work he has succeeded in writing only two lines of dialogue:

> THE OLD WOMAN: Do you think it will do?
> THE OLD MAN: It won't do by itself.[50]

Amédée and his wife, Madeleine (Madeleine again, like the wife in *Victims of Duty*), live cut off from the world. They have not left their apartment for fifteen years, and even haul their supplies through the window in a basket. Yet Madeleine is still in communication with the outside world, through her job—she works at a switchboard in the living room, where she operates a kind of telephone exchange at certain times of the day. She connects callers even to the office of the President of the Republic, communicates new traffic regulations to inquirers, and so on. The couple are on very bad terms with each other; they quarrel constantly. Madeleine is a hard, nagging creature. But the main shadow over the marriage is the presence in the next room of a corpse, the body of a young man who came to call fifteen years ago, and whom Amédée is said, but by no means with certainty, to have killed in a fit of jealousy. Perhaps the corpse is not that of the wife's lover at all. At one point, Amédée suggests that he might have left again at the time the "crime" was committed. Or again it might be that the corpse is that of a baby a neighbor once left in their care and never called for again. But why should that baby have died?

The corpse in the next room may be dead, but it is very active. Its beard and nails are growing, its eyes glow with an eerie green light, and the dead body itself is growing larger and larger. The corpse is suffering from "the incurable disease of the dead"—*geometrical progression*. As the play proceeds, this growth accelerates; the door of the next room bursts open, and a gigantic foot pushes into the room. As the corpse grows, mushrooms proliferate in the apartment—images of decay and corruption.

Who or what is the corpse that is growing so relentlessly? A flashback scene supplies some of the clues to the solution of this riddle. Amédée and Madeleine appear as a newly married couple. Amédée is loving, importunate, romantic; Madeleine is petulant, sullen, unwilling to accept his protestations of love, deflating his romantic notions. The imagery of the dialogue is clearly sexual; the situation is that of an ardent lover and a girl who regards all advances as acts of violation and rape: "Your voice is so piercing! You are deafening me! Hurting me! Don't rend my darkness! S-a-dist! S-a-dist!"[51] When Amédée's younger self hears the voices of spring, children's voices, the phantom Madeleine can merely hear "oaths and toads." The scene comes to a climax with Amédée pleading for love: "What is far can be near. What is withered can grow green again. What is separated can be reunited. What *is* no more, *will be* again," but as Amédée dreams of happiness in their house of glass (*verre*), Madeleine insists that their house is of brass (*fer*)—in other words the image of lightness, happiness, and euphoria is countered by the image of heaviness, depression, and opacity.

This flashback scene makes it fairly clear that the corpse in the next room is the corpse of the couple's dead love, the victim of their sexual incompatibility. It is a corpse made up of disgust, guilt, and regret. It poisons the atmosphere with the mushrooms of decay and decomposition—and it is growing from day to day, from hour to hour. Amédée quite clearly states that what is rotten in their home is the absence of love: "Do you know, Madeleine, if we loved each other, if we really loved each other, none of this would be important?" But

Madeleine has become hard, unsentimental, and matter of fact: "Love can't help people get rid of their troubles!"[52]

Amédée must get rid of the corpse, which threatens to burst out of the apartment. With a superhuman effort, he tries to push the endless body out of the window. As Ionesco puts it in the stage direction, the body pulled near the window should give the impression that "it is dragging the whole house with it and tugging at the entrails of the two principal characters."[53]

The third act shows Amédée dragging the body through the streets toward the Seine. He meets various people, notably an American soldier outside a bar or brothel. Amédée explains to this foreigner, with whom he is unable to communicate, that he is writing a play in which he is taking the part of the living against the dead, a play against nihilism and for a new humanism. He, Amédée, is for commitment, and believes in progress. As the scene becomes more crowded with people, girls, soldiers, policemen, Amédée continues to assure all and sundry that he is for social realism, against disintegration and nihilism. By this time the corpse has become a kind of balloon, and Amédée is already floating in the air. Madeleine wants him to come back, the mushrooms are in bloom, but Amédée floats away into the sky.

In *Amédée* we see the two basic moods of Ionesco's experience of the world side by side: heaviness and the proliferation of matter in the first two acts, lightness and evanescence in the third. As Amédée gets rid of the corpse of his dead love, that stifling presence turns into lightness and lifts him into the air. The play, which is simply labeled "Comedy in Three Acts," is a comedy of liberation, a dream of a new beginning that will abolish the past.

As in *Victims of Duty*, the polemic against the social realists runs as a secondary theme through the whole play. At one point Madeleine tells Amédée that the presence of the corpse in the next room falsifies his perception of reality, makes him see the world in a morbid light—hence his failure to write a sociological play. But, as the events of the third act show, the facts of the writer's personal life are more immediate than his social intentions. However much he protests his belief in progress and commitment, the corpse of his past love and personal memories carries him upward and pulls his feet off the ground.

Amédée contains some of Ionesco's most brilliant images. As a stage symbol of tremendous power and immediate impact the growing corpse is sure of its measure of immortality. The claustrophobic feelings of the couple's private world heightened by the echoes of the offstage voices of other tenants of the house and thrown into relief when a postman comes to deliver a letter, which plunges them both into a frenzy of fear and causes them to refuse delivery—are made brilliantly concrete. The weakness of the play lies in the third act, which is intended to be rather like the final, frantic chase in the last reel of a Keystone comedy, with soldiers and policemen pursuing each other across the stage. But this intention does not allow itself to be completely realized in the theatre. And the transition from claustrophobia to openness and lightness is a very difficult one to manage on the stage.

In the short story *Oriflamme*,[54] which constitutes a preliminary sketch for the play, the events of the last act occupy barely a page, as against about twelve pages devoted to relating the action of the first two acts. The last paragraph of the story indicates the euphoria of the final floating away even more clearly than the dramatized version:

> I still heard the Americans, who thought I was performing some sporting feat, greet me with a 'Hello, boy!' I dropped my clothes, my cigarettes; the policemen divided them between themselves. Then there was only the Milky Way that I traversed, an oriflamme [i.e., like the sacred gold-starred banner of France billowing in the wind] at headlong pace, at headlong pace.[55]

Amédée (the play) is dated Cerisy-la-Salle, August, 1953. It was first performed at the Théâtre de Babylone on April 14, 1954, under the direction of Jean-Marie Serreau. Within a few weeks of completing *Amédée*, Ionesco wrote another play, which took him only three days to finish (September 14–16, 1953) and which presents the imagery of proliferating matter with renewed force. This play is *Le Nouveau Locataire* (*The New Tenant*), and is in one act. The action consists of an empty room being filled up with the furniture of the new tenant, a mild middle-aged gentleman who seems unencumbered with worldly goods at first and takes his time carefully placing the first few pieces, but who at the end is literally buried in the unending stream of furniture, at first brought in by two moving-men, but later pouring in by itself. We learn that all the traffic is at a standstill, all the streets of Paris are blocked by more and more furniture, and the bed of the River Seine itself is filled with it.

The New Tenant is a spectacle of terrifying simplicity. Dialogue (between the tenant and the bickering, greedy concierge; between the tenant and the moving-men) is reduced to a secondary role. Primarily, this is a play of objects on the move, objects overwhelming man, stifling him in a sea of inert matter. A single poetic image is built up before our eyes, first with a certain amount of surprise, later with relentless inevitability. This is a demonstration of the possibilities of *pure* theatre: The concepts of character, conflict, plot-construction have been abandoned—and yet *The New Tenant* remains drama with mounting suspense, excitement, and poetic force. What does it mean? Is the empty room filling up with furniture, slowly at first but later with increasing speed, an image of the life of man, empty at first, but gradually cluttered up with new and repetitive experiences and memories? Or is the play merely a translation into scenic terms of the claustrophobia—the feeling of being hemmed in by heavy, oppressive matter—of the depressive, leaden moods from which Ionesco suffers?

The New Tenant was first performed by a Swedish-speaking company in Finland in 1955. It was presented at the Arts Theatre in London in November, 1956, and reached Paris only in September, 1957. Yet in spite of setbacks, in spite of the financial disasters of the first productions of his plays, Ionesco's career was making steady progress. Toward the end of 1954, the first volume of his *Théâtre* was published by Gallimard, the leading French publisher, in whose decisions Raymond Queneau, the poet and novelist who had been deeply impressed by Ionesco's first efforts, and whose own experiments with language clearly influenced Ionesco, plays an important part. Of the six plays in that first volume, only one had not yet reached the stage when it was published: *Jacques ou la Soumission*. This omission was repaired in October of the following year, 1955, when Robert Postec presented *Jacques* and another play by Ionesco, *Le Tableau* (*The Picture*), at the Théâtre de la Huchette.

Unlike *Jacques*, which was a success, *The Picture* failed to please, and Ionesco has omitted it from the second volume of his plays. But it has appeared in the *Dossiers Acénonètes du Collège de Pataphysique*, that distinguished group of followers of Jarry and his Dr. Faustroll, among whom Ionesco holds the high rank of a Transcendant Satrap (as do René Clair, Raymond Queneau, Jacques Prévert, and many other famous pataphysicians). It has also been broadcast, in a translation by Donald Watson, on the B.B.C.'s Third Programme (March 11 and 15, 1957).

The Picture is a curious play. It opens with a fat, wealthy gentleman who wants to buy a picture from a painter. They are haggling about the price; the painter wants the buyer to have a look at the picture before he names his price, but the fat gentleman wants to settle that detail first. The painter asks five hundred thousand francs at first, but is relentlessly driven down until, in the end, he is ready to settle for a mere four hundred francs. Only then does the shrewd businessman cast a glance at the picture, which represents a queen, and promptly criticizes it so savagely that the painter finally begs him to keep the picture without any payment. In fact the painter consents to pay the fat gentleman a fee for storing his picture.

The fat gentleman's old and ugly sister enters into the proceedings and is rudely treated by her brother. But the moment the painter has gone, the situation changes abruptly. Alice, the sister, becomes the tyrant and the fat gentleman is reduced to the role of a cowed schoolboy. Left to himself, the fat gentleman, who is starved for beauty and affection, works himself up into a state of frenzy about the picture. As Ionesco says in a footnote,[56] "The actor playing this part must get as erotic as the censorship permits or the spectators will tolerate." When his sister reappears, he has again become his old dominating self. He menaces his sister with a gun and finally shoots her. But instead of dying she is transformed, becoming as beautiful as the picture. An ugly woman neighbor wants to be transformed the same way. She too is shot and turned into a beautiful princess. The painter returns, admires his patron's ability to create beauty by violence, is shot himself, and becomes a Prince Charming. Shots fired into the air transform the room into a fairy palace. The fat gentleman, who alone remains as fat and ugly as he was, invites the audience to shoot at him.

Ionesco calls *The Picture* a "*guignolade*"—a Punch and Judy play. He attributes its failure at its 1955 performance to the fact that the first part, the haggling over the price with the painter, was acted realistically, as a critique of a capitalist's exploitation of an artist. "In fact, this Punch and Judy play must be acted by circus clowns in the most childish, exaggerated, idiotic manner possible. . . . The reversals of situations must happen brusquely, violently, crudely, without preparation. . . . It is only by an extreme simplification . . . that the meaning of this farce can be brought out and become acceptable through its very inacceptability and idiocy."[57] The subject of the play, according to the same note, is "metamorphosis, treated . . . parodistically, to disguise, out of bashfulness, its serious significance."[58]

It would be rash to attempt to read too much into this intentionally "idiotic" spectacle. What it seems to be driving at is the vicious circle between the crude commercialism of the Philistine businessman with his mixture of meanness and sentimentality, on the one hand, and, on the other, the supposed transcendence of this ugly world by its antithesis, a world of "beauty" redeemed by "art." But the mean are imprisoned in their own meanness: having killed the ugliness in themselves, having replaced it by what they consider its direct opposite, they merely enter a world of cheap *Kitsch*, a world of operetta with the Princesses and the Prince Charmings of the crudest erotic fantasies. If, at the end of the play, the fat gentleman begs the audience to shoot him, this is merely a variant of the situation in the rejected violent ending of *The Bald Soprano*, where the Philistine audience was to have been machine-gunned from the stage. Here the Philistine on the stage wants to be shot by the non-Philistines in the audience. And the play itself has demonstrated the futility of any such thing. Shooting, violence, cannot bring about a real transformation; the hope of changing the world or the sensibilities of people by violence is utterly vain and absurd; the changes are as idiotic as the original situation.

At the same time, the play is an experiment in the possibilities of the theatre. Ionesco once said, "I personally would like to bring a tortoise onto the stage, turn it into a race horse, then into a hat, a song, a dragoon, and a fountain of water. One can dare anything in the theatre, and it is the place where one dares the least. I want no other limits than the technical limits of stage machinery. People will say that my plays are music-hall turns or circus acts. So much the better—let's include the circus in the theatre! Let the playwright be accused of being arbitrary. Yes, the theatre is the place where one *can* be arbitrary. As a matter of fact, it is not arbitrary. The imagination is not arbitrary, it is revealing. . . . I have decided not to recognize any laws except those of my imagination, and since the imagination obeys its own laws, this is further proof that in the last resort it is not arbitrary."[59]

These two interpretations of *The Picture*, one in terms of a critique of Philistine sensibility, the other in terms of an experiment in a pure theatre of circuslike transformation-scenes, are in no way contradictory. All of Ionesco's theatre contains two strands side by side—complete freedom in the exercise of his imagination and a strong element of the polemical. His very first play, *The Bald Soprano*, was an anti-play, and as such a criticism of the existing theatre as well as of a type of dead society. The same, strongly pugnacious spirit manifests itself in Ionesco's entire œuvre, and it is therefore quite wrong, to regard him as a mere clown and prankster. Ionesco's plays are a complex mixture of poetry, fantasy, nightmare—and cultural and social criticism. In spite of the fact that Ionesco rejects, and detests, any openly didactic theatre ("I do not teach, I give testimony. I don't explain, I try to explain myself")[60] he is convinced that any genuinely new and experimental writing is bound to contain a polemical element. "The man of the avant-garde is in opposition to an existing system. . . . An artistic creation is by its very novelty aggressive, spontaneously aggressive; it is directed against the public, against the bulk of the public; it causes indignation by its unusualness, which is itself a form of indignation."[61]

Ionesco's most openly polemical play, his most direct attack against his critics, is *L'Impromptu de l'Alma, ou Le Caméléon du Berger* (English title: *Improvisation, or The*

Shepherd's Chameleon), dated Paris, 1955, and first performed
at the Studio des Champs-Elysées in February, 1956. By the
title alone, Ionesco proclaims his faith that the avant-garde is
merely the renewer of tradition—Molière's *L'Impromptu de
Versailles*, and Giraudoux's *L'Impromptu de Paris* are clearly
alluded to. And, like Molière, Ionesco puts himself on the stage
in the act of writing a play—that is, asleep with a ball-point pen
in his hand. He is visited by three learned doctors dressed in
the gowns of the pompous doctors of Molière's *Malade Imagi-
naire*, and all three called Bartholomeus—Bartholomeus I, Bartholomeus II, and Bartholomeus III. To the first of these, Ionesco explains that he is in the process of writing a play to be
called *The Shepherd's Chameleon*, which is based on a real incident: "Once, in a large country town, in the middle of the
street, during the summer, I saw a young shepherd, about
three o'clock in the afternoon, who was embracing a chameleon. . . . It was such a touching scene, I decided to turn it
into a tragic farce."[62] But, of course, this is merely the pretext,
the starting point of the play he is writing. In reality, Ionesco
explains, it will be a play about his ideas on playwriting: "You
can say I am the shepherd, if you like, and the theatre is the
chameleon. Because I have embraced a theatrical career, and
the theatre, of course, changes, for the theatre is life."[63]

Prevailed upon to read what he has written up to now,
Ionesco proceeds to read exactly what the public has seen performed—an ingenious and very characteristic mirror effect,
which is immediately reduplicated once again by the arrival of
the second Bartholomeus, who repeats the same lines as the
first; whereupon the third arrives, repeats the same lines as the
first two, asks Ionesco to read his play, Ionesco starts off with
the same opening passage. There is a new knock on the door
and it seems as though a vicious circle had been established
that would go on forever. But this time the person who
knocked is not let in, and the discussion can begin. The three
doctors are purveyors of a half-existentialist, half-Brechtian
farrago of dramatic theory, with allusions to Adamov, who discovered the Aristotelian principles before Aristotle, Sartre, and,
of course, above all, Ionesco's special *bête noire*, Brecht.

Ionesco is rescued from complete stultification by the doctors through the arrival of his charwoman (who has been

knocking at the door all the time); she represents common sense and demystification. Ionesco recovers his poise and launches into a confession of his faith as a dramatist. He condemns the three critics for having peddled truisms clothed in extravagant jargon, whereas "the critic should describe and not prescribe . . . he should only judge a work on its own terms, according to the laws that govern artistic expression, according to each work's own mythology, by penetrating into its own world. One does not set chemistry to music, one does not judge biology by the criteria of painting or architecture. . . . For my part, I believe sincerely in the poverty of the poor, I deplore it, it is real and can serve as material for the theatre; I also believe in the grave cares and anxieties that may beset the rich. But in my case it is neither from the wretchedness of the poor nor the unhappiness of the rich that I draw the substance of my drama. For me, the theatre is the projection onto the stage of the world within—it is in my dreams, my anguish, my dark desires, my inner contradictions that I reserve the right to find the stuff of my plays. As I am not alone in the world—as each one of us, in the depths of his being, is at the same time everyone else—my dreams and desires, my anguish and my obsessions do not belong to myself alone; they are part of the heritage of my ancestors, a very ancient deposit to which all mankind may lay claim."[64] At this point, Ionesco's manner becomes more and more pontifical. He begins to quote the names of German and American authorities, and is finally asked whether he is really taking himself seriously after all. Abashed, he recognizes that he has fallen into his own trap and is in danger of himself becoming didactic. He apologizes that this, in his case, is the exception, not the rule, a dig at Brecht's play *The Exception and the Rule*.

L'Impromptu de l'Alma takes us back into the thick of the controversy about the didactic, political theatre, of which the exchange with Kenneth Tynan later became one brilliant, but by no means central, episode. The main attack against Ionesco had been launched by some of the critics who had at first hailed him as a master of the new avant-garde, in the pages of such periodicals as Sartre's *Les Temps Modernes* and the influential *Théâtre Populaire*. It is no coincidence that the same number of the latter periodical (dated March 1, 1956) that contained a rather pained notice of *L'Impromptu de l'Alma* and the revival of *The Chairs* with which it shared the bill at the Studio des Champs-Elysées, also published an essay by Adamov on "Theatre, Money, and Politics," in which he made public confession of his error in having omitted the social theme from his plays that had been performed to date, and called for a revival of a historical, sociological theatre. No wonder that the review of *The Chairs* by Maurice Regnaut, in spite of high praise for direction and performance, culminates in the question, "Why, then, in spite of all this, should we too feel ourselves 'cheated'? It is because we have been provoked into taking an interest in what basically does not concern us at all. This piece has objective reality only to that extent to which the postulate of the lyrical confession is true. More than Ionesco himself, we need to believe that 'one is all people.' But the old mystification cannot long conceal the emptiness of this theatre. To transform the theatre into music is the last artistic dream of the petty bourgeois as Gorki has defined him: man who prefers himself."[65]

Thus the battle was joined between the historical, sociological, epic theatre and the lyrical, poetical theatre of the world within, the theatre of dream, mood, and being. We shall return to a discussion of these two basic points of view of the contemporary theatre in a later chapter. Here it must be noted that the final parting of the ways between Ionesco's conception and that of Brecht and his newly converted follower Adamov coincided with the breakthrough of Ionesco into the world of acceptance and success—a sure sign in the eyes of his opponents, that the bourgeoisie had at last recognized the man who best expressed their decadent point of view.

Not only in France but in other countries as well, performances of Ionesco's plays became more frequent. There were still scandals like the one in Brussels where the audience at a performance of *The Lesson* demanded their money back, and the leading actor had to escape through a back door, but also surprising successes in countries like Yugoslavia and Poland, where *The Chairs* was performed with the old couple in workmen's overalls. Within six years of the first disastrous performance of *The Bald Soprano*, Ionesco had arrived.

Being an accepted author involved Ionesco in some strange

adventures that might have come straight out of one of his own plays. In May, 1957, some London papers reported that "the Duke and Duchess of Windsor and ten other guests were present at a remarkable theatre performance given recently in the Paris home of the Argentine millionaire, M. Anchorena"[66] and that the play presented had been by Ionesco, with music specially composed by Pierre Boulez. A few days later, London papers speculated on the possibility that this play, *Impromptu pour la Duchesse de Windsor*, might be performed in England, but, as the *Daily Mail* put it, "It's going to cause some headaches" to the Lord Chamberlain. The *Evening News* of the same day, May 31, 1957, even spoke of the Duchess of Windsor having refused permission to have the little play performed in London. Yet, according to the *Daily Mail* again, Ionesco had commented that the Duke and Duchess "seemed quite amused."

In fact Ionesco's second *Impromptu* is a very slight, but witty and utterly harmless party joke: a short scene in which The Lady of the House discusses with the author and an actress what they might present to amuse the Duke and Duchess of Windsor. This leads to a discussion of Ionesco's own work and of his favorite theme of the identity of comedy and tragedy. When The Lady of the House asks Ionesco not to present "a sad play, one of those modern dramas like those by Beckett or Sophocles, which might make people cry," he answers, "Sometimes, Madame, comedies make people cry even more than dramas . . . the comedies that I write. When I want to write a tragedy I make them laugh, when I write a comedy, I make them cry."[67] There is also a very amusing nonsense version of English history as seen by a Frenchman, and an equally characteristic sequence of semantic misunderstandings about spirits: when offered a glass of whiskey by The Lady of the House, the author maintains that it is gin, while the actress tastes it and pronounces it Bénédictine. When the author, out of politeness, comes round to accepting it as whiskey, the others, also from politeness, accept each others' interpretations, increasing the confusion. The discussion of what might amuse the royal guests finally ends in complete deadlock and the piece concludes with the apologies of the hostess. As, according to the *Evening Standard*, Mme. Marcel

Achard, the wife of the playwright, remarked after the performance, "Only Ionesco could have handled such a delicate subject." Salvador Dali, another of the privileged number of guests, merely remarked, "It was most moving."

The composition of such a lighthearted trifle did not distract Ionesco overmuch from more ambitious and artistically more rewarding objectives. In November, 1955, the *Nouvelle Revue Française* had published a short story by him that was later to grow into one of his major plays. (Altogether four of Ionesco's plays are elaborations of drafts written in the form of stories: *Une Victime du Devoir*, published in the review *Medium*, later became *Victims of Duty*; *Oriflamme*, in the *Nouvelle Revue Française*, February, 1954, became *Amédée*; *Rhinocéros*, in *Les Lettres Nouvelles*, September, 1957; and *La Photo du Colonel*, in *La Nouvelle Revue Française*, November, 1955.) This particular story was *La Photo du Colonel (The Photograph of the Colonel)*,[68] which became the basis of the play Ionesco completed during a stay in London in August, 1957—*Tueur Sans Gages*, entitled in the English translation *The Killer*, which does not quite do justice to the implications of the French, which means *Killer Without Reward* (or payment); that is, a gratuitous, purposeless killer.

Tueur Sans Gages is Ionesco's second three-act work, and not only one of his most ambitious, but also probably his finest play. Bérenger, its hero, is a Chaplinesque little man, simple, awkward, but human. As the play opens, he is being shown round an ambitious new housing project by its creator, the municipal architect. This is a beautiful new quarter of the town, well-designed, with pleasant gardens and a pond. What is more, as the architect explains, permanent sunshine is built into the project; however much it may rain in other parts of the city, the moment you cross the boundary of the *cité radieuse*, the radiant city, you enter a climate of perpetual spring.

Bérenger, who never realized that such perfection of modern design or planning existed, and who strayed into this new world by pure chance, is deeply moved. But why, he asks, are the streets of this lovely quarter so deserted? He is shattered to hear that the inhabitants have either left or have locked themselves into their houses, because a mysterious killer is abroad in this happy place, who lures his victims to their death by promising to show them "the photograph of the colonel." The architect, who reveals that he also exercises the functions of a police commissar and those of a doctor, cannot understand Bérenger's horror at his revelation. After all, the world is full of misery: "Children murdered, starved old men, widows in distress, orphans, people in agony, judicial errors, houses that collapse on their inhabitants . . . mountains that come down in landslides . . . massacres, floods, dogs run over by cars—that's how the journalists earn their daily bread." Bérenger is appalled. And when news comes that among the latest victims is Mlle. Dany, the architect's young secretary, whom he had just met and with whom he had fallen in love, he resolves to track down the killer.

The second act opens in Bérenger's dingy room, where a visitor, Edouard, is silently waiting for him. Outside we hear the voices of the inhabitants of the block conversing in absurd fragments of small talk: a teacher giving a nonsensical history lesson; an efficiency expert calculating the money to be saved by stopping employees from going to the lavatory five times each day and making them concentrate these natural functions into one session of four and a half hours per month instead; old men talking of old times—a whole symphony of grotesque snippets of talk that take up and expand the voices on the landing heard offstage in *Amédée*. Bérenger returns, tells Edouard the horrible news about the killer, and is astonished to find that Edouard, in fact everybody, has long known about him, that everyone is used to the idea that such a killer is abroad. Edouard's briefcase opens and is revealed to contain the implements of the killer—the knickknacks he pretends to be selling, stacks of photos of a colonel, even the killer's identity card. Edouard says he must have picked up the briefcase by mistake, but mysteriously he has further evidence in his coat pocket—the diary of the killer, a map on which the exact spots of past and even future murders are marked. Bérenger wants to go to the police. Edouard is reluctant. Finally they go, but Edouard leaves the briefcase behind.

In the street a political meeting is in progress; a monstrous woman, *la mère Pipe*, described as the keeper of the public geese and resembling Bérenger's concierge, makes a speech composed of totalitarian clichés. In the world after her victory, everything will be different, at least in name, although the substance of things will remain the same. Tyranny will then be called liberty, occupation will be called liberation. A drunk interrupts the speech; he represents the opposite (Ionesco's own) point of view—the real revolution, he argues, as Ionesco did in his final reply to Tynan, is made not by politicians but by artists and thinkers like Einstein, Breton, Kandinsky, Picasso, who change mankind's way of seeing and thinking. In a Punch and Judy fight, the drunk is knocked out. Bérenger discovers that the briefcase has been lost. In a nightmare sequence, he tries to wrest similar briefcases from the hands of passers-by, attempts to interest the police in finding the killer, but the police have more important things to do. They have to control the traffic.

Bérenger is alone. He walks through the empty streets, the décor changing as he progresses. Suddenly he finds himself face to face with a grinning, giggling dwarf in shabby clothes. He knows that this is the killer. In a long speech (covering about ten closely printed pages in the French edition), Bérenger tries to persuade the killer, who is obviously a degenerate idiot, to desist from his murderous and senseless activity. He uses every known argument for philanthropy and goodness—patriotism, self-interest, social responsibility, Christianity, reason, the vanity of all activity, even that of murder. The killer never speaks a word, he merely giggles idiotically. In the end Bérenger pulls out two old guns and tries to kill the killer but he cannot do it. He drops the guns and silently submits to the killer's raised knife.

In a note, Ionesco underlines the intention of this last scene, which, as he says, "is a short act in itself." The speech should be presented in a manner designed "to bring out the gradual breaking down of Bérenger, his falling apart and the vacuity of his own rather commonplace morality, which collapses like a leaking balloon. In fact Bérenger finds within himself, in spite of himself and against his own will, arguments in favor of the killer."[69] The killer (who, Ionesco suggests in a stage direction, might not be seen at all, only his giggle being heard in the shadows), represents the inevitability of death, the absurdity of human existence itself. This is the murderous presence that lurks behind even the most euphoric moods of lightness and radiant happiness and turns them back into the cold, gray rainy November of our everyday existence.

In the first act, Bérenger describes at length the experience the *cité radieuse* expresses—the warmth that in former times used to fill his soul from within, the indescribable feeling of euphoria and light that made him cry out with joy, "I am, I am, everything is, everything is!" And then suddenly a feeling of emptiness invaded his soul as at the moment of a tragic separation, "old women came out of their courtyards and pierced my ears with their loud, vulgar voices; dogs barked; and I felt myself abandoned among all these people, all these things." This is the mood we are presented with in the second act in the symphony of gossiping voices in the courtyard, and later in the horrible political meeting, in the traffic regulated by policemen. It is the realization, accepted by everybody else —that life is futile in the face of inevitable death—which changes euphoria into depression. Death is the photograph of the colonel, which exercises such a fatal fascination on the killer's victims. No argument of morality or expediency can prevail against the half-witted, idiotic futility of the human condition.

Once again the whole play elaborates a single poetic image, but this time its power is sustained and deepened as the action proceeds and, in contrast to the decline of tension in the third act of *Amédée*, the final scene of *Tueur Sans Gages* is so brilliant a tour de force that it is capable of forming a climax even after the astonishing poetic invention of the *cité radieuse* in the first scene.

It is significant that the last brilliant speech is hardly foreshadowed in the short story that was the germ of the play. There the hero merely realizes that "no words, friendly or authoritative, could have convinced him; all the promise of happiness, all the love in the world, could not have reached him; beauty would not have made him relent, nor irony have shamed him, nor all the wise men in the world make him comprehend the vanity of crime as well as charity." The translation of this brief paragraph into a breathtakingly dramatic speech shows Ionesco's immense power as a dramatist.

There is another element not present in the short story of

1955 that occupies an important place in the play of 1957—the political meeting and the argument about the true revolution. This is a measure of Ionesco's growing preoccupation with the polemic against his Left Wing critics. It might be argued that the introduction of this anti-political—but for that very reason itself political—element distracts from the main poetic image of the play. After all, the *cité radieuse* of the opening scene is a more powerful argument for the same position. It is an image of a world in which all social problems have been solved, all irritation eliminated; and yet, even there, the presence of death makes life futile and absurd. On the other hand, the crowd scenes, with their nightmare tumult and agitation, are a legitimate extension of the images of proliferation and heaviness in Bérenger's diagnosis of his depressive mood.

Tueur Sans Gages was staged with considerable success at the Théâtre Récamier in February, 1959. When it reached New York in April, 1960, it met with less understanding and had to close after a few performances. Brooks Atkinson found the third act "bad theatre writing" because the last scene is static and therefore "unbearable nervously as well as esthetically."[70] Yet this is precisely what the scene is supposed to be—unbearable. For in spite of its being laced with a bitter, farcically tragic humor, Ionesco's is a far harsher convention of the theatre than one based on mere pleasantness. The mixture of the farcical and the tragic also confronts the public with an entirely new convention; no wonder Brooks Atkinson found the play an accumulation of "helter-skelter gibes." Within its own terms of reference, *Tueur Sans Gages* is a work of classical purity of style as well as language—at least in the original French.

Tueur Sans Gages, moreover, is not only based on a brilliant over-all conception, it is full of the most felicitous touches of detail: the *cité radieuse*, for example, has such perfect built-in sunshine that to produce plants that need rain, special glass houses have to be provided. The architect, showing Bérenger round the new quarter, continues his office routine on a telephone he casually pulls out of his pocket. The architect's secretary, Mlle. Dany, cannot stand her office routine and decides to quit. This is the reason for her murder—the killer does not attack municipal employees, and by choosing freedom she chooses death. But the architect merely shrugs his shoulders at people's mania, "the mania of the victims always to return to the place of the crime." Among the killer's implements in Edouard's briefcase there is a box that has another box inside it, which in turn has another inside it, and so on ad infinitum. In the crowd at the political meeting, a little old man asks the way to the Danube, although he is aware of being in Paris and is in fact a Parisian. All this is a wealth of invention that helps to conjure up Ionesco's own peculiar world of nightmare, Chaplinesque humor, and wistful tenderness. *Tueur Sans Gages* must rank as one of the major works of the Theatre of the Absurd.

Before *Tueur Sans Gages* had its first stage performance, Ionesco revealed that he had completed another full-length play, *Rhinocéros*. On November 25, 1958, he gave a public reading of the third act at the *Vieux-Colombier*, after having told the audience that "a play is made to be acted, not to be read. If I were you, I should not have come." By the following spring the play had appeared in book form (but in a note in the *Cahiers du Collège de Pataphysique*,[71] Ionesco insisted that his publishers had got the title wrong by calling the play *Le Rhinocéros* instead of simply *Rhinocéros*). On August 20, 1959, the play, already translated into English by Derek Prouse, had its first performance—on the radio, in the B.B.C.'s Third Programme; on November 6, it had its world première on the stage in Düsseldorf; on January 25, 1960, it opened at the Odéon in Paris, directed and acted by Jean-Louis Barrault, and on April 28, of the same year at the Royal Court in London, directed by Orson Welles, with Sir Laurence Olivier as Bérenger. The era of Ionesco's international acceptance as a major figure in the theatre undoubtedly dawned with *Rhinocéros*.

Rhinocéros again has Bérenger as its hero—inexplicably, if we assume that Bérenger was killed at the end of *Tueur Sans Gages;* an assumption, however, that is by no means a certainty, for, after all, the short story *The Photograph of the Colonel* is narrated in the first person singular, proof that its hero lived to tell the tale, and in the play the curtain falls before any fatal blow has been struck. But these pataphysical speculations are in vain if the character of Bérenger in the two plays is compared, for then a subtle difference between the two is certain to be detected. The Bérenger of *Rhinocéros* is less somber, though more dissipated; more poetical, though less idealistic than the Bérenger of *Tueur Sans Gages*. While the latter lives in Paris, the former inhabits a small provincial city. In short, they are not necessarily the same person; or it may be that the Bérenger of *Rhinocéros* is a younger Bérenger, in an earlier phase of his career.

The Bérenger of *Rhinocéros* works (as Ionesco did at one time) in the production department of a firm of law publishers. He is in love with a colleague, Mlle. Daisy (whose name curiously resembles that of the first Bérenger's love, Dany); he has a friend named Jean. On a Sunday morning the two are involved in an incident in which one, or perhaps two, rhinos are observed, or believed to be observed, charging down the main street of the town. Gradually more and more rhinos appear. They are the inhabitants who have been infected by a mysterious disease, rhinoceritis, which not only makes them change into rhinos but actually makes them want to turn themselves into these strong, aggressive, and insensitive pachyderms. At the end, only Bérenger and Daisy remain human in the whole town, then even Daisy cannot resist the temptation of doing what came naturally to all the others. Bérenger is left alone, the last human being, and defiantly proclaims his intention never to capitulate.

It has been said that *Rhinocéros* represents Ionesco's feelings before he left Rumania in 1938, when more and more of his acquaintances adhered to the Fascist movement of the Iron Guard. As he himself has said, "As usual, I went back to my personal obsessions. I remembered that in the course of my life I have been very much struck by what one might call the current of opinion, by its rapid evolution, its power of contagion, which is that of a real epidemic. People allow themselves suddenly to be invaded by a new religion, a doctrine, a fanaticism. . . . At such moments we witness a veritable mental mutation. I don't know if you have noticed it, but when people no longer share your opinions, when you can no longer make yourself understood by them, one has the impression of being confronted with monsters—rhinos, for example. They have that mixture of candor and ferocity. They would kill you with the best of consciences. And history has shown us during the last quarter of a century that people thus transformed not only resemble rhinos, but really become rhinoceroses."[72]

During the first performance at the Düsseldorf Schauspielhaus, the German audience instantly recognized the arguments used by the characters who feel they must follow the trend as those they themselves had heard, or used, at a time when people in Germany could not resist the lure of Hitler. Some of the characters in the play opt for a pachydermatous existence because they admire brute force and the simplicity that springs from the suppression of overtender humanistic feelings; others do so because one can try to win the rhinos back to humanity only by learning to understand their way of thinking; still others, notably Daisy, simply cannot bear being different from the majority. Rhinoceritis is not only the disease of the totalitarians of the Right as well as of the Left, it is also the pull of conformism. *Rhinocéros* is a witty play. It abounds in brilliant touches, and—unlike most plays by Ionesco—it seems easily understood. The London *Times* headed its review of *Rhinocéros*, "Ionesco Play All Easily Comprehensible."[73]

Yet, is it really as easily comprehensible as all that? As Bernard Francueil pointed out in an ingenious article in the *Cahiers du Collège de Pataphysique*,[74] Bérenger's final confession of faith and his previous assertions of the superiority of human beings over rhinos curiously resemble the cries of "Long live the white race!" in *L'Avenir Est dans les Œufs* and in *Victimes du Devoir*. If we examine Bérenger's final reasoning with his friend Dudard, we find that he defends his desire to remain human with the same recourse to *instinctive* feelings that he condemns in the rhinos, and when he notices this error, he merely corrects himself by replacing instinct with intuition. Moreover, at the very end, Bérenger bitterly regrets that he seems unable to change into a rhinoceros! His final defiant profession of faith in humanity is merely the expression of the fox's contempt for the grapes he could not have. Far from being a heroic last stand, Bérenger's defiance is farcical and tragicomic, and the final meaning of the play is by no means as simple as some critics made it appear. What the play conveys is the absurdity of defiance as much as the absurdity of conformism, the tragedy of the individualist who cannot join the happy throng of less sensitive people, the artist's feeling as an outcast, which forms the theme of writers like Kafka and Thomas Mann. In a sense, Bérenger's situation at the end of *Rhinocéros* resembles that of the victim of another metamorphosis, Kafka's Gregor Samsa. Samsa was transformed into a giant bug while the rest of humanity remained normal; Bérenger, having become the last human being, is in exactly the same position as Samsa, for now that being a rhinoceros is normal, to be human is a monstrosity. In his last speech, Bérenger deplores the whiteness and flabbiness of his skin and longs for the hardness and dark-green color of the pachyderm's armor. "I am a monster, just a monster," he cries, before he finally decides to make a stand for humanity.

If *Rhinocéros* is a tract against conformism and insensitivity (which it certainly is), it also mocks the individualist who merely makes a virtue of necessity in insisting on his superiority as a sensitive, artistic being. That is where the play transcends the oversimplification of propaganda and becomes a valid statement of the fatal entanglement, the basic inescapability and absurdity of the human condition. Only a performance that brings out this ambivalence in Bérenger's final stand can do justice to the play's full flavor.

After ten years as a playwright, Ionesco has been drawn into the mid-twentieth-century rat race of success. He has become a much-traveled man, addressing an international congress on the avant-garde theatre at Helsinki, opening a new theatre with a performance of one of his plays in Brazil, lecturing at Copenhagen, writing the narration for an avant-gardist Polish cartoon-film (*Monsieur Tête*, winner of the Prix de la Critique at the Tours Festival of 1959), discussing the writing of a musical with an American producer.

It is a sure sign of real genius that it remains unspoiled by success. Ionesco has certainly remained unchanged—a smiling little man with a clown's face and large, round, sad eyes; friendly, accessible, eager to help the importunate seeker for information he must have given to dozens of others, and continuing to translate his fears and fantasies into the concrete poetry of the stage. However trifling some of his products may be in length, they have the authentic Ionesco charm—the little

sketch *Scène à Quatre,* for example (performed at the Spoleto
Festival in June, 1959),[75] which seems to have been intended
as a kind of anticipation of a summit meeting and, as it turned
out, was uncannily prophetic. The short scene shows three
gentlemen—Dupont, Durand, and Martin—each dressed like
the other, engaged in heated but completely pointless argument, in which the only recognizable idea is the warning, *"Attention aux pots de fleurs!"* ("Be careful with the flowerpots!").
When a beautiful lady appears on the scene, all three try to
introduce her as their fiancée and to present a flowerpot
to her. As a result, all the flowerpots are broken, and the lady
is severely mauled and her clothes torn off. Was the beautiful
lady intended to represent peace?

Another trifling but charming creation by Ionesco is his first
ballet, performed with choreography by Deryk Mendel, the
interpreter of Beckett's mimeplays, at the Théâtre de l'Etoile
in April, 1960. It is called *Apprendre à Marcher,* and shows a
young man who collapses and is won back from paralysis in a
wheelchair, to the full use of his limbs and virtuosity as a
dancer, by a beautiful nurse. The hospital has changed into
a luminous garden. The nurse wants to embrace the young
man she has taught to walk and to dance, but he ascends an
endless staircase of light that has opened up in the back, and
disappears from view. The nurse is heartbroken; indignantly
the doctor makes her put on her nurse's uniform again.

While traveling from capital to capital and writing such
charming trifles, Ionesco continued to work on his next major
play, in which Bérenger is again the principal character. Again
it is a play in one long act. It shows Bérenger as the king of
a dream country and ends with his death.

Ionesco's flowering into a dramatist of world-wide fame has
been an astonishing phenomenon. He did not begin writing
The Bald Soprano until he was thirty-six. It is a case of a
long-pent-up power of expression, which had been seeking for
the right form, suddenly finding its true medium—dialogue.
The ready-made dialogue of the English primer revealed to
Ionesco where his true vocation lay—in the theatre that he had
disliked hitherto, precisely because its prevailing convention
ran counter to his own personal dramatic perceptions and in-

tuitions. He had been *writing* all his life, as he confesses in the fragment of his diaries for 1939 that has been published,[76] but the reflections and notes he put down did not amount to more than a personal record. Yet in the same extract from Ionesco's diary we already find him jotting down the idea for a dramatic sketch—a woman talking to a man offstage, and enacting what is obviously a highly emotional scene entirely in fragments of clichés and repetitions of the same stereotyped phrases, without the reader (or spectator) ever knowing what is actually at issue. This short sketch shows that Ionesco's mind was running along the lines of his later dramatic writing ten years before his encounter with the *Assimil* method finally sparked off his latent powers as a dramatist.

Ionesco is a highly intuitive writer. He himself described his method of work in a slightly bantering and exaggerated, but nevertheless convincing, way when he said:

> It is obviously difficult to write a play; it requires considerable physical effort. One has to get up, which is tiresome, one has to sit down, just when one had got used to the idea of standing up, one has to take a pen, which is heavy, one has to get some paper, which one cannot find, one has to sit at a table, which often breaks down under the weight of one's elbows. . . . It is relatively easy, on the other hand, to compose a play without writing it down. It is easy to imagine it, to dream it, stretched out on the couch between sleep and waking. One only has to let oneself go, without moving, without controlling oneself. A character emerges, one does not know whence; he calls others. The first character starts talking, the first retort is made, the first note has been struck, the rest follows automatically. One remains passive, one listens, one watches what is happening on the inner screen. . . .[77]

Ionesco regards spontaneity as an important creative element. "I have no ideas before I write a play. I have them when I have written the play or while I am not writing at all. I believe that artistic creation is spontaneous. It certainly is so for me."[78] But this does not mean that he considers his writing to be meaningless or without significance. On the contrary, the workings of the spontaneous imagination are a cognitive process, an exploration. "Fantasy is revealing; it is a method of cognition: everything that is imagined is true; nothing is true if it is not imagined."[79] Everything that springs from the imagination expresses a psychological reality: "Because the artist apprehends reality directly, he is a true philosopher. And it is from the range, the depth and the sharpness of his truly philosophical vision that his greatness springs."[80]

The spontaneity of the creative vision is in itself an instrument of philosophical exploration and discovery. But spontaneity does not mean artlessness; the true artist has mastered his technical means to such an extent that he can apply them without conscious reflection, just as a good ballet dancer has so thoroughly mastered the technique of dancing that she can concentrate wholly on expressing the music and the feelings of the character she portrays. Ionesco is far from neglecting the formal aspects of playwriting—he is a master craftsman and a classicist. He believes that "the aim of the avant-garde should be to rediscover—not invent—in their purest state the permanent forms and forgotten ideals of the theatre. We must cut through the clichés and break free from a hidebound 'traditionalism'; we must rediscover the one true and living tradition."[81]

This is why Ionesco is preoccupied with isolating the "pure" elements of theatre, with discovering and laying bare the mechanism of action even if it is devoid of sense. This is why, although he does not like Labiche, he is fascinated by Feydeau and was astonished to find some similarities to his own plays in Feydeau's farces—"not in the subject matter but in the rhythm. In the organization of a play like *La Puce à l'Oreille*, for example, there is a kind of acceleration of movement, a progression, a kind of madness. In it one might discover the essence of theatre, or at least the essence of the comic. . . . For, if Feydeau pleases, it is not for his ideas (he has none) nor for the stories of his characters (they are silly); it is this madness, this seemingly regulated mechanism that, however, comes apart through its very progression and acceleration."[82]

Ionesco compares his classicism, his attempt to rediscover "the mechanism of the theatre in its pure state" with this principle of acceleration in Feydeau's farces: "In *The Lesson*, for example, there is no story, but there is a progression nevertheless. I try to bring about a progression by a kind of progressive condensation of states of mind, of a feeling, a situation, an anxiety. The text is merely a pretext for the acting of the cast, starting from the comic toward a progressive heightening. The text is merely a prop, a pretext for this intensification."[83] From *The Bald Soprano* to *Rhinocéros*, this condensation and intensification of the action represent the basic formal principle, the shape of Ionesco's plays, in contrast to those of Beckett and Adamov (until his breach with the Theatre of the Absurd), which have a circular shape, returning to the initial situation or to its equivalent, a zero point from which the preceding action is seen to be futile, so that it would have made no difference if it had never happened. It is true that *The Bald Soprano* and *The Lesson* end as they started—with the Martins (or, in the Paris production, the Smiths) beginning to speak the same dialogue we heard at the beginning of the play, and with a new pupil arriving for a new lesson. But in the case of *The Bald Soprano* this ending is an afterthought; Ionesco's original intention was to top the pandemonium of the final scene by a direct aggression against the audience. And in *The Lesson* we know that the forty-first pupil of that day will be murdered in the same frenzied fashion as the fortieth—that there will be another inevitable, and even more frenzied, climax. This in fact is the pattern of most of Ionesco's plays: we find the same acceleration and accumulation in the obscene final frenzy of *Jacques* as well as in the growing proliferation of furniture in *The New Tenant*, in the more and more crowded room in *The Chairs*, and in the growing number of transformations in *Rhinocéros*.

Intensification, accumulation, and progression, however, must not, Ionesco insists, be confounded with the storyteller's endeavor to build action toward a climax. In the narrative, the climax leads toward the final solution of a problem. And Ionesco detests "the reasoning play, constructed like a syllogism, of which the last scenes constitute the logical conclusion of the introductory scenes, considered as premises."[84] Ionesco repudiates the well-made, storytelling play:

I do not write plays to tell a story. The theatre cannot be epic . . . because it is dramatic. For me, a play does not

consist in the description of the development of such a story—
that would be writing a novel or a film. A play is a structure
that consists of a series of states of consciousness, or situations, which become intensified, grow more and more dense,
then get entangled, either to be disentangled again or to end
in unbearable inextricability.[85]

To the elegant, logical construction of the well-made play,
Ionesco opposes, instead, the demand for intensity, the gradual
heightening of psychological tensions. To bring this about, the
author, in Ionesco's view, is bound by no rule or restraint:

> Everything is permitted in the theatre: to bring characters
> to life, but also to materialize states of anxiety, inner pres-
> ences. It is thus not only permitted, but advisable, to make
> the properties join in the action, to make objects live,
> to animate the décor, to make symbols concrete. Just as
> words are continued by gesture, action, mime, which, at the
> moment when words become inadequate, take their place,
> the material elements of the stage can in turn further
> intensify these.[86]

Language is thus reduced to a relatively minor function.
According to Ionesco, the theatre cannot hope to challenge
those forms of expression in which language is entirely autonomous—the discursive speech of philosophy, the descriptive
language of poetry or fiction. For this, he argues, the use
of language in the theatre is too narrowly circumscribed to
language as "dialogue, words in combat, in conflict."[87] But
language is regarded not as an end in itself but as merely one
element among many in the theatre; the author can treat it
freely, he can make the action contradict the text, or can let
the language of the characters disintegrate altogether. And
this too is a device serving the pattern of intensification that
underlies Ionesco's theatre. Language can be turned into
theatrical material by "carrying it to its paroxysm. To give the
theatre its true measure, which lies in going to excess, the
words themselves must be stretched to their utmost limits, the
language must be made almost to explode, or to destroy itself
in its inability to contain its meanings."[88]

The pattern of Ionesco's plays is one of intensification, ac-

celeration, accumulation, proliferation to the point of paroxysm, when psychological tension reaches the unbearable—the
pattern of orgasm. It must be followed by a release that
relieves the tension and substitutes a feeling of serenity. This
liberation takes the form of laughter. And that is why Ionesco's
plays are comic.

"As far as I am concerned," says Ionesco, "I have never been
able to understand the difference that is made between the
comic and the tragic. As the comic is the intuition of the absurd,
it seems to me more conducive to despair than the tragic.
The comic offers no way out. I say 'conducive to despair,' but
in reality it is beyond despair or hope."[89] But this is precisely
the liberating effect of laughter: "Humor makes us conscious,
with a free lucidity, of the tragic or desultory condition of man.
. . . It is not only the critical spirit itself . . . but . . . humor
is the only possibility we possess of detaching ourselves—yet
only after we have surmounted, assimilated, taken cognizance
of it—from our tragicomic human condition, the malaise of being. To become conscious of what is horrifying and to laugh
at it is to become master of that which is horrifying. . . .
Logic reveals itself in the illogicality of the absurd of which
we have become aware. Laughter alone does not respect any
taboo, laughter alone inhibits the creation of new anti-taboo
taboos; the comic alone is capable of giving us the strength to
bear the tragedy of existence. The true nature of things,
truth itself, can be revealed to us only by fantasy, which is
more realistic than all the realisms."[90]

Yet if Ionesco again and again insists on the exploratory,
cognitive function of his theatre, one must always keep in mind
what *kind* of cognition it is he wants to communicate. Bewildered critics first confronted with a Ionesco play like *The
Chairs* or *The Killer* are apt to ask what these plays seek to
demonstrate; after all, we all *know* that people have difficulty
in communicating their personal experience, we know that
death is inevitable. Once the audience has realized what the
author is driving at, the play should end. But it is not the
conceptual, formulated *moral* that Ionesco tries to communicate, it is his experience, *what it feels like* to be in the situations concerned. It is precisely against the fallacy that the
fruits of human experience can be transmitted in the form

of pre-packed, neatly formulated conceptual pills that his theatre is directed. That is why his criticism, his savage satire, tries to destroy the rationalistic fallacy that language alone, language divorced from experience, can communicate human experience from one person to another. This, if it can be done at all, can be accomplished only through the creative act of the artist, the poet who can transmit something of his own experience by making another human being capable of feeling what the artist, the poet had himself experienced.

No amount of clinical description can convey what it feels like, let us say, to be in love. A young person may have been told, may think he knows what it will be like, but when he really does have the experience, he will realize that any merely intellectual knowledge of it was not knowledge in any real sense. A poem, on the other hand, or a piece of music, can convey, to however limited an extent, the reality of feeling and experience. In the same way, Ionesco in a play like *The Killer* is not, as some critics thought, trying to tell us through three long acts that death is inevitable, he is trying to make us experience with him *what it feels like* to be grappling with this basic human experience; what it feels like when at the end we have to face the harsh truth that there is no argument, no rationalization that can remove that stark, final fact of life. When Bérenger, at the end, submits to the knife of the killer, he has finally fought through to the recognition that we must face death without evasion, prettification, or rationalization—and this is the equivalent of a mystical experience. It is true that the other characters in the play, the architect or Edouard, also accept the presence of the killer in their midst as inevitable. The difference is that they do so out of thoughtlessness, lack of imagination, superficial complacency; they have not grasped what it means to experience the presence of death, and, failing to face the issue of death, they are not fully alive. To wake up the audience, to deepen their awareness of the human condition, to make them experience what Bérenger experiences is the real purpose of Ionesco's play.

We do not expect to receive new information in a poem; a moving poem on time or the inevitability of death is not rejected by critics merely because it is not telling us any new truths. Ionesco's theatre is a poetic theatre, a theatre concerned with the communication of the experience of states of being, which are the most difficult matters to communicate; for language, consisting largely of prefabricated, congealed symbols, tends to obscure rather than to reveal personal experience. Whan A. says, "I am in love," B. will understand by it merely what *he* has experienced, or expects to experience, which may be something entirely different in kind and intensity, and so A., instead of having communicated *his* sense of being, has merely triggered off B.'s own mode of feeling. No real communication has taken place. Both remain imprisoned, as before, in their own experience. That is why Ionesco has spoken of his own work as an attempt to communicate the incommunicable.

If, however, language, because it is conceptual, and therefore schematic and generalized, and because it has hardened into depersonalized and fossilized clichés, is a hindrance rather than a means toward such genuine communication, the breakthrough into the other human being's consciousness of the poet's mode of feeling and experience has to be attempted on a more basic level, the pre- or sub-verbal level of elementary human experience. This is what the use of imagery and symbolism achieves in lyrical poetry, combined with such elements as rhythm, tonal quality, and association of words. In Ionesco's theatre the same approach is attempted through the use of basic human situations that will evoke a direct and almost physical response, such as Punch hitting the policeman in the puppet show, circus clowns falling off chairs, or the characters in a silent film throwing custard pies into each other's faces. All these evoke a direct, visceral response in audiences. And by combining such basically evocative emotional images into more and more complex structures, Ionesco gradually forges his theatre into an instrument for the transmission of more complex basic human situations and experiences.

In this he may not always be equally successful, but in plays like *The Lesson, The Chairs, Jacques,* the first two acts of *Amédée, The New Tenant,* and *Victims of Duty* he has triumphantly succeeded in putting his own experience on the stage and getting it across to the audience. It may be true that, on the whole, such basic, though multivalent and com-

plex, states of mind lend themselves better to brief statement
in the form of one-act plays or even sketches than to full-length
plays. Yet a play like *The Killer* shows that it is possible to
interweave a number of such basic images of experience into
a more complex structure. *Rhinocéros,* which also shows
Ionesco's ability to sustain a longer form, is perhaps too much
of a tract, too closely approximating to a *pièce à thèse,* to
serve as an argument in this context.

Of course, the traditional theatre too has always been an
instrument for communicating the basic experiences of humanity. But this element has often been subordinated to other
functions, such as the telling of a story or the discussion of
ideas. Ionesco is attempting to isolate this one element—which
he regards as the one that constitutes the theatre's supreme
achievement, and in which it excels all other forms of artistic
expression—and to restore a *pure,* entirely theatrical theatre.

The technical inventiveness Ionesco displays in trying to
achieve his end is truly astonishing. In *The Bald Soprano*
alone, his first and in many ways simplest play, Alain Bosquet
has isolated no fewer than thirty-six "recipes of the comic,"[91]
ranging from the negation of action (i.e., scenes in which nothing happens), loss of identity of characters, the misleading title, mechanical surprise, repetition, pseudo-exoticism,
pseudo-logic, abolition of chronological sequence, the proliferation of doubles (i.e., a whole family all called Bobby Watson),
loss of memory, melodramatic surprise (the maid says, "I am
Sherlock Holmes"), coexistence of opposing explanations for
the same thing, discontinuity of dialogue, and the raising of
false expectations, to purely stylistic devices like cliché, truism,
onomatopoeia, Surrealist proverbs, nonsense use of foreign
languages, and complete loss of sense, the degeneration of
language into pure assonance and sound patterns.

A good many other characteristic devices from Ionesco's
later plays could be added to this list—above all, the animation and proliferation of objects, the loss of homogeneity of
individual characters who change their natures in front of our
eyes, the various mirror effects in which the play itself becomes
an object of discussion within the play, the use of offstage
dialogue to suggest the isolation of the individual in a sea of
irrelevant small talk, the loss of distinction between animate

and inanimate objects, the contradiction between the implied description and actual appearance of characters (the young girl who is in fact a mustachioed gentleman, in *Maid to Marry;* the genius who has no head, in *The Leader*), the use of on-stage metamorphosis (in *The Picture* and *Rhinocéros*), and a host of others.

What, then, are the basic situations and experiences that Ionesco wants to communicate by the use of this wealth of comic—and tragicomic—invention? Ionesco's theatre has two fundamental themes, which often coexist in the same play. The lesser of these is the protest against the deadliness of present-day mechanical, bourgeois civilization, the loss of real, *felt* values, and the resulting degradation of life. Ionesco attacks a world that has lost its metaphysical dimension, in which human beings no longer feel a sense of mystery, of reverent awe in facing their own existence. Behind the violent mockery of fossilized language, there stands a plea for the restoration of a poetic concept of life:

> When I wake up, on a morning of grace, from my nocturnal sleep as well as from the mental sleep of routine, and I suddenly become aware of my existence and of the universal presence, so that everything appears strange, and at the same time familiar to me, when the astonishment of being invades me—these sentiments, this intuition belong to all men, of all times. We can find this state of mind expressed in almost the same words by all poets, mystics, philosophers, who feel it in exactly the same way I do. . . .[92]

But if Ionesco savagely assails a mode of life that has banished mystery from existence, this does not mean that he regards a full awareness of the implications of human existence as a state of euphoria. On the contrary, the intuition of being that he tries to communicate is one of despair. The main themes that recur in his plays are those of the loneliness and isolation of the individual, his difficulty in communicating with others, his subjection to degrading outside pressures, to the mechanical conformity of society as well as to the equally degrading internal pressures of his own personality—sexuality and the ensuing feelings of guilt, the anxieties arising from the uncertainty of one's own identity and the certainty of death.

If the basic pattern in Beckett's plays is pairs of interdependent, complementary personalities, and in Adamov's theatre pairs of contrasting extrovert-introvert men, Ionesco's most frequently recurring basic pattern is the married couple, the family—Mr. and Mrs. Smith, Amédée and Madeleine, Choubert and his Madeleine, the old man and his wife in *The Chairs*, the Jacques family in *Jacques* and *The Future Is in Eggs*, the professor and his maid (who is both wife and mother to him) in *The Lesson*, the rich man and his sister in *The Picture*. In this basic pattern, the woman usually plays the part of an admiring, but nagging, supporter of the husband. In Ionesco's later plays, Bérenger is a lonely and isolated individual, but he is also, in each case, in love with the ideal of an understanding young workingwoman, Dany-Daisy, who combines grace, beauty, and *savoir-faire*.

Ionesco's characters may be isolated and lonely in a metaphysical sense, but they are by no means the tramps and outcasts of Beckett and Adamov, and this, in some sense, increases the despair and absurdity of their isolation—they are lonely in spite of being members of what ought to be an organic community. Yet, as we see above all in *Jacques*, the family is the agent of society's pressures toward conformity, which not even the sweet and loving Daisy can resist in *Rhinocéros*.

Nevertheless, the presence of companionship and family relationships lightens the despair of Ionesco's world. It would be wrong to regard his attitude as wholly pessimistic. He wants to make existence authentic, fully lived, by putting man face to face with the harsh realities of the human condition. But this is also the way to liberation. "To attack the absurdity (of the human condition) is," Ionesco once said, "a way of stating the possibility of non-absurdity. . . . For where else would there be a point of reference? . . . In Zen Buddhism there was no direct teaching, only the constant search for an opening, a revelation. Nothing makes me more pessimistic than the obligation not to be pessimistic. I feel that every message of despair is the statement of a situation from which everybody must freely try to find a way out."[93]

The very statement of the desperate situation, the ability it gives the spectator to face it with open eyes, constitutes a catharsis, a liberation. Are not Oedipus and Lear confronted

with the full despair and absurdity of their human condition?
Yet their tragedies are liberating experiences.

Ionesco himself has always opposed the idea that, as an
avant-garde author, he stands outside the main stream of
tradition. He insists that the avant-garde is a mere rediscovery
of submerged parts of the main tradition. And so, while he
admits that Corneille bores him, that he finds Schiller unbearable, Marivaux futile, Musset thin, Vigny unactable, Victor
Hugo ridiculous, Labiche unfunny, Dumas *fils* laughably
sentimental, Oscar Wilde facile, Ibsen heavy, Strindberg
clumsy, Pirandello outmoded, Giraudoux and Cocteau superficial, he does see himself as part of a tradition including
Sophocles and Aeschylus, Shakespeare, Kleist, and Buechner,
precisely because these authors are concerned with the human
condition in all its brutal absurdity.

Only time can show to what extent Ionesco will become
part of the main stream of the great tradition. What is certain,
however, is that his work constitutes a truly heroic attempt to
break through the barriers of human communication.

Chapter Four

JEAN GENET: A HALL OF MIRRORS

In the most personal of his books, the autobiographical *Journal du Voleur* (*The Thief's Journal*), Jean Genet describes how he once came across Stilitano, the tall, handsome, one-handed Serbian pimp, thief, and drug peddler who was one of the heroes of his youth, lost in a hall of mirrors on a fairground. It was one of those labyrinths constructed partly of mirrors, partly of panes of transparent glass that are arranged in such a way that the crowd outside can watch the antics of those who are trying to find their way out of the maze. And so Genet could observe Stilitano caught like a trapped animal, could see, but not hear, him uttering enraged curses while the large throng of bystanders outside were splitting their sides with laughter:

> Stilitano was alone. Everyone had found the way out except he. Strangely the universe veiled itself for me. The shadow that suddenly fell over things and people was the shadow of my solitude confronted with this despair, for, no longer able to shout, to butt himself against the walls of glass, resigned at being a mockery for the gaping crowd, Stilitano had crouched down on the floor, refusing to go on. . . .[1]

This image of man caught in a maze of mirrors, trapped by the reflections of his own distorted image, trying to find the way to make contact with the others he can see around him but being rudely stopped by barriers of glass (which Genet himself used in his ballet scenario *Adam Miroir*), also sums up the essence of Genet's theatre: a series of plays concerned with expressing his own feeling of helplessness and solitude when confronted with the despair and loneliness of man caught in the hall of mirrors of the human condition, inexorably trapped by an endless progression of images that are merely his own distorted reflection—lies covering lies, fantasies battening upon fantasies, nightmares nourished by nightmares within nightmares.

In the whole long line of *poètes maudits* that runs through French literature, like a red thread, from Villon to Sade to Verlaine, Rimbaud, and Lautréamont, Jean Genet is surely among the most extraordinary. "On the planet Uranus," he writes, "it seems the atmosphere is so heavy . . . that the animals drag themselves about crushed by the weight of the gases. It is with these humiliated creatures always crawling on their bellies that I want to mingle. If in the transmigration of souls I am granted a new dwelling place, I shall choose that cursed planet to inhabit it with the convicts of my race."[2]

Jean Genet was born in Paris on December 19, 1910. He was abandoned by his mother and brought up by peasant foster parents in the Morvan, in the north of the Massif Central. When he reached the age of twenty-one he was given his birth certificate. From it he learned that his mother had been called Gabrielle Genet and that he had been born at 22 Rue d'Assas, behind the Luxembourg Gardens. When he went to find the house, he discovered it was a maternity hospital.

In his monumental study of Genet, surely one of the most astonishing books of our age, Jean-Paul Sartre has described how, at the age of ten, the little boy, who had till then been considered pious and docile, was accused of stealing, and how, being described as a thief, he resolved to *be* a thief. For Sartre this was the great act of existential choice. Genet himself puts the matter in a slightly less philosophical way: "It was not at any particular period of my life that I decided to be a thief. My laziness and my daydreaming having led me to the *maison correctionelle* at Mettray, where I was to stay till I was twenty-one, I escaped, and to gain the signing-up bonus, joined up for five years. After a few days [in the Foreign Legion] I deserted, taking with me the suitcases of some Negro officers. For a time I loved stealing, but prostitution appealed more to my easygoing ways. I was twenty. . . ."[3]

But in the essential point of existential choice, Genet's

account agrees with Sartre's: "Abandoned by my family, I found it natural to aggravate this fact by the love of males, and that love by stealing, and stealing by crime, or the complicity with crime. Thus I decisively repudiated a world that had repudiated me."[4]

Between 1930 and 1940, Genet led the life of an itinerant delinquent. After a stay in the Barrio Chino of Barcelona, among beggars and pimps, he went back to France, made his first acquaintance with French prisons, and then went to Italy. Via Rome, Naples, and Brindisi, he reached Albania. Refused a permit to land at Corfu, he passed into Yugoslavia, Austria, Czechoslovakia. In Poland he tried to pass forged banknotes, was arrested, and eventually expelled. In Hitler's Germany he felt out of place: "Even on Unter den Linden I had a feeling of being in a camp organized by bandits. . . . This is a nation of thieves, I felt. If I steal here, I accomplish no special act that could help me to realize myself. I merely obey the habitual order of things. I do not destroy it."[5] And so he hastened on into a country that still obeyed the conventional moral code and therefore enabled an outlaw to feel himself outside an established order. He went to Antwerp, where he remained for some time before returning to France.

While France was occupied by the Germans, Genet was in and out of prison. It was prison that made him into a poet. Once, he told Sartre, while still on remand, he was, by mistake, given prison clothes and pushed into a cell in which all the other prisoners, also not yet convicted, still had their ordinary clothes. He was thus exposed to ridicule and contempt. Among these prisoners there was one "who made poems to his sister, idiotic and self-pitying poems that were much admired. In the end . . . I declared that I was able to make poems just as good. They dared me and I wrote the *Condamné à Mort*"[6] —a long and solemn elegy dedicated to the memory of Maurice Pilorge, executed for the murder of his friend at the prison of Saint-Brieuc on March 17, 1939.

This poetry has a strange ritualistic, incantatory quality. It has the dark splendor of a religious act, as if the verses were a magic formula by which the dead man could be brought back to life. The same quality is present in the four long prose poems (for they are prose poems rather than novels, as they are most often called) Genet wrote between 1940 and 1948: *Notre-Dame-des-Fleurs* (dated from Fresnes prison, 1942), *Miracle de la Rose* (dated from La Santé and Tourelles prisons, 1943), *Pompes Funèbres,* and *Querelle de Brest.* All these books are in the form of stories set in a world of homosexual outlaws. Yet they are not novels, because, as Genet himself told Sartre, "none of my characters ever makes a decision by himself";[7] in other words, the characters are mere emanations of the whim of their creator. These books are in fact the erotic fantasies of a prisoner, the daydreams of a solitary outcast of society, who is resolved to live up to the pattern he feels society has imposed upon him. No wonder that in these books there is a curious mixture of lyrical beauty and the most sordid subject matter.

"I am reproached," Genet writes in *Journal du Voleur,* "with using properties like fairground shacks, prisons, flowers, the loot of sacrilege, railroad stations, frontiers, opium, sailors, ports, public lavatories, funerals, rooms in slums, in order to obtain mediocre melodramatic effects and to mistake poetry for a facile picturesqueness. What am I to reply? I have already said how much I love the outlaws who have no other beauty except that of their bodies. The properties that have been named are impregnated with the violence of men, with their brutality. . . ."[8]

Genet's narrative prose, erotic, scabrous, scatological, is at the same time highly poetic, with a solemn inverted religious atmosphere—a world literally turned upside down, in which the dedicated pursuit of the abject is carried out with the devotion of sainthood. In his essay entitled, for that very reason, *Saint Genet,* Sartre has gone so far as to draw a comparison between St. Teresa of Avila and Genet, and has reached the conclusion that if sainthood consists of carrying humility to the total acceptance of the sinfulness of the human condition, the annihilation of all pride before the absolute, Genet's claim to sainthood is the better.

Be that as it may, in writing down his erotic fantasies, in transmuting daydreams into written sentences with their own rhythm, color, and inherent demand for objective craftsmanship, Genet learned to master his dream world. As Sartre says, "By infecting us with his evil, Genet delivers himself from it. Each of his books is a cathartic crisis of possession, a psychodrama; it seems as though each book merely reproduced the preceding one, just as his new love affairs merely repeat his former ones. But with each book this possessed man becomes a little more the master of the demon that possesses him. Ten years of literature are equivalent to a psychoanalytic cure."[9]

It is significant that in this process of gradual mastery of his obsessions, Genet progressed from poetry to narrative prose and, finally, to the dramatic form.

This amounts to a progression from the most subjective to the more objective forms of writing. By the time he was completing his *Journal du Voleur* (about 1947), Genet was able to say, "I have been writing books for the last five years. I can say that I have done so with pleasure, but I have finished with it. By writing, I have obtained what I had been looking for. . . ."[10] Since then Genet has written no more prose narratives. But he continues to write plays. And it is only in his plays that he has been able to free himself from purely autobiographical subject matter, the world of prisons and homosexual outlaws.

Genet's first play, *Haute Surveillance* (*Deathwatch*), is still anchored in that world. It is a long one-act play set in a prison cell. Its theme is the one that pervades Genet's narrative prose—the hierarchy of crime. In Genet's daydreams, the prison is the equivalent of a royal palace: "To the prisoner, the prison offers the same sense of security that a royal palace offers to the guest of a king. . . . The rigor of the rules, their narrowness, their precision are of the same essential quality as the etiquette of a royal court, the exquisite but tyrannical politeness of which a guest at court is the object."[11]

For Genet there is also a rigid order in the precedence of the prisoners. In *Deathwatch* the occupant of the highest rung of the ladder is out of sight. He is Boule-de-Neige (Snowball), a convicted murderer, a Negro. The occupants of the cell where the action takes place bathe in the reflected glory of this idol. There are three of them: Yeux-Verts (Green Eyes) is also a murderer, but of lesser rank than Snowball, who murdered for gain, while Green Eyes merely killed a prostitute in a moment when he had lost self-control. Lefranc is a thief, and Maurice, only seventeen years old, a juvenile delinquent. (In the French edition of the play, Green Eyes is described as "very beautiful," Maurice as "small, handsome," and Lefranc as "tall, beautiful." These indications, highly characteristic of Genet, are coyly omitted in the American edition.)

The plot of *Deathwatch* turns on the relationship among the three prisoners. Maurice adores Green Eyes, who knows that he will be convicted of murder and is likely to be executed. Lefranc, who has been writing letters to Green Eyes' wife because Green Eyes himself is illiterate, is jealous of Maurice. He has been using the letters he wrote to Green Eyes' wife to try to seduce her away from her husband, not so much to get her himself as to break her relationship with Green Eyes. When Green Eyes finds out about this, he suggests that either Maurice or Lefranc should kill her after their release, which is due within a matter of days. Which of the two will have the guts to become a murderer for the sake of their idol and risk the guillotine, as he does? But then Green Eyes breaks down. He tells the story of the murder he committed—he killed a prostitute in a sadistic fury he could not help. When the guard brings him a gift of cigarettes from the authentic murderer, Snowball, he bequeaths his wife to the guard. The young hero-worshiper Maurice is deeply disappointed at the disintegration of his hero. To show that he, too, is a really tough, hardened criminal, Lefranc, whom Maurice has taunted with the fact that he will never be one of them ("You are not our kind. You'll never be. Even if you killed a man"),[12] strangles the boy in cold blood. Green Eyes still refuses to regard Lefranc as an authentic killer. "I didn't want [my crime]," he says. "It chose me." Lefranc, on the other hand, insists, "My misfortune comes from something deeper. It comes from myself." Green Eyes wants nothing to do with him. The play ends with Lefranc's realization, "I really am all alone!"

Thus Genet's first play is largely a dramatized form of the type of story he tells in his lyrical narratives about the lives of criminals and convicts. On the surface the play looks like a somewhat heightened and stylized prison epic; it could be the scenario of one of Hollywood's prison movies, except that it is frankly amoral. Yet the author's intention is far from straightforward naturalism. The stage directions at the be-

ginning read: "The entire play unfolds as in a dream. . . .
The movements of the actors should be either heavy or else
extremely and incomprehensibly rapid, like flashes of lightning."[13] In other words, Genet wants to make it clear that
the play is not intended to represent real events, but is a daydream, a prisoner's fantasy come to life, the product of a feverish imagination.

And in its strange, inverted, upside-down way, the subject
of Genet's daydream resembles that of so many of Thomas
Mann's and Kafka's stories. Lefranc is the outcast who tries
to emulate the authentic, instinctive beauty and intuitive belonging together of uncomplicated human beings who simply
are themselves, who do not have to will themselves into being.
But even when he forces himself to overcome his weakness and
accomplishes the act that is to make him their equal, they
reject him. Nothing he can do can make him be accepted.
Green Eyes is illiterate—his misfortune chose him. Lefranc can
read and write—he chooses his misfortune. But it is this consciousness that puts him beyond the pale. It is through being
aware of himself that he is caught, as the man lost in the hall
of mirrors is lost among the reflections of his own image.

Genet's second play, *Les Bonnes* (*The Maids*), his first to
be performed, takes us much deeper into this hall of mirrors.
This is Genet's first work in which he freed himself, at least
outwardly, from the narrow confines of a world of prisoners.

The Maids opens in a Louis XV bedroom in which an elegant lady is being dressed by her maid, whom she calls
Claire. The lady is haughty, the maid servile. But the two visibly taunt each other. In the end the maid slaps the lady. Suddenly an alarm clock rings; in a flash the whole scene collapses. The lady is seen to be no lady at all, but one of two
maids who have been playing at lady and maid in the absence
of the real lady. And in fact the maid who has been called
Claire is not Claire at all but Solange, and it was Claire who
acted the part of the lady, and treated her sister as the lady
treats Claire.

Whenever their lady is out, the two maids enact the fantasy
game of servility and final revolt against her, each playing the
lady in turn. For they are bound to their lady, who is younger
and more beautiful than they, by a mixture of affection, erotic

love, and deep hatred. They have just caused the arrest of Monsieur, the lady's lover, by writing anonymous letters to the police. The telephone rings; Monsieur is out on bail. The maids are terrified. Now their denunciation will be found out. They decide to kill the lady when she returns. They will pour poison into her tea. The lady arrives. They keep the news of Monsieur's release from her, but just as she is about to drink the poisoned tea, she notices that the receiver of the telephone is off, and one of the maids lets the news of Monsieur's release slip out. The lady will no longer drink her tea; she hurries off to meet her lover. The maids are left alone. They resume the game of lady and maid. Claire again plays the lady and demands that she be served the poisoned cup of tea. Solange has once before failed to kill the lady. Now Claire is going to show her courage. She drinks the poison and dies in the role of the lady.

The two maids are linked by the love-hatred of being each other's mirror images. As Claire says, "I'm sick of seeing my image thrown back at me by a mirror, like a bad smell. You're my bad smell."[14] At the same time, in the role of the lady, Claire sees the whole race of servants as the distorting mirror of the upper class: "Your frightened, guilty faces, your puckered elbows, your outmoded clothes, your wasted bodies, only fit for castoffs! You're our distorting mirrors, our loathsome vent, our shame, our dregs!"[15] Thus what they hate seeing reflected in each other is the distorted reflection of the world of the secure masters, which they adore, ape, and loathe.

But Genet's hall of mirrors is even more tortuous. When Louis Jouvet undertook to produce *The Maids* in 1947, Genet at first insisted that the three women who make up the cast be played by men. As he had put it in his very first narrative, *Notre-Dame-des-Fleurs,* "If I ever had to stage a play with women's parts in it, I should insist that these parts should be played by young men, and I would inform the public of it by a poster that would stay attached at the right or left of the set throughout the performance."[16] And so, in fact, the maids and their lady are young men.

As Sartre has pointed out in his brilliant analysis of *The Maids,* the play reproduces almost exactly the situation we find in *Deathwatch.* Monsieur, the absent master criminal, corresponds to Snowball, the absent murderer hero. Madame, whose beauty and wealth are a reflection of Monsieur's glory, stands for Green Eyes, and the two maids represent the two lesser figures, Maurice and Lefranc, who both love and hate to see their own inadequacy reflected in the greater glory of their hero. Just as Lefranc murders Maurice to prove himself the equal of Green Eyes, Claire braves death by forcing Solange to serve her the poisoned cup of tea. We are back in the daydream of the prisoner, the fantasy of the outcast who makes futile efforts to reach the world of acceptance and belonging.

But the lady and her lover, the masters of the maids, do not stand merely for a higher order in the hierarchy of convicts, as Snowball and Green Eyes do in *Deathwatch*. They are also an image of respectable society itself, the closed world of *les justes*, from which the orphaned foundling Genet had felt himself excluded and rejected as a monstrosity. The revolt of the maids against their masters is not a social gesture, a revolutionary action; it is tinged with nostalgia and longing, like the revolt of the fallen angel Satan against the world of light from which he is forever banished. That is why this revolt finds its expression not in protest but in ritual. Each of the maids in turn acts the part of the lady, expressing her longing to *be* the lady, and each in turn takes it upon herself to act the other maid, progressing from adoration and servility to abuse and violence—the discharge of all the hatred and envy of the outcast who sees himself as a rejected lover. This ritual, as Sartre points out, is a kind of Black Mass—the wish to murder the loved and envied object congealed and forever repeated as a ceremonial, stereotyped action. Such a ritual is frustration become flesh—an action that will never be performed in the real world is repeated over and over as a mere game. And not even this ritual ever reaches its natural climax. The lady always returns before that. As Sartre sees it, this failure is, as it were, subconsciously built into the ritual. The game is played in such a way that the time wasted on the preliminaries is always too long for the climax ever to be reached.

The ritual of wish-fulfillment is an act that is wholly absurd—it is futility mirroring itself; the wish to accomplish something which can never bridge the gulf that separates the dream from reality; the sympathetic magic of the primitive who is unable to face the cold, implacable hardness of the real world. Such ritual belongs in the world of neurosis and compulsive obsessions. It is the expression of a withdrawal from life.

The concept of the ritual act, the magical repetition of an action deprived of reality, is the key to any understanding of Genet's theatre. He himself has described his ideal of the union of the ritual with the dramatic in the letter to the publisher Pauvert that serves as preface to one of the editions of *The Maids*.

> On a stage almost like ours, on a platform, it was a matter of reconstructing the end of a meal. From that starting point that one can hardly discover in it any more, the highest modern drama has found expression through two thousand years and every day in the sacrifice of the Mass. The starting point disappears under the profusion of ornaments and symbols. . . . A performance that would not act on my soul would be in vain. . . . No doubt it is one of the functions of art to replace religious faith by the effective ingredient of beauty. At least this beauty must have the power of a poem, that is to say of a crime. But let that pass.[17]

Genet rejects the theatre as mere entertainment. He does not believe that in our Western world the theatre could ever have the effect of a real communion, a real link between human beings. He recalls that Sartre once told him that he had experienced that kind of effect in a theatrical performance only once—during a Christmas play in a prisoner-of-war camp, when the nostalgia of a French play on the stage suddenly re-created France herself, the homeland and its mystical unity, not on the stage but in the auditorium. But, says Genet, "I don't know what the theatre will be like in a Socialist world. I can understand better what it would be like among the Mau Mau, but in the Western world, more and more touched by death and turned toward it, it can only refine itself in the 'reflection' of a comedy of a comedy, the reflection of reflection which a ceremonious rendering could make exquisite and close to invisibility. If one has chosen to contemplate oneself dying deliciously, one must rigorously pursue and arrange the funeral symbols. Or choose to live and discover the Enemy.

For me there will never be an Enemy anywhere, there will never be a homeland, not even an abstract and interior one. If I am moved, it will be by the nostalgia of what my homeland once was. Only a theatre of shadows can still touch me."[18]

Genet's theatre, in a very real sense, is a Dance of Death. If in Ionesco's theatre death is always present, in the sense that the fear of extinction pervades its sense of being, in Genet's theatre the world of being exists only as a nostalgic memory of life in a world of dream and fantasy. Sartre observes on the very first page of his monumental study of Genet, "Genet is nothing but a dead man; if he still seems to live, he does so only in that larval existence that certain peoples ascribe to their dead in their tombs. All his heroes have died at least once in their life."[19]

Genet's game of mirrors—in which each apparent reality is revealed as an appearance, an illusion, which in turn is revealed as again part of a dream or an illusion, and so on, ad infinitum—is a device to uncover the fundamental absurdity of being, its nothingness. The fixed point from which we feel we can safely watch the world, made up of deceptive appearances perhaps, but always reducible to an ultimate reality, is itself shown to be a mere reflection in a mirror, and the whole structure collapses. The first *coup de théâtre* in *The Maids* is a case in point. We have seen a great lady being dressed by her maid, Claire; accustomed as we are to follow the exposition of a play we are memorizing these relationships. But suddenly, on the ringing of an alarm clock, the fixed point of reference vanishes—what had appeared to be the lady is Claire, the maid; what had appeared to be Claire now turns out to be Solange; what appeared to be the opening scene of a conventional play is revealed to be a piece of ritual play-acting within a play.

"This moment," as Sartre puts it in the technical language of his Existentialist philosophy, "in which the lights flicker, when the volatile unity of the being of non-being and the non-being of being is achieved in semi-darkness—this perfect and perverse instant makes us realize, from within, the mental attitude of Genet when he dreams: it is the moment of evil. For in order to be sure of never making *good use* of appearance, Genet wants his fancies, at two or three stages of derealization, to reveal themselves in their nothingness. In this pyramid of fantasies, the ultimate appearance derealizes all others."[20] Or, as Genet himself puts it in describing what he was trying to do in *The Maids*, "I tried to establish a *distantiation* which, in allowing a declamatory tone, would carry the theatre into the theatre. I thus hoped also to obtain the abolition of characters . . . and to replace them by symbols as far removed as possible, at first, from what they are to signify, and yet still attached to it in order to link by this sole means author and audience; in short, to make the characters on the stage merely the metaphors of what they were to represent. . . ."[21] Thus the characters themselves are only characters in appearance— they are mere symbols, reflections in a mirror, dreams within a dream.

When *The Maids* had its first performance at the Athénée in Paris on April 17, 1947, under the direction of France's foremost actor, Louis Jouvet, it seemed that Genet had finally established himself in the world of respectability. His narrative prose was already circulating in privately printed editions. In fact it was Jouvet who had suggested to Genet that he should write the play. "Commissioned by an actor famous in his time, my play was written out of vanity, but in boredom."[22] Brilliantly produced in a set of breathtaking beauty designed by Christian Bérard, *The Maids* achieved considerable success. But Genet had not yet redeemed himself completely. In 1948 he was faced with the prospect of a sentence of life imprisonment. It was only a petition signed by a number of great literary figures, Sartre and Cocteau among them, that, in the end, persuaded the President of the Republic to grant him a pardon.

He started writing a film and worked on it for a number of years. But it was not produced. One of France's leading publishers began to publish a monumental edition of his works; the first volume appeared in 1951, Sartre's great introductory study in 1952, a further volume in 1953. But Genet seemed to have stopped writing for the theatre. In fact he was reported to have forsworn the theatre after his experience with *The Maids* and *Deathwatch* (first produced at the Théâtre des Mathurins in February, 1949). In his letter to Pauvert about *The Maids*, he speaks of his dislike of the theatre and its world: "The poet who [would venture into it] would find ranged against him the haughty stupidity of the actors and theatre people. One cannot expect anything from a profession that is exercised with so little seriousness and reverence. Its starting point, its *raison d'être*, is exhibitionism."[23] But, by 1956 Genet had written another play, *Le Balcon* (*The Balcony*).

The events that surrounded the first production of this play show that in the intervening years Genet had by no means acquired a more charitable opinion of actors and stage people. *The Balcony* had its world première on April 22, 1957, in London at the Arts Theatre Club, open to members only and therefore not subjected to the Lord Chamberlain's censorship. The same issues of the London papers that reviewed the play also contained the story of how the author had been banned from the theatre after he had violently objected to the way it was being produced. Peter Zadek, the young English director who had directed a French performance of *The Maids* in London as early as 1952, and had later staged its first performance in English, was accused by Genet of having vulgarized *The Balcony*.

"My play was set in a brothel of noble dimensions," he was quoted as having said. "Peter Zadek has put on the stage a brothel of petty dimensions."[24] And Bernard Frechtman, Genet's excellent American translator, was cited as having commented, "[The scenes in the brothel] should be presented with the solemnity of a Mass in a most beautiful cathedral. Mr. Zadek has transformed it into just an ordinary brothel."[25] A few days later, Peter Zadek gave his own account of the controversy in a finely argued and magnanimous article, in which he paid tribute to Genet as an artist: "It is this complete inability to compromise with his vision that makes of Genet one of the great poet-dramatists of our century."[26] Zadek explained Genet's outburst as a manifestation of his preoccupation with the borderline between fantasy and reality: "Genet's whole life seems to repeat the pattern of the visionary who tries to make 'his fantasy penetrate into the reality of the world.' But the world has always crucified visionaries, and 'St. Genet' is no exception. . . . For him his own perfect dream of *The Balcony* was reality, and in an effort to make this concrete, our reality, the production of the play on a stage, with actors, had to be sacrificed."[27]

The conflict over the London production of *The Balcony* (which admittedly was a brave attempt in a small theatre and with modest means) was more than merely a picturesque incident in the life of a colorful and eccentric playwright. It illuminates the essence of Genet's whole approach—the deep inner tension arising from his search for something absolute, beautiful, a sacramental element in an inverted system of values in which evil is the greatest good, and the beautiful blooms in a soil of excrement and sordid crime. That is why it was not at all paradoxical for Genet to demand that his fantasies of sex and power should be staged with the solemnity and the outward splendor of the liturgy in one of the world's great cathedrals, while at the same time insisting to the director that the production should be "vulgar, violent, and in bad taste"[28] and assuring him that "if anybody tells you that you have produced this play in good taste, you will have failed. My tarts must look like the worst prostitutes in the world."[29] To live up to such demands is clearly very difficult, if not impossible.

As a matter of fact, the London production of *The Balcony*, although it contained many mistakes, weaknesses, and cuts of important passages, in some ways managed to put the play as a whole across the footlights in a more complete manner than Peter Brook's infinitely more polished, splendidly designed, and magnificently cast first French production, at the Théâtre du Gymnase in May, 1960. The slower pace resulting from the more faithful execution of the author's intention made the performance drag to such an extent that after the first night the very essential and central scene among the revolutionaries, although rehearsed and included in the première, was omitted (as it was in the New York production of March, 1960), thus depriving the final climax of the play of a point essential to its understanding. But then, at the time of the first night in Paris, Genet had become wary enough to have gone to Greece to nurse his rheumatism.

The Balcony carries the organic development of Genet's approach forward by an important step. Again, at the beginning, we have the ground pulled out from under our feet. The play opens with a magnificently robed bishop discoursing in high-flown theological language. But hardly have we adjusted ourselves to the idea that we are watching a bishop when it becomes brutally clear that we are not in a bishop's palace but in a brothel, and that the man concerned is not a bishop but a gasman who has paid the madam for the satisfaction of indulging himself in his fantasies of sex and power. Madame Irma's brothel, the Grand Balcony, is a palace of illusions—a hall of mirrors. Here men can indulge their most secret daydreams: They can see themselves as a judge meting out punishment to a girl thief; as a general feeling himself loved by his favorite steed, who is also a beautiful girl; as a leper being miraculously cured by the Madonna in person; as a dying Foreign Legionnaire being succored by a beautiful Arab maiden. The props for all the ever-recurring fantasies of grandeur are available at Madame Irma's establishment, which is thus not only a hall of mirrors, in the metaphorical as well as the actual sense (there are mirrors everywhere that multiply the images of self-heroization), but also a kind of theatre, with Madame Irma as its producer and impresario.

The plot of the play arises from the fact that the country in which the Grand Balcony is situated is in the throes of revolution. Machine-gun fire is heard throughout the first scenes. The revolutionaries want to destroy the established structure of power, represented as it is by the image of the country's Queen, chaste and remote, her bishops, her judges, and her generals. One of the inmates of Madame Irma's establishment, a girl called Chantal, has fallen in love with the leader of the revolutionaries, a plumber whom she met while he was doing some repairs at the Grand Balcony; she herself has become a kind of symbol of the revolution, its Joan of Arc. The fight against the revolution is led by the Chief of Police, who is the real power in the land, representing the modern apparatus of dictatorship, the wielder of totalitarian and terroristic power. The Chief of Police knows, however, that power is not a matter of torture and physical force, but ultimately a question of domination over people's minds. Such ascendancy expresses itself best in the secret fantasies of human beings; only when there will be a demand in Madame Irma's brothel for the trappings of the totalitarian Police Chief will he feel secure. Anxiously he keeps inquiring whether anyone has yet asked for this particular setting in the brothel. Everything is prepared for that day, but nobody has yet wanted to dream of this brand of grandeur.

We meet the revolutionaries in a scene that sets the counterpoint to the world of the Grand Balcony, but there, too, power is based on sex fantasies. Some of the rebels want to build up Chantal into a kind of trademark of the revolution, the beautiful girl leading the attack, singing rousing tunes to fire the men to greater exertions. Roger, the leader, resists these demands but has to yield in the end, protesting, "I didn't carry you off, I didn't steal you for you to become a unicorn or a two-headed eagle." But Chantal goes nevertheless.

The royal palace is blown up, the Queen and her court swept away. An envoy from the palace appears at the Grand Balcony. Only if the people can be made to believe that the age-old symbols of power are intact can the day still be saved. Will Madame Irma assume the part of the Queen, and her customers—the men who dressed up as bishop, general, and judge —assume these roles in earnest? Madame Irma and her customers consent. Solemnly they appear on the balcony and bow to the crowd. Chantal rushes up to the balcony and is killed by a shot from below. A stray bullet? Or a shot fired by the revolutionaries themselves to turn her into a myth? Or was it the bishop, who wanted to turn her into one of his saints?

The revolution has been defeated. But "bishop," "general," and "judge," having to exercise their power in the real world, are weary and nostalgic for their fantasies. When they try to assert the reality of their functions, the Chief of Police rudely reminds them that it is he who holds the real power. Yet he, too, still longs for the day when his function will be invested with the dignity of being the center of erotic dreams. He is having an immense mausoleum constructed for himself, in the hope that this will bring him nearer to his goal. He is trying to evolve a symbol for his dignity that will stir men's imagination. He has rejected the executioner's red coat and axe. His newest idea is that he should be represented by a gigantic phallus.

The first customer who wants to dress up as a Chief of Police arrives. It is Roger, the leader of the defeated revolutionaries. Anxiously Irma (now the Queen) and her dignitaries watch the scene through the intricate apparatus of mirrors and periscopes that enable the madam of the brothel to see what goes on in all the private rooms. Roger enacts his own fantasy of power and torture, but finally, exclaiming, "Since I'm playing the Chief of Police . . . I've a right to lead the character I have chosen to the very limit of his destiny—no, of mine—of merging his destiny with mine," he pulls out a knife and castrates himself. The Chief of Police, satisfied that his image has become enshrined in the fantasies of the people, has himself immured in his tomb—or its representation in the brothel. Bursts of machine-gun fire are heard. A new revolution is in progress. Madame Irma dismisses her customers, divests herself of her royal dignity, and prepares to return to her old role of the keeper of a house of illusions.

In the stage directions for *Deathwatch*, Genet had to insist that it should be acted as a dream. In *The Balcony* there is no need for such specific instructions. It is quite clear that the play represents a world of fantasy about a world of fantasy; Genet's dream about the essential nature of power and sex, which, to him, have the same roots; his wish-fantasy about the true nature of judges, policemen, officers, and bishops. The outcast child, repudiated by society and not recognizing any of its codes, unable to understand the motives of the organs of the state's coercive apparatus, weaves its own fantasy about the motives of the men who have acted as the instruments of the state. The outcast comes to the conclusion that these men are expressing their sadistic drive for domination, and that they are using the awful symbolism with which they are surrounded, the ritual and ceremonial of courtroom, army, and church, to buttress and secure their domination. Thus sex, which to Genet is essentially a matter of domination and submission; the power of the state, which manifests itself in the domination of the prisoner by the court and its policemen; and the romantic ceremonial, the manifestation of myth in sex as well as in power, are basically one.

A feeling of helplessness when confronted with the vast intricacy of the modern world, and the individual's impotence in making his own influence felt on that intricate and mysterious machinery, pervades the consciousness of Western man today. A world that functions mysteriously outside our conscious control, must appear absurd. It has lost the metaphysical motivation of a religious or historical purpose; it has ceased to make sense. The convict who is being physically separated from the outside world has literally been deprived of any means to make his presence felt, to make an impact on reality; in that sense the convict experiences the human condition in our time more intensely and more directly than any of us. He, or at least a convict of Genet's sensibility and power of expression, can therefore become the spokesman for the unspoken thoughts, the subconscious malaise of Western man.

Genet's vision in *The Balcony* may be vindictive, and distorted by the outcast's violent rage at society, but it has its validity nevertheless. It would be wrong to criticize the play on the ground that the analysis of the workings of society it presents is manifestly false, that the church, the law, and the defense forces have other functions than merely those of giving expression to the lust for power of those holding responsible positions in their hierarchies (although these motives no doubt play a powerful part in the psychology of lawyers, bishops, and generals). Genet is not concerned with giving such an analysis. He is projecting the feeling of impotence of the individual caught up in the meshes of society, he is dramatizing the often suppressed and subconscious rage of the "I" alone and terrified by the anonymous weight of the nebulous "they." It is this helplessness, this impotence, that seeks an outlet in the substitute explanation of myth and daydreams. They try to bring back meaning and purpose into the universe, yet they are bound to collapse again and again. Reality is an unattainable goal. Nothing the individual can do can have meaning in a world on the brink of annihilation for reasons and by means that the individual is unable to grasp and over which he appears to have no control.

The revolutionaries in *The Balcony* try to abolish a system of power based on mythical images. But in the very act of trying to break out of the iron ring of myth into the world of reality beyond it, they are compelled to construct their own myth. For it is by the fantasies of the masses that society is kept going. Chantal, who escaped from Madame Irma's brothel because she could not bear prostituting herself for the fantasies of impotent little men trying to partake of the feeling of power and sexual potency they felt deprived of in reality by escaping into a world of make-believe, is inevitably turned into an object of myth, a sexual image designed to lure the cannon fodder of the revolution to its death. And after her own self-sacrifice in that heroic part, Chantal, the mythical Joan of Arc, is without difficulty appropriated by the fake bishop as part of his own liturgy. (It is noteworthy that Brecht, whose work Genet is unlikely to have known, uses exactly the same image. His saintly revolutionary girl in *St. Joan of the Stockyards* is canonized by the capitalists immediately after her death.)

In the end, the leader of the revolutionaries himself faces the truth about his own motivation. The reality he wanted to break into was the reality of power, the power represented by the secret-information service and terroristic methods of the modern totalitarian state. That is why he wants to satisfy his frustrated craving by coming to the brothel to seek satisfaction in impersonating the Chief of Police. But, at the same time, he feels guilty about this realization, and is filled with a furious desire for revenge. His act of self-castration while impersonating the Police Chief is an ambivalent one; he wants to punish himself for his desire for power, and at the same time punish the Police Chief vicariously by an act of sympathetic magic. Power and virility being equated in Roger's mind as well as in Genet's, the Police Chief himself having chosen a gigantic phallus as his heraldic symbol, such an act of sympathetic magic is bound to be an act of emasculation.

Roger, although he makes only two relatively brief appearances in a long play, is the real hero of *The Balcony*. His role is analogous to that of Lefranc in *Deathwatch* and of Claire in *The Maids*. Lefranc tries to escape from his isolation and rejection by committing a murder. He fails and falls back into even more complete loneliness. Claire, having failed to murder her lady, kills herself while pretending to be the lady, in exactly the same way that Roger castrates the Chief of Police by proxy. As Claire, who really wants to become the lady whom she both loves and hates, both fulfills her craving by impersonating the loved character and punishes herself for that craving by killing herself, so Roger acknowledges his desire to *be* the Police Chief while punishing the Police Chief in his own person. But neither Claire nor Roger can break out into reality. Claire can neither become like her lady in reality nor kill her in reality. Roger can neither attain power through revolution nor really punish the Police Chief by sympathetic magic. On the contrary, his action puts the final seal on the consecration of the ritual acceptance of the figure of the Chief of Police in the pantheon of mankind's fantasies of sex and power. Instead of smashing a mirror to reach the outside world, Roger has merely added another cabinet of mirrors to the many others that serve to reflect the fake images of little men dreaming of real power.

This analysis of myth and dream is itself quite clearly a dream and a myth. Even more than in *Deathwatch* and *The Maids,* the audience is left in no doubt that they are not meant to take any of the events they see as real. There are no characters in the conventional sense in *The Balcony,* merely the images of basic urges and impulses. Nor is there, strictly speaking, a plot. Essentially the play is a series of rituals, followed by their equally ritual debunking—the customers of the brothel performing their rites, the ritual presentation of the new hierarchy of power, the ritual castration of the frustrated revolutionary. The plot structure needed to link these ceremonial acts together is the weakest part of the play. That is why all critics agree that the final part is too long and less impressive than the opening of the play. It is here that the figures of fantasy are briefly supposed to be shown exercising real power, but in fact they do nothing concrete beyond discussing the relative merits of their myths and posing for press photographers—i.e., exhibiting themselves to the populace. Here Genet himself clearly fails to achieve the breakthrough into reality. On the other hand, the ceremonial or mock-ceremonial parts of the play are superb both as theatre (witness the triumphant use of the cothurnus to make the dream images of little men appear as gigantic figures) and in the splendor of their language.

This unevenness springs from Genet's basic dilemma. He strives for a theatre of ritual, but ritual is the regular repetition of mythical events and, as such, closely akin to sympathetic magic. It endeavors to influence the real world either by re-enacting the key happenings that have shaped that world or (as in fertility rites) by performing in an exemplary manner what is hoped will be happening in abundance. A theatre as ritual and ceremonial like the theatre of ancient Greece presupposes a valid and vital body of beliefs and myths. And this is precisely what our own civilization lacks. Hence in *The Balcony* Genet is faced with the need to provide a plot structure that will furnish the rationale for his mock-liturgy and mock-ceremonial. And he has not quite succeeded in integrating plot and ritual.

In *Les Nègres* (*The Blacks*) he has found an extremely ingenious solution to this problem. Here he presents a play, labeled a *clownerie* (a clown show), which is entirely ritual and therefore needs no plot devices at all. A group of Negroes performs the ritual re-enactment of its resentments and feelings of revenge before a white audience. As Genet insists, in a prefatory note to the play, it would lose its *raison d'être* if there were not at least one white person in the audience. "But what if no white person accepted? Then let white masks be distributed to the black spectators as they enter the theatre. And if the blacks refuse the masks, then let a dummy be used."[30] In other words, the presence—even the merely ritual, symbolic presence—of at least one white spectator is indispensable to this particular ritual.

The Negro actors performing this ritual are divided into two groups: those who appear as Negroes and will enact the Negroes' fantasy, and those who appear grotesquely, and visibly, masked, to represent the Negroes' fantasy about the white man's reaction to the Negro world. The white audience in the theatre is confronted by a grotesque mirror image of itself on the stage. The Negro actors stand between two audiences of whites. The stage audience consists, however, of the Negroes' fantasy image of the white man, embodied in the hierarchy of power in a colonial society—the queen, haughty and remote; her governor; her judge; her missionary; and her valet, who plays the part of the artist or intellectual who lends his services to the hierarchy of power while not strictly belonging to it. It is significant that queen, judge, bishop, and general (the governor is a military man) are identical with the figures of the hierarchy of power in *The Balcony*.

In front of this audience of their own projected image of the structure of alien rule, the group of Negroes enacts its fantasies of resentment. The central part of the ritual is a fantasy of the ritual murder of a white woman, elaborately and lovingly imagined in lurid detail. It is this white woman who is supposed to be inside the coffin that stands in the center of the stage. For, as one of the Negroes puts it, "we must deserve their [i.e., the whites'] reprobation and get them to deliver the judgment that will condemn us."[31] At first the Negro named Village, who is supposed to have committed the murder, describes the victim as an old crone they found drunk and helpless by the docks and then strangled. Later, when the actual murder is lovingly reconstructed, the victim becomes a buxom white woman who has been so seduced by her black visitor's superior sexual attractions that she has invited him into her bedroom, where she was both violated and strangled. As an additional touch of irony, the Negro who has to enact the raped white woman is supposed in private life to be a black priest, Diouf. After his ritual murder, he takes his place among the other "whites" on the platform backstage.

After the Negroes have acted out their hatred and resentment, but also their feeling of guilt, the next phase follows—the fantasy of final liberation. The queen and her court descend, as though engaged on a punitive expedition to the colony. They are trapped and ignominiously put to death by the blacks, the missionary bishop is castrated. Thanking the Negro actors who have impersonated the whites, Archibald, who acts as the stage manager throughout the play, sums up the significance of the ritual: "The time has not yet come for presenting dramas about noble matters. But perhaps they suspect what lies behind this architecture of emptiness and words. We are what they want us to be. We shall therefore be it to the very end, absurdly."[32]

The spectacle of this ritual representation of the Negroes' feelings about the whites has been made grotesquely clownish to render it bearable to an audience of whites. In opening the proceedings, Archibald informs the spectators, "In order that you may remain comfortably settled in your seats in the presence of the drama that is already unfolding here—in order that you be assured that there is no danger of such a drama's worming its way into your precious lives—we shall even have the decency—a decency learned from you—to make communication impossible. We shall increase the distance that separates us—a distance that is basic—by our pomp, our manners, our insolence. For we are also actors."[33] Hence the play takes the form of a ritual ceremony rather than being a direct discussion of the color problem or colonialism. In ritual, meaning is expressed by the repetition of symbolic actions. The participants have a sense of awe, of mysterious participation rather than of conceptual communication. The difference is merely that here the audience sees a grotesque parody of a ritual, in which the bitterness that is to be communicated emerges from clowning and derision.

Yet this is only the initial deception in this complex hall of mirrors. As the action proceeds, the audience is made aware that something else, something more real than the ritual concerned, is happening offstage. One of the characters, Ville de Saint-Nazaire (or Newport News, in the translation), who was sent off with a revolver in the opening scene, returns toward the end and reports that a Negro traitor has been tried and executed. So the whole elaborate performance given on the stage is revealed as a blind, an illusion enacted as a diversion to distract attention from the real action behind the scenes. We have seen a ritual of the murder of a white woman, but the reality was the trial and execution of a Negro—a Negro traitor.

It is on the entrance of Ville de Saint-Nazaire with the news of the traitor's execution that the actors who have been impersonating the white court remove their masks and reveal themselves as Negroes. It is only after they have heard the news that a new revolutionary delegate has been sent to Africa, to resume the work of the executed traitor, that they put on their masks again and enact the execution and torture of the white oppressors.

So the whole ritual of revenge was a grotesque diversion. Or was it? For we know that Ville de Saint-Nazaire is also an actor, and that nothing real has been going on behind the scenes—that in fact the theatrical performance is more real than the pretended reality of execution and revolution. Whether intended by Genet or not, the pretense at political action behind the smokescreen of a grotesque performance is merely another reflection in a chain of mirages.

Moreover, we know full well that the Negroes on the stage

stand for more than simply Negroes. Just as the servant girls in *The Maids*, even if acted by women, are really meant to be boys playing women, but representing a world of men, the Negroes in *The Blacks*, acted by Negroes, are not really Negroes. As Genet himself puts it in a cryptic prefatory note to the play, "One evening an actor asked me to write a play for an all-black cast. But what exactly is a black? First of all, what is his color?"[34] The Negroes in the play are an image of all outcasts of society; they stand, above all, for Genet himself, who, when called a thief at the age of ten, decided "to be what they want us to be." Or as Archibald puts it, "On this stage we are like guilty prisoners who play at being guilty."[35] The blacks are again the convicts, the prisoners who, deprived of the chance to partake of the real world, dream their dreams of guilt and revenge—including the trial and execution of traitors.

"We—you and I," says Village, "were moving along the edges of the world, out of bounds. We were the shadow, or the dark interior, of luminous creatures. . . ." When he speaks these lines, Village is talking about his love for Virtue, the black prostitute. For a moment when that love was kindled, he was at the threshold of reality: "When I beheld you, suddenly—for perhaps a second—I had the strength to reject everything that wasn't you and to laugh at the illusion. But my shoulders are very frail. I was unable to bear the weight of the world's condemnation. And I began to hate you when everything about you would have kindled my love and when love would have made men's contempt unbearable, and their contempt would have made my love unbearable. The fact is, I hate you."[36]

Being denied the dignity of man, the outcasts, the blacks, are denied the emotions of the real world. Yet at the end of the play, when the grotesque ritual has dissolved, Village and Virtue remain alone on the stage. And Village tries to learn the gestures of love, hard though they may be to learn. This is the first gleam of hope in Genet's dark theatre—two of his characters who have found the courage to break out of the vicious circle of daydreaming and establish genuine human contact through love. Or is this too optimistic an interpretation? Is this happy end only itself a fantasy of wish-fulfillment, and false as such? It does not seem so. The final tableau of *The*

Blacks shows the whole cast standing at the back of the stage, with only Virtue and Village turning their backs to the audience and walking toward their fellow actors to the strains of the minuet from *Don Giovanni*. So the lovers *have* turned their backs on the world of illusion.

The Blacks was written in 1957 and first performed by a troupe of Negro actors, Les Griots, under the direction of Roger Blin, at the Théâtre de Lutèce on October 28, 1959. Brilliantly acted, the play achieved considerable success and had a run of several months, although it bewildered a large part of the audience and a good many of the critics.

In spite of his often professed contempt for the theatre as a place to work in, and for actors as artists, Genet seems to have abandoned writing novels and prose narratives altogether and to have finally settled down as a dramatist. His latest play, *Les Paravents (The Screens,* 1961), presents his acid comment on the Algerian war. At first sight it might appear as though Genet was following the development of Adamov in abandoning the Theatre of the Absurd and turning into a political realist. But this is not really the case, although *Les Paravents* certainly shows where Genet's sympathy lies in the conflict he has chosen as his theme. In fact, *Les Paravents* resumes and restates the subject of *Les Nègres*, and, on the whole, less successfully. The play, which manipulates a very large number of characters, again sees the poorest of the poor, the Algerian peasants, as outcasts of society fighting a desperate battle against the powers that be—the authorities, *les justes*. But whereas *Les Nègres* concentrated the action in a powerful poetic image, *Les Paravents* scatters it over a vast open-air stage (Genet insists that the play must be performed in the open air) rising in four tiers. The action is to take place, often on several tiers at the same time, in front of a wide variety of screens that are to be rolled on stage on silent rubber wheels. The indication of the background for each scene is to appear painted on these screens, and will in certain cases be drawn on them by the actors themselves. The cast list comprises almost a hundred characters, but Genet specifies that each actor should play five or six parts.

The focal point of this wide canvas is occupied by Saïd, the poorest of all Arabs, so poor in fact that he can afford to marry only the ugliest girl, Leila. Saïd's mother dominates Saïd as well as the action of the play; she is, as mother figures usually are in Genet's work, a highly ambivalent character. Saïd and his mother are involved in the rebellion; the mother is killed and appears on the uppermost tier of the stage, together with a whole row of other dead, who look down on the action like the masked figures of the whites in *Les Nègres*. The life of an Arab village—with its cadi, its brothel, its market, its *colons*, its policemen—is vividly evoked. Grotesque caricatures of French soldiers perform cruel and scurrilous antics. But the anti-colonial tendency of the play is largely overlaid by a profusion of images of an anal eroticism that had not hitherto appeared so openly in Genet's dramatic works, although it has always been present in his prose fiction. On this score, and on that of its diffuseness, *Les Paravents* appears less successful than Genet's earlier plays. It clearly cannot be performed in France while the Algerian conflict remains unsettled. It had its world première, in a much cut version, in West Berlin in May 1961.

It is as yet not quite clear whether *Les Paravents* forms part of the cycle of seven plays on which Genet is said to be working, or whether it stands outside it as a topical comment on the times. Genet is also reported to have completed a film script for the avant-gardist director Georges Franju. Its title is *Mademoiselle, ou Les Rêves Interdits* (*Mademoiselle, or The Forbidden Dreams*), and it is said to deal with a young girl schoolteacher who is also an incendiary.

In writing for the theatre, Genet has achieved what all his characters (with the possible exception of Village and Virtue) have failed to achieve—he has broken through the vicious spiral of daydream and illusion, and by putting his fantasies onto the stage—concrete, brutal, and disturbing—he has succeeded in making his impact on the real world, if only by leaving an audience of *les justes* deeply stirred and disgusted. As Sartre puts it in summing up Genet's astonishing career, "In willing himself to be a thief to the utmost limit, Genet plunges into dream; in willing his dream to the point of madness, he makes himself a poet; in willing poetry to the final triumph of the word, he becomes a man; and the man has become the truth of the poet, just as the poet had been the truth of the thief."[37]

If the young outcast's anti-social acts were attempts to revenge himself on society, to destroy the whole of its fabric in symbolic acts of sympathetic magic, his activity as a writer is a direct continuation of this protest by other and more efficacious means. "If," as Sartre points out, "Genet, confined as he is in a world of fantasy by the pitiless order of things [i.e., an outcast who can have no impact on the real world], renounced his attempt to scandalize by the action of a thief? . . . If he made . . . the imaginary sphere a permanent source of scandal? If he could bring it about that his dreams of impotence tapped, in their very impotence, an infinite power and, in defiance of all the police forces of the world, put society as a whole in question? Would he not, in that case, have found a point of junction for the imaginary and the real, the ineffective and the effective, the false and the true, the right to act and the action?"[38]

It is clear that in confronting society itself in the theatre, rather than as solitary readers of his narrative prose, Genet comes far closer to his objective. Here a group of living people constituting a collective unity—the audience—is confronted with the secret world of the dreams and fantasies of the outcast. What is more, the audience, by experiencing the impact of what they see, even if that impact takes the form of horror and disgust, is forced to recognize its own psychological predicament, monstrously heightened and magnified though it be, there in front of it on the stage. The fact that a large part of the audience may have been drawn into the theatre by rumors that the spectacle will be scandalous or pornographic only increases this effect of shock. For here the prurient among *les justes* will find that their own fantasies are not so dissimilar from those of the self-confessed outcast.

Genet's theatre may lack plot, character, construction, coherence, or social truth. It undoubtedly has psychological truth. His plays are not intellectual exercises (cleverly though they are constructed) but the projections of a world of private myth, conceived as such in the pre-logical modes of thought that are the hallmark of the sphere of myth and dream; hence the prevalence of magical modes of action in Genet's plays— the identification of subject and object, symbol and reality, word and concept, as well as, in some instances, the divorce of the name from the thing it signifies; the objectification of the word. (Genet once told Sartre that he hated roses, but loved the word "rose.") In the world of prelogical thought, dream, and myth, language becomes incantation instead of communication; the word does not signify a concept but magically conjures up a thing—it becomes a magical formula. Desire and love express themselves in the wish for possession through identification and incorporation of the beloved object. Incantation, magical substitution, and identification are the essential elements of ritual. It is the use of language as incantatory magic—the objectification of words—that makes Genet's theatre, in spite of its harshness and scabrous content, into a truly poetical theatre, a translation, as it were, of Baudelaire's *Fleurs du Mal* into dramatic imagery.

Genet's theatre is, profoundly, a theatre of social protest. Yet, like that of Ionesco and of Adamov before his conversion to epic realism, it resolutely rejects political commitment, political argument, didacticism, or propaganda. In dealing with the dream world of the outcast of society, it explores the human condition, the alienation of man, his solitude, his futile search for meaning and reality.

Although Genet's theatre differs in many aspects of method and approach from that of the other dramatists discussed in this book, it bears many of the essential hallmarks that they have in common—the abandonment of the concepts of character and motivation; the concentration on states of mind and basic human situations, rather than on the development of a narrative plot from exposition to solution; the devaluation of language as a means of communication and understanding; the rejection of didactic purpose; and the confrontation of the spectator with the harsh facts of a cruel world and his own isolation. As such *The Balcony* and *The Blacks* can with certainty, *The Maids* with a good deal of probability, be regarded as examples of the Theatre of the Absurd.

word and concept as well as, in some instances, the divorce

Chapter Five

PARALLELS AND PROSELYTES

By its very nature, the Theatre of the Absurd is not, and
never can be, a literary movement or school, for its essence
lies in the free and unfettered exploration by each of the writers
concerned of his own individual vision. Yet the wide response
these, at first sight baffling and uncompromisingly difficult,
plays have evoked shows not only how closely they express the
preoccupations of our age, but also how great is the yearning
for a new approach to the theatre. In turning their backs on the
psychological or narrative theatre, and in refusing to conform
to any of the old-established recipes for the "well-made play,"
the dramatists of the Theatre of the Absurd are, each in his
own way and independent of the others, engaged in establishing a new dramatic convention. In this enterprise of trial and
error and ceaseless experimentation, the four dramatists whose
work has been examined in some detail in this book by no
means stand alone. A number of writers of their own generation have been experimenting on parallel lines, and a growing
number of younger dramatists have been encouraged by the
success of some of the work of Beckett, Ionesco, or Genet to
develop their own personal idiom in a similar convention. A
survey (which does not claim to be complete) of the experiments of these contemporaries and followers of the masters of
the new convention may show the possible future lines of
development.

The writer whose work represents the most comprehensive
range of experiment in this field is undoubtedly Jean Tardieu
(born in 1903), who, older than Beckett, Adamov, Genet, and
Ionesco, was already well-known as a poet before the Second
World War. Having tried to write plays in his early youth,

Tardieu turned to an austere style of lyrical poetry based on Mallarmé, and became known as the author of the best French translations of the poems of Hölderlin. After the war, he turned to experiments with language, in the vein of Jacques Prévert and Raymond Queneau, and to exploring the limits of the possibilities of the theatre. He joined the staff of the French Radio and Television Service after the end of the war, became head of its experimental workshop, the *club d'essai*, and started to write experimental plays in 1947, at about the time Beckett, Adamov, Genet, and Ionesco also made their first steps as dramatists—a curious instance of the *Zeitgeist* at work.

Tardieu's dramatic experiments, which have been published in two volumes—*Théâtre de Chambre* (1955) and *Poèmes à Jouer* (1960)—are mostly on a very small scale. Many of them are short cabaret sketches rather than even one-act plays, but their range is wider than that of any other dramatist of the Absurd, extending from the fantastic and eerie to the purely lyrical, and beyond it into the sphere of a wholly abstract theatre in which language loses all conceptual content and merges into music.

The earliest of the sketches in *Théâtre de Chambre* anticipate Ionesco. *Qui Est Là?* (dated 1947, and earlier than *The Bald Soprano*) starts with exactly the same situation—a family of father, mother, and son seated around the dinner table. The father is interrogating his wife and son about their activities during the day, but as he clearly knows the answers already, he supplies them himself without waiting for any information from those he has questioned:

> What did you do this morning? I went to school. And you? I went to the market. What did you get? Vegetables, more expensive than yesterday, and meat, cheaper. Just as well, one makes up for the other. And you, what did the teacher tell you? That I was making good progress. . . . [1]

A mysterious woman appears who warns the father of an approaching danger. There is someone at the door. The father opens it. A huge man stands outside. He strangles the father and carries his corpse away. The mysterious woman invites the wife to look out of the window. There are dead bodies outside as far as the eye can see. The father's body is among them.

The son calls the father; he rises from the dead and returns to the room. The wife asks, "Who killed you?" The father replies, "It was not a human being." "Who are you?" asks the wife. "I am not a human being," replies the dead man. "Who were you?" "Nobody."

The lesson of the little play seems to be the need to search for the human image that is not yet alive within any of us, but that we might find one day. In the words of the mysterious woman visitor, who concludes the play, "The window is lighting up. Someone approaches. Let us wait!"[2] *Qui Est Là?* is an attempt to produce a poetic image of the situation at the end of the war—man faced with the fact that the routine of a bourgeois existence is as inhuman as the mass killing of the battlefields and concentration camps, and the need for finding a new, fully human way of life. . . .

If Tardieu's first sketch of this type reproduces the opening situation and—to some extent—the message of *The Bald Soprano*, it is even more curious that his second short play, *La Politesse Inutile*—also dated 1947—should open with the professor-pupil situation of *The Lesson*. Yet here the similarity is purely superficial. The professor is saying goodbye to a young man off to his exams. He impresses on him that it is not what he knows that matters but what he *is*. When the pupil has left, another visitor, a vulgar and sinister individual, enters. He receives the professor's elaborate Old World politeness with a show of extravagant rudeness and finally slaps him savagely. The professor picks himself up and addresses the audience:

I shall not explain this story to you. No doubt it happened very far from here, at the bottom of a bad memory. It is from there that I come to warn you and to convince you. . . . Shush! There is someone asleep here who might overhear me. . . . I'll come back . . . tomorrow.[3]

The same dream, or nightmare, quality characterizes a good many of Tardieu's earlier sketches. In *Le Meuble*, an inventor is trying to sell a buyer, offstage, a fabulous piece of furniture that is designed to perform any conceivable service, including recitations of Musset's poems. But gradually the machine gets out of hand; instead of Musset it sings doggerel verse and finally it pulls out a revolver and kills the buyer. If this sketch is reminiscent of Ionesco or Adamov, *La Serrure* has over-tones of Genet. In a brothel, a customer is awaiting the fulfill-ment of his dreams—to see his beloved girl through an outsize keyhole. In ecstasy, the client describes what he sees as the girl discards one garment after another. Yet even after she has reached a state of complete nudity she goes on undressing, dis-carding her cheeks, her eyes, and other parts of her body until only the bare skeleton remains. Unable to control himself any more, the customer rushes against the door and falls down dead. The madam appears: "I think . . . the gentleman . . . is satisfied."

A similar motif appears in *Faust et Yorick*, which also ex-periments with the representation of the flow of time in the manner of Thornton Wilder's *The Long Christmas Dinner*. Faust, a scientist, spends his life looking for an example of a more highly developed skull, which will represent the next stage of human evolution. We see him getting married, his child becoming a woman, Faust growing old, always neglect-ing his family to find that skull. He dies without having found it. Yet the skull he has been looking for all his life is his own.

In *Le Guichet*, one of the longer pieces in *Théâtre de Chambre*, we are in a world of Kafkaesque bureaucracy. A man comes to an information office to ask about the time of a train. He is subjected to a rigid cross-examination about his whole life. Finally the official behind the counter draws up the man's horoscope and informs him that he will be killed on leaving the office. He leaves and is promptly run over.

In all these sketches, Tardieu is exploring the possibilities of reproducing a dreamlike atmosphere on the stage. In others he is more openly experimental and even didactic in trying out what can, or cannot, be done with various stage conven-tions, such as the use of asides (*Oswald et Zenaide, ou Les Apartés*—what an engaged couple say to each other, and what they think) or monologues (*Il Y Avait Foule au Manoir, ou Les Monologues*—a crowded stage suggested by a succession of monologues that could be spoken by a single actor), or in demonstrating the relativity of language (*Ce Que Parler Veut Dire, ou Le Patois des Familles*—each family has its private slang) or manners (*Un Geste pour un Autre*—a world traveler demonstrates how the most absurd behavior is regarded as exquisite good manners in distant civilizations). These didactic sketches, which take the form of illustrated lectures, are Tardieu's least successful efforts—they recall the more hackneyed procedures of the little revue.

Tardieu's most interesting experiments are those in which he explores the possibilities of a wholly abstract theatre. *Eux Seuls Le Savent*, for example, presents a highly dramatic action that remains wholly unexplained. We see the characters engaged in violent quarrels referring to hidden motives and guilty secrets, without ever learning what these are or even in what relationship the four people involved stand to each other. "Only they know it." By presenting a wholly motiveless action that still holds the public's attention, Tardieu is in fact demonstrating the possibility of pure, plotless theatre.

But he goes further than this. Two of the short pieces in *Théâtre de Chambre* (*La Sonate et les Trois Messieurs* and *Conversation-Sinfonietta*) attempt an approximation of dialogue to music. In *La Sonate* we have three gentlemen, labeled A., B., and C., engaged in a conversation the subject of which remains undefined but which evokes a certain type of image, tempo, and rhythm to correspond to the notations of a sonata: first movement, Largo (slow, nostalgic description of an expanse of water); second movement, Andante (more animated discussion—what was it that they have seen?); third movement, Finale (animation leading to a dying fall). *Conversation-Sinfonietta* repeats the same experiment with six voices (two basses, two contraltos, a soprano, and a tenor) under the direction of a conductor. Again there are three movements: Allegro ma non troppo, Andante sostenuto, and Scherzo vivace. The text consists of the most banal fragments of small talk: "*Bonjour, Madame!*" "*Bonjour, Monsieur!*" or "*Mais oui, mais oui, mais oui, mais oui*" followed by "*Mais non, mais non, mais non, mais non!*" or lists of foods liked by the speakers, with directions as to how they are to be cooked.

Having explored the possibilities of constructing the equivalent of a symphonic poem from disjointed elements of language, Tardieu took the logical step forward. In the second volume of his collected plays, we find the results of this development.

Les Amants du Métro (*The Lovers in the Subway*), written

in 1951, is described in the subtitle as "a comic ballet without dance and without music"; that is, language in movement is to take the place of both the music and the dancing.

The first scene is a Métro station. The small talk of the waiting passengers has a thematic relationship to the main subject, the meeting of the two lovers. Two gentlemen deeply immersed in their books collide and introduce their reading matter to each other—"St. Paul!", "Marquis de Sade!"—while a student tells his girl the story of Hero and Leander. The lovers themselves are introduced in a passage of abstract dialogue simulating a waltz rhythm: *"Un, deux, trois, amour." "Un, deux, trois, Adour." "Un, deux, trois, toujours,"* and so on. Later, when the lovers quarrel, they do so in strings of women's names: "Emma! Eloa! Héloise! Diotima! Georgia! Hilda!" and so on.

In the second scene, the lovers are inside a Métro carriage, separated by a crowd of other passengers, who represent the anonymity and hostility of mass society. Another Leander, the hero has to cross this sea of puppetlike fellow men. When he has finally managed to reach his beloved, she too has relapsed into the depersonalized anonymity of the crowd. Only when he violently slaps her face does she wake up and become an individual again.

As an experiment with the expressive possibilities of language, even when almost wholly empty of conceptual content, *Les Amants du Métro* is a fascinating tour de force; it shows the richness of the textural and rhythmic possibilities of language, as well as the feasibility of a purely poetic, as distinct from discursive, use of dramatic dialogue, which replaces the exchange of ideas or information between the characters by the striking up and development of poetic images and themes by a new logic of association.

This idea is carried a step further by Tardieu in *L'A.B.C. de Notre Vie* (*The A.B.C. of Our Life*), written in 1958 and first performed on May 30, 1959. Tardieu describes this as "a poem for acting," and it is built strictly in the form of a concerto. A protagonist has the main solo part, the individual man, a day in whose life among the crowd of the great city is the subject matter of the poem, starting with his awakening from his dreams in the morning and ending with his return to

sleep at night. The choral part consists of the indistinct murmur of the crowd, against which articulated parts of sentences
rise and fall. Two further characters, Monsieur Mot and Madame Parole (Mr. Word and Madame Speech), illustrate the
proceedings by reciting strings of words from the dictionary,
which, the author states, are "musical notes or touches of
color" rather than concepts. Other solo parts include a couple
of lovers, a criminal, the voices of dreaming women. Three
themes are interwoven in the movements of this concerto-in-
words: the individual's illusion of his uniqueness against the
indistinct murmur of the mass to which he belongs; the power
of love to take man out of the flow of time and to make him
into a true individual; and, finally, the recognition of man's
rootedness in humanity as a whole—"*Humanité, tu es mon
paysage.*" The murmuring of the mass becomes one of the
sounds of nature, like the wind in the forest, like the waves
of the sea.

In another "poem for acting," *Rhythme à Trois Temps, ou
Le Temple de Ségeste* (*Rhythm in Three-Time, or The Temple of Segesta*), written in 1958, Tardieu has tried to reproduce the feelings of a traveler when he first sees the Greek
temple of Segesta. Six girls represent the six columns that face
the traveler as he approaches, a voice offstage embodies the
traveler's feelings. The girls express calm and immutability, the
ecstatic traveler is rhapsodic and emotional. Both *L'A.B.C.
de Notre Vie* and *Rhythme à Trois Temps* were accompanied
at their first production by musical quotations from the works
of Anton Webern.

In exploring the limits of the theatre, Tardieu has even tried
to write a short play in which no characters at all appear: *Une
Voix Sans Personne* (*A Voice Without Anyone*). The stage
represents an empty room. A voice offstage recalls the memory
of a room once familiar; the lighting onstage changes in accordance with the moods recalled. Only occasionally, a
woman's voice is heard, like an echo from the past. This is
certainly an interesting and ingenious, though by no means
conclusive, experiment; it merely proves that lighting and décor have a part to play in creating poetry on the stage. But
this has never been in need of proof.

On the same program with *Une Voix Sans Personne* at

the tiny Théâtre de la Huchette in 1956, Tardieu presented his nearest approximation to a straight play, *Les Temps du Verbe, ou Le Pouvoir de la Parole* (*The Tenses of the Verb, or The Power of Speech*), two acts designed to demonstrate the thesis that the tenses of the verb govern our standpoint in time. The rather melodramatic plot concerns Robert, who has lost his wife in an automobile accident. He has withdrawn from the present, lives in the past, and speaks exclusively in the past tense. When he dies, his body is found to be that of a man who died a long time ago. As the body lies on the empty stage, the moment just before the accident comes to life again. Robert hears the voices of his wife and his niece speaking in the future tense. At that moment before his wife was killed, she still had a future, but "Past, present, future, which is true? Everything partakes of each at the same time! Everything fades away, but everything remains—and everything remains unfinished!"[4]

The volume of Tardieu's *Poèmes à Jouer* concludes with his earliest dramatic effort, the verse play *Tonnerre Sans Orage, ou Les Dieux Inutiles* (*Thunder Without Storm, or The Useless Gods*), dated 1944. This outwardly conventional poetic one-act play might almost be a program note on the subject matter of the Theatre of the Absurd. On the threshold of death, Asia, the mother of the titan Prometheus, reveals to her grandson Deucalion that the gods do not exist. She herself invented the myth of their existence to curb Prometheus's ambition when he was young. But far from inducing him to submit to higher powers, the supposed existence of the gods spurred Prometheus into his lifelong struggle against them. Deucalion tells Prometheus what he has learned, but Prometheus, who is about to unleash a conflagration that will destroy the gods, and the world with them, can no longer stop events from taking their course. Deucalion sails away into the unknown, "seeking in the reflection of the two abysses an alliance with my new god—nothingness,"[5] while Prometheus remains behind alone:

> I know, I know full well henceforth
> In the superb desert of the night,
> Which is the god I threaten:
> It is myself, Prometheus![5]

It is in the light of this recognition of the absurdity of the human situation in a godless world that we must see Tardieu's impressive experimental work; it is an attempt to find a means of expression adequate to represent man's efforts to situate himself in a meaningless universe. Being avowedly experimental, Tardieu's plays, though some of them contain poetry of great distinction, cannot claim to be judged as works of art in their own right. They are explorations, materials for research from which valuable experience can be gained for the creation of works of art that Tardieu himself, or others, making use of his research, might build on the foundations he has provided. This is not to deny Tardieu's very considerable achievement, but rather to emphasize his importance. Here is a playwright's playwright, a dedicated pioneer bent on enlarging the vocabulary of his art. Alone among the playwrights of the avant-garde, Tardieu can claim that his work spans the entire gamut of exploration. He straddles the poetic theatre of Schehadé as well as the sardonic anti-theatre of Ionesco and the psychological dream world of Adamov and Genet. But by its very awareness, its experimental consciousness, its playfulness in trying out new devices, Tardieu's work misses the obsessive compulsiveness, and thus the hypnotic power, the inevitableness, of some of the masterpieces of the Theatre of the Absurd.

If Tardieu's experiments pursue a course parallel to, but independent of, the development of the main stream of the new convention, the single play by Boris Vian (1920–59) that falls within it clearly shows the signs of the direct influence of Ionesco, his fellow satrap in the Collège de Pataphysique. This play, Les Bâtisseurs d'Empire (The Empire Builders), was first performed in Jean Vilar's experimental Théâtre Récamier on December 22, 1959, six months after the tragic death of its author. Boris Vian was one of the most remarkable figures of the postwar period in Paris. Engineer, jazz trumpeter, chansonnier, film actor, novelist, wit, jazz critic; one of the great characters of the Existentialist bohemia of the caves around Saint-Germain-des-Prés; translator of Raymond Chandler, Peter Cheney, James Cain, Nelson Algren, Strindberg, and the memoirs of General Omar N. Bradley; iconoclast and condemned pornographer; science-fiction expert, and dramatist, Boris Vian seems an epitome of his time—sardonic, practical, a working technician and inventor of gadgets, a violent enemy of cant, and at the same time a sensitive poet, an artist concerned with the ultimate reality of the human condition.

Boris Vian's first play, *L'Equarrissage Pour Tous* (which might be rendered in English as *Knackery Made Easy*—written in 1946–47 and first performed in 1950), already shows him as a master of a bitter, black humor, although the play, a tragicomic farce, still fits into a traditional pattern, in spite of the fact that Jean Cocteau greeted it as an event comparable to Apollinaire's *Les Mamelles de Tirésias* and his own *Mariés de la Tour d'Eiffel*. Described as "a paramilitary vaudeville in one long act," *L'Equarrissage Pour Tous* takes place in a knacker's yard at Arromanches on the day of the Allied landings there, June 6, 1944. While the knacker's eccentric family go about their peaceful business of horse-slaughtering and arranging the marriage of one of their daughters to a German soldier, the place is continually invaded by military personnel of various nations, ranging from a Japanese parachutist to a Soviet Russian woman soldier, who inexplicably is one of the daughters of the house. There are also numerous Americans and members of the Free French forces. The hilarious and bawdy proceedings end when the knacker's house is blown up to make room for the glorious rebuilding schemes of the future. By this time the whole family has been killed, and the curtain falls to the strains of the "Marseillaise."

So soon after the war, this sardonic play provoked veritable howls of indignation from all sides, particularly for its irreverent portrayal of members of the Free French forces, although they are expressly shown as opportunists who have joined the Resistance only that very day, and spend their time looking for cars they can requisition. In fact, the play is as harmless a piece of satire as it is a brilliant example of *l'humour noir* at its blackest.

Les Bâtisseurs d'Empire also has its touches of humor, but is a play of an altogether different kind—a poetic image of mortality and the fear of death. Its three acts show a family on the run from a mysterious but terrifying noise, which they try to escape by moving onto a higher and higher floor, into

an ever-smaller apartment. In Act I, father, mother, daughter
Zénobie, and their maid, Cruche, are shown taking possession
of a two-room apartment. In Act II they are one floor higher,
in a one-room apartment. The maid leaves them, and their
daughter, who has gone to the landing, cannot return to them
when the door mysteriously closes. Only the father and mother
are left. The world becomes narrower and narrower for them.
In the third act the father is seen entering a tiny attic room,
so terrified of the noise that he barricades the entrance before
his wife can get to him. He is alone. But the noise, the terrifying noise of the approach of death, cannot be excluded. And
now there is nowhere the father can escape to. He dies.

Apart from the characters named, who have speaking parts,
there is a mysterious, silent character, a half-human being,
called a *schmürz*, "covered in bandages, dressed in rags, one
arm in a sling, he holds a walking stick in the other. He limps,
bleeds, and is ugly to look at."[6] This silent figure seems not
to be noticed by the characters. Nevertheless they constantly
rain brutal blows on him.

Simple in structure and relentless in its progression, *Les
Bâtisseurs d'Empire* is a powerful and very personal statement.
Proud as we are, confident that we are building our own world,
our personal empire on earth, we are in fact constantly on the
run; far from growing wider, our world contracts. As we approach death, we get more and more lonely, our range of
vision and action becomes more and more narrow. It is increasingly difficult to communicate with the younger generation,
and the subterranean noise of death grows louder and louder.

All this is clear enough. But what does the *schmürz* stand
for? It is perhaps significant that Boris Vian wrote some of his
contributions to the more popular magazines under the pseu-
donym Adolphe Schmürz. There can be little doubt that *Les
Bâtisseurs d'Empire* dramatizes Vian's own feelings. He knew
he was suffering from a serious heart condition, the aftereffect
of a fever attack. He had to give up playing his beloved jazz
trumpet: "Each note played on the trumpet shortens my life
by a day," he said. It was his own life he saw narrowing. Does
the *schmürz* therefore stand for the mortal part of ourselves
that we brutally flog and maltreat without noticing what we
are doing? The fact that the *schmürz* collapses and dies just

before the hero of the play does points in this direction. On the other hand, after the hero's death other *schmürzes* are seen invading the stage. Are they the messengers of death and is the hero's own *schmürz* his own death, silently waiting for him, thoughtlessly flogged by the hero when he is *not* aware of his own mortality? Or is *schmürz*, derived from the German word for pain—*Schmerz*—simply the silent, ever-present pain of heart disease?

Boris Vian died on June 23, 1959, while watching a private preview of a film based on one of his books. There had been a good deal of controversy about the adaptation and he had not been invited to attend, but had merely sneaked in.

In *Les Bâtisseurs d'Empire* the flight from death takes the form of trying to escape upward. The same image appears in the opposite direction in a remarkable play by Dino Buzzati (born in 1906), the eminent Italian novelist and journalist on the staff of the *Corriere della Sera* in Milan. This play, first performed by the Piccolo Teatro, Milan, in 1953, and in Paris in an adaptation by Camus in 1955, is *Un Caso Clinico*. In two parts (thirteen scenes), it shows the death of a middle-aged businessman, Giovanni Corte. Busy, overworked, tyrannized but pampered as the family's breadwinner, whose health must be preserved, he is disturbed by hallucinations of a female voice calling him from the distance and by the specter of a woman that seems to haunt his house. He is persuaded to consult a famous specialist, and goes to see him at his ultramodern hospital. Before he knows what has happened, he is an inmate of the hospital, about to be operated on. Everybody reassures him—this hospital is organized in the most efficient modern manner; the people who are not really ill, or merely under observation, are on the top floor, the seventh. Those who are slightly less well are on the sixth; those who are ill, but not really badly, are on the fifth; and so on downward in a descending order to the first floor, which is the antechamber of death.

In a terrifying sequence of scenes, Buzzati shows his hero's descent. At first he is moved to the sixth floor merely to make room for someone who needs his private ward more than he does. Further down, he still hopes that he is merely going down to be near some specialized medical facilities he needs, and before he has fully realized what has happened, he is so far down that there is no hope of escape. He is buried among the outcasts who have already been given up, the lowest class of human beings—the dying. Corte's mother comes to take him home, but it is too late.

Un Caso Clinico is a remarkable and highly original work, a modern miracle play in the tradition of *Everyman*. It dramatizes the death of a rich man—his delusion that somehow he is in a special class, exempt from the ravages of illness; his gradual loss of contact with reality; and, above all, the imperceptible manner of his descent and its sudden revelation to him. And in the hospital, with its rigid stratification, Buzzati has found a terrifying image of society itself—an impersonal organization that hustles the individual on his way to death, caring for him, providing services, but at the same time distant, rule-ridden, incomprehensible, and cruel. While *Les Bâtisseurs d'Empire* shows man in active flight from death, *Un Caso Clinico* depicts him gradually overtaken by old age and illness, while totally unaware of what is happening. In the gradual process of dying, man loses his personality. Looking at the raincoat he wore at the height of his powers, Corte says, "Once Corte, the engineer, wore this fine raincoat. . . . Do you remember him? A dynamic man, sure of himself . . . how sure he was of himself, do you remember . . . ?"[7]

Buzzati, the author of an outstanding Kafkaesque novel (*Il Deserto dei Tartari*) and many short stories in a similar vein, has followed *Un Caso Clinico* with another play, *Un Verme al Ministero* (*A Worm at the Ministry*), which, however, belongs to a different theatrical convention. It is a political satire on a totalitarian revolution, reminiscent of Orwell's *1984* but with a curiously mystical ending—the appearance of a Christ-like figure at the moment when the turncoat bureaucrat is about to insult the Crucifix to prove his sincerity in supporting the atheist dictatorship.

Another interesting Italian contribution to the Theatre of the Absurd is that of Ezio d'Errico (born in 1892). A man of many parts, d'Errico had made a name as a painter and a writer of thrillers in the vein of Simenon, art critic, film writer, and journalist, when, in 1948, he turned to writing plays. His output of well over twenty plays since then has been varied, but has gradually veered in the direction of the Theatre of the Absurd. The starting point here is a criticism of the modern world, which, in *Il Formicaio* (*The Anthill*), appears as a grotesque, dehumanized place in which the hero, Casimiro, ends up by losing not only his individuality but even the gift of articulate speech. *Tempo di Cavallette* (*Time of the Locusts*) shows postwar Italy as a ruined village inhabited by selfish opportunists. When Joe, the Italo-American, arrives to share his wealth with the people of his homeland, he is murdered by a pair of juvenile delinquents. He reappears as a Christ-like figure, but the inhabitants are destroyed in a holocaust—of locusts or of atom bombs?—which incinerates the ruins of the village. Only a little boy survives, the hope of a new world. *Tempo di Cavallette* had its first performance at Darmstadt in the spring of 1958, in German.

D'Errico's experimental plays seem to have daunted the theatres of his native Italy, for his most important play to date in the convention of the Theatre of the Absurd, *La Foresta* (*The Forest*), also had its first stage appearance in German— on September 19, 1959, in Kassel.

The forest of the title consists of the grotesque relics of a mechanical civilization: broken telegraph poles, a derelict petrol pump, pylons and gallows growing out of a soil of concrete. In the spring, "the concrete burgeons like a mold, a filthy mold that rises, stratifies, and invades everything."[8] The people inhabiting this forest, from which there is no way out, are lost souls. Like the tramps in *Waiting for Godot*, they are hoping for a miracle, a liberation that will never happen. From time to time a train is heard passing in the distance and a ticket collector appears—he is an image of death. Those whose tickets have run out must die.

Among the derelicts are an old professor; a man of the world, and his ex-prostitute mistress; a vintner who in some ways represents Christianity and who struggles to hold on to his faith; a general whose family was killed in an air raid while he was directing operations at the front, and who lost his military unconcern with death when he saw the ruins under which they were buried; and a young poet who lost contact with reality when he was forced to take a humdrum job to support his family—he conducts animated and agonizing conversations with unseen characters whose replies take the form of improvisations on the saxophone and the violin.

The main action of the play turns round the efforts of Margot, the ex-prostitute (who was forced into prostitution when captured by enemy troops during the war), to redeem the young poet. But when she offers him her love and invites him to flee, he cannot bear to return to reality, and kills himself. Margot reproaches herself for having offered romantic notions of love to the boy, rather than winning him back to reality with her body, and she goes mad. The vintner reaffirms his faith that man is not abandoned by the deity, but the play ends with the radio idiotically bawling out the morning gymnastics, and Max, Margot's lover, mechanically performing the grotesque exercises it prescribes.

The forest of concrete is an apt poetic image of an industrial civilization, and the characters who inhabit it are all sufferers from its scourges—war, intellectual pride, the suppression of the poetic impulse by commercial pressures, religious doubt, and all the horrors of the concentration camp. (Max was forced under torture to betray his best friend, the friend left him his vast fortune, and he is now roaming the world to escape from his memories. Margot was tortured and forced to become a prostitute for the troops during the war.) The play is the passionate outcry of a romantic against the deadening of sensibilities, the loss of contact with organic nature, that the spread of a civilization of concrete and iron has brought about.

D'Errico's dream world, absurd and harsh though it may be, has a wistful poetic symbolism, a softness that sometimes verges on sentimentality. In the work of another Latin writer, Manuel de Pedrolo (born in 1918), we are in the presence of an intelligence of almost geometrical austerity. De Pedrolo would by now be better known outside his native country but for the fact that he writes in a language—Catalan—that is little understood even by those in the English-speaking world who would normally have access to French, Spanish, or German. He is a prolific novelist and short-story writer, and also the author of a number of plays, some of which fall into the convention of the Theatre of the Absurd. After fighting in the Spanish Civil War, on the losing side, he has worked as elementary-schoolteacher, insurance agent, salesman, translator, and publisher's reader. He has gained an impressive number of literary prizes.

De Pedrolo's one-act play *Cruma* (first performed in Barcelona on July 5, 1957), is a study in human isolation. "Cruma" is the name of an Etruscan measure or measuring instrument[9] and the play shows an attempt to measure the human situation by standards that have become inoperative and meaningless. In an empty and bare-walled corridor that seems part of a larger apartment, a man who is at home there—and is therefore called "the resident"—is about to measure the dimensions of the walls. He is joined by a visitor who helps him in this work—which is in vain, because they discover that the measuring tapes they are using are blank, without markings or figures.

The situation of the resident in the corridor of his apartment is as mysterious as that of the two tramps on their road in *Waiting for Godot*. The resident is unaware of an outside world. He does not know how the objects he uses have reached him. The visitor notices that he is using an ashtray, and asks him where he got it. "I don't know," the resident replies. "Someone brought it and now it is here." The visitor warns him, "If you are not careful, objects will invade your life."[10] The visitor, too, is oblivious of the outside world, although, as the resident reminds him, he must have come from outside.

It is in the same dreamlike atmosphere that the two are brought into contact with other characters. Voices are heard outside calling a woman's name, Nagaio. A girl passes through the corridor but is barely noticed by the resident and the visitor. When the visitor, who wants to wash his hands, opens the door to the bathroom, a stranger emerges, whom the resident takes for the visitor, a misunderstanding that makes communication almost impossible. Nagaio, the woman whom the voices have been heard calling, is seen when the window is opened in an apartment on the other side of the courtyard. Again the resident and the visitor find it difficult to communicate with her, but the stranger immediately makes friends with her and arranges a date. The stranger also has no difficulty in establishing contact with the girl, who again traverses the corridor. He decides to go out with this girl, instead of Nagaio. When the girl disappears behind a curtain leading into one of the rooms, he wants to follow her, but the curtain has turned into a solid door. The resident is able to open the door and let him reach the girl. Resident and visitor are left alone. They try to understand what has happened, and come to the conclusion that the strange beings who have disturbed them do not exist. But then they themselves cannot claim that they exist in reality. This being settled, they can return to their work. There is a knock at the door. As the resident goes to open it, the curtain falls.

This strange short play poses the problem of the reality of the "others" and the possibility of establishing contact with them. Each character represents a different level of being. The resident occupies one end of the scale—he is an authentic being exploring his own world, hence unable to relate himself to others, unable even to distinguish his friend from a stranger. On the other end of the scale is the young girl—she exists only insofar as others want her. The other three characters represent intermediary steps on this scale. The greater the *inner* reality or authenticity of a human being, the less able he is to establish contact with the outside world, in its crudity and deceptiveness. And yet this interior solitude is bound to be disturbed; at the end of the play, the whole cycle of invasions from the inauthentic, everyday world is about to begin anew.

De Pedrolo's second, and more ambitious, play in this convention, *Homes i No* (*Humans and No;* first performed in Barcelona on December 19, 1958), is described by the author as "an investigation in two acts." The stage is divided into three parts by two screens of iron bars; in the compartment in the middle, the prison guard, a strange inhuman being called No, watches over the inmates of the cells to the left and right. No has fallen asleep, and the two couples, Fabi and Selena in one cage, Bret and Eliana in the other, try to overpower their jailer. But he awakes in time. The attempt of the two human couples to break out from behind the bars that imprison them fails. But the human beings, now that they have become conscious of the possibility of escape, have high hopes that someday they will succeed—and if not they themselves, their children.

In the second act, the two couples are joined by a son, Feda, in one case, and in the other by a daughter, Sorne. Feda and Sorne are in love and resolve to do all they can to break out from the cages that prevent them from being united. They undertake a thorough examination of their prison and find that on the far side the cells end in an unbridgeable abyss. Their parents had been so fascinated by No that they had never even taken the trouble to explore the other side of their prison. Yet there seems no escape that way. Hence the young people concentrate on the back wall, and discover that this is by no means as solid as it seemed but has, rather, the appearance of a kind of curtain. Shall they tear that curtain down? No, the inhuman jailer is deeply perturbed, and begs them not to do so. If they do, it will be the end for them. Death? No, much worse. As the tension grows, Feda finally decides to take the risk and they tear the curtain down. Behind it there is another row of bars, which not only close their respective cells but reveal that No himself is merely a prisoner in a third cell. Behind this new row of bars sit three new jailers clad in black, silent and motionless. No has been a prisoner himself, but as Feda exclaims, "even more so, because he knew it!"[11]

Homes i No is indeed an investigation—an investigation into the problem of liberty. Man is imprisoned in an infinitely receding series of enclosures. Whenever he thinks that he has broken through one of these barriers (the barrier of superstition, the barrier of myth or tyranny, or the inability to master nature), he finds himself face to face with a new barrier (the metaphysical anguish of the human condition, death, the relativity of all knowledge, and so on). But the struggle to overcome the new row of iron bars continues; it must go on, even if we know in advance that it will reveal only a further barrier beyond.

In the simplicity of its conception, and in the complete merging of the philosophical idea with its concrete representation in terms of a stage picture, *Homes i No* must occupy a high place among the most successful examples of the Theatre of the Absurd. Manuel de Pedrolo has completed a number of further plays in this convention. If they maintain the promise of his first attempts, he will take his place among the major exponents of the genre.

Another Spaniard who may well be able to claim such a place is Fernando Arrabal, who was born in Melilla (formerly Spanish Morocco) in 1932, completed his law studies at Madrid, but has been living in France since 1954, and writing his plays in French. Arrabal's world derives its absurdity not, like that of de Pedrolo, from the despair of the philosopher trying to probe the secrets of being, but from the fact that his characters see the human situation with uncomprehending eyes of childlike simplicity. Like children, they are often cruel because they have failed to understand, or even to notice, the existence of a moral law; and, like children, they suffer the cruelty of the world as a meaningless affliction.

Arrabal's first play, *Pique-nique en Campagne* (the title is a cruel pun—it might be taken to mean "picnic in the country," but actually stands for "picnic on the battlefield"), already clearly shows this approach. He wrote the play at the age of twenty, under the influence of the news from the Korean War. This short one-act play shows a soldier, Zapo, isolated in the front line of the fighting. His father and mother, who are too simple to grasp the ferocity of modern war, arrive to visit him, so that they can have a Sunday picnic together. When an enemy soldier, Zepo, turns up, Zapo takes him prisoner, but later invites him to join the picnic. As the party gaily proceeds, a burst of machine-gun fire wipes out all the participants.

This is Chaplinesque comedy without the redeeming happy end; it already contains the highly disturbing mixture of innocence and cruelty so characteristic of Arrabal. This is also the atmosphere of *Oraison*, a *drame mystique* in one act, which opens the volume of Arrabal's *Théâtre*, published in 1958. A man and a woman, Fidio and Lilbé (notice the baby talk of the names), sit by a child's coffin discussing ways and means of being good—from today. Lilbé cannot grasp what it means to be good:

LILBÉ: Shall we not be able to go and have fun, as before, in the cemetery?
FIDIO: Why not?
LILBÉ: And tear the eyes out of the corpses, as before?
FIDIO: No, not that.
LILBÉ: And kill people?

FIDIO: No.

LILBÉ: So we'll let them live?

FIDIO: Obviously.

LILBÉ: So much the worse for them.[12]

As this discussion on the nature of goodness proceeds, it is gradually revealed that Fidio and Lilbé are sitting by the coffin of their own child, whom they have killed. Naïvely they discuss the example of Jesus, and come to the conclusion that they will have a try at being good, although Lilbé foresees the likelihood that they will get tired of it.

In *Les Deux Bourreaux* (*The Two Executioners*), we are faced with an analogous situation, but here conventional morality is more directly attacked as self-contradictory. A woman, Françoise, comes with her two sons, Benoît and Maurice, to denounce her husband to the two executioners of the title. He is guilty of some unspecified crime. Françoise, who hates him, wants to witness his being tortured in the next room. She rejoices in his sufferings, and even rushes into the torture chamber to put salt and vinegar on his wounds. Benoît, who is a dutiful son of his mother, accepts her behavior, but Maurice protests. Maurice is thus a bad son, who disobeys his mother and hurts her. When the father finally dies of his tortures, Maurice persists in accusing his mother of having caused his death, yet finally he is persuaded into the path of duty. He asks to be forgiven for his insubordination, and as the curtain falls the mother and her sons embrace.

In *Fando et Lis*, a play in five scenes, Fando is pushing his beloved, Lis, who is paralyzed, in a wheelchair. They are on the road to Tar. Fando loves Lis dearly, and yet, at the same time, he resents her as a burden. Nevertheless he tries to amuse her by playing her the only thing he knows on his drum, the Song of the Feather. They meet three gentlemen with umbrellas, who are also on the way to Tar, a place that they, like Fando and Lis, find it almost impossible to reach. Instead of getting to Tar, they always arrive back in the same place. Fando proudly displays Lis's beauty to the three gentlemen, raising her skirt to show off her thighs, and inviting them to kiss her. Fando loves Lis, but he cannot resist the temptation to be cruel to her. In Scene 4, we learn that, to show her off to the gentlemen, he left her lying naked in the open all night. Now she is even more ill than before. Fando has her in chains, and puts handcuffs on her, just to see whether she can drag herself along with them. He beats her. Falling down, she breaks his little drum. He is so furious that he beats her unconscious. When the three gentlemen arrive, she is dead. The last scene shows the three gentlemen with umbrellas confusedly discussing what has happened. Fando appears with a flower and a dog—he promised Lis that when she died he would visit her grave with a flower and a dog. The three gentlemen decide to accompany him to the cemetery. After that the four of them can try to make their way to Tar.

In its strange mixture of *commedia dell'arte* and Grand Guignol, *Fando et Lis* is a poetic evocation of the ambivalence of love, the love a child might have for a dog, which is cuddled and tormented in turn. By projecting the emotions of childhood into an adult world, Arrabal achieves an effect that is both tragicomic and profound, because it reveals the truth hidden behind a good deal of adult emotion as well.

Arrabal's most ambitious play to date is *Le Cimetière des Voitures (The Automobile Graveyard)*, a play in two acts, which attempts no less than a reconstruction of the passion of Christ seen through Arrabal's childlike eyes and placed in a grotesque landscape of squalor. The scene is a derelict graveyard of old motorcars, which is, however, run on the lines of a luxury hotel. A valet, Milos, provides the service—breakfast in bed and a kiss from Dila, the prostitute, for every gentleman before he falls asleep. The hero, Emanou (i.e., Emanuel), a trumpet player, is the leader of a group of three musicians: his companions are Topé, the clarinetist, and Fodère, the saxophone player, a mute modeled on Harpo Marx. Emanou, like Fidio in *Oraison* wants to be good. This desire expresses itself in his providing music for dancing to the inmates of the automobile graveyard every night, although the playing of musical instruments is strictly forbidden by the police. Throughout the play, two indefatigable athletes, a man, Tiossido, and an elderly woman, Lasca, cross the scene in a grotesque show of sportsmanship. In the second act, these two are revealed as police agents who are after Emanou. They pay Topé to betray his master for money—he will identify him by a kiss. When this happens, the mute Fodère denies him by vigorously shaking his head as he is asked whether he knows Emanou. Emanou is savagely beaten and taken away, dying, his arms tied to the handle bars of a bicycle. The grotesque high life of the automobile graveyard continues.

Emanou's desire to be good is shown as a vague wish rather than a rational conviction. He recites his creed of goodness mechanically: "When one is good, one feels a great interior joy, born from the peace of the spirit that one knows when one sees oneself similar to the ideal image of man," but by the end of the play he seems to have forgotten this text and gets into a complete muddle when trying to recite it. At the same time, he earnestly discusses with his disciples whether it would not be more profitable to take up another profession—such as stealing or murder—and decides against these occupations merely on the ground that they are too difficult. When Dila tells him that she too wants to be good, Emanou replies, "But you are good already; you allow everybody to sleep with you."[13]

Although the parallels between Emanou and Christ are made so obvious as to border on the blasphemous (he was born in a stable, his father was a carpenter, he left home at the age of thirty to play the trumpet), the play achieves an impression of innocence—the search for goodness pursued with total dedication in a universe that is both squalid and devoid of meaning. In such a world there cannot be any understandable ethical standards and the pursuit of goodness becomes an enterprise tragic in its absurdity, as absurd as the strenuous running of the police spies in the pursuit of sportsmanship.

Arrabal's preoccupation with the problem of goodness—the relationship between love and cruelty, his questioning of all accepted ethical standards from the standpoint of an innocent who would be only too eager to accept them if only he could understand them—is reminiscent of the attitude of Beckett's tramps in *Waiting for Godot*. Arrabal, who insists that his writing is the expression of his personal dreams and emotions, acknowledges his deep admiration for Beckett. But although he has translated some of Adamov's plays into Spanish, he does not think that he has been influenced by him.

Arrabal's published plays are intensely human. Yet he is also greatly interested in developing an abstract theatre that would eliminate any human content altogether. In his *Orchéstration Théâtrale* (first performed under the direction of Jacques Poliéri in the fall of 1959), he has tried to create a dramatic spectacle consisting entirely of the movements of abstract three-dimensional shapes, some of which were mechanical devices, while others were moved by dancers. The formal world of this strange spectacle was based on the inventions of Klee, Mondrian, Delauney, and the mobiles of Alexander Calder. Arrabal is convinced that the incongruities of mechanical movement are a potential source of highly comic effects. The script of *Orchéstration Théâtrale*, which contains no dialogue whatever, resembles the notation of a gigantic game of chess (Arrabal is a passionate chess player) and is illustrated by fascinating colored diagrams. The difficulties of putting this daring conception on the stage within the means of a struggling avant-garde company proved so formidable that the lack of public acclaim achieved by the experiment is by no means conclusive proof of the impossibility of an abstract mechanical theatre.

Another experiment by a foreign author living in France that contains the promise of a widening of scope of the convention of the Theatre of the Absurd, is a play by a young Israeli, Amos Kenan, which Roger Blin directed and which had its first performance in French at the Théâtre de Lutèce on October 28, 1960. *Le Lion*, translated from the Hebrew by the author and Christiane Rochefort,[14] clearly shows the influence of Ionesco in its disregard for any congruity between the nature and the physical appearance of the characters. The cast list of three consists of "the baby, aged about fifty," "the woman, aged about thirty," who treats the baby as her own child, and "the chauffeur, aged about twenty." The three characters, all of whom are never together on the stage at the same time, are in constant flux. From being a baby in a playpen, the fifty-year-old brusquely changes into a general directing a battle and an industrial tycoon engaged in vast building operations. The chauffeur, who has been driving him around on this inspection tour of battlefield and factory, turns into a burglar who breaks into the woman's house, where he is made to help himself to all valuables and makes love to the woman, who has previously been shown as the baby-tycoon's mistress, being served by him in a shoe shop. In the final scene, the woman is again the mother trying to make the baby eat its cream. But the baby insists that he is now a lion.

What does all this amount to? The play seems to be an attempt to produce a synoptic view of human emotions by abolishing the sequence of time. The baby already contains the general and the general is still in many respects a baby, and both, with their aggressive instincts, are also, at the same time, a lion. The woman is mother, distantly adored mistress, and sensuous accomplice of the burglar, who, in turn, at one point is the servile subordinate of the general, then becomes the innocent victim of persecution, and then again a tough criminal. If we saw the life of our fellow men all at once rather than in a time sequence, the play argues, we would be struck by the simultaneous coexistence of such seemingly contradictory characteristics.

Le Lion shared the double bill at the Théâtre de Lutèce with a play by an already established writer of acknowledged eminence, most of whose work lies outside the scope of this book, Max Frisch (born in 1911), the important German-Swiss dramatist and novelist. The play in question, *Biedermann und die Brandstifter* (*Biedermann and the Incendiaries*), first produced in the original German at the Zürich Schauspielhaus on March 29, 1958, is Frisch's first excursion into the realm of *humour noir* and the Theatre of the Absurd. Frisch and his compatriot, Friedrich Duerrenmatt, without doubt the leading dramatists of the German-speaking world today, have developed a dramatic idiom of their own, a style that owes a great deal to Bernard Shaw, Thornton Wilder, and Bertolt Brecht, and one that might perhaps most aptly be described as a theatre of intellectual fantasy, airing contemporary problems in a vein of disillusioned tragicomedy. In being a sardonic commentary on a contemporary political phenomenon, *Biedermann und die Brandstifter* clearly belongs in this vein, but in the parodistic treatment of the subject and its resolute pursuit of the absurd, the play also shows the influence of the Theatre of the Absurd.

Labeled a "didactic play without a lesson," *Biedermann und die Brandstifter* tells, in six scenes and an epilogue, the cautionary tale of a highly respectable bourgeois (Biedermann means precisely this in German), a manufacturer of hair lotion, whose house is invaded by a trio of shady characters. Biedermann knows that his home town has been the scene of a series of incendiary acts that are the work of men who have sought shelter in various houses, on the ground that they are homeless. He soon suspects that his guests are incendiaries, but even when they openly stack drums of gasoline in his attic, even when they fix fuses and detonators in front of his own eyes, he believes that they will not set fire to his house, and to the whole town, if only he treats them nicely and invites them to a special dinner of goose and red cabbage. As one of the incendiaries sums up the situation, "Jocularity is the third-best kind of camouflage; the second-best is sentimentality. . . . But the best and safest camouflage is still the pure, naked truth. Funnily enough, no one believes it. . . ."[15]

Biedermann is shown as heartless and brutal. He has driven one of his employees to suicide by dismissing him after years of faithful service, but at the same time he sees himself as an affable fellow who knows how to charm people. And this is his undoing. Two of the incendiaries, though depicted as victims of the social order, are destructive purely for the sake of destructiveness and the feeling of power they get from seeing things burn. The third is an intellectual who thinks he is serving some abstract principle. When the fuses are about to be lit, the intellectual rats on his fellow conspirators, having discovered that they are not interested in his ideological rationalizations of destruction. But Biedermann does not believe this warning either. When the incendiaries find that they are out of matches, he obligingly hands them his own, so that they can light the fuse that burns his house, his wife, himself, and the whole town.

The civilization that is being destroyed is one in which "most people believe not in God but in the fire brigade."[16] And the play is framed by a burlesque pseudo-Greek chorus of firemen, who are constantly affirming their readiness to intervene. In the epilogue, Biedermann and his wife are in hell, but in this unmetaphysical age the Devil himself (who is revealed as one of the incendiaries) refuses to conduct a hell for people like Biedermann. As the destroyed city has been rebuilt "more beautiful than before," it seems that life can go on.

Biedermann und die Brandstifter is more than just a very telling piece of political satire. The political satire is certainly there: Biedermann's situation, according to Hans Baenziger, the author of an excellent study of Frisch, is based on the situation of President Beneš of Czechoslovakia, who took the Communists into his government although he knew that they were bent on destroying the country's independence.[17] It is also the situation of the German intellectuals who thought that Hitler did not mean what he said when he spoke of war and conquest, and so allowed him to start a world conflagration. And it is also, in a sense, the situation of the world in the age of the hydrogen bomb, when the attics of the world's major powers are stored with very highly inflammable and explosive material. But beyond this purely political aspect, Frisch's play describes the state of mind of the family in Ionesco's *The Bald Soprano* and *Jacques*—the dead world of routine and empty bonhomie, where the destruction of values has reached a point where the bewildered individual can no longer distinguish between the things that ought to be preserved and those that should be destroyed. The fire brigade is ready, but there is no one left who can recognize the incendiaries as dangerous, and so the measures taken to prevent the fire are bound to fail. What is more, in a world of dead routine, of unceasing consumption and production, the destruction of a civilization will be felt merely as a beneficial way of clearing the ground for a new building boom—so that production and consumption can continue.

The Theatre of the Absurd has struck a responsive chord in the German-speaking world, where the collapse of a whole civilization, through the rise and fall of Hitler, has made the loss of meaning and cohesion in men's lives more evident than elsewhere. The major dramatists of the Absurd have been more successful in Germany than anywhere else to date. Yet so total has been the vacuum left by Hitler that it has taken a long time for a new generation of dramatists to arise. (Hence the leading position occupied by two Swiss dramatists in the contemporary German-speaking theatre.) Nevertheless, the breakthrough of a new generation of writers has started.

Wolfgang Hildesheimer (born in 1916), one of the first German dramatists to take up the idiom of the Theatre of the Absurd, spent the war years, significantly enough, in exile abroad, and is still an Israeli citizen. Originally a painter, Hildesheimer started his career as a dramatist with a series of witty and fantastic radio plays—picaresque tales of forgers, grotesque Balkan countries, and Oriental romance. The step from this type of intellectual thriller to the Theatre of the Absurd seems a natural development. Hildesheimer regards the Theatre of the Absurd, as he has pointed out in a brilliantly argued lecture on the subject,[18] as a theatre of parables. Admittedly, "the story of the prodigal son is also a parable. But it is a parable of a different kind. Let us analyze the difference—the story of the prodigal son is a parable deliberately conceived to allow an indirect statement (that is, to give the opportunity to reach a conclusion by analogy), while the 'absurd' play becomes a parable of life precisely through the intentional omission of any statement. For life, too, makes no statement."[19]

Hildesheimer's collected volume of the plays that illustrate his conception of the Theatre of the Absurd has the title *Spiele in denen es dunkel wird (Plays in Which Darkness Falls)*.[20] This is literally the case. As each of the three plays unfolds, the light fades. In *Pastorale, oder Die Zeit für Kakao (Pastoral, or Time for Cocoa)*, some elderly characters disport themselves in a strange syncopation of dialogue concerned with business matters and stock-exchange deals, with artistic and poetic overtones (a mixture very characteristic of the tone of West German society today). As the light grows darker, summer turns into autumn and winter, and death overtakes the president of a big company, a consul, and a mining engineer.

In *Landschaft mit Figuren (Landscape with Figures)*, a painter is shown at work painting the portraits of a group of equally empty and pretentious characters—a great but aging lady, her gigolo, and an elderly tycoon. Here too the characters pass from middle to old age before our eyes until they die, are neatly packed into boxes, and sold to a collector—so that the characters themselves have become their own portraits. As this work proceeds, a glazier is putting new panes of glass into the studio windows. It is through them that the light gradually becomes dark. But at the end the painter and his wife are as young as they were in the beginning, and as they are left alone, the mauve panes of glass fall to the ground and the stage is once more bathed in light.

The glazier appears again in *Die Uhren* (*The Clocks*), but this time the panes of glass he puts into the windows of a room inhabited by a man and wife are jet black and impenetrable. As the work proceeds, the couple relive scenes from their life together; toward the end a salesman comes who sells them a profusion of clocks of all kinds. And at the final curtain the man and his wife are inside the clocks, making ticking noises.

These dramatic parables are impressive poetic statements, even though they are far from being free from rather obviously drawn analogies and somewhat facile conclusions.

Hildesheimer's parable plays are gentle and elegant. The theatre of Günter Grass (born in 1927) is of a far rougher texture. Grass also started his career as a painter. His plays are like the canvases of Bosch or Goya brought to life—violent and grotesque. In *Onkel, Onkel* (*Uncle, Uncle*), we meet Bollin, a young man single-mindedly dedicated to murder, who is always shown as failing because his intended victims display no fear of him. The little girl under whose bed he has hidden takes no notice of him when he emerges, but merely asks him to help her with her crossword puzzle; the gamekeeper he traps in the woods continues to instruct two city children in the botany of forest trees and methods of escape; the film star whom he wants to kill in her bathtub drives him away with her foolish chatter; and in the end two children steal Bollin's revolver and shoot *him* dead.

In *Zweiunddreissig Zähne* (*Thirty-two Teeth*), we meet a schoolmaster as single-minded as Bollin—for him tooth hygiene overrides all other passions. *Hochwasser* (*The Flood*) shows a family fleeing from the rising water onto the top floor of their house and then to the roof, where they meet a pair of philosophical rats. As the waters recede and they return to routine lives in a ruined home, they regret losing the excitement and the corrupt figures of fantasy they met during the emergency.

The short play *Noch Zehn Minuten bis Buffalo* (*Ten Minutes to Buffalo*) presents an ancient toy locomotive passing through a nonsense landscape accompanied by nautical conversation and never getting to Buffalo at all.

Günter Grass's most interesting play, however, *Die Bösen Köche* (*The Wicked Cooks*), is an ambitious attempt to transmute a religious subject into poetic tragicomedy. Cooks proliferate on the stage—there are two rival factions of cooks and they are after the secret of a mysterious gray soup consisting of ordinary cabbage soup with the addition of a special kind of ashes. The holder of this secret is known as the Count, although his real name is the very ordinary one of Herbert Schymanski. The cooks make a bargain with the Count. He can marry Martha, the nurse, if he promises to let them in on his secret. But when they demand that he keep his part of the bargain, the Count has forgotten the recipe. "I have told you often enough, it is not a recipe but an experience, living knowledge, continuous change. You should be aware of the fact that no cook has ever succeeded in cooking the same soup twice. . . . The last months, this life with Martha . . . has made this experience superfluous. I have forgotten it."[21] Unable to fulfill their part of the bargain, the Count and Martha kill themselves. There can be little doubt that an analogy to the Passion pervades the play. Martha washes the Count's feet shortly before he dies, and there is an association between the mysterious food and the Eucharist, which, after all, was instituted in the course of, and is symbolized by, a meal.

Günter Grass wrote most of his plays before 1957. He has since then achieved a major success with a vast and grotesquely exuberant novel, *Die Blechtrommel* (1959), but it is to be hoped that he will not abandon the theatre altogether.

Another notable novelist who also started his career as a painter and who has also ventured into the field of the Theatre of the Absurd is Robert Pinget (born in 1919). Pinget is a native of Geneva who now lives in Paris. He studied law, painted, taught French in England for a while, and became one of the leading figures in the group of "new novelists" around Alain Robbe-Grillet. Pinget is a close friend of Samuel Beckett and his play *Lettre Morte* (*Dead Letter*) shared the bill with Beckett's *Krapp's Last Tape* at the Théâtre Récamier in the spring of 1960.

Lettre Morte takes up the theme of Pinget's novel *Le Fiston* (1959), which is in the form of a letter addressed by an abandoned father to his prodigal son; the father does not know where his son has gone, so the letter cannot be sent off and remains a "dead letter." *Le Fiston* tries to reproduce the rambling, ill-organized shape of an endless epistle, added to from day to day; the book lacks even pagination, thus increasing the reader's illusion that he is reading a real letter composed by a besotted old man. The play, *Lettre Morte*, puts that same old man, Monsieur Levert, on the stage. It is as though the author had become so obsessed with the reality of the long letter that he had to see the man who wrote it before his eyes in the flesh. We see Monsieur Levert in two situations—in the bar, opening his heart to the bartender, and in the post office, trying to persuade the clerk behind the counter to have another good look to see whether there isn't somewhere, after all, a letter from his lost son that might have gone astray. But the bartender and the post-office clerk are played by the same actor, the counter of the post office is the same as that of the bar. The old man is waiting without real hope, like the tramps in *Waiting for Godot*. He is continually racking his brain to find the reason why his son has left him, what he has done wrong to lose his affection. Outside, a funeral procession passes. Monsieur Levert is waiting for death. In a short scherzo in this symphony of melancholy and regret two of the actors of an itinerant company come into the bar and playfully repeat passages from the sentimental bedroom farce they have been performing that night. The play is called *The Prodigal Son*, and it deals with a father who writes letters to his son, imploring him to return. Whereupon he *does* return. Here the worn-out convention of boulevard theatre, where everything happens as it should, is cruelly confronted with that of the Theatre of the Absurd where nothing happens at all and where the lines of dialogue do not flit wittily to and fro like ping-pong balls but are as repetitious and inconclusive as in real life—and hence as absurd as reality in a meaningless world is bound to be.

Pinget's second attempt at the dramatic form is a short

radio play, *La Manivelle* (translated under the title *The Old Tune* by Samuel Beckett, and first broadcast in the B.B.C.'s Third Programme on August 23, 1960), in which the absurdity of real speech is carried to the extreme: two old men, an organ-grinder and his friend, are talking about the past. The conversation rambles from subject to subject, and each of the old men comes out with some choice bit of his past life. The trouble is that the other immediately contradicts the truth of that information, so that each one's recollection of his own past life is called into question. The past of each of these two old men mutually cancels out the other. What are they left with? Was their past life a mere illusion? As the two stand talking in the street, the sounds of modern traffic almost drown their recollections. Eventually, however, the handle of the barrel organ that had jammed (hence the title of the French original) turns again, and the old tune rises triumphantly above the traffic, perhaps a symbol that the old tune of memory, however rickety and uncertain, still prevails.

This short radio play, brilliantly translated by Beckett into an Irish idiom, creates, out of fragments that in their strict naturalness are incoherent to the point of imbecility, a strange texture of nostalgic associations and lyrical beauty. For there is no real contradiction between a meticulous reproduction of reality and a literature of the Absurd. Quite the reverse. Most real conversation, after all, is incoherent, illogical, ungrammatical, and elliptical. By transcribing reality with ruthless accuracy, the dramatist arrives at the disintegrating language of the Absurd. It is the strictly logical dialogue of the rationally constructed play that is unrealistic and highly stylized. In a world that has become absurd, transcribing reality with meticulous care is enough to create the impression of extravagant irrationality.

This is also the method of one of the most promising exponents of the Theatre of the Absurd in the English-speaking world, Harold Pinter (born in 1930). The son of a Jewish tailor in Hackney, in East London, Pinter started writing poetry for little magazines in his teens, studied acting at the Royal Academy of Dramatic Art and the Central School of Speech and Drama, and, under the stage name David Baron, embarked on an acting career, which led him around Ireland in a Shakespearean company and to years of strenuous work in provincial repertory. After starting on a novel, *The Dwarfs*, which he did not finish, he began to write plays in 1957. He himself has told the story of how he mentioned an idea for a play to a friend of his who was working in the drama department of Bristol University. The friend liked the idea so much that he wrote to Pinter asking for the play, adding that if the university was to perform it, he would have to send the manuscript within a week. "So I wrote back and told him to forget about the whole thing. And then I sat down and wrote it in four days. I don't quite know how it happened, but it did."[22]

This rapidly and spontaneously written one-act play, *The Room* (first performed at Bristol University in May, 1957), already contains a good many of the basic themes and a great deal of the very personal style and idiom of Pinter's later and more successful work—the uncannily cruel accuracy of his reproduction of the inflections and rambling irrelevancy of everyday speech; the commonplace situation that is gradually invested with menace, dread, and mystery; the deliberate omission of an explanation or a motivation for the action. The room, which is the center and chief poetic image of the play, is one of the recurring motifs of Pinter's work. As he himself once put it, "Two people in a room—I am dealing a great deal of the time with this image of two people in a room. The curtain goes up on the stage, and I see it as a very potent question: What is going to happen to these two people in the room? Is someone going to open the door and come in?"[23] The starting point of Pinter's theatre is thus a return to some of the basic elements of drama—the suspense created by the elementary ingredients of pure, pre-literary theatre: a stage, two people, a door; a poetic image of an undefined fear and expectation. When asked by a critic what his two people in his room are afraid of, Pinter replied, "Obviously they are scared of what is outside the room. Outside the room there is a world bearing upon them which is frightening. I am sure it is frightening to you and me as well."[24]

In this case, the room is inhabited by Rose, a simple-minded old woman whose husband, Bert, never speaks to her although he is pampered and fed with overwhelming motherliness. The room is in a vast house; outside it is winter and night. Rose sees the room as her only refuge, her only security in a hostile world. This room, she tells herself, is just right for her. She would not like to live downstairs in the basement, where it is cold and damp. The room becomes an image of the small area of light and warmth that our consciousness, the fact that we exist, opens up in the vast ocean of nothingness from which we gradually emerge after birth and into which we sink again when we die. The room, this small speck of warmth and light in the darkness, is a precarious foothold; Rose is afraid that she may be driven from it. She is not sure of the place of her room in the scheme of things, how it fits into the house. When she asks Mr. Kidd, whom she takes for the landlord but who may be merely a caretaker, how many floors there are in the house, even he is vague about the matter: "Well, to tell you the truth, I don't count them now."[25] Mr. Kidd is an old, doddering man, vague about his own origins: "I think my mum was a Jewess. Yes, I wouldn't be surprised to learn that she was a Jewess."[26]

Rose's husband and Mr. Kidd leave. Rose remains alone. The door assumes all the menace of an opening into the vague unknown of the house, with its uncertain number of floors, the night and the winter outside. And when Rose finally opens the door to take the refuse out, two people are seen standing outside it. A moment of genuine terror has been produced with the utmost economy of means. And even though the strangers are merely a young couple looking for the landlord, the atmosphere of terror is kept up. They are looking for a room, they have heard there is a good room to let in that very house. Wandering through the empty house, they heard a voice in the dark basement, confirming that there was a room to let. As a matter of fact it was No. 7—Rose's room.

The strangers leave. Mr. Kidd returns. There is a man downstairs who wants to see Rose. He has been there for days, waiting for Rose's husband to leave, just lying there in the basement. Mr. Kidd goes out. Rose is left alone. Again the door becomes the focal point of a nameless menace. It opens. A blind Negro enters. His name is Riley. He has a message for Rose: "Your father wants you to come home. Come home, Sal."[27] We know the woman is called Rose. But she does not deny being called Sal. She merely insists, "Don't call me that." Bert, Rose's husband, returns. He, who has not spoken throughout the entire first scene, now speaks: "I got back all right." Again, a real *coup de théâtre* is brought about by the simplest of devices. Bert speaks about the menace of the dark and how his beloved van got him back. Then he notices the Negro. He upsets the chair on which he is sitting and beats him savagely until he remains motionless. Rose clutches her eyes. She has gone blind.

The Room shows not only the main characteristics of Pinter's style fully formed; the weaknesses it displays also allow us to judge how he gradually learned to avoid the temptations into which he fell in his first bout of spontaneous enthusiasm. The weakness of *The Room* is clearly its lapse from horror, built up from elements of the commonplace, into crude symbolism, cheap mystery, and violence. The blind Negro with the message from the father calling his daughter home, the killing of this near-parody of a death symbol by the jealous husband, and Rose's own blinding—all these are melodramatic devices that are out of keeping with the subtly built-up terrors of the opening scenes. Here mystery becomes threadbare mystification.

Pinter's second one-act play still contains this element of mystification, but already it is far more subtly and wittily used. In *The Dumb Waiter* (written in 1957, first performed at the Hampstead Theatre Club, in London, on January 21, 1960), we again have a room with two people in it—and the door that opens on the unknown. The two men in this dingy basement room are two hired killers employed by a mysterious organization to go around the country and assassinate their employers' victims. They are given an address and a key and told to wait for instructions. Sooner or later their victim arrives, they kill him or her, and drive off. They don't know what happens then: "Who clears up after we have gone? I am curious about that. Who does the clearing up? Maybe they don't clear up. Maybe they just leave them there, eh? What do you think?"[28]

Ben and Gus, the two gunmen, are very nervous. They want to make tea but are frustrated. They have no matches. An envelope with matches is mysteriously pushed under the door. But even then they don't have the shilling to put into the gas

meter. At the back of the basement room there is a serving
hatch, a "dumb waiter"—this must have been the kitchen of a
restaurant at one time. Suddenly this contraption begins to
move; an order on a piece of paper comes down: "Two
braised steak and chips. Two sago puddings. Two teas without sugar." The two gunmen, anxious not to be discovered, are
pathetically eager to fill this mysterious order from above. They
search their pockets for bits of food and send up a packet of
tea, a bottle of milk, a bar of chocolate, an Eccles cake, a
packet of potato chips. But the dumb waiter comes back for
more. It demands more and more complicated dishes, Greek
and Chinese specialties. The two men discover a speaking
tube next to the dumb waiter, and Ben establishes contact
with the powers above. He hears that "the Eccles cake was
stale, the chocolate was melted, the biscuits were mouldy."[29]
When Gus goes out to get a glass of water, the speaking tube
comes to life again. Ben gets his final instructions from above.
They are to kill the next man who enters. It is Gus. He is
stripped of jacket, waistcoat, tie, holster, and revolver. It is
Gus who is the next victim.

The Dumb Waiter brilliantly fulfills Ionesco's postulate in
completely fusing tragedy with the most hilarious farce. It
also succeeds in making the mysterious supernatural ingredient, which was merely sentimental in The Room, into an
additional element of comedy: the spectacle of the heavenly
powers bombarding two solemn gunmen with demands for
"macaroni pastitsio, ormitha macarounada, and char siu and
bean sprouts" is wildly funny. Yet the main element of comedy
is provided by the brilliant small talk behind which the two
men hide their growing anxiety. These discussions of which
football team is playing away on that particular Saturday,
whether it is correct to say "light the kettle" or "light the gas,"
the desultory discussions of trivial news in the evening paper
are utterly true, wildly comic, and terrifying in their absurdity.

Pinter's first full-length play, The Birthday Party, combines
some of the characters and situations of The Room and The
Dumb Waiter while, for the first time, omitting the melodramatic, supernatural element—without any loss of mystery or
horror. The safe and warm haven of The Room has here become a dingy seaside boarding house kept by a slovenly but

motherly old woman, Meg, who has many of the features of Rose in the earlier play. Meg's husband, Petey, is almost as silent as Rose's husband Bert. But he lacks Bert's brutality. He is a kindly old man, employed as a deck-chair attendant on the promenade. Ben and Gus, the two gunmen of *The Dumb Waiter*, reappear as a sinister pair of strangers—an Irishman, brutal and silent, and a Jew, full of false bonhomie and spurious worldly wisdom. But there is a new central character —Stanley, a man in his late thirties, indolent and apathetic, who has somehow found refuge in Meg's boarding house, which has not had any other visitor for years. Meg treats him with a motherliness so stifling as to be almost incestuous. Little is known about his past, except for a clearly apocryphal story that he once gave a piano recital at Lower Edmonton. It was a great success. But then, at his next concert, "they carved me up. Carved me up. It was all arranged, it was all worked out. My next concert. Somewhere else it was. In winter. I went down there to play. Then, when I got there, the hall was closed, the place was shuttered up, not even a caretaker. They'd locked it up. . . . A fast one. They pulled a fast one. I'd like to know who was responsible for that. . . . All right, Jack, I can take a tip."[30] Though Stanley is dreaming of a world tour, it is clear that he is taking shelter from a hostile world in Meg's sordid seaside haven.

Then, as in the two earlier plays, the door opens. Two sinister visitors, Goldberg and McCann, want a room in Meg's boarding house. It soon becomes clear that they are after Stanley. Are they the emissaries of some secret organization he has betrayed? Or male nurses sent out to fetch him back to an asylum he has escaped from? Or emissaries from another world, like the blind Negro in *The Room*? This question is never answered. We see them merely organizing a birthday party for Stanley who insists that it is not his birthday, and brainwashing him in a terrifying but nonsensical cross-examination:

GOLDBERG: You verminate the sheet of your birth.
MC CANN: What about the Albigensist heresy?
GOLDBERG: Who watered the wicket in Melbourne?
MC CANN: What about the blessed Oliver Plunkett?

GOLDBERG: Speak up, Webber. Why did the chicken cross the road?

STANLEY: He wanted to—he wanted to—he wanted to—

MC CANN: He doesn't know!

GOLDBERG: Why did the chicken cross the road?

STANLEY: He wanted . . .

MC CANN: He doesn't know. He doesn't know which came first!

GOLDBERG: Which came first?

MC CANN: Chicken? Egg? Which came first?

GOLDBERG and MC CANN: Which came first? Which came first? Which came first?[31]

The birthday party proceeds—with Meg, oblivious of what is going on, grotesquely playing the belle of the ball; with Goldberg, who seems to have a large number of different names, seducing the dumb blonde from next door—until eventually it culminates in a game of blindman's buff. Stanley, whose glasses have been snatched by McCann, becomes more and more hysterical, tries to strangle Meg, and is finally driven upstairs by the two sinister strangers.

In the third act, Goldberg and McCann take Stanley away in a big black car. He is now dressed in a black jacket and striped trousers, has a clean collar, wears a bowler hat, carries his broken glasses in his hand, and has become speechless and blank, like a puppet. When Meg comes down, she is still dreaming of the wonderful party and does not realize what has happened.

The Birthday Party has been interpreted as an allegory of the pressures of conformity, with Stanley, the pianist, as the artist who is forced into respectability and pin-stripe trousers by the emissaries of the bourgeois world. Yet the play can equally well be seen as an allegory of death—man snatched away from the home he has built himself, from the warmth of love embodied by Meg's mixture of motherliness and sexuality, by the dark angels of nothingness, who pose to him the question of which came first, the chicken or the egg. But, as in the case of *Waiting for Godot*, all such interpretations would miss the point; a play like this simply explores a situation that, in itself, is a valid poetic image that is immediately seen as relevant and true. It speaks plainly of the individual's pathetic search for security; of secret dreads and anxieties; of the terrorism of our world, so often embodied in false bonhomie and bigoted brutality; of the tragedy that arises from lack of understanding between people on different levels of awareness (the subject of Pedrolo's *Cruma*). Meg's warmth and love can never reach Stanley, who despises her stupidity and slatternliness, while, on the other hand, Meg's husband Petey is tongue-tied almost to the point of imbecility, so that his evident warmth and affection remain unexpressed and bottled up.

The possibility of an over-all allegorical interpretation of a play like *The Birthday Party* would presuppose that the play had been written to express a preconceived idea. Pinter emphatically denies that he works in this manner: "I think it is impossible—and certainly for me—to start writing a play from any kind of abstract idea. . . . I start writing a play from an image of a situation and a couple of characters involved, and these people always remain for me quite real; if they were not, the play could not be written."[32]

For Pinter, there is no contradiction between the desire for realism and the basic absurdity of the situations that inspire him. Like Ionesco, he regards life in its absurdity as basically funny—up to a point. "Everything is funny; the greatest earnestness is funny; even tragedy is funny. And I think what I try to do in my plays is to get to this recognizable reality of the absurdity of what we do and how we behave and how we speak."[33]

Everything is funny until the horror of the human situation rises to the surface: "The point about tragedy is that it is *no longer funny*. It is funny, and then it becomes no longer funny."[34] Life is funny because it is arbitrary, based on illusions and self-deceptions, like Stanley's dream that he is going on a world tour as a pianist, because it is built out of pretense and the grotesque overestimation each individual makes of himself. But in our present-day world, everything is uncertain and relative. There is no fixed point; we are surrounded by the unknown. And "the fact that it is verging on the unknown leads us to the next step, which seems to occur in my plays. There is a kind of horror about and I think that this horror and absurdity go together."[35]

The area of the unknown that surrounds us includes the motivation and background of the characters. What Pinter, in his search for a higher degree of realism in the theatre, rejects in the "well-made play" is precisely that it provides too much information about the background and motivation of each character. In real life, we deal with people all the time whose early history, family relationships, or psychological motivations we totally ignore. We are interested if we see them involved in some dramatic situation. We stop and look in fascination at a quarrel in the street even if we do not know what is at issue. But there is more to this rejection of an overdefined motivation of characters in drama than the desire for realism. There is the problem of the *possibility* of ever knowing the real motivation behind the actions of human beings who are complex and whose psychological makeup is contradictory and unverifiable. One of Pinter's major concerns as a dramatist is precisely that of the difficulty of verification. In a note inserted in the program of the performance of his two one-act plays at the Royal Court Theatre in London in March, 1960, Pinter stated this problem as follows:

> The desire for verification is understandable but cannot always be satisfied. There are no hard distinctions between what is real and what is unreal, nor between what is true and what is false. The thing is not necessarily either true or false; it can be both true and false. The assumption that to verify what has happened and what is happening presents few problems I take to be inaccurate. A character on the stage who can present no convincing argument or information as to his past experience, his present behaviour or his aspirations, nor give a comprehensive analysis of his motives, is as legitimate and as worthy of attention as one who, alarmingly, can do all these things. The more acute the experience the less articulate its expression.[36]

The problem of verification in Pinter's theatre is closely linked with his use of language. Pinter's clinically accurate ear for the absurdity of ordinary speech enables him to transcribe everyday conversation in all its repetitiveness, incoherence, and lack of logic or grammar. The dialogue of Pinter's plays is a casebook of the whole gamut of *non sequiturs* in small talk; he registers the delayed-action effect resulting from differences in the speed of thinking between people—the slower-witted character is constantly replying to the penultimate question while the faster one is already two jumps ahead. There are also the misunderstandings arising from inability to listen; incomprehension of polysyllabic words used for show by the more articulate characters; mishearings; and false anticipations. Instead of proceeding logically, Pinter's dialogue follows a line of associative thinking in which sound regularly prevails over sense. Yet Pinter denies that he is trying to present a case for man's inability to communicate with his fellows. "I feel," he once said, "that instead of any inability to communicate there is a deliberate evasion of communication. Communication itself between people is so frightening that rather than do that there is continual cross-talk, a continual talking about other things, rather than what is at the root of their relationship."[37]

The Birthday Party was Pinter's first play to get a professional performance in London. (It opened at the Arts Theatre in Cambridge on April 28, 1958, and was transferred to the Lyric, in Hammersmith, in May.) The play failed at first, but could not be kept down. Pinter himself directed it in Birmingham in January, 1959. It achieved a brilliant success in an excellent performance by the Tavistock Players at the Tower Theatre, in Canonbury, London, in the spring of the same year, and was seen by millions of British viewers in an exciting television performance early in 1960.

The impact of so strange and demanding a play on the mass audience of television was fascinating. While viewers were clearly exasperated by the lack of the cheap and obvious motivation to which they were used in their daily fare, they were also visibly intrigued. For days one could hear people in buses and canteens eagerly discussing the play as a maddening but deeply disturbing experience. *The Birthday Party* reached the United States in July, 1960, when it was very successfully staged by the Actors' Workshop in San Francisco.

Much of Pinter's astonishingly rich output since he started writing plays in 1957 has been for radio and television. In the radio play *A Slight Ache* (first performed on the B.B.C.'s Third Programme, on July 29, 1959), Pinter makes brilliant use of the limitations of the medium. Of the three characters in the play, only two speak. The third remains entirely silent and is thus invested with the terror of the unknown. An old couple, Edward and Flora, are disturbed by the mysterious presence of a matchseller at the back gate of their house. He has been standing there for weeks, holding his tray without ever selling anything. They finally call him into their house. But whatever they say to him, he remains silent. As though challenged by the stubborn absence of any reaction, Edward begins to tell the man his life story. Edward insists that he is not frightened, but he is, and goes to get some fresh air in the garden. Now it is Flora's turn to address the silent visitor with a flood of reminiscences and confessions. She even talks of sex, being clearly attracted and repelled by the old tramp. "I'm going to keep you, you dreadful chap, and call you Barnabas." Like Meg in *The Birthday Party*, Flora's attitude toward the old man is a mixture of sexuality and motherliness. Edward becomes violently jealous. It is his turn again to address Barnabas. As he still fails to elicit any reaction, he becomes more and more personal while visibly disintegrating. The play ends with Flora installing Barnabas in the house and sending Edward away: "Edward! Here is your tray!"[38] The tramp and the husband have changed places.

There is a curious affinity between the silent matchseller in *A Slight Ache* and Ionesco's Killer, whose silence also leads his antagonist, Bérenger, to paroxysms of eloquence and eventual disintegration. Here, as there, the silent character acts as a catalyst for the projection of the other's deepest feelings. Edward, in projecting his thoughts, is confronted with his inner emptiness and disintegrates, while Flora projects her still vital sexuality and changes partners. Yet as the silent matchseller is never heard, not even in the inarticulate giggle of the Killer, he might equally well be a figment of the old people's imagination. The audience of the radio play will never be able to verify whether he was real or not. But *A Slight Ache* also proved effective when produced on the stage (Arts Theatre, London, January 18, 1961).

The element of mystery is almost entirely absent in Pinter's second radio play, *A Night Out* (first broadcast in March, 1960, on the Third Programme; television version on A.B.C. Television, April, 1960), and in the television play *Night School* (first broadcast by Associated Rediffusion TV in July, 1960). In both of these plays, as in a number of short revue sketches he wrote at about the same time, Pinter relies entirely on his mastery of real-life idiom to produce a feeling of the absurdity and futility of the human condition.

A Night Out tells of the adventures of a repressed clerk, Albert Stokes, who is kept on his mother's apron strings and stifled by a possessiveness reminiscent of Meg's motherliness toward Stanley, or Flora's toward the enigmatic matchseller. Albert has been invited to an office party. He breaks loose from his mother and goes to the party, where his office rival causes him embarrassment by egging on the girls to draw him out. He is accused of having "interfered" with one of the girls, returns home, is received with nagging by his mother, loses his temper, throws something at her, and leaves, thinking that he has killed her. A prostitute takes him to her room, but when she too nags him about spilling cigarette ash on her carpet, he terrifies her with an outburst of temper and runs away. Returning home in the morning, he finds his mother alive but somewhat chastened by his aggressiveness. Has he really broken free during his night out? The question is left unanswered.

A Night Out is only seemingly simple. It is, in fact, extremely subtly constructed in suggesting Albert's predicament through a series of repetitions. The prostitute, in nagging Albert, repeats not only his situation with his mother but also, in making advances to him, his embarrassed situation when confronted with the girls at the party. Thus the scene with the prostitute focuses Albert's double predicament as a mother's boy—his inability to resist his mother and his timidity toward the other sex. In going to the prostitute's room, he has run away from both his mother and the party, yet there once again he encounters all he was trying to escape from.

The television play *Night School* returns to another of Pinter's main preoccupations—a room of one's own as a symbol for one's place in the world. Walter, on his return from prison for forging entries in post-office saving books, finds that his two old aunts have let his room. He is horrified to learn that it is now occupied by a girl, Sally, who describes herself as a schoolteacher and who goes out at night a good deal—allegedly to study foreign languages at night school. While fetching some things from his room, Walter discovers that the girl is in fact a night-club hostess. Although there is a good chance that he might make friends with Sally and thus regain his bed by having an affair with her or even marrying her, Walter asks a shady businessman friend of his aunts' to trace the night club in which she is working. Solto, the businessman, finds the girl, hopes to have an affair of his own with her, and inadvertently reveals that Walter sent him to spy her out. When Solto reports back to Walter, he conceals the fact that he has found the girl. But Sally, who now knows that Walter wanted to expose her, leaves. In wanting too badly to regain his room, Walter has lost the chance of winning the girl who might have given him a real place in the world. *Night School* also touches on the problem of verification and identity—to impress Sally, Walter makes himself out to be a romantic gunman; Sally herself pretends to be a teacher. These pretenses prevent Walter and Sally from establishing a true relationship.

The fight for a room of one's own is also the theme of Pinter's second full-length stage play, which brought him his first great success with the public—*The Caretaker* (first performed at the Arts Theatre Club, London, on April 27, 1960). This is a play in three acts, with three characters. The room in question is in a decaying property inhabited by Aston, a kindly but somewhat slow-witted man in his thirties. As the play opens, Aston has brought a visitor for the night—Davies, an old tramp he has rescued out of a fight at some café where he had been working. Davies has lost not only his place in the world—he is homeless—but also his identity. He soon confesses that while his real name *is* Davies, he has been using the name Jenkins for years. To prove his identity, he would have to get his papers. But he left them with a man, years ago, down in Sidcup. The trouble is he cannot get down to Sidcup because he has no suitable shoes, and because the weather is never good enough.

Davies is vain, irascible, evasive, and prejudiced. He could stay with Aston and his younger brother, Mick, who owns the place and dreams of converting it into modern flats. Davies is almost offered the job of caretaker there. But he cannot resist the temptation to play the two brothers off against each other, to try to gain the upper hand when the kindly Aston has, in a bout of confidence, revealed that he once received electric-shock treatment in a mental hospital. And so Davies is a personification of human weakness. His need for a place in the world is pathetically obvious, but he is unable to subdue his own nature enough to impose upon himself the minimum of self-discipline that would help him obtain it. As Mick says to him when he finally turns him out, "What a strange man you are. Aren't you? You're really strange. Ever since you come into this house, there's been nothing but trouble. Honest. I can take nothing you say at face value. Every word you speak is open to any number of different interpretations. Most of what you say is lies. You're violent, you're erratic, you're just completely unpredictable. You're nothing else but a wild animal, when you come down to it. You're a barbarian."[39]

It is a measure of Pinter's power as a playwright that the final scene, in which Davies vainly pleads to be given another chance, is almost unbearably tragic. After Davies has been shown in all his abject unreliability, clearly undeserving of the charity offered to him by the brothers, his ejection from the dingy room that could have become his world assumes almost the cosmic proportions of Adam's expulsion from Paradise. Davies's lying, his assertiveness, his inability to resist any chance to impose himself as superior, are, after all, mankind's original sin—hubris, lack of humility, blindness to our own faults.

The Caretaker achieves this quality of universality and tragedy without any of the tricks of mystery and violence that Pinter used in his earlier plays to create an atmosphere of poetic terror. Even Davies's myth of the impossible journey to Sidcup remains within the bounds of strict realism. It represents simply a form of self-deception and grotesque evasion on Davies's part. Anyone can see through it, but Davies is too self-indulgent a character to notice how the rationalization of his apathy and inability to help himself deceives no one except perhaps himself.

Pinter has revealed that originally he wanted to bring in

violence: "The original idea . . . was . . . to end the play
with the violent death of the tramp. . . . It suddenly struck
me that it was not necessary. And I think that in this play . . .
I *have* developed, that I have no need to use cabaret turns and
blackouts and screams in the dark to the extent that I enjoyed
using them before. I feel that I can deal, without resorting to
that kind of thing, with a human situation. . . . I do see this
play as merely . . . a particular human situation, concerning
three particular people and not, incidentally . . . symbols."[40]

Much in *The Caretaker* is very funny, and the long run of
the play has been attributed in some quarters to the public's
laughter over Pinter's devastatingly accurate rendering of
lower-class speech. In a letter to the London *Sunday Times*,
Pinter takes issue with this and clarifies his own views on the
relation between tragedy and farce in the play:

An element of the absurd is, I think, one of the features of
[*The Caretaker*], but at the same time I did not intend it to
be merely a laughable farce. If there had not been other
issues at stake, the play would not have been written.
Audience reaction can't be regulated, and no one would
want it to be; nor is it easy to analyze. But where the comic
and the tragic (for want of a better word) are closely interwoven, certain members of an audience will always give
emphasis to the comic as opposed to the other, for by so
doing they rationalize the other out of existence. . . .
Where this indiscriminate mirth is found, I feel it represents a cheerful patronage of the characters on the part of
the merrymakers, and thus participation is avoided. . . . As
far as I'm concerned *The Caretaker* is funny up to a point.
Beyond that point it ceases to be funny, and it was because
of that point that I wrote it.[41]

In fact, *The Caretaker* has passages of genuine poetry—
Aston's great speech about the shock treatment, or Mick's description of his plans for redecorating the old house, which
transmutes the jargon of contemporary brand names into a
dreamlike world of wish-fulfillment:

You could have an off-white pile linen rug, a table in . . .
afromosia teak veneer, sideboard with matt black drawers,

curved chairs with cushioned seats, armchairs in oatmeal tweed, beech-frame settee with woven sea-grass seat, white-topped heat-resistant coffee table, white tile surround. . . .[42]

Pinter is one of the first poets to have recognized the potentialities of laminated plastics or power tools. Mick's brother, Aston, is that typical mid-twentieth-century species of Western man, a do-it-yourself mechanic and handyman. He is constantly fixing some electrical appliance. And he too, in his slower way, extracts poetry from technical jargon:

DAVIES: What's that then, exactly, then?

ASTON: A jig saw? Well, it comes from the same family as the fret saw. But it's an appliance, you see. You have to fix it on to a portable drill.

DAVIES: Ah, that's right. They're very handy.

ASTON: They are, yes.

DAVIES: What about a hack-saw?

ASTON: Well, I've got a hack-saw, as a matter of fact.

DAVIES: They're handy.

ASTON: Yes. . . . So's a keyhole saw. . . .[43]

The laughter of the audience during the long run of *The Caretaker* was by no means merely patronizing. It was also the laughter of recognition. It is not often that the theatregoer is confronted with his own language and preoccupations, even though they are exaggerated and heightened to point up the absurdity of the primitive, magical satisfaction most of us derive from being able to name and thus to master the bewildering array of gadgets with which we are surrounding ourselves. In a world that is increasingly deprived of meaning, we seek refuge in being experts in some narrow field of irrelevant knowledge or expertise. In trying to become master of some electrical appliance, Aston is seeking to get a foothold on reality. His breakdown, which led to his receiving shock treatment, was due to a loss of contact with reality and with other people: "They always used to listen. I thought . . . they understood what I said. I mean I used to talk to them. I talked too much. That was my mistake."[44]

Because he suffered from hallucinations, because he felt he

could see things with a strange clarity, he was subjected to the horror of the mental hospital. He tried to retain his super-lucidity, he appealed to his mother, "but she signed their form, you see, giving them permission." Aston is the poet whom society crushes under the weight of its machinery of legal forms and bureaucracy. His hallucinations, his clear visions having been wiped from his brain, Aston is reduced to seeking satisfaction in the way most citizens of our affluent society obtain what poetry they can out of life, by tinkering about the house: ". . . so I decided to have a go at decorating it, so I came into this room, and I started to collect wood, for my shed, and all these bits and pieces, that I thought might come in handy for the flat, or around the house, sometime."[45]

In the radio play *The Dwarfs* (first performed on the Third Programme on December 2, 1960), Pinter amplifies Aston's experience. Len, the hero of *The Dwarfs*, also suffers from hallucinations—he sees himself as belonging to a gang of dwarfs whom he feeds with tidbits of rat meat. He fears these dwarfs, resents having to work for them, and yet, when the dream world recedes, he feels it a loss to be deprived of the warmth and the cozy litter of their squalid yard: "They've cut me off without a penny. And now they've settled down to a wide-eyed kip, cross-legged by the fire. It's unsupportable. I'm left in the lurch. Not even a stale frankfurter, a slice of bacon rind, a leaf of cabbage, not even a mouldy piece of salami, like they used to sling me in the days when we told old tales by suntime. . . . Now all is bare. All is clean. All is scrubbed. There is a lawn. There is a shrub. There is a flower."[46]

Len has two friends who are invading his room, Pete and Mark, each of whom is trying to play him off against the other. Len's room, like his sense of reality, is subject to constant change: "The rooms we live in . . . open and shut. . . . Can't you see? They change shape at their own will. I wouldn't grumble if only they would keep to some consistency. But they don't. And I can't tell the limits, the boundaries which I've been led to believe are natural."[47]

The Dwarfs, based on Pinter's unfinished novel, is a play without a plot; it is a set of variations on the theme of reality and fantasy. As Pete tells Len, "The apprehension of experience must obviously be dependent upon discrimination if it's to be considered valuable. That's what you lack. You've got no idea how to preserve a distance between what you smell and what you think about it. . . . How can you hope to assess and verify anything if you walk about with your nose stuck between your feet all day long?"[48] And yet Pete, who makes this plea for realism, follows it up by telling Len about a dream of his own—people's faces peeling off them in a panic on the underground.

The Dwarfs, although outwardly simple and without any of Pinter's earlier tricks and mystifications, is a complex and difficult play. It is also one of his most personal statements. Len's world of the dwarfs is that of Aston, or Stanley in *The Birthday Party*. All three have the same experience in common—they have been expelled from their private world, squalid but cozy, in which they could indulge their personal vision. Stanley is carried off by force in the midst of highly allegorical happenings; Aston and Len lose their vision in a process of healing that is also a catastrophic loss of a dimension of their lives—the dimension of fantasy or poetry, the ability to look behind the scenes of the commonplace, everyday world.

Pinter's theatre is essentially a poetic theatre, more so than the euphuistic verse drama of some of his contemporaries. Pinter, who acknowledges the influence of Kafka and Beckett, is, like these two writers, preoccupied with man at the limit of his being. As Len says in *The Dwarfs*, "The point is, who are you? Not why or how, not even what. . . . You are the sum of so many reflections. How many reflections? Whose reflections? Is that what you consist of? What scum does the tide leave? What happens to the scum? When does it happen? I've seen what happens. . . . The scum is broken and sucked back. I don't see where it goes, I don't see when, what do I see, what have I seen? What have I seen, the scum or the essence?"[49]

It is this preoccupation with the problem of the self that separates Harold Pinter from the social realists among the young British playwrights of his generation with whom he shares the ability to put contemporary speech onto the stage. When Kenneth Tynan reproached him in a radio interview for writing plays unconcerned with ideas and showing only a very limited aspect of the life of their characters, omitting their politics, ideas, and even their sex life, Pinter replied that he was dealing with his characters "at the extreme edge of their living, where they are living pretty much alone";[50] at a point, that is, when they are back in their rooms, confronted with the basic problem of being.

We see Pinter's characters in the process of their essential adjustment to the world, at the point when they have to solve their basic problem—whether they will be able to confront, and come to terms with, reality at all. It is only after they have made this fundamental adjustment that they will be able to become part of society and share in the games of sex or politics. Pinter repudiates the suggestion that in so presenting them he is unrealistic. After all, he maintains, his plays deal with a short, if climactic, period in the lives of his characters, a few days or, in the case of *The Caretaker*, a fortnight. "We are only concerned with what is happening then, in this particular moment of these people's lives. There is no reason to suppose that at one time or another they did not listen at a political meeting . . . or that they haven't ever had girl friends"[51] or been concerned with ideas.

It is the intriguing paradox of Pinter's position that he considers himself a more uncompromising, ruthless realist than the champions of "social realism" could ever be. For it is they who water down the reality of their picture of the world by presupposing that they have solutions for problems that have not yet been solved—and that may well be insoluble—or by implying that it is possible to *know* the complete motivation of a character, or, above all, by presenting a slice of reality that is less essential, and hence less real, less true to life, than a theatre that has selected a more fundamental aspect of existence. If life in our time is basically absurd, then any dramatic representation of it that comes up with neat solutions and produces the illusion that it all "makes sense," after all, is bound to contain an element of oversimplification, to suppress essential factors, and reality expurgated and oversimplified becomes make-believe. For a dramatist of the Absurd, like Harold Pinter, the political, social, realist play loses its claim to realism by focusing its attention on inessentials and exaggerating their importance, as though, if only some limited objective were reached, we could live happily forever after. And by choosing the wrong slice of life altogether, it falls into the same error as the drawing-room comedy that ends when boy gets girl—at the very point when their real problems, marriage and the process of aging, begin. After the social realist has established the need for his reform, the basic problems of existence remain—loneliness, the impenetrable mystery of the universe, death.

On the other hand, Pinter was indignant when a critic took him to task for introducing a character whose antecedents are clearly stated in the television play *Night School,* arguing that a true Pinter character should come from nowhere rather than from prison. Pinter considers *Night School* an experiment in a lighter vein and resents being told by others that a true Pinter play *must* deal exclusively in mysterious and wholly unmotivated events.

Pinter has been writing plays only since 1957. The quantity of his output and his rise to success are truly astonishing, but he is far too young to allow anything like a summing up of his achievement or a final verdict on his place in British drama. Yet it is possible, even on the basis of what is still an early phase of his development, to say that he has already won himself an important place among the playwrights of this century. His mastery of language, which has opened up a new dimension of English stage dialogue; the economy of his technique; the accuracy of his observation; the depth of his emotion; the freshness and originality of his approach; the fertility of his invention; and, above all, his ability to turn commonplace lower-class people and events into a profoundly poetical vision of universal validity justify the very highest hopes for his future development.

If Pinter's plays transmute realism into poetic fantasy, the work of Norman Frederick Simpson (born in 1919) is philosophical fantasy strongly based on reality. N. F. Simpson, an adult-education lecturer who lives in London, first came into prominence by winning one of the prizes in the *Observer's* 1957 playwriting competition with *A Resounding Tinkle* (first performed in a much shortened version at the Royal Court Theatre, London, on December 1, 1957). Although Simpson's work is extravagant fantasy in the vein of Lewis Carroll, and is

compared by the author himself to a regimental sergeant-
major reciting "Jabberwocky" over and over again through
a megaphone,[52] it is nevertheless firmly based in the English
class system. If Pinter's world is one of tramps and junior
clerks, Simpson's is unmistakably suburban.

A Resounding Tinkle takes place in the living room of the
bungalow inhabited by Mr. and Mrs. Paradock (the Paradocks, in fact), and the action, however wild and extravagant
it becomes, always remains firmly rooted in the world of the
English suburban lower middle class. The Paradocks have ordered an elephant from the store, but they don't like it because it is several sizes too large for a private house ("It's big
enough for a hotel"), so they exchange it for a snake ("You
can have them lengthened but we shan't bother")—two transactions only slightly more absurd than the pointless buying
and exchanging of furniture practiced in these circles.

The Paradocks invite some comedians to entertain them at
home—which is only slightly more extravagant than getting
them on the television. Their son Don comes home, but has
turned into a young woman ("Why, you've changed your
sex")—but then sex is not all that important in the restrained
world of the suburbs. The Paradocks and their guests, the two
comedians, get drunk on nectar and ambrosia. They listen to
a religious service on the radio which comes from "the Church
of the Hypothetical Imperative in Brinkfall"[53] but is delivered
in "a voice of cultured Anglican fatuity"[54] while enjoining lis-
teners to "make music, water, love, and rabbit hutches"[55] and
making them pray: "Let us laugh with those we tickle. . . .
Let us weep with those we expose to tear gas. Let us throw
back our heads and laugh at reality, which is an illusion caused
by mescalin deficiency; at sanity, which is an illusion caused
by alcohol deficiency; at knowledge, which is an illusion
caused by certain biochemical changes in the human brain
structure during the course of human evolution. . . . Let us
laugh at thought, which is a phenomenon like any other. At
illusion, which is an illusion, which is a phenomenon like any
other. . . ."[56]

Nonsense and satire mingle with parody, but the serious
philosophical intent is again and again brought into the open.
The two comedians learnedly discuss Bergson's theory of

laughter ("We laugh every time a person gives us the impression of being a thing"), and Mr. Paradock promptly puts the theory to the test by having himself plugged into the electricity supply and converting himself into a mechanical brain, which, however, in spite of being fed with data, fails to produce the correct results—because of a short circuit.

The author appears from time to time, apologizing for the shortcomings of the play, which came to him in Portuguese, a language that unfortunately he does not know too well. "I lay claim," he announces, "to no special vision, and my own notions as to what I have in mind here may well fall pitifully short of your own far better notions. No. I am the dwarf in the circus—I give what scope I can to such deficiencies as I have."[57] And in the final summing up of "an odd evening," the author draws the attention of the public to the comforting fact that "the retreat from reason means precious little to anyone who has never caught up with reason in the first place. It takes a trained mind to relish a *non sequitur*."[58] And so it does. N. F. Simpson's plays are highly intellectual entertainments. They lack the dark obsessiveness of Adamov, the manic proliferation of things in Ionesco, or the anxiety and menace of Pinter. They are spontaneous creations that often rely on free association and a purely verbal logic ("The small of my back is too big, Doctor") and lack the formal discipline of Beckett. As Simpson himself put it in one program note, "From time to time parts of the play may seem about to become detached from the main body. No attempt, well intentioned or not, should be made from the audience to nudge these back into position while the play is in motion. They will eventually drop off and are quite harmless."[59]

But for all this looseness of construction and spontaneity, Simpson's world bears the mark of the fantasies of an eminently sane, intelligent man with deep learning and a delicious sense of humor. "I think life is excruciatingly funny," he once said. "People traveling every day on the tube and doing things which are a means to an end but become ends in themselves, like buying cars to get about at weekends and spending every weekend cleaning them."[60]

The prayers and responses in the short, one-act version of

A Resounding Tinkle seem to sum up the purpose of Simpson's endeavors:

PRAYER: Give us light upon the nature of our knowing. For the illusions of the sane man are not the illusions of the lunatic, and the illusions of the flagellant are not the illusions of the alcoholic, and the illusions of the delirious are not the illusions of the lovesick, and the illusions of the genius are not the illusions of the common man:

RESPONSE: Give us light that we may be enlightened.

PRAYER: Give us light that, sane, we may attain to a distortion more acceptable than the lunatic's and call it truth:

RESPONSE: That, sane, we may call it truth and know it to be false.

PRAYER: That, sane, we may know ourselves, and by knowing ourselves may know what it is we know.

RESPONSE: Amen.[61]

There could hardly be a better statement of the objectives not merely of Simpson himself but of the Theatre of the Absurd.

The exploration of the relativity of our vision of the world, according to the individual's preoccupations, obsessions, and circumstances, is the subject of Simpson's second play, *The Hole* (performed in a double bill at the Royal Court, with the shortened version of *A Resounding Tinkle*, in December, 1957). Here a group of characters congregates around a hole in the street, discussing what it might be, each of them in turn seeing different things happening in its dark opening.

The crowd gradually congregates round a "visionary" who has settled down on a campstool with blankets and a supply of food to watch for an unspecified event of religious connotation, which he says is imminent down there—the solemn unveiling of a great window whose many-colored glass will stain the white radiance of eternity. The visionary admits that it was once his ambition "to have a queue stretching away from me in every direction known to the compass,"[62] but he has now toned down his expectations; he will be satisfied if he becomes the nucleus of a more modest queue.

Other, more commonplace characters arrive and watch the hole, projecting in turn their preoccupations—the whole content of their minds—onto the blank darkness of the mysterious opening. The discussion around the hole thus becomes a survey of the fantasy life of an English suburb. It starts with sports, ranging from dominoes to cricket, boxing, and golf; proceeds to nature, turning the hole into an aquarium housing a variety of species of fish that can be discussed with expertise; then turns to crime and punishment and violent demands for torture, execution, and revenge; and, having aroused the emotions of all concerned, culminates in fantasies of a political nature—the violence of both chauvinism and revolutionary action. After all this, a workman emerges from the hole and informs the bystanders that it contains a junction box of the electricity supply.

The intellectual among the crowd, Cerebro, is ready to accept this sobering fact and consoles himself with the thought that, after all, something is positively known about junction boxes. But his antagonist, Soma, who plays Stalin to Cerebro's Marx, seeing the potentialities of power and mass emotion, accuses him of wanting "to take away all the mystery, all the poetry, all the enchantment." Gradually the sober, positive truth is reinvested with metaphysical significance. Even Cerebro indulges in pseudo-logical speculations on whether one should speak of the cables' going in, or coming out, of the junction box, while Soma turns the crowd into a meeting celebrating the religious rites of a cult of electrical generation. The technological facts have been turned back into vague emotional mumbo-jumbo. The visionary alone remains on the scene, still waiting for the colored glass that will stain the white radiance of eternity.

The Hole is a philosophical fable. In his third play, *One Way Pendulum*, Simpson combines this theme with the suburban nonsense world of *A Resounding Tinkle*. When asked for the meaning of the title, he is reported to have replied that it is merely a name, like London or Simpson. In fact it is a kind of signpost indicating that the contents of the play are paradoxical. During its first run at the Royal Court Theatre, where it opened (after a tryout in Brighton) on December 22, 1959, the play was subtitled "An Evening of High Drung and Slarrit." When it was transferred to the West End, this somewhat esoteric description was replaced by the more readily understandable "A Farce in a New Dimension."

As in *The Hole*, a group of characters is presented, each of whom is preoccupied with a private world of fantasy. As Simpson himself put it in a radio interview, "In these plays each man is an island. The whole point about the relationship in the family is that everyone is in fact preoccupied with his own interests and makes very little contact, except superficially, with the other characters in the play."[63] The family in question are the Groomkirbys. Arthur Groomkirby, the father of the family, earns his living as a private-enterprise keeper of parking meters, a highly appropriate profession to choose in present-day Britain. Like all good suburban fathers he has a hobby. He combines an interest in the law with a passion for do-it-yourself carpentry, and constructs, in the course of the play, a very lifelike replica of the court at the Old Bailey in his own living room.

Arthur's son, Kirby Groomkirby, who has trained himself by the Pavlov method and is unable to have a meal without having heard first the bell of a cash register, is engaged on a gigantic educational enterprise—he wants to teach five hundred "speak-your-weight" weighing machines to sing the "Hallelujah" chorus from the *Messiah*. Being of a logical mind, he argues that if these machines can speak, they must be capable of learning to sing as well. And he is making progress. Once he has taught the machines to sing, he hopes to transport them to the North Pole, where they would attract large crowds of people eager to hear them. These multitudes might then be induced to jump all at the same moment, thereby tilting the axis of the earth, and causing an ice age in Britain, which would lead to the death of many people. Kirby needs many deaths, for he likes to wear black, but, being logical, he needs deaths to give him an opportunity to don his mourning attire.

The teen-age daughter of the family, Sylvia, is also preoccupied with death, or rather she wants to be, having been given a skull as a *memento mori*. But she finds that the skull does not work; it fails to remind her of death. On the other hand, Sylvia is deeply dissatisfied with the human condition. She cannot understand why her arms are not long enough to reach her knees; she cannot see the logic of the construction of human bodies. There is an old aunt who sits in a wheelchair and is, on Bergsonian principles, treated as a thing rather than a human being. Only the mother of the family, Mabel, is wholly matter-of-fact, not surprised by anything that goes on around her, and herself highly eccentric in her sanity. The charwoman she employs, Myra Gantry, is used by her to eat up surplus food, which is hard work, since much is left over.

In the second act, the homemade Old Bailey at the Groom-kirbys' house suddenly fills with judge, prosecutor, and defense counsel, and while the household goes on with its routine, a trial develops. Arthur Groomkirby is called as a witness and subjected to a fantastic cross-examination, which undermines his alibi by proving that there are millions of places he has *not* been to at a given moment, making the probability that he has not been in a particular place so small as to be negligible. After a nightmare game of three-handed whist with the judge, Arthur Groomkirby returns to the proceedings. Only now is it announced that the accused is his own son, who has killed forty-three people in order to be able to wear mourning for them. Although it is proved that he has committed these murders, he is acquitted because, as a mass murderer could be sentenced for only one crime, this would mean cheating the law of its retribution for the others. Hence he is discharged.

The play ends with Arthur Groomkirby preparing himself to act as the judge in his own courtroom—apparently with little chance of success.

One Way Pendulum owed its considerable success with the public to the sustained inventiveness of its nonsense and, in particular, to the brilliant parody of British legal procedure and language in the court scene, which occupies almost the whole of the second act. In fact, however, the play is far less amiable than it appears at first sight. What seems little more than a harmless essay in upside-down logic is essentially a ferocious comment on contemporary British life.

The play portrays a suburban family living so wrapped up in its private fantasies that each of its members might be inhabiting a separate planet. It also hints at the connection between the reticences—the mutual tolerance that allows each of the Groomkirbys to plant his weird preoccupations in the middle of the living room—and the deep undercurrents of cruelty and sadism that lie behind such a society. Kirby's Pavlovian self-conditioning is a key image of the play; it stands for the automatism induced by habit on which the suburban commuting world rests. To lead an emotional life, Kirby has to stun himself into unconsciousness; only then can he indulge in sex. When waked out of one of these stupors by his Pavlovian cash-register bell, he angrily exclaims, "I might have been dreaming. . . . Might have stopped me stone dead in the middle of an orgasm!"[64]

Habit and social convention are the great deadeners of the inauthentic society. To find a social justification for wearing black, Kirby turns into a mass murderer. Repression and habit, however, are always accompanied by guilt, hence the appearance of the courtroom in the middle of the Groomkirbys' suburban world. The proceedings may be hilarious parody, but the trial that is being conducted has its affinities with Kafka's trial of another guilty petty bourgeois. In the eerie three-handed whist game during the recess, the judge assumes an almost satanic tinge. Mr. Groomkirby faces him with earplugs in his ears. When sent out by the judge to see if it is light, he reports back that he kept his eyes shut, as he does not intend "to be blinded suddenly by the sunrise." At one point he loses the power of speech, and when the judge savagely asks him, "Are you dentally fit?" he has no answer. No wonder that after this nightmare orgy of guilt, he greets the dawn with "monumental relief."

The actual proceedings of the court are, in comparison, reassuring. They may express deep feelings of guilt, but at the same time they provide a lightning conductor in their total irrelevance to life through the formalism of reasoning in a vacuum. Here Simpson needed only a minimum supply from his rich fund of comic invention to turn reality into satire. On one level, his Old Bailey is a fantasy of guilt in a suburban world of respectability; on another level it is a powerful satirical image of tradition running down in formalistic irrelevance. *One Way Pendulum* portrays a society that has become absurd because routine and tradition have turned human beings into Pavlovian automata. In that sense, Simpson is a more powerful social critic than any of the social realists. His work is proof that the Theatre of the Absurd is by no means unable to provide highly effective social comment.

The work we have surveyed in this chapter shows that the Theatre of the Absurd has had its impact on writers in France, Italy, Spain, Germany, Switzerland, Israel, and Great Britain. The relative absence of dramatists of the Absurd in the United States, however, is puzzling, particularly in view of the fact that certain aspects of American popular art have had a decisive influence on the dramatists of the Absurd in Europe (see the following chapter).

But the reason for this dearth of examples of the Theatre of the Absurd in the United States is probably simple enough—the convention of the Absurd springs from a feeling of deep disillusionment, the draining away of the sense of meaning and purpose in life, which has been characteristic of countries like France and Britain in the years after the Second World War. In the United States there has been no corresponding loss of meaning and purpose. The American dream of the good life is still very strong. In the United States the belief in progress that characterized Europe in the nineteenth century has been maintained into the middle of the twentieth. There have been signs, particularly since the shock administered by the Russian successes in the space race, that disillusion and frustration might become a factor in the American scene, but the rise of phenomena like the beat generation has been marginal compared to parallel developments in Europe.

It is certainly significant that such a notable work of the American avant-garde as Robert Hivnor's *Too Many Thumbs*, which has been compared to the fantasies of Ionesco, is in fact an affirmation of a belief in progress and the perfectability of man. It shows a chimpanzee compressing his evolution to the status of man—and far beyond that, to complete spirituality—into a matter of months. The fantasy is there, but certainly no sense of the futility and absurdity of human endeavor.

On the other hand, Edward Albee (born in 1928) comes into the category of the Theatre of the Absurd precisely because his work attacks the very foundations of American optimism. His first play, *The Zoo Story* (1958), which shared the bill at the Provincetown Playhouse with Beckett's *Krapp's Last Tape*, already showed the forcefulness and bitter irony of his approach. In the realism of its dialogue and in its subject matter—an outsider's inability to establish genuine contact with a

dog, let alone any human being—*The Zoo Story* is closely akin
to the work of Harold Pinter. But the effect of this brilliant
one-act duologue between Jerry, the outcast, and Peter, the
conformist bourgeois, is marred by its melodramatic climax;
when Jerry provokes Peter into drawing a knife and then im-
pales himself on it, the plight of the schizophrenic outcast is
turned into an act of sentimentality, especially as the victim
expires in touching solicitude and fellow feeling for his involuntary murderer.

But after an excursion into grimly realistic social criticism
(the one-act play *The Death of Bessie Smith,* a re-creation of
the end of the blues singer Bessie Smith in Memphis in 1937;
she died after an auto accident because hospitals reserved for
whites refused to admit her), Albee has produced a play that
clearly takes up the style and subject matter of the Theatre of
the Absurd and translates it into a genuine American idiom.
The American Dream (1959–60; first performed at the York
Playhouse, New York, on January 25, 1961) fairly and
squarely attacks the ideals of progress, optimism, and faith in
the national mission, and pours scorn on the sentimental ideals
of family life, togetherness, and physical fitness; the euphemistic language and unwillingness to face the ultimate facts of
the human condition that in America, even more than in Europe, represent the essence of bourgeois assumptions and attitudes. *The American Dream* shows an American family—
Mommy, Daddy, Grandma—in search of a replacement for the
adopted child that went wrong and died. The missing member
of the family arrives in the shape of a gorgeous young man,
the embodiment of the American dream, who admits that he
consists only of muscles and a healthy exterior, but is dead
inside, drained of genuine feeling and the capacity for experience. He will do anything for money—so he will even consent
to become a member of the family. The language of *The
American Dream* resembles that of Ionesco in its masterly
combination of clichés. But these clichés, in their euphemistic,
baby-talk tone, are as characteristically American as Ionesco's
are French. The most disagreeable verities are hidden behind
the corn-fed cheeriness of advertising jingles and family-maga-
zine unctuousness. There are very revealing contrasts in national coloring of different versions of the absurd cliché—the

mechanical hardness of Ionesco's French platitudes; the flat, repetitive obtuseness of Pinter's English nonsense dialogue; and the oily glibness and sentimentality of the American cliché in Albee's promising and brilliant first example of an American contribution to the Theatre of the Absurd.

Jack Gelber's *The Connection* (1959) skillfully blends jazz with Beckett's theme of waiting. The image of the drug addicts waiting for the arrival of the messenger carrying their drug is a powerful conception. The presence of a jazz quartet improvising onstage lends the play a fascinating element of spontaneity, and the dialogue has a lyricism of pointlessness that equals much of the best writing in the Theatre of the Absurd. But the play is marred by a laborious superstructure of pretense at realism. Author and director appear, and go to great lengths to convince the audience that they are seeing real drug addicts; two film cameramen who are supposed to record the events of the evening are involved in the action, and one is actually seduced into drug-taking. And, finally, the strange, spontaneous, poetic play culminates in a plea for a reform of the drug laws. *The Connection*, brilliant as it is in parts, founders in its uncertainty as to which convention it belongs to—the realist theatre of social reform or the Theatre of the Absurd.

How difficult it seems in America to use the convention of the Theatre of the Absurd is also illustrated by Arthur L. Kopit's intriguing play *Oh Dad, Poor Dad, Mamma's Hung You in the Closet and I'm Feeling So Sad* (1960), which takes the oblique approach of parody. Described as "A Pseudo-Classical Farce in a Bastard French Tradition," the play projects a young man's feelings about a dominating mother who tries to deprive him of contact with the outside world. But by treating the horrible mother, who travels with her stuffed dead husband in a coffin, and the retarded son, who finally strangles the girl who is ready to make love to him, with a parodistic snigger that deprives the playwright of the possibility of introducing genuine tragicomic effects (like those used by Ionesco in *Jacques*, or Adamov in *As We Were*), the author merely underlines the painfully Freudian aspects of his fantasy. In seeming to say, "Don't take this seriously, I am only piling on the horror for the sake of fun!" Kopit spoils his opportunity to transmute his material into a grotesque poetic image. On the other hand, there is enough evidence of his genuine concern with the problem of the play to prevent it from being a mere parodistic joke, and *Oh Dad, Poor Dad*, written while its author was still an undergraduate at Harvard, shows considerable promise. Only time will show whether Kopit will take the plunge into the Theatre of the Absurd or revert to the psychological thrillers of Broadway.

Chapter Six

THE TRADITION OF THE ABSURD

It may seem strange that the chapter that tries to trace an outline of the tradition on which the Theatre of the Absurd is based should follow rather than precede the account of its present exponents. But the history of ideas, like most other history, is essentially a search for the origins of the present, and hence changes as the configurations of the present alter its shape. We cannot look for the germs of a current phenomenon like the Theatre of the Absurd without first having defined its nature sufficiently to be able to discern which of the recurring elements that combine and recombine in the kaleidoscopic patterns of changing tastes and outlooks it is made up of. Avantgarde movements are hardly ever entirely novel and unprecedented. The Theatre of the Absurd is a return to old, even archaic, traditions. Its novelty lies in its somewhat unusual combination of such antecedents, and a survey of these will show that what may strike the unprepared spectator as iconoclastic and incomprehensible innovation is in fact merely an expansion, revaluation, and development of procedures that are familiar and completely acceptable in only slightly different contexts.

It is only from the set expectations of the naturalistic and narrative convention of the theatre that the man in the stalls will find a play like Ionesco's *The Bald Soprano* shocking and incomprehensible. Let the same man sit in a music hall, and he will find the equally nonsensical cross-talk of the comedian and his stooge, which is equally devoid of plot or narrative content, perfectly acceptable. Let him take his children to one of the ever-available dramatizations of *Alice in Wonderland*, and he will find a venerable example of the traditional Theatre of the Absurd, wholly delightful and not in the least obscure. It is only because habit and fossilized convention have so narrowed the public's expectation as to what constitutes theatre proper that attempts to widen its range meet with angry protests from those who have come to see a certain closely defined kind of entertainment and who lack the spontaneity of mind to let a slightly different approach make its impact on them.

The age-old traditions that the Theatre of the Absurd displays in new and individually varied combinations—and, of course, as the expression of wholly contemporary problems and preoccupations—might perhaps be classed under the headings of:

"Pure" theatre; i.e., abstract scenic effects as they are familiar in the circus or revue, in the work of jugglers, acrobats, bullfighters, or mimes.

Clowning, fooling, and mad-scenes.

Verbal nonsense.

The literature of dream and fantasy, which often has a strong allegorical component.

These headings often overlap; clowning relies on verbal nonsense as well as on abstract scenic effects, and such plotless and abstract theatrical spectacles as *trionfi* and processions are often charged with allegorical meaning. But the distinctions between them serve to clarify the issue in many instances and are useful in isolating the different strands of development.

The element of "pure," abstract theatre in the Theatre of the Absurd is an aspect of its anti-literary attitude, its turning away from language as an instrument for the expression of the deepest levels of meaning. In Genet's use of ritual and pure, stylized action; in the proliferation of things in Ionesco; the music-hall routines with hats in *Waiting for Godot;* the externalization of the characters' attitudes in Adamov's earlier plays; in Tardieu's attempts to create theatre from movement and sound alone, and in the ballets and mimeplays of Beckett and Ionesco, we find a return to earlier nonverbal forms of theatre. Theatre is always more than mere language. Language alone can be read, but true theatre can become manifest only in performance. The entry of the bullfighters into the arena, the procession of the participants at the opening of the Olympic Games, the state drive of the sovereign through the streets of his capital, the meaningful actions of the priest in celebrating the Mass—all these contain powerful elements of pure, abstract theatrical effects. They have deep, often metaphysical meaning and express more than language could. These are the elements that distinguish any stage performance from the reading of a play, elements that exist independent of words, as in the performance of Indian jugglers that made Hazlitt marvel at the possibilities of man and gave him an insight into his nature: "Is it then a trifling power we see at work, or is it not something next to miraculous? It is the utmost stretch of human ingenuity, which nothing but the bending of the faculties of body and mind to it from the tenderest infancy, with incessant, ever-anxious application up to manhood, can accomplish, or make even a slight approach to. Man, thou art a wonderful animal, and thy ways past finding out! Thou canst do strange things, but thou turnest them to little account!"[1] This is the strange metaphysical power of the concreteness and skill in theatrical performance, which Nietzsche spoke of in *The Birth of Tragedy*: "The myth by no means finds its adequate objectification in the spoken word. The structure of the scenes and the visible imagery reveal a deeper wisdom than that which the poet himself is able to put into words and concepts."[2]

There has always been a close relationship between the performers of wordless skills—jugglers, acrobats, tightrope walkers, aerialists, and animal trainers—and the clown. This is a powerful and deep secondary tradition of the theatre, from which the legitimate stage has again and again drawn new strength and vitality. It is the tradition of the *mimus*, or mime, of antiquity, a form of popular theatre that coexisted with classical tragedy and comedy and was often far more popular and influential. The *mimus* was a spectacle containing dancing, singing, and juggling, but based largely on the broadly realistic representation of character types in semi-improvised spontaneous clowning.

Hermann Reich, the great historian and partial rediscoverer

of the *mimus* from obscure sources, tried to trace the line of succession from the Latin *mimus* through the comic characters of medieval drama to the Italian *commedia dell'arte* and to Shakespeare's clowns. And while much of his evidence for the *direct* handing on of the tradition has been discredited in the half century since the publication of his monumental work, the deep *inner* connection of all these forms remains a self-evident fact.

In the mimeplay of antiquity, the clown appears as the *moros* or *stupidus;* his absurd behavior arises from his inability to understand the simplest logical relations. Reich quotes the character[3] who wants to sell his house and carries one brick about with himself to show as a sample—a gag which is also attributed to the Arlecchino of the *commedia dell'arte.* Another such character wants to teach his donkey the art of going without food. When the donkey finally dies of starvation, he says, "I have suffered a grievous loss; when my donkey had learned the art of going without food, it died."[4] Another such moronic character dreams that he stepped on a nail and hurt his foot. Thereupon he puts a bandage round his foot. His friend asks him what has happened and, when told that he had only dreamed he stepped on a nail, he replies, "Indeed, we are rightly called fools! Why do we go to sleep in bare feet?"[5]

Such grotesque characters appeared in the *mimus* within a crudely realistic convention, but, characteristically, these plays, which were often half improvised, were not bound by any of the strict rules of the regular tragedy or comedy. There was no limitation on the number of characters; women appeared and played leading parts; the unities of time and place were not observed. Apart from plays with prearranged plots (*hypotheses*), there were shorter performances that remained without plot and consisted of animal imitations, dances, or juggling tricks (*paegnia*). In later antiquity, fantastic plots with dreamlike themes became prevalent. Reich quotes Apuleius as saying, "*Mimus hallucinatur,*" and adds, "We shall have to think not only of the lower meaning of *hallucinari* as 'talking at random, talking nonsense,' but also of its more elevated meaning of 'dreaming, to talk and think strange things.' Indeed, with all its realism, the *mimus* not infrequently contained curious dreams and hallucinations, as in the plays of Aristophanes. In a gloss to Juvenal, the mimes are called *paradoxi*. And in fact everything fantastic is paradoxical, as are also the *mimicae ineptiae*, clowning and foolery. The expression probably refers to both these aspects. Thus, in the *mimus*, high and low, serious, even horrifying matters are miraculously mingled with the burlesque and humorous; flat realism with highly fantasticated and magical elements."[6]

Little of the *mimus* has been preserved. Most of its plays were improvised and even those that were written down were not thought respectable enough to be copied and handed on. In the dramatic literature of antiquity that has come down to us, only the theatre of Aristophanes contains the same freedom of imagination and the mixture of fantasy and broad comedy that characterized the wild and vulgar mime plays. Yet for all their brilliance of invention, the plays of Aristophanes have had little impact on the development of at least the regular, literary drama. If their spirit lived on, it did so in that other stream of the tradition of the theatre—the anti-literary, improvised folk theatre, which was always equally unfettered in its topical comment, equally irreverent and extravagant.

It is this stream of tradition that was kept alive throughout the Middle Ages—while the schoolmen copied the comedies of Plautus and Terence—by itinerant *ioculatores* and clowns, who were the direct descendants of the Roman mimes. Their clowning and fooling reappear in the comic characters, often as Devils and personified vices, of French and English mystery plays; in the numerous farces of French medieval literature; and in the German *Fastnachtsspiele*.

Another descendant of the *mimus* of antiquity was the court jester: "The long stick he carries was the wooden sword of the comic actor in ancient times."[7] And both clowns and court jesters appear in the comic characters of Shakespeare's theatre. This is not the place for a detailed study of Shakespearean clowns, fools, and ruffians as forerunners of the Theatre of the Absurd. Most of us are too familiar with Shakespeare to notice how rich his plays are in precisely the same type of inverted logical reasoning, false syllogism, free association, and the poetry of real or feigned madness that we find in the plays of Ionesco, Beckett, and Pinter. This is not to make any claim that these latter-day playwrights should be compared to

Shakespeare, but merely to point out that both the fantastic and the nonsensical have quite a respectable and generally accepted tradition.

These elements in Shakespeare are merely parts of the whole, embedded in a rich amalgam of the poetic and literary, the popular and the vulgar, but they are present nevertheless —in the earthy vulgarity of the low type of moron like Bernardine in *Measure for Measure* who refuses to attend his own execution because he has a hangover; in the naïve stupidity of Launce in *Two Gentlemen of Verona;* in the childishness of Launcelot Gobbo, or the melancholy madness of Feste, or the Fool in *King Lear.* There is also in Shakespeare the personification of the subconscious part of man in great archetypal characters like Falstaff or Caliban, and the exalted madness of Ophelia, Richard II, and Lear—real descents into the realms of the irrational. Again, in a play like *A Midsummer Night's Dream,* there is the savage parody of conventional poetic language in the artisans' play, and Bottom's transformation into an ass is used to reveal his true animal nature. But, above all, there is in Shakespeare a very strong sense of the futility and absurdity of the human condition. This is particularly apparent in the tragicomic plays like *Troilus and Cressida,* where both love and heroism are cruelly deflated, but it underlies most of Shakespeare's conception of life:

> As flies to wanton boys, are we to the gods;
> They kill us for their sport.

If in Shakespeare's theatre elements of a vulgar, spontaneous, and in many ways irrational folk tradition broke into literature (though the presence of these very elements delayed Shakespeare's acceptance as a serious, regular poet for a very long time), the tradition of spontaneous drama outside the realm of literature continued and flourished in Italy in the *commedia dell'arte.* Whether Reich's contention that there is a direct link between the *mimus* and the improvised *commedia dell'arte*—with the Roman Sannio appearing as Zanni (in English popular drama—Zany) and Scapin—is correct or not, the deep affinity between the two genres is evident. They meet the same very human demand for fooling, the release of inhibitions in spontaneous laughter. Many of the traditional *lazzi*—the verbal and nonverbal gags of the *commedia dell'arte*—bear a close family resemblance to those of the *mimus*. Here again we have the stupid simpleton who cannot understand the meaning of the most common terms and becomes entangled in endless semantic speculations and misunderstandings. The recurring types of the sly and lecherous servant, the braggart, the glutton, the senile old man, and the spurious scholar project the basic urges of the human subconscious onto the stage in images as powerful as they are coarse. Basically simple, this theatre depends a great deal on the sheer professional skill of the performers. As Joseph Gregor points out, "Only if we imagine these, in themselves hackneyed, motifs presented in an almost superhuman confusion; the jokes, in themselves stupid enough, delivered with superhuman dexterity of tongue; the acrobatics performed with superhuman skill, can we get an idea of this theatre."[8]

So strong was the appeal of the *commedia dell'arte* that it has, in various guises, survived into the present. In France it was absorbed into legitimate drama through the work of such dramatists as Molière and Marivaux. But, in an unliterary form, it also persisted in the pantomimes of the *funambules*, where Debureau created his archetypal figure of the silent, pale, lovesick Pierrot. In England, it was the harlequinade that kept the tradition of the *commedia dell'arte* alive well into the nineteenth century, when it reached a peak in the inspired clowning of Grimaldi. The harlequinade formed the basis of the later English pantomime, which, in a somewhat modified shape, continues to this day as an irrepressible form of truly vulgar folk theatre.

Other elements of the harlequinade merged into the tradition of the English music hall and American vaudeville, with its cross-talk comedians, tap-dancers, and comic songs. The greatest performers of this genre reached heights of tragicomic pathos that left much of the contemporary legitimate theatre far behind. One of the greatest of these was Dan Leno, of whom Max Beerbohm wrote, "That face puckered with cares . . . that face so tragic, with all the tragedy that is writ on the face of a baby monkey, yet ever liable to relax its mouth into a sudden wide grin and to screw up its eyes to vanishing point over some little triumph wrested from Fate, the tyrant; that poor little personage, so 'put upon' yet so plucky with his squeaking voice and his sweeping gestures; bent but not broken; faint but pursuing; incarnate of the will to live in a world not at all worth living in—surely all hearts went always out to Dan Leno."[9] Dan Leno's patter sometimes contained passages of almost philosophical nonsense strongly reminiscent of the Theatre of the Absurd, when, for example, he asked, "Ah, what is man? Wherefore does he why? Whence did he whence? Whither is he withering?"[10]

And so the line from the *mimus* of antiquity, through the clowns and jesters of the Middle Ages and the Zanni and Arlecchini of the *commedia dell'arte,* emerges in the comedians of music hall and vaudeville from which the twentieth century derived what will in all probability be regarded as its only great achievement in popular art—the silent-film comedy of the Keystone Cops, Charlie Chaplin, Buster Keaton, and a host of other immortal performers. The type of gag and the fast-and-furious timing of the grotesque comedy of the silent cinema stems directly from the clowning and acrobatic dancing of music hall and vaudeville. But the superhuman dexterity of movement of which Gregor spoke in describing the effect of the *commedia dell'arte* is even further and more miraculously enhanced by the magic of the screen.

The silent-film comedy is without doubt one of the decisive influences on the Theatre of the Absurd. It has the dreamlike strangeness of a world seen from outside with the uncomprehending eyes of one cut off from reality. It has the quality of nightmare and displays a world in constant, and wholly purposeless, movement. And it repeatedly demonstrates the deep poetic power of wordless and purposeless action. The great performers of this cinema, Chaplin and Buster Keaton, are the perfect embodiments of the stoicism of man when faced with a world of mechanical devices that have gone out of hand.

The coming of sound in the cinema killed the tempo and fantasy of that heroic age of comedy, but it opened the way for other aspects of the old vaudeville tradition. Laurel and Hardy, W. C. Fields, and the Marx Brothers also exercised their influence on the Theatre of the Absurd. In Ionesco's *The Chairs* the old man impersonates the month of February by "scratching his head like Stan Laurel,"[11] and Ionesco himself told the audience at the American première of *The Shepherd's Chameleon* that the French Surrealists had "nourished" him but that the three biggest influences on his work had been Groucho, Chico, and Harpo Marx.[12]

With the speed of their reactions, their skill as musical clowns, Harpo's speechlessness, and the wild Surrealism of their dialogue, the Marx Brothers clearly bridge the tradition between the *commedia dell'arte* and vaudeville, on the one hand, and the Theatre of the Absurd, on the other. A scene like the famous one in *A Night at the Opera* in which more and more people stream into a tiny cabin on an ocean liner has all the mad proliferation and frenzy of Ionesco. Yet the Marx Brothers are clearly recognizable representatives of the ancient and highly skilled tribe of itinerant clowns. They belong to the same category as the great W. C. Fields, also a brilliant Surrealist comedian and at the same time a skilled juggler, and the equally great Grock, who was both an acrobat and an astonishingly accomplished musician.

In the cinema at present, only one worthy representative of this art is still active, and he, if anything, is too conscious and sophisticated an artist and thus lacks some of the glorious naïveté and vulgarity of his predecessors. Still, Jacques Tati's Monsieur Hulot is a figure helplessly enmeshed in the heartless mechanical civilization of our time. Tati's approach is closely related to that of the Theatre of the Absurd, particularly in his deflation of language by using dialogue mostly as an indistinct background murmur, and his subtle introduction of highly charged symbolical imagery, as in the masterly final scene of *Mon Oncle*, where his departure from an insanely mechanized and busy airport is subtly raised into an image of death.

The tradition of the *commedia dell'arte* reappears in a number of other guises. Its characters have survived in the puppet theatre and the Punch and Judy shows, which also, in their own way, have influenced the writers of the Theatre of the Absurd.

In Central Europe, the tradition of the *commedia dell'arte* merged with that of the clowns and ruffians of Elizabethan England to produce a long line of Pickelherrings, Hans Wursts,

and other coarse comic characters who dominated the folk
theatre of the seventeenth and eighteenth centuries. In the
Austrian folk theatre, this tradition fused with another line of
development, that of the baroque spectacle play and the allegorical drama of the Jesuits, to produce a genre combining
clowning with allegorical imagery that foreshadows many elements of the Theatre of the Absurd. This is the genre of which
Schikaneder's libretto for Mozart's *The Magic Flute* is an un-
distinguished example, and which found its greatest master in
the Viennese actor-playwright Ferdinand Raimund (1790–
1836). In Raimund's theatre, which has remained relatively
unknown outside Austria, owing to the strongly local color of
its language, we find scenes in which broad comedy merges
into naïve poetic allegory. In *Der Bauer als Millionär (The
Peasant as Millionaire)*, the vulgar, broadly comical new-rich
millionaire Wurzel is confronted with his own youth, in the
shape of a lovely boy who ceremoniously takes leave of him,
whereupon Old Age is heard knocking at the door and, when
refused entry, breaks it down. Here, as in the best examples
of the Theatre of the Absurd, the human condition is presented
to us as a concrete poetic image that has become flesh on the
stage and that is at the same time broadly comic and deeply
tragic.

Raimund's successor as the dominant figure of the Viennese
folk theatre, Johann Nestroy (1801–1862), also wrote allegorical tragicomedies in this vein, but he excelled as a master of linguistic absurdity and as a ruthless parodist of pretentious
drama, thus also anticipating some of the characteristics of the
Theatre of the Absurd. Most of Nestroy's dialogue is untrans-
latable, since it is in broad dialect, full of local allusions, and
based on elaborate multiple puns. But in a short passage like
the following from his *Judith und Holofernes* (1849–a parody
of Hebbel's *Judith*), it might be possible to get a glimpse of
his Surrealist quality:

> I am nature's most brilliant piece of work [boasts the
> great warrior Holofernes]; I have yet to lose a battle; I am
> the virgin among generals. One day I should like to pick a
> fight with myself, just to see who is stronger—I or I?[13]

On a more literary level, the traditions of the *commedia*

dell'arte and that of Shakespeare's clowns unite in another forebear of the Theatre of the Absurd, Georg Büchner (1813–1837), one of the greatest dramatists of the German-speaking world. Büchner's delightful comedy *Leonce und Lena* (1836), which is inscribed with a motto from *As You Like It:*

> O that I were a fool,
> I am ambitious for a motley coat . . .[14]

deals with the futility of human existence that can be relieved only by love and the ability to see oneself as absurd. As Valerio says, in language derived from that of Shakespeare's fools:

> The sun looks like an inn sign and the fiery clouds above it like an inscription—Tavern of the Golden Sun. The earth and the water below are like a table on which wine has been spilled, and we lie on it like playing cards with which God and the Devil play, out of boredom, and you are a playing-card king and I a playing-card knave, and all that is lacking is a queen, a beautiful Queen with a gingerbread heart on her breast.[15]

The same Büchner who wrote this gently resigned comedy of autumnal clowning is also one of the pioneers of another type of the Theatre of the Absurd—the violent, brutal drama of mental aberration and obsession. *Woyzeck,* which he left unfinished when he died, at the age of twenty-three, in 1837, is one of the first plays of world literature to make a tormented creature, almost feeble-minded and beset by hallucinations, the hero of a tragedy. In the grotesque nightmare figures that torture the helpless Woyzeck (above all the doctor who subjects him to scientific experiments), and in the violence and extravagance of its language, *Woyzeck* is one of the first modern plays —the germ of much of Brecht, German Expressionism, and of the dark strain of the Theatre of the Absurd exemplified by Adamov's early plays.

Büchner's contemporary, Christian Dietrich Grabbe (1801–1836), may not have had Büchner's genius, but he too belongs in the group of the *poètes maudits* who have influenced the Theatre of the Absurd. His comedy *Scherz, Satire, Ironie und Tiefere Bedeutung* (*Joke, Satire, Irony and Deeper*

Meaning), in which the Devil visits the earth and is mistaken for a maiden-lady novelist, is a masterpiece of *humour noir* and was translated into French by Alfred Jarry himself (under the title *Les Silènes*).

From Grabbe and Büchner, the line of development leads straight to Wedekind, the Dadaists, German Expressionism, and the early Brecht.

But before we turn to these and other direct antecedents of the Theatre of the Absurd, we must take up the story of another of the strains that have contributed to the peculiar quality of its plays—the literature of verbal nonsense.

"Delight in Nonsense," says Freud in his study of the sources of the comic,[16] "has its root in the feeling of freedom we enjoy when we are able to abandon the strait jacket of logic." At the time Freud wrote his essay, more than fifty years ago, he hastened to add that this delight "is covered up in serious life almost to the point of disappearance," so that he had to find evidence for it in the child's delight in stringing words together without having to bother about their meaning or logical order, and in the fooling of students in a state of alcoholic intoxication. It is certainly significant that today, when the need to be rational in "serious, adult life" has become greater than ever, literature and the theatre are giving room in increasing measure to that liberation through nonsense which the stiff bourgeois world of Vienna before the First World War would not admit in any guise.

Yet nonsense literature and nonsense poetry have provided lustful release from the shackles of logic for many centuries. Robert Benayoun opens his fascinating *Anthologie du Nonsense* with French scholastic nonsense poetry of the thirteenth century. And so we read in the *Fatrasies* of Philippe de Rémi, Sire de Beaumanoir (1250–1296), of a sour herring that laid siege to the city of Gisor, and of an old shirt that wanted to plead in court:

> *Une vieille chemise*
> *Avait pris à tâche*
> *De savoir plaider,*
> *Mais une cerise*

> *Devant elle s'est mise*
> *Pour la vilipender.*
> *Sans une vieille cuillère*
> *Qui avait repris haleine*
> *En apportant un vivier,*
> *Toute l'eau de la Tamise*
> *Fût entrée en un panier.*[17]

Though this may be among the earliest preserved examples of nonsense verse, we can be sure that nonsense rhymes have been sung to children and chanted by adults since the earliest times. There is a magic about nonsense, and magic formulas often consist of syllables that still have rhyme or rhythm but have lost any sense they may originally have contained.

The nursery rhymes of most nations include a large number of nonsense verses. In their *Oxford Dictionary of Nursery Rhymes*, Iona and Peter Opie produce evidence for versions of that great nonsense rhyme "Humpty Dumpty" from as far afield as Germany, Denmark, Sweden, France, Switzerland, and Finland. And in their study *The Lore and Language of School Children*, the same authors have collected nonsense rhymes still being handed on by word of mouth among British school children—proof that the need for liberation from the constraints of logic is as powerful now as it was in Freud's day or in the thirteenth century.

The literature of verbal nonsense expresses more than mere playfulness. In trying to burst the bounds of logic and language, it batters at the enclosing walls of the human condition itself. This is the impulse behind the exuberant vision of perhaps the greatest of the masters of nonsense prose and verse, François Rabelais, when he imagined a world of giants with superhuman appetites, a world he described in language so rich and extravagant that it transcends the relative poverty of the real world and opens up a glimpse into the infinite. To the poverty of sense and its restrictions, Rabelais opposed a vision of infinite freedom, which goes far beyond the rule of his humanist Abbeye de Thelème, *"Fay ce que vouldras,"* but includes the freedom to create new concepts and new worlds of the imagination.

Verbal nonsense is in the truest sense a metaphysical en-

deavor, a striving to enlarge and to transcend the limits of the
material universe and its logic:

> Like to the mowing tones of unspoke speeches
> Or like two lobsters clad in logick breeches;
> Or like the gray fleece of a crimson catt,
> Or like the moone-calf in a slipshodd hatt;
> Or like the shadow when the sun is gone,
> Or like a thought that nev'r was thought upon:
>> Even such is man who never was begotten
>> Untill his children were both dead and rotten. . . .[18]

sang Richard Corbet (1582–1635), Ben Jonson's friend and
at one time Bishop of Oxford. And it is precisely the desire to
grasp the shadow when the sun is gone, or to hear the tones
of the unspoken speeches of mankind, that lies behind the impulse to speak nonsense. It is thus no coincidence that the
greatest masters of English nonsense should have been a lo-
gician and mathematician, Lewis Carroll, and a naturalist,
Edward Lear. These two fascinating writers offer infinite material for aesthetic, philosophical, and psychological inquiry. In
our context here, it will be enough if attention is drawn to the
connection between language and being in their work.

Both Lear and Carroll are great inventors of unheard-of
creatures that receive their existence from their *names*. Lear's
Nonsense Botany, for example, contains flowers like the "Tickia
Orologica," with blossoms in the form of pocket watches; or the
"Shoebootia Utilis," which grows boots and shoes; or the
"Nasticreechia Krorluppia," which consists of a stem up which
nasty creatures crawl. Yet these inventions pale before the
poetry of Lear's greatest nonsense songs, like "The Dong with
a Luminous Nose," who lives by the great Gromboolian Plain
and was once visited by the Jumblies, who went to sea in a
sieve; or the Yonghy-Bonghy-Bo, who inhabits the "Coast of
Coromandel where the early pumpkins blow," or the Pobble,
who has no toes—all the spontaneous creations of fantasy freed
from the shackles of reality and therefore able to create by
the act of naming.

There is, of course, also a destructive, brutal streak in Lear.
Countless characters in his Limericks are being smashed, de-
voured, killed, burned, and otherwise annihilated:

> There was an Old Person of Buda,
> Whose conduct grew ruder and ruder;
> Till at last, with a hammer, they silenced his clamour,
> By smashing that Person of Buda.

In a universe freed from the shackles of logic, wish-fulfillment will not be inhibited by considerations of human kindness. Yet here too the fate of the characters is ruled by the names of the places they inhabit. If the old person of Buda had to die because of rudeness, this was entirely a geographical accident. For

> There was an Old Person of Cadiz
> Who was always polite to all ladies,

which, incidentally, did not prevent him from being drowned in the exercise of his good manners. As in the Theatre of the Absurd, and, indeed, as in the vast world of the human subconscious, poetry and cruelty, spontaneous tenderness and destructiveness, are closely linked in the nonsense universe of Edward Lear.

But is the arbitrariness of a world determined by the assonance of names less cruel than the real world, which determines the fate of its inhabitants by the accidents of birth, race, or environment?

> There was an old man of Cape Horn
> Who wished he had never been born;
> So he sat on a chair, till he died of despair,
> That dolorous Man of Cape Horn.

That is why, in Lewis Carroll's nonsense world, there are creatures that try to break the determinism of meaning and significance, which cannot be shaken off in reality:

"When I use a word," Humpty Dumpty said, in rather a scornful tone, "it means just what I choose it to mean—neither more nor less."

"The question is," said Alice, "whether you *can* make words mean so many different things."

"The question is," said Humpty Dumpty, "which is to be master—that's all."

This mastery over the meaning of words can be lost when the inexpressible is encountered. That is what happened to the Banker in *The Hunting of the Snark* when he met a Bandersnatch:

To the horror of all who were present that day
He uprose in full evening dress,
And with senseless grimaces endeavoured to say
What his tongue could no longer express.

Down he sank in his chair—ran his hands through his hair—
And chanted in mimsiest tones
Words whose utter inanity proved his insanity,
While he rattled a couple of bones.

The Hunting of the Snark is an expedition into the unknown —to the limits of being. When the hero of the poem, the Baker, finally encounters a Snark, it *is* a Boojum, and contact with a Boojum means that one vanishes away into nothingness. There is, in Lewis Carroll, a curious yearning for the void where both being and language cease.

As Miss Elizabeth Sewell suggests in her fascinating study of Lear and Carroll, *The Field of Nonsense,* one of the most significant passages in *Through the Looking-Glass* is Alice's adventure in the wood where things have no names. In that wood, Alice herself forgets her own name: "Then it really *has* happened, after all! And now, who am I? I *will* remember, if I can! I'm determined to do it!" But she has forgotten her name and thus her identity. She encounters a fawn that has also forgotten its identity and "so they walked on together through the wood, Alice with her arms clasped lovingly round the soft neck of the fawn, till they came out into another open field, and here the fawn gave a sudden bound into the air, and shook itself free from Alice's arm. 'I'm a fawn!' it cried out in a voice of delight. 'And, dear me! You're a human child!' A sudden look of alarm came into its beautiful brown eyes, and in another moment it had darted away at full speed."

Miss Sewell comments, "There is a suggestion here that to lose your name is to gain freedom in some way, since the nameless one would be no longer under control. . . . It also suggests that the loss of language brings with it an increase in loving

unity with living things."[19] In other words, individual identity
defined by language, having a name, is the source of our
separateness and the origin of the restrictions imposed on our
merging in the unity of being. Hence it is through the destruction of language—through nonsense, the arbitrary rather than
the contingent naming of things—that the mystical yearning for
unity with the universe expresses itself in a nonsense poet like
Lewis Carroll.

This metaphysical impulse is even more clearly visible in
Christian Morgenstern (1871–1914), the German nonsense
poet. More openly philosophical than Lear or Carroll, Morgenstern's nonsense verse is frequently based on his taking all
concepts as equally real. In "Der Lattenzaun" ("The Wooden
Fence"), for example, an architect takes the spaces between
the boards of the fence and uses this material to build a house:

> The fence was utterly dumfounded:
> Each post stood there with nothing round it.
>
> A sight most terrible to see.
> (They charged it with indecency.)[20]

There is also a strong streak of *humour noir* in Morgenstern's
Galgenlieder (*Songs from the Gallows*), with their grotesque
mixture of punning and cosmic fear—a knee wandering through
the world on its own, since the man to whom it once belonged
was destroyed all around it in some war; a dead man's shirt
crying in the wind; or a piece of sandwich paper that, lying
in a lonely wood in the snow,

> . . . Commenced, from fright, there is no doubt,
> To think, commenced, began, set out
>
> To think, just think, what here combined,
> Received (by fear)—a thinking mind . . .[21]

thereby anticipating Heidegger's philosophy of being (the
poem was first published in 1916) but being eaten by a bird
in the end.

Like Edward Lear, Morgenstern was an inveterate inventor
of new species of animals; like Lewis Carroll, he attempted to
write poetry in a language wholly his own:

Kroklowafzi? Sememeṁil
Seiokronto—prafriplo:
Bifzi, bafzi; hulaleṁi:
quasti, bast, bo . . .
Lalu lalu lalu la![22]

Edward Lear, Lewis Carroll, and Christian Morgenstern are
the most important among a host of poets who have found an
outlet in nonsense. A surprising number of major, otherwise
wholly serious, poets have occasionally written nonsense verse;
they range from Samuel Johnson and Charles Lamb to Keats
and Victor Hugo. The limits of nonsense verse are fluid. Do
the outrageously witty rhymes of Byron's *Don Juan* belong to
nonsense, or the fantastic puns and assonances of Thomas
Hood? Do the brilliantly illustrated verse stories of Wilhelm
Busch, that static anticipator of the cartoon film, rank as nonsense? Or the cruel verses that accompany Struwwelpeter? Or
Hilaire Belloc's *Cautionary Tales?* All these contain some of
the elements of the true nonsense universe—its exuberance or
its cruelty, which is also an outstanding feature of Harry Graham's *Ruthless Rhymes* or Joachim Ringelnatz's *Kutteldad-
deldu* and *Kinder-Verwirr-Buch.*

The field of nonsense prose is equally large, extending from
Laurence Sterne to the aphorisms of Lichtenberg, from Charles
Nodier to Mark Twain and Ambrose Bierce. There are also the
delightful nonsense playlets of Ring Lardner (1885–1933),
which Edmund Wilson has compared to the work of the
Dadaists but which nevertheless basically belong to the Anglo-
Saxon tradition of nonsense prose. Though written in dramatic
form, and even occasionally performed, these miniature masterpieces of the art of gentle *non sequitur* are not really plays.
Some of their funniest lines occur in the stage directions, so
that the little plays become more effective when read than
when seen. How, for example, is a stage direction like the following, in *Clemo Uti (The Water Lilies),* to be acted?

(Mama enters from an exclusive waffle parlor. She exits
as if she had had waffles.)

For all its amiable inconsequence, the dialogue of these
short plays, like most writing based on free association, has

its psychological relevance in returning again and again to basic human relations. In *The Tridget of Griva*, one of the characters (who are sitting in rowboats pretending to fish) asks another, "What was your mother's name before she was married?" and receives the reply, "I didn't know her then." In *Dinner Bridge*, one of the characters reveals that his first wife is dead. He is asked, "How long were you married to her?" and retorts, "Right up to the time she died." In *I Gaspiri* (*The Upholsterers*), one stranger asks another, "Where was you born?" and is told, "Out of wedlock," whereupon the first stranger comments, "That's a mighty pretty country around there." When asked, in turn, whether *he* is married, he answers, "I don't know. There's a woman living with me, but I can't place her."

Ring Lardner's nonsense is closely related to the nonsense monologues of Robert Benchley. Another among the large number of brilliant American practitioners of nonsense prose is S. J. Perelman, who was responsible for some of the best dialogue in the Marx Brothers films and who has therefore directly influenced the Theatre of the Absurd.

Most nonsense verse and prose achieve their liberating effect by expanding the limits of sense and opening up vistas of freedom from logic and cramping convention. There is, however, another kind of nonsense, which relies on a contraction rather than an expansion of the scope of language. This procedure, much used in the Theatre of the Absurd, rests on the satirical and destructive use of cliché—the fossilized débris of dead language.

The foremost pioneer of this type of nonsense is Gustave Flaubert, who was greatly preoccupied with the problem of human stupidity and composed a dictionary of cliché and automatic responses, the *Dictionnaire des Idées Reçues*, which appeared as an appendix to his posthumously published novel *Bouvard et Pécuchet*. Additional entries have since come to light, and the dictionary now contains no fewer than nine hundred and sixty-one articles, listing in alphabetical order the most common clichés, conventional misconceptions, and accepted associations of ideas of the nineteenth-century French bourgeois: "Money—the root of all evil," as well as "Diderot—

always followed by d'Alambert," or "Jansenism—one does not know what it is, but it is very chic to talk about it."

James Joyce followed Flaubert in working a whole encyclopedia of English clichés into the Gertie McDowell-Nausikaa episode of *Ulysses*. And the Theatre of the Absurd, from Ionesco to Pinter, continues to tap the inexhaustible resources of comedy discovered by Flaubert and Joyce in the storehouse of clichés and ready-made language.

Equally basic among the age-old traditions present in the Theatre of the Absurd is the use of mythical, allegorical, and dreamlike modes of thought—the projection into concrete terms of psychological realities. For there is a close connection between myth and dream; myths have been called the collective dream images of mankind. The world of myth has almost entirely ceased to be effective on a collective plane in most rationally organized Western societies (it was most effectively in evidence in Nazi Germany, and remains so in the countries of totalitarian Communism), but, as Mircea Eliade points out, "at the level of *individual experience* it has never completely disappeared; it makes itself felt in the dreams, the fantasies and the longings of modern man."[23] It is these longings that the Theatre of the Absurd seeks to express. As Ionesco put it in one of his most impassioned pleas for his kind of theatre:

> The value of a play like Beckett's *Endgame* . . . lies in its being nearer to the Book of Job than to the boulevard theatre or the *chansonniers*. That work has found again, across the gulf of time, across the ephemeral phenomena of history, a less ephemeral archetypal situation, a primordial subject from which all others spring. . . . The youngest, the most recent works of art will be recognized by, and will speak to, all epochs. Yes, it is King Solomon who is the leader of the movement I follow; and Job, that contemporary of Beckett.[24]

The literature of dreams has always been strongly linked with allegorical elements; after all, symbolic thought is one of the characteristics of dreaming. *Piers Plowman*, Dante's *Divine Comedy*, Bunyan's *Pilgrim's Progress*, and William Blake's prophetic visions are essentially allegorical dreams. The allegorical element can often become mechanically intellectualized and pedantic, as in some of the *autos sacramentales* of the Spanish baroque theatre, or it can retain its poetic quality while maintaining its meticulously worked-out correspondences, as does Spenser's *Faerie Queene*.

In the theatre it is not always easy to trace the dividing line between the poetic representation of reality and the opening up of a dream world. Shakespeare's *A Midsummer Night's Dream* deals with dreams and delusions, Bottom's metamorphosis, and the lovers' bewitchment, but at the same time the whole play is itself a dream. The plot of *A Winter's Tale* appears impossibly labored and mannered if taken as real, but will immediately fall into place and become moving poetry, if the play is seen as a dream of guilt redeemed in a glorious fantasy of wish-fulfillment. In fact, the Elizabethan theatre in some ways shares Genet's conception of the hall of mirrors, in that it sees the world as a stage and life as a dream. If Prospero says, "We are such stuff as dreams are made on, and our little life is rounded with a sleep," he himself is part of a fairy-tale play of dreamlike quality. If the world is a stage, and the stage presents dreams, it is a dream within a dream.

The same idea appears in the theatre of Calderón, not only in a play like *La Vida Es Sueño*, in which life is equated with a dream, but also in a great allegorical vision like *El Gran Teatro del Mundo*, which presents the world as a stage on which each character plays the part assigned to him by the creator, the author of the world. The characters enact their life upon the stage of the world as in a dream from which death is the awakening into the reality of eternal salvation or damnation. Calderón's play is said to be based on a text by Seneca (*Epistolae LXXVI* and *LXXVII*) in which occurs the image of the great of this world being no better than actors who have to return their insignia of power after leaving the stage.

In another great allegorical drama of the baroque period, the German Jesuit Jakob Bidermann's *Cenodoxus* (1635), which shows devils and angels fighting for the hero's soul, the choir sings in the hour of death:

Vita enim hominum
Nihil est, nisi somnium.

The baroque plays of extravagant cruelty, of which the
tragedies of John Webster, and Cyril Tourneur's *The Reveng-
er's Tragedy* are the best-known examples, are dreams of another kind—savage nightmares of suffering and revenge.

With the decline of the fashion for allegory, the element of
fantasy begins to dominate—in such satirical fantasies as Swift's
Gulliver's Travels or in Gothic novels like Walpole's *The
Castle of Otranto,* in which a mysterious helmet crashes into
the castle with the dreamlike inevitability of the growing
corpse invading Amédée's apartment in Ionesco's play. If the
dream world of baroque allegory was symbolical but strictly
rational, the dream literature of the eighteenth and early nineteenth centuries makes increasing use of fluid identities, sudden
transformations of characters, and nightmarish shifts of time
and place. E. T. A. Hoffmann, Gérard de Nerval, and Barbey
d'Aurevilly are the masters of this genre. Their fantastic tales
may have appeared to their contemporaries as a kind of science
fiction; today they are seen to be essentially dreams and fantasies, projections of aggression, guilt, and desire. The extravagant, orgiastic fantasies of the Marquis de Sade are even more
clearly projections of a psychological reality in the form of
literary fantasy.

In dramatic literature, the dream motif also appears, in the
form of real events that are made to look like a dream to the
simpleton who is put through them—on the lines of Sly's adventure in the frame-plot of *The Taming of the Shrew,* or in
such great and savagely ruthless comedies as Ludvig Holberg's
Jeppe paa Bjerget (1722). The drunken peasant Jeppe is first
made to believe, when waking in the Baron's castle, that he is
in Paradise, but later he has another awakening—on the gallows. Goethe ventured into a real dream world in the two
Walpurgis Night scenes in the first and second parts of *Faust,*
and there are scenes of dreamlike fantasy in Ibsen's *Peer Gynt;*
Madach's *The Tragedy of Man,* one of the masterpieces of
Hungarian drama, centers on Adam's dream of the coming
history and extinction of mankind; but the first to put on the
stage a dream world in the spirit of modern psycholog-

ical thinking was August Strindberg. The three parts of *To Damascus* (1898–1904), *A Dream Play* (1902), and *The Ghost Sonata* (1907) are masterly transcriptions of dreams and obsessions, and direct sources of the Theatre of the Absurd.

In these plays the shift from the objective reality of the world of outside, surface appearance to the subjective reality of inner states of consciousness—a shift that marks the watershed between the traditional and the modern, the representational and the Expressionist projection of mental realities—is finally and triumphantly accomplished. The central character in *To Damascus* is surrounded by archetypal figures—the woman, who represents the female principle in his life; the other man, who is his eternal, primordial enemy—as well as by emanations of his own personality: the tempter, who represents his evil tendencies; the confessor and the beggar, who stand for the better sides of his self. In the same way, the stage space that encloses these figures is a mere emanation of the hero's, or the author's, mental states—the sumptuous banquet at which he is entertained by the government as a great inventor suddenly turns into an assembly of disreputable outcasts who mock him because he cannot pay the bill. As Strindberg says in the introductory note to *A Dream Play*:

> In this dream play, as in his former dream play *To Damascus*, the author has sought to reproduce the disconnected but apparently logical form of a dream. Anything can happen; everything is possible and probable. Time and space do not exist. On a slight groundwork of reality, imagination spins and weaves new patterns made up of memories, experiences, unfettered fancies, absurdities, and improvisations. The characters are split, double and multiply; they evaporate, crystallize, scatter, and converge. But a single consciousness holds sway over them all—that of the dreamer. For him there are no secrets, no incongruities, no scruples and no law. . . .[25]

While *To Damascus* leads up to a solution of religious faith and consolation, *A Dream Play* and *The Ghost Sonata* show a world of grim hopelessness and despair. Indra's daughter, in *A Dream Play*, learns that to live is to do evil, while the world of *The Ghost Sonata* is a charnelhouse of guilt, obsession, madness, and absurdity.

It is a significant and somewhat paradoxical fact that the development of the psychological subjectivism that manifested itself in Strindberg's Expressionist dream plays was the direct and logical development of the movement that had led to naturalism. It is the desire to represent reality, all of reality, that at first leads to the ruthlessly truthful description of surfaces, and then on to the realization that objective reality, surfaces, are only part, and a relatively unimportant part, of the real world. This is where the novel takes the leap from the meticulous descriptions of Zola to the even more meticulous and microscopic description of the world, as reflected in the mind of one observer, in the work of Proust. In the same way, Strindberg's development led from his early historical plays to the romantic dramas of the eighties to the ruthless naturalism of obsessive pictures of reality like *The Father*, and from there to the Expressionistic dream plays of the first decade of the new century.

The development of James Joyce was analogous on a different plane. In his youth he learned Norwegian to be able to read Ibsen in the original, and in his early play *Exiles*, and in his meticulously observed Dublin stories, he tried to capture the surface of the real world, until he decided that he wanted to record an even more total reality in *Ulysses*. The Nighttown episode in this novel, written in the form of a dream play, is one of the great early examples of the Theatre of the Absurd. Bloom's dream of grandeur and degradation, and Stephen's dream of guilt are here merged in swiftly changing scenes of grotesque humor and heartbreaking anguish.

It is no coincidence that almost forty years after Joyce completed *Ulysses*, there should have been several, by no means unsuccessful, attempts to stage *Ulysses*, and the Nighttown sequence in particular.[26] For by that time the success of Beckett and Ionesco had made it possible to stage Joyce's scenes, which not only anticipate the Theatre of the Absurd but in many ways surpass it in boldness of conception and originality of invention.

Joyce's *Finnegans Wake* also anticipates the Theatre of the Absurd's preoccupation with language, its attempt to penetrate to a deeper layer of the mind, closer to the subconscious matrix of thought. But here too Joyce has in many respects gone further and probed deeper than a later generation.

If the dream allegories of the Middle Ages and the baroque period expressed a stable and generally accepted body of belief and thus concretized the acknowledged myths of their age, writers like Dostoevski, Strindberg, and Joyce, by delving into their own subconscious, discovered the universal, collective significance of their own private obsessions. This is also true of Franz Kafka, whose impact on the Theatre of the Absurd has been as powerful and direct as that of Strindberg and Joyce.

Kafka's short stories and unfinished novels are essentially meticulously exact descriptions of nightmares and obsessions —the anxieties and guilt feelings of a sensitive human being lost in a world of convention and routine. The images of Kafka's own sense of loss of contact with reality, and his feelings of guilt at being unable to regain it—the nightmare of K. accused of a crime against a law he has never known; the predicament of that other K., the surveyor, who has been summoned to a castle he cannot penetrate—have become the supreme expression of the situation of modern man. As Ionesco observes in a short but illuminating essay on Kafka:

> This theme of man lost in a labyrinth, without a guiding thread, is basic . . . in Kafka's work. Yet if man no longer has a guiding thread, it is because he no longer wanted to have one. Hence his feeling of guilt, of anxiety, of the absurdity of history.[27]

Although Kafka is known to have been greatly attracted by the theatre, only one short dramatic fragment by him is extant, *Der Gruftwächter* (*The Guardian of the Crypt*), the opening scene of an unfinished play, in which a young prince summons the old guardian of the mausoleum where his ancestors are buried, and is told by the old man about the terrifying fight he has each night with the spirits of the departed, who want to leave the prison of their tomb and invade the world of the living.

Yet even if Kafka's own modest attempt to write a play came to nothing, the directness of his narrative prose, the concrete clarity of its images and its mystery and tension, have proved a constant temptation to adapters who felt that it was ideal material for the stage. Perhaps most important among a whole series of such adaptations of Kafka's novels and stories was *The Trial* by André Gide and Jean-Louis Barrault, which opened at the Théâtre de Marigny on October 10, 1947.

This was a production that deeply stirred its public. It came at a peculiarly propitious moment—shortly after the nightmare world of the German occupation had vanished. Kafka's dream of guilt and the arbitrariness of the powers that rule the world was more for the French audience of 1947 than a mere fantasy. The author's private fears had become flesh, had turned into the collective fear of nations; the vision of the world as absurd, arbitrary, and irrational had been proved a highly realistic assessment.

The Trial was the first play that fully represented the Theatre of the Absurd in its mid-twentieth-century form. It preceded the performances of the work of Ionesco, Adamov, and Beckett, but Jean-Louis Barrault's direction already anticipated many of their scenic inventions and united the traditions of clowning, the poetry of nonsense, and the literature of dream and allegory. As one bewildered critic put it at the time, "This is not a play, so much as a sequence of images, phantoms, hallucinations." Or, in the words of another, "This is cinema, ballet, pantomime, all at once. It reminds one of film montage, or of the illustrations in a picture book."[28]

In using a free, fluid, and grotesquely fantastic style of production, Jean-Louis Barrault fused Kafka's work with a style in which he himself had been nurtured and which is in the direct literary and stage lineage of the Theatre of the Absurd—the tradition of the iconoclasts: Jarry, Apollinaire, the Dadaists, some of the German Expressionists, the Surrealists, and the prophets of a wild and ruthless theatre, like Artaud and Vitrac.

This was the movement that began on that memorable evening of December 10, 1896, when Jarry's *Ubu Roi* opened at Lugné-Poë's Théâtre de l'Œuvre and provoked a scandal as violent as the famous battle at the first night of Victor Hugo's *Hernani*, in 1830, which opened the great dispute about Romanticism in the French theatre.

Alfred Jarry (1873–1907) is one of the most extraordinary and eccentric figures among the *poètes maudits* of French literature; when he died he was regarded as little more than one of those bizarre specimens of the Paris *Bohème* who merge their lives and their poetry by turning their own personalities into grotesque characters of their own creation that disappear when they perish, as Jarry did, from overindulgence in absinthe and dissipation. Yet Jarry left an œuvre that has been exerting a growing influence ever since he died and that still continues to increase.

Wild, extravagant, and uninhibited in his use of language, Jarry belongs to the school of Rabelais, but his imagery also owes much to the dark, brooding, haunted dream world of that other perverse and unhappy *poète maudit*, Isidore Ducasse, who called himself the Comte de Lautréamont (1846–1870) and was the author of that masterpiece of the Romantic agony, *Les Chants de Maldoror*, which later became the inspiration of the Surrealists. Jarry also owes much to Verlaine, Rimbaud, and, above all, Mallarmé, in whose writings on the theatre there are a number of scattered pleas for a revolt against the rational, well-made play of the *fin de siècle*. As early as 1885, Mallarmé demanded a theatre of myth that would be wholly un-French in its irrationality, with a story "freed of place, time, known characters," for "the century, or our country that exalts it, has dissolved the myths by thought. Let us remake them!"[29]

Ubu Roi certainly created a mythical figure and a world of grotesque archetypal images. Originally the play had been a schoolboy prank aimed at one of the teachers at the *lycée* in Rennes where Jarry was a pupil. This teacher, Hébert, was the butt of much ridicule and had been nicknamed Père Héb, or Père Hébé, and later Ubu. In 1888, when Jarry was fifteen, he wrote a puppet play about the exploits of Père Ubu and performed it for the benefit of his friends.

Ubu is a savage caricature of a stupid, selfish bourgeois seen through the cruel eyes of a schoolboy, but this Rabelaisian character, with his Falstaffian greed and cowardice, is more than mere social satire. He is a terrifying image of the animal nature of man, his cruelty and ruthlessness. Ubu makes himself King of Poland, kills and tortures all and sundry, and is finally chased out of the country. He is mean, vulgar, and incredibly brutal, a monster that appeared ludicrously exaggerated in 1896, but was far surpassed by reality by 1945. Once again, an intuitive image of the dark side of human nature that a poet had projected onto the stage proved prophetically true.

Jarry consciously intended his monstrous puppet play, which was acted by a cast clad in highly stylized, wooden-looking costumes, in a décor of childish naïveté, to confront a bourgeois audience with the horror of its own complacency and ugliness:

I wanted the stage to stand, as soon as the curtain went up, before the public like one of those mirrors in the fairy tales of Madame Leprince de Beaumont, where the vicious villain sees himself with bull's horns and a dragon's body, the exaggerations of his own vicious nature. And it is by no means astonishing that the public was stupefied at the sight of its ignoble double, which had never before been presented to it in its entirety, made up, as M. Catulle Mendès has excellently put it, "of the eternal imbecility of man, his eternal lubricity, his eternal gluttony, the baseness of instinct raised to the status of tyranny; of the coyness, the virtue, the patriotism, and the ideals of the people who have dined well."[30]

The public was indeed stupefied. As soon as Gémier, who played Ubu, had uttered the opening line, "*Merdre!*" the storm broke loose. It was fifteen minutes before silence could be re-established, and the demonstrations for and against continued throughout the evening. Among those present were Arthur Symons, Jules Renard, W. B. Yeats, and Mallarmé. Arthur Symons has left a description of the décor and production:

The scenery was painted to represent, by a child's convention, indoors and out of doors, and even the torrid, temperate, and arctic zones at once. Opposite you, at the back of the stage, you saw apple trees in bloom, under a blue sky, and against the sky a small closed window and a fireplace . . . through the very midst of which . . . trooped in and out the clamorous and sanguinary persons of the drama. On the left was painted a bed, and at the foot of the bed a bare tree and snow falling. On the right there were palm trees . . . a door opened against the sky, and beside the door a skeleton dangled. A venerable gentleman in evening dress . . . trotted across the stage on the points of his toes between every scene and hung the new placard [with the description of the place where the action was laid] on its nail.[31]

Yeats rightly sensed that the scandalous performance he attended marked the end of an era in art. In his autobiography, *The Trembling Veil,* he left an exact description of what he felt when confronted with Jarry's grotesque drama, with its stark colors and deliberate rejection of delicate nuances:

The players are supposed to be dolls, toys, marionettes, and now they are all hopping like wooden frogs, and I can see for myself that the chief personage, who is some kind of King, carries for sceptre a brush of the kind that we use to clean a closet. Feeling bound to support the most spirited party, we have shouted for the play, but that night at the Hôtel Corneille I am very sad, for comedy, objectivity, has displayed its growing power once more. I say: "After Stéphane Mallarmé, after Paul Verlaine, after Gustave Moreau, after Puvis de Chavannes, after our own verse, after all our subtle colour and nervous rhythm, after the faint mixed tints of Conder, what more is possible? After us the Savage God."[32]

Yet Mallarmé, whom Yeats invoked as one of the masters of subtle nuance, congratulated Jarry:

You have put before us, with a rare and enduring glaze at your finger-tips, a prodigious personage and his crew, and this as a sober and sure dramatic sculptor. He enters into the repertoire of high taste and haunts me.[33]

Another among those present on that memorable first night was Jacques Copeau, one of the greatest creative artists of the modern French theatre—he was then seventeen years of age. Almost half a century later he summed up the significance of the event:

. . . in my view the chief claim of the Théâtre de

l'Œuvre to the gratitude of the friends of the art of the
theatre [lies in] the presentation of *Ubu Roi* in a cacophony
of birdcalls, whistles, protests and laughter. . . . The
schoolboy Jarry, to mock a professor, had without knowing
it created a masterpiece in painting that somber and oversimplified caricature with brushstrokes in the manner of
Shakespeare and the puppet theatre. It has been interpreted
as an epic satire of the greedy and cruel bourgeois who
makes himself a leader of men. But whichever sense is attributed to the piece, *Ubu Roi* . . . is "hundred per cent
theatre," what we today would call "pure theatre," synthetic
and creating on the margin of reality, a reality based on
symbols.[34]

And so a play that had only two performances in its first run
and evoked a torrent of abuse appears, in the light of subsequent developments, as a landmark and a forerunner.

Jarry himself more and more assumed the manner of speaking of Ubu, who makes an appearance in a number of his
subsequent works (as indeed he had in the earlier *Les Minutes
de Sable Mémorial* and *César-Antechrist*, a strange cosmic
fantasy that mixes mystical and heraldic elements with Ubu's
kingship of Poland in its third, terrestrial act). In 1899, 1901,
and 1902, Jarry published Almanachs of Père Ubu, while a
full-scale sequel to *Ubu Roi, Ubu Enchaîné*, appeared in 1900.
In this play, Ubu has arrived in exile in France, where, in
order to be different in a country of free men, he turns himself
into a slave.

Some of Jarry's most important works appeared only after
his death, notably *Gestes et Opinions du Docteur Faustroll*
(1911), an episodic novel modeled on Rabelais in which the
hero, whose nature is indicated by his name, is half Faust,
half troll (Jarry knew the Scandinavian nature sprite from
Ibsen's *Peer Gynt*), and is the chief spokesman of the science
of pataphysics. Originally it was Ubu who professed himself a
doctor of pataphysics (in his first appearance in *Les Minutes
de Sable Mémorial*), simply because Hébert had been a phys-
ics teacher. But what had started as a mere burlesque of science later turned into the basis of Jarry's own aesthetics. As
defined in *Faustroll*, pataphysics is:

. . . the science of imaginary solutions, which symbolically attributes the properties of objects, described by their virtuality, to their lineaments.[35]

In effect, the definition of a subjectivist and expressionist approach that exactly anticipates the tendency of the Theatre of the Absurd to express psychological states by objectifying them on the stage. And so Jarry, whose memory is kept green by the College of Pataphysics, of which Ionesco, René Clair, Raymond Queneau, and Jacques Prévert are leading members and in which the late Boris Vian played an important part, must be regarded as one of the originators of the concepts on which a good deal of contemporary art, and not only in literature and the theatre, is based.

Something of the verve and extravagance of *Ubu* can be found in another play that caused an almost comparable scandal nearly twenty years later—Guillaume Apollinaire's *Les Mamelles de Tirésias* (*Tiresias's Breasts*), staged at the Théâtre Maubel in Monmartre on June 24, 1917. In his preface to the play, Apollinaire claims that most of it was written much earlier, in 1903. Apollinaire, who knew Jarry well, was a friend of the young painters of genius who founded the Cubist school and became one of its most influential critics and theoreticians. He labeled *Les Mamelles de Tirésias* "*drame surréaliste*," and can thus claim to have been the first to invent a term that later became the hallmark of one of the important aesthetic movements of the century.

However, Apollinaire's use of the term is quite different from the meaning it was given in the writings of André Breton, which defined Surrealism in its later sense. Here is Apollinaire's explanation of the term:

To characterize my drama, I have used a neologism, for which I hope to be forgiven, as it does not happen often that I do such a thing, and I have coined the adjective "Surrealist," which does not mean symbolical . . . but rather well defines a tendency of art that, if it is no newer than anything else under the sun, has at least never been utilized to formulate an artistic or literary creed. The idealism of the dramatists who succeeded Victor Hugo sought likeness to nature in a conventional local color that corresponds to

the *trompe-l'œil* naturalism of the comedies of manner.
. . . To attempt, if not a renovation of the theatre, at least
a personal effort, I thought one should return to nature itself,
but without imitating her in the manner of the photographers. When man wanted to imitate the action of walking,
he created the wheel, which does not resemble a leg. He
has thus used Surrealism without knowing it. . . .[36]

Surrealism for Apollinaire was an art more real than reality,
expressing essences rather than appearances. He wanted a theatre that would be "modern, simple, rapid, with the shortcuts
and enlargements that are needed to shock the spectator."[37]

Les Mamelles de Tirésias is a grotesque vaudeville that purports to have a serious political message—it advocates the radical repopulation of France, decimated by war and the emancipation of women. The Tiresias of the title starts out as a
woman called Thérèse, who wants to enter politics, the arts,
and a number of other masculine occupations and decides to
turn into a man—an operation accomplished by the release of
her breasts, which float into the air as colored toy balloons.
Her husband thereupon decides to fulfill the function of Thérèse, who has now become Tiresias. In Act II, he has succeeded in producing forty thousand and forty-nine children,
simply by wanting them very hard. In the end, his wife returns
to him. All this takes place in Zanzibar, in front of the people
of Zanzibar, represented by a single actor who never says a
word but sits by a table equipped with all kinds of instruments
suitable for the production of noises—from guns, drums, and
castanets to pots and pans that can be broken with a bang.
The play is preceded by a prologue in which the director of
the company of actors presenting it sums up Apollinaire's dramatic creed:

For the theatre should not be a copy of reality
It is right that the dramatist should use
All the mirages at his disposal . . .
It is right that he should let crowds speak inanimate objects
If he so pleases
And that he no longer should reckon with time
Or space
His universe is the play

Within which he is God the Creator
Who disposes at will
Of sounds gestures movements masses colors
Not merely in order
To photograph what is called a slice of life
But to bring forth life itself in all its truth . . .[38]

Apollinaire's play *Couleur du Temps* (*The Color of Time*), which was in rehearsal when he died of Spanish influenza on November 9, 1918 (the day of the Armistice), though very different from *Les Mamelles de Tirésias*, also creates its own universe. It is a curious verse play in which a group of aviators escape from the war; arrive at the South Pole, where they want to find eternal peace; discover a beautiful woman frozen into the ice; and kill each other fighting for her—another allegorical dream that, coming from the author of *Tirésias*, testifies to the close connection between the grotesque nonsense of that play and the atmosphere of myth in this.

The Paris *Bohème* of Jarry and Apollinaire was a world in which painting, poetry, and theatre mingled, and the efforts to find a modern art overlapped. The décor for *Ubu Roi* had been painted by Jarry himself with the aid of Pierre Bonnard, Vuillard, Toulouse-Lautrec, and Sérusier.[39] Apollinaire was the advocate and propagandist of the Cubist movement, and a friend and companion of Matisse, Braque, and Picasso. The fight to transcend the conception of art as mere mimesis, imitation of appearances, was carried forward on a broad front, and the Theatre of the Absurd is as much indebted to the collages of Picasso or Juan Gris and the paintings of Klee (the titles of which are often little nonsense poems) as to the work of its literary forebears.

The Dada movement, which began in Zürich during the war, among French, German, and other European refugees and conscientious objectors and which thus merged a Parisian with a Central European tradition, also mingled writers, painters, and sculptors. On February 2, 1916, the Zürich papers announced the formation of the Cabaret Voltaire. On February 5, the first evening's entertainment was provided by Tristan Tzara (born in 1896), the young Rumanian poet, reading his own work. Hugo Ball (1886–1927) and his wife,

Emmy Hennings (1885–1948); Richard Huelsenbeck (born in 1892); Hans Arp, the sculptor and poet (born in 1887); and the painter Marcel Janco, another Rumanian (born in 1895), were the other founder-members of the movement, which owed its name to a lucky dip into a French dictionary. Huelsenbeck and Ball, looking for a name for a singer in the cabaret, came across the word "*dada*"—hobbyhorse. The aim of the Dadaists was the destruction of art, or at least the conventional art of the bourgeois era that had produced the horrors of war.

The program of the Cabaret Voltaire at No. 1 Spiegelgasse, in the old town of Zürich—right opposite house No. 6, inhabited by Lenin, who must have been disturbed every evening by the noisy goings on there—was on a modest scale—songs, recitations of poetry, short sketches, an occasional play. Here the tradition of the literary cabarets of Munich, where Wedekind and his circle had cultivated an impertinent and witty kind of chanson, merged with the French tradition of popular song that had produced Yvette Guilbert and Aristide Bruant. Hugo Ball's diary lists readings of poems by Kandinsky, songs by Wedekind and Bruant, music by Reger and Debussy. Arp read from *Ubu Roi;* Huelsenbeck, Tzara, and Janco performed a *Poème Simultan,* a simultaneous recitation of three different poems, producing an indistinct and inarticulate murmur, "showing the struggle of the *vox humana* with a threatening, entangling, and destroying universe whose rhythm and sequence of noise is inescapable."[40] In June, 1916, the Dadaists published what remained the only number of a periodical, *Cabaret Voltaire,* which included contributions by Apollinaire, Picasso, Kandinsky, Marinetti, Blaise Cendrars, and Modigliani.

The first play performed at a Dada soirée, in new and larger premises, was *Sphinx und Strohmann* by the Austrian painter Oskar Kokoschka (born in 1886). Marcel Janco was responsible for directing the play, and he designed the masks. Hugo Ball, who played one of the leading parts, has described the strange performance in his diary under the date of April 14, 1917:

> The play was acted . . . in tragic body-masks; mine was so large that I could comfortably read my part inside it.

The head of the mask was lit up electrically, and it must have made a rather strange effect in the darkened auditorium, with light coming from the eyes. . . . Tzara, in the back room, was responsible for thunder and lightning as well as having to say "Anima, sweet Anima" as the voice of the parrot. But he was also looking after entrances and exits, thundered and lightninged in the wrong places, and gave the impression that this was a special effect intended by the director, an intended confusion of backgrounds. . . .[41]

Kokoschka's play, labeled by the author "a curiosity," is a remarkable example of early Expressionism (it had already been given an improvised performance at the Vienna School of Arts and Crafts in 1907). Its theme revolves around Mr. Firdusi, who is in love with Anima, the female soul. Kautschukmann (Rubber Man), a "snake man" and obviously the embodiment of evil, pretends he is a doctor who can cure Firdusi of his love. Firdusi's head is turned by love, which means that it is actually turned backward on his straw body. So even when he is face to face with Anima, he cannot see her. The cure of love is death. Kautschukmann makes Firdusi jealous by letting the parrot call on sweet Anima, and as he cannot turn his head to see what is really happening, he dies of grief. A chorus of top-hatted gentlemen with holes instead of faces quickly pronounces a series of nonsense aphorisms, and Death, who alone among all the characters has the appearance and costume of an entirely ordinary human being, leaves with Anima, whom he "attempts to console, with good results."[42]

Tzara noted in his diary, "This performance decided the role of our theatre, which will leave the direction to the subtle invention of the explosive wind [of spontaneity], with the scenario in the auditorium, visible direction, and grotesque means—the Dadaist theatre."[43] But in spite of these high hopes for Dada in the theatre, the movement never produced a real impact on the stage. And this is not surprising. Dada was essentially destructive and so radical in its nihilism that it could hardly be expected to be creative in an art form that necessarily relies on constructive co-operation. As Georges Ribemont-Dessaignes, one of the leading French exponents of Dada, recognizes in his autobiography, "Dada consisted of opposing, incompatible, explosive tendencies. To destroy a world so as to put another in its place *in which nothing more exists*, that was, in fact, the watchword of Dada."[44]

The plays the Dadaists produced and largely performed themselves are essentially nonsense poems in dialogue form, accompanied by equally nonsensical business and decorated with bizarre masks and costumes. The Dada manifestation at the Théâtre de l'Œuvre in Paris (which had become the center of Dada after the end of the war) on March 27, 1920, presented a selection of plays that included *La Première Aventure Céleste de M. Antipyrine* (*The First Celestial Adventure of M. Antipyrine*), by Tzara, in which a "parabola" recites verses that contain lines like:

This bird has come white and feverish as
from which regiment comes the clock? from that music
    humid as
M. Cricri receives the visit of his fiancée at the hospital
in the Jewish cemetery the graves rise like snakes
Mr. Poet was an archangel—really
he said that the druggist resembled the butterfly
and our Lord and that life is simple like a bumbum
like the bumbum of his heart.[45]

Ribemont-Dessaignes's *Le Serin Muet* (*The Silent Canary*), which was performed on the same occasion by André Breton, Philippe Soupault, and Mlle. A. Valère, had one of the characters perched on top of a ladder, while another was a Negro who believes he is the composer Gounod and has taught all his compositions to his mute canary, who sings them most beautifully without uttering a sound. Similarly bizarre and largely improvised plays performed at this manifestation were *S'Il Vous Plaît* (*If You Please*), by Breton and Soupault, and *Le Ventriloque Désaccordé* (*The Out of Tune Ventriloquist*), by Paul Dermée. Lugné-Poë, the director of the Œuvre, who had performed *Ubu* twenty-five years earlier, was so delighted with the *succès de scandale* of this Dada manifestation that he asked for more Dada plays. Ribemont-Dessaignes was the only one who responded to the offer. He composed a play called *Zizi de Dada*, "of which the manuscript is lost. The Pope was in it, enclosed in a chalk circle from which he could not leave . . .

but what happened? Even the memory of it is lost!"[46] Lugné-Poë gave the piece careful consideration, but rejected it in the end as being somewhat improper.

At a second Dada manifestation at the Salle Gaveau, on May 26, 1920, the program included another play by Tzara, *La Deuxième Aventure Céleste de M. Antipyrine (M. Antipyrine's Second Celestial Adventure)*; another sketch by Breton and Soupault, *Vous M'Oublierez (You Will Forget Me)*; a piece by Aragon, *Système DD*; and *Vaseline Symphonique*, by Tzara, a cacophony of inarticulate sounds, performed by an ensemble advertised as twenty strong, that aroused the protests of Breton, who did not like being reduced to the role of a musical instrument. Among the other participants in that evening's entertainment were Picabia and Eluard.

Most successful among the Dadaist plays was Tzara's three-act piece *Le Cœur à Gaz (The Gas Heart)*, first performed June 10, 1921, at the Studio des Champs-Elysées, a weird recitation by characters representing parts of the body—the ear, the neck, the mouth, the nose, and the eyebrow. Ribemont-Dessaignes confesses that he cannot remember the performance because, clearly, he did not see it. Yet he appeared in the play in the part of the mouth, together with Soupault, Aragon, Benjamin Péret, and Tzara himself, in the part of the eyebrow. *Le Cœur à Gaz* is a piece of "pure theatre" that derives its impact almost entirely from the subtle rhythms of its otherwise nonsensical dialogue, which, in the use of the clichés of polite conversation, foreshadows Ionesco.

Tzara himself called the play "the biggest swindle of the century in three acts," which "will make happy only the industrialized imbeciles who believe in the existence of men of genius. The actors are asked to give to this piece the attention due to a masterpiece of the power of *Macbeth* or *Chantecler*, but to treat the author, who is not a genius, with little respect and to note the lack of seriousness of the text, which contributes nothing new to the technique of the theatre."[47] A revival of *Le Cœur à Gaz* with professional actors at the *Théâtre Michel* on July 6, 1923, led to one of the most memorable battles of the declining years of Dadaism, with Breton and Eluard jumping onto the stage and being thrown out after hand-to-hand fighting.

More substantial than any of these short plays, whose main function was to shock a bourgeois audience, are two works by Ribemont-Dessaignes that really try to create a poetic universe with validity on the stage. *L'Empéreur de Chine* (*The Emperor of China*), written in 1916, and *Le Bourreau du Pérou* (*The Executioner of Peru*), published in 1928.

The first of these deals with the themes of sexuality, violence, and war. The heroine, Onane, Princess of China, is a willful and cruel sex-kitten; her father Espher, who becomes Emperor of China, a sadistic tyrant. Onane is accompanied by two slaves, Ironique and Equinoxe, who arrive in the opening scene in cages, as presents from the Emperor of the Philippines. They are eccentrically dressed in top hats, kilts, and tuxedo jackets. Ironique has his left eye bandaged, Equinoxe his right eye, so that they have to look at the world together. War and torture play a great part in the action. The Minister of Peace takes up the study of strategy and becomes Minister of War, and scenes of rape and violence follow. Only those women who drink the blood of those already killed will be spared by the soldiers. In the end, the bureaucrat Verdict kills Onane, who is in love with him. The final scene is a duet of nonsense words by the two slaves. The final lines are:

IRONIQUE: When love dies . . .

EQUINOXE: Urine.

VOICE OF VERDICT (in the shadows): God.

IRONIQUE: Constantinople.

EQUINOXE: An old woman died of starvation yesterday in Saint-Denis.[48]

L'Empéreur de Chine is a powerful play that combines the elements of nonsense and violence which characterize the Theatre of the Absurd. Its weakness lies in the insufficient blending of its elements into an organic whole, and in the length of its somewhat rambling design.

Le Bourreau du Pérou expresses preoccupations similar to those of the earlier play. The government abdicates and hands the sacred seals of state to the hangman, and a period of gratuitous murder and execution ensues. Here again, in a curious way, the free flow of the imagination and the release of the subconscious fantasies of a poet assume a prophetic content. The outbreak of violence in the era of the Second World War is exactly forecast by *L'Empéreur de Chine* and even more drastically by *Le Bourreau du Pérou*. It is as though the destructiveness of the Dadaists were a sublimated release of the same secular impulse toward aggression and violence that found expression in the mass murders of the totalitarian movements.

While Dadaism had shifted its center of gravity to Paris after the end of hostilities, other members of the Zürich circle went back to Germany, transplanting the movement to Berlin and Munich, where it merged and coexisted with the powerful stirrings of German Expressionism. The dramatic products of the Expressionist movement were on the whole too idealistic and politically conscious to rank as forerunners of the Theatre of the Absurd, with which, however, they share the tendency to project inner realities and to objectify thought and feeling. The only major writer among the Expressionists who definitely belongs to the antecedents of the Theatre of the Absurd is Yvan Goll (1891–1950), who, born in the disputed territory of Alsace-Lorraine, had gone to Switzerland at the outbreak of the war. There he met Arp and other members of the Dadaist circle. Later he went to Paris. Goll, who described himself as without a homeland, "Jewish by destiny, born in France by chance, described as a German by a piece of stamped paper,"[49] became a bilingual poet who sometimes wrote in French, sometimes in German.

Goll's dramatic work during his Expressionist-Dadaist period was written in German. Clearly under the influence of Jarry and Apollinaire, Goll was also greatly impressed with the possibilities of the cinema. *Die Chaplinade* (1920), which he describes as a "film poem," is a highly imaginative combination of poetry and film images. Charlie Chaplin's little tramp is its hero. Chaplin's image comes to life on a poster, escapes from the billsticker, who tries to pin him back, and floats through a series of dreamlike, filmlike adventures, accompanied by a doe (which turns into a beautiful girl and is killed by a huntsman). He is involved in revolutions and riots and finally returns to his poster. This is a beautiful work, probably the first to recognize the poetry and poetic potentialities of the cinema.

During the same year, 1920, Goll published two plays under the joint title *Die Unsterblichen* (*The Immortals*), which he subtitled *Überdramen*, or superdramas, in the sense in which Apollinaire used the term *drame surréaliste* in his subtitle for *Tirésias*. In his preface, Goll explains his conception of a new kind of theatre. In Greek drama, the gods measured themselves against human beings; theatre was a vast enlargement of reality onto a superhuman scale. But in the nineteenth century, plays sought to be nothing but "interesting, challenging in the manner of an advocate [of a cause] or simply descriptive, imitative of life, not creative."[50] The dramatist of the new age must again find a way to penetrate behind the surface of reality:

> The poet must again know that there are worlds quite different from that of the five senses: a superworld (*Überwelt*). He must come to grips with it. This will by no means be a relapse into the mystical or the romantic or the clowning of the music hall, although it has something in common with all of these—the probing into a world beyond the senses. . . . It has been quite forgotten that the stage is nothing but a magnifying glass. Great drama has always known this—the Greek walked on the cothurnus; Shakespeare spoke with giant spirits of the dead. It has been quite forgotten that the first symbol of the theatre is the mask. . . . In the mask there lies a law and this is the law of the theatre—the unreal becomes fact. For a moment it is proved that the most banal can be unreal and "divine" and that precisely in this there lies the greatest truth. Truth is not contained in reason; it is found by the poet, not the philosopher. . . . The stage must not only work with "real" life; it becomes "surreal" when it is aware of the things behind the things. Pure realism was the greatest lapse in all literature.[51]

The theatre must not be just a means to make the bourgeois comfortable, it must frighten him, turn him into a child again. "The simplest means is the grotesque, but without inciting to laughter. The monotony and stupidity of human beings are so enormous that they can be adequately represented only by enormities. Let the new drama be an enormity."[52] To create the effect of masks in our technical age, the stage must use the techniques of recording, electrical posters, mega-phones. The characters must be caricatures in masks and on stilts.

This is an impressive manifesto, which accurately describes many of the features and the aims of the Theatre of the Absurd. Yet the two plays in which Goll sought to translate these ideas into action are disappointing. *Der Unsterbliche*, in two acts, shows a musician of genius who loses his mistress to a tycoon and sells his soul to him for a large sum of money. His soul is abstracted in the process of filming it, making him immortal. In the second act, the musician's mistress desperately seeks him, but flirts with the bridegroom of a newly married couple who come to be photographed by her tycoon-husband. In the end, Sebastian, the musician, comes to life again—on film, crying out for her—but she finally departs with an officer. Although the play uses the technique of projected stills and film, and some of the characters appear as grotesque masks, its contents are, after all, the old romantic, sentimental clichés of the artist who loses his soul to commerce and the beloved woman who cannot resist money or power.

The second *Überdrama, Der Ungestorbene* (*The Not Yet Dead*), deals with the very similar dilemma of the philosopher who wants to improve the world and lectures on eternal peace. This time his wife, who sits at the box office of the lecture hall, is seduced by a journalist who battens on the thinker, and persuades him, for the sake of sensationalism, to die in public, to prove that he is serious about progress. But after his public death for humanity is advertised, the philosopher fails to die. Nevertheless, the newspaper still proclaims that he has died for humanity. In the end, his wife returns and he launches a new series of lectures, this time on "The hygienic conditions of bedbugs in hotels." Again a good many technical devices are used by Goll to translate his ideas into stage reality —the mad dance of modern publicity is expressed in a dance of advertising columns, the public at the hero's lectures is represented by a monstrous giant figure, a student throws his brain on the floor and later picks it up again and puts it back in his head—but again the Surrealist devices cannot hide the lack of originality of the basic idea, the commercialization of idealism by the press.

The same discrepancy between the modernity of the means of expression employed and the tameness of the contents characterizes Goll's most ambitious attempt in this genre, the "satirical drama" *Methusalem, oder Der Ewige Bürger* (*Methusalem, or The Eternal Bourgeois*). Again the theoretical preface is far more original than the play itself:

> The modern satirist must seek new means of provocation. He has found them in "Surrealism" (*Überrealismus*) and in "a-logic." Surrealism is the strongest negation of realism. The reality of appearance is unmasked in favor of the truth of being. "Masks"—rough, grotesque, like the emotions of which they are the expression. . . . A-logic is the most spiritual form of humor, and thus the best weapon against the clichés that dominate our whole life. . . . So as not to be a tearful pacifist or salvationist, the poet must perform a few somersaults to make you into children again. For this is his aim—to give you some dolls, to teach you to play and then to throw the sawdust of the broken doll into the wind.[53]

But *Methusalem,* witty and charming though it is, proves to be little more than the conventional satire against the *Spiessbürger* with his shoe factory and his greedy, businesslike son, who instead of a mouth has the mouthpiece of a telephone, whose eyes are five-mark pieces, and whose forehead and hat consist of a typewriter topped by radio antennas. Again there is the student-idealist who is a poet and a revolutionary and seduces Methusalem's daughter, and who in one scene appears split into three parts—his "I," his "Thou," and his "He." The student is killed in a duel with Methusalem's son, but in the last scene he is alive again; has married the daughter, who has given birth to his child; and is on the point of becoming a bourgeois himself. For revolutions end "when the others no longer have villas," and new revolutions start "when we have got one." And the outcome of all the romantic love is the young mother's cry: "If only [our son] would not piss so much!"

Again Goll uses film in a sequence of Methusalem's dreams. In another dream sequence, the animals that adorn his household, alive or dead, call for a revolution against the tyranny of man. Dead characters come to life to show that life always goes on in one form or another, and that the theatre can never furnish valid, final solutions. But the most successful parts of this ambitious play, which was published with illustrations by Georg Grosz, the leading German Dadaist painter, and performed in 1924 in masks designed by him, are the dialogues of the bourgeois and his guests, which consist entirely of clichés, and thus anticipate Ionesco. This fact, surely, reveals Goll's mistake: he, who was a great and sensitive lyric poet and a master of language, fell victim to the seduction of new techniques, and, in subordinating his imagination to the demands of masks and film, he failed to transmute his material into the new poetry of the Absurd, which he had so clearly foreseen and so effectively formulated in theory. Perhaps Goll was too tender and gentle a soul to be able to live up to the harshness of his satirical objectives.

Among Goll's German contemporaries, the one who came nearest to the realization of a theatre as cruel and grotesque as the one Goll had postulated was Bertolt Brecht, who hailed Goll's first published plays in a review published in December, 1920, calling him the Courteline of Expressionism. In the course of his development from anarchic poetic drama, in the style of Büchner and Wedekind, toward the austerity of the Marxist didacticism of his later phase, Brecht wrote a number of plays that come extremely close to the Theatre of the Absurd, both in their use of clowning and music-hall knockabout humor and in their preoccupation with the problem of the identity of the self and its fluidity.

Brecht was deeply influenced by the great Munich beer-hall comedian Karl Valentin, an authentic heir of the harlequins of the *commedia dell'arte*. In Brecht's one-act farce *Die Hochzeit* (*The Wedding*), written circa 1923, the collapse of pieces of furniture externalizes the rottenness of the family in which the wedding takes place, in exactly the way that objects express inner realities in the plays of Adamov and Ionesco while, at the same time, giving an opportunity for broad music-hall gags.

In a far more serious vein, Brecht's most enigmatic play, and one of his greatest, *Im Dickicht der Städte* (*In the Jungle of Cities*), written 1921–23, foreshadows the Theatre of the Absurd in its deliberate rejection of motivation. The play shows

a fight to the death between two men, Garga and Shlink, who
are linked in a strange relationship of love-hatred. It opens
with Shlink's attempt to buy Garga's opinion of a book. He
offers Garga, who is employed in a lending library, a large
sum of money to make him declare that he likes a book for
which he has expressed a dislike. From this point, the fight
develops; it is always a matter of making the one man ac-
knowledge the other's superiority through forcing him into
either gratitude or aggression. All this takes place in a grotesque Chicago of gangsters and lynching mobs.

Im Dickicht der Städte not only deals with the impossibility
of knowing the motivation of human beings in their actions
(thus anticipating the techniques of Pinter), it also presents
the problem of communication between human beings, which
preoccupies Beckett, Adamov, and Ionesco. The fight between
Shlink and Garga is essentially an attempt to achieve contact.
At the end they recognize the impossibility of such contact,
even through conflict. "If you crammed a ship full of human
bodies till it burst, the loneliness inside it would be so great that
they would turn to ice . . . so great is our isolation that even
conflict is impossible."[54]

The "comedy" *Mann Ist Mann* (*Man Equals Man*), written
1924–25, describes the transformation of a meek little man
into a ferocious soldier. Here Brecht uses the techniques of
the music hall again. The transformation scene, in which the
victim is induced to commit what he believes to be a crime, is
tried, sentenced, and made to think that he has been shot
(after which he is resurrected in his new personality), is presented like a variety act—a series of conjuring tricks. In productions of this play Brecht used stilts and other devices to
turn the British colonial soldiers who perform the transformation into huge monsters. *Mann Ist Mann* anticipates the Theatre of the Absurd in its thesis that human nature is not a
constant, and that it is possible to transform one character into
another in the course of a play.

The recent publication of a hitherto unpublished poem by
Brecht has thrown an interesting light on the connection between *Mann Ist Mann* and his earlier *Im Dickicht der Städte*.
This poem comes from an early draft-play, *Der Grüne Garraga* (*Green Garraga*), and deals with a citizen, Galgei, who

was turned into another human being. Thus Galy Gay, the victim of *Mann Ist Mann*, was originally identical with Garga, the victim of aggression in *Im Dickicht der Städte*. And in fact Shlink's attempt to buy Garga's opinion is an attempt to rob him of his personality, just as Galy Gay is robbed of his personality in the later play. Both plays are about the appropriation of human personality by a stronger personality—the stealing of one's identity, as a form of rape. And this is one of the themes of the Theatre of the Absurd as well: Ionesco's *Jacques, ou La Soumission* is a clear case in point.

In Brecht's short interlude (written to be performed in the entr'acte of *Mann Ist Mann*) *Das Elephantenkalb* (*The Baby Elephant;*) 1924–25, the automatic writing of Surrealism is as much anticipated as the problem of shifting identity. A baby elephant, accused of having murdered its mother, can prove that the mother is not dead at all and is not its mother in any case. Yet the case is proved and the baby elephant found guilty. This is pure anti-theatre, and dramatizes its author's subconscious mind as ruthlessly as Adamov's early plays project *his* neurosis.

Like Adamov, Brecht later rejected this phase of his artistic development. Like Adamov, he turned toward a socially committed and, at least in outward intention, fully rational theatre. Yet Brecht's case also shows that the irrational Theatre of the Absurd and the highly purposeful politically committed play are not so much irreconcilable contradictions as, rather, the obverse and reverse side of the same medal. In Brecht's case, the neurosis and despair that were given free rein in his anarchic and grotesque period continued as actively and as powerfully behind the rational façade of his political theatre, and provide most of its poetic impact.

In fact, Kenneth Tynan in quoting Brecht to Ionesco as an example of his socially committed ideal, and Ionesco in attacking Brecht as the embodiment of the arid ideological theatre, are both equally wide of the mark. Brecht was one of the first masters of the Theatre of the Absurd, and his case shows that the *pièce à thèse* stands or falls not by its politics but by its poetic truth, which is beyond politics, since it proceeds from far deeper levels of the author's personality. Brecht's personality contained a strong element of anarchy and despair. Hence even in his politically committed period, the picture he presented of the capitalist world was essentially negative and absurd: the universe of *The Good Woman of Setzuan* is ruled by imbecile gods, that of *Puntila* is modeled on a Chaplinesque formula of slapstick, and in *The Caucasian Chalk Circle* justice is done only by the unlikeliest of accidents.

While in Germany the impulse behind Dadaism and Expressionism had flagged into the *Neue Sachlichkeit* by the middle twenties, and the whole modern movement was swallowed up in the intellectual quicksands of the Nazi period in the thirties, the line of development continued unbroken in France. The destructiveness of Dadaism had cleared the air. Dada was reborn in a changed form in the Surrealist movement. Where Dada was purely negative, Surrealism believed in the great, positive, healing force of the subconscious mind. As André Breton put it in his famous definition of the word in the first Surrealist manifesto of 1924, Surrealism was a "pure psychic automatism by which it is proposed to express, verbally, in writing, or in any other way, the real functioning of thought."

This is not the place to trace in detail the fascinating story of the struggles and internal conflicts of the Surrealist movement or its achievements in poetry or painting. In the theatre, the harvest of Surrealism proved a meager one. The stage is far too deliberate an art form to allow complete automatism in the composition of plays. It is most unlikely that any of the plays we can today class as Surrealist were written in the way Breton ideally wanted them composed.

Louis Aragon's volume *Le Libertinage* (1924) contains two such plays. *L'Armoire à Glace un Beau Soir* (*The Mirror-Wardrobe One Beautiful Evening*) is a charming sketch. In the prologue we meet an assortment of fantastic characters. A soldier meets a nude woman, the President of the Republic appears with a Negro general, Siamese twin sisters appeal to the President for permission to marry separately. A man on a tricycle passes; his nose is so long that he has to lift it when he wants to speak; Théodore Fraenkel (a member of the Surrealist circle) introduces a fairy. The play proper opens with the familiar scene of a husband returning home, while his wife nervously eyes the wardrobe, implores him not to go near it, and gives every indication that her lover is hidden inside it. After suspense and jealousy have been built up into an atmosphere of sexual excitement, the couple disappear into the next room. Finally, after a long and charged pause, the husband returns with his clothes in disorder and opens the cupboard. Out march all the fantastic characters of the prologue in solemn procession. The President of the Republic sings a nonsense song.

Au Pied der Mur (*At the Foot of the Wall*), Aragon's second play in *Le Libertinage*, uses the same method—a fairly conventional action interrupted by Surrealist interludes. The main plot is romantic to the point of ridiculousness. A young man, who has been left by his mistress, forces the maid in the country inn where he has sought refuge to kill herself to prove her love for him. In the second act, the young hero, Frédéric, and his mistress roam the high mountains of the Alps, and finally Frédéric faces the narrator of the framework scenes as his own double. The appearance of fairies and Parisian workmen in overalls cannot disguise the fact that basically this is a romantic play in the vein of Musset or Victor Hugo, revealing, through its modernistic trappings, Aragon's essential traditionalism, which later also emerged in his beautiful wartime poetry and his monumental social novels.

Aragon and Breton jointly wrote a play, *Le Trésor des Jésuites* (*The Treasure of the Jesuits*), from which they both dissociated themselves after Aragon's break with the Surrealist movement, and which has therefore never been republished. One of the most remarkable features of this play is that, more than ten years before, it forecast the outbreak of the Second World War in 1939, substantiating Breton's claim that the Surrealist method of automatic writing awakens powers of prophecy and clairvoyance.

More important than most of the dramatic production within the Surrealist movement was the work some of its members produced after they had left, or been expelled from it. Antonin Artaud (1896–1948), one of the finest of the Surrealist poets and also a professional actor and director who became the most powerful seminal influence on the modern French theatre, and Roger Vitrac (1899–1952), the ablest dramatist to emerge from Surrealism, were both banished from the circle by Breton because they had yielded to unworthy commercial instincts, to the extent of wanting to produce Surrealist plays in the framework of the professional theatre. Artaud and Vitrac were proscribed by Breton toward the end of 1926. They became associates in a venture appropriately named the Théâtre Alfred Jarry, which opened on June 1, 1927, with a program that included a one-act play by Artaud, *Ventre Brûlé, ou La Mère Folle* (*Upset Stomach, or The Mad Mother*), and Vitrac's *Les Mystères de l'Amour* (*The Mysteries of Love*).

Les Mystères de l'Amour (three acts, five scenes) is probably the most sustained effort to write a truly Surrealist play. It could well be the product of automatic writing, consisting, as it does, largely of the tender and sadistic fantasies of two lovers. The author himself appears at the close of the first scene. He has tried to commit suicide by shooting himself, and enters bathed in blood but shaking with helpless laughter. At the end, he reappears, none the worse for his experience. Lloyd George and Mussolini also form part of the cast, and Lloyd George in particular appears in a gruesome light—he is sawing off heads and trying to dispose of fragments of corpses. The sets are modeled on Surrealist paintings. Thus, the fourth scene represents, at the same time, a railway station, a dining car, the seashore, a hotel hall, a draper's shop, and the main square of a provincial town. Past, present, and future merge in dreamlike fashion, the actual and the potential are inextricably interwoven. Yet in this chaos there are passages of remarkable poetic power. At one point, in a dialogue between the hero, Patrice, and the author, the basic theme of the Theatre of the Absurd, the problem of language, is squarely faced:

THE AUTHOR: Your words make everything impossible, my friend.

PATRICE: Then make a theatre without words.

THE AUTHOR: But, my dear sir, have I ever wanted to do anything else?

PATRICE: You have: you have put words of love into my mouth.

THE AUTHOR: You ought to have spat them out.

PATRICE: I tried, but they changed into shots or vertigo.
THE AUTHOR: That is not my fault. Life is like that.[55]

Vitrac's second Surrealist play, *Victor, ou Les Enfants au Pouvoir* (*Victor, or Power to the Children*), first performed under Artaud's direction on December 24, 1924, has already left the chaos of pure automatism behind and adopts the convention of the farcical and fantastic drawing-room comedy we find again in Ionesco's work. Victor is a boy of nine, seven feet tall and with the intelligence of an adult. He and his six-year-old girl friend Esther are the only rational beings in a family of mad puppetlike adults. Victor's father has an affair with Esther's mother, but the children expose the lovers, and Esther's father hangs himself. One of the characters is a woman of breathtaking beauty but disconcerting carminative incontinence. In the end, Victor dies of a stroke on his ninth birthday and his parents commit suicide. As the maid rightly points out in the last line of the play, *"Mais, c'est un drame!"*[56]

Victor anticipates Ionesco in many ways: the banality of a cliché-laden language is parodied when one of the characters reads genuine extracts from *Le Matin* of September 12, 1909; there is a similar mixture of the parody of the conventional theatre and pure absurdity. Yet Vitrac's play lacks the sense of form and the poetry that gives Ionesco's madness its method —and its charm. Here the blending of the elements is not complete, the nightmare alternates with the students' rag.

Vitrac's later plays return to a more traditional form, but some of them still bear traces of his Surrealist experience. Even so sociological and political a play as *Le Coup de Trafalgar* (a picture of a slice of Parisian society before, during, and after the First World War, first performed in 1934) shows traces of a delightful crazy humor, while in *Le Loup-Garou* (*The Were-wolf*), a comedy that takes place in a fashionable mental hospital, the author's Surrealist experience is clearly detectable in his mastery of the technique of lunatic dialogue.

Antonin Artaud directed Vitrac's Surrealist plays and is the author of one or two remarkable dramatic sketches, but his real importance for the Theatre of the Absurd lies in his theoretical writings and in his practical experiments as a producer. One of the most extraordinary men of his age, actor, director,

prophet, blasphemer, saint, madman—and a great poet—
Artaud's imagination may have outrun his practical achievement in the theatre. But his vision of a stage of magic beauty
and mythical power remains, to this day, one of the most active leavens in the theatre. Although he had worked under
Dullin and had directed the performances of the short-lived
Théâtre Alfred Jarry, Artaud's revolutionary conception of the
theatre crystallized only after he had seen the Balinese dancers at the Colonial Exhibition of 1931. He formulated his ideas
in a series of impassioned manifestoes later collected in the
volume Le Théâtre et Son Double (1938).

Diagnosing the confusion of his time as springing from the
"rupture between things and words, between things and the
ideas that are their representation"[57] and rejecting the psychological and narrative theatre, with its "preoccupation with personal problems,"[58] Artaud passionately called for a return to
myth and magic, for a ruthless exposure of the deepest conflicts of the human mind, for a "Theatre of Cruelty." "Everything that acts is a cruelty. It is upon this idea of extreme
action, pushed beyond all limits, that theatre must be rebuilt."[59] By confronting the audience with the true image of
their internal conflicts, a poetic, magical theatre would bring
liberation and release. "The theatre restores to us all our dormant conflicts and all their powers, and gives these powers
names we hail as symbols—and behold! Before our eyes is
fought a battle of symbols . . . for there can be theatre only
from the moment when the impossible really begins and when
the poetry that occurs on the stage sustains and superheats the
realized symbols."[60]

This amounts to a complete rejection of realism and a demand for a theatre that would project collective archetypes:
"The theatre will never find itself again . . . except by furnish-
ing the spectator with the truthful precipitate of dreams, in
which his taste for crime, his erotic obsessions, his savagery,
his chimeras, his utopian sense of life and matter, even his
cannibalism pour out on a level not counterfeit and illusory,
but interior. In other terms, the theatre must pursue by all its
means a reassertion not only of all the aspects of the objective
and descriptive external world but of the internal world; that
is, of man considered metaphysically."[61]

Under the influence of the powerful impression made on him by the subtle and magical poetry of the Balinese dancers, Artaud wanted to restore the language of gesture and movement to make inanimate things play their part in the action, and to relegate dialogue (which "does not belong specifically to the stage, it belongs to books")[62] to the background. Quoting the music hall and the Marx Brothers as well as the Balinese dancers, he called for a true language of the theatre, which would be a wordless language of shapes, light, movement, and gesture: "The domain of the theatre is not psychological but plastic and physical. And it is not a question of whether the physical language of theatre is capable of achieving the same psychological resolutions as the language of words, whether it is able to express feelings and passions as well as words, but whether there are not attitudes in the realm of thought and intelligence that words are incapable of grasping and that gestures and . . . a spatial language attain with more precision."[63]

The theatre should aim at expressing what language is incapable of putting into words. "It is not a matter of suppressing speech in the theatre but of changing its role, and especially of reducing its position."[64] "Behind the poetry of the texts, there is the actual poetry, without form and without text.[65] . . . For I make it my principle that words do not mean everything, and that by their nature and defining character, fixed once and for all, they arrest and paralyze thought instead of permitting it and fostering its development. . . . I am adding another language to the spoken language, and I am trying to restore to the language of speech its old magic, its essential spellbinding power."[66]

In theory, Artaud had formulated some of the basic tendencies of the Theatre of the Absurd by the early nineteen-thirties. But he lacked the opportunity either as dramatist or as a director to put these ideas into practice. His only chance to achieve his aims came in 1935, when he found the backers to give a performance of his Théâtre de la Cruauté. He decided to make his own adaptation of the gruesome story of the Cenci, which Stendhal had written as a story and which Shelley had made into a tragedy. But in spite of some beautiful points of detail, the performance was a failure. Artaud himself played the part of Count Cenci. His ritual chanting of the text was intriguing, but it did not convince the audience. Financial failure followed and played its part in driving Artaud into abject poverty, despair, and long spells of insanity. Jean-Louis Barrault, then twenty-five years old, acted as the secretary of the production, and Roger Blin, one of the most important directors in the Theatre of the Absurd, assisted Artaud as director and played the part of one of the hired assassins.

Artaud, who made his debut as an actor under Lugné-Poë at the Théâtre de l'Œuvre; who knew and acted with Gémier, the first Ubu; who appeared in 1924 in Yvan Goll's *Methusalem* when it was performed in Paris; Artaud, who was befriended by Adamov in the period of his mental illness, forms the bridge between the pioneers and today's Theatre of the Absurd. Outwardly his endeavors ended in utter failure and mental collapse. And yet, in some sense, he triumphed.

Another important poet who emerged from the Surrealist movement was Robert Desnos (1900–1945), the author of elegiac and nonsense verse, recorder of delicate and dreadful dreams, and writer of numerous Surrealist film scenarios that were never made into films. His only dramatic work is *La Place de l'Etoile*, written as early as 1927, revised shortly before his arrest and deportation in 1944, and published after his tragic death in the concentration camp of Theresienstadt, where he was found emaciated and dying at the end of hostilities.

La Place de l'Etoile is a punning title; it refers not to the Paris landmark but to the starfish, which is the poetic symbol of the dreams and desires of its hero, Maxime. People ask Maxime to give them his starfish, and he refuses. But when he does give it away to the woman he loves, not only does a policeman come almost immediately to bring it back, having found it in the street below his window, but groups of people come and bring him more and more starfish. Twelve waiters enter with twelve starfish on silver platters, and the streets of the town are so full of starfish that one can barely walk.

La Place de l'Etoile is also a romantic love story of Maxime and two women, Fabrice and Athénais, but in its dreamlike atmosphere, in the conversations of drinkers in a bar, which provide a kind of Greek chorus, the play foreshadows much of the Theatre of the Absurd. Desnos gave the play the sub-title *Antipoème*, and thus anticipated Ionesco's *anti-pièce*.

So strong was the tendency of the times and the influence of the pioneers of abstract art in painting and sculpture that even outside the Surrealist movement attempts were made to break the conventions of the naturalistic theatre. Jean Cocteau experimented with a theatre of pure movement. *Parade,* devised by Cocteau with décor by Picasso and music by Satie (who was a master of *humour noir* in his own right), and performed by the Diaghilev Ballet Russe in 1917, is a return to the circus and music hall, while Cocteau's *Le Bœuf sur le Toit (The Steer on the Roof,* 1920), with décor by Dufy and music by Milhaud, was performed by such famous music-hall actors as the three Fratellinis. *Les Mariés de la Tour Eiffel (The Married Couple of the Eiffel Tower,* 1921) is a mimeplay and ballet accompanied by narration spoken by actors in the costumes of giant phonographs.

Although most of Cocteau's later work oscillates between the heavily romantic and the merely playful, it bears the stamp of his preoccupation with some of the basic elements of an abstract and dreamlike theatre, most clearly perhaps in his poetic and haunting films, from *Le Sang d'un Poète (The Blood of a Poet)* to *La Belle et la Bête (Beauty and the Beast); Orphée,* with its brilliantly realized images of the land of the dead; and the final *Testament d'Orphée.* Ionesco has paid tribute to Cocteau for precisely his playfulness and baroque taste: "I think Jean Cocteau has been reproached for having merely touched upon grave problems lightly. I feel that this is wrong; he raises them in a moon-struck, enchanted décor. He has been reproached for an impurity of style, his fairyland of cardboard stage sets. It is precisely his confetti that I love, his serpentines, his baroque fairground sphinxes. As everything is but a mirage and life a fairground, it is not amiss that there should be sphinxes and that there should be a kind of fair. Nothing expresses better than these itinerant and precarious festivities the precariousness of life, the fragility of beauty, evanescence."[67]

A play that clearly anticipates Ionesco's onslaught on the bourgeois family and that originated in Cocteau's circle is *Les*

Pélicans (*The Pelicans*, 1921), by that precocious genius Raymond Radiguet (1903–1923). In two short acts we meet the Pelican family, anxious to do great deeds to make their name so famous that it will no longer sound ridiculous. The lady of the house comes riding in on the back of her swimming teacher, who does not know how to swim but has an affair with her. The son tries to become a jockey, and the daughter, wanting to commit suicide, wins a skating trophy on the frozen Seine. The play ends with a grotesque family group.

At about this time, Armand Salacrou, who later became a leading playwright in a robust stage idiom, wrote some delicate near-Surrealist plays intended to be read rather than acted. Most of these are lost, but *Les Trente Tombes de Judas* (*The Thirty Tombs of Judas*) and *Histoire de Cirque* (*Circus Story*) escaped destruction and have recently been reprinted.[68] Set in a dance hall and a circus, these little plays combine the traditions of clowning and the dream—oranges spout blood, strange plants grow before our eyes, and the circus tent vanishes to let the lovesick youth die in a snowstorm.

In 1924, while still boys at school, René Daumal (1908–1944) and Roger Gilbert-Lecomte (1907–1943) composed a series of miniature playlets, in a truly Jarryesque spirit, which have been published under the auspices of the Collège de Pataphysique, with the title *Petit Théâtre*. They are delightful nonsense and wholly beyond interpretation. Both authors developed into considerable poets. Daumal carried his exploration of the dark regions of the soul to the point of repeatedly committing a kind of controlled suicide by inhaling toxic fumes so that he could reach the frontiers of life. He is regarded as one of the most authentic followers of Jarry, and his memory is cultivated by the Collège de Pataphysique.

Even more important as a nonsense dramatist among the pataphysical heroes is Julien Torma (1902–1933), another poetic vagabond and *poète maudit* who drifted through life with sovereign unconcern until he disappeared in the Austrian Alps, walking out of his hotel never to return. Torma, who despised the Surrealists for their publicity-seeking and exploitation of their personalities, wrote some extraordinary nonsense plays. *Coupures* (*Cuts*), "a tragedy in nine scenes," and the one-act play *Lauma Lamer* appeared during his lifetime in a limited edition of two hundred copies. His most ambitious play, *Le Bétrou*, was posthumously published by the Collège de Pataphysique.

Coupures is remarkable chiefly for a character who speaks all the stage directions and is presented as a god who arbitrarily dominates the action. He is called Osmur and evidently represents fate in all its absurdity. After the play has ended, Osmur is pulled offstage on a wheeled platform and revealed as a mere mechanism. In accordance with this, the action itself, dictated by a mechanical and senseless mechanism, cannot make sense, except that it shows images of eroticism and violence. *Lauma Lamer* is a nautical nonsense play. The hero of *Le Bétrou* (which is in four acts, numbered backward from minus three to zero) is a strange creature who inspires his numerous wives with terror. The Bétrou speaks in inarticulate stammers and has his utterances interpreted by an astronomer. At the end of the second act (or, rather, Act Minus 2), practically all the characters have been killed by the Bétrou, but they are resuscitated in the next act (Minus 1), to be killed again; are again alive and kicking in the final act (Zero), in which the action reaches its appointed end—the quantity of nothingness.

There is an element of suspense here—the Bétrou is being taught to speak and reaches a point where he can imitate certain animal noises. This, however, somehow seems to diminish his power. He flees in disorder, and the play ends in chaos. As the learned pataphysical editors explain, "The essential element of the play is in the psychological paralysis that reigns everywhere and in the '*phraséolalie*,' or, if one wanted to put it like that, in the verbal material which dominates everything and is the veritable destiny."[69] This is analogous to the dominance of language over fate in nonsense poets like Lewis Carroll, Edward Lear, and Christian Morgenstern.

Torma explained his ideas in clearer language in a slim little volume of aphorisms, *Euphorismes* (1926), a remarkable book the copy of which in the Bibliothèque National is inscribed by Torma with a dedication to Max Jacob: "If God existed, you could not invent him!" Some of the aphorisms probe into the ethics of homosexuality, but others contain a resolute rejection of language. "As soon as one speaks, there is a stink of the social,"[70] or even more drastically, "To express oneself . . . the word itself borrows the scatosociological urge and consecrates it as the model of elocution,"[71] so that language becomes "caca-phony." Hence Torma's endeavor to "give back to thought the fundamental and *unthinkable* ambiguity, which, however, *is* reality—to deossify language and to *leave* literature."[72]

Torma, who knew and corresponded with Daumal and Desnos, is a writer's writer and will probably never be read outside a narrow circle of enthusiastic connoisseurs of poetic nonsense. He did not want to have an impact or to be taken seriously: "I am neither a man of letters nor a poet. I do not even pretend to be interested, I just amuse myself. . . . For me even the admission of tragic silences is too much. I don't have any confessions to make, I do nothing in particular—just as I have perpetrated these poems, lightly."[73] He was one of the few who had the courage to take their recognition of the absurdity of the human condition to its logical conclusion—he refused to take anything seriously, least of all himself. The casual manner of his death shows that this attitude was anything but a pose.

As strange and eccentric as Torma and, in his own peculiar way, as influential on contemporary writing, was Raymond Roussel (1877–1933). Immensely rich, he traveled all over the world without taking the trouble to look at it. Having arrived at Peking, he drove once through the town and then locked himself in his hotel room. When the ship he traveled on lay in the harbor of Tahiti, he remained in his cabin, writing, not even looking out of the porthole. In his writings as well, Roussel aimed at excluding the real world completely. He wanted to construct a world entirely his own and based, like that of Torma or the nonsense poets, on the logic of assonance and verbal association.

Some of Roussel's novels are constructed on the principle of two cornerstone sentences, similar in sound but different in sense, which he made into the opening and closing phrases of the book and then tried to link by a chain of propositions that would constitute an unbroken sequence of such verbal logic—a logic of metaphor, pun, homonym, association of ideas, and anagrams. The same internal logical mechanisms actuate his plays, *L'Etoile au Front* (*The Star on the Forehead*, 1924) and *La Poussière de Soleils* (*Sun Dust*, 1926).

These long and complicated plays, which he had produced at his own expense and which were performed to gales of derisive laughter, must be among the most undramatic dramas ever written. They consist almost exclusively of chains of very complicated and fantastic stories that the characters tell each other in a curiously static, stilted language. Roussel's theatre is more truly "epic" than Brecht's and infinitely more anti-theatrical than anything that Ionesco has ever written. At the same time, the incredible fantasy of Roussel's invention, combined with an involuntary primitivism that make him the Douanier Rousseau of the theatre, gives his work an almost hypnotic power and has made him the idol of Surrealists and pataphysicians. Roussel committed suicide—in Palermo—in 1933.

From Apollinaire to the Surrealists and beyond, an extremely close link has always existed between the pioneers of painting and sculpture and the avant-garde of poets and dramatists. Beckett has written a sensitive study of the abstract painter Bram Van Velde,[74] and Ionesco is a friend of Max Ernst and Dubuffet. The influence of some of the leading painters of the age on the Theatre of the Absurd is clearly discernible in the imagery and décor of its plays (*vide*, the girl with three noses in Ionesco's *Jacques*).

Moreover, a good many of the painters and sculptors of our time have ventured into the field of avant-garde poetry or drama. We have already referred to Kokoschka's pioneering Dadaist play, which he followed up with a number of other dramatic experiments. The great German Expressionist sculptor Ernst Barlach (1870–1938) also wrote a series of haunting plays that anticipate some of the dreamlike, mythical features of the Theatre of the Absurd. And Picasso is the author of two avant-gardist plays, *Le Désir Attrapé par la Queue* (*Desire Caught by the Tail*, 1941) and the thus far unpublished *The Four Little Girls* (1952).

The first of these, which was given a public reading on March 19, 1944, under the direction of Albert Camus and with the participation of Simone de Beauvoir, Jean-Paul Sartre, Michel Leiris, Raymond Queneau, and other distinguished personalities of the world of literature and the arts, consists, like Tzara's *Le Cœur à Gaz*, of dialogues between disembodied feet (some of which monotonously complain of chilblains) and other dehumanized characters. There is little plot, but the action reflects wartime worries in its preoccupation with images of cold and of food shortages. In its mixture of humor and grimness, the little play says what one of Picasso's paintings would say if it came to life for a moment and could speak. It has the playfulness and the sensuality of its master's style.

The same seems to apply to *The Four Little Girls,* from which Roland Penrose quotes in his biography of Picasso, and which contains stage directions like, "Enter an enormous winged white horse dragging its entrails, surrounded by wings, an owl perched on its head; it stands for a brief moment in front of the little girl, and then disappears at the other end of the stage."[75]

The modern movement in painting and the Theatre of the Absurd meet in their rejection of the discursive and narrative elements, and in their concentration on the poetic image as a concretization of the inner reality of the conscious and subconscious mind and the archetypes by which it lives.

In Spain—the homeland of Picasso and Goya, the country of the allegorical *autos sacramentales* and the baroque poetry of Quevedo and Góngora—some of the tendencies of the Surrealists found their literary parallels in the work of two important dramatists.

Ramón del Valle-Inclán (1866–1936), a great novelist and dramatist practically unknown outside Spain, from about 1920 onward developed a style of dramatic writing that he called *esperpento* (the grotesque or ridiculous), in which the world is depicted as inhabited by tragicomic, almost mechanically actuated marionettes. As Valle-Inclán explained it, the artist can see the world from three different positions. He can look upward, as if on his knees before it, and present an idealized, reverent picture of reality; he can confront it standing on the same level, which will lead to a realistic approach; or he can see the world from above—and from this distant vantage point it will appear ridiculous and absurd, for it will be seen as through the eyes of a dead man who looks back on life. Valle-Inclán's *esperpentos*, notably *Las Galas del Defunto* (*The Gala of Death*) and *Los Cuernos de Don Friolera* (*The Horns of Don Friolera*), written about 1925, are bitter caricatures of life in which deformed and ugly lovers are pursued by witless and ridiculous husbands while the rules and mannerisms of society appear as mechanical and dehumanized as machines gone mad and functioning in a void. Among the younger dramatists of the Absurd, Arrabal acknowledges Valle-Inclán as an important influence on his work.

In a gentler and more poetic mood, some of the plays of Federico García Lorca clearly show the influence of the French Surrealists. Less well known and earlier than Lorca's great realistic tragedies, these include the charming short scenes of *Teatro Breve* (*Short Theatre*, 1928), one of which, *El Paseo de Buster Keaton* (*Buster Keaton's Walk*), openly derives from the American silent film (like Goll's *Chaplinade*); the puppet play *Retablillo de Don Cristobal* (*The Little Altar Piece of Don Cristobal*, 1931), with its charming brand of slapstick and outspokenness derived from Andalusian folk entertainment; the more intellectualized Surrealism of *Asi que Pasen Cinco Años* (*So Pass Five Years*, 1931), a legend of time, in a dream idiom; and the two scenes from an unfinished play *El Publico* (*The Public*, 1933) that are very near to the Theatre of the Absurd, especially the first, in which a Roman emperor is confronted with two nonhuman characters, one wholly covered in vines, the other wholly covered in golden bells.

In the English-speaking theatre, the influence of Dadaism and Surrealism has been slight. Gertrude Stein wrote a number of pieces she described as "plays," but most of them are short abstract prose poems in which single sentences or short paragraphs are labeled Act I, Act II, and so on. Even a work like *Four Saints in Three Acts,* which has been staged successfully as a ballet opera (with choreography by Frederick Ashton and music by Virgil Thomson), is essentially an abstract prose poem on which elements of "pure theatre" can be imposed in a more or less arbitrary fashion. When, toward the end of her life, Gertrude Stein wrote a play with a plot and dialogue, *Yes Is for a Very Young Man*, it turned out to be a fascinating but essentially traditional piece of work about the French Resistance and an American expatriate lady's unspoken affection for a young French Resistance fighter, written in a mildly Steinian idiom.

In some ways, F. Scott Fitzgerald's play *The Vegetable*, which was staged, and failed dismally, in November, 1922, must be regarded as an early example of the Theatre of the Absurd, at least in its middle part, which gives a grotesque nonsense version of life at the White House. But this satirical sequence of scenes is laboriously motivated in the first act by making the hero, Jerry Frost, drunk on bootleg liquor so as to justify the satire as an alcoholic nightmare; in the third act the action is equally laboriously brought back to earth. *The Vegetable* is an attempt to leave the naturalistic convention, and fails by remaining firmly anchored within it.

This pitfall has been brilliantly avoided in E. E. Cummings' *him* (1927), one of the most successful plays in the Surrealist style, and far more integrated as an artistic whole than the majority of the French Surrealist plays of the period. Here a spiritual odyssey of a man and a woman is embedded in a dreamlike sequence of fairground scenes and fantastic incidents. Eric Bentley has given an ingenious interpretation of the play as the fantasy of the heroine, Me, "who is lying under an anaesthetic awaiting the birth of a child,"[76] so that the play revolves around the story of Me and Him, "a young American couple and their quest for reality." The chorus of weird sisters talking a nonsense language; the vaudeville scenes of fairground barkers and soap-box salesmen; the skits on gangster films, popular ballads, Americans in Europe, and Mussolini's Italy, all fit beautifully into this interpretation. Bentley, however, also quotes Cummings' dialogue between the Author and the Public, in which the author says, ". . . so far as you are concerned 'life' is a verb of two voices, active, to do, and passive, to dream. Others believe doing to be only a kind of dreaming. Still others have discovered (in a mirror surrounded with mirrors) something harder than silence but softer than falling: the third voice of 'life' which believes itself and which cannot mean because it is."[77]

This, surely, is a perfect statement of the philosophy of

the Theatre of the Absurd, in which the world is seen as a hall of reflecting mirrors, and reality merges imperceptibly into fantasy.

The Theatre of the Absurd is part of a rich and varied tradition. If there is anything really new in it, it is the somewhat unusual combination of different strands of various familiar basic attitudes of mind and literary idiom, and, above all, the fact that for the first time this approach has met with a wide response from a broadly based public. This is a characteristic not so much of the Theatre of the Absurd as of its epoch. Surrealism admittedly lacked the qualities that would have been needed to create a real Surrealist drama; but this may have been due as much to the lack of a real need for such a theatre on the part of the public as to a lack of interest or application on the part of the writers concerned. They were ahead of their time; now the time has caught up with the avantgarde of the twenties and thirties, and the theatre Jarry and Cummings created has found its public.

THE SIGNIFICANCE OF THE ABSURD

When Nietzsche's Zarathustra descended from his mountains to preach to mankind, he met a saintly hermit in the forest. This old man invited him to stay in the wilderness rather than go into the cities of men. When Zarathustra asked the hermit how he passed his time in his solitude, he replied:

I make up songs and sing them; and when I make up songs I laugh, I weep, and I growl; thus do I praise God.

Zarathustra declined the old man's offer and continued on his journey:

But when he was alone, he spoke thus to his heart: "Can it be possible! This old saint in the forest has not yet heard that God is dead!"[1]

Zarathustra was first published in 1883. The number of people for whom God is dead has greatly increased since Nietzsche's day, and mankind has learned the bitter lesson of the falseness and evil nature of some of the cheap and vulgar substitutes that have been set up to take His place. And so, after two terrible wars, there are still many who are trying to come to terms with the implications of Zarathustra's message, searching for a way in which they can, with dignity, confront a universe deprived of what was once its center and its living purpose, a world deprived of a generally accepted integrating principle, which has become disjointed, purposeless—absurd.

The Theatre of the Absurd is one of the expressions of this search. It bravely faces up to the fact that for those to whom the world has lost its central explanation and meaning, it is no longer possible to accept art forms still based on the con-

tinuation of standards and concepts that have lost their validity;
that is, the possibility of knowing the laws of conduct and ultimate values, as deducible from a firm foundation of revealed certainty about the purpose of man in the universe.

In expressing the tragic sense of loss at the disappearance
of ultimate certainties the Theatre of the Absurd, by a strange
paradox, is also a symptom of what probably comes nearest
to being a genuine religious quest in our age: an effort, however timid and tentative, to sing, to laugh, to weep—and to
growl—if not in praise of God (whose name, in Adamov's
phrase, has for so long been degraded by usage that it has lost
its meaning), at least in search of a dimension of the Ineffable;
an effort to make man aware of the ultimate realities of his
condition, to instill in him again the lost sense of cosmic wonder
and primeval anguish, to shock him out of an existence that
has become trite, mechanical, complacent, and deprived of the
dignity that comes of awareness. For God is dead, above all,
to the masses who live from day to day and have lost all contact with the basic facts—and mysteries—of the human condition with which, in former times, they were kept in touch
through the living ritual of their religion, which made them
parts of a real community and not just atoms in an atomized
society.

The Theatre of the Absurd forms part of the unceasing endeavor of the true artists of our time to breach this dead wall
of complacency and automatism and to re-establish an awareness of man's situation when confronted with the ultimate
reality of his condition. As such, the Theatre of the Absurd
fulfills a dual purpose and presents its audience with a two-
fold absurdity.

On the one hand, it castigates, satirically, the absurdity of
lives lived unaware and unconscious of ultimate reality. This
is the feeling of the deadness and mechanical senselessness of
half-unconscious lives, the feeling of "human beings secreting
inhumanity," which Camus describes in *The Myth of Sisyphus:*

> In certain hours of lucidity, the mechanical aspect of their
> gestures, their senseless pantomime, makes stupid every-
> thing around them. A man speaking on the telephone behind
> a glass partition—one cannot hear him but observes his triv-

ial gesturing. One asks oneself, why is he alive? This malaise in front of man's own inhumanity, this incalculable letdown when faced with the image of what we are, this "nausea," as a contemporary writer calls it, also is the Absurd.[2]

This is the experience that Ionesco expresses in plays like *The Bald Soprano* or *The Chairs*, Adamov in *La Parodie*, or N. F. Simpson in *A Resounding Tinkle*. It represents the satirical, parodistic aspect of the Theatre of the Absurd, its social criticism, its pillorying of an inauthentic, petty society. This may be the most easily accessible, and therefore most widely recognized, message of the Theatre of the Absurd, but it is far from being its most essential or most significant feature.

Behind the satirical exposure of the absurdity of inauthentic ways of life, the Theatre of the Absurd is facing up to a deeper layer of absurdity—the absurdity of the human condition itself in a world where the decline of religious belief has deprived man of certainties. When it is no longer possible to accept simple and complete systems of values and revelations of divine purpose, life must be faced in its ultimate, stark reality. That is why, in the analysis of the dramatists of the Absurd in this book, we have always seen man stripped of the accidental circumstances of social position or historical context, confronted with the basic choices, the basic situations of his existence: man faced with time and therefore waiting, in Beckett's plays or Gelber's, waiting between birth and death; man running away from death, climbing higher and higher, in Vian's play, or passively sinking down toward death, in Buzzati's; man rebelling against death, confronting and accepting it, in Ionesco's *Tueur Sans Gages;* man inextricably entangled in a mirage of illusions, mirrors reflecting mirrors, and forever hiding ultimate reality, in the plays of Genet; man trying to establish his position, or to break out into freedom, only to find himself newly imprisoned, in the parables of Manuel de Pedrolo; man trying to stake out a modest place for himself in the cold and darkness that envelop him, in Pinter's plays; man vainly striving to grasp the moral law forever beyond his comprehension, in Arrabal's; man caught in the inescapable dilemma that strenuous effort leads to the same result as passive indolence—complete futility and ultimate death —in the earlier work of Adamov; man forever lonely, immured in the prison of his subjectivity, unable to reach his fellow man, in the vast majority of these plays.

Concerned as it is with the ultimate realities of the human condition, the relatively few fundamental problems of life and death, isolation and communication, the Theatre of the Absurd, however grotesque, frivolous, and irreverent it may appear, represents a return to the original, religious function of the theatre—the confrontation of man with the spheres of myth and religious reality. Like ancient Greek tragedy and the medieval mystery plays and baroque allegories, the Theatre of the Absurd is intent on making its audience aware of man's precarious and mysterious position in the universe.

The difference is merely that in ancient Greek tragedy—and comedy—as well as in the medieval mystery play and the baroque *auto sacramental,* the ultimate realities concerned were generally known and universally accepted metaphysical systems, while the Theatre of the Absurd expresses the absence of any such generally accepted cosmic system of values. Hence, much more modestly, the Theatre of the Absurd makes no pretense at explaining the ways of God to man. It can merely present, in anxiety or with derision, an individual human being's intuition of the ultimate realities as he experiences them; the fruits of one man's descent into the depths of his personality, his dreams, fantasies, and nightmares.

While former attempts at confronting man with the ultimate realities of his condition projected a coherent and generally recognized version of the truth, the Theatre of the Absurd merely communicates one poet's most intimate and personal intuition of the human situation, his own *sense of being,* his individual vision of the world. This is the *subject matter* of the Theatre of the Absurd, and it determines its *form,* which must, of necessity, represent a convention of the stage basically different from the "realistic" theatre of our time.

As the Theatre of the Absurd is not concerned with conveying information or presenting the problems or destinies of characters that exist outside the author's inner world, as it does not expound a thesis or debate ideological propositions, it is not concerned with the representation of events, the narration of the fate or the adventures of characters, but instead with the presentation of one individual's basic situation. It is a theatre of situation as against a theatre of events in sequence, and therefore it uses a language based on patterns of concrete images rather than argument and discursive speech. And since it is trying to present a sense of being, it can neither investigate nor solve problems of conduct or morals.

Because the Theatre of the Absurd projects its author's personal world, it lacks objectively valid characters. It cannot show the clash of opposing temperaments or study human passions locked in conflict, and is therefore not dramatic in the accepted sense of the term. Nor is it concerned with telling a story in order to communicate some moral or social lesson, as is the aim of Brecht's narrative, "epic" theatre. The action in a play of the Theatre of the Absurd is not intended to tell a story but to communicate a pattern of poetic images. To give but one example: Things happen in *Waiting for Godot*, but these happenings do not constitute a plot or story; they are an image of Beckett's intuition that *nothing really ever happens* in man's existence. The whole play is a complex poetic image made up of a complicated pattern of subsidiary images and themes, which are interwoven like the themes of a musical composition, not, as in most well-made plays, to present a line of development, but to make in the spectators' mind a total, complex impression of a basic, and static, situation. In this, the Theatre of the Absurd is analogous to a Symbolist or Imagist poem, which also presents a pattern of images and associations in a mutually interdependent structure.

While the Brechtian epic theatre tries to widen the range of drama by introducing narrative, epic elements, the Theatre of the Absurd aims at concentration and depth in an essentially lyrical, poetic pattern. Of course, dramatic, narrative, and lyrical elements are present in all drama. Brecht's own theatre, like Shakespeare's, contains lyrical inserts in the form of songs; even at their most didactic, Ibsen and Shaw are rich in purely poetic moments. The Theatre of the Absurd, however, in abandoning psychology, subtlety of characterization, and plot in the conventional sense, gives the poetical element an incomparably greater emphasis. While the play with a linear plot describes a development in time, in a dramatic form that presents a concretized poetic image the play's extension in time is purely incidental. Expressing an *intuition in depth,* it should ideally be apprehended *in a single moment,* and only because it is physically impossible to present so complex an image in an instant does it have to be spread over a period of time. The formal structure of such a play is, therefore, merely a device to express a complex total image by unfolding it in a sequence of interacting elements.

The endeavor to communicate a total sense of being is an attempt to present a truer picture of reality itself, reality as apprehended by an individual. The Theatre of the Absurd is the last link in a line of development that started with naturalism. Once the idealistic, Platonic belief in immutable essences—ideal forms that it was the artist's task to present in a purer state than they could ever be found in nature—had foundered in the aftermath of the rise of the philosophy of Locke and Kant, which based reality on perception and the inner structure of the human mind, art became mere imitation of external nature. Yet the imitation of surfaces was bound to prove unsatisfying and this inevitably led to the next step— the exploration of the reality of the mind. Ibsen and Strindberg exemplified that development during the span of their own lifetime's exploration of reality. James Joyce began with minutely realistic stories and ended up with the vast multiple structure of *Finnegans Wake.* The work of the dramatists of the Absurd continues the same development. Each of these plays is an answer to the questions "How does this individual feel when confronted with the human situation? What is the basic mood in which he faces the world? What does it feel like to be him?" And the answer is a single, total, but complex and contradictory poetic image—one play—or a succession of such images, complementing each other—the dramatist's *œuvre.*

Any really fundamental analysis of reality as perceived by man leads to the recognition that any attempt at communicating what we perceive and feel consists of the dissection of a momentary, simultaneous intuition of a complex of perceptions into a *sequence* of atomized concepts structured in time within a sentence, or a sequence of sentences. To convert our perception into conceptual terms, into logical thought and language, we perform an operation analogous to the scanner that analyzes the picture in a television camera into rows of single impulses. The poetic image, with its ambiguity and its simultaneous evocation of multiple elements of sense associations, is one of the methods by which we can, however imperfectly, communicate the reality of our intuition of the world.

The highly eccentric German philosopher Ludwig Klages —who is almost totally unknown, and quite unjustly so, in the English-speaking world—formulated a psychology of perception based on the recognition that our senses present us with images (*Bilder*) built up of a multitude of simultaneous impressions that are subsequently analyzed and disintegrated in the process of translation into conceptual thinking. For Klages, this is part of the insidious action of critical intellect upon the creative element of the mind—his philosophical magnum opus is called *Der Geist als Widersacher der Seele* (*The Intellect as Antagonist of the Soul*)—but however misguided his attempt to turn this opposition into a cosmic battle between the creative and the analytical may have been, the basic idea that conceptual and discursive thought impoverishes the ineffable fullness of the perceived image remains valid, at least as an illustration of the problem of what it is that is being communicated in poetic imagery.

And it is in this striving to communicate a basic and as yet undissolved totality of perception, an intuition of being, that we can find a key to the devaluation and disintegration of language in the Theatre of the Absurd. For if it is the translation of the total intuition of being into the logical and temporal sequence of conceptual thought that deprives it of its pristine complexity and poetic truth, it is understandable that the artist should try to find ways to circumvent this influence of discursive speech and logic. Here lies the chief difference between poetry and prose: Poetry is ambiguous and associative, striving to approximate the wholly unconceptual language of music. The Theatre of the Absurd, in carrying the same poetic endeavor into the concrete imagery of the stage, can go further than pure poetry in dispensing with logic, discursive thought, and language. The stage is a multidimensional medium; it allows the simultaneous use of visual elements, movement, light, and language. It is, therefore, particularly suited to the communication of complex images consisting of the contrapuntal interaction of all these elements.

In the "literary" theatre, language remains the predominant component. In the anti-literary theatre of the circus or the music hall, language is reduced to a very subordinate role. The Theatre of the Absurd has regained the freedom of using language as merely one—sometimes dominant, sometimes submerged—component of its multidimensional poetic imagery. By putting the language of a scene in contrast to the action, by reducing it to meaningless patter, or by abandoning discursive logic for the poetic logic of association or assonance, the Theatre of the Absurd has opened up a new dimension of the stage.

In its devaluation of language, the Theatre of the Absurd is in tune with the trend of our time. As George Steiner has pointed out in two radio talks entitled *The Retreat from the Word*, the devaluation of language is characteristic not only of the development of contemporary poetry or philosophical thought but, even more, of modern mathematics and the natural sciences. "It is no paradox to assert," Steiner says, "that much of reality now begins *outside* language.[3] . . . Large areas of meaningful experience now belong to non-verbal languages such as mathematics, formulae, and logical symbolism. Others belong to 'anti-languages' such as the practice of non-objective art or atonal music. The world of the word has shrunk."[4] Moreover, the abandonment of language as the best instrument of notation in the spheres of mathematics and symbolic logic goes hand in hand with a marked reduction in the popular belief in its practical usefulness. Language appears more and more as being in contradiction to reality. The trends of thought that have the greatest influence on contemporary popular thinking all show this tendency.

Take the case of Marxism. Here a distinction is made between *apparent* social relations and the social *reality* behind them. Objectively, an employer is seen as an exploiter, and therefore an enemy, of the working class. If an employer therefore says to a worker; "I have sympathy with your point of view," he may himself believe what he is saying, but objectively his words are meaningless. However much he asserts his sympathy for the worker, he remains his enemy. Language here belongs to the realm of the purely subjective, and is thus devoid of objective reality.

The same applies to modern depth psychology and psychoanalysis. Every child today knows that there is a vast gap between what is consciously thought and asserted and the psychological reality behind the words spoken. A son who tells his father that he loves and respects him is objectively bound to be, in fact, filled with the deepest Oedipal hatred of his father. He may not know it, but he means the opposite of what he says. And the subconscious has a higher content of reality than the conscious utterance.

The relativization, devaluation, and criticism of language are also the prevailing trends in contemporary philosophy, as exemplified by Wittgenstein's conviction, in the last phase of his thinking, that the philosopher must endeavor to disentangle thought from the conventions and rules of grammar, which have been mistaken for the rules of logic. "A *picture* held us captive. And we could not get outside it, for it lay in our language, and language seemed to repeat it to us inexorably. . . . Where does our investigation get its importance from, since it seems only to destroy everything interesting; that is, all that is great and important? (As it were, all the buildings, leaving behind only bits of stone and rubble.) What we are destroying is nothing but houses of cards, and we are clearing up the ground of language on which they stand."[5] By a strict criticism of language, Wittgenstein's followers have declared large categories of statements to be devoid of objective meaning. Wittgenstein's "word games" have much in common with the Theatre of the Absurd.

But even more significant than these tendencies in Marxist, psychological, and philosophical thinking is the trend of the times in the workaday world of the man in the street. Exposed to the incessant, and inexorably loquacious, onslaught of the mass media, the press, and advertising, the man in the street becomes more and more skeptical toward the language he is exposed to. The citizens of totalitarian countries know full well that most of what they are told is double-talk, devoid of real meaning. They become adept at reading between the lines; that is, at guessing at the reality the language conceals rather than reveals. In the West, euphemisms and circumlocutions fill the press or resound from the pulpits. And advertising, by its constant use of superlatives, has succeeded in devaluing language to a point where it is a generally accepted axiom that most of the words one sees displayed on billboards or in the colored pages of magazine advertising are as meaningless as the jingles of television commercials. A yawning gulf has opened between language and reality.

Apart from the general devaluation of language in the flood of mass communications, the growing specialization of life has made the exchange of ideas on an increasing number of subjects impossible between members of different spheres of life which have each developed its own specialized jargon. As Ionesco says, in summarizing and enlarging on, the views of Antonin Artaud:

> As our knowledge becomes separated from life, our culture no longer contains ourselves (or only an insignificant part of ourselves), for it forms a "social" context into which we are not integrated. So the problem becomes that of bringing our life back into contact with our culture, making it a living culture once again. To achieve this, we shall first have to kill "the respect for what is written down in black and white" . . . to break up our language so that it can be put together again in order to re-establish contact with "the absolute," or, as I should prefer to say, "with multiple reality"; it is imperative to "push human beings again toward seeing themselves as they really are."[6]

That is why communication between human beings is so often shown in a state of breakdown in the Theatre of the Absurd. It is merely a satirical magnification of the existing state of affairs. Language has run riot in an age of mass communication. It must be reduced to its proper function—the expression of authentic content, rather than its concealment. But this will be possible only if man's reverence toward the spoken or written word as a means of communication is restored, and the ossified clichés that dominate thought (as they do in the limericks of Edward Lear or the world of Humpty Dumpty) are replaced by a living language that serves it. And this, in turn, can be achieved only if the limitations of logic and discursive language are recognized and respected, and the uses of poetic language acknowledged.

The means by which the dramatists of the Absurd express their critique—largely instinctive and unintended—of our disintegrating society are based on suddenly confronting their audiences with a grotesquely heightened and distorted picture of a world that has gone mad. This is a shock therapy that achieves what Brecht's doctrine of the "alienation effect" postulated in theory but failed to achieve in practice—the inhibition of the audience's identification with the characters on the stage (which is the age-old and highly effective method of the traditional theatre) and its replacement by a detached, critical attitude.

If we identify ourselves with the main character in a play, we automatically accept his point of view, see the world in which he moves with *his* eyes, feel *his* emotions. From the standpoint of a didactic, Socialist theatre, Brecht argued that this time-honored psychological link between the actor and the audience must be broken. How could an audience be made to see the actions of the characters in a play *critically* if they were made to adopt their points of view? Hence Brecht, in his Marxist period, tried to introduce a number of devices designed to break this spell. Yet he never completely succeeded in achieving his aim. The audience, in spite of the introduction of songs, slogans, nonrepresentational décor, and other inhibiting devices, continues to identify with Brecht's brilliantly drawn characters and therefore often tends to miss the critical attitude Brecht wanted it to assume toward them. The old magic of the theatre is too strong; the pull toward identification, which springs from a basic psychological characteristic of human nature, is overwhelming. If we see Mother Courage weep for her son, we cannot resist feeling her sorrow and therefore fail to condemn her for her acceptance of war as a business, which inevitably leads to the loss of her children. The finer the characterization of a human being on the stage, the more inevitable is this process of identification.

In the Theatre of the Absurd, on the other hand, the audience is confronted with characters whose motives and actions remain largely incomprehensible. With such characters it is almost impossible to identify; the more mysterious their action and their nature, the less human the characters become, the more difficult it is to be carried away into seeing the world from their point of view. Characters with whom the audience fails to identify are inevitably comic. If we identified with the figure of farce who loses his trousers, we should feel embarrassment and shame. If, however, our tendency to identify has been inhibited by making such a character grotesque, we laugh at his predicament. We see what happens to him from the outside, rather than from his own point of view. As the incomprehensibility of the motives, and the often unexplained and mysterious nature of the characters' actions in the Theatre of the Absurd effectively prevent identification, such theatre is a comic theatre in spite of the fact that its subject matter is somber, violent, and bitter. That is why the Theatre of the Absurd transcends the categories of comedy and tragedy and combines laughter with horror.

But, by its very nature, it cannot provoke the thoughtful attitude of detached social criticism that was Brecht's objective. It does not present its audience with sets of social facts and examples of political behavior. It presents the audience with a picture of a disintegrating world that has lost its unifying principle, its meaning, and its purpose—an absurd universe. What is the audience to make of this bewildering confrontation with a truly alienated world that, having lost its rational principle, has in the true sense of the word gone mad?

Here we are face to face with the central problem of the effect, the aesthetic efficacy and validity, of the Theatre of the Absurd. It is an empirical fact that, in defiance of most of the accepted rules of drama, the best examples of the Theatre of the Absurd are effective as theatre—the convention of the Absurd *works*. But *why* does it work? To some extent, the answer has been given in the foregoing account of the nature of comic and farcical effects. The misfortunes of characters we view with a cold, critical, unidentified eye *are* funny. Stupid characters who act in mad ways have always been the butt of derisive laughter in the circus, the music hall, and the theatre. But such comic characters usually appeared in a rational framework, and were set off by positive characters with whom the audience could identify. In the Theatre of the Absurd, the whole of the action is mysterious, unmotivated, and at first sight nonsensical and mad.

The alienation effect in the Brechtian theatre is intended to activate the audience's critical, intellectual attitude. The Theatre of the Absurd speaks to a deeper level of the audience's mind. It activates psychological forces, releases and liberates hidden fears and repressed aggressions, and, above all, by confronting the audience with a picture of disintegration, it sets in motion an active process of integrative forces in the mind of each individual spectator.

As Eva Metman says in her remarkable essay on Beckett:

> In times of religious containment, [dramatic art] has shown man as protected, guided, and sometimes punished by [archetypal] powers, but in other epochs it has shown the visible tangible world, in which man fulfills his destiny, as permeated by the demonic essences of his invisible and intangible being. In contemporary drama, a new, third orientation is crystallizing in which man is shown not in a world into which the divine or demonic powers are projected but alone with them. This new form of drama forces the audience out of its familiar orientation. It creates a vacuum between the play and the audience so that the latter is compelled to experience something itself, be it a reawakening of the awareness of archetypal powers or a reorientation of the ego, or both. . . .[7]

One need not be a Jungian or use Jungian categories to see the force of this diagnosis. Human beings who in their daily lives confront a world that has split up into a series of disconnected fragments and lost its purpose, but who are no longer aware of this state of affairs and its disintegrating effect on their personalities, are brought face to face with a heightened representation of this schizophrenic universe. "The vacuum between what is shown on the stage and the onlooker has become so unbearable that the latter has no alternative but either to reject and turn away or to be drawn into the enigma of the plays in which nothing reminds him of any of his purposes in and reactions to the world around him."[8] Once drawn into the mystery of the play, the spectator is compelled to come to terms with his experience. The stage supplies him with a number of disjointed clues that he has to fit into a meaningful pattern. In this manner, he is forced to make a creative effort of his own, an effort at interpretation and integration. The time has been made to appear out of joint; the audience of the Theatre of the Absurd is being compelled to set it right, or, rather, by being made to see that the world has become absurd, in acknowledging that fact takes the first step in coming to terms with reality.

The madness of the times lies precisely in the existence, side by side, of a large number of unreconciled beliefs and attitudes—conventional morality, for example, on the one hand, and the values of advertising on the other; the conflicting claims of science and religion; or the loudly proclaimed striving of all sections for the general interest when in fact each is pursuing very narrow and selfish particular ends. On each page of his newspaper, the man in the street is confronted with a different and contradictory pattern of values. No wonder that the art of such an era shows a marked resemblance to the symptoms of schizophrenia. But it is not, as Jung has pointed out in an essay on Joyce's *Ulysses,* the artist who is schizophrenic: "The medical description of schizophrenia offers only an analogy, in that the schizophrenic has apparently the same tendency to treat reality as if it were strange to him, or, the other way around, to estrange himself from reality. In the modern artist, this tendency is not produced by any disease in the individual but is a manifestation of our time."[9]

The challenge to make sense out of what appears as a senseless and fragmented action, the recognition that the fact that the modern world has lost its unifying principle is the source of its bewildering and soul-destroying quality, is therefore more than a mere intellectual exercise; it has a therapeutic effect. In Greek tragedy, the spectators were made aware of man's forlorn but heroic stand against the inexorable forces of fate and the will of the gods—and this had a cathartic effect upon them and made them better able to face their time. In the Theatre of the Absurd, the spectator is confronted with the madness of the human condition, is enabled to see his situation in all its grimness and despair, and this, in stripping him of illusions or vaguely felt fears and anxieties, enables him to face it consciously, rather than feel it vaguely below the surface of euphemisms and optimistic illusions. And this, in turn, results in the liberating effect of anxieties overcome by being formulated. This is the nature of all the gallows humor and *humour noir* of world literature, of which the Theatre of the Absurd is the latest example. It is the unease caused by the presence of illusions that are obviously out of tune with reality that is dissolved and discharged through liberating laughter at the recognition of the fundamental absurdity of the universe. The greater the anxieties and the temptation to indulge in illusions, the more beneficial is this therapeutic effect—hence the success of *Waiting for Godot* at San Quentin. It was a relief for the convicts to be made to recognize in the tragicomic situation of the tramps the hopelessness of their own waiting for a miracle. They were enabled to laugh at the tramps—and at themselves.

As the reality with which the Theatre of the Absurd is concerned is a psychological reality expressed in images that are the outward projection of states of mind, fears, dreams, nightmares, and conflicts within the personality of the author, the dramatic tension produced by this kind of play differs fundamentally from the suspense created in a theatre concerned mainly with the revelation of objective characters through the unfolding of a narrative plot. The pattern of exposition, conflict, and final solution mirrors a view of the world in which solutions are possible, a view based on a recognizable and generally accepted pattern of an objective reality that can be apprehended so that the purpose of man's existence and the rules of conduct it entails can be deduced from it.

This is true even of the lightest type of drawing-room comedy, in which the action proceeds on a deliberately restricted view of the world—that the sole purpose of the characters involved is for each boy to get his girl. And even in the darkest pessimistic tragedies of the naturalistic or Expressionist theatres, the final curtain enables the audience to go home with a formulated message or philosophy in their minds: the solution may have been a sad one, but it was a rationally formulated conclusion nevertheless. This, as I pointed out in the introduction, applies even to the theatre of Sartre and Camus, which is based on a philosophy of the absurdity of human existence. Even plays like *Huis Clos* (*No Exit*), *Le Diable et le Bon Dieu* (*Lucifer and the Lord*), and *Caligula* allow the audience to take home an intellectually formulated philosophical lesson.

The Theatre of the Absurd, however, which proceeds not by intellectual concepts but by poetic images, neither poses an intellectual problem in its exposition nor provides any clear-cut solution that would be reducible to a lesson or an apothegm. Many of the plays of the Theatre of the Absurd have a circular structure, ending exactly as they began; others progress merely by a growing intensification of the initial situation. And as the Theatre of the Absurd rejects the idea that it is possible to motivate all human behavior, or that human character is based on an immutable essence, it is impossible for it to base its effect on the suspense that in other dramatic conventions springs from awaiting the solution of a dramatic equation based on the working out of a problem involving clearly defined quantities introduced in the opening scenes. In most dramatic conventions, the audience is constantly asking itself the question "What is going to happen next?"

In the Theatre of the Absurd, the audience is confronted with actions that lack apparent motivation, characters that are in constant flux, and often happenings that are clearly outside the realm of rational experience. Here, too, the audience can ask, "What is going to happen next?" But then *anything* may happen next, so that the answer to this question cannot be worked out according to the rules of ordinary probability based on motives and characterizations that will remain constant throughout the play. The relevant question here is not so much what is going to happen next but what *is* happening? "What does the action of the play represent?"

This constitutes a different, but by no means less valid, kind of dramatic suspense. Instead of being provided with a *solution*, the spectator is challenged to formulate the *questions* that he will have to ask if he wants to approach the meaning of the play. The total action of the play, instead of proceeding from Point A to Point B, as in other dramatic conventions, gradually builds up the complex pattern of the *poetic image* that the play expresses. The spectator's suspense consists in waiting for the gradual completion of this pattern which will enable him to see the image as a whole. And only when that image is assembled—after the final curtain—can he *begin* to explore, not so much its meaning as its structure, texture, and impact.

It is certainly arguable that this new kind of suspense represents a higher level of dramatic tension and evokes a more satisfying, because more challenging, aesthetic experience in the audience. Of course, the poetic qualities of great drama, of Shakespeare, Ibsen, and Chekhov, have always provided the audience with a deeply complex pattern of poetic association and significance; however simple the motivations may appear to be on the surface, the profound intuition with which the characters are drawn, the multiple planes on which the action proceeds, the complex quality of truly poetic language combine in a pattern that transcends any attempt at a simple and rational apprehension of the action or its solution. The suspense in a play like *Hamlet* or *The Three Sisters* does *not* lie in an anxious expectation of how these plays will *end*. Their eternal freshness and power lie in the inexhaustible quality of the poetic and infinitely ambiguous image of the human condition they present. In a play like *Hamlet*, we do indeed ask, "What is happening?" And the answer clearly is that it is not just a dynastic conflict or a series of murders and sword fights. We are confronted with a projection of a psychological reality and with human archetypes shrouded in perpetual mystery.

This is the element the Theatre of the Absurd (without making any claim at reaching the heights the greatest dramatists have attained with intuition and the richness of their creative capacity) has tried to make the core of its dramatic convention. If Ionesco, in seeking to trace the tradition to which he belongs, singles out the scenes of Richard II's loneliness and degradation, it is because they are such poetic images of the human condition:

> All men die in solitude; all values are degraded in a state of misery: that is what Shakespeare tells me. . . . Perhaps Shakespeare wanted to relate the story of Richard II: if he had narrated merely that, the *story of another human being*, it would not have moved me. But Richard II's prison is not a truth that has been overtaken by the flow of history.

Its invisible walls still stand, while so many philosophies, so many ideologies have crumbled forever. All this endures because this language is the language of living evidence, and not that of discursive and demonstrative thought. It is the theatre which provides this eternal and living presence; it corresponds, without doubt, to the essential structure of the tragic truth, of stage reality. . . . This is a matter of archetypes of the theatre, of the essence of the theatre, of the language of the theatre.[10]

It is this language of stage images that embody a truth beyond the power of mere discursive thought which the Theatre of the Absurd places at the center of its endeavor to build a new dramatic convention, subordinating all other elements of stage-craft to it.

But if the Theatre of the Absurd concentrates on the power of stage imagery, on the projection of visions of the world dredged up from the depth of the subconscious; if it neglects the rationally measurable ingredients of the theatre—the highly polished carpentry of plot and counterplot of the well-made play, the imitation of reality which can be measured against reality itself, the clever motivation of character—how can it be judged by rational analysis, how can it be subjected to criticism by objectively valid standards? If it is a purely subjective expression of its author's vision and emotion, how can the public distinguish the genuine, deeply felt work of art from mere impostures?

These are the old questions that have been asked about each phase in the development of modern art and literature. That they are questions of real relevance is clear to anyone who has seen the bewildered attempts of professional critics to come to terms with works in any of these new conventions—the art critics who miss the quality of "classical beauty" in Picasso's grimmer pictures, as well as the drama critics who dismiss Ionesco or Beckett because their characters lack verisimilitude or transgress the rules of polite behavior that are to be expected in drawing-room comedy.

But all art is subjective, and the standards against which the critics measure success or failure are always worked out *a posteriori* from an analysis of accepted and empirically successful works. In the case of a phenomenon like the Theatre of the Absurd, which is the outcome not of the conscious pursuit of a collectively worked-out program or theory (as the Romantic movement was, for example) but of an unpremeditated response by a number of independent authors to tendencies inherent in the general movement of thought in a period of transition, we have to analyze the works themselves and find the tendencies and modes of thought they express, in order to gain a picture of their artistic purpose. And once we have gained a clear idea of their general tendency and aim, we can arrive at a perfectly valid judgment of how they measure up to what they have set out to do.

If in the course of this book, therefore, we have established that the Theatre of the Absurd is concerned essentially with the evocation of concrete poetic images designed to communicate to the audience the sense of perplexity that their authors feel when confronted with the human condition, we must judge the success or failure of these works by the degree to which they succeed in communicating this mixture of poetry and grotesque, tragicomic horror. And this in turn will depend on the quality and power of the poetic images evoked.

How can we assess the quality of a poetic image or a complex pattern of such images? Of course, as in the criticism of poetry, there will always be a subjective element of taste or personal responsiveness to certain associations, but on the whole it is possible to apply objective standards. These standards are based on such elements as suggestive power, originality of invention, and the psychological truth of the images concerned; on their depth and universality; and on the degree of skill with which they are translated into stage terms. The superiority of complex images like the tramps waiting for Godot, or the proliferation of chairs in Ionesco's masterpiece, over some of the more childish pranks of the early Dadaist theatre is as evident as the superiority of Eliot's *Four Quartets* over the doggerel on a Christmas card, and for the same self-evident and purely objective reasons—higher complexity, greater depth, more brilliant and sustained invention, and infinitely greater craftsmanship. Adamov himself rightly puts a play like *Le Professeur Taranne* above a play on a similar subject like *Les Retrouvailles* because the former sprang from a genuine dream image while the latter was artificially contrived. The criterion here is that of psychological truth, and even if we did not have the author's own evidence, we could deduce the greater psychological truth, and hence the greater validity, of *Le Professeur Taranne* from an analysis of its imagery. It is clearly more organic, less symmetrical and less mechanically constructed, far more intense and coherent, than the imagery of the later play.

Touchstones of judgment such as these—depth, originality of invention, psychological truth—may not perhaps be reducible to quantitative terms, but they are no less objective than the same criteria applied to making the distinction between a Rembrandt or a mannerist painting, or between a poem of Pope's and one of Settle's.

Valid criteria certainly exist to assess the success of works within the category of the Theatre of the Absurd. It is more difficult to place the best works in this convention into a general hierarchy of dramatic art as a whole, but this, in any case, is an impossible task. Is Raphael a greater painter than Brueghel, Miró a greater painter than Murillo? While it is clearly futile to argue, as is so often done in discussing abstract painting or the works of the Theatre of the Absurd, whether such apparently effortless products of the imagination deserve the title of works of art simply because they lack the sheer effort and ingenuity that go into a group portrait or a well-made play, it is worthwhile to refute some of these popular misconceptions.

It is *not* true that it is infinitely more difficult to construct a rational plot than to summon up the irrational imagery of a play of the Theatre of the Absurd, just as it is quite untrue that any child could draw as well as Klee or Picasso. There is an immense difference between artistically and dramatically valid nonsense and just nonsense. Anyone who has seriously tried to write nonsense verse or to devise a nonsense play will confirm the truth of this assertion. In constructing a realistic plot, as in painting from a model, there is always reality itself and the writer's own experience and observation to fall back on—characters one has known, events one has witnessed. Writing in a medium in which there is complete freedom of invention, on the other hand, requires the ability to *create* images and situations that have no counterpart in nature while, at the same time, establishing a world of its own, with its own inherent logic and consistency, which will be instantly acceptable to the audience. Mere combinations of incongruities produce mere banality. Anyone attempting to work in this medium simply by writing down what comes into his mind will find that the supposed flights of spontaneous invention have never left the ground, that they consist of incoherent fragments of reality that have not been transposed into a valid imaginative whole. Unsuccessful examples of the Theatre of the Absurd, like unsuccessful abstract painting, are usually characterized by the transparent way in which they still bear the mark of the fragments of reality from which they are made up. They have not undergone that sea change through which the merely *negative* quality of *lack* of logic or verisimilitude is transmuted into the *positive* quality of a new world that makes imaginative sense in its own right.

Here we have one of the real hallmarks of excellence in the Theatre of the Absurd. Only when its invention springs from deep layers of profoundly experienced emotion, only when it mirrors real obsessions, dreams, and valid images in the subconscious mind of its author, will such a work of art have that quality of truth, of instantly recognized general, as distinct from merely private, validity that distinguishes the vision of a poet from the delusions of the mentally afflicted. This quality of depth and unity of vision is instantly recognizable and beyond trickery. No degree of technical accomplishment and mere cleverness can here, as in the sphere of representational art or drama, cover up the poverty of the inner core of the work in question.

To write a well-made problem play or a witty comedy of manners may therefore be more laborious or require a higher degree of ingenuity or intelligence. On the other hand, to invent a generally valid poetic image of the human condition requires unusual depth of feeling and intensity of emotion, and a far higher degree of genuinely creative vision—in short, inspiration. It is a widespread but vulgar fallacy that bases a hierarchy of artistic achievement on the mere difficulty or laboriousness of the process of composition. If it were not futile from the outset to argue in terms of position on a scale of values, such a scale could be based only on the quality, the universal validity, the depth of vision and insight of the work itself, whether or not it was produced in decades of patient plodding or in a flash of inspiration.

The criteria of achievement in the Theatre of the Absurd are not only the quality of invention, the complexity of the poetic images evoked, and the skill with which they are combined and sustained but also, and even more essentially, the *reality* and *truth* of the vision these images embody. For all its freedom of invention and spontaneity, the Theatre of the Absurd is concerned with communicating an experience of being, and in doing so it is trying to be uncompromisingly honest and fearless in exposing the reality of the human condition.

This is the consideration from which it is possible to resolve the controversy between the "realistic" theatre and the Theatre of the Absurd. Kenneth Tynan rightly argued in his debate with Ionesco that he expected what an artist communicated *to be true.* But Ionesco, in asserting that he was concerned with communicating *his personal vision,* in no way contradicted Tynan's postulate. Ionesco also strives to tell the truth—the truth about his intuition of the human condition. The truthful exploration of a psychological, inner reality is in no way less true than the exploration of an outward objective reality. Indeed, the reality of vision is more immediate and nearer to the core of experience than any description of an objective reality. Is a painting of a sunflower by van Gogh less real, less objectively true, than a picture of a sunflower in a textbook of botany? In some senses, perhaps, but certainly not in others. And the van Gogh painting will have a higher level of truth and reality than any scientific illustration, even if van Gogh's sunflower has the wrong number of petals.

Realities of vision and perception are as real as quantitatively verifiable external realities. There is no real contradiction between what claims to be a theatre of objective reality and a theatre of subjective reality. Both are equally realistic—but concerned with different aspects of reality in its vast complexity.

This also disposes of the apparent conflict between an ideological, politically oriented theatre and the seemingly apolitical, anti-ideological Theatre of the Absurd. A *pièce à thèse* on, say, as important a subject as capital punishment will try to present a set of arguments and circumstances to illustrate its case. If the circumstances presented are *true*, the play will be convincing. If they are obviously biased and manipulated, it will fail. But the test of the truth of the play must lie ultimately in its ability to communicate the truth of the *experience* of the characters involved. And here the test of its truth and realism will ultimately coincide with its *inner reality*. However correct the statistics and descriptive details of the play may be, its dramatic truth will depend on the author's ability to convey the victim's fear of death, the human reality of his predicament. And here, too, the test of truth will lie in the creative ability, the poetic imagination of the author. And this is precisely the criterion by which we can judge the truth of the wholly subjective creations of a theatre not concerned with social realities.

The contradiction does not lie between realistic and unrealistic, objective and subjective, theatre but merely between poetic vision, poetic truth, and imaginative reality on the one hand, and arid, mechanical, lifeless, poetically untrue writing on the other. A *pièce à thèse* written by a great poet like Brecht is as true as an exploration of private nightmares like Ionesco's *The Chairs*. And paradoxically some plays by Brecht in which the poet's truth has proved stronger than the thesis may be *politically* less effective than that very play by Ionesco, which does attack the absurdities of polite society and bourgeois conversation.

In trying to deal with the ultimates of the human condition not in terms of intellectual understanding but in terms of communicating a metaphysical truth through a living experience, the Theatre of the Absurd touches the religious sphere. There is a vast difference between *knowing* something to be the case in the conceptual sphere and *experiencing* it as a living reality. It is the mark of all great religions that they not only possess a body of knowledge that can be taught in the form of cosmological information or ethical rules but that they also communicate the essence of this body of doctrine in the living, recurring poetic imagery of ritual. It is the loss of the latter sphere, which responds to a deep inner need in all human beings, that the decline of religion has left as a deeply felt deficiency in our civilization. We possess at least an approximation to a coherent philosophy in the scientific method, but we lack the means to make it a living reality, an experienced focus of men's lives. That is why the theatre, a place where men congregate to experience poetic or artistic insights, has in many ways assumed the function of a substitute church. Hence the immense importance placed upon the theatre by totalitarian creeds, which are fully aware of the need to make their doctrines a living, experienced reality to their followers.

The Theatre of the Absurd, paradoxical though this may appear at first sight, can be seen as an attempt to communicate the metaphysical experience behind the scientific attitude and, at the same time, to supplement it by rounding off the partial view of the world it presents, and integrating it in a wider vision of the world and its mystery.

For if the Theatre of the Absurd presents the world as senseless and lacking a unifying principle, it does so merely in the terms of those philosophies that start from the idea that human thought *can* reduce the totality of the universe to a complete, unified, coherent system. It is only from the point of view of those who cannot bear a world where it is impossible to know why it was created, what part man has been assigned in it, and what constitutes right actions and wrong actions that a picture of the universe lacking all these clear-cut definitions appears deprived of sense and sanity, and tragically absurd. The modern scientific attitude, however, rejects the postulate of a wholly coherent and simplified explanation that must account for all the phenomena, purposes, and moral rules of the world. In concentrating on the slow, painstaking exploration of limited areas of reality by trial and error—by the construction, testing, and discarding of hypotheses—the scientific attitude cheerfully accepts the view that we must be able to live with the realization that large segments of knowledge and experience will remain for a long time, perhaps forever, outside our ken; that ultimate purposes cannot, and never will be, known; and that we must therefore be able to accept the fact that much that earlier metaphysical systems, mythical, religious, or philosophical, sought to explain must forever remain unexplained. From this point of view, any clinging to systems of thought that provide, or purport to provide, complete explanations of the world and man's place in it must appear childish and immature, a flight from reality into illusion and self-deception.

The Theatre of the Absurd expresses the anxiety and despair that spring from the recognition that man is surrounded by areas of impenetrable darkness, that he can never know his true nature and purpose, and that no one will provide him with ready-made rules of conduct. As Camus says in *The Myth of Sisyphus*:

> The certainty of the existence of a God who would give meaning to life has a far greater attraction than the knowledge that without him one could do evil without being punished. The choice between these alternatives would not be difficult. But there is no choice, and that is where the bitterness begins.[11]

But by facing up to anxiety and despair and the absence of divinely revealed alternatives, anxiety and despair can be overcome. The sense of loss at the disintegration of facile solutions and the disappearance of cherished illusions retains its sting only while the mind still clings to the illusions concerned. Once they are given up, we have to readjust ourselves to the new situation and face reality itself. And because the illusions we suffered from made it more difficult for us to deal with reality, their loss will ultimately be felt as exhilarating. In the words of Democritus that Beckett is fond of quoting, "Nothing is more real than Nothing."

To confront the limits of the human condition is not only equivalent to facing up to the philosophical basis of the scientific attitude, it is also a profound mystical experience. It is precisely this experience of the ineffability, the emptiness, the nothingness at the basis of the universe that forms the content of Eastern as well as Christian mystical experience. For if Lao-tzu says, "It was from the nameless that Heaven and Earth sprang, the named is but the mother that rears the ten thousand creatures, each after its kind,"[12] St. John of the Cross speaks of the soul's intuition "that it cannot comprehend God at all,"[13] and Meister Eckhart expresses the same experience in the words, "The Godhead is poor, naked, and empty, as though it were not; it has not, wills not, wants not, works not, gets not. . . . The Godhead is as void as though it were not."[14] In other words, in facing man's inability ever to comprehend the meaning of the universe, in recognizing the Godhead's total transcendence, His total otherness from all we can understand with our senses, the great mystics experienced a sense of exhilaration and liberation. This exhilaration also springs from the recognition that the language and logic of cognitive thought cannot do justice to the ultimate nature of reality. Hence a profoundly mystical philosophy like Zen Buddhism bases itself on the rejection of conceptual thinking itself:

> The denying of reality is the asserting of it,
> And the asserting of emptiness is the denying of it.[15]

The recent rise of interest in Zen in Western countries is an expression of the same tendencies that explain the success of the Theatre of the Absurd—a preoccupation with ultimate realities and a recognition that they are not approachable through conceptual thought alone. Ionesco has been quoted as drawing a parallel between the method of the Zen Buddhists and the Theatre of the Absurd,[16] and in fact the teaching methods of the Zen masters, their use of kicks and blows in reply to questions about the nature of enlightenment and their setting of nonsense problems, closely resemble some of the procedures of the Theatre of the Absurd.

Seen from this angle the dethronement of language and logic forms part of an essentially mystical attitude toward the basis of reality as being too complex and at the same time too unified, too much of one piece, to be validly expressed by the analytical means of orderly syntax and conceptual thought. As the mystics resort to poetic images, so does the Theatre of the Absurd. But if the Theatre of the Absurd presents analogies with the methods and imagery of mysticism, how can it, at the same time, be regarded as expressing the skepticism, the humble refusal to provide an explanation of absolutes, that characterize the scientific attitude?

The answer is simply that there is no contradiction between the recognition of the limitations of man's ability to comprehend all of reality by integrating it in a single system of values and the recognition of the mysterious and ineffable oneness, beyond all rational comprehension, that, once experienced, gives serenity of mind and the strength to face the human condition. These are in fact two sides of the same medal—the mystical experience of the absolute otherness and ineffability of ultimate reality is the religious, poetic counterpart to the rational recognition of the limitation of man's senses and intellect, which reduces him to exploring the world slowly by trial and error. Both these attitudes are in basic contradiction to systems of thought, religious or ideological (e.g., Marxism), that claim to provide complete answers to all questions of ultimate purpose and day-to-day conduct.

The realization that thinking in poetic images has its validity side by side with conceptual thought and the insistence on a clear recognition of the function and possibilities of each mode does not amount to a return to irrationalism; on the contrary, it opens the way to a truly rational attitude.

Ultimately, a phenomenon like the Theatre of the Absurd does not reflect despair or a return to dark irrational forces but expresses modern man's endeavor to come to terms with the world in which he lives. It attempts to make him face up to the human condition as it really is, to free him from illusions that are bound to cause constant maladjustment and disappointment. There are enormous pressures in our world that seek to induce mankind to bear the loss of faith and moral certainties by being drugged into oblivion—by mass entertainments, shallow material satisfactions, pseudo-explanations of reality, and cheap ideologies. At the end of that road lies Huxley's Brave New World of senseless euphoric automata. Today, when death and old age are increasingly concealed behind euphemisms and comforting baby talk, and life is threatened with being smothered in the mass consumption of hypnotic mechanized vulgarity, the need to confront man with the reality of his situation is greater than ever. For the dignity of man lies in his ability to face reality in all its senselessness; to accept it freely, without fear, without illusions—and to laugh at it.

That is the cause to which, in their various individual, modest, and quixotic ways, the dramatists of the Absurd are dedicated.

NOTES

Notes to Introduction

1. *San Quentin News,* San Quentin, Calif., November 28, 1957.
2. Ibid.
3. *Theatre Arts,* New York, July, 1958.
4. Ibid.
5. *San Quentin News,* November 28, 1957.
6. Albert Camus, *Le Mythe de Sisyphe* (Paris: Gallimard, 1942), p. 18.
7. Eugène Ionesco, "Dans les Armes de la Ville," *Cahiers de la Compagnie Madeleine Renaud-Jean-Louis Barrault,* Paris, No. 20, October, 1957.

Notes to Chapter One

1. Samuel Beckett, *Murphy* (New York: Grove Press, no date), p. 269.
2. Beckett, *Proust* (New York: Grove Press, no date), p. 57.
3. Beckett, quoted by Harold Hobson, "Samuel Beckett, Dramatist of the Year," *International Theatre Annual,* No. 1 (London: John Calder, 1956).
4. Peggy Guggenheim, *Confessions of an Art Addict* (London: André Deutsch, 1960), p. 50.
5. Beckett, "Dante . . Bruno . Vico . . Joyce," in *Our Examination round his Factification for Incamination of Work in Progress* (Paris: Shakespeare & Co., 1929), p. 13.

6. *Letters of James Joyce*, ed. Stuart Gilbert (London: Faber & Faber, 1957), pp. 280–81.

7. *Proust*, p. 46.

8. Ibid., p. 47.

9. Beckett, *More Pricks Than Kicks* (London: Chatto & Windus, 1934), p. 43.

10. Richard Ellmann, *James Joyce* (New York: Oxford University Press, 1959), p. 661.

11. Ibid., p. 662.

12. Guggenheim, *op. cit.*, p. 50.

13. *More Pricks Than Kicks*, p. 32.

14. Niklaus Gessner, *Die Unzulänglichkeit der Sprache* (Zurich: Juris Verlag, 1957), p. 32.

15. Letter from Herbert Blau to members of San Francisco Actors' Workshop, dated London, October 28, 1959.

16. Claude Mauriac, *L'Alittérature Contemporaine* (Paris: Albin Michel, 1958), p. 83.

17. Alan Schneider, "Waiting for Beckett," *Chelsea Review*, New York, Autumn, 1958.

18. Beckett, *Waiting for Godot* (London: Faber & Faber, 1959), p. 41.

19. Ibid., p. 37.

20. Ibid., p. 34.

21. Gessner, *op. cit.*, p. 37.

22. *Waiting for Godot*, p. 33.

23. Eric Bentley, *What Is Theatre?* (Boston: Beacon Press, 1956), p. 158.

24. Honoré de Balzac, *Œuvres Complètes* (Paris, 1866), XIX.

25. *Proust*, pp. 2–3.

26. Ibid., pp. 4–5.

27. Ibid., p. 13.

28. *Waiting for Godot*, p. 48.

29. Ibid., p. 88.

30. Ibid., p. 32.

31. Ibid., p. 89.

32. Ibid., p. 91.

33. Beckett, *En Attendant Godot* (Paris: Les Editions de Minuit, 1952), p. 30.

34. *Waiting for Godot*, p. 18.

35. Beckett, quoted by Harold Hobson, *op. cit.*, and by Alan Schneider, *op. cit.*

36. *Waiting for Godot*, p. 11.

37. Ibid., pp. 12–13.

38. Ibid.

39. Ibid., p. 31.

40. Ibid., pp. 73–74.

41. Ibid., pp. 83–84.

42. Ibid., p. 42.

43. Ibid., p. 10.

44. Ibid., p. 18.

45. Ibid., p. 20.

46. Ibid., p. 80.

47. Ibid., p. 34.

48. Eva Metman, "Reflections on Samuel Beckett's Plays," *Journal of Analytical Psychology*, London, January, 1960, p. 51.

49. *Waiting for Godot*, p. 91.

50. *Proust*, p. 8 [my italics—M.E.].

51. Ibid., p. 9.

52. *Waiting for Godot*, p. 64.

53. Ibid., pp. 62–63.

54. Jean-Paul Sartre, *L'Etre et le Néant* (Paris: Gallimard, 1943), p. 111.

55. Beckett, *Watt* (Paris: Olympia Press, 1958), pp. 144–45.

56. Ibid., p. 146.

57. Beckett, *Endgame* (New York: Grove Press, 1958), p. 43.

58. Ibid., p. 38.

59. Ibid., p. 14.

60. Ibid., p. 68.

61. Ibid., p. 75.

62. Ibid., p. 13.

63. Ibid., p. 56.

64. Ibid., p. 69.

65. Ibid., p. 78.

66. Ibid., p. 79.

67. Ibid., p. 81.

68. Nikolai Evreinov, *The Theatre of the Soul,* Monodrama, trans. M. Potapenko and C. St. John (London, 1915).

69. *Endgame,* p. 44.

70. Ibid., p. 1.

71. Lionel Abel, "Joyce the Father, Beckett the Son," *The New Leader,* New York, December 14, 1959.

72. *Endgame,* p. 78.

73. Beckett, *Fin de Partie* (Paris: Les Editions de Minuit, 1957), pp. 103–5.

74. *Endgame,* p. 79.

75. Beckett, *Malone Dies,* in *Molloy. Malone Dies. The Unnamable* (London: John Calder, 1959), p. 193.

76. *Murphy,* p. 246.

77. Metman, *op. cit.,* p. 58.

78. Beckett, *Act Without Words I,* in *Krapp's Last Tape and Other Dramatic Pieces* (New York: Grove Press, 1960).

79. *Endgame,* p. 57.

80. Beckett, *All That Fall,* in *Krapp's Last Tape,* p. 53.

81. Ibid., p. 74.

82. Ibid., p. 88.

83. Beckett, *Krapp's Last Tape* in *op. cit.,* p. 25.

84. Ibid., p. 28.

85. Beckett, *Embers,* in *Krapp's Last Tape,* p. 115.

86. Ibid., p. 121.

87. Ibid., p. 111.

88. Beckett, *Molloy,* in *Molloy. Malone Dies. The Unnamable,* p. 50.

89. *Murphy,* p. 40.

90. *Molloy,* p. 28.

91. Beckett, *The Unnamable,* in *Molloy. Malone Dies. The Unnamable,* p. 316.

92. *Endgame,* pp. 32–33.

93. *Waiting for Godot,* p. 61.

94. *Endgame,* p. 70.

95. *Molloy,* p. 64.

Notes to Chapter Two

1. Arthur Adamov, *L'Aveu* (Paris: Editions du Sagittaire, 1946), p. 19.

2. Ibid., p. 23.

3. Ibid., pp. 25–26.

4. Ibid., p. 28.

5. Ibid., p. 42.

6. Ibid., p. 45.

7. Ibid., p. 45.

8. Adamov, "The Endless Humiliation," trans. Richard Howard, *Evergreen Review*, New York, II, 8 (1959), pp. 64–95.

9. *L'Aveu*, p. 69; "The Endless Humiliation," p. 75.

10. Carl Gustav Jung, *Le Moi et l'Inconscient*, trans. Adamov (Paris: 1938).

11. *L'Aveu*, p. 57; "The Endless Humiliation," p. 67.

12. *L'Aveu*, p. 58; "The Endless Humiliation," p. 67.

13. *L'Aveu*, p. 106.

14. Ibid., p. 110.

15. Ibid., p. 114.

16. Ibid., p. 115.

17. Adamov, "Une Fin et un Commencement," *L'Heure Nouvelle*, No. 1 (Paris: Editions du Sagittaire, 1946), p. 17.

18. Adamov, "Assignation," *L'Heure Nouvelle*, No. 2, p. 3.

19. Ibid., footnote on p. 6.

20. "Une Fin et un Commencement," p. 16.

21. "Le Refus," *L'Heure Nouvelle*, No. 2, footnote on p. 6.

22. Ibid.

23. Adamov, *Théâtre II* (Paris: Gallimard, 1955), "Note Préliminaire," p. 8.

24. Ibid.

25. Ibid., p. 9.

26. Adamov, *La Parodie. L'Invasion* (Paris: Charlot, 1950), p. 22.

27. *L'Aveu*, p. 85; "The Endless Humiliation," p. 85.

28. Adamov, *Théâtre I* (Paris: Gallimard, 1953), p. 86.

29. Ibid., p. 94.

30. *La Parodie. L'Invasion*, p. 16.

31. Adamov, quoted by Carlos Lynes, Jr., "Adamov or le 'sens littéral' in the Theatre," *Yale French Studies*, No. 14, Winter, 1954-55.

32. *Théâtre I*, p. 107.

33. *La Parodie. L'Invasion*, p. 22.

34. Ibid., p. 23.

35. *Théâtre II*, p. 11.

36. Ibid., p. 12.

37. Ibid., p. 13.

38. Maurice Regnaut, "Arthur Adamov et le Sens du Fétichisme," Cahiers Renaud-Barrault, Nos. 22-23, May, 1958.

39. *Théâtre II*, p. 14.

40. Adamov, "As We Were," trans. Richard Howard, *Evergreen Review*, I, 4 (1957).

41. *Théâtre II*, p. 15.

42. Ibid., p. 15.

43. Ibid., p. 17.

44. *Théâtre I*, p. 136.

45. "Qui êtes-vous Arthur Adamov?" *Cité Panorama* (Program Bulletin of Planchon's Théâtre de la Cité), Villeurbanne, No. 9, 1960.

Notes to Chapter Three

1. Kenneth Tynan, "Ionesco, Man of Destiny?" *The Observer*, London, June 22, 1958.

2. Ionesco, "The Playwright's Role," *The Observer*, June 29, 1958.

3. Ibid.

4. Ibid.

5. Tynan, "Ionesco and the Phantom," *The Observer*, July 6, 1958.

6. Ionesco, "Le Cœur n'est pas sur la Main," *Cahiers des Saisons*, Paris, No. 15, Winter, 1959.

7. Ibid.

8. Ionesco, "Lorsque j'écris . . . ," *Cahiers des Saisons*, No. 15.

9. Ionesco, "Expérience du Théâtre," *Nouvelle Revue Française*, Paris (February 1, 1958), p. 253.

10. Ionesco, "Printemps 1939. Les Débris du Souvenir. Pages de Journal," *Cahiers Renaud-Barrault*, No. 29, February, 1960, p. 104.

11. Ibid., p. 108.

12. "Lorsque j'écris . . ."

13. "Printemps 1939," *loc. cit.*, p. 98.

14. Ibid., p. 103.

15. "Expérience du Théâtre," *loc. cit.*, p. 247.

16. Ibid., p. 253.

17. Lutembi, "Contribution à une étude des sources de la Cantatrice Chauve," *Cahiers du Collège de Pataphysique*, 8–9, 1953.

18. Ionesco, "La Tragédie du Langage," *Spectacles*, Paris, No. 2, July, 1958.

19. Ibid.

20. Ibid.

21. Nicolas Bataille, "La Bataille de la Cantatrice," *Cahiers des Saisons*, No. 15.

22. "Expérience du Théâtre," *loc. cit.*, p. 258.

23. Ibid., pp. 258–59.

24. *The Observer*, July 14, 1958.

25. "Expérience du Théâtre," *loc. cit.*, p. 268.

26. Ionesco, "The World of Ionesco," *International Theatre Annual*, No. 2 (London: Calder, 1957).

27. Ionesco, "The Tragedy of Language," *The Tulane Drama Review*, Spring 1960.

28. Ionesco, "Le Point du Départ," *Cahiers des Quatre Saisons*, Paris, No. 1.

29. Ionesco, Preface to *Les Possédés*, adapted from Dostoevski by Akakia Viala and Nicolas Bataille (Paris: Editions Emile-Paul, 1959).

30. Ibid.

31. Ibid.

32. Jacques Lemarchand, Preface to Ionesco, *Théâtre I.*

33. P. A. Touchard, "La Loi du Théâtre," *Cahiers des Saisons*, No. 15.

34. Letter from Ionesco to Sylvain Dhomme, quoted by F. Towarnicki, "Des *Chaises* vides . . . à Broadway," *Spectacles*, Paris, No. 2, July, 1958.

35. J. Anouilh, "Du Chapitre des Chaises," *Figaro*, Paris, April 23, 1956.

36. Ionesco, *Victims of Duty*, in *Plays*, Vol. II (London: Calder; New York: Grove Press), p. 119.

37. Ibid., pp. 158–59.

38. Ibid., p. 162.

39. Ibid., p. 159.

40. Sartre, *L'Etre et le Néant*, p. 60.

41. Ibid., p. 85.

42. S. Doubrovsky, "Le Rire d'Eugène Ionesco," *Nouvelle Revue Française*, February, 1960.

43. Ibid.

44. "Le Point du Départ."

45. Ibid.

46. Ionesco, *Théâtre I* (Arcanes, Paris, 1953). Trans. Sasha Moorsom, *The Motor Show*, in *3 Arts Quarterly*, London, No. 2, Summer, 1960.

47. Ionesco, *La Jeune Fille à Marier*, in *Théâtre II*. Trans. Donald Watson, in *The Killer and Other Plays* (London: Calder; New York: Grove Press, 1960), p. 158.

48. Ionesco, *Le Maître*, in *Théâtre II*. Trans. Derek Prouse, *The Leader*, in *Plays IV* (London: Calder; New York: Grove Press, 1960).

49. Ionesco, interview in *L'Express*, January 28, 1960.

50. Ionesco, *Amédée*, trans. Donald Watson, *Plays II* (London: Calder; New York: Grove Press, 1958), p. 8.

51. Ibid., p. 48.

52. Ibid., pp. 52–53.

53. Ibid., p. 62.

54. Ionesco, "Oriflamme," *Nouvelle Revue Française*, February, 1954.

55. Ibid.

56. Ionesco, *Le Tableau*, in *Dossiers Acénonètes du Collège de Pataphysique*, No. 1, 1958, p. 44.

57. Ibid., p. 5.

58. Ibid.

59. "Eugène Ionesco ouvre le feu," *World Theatre*, VIII, 3, Autumn, 1959.

60. Ionesco, "Pages de Journal," *Nouvelle Revue Française*, February, 1960.

61. "Eugène Ionesco ouvre le feu."

62. Ionesco, *Improvisation*, trans. Donald Watson, *Plays III* (London: Calder; New York: Grove Press, 1960), pp. 112–13.

63. Ibid., pp. 113–14.

64. Ibid., pp. 149–50.

65. *Théâtre Populaire*, Paris, No. 17, March 1, 1956, p. 77.

66. Sam White, "Paris Newsletter," *Evening Standard*, London, May 24, 1957.

67. Ionesco, *Impromptu pour la Duchesse de Windsor*, manuscript, pp. 6–7.

68. Trans. Stanley Read, *Evergreen Review*, I, 3, 1957.

69. *The Killer*, loc. cit., p. 9.

70. *New York Times*, April 3, 1960.

71. *Cahiers du Collège de Pataphysique*, Dossier 7, 1959.

72. Ionesco, interview with Claude Sarraute, *Le Monde*, January 17, 1960.

73. *The Times*, London, April 29, 1960.

74. *Cahiers du Collège de Pataphysique*, Dossiers 10–11, 1960.

75. *Cahiers du Collège de Pataphysique*, Dossier 7, 1959; also in *L'Avant-Scène*, December 15, 1959. Trans. Donald Allen, "Foursome," *Evergreen Review*, No. 13, May–June, 1960.

76. "Printemps 1939," loc. cit., p. 98.

77. Preface to *Les Possédés*.

78. "Expérience du Théâtre," loc. cit., p. 268.

79. Ionesco, "La Démystification par l'Humour Noir," *L'Avant-Scène*, February 15, 1959.

80. "Expérience du Théâtre," loc. cit., p. 270.

81. "The World of Ionesco."

82. Interview in *L'Express*, January 28, 1960.

83. Ibid.

84. Ionesco, "Théâtre et Anti-Théâtre," *Cahiers des Saisons*, No. 2, October, 1955.

85. "Pages de Journal," loc. cit., p. 231.

86. "Expérience du Théâtre," loc. cit., p. 262.

87. Ibid.

88. Ibid.

89. Ibid., p. 260.

90. "La Démystification par l'Humour Noir."

91. Alain Bosquet, "Le Théâtre d'Eugène Ionesco, ou Les 36 Recettes du Comique," *Combat*, Paris, February 17, 1955.

92. "Expérience du Théâtre," *loc. cit.*, p. 264.

93. Ionesco, quoted by Towarnicki, *Spectacles*.

Notes to Chapter Four

1. Jean Genet, *Journal du Voleur* (Paris: Gallimard, 1949), p. 282.

2. Ibid., p. 47.

3. Ibid., p. 48.

4. Ibid., p. 92.

5. Ibid., p. 131.

6. Sartre, *Saint Genet, Comédien et Martyr* (Paris: Gallimard, 1952), p. 397.

7. Ibid., p. 421.

8. *Journal du Voleur*, p. 283.

9. *Saint Genet*, p. 501.

10. *Journal du Voleur*, p. 47.

11. Ibid., p. 93.

12. Genet, *Deathwatch*, in *The Maids-Deathwatch*, trans. Bernard Frechtman (New York: Grove Press, 1954), p. 128.

13. Ibid., pp. 103-4.

14. *The Maids*, p. 61.

15. Ibid., p. 86.

16. Genet, *Notre-Dame-des-Fleurs* in *Œuvres Complètes*, Vol. II (Paris: Gallimard, 1951), p. 119.

17. Genet, letter to Pauvert, in Genet, *Les Bonnes-L'Atelier d'Alberto Giacometti* (Décines [Isère], L'Arbalète, 1958), pp. 145-46.

18. Ibid., p. 147.

19. *Saint Genet*, p. 9.

20. Sartre, introduction to *The Maids-Deathwatch*, p. 30.

21. Genet, letter to Pauvert, p. 144.

22. Ibid.

23. Ibid., p. 142.

24. *The News Chronicle*, London, April 23, 1957.

25. *The News Chronicle*, London, April 24, 1957.

26. *The New Statesman*, London, May 4, 1957.

27. Ibid.

28. Ibid.

29. *Picture Post*, London, May 11, 1957.

30. Genet, *The Blacks*, trans. Bernard Frechtman (New York: Grove Press, 1960), p. 11.

31. Ibid., p. 39.

32. Ibid., p. 127.

33. Ibid., p. 22.

34. Ibid., p. 10.

35. Ibid., p. 47.

36. Ibid., p. 44.

37. *Saint Genet*, p. 535.

38. Ibid., p. 388.

Notes to Chapter Five

1. Jean Tardieu, *Théâtre de Chambre* (Paris: Gallimard, 1955), p. 10.

2. Ibid., p. 14.

3. Ibid., p. 23.

4. Tardieu, *Théâtre II: Poèmes à Jouer* (Paris: Gallimard, 1960), p. 163.

5. Ibid., pp. 240–41.

6. Boris Vian, *Les Bâtisseurs d'Empire* (Paris: L'Arche, 1959), p. 8.

7. Dino Buzzati, *Un Caso Clinico* (Milan: Mondadori, 1953), p. 182.

8. Ezio d'Errico, *La Foresta*, in *Il Dramma* (Turin: November, 1959), p. 9.

9. See Pallotino, *The Etruscans* (Penguin Books, 1953), p. 246.

10. Manuel de Pedrolo, *Cruma*, in *Premi Joan Santamaria 1957* (Barcelona: Editoral Nereida, 1958), p. 14.

11. De Pedrolo, *Homes i No*, in *Quaderns de Teatre A.D.B.*, No. 2 (Barcelona: 1960), p. 24.

12. Fernando Arrabal, *Théâtre* (Paris: Julliard, 1958), pp. 13–14.

13. Ibid., p. 152.

14. Amos Kenan, *Le Lion*, in *Les Lettres Nouvelles*, Paris, March–April, 1960.

15. Max Frisch, *Biedermann und die Brandstifter* (Berlin and Frankfurt: Suhrkamp, 1958), p. 78. Based on a radio play broadcast by Bayrischer Rundfunk, Munich, in March, 1953; published as *Herr Biedermann und die Brandstifter* (Hamburg: Hans Bredow Institut, 6th ed., 1959).

16. *Biedermann und die Brandstifter*, p. 20.

17. Hans Baenziger, *Frisch und Duerrenmatt* (Bern and Munich: Francke, 1960), p. 100.

18. Wolfgang Hildesheimer, "Erlanger Rede über das absurde Theater," *Akzente*, Munich, No. 6, 1960.

19. Ibid.

20. Hildesheimer, *Spiele in denen es dunkel wird* (Pfullingen: Neske, 1958).

21. Günter Grass, *Die Bösen Köche*, stage manuscript, p. 101.

22. Harold Pinter, interview with Kenneth Tynan, B.B.C. Home Service, October 28, 1960.

23. Pinter, interview with Hallam Tennyson, B.B.C. General Overseas Service, August 7, 1960.

24. Pinter interview with Tynan.

25. Pinter, *The Room*, in *The Birthday Party and Other Plays* (London: Methuen, 1960), p. 102.

26. Ibid., p. 103.

27. Ibid., p. 118.

28. Pinter, *The Dumb Waiter*, loc. cit., p. 150.

29. Ibid.

30. Pinter, *The Birthday Party*, p. 23.

31. Ibid., pp. 54–55.

32. Pinter interview with Tynan.

33. Pinter interview with Tennyson.

34. Ibid.

35. Ibid.

36. Program note for performance of *The Room* and *The Dumb Waiter*, Royal Court Theatre, London, March, 1960.

37. Pinter interview with Tynan.

38. Pinter, *A Slight Ache*, in *Tomorrow*, Oxford, No. 4, 1960. Also in *A Slight Ache and Other Plays* (London: Methuen, 1961).

39. Pinter, *The Caretaker* (London: Methuen), p. 77.

40. Pinter interview with Tynan.

41. *The Sunday Times*, August 14, 1960.

42. *The Caretaker*, p. 63.

43. Ibid., p. 25.

44. Ibid., p. 57.

45. Ibid., p. 60.

46. Pinter, *The Dwarfs* in *A Slight Ache and Other Plays* (London: Methuen, 1961), p. 116.

47. Ibid., p. 97.

48. Ibid., p. 99.

49. Ibid., p. 111.

50. Pinter interview with Tynan.

51. Ibid.

52. N. F. Simpson, *A Resounding Tinkle*, in *New English Dramatists 2* (Penguin Books, 1960), p. 8. First published in *The Observer Plays*, ed. Kenneth Tynan (London: Faber & Faber, 1958).

53. *A Resounding Tinkle* (short version), unpublished acting manuscript, p. 25.

54. *A Resounding Tinkle*, published version, p. 99.

55. Ibid., p. 100.

56. Ibid., p. 110.

57. Ibid., p. 130.

58. Ibid., p. 139.

59. Simpson, quoted by Penelope Gilliat, "Schoolmaster from Battersea," *Manchester Guardian*, April 14, 1960.

60. Simpson, quoted in *London Daily Mail*, February 25, 1960.

61. *A Resounding Tinkle* (short version), p. 25.

62. Simpson, *The Hole*, unpublished acting manuscript, p. 1.

63. Simpson interview, B.B.C. General Overseas Service, March 6, 1960.

64. Simpson, *One Way Pendulum* (London: Faber & Faber, 1960), p. 50.

Notes to Chapter Six

1. William Hazlitt, "The Indian Jugglers," *Table Talk* (London and New York: Everyman's Library), p. 78.

2. Friedrich Nietzsche, *Die Geburt der Tragödie*, in *Werke*, Vol. I, ed. Schlechta (Munich: Hanser), p. 94.

3. Hermann Reich, *Der Mimus*, Vol. I (Berlin: 1903), p. 459.

4. Ibid., p. 460.

5. Ibid.

6. Ibid., pp. 595–96.

7. E. Tietze-Conrat, *Dwarfs and Jesters in Art* (London: Phaidon, 1957), p. 7.

8. Joseph Gregor, *Weltgeschichte des Theaters* (Vienna: Phaidon, 1933), p. 212.

9. Max Beerbohm, *Around Theatres* (London: Rupert Hart-Davis, 1953), p. 350.

10. Quoted by Colin McInnes, *The Spectator*, London, December 23, 1960.

11. Ionesco, *The Chairs*, p. 115.

12. *Time*, December 12, 1960.

13. Johann Nestroy, *Judith und Holofernes*, Scene 3, in *Sämtliche Werke*, Vol. IV, ed. Brukner and Rommel (Vienna: Schroll), p. 167.

14. Shakespeare, *As You Like It*, II, 7.

15. Georg Buechner, *Leonce und Lena*, Act II, Scene 2.

16. Freud, *Der Witz und Seine Beziehung zum Unbewussten* (1905), paperback edition (Frankfurt: Fischer, 1958), p. 101.

17. Robert Benayoun, *Anthologie du Nonsense* (Paris: Pauvert, 1957), p. 36.

18. Richard Corbet, "Epilogus Incerti Authoris," *Comic and Curious Verse*, ed. J. M. Cohen (Penguin Books), p. 217.

19. Elizabeth Sewell, *The Field of Nonsense* (London: Chatto & Windus, 1952), p. 128.

20. Christian Morgenstern, "Der Lattenzaun," trans. R. F. C. Hull, *More Comic and Curious Verse*, ed. J. M. Cohen (Penguin Books, 1956), p. 49.

21. Morgenstern, "Das Butterbrotpapier," trans. A. E. W. Eitzen, *Das Mondschaf* (Wiesbaden: Insel, 1953), p. 19.

22. Morgenstern, "Das Grosse Lalulā," *Alle Galgenlieder* (Wiesbaden: Insel, 1950), p. 23.

23. Mircea Eliade, *Myths, Dreams and Mysteries* (London: Harvill Press, 1960), p. 27.

24. Ionesco, "Lorsque j'écris . . . ," p. 211.

25. August Strindberg, *A Dream Play*, in *Six Plays of Strindberg*, trans. Sylvia Sprigge (New York: Doubleday Anchor Books, 1955), p. 193.

26. James Joyce, *Ulysses in Nighttown*, adapted by Marjorie Barkentin under supervision of Padraic Colum; first perf. New York, June 5, 1958. (New York: Random House Modern Library Paperbacks, 1958.) See *Bloomsday*, another dramatization of *Ulysses*, by Alan MacClelland.

27. Ionesco, "Dans les Armes de la Ville," *Cahiers Renaud-Barrault*, No. 20, October, 1957, p. 4.

28. Quoted by André Franck, "Il y a dix ans . . . ," *loc. cit.*, p. 35.

29. Stéphane Mallarmé, "Richard Wagner, Rêverie d'un poète Français," in *Œuvres* (Bibliothèque de la Pléiade), pp. 544–45.

30. Alfred Jarry, "Questions de Théâtre," in *Ubu Roi* (Lausanne: Henri Kaeser, 1948), p. 158.

31. Arthur Symons, *Studies in Seven Arts*, quoted by Roger Shattuck, *The Banquet Years* (London: Faber & Faber, 1959), p. 161.

32. W. B. Yeats, *Autobiographies* (London: Macmillan, 1955), pp. 348–49.

33. Mallarmé, undated letter to Jarry, in Mallarmé, *Propos sur la Poésie*, ed. H. Mondor, quoted in J. Robichez, *Le Symbolisme au Théâtre* (Paris: L'Arche, 1957), pp. 359–60.

34. Jacques Copeau, *L'Art du Théâtre* (Montreal: Editions Serge, 1944), p. 149.

35. Jarry, *Gestes et Opinions du Docteur Faustroll* (Paris: Fasquelle, 1955), p. 32, trans. in *Evergreen Review*, No. 13, 1960, p. 131.

36. Guillaume Apollinaire, Preface to *Les Mamelles de Tirésias*, *Œuvres* (Pléiade), pp. 865–66.

37. Ibid., p. 868.

38. Ibid., p. 882.

39. Shattuck, *op. cit.*, p. 161.

40. Hugo Ball, "Dada Tagebuch," in Arp-Huelsenbeck-Tzara, *Die Geburt des Dada* (Zürich: Arche, 1957), p. 117.

41. Ibid., p. 139.

42. Oskar Kokoschka, *Sphinx und Strohmann*, in *Schriften 1907–1955* (Munich: Albert Langen, 1956), p. 167.

43. Tristan Tzara, "Chronique Zurichoise," in *Die Geburt des Dada*, p. 173.

44. Georges Ribemont-Dessaignes, *Déjà Jadis* (Paris: Julliard, 1958).

45. Tzara, *Première Aventure Céleste de M. Antipyrine* (Collection Dada, Zürich, 1916); extract in Tzara, *Morceaux Choisis* (Paris: Bordas, 1947).

46. Ribemont-Dessaignes, *op. cit.*, p. 73.

47. Tzara, *Le Cœur à Gaz* (Paris: GLM, 1946), p. 8.

48. Ribemont-Dessaignes, *L'Empéreur de Chine, suivi de Le Serin Muet* (Paris: Sans Pareil, Collection Dada, 1921), p. 127.

49. Yvan Goll, autobiographical note, in K. Pinthus, *Menschheitsdämmerung* (Berlin: Rowohlt, 1920), p. 292.

50. Goll, Preface to *Die Unsterblichen*, in *Dichtungen* (Neuwied: Luchterhand, 1960), p. 64.

51. Ibid., pp. 64–65.

52. Ibid., p. 65.

53. Goll, *Methusalem*, in *Schrei und Bekenntnis*, ed. K. Otten (Neuwied: Lucherhand, 1959), pp. 426–27.

54. Bertolt Brecht, *Im Dickicht der Städte, Stuecke I* (Frankfurt: Suhrkamp, 1953), pp. 291–92.

55. Roger Vitrac, *Les Mystères de l'Amour*, in *Théâtre II* (Paris: Gallimard, 1948), p. 56.

56. Vitrac, *Victor, ou Les Enfants au Pouvoir*, in *Théâtre I* (Paris: Gallimard, 1946), p. 90.

57. Antonin Artaud, *The Theater and Its Double*, trans. Mary Caroline Richards (New York: Grove Press, 1958), p. 7.

58. Ibid., p. 42.

59. Ibid., p. 85.

60. Ibid., p. 28.

61. Ibid., p. 93.

62. Ibid., p. 37.

63. Ibid., p. 71.

64. Ibid., p. 73.

65. Ibid., p. 78.

66. Ibid., pp. 110–11.

67. Ionesco, "Pour Cocteau," *Cahiers des Saisons*, No. 12, October, 1957.

68. Armand Salacrou, *Pièces à Lire*, in *Les Œuvres Libres*, Paris, No. 173, October, 1960.

69. J. H. Sainmont, H. Robillot, A. Templenul, Introduction to J. Torma, *Le Bétrou*, Collège de Pataphysique, Year 83 of the pataphysical era (1956), p. 14.

70. Torma, *Euphorismes* (Paris: 1926), p. 37.

71. Ibid., p. 36.

72. Ibid., p. 39.

73. Ibid.

74. Beckett, Georges Duthuit, Jacques Putman, *Bram Van Velde* (New York: Grove Press, 1960).

75. R. Penrose, *Picasso: His Life and Work* (London: Gollancz, 1955), p. 335.

76. Eric Bentley, Notes to *him* in *From the Modern Repertoire*, II (Indiana University Press, 1957), p. 487.

77. E. E. Cummings, quoted by Bentley, *op. cit.*, p. 487.

Notes to Chapter Seven

1. Nietzsche, *Also Sprach Zarathustra*, in *Werke*, Vol. II (Munich: Hanser, 1955), p. 279.

2. Camus, *Le Mythe de Sisyphe*, *loc. cit.*, p. 29.

3. George Steiner, "The Retreat from the Word: I," *The Listener*, London, July 14, 1960.

4. Steiner, "The Retreat from the Word: II," *loc. cit.*, July 21, 1960.

5. Ludwig Wittgenstein, *Philosophical Investigations: I* (Oxford: Blackwell, 1958), pp. 48–48e.

6. Ionesco, "Ni un Dieu, ni un Démon," *Cahiers Renaud-Barrault*, No. 23, May, 1958, p. 131.

7. Eva Metman, "Reflections on Samuel Beckett's Plays," *op. cit.*, p. 43.

8. Ibid.

9. Jung, "Ulysses," quoted by Metman, *loc. cit.*, p. 53.

10. Ionesco, "Expérience du Théâtre," *loc. cit.*, p. 266.

11. *Le Mythe de Sisyphe*, p. 94.

12. Lao-tzu, quoted by Aldous Huxley, *The Perennial Philosophy* (London: Chatto & Windus, 1946), p. 33.

13. St. John of the Cross, quoted by Huxley, *op. cit.*

14. Meister Eckhart, quoted by Huxley, *op. cit.*

15. Seng-t'san, "On Believing in Mind," quoted by Suzuki, *Manual of Zen Buddhism* (London: Rider, 1950), p. 77.

16. Ionesco, quoted by Towarnicki, *Spectacles* No. 2, July, 1958.

BIBLIOGRAPHY

1. THE DRAMATISTS OF THE ABSURD

ADAMOV, Arthur

PLAYS:

Théâtre, 2 vols., Paris: Gallimard, Vol. I, 1953, Vol. II, 1955.
Vol. I contains *La Parodie, L'Invasion, La Grande et la Petite Manoeuvre, Le Professeur Taranne, Tous contre Tous* (*Le Professeur Taranne* trans. by A. Bermel in *Four Modern French Comedies*, New York: Capricorn Press, 1960).
Vol. II contains *Le Sens de la Marche, Les Retrouvailles, Le Ping-Pong* (*Le Ping-Pong* trans. by Richard Howard, New York: Grove Press, 1959).

SEPARATELY PUBLISHED PLAYS:

La Parodie, L'Invasion, précédées d'une lettre d'André Gide, et des témoignages de René Char, Jacques Prévert, Henri Thomas, Jacques Lemarchand, Jean Vilar, Roger Blin, Paris: Charlot, 1950.

Paolo Paoli, Paris: Gallimard, 1957. Eng. trans. by Geoffrey Brereton, London: Calder, 1959.

Les Ames Mortes, d'après le poeme de Nicolas Gogol, Paris: Gallimard, 1960.

Comme nous avons été in *Nouvelle Revue Française*, Paris: March 1953. Eng. trans., *As We Were*, by Richard Howard, New York: *Evergreen Review*, No. 4, 1957.

Théâtre de Societé. Scènes d'Actualité, Paris: Les Editeurs Français Réunis, 1958, contains three short sketches by Adamov: *Intimité, Je ne suis pas Français, La Complainte du Ridicule*.

En Fiacre, radio play, unpublished ms., 1959.

Le Printemps 71, Paris: *Théâtre Populaire*, No. 40, 1960.

OTHER WRITINGS:

L'Aveu, Paris: Sagittaire, 1946. One section of this autobiographical confession trans. by Richard Howard: "The Endless Humiliation," New York: *Evergreen Review*, No. 8, Spring 1958.

"Assignation," Paris: *L'Heure Nouvelle*, No. I, 1945.

"Une Fin et un Commencement," Paris: *L'Heure Nouvelle*, No. II, 1946.

"Le Refus," Paris: *L'Heure Nouvelle*, No. II, 1946.

ADAMOV, Arthur (cont'd)

Auguste Strindberg, Dramaturge, Paris: L'Arche, 1955.

"Théâtre, Argent et Politique," Paris: *Théâtre Populaire*, No. 17, March 1956.

"Parceque je l'ai beaucoup aimé . . ." (on Artaud), *Cahiers de la Compagnie M. Renaud-J. L. Barrault*, No. 22–23, May 1958.

Anthologie de la Commune (edited by Adamov), Paris: Ed. Sociales, 1959.

TRANSLATIONS BY ADAMOV:

Rilke, *Le Livre de la pauvreté et de la Mort*, Algiers: 1941.

Buechner, *Théâtre Complet*, trans. by Adamov and Marthe Robert.

Dostoyevsky, *Crime et Châtiment*.

Jung, *Le Moi et l'Inconscient*, Paris: 1938.

Gogol, *Les Ames Mortes*, Lausanne: La Guilde du Livre.

Chekhov, *L'Esprit des Bois*, Paris: Gallimard (in the series "Le Manteau d'Arlequin").

Chekhov, *Théâtre*, Paris: Club Français du Livre.

Strindberg, *Le Pelican*, Paris: *Théâtre Populaire*, No. 17, March 1956.

Strindberg, *Père*, Paris: L'Arche, 1958.

Kleist, *La Cruche Cassée*, Paris: *Théâtre Populaire*, No. 6, March–April 1954.

Gorki, *Théâtre*, Paris: L'Arche.

ON ADAMOV:

Lynes, Carlos, Jr., "Adamov or 'le sens littéral' in the Theatre," *Yale French Studies*, No. 14, Winter 1954–55.

Regnaut, Maurice, "Arthur Adamov et le sens du fétichisme," *Cahiers de la Compagnie M. Renaud-J. L. Barrault*, No. 22–23, May 1958.

ALBEE, Edward

PLAYS:

The Zoo Story (1958), New York: *Evergreen Review*, No. 12, March–April 1960.

The American Dream, A Comedy (1959–60), New York: *Mademoiselle*, November 1960.

The Sandbox (1959).

The Death of Bessie Smith (1959).

The last two plays, together with *The Zoo Story*, published by Coward-McCann, New York: 1960.

ARRABAL, Fernando

PLAYS:

Théâtre, Paris: Julliard, 1958. Contains *Oraison, Les Deux Bourreaux, Fando et Lis, Le Cimetière des Voitures* (two of these plays trans. in *The Automobile Graveyard/The Executioners*, New York: Grove Press, 1960.

Pique-nique en Campagne, in *Les Lettres Nouvelles*, No. 58, March 1958. Eng. trans., *Picnic on the Battlefield*, by James Hewitt, New York: *Evergreen Review*, No. 15, November–December 1960.

Le Tricycle (unpublished).

Guernica (unpublished).

Orchéstration théâtrale (unpublished).

ON ARRABAL:

Morrissett, Ann, "Dialogue with Arrabal," New York: *Evergreen Review*, No. 15, November–December 1960.

Serreau, Geneviève, "Un nouveau style comique: Arrabal," Paris: *Lettres Nouvelles*, No. 65, November 1958. Trans. New York: *Evergreen Review*, No. 15, November–December 1960.

BECKETT, Samuel

PLAYS:

En attendant Godot, Paris: Ed. de Minuit, 1952. Trans. by author: U.S. edition, *Waiting for Godot*, New York: Grove Press, 1954. Eng. edition, London: Faber & Faber, 1955.

Fin de Partie suivi de *Acte sans Paroles*, Paris: Ed. de Minuit, 1957. Trans. by author: U.S. edition, *Endgame* followed by *Act without Words*, New York: Grove Press, 1958. Eng. edition, London: Faber & Faber, 1958.

All That Fall, London: Faber & Faber, 1957 (U.S. edition: see below).

Krapp's Last Tape and Embers, London: Faber & Faber, 1959.

Krapp's Last Tape and Other Dramatic Pieces, New York: Grove Press, 1960. Contains *Krapp's Last Tape, All That Fall, Embers, Act without Words I, Act without Words II.*

NARRATIVE PROSE:

More Pricks than Kicks, London: Chatto & Windus, 1934. One story, "Dante and the Lobster," New York: *Evergreen Review*, No. 1.

Murphy, London: Routledge, 1938. New edition, New York: Grove Press, n.d.

Watt, Paris: Olympia Press, 1958.

Molloy, Paris: Ed. de Minuit, 1951.

Malone meurt, Paris: Ed. de Minuit, 1951.

L'Innommable, Paris: Ed. de Minuit, 1953.

Three Novels, London: Calder, 1959. Contains *Molloy*, trans. by Patrick Bowles, *Malone Dies* and *The Unamable*, trans. by author.

Nouvelles et Textes pour Rien, Paris: Ed. de Minuit, 1955. A story trans. by Richard Seaver and author: *The End*, New York: *Evergreen Review*, No. 15, November–December 1960.

Text for Nothing I, trans. by author, New York: *Evergreen Review*, No. 9, Summer 1959.

BECKETT, Samuel (cont'd)

>   *From an Abandoned Work,* London: Faber & Faber, 1957.
>   Also in *Evergreen Review,* No. 3, New York: 1957.

>   *Comment c'est,* Paris: Ed. de Minuit, 1961. An extract from
>   an earlier version of this novel, "L'Image" in *X,* No. 1, Lon-
>   don: November 1959. Another extract trans. by author,
>   "From an Unabandoned Work," New York: *Evergreen Re-
>   view,* No. 14, September–October 1960.

VERSE:

>   *Whoroscope,* Paris: The Hours Press, 1930.
>   *Echo's Bones,* Paris: Europa Press, 1935.
>   "Trois Poèmes," in *Cahiers des Saisons,* No. 2, October 1955.

ESSAYS:

>   *Proust,* London: Chatto & Windus (Dolphin series), 1931.
>   Reprinted New York: Grove Press, n.d.

>   "Dante . . Bruno . Vico . . Joyce" in *Our Exagmination
>   round his Factification for Incamination of Work in Progress,*
>   Paris: Shakespeare & Co., 1929.

>   *Bram van Velde,* New York: Grove Press, 1960.

ON BECKETT:

>   Abel, Lionel, "Joyce the Father, Beckett the Son," New York:
>   *The New Leader,* December 14, 1959.

>   Bentley, Eric, *What Is Theatre?,* Boston: Beacon Press, 1956.

>   Ellmann, Richard, *James Joyce,* New York: Oxford University
>   Press, 1959.

>   Gessner, N., *Die Unzulaenglichkeit der Sprache,* Zürich: Juris,
>   1957.

>   "Godot Gets Around," New York: *The Theatre Arts,* July 1958.

>   Guggenheim, Peggy, *Confessions of an Art Addict,* London:
>   André Deutsch, 1960.

>   Hobson, Harold, "Samuel Beckett, Dramatist of the Year,"
>   London: *The International Theatre Annual,* No. I, Calder,
>   1956.

>   Joyce, James, *Letters* (ed. by Stuart Gilbert), London: Faber
>   & Faber, 1957.

>   Kern, Edith, "Drama Stripped for Inaction: Beckett's *Godot,*"
>   *Yale French Studies,* No. 14, Winter 1954–55.

>   Levy, Alan, "The Long Wait for Godot," New York: *Theatre
>   Arts,* August 1956.

>   Mauriac, Claude, *L'Alittérature Contemporaine,* Paris: Albin
>   Michel, 1958.

>   "Messenger of Gloom" (Profile), London: *The Observer,* No-
>   vember 9, 1958.

>   Metman, Eva, "Reflections on Samuel Beckett's Plays," Lon-
>   don: *The Journal of Analytical Psychology,* January 1960.

>   San Quentin, Cal.: *San Quentin News,* Vol. XVII, No. 24,
>   November 28, 1957.

>   Schneider, Alan, "Waiting for Beckett," New York: *Chelsea
>   Review,* Autumn 1958.

BUZZATI, Dino
PLAYS:
Un Caso Clinico, Commedia in 2 tempi e 13 quadri, Milan: Mondadori, 1953 (No. 85 in the series "La Medusa degli Italiani").
Un Verme al Ministero, Turin: *Il Dramma*, No. 283.

d'ERRICO, Ezio
PLAYS:
La Foresta, Turin: *Il Dramma*, No. 278.
Tempo di Cavalette, Turin: *Il Dramma*, No. 261.
Il Formicaio (stage manuscript).
ON d'ERRICO:
Trilling, Ossia, "Enzio d'Errico—a new Pirandello?", London: *Theatre World*, April 1958.

FRISCH, Max
PLAYS:
Biedermann und die Brandstifter, Berlin/Frankfurt: Suhrkamp, 1958. This is the stage version, based on an earlier radio play, *Herr Biedermann und die Brandstifter*, first broadcast by Bayrischer Rundfunk, Munich: 1953, published Hamburg: Hans Bredow Institut, 6th edition: 1959.
ON FRISCH:
Baenziger, Hans, *Frisch und Duerrenmatt*, Berne: Francke, 1960.
Ziskoven, Wilhelm, "Max Frisch" Frankfurt: *Zur Interpretation des modernen Dramas* (edited by Rolf Geissler), Diesterweg, n.d. (1960).
These two exhaustive studies also contain bibliographical data on Frisch's numerous other plays which do not fall into the category of the Theatre of the Absurd.

GELBER, Jack
PLAYS:
The Connection (Introduction by Kenneth Tynan), New York: Grove Press, 1960.

GENET, Jean
PLAYS:
Haute Surveillance, Paris: Gallimard, 1949. Trans., *Deathwatch*, by B. Frechtman in *The Maids/Deathwatch*, New York: Grove Press, 1954. English edition, *Deathwatch*, London: Faber & Faber, 1961.
Les Bonnes, Décines, L'Arbalète, 1948. A new edition, containing the first and the revised version of the play: *Les Bonnes, Les deux versions précédées d'une lettre de l'auteur*, Sceaux, Pauvert, 1954. (The first version as performed at

GENET, Jean (cont'd)

the Athénée in 1946, the second as performed at the Théâtre de la Huchette in 1954.) The second version is also reprinted in *Les Bonnes & L'Atelier d'Alberto Giacometti*, Décines, L'Arbalète, 1958, which also contains "L'Enfant Criminel" (a suppressed radio talk) and "Le Funambule" (prose reflections). Translation of *Les Bonnes: The Maids*, trans. by B. Frechtman in *The Maids/Deathwatch*, New York: Grove Press, 1954. English edition, London: Faber & Faber, 1957.

Le Balcon (first version: 15 scenes), Décines, L'Arbalète, 1956, (second version: 9 scenes) Décines, L'Arbalète, 1960. Translation: *The Balcony*, trans. by B. Frechtman, New York: Grove Press, 1960. English edition, London: Faber & Faber, 1960.

Les Nègres, Clownerie, Décines, L'Arbalète, 1958. Second edition illustrated with photographs of the Paris performance and an introductory note by Genet, 1960. Translation: *The Blacks, A Clown Show*, trans. by B. Frechtman, New York: Grove Press, 1960. English edition, London: Faber & Faber, 1960.

Les Paravents, Décines, Marc Barbézat (L'Arbalète), 1961.

OTHER WRITINGS:

Journal du Voleur, Paris: Gallimard, 1949. A translation, *The Thief's Journal*, trans. by B. Frechtman, Paris: Olympia Press, 1954.

Oeuvres Complètes, Vol. II, Paris: Gallimard, 1951. Contains *Notre-Dame des Fleurs, Le Condamné à Mort, Miracle de la Rose, Un Chant d'Amour*.

Oeuvres Complètes, Vol. III, Paris: Gallimard, 1953. Contains *Pompes Funèbres, Le Pêcheur du Suquet, Querelle de Brest*.

ON GENET:

Abel, Lionel, "Metatheater," New York: *Partisan Review*, Spring 1960.

Bataille, Georges, *La Littérature et le Mal*, Paris: Gallimard, 1957.

Duvignaud, Jean, "Roger Blin aux prises avec le Nègres de Jean Genet," Paris: *Les Lettres Nouvelles*, October 28, 1959.

Sartre, Jean-Paul, *Saint Genet, Comédien et Martyr* (Vol. I of Genet, *Oeuvres Complètes*), Paris: Gallimard, 1952.

GRASS, Güenter

PLAYS:

Die boesen Koeche (stage manuscript).

Onkel, Onkel (stage manuscript).

Noch zehn Minuten bis Buffalo (stage manuscript).

Zweiunddreissig Zaehne (stage manuscript).

Hochwasser (stage manuscript).

OTHER WRITINGS:

Die Blechtrommel (novel), Neuwied: Luchterhand, 1959.
Gleisdreieck (poems), Neuwied: Luchterhand, 1960.

HILDESHEIMER, Wolfgang

Spiele in denen es dunkel wird, Pfullingen, Neske, 1958. Contains: *Pastorale oder Die Zeit fuer Kakao, Landschaft mit Figuren, Die Uhren.*

"Erlanger Rede ueber das absurde Theater," Munich: *Akzente*, No. 6, 1960.

Hildesheimer's radio plays include: *Das Ende kommt nie, Begegnung im Balkanexpress, Prinzessin Turandot* (stage version: *Der Drachenthron*), *An den Ufern der Plotinitza, Das Atelierfest, Die Bartschedelidee, Herrn Walsers Raben.*

IONESCO, Eugène

PLAYS:

La Cantatrice Chauve (written 1948, first performance 1950), in *Théâtre I* (Arcanes), also *Théâtre I* (Gallimard). Translations: *The Bald Soprano*, trans. by Donald M. Allen, in *Plays I* (New York: Grove Press), *The Bald Prima Donna*, trans. by Donald Watson, in *Plays I* (London: Calder).

La Leçon (written 1950, first performance 1951), in *Théâtre I* (Arcanes), also *Théâtre I* (Gallimard). Translations: *The Lesson*, trans. by Donald M. Allen, in *Plays I* (New York: Grove Press), trans. by Donald Watson, in *Plays I* (London: Calder).

Jacques ou La Soumission (written 1950, first performance 1955), in *Théâtre I* (Arcanes), also *Théâtre I* (Gallimard). Translations: *Jack or the Submission*, trans. by Donald M. Allen, in *Plays I* (New York: Grove Press), *Jacques or Obedience*, trans. by Donald Watson, in *Plays I* (London: Calder).

Les Chaises (written 1951, first performance 1952), in *Théâtre I* (Gallimard). Translations: *The Chairs*, trans. by Donald M. Allen, in *Plays I* (New York: Grove Press), trans. by Donald Watson, in *Plays I* (London: Calder).

Le Salon de l'Automobile (first performance 1951), in *Théâtre I* (Arcanes). Translations: *The Motor Show*, trans. by Sasha Moorsom, in *3 Arts Quarterly*, London: No. 2, Summer 1960.

L'Avenir est dans les Oeufs ou Il faut de tout pour faire un monde (written 1951, first performance 1957), in *Théâtre II*. Translation: *The Future is in Eggs or It Takes All Sorts to Make a World*, trans. by Derek Prouse, in *Plays IV*.

Victimes du Devoir (written 1952, first performance 1953), in *Théâtre I* (Gallimard). Translation: *Victims of Duty*, trans. by Donald Watson, in *Plays II*.

Amédée ou Comment s'en débarrasser (written 1953, first performance 1954), in *Théâtre I* (Gallimard). Translation: *Amédée or How to Get Rid of It*, trans. by Donald Watson, in *Plays II*.

IONESCO, Eugène (*cont'd*)

Le Nouveau Locataire (written 1953, first performance 1955), in *Théâtre II*. Translation: *The New Tenant*, trans. by Donald Watson, in *Plays II*.

Les Grands Chaleurs (first performance 1953), based on a play by Caragiale, unpublished.

La Jeune Fille à Marier (first performance 1953), in *Théâtre II*. Translation: *Maid to Marry*, trans. by Donald Watson, in *Plays III*.

Le Maître (first performance 1953), in *Théâtre II*. Translation: *The Leader*, trans. by Derek Prouse, in *Plays IV*.

Le connaissez-vous? (first performance 1953), unpublished.

La Nièce-Epouse (first performance 1953), unpublished.

Le Rhume Onirique (first performance 1953), unpublished.

Le Tableau (first performance 1955), in *Dossiers du Collège de Pataphysique*, No. 1, 1958. Translation: *The Picture*, trans. by Donald Watson, unpublished, broadcast in BBC, Third Programme, March 11, 1957.

L'Impromptu de l'Alma ou Le Caméléon du Berger (written 1955, first performance 1956), in *Théâtre II*. Translation: *Improvisation or The Shepherd's Chameleon*, trans. by Donald Watson, in *Plays III*.

Impromptu pour la Duchesse de Windsor (written 1957, first performance 1957), unpublished. Trans. by Donald Watson, unpublished.

Tueur sans Gages (written 1957, first performance 1959), in *Théâtre II*. Translation: *The Killer*, trans. by Donald Watson, in *Plays III*.

(Le) Rhinocéros (the definite article on the title page is an error committed by the publishers) (written 1958, first performance 1959), Paris: Gallimard, 1959 (in the series *Le Manteau d'Arlequin*). Translation: *Rhinoceros*, trans. by Derek Prouse, in *Plays IV*.

Scène à Quatre (written 1959, first performance 1959), in *Dossiers du Collège de Pataphysique*, No. 7, 1959, also in *Avant-Scène*, Paris: No. 210, December 15, 1959. Translation: *Foursome*, trans. by Donald M. Allen, New York: *Evergreen Review*, No. 13, May–June 1960.

Apprendre à Marcher, Ballet, unpublished. (First performance 1960.)

Les Salutations (Opening scene of an as yet uncompleted play, *Scène à Sept*), Paris: *Les Lettres Françaises*, No. 805, December 31, 1960.

COLLECTED EDITIONS:

Théâtre I, Paris: Arcanes, 1953 (in the series "Locus Solus"). Contains *La Cantatrice Chauve, La Leçon, Jacques ou La Soumission, Le Salon de l'Automobile*. A second volume of this edition, announced as being in preparation in 1953 did not appear. It was to contain *Les Chaises, Victimes du Devoir, La Nièce-Epouse, La Jeune Fille à Marier.*

Théâtre I, Paris: Gallimard, 1954. Contains Preface by Jacques Lemarchand, *La Cantatrice Chauve, La Leçon, Jacques ou La Soumission, Les Chaises, Victimes du Devoir, Amédée.*

Théâtre II, Paris: Gallimard, 1958. Contains *L'Impromptu de l'Alma, Tueur sans Gages, Le Nouveau Locataire, L'Avenir est dans les Oeufs, Le Maître, La Jeune Fille à Marier.*

ENGLISH TRANSLATIONS:

Ionesco's plays in four volumes have been published by Grove Press, New York, and John Calder, London. The first volume of these editions differs; volumes two, three and four are identical.

Vol. I, U.S. edition, trans. by Donald M. Allen, contains *The Bald Soprano, The Lesson, Jack or the Submission, The Chairs.* English edition, trans. by Donald Watson, contains *The Lesson, The Chairs, The Bald Prima Donna, Jacques or Obedience.*

Vol. II, trans. by Donald Watson, contains *Amédée or How to Get Rid of It, The New Tenant, Victims of Duty.*

Vol. III, trans. by Donald Watson, contains *The Killer, Improvisation or The Shepherd's Chameleon, Maid to Marry.*

Vol. IV, trans. by Derek Prouse, contains *Rhinoceros, The Leader, The Future is in Eggs.*

SHORT STORIES:

Une Victime du Devoir (written 1952), published Paris: *Medium,* January 1955; also Paris: *Cahiers des Saisons,* No. 24, Winter 1961. Basis of *Victimes du Devoir.*

Oriflamme, in *Nouvelle Revue Française,* February 1954. Basis of *Amédée.* Translation: *Flying High,* New York: *Mademoiselle,* 1957.

La Photo du Colonel in *Nouvelle Revue Française,* November 1955. Translation: *The Photograph of the Colonel,* trans. by Stanley Read in *Evergreen Review,* No. 3, 1957. Basis of *Tueur sans Gages.*

Rhinocéros in *Lettres Nouvelles,* September 1957. Also Paris: *Cahiers Renaud-Barrault,* No. 29, February 1960. Translation: Donald M. Allen, New York: *Mademoiselle,* March 1960.

ESSAYS AND OTHER PROSE WRITINGS:

"L'invraisamblable, l'insolite, mon univers . . ," Paris: *Arts,* August 14, 1953. Also in *Cahiers des Saisons,* No. 15, Winter 1959, under the title: "Je n'ai jamais réussi . . ."

"Le Point de Départ," *Cahiers des Quatre Saisons,* No. 1, August 1955. (This periodical changed its title to *Cahiers des Saisons* from No. 2, October 1955.) Translation: L. C. Pronko, New York: *Theatre Arts,* June 1958. Donald Watson, in *Plays I,* London: Calder.

IONESCO, Eugène (cont'd)

"Théâtre et Anti-Théâtre," *Cahiers des Saisons*, No. 2, October 1955. Translation: L. C. Pronko, New York: *Theatre Arts*, June 1958.

"Mes pièces ne prétendent pas sauver le monde," Paris: *L'Express*, October 15–16, 1955.

"Mes Critiques et Moi," Paris: *Arts*, February 22, 1956.

"Gammes" (nonsense aphorisms), *Cahiers des Saisons*, No. 7, September 1956.

"There Is No Avant-garde Theater" (trans. by Richard Howard), New York: *Evergreen Review*, No. 4, 1957.

"The World of Eugène Ionesco," London: *International Theatre Annual*, No. 2, ed. by Harold Hobson, Calder, 1957. Also, *Tulane Drama Review*, October 1958.

"Olympie" (prose poem), *Cahiers des Saisons*, No. 10, April–May 1957.

"Pour Cocteau," *Cahiers des Saisons*, No. 12, October 1957.

"The Theatre" (talk in BBC Third Programme, July 1957). An early version of "Expérience du Théâtre" (see below).

"Dans les armes de la Ville" (on Kafka), *Cahiers Renaud-Barrault*, No. 20, October 1957.

"Qu'est-ce que l'avant-garde en 1958," *Lettres Françaises*, April 10, 1958; also, *Cahiers des Saisons*, No. 15, Winter 1959, under the title: "Lorsque j'écris . . ."

"Expérience du Théâtre," *Nouvelle Revue Française*, February 1958. Translation: L. C. Pronko, "Discovering the Theatre," *Tulane Drama Review*, September 1959.

"Ni un Dieu ni un Démon" (on Artaud), Paris: *Cahiers Renaud-Barrault*, No. 22–23, May 1958.

"Reality in Depth," London: *Encore*, May–June 1958.

"The Playwright's Role," *The Observer*, June 29, 1958. The entire controversy with Kenneth Tynan is reproduced as "Controverse londonienne" in *Cahiers des Saisons*, No. 15, Winter 1959.

"La Tragédie du Langage," Paris: *Spectacles*, No. 2, July 1958. Translation: Jack Undank, "The Tragedy of Language," *Tulane Drama Review*, Spring 1960.

"Préface" to *Les Possédés*, adapted from the novel by Dostoevsky by Akakia Viala and Nicolas Bataille, Paris: Émile-Paul, 1959.

"Le Coeur n'est pas sur la main," *Cahiers des Saisons*, No. 15, Winter 1959 (reply to Kenneth Tynan not published by *The Observer*).

"Naissance de la Cantatrice," *Cahiers des Saisons*, No. 15, Winter 1959.

"La Démystification par l'Humour Noir," Paris: *L'Avant-Scène*, February 15, 1959.

"Eugène Ionesco ouvre le Feu" (with parallel English translation), Paris: *World Theatre*, Vol. VIII, No. 3, Autumn 1959.

Interview with Claude Sarraute, *Le Monde*, January 17, 1960.

Interview with himself, *France-Observateur*, January 21, 1960. Reprinted in *Dossiers du Collège de Pataphysique*, No. 10–11, 1960.

Interview, Paris: *L'Express*, January 28, 1960.

"Pages de Journal," *Nouvelle Revue Française*, February 1960.

"Printemps 1939. Les Débris du Souvenir. Pages de Journal," *Cahiers Renaud-Barrault*, No. 29, February 1960.

"Propos sur mon Théâtre et sur les Propos des Autres," Brussels: *L'VII*, No. 3, 1960.

"Le Rhinocéros à New York," Paris: *Arts*, February 1961.

"Some Recollections of Brancusi," trans. by John Russell, *The London Magazine*, April 1961.

ON IONESCO:

Abenteuer Ionesco, Das. Beitraege zum Theater von Heute (with contributions by Ionesco, A. Schulze Vellinghausen and Rudolf Sellner), Zürich: Verlag & H. R. Stauffacher, 1958.

Anouilh, Jean, "Du Chapitre des Chaises," Paris: *Le Figaro*, April 23, 1956.

Bataille, Nicolas, "La Bataille de la Cantatrice," Paris: *Cahiers des Saisons*, No. 15, Winter 1959.

Bentley, Eric, "Ionesco, Playwright of the Fifties," New York: *Columbia Daily Spectator*, March 11, 1958.

Bosquet, Alain, "Le Théâtre d'Eugène Ionesco ou les 36 Recettes du Comique," Paris: *Combat*, February 17, 1955.

Coe, Richard, *Ionesco*, Edinburgh and London: Oliver & Boyd, 1961. (No. 5 in the series "Writers and Critics.")

Doubrovsky, Serge, "Ionesco and the Comedy of the Absurd," *Yale French Studies*, No. 23, Summer 1959. Also, *Nouvelle Revue Française*, February 1960, under the title, "Le Rire d'Eugène Ionesco."

Duvignaud, Jean, "La Dérision," Paris: *Cahiers Renaud-Barrault*, No. 29, February 1960.

Francueil, Bernard, "Digression automobile & Dilectus quemadmodum filius unicornium" (review of *Rhinocéros*), *Dossiers du Collège de Pataphysique*, No. 10–11, 1960.

Laubreaux, R., "Situation de Ionesco," *Théâtre d'Aujourd'hui*, January–February 1959.

Lerminier, Georges, "Clés pour Ionesco," Paris: *Théâtre d'Aujourd'hui*, September–October 1957.

Lutembi, "Contribution à une étude des sources de la Cantatrice Chauve," *Cahiers du Collège de Pataphysique*, 8–9, 1953.

Marcel, Gabriel, "La Crise du Théâtre et le Crépuscule de l'Humanisme," *Revue Théâtrale*, No. 39.

Robbe-Grillet, Alain, "Notes," *Critique*, January 1953.

IONESCO, Eugène (cont'd)

Roud, Richard, "The Opposite of Sameness," London: *Encore*, June–July 1957.

Saroyan, William, "Ionesco," New York: *Theatre Arts*, July 1958.

Saurel, Renée, "Ionesco ou Les Blandices de la Culpabilité," Paris: *Les Temps Modernes*, No. CIII, 1954.

"School of Vigilance, A," London: *The Times Literary Supplement*, March 4, 1960.

Touchard, P. A., "La Loi du Théâtre," Paris: *Cahiers des Saisons*, No. 15, Winter 1959.

Touchard, P. A., "Un Nouveau Fabuliste," Paris: *Cahiers Renaud-Barrault*, No. 29, February 1960.

Towarnicki, F., "Des Chaises vides . . . à Broadway," *Spectacles*, No. 2, July 1958.

KENAN, Amos

Le Lion (translated from the Hebrew by Christiane Rochefort and the author), Paris: *Les Lettres Nouvelles* (new series), No. 1, March–April 1960.

KOPIT, Arthur L.

Oh Dad, Poor Dad, Mamma's Hung You in the Closet and I'm Feeling So Sad. A Pseudoclassical Tragifarce in a bastard French tradition, New York: Hill and Wang, 1960.

PEDROLO, Manuel de

Cruma in *Premi Joan Santamaria 1957*, Barcelona. Editorial Nereida, 1958.

Homes i No, Barcelona: *Quaderns de Teatre*, No. 2, 1960.

PINGET, Robert

PLAYS:

Lettre Morte, Paris: Ed. de Minuit, 1959.

La Manivelle, pièce radiophonique (with parallel translation by Samuel Beckett, *The Old Tune*), Paris: Ed. de Minuit, 1960.

Clope (in manuscript).

PINTER, Harold

The Birthday Party and Other Plays, London: Methuen, 1960. Contains *The Room, The Dumb Waiter, The Birthday Party*.

The Caretaker, London: Methuen, 1960.

A Slight Ache and Other Plays, London: Methuen, 1961. Contains *A Slight Ache, A Night Out, The Dwarfs* and the revue sketches *Trouble in the Works, The Black and White, Request Stop, Last to Go* and *Applicant*.

Night School, television play, unpublished.

The Collection, television play, unpublished.

SIMPSON, Norman Frederick
> *A Resounding Tinkle* in *The Observer Plays* (anthology of prize-winning entries in a playwriting competition), London: Faber & Faber, 1958. Reprinted in *New English Dramatists 2*, Harmondsworth: Penguin Books, 1960. Shorter stage version as performed at the Royal Court Theatre, London, unpublished manuscript.
> *The Hole*, stage manuscript.
> *One Way Pendulum, A Farce in a New Dimension*, London: Faber & Faber, 1960.
> *The Form*, unpublished.
> *Gladly Otherwise*, revue sketch, unpublished.
> *The Overcoat* (short story), London: *Man about Town*, December 1960.

TARDIEU, Jean
> *Théâtre de Chambre I*, Paris: Gallimard, 1955. Contains *Qui est là?, La Politesse Inutile, Le Sacre de la Nuit, Le Meuble, La Serrure, Le Guichet, Monsieur Moi, Faust et Yorick, La Sonate et les trois Messieurs ou Comment parler Musique, La Societé Apollon ou Comment parler des Arts, Oswald et Zenaïde ou Les Apartés, Ce que Parler veut dire ou Le Patois des Familles, Il y avait foule au manoir ou Les Monologues, Eux seuls le savent, Un Geste pour un autre, Conversation-Sinfonietta.*
> *Théâtre II: Poèmes à jouer*, Paris: Gallimard, 1960. Contains *L'A.B.C. de Notre Vie, Rhythme à Trois Temps ou Le Temple de Segeste, Une Voix sans Personne, Les Temps du Verbe ou Le Pouvoir de la Parole, Les Amants du Métro, Tonnerre sans Orage ou Les Dieux Inutiles.*

ON TARDIEU:
> Jacottet, Philippe, "Note à propos de Jean Tardieu," *Nouvelle Revue Française*, July 1960.

VIAN, Boris
> A full bibliography of Vian's numerous writings, Paris: *Dossiers du Collège de Pataphysique*, No. 12, 1960. This issue also contains critical and biographical studies of Boris Vian.

PLAYS:
> *L'Équarrissage pour tous*, Paris: Toutain, 1950. Apart from extracts from notices of the performance, this also contains "Salut à Boris Vian" by Cocteau, and a second short play, *Le dernier des Métiers, Saynètes pour Patronages.*
> *L'Équarrissage pour tous* is reprinted in *Paris Théâtre*, Paris: No. 66, 1952.

VIAN, *Boris* (*cont'd*)

Les Bâtisseurs d'Empire ou Le Schmürz, *Dossiers du Collège de Pataphysique*, No. 6, 1959. Also in the series "Collection du Répertoire du TNP," Paris: L'Arche, 1959.

2. BACKGROUND AND HISTORY OF THE THEATRE OF THE ABSURD

GENERAL WORKS

BARNES, HAZEL, *The Literature of Possibility*, Lincoln, Nebraska: University Press, 1959.

BEIGBEDER, MARC, *Le Théâtre en France depuis la Libération*, Paris: Bordas, 1959.

BERGEAUD, JEAN, *Je choisis . . mon théâtre. Encyclopédie du Théâtre Contemporain*, Paris: Odilis, 1956.

BERGSON, HENRI, *Le Rire. Essai sur la Signification du Comique*, in *Oeuvres*, Paris: Presses Universitaires de France, 1959.

BOISDEFFRE, PIERRE DE, *Une Histoire Vivante de la Littérature d'Aujourd'hui*, Paris: Le Livre Contemporain.

CAMUS, ALBERT, *Le Mythe de Sisyphe*, Paris: Gallimard, 1942.

CRUICKSHANK, JOHN, *Albert Camus and the Literature of Revolt*, New York: Oxford University Press, 1959.

Dictionnaire des Hommes de Théâtre Français Contemporains (tome I: Directeurs, Animateurs, Historiens, Critiques). Paris: Librairie Théâtrale, 1957.

ECO, UMBERTO, "L'Oeuvre Ouverte ou La Poétique de l'Indétermination," *Nouvelle Revue Française*, July and August 1960.

EVREINOV, NIKOLAI, *The Theatre of the Soul, Monodrama*, trans. by M. Potapenko and C. St. John, London: 1915.

FOWLIE, WALLACE, *Dyonisus in Paris. A Guide to Contemporary French Theatre*, New York: Meridian, 1960.

FREUD, SIGMUND, *Der Witz und seine Beziehung zum Unbewussten* (1905), paperback reprint, Frankfurt: S. Fischer, 1958.

GREGOR, JOSEPH, *Weltgeschichte des Theaters*, Vienna: Phaidon, 1932.

GROSSVOGEL, DAVID, *The Selfconscious Stage in Modern French Drama*, New York: Columbia University Press, 1958.

HUXLEY, ALDOUS (editor), *The Perennial Philosophy*, London: Chatto & Windus, 1946.

MALLARMÉ, STÉPHANE, *Crayonné au Théâtre*, in *Oeuvres Complètes*, Paris: Bibl. de la Pléiade, 1945.

NIETZSCHE, *Die Geburt der Tragoedie* and *Also sprach Zarathustra*, in *Werke*, ed. by Schlechta, Munich: Hanser, Vol. I and II, 1955.

POUND, EZRA, *Literary Essays*, ed. by T. S. Eliot, London: Faber & Faber, 1954.

SARTRE, JEAN-PAUL, *L'Etre et le Néant*, Paris: Gallimard, 1943.

STEINER, GEORGE, "The Retreat from the Word," London: *The Listener*, July 14 and 21, 1960.

SUZUKI, D., *Manual of Zen Buddhism*, London: Rider, 1950.

Théâtre Populaire, "Du Coté de l'Avant-Garde" (special number on the avant-garde theatre), No. 18, May 1956.

WITTGENSTEIN, LUDWIG, *Philosophical Investigations*, Oxford: Blackwell, 1958.

PURE THEATRE, CLOWNING, COMMEDIA DELL'ARTE, MUSIC HALL, etc.

BEERBOHM, MAX, "Dan Leno" in *Around Theatres*, London: Hart-Davies, 1953.

BUECHNER, GEORG, *Werke und Briefe*, Leipzig: Insel, 1958.

CRICHTON, KYLE, *The Marx Brothers*, London: Heinemann, 1951.

DISHER, WILLSON, *Clowns and Pantomimes*, London: Constable, 1925.

GRABBE, CHRISTIAN DIETRICH, *Werke*, ed. by Wukadinowic, 2 vols., Berlin: Bong, n.d.

HAZLITT, WILLIAM, "The Indian Jugglers," *Table Talk*, London and New York: Everyman's Library.

HOLZER, RUDOLF, *Die Wiener Vorstadtbuehnen*, Vienna: 1951.

LEA, K. M., *Italian Popular Comedy. A Study in the Commedia dell'Arte*, Oxford: 1934.

MACINNES, COLIN, "Wherefore Does He Why?" (on Dan Leno), London: *The Spectator*, December 23, 1960.

MC KECHNIE, SAMUEL, *Popular Entertainment through the Ages*, London: Sampson Low, n.d.

NESTROY, JOHANN, *Saemtliche Werke*, ed. by Brukner and Rommel, Vienna: Schroll, 15 vols., 1924–30.

RAIMUND, FERDINAND, *Werke*, ed. by Castle, Leipzig: Hesse & Becker, n.d.

REICH, HERMANN, *Der Mimus*, Vol. I (in two tomes) (no further volumes appeared), Berlin: Weidmann, 1903.

TIETZE-CONRAT, E., *Dwarfs and Jesters in Art*, London: Phaidon, 1957.

WOOD, J. HICKORY, *Dan Leno*, London: Methuen, 1905.

NONSENSE POETRY AND NONSENSE PLAYS

BELLOC, HILAIRE, *Cautionary Verses*, London: Duckworth, 1940.

BENAYOUN, R., *Anthologie du Nonsense*, Paris: Pauvert, 1957.

BRETON, ANDRÉ, *Anthologie de l'Humour Noir*, Paris: Sagittaire, 1950.

BUSCH, WILHELM, *Saemtliche Werke*, Guetersloh: Bertelsmann, n.d., 2 vols.

CARROLL, LEWIS, *Complete Works*, London: Nonesuch. New York: Random House, 1939.

COHEN, J. M., *Comic and Curious Verse*, Harmondsworth: Penguin, 1952.

COHEN, J. M., *More Comic and Curious Verse*, Harmondsworth: Penguin, 1956.

FLAUBERT, GUSTAVE, *Dictionnaire des Idées Reçues* (augmented with newly discovered entries), Paris: Aubier, 1951.

LARDNER, RING

  NONSENSE PLAYS:

  The Tridget of Griva, unpublished (extract in Elder, see below).

  Dinner Bridge (1927), *New Republic*, July 20, 1927, also in *First and Last*, New York: Scribner, 1934.

  I Gaspiri (The Upholsterers) (1924) in *Chicago Literary Times*, February 15, 1924, also in *What of It?*, New York: Scribner, 1925.

  Clemo-Uti/The Water Lilies in *What of It?*, New York: Scribner, 1925.

  Cora or Fun at the Spa, in *Vanity Fair*, June 1925.

  Quadroon. A Play in Four Pelts which May All Be Attended in One Day or Missed in a Group, *The New Yorker*, December 19, 1931.

  Abend di Anni Nouveau, New York: *The Morning Telegraph*, 1928–29.

  ON LARDNER:

  Elder, Donald, *Ring Lardner*, New York: Doubleday, 1956.

LEAR, EDWARD, *The Complete Nonsense of Edward Lear*, ed. by Holbrook Jackson, London: Faber & Faber, 1947.

MORGENSTERN, CHRISTIAN, *Alle Galgenlieder*, Wiesbaden: Insel, 1950.

MORGENSTERN, CHRISTIAN, *Das Mondschaf*, deutsch und englisch (English versions by A. E. W. Eitzen), Wiesbaden: Insel, 1953.

OPIE, IONA and PETER, *The Oxford Dictionary of Nursery Rhymes*, Oxford: 1951.

OPIE, IONA and PETER, *The Lore and Language of Schoolchildren*, Oxford: 1959.

RINGELNATZ, JOACHIM, *Kinder-Verwirr-Buch*, Berlin: Rowohlt, 1931.

RINGELNATZ, JOACHIM, *Turngedichte*, Munich: Kurt Wolff, 1923.

RINGELNATZ, JOACHIM, *Kuttel-Daddeldu*, Berlin: Rowohlt, 1930.

SEWELL, E., *The Field of Nonsense*, London: Chatto & Windus, 1952.

DREAM PLAYS AND ALLEGORIES

BIDERMANN, JAKOB, *Cenodoxus der Doktor von Paris,* in *Deutsche Dichtung des Barock,* ed. by Edgar Hederer, Munich: Hanser, n.d.

CALDERON DE LA BARCA, PEDRO, *Autos Sacramentales,* Vol. III of *Obras Completas,* Madrid: Aguilar, 1945–52.

ELIADE, MIRCEA, *Myths, Dreams and Mysteries,* London: Harvill, 1960.

GREGOR, JOSEPH, *Das Spanische Welttheater,* Vienna: Riechner, 1937.

HOLBERG, *Comoedierne,* ed. by Bull, Kristiania: 1922–25.

HONIG, EDWIN, *Dark Conceit. The Making of Allegory,* Chicago: Northwestern University Press, 1959, London: Faber & Faber, 1960.

JOYCE, JAMES. Stage adaptations of Ulysses:
   Ulysses in Nighttown, ad. for the stage by Marjorie Barkentin under the supervision of Padraic Colum, New York: Random House, Modern Library Paperbacks, 1958.
   Bloomsday, ad. by Alan Maclelland, London: Ace Books, 1961.

KAFKA, FRANZ, *Der Gruftwaechter* (dramatic fragment) in *Beschreibung eines Kapmpfes,* New York: Schocken, 1946.

KAFKA, FRANZ, adapted by GIDE, ANDRÉ and BARRAULT, JEAN-LOUIS, *Le Procès,* Paris: Gallimard, 1947.

Franz Kafka du Procès au Château, special number of *Cahiers Renaud-Barrault,* No. 20, Paris: October 1957.

LOPE DE VEGA, *Obras Escogidas,* 3 vols., Madrid: Aguilar, 1952–55. Contains Lope's principal *Autos Sacramentales.*

MADACH, IMRE, *Az Ember Tragédiája,* Budapest: Franklin, n.d.

STRINDBERG, AUGUST, *Samlade Skrifter,* 55 vols., Stockholm: Bonnier, 1911–21.

STRINDBERG, AUGUST, *A Dream Play* and *The Ghost Sonata* in *Six Plays of Strindberg,* trans. by E. Sprigge, New York: Doubleday, Anchor Books, 1955.

DADAISM, SURREALISM, PATAPHYSICIANS,
and their forerunners and followers

APOLLINAIRE, GUILLAUME
   PLAYS:
      Les Mamelles de Tirésias/Couleur du Temps in *Oeuvres Poétiques,* Paris: Pléiade, 1956.

ARAGON, LOUIS
   PLAYS:
      L'Armoire à Glace un beau Soir and *Au Pied du Mur* in *Le Libertinage,* Paris: Gallimard, 1924.
      with BRETON, ANDRÉ, *Le Trésor des Jésuites* in *Variétés,* Brussels: June 1929.

ARTAUD, ANTONIN

Oeuvres Complètes, Vol. I, Paris: Gallimard, 1956. (The publication of the other four volumes planned for the complete edition was delayed owing to copyright disputes.) The first volume contains the short play Le Jet de Sang. Vol. IV was planned to contain: Ventre Brûlé ou La Mère Folle and Les Cenci.

Le Théâtre et son Double, Paris: Gallimard, 1938. English translation: The Theatre and Its Double, trans. by C. Richards, New York: Grove Press, 1958.

Lettres à Jean-Louis Barrault, Paris: 1952. (Contains a study of Artaud's theatre by Paul Arnold.)

Antonin Artaud et le Théâtre de notre Temps, Paris: special issue of Cahiers Renaud-Barrault, No. 22–23, May 1958.

Antonin Artaud ou La Santé des Poètes, Jarnac: special number of La Tour du Feu, December 1959.

BARLACH, ERNST, Das Dichterische Werk, Band I: Dramen, Munich: Piper, 1956.

BRECHT, BERTOLT, Stuecke, 12 vols., Frankfurt: Suhrkamp, 1954–60.

COCTEAU, JEAN

Les Mariés de la Tour Eiffel in Théâtre I, Paris: Gallimard, 1948.

Parade and Le Boeuf sur le toit in Nouveau Théâtre de Poche, Monaco: Ed. du Rocher, 1960.

Orphée, Paris: Stock, 1927.

Le Sang d'un Poète (film), Paris: Marin, 1948.

CUMMINGS, E. E.

him in From the Modern Repertoire, Series Two, ed. by Eric Bentley, Indiana University Press, 1957.

Bentley, Eric, "Notes to him," ibid.

Norman, Charles, The Magic Maker, New York: Macmillan, 1958.

DADA

Arp/Huelsenbeck/Tzara, Die Geburt des Dada, Zürich: Arche, 1957.

Mehring, Walter, Berlin Dada, Zürich: Arche, 1959.

Huelsenbeck, Richard, Mit Witz, Licht und Gruetze, Wiesbaden: Limes, 1957.

DAUMAL, RENÉ and GILBERT-LECOMTE, ROGER, Petit Théâtre, Paris: Collège de Pataphysique, 1957.

DESNOS, ROBERT

La Place de l'Étoile, Antipoème, Rodez: Collection Humour, 1945.

Domaine Publique, collected poems, Paris: Gallimard, 1953.

Berger, Pierre, Robert Desnos, Paris: Seghers, 1960. Essay on Desnos and anthology of his works. (No. 16 in the series "Poètes d'Aujourd'hui.")

EXPRESSIONISMUS. Literatur und Kunst, 1910–1923.

Catalogue of an Exhibition at the Schiller Museum at Marbach,

West Germany, May 8–October 31, 1961, ed. by B. Zeller, Marbach: 1960. (A very full bibliography of Expressionism, with biographical notes on all important authors).

FITZGERALD, F. SCOTT

The Vegetable or From President to Postman, New York: Scribner, 1923.

Mizener, Arthur, *This Side of Paradise*, London: Eyre & Spottiswoode, 1951.

GOLL, YVAN

Die Chaplinade

Die Unsterblichen: Zwei Ueberdramen. 1. Der Unsterbliche. 2. Der Ungestorbene.

Melusine

The above are reprinted in GOLL, *Dichtungen*, ed. by Claire Goll, Neuwied: Luchterhand, 1960.

Methusalem in *Schrei und Bekenntnis*. Expressionistisches Theater (anthology of Expressionist Plays), ed. by K. Otten, Neuwied: Luchterhand, 1959.

Romains, Jules/Brion, Marcel/Carmody, F./Exner, R., *Yvan Goll*, Paris: Seghers, 1956. (No. 50 in the series "Poètes d'Aujourd'hui"—anthology and critical essays.)

JARRY, ALFRED

Oeuvres Complètes, Monte Carlo and Lausanne: 1948.

Ubu Roi/Ubu Enchaîné/Paralipomènes d'Ubu/Questions de Théâtre/Les Minutes de Sable Mémorial/César-Antechrist/Poésies/L'Autre Alceste, Lausanne: Henri Kaeser, 1948. (Collection of all Ubu-esque writings.)

Ubu Roi, trans. by Barbara Wright in *Four Modern French Comedies*, New York: Capricorn Books, 1960.

Ubu, version pour la scene (acting edition of *Ubu Roi* and *Ubu Enchaîné* adapted for performance as one play at the *Théâtre National Populaire*), Paris: L'Arche, 1958.

Gestes et Opinions du Docteur Faustroll, Paris: Fasquelle, 1955.

XII Arguments de Alfred Jarry sur le Théâtre in *Dossiers du Collège de Pataphysique*, No. 5, 1959.

KOKOSCHKA, OSKAR, *Schriften 1907–1955*, Munich: Langen, 1956.

LAUTRÉAMONT, COMTE DE (Isidore Ducasse), *Oeuvres Complètes*, Paris: Corti, 1946.

LORCA, FEDERICO GARCIA, *Obras Completas*, Madrid: Aguilar, 1955.

NADEAU, MAURICE, *Histoire du Surréalisme*, Paris: Ed. du Seuil, 1945.

PICASSO, PABLO

Le Désir attrapé par la Queue, in *Messages II*, Paris: 1944. Also in book form as No. 23 of the collection "Métamorphoses," Paris: Gallimard, 1949. Translation: *Desire Caught by the Tail*, trans. by B. Frechtmann, London: Rider, 1950.

PICASSO, Pablo (cont'd)
Penrose, Roland, *Picasso, His Life and Work*, London: Gollancz, 1955.

PINTHUS, KURTH, *Menschheitsdaemmerung* (one of the first anthologies of Expressionist Poetry), Berlin: Rowohlt, 1920. Reissue, with new introduction and new biographical and bibliographical material, Hamburg: Rowohlt, 1959.

RADIGUET, RAYMOND
Les Pélican, pièce en deux actes, in *Oeuvres Complètes*, Vol. I, Paris: Club des Libraires de France, 1959.

RIBEMONT-DESSAIGNES, GEORGES
L'Empereur de Chine suivi de Le Serin Muet, Paris: Sans Pareil, 1921.
Le Bourreau de Pérou, Paris: Sans Pareil, 1928.
Déjà Jadis (memoirs), Paris: Julliard, 1958.

ROBICHEZ, J., *Le Symbolisme au Théâtre. Lugné-Poë et les débuts de l'Oeuvre*, Paris: L'Arche, 1957.

ROUSSEL, RAYMOND
PLAYS:
L'Étoile au Front, Paris: Lemerre, 1925.
La Poussière de Soleils, Paris: Lemerre, 1927.
Rousselot, Jean, *Raymond Roussel et le toute-puissance du langage*, Paris: *La Tour St. Jacques*, March–April 1957.

SALACROU, ARMAND
SURREALIST PLAYLETS:
Pièces à Lire: Les trente Tombes de Judas, Histoire de Cirque in *Les Oeuvres Libres*, Paris: No. 173, October 1960.

SHATTUCK, ROGER, *The Banquet Years*, London: Faber & Faber, 1959. (Contains outstanding studies of Apollinaire and Jarry.)

SOKEL, WALTER H., *The Writer in Extremis: Expressionism in Twentieth Century German Literature*, Stanford University Press, 1959.

STEIN, GERTRUDE
DRAMATIC WORKS:
Four Saints in Three Acts, New York: Random House, 1934.
Geography and Plays, Boston: Four Seas, 1922.
Doctor Faustus Lights the Lights
In Savoy or Yes Is for a Very Young Man, London: Pushkin Press, 1946.

TORMA, JULIEN
Coupures, tragédie, suivi de Lauma Lamer, Paris: Pérou, 1926.
Euphorismes (no publisher indicated), 1926.
Le Bétrou, drame en IV actes, Paris: Collège de Pataphysique, 1956.
"Hommage à Torma" (biographical, bibliographical and critical studies by various hands) in *Cahiers du Collège de Pataphysique*, No. 7, 1952.

TZARA, TRISTAN

  PLAYS:

    La Première Aventure Céleste de M. Antipyrine, Zürich, Collection Dada, 1916.

    La Deuxième Aventure Céleste de M. Antipyrine, Paris: Réverbère, 1938.

    Le Coeur à Gaz, Paris: GLM, 1946.

    La Fuite, Paris: Gallimard, 1947.

VITRAC, ROGER

    Théâtre, 2 vols. Paris: Gallimard, 1946.

      Vol. I contains *Victor ou Les Enfants au Pouvoir, Le Coup de Trafalgar, Le Camelot.*

      Vol. II contains *Les Mystères de l'Amour, Les Demoiselles du Large, Le Loup Garou.*

VALLE-INCLAN, RAMON DEL

  ESPERPENTOS:

    Martes de Carnaval, Esperpentos, in *Opera Omnia*, vol. 24, Madrid: Editorial Rua Nueva, 1943. Contains *Las Galas del Difunto, Los Cuernos de Don Friolera, La Hija del Capitan.*

YEATS, W. B., *Autobiographies*, London: Macmillan, 1955.

INDEX

ANCHOR BOOKS

DRAMA

MUSIC

ANCHOR BOOKS

FICTION

CLASSICS AND HUMANITIES

ANCHOR BOOKS

AMERICAN HISTORY AND STUDIES

ANCHOR BOOKS

EDUCATION

LINGUISTICS AND LANGUAGE

ANCHOR BOOKS

ART AND ARCHITECTURE